D0977011

1,000 Places To See Before You Die®

The New Full-Color Second Edition

by **PATRICIA SCHULTZ**

WORKMAN PUBLISHING, NEW YORK

An Important Note to Readers

Though every effort has been made to ensure the accuracy and timeliness of the information contained in this book, it may change at any time for many reasons, including market forces, political and economic conditions, and weather. Readers should be sure to call or e-mail ahead for confirmation of information when making any travel plans. The author, editors, and publisher shall not be responsible for any travel conditions experienced by readers resulting from changes in information provided in this book. If you discover any out-of-date or incorrect information in the book, we would appreciate it if you would let us know via our website, www.1000places.com.

Published simultaneously in Canada by Thomas Allen & Son Limited.

Library of Congress Cataloging-in-Publication Data is available.

ISBN 978-0-7611-5686-4 (pb); 978-0-7611-6337-4 (hc)

Design by Orlando Adiao and Lidija Tomas

Workman Publishing Company, Inc.
225 Varick Street
New York, NY 10014-4381
www.workman.com

Printed in the United States of America
First printing October 2011

10 9 8 7 6 5 4 3 2 1

Better to see
something once
than to hear about it
a thousand times.

—ASIAN PROVERB

Dedication

To Nick, whose big heart and
light-up-the-room personality make every trip a joy.

To my sister Roz, her husband Ed,
and their children Star, Corey, and Brittany—
they are the reason that home is always on my short list
of favorite places in the world.

And to our wonderful parents,
who always fostered my insatiable love of travel.

ACKNOWLEDGMENTS

I want to thank the gods of karma who long ago nudged me into the orbit of Peter and Carolan Workman, who have loved and nurtured this book every bit as much as I. If the outreach and response to the original edition have exceeded all our expectations, it is because I stand on the shoulders of these giants. Those who think I've had my hands full these last few years while revising the book—well, they should see my heart. My deepest thanks to the Workmans and the Workman Publishing team. They have become my family and friends.

This collaborative makeover of *1,000 Places* was spearheaded by my editrix extraordinaire, Margot Herrera, who by now has a number of these 1,000 tomes under her belt. Yet she approaches each one with a fresh eye and an inexhaustible reservoir of enthusiasm and patience: When I grow up I want to have her unflappable outlook and optimist's soul. Her new right hand, Heather Schwedel, took 5 minutes to settle in and roll up her sleeves—and then became the poster child for steadfast, earnest, and reliable assistance that helped us make this volume better. I am also grateful to editor-in-chief Suzie Bolotin, for championing the book and giving Margot and Heather the support they needed.

The publicity team of Oleg Lyubner and Selina Meere have jumped through hoops to make sure the book is on everyone's lips, while Bob Miller, Savannah Ashour, Andrea Fleck-Nisbet, David Schiller (who wears many invaluable hats), and Marissa Hussey helped oversee the exciting expansion into the realm of apps and the electronic world. Jessica Weiner created marketing partnerships that ensure the excitement will keep on giving.

My gratitude to Kristina Peterson, who made sure the original *1,000 Places* was reborn in 25 translations—whether I am in a bookstore in Istanbul or in Rio, I thrill to see my book being enjoyed by travelers around the world. And much appreciation to licensing manager Pat Upton, who made many good things come to pass, as well as to special sales goddess Jenny Mandel and her associate Emily Krasner.

Kudos to Janet Vicario for her beautiful art direction and to talented and indefatigable designers Orlando Adiao (who has a bottomless well of patience and good cheer) and Lidija Tomas. Also to photo editor Anne Kerman and her able staff, who surmounted the Herculean challenge of handpicking the images needed to make this new-and-improved color version as intoxicating and irresistible as possible.

Production editor Carol White combed through every pass with eagle eyes and total commitment; copy editor Judit Bodnar sharpened the manuscript with fact-checking and clarifying questions, plus made sense of the spellings of curious names in countless languages; and managing editor Peggy Gannon created the all-important schedules (and then made sure we stuck to them).

Thanks to Barbara Peragine for working typesetting miracles, to Doug Wolff for overseeing the printing of the book, and to freelance editor Hilary Sterne, whose involvement in almost every phase was invaluable. My gratitude to Adam Greene, who graciously gave over his restaurant Snack Taverna for a photo shoot.

An especially sincere and heartfelt thank-you to travel veterans and friends Caren Banks, Anitra Brown, Bill McCrae, and Elizabeth Ragagli for embracing the project as if it were their own and being available and supportive from beginning to end. To Alison D'Amato, Giema Tsakuginow, and Charlene Lamberis: Thanks for helping me create a research archive and organize my life. And all my love to Nick Stringas for—among countless other things—keeping me from coming unglued.

The team of road warriors whose expertise I was able to call upon for destinations from Alaska to Zimbabwe comprise a remarkable group of individuals—bright, knowledgeable, cultured, and fun—proving that kindred adventurers always find each other in life: Brett Atkinson (New Zealand, Southeast Asia, and the Czech Republic), Greg Bloom (Uzbekistan, Turkmenistan, Ukraine), Rodney Bolt (the Netherlands), Stephen Brewer (Greece and Italy), Mark Chestnut (Brazil and Chile), Paul Clammer (Haiti), Beth Connelly (Germany, Austria, Switzerland), Laura Del Rosso (Mexico), Christine Del Sol (Mexico), David Else (the U.K.), Andrew Evans (Antarctica, South Georgia, the Falkland Islands, and Greenland), Stephen Fallon (London, Paris, Eastern Europe, and Turkey), John Fischer (Hawaii), Andrew Forbes and Colin Hinshelwood (Indonesia), Bob Friel (the Caribbean), Bill Goodwin (South Pacific Islands), Michael Grosberg (the Philippines and Myanmar), Patricia Harris and David Lyons (Portugal and Spain), Lynn Hazelwood (New York City), Jen Johnston (the U.S.A.), Brian Johnstone (Australia and China), David Kaufman (Israel and the Middle East), Michael Kohn (Uzbekistan, Kyrgyzstan, and Tajikistan), Michael Luongo (Argentina and much of South America), Antony Mason (Belgium), Michael McDermott and Jenny Shannon Harkins (Ireland), Nancy McKeon (Washington, D.C.), Sally McLaren (Kyoto), Leif Pettersen (Romania), Simon Richmond (Japan and Malaysia), Regis St. Louis (Australia, the Baltics, Iceland, Russia, Finland, and Brazil), AnneLise Sorensen (Scandinavia), David Stanley (the South Pacific), Aaron Starmer (for lots of miscellaneous fact-checking and research around the world), Mimi Tompkins (France and way beyond), and Neil Wilson (Georgia, Malta).

And to everyone I've ever met along the way who made a difference.

Contents

BONUS INDEXES! *Go to www.1000places.com/indexes to access the following 12 thematic indexes, which are organized by type of experience: Active Travel, Wildlife, and Adventure • Ancient Worlds: Pyramids, Ruins, and Lost Cities • Culinary Experiences • Festivals and Special Events • Glories of Nature: Gardens, Parks and Wilderness Preserves, and Natural Wonders • Gorgeous Beaches and Getaway Islands • Hotels, Resorts, Eco-lodges, and Inns • Living History: Castles and Palaces, Historical Sites • Roadways, Railways, and Waterways • Sacred Places • Splendor in the Glass: Bars and Pubs, Vineyards and Wineries, Breweries and Distilleries • Unrivaled Museums*

Introduction

The World Revisited

As I write this introduction, my nieces are in Iceland. I imagine them enjoying a hot soak in the Blue Lagoon under the midnight sun, driving through a vast, empty countryside of stark, otherworldly beauty—slowing down to let wild horses cross the two-lane road and stopping to order lunch from menus in a language they cannot pronounce. They are sending me e-mails (the postcards of today) and posting Facebook updates (how things have changed!), and I can feel their excitement and their sense of wonder. They will return home exhilarated, having felt firsthand how travel opens up your whole world while nurturing a newfound appreciation for everything you've left behind. There really is no downside to travel, save a little jet lag and a dented bank account. A small price to pay for a million-dollar experience.

Wanderlust—I like to think of it as wanderlove—has always coursed through my veins. To paraphrase Winston Churchill, I never felt an hour spent in the seat of an airplane (or bus, tuk-tuk, car, or bullet train) was an hour wasted. As a toddler I realized that a whole big world awaited every time our family locked the front door and piled into the station wagon for the Jersey shore (yes, that one, but before its reputation was compromised). Playing Risk on the living room floor introduced me to places with names like Madagascar and Siam. It wasn't the game's promise of world domination that enticed me, but the far reaches of a planet so big and exotic and rich with romance that it felt like make-believe to me.

My first true "aha!" moment happened when I was 15 and my parents agreed to let me visit a high school friend who lived with her family in Santo Domingo, the capital of the Dominican Republic. I was too naïve at the time to grasp the importance of the beautiful and historically rich "City of Firsts." (As the first colonial outpost in the Americas, Santo Domingo was the site of the first street, the first cathedral, the first fortress.) But there was no escaping the impact of my personal firsts: my first total immersion in a foreign language and culture, my first brush with salsa and merengue (their vibrant sound was everywhere), my first taste of avocados from the backyard tree, my first guitar lesson. My love and fascination for all things Latino was born during that formative and enlightening stay. I didn't return to Santo Domingo until this past year, more than 40 years later: It was like running into your first love, with all the dormant memories rushing back. Like me, the city had grown and changed and was almost unrecognizable. But it reminded me of how I had arrived—a wide-eyed innocent abroad—and left with a jolted curiosity that has been stuck in high gear ever since. As Herman Melville wrote in *Moby Dick,* I had "an everlasting itch for things remote."

It is rare that I return to a place where I have already been: There are simply too many places I haven't yet seen. When asked what my favorite trip was, I used to think it was the most recent, the one still the most vivid in my memory. But now I realize it is my next one. I always have a next one—or four—lined up before my suitcase is unpacked. I have been my own best customer, embracing the carpe-diem see-it-now spirit of *1,000 Places*, and have spent the years since the book's initial release in 2003 gathering more places to fill the pages of this edition. I'm sure I'll upset a lot of people who found the first list overwhelming. Now here I am, with a revision that I consider an entirely new book. There are 200-some brand-new entries, including 28 countries new to this edition. Some of these nations had simply not been on my radar before (Ghana, Nicaragua, South Korea); others were still reeling from the early days of independence from the Soviet Union (Estonia, Ukraine, Slovakia) when I was writing the original book. At that point, they were poorly equipped to welcome tourism, but today they guarantee visits that are a revelation. And then there are the many destinations that space requirements forced me to leave out of the original book in countries already well represented—I half-jokingly said I would save them for a sequel. Well, here they are: the Mani Peninsula in Greece, Chile's lake district, India's Golden Temple of Amritsar, the stuck-in-time Pleasantville Shaker Village in Kentucky, and the Mendoza wine country in Argentina, among others.

Arriving at this revision's final list of places was even more exciting and terrifying than with the original book—I mean, how many more opportunities was I going to have to get my Life List straight? To have carte blanche to compile an eclectic and all-encompassing list of far-flung gems like the man-made wonder of Petra and the overwhelming natural beauty of Patagonia, together with hedonistic beauties such as Brazil's Trancoso and the inimitable Seychelles island of La Digue? Well, that was a challenge for sure, but a whole lot of fun as well. I followed my heart and my gut, aiming for a glorious compilation of places both grand and humble, iconic and unsung. Drawing from a lifetime of wandering, I had nurtured an internal meter along the way that set off an alert when I was approaching something of particular beauty and awe—sometimes heart-stopping in its impact (think of thundering Victoria Falls of Zambia and Zimbabwe or the remarkable Military Tattoo in the shadow of Edinburgh's Castle), other times quietly and timelessly standing apart from the ordinary and waiting for our attention (the desolate and wind-blown Aran Islands off Ireland's west coast or a sunset sail through the Mekong Delta before it empties into the South China Sea).

But this list is much more than just my visceral response to the planet and its wonders. The amount of research I do before each trip would surprise those who think that when you book your ticket, your work is done. I read everything I can get my hands on, and have never met a guidebook

I didn't like: There is always some tidbit or trivia that catches my fancy, and I enjoy the sense of excitement in the author's words when sharing a discovery or secret—I hope you will hear the same in mine.

Before you do the math (how did I add 200-some new entries but still keep my original 1,000 favorites?), I should first explain that rethinking and reorganizing the book allowed me to open up new pages to fill with new adventures. I thoroughly deconstructed and then rewrote the wealth of information from the first *1,000 Places*, creating a whole new tantalizing homage to the world's bounty. Instead of featuring single locations as I had in the original, I have now merged two—and sometimes more—destinations into a single, more comprehensive piece, creating an embellished travel experience (in many cases a mini-itinerary). The original entries about gorgeous Shoal Bay Beach and the iconic hotels of Anguilla have become part of one entry that showcases the entire island: It is small enough to drive around in a day, and now you'll know where to stop along the way.

This book is a grab bag of all those wonders, a glorious mix of the unfamiliar and the predictable, a reminder that even in this global age of a homogenizing world, there are still remarkable and wonderful things to behold. In each of these thousand places, I hope I have imbued that same simple sense of wonder—like that of my nieces' Iceland odyssey or my journey to Santo Domingo when I first understood how far I could reach.

Who was it that said "You can't have a narrow mind if you have a fat passport"? I think travel makes you a better person and a more aware global citizen. I know that I cherish it as a privilege and a gift—it lifts me up, lightens me, expands me. Most important, and most simply, travel brings us joy. So, what are you waiting for? If you're waiting for a special occasion to make your next trip happen, then consider this: The day you get off the couch and head for the airport, that's the special occasion.

How This Book Is Organized

For the purposes of this book, I've divided the world into eight regions, which are further subdivided geographically:

- **Europe:** Great Britain and Ireland, Western Europe, Eastern Europe, Scandinavia
- **Africa:** North Africa, West Africa, East Africa and Southern Africa, the Islands of the Indian Ocean
- **The Middle East**
- **Asia:** East Asia, South and Central Asia, Southeast Asia
- **Australia, New Zealand, and the Pacific Islands**
- **The United States of America and Canada:** Subdivided by state or province
- **Latin America:** Mexico and Central

America, South America and Antarctica
- **The Caribbean, the Bahamas, and Bermuda**

Within these divisions, entries are further divided by country (see the table of contents for a quick reference), and within each country they're organized alphabetically by region or town. If you'd like to learn about destinations by type of experience, visit www.1000places.com/indexes, where you'll find 12 thematic indexes, including Gorgeous Beaches and Getaway Islands, Unrivaled Museums, and Sacred Places.

At the end of each entry is practical information that will help you in planning a trip—including telephone numbers, web addresses, and prices of the sites mentioned. But remember: Since travel information is always subject to change, you should confirm by phone or e-mail before you leave home.

How the Listings Are Organized

Here's a run-through of the information you'll see at the end of most of the entries.

Where

The distance of the site from a major city or airport.

Visitor info

The official website of the region's board of tourism.

Info and/or the Names of the Sites within the entry

The telephone and web address of the entry sites.

A note on phone numbers: All phone numbers in the book are listed with their country codes, so to call any of them from your home country, you simply have to dial your international access code (011 in the U.S. and Canada; 0011 in Australia; 00 in the U.K., Ireland, and New Zealand; etc.), then the listed number. U.S. and Canadian telephone numbers are listed without the country code; to call these countries from outside their borders, simply add the number "1" at the beginning, after dialing your international access code. In many countries, you must add a 0 before the local number when calling within the borders. (Naturally, you do not need to dial the country code in these instances.)

How

"How" includes information on recommended outfitters or operators who offer tours, treks, cruises, safaris, and other packages or customized travel to or within the destination.

Where to Stay

Hotels and inns listed under this head, though not discussed in the entry text, are good lodging recommendations located near the topic of the entry.

Cost

I've listed prices for all hotels, restaurants, and organized trips discussed in the entry, based on the following parameters:

Hotels: Listed hotel costs are per standard double room, unless noted otherwise. Where available, hotel entries include information for peak and off-peak seasons.

Complimentary breakfasts are not mentioned. Remember that many hotels are flexible with their prices—sometimes extremely so—offering various discounts to keep occupancy high throughout the year. Always make sure to check for special promotions on the hotel website and/or ask about them by phone.

Some hotels and resorts (and many safari lodges and camps and eco-lodges) post rates that are per person based on double occupancy and include breakfast and dinner (and sometimes lunch). For these I have noted prices that are per person, inclusive. When more amenities are included, such as guided tours, use of recreational facilities, lectures, classes, etc., it's noted as all-inclusive.

TRIPS/TREKS/EXCURSIONS/CRUISES: Trip costs are usually given in total, per person, based on double occupancy. They are noted as all-inclusive when accommodations, meals, land or water transportation, amenities, etc., are included. When these are only partially included, it's noted as inclusive. Airfare is not included unless specifically stated.

RESTAURANTS: Meal prices listed are per person and represent the approximate total cost of a three-course a la carte meal without wine. The price of a prix-fixe menu is given when it is the only offering or is particularly recommended. Costs are rarely given for bars, pubs, or cafés.

WHEN

For the most part, "When" indicates seasonal closings. It will *not* appear if the establishment is open year-round, or if the seasonal closing is brief (less than 6 weeks). For package trips, "When" includes the months that the outfitter offers a particular trip.

In general, it's wise to contact hotels, restaurants, and attractions if traveling during off-season months to confirm that they are open, and also to bear in mind peak season crowds or large local or cultural holidays when hotels at your destination may be full. The Bank Holidays of the World website (www.bank-holidays.com) maintains a worldwide database of public holidays during which you may encounter crowds or closures.

BEST TIMES

For most entries, I've listed the best months to visit, taking into account weather, local festivals, sports and leisure opportunities, peak tourist crowds, and other significant events. When no "Best times" are listed, the reason is the place is "wonderful anytime." For example, it is always a good time to visit the Louvre in Paris!

Travel Safety

This book represents travel opportunities in an ideal, peaceful world. However, that's not the world we live in today. Travelers will generally be perfectly safe visiting most of the destinations discussed, but a few places may pose some risk, either currently or in the future. Therefore, before making plans to travel to destinations with which you're not familiar, be sure to do your homework, especially if you will be traveling alone. The U.S. Department of State maintains travel advisories on its website at www

.travel.state.gov. Other information listed includes a general overview of each country, entry requirements for U.S. citizens, and information on health, safety, crime, and other travel issues.

The British Foreign & Commonwealth Office maintains similar information on its website, www.fco.gov.uk, in the "Travel and living abroad" section.

Travel Documents

In addition to a valid passport, many countries listed in this book require that foreign citizens obtain travel visas in advance of their trip. U.S. citizens can look online at www.travel.state.gov, which notes the documentation required for each country and provides a link to the country's embassy. British citizens should go to www.fco.gov.uk.

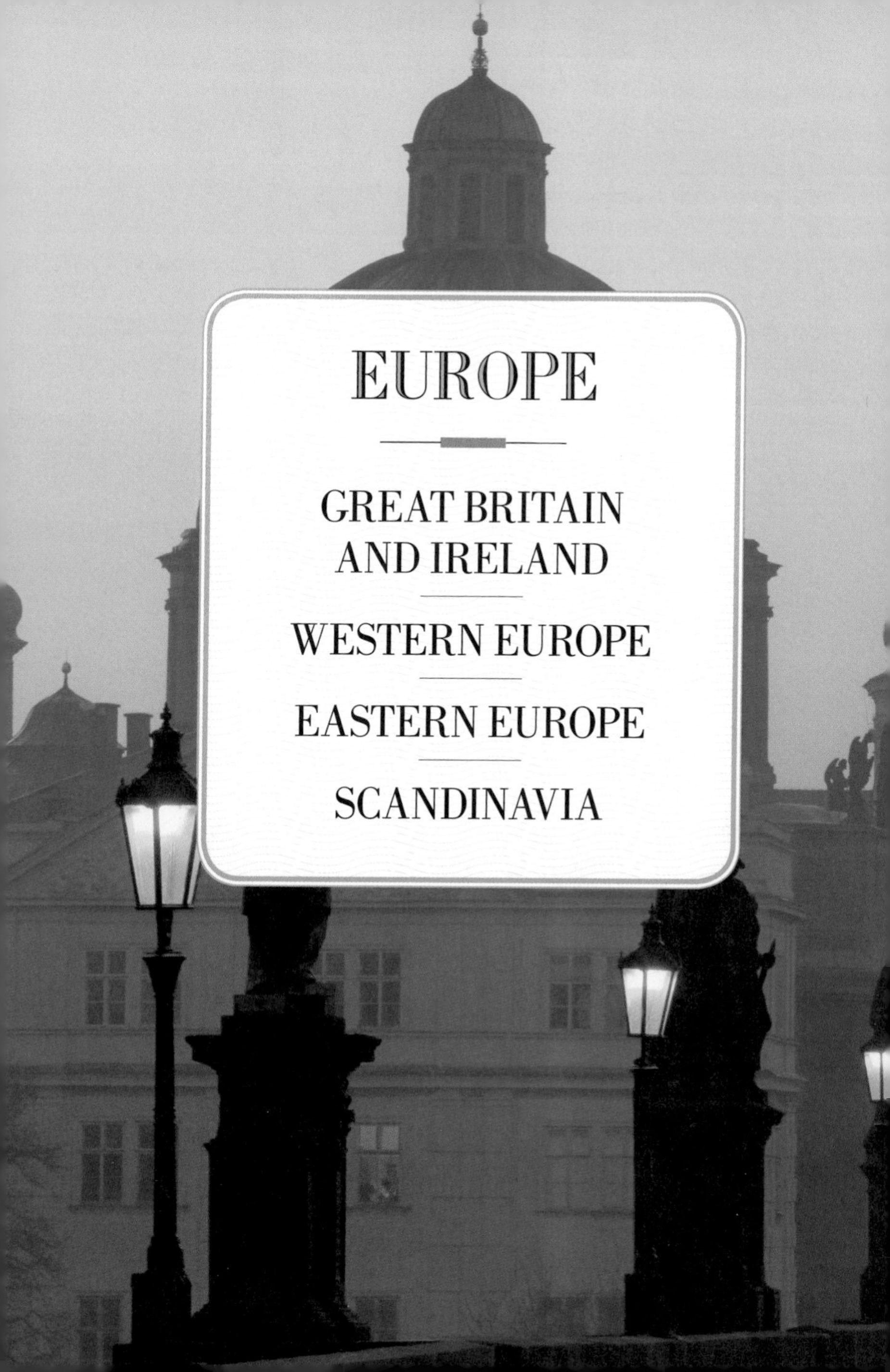
EUROPE
GREAT BRITAIN AND IRELAND
WESTERN EUROPE
EASTERN EUROPE
SCANDINAVIA

ARCTIC OCEAN
Reykjavík
ICELAND
Faroe Islands
Greenland
0 200 400 MILES
0 322 644 Kilometers
NORWEGIAN SEA
NORWAY
SWEDEN
FINLAND
KOLA PENINSULA
URAL MOUNTAINS
N
S
E
W
0 200 400 MILES
0 322 644 Kilometers
Oslo
Stockholm
BALTIC SEA
Helsinki
Tallinn
ESTONIA
Riga
LATVIA
LITHUANIA
Vilnius
RUSSIA
Moscow
Volga
N. IRELAND
SCOTLAND
NORTH SEA
IRELAND
Dublin
UNITED KINGDOM
DENMARK
Copenhagen
NETHERLANDS
WALES
London
ENGLAND
Amsterdam
The Hague
Brussels
Elbe
Berlin
POLAND
Warsaw
Minsk
BELARUS
ATLANTIC OCEAN
GERMANY
Paris
Prague
CZECH REP.
Kiev
UKRAINE
CARPATHIANS
1 BELGIUM
2 LUXEMBOURG
3 SWITZERLAND
4 LIECHTENSTEIN
5 SLOVENIA
6 CROATIA
7 BOSNIA-HERZEGOVINA
8 SERBIA
9 MONTENEGRO
10 MACEDONIA
Loire
FRANCE
Danube
SLOVAKIA
Vienna
Bratislava
MOLDOVA
Bay of Biscay
Bern
ALPS
AUSTRIA
Budapest
HUNGARY
Ljubljana
Zagreb
ROMANIA
Belgrade
Bucharest
GEORGIA
Tbilisi
PORTUGAL
Madrid
PYRENEES
MONACO
Sarajevo
Danube
BLACK SEA
Lisbon
Tagus
SPAIN
ANDORRA
Corsica
Rome
ITALY
BULGARIA
Balearic Islands
Sardinia
Strait of Gibraltar
MEDITERRANEAN SEA
ALBANIA
GREECE
Sicily
Athens
Crete
MALTA
CYPRUS

GREAT BRITAIN AND IRELAND

Hallowed Seat of Academia

CAMBRIDGE UNIVERSITY

Cambridgeshire, England

Cambridge is one of Europe's oldest centers of learning—with its first college founded in 1284—and one of the most prestigious as well. Its 31 colleges have produced alumni as varied as John Milton, Stephen Hawking, Iris Murdoch, Isaac Newton, Charles Darwin, and Oliver Cromwell, and it consistently ranks among the world's top universities.

Greatest of all its historic sights is King's College Chapel, called by Henry James "the most beautiful [chapel] in England." Begun in 1441, it remains the country's finest example of the late-Gothic English style known as Perpendicular. Rubens's 17th-century *Adoration of the Magi* hangs behind the main altar, softly lit by vast 16th-century stained-glass windows beneath an awe-inspiring fan-vaulted ceiling. If you're here on Christmas Eve and join the long line early, you may get to attend the much-loved Festival of Nine Carols and Lessons sung by a student choir, a tradition since 1918.

In spring and summer enjoy a classic view of the chapel from the Backs, the mile-long strip of emerald green lawns along the banks of the lovely River Cam, where "punting"—floating on a wooden, flat-bottomed boat slowly maneuvered by a pole—is a pastime not to be missed. Be sure to include a visit to the Fitzwilliam Museum, one of Britain's oldest and finest public art museums. Its prize collection centers around 17th-century Dutch art, enriched with masterpieces by everyone from Titian and Michelangelo to the French Impressionists.

Wander down the town's narrow lanes lined with cluttered bookstores, historic inns, and pubs, and quench your thirst at the Eagle, where students have been propping up the bar for centuries. Then retire to the nearby Hotel du Vin, a stylish, modern lodging option in a medieval former university building, today well known for its classic bistro. Or leave the city behind and stay at the Hotel Felix, a large Victorian manse about a mile from the town center, with sleek contemporary rooms and an excellent restaurant.

WHERE: 55 miles/88 km north of London. **VISITOR INFO:** www.visitcambridge.org. **FITZWILLIAM MUSEUM:** Tel 44/1223-332-900; www.fitzmuseum.cam.ac.uk. **HOTEL DU VIN:** Tel 44/1223-227-330; www.hotelduvin.com. *Cost:* from $225; dinner $45. **HOTEL FELIX:** Tel 44/1223-277-977; www.hotelfelix.co.uk. *Cost:* from $195; dinner $50. **BEST TIME:** May–Sep for nicest weather.

The River Cam flows through the heart of the university.

A Walled City and Architectural Feast

CHESTER

Cheshire, England

The city of Chester boasts a broad and intriguing cross-section of English history stretching back more than 2,000 years. It was important in Roman times (the remains of the country's largest amphitheater are here), then again in the Middle Ages, and once more during an 18th-century revival that inspired author James Boswell to write in 1779: "It pleases me more than any town I ever saw." Chester still has much to show for its historical heydays. A well-preserved fortified wall, constructed during the Roman period and rebuilt over the following centuries, surrounds much of the city. Its ramparts are topped by a 2-mile footpath, providing a lovely vantage point on the pinkish red sandstone tower and spires of the medieval cathedral and passing the 19th-century Eastgate, where Chester's famous wrought-iron clock tower proudly stands.

Within the walls is one of England's best collections of half-timbered buildings, some of their façades a riot of black-and-white patterns. Especially famous are the Rows: highly decorated two-story buildings with connecting walkways above street level. After a day full of history and architecture, repair to the serenity of the city's premier hotel, the Chester Grosvenor. This Tudor-style building in the heart of the historic neighborhood is owned by the Duke of Westminster's Grosvenor Estate and traces its origins to the reign of Queen Elizabeth I. Its sophisticated Simon Radley restaurant, named after its noted chef, is one of the finest in the region. If you prefer relaxing away from the center's bustle, the Stone Villa, in the neighborhood of Hoole, is a friendly ten-room guesthouse with a professional and welcoming staff. It is less than a mile from the historic sites, a pleasant 15-minute walk.

WHERE: 207 miles/333 km northwest of London. **CHESTER GROSVENOR:** Tel 44/1244-324-024; www.chestergrosvenor.com. *Cost:* from $390; dinner $105. **STONE VILLA:** Tel 44/1244-345-014; www.stonevillachester.co.uk. *Cost:* from $115. **BEST TIMES:** May–Sep for pleasant weather; Jul (typically) for the classical Summer Music Festival.

Treasures at the End of the Earth

LAND'S END

Cornwall, England

Land's End is the far southwestern tip of the English mainland, where the country plunges over sheer cliffs and into the Atlantic. Once the ancient kingdom of Kernow, now the county of Cornwall, this timeless landscape is rich in history and atmosphere. Once upon a time, a lonely pub called the First-and-Last Inn stood here; now there's a theme park, but the natural scenery never fails to be awe-inspiring.

St. Michael's Mount is dedicated to the archangel of the same name, who is said to have appeared here in a vision in the year 495.

A few miles east is the fantastical castle-topped island of St. Michael's Mount, attached to the mainland by nothing more than a cobbled causeway that's covered at high tide. It was originally created in 1135 as a sister abbey to the more famous Mont St-Michel across the English Channel in Normandy (see p. 110). The arduous climb to the top, rising 250 feet from the sea, is well worth it for the dazzling views. Nearby, on the mainland, is Penzance, the westernmost town in England, a workaday port famous as the home of Gilbert and Sullivan's singing pirates. Hidden away in a narrow lane is the Abbey Hotel, a historic building that 1960s supermodel Jean Shrimpton turned into one of the most eclectic and charming hotels around. For more history, plus a pint of Cornish ale, visit the Turk's Head, an old pub in the center of town, famously damaged—along with much of old Penzance—during a Spanish invasion in 1595, but thriving today.

Ferries leave from Penzance for the Isles of Scilly, a group of 100-plus mostly uninhabited rocky islands. Warmed by the Gulf Stream, they feature unspoiled beaches, exotic palms, and swarms of rare sea birds. You'll even find world-famous subtropical gardens on the island of Tresco. The only place worth staying on this car-free escape is also one of its highlights: The Island House offers a seasonal sailing school, noted gardens, and open views of the sea and other islands.

Northeast of Land's End is the little holiday resort and harbor town of St. Ives, where an almost Mediterranean quality of light has attracted artists for many years. A Cubist tumble of well-kept white cottages overlooks a bay, and art galleries and artisans' shops line the narrow streets. London's Tate Gallery has an offshoot here in a handsome rotunda above the sea. Nearby is the Barbara Hepworth Museum and Sculpture Garden, studio and home of St. Ives's leading artist, who, together with her husband, painter Ben Nicholson, helped establish this port town as a haven for avant-garde and abstract artists in the 1930s. After browsing the galleries or riding the surf, relax at one of St. Ives's best hotels, Primrose Valley, a delightfully stylish, friendly option on the seafront.

Where: 332 miles/534 km southwest of London. **St. Michael's Mount:** www.stmichaelsmount.co.uk. **Abbey Hotel:** Tel 44/1736-366-906; www.theabbeyonline.co.uk. *Cost:* from $195. *When:* closed early Jan–late Mar. **Island House:** Tel 44/1720-423-008; www.tresco.co.uk. *Cost:* from $400, inclusive. **Tate St. Ives:** Tel 44/1736-796-226; www.tate.org.uk/stives. **Primrose Valley Hotel:** Tel 44/1736-794-939; www.primroseonline.co.uk. *Cost:* from $150 (off-peak), from $195 (peak). **Best times:** Apr–Oct for best weather; Sep for St. Ives September Festival for music and art.

Tropical Air and Mediterranean Flavors

Padstow and St. Mawes

Cornwall, England

On the ruggedly beautiful north coast of Cornwall is the friendly port of Padstow. This is one of the region's oldest towns, founded in the 6th century and quaint enough to attract those en route to Land's End (see p. 4).

But most visitors come explicitly to dine at the Seafood Restaurant, a light, airy, plant-filled restaurant housed in a former quayside grain warehouse. Diners thrill to classic dishes (grilled Dover sole, local oysters) and imaginative adaptations (a light bouillabaisse, seafood ravioli) alike. Chef-owner, author, BBC food-series personality, and pioneering seafood guru Rick Stein is perhaps best known for his signature fruits de mer plate, handpicked off the trawlers bobbing outside. Devotees can stay overnight in rooms above the restaurant or at one of Stein's other stylish and comfortable accommodations in town.

Another wondrous example of nature's bounty can be enjoyed about 15 miles south of Padstow at the Eden Project, where two giant greenhouses (the largest in the world) form a unique oasis of trees and plants. Conceived in the 1990s by Tim Smit, the project was completed in 2001, and today it is one of the most visited sites in the region. The larger is the moist, tropical biome, where palms and giant bamboo grow as well as commercial crops such as bananas, coffee, and rubber. Raised wooden walkways take visitors past a plunging waterfall. Next door, the Mediterranean biome is warm and dry, with plants that thrive in more arid conditions, including olive trees and grape vines.

An easy half-hour drive along the Cornish Riviera leads to the picturesque fishing village of St. Mawes and the Hotel Tresanton. Here, Olga Polizzi (scion of England's most famous hotel dynasty, the Fortes) has created a boutique hotel above the sea with breezy terraces, gorgeous views, and a simple but superb restaurant specializing in local ingredients with hints of Spanish and Italian influence.

Where: 250 miles/400 km southwest of London. **The Seafood Restaurant:** Tel 44/1841-532-700; www.rickstein.com. *Cost:* from $150; dinner $75. **Eden Project:** Tel 44/1726-811-911; www.edenproject.com. **Hotel Tresanton:** Tel 44/1326-270-055; www.tresanton.com. *Cost:* from $325; dinner $60. **Best time:** Apr–Oct for finest weather.

The "Palace of the Peak" in the Heart of England

Chatsworth House

Bakewell, Derbyshire, England

Of the many historic "Stately Homes" and "Great Houses" enriching England's countryside, Chatsworth is one of the most impressive. The centuries-old seat of the dukes of Devonshire, this Baroque palace was built in the late 17th century and has some 300 rooms, the most spectacular of which are open to the public. Lavish state apartments are decorated with a wealth of treasures, and the chapel features one of the finest Baroque interiors in all of England. The prodigious art collection includes paintings by such masters as Tintoretto, Veronese, and Rembrandt, enhanced with more contemporary works, including portraits by Lucian Freud.

Alongside the house is a 100-acre garden landscaped by the famed Lancelot "Capability" Brown in the 1760s; a century later, the equally esteemed Joseph Paxton transformed it into one of the most celebrated gardens in all of Europe. A highlight is the stepped Cascade waterfall along with the seasonally changing display of contemporary sculptures. Surrounding the property are another thousand acres of parkland, where herds of deer graze on the grassy plain by the river, and a steep wooded hillside provides the backdrop.

Beyond the manicured Chatsworth lies a very different landscape: the craggy moors and limestone dales of the Peak District, England's oldest national park. The little market town of Bakewell lies just a few miles away; it is famous across England as the birthplace of the Bakewell Pudding. Every local tearoom and bakery claims to make the best, but start your quest at the Old Original Bakewell Pudding Shop to sample the goods eaten hot, with custard or cream, or choose among the various renditions if you're in town for the busy outdoor market on Monday.

WHERE: 150 miles/241 km north of London. Tel 44/1246-565-300; www.chatsworth.org. **OLD ORIGINAL BAKEWELL PUDDING SHOP:** Tel 44/1629-812-193; www.bakewellpuddingshop.co.uk. **BEST TIMES:** May and Sep for the gardens; Mon for market day in Bakewell.

A team of 18 gardeners works to maintain Chatsworth House's historic grounds, with the help of some four-legged friends.

Luxurious Stays in Romantic Countryside

DARTMOOR

Devon, England

England's Southwest Peninsula—and especially the county of Devon—is renowned as a green and lush destination. Fertile conditions and a long farming heritage explain why it's the home of Devon cream and the sacrosanct tradition of sitting down to a Devonshire tea. At the center of this bucolic idyll, though, lies a very different landscape: the high hills and rocky outcrops of Dartmoor, with 368 square miles of countryside protected as one of England's many national parks. Surrounding its wild, dramatic moors are delightful wooded valleys, where streams and rivers meander along or plunge over waterfalls. A maze of footpaths is perfect for strolls or more energetic hikes. Other activities include excellent trout fishing and visiting Dartmoor's famous country houses and gardens.

Chagford is a good base for exploring the park. It is also where you'll find the secluded and elegant Gidleigh Park, a Tudor-style mansion built in 1928 on over 100 magnificent acres. From the terraced patio, guests hear only the rushing waters of the North Teign River. Gidleigh Park is also one of the country's finest eating establishments, with chef Michael Caines at the helm since 1994 and featuring an unrivaled wine cellar.

Anglers revere the Arundell Arms, an old coach inn, just to the west of Dartmoor in the village of Lifton. It has been a premier fishing hotel for more than half a century, with 20 miles of private access to the River Tamar, one of the best salmon rivers in England and home to wild brown trout and sea trout too. Exceptional cuisine and delightful accommodations add to the experience, making the Arundell Arms a standout among a vanishing breed of well-heeled sporting hotels.

Or exchange river for sea: Head south of Dartmoor to the coast and the Burgh Island Hotel, a romantic Art Deco retreat that conjures up the Jazz Age, located on its own 26-acre private island off the southern coast of Devon (the closest mainland village is Bigbury-on-Sea). It holds a special place in history too: The Duke of Windsor and Wallis Simpson escaped the attention of the world here, Noël Coward sipped gin cocktails at the bar, and Agatha Christie (who was born in Devon) wrote *And Then There Were None* during a visit in the early 1930s.

WHERE: 230 miles/384 km southwest of London. **VISITOR INFO:** www.dartmoor.co.uk. **GIDLEIGH PARK:** Tel 44/1647-432-367; www.gidleigh.com. *Cost:* from $510; dinner $150. **ARUNDELL ARMS:** Tel 44/1566-784-666; www.arundellarms.com. *Cost:* from $270. **BURGH ISLAND HOTEL:** Tel 44/1548-810-514; www.burghisland.com. *Cost:* from $600, inclusive. **BEST TIMES:** Apr–Sep; May for wildflowers; Aug for heather on the moor turning purple.

Where the Moors Meet the Sea

EXMOOR

Devon and Somerset, England

In a beautiful corner of the West Country, where Somerset becomes Devon, sits the dramatic and romantic landscape of Exmoor National Park. On the high hills, bare of trees, are the remains of Bronze Age settlements, while streams and rivers cut steep-sided valleys down to the sea—most famously, the boulder-scattered Valley of the Rocks.

Just north of the Valley of the Rocks, the rolling hills suddenly meet the sea at the Bristol Channel, with Wales beyond. The landscape is cut as if by a giant knife, with cliffs plummeting to the surf below. Tucked into a bay are the twin Victorian towns of Lynmouth and Lynton, linked by a century-old funicular railway, which uses cables and the power of water to carry passengers up and down the steep cliff face. Near the harbor is the Rising Sun, a 14th-century smugglers' inn of crooked beams, uneven floors, and thick walls. Percy Bysshe Shelley supposedly chose the inn's private thatch-roofed cottage for his honeymoon with his first wife, Harriet, in 1812; it is a cozy refuge with a four-poster bed, lovely views of the quaint little harbor and its bobbing boats, and "a climate so mild," wrote Shelley, "that myrtles of immense size twine up our cottage, and roses bloom in the open air in winter." From here myriad footpaths make the perfect starting point for inland forays onto the sweeping moors of the national park; the coastal path will take you to the sheer face of Countisbury Cliffs, which at 1,200 feet are the highest in England. Enjoy bracing sea winds and breathtaking scenery before ambling back "home" to the lovely Rising Sun, whose smiling staff and warm fireplace make the restaurant's freshly caught salmon and lobster taste extra scrumptious.

Where: 200 miles/320 km southwest of London. **Visitor info:** www.visit-exmoor.co.uk. **The Rising Sun Hotel:** Tel 44/1598-753-223; www.risingsunlynmouth.co.uk. *Cost:* from $210; dinner $35. **Best time:** Sep–Nov for heather at its most beautiful.

The European Circuit's Summertime Standout

Glyndebourne Festival

Lewes, East Sussex, England

For true opera fans, summer in Europe remains sacred, with no lovelier setting than at the renowned Glyndebourne Festival, amid the green hills of the Sussex Downs. The cream of British society has been flocking here since 1934, to a grand country estate whose small but charming old opera house was replaced in 1994 by a much larger, modern theater with excellent acoustics. Even skeptical old-timers love the new building, and more seating means tickets are somewhat less difficult to come by. Serious aficionados know they'll find world-class standards in the festival's innovative repertoire, which offers a little of everything for everyone, performed by international artists both established and emerging. The festival also provides the social season's highlight: the ritual evening picnic enjoyed on a garden-framed lawn that stretches before the graceful neo-Elizabethan manor, private home of the festival founder's son. Sheep and cows graze within sight while musicians tune up in the background.

To get there, hop on the train from London for the one-hour trip to the charming country town of Lewes, from which Glyndebourne is just 3 miles by taxi. Or book a room at one of the many small historic hotels in Lewes, such as the Shelleys (formerly in the family of poet Percy Bysshe Shelley), a polished favorite located in a 1588 town house on the main street. The hotel's garden offers views of the Sussex Downs, while the restaurant serves award-winning food in a relaxed and traditional setting.

The 400-year-old creeper-covered Gravetye Manor, a 20-mile drive out of town, is the perfect luxurious match for Glyndebourne. It is one of the oldest baronial manors in Sussex, filled with comfortable furniture and surrounded by famously gorgeous gardens. It also has one of the area's best chefs (who packs a fantastic gourmet picnic hamper for the opera).

Where: 55 miles/88 km south of London. Tel 44/1273-813-813; www.glyndebourne.com. *Cost:* tickets $50–$375. *When:* late May–Aug. **The Shelleys:** Tel 44/1273-472-361; www.the-shelleys.co.uk. *Cost:* from $185 (off-peak), $285 (peak); dinner $55. **Gravetye Manor:** Tel 44/1342-810-567; www.gravetyemanor.co.uk. *Cost:* from $380; dinner $60.

Timeless Tableau of the English Countryside

THE COTSWOLDS

Gloucestershire, Worcestershire, and Oxfordshire, England

The Cotswolds is the quintessence of rural England, stretching about 100 miles between Bath and Stratford-upon-Avon (see pp. 26 and 28) and marked on its western side by a steep slope called the Cotswold Edge.

Sheep graze in the fields, as they have for centuries; wool was the key commodity here in the Middle Ages, and almost every once-prosperous town in the region has a Sheep Street and an impressive church or cathedral built with the industry's profits. Most of the villages are constructed from the local honey-colored stone and have preserved their character despite being unabashedly devoted to tourism.

Turrets and gargoyles grace Broadway Tower.

At the northern end of the hills sits pristine Chipping Campden, with its showpiece main street and famous 10-acre Hidcote Gardens. Nearby is the deservedly popular village of Broadway, its architecturally striking High Street lined with antiques stores. Removed from Broadway's hubbub, Buckland Manor hotel is a former Elizabethan home that is surprisingly unfussy despite a superb dinner elegantly served amid silver domes and candlelight. It's a 3-mile hike to Broadway Tower, the highest point around and a favorite picnic spot.

Continue south, to the towns of Stow-on-the-Wold, Moreton-in-Marsh, and Bourton-on-the-Water sitting astride the Fosse Way, an ancient Roman road. Like Broadway, Stow is famous for its antiques shops, while Bourton's streams have earned it the nickname "the Venice of the Cotswolds." The nearby village of Bibury was chosen by William Morris, father of the Arts and Crafts Movement, as the most beautiful in England.

The Cotswolds is a prime area for walkers, whether they seek gentle riverside strolls or more serious hikes. One of the most popular long-distance trails is the Cotswold Way, a clearly marked path along the crest of the Cotswold Edge from Bath to Chipping Campden. The whole 102-mile route is usually completed in 7 to 10 days, with hikers lodging at comfortable inns or B&Bs along the way; for a shorter trek, follow the beautiful section of path north of Winchcombe.

A more relaxing tour lets you saunter along the tranquil valleys of the rivers Colne or Windrush. On the banks of the latter, the old market town of Burford offers another enticing place to stay: the 15th-century inn The Lamb, with traditionally decorated rooms and a great restaurant. Top off your tour of this region with a stay in the spa town of Cheltenham (just to the west of the Cotswolds), with its beautiful Regency-era Promenade, gardens, and famous horse-racing festival.

WHERE: 140 miles/225 km from London. **BUCKLAND MANOR:** Tel 44/1386-852-626; www.bucklandmanor.co.uk. *Cost:* from $340; dinner $75. **THE LAMB:** Tel 44/1993-823-155; www.cotswold-inns-hotels.co.uk. *Cost:* from $250; dinner $50. **BEST TIMES:** May–Oct for nice weather and numerous town fairs; Mar for the Cheltenham Festival, which includes the Gold Cup horse race.

Queens of the High Seas

CUNARD'S CRUISE LINERS

Southampton, Hampshire, England

In 1840, Samuel Cunard secured the first contract to carry mail by steamship between Britain and America, and to this day the cruise line that bears his name remains the most recognized in the world. The first ships were paddle steamers, the fastest vessels of their time, serving the route from Liverpool in England to Halifax and Boston in North America. In the early years of the 20th century, Cunard's flagships on the transatlantic route were the *Mauretania* and the *Lusitania,* the latter tragically sunk at the outset of World War I.

By the 1960s, though airplanes were taking over transatlantic travel, Cunard's flagship was the *Queen Elizabeth 2* (usually shortened to *QE2*), a classic ocean liner built specifically for the North Atlantic passage. For more than 30 years the *QE2* was the only ship sailing that route on a regular schedule. Carrying about 1,800 passengers, she was the epitome of luxury, strength, and speed in an age of jetliners and more prosaic cruise ships, delivering an old-fashioned Atlantic crossing filled with white-glove service, informal lectures, a preponderance of eating options, idle hours in the top-drawer spa or library, and much gazing out over the rail at the high seas.

In 2003, *QE2* sailed her last transatlantic voyage, replaced by her younger—but much larger and more luxurious—sibling *Queen Mary 2.* The *Queen Victoria* joined the fleet in 2007, and a brand-new *Queen Elizabeth* followed in 2010. The three Cunard Queens cruise the world from the Caribbean to the Baltic, while the *Queen Mary 2* continues the original Cunard legacy as the only ship to consistently ply the historic transatlantic route between Southampton and New York on a regular schedule.

WHERE: westbound departures from Southampton, 80 miles/130 km southwest of London. Eastbound departures from Brooklyn, NY. In England, tel 0845-3565-555; www.cunard.co.uk; in the U.S., tel 800-728-6273; www.cunard.com. *Cost:* 7-night transatlantic crossings on the *QM2,* from $845. **WHEN:** year-round Cunard itineraries; Apr–Nov for transatlantic crossings on the *QM2.*

A Medieval Wonder That Still Surprises

WINCHESTER CATHEDRAL

Winchester, Hampshire, England

Work first began on Winchester Cathedral in 1079, on the site of an even older Saxon church, to create what would be the longest cathedral in existence (526 feet), famous as well for its soaring 12-bay nave.

The surrounding city of Winchester, which still feels like a market town, is even older than the cathedral. As capital of the Anglo-Saxon kingdom of Wessex and the seat of legendary King Alfred the Great, Winchester was a major religious, political, and commercial center in the 9th century. Be sure to visit the Great Hall, another medieval masterpiece in town, where King Arthur's iconic Round Table is displayed, a potent centerpiece of English mythology and literature.

While slightly austere on the outside, the cathedral has a grand and awe-inspiring interior. Lovers of classic English literature can pay a visit to the tomb of novelist Jane Austen (1775–1817) in a quiet corner of the church. They may combine a Winchester excursion with a visit to Chawton Cottage, her pleasant country home 15 miles west of town. Now the Jane Austen's House Museum, this is where many of her greatest works—including *Emma* and *Persuasion*—were penned. Victorian author Thomas Hardy (1840–1928) hailed from the neighboring county of Dorset and also mined this bucolic area for literary inspiration. He revived the historic name of Wessex in works such as *The Return of the Native* and *Far from the Madding Crowd* and renamed many local towns and cities—Dorchester became "Casterbridge" and Winchester "Wintoncester," where Tess (as in *Tess of the d'Urbervilles*) was executed.

Walkers can get a taste of the landscape by following the South Downs Way from Winchester eastward toward Beacon Hill or the village of Exton. For more of a challenge, follow this national trail 107 miles, all the way to Eastbourne in Sussex and the famous white cliffs of the Seven Sisters.

The interior contains original medieval tiles and wall paintings.

You'd do well to check into Lainston House Hotel, a stately old redbrick mansion dating from 1683, set among fabulous gardens and famously featuring a mile-long avenue of lime trees. The food and service are the principal draws, while the atmosphere is relaxed and inspiring, with log fires in winter and croquet on the lawn in summer.

WHERE: 72 miles/116 km southwest of London. **VISITOR INFO:** www.winchester-cathedral.org.uk. **JANE AUSTEN'S HOUSE:** Tel 44/1420-83262; www.jane-austens-house-museum.org.uk. **LAINSTON HOUSE HOTEL:** Tel 44/1962-776-088; www.lainstonhouse.com. *Cost:* from $255; dinner $80. **BEST TIMES:** 2nd and last Sun of every month for market.

A Retreat for Royal R&R

OSBORNE HOUSE

Isle of Wight, England

The Isle of Wight lies off the southern coast of England, a short ferry ride from the major ports of Southampton and Portsmouth, or, more scenically, from the little harbor town of Lymington. The island's name is derived from Vectis, the name given to it by the Romans when they settled here some 2,000 years ago. In the 19th century, Charles Dickens was drawn to its sandy beaches and dramatic cliffs, while another man of letters, poet Alfred Lord Tennyson, spent time strolling the hills overlooking the sea.

A compact 23 by 13 miles, it is a favorite summer destination of the British. Its most visited site is Osborne House, the cherished home of Queen Victoria and Prince Albert that was constructed at Victoria's own expense as a seaside retreat in 1845. It was here that they managed to leave royal responsibilities behind, enjoying long walks and informal family dinners with their nine children. Grief-stricken at Albert's death in 1861 at the age of 42, Victoria requested that everything remain exactly as it had been in his final days. Family mementos fill the bedroom where the queen died in 1901.

A few miles south of Osborne House is the island's capital, Newport, and 11th-century Carisbrooke Castle. The best-preserved Norman castle in the country, it provides spectacular views for those who climb to the top of the keep. A less enthusiastic visitor, Charles I, was held hostage here by Oliver Cromwell in 1647 pending execution: His attempt to escape was foiled when he got stuck between the iron window bars.

The island is crisscrossed with hiking trails, including the 67-mile Coastal Path, which encircles the island. A favorite section crosses Tennyson Down, past a monument celebrating the poet, then continues to the western tip of the island for outstanding views of the Needles, three offshore rock pinnacles battered by the waves of the English Channel.

If you cross to the island from the New Forest (see p. 30) via the Lymington ferry, stop at the George Hotel in the historic town of Yarmouth. Dating from 1764, it is known for its traditional ambience, waterfront location, and the fine Brasserie restaurant, making this old inn a popular choice.

WHERE: 90 miles/145 km southwest of London. **VISITOR INFO:** www.islandbreaks.co.uk. **OSBORNE HOUSE:** Tel 44/1983-200-022; www.english-heritage.org.uk. **GEORGE HOTEL:** Tel 44/1983-533-814; www.thegeorge.co.uk. *Cost:* from $285; dinner $60. **BEST TIME:** early Aug for the yachting festival Cowes Week.

The Mother Church of the Anglican World

CANTERBURY CATHEDRAL

Canterbury, Kent, England

The seat of the Anglican Church, Canterbury Cathedral is one of the most beautiful in all of England, and also among the country's holiest pilgrimage sites, thanks to a seminal incident in British history that took place here in 1170: Archbishop Thomas Becket was cruelly murdered in the cathedral by four knights allegedly following the orders of King Henry II. Becket was canonized 3 years later, while a repentant Henry established the cathedral as the center of English Christianity.

The surrounding city of Canterbury, located on the main route from London to the English Channel port of Dover, was already an important town in ancient Roman times. It gained further favor when, in A.D. 597, St. Augustine was sent by Pope Gregory the Great to convert the heathen Anglo-Saxons to

Christianity; St. Augustine established Canterbury as his base, and became first Archbishop of Canterbury. Canterbury's importance as a religious center was then immortalized by the great 14th-century English poet Geoffrey Chaucer in his epic poem *The Canterbury Tales*, told by a group of pilgrims traveling from London to St. Thomas Becket's shrine.

Much of Canterbury was destroyed during a 1942 World War II air raid, but the cathedral remained largely unscathed, including its outstanding 12th- and 13th-century stained-glass windows, which locals temporarily removed for safekeeping. The most important are considered to be the Great West Window, the Bible Windows, and the suitably named Miracle Windows, while the spot where Becket died is now marked by a solitary candle.

Stained-glass panels depict biblical figures.

Many modern-day pilgrims come to Canterbury by train as a day trip from London. Others spend the night at the Abode Canterbury, a boutique hotel very near the cathedral, offering contemporary luxury in a building that dates back to the 16th century. Day-trippers should at least linger for a meal at the excellent hotel restaurant under the supervision of the acclaimed chef Michael Caines before catching the last train back to London.

WHERE: 56 miles/90 km southeast of London. www.canterbury-cathedral.org. **ABODE CANTERBURY:** Tel 44/1227-766-266. www.abodehotels.co.uk/canterbury. *Cost:* from $180; dinner $60. **BEST TIMES:** Sat–Sun, 2:30 P.M. and Mon–Fri, 4:30 P.M. for Evensong.

A Magnificent Pile of Medieval Origin

LEEDS CASTLE

Maidstone, Kent, England

Like a lady of the lake, Leeds Castle appears as if a mirage, its buff-colored stone and crenellated towers reflected in the distinctive waters of the ornamental pond and moat. Described by historian Lord Conway as the loveliest castle in the world, it is historically noteworthy as well as visually striking. Construction began in the 12th century (replacing a wooden structure built in the 9th century), when the site was known as Esledes. It was much loved as a royal residence, not unlike Balmoral today (see p. 40), from 1278, when it was given to Edward I by a wealthy courtier seeking favor. Henry VIII enjoyed spending time here, and he invested much effort and money in expanding and redecorating it to look more like a royal palace and less like a military fortress. For many years it was a dower castle: six queens called it their favorite residence. Its lake-like moat is unlike any other castle setting in England.

The castle stands at the heart of 500 acres of gardens and parkland that are perfect for country walks; it includes an aviary opened in 1988 that is considered one of the best in the country. Then there is the unlikely Dog Collar Museum (dogs once played an important role in guarding the grounds): It sounds like an oddity but winds up being a highlight for many visitors. The collection spans a period of 400 years, and some of the collars are veritable works of art.

WHERE: 40 miles/64 km southeast of London (not to be confused with the city of Leeds in Yorkshire, in northern England). Tel 44/1622-765-400; www.leeds-castle.com. **BEST TIME:** Apr–Jun for the gardens.

Eden on London's Doorstep

SISSINGHURST CASTLE GARDEN

Sissinghurst, Kent, England

Situated southeast of London, the wealthy and fertile county of Kent lives up to its affectionate nickname of "The Garden of England." The most renowned gardens in this "Garden"—and some of the most beloved in a nation besotted with them—are found at Sissinghurst. Vita Sackville-West—Bloomsbury writer and famed eccentric—added "inspired gardener" to her list of talents in the 1930s when she spectacularly transformed the grounds around the house where she lived with her diplomat husband Harold Nicolson with a series of gardens within gardens, each one based on a family of plants or a single color.

Most famous, and imitated around the globe to this day, is her White Garden, which reaches its zenith in June. Nearby, the Rose Garden, whose old Bourbon, centifolia, and moss varieties are world renowned, bursts forth in June and July, while the Cottage Garden, a riot of red, yellow, and orange flowers, is at its best in the fall. Despite the many visitors who take advantage of Sissinghurst's relative proximity to London, the gardens are still an oasis of serenity and beauty. Little remains of the original "castle," in reality an Elizabethan manor house, but the standing ruins—including a gateway flanked by a pair of towers—add a touch of atmosphere, while the parkland surrounding the gardens is perfect for sylvan strolls.

If time allows for a detour within Kent, head 10 miles south to Knole House, a castellated stately home dating from 1456. For much of the 18th and 19th century, a small part of the 365-room house served as the residence of the Sackville family, and the remaining chambers—containing decorations, furniture, and works of art little changed over 300 years—are the highlight of a visit today.

WHERE: near Cranbrook, which is 53 miles/85 km southeast of London. Tel 44/1580-710-700; www.nationaltrust.org.uk. *When:* estate year-round; garden mid-Mar–Oct. **KNOLE HOUSE:** Tel 44/1732-450-608; www.nationaltrust.org.uk. *When:* house Mar–Oct; garden Apr–Sep. **BEST TIME:** Jun–Jul for most gardens, though every month holds its beauty.

Sissinghurst's Elizabethan tower rises above the flora.

Glorious Walking and Delicious Repasts

THE LAKE DISTRICT

Lancashire and Cumbria, England

The poet William Wordsworth described England's Lake District as "the loveliest spot that man has ever known." It is at once pastoral and wild, graced with some 15 principal lakes and dozens of lesser ones, with high mountains (including England's highest summit, the 3,210-foot Scafell Pike), steep-sided "fells" (hills), and grazing sheep everywhere in between. The 880-square-mile region is protected as a national park and is a favorite with hikers. The 70-mile Cumbria Way unfurls across the heart of the district, and there are countless shorter options, from lakeside strolls to hardy hilltop hikes. Immortalized on canvas and in literature, the land was the birthplace of English Romanticism.

The best-known lake in the region, as well as the largest in the country and the southern gateway to the area, is Windermere, a glistening sliver of water some 10 miles long nestled between the hills and mountains. Its shores, especially around the town of Bowness-on-Windermere, have been a popular holiday destination since the arrival of the railway in Victorian times.

The village of Grasmere is where Wordsworth lived with his wife and sister at Dove Cottage, built in the 17th century and now a museum. The poet laureate was buried here in 1850 in the graveyard of the village church. To enjoy Grasmere's romantic atmosphere in the late afternoon or evening, stay at the Harwood Hotel, a grand Victorian house in the center of the village, with just six modern and well-appointed rooms.

Further on is Ullswater, which Wordsworth described as "perhaps . . . the happiest combination of beauty and grandeur, which any of the lakes affords," and where he beheld his famous "host of golden daffodils." In summer, a restored 19th-century steamer plies the 9-mile length of the lake, the second largest in the district and one of the less developed.

Long and narrow, Windermere is a ribbon lake.

On Ullswater's relatively secluded eastern shore is Sharrow Bay Country House Hotel, renowned for its exceptional views. Grand and historic, this 24-bedroom hotel has classic waterfront gardens, along with sumptuous teas and inspired dinners (desserts are a favorite tradition here), the finest service, and a welcoming ambience.

WHERE: Grasmere is 280 miles/451 km northwest of London. **VISITOR INFO:** www.golakes.co.uk. **DOVE COTTAGE & THE WORDSWORTH MUSEUM:** Tel 44/15394-35544; www.wordsworth.org.uk. **HARWOOD HOTEL:** Tel 44/15394-35248; www.harwoodhotel.co.uk. *Cost:* from $165. **SHARROW BAY COUNTRY HOUSE HOTEL:** Tel 44/17684-86301; www.sharrowbay.com. *Cost:* from $440. **BEST TIMES:** Mar–Apr for Ullswater's blooming daffodils; Apr–Jun for biggest variety of flowers; Jun–Aug for least rainfall; Aug for Lake District Music Festival; Sep–Oct for fall colors.

"London is the epitome of our times and the Rome of today."—Ralph Waldo Emerson

London

England

London claims to be the capital of 21st-century Europe, and most will agree; at times it feels like anything of any importance in art, music, and fashion starts, finishes, or is taking place here. But today's London is not just a mecca for modernity: It remains very much a city of pomp and pageantry, where history and tradition are not only prized, they are integrated into daily life.

Top Attractions

British Museum—Unless you have a week to walk the 2 miles of corridors leading to many of the 7 million objects on display, head for the Elgin Marbles (which once decorated the Parthenon in Athens; see p. 156), the Rosetta Stone, the Egyptian mummies, the Samurai armor, and the Portland Vase. Or join one of the free eyeOpener tours, which focus on different areas of the museum's collection: They last about 30 minutes and depart throughout the day. **Info:** Tel 44/20-7323-8000; www.britishmuseum.org.

Buckingham Palace—When the queen is away from her London residence and workplace from late July to September, parts of the 775-room landmark—including the Throne Room, the 155-foot-long Picture Gallery, and the magnificent Grand Staircase designed by architect John Nash for George IV—are open to the public. The Changing of the Guard takes place at 11:30 A.M. daily or on alternate days depending on the month. **Info:** Tel 44/20-7766-7300; www.royalcollection.org.uk.

Hampton Court Palace—A royal palace for more than two centuries, Hampton Court was home to Henry VIII and five of his six wives. Christopher Wren added extensions in the late 17th century, and the result is a delightful blend of Tudor and English Baroque architecture. The palace is surrounded by some 60 landscaped acres of gardens and a centuries-old maze of tall hedges—it takes 20 minutes on average to reach the center. **Where:** 13 miles/22 km southwest of London, in East Molesey, Surrey. Tel 44/20-3166-6000; www.hrp.org.uk.

Hyde Park and Kensington Gardens—At 350 acres, Hyde Park is London's largest royal park and was once the favorite hunting ground of Henry VIII. Today it hosts open-air concerts, royal events, and, in summer, sunbathers and picnickers. The Serpentine,

At Buckingham Palace, the Queen's Guard, wearing red tunics and bearskin hats, is responsible for protecting the sovereign.

an L-shaped lake, separates it from well-manicured Kensington Gardens, with its necklacelike Princess Diana Memorial Fountain and nearby Kensington Palace. **Info:** Tel 44/20-7298-2000; www.royalparks.org.uk.

Prince Charles married Lady Diana Spencer at St. Paul's Cathedral in 1981.

London Eye—The world's tallest Ferris wheel, offering views on a clear day some 25 miles in every direction, the Eye is London's newest and most visible landmark. Ride in one of its 32 glass-enclosed gondolas that take a graceful half hour to complete a revolution. **Info:** Tel 44/871-781-3000; www.londoneye.com.

National Gallery—One of the world's largest and best art collections, the National Gallery exhibits more than 2,000 works representing every major European school from the mid-13th through the 19th centuries. Free, centrally located, and on everyone's short list, the gallery can be overwhelmingly crowded; the savvy visit on weekday mornings and on Friday evenings, when it stays open late. **Info:** Tel 44/20-7747-2885; www.nationalgallery.org.uk.

St. Paul's Cathedral—This 17th-century masterpiece of Sir Christopher Wren (who, along with a host of other notables, is buried in its crypt) is located in the heart of the historic financial district known as the City. The great dome offers a wonderful 360-degree view of London; encircling its interior is the Whispering Gallery—watch what you say! **Info:** Tel 44/20-7236-4128; www.stpauls.co.uk.

Tate Modern and Tate Britain—The Tate Modern, London's largest repository of modern art, houses British and foreign works from 1900 to the present in a converted power station. It is especially known for its (often participatory) special exhibits in the enormous Turbine Hall. Its sister gallery, the Tate Britain, displays British classics dating back to the 16th century and hosts the annual (and usually controversial) Turner Prize in visual art. **Info:** Tel 44/20-7887-8000; www.tate.org.uk.

Tower of London—Begun in the 11th century by William the Conqueror, the Tower of London is actually a castle with assorted towers. It contains the Crown Jewels (including the 530-carat Star of Africa diamond, aka Cullinan I, and Queen Victoria's Imperial State Crown, studded with more than 3,000 jewels), the macabre Scaffold Site (where Anne Boleyn was beheaded), and many other exhibits watched over by the colorful Beefeater Guards. **Info:** Tel 44/20-3166-6000; www.hrp.org.uk.

Victoria and Albert Museum—Opened in 1852, the largest decorative arts museum in the world exhibits objects from all corners of the globe. Among its treasures is the largest collection of Italian sculpture outside Italy and the superbly renovated Medieval and Renaissance Galleries as well as 15 galleries that pay tribute to 16th–19th century Britain. **Info:** Tel 44/20-7942-2000; www.vam.ac.uk.

Westminster Abbey—This English Gothic house of worship, administered directly by the Crown, has been the site of all but two British coronations since 1066. The Henry VII Lady Chapel, completed in 1509, is one of the loveliest in Europe. The world caught a glimpse of its beauty during the 2011 wedding of Prince William and Kate Middleton. Poets' Corner has monuments to, and/or the tombs of, Chaucer, Tennyson, Browning, and Dickens, among many others. A lovely way of visiting the abbey is to attend a service, in particular evensong at 5 P.M. on weekdays and 3 P.M. on the weekend. **Info:** Tel 44/20-7222-5152; www.westminster-abbey.org.

Other Must-Dos

A Night at the Theater—In the West End, 50-plus theaters promise some of the best and most varied theatergoing in the English-speaking world, be it serious drama or a rafter-rising musical. Shakespeare's Globe is a faithful re-creation of the original 1599 Elizabethan theater, complete with thatched roof and productions staged as they were in the Bard's lifetime. The Royal Shakespeare Company, based in Stratford-upon-Avon also performs at various theaters in London, while some of the city's best contemporary theater is staged in a trio of modern auditoriums that make up the National Theatre. **Info:** www.londontheatre.co.uk. **Shakespeare's Globe:** Tel 44/20-7902-1400; www.shakespeares-globe.org. **Royal Shakespeare Company:** Tel 0844/800-1110; www.rsc.org.uk. **National Theatre:** Tel 44/20-7452-3000; www.nationaltheatre.org.uk.

An Evening of Music—The church of St. Martin-in-the-Fields hosts classical music concerts, jazz sessions, and evensong in its elegant early-18th-century setting. From mid-July to mid-September, the beautiful Royal Albert Hall serves as the setting for the Promenade Concerts, aka the "Proms," featuring orchestras from around the world: The Last Night of the Proms is a high note. A top venue for chamber music, Wigmore Hall is celebrated for its near-perfect acoustics, beautiful Art Nouveau décor, and great variety of concerts and recitals. **St. Martin-in-the-Fields:** Tel 44/20-7766-1100; www.stmartin-in-the-fields.org. **Royal Albert Hall:** Tel 44/20-7589-8212; www.royalalberthall.com. **Wigmore Hall:** Tel 44/20-7935-2141; www.wigmore-hall.org.uk.

British Library—Visit its treasure-laden John Ritblat Gallery for a close-up look at the original Magna Carta, *Beowulf,* Shakespeare's First Folio, and lyrics to Beatles songs written on the back of a Lufthansa envelope. There is more than just writing: Lift one of the headsets in the gallery to hear such notables as James Joyce reading from *Ulysses* or Thomas Edison recording sound for the first time. **Info:** Tel 44/20-7412-7000; www.bl.uk.

Kew Gardens—London's vast 300-acre indoor/outdoor Royal Botanic Gardens boast an estimated 38,000 species of plants as well as the world's largest orchid collection and the Palm House and Temperate House conservatories. Within the gardens, 17th-century Kew Palace, favorite home-away-from-home for George III, has reopened its doors after almost a decade under renovation. **Where:** 8 miles/13 km southwest of London. Tel 44/20-8332-5000; www.rbgkew.org.uk.

National Portrait Gallery—The first museum in the world devoted to portraits when it opened in 1856, it is dedicated to collecting "the likenesses of famous British men and women," from Hans Holbein the Younger's Henry VIII portraits to Andy Warhol's silkscreens of Mick Jagger and the queen. The ground floor shows contemporary personalities—from writers to actors to boy bands—in various mixed media. **Info:** Tel 44/20-7306-0055; www.npg.org.uk.

Regent's Park—The most classically beautiful and manicured of London's parks, Regent's Park was designed by John Nash as an estate with dozens of villas for the aristocracy. Today it offers some of London's most beautiful flower gardens, hundreds of deck chairs for sunbathing (when the sun cooperates), and open-air Shakespeare at Queen Mary Gardens in summer. **Info:** Tel 44/20-7298-2000; www.royalparks.org.uk.

Shopping—Fortnum & Mason is the world's most elite grocery store. Floris has been London's leading perfumer and purveyor of toiletries since it opened in 1730. Turnbull and Asser is the place for bespoke shirts while Liberty sells its famous fine-patterned prints and fabrics (especially scarves) in unique Art Nouveau surroundings. As much a cultural experience as a shopping spree, Harrods is the king of department stores; its elaborate

Food Halls sell "everything for everybody," and the fourth floor's Georgian Restaurant is where to go for afternoon tea. Or try the Fifth Floor Café of Harvey Nichols, London's most fashionable department store, another good place to recharge. **Fortnum & Mason:** Tel 44/20-7734-8040; www.fortnumandmason.com. **Floris:** Tel 44/20-7930-2885; www.florislondon.com. **Turnbull and Asser:** Tel 44/20-7808-3000; www.turnbullandasser.com. **Liberty:** Tel 44/20-7734-1234; www.liberty.co.uk. **Harrods:** Tel 44/20-7730-1234; www.harrods.com. **Harvey Nichols:** Tel 44/20-7235-5000; www.harveynichols.com.

Hitting the markets—In Notting Hill, Portobello Market is the granddaddy of all London street markets. Thousands of stalls sell antiques, collectibles, and vintage clothing, with Friday to Sunday the busiest days. On weekends Camden Market offers an unpredictable jumble of both junk and food (and the odd diamond in the rough). South of Tower Bridge, Bermondsey Market is a proper flea market, held every Friday, and scoured before dawn by dealers. Just south of London Bridge and known as "London's Larder" since the 13th century, Borough Market is by far the city's best food market. **Portobello Market:** www.portobellomarket.org. **Camden Market:** www.camdenlock.net. **Bermondsey Market:** www.bermondseysquare.co.uk/antiques.html. **Borough Market:** www.boroughmarket.org.uk.

Harrods is the United Kingdom's largest department store.

Sir John Soane's Museum—Hogarth originals and Piranesi drawings are part of an eccentric collection in the charmingly chaotic home of the 19th-century architect, famous for designing the Bank of England. Time your visit for the first Tuesday of the month when the interior is lit by candles. **Info:** Tel 44/20-7405-2107; www.soane.org.

Wallace Collection—Bequeathed to the nation by the widow of art connoisseur Sir Richard Wallace in 1897, this museum is housed in a lovely Italianate mansion and includes works by Titian, Rubens, Velázquez, and Gainsborough and the largest collection of English armor in the country. **Info:** Tel 44/20-7563-9500; www.the-wallace-collection.org.uk.

Special Events

On a Saturday in early or mid June, Trooping the Colour is the official celebration of the queen's birthday, with all the queen's horses and all the queen's men departing from Buckingham Palace. For more tradition, head for the Royal Ascot Races, held in Berkshire in June, as famous for millinery finery and appearances by the royal family as for the races themselves (30 over a 5-day period). Held in late June–early July, the Wimbledon Lawn Tennis Championships is one of the tennis world's most prestigious tournaments. And in a gardening-mad nation, the grand event of the season is the Olympics of gardening, a monumental 4-day horticultural orgy in May called the Chelsea Flower Show organized by the Royal Horticultural Society. **Trooping the Colour:** www.trooping-the-colour.co.uk. **Royal Ascot Races:** www.ascotco.uk. **Wimbledon Tennis Championship:** www.wimbledon.com. **Chelsea Flower Show:** Tel 44/845-260-5000; www.rhs.org.uk.

Where to Stay

Aster House—This gem of a B&B in the heart of South Kensington wins hands down for its comfortable accommodations, consistently warm welcome, and delightful garden. Breakfast is served buffet style in the sunlit conservatory. **Info:** Tel 44/20-7581-5888; www.asterhouse.com. *Cost:* from $290.

BLAKE'S—This classic South Kensington hostelry cobbled from five Victorian terrace houses sets the standard by which all other boutique hotels in London are judged. Expect daring color schemes, an opulent atmosphere, a who's-who clientele, and top-drawer service. **INFO:** Tel 44/20-7370-6701; www.blakes hotels.com. *Cost:* from $300 (off-peak), from $420 (peak).

CHARLOTTE STREET HOTEL—London's first and still favorite boutique hotel combines the best of contemporary English style, facilities, and extras. Its location north of Oxford St. in Fitzrovia means you'll find lots of media and fashion types at its popular Oscar bar. **INFO:** Tel 44/20-7806-2000; www.charlottestreet hotel.com. *Cost:* from $390.

CLARIDGE'S—This bastion of tradition is so much a part of the old establishment, it functions as a kind of annex to Buckingham Palace, unflappably hosting heads of state, yet somehow it manages to be unstuffy. Come for afternoon tea or a port in the Art Deco Reading Room, or dine at celebrity chef Gordon Ramsay's in-house restaurant. **INFO:** Tel 44/20-7629-8860; www.claridges.co.uk. *Cost:* from $880 (off-peak), from $995 (peak); dinner $145.

CONNAUGHT—With 90 luxuriously appointed rooms and suites, the Connaught is a "baby grand" hotel in size and home to French culinary star and media darling Hélène Darroze and her sef-named restaurant. If you've never stayed at Buckingham Palace, stay (or dine) here for the next-best thing. **INFO:** Tel 44/20-7499-7070; www.the-connaught.co.uk. *Cost:* from $550 (off-peak), from $850 (peak); dinner $150.

PORTOBELLO HOTEL—The Portobello in Notting Hill has been a favorite with celebrities over the years, and you'll either love or hate the quirky style and eccentric touches that reflect the nearby Portobello Market. A real plus is the popular in-house bar that is open till the very wee hours. **INFO:** Tel 44/20-7727-2777; www.portobello-hotel.co.uk. *Cost:* from $375.

EATING & DRINKING

AFTERNOON TEA—Nowhere is Britain's most sacrosanct daily custom performed with more reverence or flair than at the rococo Palm Court of the Ritz Hotel. Dainty finger sandwiches complement fresh-baked scones with homemade strawberry jam and clotted cream as well as an array of bite-size tea cakes and fancy pastries. Less formal but served at the very place where the tradition is said to have originated is tea at the Langham Hotel's own splendid Palm Court. For style on a budget, you can't beat a cuppa with all the trimmings at the Orangery, an 18th-century conservatory on the grounds of Kensington Palace. **THE RITZ LONDON:** Tel 44/20-7493-8181; www.theritzlondon.com. *Cost:* $60. **LANGHAM HOTEL:** Tel 44/20-7636-1000; http://london.langhamhotels.co.uk. *Cost:* $60. **THE ORANGERY:** Tel 44/20-3166-6112; www.hrp.org.uk. *Cost:* $25.

BIBENDUM—This hot spot offers an eclectic, modern, consistently inventive menu served in Michelin House, an Art Nouveau masterpiece. The separate, very popular Bibendum Oyster Bar and Café are at street level amidst more splendid architecture. **INFO:** Tel restaurant 44/20-7581-5817, oyster bar 44/20-7589-1480; www.bibendum.co.uk. *Cost:* restaurant $85, oyster bar $69, café $15.

GEALES—A lot more posh now than when it opened in Notting Hill on the eve of World War II, this neighborhood place is still your best bet for fish-and-chips, though the menu now includes other fare like fish pie and even steak. **INFO:** Tel 44/20-7727-7528; www.geales.com. *Cost:* dinner $45.

GORDON RAMSAY—Mr. Ramsay's renowned flagship eatery serves "modern European" cuisine. The dishes are innovative and complex, on the order of pressed foie gras marinated in white port and salt marsh lamb with crystallized walnuts and cumin.

(Another location is at Claridge's Hotel; see above.) **Info:** Tel 44/20-7352-4441; www.gordonramsay.com. *Cost:* dinner $140.

The Ivy—This is still one of the most difficult tables to book, with its glamorous 1930s décor, high-energy buzz, great people-watching, and consistently excellent (if predictable) food—from the reinvented fish-and-chips and Ivy hamburger to the signature salmon cakes. **Info:** Tel 44/20-7836-4751; www.theivy.co.uk. *Cost:* $75.

Oxo Tower Restaurant—Breathtaking views of St. Paul's and the illuminated Thames are the real attractions here, although the modern European and fusion cuisine get solid reviews. The neighboring brasserie serves similar though less stratospherically priced dishes. **Info:** Tel 44/20-7803-3888; www.harveynichols.com. *Cost:* restaurant $95, brasserie $70.

Pubs—London is awash in "public houses," where the welcome—and the ale—is always warm. The only surviving galleried 17th-century coaching inn, George Inn is an atmospheric pub offering food as well as drink. Once the mess hall of the Duke of Wellington's Grenadier Guards and reputedly haunted by one of them, the Grenadier serves a mean Bloody Mary and is always crowded and convivial; its beef Wellington is a favorite. The Red Lion, built in 1821 and redesigned in the 1870s, is the ultimate Victorian pub—small, intimate, and dedicated to the fine art of drinking. **George Inn:** Tel 44/20-7407-2056. **Grenadier:** Tel 44/20-7235-3074. **Red Lion:** Tel 44/20-7930-2030.

The River Café—The simple-made-chic, always seasonal Italian menu is the lure here, as is the chance to eat outdoors by the Thames in warm weather. An iconic venue that spawned a legendary cookbook and a generation of influential chefs, the River Café is popular for signature dishes such as mushroom risotto. **Info:** Tel 44/20-7386-4200; www.rivercafe.co.uk. *Cost:* dinner $95.

Rules—London's oldest restaurant, Rules was established as an oyster bar in 1798. Oysters are still a house specialty, along with game from its own estate, with a setting that's unapologetically late 1700s. **Info:** Tel 44/20-7836-5314; www.rules.co.uk. *Cost:* dinner $75.

Day Trips

Oxford—Although the city of Oxford dates back to the 12th century, it is the university—collectively formed of 38 colleges—that draws visitors and has given the city its identity and character since it first opened its doors in 1263. The buildings are like a textbook of English architecture, making Oxford a visually fascinating and excellent walking city. Visit the history-steeped students' drinking halls (for starters, the well-known 13th-century Bear Inn) or peek into the Ashmolean Museum, a treasure trove of fine art and antiquities that first opened in 1683. In the center of town but with a country inn ambience, the 17th-century Old Parsonage is the hotel of choice. For a complete about-face, head to the country and the Le Manoir aux Quat'Saisons and enjoy the extraordinary talents of world-renowned French chef Raymond LeBlanc; stay the night in an exquisitely decorated guest room. **Where:** 57 miles/92 km northwest of London. **Old Parsonage Hotel:** Tel 44/1865-310-210; www.oldparsonage-hotel.co.uk. *Cost:* from $350. **Le Manoir aux Quat'Saisons:** Tel 44/1844-278881; www.manoir.com. *Cost:* from $770; dinner $155.

Windsor Castle—Windsor is the oldest and—with 1,000 rooms—largest occupied castle in the world. Since its construction began under William the Conqueror almost a millennium ago, it has been home to eight successive royal houses, including that of the present queen, Elizabeth II, who spent much of her childhood here and has dubbed it her favorite residence. Highlights include the Changing of the Guard; Queen Mary's Dolls' House; the Great Kitchen; and the Gothic jewel of St. George's Chapel, which, like Westminster Abbey (see p. 18), contains the tombs of many English monarchs. Henry VIII and his third wife, Jane Seymour, lie here. **WHERE:** 23 miles/37 km west of London. Tel 44/1753-831-118; www.royalcollection.org.uk.

THE ROYAL PAVILION, BRIGHTON—The star attraction of Brighton, London's favorite seaside getaway, is the Royal Pavilion, a pseudo-Oriental pleasure palace begun in the late 1700s and enlarged by the prince regent, later King George IV. The fantasy structure of minarets and Moorish domes on the outside hide a whimsical chinoiserie interior, one of the most ornate in Europe. Always loved for its bracing breezes, the naughty postcards, and the fish-and-chips one finds while promenading along the 3-mile-long amusement-lined Brighton Pier, the city now boasts cafés, antiques shops, and galleries in the tight-knit alleyways called the Lanes. Look for English's of Brighton, a long-time institution known for its no-fuss super-fresh fish and oysters on the half-shell. **WHERE:** 51 miles/82 km south of London. **ROYAL PAVILION:** Tel 44/1273-290-900; www.brighton-hove-rpml.org.uk. **ENGLISH'S OF BRIGHTON:** Tel 44/1273-327-980; www.englishs.co.uk. *Cost:* dinner $60.

Ancient Rome's Line in the Sand

HADRIAN'S WALL

Hexham, Northumberland, England

Where legions once marched, sheep now peacefully graze. A few sections are all that remain of this dividing wall that was constructed some 1,800 years ago as the demarcation line for the northwesternmost border of Rome's mighty empire. Named after Emperor Hadrian (A.D. 76–138), who ordered its construction, the wall spanned 73 miles across England, between Bowness-on-Solway on the west coast (beyond Carlisle) and Wallsend on the east coast (beyond Newcastle), with major forts and smaller "mile-castles" dotted along its length. Work was begun in 121 by some 18,000 soldiers and indentured slaves, and was abandoned around the year 400 as the Roman Empire crumbled.

Today, the wall is Britain's largest ruin dating from the Roman era and is one of northern Europe's most impressive and important Roman sites. The best-preserved chunk is a 10-mile stretch in Northumberland, to the east of Carlisle and within striking distance of England's much-visited Lake District (see p. 16). Also in this area are some of the region's finest Roman forts, including Birdoswald, Vindolanda, and Housesteads, all with attached museums giving a fascinating insight into daily life on the wall for Roman soldiers.

Walk beside the wall for a mile or two or hike its entire length on the Hadrian's Wall

The wall was one of the Roman empire's greatest engineering feats.

Path—one of England's most popular national trails. Or rent a bike and sample the equally popular Hadrian's Cycleway.

South of the ancient wall sit several modern towns, including Haltwhistle, which claims to be the geographic midpoint of the country, a fact celebrated by the Centre of Britain Hotel. Dating from the 15th century, the hotel combines classic and contemporary style with a friendly welcome and good service. For more history and greater creature comforts, retreat to nearby Langley Castle Hotel, about 7 miles east of Haltwhistle in the village of Langley-on-Tyne. Built in 1350 during the reign of King Edward III, its turreted 7-foot-thick walls and original medieval stained-glass windows and spiral staircases enchantingly evoke the past. It's a pocket of modern luxury complete with an acclaimed restaurant.

Where: Hadrian's Wall is between Carlisle and Newcastle, about 250 miles/400 km north of London. **Visitor info:** www.hadrians-wall.org; www.nationaltrail.co.uk/hadrianswall. **Centre of Britain Hotel:** Tel 44/1434-322-422; www.centre-of-britain.org.uk. *Cost:* from $120. **Langley Castle Hotel:** Tel 44/1434-688-888; www.langleycastle.com. *Cost:* from $250; dinner $60. **Best time:** Apr–Oct for pleasant weather.

The Thrill of the Hunt

The International Antiques and Collectors Fair

Newark-on-Trent, Nottinghamshire, England

Think antiques-lover's paradise and you think of London. But where do the umpteen antiques dealers that fill the stalls and stores of Portobello Road and Camden Passage replenish their stock? At Newark's Antiques and Collectors Fair, the largest in all of Europe filling an 86-acre showground with up to 4,000 vendors' stands and stalls.

Antiques hunters and collectors will find the 2-day fair—held six times yearly—both a joy and an endurance test, with stalls stretching to infinity and the widest range of antiques and collectibles imaginable on sale. Sellers arrive from throughout Britain and Europe, attracting buyers and the merely curious from all over the world. Most dealers are savvy merchants, so fantastic deals are not likely (though by no means impossible), but those arriving promptly when the gates open might happen upon a choice find. To avoid a predawn start on a day trip from London, stay overnight at the small and charming Grange Hotel. Its amiable hosts provide a warm welcome, and the beautiful and tranquil garden is the perfect place to recover after a hectic morning of bartering.

In addition to the hope of the ultimate find, the crowds come for the enormous range and variety of wares. Those with little intention to buy will enjoy this as an enormous cultural outing: Since the British traveled so extensively and far afield during colonial days, shopping English antiques is like shopping the world.

Where: 108 miles/174 km north of London. **Visitor info:** www.iacf.co.uk/newark. **Grange Hotel:** Tel 44/1636-703-399; www.grangenewark.co.uk. *Cost:* from $150. **When:** Feb, Apr, Jun, Aug, Oct, and Dec.

England's Most Perfect Baroque Palace

Blenheim Palace

Woodstock, Oxfordshire, England

Of England's countless stately homes, Blenheim is the most celebrated. Its size and opulence are testimony to its wealth of history: It was the gift of a grateful Queen Anne to General John Churchill, first Duke of Marlborough, after his crushing defeat of the French in 1704 at the Bavarian village of Blenheim. In 1874, a boy called Winston Churchill was born here; he went on to become Sir Winston, Britain's Prime Minister during World War II. Designed by leading architect of the day Sir John Vanbrugh and regarded as the finest Baroque construction in Britain, the lavish palace—impersonal in scale—is England's answer to Versailles.

Although the house has changed little since its completion in 1722, much of the 2,000 acres of park and gardens were transformed in the 1760s by Lancelot "Capability" Brown, the great landscape gardener. Many visitors come today to try their luck in the famous Marlborough Maze, the world's largest hedge maze.

Within walking distance of Blenheim Palace, Feathers Inn in Woodstock promises outstanding meals and stylish rooms in a country setting that belies London's proximity. Nearby is the equally historic Star Inn, a cozy pub on the town's main square, with excellent food and comfortable rooms upstairs.

Where: 62 miles/101 km northwest of London. **Visitor info:** www.blenheimpalace.co.uk. **Feathers Inn:** Tel 44/1993-812-291; www.feathers.co.uk. *Cost:* from $230; dinner $70. **Star Inn:** Tel 44/1993-811-373; www.thestarinnwoodstock.co.uk. *Cost:* from $135; dinner $30. **Best times:** Apr–May for gardens at their peak; Sep–Oct for fall colors in the parkland.

Gastronomic Getaway

Ludlow

Shropshire, England

Every proud patriot has a running list of contenders for his or her country's "prettiest little town." On many an Anglophile's list, Ludlow is sure to be at the top. With a population of less than 10,000 people, this market town sits contentedly in a quiet, mellow region of pastoral scenery along England's Welsh border, an area known as The Marches (an ancient word derived from "the edge" or "frontier"). Ludlow still feels very much on the edge of England, and it takes some patience to get there, though there's a benefit—the town has thus far blessedly escaped the common blight of bus tours, urban sprawl, and shopping malls. Swans glide on the River Teme that encircles it, spanned by medieval bridges that were a frequent subject for J.M.W. Turner's paintings.

The imposing Ludlow Castle went up in 1094 upon orders from the Earl of Shrewsbury and the cobbled streets are distinguished by elegant Georgian and Jacobean houses.

In recent years, Ludlow has established itself as an epicurean center, with a market held four days per week, specialty food stores, and a number of excellent places to eat, from high-profile restaurants to comfortable bistros and cozy inns—a surprisingly varied selection for an unassuming country outpost. The town is at the forefront of the UK's Slow Food movement, and the high point of the year is the annual Food and Drink Festival.

Leading restaurants include Mr. Underhills and La Becasse—the former a riverside inn specializing in refined British fare and the latter leaning toward French cuisine in a handsome oak-lined dining room. Both pride themselves on using local ingredients and standards that are exceptional. They are each within walking distance of the Merchant House, offering comfortable lodgings in just two rooms. The friendly owners maintain the town's culinary traditions with a fine breakfast, and they're a mine of information about local history and gastronomic haunts.

Where: 160 miles/257 km northwest of London. **Mr. Underhills:** Tel 44/1584-874-431; www.mr-underhills.co.uk. *Cost:* dinner $85. **La Becasse:** Tel 44/1584-872-325; www.labecasse.co.uk. *Cost:* 3-course dinner $95. **The Merchant House:** Tel 44/1584-875-438; www.merchanthouse.co.uk. *Cost:* from $140. **Best times:** Mon, Wed, Fri, Sat for Ludlow Market; 2nd and 4th Thurs for Ludlow's Food and Produce Market; late Jun–early Jul for the 2-week Ludlow Festival featuring Shakespeare; 2nd weekend of Sep for Ludlow Food and Drink Festival.

Britain's Most Historic Spa Town

Bath

Somerset, England

Legend has it that an ancient Celtic king first discovered the healing properties of the thermal waters here; then, between A.D. 50 and 300, the Romans built elaborate saunas, temples, and bathhouses around the hot springs. More than a millennium later, in 1702, Queen Anne's visit launched the city's rebirth as the country's premier spa town. Throughout the 18th century, English high society would come here for the season to "take the waters" as depicted in the novels of Jane Austen. The flourish of grand architecture that followed transformed Bath into what is today Britain's most perfectly and beautifully preserved Georgian city. Relaxed and refined, the city is a gracious host, with wonderful antiquing, shopping, and dining.

A terrace overlooks the Great Bath, the baths' centerpiece.

The city's historic heart is still its Roman baths, among Britain's finest classical ruins.

Overlooking them is the 18th-century Pump Room, a noted restaurant and one of the greatest temples to old-fashioned English teatime, where you can still see the fountain of natural mineral waters that visitors enjoyed in the Georgian heyday. The 16th-century Bath Abbey is nearby, and it's a short walk to The Circus, one of the city's most impressive sites: 33 perfectly matching yet subtly differentiated houses forming a huge Colosseum-inspired circle, designed by John Wood the Elder, orchestrator of Bath's architectural golden days.

In 1775 his son John Wood the Younger designed the equally spectacular Royal Crescent, a huge semi-ellipse of 30 identical stone houses overlooking Royal Victoria Park, on what is hailed as the most majestic street in Britain. Stop by for tea at the Royal Crescent, Bath's most patrician hotel.

Just north of The Circus on Russel Street—another charming row of honey-colored houses—is the stylish, yet casual and slightly eccentric, Queensberry Hotel. Or cross the park below the Royal Crescent to reach Brooks Guesthouse, a small, quiet hotel with a historic ambience.

After enjoying life in town, retire to Ston Easton Park, a stately Palladian mansion rebuilt in 1740, set in impeccably maintained gardens and parkland, 20 minutes outside of Bath. This is a period gem of the highest order, an unforgettable country retreat with traditionally decorated bedrooms and lounges and one of the finest restaurants in the region.

WHERE: 115 miles/185 km west of London. **VISITOR INFO:** www.visitbath.co.uk. **PUMP ROOM:** Tel 44/1225-444-477; www.romanbaths.co.uk *Cost:* tea $30. **ROYAL CRESCENT HOTEL:** Tel 44/1225-823-333; www.royalcrescent.co.uk. *Cost:* from $300. **QUEENSBERRY HOTEL:** Tel 44/1225-447-928; www.thequeensberry.co.uk. *Cost:* from $200; dinner $65. **BROOKS GUESTHOUSE:** Tel 44/1225-425-543; www.brooksguesthouse.com. *Cost:* from $135. **STON EASTON PARK:** Tel 44/1761-241-631; www.stoneaston.co.uk. *Cost:* from $275; dinner $70. **BEST TIMES:** May–Sep for nicest weather; late May–early Jun for Bath International Music Festival.

A Standout in England's Smallest City

WELLS CATHEDRAL

Wells, Somerset, England

In the heart of the sleepy rural county of Somerset is England's smallest city, delightful little Wells. A settlement since Saxon times, Wells reached its pinnacle of prestige around the 12th century, when the magnificent Cathedral Church of St. Andrew was built to reflect the city's affluence. Over the following years, Wells gradually fell into a centuries-long slumber that would preserve its character and heritage for today's visitors.

Although St. Andrew is one of Britain's smallest cathedrals, it dwarfs the perfectly preserved surrounding streets that spread out in its shadow. A special feature is the cathedral's west front, heavily ornamented with six tiers of 365 carved life-size figures that comprise the most extensive surviving array of medieval sculpture in Britain. Completed in the early 13th century, they illustrated biblical stories for the illiterate masses. The front's twin towers were not added until the late 14th century, yet look as if they were always meant to be there. England's (and the world's) second oldest clock, built in 1392, is found in the interior's north transept, announcing the hour with a fanfare of tilting knights on armored steeds.

After marveling at the cathedral, check into the charming Swan Hotel, a former coaching inn whose interior of baronial log fireplaces, beamed ceilings, rich wood paneling, and heavy four-poster beds evokes its 500 years of history. Enjoy views of the cathedral from its highly regarded restaurant, a perfect spot for lunch or dinner. Or drive a little way out of town to Stoberry House, a small hotel with luxurious rooms, contemporary sculptures in the garden, and unbeatable vistas across the green fields to Wells and the cathedral.

Also visible about 6 miles away is the hill of Glastonbury Tor, thought to be variously the mythical Isle of Avalon, the last resting place of legendary King Arthur, a meeting place for fairies, a holy spot visited by Joseph of Arimathea (uncle of Jesus), or a beacon for UFOs. Below lies the town of Glastonbury. The gigantic Glastonbury Festival, an annual celebration of rock and folk music, takes its name from the town but since 1970 has been held in the nearby village of Piton.

WHERE: 120 miles/193 km southwest of London. **SWAN HOTEL:** Tel 44/1749-836-300; www.swanhotelwells.co.uk. *Cost:* from $225; dinner $40. **STOBERRY HOUSE:** Tel 44/1749-672-906; www.stoberry-park.co.uk. *Cost:* from $95. **BEST TIMES:** May–Oct for the nicest weather; late Jun for Glastonbury Festival.

Drama and Ghosts at Shakespeare's Birthplace

STRATFORD-UPON-AVON

Warwickshire, England

The timeless appeal and universality of William Shakespeare's literary work have long made his hometown, Stratford-upon-Avon, a point of pilgrimage. With streets of historic half-timbered houses and an air of genial prosperity, it would likely draw visitors even without the fame of the town's native son. In and around Stratford are five houses with connections to the Bard, including the house where he was born in 1564 (the exact date is unrecorded, but he was baptized on April 26, so his birth date is estimated as April 23) and the cottage of his wife, Anne Hathaway. Also on the required circuit is the 13th-century Trinity Church, where Shakespeare and his family were buried (he died on April 23 at the age of 52).

But the zenith of any visit is enjoying a performance by the Royal Shakespeare Company, one of the finest repertory troupes in the world. Of the three theaters in town, most classics are performed at the Royal Shakespeare Theatre; there are weekly matinees for those heading back to London in time for dinner. The Elizabethan-style Swan Theatre was reconstructed along the lines of Shakespeare's original Globe Theatre, and The Other Place is a more intimate venue for experimental productions.

In between sightseeing venues, stop for a pint at a historic pub such as the Windmill, which is old enough to have been frequented by Shakespeare himself, or the Black Swan, affectionately known by all as "the Dirty Duck" and a favorite spot for actors, pre- or postperformance.

After a day in town or an evening at the theater, relax at the Swan's Nest Hotel, a grand old redbrick house dating from the 17th century, where guests can enjoy a drink on the terrace overlooking the river as real swans glide by. Or travel 5 miles in the direction of Alderminster to the magnificent Ettington Park Hotel, a stately neo-Gothic home set on 40 acres of deer-inhabited parkland and manicured gardens on the banks of the River Stour. This 19th-century country house has long been associated with the Shirley family (Shakespeare's Hal speaks of a "valiant Shirley" in *Henry IV Part I*), and family ghosts linger, but guests will be hard pressed to find a more welcoming place.

WHERE: 90 miles/145 km northwest of London. **VISITOR INFO:** www.shakespeare-country.co.uk. **THEATERS:** ticket hotline, tel 0844-800-1110; www.rsc.org.uk. *When:* theater season is Mar–Nov. **SWAN'S NEST HOTEL:** Tel 44/1789-266-804; www.macdonaldhotels.co.uk/swansnest. *Cost:* from $165. **ETTINGTON PARK HOTEL:** Tel 44/1789-450-123; www.ettingtonpark.co.uk. *Cost:* from $225 (off-peak), from $310 (peak). **BEST TIME:** A festival of Bard-related events takes place the weekend closest to Apr 23, traditionally celebrated as the date of Shakespeare's birth and death.

England's Finest Feudal Castle

WARWICK CASTLE

Warwick, Warwickshire, England

After more than 9 centuries at the heart of British history, the magnificent feudal fortress of Warwick is still the country's finest medieval castle. Built in 1068 by William the Conqueror, just 2 years after the seminal Battle of Hastings, its commanding position on an escarpment above the River Avon was described as "the most noble site in England" by Sir Walter Scott.

Originally built to keep out unwanted "guests," Warwick Castle is now more visited than any other English house in private hands, and the second most visited castle after Windsor (see p. 22). These modern-day invaders come to see the finely preserved historic structure, of course, but also to be entertained by numerous attractions such as the Pageant Playground and Castle Dungeon. Crowds can be big during school vacation time, but guards at the gate keep the long lines moving within the monumental Norman walls.

Inside the castle are fascinating displays, including one of Europe's most important collections of medieval armor and weaponry, as well as paintings by such old masters as Rubens and Van Dyck. The castle's bellicose character is best viewed from outdoors, where peacocks preen on 60 acres of grounds, landscaped in the 18th century by Lancelot "Capability" Brown.

For a much more serene historical experience, it's just 5 miles north to Kenilworth Castle. Overshadowed by its more famous neighbor and 50 years younger, it's nevertheless an impressive ruin, and its history is just as intriguing. Previous owners include "Bad" King John in the early 13th century followed by John of Gaunt and Robert Dudley, believed by some to have been a secret lover of Elizabeth I. Fast-forward to the 19th century and Sir Walter Scott, who was as impressed with Kenilworth as he was with Warwick: His novel *Kenilworth* put the castle on the tourist map in the Victorian era.

WHERE: 92 miles/148 km northwest of London. **VISITOR INFO:** www.warwick-castle.co.uk; www.kenilworthweb.co.uk.

A Masterpiece of Medieval Technology

Salisbury Cathedral

Salisbury, Wiltshire, England

The 19th-century paintings of Turner and Constable familiarized the world with Salisbury Cathedral and its remarkable 404-foot spire, the tallest in the country and an iconic image of England. The cathedral was begun in 1220 and was completed in a record 38 years (the spire was added toward the end of the century) making Salisbury the most architecturally unified of all the great European cathedrals and the very pinnacle of what is known as the Early English or pointed Gothic style.

Inside is the oldest working clock in the world, dating back to the 1300s. It's a strange mechanical contraption with no dial, designed to strike a bell to mark the passing hours. Climb up the spire's internal steps for a striking view across the attractive and lively market town of Salisbury in the direction of Salisbury Plain and Stonehenge (see next page), Wiltshire's other significant site.

To the south of the cathedral, on the other side of the River Avon and about a mile from the center of town, the lovely old 13th-century Rose and Crown Inn has welcomed pilgrims and wayfarers since its earliest days, with hand-hewn beams and a genial sense of hospitality still firmly intact. It's an inviting place to spend the afternoon, with views of a lawn stretching down to the river—a veritable Turner canvas come to life, with the cathedral's soaring spire in full sight.

Drive about 20 miles south from Salisbury through the New Forest—once the private hunting ground of medieval kings and now one of England's newest national parks—to New Milton and Chewton Glen, a neo-Georgian country manor hotel distinguished by an air of well-being and known for its impeccable standards of service and quality. Nothing ruffles the feathers of the extremely amiable staff at this grand, green-shuttered, ivy-clad home where croquet on the front lawn is one of myriad amenities.

The cathedral houses an original Magna Carta.

Where: 90 miles/145 km southwest of London; www.salisburycathedral.org.uk. **Rose and Crown Inn:** Tel 44/1722-359-999; www.legacy-hotels.co.uk/legacy-roseandcrown. *Cost:* from $140. **Chewton Glen Hotel:** Tel 44/1425-275-341; in the U.S., tel 800-344-5087; www.chewtonglen.com. *Cost:* from $490; dinner $90. **Best times:** Tues and Sat for the outdoor Salisbury Charter Market; Apr–Oct for the New Forest at its best; late May–early Jun for Salisbury Festival, an arts and cultural event.

One of the World's Great Mysteries

STONEHENGE

Wiltshire, England

Britain's best-known prehistoric site, Stonehenge is still as magical, mystical, and mysterious as it was probably always meant to be—but only if you catch it between tour bus caravans. No one knows for sure the reason for Stonehenge, although it is fairly certain that ancient Neolithic and Bronze Age peoples built this stunning collection of artfully placed rocks over a very long period, then used the site for rituals or ceremonies pertaining to the sun and perhaps also as a calendar. In the 17th century, the widely held view that the circle was somehow connected to the Celtic druids took hold and has never died, even though it has since been proved that Stonehenge predates the priestly cult by at least 1,500 years and probably more.

The massive trilithons—two upright stones with a lintel across the top—were assembled some 4,000 years ago. Some of the standing stones weigh up to 50 tons, and experts estimate that to move each one into position took more than 1,000 men. Scholars disagree about where the stones came from (some say southwest Wales) and how they got to the windswept Salisbury Plain. Modern researchers believe they were to be put together in three distinct stages (two of which were never completed), in alignments made possible by sophisticated builders with a knowledge of astronomy, mathematics, and engineering unparalleled anywhere in Europe at that time. Today, thousands of visitors gravitate here, especially for the summer and winter solstice, including many modern-day druids and followers of other pagan religions.

Not as famous as Stonehenge but more powerful for their simplicity, the nearby Avebury Stone Circles, some 20 miles north, were erected 500 years before Stonehenge was completed. Uncrowded and more accessible, they consist of circles of 100 massive stones.

WHERE: 85 miles/137 km southwest of London. **VISITOR INFO:** www.english-heritage.org.uk. **BEST TIMES:** early morning or late afternoon to avoid crowds; summer and winter solstices (usually sunrise on Jun 21 and Dec 22), and spring and fall equinoxes (the halfway points between the solstices).

A Stroll Through a Classical Painting

STOURHEAD GARDEN

Stourton, Wiltshire, England

Lying between gentle hills in the bucolic county of Wiltshire, Stourhead is arguably England's finest and best-known example of 18th-century English landscape gardening, confirmation that no other country holds a candle to

England's horticultural expertise and passion. Stourhead's poetic grounds—inspired by the paintings of Claude Lorrain and Gaspard Poussin—are punctuated with a neoclassical Pantheon, a grotto, and temples built to Flora and Apollo, creating a classical effect that is much mimicked around the world.

The Stourhead estate was owned by the wealthy Hoare family from the early 18th century, and the gardens were created between 1740 and 1780 by Henry ("the Magnificent") Hoare. After a grand tour of the Mediterranean, he decided to relandscape his estate's 100-acre grounds upon his return home. Although Stourhead is beautiful all year long, it perhaps offers the most romantic walks in early fall, along the footpaths that wind around a chain of small man-made lakes, and in summer, when its famous dells of rhododendrons and camellias are in full bloom.

The gardens surround Stourhead House, an 18th-century Palladian-style mansion, where many beautiful rooms are also open to the public. Within strolling distance of the gardens' main gate, the Spread Eagle Inn is a local institution, known for its leisurely dinners of traditional cooking and five comfortable rooms decorated with antiques.

WHERE: 112 miles/180 km southwest of London. Tel 44/1747-841-152; www.nationaltrust.org.uk. *When:* garden open daily; house open mid-Mar–Oct. **SPREAD EAGLE INN:** Tel 44/1747-840-587; www.spreadeagleinn.com. *Cost:* from $155; dinner $40. **BEST TIMES:** Mar–Apr for daffodils; May–Jun for garden in full bloom; Oct for fall colors.

Grand, Stately, Elegant

CASTLE HOWARD

York, Yorkshire, England

Although best known today as the location for BBC TV's 1981 adaptation of Evelyn Waugh's classic novel *Brideshead Revisited* and for the 2008 movie of the same name, since the early 18th century Castle Howard has been considered to be one of the largest and most august privately owned homes in the British Isles. Though not really a castle, it stands on the former site of one amid 1,000-acre parkland and gardens. The Howard family, whose descendants still reside there today, saw in then-inexperienced architect Sir John Vanbrugh the talent that would later secure him the commission to create the lavish Blenheim Palace near Oxford (see p. 25). The main body of Castle Howard was completed in 1715, including its signature gilt Great Hall, rising 70 feet from floor to dome. The 160-foot, aptly named Long Gallery is the castle's other highlight, lined with a large number of portraits of Howard ancestors by Holbein and other artists.

The Howard family has made the castle their home for more than 300 years.

For more history, unpack your bags at the Old Lodge Hotel, a Tudor mansion on the edge of the nearby market town of Malton, below the heather-clad hills of the North York Moors National Park. Or head south to handsome Middlethorpe Hall & Spa, on the outskirts of York (see below), one of the grandest country hotels in northern England. Commissioned in 1699, the same year as Castle Howard, this elegant William III–style inn is surrounded by 26 impeccable acres of parkland that border York's famous racecourse, and is the perfect jumping-off point for a tour of Yorkshire.

WHERE: 15 miles/24 km northeast of York. Tel 44/1653-648-444; www.castlehoward.co.uk. *When:* house open mid-Mar–Oct; garden, year-round. **OLD LODGE HOTEL:** Tel 44/1653-690-570; www.theoldlodgemalton.co.uk. *Cost:* from $180. **MIDDLETHORPE HALL HOTEL:** Tel 44/1904-641-241; www.middlethorpe.com. *Cost:* from $240 (off-peak), from $300 (peak). **BEST TIMES:** May for rhododendrons in Castle Howard's gardens; May–Oct for racing season; Sep–Oct for fall colors on the moors.

An Ancient City's Crowning Glory

YORK MINSTER

York, Yorkshire, England

The historic city of York is surrounded by 3 miles of beautifully preserved, centuries-old defensive walls: Strolling along its wall-top walkway is one of England's finest pleasures. Within lies an architecture-rich city, with all paths leading to its famous showpiece cathedral, the Minster. A wonder of Gothic architecture, it is the largest medieval cathedral in Great Britain and the second largest Gothic cathedral in northern Europe (only Cologne's is larger; see p. 150). Measuring 500 feet from end to end, its nave is the widest in England, and the choir is the second-highest after Canterbury (see p. 13). The whole structure took more than 250 years to build, from around 1220 to 1472, on a site where previous cathedrals and churches had stood, possibly as far back as 627. The central tower is almost 200 feet high, and a breath-sapping climb up the 275-step spiral staircase provides the chance to appreciate both the scale of this massive building (offset by stunning views of the Yorkshire moors beyond) and the sophisticated engineering genius of the buttresses that hold it up.

Best known of the Minster's 128 immense stained-glass windows is the Rose Window, commemorating the end of the War of the Roses. Above the main entrance is the Great West Window, dubbed "the Heart of Yorkshire" and renowned for its particularly fine tracery. Most amazing of all is the Great East Window, behind the altar. At 1,680 square feet—bigger than a tennis court—it's the largest single medieval stained-glass window in the world.

Surrounding the Minster is a web of narrow streets and cobblestone alleyways lined with half-timbered houses, many at least 500 years old. Quite a few of the older thoroughfares are called "gates"—Stonegate, Colliergate, and so on—from the Norse word *gata,* meaning "street," a constant reminder of York's Viking past. The Viking period is celebrated at the extremely popular Jorvik Center, which transports visitors back to the year 975, long before the Minster's first block was laid.

WHERE: 203 miles/327 km north of London. Tel 44/1904-557-216; www.yorkminster.org. **JORVIK CENTER:** Tel 44/1904-643-211; www.vikingjorvik.com. **WHERE TO STAY:**

The stylish boutique Marmadukes Hotel is a short walk from the Minster. Tel 44/1904-640-101; www.marmadukesyork.com. *Cost:* from $115. **Best times:** Apr–Sep for pleasant weather, with Aug especially busy; mid- to late Feb for Viking Festival; Jul for Early Music Festival; Jul–Aug for height of York's famous horse races.

Reliving the Grand Days of Travel

Balmoral Hotel and the Royal Scotsman

Edinburgh, Scotland

Standing proudly at the end of Edinburgh's mile-long, shop-lined Princes Street is the historic and undeniably palatial Balmoral Hotel. Built in 1902 as a railway hotel, it is now one of the city's most elegant landmarks, complete with kilted doormen at its entrance. Guests can daydream their way through afternoon tea in the Drawing Room, eat like kings and queens in the refined surrounds of the Number One restaurant, or sample the bounty of Scotland's best distilleries in the high-ceilinged Bollinger Bar in the Palm Court.

The hotel's clock tower is a landmark in Edinburgh's skyline.

The Balmoral's ornate clock tower is a city landmark, always turned 2 minutes ahead so guests don't miss their train at the adjacent Waverly Station. Head there for a grand tour of quintessential Scotland aboard *The Royal Scotsman,* which lets you choose from 2- to 7-night itineraries through the Highlands and beyond. You and 35 fellow passengers will travel in the relaxed and romantic ambience of the Edwardian era on an Orient Express train. From the kilted piper who greets you on the station platform to the restored grandeur of the mahogany-paneled parlor car and richly refurbished private compartments, the attention to detail is everywhere. You'll journey through glens and mountain passes on remote and little-used railway lines with frequent stops to visit castles, distilleries, and scenic harbor towns. The elegant dining cars host excellent meals reflecting the local bounty, from full Scottish breakfasts to dinners featuring loch prawns, smoked salmon, or rack of lamb. The wine selection is surpassed only by the whisky tastings; enjoy your dram or two to the full—you'll not be driving home tonight.

Where: 375 miles/603 km north of London. **Balmoral Hotel:** Tel 44/131-556-2414; in the U.S., 888-667-9477; www.thebalmoralhotel.com. *Cost:* from $600; dinner at Number One $90. ***The Royal Scotsman:*** In the U.K., tel 0845–217-0799; in the U.S., 800-524-2420; www.royalscotsman.com. *Cost:* options begin with a 2-night tour of the Highlands from $3,720, all-inclusive. *When:* May–Oct. **Best time:** May–Sep for nicest weather.

Heart and Soul of Historic and Cultural Scotland

Edinburgh Castle and Festivals

Edinburgh, Scotland

One of Europe's loveliest capital cities, Edinburgh owes much of its character and good looks to its showcase landmark, Edinburgh Castle, atop the craggy remains of an ancient volcano overlooking the surrounding city. This sprawling structure has played many roles: fortress, military garrison, state prison. But its zenith was as royal palace, and today visitors come to see the Honours of Scotland (the Scottish crown jewels). The oldest regalia in Europe, they include the Scottish crown, scepter, and sword of state. Other highlights here include the royal chambers—used until the king permanently moved to England in 1603—where Mary, Queen of Scots, gave birth to James VI of Scotland, who would rule England as James I.

From the castle, the famous streets of the Royal Mile lead down toward the Palace of Holyroodhouse—the official residence of the British monarch in Scotland, and more simply called Holyrood Palace. Branching off this noble thoroughfare are the narrow lanes and alleyways of the Old Town that still evoke the Middle Ages. Among the many historic buildings is The Scotsman, once the headquarters of the newspaper of the same name and now a history-steeped hotel. The exterior is a fantastical mix of Baroque and Gothic styles, with castlelike towers and turrets and stained glass, while the inside retains many original features, such as oak-paneled walls.

For a change of scene and century, cross the bridge below the castle to the orderly streets and squares of New Town. Here you'll find the classic Caledonian Hotel—enveloped in Edwardian splendor and renowned for its views of the medieval skyline and spires of the Royal Mile—and, of course, the castle, most romantic when brightly illuminated at night.

Every August, all eyes are on this venerable city for the Edinburgh International Festival, a world-class extravaganza of music, drama, and dance founded in 1947 that transforms the sleepy, historic city into a vibrant cultural epicenter. Garnering equal attention is the Edinburgh Festival Fringe, its amateur offshoot that is almost as old; you can expect the unexpected from thousands of performers in hundreds of venues, from pubs to churches. In contrast, the well-ordered display of the nighttime Edinburgh Military Tattoo, also held in August, is possibly the world's most outstanding military spectacle, augmented by its dramatic floodlit setting on a castle esplanade.

As lively as the summer festivities is New Year's Eve. Known as Hogmanay throughout Scotland, it's celebrated with special fervor in Edinburgh, which hosts Europe's greatest street party, with song and dance carrying through the night and well into the morning.

Visitor info: www.edinburgh.org. **Edinburgh Castle:** www.edinburghcastle.gov.uk. **The Scotsman:** Tel 44/131-556-5565; www.thescotsmanhotel.co.uk. *Cost:* from $235 (off-peak), from $565 (peak). **Caledonian Hilton Hotel:** Tel 44/131-222-8888; www.hilton.co.uk/caledonian. *Cost:* from $240. **Edinburgh festivals:** www.edinburghfestivals.co.uk. **Best times:** May–Sep for best weather; Aug–early Sep for major festivals.

Fine Design and High Style in Scotland's Second City

Mackintosh's Glasgow

Glasgow, Scotland

Just as Barcelona is associated with the architecture of Gaudí and London linked to the churches of Christopher Wren, Glasgow is proudly home to the work of Scotland's best-known architect-designer, Charles Rennie Mackintosh (1868–1928). His style, characterized by curves and floral motifs, is often regarded as the epitome of Art Nouveau; but he's also cited as an Art Deco influence thanks to the clean lines and abstract shapes he favored. His major achievement, heralded as one of Europe's finest examples of Modernism, is the Glasgow School of Art, completed in 1899 when Mackintosh was just 32. The only church he ever designed is at Queen's Cross; it's now headquarters for the Charles Rennie Mackintosh Society, which organizes tours of all his key sites.

Mackintosh's tearooms were renowned, and he ultimately became as known for his furniture designs as for his architecture. Experience both at the Willow Tearoom on Sauchiehall Street; some of the tables and chairs may be reproductions, but the atmosphere is authentic. Ask to be seated in the Room de Luxe, an Art Nouveau fantasy.

Beyond specific addresses, the artist's inimitable style remains vividly alive throughout town—from designs found on wrought-iron gates and decorative motifs used on restaurant menus to the ubiquitous, stylized rose that has become a kind of Glasgow logo.

Also emblematic of the city is the Grand Central Hotel, another Glasgow landmark, built in 1883 next to the main train station and newly refurbished. Fans of architecture and design will also appreciate the elegant style of the Hotel du Vin at One Devonshire Gardens. You may need to ring the front doorbell upon arrival, but it will be the last time you'll lift a finger here. Five exquisitely renovated Victorian town houses have been connected to create a chic jewel box, where superb service and a much touted restaurant (and a whisky bar with more than 300 varieties) may tempt you to see not a whit of Glasgow beyond its gorgeous walls.

Tea at the Willow offers the chance to experience a bygone era amid Mackintosh's design.

Where: 40 miles/64 km west of Edinburgh. **Visitor info:** www.visitglasgow.com. **Charles Rennie Mackintosh Society:** Tel 44/141-946-6600; www.crmsociety.com. **Willow Tearoom:** Tel 44/141-353-5500; www.willowtearooms.co.uk. **Grand Central Hotel:** Tel 44/141-240-3700; www.principal-hayley.com. *Cost:* from $160. **Hotel du Vin:** Tel 44/141-339-2001; www.hotelduvin.com. *Cost:* from $180 (off-peak), from $240 (peak); dinner $50. **Best times:** May–Sep for pleasant weather; Jan for Celtic Connections, one of the world's largest folk and traditional music festivals; Jun for West End Festival of music and the arts.

Mountains and Monuments in Scotland's Northeast

THE CASTLE TRAIL

Grampian Mountains, Scotland

A long history of battles, clan rivalries, and English invasions manifests itself in the 1,000-plus castles dotting Scotland's landscape. Some are evocative ruins or little more than long-forgotten mounds in the heather, while others appear as sturdy and foreboding as the day they were built. Many remain inhabited after being flamboyantly refurbished in the Victorian era, when Scotland's land-owning classes rediscovered a penchant for the turrets and towers of baronial architecture.

One of the greatest concentrations of castles can be found in Scotland's northeast, the eastern foothills of the Grampian Mountains inland from the "granite city" of Aberdeen. Fourteen of the finest examples have been linked to form the Castle Trail, a signposted route for drivers that's similar to the Whisky Trail of Speyside (see p. 42), farther to the west. Whether the castles are managed by public trusts or in private hands, all are open to the public.

The impressive collection includes the Delgatie Castle, one of the oldest in Scotland (A.D. 1030), and the ruins of the 13th-century Kildrummy Castle. The most lavishly restored—now grand, stately homes—are Castle Fraser, Crathes Castle, and Fyvie Castle; many are surrounded by impressive gardens that add an extra layer of splendor to any tour of the Grampian region.

Exploring beyond the formal Castle Trail, fortress fans can enjoy the dramatic ruins of Slains Castle, said to have inspired Bram Stoker to write *Dracula*. Possibly the most dramatic location of all is the cliff-top towers and battlements of Dunnottar, where Franco Zeffirelli chose to film *Hamlet* in 1990.

Another literary landmark can be found to the northwest, at 700-year-old Castle Cawdor, which has a famous connection to Shakespeare's Macbeth (though Macbeth is supposed to have reigned some 3 centuries before the castle was built). Balmoral Castle, in the south of the region, is perhaps the best-known of all. It was the "dear paradise" of Queen Victoria, and remains the private summer residence of the British sovereign.

Maintain the theme by checking into the Castle Hotel at Huntly, a fine old mansion originally built for the Dukes of Gordon near the castle that provided its name as well as much of the building's stone. (Huntly Castle itself, by the way, is yet another impressive ruin on the trail.) For a livelier setting, turn to the 19th-century landmark Douglas Hotel in Aberdeen, where a nearby harbor hosts fishing boats bringing in catches from the Arctic waters and ferries departing for the islands of Orkney (see p. 44) and Shetland.

Drum Castle's square tower was built in the 13th century.

WHERE: Aberdeen is 125 miles/201

km north of Edinburgh. **VISITOR INFO:** www.aberdeen-grampian.com. **CASTLE TRAIL:** 3 main loops, in total about 150 miles/241 km long. **CASTLE HOTEL:** Tel 44/1466-792-696; www.castlehotel.uk.com. *Cost:* from $180. **DOUGLAS HOTEL:** Tel 44/1224-582-255; www.aberdeendouglas.com. *Cost:* from $210. **BEST TIME:** Apr–Sep for nicest weather.

Islands at the Edge of the Sea

THE HEBRIDES

Scotland

Off the crenellated northwest coast of Scotland lie the islands of the Hebrides. Divided neatly into two areas—Inner and Outer Hebrides—they are as representative of Scotland as are the Highlands but manage to feel a world apart. The landscape of the Inner Hebrides never fails to impress, with high mountains dropping precipitously to the rocky shores and narrow sea-lochs cutting deep inland. On the island of Mull you'll find the dark, rocky peak of Ben Mor and the scenic port of Tobermory, with its waterfront of gaily painted houses. Nearby is the sacred isle of Iona, with the less-than-holy-sounding islands of Muck and Rum nearby.

But the most famous of all the Inner Hebrides is the Isle of Skye—one of Scotland's largest islands at over 530 square miles, as well as the closest to the mainland. Such proximity brought the inevitable arrival of a bridge in the 1990s, putting an end to the ferry service that had run since the 17th century. Yet Skye retains its air of mystery and otherworldliness. The perfect place to drink it all in is at Kinloch Lodge, in the beautiful southern corner of the island. Built in 1680 as a hunting lodge, this elegant yet unpretentious hotel is today the home of Lord Macdonald, high chief of the Clan Donald, and his wife, Claire, a leading authority on Scottish cooking. Her passion is on display in the dinners served in the elegant restaurant, lined with ancestral portraits, where non-guests are welcome.

Farther to the west are the Outer Hebrides, also called the Western Isles, a wild and remote region that's still relatively untrammeled by tourism. The main islands include Barra, Benbecula, and the connected pair of Lewis and Harris. Rugged topography and frequent rain mean many freshwater lochs, and the view from the top of an Outer Hebridean mountain is of a complex landscape where land and sea become intertwined.

For travelers with a taste for adventure, an end-to-end road and ferry tour of the island chain is a must. Be sure to stop for a night at the Hotel Hebrides, a boutique hotel on the Isle of Harris, with unexpectedly sleek, contemporary rooms and an excellent restaurant specializing in Scottish seafood.

Or take to the sea and view the powerful, bleak, and mystical beauty of the islands from the deck of the *Hebridean Princess.* The romantic, five-star vessel is more like an opulent country-house hotel famed for its service than a cruise ship. (The Queen charters it for family sailings.) It carries just 50 very cosseted passengers who lounge in the handsome, chintz-draped cabins (some with private balconies), dine on superb smoked salmon and island-raised lamb, and sample an impressive variety of Scotch whisky.

WHERE: Oban is the gateway to the Hebrides, 124 miles/200 km northwest of

Edinburgh. **VISITOR INFO:** www.visithebrides.com. **KINLOCH LODGE:** Tel 44/1471-833-333; www.kinloch-lodge.co.uk. *Cost:* from $320, inclusive; 4-course dinner $90. **HOTEL HEBRIDES:** Tel 44/1859-502-364; www.hotel-hebrides.com. *Cost:* from $87; dinner $45. ***HEBRIDEAN PRINCESS:*** Tel 44/1756-704-700; in the U.S., 877-600-2648; www.hebrideancruises.com. *Cost:* 7-night cruise from $3,200; 4- to 10-day cruises available in Scotland and beyond. Originates in Oban. *When:* Mar–Nov. **BEST TIMES:** May–Sep for best weather; mid-Jul for Lewis Highland Games; early Aug for Skye Highland Games.

A Warm Welcome Among the Lochs and Glens

ARGYLL HIGHLANDS

Highlands, Scotland

Halfway along Scotland's filigree western coastline is the dramatic region of Argyll, where hills, glens, forests, and mountains stretch from the remote Ardnamurchan Peninsula, down to the Mull of Kintyre Lighthouse.

Islands such as Colonsay, Mull, and Jura are just a ferry hop away across narrow straits, and slender fjordlike inlets dissect the landscape. All across Argyll, the lines between island and mainland become wonderfully blurred.

The main town in the region is Oban ("the gateway to the isles"); from there, ferries cross to the islands of the Inner and Outer Hebrides (see previous page). Check in to Alt na Craig House, a stylish, six-room guesthouse set in large gardens on the edge of town, with great views of the bay and out toward the islands.

If driving to Oban from Edinburgh or Glasgow, be sure to take the scenic route that cuts across the heart of the Argyll Highlands, through Glen Aray and past the beautiful (and suitably named) Loch Awe. Pause at the handsome town of Inveraray (the ancient capital of Argyll) to admire Inveraray Castle, home of the Duke of Argyll, or detour down the western shore of Loch Fyne to the 90 acres of lush greenery at Crarae Gardens. Don't miss lunch at the Loch Fyne Oyster Bar near Cairndow, an unassuming place founded in the 1980s as a roadside shed that later spawned a chain of seafood restaurants across Britain.

North of Oban, the road continues alongside the wildly beautiful banks of Loch Linnhe and to the village of Port Appin, home to the intimate Airds Hotel. Once an inn serving ferry passengers headed out to the islands, it's now a peaceful vacationers' retreat with ample corners for relaxation: in the garden with its views of the loch, fireside in the lounge, or in the restaurant or bar, where you'll enjoy excellent local fare and malt whiskies.

Inverlochy Castle can be found another 20 miles beyond Port Appin, across Argyll's northern border and near the town of Fort William. This is where Queen Victoria, no stranger to the allure of the Highlands, stayed in 1873 and famously wrote: "I never saw a lovelier or more romantic spot." Set in a magnificent landscape, the former baronial castle, set on 500 acres of private land, is now a grand 17-room hotel awash with antique furniture, floral drapes, and overstuffed chairs. One of Britain's most special country retreats, it offers visitors a taste of life as lived by a noble monarch.

WHERE: 120 miles/200 km northwest of Edinburgh. **VISITOR INFO:** www.visitscottishheartlands.com. **ALT NA CRAIG HOUSE:** Tel

44/1631-564-524; www.guesthouseinoban.com. *Cost:* from $195. **Loch Fyne Oyster Bar:** Tel 44/1499-600-482; www.lochfyne.com. *Cost:* lunch $30. **Airds Hotel:** Tel 44/1631-730-236; www.airds-hotel.com. *Cost:* from $450, inclusive; dinner $80. **Inverlochy Castle:** Tel 44/1397-702-177; in the U.S., 888-424-0106; www.inverlochycastlehotel.com. *Cost:* from $520 (off-peak), from $715 (peak); 4-course prix-fixe dinner $110. **Best time:** May–Sep for the finest weather.

Scotland's longest lake, Loch Awe, stretches over 20 miles.

Hammers, Heavies, and Ancient Traditions

Highland Games

Braemar, Highlands, Scotland

Blazing with brightly colored tartans and ringing with the sound of bagpipes, the Highland Games are unique sporting and cultural events celebrating all things Scottish, and are held in towns throughout the Highlands every summer. The games, or "gatherings," go back at least 900 years. They originated as county fairs with competitions providing clan chiefs the chance to observe the physical prowess of the area's most promising young lads. The tradition continues today, as a breed of tough, kilted Scotsmen known as Heavies engage in traditional sports such as "throwing the hammer," "putting the stone," and the gatherings' prime event, "tossing the caber"—heaving a 20-foot tree trunk weighing upward of 130 pounds. Alongside the traditional musclebound displays, there are foot races and long-jump competitions, plus all kinds of Highlands dancing and music, and a wee bit of whisky to help the celebrations along.

Of Scotland's 40-plus annual gatherings, those at Braemar are among the most renowned. In the 19th century, Queen Victoria used to come to watch from her nearby Scottish residence of Balmoral Castle, and the current royal family maintains the tradition, with the men donning kilts for the occasion. The monarch is honored as Chieftain of the Braemar Gathering.

If watching the Highland dancers and athletes tires you out or stirs up your appetite, a night at the Auld Kirk in the charming little town of Ballater, a few miles east of Braemar, will reinvigorate the senses. This former Victorian-era church is now a fine restaurant, with many of the original ecclesiastical details still in place, making it an intriguing setting in which to enjoy modern Scottish cuisine. And though the emphasis here is on food, six welcoming bedrooms are hidden away in the Kirk's upper floor, providing a perfect place to prolong the experience.

Braemar: 80 miles/129 km north of Edinburgh. **Visitor info:** www.braemargathering.org. **When:** Gatherings are held across Scotland late May–Sep; Braemar Gathering is 1st Sat in Sep. **The Auld Kirk:** Tel 44/1339-755-762; www.theauldkirk.co.uk. *Cost:* from $180; dinner $50.

Magnificent Home of a Mythical Monster

Loch Ness

Highlands, Scotland

The deep waters of Loch Ness lie in a giant gash in the earth's surface—a 60-million-year-old diagonal fault line that almost splits Scotland in two, with the Highland capital of Inverness at its northern end. Measuring 24 miles long and 755 feet deep, it's one of the largest "lochs" (lakes) in Scotland, but its main claim to fame remains almost exclusively as home to the mythic Loch Ness Monster.

Resembling an aquatic dinosaur, and said to have descended from a forebear trapped within the waters back in geological times, this beast was allegedly first spotted in 565 by St. Columba, the man credited with introducing Christianity to Scotland. Centuries later, the monster was given the Latin title *Nessiteras rhombopteryx* (quickly shortened to Nessie) and has held the world's imagination ever since. An ancient legend predicts a violent end for the region if the monster is ever captured, but researchers using sophisticated underwater technology and sonar-rigged mini-submarines continue their quest nonetheless and have recorded large, moving underwater objects they could not explain. They are still spurred on by reports of sightings from 1961, when 30 visitors said they saw the monster just before an explosion that sank their craft, and 1973, when a local monk claimed a viewing.

Whether you believe in the creature or not (many suggest that Scotland's age-old love of whisky may have something to do with the sightings), a glimpse of the beautiful glacier-gouged lake and the crumbling ruins of Urquhart Castle atop a small promontory is not to be missed. Take the less-trafficked road along the eastern shore to the village of Foyers and the striking waterfalls nearby. Or, from the settlement of Drumnadrochit (where the Loch Ness Centre & Exhibition is a fun place to spend an hour), aim westward and follow the road through peaceful Glen Urquhart, eventually reaching remote Glen Affric, one of the most scenic valleys in all Scotland.

Back in the "Highland capital" of Inverness, check into the Rocpool Reserve Hotel, an excellent little luxury option in the heart of the city. The décor is contemporary and the food at Chez Roux Restaurant is first-class. Alternatively, opt for the larger Loch Ness Country House Hotel at Dunain Park, just south of Inverness on the road to the loch, complete with cozy drawing rooms, log fires, and a beautiful outdoor garden. It's worth going the extra mile down the west side of the loch to the village of Invermoriston and the Old Manse. This warm, family-run B&B has just two romantic guest bedrooms, each with a private Victorian-style lounge and beautiful formal gardens surrounded by woodland.

Where: Inverness is 171 miles/275 km north of Edinburgh. **Visitor info:** www.visitlochness.com. **Rocpool Reserve Hotel:** Tel 44/1463-240-089; in the U.S., 866-376-7831; www.rocpool.com. *Cost:* from $320; dinner $55. **Loch Ness Country House Hotel:** Tel 44/1463-230-512; www.lochnesscountryhousehotel.co.uk. *Cost:* from $240; dinner $50. **Old Manse:** Tel 44/1320-351-296; www.theoldmanse-lochness.co.uk. *Cost:* from $180. **Best times:** May–Sep for nice weather; end of Jul for Inverness Highland Games; Sep–Oct for fall colors in Glen Affric.

Water of Life

The Malt Whisky Trail

Speyside, Highlands, Scotland

Just as true Champagne can come only from the Champagne region in France (see p. 107), authentic Scotch malt whisky (spelled without an "e" and from the Gaelic *uisge beatha* meaning "water of life") must be made on its native soil. There are distilleries all over Scotland—at any given time there are 18.5 million barrels of maturing whiskies—but the most celebrated home of whisky is the Highland region, and the very epicenter is Speyside—the valley of the River Spey—to the north of the Grampian Mountains. Here the finest examples of Scotland's amber spirits have been produced for centuries.

Glenfiddich is still owned by the family that founded it.

Coming from the south, the gateway to the area is Grantown-on-Spey, where you can pick up the Malt Whisky Trail—a signposted route for drivers that leads to some of the most memorable spots at which to discover the mystery of the malt. These include the Glenfiddich Distillery in Dufftown, the whisky-making capital of the Western world; the Glenlivet Distillery, in the village of the same name; and Cardhu and Glen Grant, both near the town of Aberlour. Nearby are other companies, well known to whisky aficionados, such as Glen Moray, in Elgin, and Benromach, near Forres, as well as several smaller and lesser-known distilleries that all make tempting detours.

Each whisky made in Speyside has a distinct flavor, as a visit to a number of distilleries will prove. The use of pure water is key, as is the quality of the barley and the amount of peat used to stoke the fire used in the production. To fully appreciate these nuances, connoisseurs delight in sampling a range of single malts—as opposed to blended whisky, which is the marriage of single malts and "neutral" spirits and regarded as an inferior product. Keep to the genuine article, though, and after a few wee drams you'll find the distinction between one amber elixir and the next may get a little cloudy.

Designated drivers can take their charges to Cawdor Cottages, a location hard to beat for either history or style. Set within the 50-square-mile estate belonging to the 1375 Cawdor Castle, just west of Forres, its five cottages have been decorated with flawless taste by Lady Cawdor, a former fashion-magazine editor. Or base yourself at the other end of the whisky trail, in Grantown-on-Spey, where small and friendly Dunallan House is a lovingly restored Victorian villa on a quiet street near the edge of town.

Where: 100 miles/161 km north of Edinburgh. **Visitor info:** www.maltwhiskytrail.com. **Cawdor Cottages:** Tel 44/1667-402-402; www.cawdor.com. *Cost:* 3-night stay from $490 (off-peak), from $730 (peak). **Dunallan House:** Tel 44/1479-872-140; www.dunallan.com. *Cost:* from $90. **Best times:** May–Sep for pleasant weather; May and Sep for Spirit of Speyside Whisky Festival.

In the Footsteps of Rob Roy and Braveheart

Loch Lomond and the Trossachs

Scotland

Just beyond the city limits of Glasgow, the hills, lochs, and glens of the Trossachs ("bristly country") provide an enticing first taste of the classic Scottish wildness usually associated with the more mountainous country farther north. This is where the Highlands meet the heather-clad Lowlands, whose centerpiece is Loch Lomond, the largest and most famous of Scotland's fjordlike lakes.

It was here that Rob Roy ("Red Robert") MacGregor—a real-life, 18th-century cattle dealer, Highlander, and outlaw—became a Scottish folk hero akin to England's Robin Hood. His fame spread far beyond Scotland thanks mainly to Sir Walter Scott's 1817 *Rob Roy*, a major blockbuster of its time.

Scott also found inspiration in the beauty of nearby Loch Katrine, where he set his narrative poem "The Lady of the Lake." Both it and Loch Lomond (and dozens of others) lie within the 720-square-mile Trossachs National Park—Scotland's first national park, established in 2002. Visitors come to hike and bike before stepping aboard the SS *Sir Walter Scott,* a small, century-old steamboat that plies the serene waters of Loch Katrine, which mirrors the forested shores beyond.

More heroes of Scotland's turbulent history are recalled just a few miles east of the Trossachs at Stirling Castle, the country's most significant stronghold: "He who holds Stirling, holds Scotland," goes an ancient adage. Dating from the 12th century and second only to Edinburgh Castle (see p. 35) in grandeur, it was the residence of the infant Mary, Queen of Scots: She was crowned here in 1543 at the age of 9 months. Just beyond is the National Wallace Monument, an impressive neo-Gothic tower overlooking the battlefield where William Wallace, legendary leader of Scotland's struggle for independence (and better known as Braveheart), fought against the English in the 13th century.

The only struggle you'll face is deciding where to stay. Monachyle Mhor, a remote, 18th-century farmhouse in the heart of the Trossachs has been transformed into a stylish family-run hotel with a celebrated restaurant that attracts foodies from miles around. Make time to visit the grave of Rob Roy in the churchyard of nearby Balquhidder as well as the charming town of Callander, situated neatly between Stirling and the Trossachs.

For a sampling of baronial life, there's the Cameron House, a grand castle-turned-hotel on the banks of Loch Lomond. In addition to its elegant rooms and tempting choice of bars and restaurants, the adjoining championship-standard Carrick course lets golfers test their skills. The best view in the house is from the spa's pool on the rooftop terrace.

Where: Callander is 50 miles/80 km northwest of Edinburgh. **Visitor info:** www.lochlomond-trossachs.org. **SS *Sir Walter Scott* and Loch Katrine:** Tel 44/1877-332-000; www.lochkatrine.com. *When:* Apr–Oct. **Stirling Castle:** 44/1786-450-000; www.stirlingcastle.gov.uk. **Monachyle Mhor:** Tel 44/1877-384-622; www.mhor.net. *Cost:* from $300; 5-course dinner $70. **Cameron House:**

Tel 44/1389-755-565; www.cameronhouse.co.uk. *Cost:* from $180 (off-peak), $450 (peak); dinner $65. **Best times:** May–Sep for finest weather; 2nd Sun in Jul for Stirling Highland Games; last weekend in Jul for Callander Highland Games; Sep for autumn colors.

Scotland's Rocky Northern Outpost

Orkney Islands

Scotland

Disconnected from the mainland by 6 miles of North Atlantic waters, the 67 islands that make up Scotland's remote Orkney archipelago are often figuratively—and literally—off the map. Their history is unconnected from the rest of the country's too: The islands have been part of Scotland only since the 1470s. Before that they were under Norwegian rule—a legacy of the Viking era, when Nordic peoples settled here and used the islands as a base for raids against other parts of Scotland. The Orkneys' Neolithic sites, from a much earlier period, are some of the best preserved in Europe. These include the village of semi-underground stone houses at Skara Brae and the mysterious standing stones known as the Ring of Brodgar.

Some 20 stones of the original 60 form the Ring of Brodgar, thought to have been erected more than 4,000 years ago.

Ferries run from Aberdeen, on the Scottish mainland, to Kirkwall, the small but surprisingly lively Orkney capital on the island of Mainland—one of just 20 that are inhabited. Set up base at the small and impeccably styled Albert Hotel, with clean lines and contemporary furniture and a famously welcoming bar. Or go for the more traditional décor of four-poster beds and antique accents at the Lynnfield Hotel, close to the island's distillery (it produces Orkney's finest export, Highland Park Whisky).

If Mainland isn't remote enough, the little island of Shapinsay is another ferry ride away. Thanks to a largely flat topography and fertile soil, it's given over mostly to cattle and sheep rearing, and its small size makes it possible to walk around in a day. Secluded beaches and seal- and bird-watching (with some 300 species of the latter identified) are among the attractions, with a sound track of the bleating of lambs and the cries of seagulls against the ocean waves.

As you walk, you cannot fail to spot Balfour Castle, a major landmark of Shapinsay with its famous seven spires. Built in 1848 by local landowner Thomas Balfour, today the whole castle can be rented out for exclusive use by groups of 6 to 18. Days are spent fishing at sea or playing croquet on the lawn, but Balfour Castle's best-known activity is shooting, particularly the specialty of "wildfowling" (for ducks and geese), which attracts hunting devotees from around the world.

Where: Mainland is 182 miles/293 km north of Aberdeen. **Visitor info:** www.visitorkney.com. **Albert Hotel:** Tel 44/1856-876-000; www.alberthotel.co.uk. *Cost:* from

$190. **Lynnfield Hotel:** Tel 44/1856-872-505; www.lynnfield.co.uk. *Cost:* from $175. **Balfour Castle:** Tel 44/1856-711-282; www.balfourcastle.co.uk. *Cost:* from $4,300 per day for a group of 6 guests, all-inclusive. **Best times:** Jun–Sep for nicest weather; Mar–Oct for birdlife; May for Orkney Traditional Folk Music festival.

Birthplace of the Royal and Ancient Game

Scottish Golf

Scotland

There are more than 550 courses in Scotland—more per capita than in any other country in the world—and they're some of the globe's finest. Many are true "links" courses, a term derived from the old Scottish word for coastal dunes and scrubby undergrowth; it's where trees are rare, bunkers are frequent, and unpredictable winds pose an additional hazard.

Officially recorded in 1552, golf is believed by historians to have originated in Scotland as a diversion for the bored aristocracy as early as the 14th century. You'll feel like nobility yourself at the grand, storied hotels near many of the courses, where the raison d'être is to indulge guests with as much top-notch playing as the long hours of daylight will permit—with luxurious après-golf accommodations to boot.

The Old Course at St. Andrews is the world's most legendary temple of golf, which explains why you sometimes need to reserve tee times up to a year in advance. To relax after your round, the 22-room St. Andrew's Golf Hotel offers excellent bay and links views plus a knowledgeable staff to help make your golf arrangements.

Near Edinburgh is the distinguished Muirfield, where top-level tournaments, including 11 Amateur Championships and 15 Open Championships, have been played over the years. Overlooking the fairways is the elegant Edwardian Greywalls Hotel, designed in 1901 by Edwin Lutyens (responsible for building much of New Delhi) and exuding the warmth of a private home.

Scotland's other hallowed greens include Gleneagles, with its venerable Queen's and King's courses and its PGA Centenary Course, designed by Jack Nicklaus, all framed by remarkable scenery. Beyond the Highland city of Inverness is the Royal Dornoch Golf Club; at just 6 degrees short of the Arctic Circle, it is the most northerly of the world's great courses as well as the third oldest on record. The historic club at Turnberry offers three magnificently situated coastal courses and even has its own lighthouse, while Carnoustie (6 miles east of Dundee) has a reputation for being treacherous—though world champions call it the best in Britain.

Visitor info: http://golf.visitscotland.com. **St. Andrews:** Tel 44/1334-466-666; www.standrewsgolf.org. *Cost:* greens fees for Old Course $105 (off-peak), $210 (peak). **St. Andrews Golf Hotel:** Tel 44/1334-472-611; www.standrews-golf.co.uk. *Cost:* from $300. **Muirfield:** Tel 44/1620-842-123; www.muirfield.org.uk. *Cost:* greens fees for visitors $285. **Greywalls Hotel:** Tel 44/1620-842-144; www.greywalls.co.uk. *Cost:* from $375. **Other courses:** www.gleneagles.com; www.royaldornoch.com; www.turnberry.co.uk; www.carnoustiegolflinks.co.uk. **Best time:** May–Sep for nicest weather conditions, although greens fees rise during this period.

Bookworm's Delight

HAY-ON-WYE

Mid Wales, Wales

Astride the border between England and Wales is compact little Hay-on-Wye. Often simply called Hay (the suffix comes from the River Wye, which flows through the town), this is the world's capital of antiquarian and secondhand books, and a monument to British eccentricity.

Hay was once a sleepy market town surrounded by sheep-grazed hills. Then along came Richard Booth in the 1960s, determined to reverse its economic decline by converting an empty building into the town's first bookstore. Thanks to his perseverance (and some successful publicity stunts, such as declaring Hay an independent nation), book buyers came in droves, and the town with a population of 2,000 now has more than 30 bookstores stocking millions of titles among them.

Hay's annual Festival of Literature, known to bibliophiles everywhere, is the largest gathering of its type in Britain, with writers and poets coming from around the world to give readings and hold informal discussions about their work. (Guest speakers have included Bill Clinton, who famously called it "the Woodstock of the mind.") Such is its success that satellite Hay Festivals now take place in locations as varied as Belfast, Cartagena, and Beirut.

Bookstores flourish in this small Welsh town.

After trawling the endless shelves looking for an elusive title, rest your legs at the Old Black Lion, one of Hay's most venerable pubs and restaurants. There are comfortable rooms upstairs, and breakfasts are especially good.

Or leave the town behind and travel into the 500-square-mile Brecon Beacons National Park, a broad range of rolling whaleback hills that separate the tranquil farmland and empty moors of Mid Wales from the industrialized valleys of the southeast. The main town, Brecon, is a good base for explorations, and it's home to a Hay sibling event: the annual Brecon Jazz Festival.

Stop at the White Swan Inn in Llanfrynach, about 15 miles south of Hay; the food is excellent, and the friendly ambience may tempt you to linger on one of the fireside sofas. Or head 10 minutes west from Hay to Llangoed Hall, a country hotel with a rich history (some parts date back to the 1600s) and several distinguished past owners, including the architect of Portmeirion (see p. 49) and Sir Bernard Ashley, cofounder, with wife, Laura, of the company that still bears her name. If you can tear yourself away from the delightfully decorated rooms, not to mention the fine restaurant, the River Wye wends its way through the hotel grounds (providing guests with some of the best salmon and trout fishing in Britain), while the 10 acres of pristine gardens offer views across to the dramatic Brecon Beacons on the horizon.

WHERE: 150 miles/245 km northwest of

London. **Visitor info:** www.hay-on-wye.co.uk. **Old Black Lion:** Tel 44/1497-820-841; www.oldblacklion.co.uk. *Cost:* from $135; dinner $45. **Brecon Beacons National Park:** www.breconbeacons.org. **White Swan:** Tel 44/1874-665-276; www.the-white-swan.com. *Cost:* dinner $50. **Llangoed Hall:** Tel 44/1874-754-525; www.llangoedhall.com. *Cost:* from $315; dinner $75. **Best times:** May–Sep for pleasant weather; late May–early Jun for Hay Festival; mid-Aug for Brecon Jazz Festival.

Stalwart Symbols of the Past

The Castles of North Wales

North Wales, Wales

No other country on earth has as many castles per square mile as Wales. From Roman garrisons and Norman strongholds to medieval forts and fanciful follies of the Victorian era, the history of Wales is writ large in some 600 solid piles of stone. The finest collection of fortresses is in north Wales, most of them constructed at the end of the 13th century by England's empire-building King Edward I to impress and ultimately subdue the fiery Welsh.

If you're driving from England, the mighty Conwy Castle will likely be your first stop; as well as admiring the castle itself, be sure to take a walk along the perfectly preserved defensive walls that surround the medieval town. Just 10 miles to the west, on the island of Anglesey (Wales's largest, and where Will and Kate live part-time), the towers and battlements of Beaumaris Castle overlook the waters of Conwy Bay. Farther south is the dramatic ruin of Harlech Castle—inspiration for "Men of Harlech," an unofficial Welsh national anthem.

But the greatest of all is the crenellated Caernarfon Castle, with its distinctive octagonal towers. Edward II, born here in 1284, was given the honorary title of Prince of Wales as a clear symbol to the Welsh that the English were in charge, and to this day it is a title conferred on the eldest son of the reigning British monarch. The investiture of Prince Charles, the current Prince of Wales, took place at Caernarfon in 1969 amid great pomp and ceremony.

In sharp contrast to foreboding castle battlements are the genteel surrounds of Bodnant Garden, a few miles south of Conwy in Tay-y-Cafn, overlooking the Conwy Valley. It is one of the country's most luxuriant gardens, particularly when seen against the postcard-perfect backdrop of the mountains of Snowdonia (see p. 50). Fragrantly covering around 80 acres, the plantings are arranged in formal Italian-style terraces near the manor house and lead down to a woodland of colorful flowers, exotic shrubs, magnificent trees, and rock arrangements.

Nearby Bodysgallen Hall, housed in a 17th-century building, offers similar vistas of Snowdonia; its antiques-furnished interiors, leavened with just the right modern touches, create a bucolic retreat.

At the historic and more informal Groes Inn, near Conwy, a traditional British pub is the unexpected setting for truly exceptional food and 14 comfortable rooms, some with balconies overlooking the surrounding Welsh countryside. Meanwhile, more refined dining is the draw at Seiont Manor Hotel, near

Caernarfon. After dinner relax by the fire in the cozy lounge or stroll by moonlight in the delightful gardens.

Where: Conwy is 210 miles/340 km northwest of London. **Visitor info:** www.gonorthwales.co.uk. **Castle info:** www.cadw.wales.gov.uk. **Bodnant Garden:** Tel 44/1492-650-469; www.bodnantgarden.co.uk. *When:* closed Dec–Jan. **Bodysgallen Hall:** Tel 44/1492-584-466, www.bodysgallen.com. *Cost:* from $225; dinner $60. **Groes Inn:** Tel 44/1492-650-545; www.groesinn.com. *Cost:* from $185; dinner $45. **Seiont Manor Hotel:** Tel 44/845-072-7550; www.handpickedhotels.co.uk. *Cost:* from $120; dinner $60. **Best times:** May–Sep for pleasant weather; Mar–Apr and Oct for Bodnant Garden at its finest.

Olympics of Welsh Culture

International Musical Eisteddfod

Llangollen, North Wales, Wales

Wales is known as "the Land of Song." Its tradition of poetry and music stretches back to the ancient Celtic era and is symbolized by the harp, the country's best-known instrument, in the same way that bagpipes represent Scotland. In more recent times, a vital part of Welsh culture has become that of male choirs—a tradition originating in the south Wales collieries of the mid-19th century and remaining strong today. It is said that when a Welsh male choir bursts into song, the audience bursts into tears, and the harmonies of the very best ensembles—a kind of aural waterfall—certainly seems spiritual.

Traditional poetry, harp music, male choirs, and much more are major attractions at eisteddfods (the plural in Welsh is *eisteddfodau*), festivals of Welsh music and language which trace their roots back to a 12th-century Celtic tradition of traveling bards. Today, eisteddfods are held annually across the country, with many of the events judged and winners declared in various categories. The pinnacle is the National Eisteddfod of Wales (*Eisteddfod Genedlaethol Cymru*), the largest gathering of competitive poetry and song in Europe. It is a totally Welsh-speaking festival (with headphone translations available for non-Welsh speakers) that's held in a different town every year, usually alternating between the north and the south.

In contrast, the International Musical Eisteddfod is held at the same venue every year—the town of Llangollen, with more than 4,000 performers of instrumental music, song, and dance from 50 countries around the world, often appearing in colorful national costume. It is recognized as one of the world's greatest music festivals. Competitive events are held during the day, with evenings given over to concerts, all of it intending to promote Wales's place in the wider world as well as global peace and harmony.

Where: Llangollen is 190 miles/308 km northwest of London. **Visitor info:** www.llangollen.org.uk. **National Eisteddfod:** www.eisteddfod.org.uk. *When:* 1 week, early Aug. **Llangollen International Musical Eisteddfod:** Tel 44/1978-862-001; www.international-eisteddfod.co.uk. *When:* 1 week, early Jul.

Nature's Beauty and One Man's Legacy

LLŶN PENINSULA

North Wales, Wales

Jutting out from northwest Wales is a very special corner of the country: the Llŷn Peninsula (or Lleyn, its English name). It's a popular holiday destination, thanks to an unspoiled rural landscape and a sandy, picturesque coastline.

Seaside resorts on the south side of the peninsula, such as Abersoch and Pwllheli, overlook the waters of Tremadoc Bay and are thus sheltered from the weather. To the north, the coast is rockier, with beaches such as Trefor and Nefyn Bay overlooked by the distinctive range of conical hills—including the three summits of Yr Eifl—that dominate the skyline. With a landscape like this, it comes as no surprise that much of the Llŷn Peninsula is designated as an Area of Outstanding Natural Beauty, a protection given to locations in England and Wales, second in importance only to national parks.

Portmeirion took its inspiration from southern Italy.

Near Pwllheli is one of the Llŷn Peninsula's gems, Plas Bodegroes, a handsome Georgian manor-house-turned-hotel whose quiet is broken only by birdsong. The emphasis here falls firmly on the cuisine—it's a "restaurant with rooms" more than a hotel, and it's one of the best places to eat in the country, serving temptations such as seared Nefyn Bay scallops with Carmarthen ham and butter pudding served with Welsh whisky ice cream.

At the far southeastern part of the peninsula is the historic town of Criccieth, with its 13th-century castle, one of the many constructed or strengthened in this region by King Edward I of England; other examples are Conwy and Caernarfon (see p. 47). Also here is the Moelwyn, another "restaurant with rooms," where the fabulous sea views from the vast picture windows are as enticing as the menu.

Nearby, the village of Portmeirion, more redolent of southern Italy than Wales with its campanile and piazzas, stands atop a wooded hillside with romantic views of sea, sand, and mountains. Reportedly inspired by a trip to Portofino, Welsh architect Sir Bertram Clough Williams-Ellis built the village in pieces, from 1925 to 1975, when it was completed on his 90th birthday.

At the edge of the village, down by the sea, is the Hotel Portmeirion, one of the architect's early ventures. Inaugurated in 1926, it reopened in 1990 after a major fire and has since been refurbished to its original charm, with an interior that's both opulent and informal. Noël Coward was inspired to write *Blithe Spirit*, his most ethereal play, while staying here.

WHERE: 200 miles/324 km northwest of London. **VISITOR INFO:** www.llyn.info. **PLAS BODEGROES:** Tel 44/1758-612-363; www.bodegroes.co.uk. *Cost:* from $240; dinner $67. **MOELWYN:** Tel 44/1766-522-500; www.themoelwyn.co.uk. *Cost:* from $110; dinner $35. **HOTEL PORTMEIRION:** Tel 44/1766-770-000; www.portmeirion-village.com. *Cost:* from $235 (off-peak), from $390 (peak), inclusive. **BEST TIMES:** May–Sep for nicest weather; May, Jun, Sep, and Oct for local festivals.

Arthurian Mountains and Victorian Railways

Snowdonia National Park

North Wales, Wales

Wales is as famed for stunning landscapes as for its historic castles, and the mountains of Snowdonia offer unparalleled grandeur and beauty. Dominating the scenery of northern Wales and protected as a national park (the first of three in the country), the area takes its name from Snowdon, at 3,560 feet the highest point in Wales (and higher than anything in England). According to myth, this rugged peak is watched over by the spirit of King Arthur, while underneath the rocky slopes his Knights of the Round Table lie sleeping. Its Welsh name, Yr Wyddfa, means "tomb," referring to the grave of Rhita Gawr, the legendary giant slain by King Arthur.

Unlike in many other countries, the national parks of Britain are inhabited, and Snowdonia is no exception—it is home to over 26,000 people. One of the villages within its rugged terrain, Llanberis, is the departure point for a 3-hour trek to the summit. A more relaxing ascent is on the Snowdon Mountain Railway, installed for Victorian sightseers a century ago with steam-powered locomotives still going strong today. Trains stop just 70 feet below the peak, leaving an easy climb for the final stage. From the top, on a clear day, you can see much of the park's 840 square miles and as far as Ireland's Wicklow Mountains (see p. 75), 90 miles away across the Irish Sea.

There are endless opportunities to hike and bike on marked trails amid a vast range of spectacular scenery and wildlife. For train buffs, there are other narrow-gauge steam railways within the park; most were originally built to transport slate from quarries on the high ground to harbors on the coast, but now they provide entertaining rides through the Welsh countryside, connecting tiny villages and remote stations, such as Dduallt, still not accessible by car.

Within the southern range of the park, about 20 miles south of Llanberis, in the village of Talsarnau, is Maes-y-Neuadd, a handsome 14th-century manor house (with more recent 16th- and 18th-century additions). Offering a range of room styles from traditional to more contemporary, it's the perfect base from which to explore the mountains and railways, as well as Harlech Castle (see p. 47), just 3 miles away. The restaurant offers freshly prepared meals made with ingredients from the hotel's own garden or locally sourced that are perfectly topped with a board of specialty Welsh cheeses.

Just beyond the park's southern border in Eglwys Fach, near the historic town of Machynlleth, is Ynyshir Hall. Once owned by Queen Victoria, it's now a hideaway hotel, perfect for guests seeking luxury in a tranquil, rural location. The main house, with just nine rooms and an acclaimed restaurant, dates back to the 15th century, giving a palpable sense of royal history, with the mountains of Snowdonia still within easy reach.

Where: Llanberis is 200 miles/324 km northwest of London. **Visitor info:** www.eryri-npa.gov.uk/visiting; www.greatlittletrainsofwales.co.uk. **Hotel Maes-y-Neuadd:** Tel 44/1766-780-200; www.neuadd.com. *Cost:* from $130; dinner $55. **Ynyshir Hall:** Tel 44/1654-781-209; www.ynyshirhall.co.uk. *Cost:* from $450; dinner $120. **Best times:** May–Sep for pleasant weather; Jul–Aug is busiest.

Poetic Landscapes

DYLAN THOMAS COUNTRY

South Wales, Wales

In the county of Camarthenshire is the little coastal town of Laugharne (Talacharn), best known as the home of Dylan Thomas (1914–1953), the nation's favorite poet. A simple white cross in St. Martin's churchyard marks his grave and that of his wife, Caitlin, and there are still a few old-timers in town who remember him sitting in the bar at Brown's Hotel, where he would regularly enjoy a pint.

"The Boathouse," where he lived with Caitlin for the last years of his life, is now a museum whose quiet setting overlooking the estuary of the River Taf exudes a lyric beauty. Nearby, his writing shed is just as he left it, filled with his papers, manuscripts, and furnishings. It was here that he wrote some of his most famous works, including part of *Under Milk Wood,* his landmark "play for voices," that was translated into the classic 1972 film, shot close by, starring Elizabeth Taylor, Peter O'Toole, and the Welsh-born Richard Burton.

For a place to stay in Laugharne, the finest is Hurst House on the Marsh, a luxurious hotel just to the south of the village. Originally part of a 16th-century dairy farm, the main building is now a stylish mix of modern and traditional designs, while the restaurant has the relaxing air of a conservatory.

Thomas was born and educated east of Laugharne in Swansea, Wales's second largest city. He worked on the local newspaper there and frequented the local pubs, especially in the area known as the Mumbles. Today, his life and work are celebrated at the Dylan Thomas Centre, in an area near the city's former docks now revitalized as the Maritime Quarter; the Centre is a focal point for Thomas-related studies and regular arts events, including the annual Dylan Thomas Festival.

Thomas lived and wrote here from 1949 to 1953.

From Swansea, stretching for 15 miles into the waters of Carmarthen Bay, is the sparsely populated Gower Peninsula, a scenic enclave of green hills, rocky hillocks, and sandy, surf-pounded beaches. In the heart of this officially declared Area of Outstanding Natural Beauty is the suitably magical Fairyhill Hotel, in the village of Reynoldston. This 200-year-old country house has just eight inviting rooms, ensuring a peaceful stay, while the highly regarded restaurant lets you enjoy a taste of Wales.

WHERE: Laugharne is 180 miles/308 km west of London. **VISITOR INFO:** www.dylanthomasboathouse.com. **HURST HOUSE:** Tel 44/1994-427-417; www.hurst-house.co.uk. *Cost:* from $285; dinner $55. **FAIRYHILL HOTEL:** Tel 44/1792-390-139; www.fairyhill.net. *Cost:* from $295; dinner $70. **BEST TIMES:** May–Sep for nicest weather; late Oct–Nov for 12-day Dylan Thomas Festival, in Swansea.

In the Footsteps of Wordsworth

WYE VALLEY

Southeast Wales, Wales

For much of its southern extent, the border between England and Wales is marked by the River Wye. Starting as a small stream on the mountain of Plynlimon (Pumlumon in Welsh means "five peaks") the river flows through the remote hills of mid-Wales to reach Hay-on-Wye (see p. 46). South of here is the historic frontier town of Monmouth, with its castle built by a baron of William the Conqueror in 1067 (just a year after the seminal Battle of Hastings) and considerably damaged in the 17th century during the English Civil War.

Near Monmouth, the river is forced between cliffs and over rapids at a place called Symonds Yat, and the Wye Valley becomes narrow, with trees covering the steep slopes on both sides. On a bend in the river stand the ruins of Tintern Abbey. Centuries ago, a monk of the abbey wrote, "You will find among the woods something you never found in books," and the sense of peace and tranquility remains very much in place today.

Once a thriving center for religion and learning, and the richest abbey in Wales, it was founded in 1131 by Cistercian monks; today's soaring structure (ruined but remarkably intact in spots, and still spectacular) dates from the 13th century. Before being dissolved by Henry VIII in 1536, Tintern had grown to include an abbey church, chapter house, infirmary, and dining hall. Their remains are still clearly visible, with fine arches and traces of vast windows standing against the sky, the whole edifice an outstanding example of the medieval Gothic style.

Roofless and almost forgotten for 300 years, Tintern Abbey was rediscovered in the 18th century by artists and poets in search of picturesque locations. One such visitor was William Wordsworth; enchanted by this sylvan setting, he penned his much loved sonnet celebrating the greatness of God in nature: "And I have felt, a presence that disturbs me with the joy of elevated thoughts; a sense sublime. . . ."

Continue down the river to its mouth, where it meets the giant River Severn near the town of Chepstow. Here is another castle, built at the same time as Monmouth's, though it has weathered the years in better shape, making it one of the oldest surviving stone castles in Britain. Overlooking the river from its perch on the cliffs, its impressive towers are a reminder of the castle's strategic importance in days gone by, and a perfect finish to a tour along the beautiful River Wye.

Wordsworth and Tennyson found inspiration in Tintern Abbey.

WHERE: 120 miles/194 km west of London. **VISITOR INFO:** www.visitwyevalley.com. **WHERE TO STAY:** Small and romantic and with an acclaimed restaurant, the Crown at Whitebrook is located between Monmouth and Tintern.

Tel 44/1600-860-254; www.crownatwhitebrook.co.uk. *Cost:* from $220; dinner $85. **Best times:** late Jul for Monmouth Music Festival; late Aug for Monmouth Show, one of the largest festivals of agriculture and country life in Wales; Sep–Oct for fall colors.

Sacred Site on a Scenic Coastline

St. Davids Cathedral

Pembrokeshire, West Wales, Wales

The cathedral dedicated to the patron saint of Wales is the largest in the country—all out of proportion to the tiny town of St. Davids (population less than 2,000) in which it sits. Unlike many other cathedrals that dominate their surroundings, St. Davids is hidden away in a valley, a reminder of the days when it needed to be secluded from Viking raiders and marauding pirates. It's a short walk beyond the shops and houses of the town center, along a narrow street and through an ancient gatehouse, to reach the viewpoint overlooking the cathedral; a long flight of steps leads you down to its door.

St. David was born in this coastal corner of southwestern Wales around A.D. 500 and returned later in life to found a monastic community that grew to great importance. The cathedral, begun in the 12th century, was built in the same spot, flanked by the once magnificent Bishop's Palace, now a glorious ruin. St. David is buried here, making it Wales's most sacred site, with visitors still flocking as they did in the Middle Ages when the cathedral was one of Britain's most important places of pilgrimage.

Modern-day pilgrims may stop for earthly sustenance at Cwtch, the best restaurant in town. From the Welsh word for "snug," or "cuddle," the place entices diners with top-quality food served in smart yet informal surroundings.

The town of St. Davids is one of many settlements within the Pembrokeshire Coast National Park, comprising more than 250 miles of protected coastline. With craggy cliffs, stacks and blowholes, narrow inlets, and huddled bays, the park also contains a hinterland of rolling hills, the tranquil waterways of the Daugleddau Estuary, and the rocky peaks of the Preseli Mountains, said to be the mystical source of some of the stone menhirs that make up Stonehenge (see p. 31). Big waves and sandy beaches attract surfers and families, while hikers enjoy a network of cliff-top and seaside footpaths in the company of wildflowers and seabirds.

In the hamlet of Molleston, just outside Narberth and a gateway to the park from the east, is the Grove, one of the region's finest hotels. The 18th-century country house has been beautifully restored with just 12 rooms, a relaxed ambience, and first-class service. Other highlights include the contemporary restaurant and the exquisite garden, the latter a passion of the hotel's owners.

Where: 220 miles/356 km west of London. **Visitor info:** www.visitpembrokeshire.com. **Cwtch:** Tel 44/1437-720-491; www.cwtchrestaurant.co.uk. *Cost:* dinner $45. **The Grove:** Tel 44/1834-860-915; www.thegrove-narberth.co.uk. *Cost:* from $245 (off-peak), from $295 (peak); dinner $65. **Best times:** Mar 1 for St. David's Day; late May–Jun for St. Davids Cathedral Festival, featuring classical music; mid-Aug for Pembrokeshire County Show.

Moody Moonscapes to Stone Castles

THE COAST OF CLARE

County Clare, Ireland

A wonderland of all things rocky, the coast of County Clare runs the gamut from stone pastures and towering cliffs to a cluster of romantic castles. The area simply known as the Burren (in Irish *boireann,* or "stony place"), stretching 116 square miles below Galway Bay on Clare's northwestern edge, is a crackled landscape of steel-gray limestone exposed by the last ice age. It may seem barren at first glance, but up close, you'll see some of the nearly 1,000 species of wildflowers and plants in the only place in Europe where Mediterranean and Alpine flowers grow side by side. A well-signposted hiking trail, the 28-mile Burren Way, leads across rolling hills and winds up at Ballyvaughan and Gregans Castle Hotel, a refined manor house with a celebrated restaurant that welcomes the weary. It takes its name from the 15th-century former residence of the Prince of the Burren, across the way.

Doolin, on the coast, is Ireland's hotbed of trad (traditional) music. It is a one-street town, with more than its share of music pubs: McDermott's, McGann's, and Gus O'Conor's. Stop to wet your whistle and tap your feet before picking up the Burren Way, which winds south to the Cliffs of Moher, Ireland's most recognizable landmark. Stretching 5 miles along the Atlantic, these shale and sandstone cliffs drop more than 700 feet into the churning ocean and are home to major colonies of seabirds. Though the area is always crowded with tour buses, you can still enjoy a quiet moment if you arrive at sunset.

Contrived but nevertheless fun, raucous evenings at 15th-century Bunratty Castle, an Irish-village theme park, let you feast at eat-with-your-hands medieval banquets while seated at a torch-lit table and entertained with song. Make another castle your home for the night, at a historic hotel with exemplary service: Dromoland, the distinguished 16th-century ancestral home of the native Gaelic O'Briens, barons of Inchiquin and direct descendants of High King Brian Boru. The hotel has its own emerald green 18-hole, 410-acre golf course.

The Cliffs of Moher are among Ireland's most photographed natural wonders.

WHERE: The Burren is 33 miles/53 km north of Shannon. **VISITOR INFO:** www.discover ireland.ie. **BURREN NATIONAL PARK:** www .burrennationalpark.ie. **GREGANS CASTLE HOTEL:** Tel 353/65-707-7005; www.gregans .ie. *Cost:* from $275 (off-peak), from $350 (peak); dinner $75. *When:* closed Dec–mid-Feb. **BUNRATTY CASTLE:** Tel 353/61-36-0788; www.shannonheritage.com. *Cost:* $85. **DROMOLAND CASTLE:** Tel 353/61-36-8144; www.dromoland.ie. *Cost:* from $335 (off-peak), from $615 (peak); greens fees $130 (guests), $160 (nonguests). **BEST TIMES:** May–Jun for Burren flowers; late Feb for Doolin's trad music festival.

Heaven on the Green

IRELAND'S TEMPLES OF GOLF

Counties Clare and Kerry, Ireland

With spectacular, rolling green countryside, Ireland ranks as one of the most scenic and respected golf destinations on earth. More than 400 courses surround idyllic castle hotels (such as Adare and Dromoland; see p. 69 and previous page) and ramble across emerald pastures (see Horse Country, p. 68). Stellar courses reach from outside Dublin (the challenging championship Portmarnock Golf Links lies just 10 miles from the capital) to Donegal, to Northern Ireland (see Causeway Coast and the Kingdom of Mourne, pp. 77 and 79). But the outstanding links of Ireland's southwest remain the most visited.

Topping the wish list of many is the Ballybunion Golf Club, which graces the blustery gray coast of County Kerry. The closing stretch of its Old Course is considered among the most difficult anywhere, a "true test of golf," to quote five-time British Open champion Tom Watson. Lahinch Golf Club, in nearby County Clare, rivals its neighbor in both beauty and popularity, with an Old Course that undulates along the rugged coastline of Liscannor Bay, hiding greens, testing challengers, and earning the nickname "the St. Andrew's of Ireland," in reverence of the famed Scottish links (see p. 45). Between these two landmarks stands the much younger but equally impressive Doonbeg Golf Club. Opened in 2002, the course was designed by Greg Norman, who marveled at the mountainous dunes along Doughmore Bay and took full advantage of their natural offerings.

The riches don't end there. Waterville Links winds along Ballinskelligs Bay, and boasts inspiring views of the water and the Macgillycuddy Reeks mountain range. Killarney National Park's three courses can be found at the Killarney Golf & Fishing Club. The most revered is Killeen: Reopened in 2006, it now makes even better use of its position along Lough Leane, the largest freshwater lake of the region as well as an enchanting backdrop (and obstacle to avoid). The outstanding Arnold Palmer–designed Tralee is an invigorating course that hugs the Atlantic before snaking through towering dunes and crossing treacherous ravines, leaving its players to understand why Palmer claimed that he "designed the first nine, but surely God designed the back nine."

Ballybunion Golf Club: Tel 353/68-27146; www.ballybuniongolfclub.ie. *Cost:* greens fees from $56 (off-peak), from $90 (peak). **Lahinch Golf Club:** Tel 353/65-708-1003; www.lahinchgolf.com. *Cost:* greens fees from $140. **Doonbeg Golf Club:** Tel 353/65-905-5602; www.doonbeggolfclub.com. *Cost:* greens fees from $130 (off-peak), from $185

Ballybunion golfers must factor the coastal winds into their swings.

(peak). **Waterville Golf Links:** Tel 353/66-947-4102; www.watervillegolfclub.ie. *Cost:* greens fees from $85 (off-peak), from $210 (peak). **Killarney Golf & Fishing Club:** Tel 353/64-663-1034; www.killarney-golf.com. *Cost:* greens fees from $70. **Tralee Golf Club:** Tel 353/66-713-6379; www.traleegolfclub.com. *Cost:* greens fees $255. **How:** U.S.-based Irish Links specializes in custom-designed golf tours to all of Ireland's champion links. Tel 800-824-6538 or 203-363-0970; www.irish-links.com. **Best time:** Apr–Sep for nicest weather and when nonmembers are most welcomed.

Heavenly Music and Divine Inspiration

Cork Jazz Festival and Blarney Castle

County Cork, Ireland

Cork may be Ireland's number two city, but it hosts the country's number one jazz festival, which provides a long weekend of fun before the chill of winter settles in. The city is the south's sporting and commercial capital and is the source of two well-loved dry stouts, Murphy's and Beamish—still it is their chief competitor, Guinness, that sponsors the fest, a city staple since 1978. Beer plays a vital role in keeping the beat, though one overshadowed by the power, quality, and diversity of the music in a country in love with its musical heritage. The big-time international names perform in major venues around town, but the pubs and street corners can offer up some of the festival's most inspiring, and spontaneous, performances by up-and-coming talents. The enthusiasm for the arts also includes poetry readings, gallery shows, film screenings, and concerts showcasing hip-hop, blues, and world music. But jazz is the clear driver, so much so that a concurrent jazz festival runs in neighboring Kinsale (18 miles southwest). For a dose of traditional music, stop by An Spailpín Fánac (The Migrant Laborer), a classic Irish pub. More Irish hospitality can be found just a short walk from the city center at the Hayfield Manor, a family-run hotel that combines the warmth and charm of a 19th-century manor house with modern amenities and strikingly attentive service.

Don't miss your chance to attain the "gift of the gab" by kissing the Blarney Stone. Join the hordes that come from the distant corners of the world to clamber up the steep steps of 500-year-old Blarney Castle, 5 miles northwest of Cork. Then lie on your back over a sheer drop of 120 feet (strong-armed "holders" guarantee that there are no mishaps) to kiss a rock believed to have made its way here in 1314 from Scotland. Regardless of its origin, the stone was always believed to have special powers and remains one of the country's most enduring symbols.

Where: 76 miles/122 km southeast of Shannon. **Cork Jazz Festival:** www.corkjazzfestival.com. *When:* 4 days in late Oct. **An Spailpín Fánac:** Tel 353/21-427-7949. **Hayfield Manor Hotel:** Tel 353/21-484-5900; www.hayfieldmanor.ie. *Cost:* from $210 (off-peak), from $330 (peak). **Blarney Castle:** Tel 353/21-438-5252; www.blarneycastle.ie.htm.

From Famine to Food Revolution

CULINARY CORK

County Cork, Ireland

County Cork once saw masses of emigrants fleeing the 19th-century famine, known as the Great Hunger, but today it's the epicenter of Ireland's culinary reawakening and Slow Food movement. Its reputation as a food capital was launched when Myrtle Allen opened the restaurant at Ballymaloe House in 1964, and grew as her daughter-in-law Darina founded Ballymaloe's now famous Cookery School. With orchards, gardens, and a 100-acre farm outside its front door, Ballymaloe emphasizes cooking the freshest ingredients simply. Darina helped found the nearby farmers market in Midleton, which is known for its food festival, its former Jameson distillery with 18th-century mill, and its beloved Farmgate Restaurant.

In Cork City, Farmgate's sister café, upstairs at the famous redbrick English Market, offers breakfasts and lunches made with impeccable ingredients from the market's plethora of butchers, fishmongers, produce stands, bakeries, and cheese purveyors. Nearby, prized Café Paradiso serves dinners with locally sourced vegetables crafted into dishes by Cork native chef Denis Cotter that will tempt even stubborn meat eaters. (Beamish ice cream made with local stout meets no resistance either.) South of Cork City, seaside Kinsale, with its harbor full of bobbing boats, is called Ireland's Culinary Capital for its International Gourmet Festival every October. Great dining can be had year-round at its many fine restaurants, such as Fishy Fishy, where treats include warm seafood salad tossed with sweet-spicy sauce and haddock battered with locally brewed lager.

Cork's guesthouses welcome with excellent food too. At Longueville House, his ancestral 18th-century Georgian mansion, acclaimed chef William O'Callaghan whips up salmon, trout, lamb, pork, and game (often smoked in their private smokehouse) from his 500-acre estate. He also offers Ireland's only apple brandy. Elegant yet relaxed Ballyvolane, is another well-known Georgian inn, renovated in the Italianate style, and near the salmon-rich Blackwater River. Ballyvolane hosts four-course dinners showcasing local artisanal specialties; the proprietor's father tends the vegetable garden and livestock. Homemade cookies and cordials await visitors in each of the six guest rooms, and the kitchen can prepare picnic lunches, handy for visits to their Blackwater Salmon Fishery, which affords angling guests private access to the storied river.

WHERE: Cork City is 76 miles/123 km southeast of Shannon. **VISITOR INFO:** www.goodfoodireland.ie. **BALLYMALOE:** Tel 353/21-465-2531; www.ballymaloe.ie. *Cost:* 5-course dinner $105. **JAMESON EXPERIENCE:** Tel 353/21-461-3594; www.tours.jamesonwhiskey.com. **FARMGATE:** in Midleton, tel 353/21-463-2771, in Cork City, tel 353/21-427-8134; www.farmgate.ie. **CAFÉ PARADISO:** Tel 353/21-427-7939; www.cafeparadiso.ie. *Cost:* lunch $30. **FISHY FISHY:** Tel 353/21-4700415; www.fishyfishy.ie. *Cost:* lunch $50. **LONGUEVILLE HOUSE:** Tel 353/22-47156, in the U.S., 800-323-5463; www.longuevillehouse.ie. *Cost:* from $250; dinner $90. **BALLYVOLANE:** Tel 353/25-36349; www.ballyvolanehouse.ie. *Cost:* from $210; dinner $70. **BEST TIMES:** Sep for Skibbereen's Taste of West Cork Festival, Cork's EAT Cork Festival, and Midleton's Food and Drink Festival; Oct for Kinsale's International Gourmet Food Festival.

The Island's Northernmost Fringe

WILD DONEGAL

County Donegal, Ireland

Rural, rugged, and always breathtaking, Donegal has a distinctive, top-o'-the-world feel. Its sea-torn coastline, in Ireland's northwestern corner, faces the open ocean in the direction of Iceland (see p. 354) and Greenland (see p. 345), and its wild waves, seaside caverns, waterfalls, forests, and mountains afford boundless opportunity for outdoor adventure. Explore it all by sea kayaking, scuba diving, hiking, surfing, or wildlife-watching. You'll find whales, basking sharks, and a variety of birds from puffins to peregrine falcons here.

The 30-mile-long Slieve League peninsula has some of Europe's tallest sea cliffs. It is Donegal's dramatic highlight, with a narrow trail along its top, the heart-stopping One Man's Pass. On the same peninsula, you'll find Slí Cholmcille's Way, a marked long-distance walking route that leads to graceful Assarancagh (Eas a' Ranca) Waterfall and stunning Glengesh Pass with its verdant mountains, valleys, and striking switchbacks. (If you're not up for exploring by foot, you can always drive the pass.) Glenveagh National Park—with placid lakes, heathered bogland, grazing red deer, and golden eagles overhead—is an essential wilderness excursion with a neo-Gothic castle at its heart.

The region has tenaciously preserved its heritage. For many, Irish Gaelic is the primary language here, including on Tory Island, where the year-round population of almost 200 elect their own "king." Currently he is Patsy Dan Rogers, an original member of the Tory School of Art (a celebrated style of primitive painting) who shows up to greet all passenger ferries.

On Donegal's northern periphery, a gorgeous fjord, Lough Swilly (Lake of Shadows), cuts a deep-set inlet. Deserted beaches skirt the edges of Swilly, where Rathmullen House is found, an informal and welcoming 19th-century guesthouse set in lush gardens, whose award-winning restaurant celebrates the local bounty.

Across Swilly, the pre-Celtic fort Grianan Ailligh, restored in the 1800s, stands on a hill with magnificent views, including the Inishowen Peninsula to the north. Drive the Inis Eoghain 100, a scenic 100-mile loop, and stop at the northernmost point in Ireland, Malin Head's rocky promontory. Due to its northern location, summer skies stay light long into the night, and as autumn approaches, a rare glimpse of the aurora borealis might be seen.

WHERE: 168 miles/271 km northwest of Dublin. **VISITOR INFO:** www.discoverireland.ie/northwest. **NATIONAL TRAILS OFFICE:** www.irishtrails.ie. **RATHMULLEN HOUSE:** Tel 353/74-915-8188; www.rathmullenhouse.com.

Ireland's highest sea cliffs lie along the Slieve League peninsula.

Cost: from $215; dinner $65. *When:* Mar–Oct; weekends only Nov, Dec, and Feb. Closed Jan. **Best times:** May–Aug for nicest weather; Jul for Earagail Arts Festival; Aug for guided hill walks and bird- and whale-watching during National Heritage Week.

Flavors Along the Liffey

Edible Dublin

Dublin, Ireland

Once known solely as a pub-grub destination, Dublin has—over the last few decades—become a gastronomic contender. Frenchman Patrick Guilbaud first opened his restaurant here in 1981, underpinning his elegant French menu with the finest Irish ingredients—fillet of Wicklow lamb, Clogher Head lobster, west coast king scallops—and paving the way for a citywide culinary awakening. Restaurant Patrick Guilbaud continues its reign in the Merrion Hotel, which is composed of four conjoined 18th-century town houses that feature lavish period furnishings, rococo plasterwork ceilings, peat-burning fireplaces, and a collection of Irish art. During Art Tea, the staff serves pastries inspired by the surrounding artwork, including miniature renditions of paintings, accompanied by a harpist on Sundays.

Like his French neighbor, Kevin Thornton reveres Ireland's bounty, evident at the restaurant that bears his name in the Fitzwilliam Hotel and overlooks St. Stephen's Green. He accompanies his signature dish, slowly braised suckling pig and trotter pomme Maxine, with a sauce of *poitín,* illegal Irish moonshine, one of the world's strongest liquors.

Across the River Liffey, Chapter One Restaurant pays homage to Dublin's obsession with all things literary. An adored institution in the basement of the Dublin Writers Museum (see p. 61), the former home of whiskey distiller John Jameson, Chapter One has a refined cellar-vault ambience with stacked-stone walls, arches, and a green-veined marble bar. A charcuterie trolley with meats cured and smoked by artisans, and a chef's table with a view of the kitchen's "culinary theater," make it a standout. Dublin has another literary-themed restaurant in the casual, homey Winding Stair, named after a W. B. Yeats poem. A landmark in the 1970s, when it hosted events for the creative community, it still has a popular bookshop beside the restaurant, which showcases informal fare like Irish seafood chowder with chorizo. High ceilings, old girders, sofas, bookshelves, bentwood furniture, and a winding staircase make it heaven for hungry bookworms.

Share the Irish culture's collective love of the leaf with tea at Temple Bar's Clarence Hotel, owned by U2's Bono and The Edge. The Clarence's "enhanced" Afternoon Tea—champagne or cosmopolitans alongside traditional tea, sandwiches, and patisseries—is served beneath the 20-foot ceilings of its Tea Room Restaurant and in the Study Café, with wainscoting and antique refectory table, as well as in the Octagon Bar.

Restaurant Patrick Guilbaud: Tel 353/1-676-4192; www.restaurantpatrickguilbaud.ie. *Cost:* dinner $170. **Merrion Hotel:** Tel 353/1-603-0600; www.merrionhotel.com. *Cost:* from $260 (off-peak), from $300 (peak); Art Tea $50. **Thornton's:** Tel 353/1-478-7008; www.thorntonsrestaurant.com. *Cost:* dinner $110. **Chapter One:** Tel 353/1-873-2266;

www.chapteronerestaurant.com. *Cost:* dinner $85. **The Winding Stair:** Tel 353/1-872-7320; www.winding-stair.com. *Cost:* dinner $42. **The Clarence:** Tel 353/1-407-0800; www.theclarence.ie. *Cost:* from $160 (off-peak), from $250 (peak); afternoon tea $30. **Best time:** Jun for A Taste of Dublin Festival.

Monuments of the Republic's Revolt for Liberty

Historical Dublin

Dublin, Ireland

Strategically located at Dublin's epicenter, the General Post Office (G.P.O.) is a landmark that launched the free Irish Republic. On Easter Monday of 1916, 1,200 armed citizens who wanted a self-ruled Ireland, free from British occupation, took it over, made it their headquarters, and set up garrisons around the city. From the G.P.O.'s portico, rebel leaders announced the founding of an independent Irish state by reading their Proclamation of the Republic. Street fighting between the rebels and British armed forces, who vastly outnumbered them, lasted for close to a week. When rebel leaders surrendered, Dublin lay in ruin and the G.P.O. had burned to a mere shell. Today, it stands proudly renovated, with a sculpture of Celtic warrior Cuchulainn dedicated to the rebels, an exhibition room on the significance of the "Rising," and portico columns still bearing bullet pockmarks.

Farther out in Dublin sits Kilmainham Gaol, where British troops incarcerated most of the Rising's leaders before executing them by firing squad. That led to enormous public objection and, in turn, to the War of Independence, the Anglo-Irish Treaty (root of the later "Troubles" in Northern Ireland; see p. 76), and the founding of the Irish Free State. Tours through Kilmainham's ghostly interior and outdoor execution yard are riveting.

Arbour Hill military cemetery, where most of the executed rebel leaders were buried, lies across the River Liffey—as does the Decorative Arts and History branch of the National Museum of Ireland, an imposing Neoclassical block of stone, formerly the British Royal Military Barracks. Renamed Collins Barracks after Irish nationalist leader Michael Collins, the museum's exhibition on the Easter Rising includes an original copy of the Proclamation of the Republic.

In 1967, on the Rising's 50th anniversary, surviving rebel (and then president of Ireland) Eamon de Valera opened Dublin's Garden of Remembrance. A place for contemplating subjugation, resurrection, and freedom, the park features a cross-shaped pool with a mosaic of broken spears and shields, symbolizing the Celtic tradition of casting weapons into rivers after hostilities ended. Beyond is a stone-inscribed poem predicting Ireland's rebirth, and asking the generation of freedom to remember the "Generation of the Vision."

G.P.O.: Tel 353/1-705-8833; www.anpost.ie. **Historical sites info:** www.heritageireland.ie/en/Dublin/. **Kilmainham Gaol:** Tel 353/1-453-5984. **Arbour Hill Cemetery:** Tel 353/1-821-3021. **National Museum of Ireland:** Tel 353/1-677-7444; www.museum.ie. **Garden of Remembrance:** Tel 353/1-821-3021. **How:** Passionate historians at Rebellion Walking Tour lead groups to the locales of the Rising. Tel 353/868-583-847; www.1916rising.com. *When:* Mar–Oct. **Best time:** around Easter for the Rising's anniversary.

A Love of Language and the Written Word

Literary Dublin

Dublin, Ireland

Ireland's deep love of words stretches back to Druidic oral poetry, Celtic myth, and Ogham-alphabet writing inscribed on stone. The illuminated manuscripts of early Christian monastic scribes and traditional storytellers called *seanchaí* are part of Irish heritage too. Dublin names bridges and streets after writers, erects statues and memorials to commemorate them, and designates historical houses in their honor. It awards the world's largest literary prize every year and attracts readers and scholars to its dozens of literary pubs. In 2010, the United Nations declared Dublin an official City of Literature.

Celtic monks created the Book of Kells, now on display at Trinity College.

Trinity College has an impressive roster of alumni that includes writers Jonathan Swift, Bram Stoker, Oscar Wilde, and Samuel Beckett. Founded in 1592, it collectively holds more than 5 million volumes, with 200,000 of the oldest housed in the 18th-century Old Library's main chamber, the Long Room. The ground-floor area preserves the college's star attraction: the early medieval Book of Kells. Dating from the early 9th century, Kells depicts the Four Gospels in Latin, on 680 vellum pages, magnificently embellished with elaborate patterns and animals in rich colors.

Dubliners was the first book written by James Joyce, the city's most famous son. His masterpiece, *Ulysses,* recounts a single day in Dublin—June 16, 1904 (the same day as Joyce's first date with wife Nora)—and is the focal point of today's quirky Bloomsday festival, drawing Joyce lovers from around the world. Often dressed in Edwardian garb—boater hats and waistcoats or long skirts—and carrying parasols, these Joyceans trace every footstep of the central characters, including those of Leopold Bloom, reliving turn-of-the-last-century Dublin. Numerous other writers are connected to Dublin, and three of Ireland's four Nobel Prize winners for literature—George Bernard Shaw, W. B. Yeats (see p. 72), and Samuel Beckett—were born here. The fourth, Seamus Heaney, transplanted himself here from the north.

The Writers Museum, located in an 18th-century house next to the Irish Writers Centre, is a fine place to start your visit. The museum displays books inscribed by Joyce and Yeats (who cofounded the Abbey Theatre in 1903), plus pens, typewriters, portraits, Beckett's telephone, Brendan Behan's union card, and Shaw's signed refusal to provide an autograph.

Writers not only lived and drank here, but died in Dublin too: Satirist Jonathan Swift is buried in St. Patrick's Cathedral, where he was dean, and poet Gerard Manley Hopkins rests in Glasnevin Cemetery.

Visitor info: www.dublincityofliterature.com. **Book of Kells:** Tel 353/1-896-2320; www.bookofkells.ie. **Bloomsday:** Tel 353/1-878-8547; www.jamesjoyce.ie. **Dublin Writers Museum:** Tel 353/1-872-2077; www.writersmuseum.com. **Best times:** Jun for Dublin Writers Festival; Jun 16 for Bloomsday; Oct for Dublin Theatre Festival.

Celebrating All Things Irish

Pubs and St. Patrick's Festival

Dublin, Ireland

Dublin's greatest asset has always been its people and their gifts of music and gab. You'll find boatloads of both, along with plenty of *craic* (Irish for "sociable good times") when you join the locals in one of the city's 1,000-plus pubs. Here the thick, oil-black "Dublin gargle" (Guinness) reigns as the national drink and music is almost always a welcome by-product.

Brewed in Dublin since 1769, the "poetry in a glass" was once accompanied by advertising slogans such as "Guinness is good for you!" and inspires a reverence that may explain why Ireland boasts a yearly per capita beer consumption of 131 liters (second only to the Czech Republic; see p. 289). For the full history of Arthur Guinness and his world-famous brew, spend a few fun hours at the Guinness Storehouse, the expansive former fermentation plant built in the shape of a mammoth pint glass and packing in a museum, a brewery open for tours, a restaurant, and the glass-encased top-floor Gravity Bar, with a panoramic view of Dublin.

Live music is a tradition at O'Donoghue's.

While today's pub count might not compare to that of the mid-18th century (when Dublin had 2,000 alehouses, 300 taverns, and 1,200 brandy stores), plenty of choice places remain to draw a creamy pint of what James Joyce called "the wine of Ireland." Just steps from the River Liffey on Lower Bridge Street is the oldest pub in town, the lantern-lit Brazen Head. Born as a coaching inn in 1198 and licensed as a pub in 1661, it retains a timeworn charm and offers nightly musical performances.

Just off St. Stephen's Green, O'Donoghue's, opened in 1934, is a relative newcomer. It has always been known for its lively jam sessions, out of which sprang the '60s folk crossover success the Dubliners. A few steps from the green on Duke Street, you'll find Davy Byrne's, established in 1889 and later made famous by James Joyce as a stop along Leopold Bloom's journey in *Ulysses.* Enjoy a Gorgonzola sandwich and a glass of burgundy in tribute to Bloom's meal, or just soak up the Art Deco surroundings, complete with murals featuring the renowned scribe.

To see more writerly haunts, join the Dublin Literary Pub Crawl, a spirited and informative tour led by actors who share humorous anecdotes and recite lyrical lines by great Irish authors.

Pubs all across town kick into high gear

when March rolls around and thoughts turn to honoring St. Patrick, the venerated patron saint of the country and the Irish Diaspora, who was born in Scotland and brought to Ireland as a slave in A.D. 432. Dublin is the home of the longest annual celebration (the largest takes place in New York City). The highlight of the 5-day festival is a parade that proudly marches down O'Connell Street, featuring drill teams, floats, and delegations from around the world. Other activities include concerts, carnival rides, and the All-Ireland finals for both Gaelic football and hurling at Croke Park stadium, both held on St. Patrick's Day.

GUINNESS STOREHOUSE: Tel 353/1-408-4800; www.guinness-storehouse.com. **BRAZEN HEAD:** Tel 353/1-677-9549; www.brazenhead.com. **O'DONOGHUE'S:** Tel 353/1-660-7194; www.odonoghues.ie. **DAVY BYRNE'S:** Tel 353/1-677-5217; www.davybyrnes.com. **LITERARY PUB CRAWL:** Tel 353/1-670-5602; www.dublinpubcrawl.com. **ST. PATRICK'S FESTIVAL:** Tel 353/1-676-3205; www.stpatricksfestival.ie. *When:* 5 days surrounding Mar 17, parade on Mar 17.

Windswept Outposts of Gaelic Culture

ARAN ISLANDS

County Galway, Ireland

With an ever-dwindling population, the trio of windblown Aran Islands, off Ireland's western shore, offers a window onto centuries past. Visitors come here for the moody, starkly romantic beauty, where the primary language is Irish Gaelic and the occasional pony-and-trap cart still travels the narrow roads. Over a century ago, playwright John Millington Synge immortalized the Arans—scattered as they are with Iron Age stone forts, Neolithic wedges, early Christian churches, and *clochán*s (monastic beehive stone huts)—as "Ireland at its most exotic, colorful, and traditional." In the 17th century, when British penal laws dictated that the native Irish migrate west, many traveled all the way to these hardscrabble limestone islands, making do with the harsh terrain by turning sand and seaweed into fertile soil. Many of the Arans' approximately 1,500 current residents can be counted as their descendants.

Most tourists today visit the largest island, Inishmore *(Inis Mór)*, and Dún Aengus, the haunting ruins of a 4,000-year-old megalithic cliff fort. Every summer, the smallest island, Inisheer *(Inis Oirr)*, hosts *Craiceann* (Irish for "skin"), a traditional *bodhrán*, or drum festival. Least-visited Inishmaan *(Inis Meáin)*, the middle island, holds a charm all its own, known for its fishing nets piled on inverted *currachs* (traditional rowing boats) and a landscape divided into geometric labyrinths by endless stone walls and a population of just 200. Synge spent most of his time here, writing in a sheltered spot within a semicircle of stones and perched on a cliff edge looking over the ocean's whitecapped waves. The spot is now marked with a stone plaque reading *Cathaoir Synge* ("Synge's chair"). During summers here (a time that inspired *The Playboy of the Western World*, *Riders to the Sea*, and *The Aran Islands*), Synge lived in a thatched cottage that is now a seasonal museum filled with Synge memorabilia, and run by a descendant of his original host.

You can find a cluster of traditional B&Bs on Inishmaan, but for a unique experience, seek out the newly built Inis Meáin Restaurant & Suites. Its streamlined style complements the surroundings with a simple exterior and five spare rooms that recall the islands' monastic history, albeit luxuriously: Each has panoramic windows, an outdoor terrace, bikes, and fishing rods. Owners Marie-Therese and Ruairí de Blacam (a chef and island native) serve simple meals made with local ingredients: island vegetable soup, just-caught lobster and crab, and pudding with foraged-berry compote.

Each island holds a *Pátrún* (patron saint) festival in summertime that features boat races, donkey rides, and dancing on the piers. On June 23, known as St. John's Eve, islanders light bonfires and keep them alive long into the night, a custom that harks back to a pre-Christian summer solstice ritual once practiced all over Ireland.

WHERE: 30 miles/48 km off the coast of Galway City. **HOW:** year-round ferries from Rossaveal, outside Galway City. Tel 353/91-568-903; www.aranislandferries.com. High-season ferries from Doolin, County Clare. Tel 353/65-707-4455; www.doolinferries.com. **INIS MEÁIN RESTAURANT & SUITES:** Tel 353/86-826-6026; www.inismeain.com. *Cost:* $355; dinner $65. *When:* Apr–Oct. **BEST TIMES:** Jun 23 for St. John's Eve; Jun and Aug for Pátrún festivals; late Jun for Inisheer Craiceann.

The Wild West

CONNEMARA

County Galway, Ireland

Connemara is difficult to pinpoint: It is not a town or a valley, but a ruggedly poetic corner of County Galway, a region of Ireland known for its romantic landscape and peat bogs. Oscar Wilde called it a "savage beauty." Wild, lonely, and for the most part uninhabited, Connemara makes up the western third of the county and was once part of the biggest private estate in Ireland.

From its perch along the Atlantic, Clifden, the quaint, unofficial capital of the region, affords excellent views as well as easy access to the immensely scenic Sky Road, one of western Ireland's most delightful (and less trafficked) drives. The steep and narrow single lane twists and turns along the coastline to offer glimpses of the Twelve Bens, a dozen sharp—often mist-shrouded—gray peaks that culminate at 2,388 feet. This is the untamed heart of the Connemara National Park, 3,800 acres of heaths, grasslands, and some of Ireland's best hiking trails. Herds of red deer and Connemara ponies, the only horse breed native to Ireland, can sometimes be glimpsed roaming the hills. Near the entrance to the park, family-run Rosleague Manor, a two-story Regency home, draws those seeking comfortable quarters. It is renowned for its dinners—of seafood, local lamb, and

The ruins of Clifden Castle stand along the seashore.

home-grown vegetables—that epitomize the spirit and taste of Connemara.

Standing alone by a lake amid glorious mountains, the isolated Delphi Lodge provides access to some of the best salmon and sea trout fishing in the west. The ambience is that of a relaxed country estate, where dinners take place at a large communal table often overseen by the amiable owner and host. Although an expert angler's heaven, Delphi also caters to novices, who enjoy weekend courses, run several times a year, and nonanglers who come merely for the solitude, serenity, and verdant surroundings.

The Cashel House, a gracious estate with its own stables, offers you the region's natural wonders without leaving the property. Idyllic paths meander past award-winning gardens and through 50 stream-crossed acres of rolling hills, shaded woodland, and even a small private beach. Choose from dozing in front of a peat fire, an afternoon of biking or boating, or the glory of getting lost in a good book. Evenings bring sophisticated but unpretentious meals.

Where: Clifden is 50 miles/80 km northwest of Galway. **Connemara National Park:** Tel 353/95-41323; www.connemaranationalpark.ie. **Rosleague Manor:** Tel 353/95-41101; www.rosleague.com. *Cost:* from $195 (off-peak), from $290 (peak); dinner $45. *When:* Mar–Oct. **Delphi Lodge:** Tel 353/95-42222; www.delphilodge.ie. *Cost:* from $280; dinner $70. *When:* closed Nov–Feb. **Cashel House:** Tel 353/95-31001; www.cashel-house-hotel.com. *Cost:* $240 (off-peak), $340 (peak); dinner $70. **Best times:** in Clifden: mid-Sep for Arts Festival; 3rd Thurs in Aug for Connemara Pony Show. Fishing: Feb–May for spring salmon; Jun–Jul for grilse; Aug–Sep for sea trout.

Ireland's Most Festive Town

GALWAY

County Galway, Ireland

Poised at the edge of Europe, Galway is Ireland's unofficial arts capital. It's also been known since 1954 for celebrating the oyster, which gets its due at a massive festival in September. Foodies also make time for the short trip to the neighboring fishing village of Kilcolgan for a meal at Moran's Oyster Cottage, originally opened in 1797 and considered bivalve headquarters since 1966.

As for those pleasures not enjoyed on the half shell, Galway hosts Ireland's largest interdisciplinary arts extravaganza, with public performances including citywide dancing in the streets; a festival of medieval, Renaissance, and Baroque music; major literary events; and Ireland's leading film festival. That's not to mention the Galway Races, which attract around 150,000 horse racing fans, and a festival of Galway hookers, traditional sailboats constructed for rough seas, with races, demos of rope skills and man-overboard recovery techniques. You can sip a "Galway Hooker" of another kind while you're celebrating—an Irish Pale Ale, made at a local craft brewery.

Anglo-Normans captured the fishing village of Galway from natives in the 13th century. It then became a major port led by 14 merchant families, earning it the moniker "the City of Tribes." Traces of Galway's past linger in its Medieval Quarter, in Lynch's Castle, and in its narrow, cobbled lanes. Only one gate still stands from the medieval stone walls that used to surround the city, the

Spanish Arch, along the brisk, energetic Corrib River, which empties into Galway Bay. Today the arch leads to the Galway City Museum. Across the Corrib lies the old fishing quarter of Claddagh, where the world-famous ring—two hands clasping a crowned heart, symbolizing friendship, loyalty, and love—originated.

Near the Spanish Arch, Ard Bia ("high food") at Nimmos serves Galway's finest fare in a hewn-stone former boathouse. A café during the day and restaurant after dark, this quirky, award-winning eatery dishes up cuisine befitting Galway's international port heritage: contemporary Irish fare with faint Middle Eastern and Moroccan touches. For another taste of Galway's food-trade past, visit the church square, where you'll find Sheridan's Cheesemongers, a great shop for local and European artisanal cheeses, provisions, and wine. On Saturday mornings the square bustles with a busy farmers market.

WHERE: 52 miles/84 km north of Shannon. **VISITOR INFO:** www.discoverireland.ie. **MORAN'S:** Tel 353/91-796113; www.moransoystercottage.com. *Cost:* dinner \$50. **ARD BIA AT NIMMOS:** Tel 353/91-539897; www.ardbia.com. *Cost:* lunch \$30. **BEST TIMES:** Apr for Cúirt International Festival of Literature; May for Galway Early Music Festival; Jul for Galway Arts Festival, Galway Film Festival, Galway Races; Aug for Cruinniú na mBád (Traditional Boat Festival); Sep for International Oyster Festival.

Last Stop Before Brooklyn

DINGLE PENINSULA

County Kerry, Ireland

The westernmost point in Europe juts out fiercely and dramatically into the Atlantic: "Next parish to America," as the saying goes. The lilt of Irish Gaelic is still heard here, and Celtic monuments to ancient Christianity litter the rugged and spectacularly scenic coastline. One of many peninsulas along Ireland's west coast (see next page), the windswept Dingle Peninsula is especially raw and beautiful, extending 30 miles and from 5 to 12 miles across, providing hikers, cyclists, and motorists with a vast and visually complex expanse of water and shore. As you wind along the coastline or up and over sinuous Conor Pass, you'll take in breathtaking views of the sparsely vegetated slopes leading to the sea. Around the tip of the peninsula, you can see the seven Blasket Islands. Evacuated in 1953 and uninhabited since, they once gave rise to a unique body of literature and make for a mysterious, near-mystical destination when the sea is not too rough.

Dingle is the prettiest town in all of County Kerry, still reminiscing about its moment in the limelight when, in 1969, Robert Mitchum (and a sizable Hollywood contingent) arrived

Seaside Dingle is full of delightful shops and pubs.

to film *Ryan's Daughter.* In the cheerily painted town is a collection of pottery shops, alternative bookstores, and the country's highest pub-per-person ratio for its 2,000 residents; you can expect live, foot-tapping music most nights. Making the most of the seaside location, Out of the Blue, a small, colorful seafood-only restaurant, is open exclusively when there's a worthy fresh catch (thankfully, most of the time). It serves a delectable selection of traditional and inventive preparations and tops off the meal with scrumptious desserts. Doyle's is a friendly competitor and a longtime favorite for classics (seafood chowder) to more innovative (salmon mousse or fish tempura) in a friendly environment.

Walk home full and tipsy to the Castlewood House, a large, elegant B&B with luxurious rooms offering views of Dingle Bay and a breakfast you won't soon forget.

WHERE: 95 miles/153 km southwest of Shannon. **OUT OF THE BLUE:** Tel 353/66-915-0811; www.outoftheblue.ie. *Cost:* dinner $60. *When:* mid-Mar–Oct. **DOYLE'S:** Tel 353/66-915-2674; www.doylesofdingle.com. *Cost:* dinner $60. **CASTLEWOOD HOUSE:** Tel 353/66-915-2788; www.castlewooddingle.com. *Cost:* from $120 (off-peak), from $200 (peak). *When:* closed Dec–Feb. **BEST TIMES:** late Apr–mid-Oct for nicest weather; late Apr–early May for Féile na Bealtaine Celtic Arts festival; Aug for Regatta; late Oct for Dingle Food & Wine Festival.

A Dream Drive Along the Iveragh Peninsula

THE RING OF KERRY

County Kerry, Ireland

In a country where every drive guarantees a scenic odyssey, the famed Ring of Kerry, unfurling along a 110-mile coast-hugging road around the Iveragh Peninsula, reveals particularly breathtaking vistas of land, sea, and sky.

Couple it with neighboring Dingle Peninsula to the north (see previous page) and risk visual overload.

Most drivers begin in Killarney, an attractive village near the ivy-covered Victorian mansion Muckross House, now a museum of County Kerry folklore and history. The elegant, lakeside property serves as the entrance to car-free Killarney National Park, the county's centerpiece. Here, waterfalls, heather-covered valleys, woodlands, and abundant wildlife are highlights for cyclists, hikers, and those who choose to ride in two-wheeled, horse-drawn "jaunting cars."

For an ambitious alternative, skip the road entirely and walk the Kerry Way, a strenuous, 120-mile trek that encircles the peninsula, granting dramatic views without the crowds. You'll catch a glimpse of the craggy outlines of the mystic Skellig Islands, including Skellig Michael. Its steep, barren slopes also offer opportunities for invigorating hikes and are home to a well-preserved monastery dating back to the 7th century. Boats leave from Port Magee when the sea is calm.

Twenty miles from Killarney, you can settle into quiet, picturesque Kenmare, a 19th-century market town with a surprising profusion of high-quality dining options. Longtime favorite Packie's is a cozy bistro with a menu known for both the simple (Irish stew, rack of lamb) and the imaginative (gratin of crab and prawns). For an eclectically modern alternative, try Mulcahy's, offering a blend of international cuisine inflected with Asian touches—from steak to sushi.

The Park Hotel Kenmare is one of Ireland's most exquisite country-house hotels. Built in 1897, the gray stone manse is known for its splendid collection of antiques, original paintings, and rich tapestries. The warm, welcoming atmosphere is enhanced by a house-proud staff, and its renowned restaurant serves Irish-Continental cuisine. The Sámas (Gaelic for "sensual indulgence") Spa and the challenging 18-hole golf course (with breathtaking views) heighten the sense of luxury.

Torc Waterfall runs within Killarney National Park.

Nearby Sheen Falls Lodge sits at the head of Kenmare Bay. Guests find it hard to leave the spacious, beautifully appointed rooms to enjoy the surrounding palm trees, camellias, and fuchsias or the 15-mile stretch of private salmon fishing on the River Sheen. You'll find sophisticated cuisine highlighted by local ingredients at the lodge's wide-windowed La Cascade Restaurant, named for the view of a small, floodlit waterfall.

For a stay in town, look no further than the Brook Lane Hotel, a stylish boutique option with comfortable rooms ranging from modern to trendy and a wonderful restaurant. It puts you just a stroll away from Kenmare's pretty town center.

WHERE: Killarney is 84 miles/135 km southwest of Shannon. **VISITOR INFO:** www.killarney.ie. **MUCKROSS HOUSE:** www.muckross-house.ie. **KILLARNEY NATIONAL PARK:** www.killarneynationalpark.ie. **KERRY WAY:** www.kerryway.com. **PACKIE'S:** Tel 353/64-664-1508. *Cost:* dinner $40. **MULCAHY'S:** Tel 353/64-664-2383. *Cost:* dinner $50. **PARK HOTEL KENMARE:** Tel 353/64-664-1200; in the U.S., 800-323-5463; www.parkkenmare.com. *Cost:* from $560 (off-peak), from $700 (peak); dinner $95. *When:* closed Nov–mid-Apr. **SHEEN FALLS LODGE:** Tel 353/64-664-1600; www.sheenfallslodge.ie. *Cost:* from $435 (off-peak), from $635 (peak); dinner $90. **BROOK LANE HOTEL:** Tel 353/64-664-2077; www.brooklanehotel.com. *Cost:* from $150 (off-peak), from $246 (peak). **BEST TIMES:** Mar–Apr and Oct–Nov to avoid crowds; Aug 15 for Kenmare fair.

Riding and Golf in the Heart of Thoroughbred Country

HORSE COUNTRY

Straffan (County Kildare) and Thomastown (County Kilkenny), Ireland

South of Dublin, the rolling green pastures of counties Kildare and Kilkenny are home to many of Ireland's 300 stud farms. This is the site of the internationally famous Curragh Racecourse, where the Irish Derby, often referred to as the Churchill Downs of Ireland, is held during the last week in June. The government-owned Irish National Stud, where some of the country's most famous horses have been born and raised, is the standard for all other stud farms in the country, if not the world. This dedication reflects the Irish passion for horses, a bond that can be traced back to ancient Celtic myths. The original owner of the property had a great love for gardens, and a highlight of the farm's almost 1,000 acres are the delightfully surprising Japanese Gardens, arguably the most beautiful in Europe. The Kildare Hotel and Country Club (the "K Club"), a 19th-century manor house, is the hub of this 330-acre deluxe sporting resort, every bit as gorgeous as the Irish National Stud, with miles of bridle trails for its own stable of beauties. The alluring green isn't solely for the horses: One of the K Club's two 18-hole courses, both designed by Arnold Palmer, is consistently rated among the country's finest.

The region's other premier sporting retreat is Mount Juliet; once part of the largest private estate in Ireland, its handsome, ivy-walled stone manor house was built by the Earl of Carrick more than 200 years ago. Its 1,500 acres include unspoiled woodland, pasture, formal gardens, and—the landmark for which it is acclaimed—a manicured 18-hole championship golf course designed by Jack Nicklaus. Dubbed the "Augusta of Europe," its world-class par-72 course has hosted the Irish Open three times. Cozy, handsomely appointed bedrooms with fireplaces and large windows overlook the rolling grounds that lead to the hotel's Ballyinch Stud Farm, where Thoroughbreds graze idly in lush meadows. Riding stables provide mounts for forays on trails without end, private beats on the River Nore allow 4 miles of trout and salmon fishing, and a spa offers indulgent massages.

Those who prefer to stay in nearby Dublin can check into the historic Shelbourne Hotel. Built in 1824, it is the last survivor among Dublin's great 19th-century hotels; the Irish Constitution was drafted here in 1922. For years it's been a destination for those of wealth and pedigree, with public areas full of chandeliers, glowing fireplaces, and fine art. During August's prestigious Horse Show Week, its famous Horseshoe Bar is the only place to be.

WHERE: Irish National Stud is in Tully, 30 miles/48 km west of Dublin. Tel 353/4-552-2963; www.irish-national-stud.ie. *When:* closed mid-Dec–mid-Feb. Racing season is Mar–Oct. **KILDARE HOTEL:** Tel 353/1-601-7200; www.kclub.ie. *Cost:* from $410 (off-peak), from $550 (peak); greens fees from $130 (off-peak), from $260 (peak). **MOUNT JULIET:** Tel 353/56-777-3000; www.mountjuliet.ie. *Cost:* from $190 (off-peak), from $220 (peak); dinner $55; greens fees from $86 (off-peak), from $100 (peak). **THE SHELBOURNE HOTEL:** Tel 353/1-663-4500; www.theshelbourne.ie. *Cost:* from $275. **BEST TIMES:** May–Oct for pleasant weather; late Jun for Irish Derby in Curragh; Aug for Dublin Horse Show Week and Kilkenny Arts Festival.

Ireland's Most Charming Village

ADARE

Adare, County Limerick, Ireland

Often called Ireland's prettiest village—and certainly one of its most photographed—Adare is a snug collection of thatch-roofed cottages, Tudor-style houses, and ivied medieval ruins, with a welcoming main street that is filled with small restaurants, pubs, and a smattering of colorfully painted gift and craft shops. Odd, then, that such a quaint town would also contain Adare Manor, an astonishing Gothic pile with 52 chimneys, 365 leaded-glass windows, and turrets everywhere. Former home and seat of the Earls of Dunraven, it is now an 840-acre baronial haven for guests who relish being cosseted like descendants of royalty. Opened in 1988 as one of the country's most impressive castle hotels, it fulfills storybook standards, with colossal halls, ornate fireplaces (75 of them), enormous oil portraits, Waterford-crystal chandeliers, and grounds embellished with groomed box hedges and formal French parterre gardens. Anglers enjoy the riverside location, but the real reason to stay here is the 18-hole championship golf course designed by Robert Trent Jones Jr. in 1995. Adare Manor is also no slouch in the dining department: Excellent dinners in the oak-paneled dining room call for jacket and tie, making every evening an occasion.

For a town with a population of just 2,600, Adare is surprisingly endowed with culinary riches. The Mustard Seed, an immediate favorite when it debuted in 1985, uses local meats and organic greens to give Irish touches to European fare. It is housed in the atmospheric 19th-century Echo Lodge, a converted convent that includes 11 classic rooms as well as several modern suites in a former schoolhouse, all surrounded by 10 acres of gardens and orchards.

The Wild Geese is Adare's other stellar restaurant, where diners sip drinks by a peat fire before moving to the cozy, dollhouse atmosphere of the dining room for meals that emphasize fresh, locally sourced flavors, served in a homey environment.

Where: 25 miles/40 km northwest of Shannon. **Adare Manor:** Tel 353/61-605-200; in the U.S., 800-462-3273; www.adaremanor.com. *Cost:* from $340 (off-peak), from $630 (peak); dinner $90; greens fees $105 (off-peak), $165 (peak). **Mustard Seed at Echo Lodge:** Tel 353/69-68508; www.mustardseed.ie. *Cost:* from $230; dinner $90. **Wild Geese:** Tel 353/61-396451; www.thewild-geese.com. *Cost:* dinner $50. **Best time:** May–Oct for nicest weather.

The Fairest of Them All

Ashford Castle

Cong, County Mayo, Ireland

Ireland has no shortage of castle hotels, but Ashford Castle—an imposing flight of fancy reflected in Ireland's second largest lake, Lough Corrib—stands alone. Think turrets, drawbridge, and battlements, coupled with gracious service, canopied four-poster beds, armor-lined corridors, and crackling fires in richly paneled drawing rooms. Dating to the 13th century, the world-famous hotel served as the Guinness brewing family's private residence for almost 100 years, beginning in 1852. Ashford's George V Room and more intimate Connaught Room offer elegant dining, replete with vast windows, Waterford crystal engraved with Ashford's crest, and custom-made Wedgwood place settings. Those not checking in can dine on bistro fare in Cullen's at the Cottage, on Ashford's spectacular 300-acre grounds. Activities, such as lake fishing and cruises, golf, and falconry lessons, are open to nonguests as well. In 1952, when John Ford filmed scenes of the silver-screen classic *The Quiet Man* (with John Wayne and Maureen O'Hara) on Ashford's grounds and in the neighboring village of Cong, the cast called the flamboyant castle home.

Though County Mayo is home to the country's grandest luxury castle, its residents experienced great devastation during the Famine. A bronze memorial dedicated to its victims stands at the base of Mayo's sacred mountain, Croagh Patrick, hallowed since the era of the Celts, who celebrated their harvest festival Lughnasa on its summit every August 1. Originally called Croagh Aigh, it was renamed after the saint who fasted there for 40 days in the year 441. From his post there, St. Patrick reputedly banished "the snakes" from Ireland, likely a euphemism for eradicating much of Celtic religion and introducing Christianity. On the last Sunday of every July, tens of thousands of pilgrims (many of them barefoot) make the 3-hour climb to the 2,460-foot summit to pray and attend religious services.

Mayo's history goes back even further—over 5,000 years—at the Ceide Fields, the world's most extensive Stone Age site. Perched at the ocean's edge, Ceide's farming settlement has the oldest-known walled fields, preserved over the millennia by the bog.

These days, Mayo enjoys a solid reputation for the brown trout that thrive in the waters of Lough Conn. To angle on the lake, visit Cloonamoyne Fishery, on the grounds of Enniscoe House, the 17th-century ancestral home of Susan Kellett and her son DJ, who open its rooms and those of their farmhouses to overnight guests. Cloonamoyne can outfit you with a boat, a ghillie (guide), and equipment. Wrap up the day at Matt Molloy's pub in the popular and picturesque town of Westport. Owned by flutist Matt Molloy from the world-renowned trad band the Chieftains, the pub has a back room that is alive with music every night of the week.

WHERE: 155 miles/249 km miles west of Dublin. Tel 353/94-954-6003; www.ashford.ie. *Cost:* from $250 (off-peak), from $535 (peak). **CLOONAMOYNE FISHERY:** Tel 353/96-51156; www.cloonamoynefishery.com. *Cost:* $165 per day for motorboat and guide. *When:* Apr–Sep. **ENNISCOE HOUSE:** Tel 353/96-31112; www.enniscoe.com. *Cost:* guesthouse from $270 per night; farmhouses from $689 per week. *When:* Apr–Oct for guesthouse; year-round for farmhouses. **MATT MOLLOY'S PUB:** Tel 353/98-26655; www.mattmolloy.com. **BEST TIMES:** Apr–Jun for trout fishing; last Sun in Jul for Croagh Patrick pilgrimage; early Aug for Westport Music Festival.

Ancient History's Sacred Ground

THE BOYNE VALLEY

County Meath, Ireland

Just north of Dublin, a concentration of impressive megalithic monuments, called Brú na Bóinne, clusters along the banks of the River Boyne in County Meath. The main site, Newgrange—an immense, grass-covered mound surrounded by a retaining wall—dates to around 3200 B.C. Newgrange encloses a long, narrow stone passageway that ends in a cruciform, corbel-vaulted room, likely a tomb and royal chamber, that soars to 20 feet high. During the winter solstice, the first light of day shines into an open roof-box above the entrance lintel and slips along the passageway until it illuminates the chamber for 20 minutes. For each of six mornings around this day, ten lucky lottery winners and their ten guests win the chance to climb inside Newgrange to witness this spectacle. The rest of the year, visitors can see a light show that mimics the effect. Knowth, Newgrange's sister site, displays the greatest concentration of megalithic art in western Europe in the form of decorative circles, spirals, chevrons, and zigzags carved into huge boulders and chiseled away in raised-relief design.

Built by Hugh de Lacy, Trim Castle has changed little since its completion.

Farther down the Boyne stands Ireland's spiritual center, the Hill of Tara. Sacred since prehistoric times, Tara has strong links to Celtic myth and history as the ceremonial seat of the High Kings of Eire, who ruled for over 2 millennia, according to Irish historical record, until the 11th century. Its Stone of Destiny is reputed to be the coronation site of ancient kings, and Ireland's Five Ancient Roads led directly to Tara. Tribal clans gathered at Tara for national celebrations called *feis*, at which they passed laws, settled disputes, listened to druids, and hosted feasts. Today, on important dates from the Celtic calendar such as the summer solstice, you might find modern-day pagan worshippers celebrating on Tara's grassy, gently rising 512-foot hill. A new nearby motorway threatens Tara's structure and sanctity and compelled the Smithsonian Institution to name Tara a must-see endangered cultural treasure.

For comparatively modern history along the Boyne, visit Trim to see Ireland's largest Anglo-Norman castle. Trim Castle's keep was completed by 1206, and its massive 20-sided tower remains so striking that Mel Gibson shot parts of *Braveheart* here in 1994. In Trim, you can also hop into a hot-air balloon for sweeping views of the Boyne and the best possible vantage of Tara's raised earthworks.

WHERE: 27 miles/43 km north of Dublin. **VISITOR INFO:** www.heritageireland.ie. **BRÚ NA BÓINNE:** Tel 353/41-988-0300. **NEWGRANGE SOLSTICE LOTTERY:** by application at visitor center or e-mail brunaboinne@opw.le. *When:* Newgrange open year-round, winter solstice event Dec 18–23 at dawn. **HILL OF TARA:** Tel 353/46-902-5903. *When:* late May–mid-Sep. **IRISH BALLOON FLIGHTS:** Tel 353/46-948-3436; www.balloons.ie. *When:* Apr–Sep. *Cost:* $335. **BEST TIMES:** early Apr for Trim's Hot Air Balloon Fiesta; Dec 18–23 for winter solstice, if you have the luck of the Irish and win Newgrange's lottery.

Terrain of the Celtic Twilight

YEATS COUNTRY

County Sligo, Ireland

Steeped in mysticism and the beauty of the natural world, the writing of Nobel laureate William Butler Yeats (1865–1939) sprang from the deep impression County Sligo left on his childhood imagination during summers he spent there with his mother's family. Yeats was born in Dublin (see p. 61); however, his poems, plays, and prose were often inspired by Sligo's evocative landscapes and legends.

Sligo town holds the concentration of Yeats' museums and memorials, but what captured the writer's heart lies outside town. To understand their powerful effect on the writer, wander along Lough Gill (whose Innisfree Isle inspired one of his most famous poems) and visit the Dooney Rock and the hazel woods. Or climb the massive Knocknarea Mountain, its summit topped with Celtic Queen Maeve's limestone cairn, then continue east just over the Leitrim border to the Glencar waterfall, so smooth it almost looks like glass.

It takes time to see it all, so head 11 miles south of Sligo, and check in at Coopershill, a three-story Georgian manor house that has been in the O'Hara family for eight generations. The elegant 1774 inn exudes old-world grace in the eight spacious and beautifully furnished guest rooms as well as in the handsome dining room, where wonderful farm-to-plate meals are served by candlelight.

Yeats's final resting place is in Sligo's Drumcliffe graveyard, at St. Columba's Church. Per his wishes, his gravestone stands under the watchful gaze of Ben Bulben, the monolithic mountain reputed to be the dwelling of the Fianna tribe of Celtic warriors. Yeats, whose great-grandfather had been a rector of St. Columba's Church, wanted to be buried in the tiny village. Though he was originally interred in France in 1939, his relatives eventually had his remains returned to St. Columba's. The church's swan-shaped door handles recall Yeats's poem "The Wild Swans at Coole." His epitaph is the last lines of his poem "Under Ben Bulben." Outside the graveyard, a statue crouches as if to contemplate "He Wishes for the Cloths of Heaven," another work of Yeats's. The poem is inscribed in stone at the feet of the figure, which is draped with the sculptor's rendition of heaven's embroidered cloths.

WHERE: 128 miles/206 km northeast of Dublin. **VISITOR INFO:** www.discoverireland.ie/northwest. **COOPERSHILL HOUSE:** Tel 353/7191-65108; www.coopershill.com. *Cost:* from $285; dinner $65. **YEATS MEMORIAL BUILDING/YEATS SOCIETY:** Tel 353/7191-42693; www.yeats-sligo.com. *When:* Apr–Oct. **BEST TIME:** Jul–Aug for Yeats summer festival in Sligo town and around the county.

The Sparkle On and Off the Water

Waterford Crystal and Waterford Castle

Waterford, County Waterford, Ireland

Waterford County, in Ireland's southeast, has long been associated with the famed crystal produced here. After falling on hard times and closing down in 2009, a new factory and visitors center, the House of Waterford Crystal, opened in 2010 in the heart of town, offering tours that explore a tradition of classic and modern methods of glassmaking dating back to 1783 as well as the largest collection of Waterford crystal in the world. Thanks to its purity and intricate detail, the company's worldwide reputation endures, with one-of-a-kind pieces found in Westminster Abbey, the Kennedy Center, the White House, and, in the form of the massive ball that drops every New Year's Eve in Times Square.

When you've had your fill of the world of etched glass, float downstream along the River Suir (one of three that converge here) to

Craftsmen sculpt, cut, and engrave Waterford Crystal.

Waterford Castle, now a luxury hotel, situated on its own small island. Simply called the Island, the 300-acre spread is the castle hotel's private dominion, reachable only by 5-minute car ferry. Built on Norman foundations that date back some 800 years, the 18th-century structure is the real deal, complete with authentic turrets, gargoyles, and battlements. Pass through massive, studded oak doors to the grand hallway, where an enormous coat-of-arms has been woven into a circular carpet and where the ambience is graciously informal. And with just 19 rooms and suites, guests share their lordly domain with only a handful of other equally lucky castaways. Dine in the grand Munster Room restaurant, feasting on seasonal dishes simply prepared to bring out the natural flavors. Relax with wine from the exceptional cellar while listening to the tinkling of the house pianist. You can work off a fit-for-a-king breakfast by exploring the bridle and bicycle paths through the island's woodlands. The big draw, though, is the 18-hole, par-72 parkland course designed by Irish pro Des Smyth—making this the country's only true island golf resort.

WHERE: 102 miles/165 km southwest of Dublin. **HOUSE OF WATERFORD CRYSTAL:** Tel 353/51-317-000; www.waterfordvisitorcentre.com. **WATERFORD CASTLE:** Tel 353/51-878-203; www.waterfordcastle.com. *Cost:* from $190 (off-peak), from $315 (peak); dinner $85; greens fees from $50. **BEST TIMES:** Mar–Aug for nicest weather; Nov for Waterford International Music Festival.

Showcasing the Offbeat and Little Known

WEXFORD FESTIVAL OPERA

Wexford, County Wexford, Ireland

The best time to catch sleepy Wexford is in October, when the whole town turns out for its renowned Opera Festival. Begun in 1951, the event continues to grow in prestige and recognition, expanding its offerings with the large, state-of-the-art Wexford Opera House, opened in 2008. The festival showcases lesser-known operas and world-class performers, and employs innovative approaches, such as presenting condensed versions of classic works. Unsnobby, nonelitist, and often offbeat, it is the country's most important opera festival and one of the world's best small festivals of any kind. Myriad art exhibitions and traditional Irish music performances enthusiastically join the fray for the 3-week period, creating a lively atmosphere townwide.

Experience more of that spirit of both small-town pride and sophistication with a stay at County Wexford's most gracious inn, the exquisite Regency-style Marlfield House, in Gorey, a half hour north of town. Set amid 36 acres of gardens and parkland that are as impeccably overseen as the inn itself, this 1820 seat of the Earls of Courtown is an antiques-filled oasis of calm, with its own lake and wild fowl reserve. Enjoy fare from a refined menu in the romantic, candlelit Victorian-style conservatory added by the current owners. Filled with plants, mirrors, and the aroma of expertly prepared meals, the dining room makes the perfect setting in which to toast your stay.

For country living with a homier touch, book one of the five rooms at Ballinkeele House, an Italianate mansion in nearby Enniscorthy. It was built in 1840 for the Maher family, who operate it today as a B&B. The elegantly appointed rooms showcase period furnishings, including four-poster beds, and offer glimpses of the surrounding 350 acres, which include gardens, woodland, and a working farm. Roam the grounds, play croquet on the lawn, or cozy up to a fire in cooler months, before heading for your opera performance or while waiting for dinner at a long communal table in the deep-red, candlelit Victorian dining room. County Wexford feels so bucolic and serene, one would never know that Dublin is within easy reach.

Where: 88 miles/142 km south of Dublin. **Wexford Festival Opera:** Tel 353/53-912-2400; www.wexfordopera.com. *Cost:* tickets from \$20–\$180. *When:* 3 weeks in Oct. **Marlfield House:** Tel 353/53-942-1124; www.marlfieldhouse.com. *Cost:* from \$230 (off-peak), from \$340 (peak); dinner \$85. *When:* closed Jan–Feb. **Ballinkeele House:** Tel 353/53-913-8105; www.ballinkeele.ie. *Cost:* from \$215; dinner \$65. *When:* closed Dec–Jan. **Best time:** May–Sep for nicest weather.

Pride of the Emerald Isle

The Gardens of Wicklow

County Wicklow, Ireland

In a country known around the world for its verdant, coast-to-coast beauty, it says something that the Irish call Wicklow the "Garden of Ireland." In addition to the rolling green expanse of the Wicklow Mountains, Ireland's "little Alps," the county is home to more than 30 public gardens, from tiny half-acre cottage plots to the sprawling 47 acres of Powerscourt, Ireland's most visited garden. Its richly textured landscape includes formal flower beds, ornamental lakes, a Japanese garden, and more than 200 varieties of trees and shrubs. Expanding upon the original 13th-century castle, Powerscourt House was magnificently rebuilt in the 18th century, with the more recent addition of sweeping Italianate terraces, statuary, ironwork, and decorative items collected by the owners. Sit for a moment overlooking the gardens at the Terrace Café, a prime location with a simple menu of freshly made dishes.

Or come equipped with a picnic and strike off across the 1,000-acre estate to its waterfall, the highest in the British Isles at 398 feet. It is set in a beautifully wooded park where the Powerscourt lords introduced the first herd of Japanese sika deer to Europe. The current owners of the estate, the Slazenger family, purchased the park from the 9th

Viscount Powerscourt in 1961 and built the 36-hole Powerscourt Golf Club, ranked one of the finest in Ireland and an easy drive from downtown Dublin.

To lodge in comparable luxury, check in at the Ritz-Carlton Powerscourt, a monumental hotel located on the estate grounds and newly built in the Palladian style, with Georgian-inspired interiors and rooms granting glorious views of the countryside. A spa outfitted in slate, wood, and stone offers a dip in the Swarovski crystal–lit pool and a Garden of Inspiration massage, while the hotel's restaurant-with-a-view is overseen by renowned chef Gordon Ramsay.

Farther afield, try the gracious 19th-century Tinakilly House, a Victorian Italianate country manor built for the captain of the ship *Great Eastern,* who laid the first successful transatlantic cable in 1866. Captain Halpin's love for the sea is evident everywhere—the lobby's central staircase is a replica of one of his vessels—and nautical memorabilia fill the common rooms and guest rooms, most of which are named after famous ships. With its 7 acres of gardens adjacent to the Broadlough Bird Sanctuary, Tinakilly is serene and wonderfully romantic, with a highly rated restaurant and an abundance of country pursuits. Twenty minutes away by car lies Wicklow Mountains National Park, where you can hike a stretch of the 79-mile Wicklow Way that runs through it. The country's most important walking trail, it's one of the best ways to experience the Garden of Ireland.

WHERE: 12 miles/19 km south of Dublin. **POWERSCOURT HOUSE AND GARDENS:** Tel 353/1-204-6000; www.powerscourt.ie. **POWERSCOURT GOLF CLUB:** Tel 353/1-204-6033; greens fees from $66 (off-peak), from $160 (peak). **RITZ-CARLTON POWERSCOURT:** Tel 353/1-274-8888; www.ritzcarlton.com. *Cost:* $275 (off-peak), $450 (peak); dinner $100. **TINAKILLY HOUSE:** Tel 353/404-69274; www.tinakilly.ie. *Cost:* from $125 (off-peak), from $265 (peak); dinner $60. **WICKLOW WAY:** www.wicklowway.com. **BEST TIMES:** Apr–Jun for gardens in bloom; Jun for Wicklow Gardens Festival.

Leaving the Troubles Behind

BELFAST'S MOMENT

County Antrim, Northern Ireland

In the years since the quelling of its violent Troubles—the decades-long political conflict with Britain—Belfast has burst forth with renewed energy. The city first grew rapidly during the Industrial Revolution, thanks to its linen, tobacco, rope, and shipbuilding industries (the *Titanic* launched from its quays in 1912). In 1922, though most of Ireland obtained independence from England, six of its 32 counties remained under British rule and became Northern Ireland, with Belfast as its capital. Evidence of the schism this caused can be seen in rows of working-class housing, which during the Troubles served as canvasses for painted murals by both Republicans, aka Nationalists (mostly Catholics, who wanted the 6 counties reunited with the Republic of Ireland), and Loyalists, or Unionists (Protestants, who swore allegiance to the British crown). Today, black-taxi tours let tourists see the public art created by both sides and tell the stories behind it.

Ceasefires, peace treaties, and power sharing in government by both sides have ushered Belfast into a new era. Its Victorian heyday shines again in newly refurbished buildings, such as the Crown Liquor Saloon, across from the Grand Opera House. Here you can tuck into a plate of local Ardglass oysters and sip a pint of Guinness while marveling at extravagant craftsmanship: mosaic-tiled floors, ornate mirrors, etched glass, and elaborately patterned tin ceilings. Spend an afternoon in the Botanic Gardens' Palm House Conservatory, with its Victorian cast-ironwork and curvilinear glass, or at the block-long St. George's Market, an indoor bazaar where vendors in hundreds of stalls sell antiques, flowers, and a vast array of produce and gourmet food. The former Ulster Bank headquarters, with its 1860s Italianate façade and interior bursting with pomp and luxury, is now repurposed as the Merchant Hotel. Take tea amid the Great Room's towering black columns, gilded capitals, and carved putti. Outside, the Cathedral Quarter thrums with energy from galleries, clubs, artists' studios, and music pubs.

The food scene is also thriving. Amid minimalist décor, Deanes fuses the classic with the unexpected, in dishes like roast quail with French-toasted gingerbread. For casual fare, walk a cobblestone lane to Nick's Warehouse, an 1832 Bushmills Whiskey storehouse redone as an inviting restaurant with an open kitchen that turns out entrées such as pan-fried crab claw with fennel puree and warm peppered oranges; a plethora of wines is also on offer. Revitalization stretches to the waterfront too, the site of Belfast's 2012 celebration of *Titanic*'s centenary, with a museum about the ocean liner, galleries, theaters, and parkland on the old dockyards.

WHERE: 97 miles/156 km north of Dublin. **BLACK-TAXI TOURS:** Harper Taxi Tours, tel 44/28-90-742-711; www.harpertaxitours.com. **CROWN LIQUOR SALOON:** Tel 44/28-9024-3187; www.crownbar.com. *Cost:* lunch $24. **MERCHANT HOTEL:** Tel 44/28-9023-4888; www.themerchanthotel.com. *Cost:* from $225 (off-peak), from $350 (peak). **DEANES:** Tel 44/28-9033-1134; www.michaeldeane.co.uk. *Cost:* dinner $65. **NICK'S WAREHOUSE:** Tel 44/28-9043-9690; www.nickswarehouse.co.uk. *Cost:* dinner $50. **BEST TIMES:** Mar 17 for St. Patrick's Day; Apr–May for Cathedral Arts Festival; Jul–Aug for Festival of the People; Oct–Nov for Belfast Festival at Queen's.

Political murals painted from a Republican perspective during the period called the Troubles form the Solidarity Wall.

Nature's Masterwork

THE CAUSEWAY COAST

County Antrim, Northern Ireland

"When the world was moulded and fashioned out of formless chaos," wrote William Thackeray, "this must have been the bit left over—a remnant of chaos." Fortunately, the rugged scenery of Northern

Irish legend alleges that mythic hero Finn MacCool created the rocks as stepping-stones.

Ireland is easily traversed these days on the wonderfully scenic Causeway Coastal Route, with the first and most notable stop at the grand, strange, and astonishing Giant's Causeway. Now under the attentive auspices of the National Trust (and Northern Ireland's only UNESCO World Heritage site), this honeycomb mass along the island's northern coast is made up of more than 40,000 basalt columns (each a foot or two across) created by volcanic eruptions some 60 million years ago. Hopscotch around the tightly packed, mostly hexagonal formations—though some have four or five sides, others as many as ten—a few reach as high as 40 feet. Or wander along the cliff-top belvederes to marvel at the causeway from afar.

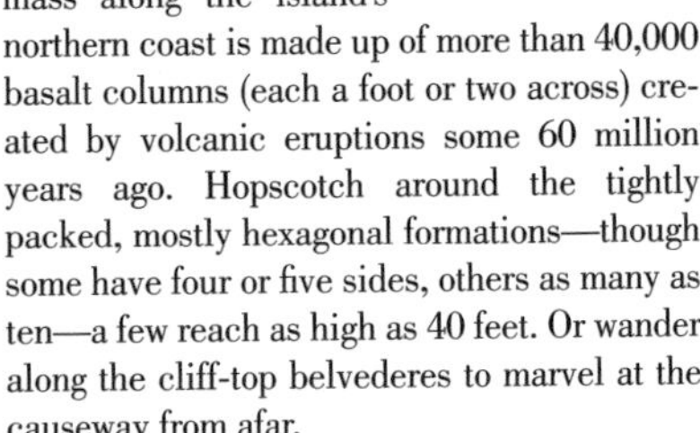

Stop for a tipple at Bushmills, Ireland's oldest-known whiskey distillery (licensed in 1608 but with historical references dating from 1276), but go easy on the amber elixir if you want to brave the Carrick-a-Rede rope bridge, a wobbly path over a 75-foot-deep watery chasm to rocky Carrick Island. Here you can savor the diverse birdlife as well as the stunning views of nearby Rathlin Island and the more distant Scottish isles. As you take in the bracing air, ponder the legend that fabled giant Finn MacCool built the Causeway as a bridge to reach his ladylove on the Scottish island of Staffa.

Next, repair to the village's Bushmills Inn, founded in the 1820s as a stopover for visitors traveling by horse and carriage to the nearby sites. Restored and updated, the rustically charming hotel offers spacious rooms, a popular restaurant, and plenty of nooks and crannies to cozy up with a good book and a locally brewed Caffey's Irish Ale.

Equally majestic surroundings are the backdrop for Royal Portrush, one of two distinguished golf courses in Northern Ireland, and consistently ranked among the world's premier destinations for the sport. Founded in 1888, Royal Portrush is the country's most spectacular and, together with its friendly rival Royal County Down in Newcastle (see next page), it is considered one of the stiffest tests of just about every club in your bag. Challenges are made easier by spectacular views of sea and cliffs, and the striking façade of the 13th-century Dunluce Castle, the largest Norman castle in the North.

The elegant Ardtara Country House, in Upperlands, offers the luxury of a remote countryside estate within easy driving distance of the Causeway and Belfast (see p. 76). The nine spacious rooms of the restored 19th-century manor house showcase antique furnishings, working fireplaces, and grand views of the expansive lawns and surrounding countryside, while the skylit dining room offers simply prepared local lamb, beef, and salmon.

Where: Giant's Causeway is 75 miles/120 km northwest of Belfast. Tel 44/28-2073-1855; www.giantscausewaycentre.com. **Bushmills Inn:** Tel 44/28-2073-3000; www.bushmillsinn.com. *Cost:* from $255. **Royal Portrush Golf Club:** Tel 44/28-7082-2311; www.royalportrushgolfclub.com; greens fees $95 (off-peak), $215 (peak). **Ardtara Country House:** Tel 44/28-7964-4490; www.ardtara.com. *Cost:* from $145; dinner $45. **Best time:** May–Oct for nicest weather.

Wuthering Heights

The Kingdom of Mourne

County Down, Northern Ireland

Made famous by the traditional Irish ballad with the lyrics "Where the Mountains o' Mourne sweep down to the sea," this distinctive granite range is Northern Ireland's highest. The tightly packed Mournes are barely 7 miles across, with a dozen of the 50-odd peaks over 2,000 feet high. It resembles "earth-covered potatoes," wrote C. S. Lewis, and is so remote (ringed by a single road, with just one other running through it) that it was neglected by both St. Patrick and the Normans and chalked up as ungovernable. Still, a web of ancient footpaths through open moorland and upland pasture makes it a rambler's paradise, offering the best hiking in Northern Ireland.

It's a safe and relatively easy climb up the highest peak, Slieve Donard (2,796 feet), where it's said that if the day is clear, you can see all the countries of the British Isles. The ascent begins near Bloody Bridge, north of the lively seaside town of Newcastle. The challenging 22-mile Mourne Wall trek wends across 15 peaks; the wall was built in the early 1900s to keep livestock away from a planned reservoir.

In the shadow of the Mournes and at the edge of the Irish Sea, the lavish Slieve Donard Hotel takes its guests back to the heyday of early-20th-century seaside resorts. The turreted, Victorian redbrick hotel is traditionally furnished, serves classic Irish cuisine, offers hiking paths that begin on the manicured grounds, and puts guests within walking distance of the world-class links of the Royal County Down Golf Club, arguably the top course in Ireland. Expect a challenge, what with changing winds, long holes, small greens, and the distraction of what many consider the world's most beautiful course.

Oysters and mussels at the informal and forever busy Mourne Seafood Bar, in nearby Dundrum, hail from the bar's very own shellfish beds. For quiet accommodations in the heart of the mountains—and with the sea at your doorstep—stay at the Glassdrumman Lodge, a converted farmhouse with attentive hosts. Rooms offer views of mountains or sea, dinners blend ingredients from the gardens, and there's a cozy lounge and an open fire.

WHERE: Newcastle is 30 miles/48 km southwest of Belfast. **SLIEVE DONARD HOTEL:** Tel 44/28-4372-1066; www.hastingshotel.com. *Cost:* from $150 (off-peak), from $220 (peak). **ROYAL COUNTY DOWN GOLF COURSE:** Tel 44/28-4372-3314; www.royalcountydown.org. *Cost:* greens fees from $80 (off-peak), from $240 (peak). **MOURNE SEAFOOD BAR:** Tel 44/28-4375-1377; www.mourneseafood.com. *Cost:* dinner $35. **GLASSDRUMMAN LODGE:** Tel 44/28-4376-8451; www.glassdrummanlodge.com. *Cost:* from $150; dinner $55. **BEST TIMES:** May–Sep for nicest weather; 3rd week in Jul for Celtic Fusion music festival.

Few roads cross the Mourne Mountains, the country's highest range.

WESTERN EUROPE

The Pinnacle of Alpine Playgrounds

Arlberg Region and Kitzbühel

Austria

Some of the choicest downhill skiing in the world can be found in the western reaches of the Austrian Alps. Wonderfully picturesque Arlberg ensures ample amounts of powder even when other resorts go bare. This area encompasses Lech, its most charming village resort, as well as Zürs, St. Anton, St. Christoph, and Stuben. In the sister hamlets of Lech-Zürs alone there are 35 lifts and cable cars serving a 65-mile ski circuit of groomed pistes and 75 miles of open, ungroomed runs, including the magnificent 12-mile Madloch tour. The ski technique named for Arlberg is practiced around the globe, and the area's schools and instructors are among the best.

Skiers in the region pioneered the Arlberg technique, but snowboarding is also popular here.

Lech's smallest and best five-star hotel, the Gasthof Post, has been run by the gracious Moosbrugger clan for three generations, and is known for its homey ambience and excellent restaurant. For après-ski fun and food, Skihütte Schneggarei is popular with the young and beautiful. In St. Anton, après-ski central, the Lux Alpinae is a cutting-edge hotel with a modern façade of glass, metal, and wood that opens into an unexpectedly cozy lobby. For the lap of luxury in quaint little St. Christoph, stay at the Arlberg Hospiz, a winter-only inn and restaurant that exudes warmth and top-notch hospitality.

While the Arlberg resorts are sought out for their unspoiled character, Kitzbühel—equidistant from Innsbruck and Salzburg—is beloved for its fashionable, glamorous atmosphere. The town's historic center of cobbled streets and pastel-painted medieval houses brims with trendy boutiques, lively casinos, and sophisticated clubs for off-mountain fun. Visitors can relax with hot chocolate and pastries at the well-known Café Praxmair. Set high on the sunny side of the Kitzbüheler Horn is the romantic and friendly Tennerhof Hotel, a quaint, converted 17th-century farmhouse. The eating is some of the best in town, so dine here even if you're lodging elsewhere.

The smooth, mighty crags behind the medieval walled town are ideal for finding your ski legs—except, perhaps, on Kitzbühel's difficult, world-famous Hahnenkamm downhill run. Heart-stopping cable car rides and 120 miles of awesome summertime hiking possibilities set it apart from other Alpine resorts.

Where: 125 miles/201 km east of Zürich, Switzerland. **Visitor info:** www.arlberg.com; www.kitzbuehel.com. **Gasthof Post:** Tel 43/ 5583-22060; www.postlech.com. *Cost:* from

$355 (off-peak), from $655 (peak). *When:* closed late Apr–mid-Jun, mid-Oct–Nov. **Lux Alpinae:** Tel 43/5446-30108; www.luxalpinae.at. *Cost:* from $175 (off-peak), from $400 room only (peak). *When:* closed late Apr–Jun, Oct–Nov. **Arlberg Hospiz:** Tel 43/5446-2611; www.hospiz.com. *Cost:* from $345. *When:* closed late Apr–Nov. **Tennerhof Hotel:** Tel 43/5356-63181; www.tennerhof.com. *Cost:* from $335; dinner $55. *When:* closed Apr–May, late Sep–mid-Dec. **Best times:** Dec–Mar for skiing; Jan for the Hahnenkamm races; Jul–Aug for hiking and biking.

Pulling the Right Strings

Austria's Music Festivals

Austria

Few countries reverberate with as many world-class music festivals as Austria. The hills *are* alive with the sound of music, beginning with the spectacular Bregenz Festival (Bregenzer Festspiele) on a vast floating stage at the edge of picturesque Lake Constance (Bodensee in German), the Alpine lake shared with Switzerland and Germany (see p. 142). Puccini's *Tosca,* Bernstein's *West Side Story,* the music of Beethoven, Shakespeare's plays: These are just samplings of the operatic, orchestral, and dramatic works performed here. The place to stay in charming Bregenz is the antiques-filled, 17th-century Hotel Deuring Schlössle, seated high on a hill overlooking the lake. The ivy-covered Baroque château has a highly regarded restaurant that has been ranked among the country's finest for years. Take a ferry across the mountain-framed lake, or for stunning panoramic views of Austria's westernmost province, ride the gondola up the 3,460-foot Pfänder Mountain.

Mozart's glorious birthplace is the appropriate venue for Europe's largest annual musical event, the Salzburg Festival (Salzburger Festspiele). More than 180 classic and contemporary performances—including operas, symphonies, recitals, and theater productions—concentrate on their native son while also offering works by other artists. Though banner events sell out well in advance, tickets to matinees for no-less-enjoyable chamber music or church concerts can be found at the last minute. (And don't dismiss the hokey but fun Sound of Music tour, still going strong.) Rest your head at the Hotel Schloss Mönchstein, a 14th-century turreted castle built as the summer escape for the archbishops of Salzburg. Surrounded by gardens and 25 acres of parkland, the 17 luxurious hilltop guest rooms feature modern amenities amid 18th-century furniture and Oriental rugs.

The most distinguished festival in the world to honor Franz Schubert is the Schubertiade, held in the charming neighboring villages of Schwarzenberg and Hohenems, about 415 miles west of Vienna. Some 70 chamber ensembles, orchestral concerts, and recitals honor the Austrian-born composer's works and the art of music-making in an intimate, idyllic setting. In nearby Hittisau, the family-run Gasthof Krone is a small hotel known for nurturing the arts; it runs free shuttles to all events during the festival.

Where: Bregenz is 126 miles/200 km northwest of Innsbruck 80 miles/129 km northeast of Zürich, Switzerland. **Bregenz Festival:** Tel 43/5574-4076; www.bregenzerfestspiele.com. *Cost:* tickets $35–$350. *When:*

4 weeks late Jul–Aug. **Hotel Deuring Schlössle:** Tel 43/5574-47800; www.schlosshotels.co.at. *Cost:* from $510 during festival; dinner $80. **Salzburg Festival:** Tel 43/662-8045500; www.salzburgerfestspiele.at. *Cost:* tickets $20–$420. *When:* 5 weeks late Jul–early Sep. **Sound of Music tours:** Tel 43/662-8832110; www.panoramatours.com. **Hotel Schloss Mönchstein:** Tel 43/662-848-5550; www.monchstein.at. *Cost:* from $510 during festival. **Schubertiade:** Tel 43/5576-72091; www.schubertiade.at. *Cost:* tickets $45–$80. *When:* 2 weeks late Jun, 2 weeks late Aug–mid-Sep. **Gasthof Krone:** Tel 43/5513-6201; www.krone-hittisau.at. *Cost:* from $180 during festival.

From Picturesque Peaks to Lakeside Splendor

Grossglockner Road and Hallstatt

Austria

Feast your eyes on the essence of Alpine beauty as you ride along the lofty Grossglockner Road, Austria's white-knuckle, breathtaking drive. Named after the country's highest peak and traversing some of Austria's most scenic regions, it was an important trading route between Germany and Italy in the Middle Ages. The road (aka Highway 107) was built between 1930 and 1935, and while most adventurous motorists strike out today from Salzburg (and head south) or from Lienz (and head north), the road actually begins in the heart of Hohe Tauern National Park. Almost 700 square miles in size, the park has 300 mountains over 9,840 feet, 246 glaciers, lush valleys, and dozens of pretty villages that provide a good meal and simple overnight lodging. Spectacular vistas of the park's centerpiece, the towering 12,460-foot-tall Grossglockner, make it hard for drivers to keep their eyes on the hairpin turns. The 47-mile strip from Bruck to Heiligenblut is the most riveting, highlighted by the Edelweiss-Spitze and Kaiser-Franz-Josefs-Höhe, two awesome peaks at 8,500 feet and 7,800 feet, respectively. Throw in the fantastic 6-mile sector called the Road of the Glaciers and you've got an unforgettable journey.

Built as a public works project, the winding Grossglockner Road opened in 1935.

Well worth a side trip on your return to Salzburg is the ancient village of Hallstatt (34 miles southeast of Salzburg), dating back centuries B.C. Perched between water and mountain, the storybook square and cluster of terraced fishermen's cottages and churches overlook a tranquil, fjordlike lake. A thrilling funicular runs up the mountain, where it's a short hike to the entrance of the world's first known salt mines, which visitors can tour.

Where: Salzburg is 157 miles/253 km west of Vienna; Lienz is 131 miles/211 km south of Salzburg. **When:** road closed Dec–Apr. **Best time:** May–Sep for nicest weather.

Historic Architecture and Modern Design

OLD GRAZ

Austria

Graz, established as the southeastern seat of the Hapsburg Empire in 1379, features one of Central Europe's best-preserved Altstädte (Old Towns). Known for its magnificent architecture from the Middle Ages and the Renaissance, it buzzes with upbeat energy, thanks to a sunny climate and three prominent universities, the oldest founded in the 16th century. Europe's largest armory is located here, with more than 30,000 pieces of every imaginable kind of armor and weaponry filling four floors of the 17th-century Landeszeughaus. Jump forward a few centuries at the curvy Kunsthaus (House of Art), Graz's newest landmark, which holds contemporary art bragging rights for its groundbreaking exhibitions. It billows up from the banks of the Mur in striking contrast to the medieval contours of the Old Town. Off the river's banks is the Murinsel (Mur Island), an artificial floating platform made of glass and steel and home to an amphitheater, playground, and trendy café-bar.

You can find a refreshing blend of antiquity and contemporary art at the Schlossberg Hotel, in two splendid 16th-century Baroque buildings; its 54 guest rooms are situated around three courtyards, providing a cloistered serenity. Ride the elevator to the hillside terrace for a spectacular view. There's more art behind the glass-and-metal façade of the sophisticated Augarten Hotel, which features a warm interior accented by chestnut-hued wood and colorful works by more than 250 contemporary artists. In its 56 gorgeous guest rooms, mid-century–modern furnishings contrast with soothingly neutral walls.

From spring until fall, a number of prestigious fairs and music festivals enliven the flagstone streets and squares, while students keep the atmospheric beer cellars, bars, and *beisls* (pubs) full. Fresh herbs and produce vie for attention with homemade cheeses and local pumpkinseed oil at the farmers market behind the opera house. One of Graz's most enticing day trips is a meander along any of the eight *weinstrassen* (wine roads) south of the city (see also the Wachau Valley, p. 90). At the Bundesgestüt (Federal Stud) in nearby Piber, visit the famous Lipizzaner horses, bred and raised here for the Spanish Riding School in Vienna (see p. 85).

Architects Peter Cook and Colin Fournier designed the organically shaped Kunsthaus art museum.

WHERE: 124 miles/200 km southwest of Vienna. **LANDESZEUGHAUS:** Tel 43/316-8017-9810. **KUNSTHAUS GRAZ:** Tel 43/316-8017-9200; www.museum-joanneum.at. **SCHLOSSBERG HOTEL:** Tel 43/316-8070; www.schlossberg-hotel.at. *Cost:* from $195. **AUGARTEN HOTEL:** Tel 43/316-208-00; www.augartenhotel.at. *Cost:* from $200. **FEDERAL STUD:** Tel 43/1-533-9031; www.piber.com. **BEST TIMES:** early Jun for Spring Festival of electronic art and music; late Sep–mid-Oct for Steierischer Herbst (Styrian Autumn) festival; late Nov–Dec for Christmas markets and Piber's Christmas Walk.

Much More than Just Mozart

Salzburg: Baroque and Modern

Austria

This golden city's High Baroque architecture is due in large part to prince-archbishop Wolf Dietrich, who reigned from 1587 to 1612. He lavished much of his wealth on rebuilding Salzburg into an Italianate city based around five plazas, dominated by the medieval Hohensalzburg Fortress atop its rocky cliff. The French-style confection of Schloss Mirabell, which he generously built for his mistress (and their 15 children), sits across the Salzach River from the opulent Residenz, historic home of the ruling prince-bishops and dating from the 12th century. The Residenz houses magnificent staterooms and a gallery of Rembrandts, Rubens, and other European masters.

As you wander the heart of Salzburg, with the famous Glockenspiel ringing out classic Mozart or Haydn, you can't miss the massive Salzburger Dom. With towers 249 feet high, the grand 17th-century cathedral is renowned for its 4,000-pipe organ and elaborate frescoes. Next to the 13th-century Stiftkirche St. Peter—the church where Mozart premiered his Great Mass in C Minor in 1783—is the bustling restaurant and beer cellar he frequented, Stiftskeller St. Peter. First mentioned in a document in A.D. 803, Austria's oldest eatery still draws crowds for candlelit dinners while costumed performers sing arias from Mozart's operas.

Indeed, it is impossible to escape the presence of Mozart here in his hometown (the Salzburg Festival celebrates his work annually; see p. 81). In Getreidegasse, the Old Town's venerable merchants' quarter, Mozart's Geburtshaus (birthplace) is a pilgrimage destination for music lovers. Now a museum, it contains many of his childhood belongings, including musical scores and his first child-size violin. A few steps away is one of the country's most glamorous hotels, the Goldener Hirsch, a 600-year-old historical monument that's ground zero during the city's various festivals and a favored choice for its excellent service and wonderful restaurant. The neighborhood is characterized by flower-bedecked arcades and inviting eateries, such as the historical Café Tomaselli, where people-watching is enjoyed over coffee and homemade pastries on a delightful cobblestone square.

Pulsing new life into this historic city are experimental restaurants, design hotels, and the brand-new hilltop Museum der Moderne. Clad in minimalist white marble and glass, it has three exhibition levels and a restaurant terrace that offers spectacular views, particularly magical at night. Down in the Old Town, French fare is served with an Austrian twist at chic Esszimmer, where a glass floor allows guests to gaze down on the flowing Almkanal. Hotel Stein, the 1399 hostelry on the banks of the Salzach River, now boasts modern rooms dressed in either neo-Baroque or animal prints, with a rooftop café that offers great views and buzzes with locals come evening. The 660-year-old Arthotel Blaue Gans blends medieval stone arches and ancient wood beams with minimalist rooms and a top-notch restaurant, both highlighted with avant-garde works from the hotel's own art collection.

Where: 186 miles/299 km southwest of

Vienna. **Stiftskeller St. Peter:** Tel 43/662-841-2680; www.haslauer.at. *Cost:* Mozart Dinner $65. **Hotel Goldener Hirsch:** Tel 43/662-8084; in the U.S., 800-325-3535; www.goldenerhirsch.com. *Cost:* from $270. **Museum der Moderne:** Tel 43/662-842-220; www.museumdermoderne.at. **Esszimmer:** Tel 43/662-870-899; www.esszimmer.com. *Cost:* dinner $85. **Hotel Stein:** Tel 43/662-874-3460; www.hotelstein.at. *Cost:* from $275. **Arthotel Blaue Gans:** Tel 43/662-842-4910; www.blauegans.at. *Cost:* from $210. **Best times:** late Jan for Mozart Week; Mar–Apr for Easter Festival; late Jul–Aug for Salzburg Festival; late Nov–Dec for Christmas Market on the Domplatz.

"The wonderful, inexhaustibly magical city, with its mysterious, soft, light-saturated air!"
—Hugo von Hofmannsthal

Vienna

Austria

A fresh breeze of creativity has been sweeping through this gracious old-world city, adding 21st-century appeal to the legacies of Beethoven, the Strausses, Freud, Klimt, and Mahler. One of the most compelling capitals of Europe, Vienna is exploding with contemporary art in the new MuseumsQuartier and emerging design districts, while forward-thinking architecture distinguishes new hotels and cutting-edge restaurants rife with culinary talent. More than ever, the romantic city on the Danube—famous for its gemütlichkeit, its cafés and dazzling confections, its coffeehouses, and its Lipizzaners—is a delightfully civilized and elegant place and a timeless destination for art, music, and culture.

Top Attractions

The Hofburg (Imperial Palace)—The Hofburg served as the seat of Hapsburg emperors for 6 centuries, through the Holy Roman Empire until the end of the monarchy (1806–1918). Each emperor made his own additions and renovations, resulting in today's sprawling complex, the official seat of the Austrian president. Among 18 wings, 19 courtyards, and 2,600 rooms, you'll find the following highlights:

The Imperial Apartments (Kaiserappartments)—Emperor Franz Josef I lived here in the late 19th and early 20th centuries. Visitors can tour his opulent private rooms, the great audience hall, and the dining rooms, richly decorated in Rococo stucco work, tapestries, and Bohemian crystal chandeliers—Vienna at its most Viennese. **Info:** Tel 43/1-533-7570; www.hofburg-wien.at.

The Michaelerkuppel tops off the Hofburg Palace.

Lipizzaner Horses of the Spanish Riding School—Founded in 1572, the Spanische Reitschule preserves classic dressage in its purest form, with frequent presentations executed with charmingly antiquated formality (including their morning exercise performed to music) that are open to the public. These horses are said to be the finest equestrian performers on earth. **Info:** Tel 43/1-533-9031; www.srs.at.

The Treasury (Schatzkammer)—This superb collection includes the imperial crowns of the Holy Roman and Austrian empires and numerous treasures from the house of Burgundy and the Order of the Golden Fleece. **Info:** Tel 43/1-525-240; www.khm.at.

Vienna Boys' Choir at the Hofburgkapelle—Linked with Vienna's musical life since 1498 and associated over the years with composers such as Mozart, Schubert, and Bruckner, members of the choir perform Sunday Mass at the Imperial Chapel (reservations are required). **Info:** www.wsk.at. *When:* Jan–Jun and Sep–Dec.

Albertina Museum—Combining a 17th-century palace and a new 14-story building, the Albertina contains one of the world's largest collections of graphic art, from the Gothic to the contemporary, plus some 25,000 architectural drawings and a major photography collection. The impressive permanent collection, including Albrecht Dürer's fabled *Hare* (1502), is complemented by important temporary exhibitions. **Info:** Tel 43/1-534-830; www.albertina.at.

Schloss Belvedere (Belvedere Palace)—This is actually two 18th-century palaces separated by landscaped gardens. The upper palace exhibits 19th- and 20th-century Viennese art, including the world's largest collection of paintings by Gustav Klimt (*The Kiss* and *Judith* among them). The lower palace showcases the Gothic and Baroque. **Info:** Tel 43/1-795-570; www.belvedere.at.

Kunsthistorisches Museum—One of the richest fine-arts museums on the planet, with works from the ancient world and all over Europe, is housed in palatial galleries across from the Hofburg Palace. The Italian and Flemish collections are especially fine, as is the world's largest collection of paintings by Pieter Brueghel the Elder, which includes his *Hunters in the Snow.* **Info:** Tel 43/1-525-244-025; www.khm.at.

MuseumsQuartier (MQ)—Once the grounds of the imperial stables and now Vienna's sprawling cutting-edge cultural complex, the MQ is home to open-air restaurants and more than 60 arts institutions, including museums, artist studios, and performance spaces. The Kunsthalle hosts contemporary exhibitions, the steel-gray Museum Moderner Kunst (MUMOK) features modern art and international design, and the limestone Leopold Museum boasts the world's largest collection of works by Egon Schiele. Recharge at the popular café Halle, in the MQ. **Info:** Tel 43/1-523-5881; www.mqw.at.

St. Charles Church (Karlskirche)—Built in the early 18th century, this Baroque masterpiece has an entrance framed by huge freestanding columns, replicas of Rome's Trajan's Column. From the top of the dome, enjoy the heavenly frescoes within and the magnificent views out over the city. **Info:** Tel 43/1-504-6187; www.karlskirche.at.

St. Stephen's Cathedral (Stephansdom)—Even after centuries of renovation and rebuilding, the Stephansdom, dedicated in 1147, retains a medieval atmosphere. Its towering Gothic spires still dominate the city skyline. Inside, it's full of monuments, sculptures, and paintings. Catacomb tours run regularly, revealing sarcophagi of former archbishops and Hapsburg emperors. **Info:** Tel 43/1-515-52-3526; www.stephanskirche.at.

Schloss Schönbrunn—Built by the Hapsburgs between 1696 and 1712, this 1,441-room summer palace was inspired by Versailles and is filled with delicate Rococo touches that set it in contrast to the starker Hofburg. Mozart performed here at age six for the Empress Maria Theresa, and Emperor Franz Joseph was born here. About 40 of its rooms are open to visitors, and the palace's park, opened to the public around 1779, is still popular for its hedge maze, reproduction Roman ruins, botanical garden, and zoo. **Info:** Tel 43/1-811-13-239; www.schoenbrunn.at.

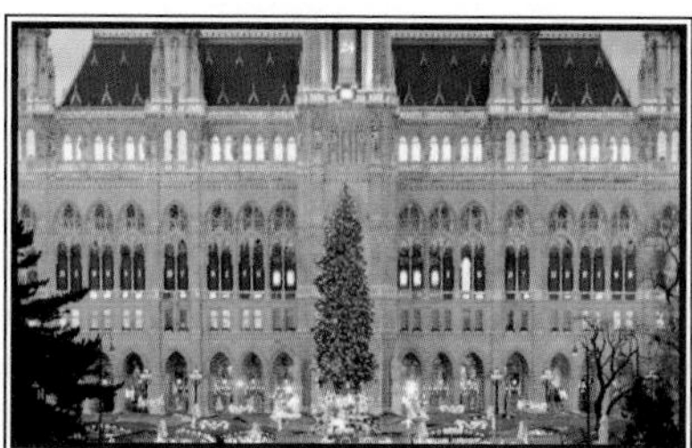

The country's most-visited Christmas market takes place at Rathausplatz, Vienna's City Hall square, during the weeks leading up to the holiday.

Other Must-Dos

Christmas in Vienna—Vienna *is* Christmas: white with snow, adorned with traditional decorations, and beautifully noncommercial. There's midnight mass at St. Stephen's, where the Vienna Boys' Choir performs Viennese carols. At City Hall's Christkindlmarkt, which dates back to 1298, hundreds of festive outdoor stands sell everything that smells and tastes of the holidays. Behind the MuseumsQuartier, the bohemian Spittelberg neighborhood's more intimate market is popular for its artisanal stalls along narrow lanes fronting Biedermeier and Baroque façades.

The Musikverein—Built in 1867, with nearly flawless acoustics, the Musikverein is one of the greatest music halls in the world. It's home to the Vienna Philharmonic, whose New Year's concert featuring the music of Johann Strauss is broadcast around the globe. The celebrated Vienna Mozart Concerts take place here and elsewhere in town, from May to October. **Info:** Tel 43/1-505-8190; www.musikverein.at.

The Staatsoper (Vienna State Opera)—Built in 1887 as the imperial court opera, the green-domed opera house is one of the world's best, offering an incredibly long season of masterworks by Verdi, Mozart, and Strauss. **Info:** Tel 43/1-514-44-2250; www.wiener-staatsoper.at.

Viennese Ball Season—Vienna takes its ball season seriously. Beginning on New Year's Eve with the Imperial Ball at the Hofburg and continuing through Fasching (Carnival) season until Lent begins, thousands of white-tied and elegant-gowned waltzers attend more than 300 formal balls. The belle of them all is the legendary Opera Ball, established by the Emperor Franz Josef in 1877 and held in the ornate Staatsoper. Tickets are easier to come by for galas hosted by the professions, including the Coffeehouse Owners' and Florists' Balls, held in such venerable venues as the Imperial Palace and City Hall. **Info:** www.vienna.info. **Opera Ball, Vienna State Opera:** Tel 43/1-514-44-2250; www.wiener-staatsoper.at. *Cost:* from $240. **Imperial Ball, Hofburg:** Tel 43/1-587-36-6623; www.kaiserball.at. *Cost:* from $180.

Where to Stay

Hotel Altstadt—This former aristocrat's home in the cobbled Spittelberg neighborhood has been carefully transformed into an elegant 42-room Viennese inn featuring contemporary art from the owner's personal collection. The newest wing, designed by renowned Italian architect Matteo Thun in 2006, features nine dramatic rooms with gray-black walls and red velvet upholstery. **Info:** Tel 43/1-522-6666; www.altstadt.at. *Cost:* from $195.

Hotel Imperial—Built in 1867 in the Renaissance style by Emperor Franz Josef for his niece and her husband, Vienna's trophy hotel is still the official hotel for state visitors. Many details remain unchanged (give or take a few multimillion-dollar renovations): priceless furnishings, marble floors, gilded balustrades, ceiling frescoes, glittering chandeliers. Guests will naturally feel as if they're being treated like Queen Elizabeth, who uttered before leaving that it was "the most beautiful hotel we have ever stayed in." **Info:** Tel 43/1-501-100; in the U.S., 800-325-3589; www.hotelimperialvienna.com. *Cost:* from $465 (off-peak), from $565 (peak).

Hotel König von Ungarn—Simple and polished, with old-world service, the 33-room

King of Hungary property is Vienna's oldest hotel, tucked away in the shadow of St. Stephen's cathedral and in operation since 1746. After a day of exploring Old Town's busy Kärnterstrasse and meandering passageways, relax over drinks in the lovely glass-ceilinged courtyard. **Info:** Tel 43/1-515-840; www.kvu.at. *Cost:* from $250.

Hotel Rathaus Wein und Design—Housed in an 1890s building with a gorgeous original iron elevator and inviting winter garden, this boutique hotel, opened in 2004, takes wine appreciation to new levels. All its 39 handsome, high-ceilinged guest rooms are stocked with professional stemware and wine-based bath products, and each room is dedicated to a top Austrian vintner who provides wines for the minibar. **Info:** Tel 43/1-400-1122; www.hotel-rathaus-wien.at. *Cost:* from $225 (off-peak), from $300 (peak).

The Ring Hotel—This chic urban hideaway behind a historic façade is known for impeccable service and laid-back luxe design. Opened in 2007, The Ring boasts a superb location on the leafy Ringstrasse, an inviting spa, and 68 spacious rooms with high ceilings and easy-on-the-eyes minimalist décor. It is the new face of Vienna's hotel array, a welcome alternative to the city's ubiquitous Imperial style. **Info:** Tel 43/1-221-22; www.theringhotel.com. *Cost:* from $280.

Hotel Sacher—Opened in 1876 by Eduard Sacher, 44 years after his father created their namesake torte (still served in the hotel's café; see below), this luxury hotel evokes pure elegance, from the plushly decorated parlor and crystal chandeliers to guest rooms with silk-covered walls and original paintings from its private collection. A roof-raising expansion in 2005 added two floors of more modern accommodations. **Info:** Tel 43/1-514-560; www.sacher.com. *Cost:* from $515 (off-peak), from $615 (peak).

Sofitel Vienna Stephansdom—Designed by Pritzker Prize–winning architect Jean Nouvel, this new glass-and-steel tower near St. Stephen's delivers 182 tasteful guest rooms furnished in minimalist crème, gray, and black, with fabulous views of the city and the Vienna Woods. The lobby features a magnificent vertical garden, covering one multistory wall with 20,000 species of vegetation, and the top floor's glass-encased Le Loft restaurant includes dazzling panoramic views. **Info:** Tel 43/1-906-160; www.sofitel-vienna.com. *Cost:* from $290 (off-peak), from $490 (peak); dinner $100.

Eating & Drinking

Demel and Sacher—Open since 1887, Demel is the high temple of Viennese pastry and one of the reasons this city is known as Europe's pastry capital, setting up an Olympic-size array of more than 60 confections in its music-box-perfect front rooms. The five-layer chocolate Anna torte and the profoundly rich chocolate Sacher torte are house specialties. Compare the goods at the Hotel Sacher's café (both insist they have the original secret recipe). Demel's usually wins out; however, Sacher's strudel (*mit Schlagobers*—with whipped cream) knows no rival. **Demel:** Tel 43/1-535-17170; www.demel.at. **Sacher:** Tel 43/1-514-560; www.sacher.com.

Ein Wiener Salon—Designed like a stylish Viennese drawing room, with midnight blue

Café Central has a long history as a favorite meeting place for Vienna intellectuals.

wallpaper and outsize portraits of Empress Maria Theresa and Emperor Francis I, this small, romantic eatery offers imaginative four- to six-course menus that change with the seasons. You might find chickpea soup with smoked duck breast and homemade celery ravioli with beetroot and caviar. **Info:** Tel 43/1-660-654-2785; www.einwienersalon .com. *Cost:* dinner $55.

The Heuriger experience—At these rustic alfresco wine taverns, sprinkled along the edge of the nearby Vienna Woods (the Wienerwald), large quantities of wine help generate an atmosphere alive with bonhomie, singing, and shameless Viennese accordion schmaltz. The simple Viennese fare typically includes hearty soups, potato dumplings, and wild game dishes. Beethoven lived at Mayer am Pfarrplatz in 1817; today it's a favorite Heuriger. **Info:** Tel 43/1-370-3361; www.pfarrplatz.at. *Cost:* dinner $40.

Hollmann Salon—Step into the city's most beautiful courtyard, where cobblestones and Baroque façades front art galleries, private homes, and this stylish restaurant. Beneath the vaulted ceilings hung with steel antler chandeliers lie long wooden tables and an open stainless-steel kitchen that bestow a chic Austrian farmhouse warmth. Three- and four-course menus are driven by seasonal local ingredients: You may find standouts such as marinated venison with baked apple pancake, honey nuts, and plum mousse and crispy carp on mashed horseradish with gherkin in piccalilli chutney. **Info:** Tel 43/1-961-196-040; www.hollmann-salon.at. *Cost:* dinner $45.

Palmenhaus—Overlooking the imperial gardens, the spectacular Art Nouveau conservatory where Emperor Franz Joseph came to relax now serves fine Austrian fare with a contemporary twist. Savor your meal amid the glass-and-steel eatery's gargantuan ancient palms. **Info:** Tel 43/1-533-1033; www.palmenhaus.at. *Cost:* dinner $45.

Steirereck im Stadtpark—One of Austria's finest and most beloved restaurants and the innovator of New Viennese Cuisine, the Steirereck offers elaborate dishes that arrive with their own recipe card and are made with fresh local produce and products from chef Heinz Reitbauer's farm. Enjoy grilled guinea fowl with porcini fig duxelles, or veal with raw marinated scallops and black salsify. At Meierei, the adjacent white-on-white dairy bar and bistro, the menu features soups, Wiener schnitzel, 120 varieties of cheese, and homemade strudels, as well as an exotic selection of milks (including horse milk and tonka bean– and geranium-flavored milks). **Info:** Tel 43/1-713-3168; www.steirereck.at. *Cost:* dinner $115; at Meierei $25.

Traditional coffeehouses—For centuries, artists and literati have been gathering at Viennese coffeehouses to linger for hours over *kaffee und kuchen* (coffee and cake), while perusing racks of newspapers or engaging in (usually) friendly debate. To this day, each coffeehouse has its own personality and devoted following. One of the city's most famous intellectual cafés remains the classic, unapologetically smoky Café Hawelka—order the signature *buchteln* (jam-filled dumplings). Adorning the walls are works artists used to pay their tabs. Since 1880, artists and musicians from the nearby Theater an der Wien have been regulars at cozy Café Sperl. Create your own niche and relax in a plush red-velvet window seat, while savoring the signature sausages and fabulous plum cake. At Café Central, famous at the turn of the last century for its literary patrons (Sigmund Freud and Robert Musil were regulars), vaulted ceilings and marble pillars evoke a majestic setting for apple strudel and a cup of frothy *wiener mélange*. At all three coffeehouses, expect superb coffee that's dense, bitter, and fresh. **Café Hawelka:** Tel 43/1-512-8230; www .hawelka.com. **Café Sperl:** Tel 43/1-586-4158; www.cafesperl.at. **Café Central:** Tel 43/1-533-376-426; www.palaisevents.at.

Winning Wines Along the Danube

The Wachau Valley

Austria

With 1,730 acres of vineyards inside the city limits, Vienna is one of the world's most unique wine regions. But for the cream of the area's wine-producing crop, head northwest to the Wachau Valley along the Danube. Though its grape-producing land represents a small percentage of the country's 120,000 acres of vineyards, the region accounts for the lion's share of top releases.

Fortified abbeys and castles crown the valley's rolling hills, on which steeply terraced vineyards alternate with forested slopes and apricot orchards. A mild climate and the beautiful Danube have made the region ideal for vine cultivation since the Romans introduced it nearly 2,500 years ago. Towpaths along the Danube allowed horses to pull ships of wine upriver, and today cyclists pedal through wine country along one of Europe's most beloved bike paths.

Dominating the region are family-owned operations that produce award-winning rieslings and grüner veltliners known for rich fruit flavors. Sample them in towns up and down the Danube, including Krems, Klosterneuburg, and Poysdorf. The region's largest winemaking community, Langenlois, boasts soil honeycombed with wine caves. The city's modern temple to wine-making is the Steven Holl–designed Loisium, a steel-clad structure that houses a hotel, wine spa, and wine-producing facilities. Guests encounter wine at every turn, with lights shaped like corks and a view of the vineyards through the hotel's transparent ground floor.

Medieval Dürnstein may be the Wachau's loveliest town, dominated by the hilltop ruins of 17th-century Kuenringer Castle, which are said to have inspired the magic kingdoms of the Brothers Grimm tales. Enjoy dinner and a glass of the local grüner veltliner on the terrace of the old-world Hotel Schloss Dürnstein, where many of the elegant rooms offer beautiful views of the river.

In the very center of town, the Hotel-Restaurant Sänger Blondel, a comfortable, charmingly old-fashioned guesthouse, has a good restaurant and delightful owners, who serve breakfast under the garden's chestnut trees. Outside town, the Melk Abbey (Stift Melk), a 1,000-year-old Benedictine monastery, showcases manuscripts and precious works of art, including the famous Melk crucifix. Short boat cruises drift through this particularly picturesque, 21-mile stretch of the Danube, a lovely day trip from Vienna.

Where: 45 miles/73 km northwest of Vienna. **Loisium:** Tel 43/2734-771-000; www.loisiumhotel.at. *Cost:* from $225. **Hotel Schloss Dürnstein:** Tel 43/2711-212; www.schloss.at. *Cost:* from $305; dinner $55. *When:* closed Nov–early Apr. **Hotel-Restaurant Sänger Blondel:** Tel 43/2711-253; www.saengerblondel.at. *Cost:* from $140; dinner $30. **Melk Abbey:** Tel 43/2752-555-225; www.stiftmelk.at. **How:** DDSG Blue Danube offers riverboat tours. Tel 43/1-588-800; www.ddsg-blue-danube.at. *When:* mid-Apr–Oct. **Best times:** early Apr for apricot blossoms; late Apr–early May for Danube Music Festival in Krems; late May for Melk Summer Festival; mid-Aug for Weissenkirchen's Riesling festival; late Aug–Nov for grape harvest and Weinherbst, the local wine cellars' harvest celebration.

Epicenter of Art and Fashion

The Rubens Trail

Antwerp, Belgium

With its port on the broad estuary of the River Scheldt, Antwerp was a trading powerhouse in the 16th and 17th centuries, a Golden Age of intellectual, commercial, and artistic life of the Low Countries. This was the era of Peter Paul Rubens, who returned from training in Italy in 1609 to enthrall his homeland with his matchless technique and dynamic composition. His great early showpieces were a pair of triptychs, *Raising of the Cross* (1610) and *Descent from the Cross* (1612), made for the Onze-Lieve-Vrouwekathedraal (Cathedral of Our Lady). It is the largest Gothic cathedral in the Low Countries, with an ornamented, 404-foot white stone tower that soars above the Grote Markt, the old town square. It is still the city's reference point, ringing its 49-bell carillon every Monday evening in the summer months.

Rubens lived in Rubenshuis from 1611 until his death.

A short walk through central Antwerp leads to the Rubenshuis, the mansion where Rubens lived and ran his busy workshop; several of his canvases are still on display here. For further insight into the time in which he lived, head for the Rockoxhuis. The home of one of Rubens's wealthy patrons, Nicolaas Rockox, it is filled with furniture, paintings, and objets d'art. Rubens provided engravings for the influential printing house founded by Christophe Plantin, whose lavish home and workshops have been converted into the intriguing Museum Plantin-Moretus. The Koninklijk Museum voor Schone Kunsten Antwerpen (KMSKA, Royal Museum of Fine Arts Antwerp) has one of the world's largest collections of Rubens's work, but is undergoing massive renovation until 2017, so its collections can only be glimpsed elsewhere, in temporary exhibitions.

The inspiration and sense of daring innovation that drove Rubens still ripples through Antwerp, today known for its diamond and fashion industries. It can also be witnessed in Antwerp's most stylish small hotel, De Witte Lelie (The White Lily), which occupies an imaginatively transformed 17th-century mansion. The elegant Hotel Rubens–Grote Markt echoes the city's historic past too and even has a rare surviving lookout tower, built in medieval times to watch out for trading ships on the River Scheldt.

Where: 34 miles/55 km north of Brussels. **Visitor info:** visit .antwerpen.be. **Rubenshuis:** Tel 32/3-201-1555; www.rubenshuis.be. **Rockoxhuis:** Tel 32/3-201-9250; www.rockoxhuis.be. **Museum Plantin-Moretus:** Tel 32/3-221-1450; http://plantin-moretus.be. **KMSKA:** Tel 32/3-238-7809; www.kmska.be. **De Witte Lelie:** Tel 32/3-226-1966; www.dewittelelie.be. *Cost:* from $320. **Hotel Rubens–Grote Markt:** Tel 32/3-222-4848; www.hotelrubensantwerp.be. *Cost:* from $185 (off-peak), from $245 (peak). **Best times:** Jul–Aug for Zomer van Antwerpen (Summer of Antwerp) festival; Aug for the Middelheim Jazz Festival; Dec for the Christmas Market in the Grote Markt.

Heavenly Brews

BEER IN BELGIUM

Belgium

In a country barely the size of New Jersey, the breadth of Belgium's unparalleled beer-brewing industry is astonishing. Some 125 breweries produce more than 800 varieties, including "white beers" made of wheat, stratospherically strong Bush beers, dark and winey Rodenbach, and the famous Trappist beers brewed for centuries under the watchful eyes of monks and, no doubt, St. Arnold, Belgium's own patron saint of beer.

Trappist monks run the historic Orval church and brewery.

The Abbaye d'Orval is one of the country's five Trappist breweries. Set in the forested hills of the Ardennes region, 100 miles south of Brussels, its ruins date to 1110; other buildings date to the 17th century. A community of monks carefully tends the beautiful grounds, medicinal herb garden, and dispensary, where the famous Orval beer is sold along with artisanal bread and cheese.

Belgium's Trappist breweries, and many of its other breweries, are not generally open to the public. One happy exception, halfway between the Abbaye d'Orval and Brussels, is the little Brasserie du Bocq. Founded in 1858 and still operated by the Belot family, it produces 10 varieties of beer. Another accessible brewery is in Bruges (see next page): De Halve Maan (The Half Moon) has been making beer since 1856; today it turns out two excellent varieties that pack a punch, Brugse Zot (6 percent ABV) and Straffe Hendrik (9 percent ABV).

Brussels lies in the Valley of the Senne, where an unusual wild, air-borne yeast called *brettanomyces* is found. This is the secret of the unique beers of Brussels called *lambic:* The warm brew is placed in copper basins open to the air, and the yeast does its work. Lambic is blended and matured to create *gueuze,* mixed with cherry juice to make *kriek,* and with caramelized sugar to make *faro*—all classic Brussels beers. You can see these processes at the atmospheric Cantillon Brewery, which doubles as the Musée Bruxellois de la Gueuze, located in the Brussels suburb of Anderlecht.

For a good variety of beer in Brussels, ask anyone for directions to the celebrated tavern La Fleur en Papier Doré, just a 5-minute walk from the Grand Place, in the Rue des Alexiens. It was a favorite haunt of the surrealists, including René Magritte. Order some tasty, traditional *bruxellois* bar food, such as *pottekeis* (light cheese spread) and *bloempanch* (blood sausage), and a few brews and you've got yourself a quintessential Belgian meal.

ABBAYE D'ORVAL: Tel 32/61-31-1261; www.orval.be. **WHERE TO STAY:** Auberge du Moulin Hideux, a refined country inn housed in a 17th-century mill, is 20 minutes from Orval. Tel 32/61-46-7015; www.moulinhideux.be. *Cost:* from $280; dinner $100. **BRASSERIE DU BOCQ:** Tel 32/82-61-0780; www.bocq.be. **DE HALVE MAAN:** Tel 32/50-44-4222; www.halvemaan.be. **MUSÉE BRUXELLOIS DE LA GUEUZE:** Tel 32/2-521-4928; www.cantillon.be. **LA FLEUR EN PAPIER DORÉ:** 32/2-511-1659; www.lafleurenpapierdore.be. *Cost:* lunch $20. **BEST TIME:** early Sep for Brussels Belgian Beer Weekend, when some 50 breweries show off their products.

A Medieval Moment Captured in Time

BRUGES

Belgium

Bruges, or Brugge, is a perfectly formed city in miniature, brimming with reminders of its age of glory in medieval times. It's the kind of place that's easy to explore on foot. Better still, take a tour in an open boat on the meandering, willow-lined canals, to learn how Bruges was once linked to the world beyond and why it is called the "Venice of the North."

This was once one of Europe's most prosperous cities, the 15th-century capital of the Dukes of Burgundy, and a busy trading hub where Italian bankers rubbed shoulders with merchants from Spain, England, and Scandinavia. Then, in the early 16th century, political power shifted away, the canals silted up, and Bruges fell into a long decline until it was rediscovered more than 300 years later.

The riches of Bruges's golden age become vividly clear at the city's small but exquisite Groeninge Museum. When Jan van Eyck painted his *Virgin with Canon Joris van der Paele* in 1436, he was depicting not just a sacred scene but also the kind of luxuries and supreme craftsmanship that surrounded him: the sumptuous textiles, the gemstones, the finely tooled armor. In a similar vein, the German-born and prolific local master Hans Memling painted six works of jewel-like precision for the chapel of Sint-Janshospitaal, the medieval hospital where they can still be seen.

Day-trippers flock to Bruges from Brussels to swarm around its medieval landmarks: the towering town belfry, the 14th-century Gothic Stadhuis (town hall), the Onthaalkerk Onze-Lieve-Vrouw (Church of Our Lady) with its white marble *Madonna and Child* by Michelangelo, and the 13th-century Begijnhof, a self-contained conventlike community that flourished for 600 years and remains a world apart. Linger overnight at the Prinsenhof, one of Bruges's many supremely comfortable hotels, this one housed in a 20th-century mansion. Or try the family-owned Alegria, a small and stylish central inn. Cozy bistros serving the regional favorite of *moules-frites* (mussels and fries) are plentiful; for a sampling from the new guard, try Restaurant Patrick Devos, where a centuries-old house is the elegant setting for first-class French cuisine cooked with a Belgian twist. Then take a stroll to the city's central square, the Burg, glorious when illuminated at night.

Canals still flow throughout Bruges, which has retained much of its medieval architecture.

WHERE: 62 miles/100 km northwest of Brussels. **VISITOR INFO:** www.brugge.be. **GROENINGE MUSEUM AND MEMLING IN SINT-JAN:** Tel 32/50-44-8743; www.brugge.be. **PRINSENHOF:** Tel 32/50-34-2690; www.prinsenhof.com. *Cost:* from $245. **ALEGRIA:** Tel: 32/50-33-0937; www.alegria-hotel.com. *Cost:* from $135. **RESTAURANT PATRICK DEVOS:** Tel 32/50-33-5566; www.patrickdevos.be. *Cost:* dinner $80. **BEST TIMES:** Mar–Nov for boat tours; May for Procession of the Holy Blood on Ascension Day (40 days after Easter); Aug for Klinkers music festival.

A Connoisseur's Nirvana

Belgian Chocolate

Brussels, Belgium

Stand outside the Leonidas shop on the Boulevard Anspach—one of the 22 Brussels outlets of this leading Belgian manufacturer—and you might think it was fast food it was selling, not luxury chocolates. But the reason the crowds gather is for the assortments of *pralines* (filled chocolates): Wrapped in a small, gilded treasure box called a *ballotin*, they make for a perfect gift, everyone's first-choice souvenir to take home. Once an indulgence of the rich, Belgian chocolate is now a favorite of the masses.

The high quality of Belgian chocolate has to do with both the raw materials used to make it and the method by which it is made. It has high levels of cocoa solids and cocoa butter and is subjected to long and intense processing. For a more detailed explanation of what makes Belgian chocolate so wonderful, visit the Musée du Cacao et du Chocolat (the chocolate museum), close to the Grand Place.

Brussels claims to be the birthplace, in 1912, of the praline—the triumph of Jean Neuhaus, who sold his confections in the Galeries Royales St-Hubert, the elegant 19th-century shopping arcade near the Grand Place. Neuhaus is now another leading brand of Belgian luxury chocolates; the third may be the most recognizable—Godiva, founded in 1926.

Godiva, along with Leonidas and Neuhaus, sell peerless chocolates, but if you are in search of smaller, artisanal brands, try the handmade chocolates by Mary, founded in 1919. They rank among the finest anywhere—the chocolatier has earned a warrant from the royal court. Mary's elegant shop—appropriately located in Rue Royale—looks like a jewelry store, with its bonbons (including 70 flavors of pralines) displayed like precious baubles. The venerable family-run *chocolatier-pâtissier* Wittamer, in the Place du Grand Sablon, founded in 1910, also has a royal warrant, and produces pralines to match their exquisite cakes. Across the square is the new kid on the block, Pierre Marcolini, who has introduced a new panache in the flavors, shapes, and packaging of his chocolates.

Musée du Cacao et du Chocolat: Tel 32/2-514-2048; www.mucc.be. **Mary:** Tel 32/2-217-4500; www.marychoc.com. **Wittamer:** Tel 32/2-512-3742; www.wittamer.com. **Pierre Marcolini:** Tel 32/2-214-1206; www.marcolini.be.

The Original Golden Wonders

Belgian Frites

Brussels, Belgium

Belgium's *pommes frites* are not french fries at all—a grievous misnomer, as this universally known and loved side order is Belgian in origin. Belgians make the best *frites* in the world: Crispy, sweet, lightly bronzed—these are the gold standard of fries. What makes Belgian frites so special? First, there's the sweet *bintje* potato they're made from. Second, and most important, the frites are twice-fried: once to cook them through, then a second time, in hotter oil, to make them golden brown and crisp, or *bien croustillantes.*

Well-made *frites* (to use the French term; *frieten* in Dutch, the other main language of Belgium) can be snacked on at any time of day, smothered with a healthy dollop of mayonnaise. They are sold from roadside stalls called *friteries* or *frietkoten.* One of the most celebrated friteries in Brussels is Maison Antoine, in the middle of Place Jourdan, a stand-at-the-counter outdoor eatery close to the district now devoted to the administration of the European Union. With 60 years of frying to its credit, it produces supreme frites and offers more than 25 sauces to go with them. In traditional friterie style, you can have add-ons like *carbonnade* (beef stew cooked with beer), *boulettes* (meatballs), sausages, burgers, or brochettes, but it is the frites that take center stage.

With the unofficial national dish of mussels and fries—*moules-frites*—the Belgians discovered a perfect marriage. They steam their mussels in simple *marinière* style (flavored with a little chopped onion, celery, carrot, parsley, bay leaf, and thyme), and then serve heaping mounds of them. Brussels's most famous place to eat moules-frites is Chez Léon, close to the Grand Place, in the original location (established 1893) of what is now an international brand: Boisterous and busy, this is as close as moules-frites come to fast food. The dish is also on the menu at some of the restaurants in and around the Place Ste-Catherine, such as the highly respected La Marée, a no-frills place that is loved by locals.

MAISON ANTOINE: Tel: 32/2-230-5456; www.maisonantoine.be. *Cost:* lunch $15. **CHEZ LÉON:** Tel 32/2-511-1415; www.chezleon.be. *Cost:* dinner $45. **LA MARÉE:** Tel 32/2-511-0040; www.lamaree-sa.com. *Cost:* dinner $45.

At the Heart of the Continent's Capital

LA GRAND PLACE

Brussels, Belgium

Few urban squares have the impact of Brussels's gigantic, one-of-a-kind Grand Square (Grote Markt in Dutch). Louis XIV of France bombarded the entire city center in 1695, destroying more than 5,000 buildings; what you see today is damage-turned-triumph. Most art historians agree with Jean Cocteau, who called it "a splendid stage." Indeed, the ornate Flemish Renaissance and Baroque façades of the powerful (and competitive) guild houses provide the perfect foil for the Gothic Hôtel de Ville (Stadhuis in Dutch, or town hall), which dates to 1449 and is the only building to have survived the destruction.

The square has been the heart of town since the 13th century, and something is always going on here: For a ringside seat, order a Trappist beer on the terrace of the Roy d'Espagne tavern, in the former guild house of the bakers. Or stop by the 17th-century brick-arched cellar of 't Kelderke and dig in to a traditional Belgian dish such as *anguilles au vert* (eels in green herb sauce). Find more refined fare at the luxurious wood-paneled restaurant La Maison du Cygne, in a building that once housed the butcher's guild.

The grand, neo-Gothic Maison du Roi is

home to the Musée de la Ville de Bruxelles, which tells the story of the city. Among the stranger items on display are examples of the 800 miniature costumes belonging to the city's mascot, the Manneken-Pis. The bronze statue and fountain depicts a little boy doing what the name suggests and is a short walk west of the Grand Place.

You can stay close to the action at the newly transformed Hotel Amigo, right behind the town hall; its name dates from the era when the Spanish ruled the Netherlands (1519–1713), but its style is sumptuous and modern, in keeping with the Rocco Forte luxury hotels. For a scaled-back alternative, consider Le Dixseptième, the former Spanish ambassador's residence, now reborn as one of Brussels's most delightful boutique hotels.

Visitor info: http://visitbrussels.be. **'t Kelderke:** Tel 32/2-513-7344; www.atgp.be. *Cost:* dinner $40. **La Maison du Cygne:** Tel 32/2-511-8244; www.lamaisonducygne.be. *Cost:* dinner $100. **Musée de la Ville de Bruxelles:** Tel 32/2-279-4350; www.brusselsmuseums.be. **Hotel Amigo:** Tel 32/2-547-4747; www.hotelamigo.com. *Cost:* from $290 (off-peak), from $450 (peak); dinner $70. **Le Dixseptième:** Tel 32/2-517-1717; www.ledixseptieme.be. *Cost:* from $225. **Best times:** Jul–Sep for nightly Music and Light Show; 1st Tues and Thurs in Jul for the Ommegang, a costumed medieval pageant; mid-Aug in even years for the Tapis de Fleurs, a "carpet" of living flowers.

In August of even-numbered years, a flower carpet of begonias is created, covering La Grand Place.

Birthplace of an Enduring Style

A Showcase of Art Nouveau

Brussels, Belgium

Brussels is a place of pilgrimage for Art Nouveau fans from all over the world, and their first stop is often the former home of seminal architect Victor Horta, who built it in the suburb of St-Gilles. Completed in 1901, it was designed down to the last detail and is a showcase of stained glass, wrought iron, and finely crafted woodwork. Today it is preserved as the Musée Horta.

The style Horta helped popularize was Art Nouveau, "new art," because, with its highly stylized organic curves and embrace of new materials, it made no reference to past styles. Horta's first experimentation—and one of the first appearances of Art Nouveau in architecture—was the Hôtel Tassel (6 Rue Paul-Émile Janson), whose groundbreaking innovations include a semiopen floor plan and an interior iron structure with ornate botanical lines. Other Art Nouveau homes by various architects can be seen in Rue Faider, Rue Defacqz, and in the streets west of the Étangs d'Ixelles. Close to the Parc du Cinquantenaire, there is the lavishly decorated Maison Cauchie (5 Rue des Francs), a rarity in that it is open to the public, and the extraordinary Maison St-Cyr (11 Square Ambiorix).

The use of Art Nouveau in commercial architecture can be admired at the iron-and-glass Old England department store, now reborn as the Musée des Instruments de Musique (le MIM). It holds a world-class collection of more than 600 musical instruments (and an inviting top-floor café-with-a-view). Be sure to pop over to the Centre Belge de la Bande Dessinée, which chronicles the history of the comic strip (Tintin, the boy reporter created by cartoonist Georges Remi, whose pen name was Hergé, may be the most famous Belgian in the world) and is housed in a fabric warehouse designed by Horta in 1903–6.

Such buildings are the rare survivors. Art Nouveau fell out of fashion after World War I, and many of the greatest examples of the movement were destroyed. Only a renewed appreciation for the style in the late 1960s turned the tide. If this makes you want to cry in your beer, go to Le Falstaff, a splendid bar-brasserie close to the Grand Place. Designed by Horta's master cabinetmaker in 1903 and retaining many of its original features, the restaurant's simple menu makes it a good choice for lunch. Or spoil yourself at Comme Chez Soi (Just Like Home), with its elegant Horta-inspired Art Nouveau décor. The artistic venue sets the mood for what many say is the city's culinary highlight.

Maison St-Cyr's impressive ironwork sets it apart.

Musée Horta: 32/2-543-0490; www.hortamuseum.be. **La Maison Cauchie:** Tel 32/2-733-8684; www.cauchie.be. **MIM:** Tel 32/2-545-0130; www.mim.fgov.be. **Centre Belge de la Bande Dessinée:** Tel 32/2-219-1980; www.comicscenter.net. **Le Falstaff:** Tel 32/2-511-8789; www.lefalstaff.be. *Cost:* lunch $40. **Comme Chez Soi:** Tel 32/2-512-2921; www.commechezsoi.be. *Cost:* dinner $120.

A Country's Best-Kept Secret

Ghent

Belgium

The water of the River Leie stands mirror-still between the old quays in the heart of Ghent. Reflections pick up the sandstone and brick stepped gables of the centuries-old guild- and warehouses, now doing a brisk business as cafés and restaurants. They once dominated a busy river port here, overseeing trade that linked Ghent to the rest of Europe and the world. From the old Sint-Michielsbrug (St. Michael Bridge), the towers and spires built during those days line up like masts in a harbor and include the Belfort, the city belfry with its 54-bell carillon, and the massive cathedral of St. Bavo that houses the multi-paneled *Adoration of the Mystic Lamb.* Painted by Jan van Eyck and his brother Hubrecht in 1432, it is one of northern Europe's outstanding cultural treasures and a witness to Ghent's medieval wealth and standing.

Ghent was the first city in Belgium to industrialize, beginning with textiles at the start of the 19th century. It acquired its much respected university in 1817, and the lavish Vlaamse Opera in 1840. Design Museum Gent (the Dutch spelling of the city's name) tracks this history through the evolution of decorative style, leading visitors through a series of chronologically furnished rooms that end with Art Nouveau, Art Deco, and post-Modernism. The impressive Stedelijk Museum voor Actuele Kunst (Municipal Museum for Contemporary Art), or SMAK, carries the story forward with the cutting-edge work that has helped spotlight Belgian art in today's international art scene.

Your lodgings can immerse you in various moments along the city's history. The Hotel Erasmus occupies a 16th-century patrician's house, simply furnished with antiques, while a 19th-century convent has been stylishly updated as the hotel called Monasterium PoortAckere. Enjoy lunch at Het Groot Vleeshuis, a 15th-century butcher's hall, which now showcases the food specialties of Eastern Flanders, of which Ghent is the capital. Or dine amid the cast-iron pillars and galleries of the Brasserie Pakhuis, a 19th-century warehouse theatrically reimagined to match the dynamism of 21st-century Ghent.

Where: 35 miles/56 km northwest of Brussels. **Visitor info:** www.visitgent.be. **Design Museum Gent:** Tel 32/9-267-9999; www.designmuseumgent.be. **SMAK:** Tel 32/9-267-1466; www.smak.be. **Hotel Erasmus:** Tel 32/9-224-2195; www.erasmushotel.be. *Cost:* from $140. **Monasterium PoortAckere:** Tel 32/9-269-2210; www.monasterium.be. *Cost:* from $165. **Het Groot Vleeshuis:** Tel 32/9-223-2324; www.grootvleeshuis.be. *Cost:* lunch $25. **Brasserie Pakhuis:** Tel 32/9-223-5555; www.pakhuis.be. *Cost:* dinner $50. **Best time:** late Jul for Gentse Feesten, a festival of music, theater, and street entertainment.

A City of Folklore

Liège

Belgium

An exhilarating wave of glass and steel greets visitors arriving by train at Gare de Liège-Guillemins these days—a characteristically sensational work by the Spanish architect Santiago Calatrava. This is prestige architecture, commissioned to place the city of Liège on the map not only as a stop along the international high-speed train network but also as a destination in itself.

The Musée Grand Curtius is representative of Liège's new dynamic. Set in a striking 17th-century mansion, it overlooks the broad River Meuse and has recently undergone massive refurbishment to take its place among Europe's important decorative-art museums. Treasures from ancient Egypt, Greece, and Rome; paintings; and antique clocks, furniture, tapestries, and glassware—even historic firearms—are beautifully lit and displayed.

For many centuries, Liège was the capital of the extensive independent territory ruled by grand prince-bishops, one legacy of which is its many fine Gothic churches. (The prince-bishops were eventually booted out in the wake of the French Revolution of 1789.) You can pick up a sense of the character of the *liègeois*—down-to-earth, independent-minded, with an irreverent sense of humor—at the famous market called La Batte, the largest in Belgium, held every Sunday morning along the north bank of the Meuse. Or drop by the popular Restaurant-Café Lequet to sample robust dishes such as *boulets à la liègeoise*—meatballs with a sweetened sauce—along with the local lager, Jupiler.

The folkloric side of Liège is wonderfully documented in a converted 17th-century convent in the historic heart of the city. The Musée de la Vie Wallonne, also recently refurbished, contains an intriguing collection of artifacts relating to past daily life in Wallonia, the French-speaking part of Belgium.

Santiago Calatrava designed the Gare de Liège-Guillemins.

WHERE: 60 miles/96 km southeast of Brussels. **VISITOR INFO:** www.liege.be. **MUSÉE GRAND CURTIUS:** Tel 32/4-221-9404; www.grandcurtiusliege.be. **RESTAURANT-CAFÉ LEQUET:** Tel 32/4-222-2134. *Cost:* dinner $30. **MUSÉE DE LA VIE WALLONNE:** Tel 32/4-237-9040; www.viewallonne.be. **BEST TIMES:** Sun mornings for La Batte market; Aug 15 for Festival de la République Libre folk festival.

Vineyards, Country Cuisine, and Half-Timbered Houses

STRASBOURG AND THE ALSACE WINE ROAD

Alsace, France

Strasbourg's magnificent Gothic cathedral, known for its off-center spire and stained-glass windows, dominates the central square of this picturesque town of half-timbered houses, canals, elite schools, and the seat of the European Parliament and Council of Europe. Admire the cathedral from the restaurant Maison Kammerzell, one of the most ornate, well-preserved medieval buildings in Europe, over a plate of delicious *choucroute alsacienne*, an earthy dish of sauerkraut, sausages, bacon, pork, and potatoes. Modernity is not absent in the city: The sleek, stylish, highly discreet Hôtel Régent Petite France stands in the historic old quarter and is a favorite with reigning presidents and visiting VIPs.

Ownership of Alsace has passed between France and Germany for centuries, most recently during World War II. The Germanic feel lingers along the Route du Vin d'Alsace (Alsatian Wine Road), which passes through one of France's premier white and dessert wine regions with 50 grand cru vineyards. Rieslings and gewürztraminers are born here, along with sylvaner, muscat, and the sparkling crémant d'Alsace. The 106-mile route runs from Strasbourg to Thann, southwest of Colmar, with the Vosges mountains to the west and the Rhine Valley to the east. It zigzags past dramatic feudal ruins and through enchanting medieval towns where convivial *winstubs* (Alsatian bistros) serve local wines and choucroute or the ambrosial pâté de foie gras, considered by many to be some of the best in the world.

Of the Wine Road's 119 gabled wine villages, Riquewihr is the showpiece, with storybook half-timbered houses, cobblestone culs-de-sac, and courtyards anchored by massive wine presses. Nearby Kaysersberg shares the prize for quaintness, and fortified Turckheim has some of the best-preserved medieval architecture in France. For glorious views of the Alsatian plains, visit the hilltop 12th-century Haut-Koenigsbourg castle. Wine

Road gastronomes love the elegant Auberge de l'Ill in Illhaeusern's idyllic riverside setting. Another star is Rouffach's hilltop Château d'Isenbourg, built over ancient, vaulted wine cellars, with an impressive Alsatian wine collection and regional cuisine.

Hunawihr, one of many small villages along the Wine Road, is set among vineyards and has a centuries-old church.

For an inn with 16th-century charm, try the Hostellerie Le Maréchal in the "Old Venice" quarter of Colmar, the attractive capital of the Wine Road region. Here you'll find the popular Musée d'Unterlinden, housed in a 13th-century convent and showcasing such masterworks as the 16th-century Issenheim Altarpiece by Matthias Grünewald.

Where: 306 miles/492 km east of Paris. **Maison Kammerzell:** Tel 33/3-88-324214; www.maison-kammerzell.com. *Cost:* dinner $50. **Régent Petite France:** Tel 33/3-88-764343; www.regent-petite-france.com. *Cost:* from $220. **Wine Road:** www.vinsalsace.com. **Auberge de l'Ill:** Tel 33/3-89-718900; www.auberge-de-l-ill.com. *Cost:* dinner $170. **Château d'Isenbourg:** Tel 33/3-89-785850; www.chateaudisenbourg.com. *Cost:* from $200. **Hostellerie Le Maréchal:** Tel 33/3-89-416032; www.hotel-le-marechal.com. *Cost:* from $150; dinner $70. **Musée d'Unterlinden:** Tel 33/3-89-201550; www.musee-unterlinden.com. **Best times:** Apr–Nov for the Wine Road; Jun and Jul in Strasbourg for Festival International de Musique; Jul for the Colmar International Music Festival; Sep–Oct for wine harvest; late Nov–Dec Strasbourg's Christmas market, the largest in France.

The Royal and Rustic in the Shadow of the Pyrenees

Biarritz and the Pays Basque

Aquitaine, France

The resort of Biarritz, on France's southwest coast near the Spanish border, has been a favorite international destination since Napoleon III built a villa here in 1855 for his Spanish bride, the Empress Eugénie. A playground first for Russian and British nobility, then for 1930s and '40s artists, writers, and glitterati, Biarritz and its lovely beaches are still a popular destination, and with some of Europe's best waves, it's the unofficial surfing and windsurfing capital of the continent.

Still tinged with past glamour, Napoleon's villa is now the elegantly refurbished Hôtel du Palais. The hotel's spacious guest rooms overlook the rugged Atlantic coastline where the mighty Pyrenees step into the Bay of Biscay. This is Pays Basque, an unofficial region that straddles the French-Spanish border. The Basque are fiercely proud of their language (Euskara), their rustic cuisine, and *pelota* (jai alai), a sport similar to racquetball but played with balls hurled by long, curved baskets. Watch a local game in the village of St-Jean-de-Luz down the coast. Or walk along its horseshoe-shaped beach, considered one of the finest in France.

To get a real taste of Basque landscape and

the new Basque cooking influenced by nouvelle cuisine in France, head inland to one of the villages in the hills, such as Aïnhoa, Ascain, or pretty Sare. The last is just 10 minutes from the sea and where you'll find the Hotel Arraya, whose bakeshop sells *gâteau basque*, a delicious tart filled with cherry confiture.

For a superb modern take on Basque cuisine, stay overnight at L'Auberge Basque in St-Pée-sur-Nouvelle, known for its striking dining room overlooking the lush countryside. The luxurious Hegia in Hasparren, about 22 miles southeast of Biarritz, is a 1746 timbered Basque country house with five rooms featuring minimalist décor. The star here is the food; guests sit in the kitchen while well-known chef Arnaud Daguin creates updated local produce-driven dishes.

Continue your Basque dining experience in the pretty medieval border village of St-Jean-Pied-de-Port on the road to Santiago, an ancient religious pilgrimage route (see p. 265). Master chef Firmin Arrambide and his son conjure up refined interpretations of Pays Basque cooking at Hôtel Les Pyrénées.

WHERE: 118 miles/190 km southwest of Bordeaux, 20 miles/32 km from the Spanish border. **HÔTEL DU PALAIS:** Tel 33/5-59-416400; in the U.S., 800-745-8883; www.hotel-du-palais.com. *Cost:* from $550 (off-peak), from $730 (peak). **HOTEL ARRAYA:** Tel 33/5-59-542046; www.arraya.com. *Cost:* from $105. *When:* closed Nov–Mar. **L'AUBERGE BASQUE:** Tel 33/5-59-517000; www.aubergebasque.com. *Cost:* from $130; dinner $85. **HEGIA:** Tel 33/5-59-517000; www.hegia.com. *Cost:* $695 (room only), $940 (with meals). **LES PYRÉNÉES:** Tel 33/5-59-370101; in the U.S., 800-735-2478; www.hotel-les-pyrenees.com. *Cost:* from $145; dinner $95. **BEST TIMES:** Jun–Sep for beach weather; Jun–Nov for surfing; early Jul for surf festival.

Basking in Historic Wine Country

BORDEAUX

Aquitaine, France

With more than 7,000 wineries and a wine-making tradition dating back to the 12th century, this fertile region and its famous Médoc, St-Émilion, and Graves vineyards rank among the top in the world.

The temperate climate is unlike other wine-growing regions in the country, thanks to Bordeaux's proximity to the Atlantic Ocean. Fortunately for visiting oenophiles, many private vineyards welcome visitors.

With its rich architectural heritage, the city has more protected buildings than any other French city except Paris; Bordeaux is the largest urban UNESCO World Heritage Site in the world. An expensive revitalization campaign polished up jewels like the Place de la Bourse and the Grand Théâtre, one of Europe's most beautiful opera houses, with the majestic and voluptuously renovated Regent Grand Hotel Bordeaux across the street. Hotels such as La Maison Bord'eaux, an elegant 18th-century building with a contemporary interior, exemplify the city's new energy. Even French cuisine has been overhauled—the menu at the prestigious landmark restaurant Le Chapon Fin has been modernized. Those seeking more straightforward, hearty French food—*cuisine du terroir*—will find it at the venerable La Tupina.

Médoc, north of Bordeaux, is on a triangular, marshy peninsula on the left bank of the

Gironde estuary. It is home to some of the more fabled château wines in the country, including Margaux, Latour, Lafite-Rochschild, and Mouton-Rothschild. Rent a car and stay at the Château Cordeillan-Bages in Pauillac, an 18th-century property with a legendary restaurant serving innovative cuisine.

One of the most picturesque villages in the Bordeaux region is St-Émilion, with its steep cobblestone streets and dramatic views of small-parcel vineyards. Enjoy dinner paired with local wines by St-Émilion vintners at the aristocratic, 19th-century Château Grand Barrail estate, located on its own vineyards.

Just south of Bordeaux is the Graves region, and farther south—about 25 miles—is Sauternes, home to France's most famous sweet white. Sample it at the luxury hotel and spa Les Sources de Caudalie, and even lather it on your face as part of their renowned "vinothérapie"—antioxidant spa treatments using grapes and thermal springs. Surrounded by the vineyards of the Château Smith Haut-Lafite, the chic enclave also has a gourmet restaurant, aristocratic charm, and a wine cellar with more than 15,000 bottles: It's wine therapy at its best.

Where: 308 miles/496 km southwest of Paris. **Regent Grand Hotel Bordeaux:** Tel 33/5-57-304444; www.theregentbordeaux.com. *Cost:* from $400 (off-peak), from $480 (peak). **La Maison Bord'eaux:** Tel 33/5-56-440045; www.lamaisonbord-eaux.com. *Cost:* from $205. **Le Chapon Fin:** Tel 33/5-56-791010; www.chapon-fin.com. *Cost:* dinner $95. **La Tupina:** Tel 33/5-56-915637; www.latupina.com. *Cost:* dinner $60. **Château Cordeillan-Bages:** Tel 33/5-56-592424; in the U.S., 800-735-2478; www.cordeillanbages.com. *Cost:* from $285; dinner $125. *When:* closed mid-Dec–mid-Feb. **Château Grand Barrail:** Tel 33/5-57-553700; www.grand-barrail.com. *Cost:* from $415; dinner $80. **Les Sources de Caudalie:** Tel 33/5-57-838383; www.sources-caudalie.com. *Cost:* from $300 (off-peak), from $345 (peak); dinner $115. **Best times:** May–Jun and Sep–Oct for pleasant weather.

Brimming Markets, Medieval Hamlets, and the Lascaux Caves

Dordogne

Aquitaine, France

A "country of enchantment" is how novelist Henry Miller described the lush green *département,* or administrative division, of the Dordogne. This hilly region is rich with medieval hamlets, village markets, imposing châteaux, Romanesque churches, and tranquil rivers; it's also a great place to sample the local foie gras and hearty red wines.

The site of great battles during the Hundred Years' War, the Dordogne's most significant history is ancient, revealed underground in painted prehistoric caves, particularly those of Lascaux. Discovered in 1940 and dubbed "Périgord's Sistine Chapel," it's the world's most extraordinary repository of prehistoric wall paintings, executed by Stone Age artists around 17,000 years ago. Though permanently closed to the public in 1963 to prevent deterioration, you can tour Lascaux II, 200 yards away, a dazzlingly accurate replica. Astonishing drawings of bison, horses, boars, and bulls have been meticulously re-created using the same pigments available to Cro-Magnon man. More than 18,000 ancient artifacts are on display at the National Prehistory

Museum in the town of Les Eyzies-de-Tayac-Sireuil, in the Vézère Valley. Don't miss the Font-de-Gaume cave nearby, with original Paleolithic artwork that approaches Lascaux's in importance, or Combarelles and Rouffignac, with their bison and mammoth figures.

Of the pretty towns and walled villages dotting the landscape, a favorite is Sarlat-la-Canéda, capital of Périgord Noir and one of the best-preserved medieval towns in France. Outdoor markets brim with local and seasonal delicacies such as truffles, cèpe mushrooms, foie gras, and jars of duck confit. Soak up the charm of the riverside hotel Moulin de l'Abbaye in the pretty market town of Brantôme, north of Périgueux, or head south and enjoy delicious dishes of regional cuisine under linden trees at the Hotel Le Vieux Logis in Trémolat, a former tobacco barn, whose restaurant is considered the best in the Dordogne.

Just beyond the Dordogne border is Rocamadour, a gravity-defying village and pilgrimage site that rises up the side of a cliff. Join the throngs and climb the 216 steps to its cluster of seven medieval chapels. The most important is the Church of Notre Dame, known as the sanctuary of the Black Madonna.

WHERE: Lascaux is 270 miles/432 km southwest of Paris. **VISITOR INFO:** www.tourisme-lascaux.com. **HOW:** U.S.-based American Museum of Natural History Expeditions offers tours of the Dordogne, including Lascaux II, and other caves. Tel 800-462-8687 or 212-769-5700; www.amnhexpeditions.org. *Cost:* 9-day trip from $6,295 inclusive. Originates in Bordeaux. *When:* May and Sep. **MOULIN DE L'ABBAYE:** Tel 33/5-53-058022; in the U.S., 800-735-2478; www.moulinabbaye.com. *Cost:* from $220 (off-peak), from $350 (peak). *When:* closed mid-Nov–early Apr. **LE VIEUX LOGIS:** Tel 33/5-53-228006; in the U.S., 800-735-2478; www.vieux-logis.com. *Cost:* from $270; dinner $75. **BEST TIMES:** In Sarlat: Aug for music festival; Wed and Sat mornings for markets and Fri evenings in Jul and Aug for night market; Sat from mid-Nov to mid-Mar for truffle and foie gras markets; mid-Jan for truffle festival.

The Pastoral Birthplace of Spa Cuisine

LES PRÉS D'EUGÉNIE

Aquitaine, France

Nestled in the heart of farm country in the southwestern corner of France, the tiny backwater village of Eugénie-les-Bains is named in honor of the fashionable Empress Eugénie, consort of Napoleon III. She spent many summer weeks here in the late 1800s, charmed by the town's pastoral setting and ancient thermal springs. Long overlooked by time and tourism, the hamlet was brought back to life in 1973 with the arrival of master chef Michel Guérard and his wife, Christine. They transformed a 16-acre farm in the heart of this village near Biarritz (see p. 100) into Les Prés d'Eugénie, a luxury spa and gastronomic retreat based on his famous *cuisine minceur,* or spa cuisine, which helped spawn the nouvelle cuisine revolution. Nightly or weekly stays here comprise "cures" for losing weight or treating aching bones while indulging in gourmand calorie-conscious meals. Visitors who are of the calories-to-the-wind school can opt for Guérard's elaborate full-tilt gourmand menu.

Eugénie-les-Bains consists almost entirely of the meticulously run Guérard fiefdom: two spas (the original plus the new luxury La Ferme Thermale), three restaurants, and five charming guest hotels ranging from refined (the sumptuous Les Prés d'Eugénie Hôtel) to rustic (the simpler, country-style Maison Rose). Guests can use Eugénie-les-Bains as a base for exploring the serene forested environs, including the nearby mountain town of Pau, the birthplace of Henri IV, or the beautiful Pyrenees and Basque region to the south. But most find it hard to leave the comfort of this quiet village that once enchanted an empress and her coterie.

Where: 87 miles/140 km south of Bordeaux. Tel 33/5-58-050607; in the U.S., 800-735-2478; www.michelguerard.com. *Cost:* Les Prés d'Eugénie Hotel from $440 (off-peak), from $515 (peak); La Maison Rose from $200 (off-peak), from $285 (peak); dinner at La Ferme aux Grives $90, gourmand menu $226. **Best times:** Apr–Jun and Sep–Oct for pleasant weather.

Seaside Resorts, Fresh Oysters, and Medieval Ramparts

Brittany's Emerald Coast

Brittany, France

The rugged Emerald Coast of north Brittany (Bretagne) gets its name from the green-blue color of the sea and a dramatic landscape as precious as any gem, with moors, steep cliffs, curving sandy beaches, galloping high tides, and elegant seaside resorts. The 5,000 year-old megaliths found inland reveal the region's deep Celtic roots.

One of the best-preserved and prettiest towns in Brittany is Dinan, noted for its medieval architecture. Wander the old city's cobblestone streets or if you're visiting in July of an even year, take part in the largest medieval festival in Europe, the Fête des Ramparts. A short drive north, along the Rance River on a rocky bluff, is the elegant Belle Époque sea resort town of Dinard, popular in the 1920s with British aristocrats, artists such as Picasso, and Hollywood's elite. Among the town's many Victorian-style villas is one of the coast's most gracious inns, the Grand Hotel Barrière. Built in 1858 in the striking Second Empire style, it is distinguished by rich interiors, sculpted gardens, and views of the ramparts of St-Malo, across the Rance.

Oysters rule in Cancale, the seafood capital of Brittany.

In the 16th to 18th centuries, the elegant walled port town of St-Malo was a hot spot for sailors, corsairs, and explorers. Retreating Nazis set it on fire in 1944, but it was largely rebuilt and much of the original architectural design remains. The town castle houses a museum devoted to native son Jacques Cartier, who helped France claim Quebec (see p. 940) in the 16th century. Enjoy a cozy, friendly retreat from the summer tourist fray at Hotel Elizabeth, where breakfast is served under 400-year-old wooden beams.

Just east of St-Malo is Cancale, a picturesque fishing village known as the "Oyster Capital of Brittany." Indulge in a few, cracked open by blue apron–clad fishmongers, at the wooden stalls of the *marché aux huitres* (oyster market). The best place to enjoy a meal of the local catch is at Le Coquillage, in the elegant hotel Château Richeux, a refurbished 1920s villa in nearby Le Buot. Savor fresh dishes as you sip a chilled glass of Muscadet, enjoying the view of the bay of Mont St-Michel, where the dramatic Gothic Benedictine abbey stands (see p. 110).

Where: The Emerald Coast runs from St-Brieuc to Cancale, about 250 miles/400 km north of Paris. **Grand Hotel Barrière:** Tel 33/2-99-882626; in the U.S., 800-745-8883; www.lucienbarriere.com. *Cost:* from $200. *When:* closed Dec–Feb. **Hotel Elizabeth:** Tel 33/2-99-562498; www.st-malo-hotel-elizabeth.com. *Cost:* from $110. **Château Richeux:** Tel 33/2-99-896476; www.maisons-de-bricourt.com. *Cost:* from $235; dinner $75. **Best times:** Apr–Jun and Sep–Oct for nice weather and fewer crowds; Jul in even years for Fête des Ramparts medieval festival in Dinan; mid-Aug for France's best indie rock festival, La Route du Rock, in St-Malo; Oct for British Film Festival in Dinard.

A Trio of Island Beauties

Belle-Île, Île de Ré, and Île de Porquerolles

Brittany, Poitou-Charentes, and Provence-Alpes-Côte d'Azur, France

France has several coasts but only a handful of islands. Three in particular are wonderful places to unwind and live the local life, especially off-season. The sophisticated yet laid-back Belle-Île-en-Mer, off the coast of Brittany near Quiberon, features rugged shorelines, long, sandy beaches, grassy moors with ancient Celtic menhirs, and untrafficked dirt roads perfect for biking. Pretty pastel buildings line the port of Sauzon, on the northern tip, and the peaceful, tastefully decorated rooms of Hotel la Désirade are near the dramatic cliffs immortalized by Claude Monet.

Farther south is the chic, genteel Île de Ré, near La Rochelle, whose year-round residents make their living from oysters, salt, and wine. In August, the island becomes a favorite spot for well-heeled Parisians seeking relaxation, and its population increases twelvefold. Bike along the flat, 19-mile-long island, past whitewashed homes with green shutters and seafood shacks serving mussels cooked over pine-needle fires. Or climb the Phare des Baleines (Whales Lighthouse) for a view of the untamed Conche des Baleines, a vast, sandy beach on the north coast. The seawater and climate make the island an ideal thalassotherapy center; the best spa is at Le Richelieu, one of the island's upscale hotels also known for its excellent restaurant. The Hotel de Toiras is a classically decorated 17th-century building overlooking the St-Martin-de-Ré harbor; for a more beachy feel, try the simple but stylish Hotel L'Océan.

Visiting the 4-mile-long car-free, state-protected Mediterranean Île de Porquerolles, near Toulon, is like going back in time—the wild subtropical shoreline, forests, and beaches bounded by heather, scented myrtle, and pine trees suggest what the French Riviera (see p. 128) might have been like a century ago. With only 400 residents, hotels are limited, but the Mas du Langoustier is a good choice. Decorated in antique Provençal style, it serves sophisticated meals on an outdoor terrace, accompanied by a glass of rosé and a beautiful view.

Where: Belle-Île is 101 miles/162 km west of Nantes. Île de Ré is 295 miles/475 km southwest of Paris. Île de Porquerolles is 24 miles/39 km southeast of Toulon. **Hotel la Désirade:** Tel 33/2-97-317070; www.hotel-la-desirade.com. *Cost:* from $195 (off-peak), from $250 (peak). **Le Richelieu:** Tel 33/5-46-096070; www.hotel-le-richelieu.com. *Cost:* from $170 (off-peak), from $300 (peak). **Hôtel de Toiras:** Tel 33/5-46-354032; in the U.S., 800-735-2478; www.hotel-de-toiras.com. *Cost:* from $195 (off-peak), from $400 (peak). **Hôtel L'Océan:** Tel 33/5-46-092307; www.re-hotel-ocean.com. *Cost:* from $110. **Hôtel Mas du Langoustier:** Tel 33/4-94-583009; www.langoustier.com. *Cost:* from $275. **Best times:** May–Oct for nicest weather; late Jul–Aug for opera festival in Belle-Île, the largest in western France.

A Premier Wine Region Rich in History

Burgundy

France

Chassagne-Montrachet. Meursault. Pommard. The Burgundy region produces some of the world's finest wines. This bucolic region also helped define classic French cuisine with dishes such as *escargots* (snails) and *boeuf bourguignon* (beef Burgundy) and has more Romanesque monasteries than any other area in France. Church-owned properties were divided up after the French Revolution, leaving Burgundy with more than 4,500 small, mostly family-run wineries today.

Some of the best lie along the scenic 50-mile Route des Grands Crus that runs from Dijon to Santenay; they include Côte de Nuits and Côte de Beaune (others are Chablis, Côte de Chalonnais, Côte Maçonnais, and Beaujolais to the south). It's best to call ahead for vineyard tours in such iconic villages as Puligny-Montrachet, Vosne-Romanée, or Aloxe-Corton because not all are open to the public.

Once ruled by dukes wielding more power than kings, Burgundy's regional capital and only real city, Dijon, retains vestiges of its medieval influence, with beautiful half-timbered houses and mansions. Farther south, in the pretty 2,000-year-old town of Beaune, a lively restaurant scene has sprung up—choose from more than 500 wines at the elegant, contemporary Bistro de l'Hôtel in L'Hôtel de Beaune, or sample traditional Burgundian dishes at Ma Cuisine, an old-time favorite with wine-industry professionals. The chic Hôtel le Cep's antiques-filled rooms are named after regional grand cru wines.

The village of Saulieu, outside Beaune, helped put French cuisine on the map, thanks to the late, great chef Bernard Loiseau. His spirit lives on at the Relais Bernard Loiseau, whose restaurant continues to draw gastronomes to his healthy *cuisine légère*, showcasing local produce with little cream or butter.

Nearby, the spectacular 11th-century Basilique Ste-Madeleine—a masterpiece of light and space—perches on a hill in Vézelay with commanding views. At the foot of Vézelay in St-Père-sous-Vézelay is L'Espérance, where revered chef Marc Meneau and his wife, Françoise, gracefully combine rural ease with effortless sophistication. Enjoy peaceful surroundings by staying nearby at the

15th-century Château de Vault-de-Lugny on 100 acres of private grounds.

Among the hundreds of Romanesque churches or abbeys in Burgundy, the Abbaye de Fontenay, near Montbard, founded in 1118 by St. Bernard, is the best preserved. The abbey in the nearby town of Cluny, built in 812 and once the largest Christian building in the world, was destroyed during the French Revolution and reconstructed in the 18th century. Not content to spend a few hours in the abbeys' hallowed halls? Spend the night in the exquisitely restored 12th-century Abbaye de la Bussière and enjoy inspiring views and a contemplative atmosphere.

WHERE: Dijon is 164 miles/264 km southeast of Paris. **MA CUISINE:** Tel 33/3-80-223022. *Cost:* dinner $44. **HÔTEL LE CEP:** Tel 33/3-80-223548; www.hotel-cep-beaune.com. *Cost:* from $250. **RELAIS AND BISTRO BERNARD LOISEAU:** Tel 33/3-80-905353; in the U.S., tel 800-735-2478; www.bernard-loiseau.com. *Cost:* from $210 (off-peak), from $365 (peak); dinner $205. **L'ESPÉRANCE:** Tel 33/3-86-333910; in the U.S., 800-735-2478. *Cost:* dinner $185. **CHÂTEAU DE VAULT-DE-LUGNY:** Tel 33/3-86-340786; www.lugny.fr. *Cost:* from $340. *When:* closed mid-Nov–Mar. **ABBAYE DE LA BUSSIÈRE:** Tel 33/3-80-490229; www.abbaye-dela-bussiere.com. *Cost:* from $260 (off-peak), from $325 (peak). **BEST TIMES:** May–Oct for nice weather; late Sep for wine harvest; mid–late Nov in Beaune for wine festival; Nov for Gastronomic Fair in Dijon.

In Dijon's highly walkable historic core, the restored half-timbered houses date from the 12th through 15th centuries.

Cathedrals and Bubbly Wine

CHAMPAGNE

Champagne-Ardennes, France

Sparkling wine can come from anywhere, but Champagne with a capital "C" comes only from Champagne, a region of 75,000 vine-laden acres that produces more than 200 million bottles of the coveted bubbly each year.

Anchoring the region's rolling countryside, vineyards, and chalky plains is Reims, with its remarkable Cathédrale Notre-Dame, a graceful masterpiece of Gothic art where nearly all French kings were crowned for a thousand years beginning in 815. Visitors come to admire its richly sculpted façade and beautiful stained-glass windows by Marc Chagall.

Wine lovers head underground to the miles of caves, or wine cellars, carved out by the Romans to obtain chalk for construction and more recently used as makeshift hospital wards, schools, and bomb shelters during the two world wars. In Épernay, world-class names such as Moët et Chandon, Taittinger, Mumm, and Veuve Clicquot Ponsardin tend to their bottles (as does Pommery in Reims). They blend wine from a choice of 60 varieties, putting it through the double-fermentation process that creates Champagne and turning bottles daily for 15 months to three years to dislodge sediment.

Of the 100-plus Champagne houses here, the most famous offer guided tours and tastings. Drive or bike along the scenic Route du Champagne through vineyards and wine-producing villages such as Bouzy, Verzy, and Rilly-la-Montagne. To see more examples of the stunning Gothic cathedrals for which the region is also renowned, detour to nearby Amiens, Loan, or Soissons, all in Picardy.

The ultimate in Champagne luxury requires a stay at the world-famous Les Crayères hotel (named after the centuries-old chalk cellars) and restaurant, located just outside Reims on the 7-acre former estate of the Princess de Polignac. One of the finest château-hotels in northern France, it features high ceilings, luxurious furnishings, and impeccable grounds. Its star attraction is the gourmet restaurant Le Parc, which offers exquisite dining under the guidance of the talented young chef Philippe Mille, along with, of course, a dizzying selection of Champagnes. Or come for lunch in the more casual brasserie, Le Jardin, located in the beautiful gardens of the château.

WHERE: Reims is 90 miles/145 km east of Paris. **VISITOR INFO:** www.reims-tourisme.com. **LES CRAYÈRES:** Tel 33/3-26-828080; in the U.S., 800-735-2478; www.lescrayeres.com. *Cost:* from $490 (off-peak), from $540 (peak); dinner at Le Parc $140; lunch at Le Jardin $40. **BEST TIMES:** May–Oct for best weather; late Jun–early Aug for Les Flâneries Musicales festival in Reims; late Jul for the Champagne Route Festival, with vintners opening cellars to visitors.

The Rugged Beauty of Corsica's Cliffs and Beaches

LES CALANCHES

Gulf of Porto, Corsica, France

To the ancient Greeks, the mountainous Mediterranean island of Corsica (Corse) was Kallisté, meaning "the most beautiful." The French still call it *l'Île de Beauté,* and for good reason. Corsica's rugged coastline is dotted with sun-drenched white and gold sand beaches and picturesque coastal towns; in its wild and sparsely inhabited interior, mountainous villages are linked by roads with stunning vistas and hairpin turns.

Though a fiercely independent people proud of living in Napoleon Bonaparte's birthplace, nationalist tempers have calmed since a 2003 referendum rejected greater autonomy. Today, the island's greatest drama lies in its astonishing natural beauty, such as the outstanding cliff and rock formations of Les Calanches on the west coast at the Gulf of Porto. The hues of the weathered granite pinnacles and phantasmagorical rock outcroppings shift from orange to pink to vermilion as the light changes, contrasting with the sparkling indigo sea 3,000 feet below. Terraces of the romantic if gently worn Hôtel Roches Rouges, built in 1912, afford magnificent views. Come for acclaimed food, or stay in the pretty village of Piana overlooking the rocks.

To explore the area, take the narrow road that weaves around and past the Calanches or head into the craggy interior on a winding road to the university town of Corte, sitting between two snowcapped peaks. The town's steep, cobblestone streets are lined with cafés where you'll hear the Corsican dialect; the plunging cliffs, jagged summits, and glacial lakes surrounding the town make for exhilarating day hikes. The refurbished Hôtel Duc de Padoue, a 19th-century building on Corte's central square, is a simple but pleasant place to stay.

Corsica is a hiker's paradise, and one of the most visually arresting trails in Europe is the challenging two-week, 112-mile GR20 (for *grande randonnée*, "great hike"), a network of paths that crosses the island diagonally from the chic resort town of Calvi on the northwest coast. A more easygoing option is the Tra Mare e Monti (Across Sea and Mountains) route, running from Cargèse, south of Les Calanches, to Moriani, on the east coast. For plain old relaxation, put your feet up at the rustic and stylish beachside hotel Le Maquis, on the Gulf of Ajaccio south of the capital, named for the thick underbrush of thyme, lavender, and sage that gives Corsica yet another nickname: "the perfumed isle."

Explore Les Calanches, which jut into the Mediterranean, by hiking, by car, or on a boat tour.

WHERE: 50 miles/80 km north of Ajaccio. **VISITOR INFO:** www.visit-corsica.com. **HÔTEL ROCHES ROUGES:** Tel 33/4-95-278181; www.lesrochesrouges.com. *Cost:* from $165. **HÔTEL DUC DE PADOUE:** Tel 33/4-95-460137; www.ducdepadoue.com. *Cost:* from $120. **LE MAQUIS:** Tel 33/4-95-250555; in the U.S., 800-745-8883; www.lemaquis.com. *Cost:* $260 (off-peak), $685 (peak). **HOW:** U.S.-based Distant Journeys offers a 12-day "Tra Mare e Monti" walking tour. Tel 888-845-5781 or 207-236-9788; www.distantjourneys.com. *Cost:* $3,195, inclusive. Originates in Ajaccio. *When:* May. **BEST TIMES:** May–Jun and Sep–Oct for fine weather and no crowds; Apr–May for wildflowers.

From Giverny to Rouen and Honfleur

IMPRESSIONIST NORMANDY

Haute-Normandie, France

In the 1860s, young artists such as Claude Monet, Alfred Sisley, Pierre-Auguste Renoir, and Camille Pissarro rode the new train lines from Paris north to the pretty towns and striking coastline of Normandy. Dubbed the Impressionists, after Monet's early *Impression, Soleil Levant* (*Impression, Sunrise*), they strove to capture the beauty and changing light *en plein air* ("in the open air") of this picturesque landscape, and their radical work altered the course of 19th- and 20th-century art.

An Impressionist pilgrimage in Normandy should start in Giverny, at the home of Claude Monet. He lived and worked here from 1883 until his death in 1926, capturing the beauty of his gardens in paintings, including his famous Water Lily series. You can tour his house, now a museum, and view the still-splendid lily ponds. Works by other artists are on display at the new Museum of Impressionisms.

Nearby Rouen, where Joan of Arc was burned at the stake in 1431, is now a bustling port city. The elaborate façade of its grand cathedral inspired more than 30 of Monet's paintings, and a few hang in the city's Fine

Arts Museum, along with works by Pissarro, Renoir, and Sisley, who all spent time here.

Though the pretty port town of Honfleur, where the sea and the river Seine meet, attracted artists long before the Impressionists, in the 1860s it was base camp for the burgeoning movement. Monet, Boudin, Courbet, Corot, Sisley, and Renoir would head to the St-Siméon Farm to paint the Seine and its surroundings; some of those works, considered the forerunner to Impressionism, are displayed in Honfleur's Eugène Boudin Museum. Today La Ferme St-Siméon is a rustic yet elegant hotel and spa. Its restaurant serves Normandy specialties such as mussels and oysters and calvados (apple brandy). In the center of Honfleur, stay at the romantic, handsomely renovated La Petite Folie, a short stroll from the picturesque harbor.

Impressionists Degas, Matisse, and Courbet would travel from Honfleur along the coast to Étretat, painting its dramatic white cliffs and tall rock archways along the shoreline known as the Alabaster Coast. Artists also found inspiration along La Côte Fleurie, the 30 miles of coastline linking Honfleur and more than a dozen small towns and resorts. Trouville, the oldest seaside resort in France, has a subdued, family atmosphere, while its glamorous neighbor Deauville offers casinos, racetracks, expensive shops, and a beautiful boardwalk. Hollywood camps out at the elegant Grande Normandy Barrière and Royal Barrière hotels during the annual American Film Festival in early September. To steep yourself in local atmosphere, stay at the Hôtel Villa Joséphine, a Tudor-style country home about a block from the water, built in the late 1800s as the home of Deauville's mayor.

The bridge and water lilies of Monet's home in Giverny were famously captured in his paintings.

WHERE: Giverny is 50 miles/80 km northwest of Paris. **HOUSE OF CLAUDE MONET:** Tel 33/2-32-512821; www.giverny.org. **MUSÉE DES IMPRESSIONNISMES GIVERNY:** Tel 33/2-32- 519465; www.museedesimpressionnismes giverny.com. *When:* closed Nov–Mar. **MUSÉE DES BEAUX-ARTS DE ROUEN:** Tel 33/2-35-712840; www.rouen-musees.com. **LA FERME ST-SIMÉON:** Tel 33/2-31-817800; www.ferme saintsimeon.fr. *Cost:* from $260; prix-fixe dinner $200. **LA PETITE FOLIE:** Tel 33/6-74-394646; www.lapetitefolie-honfleur.com. *Cost:* $200. **HÔTEL VILLA JOSÉPHINE:** Tel 33/2-31-141800; www.villajosephine.fr. *Cost:* from $170. **BEST TIMES:** in Giverny: May–Aug for flowers in Monet's gardens; late Aug for International Chamber Music Festival. In Rouen: last Sun in May for Joan of Arc Festival. In Honfleur: May for Sailor's Festival; mid-Sep for Shrimp Festival. In Deauville: early Sep for American Film Festival.

A Gothic Wonder Surrounded by Galloping Tides

MONT ST-MICHEL

Haute-Normandie, France

The fortified island-village of Mont St-Michel ranks among the wonders of the Western world, drawing more than 3 million visitors a year—second in France only to the Eiffel Tower. The ancient abbey and town, on the summit of a dramatic granite outcropping rising from a flat seabed, are a marvel of engineering and sheer audacity.

Originally the site of a small oratory, built in 708 after a bishop reported a sighting of St. Michael, over several centuries the island became a complex of churches, Benedictine monasteries, ramparts, and a village. Once a pilgrimage site, an unassailable fortification, even a prison after the French Revolution, it now stands as a tribute to French medieval architecture.

Much has been made of the dangerous "galloping" tides—the highest in Europe—which can rush in as high as 45 feet, then rush out again just as quickly (the highest tide occurs 36 to 48 hours after a full moon). Many medieval pilgrims lost their lives sinking into dangerous quicksand when picking their way across the bay; a half-mile-long causeway was finally built in 1879. Over the years, silt buildup has inexorably joined Mont St-Michel to the mainland; a new dam and an elevated bridge replacing the causeway let tides circulate naturally and will return the monument to its true island state by 2015.

Avoid the crush of tourists by visiting off-season, or enjoy the silent magic of a near-deserted Mont St-Michel in late evening by dining or staying at La Mère Poulard. They've been putting up pilgrims and tourists since 1888, serving their soufflélike omelets made from a secret recipe. At the rustic Ferme Saint-Michel on the mainland, you can enjoy a menu highlighted with Normandy specialties—seafood, camembert, or Calvados brandy—with a view of Mont St-Michel illuminated at night.

WHERE: 200 miles/322 km northwest of Paris, 30 miles/48 km east of St-Malo. **LA MÈRE POULARD:** Tel 33/2-33-896868; www.merepoulard.com. *Cost:* from $220; dinner $75. **LA FERME SAINT-MICHEL:** Tel 33/2-33-584679; www.restaurant-ferme-saint-michel.com. *Cost:* dinner $38. **BEST TIMES:** May–Jun and Sep–Oct for nice weather and fewer crowds; Nov–Feb for moody, dramatic weather and to have the place to yourself.

Where the Liberation of Europe Began

NORMANDY'S D-DAY BEACHES

Haute-Normandie, France

On June 6, 1944, the Allied Forces launched Operation Overlord, the largest seaborne invasion in history. More than 6,900 ships and landing craft, 54,000 vehicles, and nearly 11,600 planes set off from the British coast through thick fog to cross the rough waters of the English Channel. Destination: the shores of Normandy, in Nazi-occupied northern France, chosen because they were less defended by the Germans than sites farther east. Although the Allies successfully caught the Nazis off-guard, the battle was bloody and the cost of human life high on the beaches code-named Omaha, Utah, Gold, Juno, and Sword—it's estimated that nearly 4,500 Allied soldiers died on the first day alone. Casualties

Germans manned the Longues-sur-Mer battery on D-day.

on both sides exceeded 400,000 for the campaign, which ran through the end of August and launched the successful Allied march across Europe that helped to end Adolf Hitler's dream of world domination.

Time has erased most of World War II's scars from this quiet coast, except for the dramatic reminder of rows and rows of stark white crosses and Stars of David marking the resting places of 9,387 American soldiers at Colleville-sur-Mer's American Cemetery. Nearly 5,000 British, Canadian, Australian, and South African troops rest at the British Cemetery at Bayeux. Near the town of Néville-sur-Mer, pieces of wrecked German bunkers and barbed wire overlook the beach, and at Arromanches, just off Gold Beach, sit the remains of the floating Mulberry Harbor, an artificial port built to receive supplies during the landing.

Several museums detail the D-day invasion, the most important and comprehensive being the Musée du Débarquement (D-day Museum) at the site of the Mulberry Harbor and the moving and informative Caen Memorial—A Center for History and Peace, about 30 miles to the south. The latter gives an overview of the invasion, set in a city that was 80 percent destroyed by Nazi bombing.

Where: 170–185 miles/274–298 km northwest of Paris. **Visitor info:** www.normandie-tourisme.fr or www.normandiememoire.com. **Musée du Débarquement:** Tel 33/2-31-223431; www.musee-arromanches.fr. **Caen Memorial:** Tel 33/2-31-060645; www.memorial-caen.fr. **Best times:** May–Jun and Sep–Oct for nice weather and fewer crowds; Jun 6 for remembrance ceremonies.

"If you are lucky enough to have lived in Paris as a young man, then wherever you go for the rest of your life, it stays with you, for Paris is a moveable feast."—Ernest Hemingway

Paris

Île-de-France, France

It's impossible to be objective about Paris, possibly the most beautiful and romantic city in the world. The architecture, manicured green spaces, bridges over Seine, café life, and joie de vivre of its soigné citizens all conspire to make the City of Light an elegant and timelessly exciting place to visit. See the key sights first, then wander down its backstreets and discover your own Paris, the birthplace of style and *savoir vivre,* where everything is magic and anything can happen.

The Arc de Triomphe stands at the western end of the Champs-Élysées.

Top Attractions

Arc de Triomphe—The largest triumphal arch in the world (163 feet high and 147 feet wide) was erected by Napoleon in 1806 to commemorate his imperial army's victories.

During World War II, both the invading Germans and the liberating Allied forces passed beneath it. It's the site of France's Tomb of the Unknown Soldier and at the top it has a viewing platform and multimedia exhibit allowing you to inspect the arch's glorious sculptures and friezes up close. **INFO:** Tel 33/1-55-377377; www.monuments-nationaux.fr.

BASILIQUE DU SACRÉ-COEUR—Planned as a votive offering after France's humiliating defeat in the Franco-Prussian War and the ensuing uprising of the Paris Commune, Sacré-Coeur was built between 1876 and 1914 in an ornate Romanesque-Byzantine style. A perpetual prayer cycle that began at the basilica's consecration in 1919 continues round-the-clock to this day. Gleaming white and with a 272-foot-high central dome, the outside of the cathedral is almost confectionary. Inside is one of the world's largest mosaics, depicting Christ with outstretched arms. The view from the dome is breathtaking; on a clear day you can see for almost 20 miles. **INFO:** Tel 33/1-53-418900; www.sacre-coeur-montmartre.com.

CENTRE GEORGES POMPIDOU—Looking like a building turned inside out so that all its brightly painted pipes and ductwork show, the bold Centre Pompidou was the original bad boy of museums when it opened in 1977 as a center for modern art. Its futurism is a bit dated today, but a late-'90s restoration freshened things up, adding 5,000 feet of exhibition space, a number of new auditoriums, and improved dining options. Attractions include the National Museum of Modern Art, with about 1,350 works on display from its massive collection. **INFO:** Tel 33/1-44-781233; www.centrepompidou.fr.

CIMETIÈRE DU PÈRE-LACHAISE—The world's most visited cemetery opened its one-way doors in 1804, and today its 69,000 ornate tombs form an open-air sculpture garden. Among the 800,000 souls who call this place "home" are Chopin, Molière, Proust, Gertrude Stein, Colette, Sarah Bernhardt, Yves Montand, Édith Piaf, and Isadora Duncan. Especially popular are the graves of Oscar Wilde and 1960s rock star Jim Morrison. **INFO:** Tel 33/1-55-258210; www.pere-lachaise.com.

Fireworks surround the tower every July 14.

TOUR EIFFEL—Possibly the most recognized structure in the world, the Eiffel Tower was built as a temporary centerpiece for the 1889 Universal Exhibition; the much maligned "metal asparagus" was saved from demolition only because, as the tallest structure in Europe at the time (1,063 feet high), it was useful as a radio tower. Today it's the symbol of Paris, providing a view of up to 40 miles from its observation platforms. On its second level at 400 feet, Alain Ducasse's restaurant Le Jules Verne gives new meaning to the term "haute cuisine"; should your budget not match those heights, dine on the first level at 58 Tour Eiffel. **INFO:** Tel 33/8-92-701239; www.tour-eiffel.fr. **LE JULES VERNE:** Tel 33/1-45-556144; www.lejulesverne-paris.com. *Cost:* dinner $190. **58 TOUR EIFFEL:** Tel 33/1-45-552004; www.restaurants-toureiffel.com. *Cost:* dinner $45.

L'HÔTEL NATIONALE DES INVALIDES (NAPOLEON'S TOMB)—This spectacular complex was originally designed in the late 17th century as a hospital and retirement home for French veterans. It features a huge military building erected around a large courtyard, an armory that was plundered at the outset of the French Revolution, and a church with a gilded Baroque dome. In 1840, Napoleon's remains were moved from the island of St. Helena, where he had died in exile in 1821, to rest in the church. In addition to the tomb, visitors can see the

Musée de l'Armée, full of weapons, uniforms, and equipment, and the Musée des Plans-Reliefs, with scale models of various French towns, fortresses, and châteaux. **Info:** Tel 33/8-10-113399; www.invalides.org.

The Louvre—Once the largest palace in the world, now one of its largest art museums, the Louvre is home to the *Mona Lisa*, the armless *Venus de Milo*, I. M. Pei's controversial glass pyramid, and some 400,000 works of art—35,000 of which are on permanent display. Stretching for half a mile along the northern banks of the Seine, the palace was initially a medieval fortress and was expanded into a luxurious royal residence. It was designated a museum immediately after the Revolution, and its collection was significantly expanded with spoils of war taken by Napoleon. Today the collections are divided into eight departments, including sculpture, paintings, and antiquities. Exit the museum and delve into the Jardin des Tuileries, gardens laid out in 1664 by André Le Nôtre, designer of the grounds at Versailles (see p. 118). They form one of Paris's loveliest promenades, dotted with statues and fountains, and link the Louvre with the Place de la Concorde. **Info:** Tel 33/1-40-205317; www.louvre.fr.

Musée National du Moyen Age—Built in the 15th century as a splendid Gothic residence for the abbot of the Cluny Abbey, the mansion now houses the Museum of the Middle Ages (aka the Cluny Museum). Following the Revolution, Alexandre du Sommerard filled it with a collection of medieval tapestries, statues, crosses and chalices, jewelry, coins, manuscripts, and more. Its most prized possession is The Lady and the Unicorn, a unique series of six late-15th-century tapestries. The site also contains the ruins of 2nd-century Roman baths. **Info:** Tel 33/1-53-737800; www.musee-moyenage.fr.

Musée d'Orsay—Housed in the Neoclassical Gare d'Orsay railroad station (built in 1900), the Musée d'Orsay exhibits works from the years 1848 to 1914, a period that saw the rise of Impressionism, Symbolism, pointillism, realism, Fauvism, and Art Nouveau. The dazzling collection includes works by Degas, Manet, Monet, Cézanne, Renoir, Matisse, and Whistler. If you get a second wind, take in the furniture, architectural drawings and models, photographs, and objets d'art. **Info:** Tel 33/1-40-494814; www.musee-orsay.fr.

Musée Picasso—With more than 3,500 drawings, engravings, paintings, ceramic works, and sculptures donated by the artist's heirs, the Picasso Museum represents the greatest single collection of the artist's work in the world. Housed in the 17th-century Hôtel Salé, the museum's collection also shows Picasso's personal art collection of such masters as Braque, Cézanne, Matisse, and Modigliani. **Info:** Tel 33/1-42-712521; www.musee-picasso.fr.

Notre Dame—A "symphony in stone," according to Victor Hugo, the Cathedral of Notre Dame is the historic, spiritual, and geographic heart of Paris. Its foundation stone was laid by Pope Alexander III in 1163, and construction was completed nearly two centuries later. A 422-step climb to the top of the north tower provides close-ups of the bestiary of gargoyles, the 13-ton bell Emmanuel in the south tower, and a magnificent 360-degree view. **Info:** Tel 33/1-42-345610; www.cathedraledeparis.com.

Ste-Chapelle—The walls of this small chapel, completed in 1248 to house Louis IX's precious collection of holy relics and one of the supreme achievements of the Middle Ages, form the largest expanse of stained glass in the world—so be sure to visit on a sunny day. Or in the evening when there are candlelit classical concerts in this Gothic jewel box. **Info:** Tel 33/1-53-406097; www.monuments-nationaux.fr.

Other Must-Dos

Cabaret—Paris's oldest bar-cabaret and a Montmartre landmark, Au Lapin Agile was frequented by Picasso and Utrillo, among others. This glimpse of Paris past has been the heart of French folk music for decades, with spirited sing-alongs after the tourists leave. In the same neighborhood and easily spotted by its trademark red windmill, the Moulin Rouge puts on much more lavish shows that were immortalized in the posters of Toulouse-Lautrec. **Au Lapin Agile:** Tel 33/1-46-068587; www.au-lapin-agile.com. **Moulin Rouge:** Tel 33/1-53-098282; www.moulinrouge.fr.

Bateaux Mouches—These glass-enclosed boats are to Paris what gondolas are to Venice—a wonderful, unabashedly touristy way to see the city from a different perspective. They ply the waters of the Seine and slip under its famous bridges, providing a glimpse of life along the quais of the refined Right and storied Left banks. **Info:** Tel 33/1-42-259610; www.bateauxmouches.com.

Île St-Louis—This small island in the middle of the Seine was created in the 17th century by joining two islets together. Since then, it's been largely residential, with stately 17th- and 18th-century mansions. One of the most romantic spots is at the western end, around Pont St-Louis and Pont Louis-Philippe. Look for Berthillon to sample its famous ice cream. **Berthillon:** Tel 33/1-43-543161; www.berthillon.fr.

Marché aux Puces de St-Ouen—A must for every flea-market lover, this enormous market consists of thousands of vendors in a dozen different sections, selling everything under the sun, including one-of-a-kind finds for early birds with sharp eyes. It's the largest in Europe, held Saturday, Sunday, and Monday—and, yes, that might be that famous American designer you see sleuthing around. **Info:** www.parispuces.com.

Musée de l'Orangerie—This small but perfectly formed museum exhibits Impressionist and Post-Impressionist paintings, pastels, watercolors, and other works, by such notables as Cézanne, Matisse, Renoir, Rousseau, Soutine, and Utrillo. The main reason for a visit, though, is to view Monet's sublime *Water Lilies,* eight enormous panels arranged in two oval rooms built exactly to the artist's specifications. **Info:** Tel 33/1-44-778007; www.musee-orangerie.fr.

Musée Rodin—Housed in the sculptor's 18th-century mansion and surrounded by gardens filled with his works, this museum is one of the most relaxing spots in Paris. *The Thinker* is instantly recognizable, but don't miss *The Burghers of Calais, The Cathedral,* and especially *The Kiss,* just about the most romantic work ever carved in stone. **Info:** Tel 33/1-44-186110; www.musee-rodin.fr.

Opéra Garnier—A Rococo wonder, this opera house completed in 1875 includes a delightful ceiling added in 1964 by Marc Chagall. Lavish performances by the National Opera, the Paris Ballet, and various orchestras promise the ultimate night on the town. **Info:** Tel 33/1-71-252423; www.opera-de-paris.fr.

Place des Vosges—The small, rose-colored brick Place des Vosges is the city's oldest and most beautiful square, planned by Henri IV in the early 17th century and entirely surrounded by arcades. Victor Hugo lived here, at No. 6, and his apartment is now a museum. **Maison de Victor Hugo:** Tel 33/1-42-721016; www.musee-hugo.paris.fr.

Where to Stay

L'Hôtel—For over a century, L'Hôtel was always the right address—or so thought Oscar Wilde, who died here in 1900 in Room 16. Following a stylish yet historically correct renovation, today it's a chic, upscale St-Germain address for a new generation of savvy travelers. **Info:** Tel 33/1-44-419900; www.l-hotel.com. *Cost:* from $380.

Hôtel du Petit Moulin—Everyone's favorite boutique hotel in the Marais, the

Little Mill (it's housed in a bakery dating back to the early 17th century) is courtesy of designer Christian Lacroix. Rooms are decorated in styles ranging from medieval and Rococo (toile de Jouy wallpaper, Louis XIV–style chairs) to modern, with large floral murals and mirrors that are just this side of kitsch. **Info:** Tel 33/1-42-741010; www.hoteldupetitmoulin.com. *Cost:* from $270.

Hôtel Sainte-Beuve—A very Parisian experience that won't break the bank, this boutique hotel off the Blvd Raspail is a 5-minute walk to the Luxembourg Gardens. The 22 guest rooms have been updated by British designer David Hicks and face a quiet street. **Info:** Tel 33/1-45-482007; www.parishotelcharme.com. *Cost:* from $230.

Palace hotels— France has a plethora of palace hotels, and Paris's Right Bank is awash in them. Step into the quiet, marbled lobby of the fabled Hôtel de Crillon, the 18th-century building where Benjamin Franklin and delegates of Louis XVI signed the treaty recognizing American independence in 1778. Crowned heads, famous entertainers, and VIPs fill the hotel's *livre d'or* (guest book) or dine at Les Ambassadeurs, one of Paris's finest restaurants. Overlooking the Tuileries garden, the Hôtel Meurice has hosted sultans and royalty for nearly two centuries. The Ritz entered the English language as a byword for elegance, and the hotel is just that, with a pink-marble Louis XV interior where you can linger for a spot of tea, a relaxing aperitif at the Hemingway Bar, or a *très haute* dinner at L'Espadon. At the Plaza Athénée, an army of discreetly professional staff provide the service expected by the discerning guests who stay here. It's located at the heart of Avenue Montaigne's famous couturiers and jewelers, and guests enjoy priority at the hotel's star-studded Alain Ducasse restaurant. **Hôtel de Crillon:** Tel 33/1-44-711500; in the U.S., 800-888-4747; www.crillon.com. *Cost:* from $1,010; prix-fixe dinner at Les Ambassadeurs $190. **Hôtel Meurice:** Tel 33/1-44-581010; in the U.S., 800-650-1842; www.meuricehotel.com. *Cost:* from $895. **Ritz Hotel Paris:** Tel 33/1-43-163030; in the U.S., 800-745-8883; www.ritzparis.com. *Cost:* from $1,035; prix-fixe dinner at L'Espadon $300. **Plaza Athénée:** Tel 33/1-53-676665; in the U.S., 800-650-1842; www.plaza-athenee-paris.com. *Cost:* from $875; prix-fixe dinner at Alain Ducasse $350.

Themed hotels—Paris's delightful themed hotels, situated largely in the quirky Marais district, put you in the thick of history, literature, and culture. If cinema is your thing, the Hôtel du 7ème Art, with its B&W-movie theme, is just the ticket, and each of its 24 rooms is charmingly different. Awaken your inner neogoth at the Hôtel St-Merry, housed in the remains of a medieval church, with one-of-a-kind rooms containing original features (the flying buttress soaring over the bed in Room 9, the choir-stall bed board in Room 12). Hôtel Caron de Beaumarchais is done up like an 18th-century *hôtel particulier*—the "private mansions" the Marais is so famous for—circa the time of the playwright Beaumarchais, who wrote *The Barber of Seville* just down the road. **Hôtel du 7ème Art:** Tel 33/1-44-548500; www.paris-hotel-7art.com. *Cost:* from $148. **Hôtel St-Merry:** Tel 33/1-42-781415; www.hotelmarais.com. *Cost:* from $160. **Hôtel Caron de Beaumarchais:** Tel 33/1-42-723412; www.carondebeaumarchais.com. *Cost:* from $210.

Eating & Drinking

Angelina and Ladurée—Replete with marble and gilt, Paris's most popular *salon de thé* is opposite the Tuileries garden. Its decadent Mont Blanc pastry takes a backseat only to the richest hot chocolate imaginable. The ornate Ladurée was established in 1862 but looks like it just stepped out of 17th-century Versailles. It is best known for its macaroons, but order just about anything on the menu to experience a confectionary epiphany, including *le baiser Ladurée*, a showstopping layered almond cake with strawberries and cream. **Angelina:** Tel 33/1-42-608200; www.groupe-bertrand.com/angelina. **Ladurée:** Tel 33/1-40-750875; www.laduree.fr.

Brasserie Lipp—Waiters still dress in black waistcoats, bowties, and long, crisp white aprons, much as they did when the place opened in 1880. The profiteroles in hot chocolate sauce are reason enough to come, especially if they're preceded by the best choucroute-and-beer combination this side of Alsace. **Info:** Tel 33/1-45-485391. *Cost:* dinner $55.

The café scene—The Left Bank's St-Germain-des-Prés is the traditional and still-fashionable hub of the café scene, offering a glimpse of Paris from Hemingway's *A Moveable Feast.* The venerable Café de Flore and next door Les Deux Magots still draw expats and homegrown intelligentsia, generations after their World War II-era heyday. A completely different take on café society, the Café Marly is discreetly housed under the colonnades of the Louvre's Richelieu wing and faces I. M. Pei's stunning glass pyramid. Come for the views, not the service. **Café de Flore:** Tel 33/1-45-485526; www.cafedeflore.com. **Les Deux Magots:** Tel 33/1-45-485525; www.lesdeuxmagots.fr. **Café Marly:** Tel 33/1-49-260660.

Sartre and Hemingway once rubbed elbows at Les Deux Magots.

Chez Janou—A French bistro the way Hollywood would imagine it, this spot just east of the Place des Vosges is perennially popular with both celebs and locals and goes the distance with its Provençal dishes and dozens of types of pastis. **Info:** Tel 33/1-42-722841; www.chezjanou.com. *Cost:* dinner $50.

Chez Toinette—You won't be the only foreigner in this cozy and romantic place in the heart of touristy Montmartre. But there are plenty of locals who come for the filet of duck with sage and honey, a longtime specialty. The friendly wait-staff is a welcome plus. **Info:** Tel 33/1-42-544436. *Cost:* dinner $40.

La Coupole—Every meal is a sentimental journey at one of the most legendary scene-making brasseries in Paris since 1927. Cherished by out-of-towners and locals alike, its platters of oysters, mussels, and other delights from the briny deep are served in a cavernous train-station-like Art Deco setting, bustling with faithful clients, who once included Man Ray, Jean-Paul Sartre, and Josephine Baker. **Info:** Tel 33/1-43-201420; www.lacoupoleparis.com. *Cost:* dinner $50.

Fauchon—This is the city's most famous food emporium and caterer. Artistically prepared window and counter displays of picture-perfect food are scrutinized as carefully as this season's runway fashions. This is one-stop-shopping for exquisitely packaged souvenirs for foodie friends back home. A tea salon and brasserie let you sample some of the goods before leaving the premises. **Info:** Tel 33/1-70-393800; www.fauchon.fr.

Guy Savoy—One of Paris's finest and most innovative restaurants is the elegant domain of a chef extraordinaire. The menus (including two 10-course tasting menus) adhere to the season's offerings: Come in the fall and you may find a dozen varieties of mushrooms. The ambience is festive, and the décor is warm, sophisticated, and comfortable, accented by the chef's own art collection. **Info:** Tel 33/1-43-804061; www.guysavoy.com. *Cost:* dinner $275; tasting menus from $355.

Jadis—The buzzword in Paris gastronomic circles these days is *néo-bistro*, describing a small, informal "new bistro" serving outstanding cuisine under the watch of a talented (and often young) chef. Jadis, with rising-star chef Guillaume Delage at the helm, is the very embodiment of the idea. Expect bistro fare with a twist that makes it near-perfect. **Info:** Tel 33/1-45-577320; www.bistrot-jadis.com. *Cost:* dinner $60.

Le Grand Véfour—For an unforgettable visual and gustatory experience, the 18th-century setting of chef Guy Martin's jewelry box restaurant is the epitome of classic French cuisine. You will leave with a better understanding of why the French are known to cook—and decorate—better than anyone else. **Info:** Tel 33/1-42-965627; www.grand-vefour.com. *Cost:* dinner $270.

Taillevent—Considered by most critics to be among the city's top restaurants, Taillevent is presided over by Valérie Vrinat, daughter of the late, consummate host Jean-Claude. Chef Alain Solivérès creates a masterful mélange of old and new. In perfect harmony with the unimpeachable menu is Taillevent's legendary wine list of more than 1,300 labels managed by four sommeliers; its wine shop is one of Paris's finest. **Info:** Tel 33/1-44-951501; www.taillevent.com. *Cost:* dinner $250.

Day Trips

Cathédrale Notre Dame de Chartres—Chartres' incomparable Gothic cathedral—the first to use flying buttresses—is known for its unrivaled stained-glass windows as well as the sculptures that decorate it inside and out. The magnificent stained glass covers an expanse of almost 28,000 square feet; its 172 jewel-like windows created by 12th- and 13th-century master artists were saved from destruction during the Revolution due to bureaucratic red tape and during World War II when they were removed piece by piece and hidden for safekeeping. The kaleidoscopic colors—ruby reds, emerald greens, rich golds, and the famous "Chartres blue"—are once again sparkling and vibrant. For the illiterate masses, they served as an illuminated "paupers' Bible," familiar narratives that could be read from bottom to top—earth to heaven. **Where:** 57 miles/91 km southwest of Paris. Tel 33/2-37-212207; www.diocese-chartres.com.

Château de Versailles—Housing the most flamboyant court since ancient Rome, France's most-visited château, Versailles, was home to the French monarchy at the height of its glory. The century-long heyday lasted from 1682, when Louis XIV brought his court of more than 6,000 here from Paris, until 1789, when Louis XVI and his queen, Marie Antoinette, were notified that revolutionary mobs were on their way. Of the palace's 700 rooms, the most famous is the 246-foot-long Galerie des Glaces (Hall of Mirrors), whose 17 large beveled mirrors reflect an equal number of arched windows. The room has witnessed everything from the marriage of Louis XVI and Marie Antoinette to the signing of the Treaty of Versailles after World War I. The elaborately Baroque Grands Appartements (State Apartments) are equally extraordinary. After exploring the palace's interior, stroll through Versailles's famous 225-acre park; the formal gardens were designed by the well-known André Le Nôtre. Rather than rush back to Paris, check into the neighboring turn-of-the-century Trianon Palace hotel for the royal pampering once reserved for guests of the Sun King and a restaurant by Gordon Ramsay. **Where:** 17 miles/28 km southwest of Paris. Tel 33/1-30-837800; www.chateauversailles.fr. **Trianon Palace Versailles:** Tel 33/1-30-845000; www.trianonpalace.com. *Cost:* from $395.

In the Footsteps of Toulouse-Lautrec

Albi

Languedoc-Roussillon, France

Historians know the well-preserved market town of Albi as the stronghold of the Cathars, an ascetic religious movement wiped out in a vicious inquisition by the Catholic Church in the 12th and 13th centuries. But to the general public, Albi is the birthplace of artist Henri de Toulouse-Lautrec, famous interpreter of bohemian life in and around Montmartre, in Paris, at the turn of the 20th century.

Born in 1864 to an aristocratic family and suffering from a genetic bone deficiency that stunted his growth, the tormented Toulouse-Lautrec fled to Paris at 18 and died at 37, leaving a vast body of work and the legacy of having created poster art. The world's most important collection of his drawings of dancers, prostitutes, and café and cabaret life is on display at Albi's impressive Musée Toulouse-Lautrec, in the austere Palais de la Berbie, a former fortress built in 1265 as a bishops' residence. Its geometric gardens were designed by André Le Nôtre, known for his gardens at the Château de Versailles (see previous page).

This small town's massive Cathédrale Ste-Cécile, built as a symbol of Catholic power after the crusade against the Cathars, houses the largest collection of Italian Renaissance paintings in a French church. The Hostellerie St-Antoine was converted from a monastery to a hotel in 1734, and work by Toulouse-Lautrec hangs on the walls, a gift from the artist to his friend the great-grandfather of the current owners. The same family runs the rural La Réserve, on the northern outskirts of town, an elegant Mediterranean-style villa overlooking the Tarn river. A short drive through countryside dotted with medieval and classical châteaux takes you to the fortified hill town of Cordes-sur-Ciel, built in the early 13th century. Isolated and picture-perfect, the tiny village appears to hover in the air on a misty day.

Nearby Toulouse, one of the fastest-growing towns in France, offers some big city energy. Nicknamed "La Ville Rose" because of its ubiquitous red brick, Toulouse was one of medieval Europe's great artistic and literary capitals. The Dominican order was formed here, and many historic churches remain in the medieval quarter; the magnificent 11th-century Basilique St-Sernin, with its multi-arched Italianate bell tower, is Europe's largest Romanesque church. Toulouse's universities and the headquarters of France's aeronautical industry have generated a vibrant café and restaurant scene. One of the more stylish choices is the celebrated Chez Michel Sarran, serving a refined interpretation of the region's hearty cuisine that respects traditional flavors.

Albi: 47 miles/76 km northeast of Toulouse. **Musée de Toulouse-Lautrec:** Tel 33/5-63-494870; www.albi-tourisme.fr. **Hostellerie St-Antoine:** Tel 33/5-63-540404; www.hotel-saint-antoine-albi.com. *Cost:* from $145 (off-peak), from $220 (peak). **La Réserve:** Tel 33/5-63-608080; in the U.S., 800-735-2478; www.lareservealbi.com. *Cost:* $245. *When:* closed Nov–Apr. **Chez Michel Sarran:** Tel 33/5-61-123232; www.michel-sarran.com. *Cost:* dinner $125. **Best times:** in Albi: Jul–Aug for classical concerts in the cathedral; Jul for guitar festival. In Toulouse: Apr for flamenco festival; Jul for contemporary dance festival; Aug for music festival.

Medieval Military Might and Serious Cassoulet

CARCASSONNE

Languedoc-Roussillon, France

Carcassonne is both a storybook medieval town and an extraordinary example of early military architecture. Built in the 6th century on Roman foundations and fortified in the 12th and 13th centuries, the city was virtually impenetrable for centuries. Restored in the 1800s, Carcassonne is surrounded by Europe's longest walls—nearly 2 miles of turrets, battlements, drawbridges, and more than 50 watchtowers.

Today, Carcassonne's streets teem with tourists in summer months. Spend the night at the elegant Hôtel de la Cité to enjoy the town during the quiet evening hours, when its walls are illuminated. A former episcopal palace built into the ancient ramparts and incorporating one of the stone watchtowers, the ivy-covered hotel has soaring ceilings, tapestries, wood paneling, and an elegant restaurant, La Barbacane, along with the more casual Chez Saskia. To escape the high-season congestion in Carcassonne's fortified upper town, known as La Cité, enjoy views of the fortress from the outdoor terrace of the tasteful, family-run Hôtel du Château, just outside the walls in the lower, newer city, the Ville Basse.

Languedoc is famous for cassoulet, a dense, hearty stew blending white beans, carrots, onions, and breadcrumbs with cubes of tender mutton (other cassoulets may use pork, sausage, or duck), then baked until perfectly crusty on top. Try it at the Château St-Martin Trencavel, just outside of Carcassonne—chef Jean-Claude Rodriguez takes the dish so seriously he founded the good-humored "Universal Academy of Cassoulet" to honor it. The academy's Cassoulet Trail encourages aficionados to sample different versions at restaurants and inns between Carcassonne and Toulouse (see p. 119).

An idyllic way to explore the region is by barge, along the picturesque Canal du Midi. This tranquil 149-mile man-made waterway, constructed in the late 19th century, passes through Carcassonne on its way to Toulouse or Sète. Barges glide through the region's back door, past pretty villages, vineyards, and magnificent châteaux and through nearly 100 canal locks.

WHERE: 55 miles/88 km southeast of Toulouse. **HÔTEL DE LA CITÉ:** Tel 33/4-8-714285; in the U.S., 800-237-1236; www.hoteldelacite.com. *Cost:* from $420; dinner at La Barbacane $115. *When:* closed late Jan–mid-Mar. **HÔTEL DU CHÂTEAU:** Tel 33/4-68-113838; www.hotelduchateau-carcassonne.com. *Cost:* from $165. **CHÂTEAU ST-MARTIN TRENCAVEL:** Tel 33/4-68-710953; www.chateausaintmartin.net. *Cost:* dinner $60. **HOW:** For

La Cité overlooks the countryside from a 1,500-foot hilltop.

barge cruises accommodating 4–10 passengers, contact U.S.-based Bargelady. Tel 800-880-0071 or 312-245-0900; www.bargeladycruises.com. *Cost:* 7-day cruise from $3,690, inclusive. *When:* Mar–Nov. **Best times:** Jul 14 for Bastille Day fireworks over the ramparts; mid-Jun–Aug for the Festival de Carcassonne of music and theater.

Where Rococo and Art Nouveau Flourished

Nancy

Lorraine, France

The capital of the Lorraine region, Nancy is one of the loveliest cities in Europe, an urban center where art and culture have long flourished. Its centerpiece is the Place Stanislas, considered France's most beautiful square. It was named for Stanisław Leszczyński, twice king of Poland and father-in-law to King Louis XV, who appointed Leszczyński Nancy's ruling Duke of Lorraine when the Duchy of Lorraine was folded back into France after many centuries as an independent enclave. Passionate about architecture and urban design, Leszczyński oversaw construction of the square from 1751–60 and turned Nancy into one of Europe's most elegant cities. Place Stanislas is the epitome of Rococo delicacy, with gilded wrought-iron gates and decorative gold railings. It integrates the classic French architecture of the surrounding buildings, including the Hôtel de Ville (Town Hall), an *arc de triomphe,* and what is today the Grand Hôtel de la Reine, a splendid 18th-century mansion with many guest rooms overlooking the square.

Also on the Place Stanislas is the outstanding Musée des Beaux-Arts, with works by Delacroix, Modigliani, and Rubens. Nearby, the Musée Lorrain, housed in the Renaissance Palais Ducal, is devoted to the art and history of the Lorraine region, whereas the Musée de l'École de Nancy showcases the Belle Époque style of Art Nouveau, one of the city's major legacies. The Nancy School, formed here in 1901, played a key role in spreading Art Nouveau worldwide, bringing together artists, artisans, and manufacturers who promoted and nurtured the new decorative style known for its use of natural shapes, flowers, vines, mythical beasts, and even insects. Art Nouveau architecture and details abound in Nancy—the city's top restaurant of note, Le Capucin Gourmand, is a fine example, with its giant chandelier and glowing mushroom lights gracing the tables. At the more casual Brasserie Excelsior, built in 1911, sensational stained glass and high ceilings complement a menu of elegantly prepared French classics, including another regional specialty—quiche Lorraine.

Where: 175 miles/285 km southeast of Paris. **Visitor info:** www.ot-nancy.fr. **Grand Hôtel de la Reine:** Tel 33/3-83-350301; www.hoteldelareine.com. *Cost:* from $130. **Musée des Beaux-Arts:** Tel 33/3-83-853072; www.ecole-de-nancy.com. **Musée Lorrain:** Tel 33/3-83-321874; www.ot-nancy.fr/musees/lorrain.php. **Musée de l'École de Nancy:** Tel 33/3-83-401486; www.ecole-de-nancy.com. **Le Capucin Gourmand:** Tel 33/3-83-352698; www.lecapu.com. *Cost:* dinner $95. **Brasserie Excelsior:** Tel 33/3-83-352457; www.brasserie-excelsior.com. *Cost:* dinner $50. **Best times:** Jul 14 for Bastille Day parade; mid-Jul–early Aug for jazz festival; first 2 weeks of Oct for classical music festival.

Pilgrimage to Mystical Waters

Lourdes

Midi-Pyrénées, France

Every year, 6 million pilgrims and visitors flock to this small town perched on the lower slopes of the Pyrenees mountains to stand where, in 1858, a local 14-year-old peasant girl named Bernadette had 18 visions of the Virgin Mary in a riverside grotto.

Lourdes is France's most visited city after Paris and the second most popular Christian pilgrimage site after St. Peter's Basilica in Rome (see p. 184). It accommodates as many as 25,000 people a day in high season while somehow maintaining a benevolent sanctity that disarms even the most skeptical. Despite dormitory-like hotels and tawdry souvenir shops selling dashboard Virgins, Lourdes can still be a moving experience, particularly during evening candlelight processions to the neo-Byzantine Basilique du Rosaire, a church built beneath the Basilique Supérieure.

The faithful and devout from around the world come to drink and bathe in the water they believe to have miraculous healing powers. After one of the Virgin Mary's apparitions (seen by no one other than Bernadette), a spring apparently welled up in the grotto and has been flowing ever since. Of some 2,500 "unexplained healings," the church has officially recognized 67 physical cures since Bernadette's death in 1879. (She was canonized in 1933.)

Where: 78 miles/126 km east of Biarritz. **Visitor info:** www.lourdes-infotourisme.com. **When:** 6 official pilgrimage dates between Easter and late Oct are the busiest; the most important is Aug 15. **Where to stay:** The 19th-century Grand Hôtel Moderne has old-world charm and is a 10-min walk from the basilica. Tel 33/5-62-941232; grandhotelmoderne.com. *Cost:* from $180. *When:* closed Nov–Mar. **Best time:** 9 P.M. Apr–Oct for the daily candlelight procession.

The Playground of Kings

Loire Valley

Pays de la Loire, France

The lush, fertile valley created by the winding Loire River has captured travelers' hearts and imaginations for centuries. Hundreds of châteaux line France's "Royal River," the highest concentration of castles in the world, each a concoction of sumptuousness and excess. The châteaux began as castle fortifications in the Middle Ages as the British and French battled over this strategic valley; they reached their pinnacle of artistic splendor during the French Renaissance, when royalty and nobility from nearby Paris turned the valley into their power base and playground.

Château de Chenonceau was built in 1513 and contains original furnishings from that period.

With 440 rooms and 365 fireplaces, Chambord, François I's favorite hunting lodge, is the largest. Gracefully spanning the River Cher, the romantic Chenonceau is an unsurpassed Renaissance masterpiece with ornamental gardens to match. Cheverny, a fine example of 17th-century elegance, is the largest Loire château and has been home to the same noble family since it was built 6 centuries ago. The regal beauty of Château d'Ussé is said to have inspired Charles Perrault to write *Sleeping Beauty*. Many lesser-known châteaux are just as special for their majestic moats, riverine locations, lush parklands, and ancestral interiors chockablock with artwork and furniture.

The valley's fertile lowlands and temperate climate make it the "Garden of France"; town markets are a gourmand's dream and inspiration for a riverside picnic. The land also nurtures some of the nation's best vineyards, producing gentle reds and fruity whites such as Chinon, Sancerre, muscadet, Vouvray, and Bourgueil, and the rosés of Anjou. Visit the wine cellars of Chinon or tour the distillery of the orange liqueur Cointreau near Angers. Or hop on a bike—few regions are better suited to cycling in terms of beauty, history, grandeur, and gentle, rolling landscapes.

Consider unpacking your bags at the Domaine des Hauts de Loire, in Onzain. Built as a hunting lodge in 1860, it has gabled, antiques-filled guest rooms and a restaurant well known for its exceptional gourmet meals. For a setting worthy of the Valley of Kings, there's magnificent Château d'Artigny, in Montbazon, outside Tours. Rebuilt in the early 1900s by perfume pioneer François Coty, its pricier palatial rooms are awash in the formal, opulent style of Versailles.

WHERE: Orléans is 80 miles/129 km southwest of Paris. **VISITOR INFO:** www.loirevalleytourism.com. **DOMAINE DES HAUTS DE LOIRE:** Tel 33/2-54-207257; in the U.S., 800-735-2478; www.domainehautsloire.com. *Cost:* from $185; dinner $140. *When:* closed Dec–Feb. **CHÂTEAU D'ARTIGNY:** Tel 33/2-47-343030; www.artigny.com. *Cost:* from $200; dinner $110. **HOW:** Toronto-based Butterfield & Robinson arranges bike trips among châteaux, villages, and vineyards. Tel 866-551-9090 or 416-864-1354; www.butterfield.com. *Cost:* weeklong trips $6,795, all-inclusive. Originate in Montbazon. *When:* May–Sep. **BEST TIME:** mid-Apr–Oct for lovely weather.

Charming Town of Thermal Springs, Music, and Art

AIX-EN-PROVENCE

Provence-Alpes-Côte d'Azur, France

Take a stroll beneath the canopy of plane trees, past gurgling Rococo fountains and stately 17th- and 18th-century buildings on the elegant Cours Mirabeau, and take in perhaps the most perfect town in Provence.

The bookshops and lively cafés lining the avenue reflect Aix-en-Provence's artistic roots; author Émile Zola grew up here and often ate at the town's most famous brasserie, Les Deux Garçons, as did his friend Paul Cézanne. Then as now, the brasserie was more noted for its people-watching than its menu.

The fashionable and aristocratic small city of Aix (pronounced ex) was founded by Romans who came for its thermal springs; today, it is filled with over 30,000 international students. Its summer classical music and opera festival is one of the most famous in Europe.

Visit Cézanne's atelier, where he painted until his death in 1906; his coat still hangs on the wall and his easel holds an unfinished picture. Nine of Cézanne's paintings hang at the Musée Granet, along with his watercolors and sketches and 600 works by artists such as Giacometti, Picasso, Matisse, Mondrian, and Léger. Pack a picnic of fresh bread, vegetables, olives, fruit, and cheeses from the bustling daily outdoor market on the Place Richelme, then head out for a day trip to the limestone Montagne Ste-Victoire. A 3-hour climb to the summit, passing the Croix (cross) de Provence near the top, provides beautiful panoramas of Provence.

For a lovely view overlooking Aix, stay at La Villa Gallici, one of the city's finest hotels, decorated with sumptuous Provençal fabrics and antiques and set in a Florentine garden of cypress and lemon trees, rose bushes, and lavender. The founders of the villa have also created the perfect *petite auberge* in town at 28 à Aix: just four rooms stylishly decorated in modern Baroque. Cézanne didn't sleep at the Hotel Cézanne, but this small, smart hotel is perfect for those who appreciate contemporary décor. For an unforgettable Provençal dining experience, enjoy inspired dishes based on local, seasonal ingredients at Le Clos de la Violette.

WHERE: 91 miles/146 km northwest of Nice. **LES DEUX GARÇONS:** Tel 33/4-42-260051. *Cost:* dinner $50. **CÉZANNE'S STUDIO:** Tel 33/4-42-210653; www.atelier-cezanne.com. **MUSÉE GRANET:** Tel 33/4-42-528832; www.museegranet-aixenprovence.fr. **HOTEL LA VILLA GALLICI:** Tel 33/4-42-232923; www.villagallici.com. *Cost:* from $400 (off-peak), from $600 (peak). **28 À AIX:** Tel 33/4-42-548201; www.28aaix.com. *Cost:* from $310 (off-peak), from $380 (peak). **HOTEL CÉZANNE:** Tel 33/4-42-911111; http://cezanne.hotelaix.com. *Cost:* from $260. **LE CLOS DE LA VIOLETTE:** Tel 33/4-42-233071; www.closdelaviolette.com. *Cost:* dinner $125. **BEST TIMES:** Apr–Oct for nice weather; late Apr for daylong carnival; mid-Jul for Aix-en-Provence Festival.

On the Trail of Van Gogh

ARLES AND LES ALPILLES

Provence-Alpes-Côte d'Azur, France

Often called the soul of Provence, Arles is a town of classic antiquities, leafy squares, and art festivals, with a well-preserved Roman amphitheater known for bullfights both bloody and bloodless. But Arles is perhaps best known as Van Gogh's place of anguish, where he painted more than 200 works during the single year of 1888, including *Sunflowers*—and where he famously cut off his ear.

The lively, café-crammed Place du Forum (laid out by Julius Caesar) is the perfect place for a *café au lait* or an *apéritif*; it's also the site of Van Gogh's iconic *Café Terrace on the Place du Forum.* Overlooking the square is the landmark Grand Hôtel Nord Pinus, its worn bohemian elegance recalling the days when Picasso, Hemingway, and Édith Piaf stayed here. This quirky hotel is a favorite among famous toreadors who take part in bullfights at Les Arènes, where gladiators once fought.

Housed in a former 17th-century convent styled like a Roman palace, the elegant Hôtel Jules César is known for its restaurant, one of the best in Arles, as well as its proximity to the popular Saturday market held just outside its doors. Capturing the energy of modern-day Arles is the creative restaurant L'Atelier, overseen by chef Jean-Luc Rabanel, who found fame at La Chassagnette, 8 miles outside Arles, in the Camargue (see next page).

After his tumultuous year in Arles, Van Gogh voluntarily committed himself to the sanatorium in nearby St-Rémy-de-Provence, today open to visitors. St-Rémy is a pretty market town in the foothills of the Alpilles ("little Alps")—jagged mounds and cliffs surrounded by hills and valleys and green with pine, cypress, and olive trees. Nestled on a craggy bluff of the Alpilles is the medieval city Les Baux (named for the mineral bauxite found here), offering spectacular views and home to the legendary restaurant and hotel L'Oustau de Baumanière, which serves exceptional cuisine in a converted 14th-century farmhouse. Nearby is the charming La Riboto de Taven, an 1835 country manor with several hotel rooms built right into the cliffs. Chef Jean-Pierre Novi creates near-perfect home-style Provençal meals in a welcoming, antiques-filled dining room.

WHERE: 20 miles/32 km south of Avignon. **GRAND HÔTEL NORD PINUS:** Tel 33/4-90-934444; www.nord-pinus.com. *Cost:* from $215. **HÔTEL JULES CÉSAR:** Tel 33/4-90-525252; www.hotel-julescesar.fr. *Cost:* from $230, dinner $70. **L'ATELIER:** Tel 33/4-90-910769; www.rabanel.com. *Cost:* dinner $75. **L'OUSTAU DE BAUMANIÈRE:** 33/4-90-543307; in the U.S., 800-735-2478; www.oustaudebaumaniere.com. *Cost:* from $270 (off-peak), from $400 (peak); dinner $130. **LA RIBOTO DE TAVEN:** Tel 33/4-90-543423; www.riboto-de-taven.fr. *Cost:* from $250; prix-fixe dinner $80. *When:* closed Nov–Mar. **BEST TIMES:** Apr–Sep for bullfighting season; Jun–Aug for Photography Festival; mid-Jul for World Music festival; late Aug for Roman Festival.

Jewel of the Vaucluse

AVIGNON

Provence-Alpes-Côte d'Azur, France

Avignon was thrust into the international spotlight as the capital of the Christian world in the 14th century when it became home to seven consecutive popes at odds with the courts in Rome. The small town swelled as fortified ramparts, bridges, the huge Palais des Papes (Papal Palace), and cardinals' residences were built. The palace has been stripped of finery, but a vibrant cultural city flourishes today, thanks to university life and the famous summer international theater and dance festival.

You'll need imagination to grasp the former splendor in the Palais des Papes, but its rich collection of medieval Christian art and sculpture is on display in the nearby Petit Palais museum. Experience great opulence at the sumptuous La Mirande hotel across from the palace. Built for a cardinal in the 1300s and decorated with 2 centuries of art, it's considered one of the finest hotels in the region and boasts one of Avignon's best restaurants. Another grand option is the Hôtel d'Europe, occupying a 16th-century residence with emperor-size rooms, which overlook the palace. Food fit for a king is served at Christian Étienne's restaurant, graced with 700-year-old frescoes; the special menus showcase a single ingredient, such as lobster or tomatoes.

Only four of 22 arches of the Pont St-Bénézet still stand, a bridge immortalized by the children's song "Sur le pont d'Avignon." In the Middle Ages, it led across the river to Villeneuve les Avignon, where more than a dozen beautiful 14th-century cardinals' residences with views over Avignon and the Rhône Valley still stand. The Prieuré hotel, originally an archbishop's palace, has 33 lovely guest rooms, some with terraces.

Constructed in 45 B.C. and used until the 4th century, Pont du Gard carried water more than 30 miles from the Eure River to Nîmes.

Equidistant from Avignon are two favorite day trips. To the west is the stunning Roman aqueduct Pont du Gard, a three-tiered feat of engineering built 2,000 years ago to deliver water to Nîmes. To the east is the pretty town of L'Isle sur la Sorgue, with its picturesque canals and waterways. Its sprawling Sunday antiques market is France's largest outside Paris.

For a quiet getaway within striking distance of Avignon, the elegant Hôtel Crillon-le-Brave is a quintessential Provençal country inn that was once the home of dukes, with views of vineyards, olive groves, and Mont Ventoux. Rows of lavender carpet the fields at the base of the mountain. Some of the prettiest fields are an hour's drive south near Sault, considered Provence's lavender capital.

WHERE: 463 miles/742 km south of Paris; 65 miles/105 km northwest of Marseilles. **LA MIRANDE:** Tel 33/4-90-142020; www.la-mirande.fr. *Cost:* from $470 (off-peak), from $570 (peak); dinner $95. **HÔTEL D'EUROPE:** Tel 33/4-90-147676; www.heurope.com. *Cost:* from $295. **CHRISTIAN ÉTIENNE:** Tel 33/4-90-861650; www.christian-etienne.fr. *Cost:* dinner $100. **LE PRIEURÉ:** Tel 33/4-90-159015; in the U.S., 800-735-2478; www.leprieure.com. *Cost:* from $275. *When:* closed Nov–Mar. **HÔTEL CRILLON-LE-BRAVE:** Tel 33/4-90-656161; in the U.S., 800-735-2478; www.crillonlebrave.com. *Cost:* from $355. **BEST TIMES:** Jul for Avignon theater festival; Jun–mid-Aug for lavender in bloom.

Wild Horses, Bulls, and Pink Flamingos

THE CAMARGUE

Provence-Alpes-Côte d'Azur, France

One of France's—and Europe's—most intriguing wildlife regions is the untamed Camargue, a government-protected habitat on France's southern coast where the Rhône River runs into the Mediterranean. In this

360-square-mile delta of pastures, wetlands, and salt flats, more than 640 species of plants and at least 500 types of birds flourish (including as many as 40,000 pink flamingos). The most dramatic sights are of the chalky-white Camargue horses and small black bulls running free, overseen by some of the last cowboys in Europe, known as *les gardians.* Ride one of these horses or watch a roundup of bulls at Le Mas de Peint, in Le Sambuc, 20 miles southeast of Arles (see p. 124), a 1,300-acre working ranch with an elegant 17th-century stone guest farmhouse. The spacious interiors are tastefully decorated; guests enjoy sophisticated dishes made from meat and produce raised on the ranch, sitting on the canopied terrace with pastoral views. Down the road, enjoy a gourmet meal or take a cooking class at La Chassagnette, a former sheepfold, where young top chef Armand Arnal conjures up gastronomic feasts with ingredients from his organic garden and the nearby Mediterranean.

Arrange your trip to Les Stes-Maries-de-la-Mer for May's Gypsy Pilgrimage, when the fishing village vibrates with the rhythms and colors of more than 20,000 Roma (*gitans* in French), who come from as far away as Hungary and Romania to sing and dance in homage to their patron saint, Sara.

As the legend goes, Sara accompanied Mary Magdalene, Martha, Marie-Jacobé, and Marie-Salomé, all followers of Jesus, in A.D. 40 after they were exiled from Judea. Their boat, without sails or oars, miraculously arrived on the shores of the town that now bears their names, and their remains are said to lie in the town's 12th-century Romanesque church. Throughout the year, the historic arena in Les Stes-Maries-de-la-Mer holds horse shows and bloodless bullfights known as *courses camarguaises,* in which toreadors try to scoop a red ribbon from the horns of a bull.

WHERE: 18 miles/24 km south of Arles. **LE MAS DE PEINT:** Tel 33/4-90-972062; www.masdepeint.com. *Cost:* from $335; dinner $100. **LA CHASSAGNETTE:** Tel 33/4-90-972696; www.lachassagnette.fr. *Cost:* dinner $75. **BEST TIMES:** Apr–May or Sep–Oct to avoid mosquito season; May for bird-watching; May 24–26 for the Gypsy Pilgrimage.

Queen of the Côte d'Azur

CANNES

Provence-Alpes-Côte d'Azur, France

The Riviera city of Cannes, host of the world's most glamorous film festival, has more to offer than just star-gazing for 12 days every May: The charming old quarter, lively food market, and beautiful beaches make this one of the nicest stops on France's Mediterranean coast.

The Hotel InterContinental Carlton Cannes, the glittering neo-Classical command post for the Cannes Film Festival, dominates La Croisette, Cannes's famous palace- and palm-studded seafront boulevard. Unless you're with Brad or Penelope, settle for a cocktail at the terrace bar or for tea during the festival frenzy, your best shot at mingling with the Riviera's beautiful set.

All along the Croisette, hotels such as Le Grand, the Martinez, and the Majestic Barrière bustle with film festival events. But venture a block behind the Majestic and you'll find the Hôtel America, a modest but reliable alternative address.

Daily life in Cannes revolves around the city's old port to the west of La Croisette and, behind it, in the old quarter, Le Suquet. Stop in at portside La Pizza, a Cannes institution, and indulge in one of 20 varieties of pizza from their wood-burning oven. Climb picturesque rue St-Antoine, lined with attractive restaurants such as Le Maschou, a tiny haven for fresh regional and seafood dishes. Also in the old quarter is Marché Forville, the vibrant Cannes food and flower market.

The Promenade de la Croisette is flanked by the Mediterranean and luxury hotels.

Nearby Mougins, 10 minutes north of Cannes on the road to the perfume capital of Grasse, offers a quiet alternative. One of southern France's lovely medieval *villages perchés*—"perched villages," or hill towns—Mougins is a peaceful enclave of cobblestone lanes and open-air markets, where Picasso lived and worked for the final 12 years of his life. Gastronomes have flocked for decades to Le Moulin de Mougins, the culinary kingdom of chef Alain Llorca housed in a 16th-century olive-oil mill.

WHERE: 16 miles/26 km southwest of Nice. **VISITOR INFO:** www.cannesfrance.ca. **HOTEL INTERCONTINENTAL CARLTON CANNES:** Tel 33/4-93-064006; in the U.S., 800-496-7621; www.intercontinental.com. *Cost:* from $200 (off-peak), from $900 (peak). **HÔTEL AMERICA:** Tel 33/4-93-067575; www.hotel-america.com. *Cost:* from $135. **LA PIZZA:** Tel 33/4-93-392256; www.crescere.fr. *Cost:* dinner $25. **LE MASCHOU:** Tel 33/4-93-396221. *Cost:* dinner $45. **LE MOULIN DE MOUGINS:** Tel 33/4-93-757824; www.moulindemougins.com. *Cost:* dinner $120. **BEST TIMES:** Jun–Aug for beach weather; mid–late May for Cannes Film Festival.

Glamour and Beauty Along the Mediterranean

THE FRENCH RIVIERA

Provence-Alpes-Côte d'Azur, France

Stretching from Marseilles to Menton at the Italian border, the French Riviera is among the world's most coveted parcels of real estate. Enticing attributes include a temperate climate, unending ocean views, beautiful seaside marinas, rustic hilltop towns, and opulent villas. Its biggest cities are some of the Mediterranean's most glamorous—Cannes, Monte Carlo (see p. 226), and Nice (see p. 133). Despite coastal overdevelopment and the crush of summer visitors, the Côte d'Azur has a magic that's made it a magnet for tourists of all social strata for centuries.

The very essence of the Riviera's allure lies in St-Tropez, the port town that's attracted the rich and famous since Brigitte Bardot starred in Roger Vadim's *And God Created Woman* here in 1956. Claim a spot of sand on the Pampelonne beach, or head to the portside Café Sénéquier, on the Quai Jean Jaurès, for nonpareil people-watching. The Pastis Hotel, a chic oasis of calm centered around a courtyard pool and just a 10-minute walk from the port, is run by British expats who bring a touch of London sophistication. The Hôtel La Ponche, a longtime favorite with well-known writers and actors, oozes a casual charm and serves top-notch Provençal dishes in a restaurant with a view of the port.

Antibes, on the Baie des Anges (Bay of Angels) facing Nice, has a quieter charm. From the 1920s to the '50s, artists such as Picasso, Matisse, and Chagall were drawn here for the light and lifestyle, and Antibes's Picasso Museum houses some of the prolific artist's most joyous works. A short distance away is Cap d'Antibes, one of the coast's most beautiful and exclusive hideaways. Bypass the pine-cloaked estates and head to the small, friendly Hôtel La Jabotte. For sheer old-world glamour, go just a few miles farther along the coast to the legendary Grand Hôtel du Cap-Ferrat at St-Jean-Cap-Ferrat—the belle of the French Riviera since it opened in 1908 on 17 acres with gorgeous Mediterranean panoramas.

More sensational views abound at the legendary gardens of the Villa Ephrussi de Rothschild, a grand mansion built in the early 1900s and modeled after Versailles. In nearby Beaulieu, the ne plus ultra Réserve de Beaulieu & Spa has hosted guests from Winston Churchill to Pablo Picasso over the years.

WHERE: St-Tropez is 69 miles/112 km west of Nice; Antibes is 19 miles/30 km west of Nice. **CAFÉ SÉNÉQUIER:** Tel 33/4-94-970090. *Cost:* dinner $50. **PASTIS HOTEL:** Tel 33/4-98-125650; www.pastis-st-tropez.com. *Cost:* from $250 (off-peak), from $640 (peak). **HÔTEL LA PONCHE:** Tel 33/4-94-970253; www.laponche.com. *Cost:* from $265 (off-peak), from $450 (peak); dinner $80. **MUSÉE PICASSO:** Tel 33/4-92-905420; www.antibes-juanlespins.com. **HÔTEL LA JABOTTE:** Tel 33/4-93-614589; www.jabotte.com. *Cost:* from $135 (off-peak), from $175 (peak). **GRAND HÔTEL DU CAP-FERRAT:** Tel 33/4-93-765050; www.grand-hotel-cap-ferrat.com. *Cost:* from $375 (off-peak), from $825 (peak). **VILLA EPHRUSSI DE ROTHSCHILD:** Tel 33/4-93-013309; www.villa-ephrussi.com. **RÉSERVE DE BEAULIEU:** Tel 33/4-93-010001; www.reservebeaulieu.com. *Cost:* from $340 (off-peak), from $870 (peak). **BEST TIME:** Jun or Sep to avoid summer crowds.

Picturesque Hilltop Villages

THE LUBERON

Provence-Alpes-Côte d'Azur, France

East of Avignon, the Luberon region in Provence offers a quintessentially French experience: touring sleepy villages perched atop rugged hills overlooking vineyards and fields of lavender. The experience has become an industry, thanks to Peter Mayle's books about Provence, set in the author's picturesque and wildly popular town of Ménerbes, with its narrow streets and dramatic views. Despite the tourist crush, Ménerbes remains one of the country's prettiest hilltop villages and a perfect base for exploring others.

Among the vineyards just outside Ménerbes is a near-perfect Provençal lodging: the relaxed and refined Bastide de Marie, an 18th-century farmhouse with country-casual décor and cuisine. Nearby Oppède-le-Vieux is a "ghost village," with ruins of a medieval fortress, workshops, and houses (dampness and darkness led residents to relocate to the valley in the 19th century).

The beautiful town of Gordes, its gray-and-white stone houses rising around a hill, is topped by a stunning Renaissance castle. In the Luberon Valley below, surrounded by rows of lavender, monks still live in the dramatic 12th-century Abbaye de Sénanque. The ancient, deserted Village de Bories is named after the 20 or so mysterious beehive huts of piled stones, lived in or used as shepherd's housing from the Bronze Age until the 18th century. For 21st-century luxury, head to the Hôtel Les Bories & Spa, just outside the center of Gordes, for an overnight stay or a massage using local herbs. Or sample those herbs in the regional dishes served in the garden of the rustic Le Clos de Gustave.

Bonnieux is one of Provence's most impressive hilltop towns, with views of three neighboring villages. Artists have long been drawn to the pretty "red village" of Roussillon, known for its blazing red cliffs and buildings of red stone mined from nearby quarries. For one of the best markets in the Luberon, head to Apt on a Saturday morning and stock up on Provençal ceramics, lavender, olives, and wine.

Where: Ménerbes is 24 miles/39 km east of Avignon. **La Bastide de Marie:** Tel 33/4-90-723020; www.labastidedemarie.com. *Cost:* from $370; dinner $80. **Hôtel Les Bories:** Tel 33/4-90-720051; www.hotellesbories.com. *Cost:* from $285. **Le Clos de Gustave:** Tel 33/4-90-720425; www.leclosdegustave.com. *Cost:* dinner $55. *When:* closed Dec–Feb. **Best times:** May–Jun and Sep–Oct for fewer tourists; mid-Jul–early Aug for the Festival de Lacoste; Sat morning for market in Apt.

Forts, Ports, Bouillabaisse, and Dramatic Cliffs

Old Marseilles and Cassis

Provence-Alpes-Côte d'Azur, France

Colorful, energetic, and slightly rough-and-tumble, Marseilles is undergoing an urban revival, helping this oldest and second largest city in France shake its seedy reputation. The home to the national anthem, "The Marseillaise," has new waterfront development and growing civic pride. One quarter of the diverse population is from North Africa, and an abundance of spice markets, hammams (bath houses), and hookah cafés recall Tunisia, Morocco, or Algeria. The Old Port, dominated by two 17th-century forts, includes dozens of cafés that serve fresh seafood and local specialties such as pastis, a 90-proof anise-flavored cousin of absinthe.

The lively fish market on the Quai des Belges sells the daily catch to restaurants serving bouillabaisse, Marseilles' signature seafood stew. Purists agree that it needs *rascasse* (scorpion fish) and at least two other types of Mediterranean fish. The 1950s-style Miramar restaurant, a city landmark overlooking the Old Port, prepares the most traditional version, while high-end L'Épuisette, on a tiny cove outside the city center, serves a more modern interpretation. The hip Café des Épices, near the Old Port, and the Bistrot d'Édouard, with its updated Mediterranean menu, cater to a growing professional class, helping to turn Marseilles into an emerging gastronomic destination.

For centuries, artists have been drawn to the light in this part of France, particularly to the unspoiled beauty of nearby Cassis, one of the prettiest coastal towns in Provence and perhaps on the Riviera (see p. 128). Surrounding vineyards produce a respected straw-white blanc de blanc; neighboring Bandol makes a rare orange rosé, its hue obtained from 8 months of aging. (Oddly, the black currant liqueur called cassis comes from Burgundy.)

Cassis is most famous for Les Calanques: dramatic white limestone cliffs with finger-shaped fjords and tableaux of sailboats, pristine beaches, and aquamarine waters. Hike the cliffs or take one of the twice-daily boat tours from the Cassis marina to visit several calanques, including the prettiest, the Calanque en Vau. The hotel Les Roches Blanches, a former private home built in 1887, with a panoramic dining room and an infinity pool, boasts a dramatic view of the port and Cap Canaille, the highest sea cliff in France.

The steep-sided inlets and coves that make up Les Calanques are now part of France's newest national park.

WHERE: Marseilles is 117 miles/189 km west of Nice. **MIRAMAR:** Tel 33/4-91-911040; www.bouillabaisse.com. *Cost:* dinner $138. **L'ÉPUISETTE:** Tel 33/4-91-521782; www.l-epuissette.com. *Cost:* dinner $125. **CAFÉ DES ÉPICES:** Tel 33/4-91-912269; www.cafedesepices.com. *Cost:* dinner $50. **BISTROT D'ÉDOUARD:** Tel 33/4-91-711652. *Cost:* dinner $45. **LES ROCHES BLANCHES:** Tel 33/4-42-010930; www.roches-blanches-cassis.com. *Cost:* from $240. **BEST TIMES:** May–Oct for pleasant weather; mid-Jun–early Jul for the Festivale de Marseilles.

A Village Perched at the Grand Canyon of France

MOUSTIERS AND LES GORGES DU VERDON

Provence-Alpes-Côte d'Azur, France

A 90-minute drive northwest of Nice along twisting mountain roads leads you to the medieval village of Moustiers-Ste-Marie, high on a limestone cliff at the western entrance of the dramatic Verdon gorge. A fast-moving stream divides the village in two—the sound of rushing waters give Moustiers an Alpine village feel.

Moustiers has been a center for *faience* (earthenware) since the 17th century, and today its narrow streets are lined with pottery shops. Escape the summer crowds with a steep climb to the 12th-century cliff-top church Notre-Dame-de-Beauvoir for beautiful vistas of the village, the Maire valley, and glacier-blue waters in the gorge below. Suspended above town from a long chain between two cliffs is a mysterious star—put there, according to legend, by a knight returning home from the Crusades.

At the base of the village is La Bastide de Moustiers, one of France's most special inns, a gourmet retreat in a former master potter's house and owned by legendary French chef Alain Ducasse. Or, stay in the charming centrally located La Bouscatière, a family-run bed-and-breakfast built into the rock with a fine restaurant and views of the town's waterfall.

One of the most spectacular natural sights in France is the Gorges du Verdon, considered Europe's Grand Canyon and a favorite spot for rock-climbing and hiking, rafting and kayaking. Use Castellane, Bauduen, or Ste-Croix-du-Verdon as a center for boating; for hiking, take the 9-mile Martell trail, a popular 9- to 12-hour route with sensational views. Windshield tourists can enjoy it all on a drive around the rim of the gorges on the Route des Cretes.

WHERE: 93 miles/150 km northwest of Nice. **LA BASTIDE DE MOUSTIERS:** Tel 33/4-92-70-47-47; www.bastide-moustiers.com. *Cost:* from $275; dinner $80. **LA BOUSCATIÈRE:** Tel 33/4-92-74-67-67; www.labouscatiere.com. *Cost:* $185; dinner $45. **BEST TIMES:** Apr–Jun and Sep–Oct to avoid crowds and for outdoor sports and hiking.

Artistic Havens in the Hills of Provence

ST-PAUL-DE-VENCE AND VENCE

Provence-Alpes-Côte d'Azur, France

The walled medieval village of St-Paul-de-Vence is a pretty, car-free hill town overlooking rugged hills and valleys high in the backcountry above Cannes (see p. 127). Its pleasures—ramparts, charming narrow streets, rich smells of rosemary, lavender, and pine—endure even when throngs ascend in high season.

St-Paul was a magnet for artists such as Picasso, Braque, Matisse, Chagall, Dubuffet, and Léger in the 1920s, who would gather at the Colombe d'Or. Today the walls of this eclectic hotel and restaurant are lined with their art. Sit by the pool, next to a tiled mural by Braque or a Calder sculpture, or enjoy Provençal dishes in the leafy courtyard decorated with a Léger mural. The Hôtel Le Saint-Paul sits close by, an enticing stylish hideaway in a converted 16th-century bourgeois home, with terraces overlooking the valley and a restaurant that takes its food seriously.

Art by the masters who lived or worked here is beautifully showcased in the impressive galleries and gardens of the Fondation Maeght. Opened in 1964, it's considered the richest collection of 20th-century art of any private museum in Europe: Its 40,000 works include more than 50 sculptures by Giacometti, 150 pieces by Miró, and art by Kandinsky, Calder, Matisse, and many others.

The unpretentious village of Vence, with one of the best outdoor markets in the region, was also an artists' haven—Marc Chagall, who lived here from 1950 until his death in 1985, produced a beautiful mosaic in Vence's 11th-century cathedral. Matisse created what he felt was his masterpiece in helping design and decorate the Chapelle du Rosaire (known as the Matisse Chapel), considered the greatest ensemble artwork of the 20th century.

Casual luxury and top-flight cuisine reign at the serene Château St-Martin, a stately retreat on the site of a 12th-century crusaders' fortress with a panoramic terrace and views of the Mediterranean. Gentler prices can be found at Auberge des Seigneurs, in the center of Vence. It has six bright, airy rooms and a popular restaurant specializing in delicious spit-roasted meats.

WHERE: 10 miles/16 km northwest of Cannes. **LA COLOMBE D'OR:** Tel 33/4-93-328002; www.la-colombe-dor.com. *Cost:* from $350 (off-peak), from $455 (peak); dinner $75. **HÔTEL LE SAINT-PAUL:** Tel 33/4-93-326525; www.lesaintpaul.com. *Cost:* from $350 (off-peak), from $550 (peak). **Fondation Maeght:** Tel 33/4-93-328163; www.fondation-maeght.com. **Château St-Martin:** Tel 33/4-93-580202; www.chateau-st-martin.com. *Cost:* from $345 (off-peak), from $565 (peak). **Auberge des Seigneurs:** Tel 33/4-93-580424; www.auberge-seigneurs.com. *Cost:* from $125; dinner $50. **Best times:** May–Oct; Jul–Aug for Nuits de la Courtine outdoor music and theater festival in St-Paul.

A Beautiful Diva on the Sea

Vieux Nice

Provence-Alpes-Côte d'Azur, France

On balmy summer nights, the warren of medieval streets of Vieux Nice and its long pedestrian thoroughfare, the Cours Saleya, are abuzz with a mix of young and old, locals and tourists. Although this is the largest city on the Riviera (see p. 128), Vieux Nice (Old Nice) has a small-town ambience. The main food and flower market evokes the colors and scents of the Provençal countryside just outside town. Nibble on *socca,* the grilled chickpea snack unique to Nice, at Chez René Socca, or choose from 50 flavors of gelato at Fenocchio. Two of the Old Town's most charming restaurants are tiny, casual Merenda and homey Acchiardo, whose hearty dishes featuring fish, tomatoes, garlic, and olives exemplify Niçoise cuisine. The only hotel in the heart of Old Town, the rustic Villa La Tour, is a modest but pleasant choice with city views from its rooftop garden.

Food aficionados seeking upscale dining head to the acclaimed Le Chantecler in the Hôtel Negresco, an elegant Italianate building west of Vieux Nice that dominates the 4-mile-long seafront Promenade des Anglais. Built in 1912 when Nice was Europe's most fashionable winter retreat, the Negresco is one of the Riviera's landmark hotels. Also standing proud on the fabled boulevard, the Palais de la Mediterranée underwent a major interior renovation by the Taittinger Champagne family in 2004 while keeping the Art Deco exterior intact.

For a special escape from Nice, make the 7-mile drive north to the dramatic medieval village of Èze, the highest of Provence's *villages perchés* (perched villages). Lunch and dinner at the formal Château de la Chèvre d'Or is served in the hotel's glass-encased restaurant, with sensational views of the Mediterranean 1,400 feet below. Another contender for an overnight stay is the more intimate and relaxed Château Eza, former residence of Sweden's Prince William, with dining on the open-air terrace.

Where: 19 miles/31 km west of Cannes. **Merenda:** no phone; to make a reservation, stop by 4 rue Terrasse. *Cost:* dinner $80. **L'Acchiardo:** Tel 33/4-93-855116. *Cost:* dinner $40. **Villa La Tour:** Tel 33/4-93-800815; www.villa-la-tour.com. *Cost:* from $75. **Hôtel Negresco:** Tel 33/4-93-166400; in the U.S., 800-745-8883; www.hotel-negresco-nice.com. *Cost:* from $350; dinner at Le Chantecler $130. **Palais de la Mediterranée:** Tel 33/4-92-147700; in the U.S., 800-888-4747; palais.concorde-hotels.com. *Cost:* from $315 (off-peak), from $495 (peak). **Château de la Chèvre d'Or:** Tel 33/4-92-106666; www.chevredor.com. *Cost:* from $440; dinner $180. **Château Eza:** Tel 33/4-93-411224; www.chateaueza.com. *Cost:* from $325 (off-peak), from $560 (peak); dinner $150. **Best times:** Feb or Mar for Carnival; late Jul for Festival de Jazz.

Excellent Wines and Inspired Cuisine

Beaujolais and The Rhône Valley

Rhône-Alpes and Provence-Alpes-Côte d'Azur, France

Scenic and unpretentious, Beaujolais is France's least crowded wine region. Nearly 100 charming wine-producing villages are set among the country's highest concentration of vineyards. Half the annual yield of 160 million bottles bears the Beaujolais AOC label, but experts laud all 12 appellations here—including Fleurie, Brouilly, Morgan, and Chiroubles—for the quality and value of their light-bodied, fruity reds, though the craze for Beaujolais nouveau is waning from overexposure and poor vintages. Many of the region's wineries line the RN6 roadway from Mâcon to Villefranche-sur-Mer.

Tourists flock to the medieval hilltop village of Pérouges, whose historic inn, the Hostellerie de Pérouges, overlooks a pretty cobbled square. For more modern-day luxury cross the drawbridge of the meticulously renovated 13th-century Château de Bagnols to a world of opulent fabrics, Renaissance-inspired frescoes, and romantic four-poster beds. Head to Vonnas, near Bourg-en-Bresse, where esteemed chef Georges Blanc holds court; his antiques-laden "traditional-nouvelle" restaurant (where the local Bresse chicken is a specialty) maintains a cellar of more than 130,000 bottles.

The Rhône Valley begins at Lyon (see p. 137), where the Rhône and Saône rivers join. This is the nation's second largest wine-growing region and also its oldest: Romans planted vines 2,000 years ago. Along the northern valley's mountainous riverbanks, vineyards of mostly syrah grapes climb steep hills for use in such wines as Crozes-Hermitage and St-Joseph. Below Valence, toward Avignon (see p. 125) in the southern Rhône Valley, lavender fields and olive, almond, and pear orchards share the gently sloping hillsides with a marvelous variety of red and white grapes, used in blends such as the renowned red of Châteauneuf-du-Pape.

In Valence, sample the ultimate French cooking at Restaurant Pic, overseen by Anne-Sophie Pic, the third generation of a family that raised traditional cuisine to a gastronomic art form. You'll dine in a rich, contemporary setting with a less pricey bistro, Le 7, next door.

Another family gourmet empire lies south of Lyons in Roanne. La Maison Troisgros has topped the world's best-dining lists for decades. Michel, son of renowned chef Pierre Troisgros, maintains the family legacy of culinary excellence, serving technically perfect dishes in hushed, minimalist surroundings.

Where: Mâcon is 209 miles/336 km south of Paris. **L'Hostellerie de Pérouges:** Tel 33/4-74-610088; www.hostelleriedeperouges.com. *Cost:* from $175. **Château de Bagnols:** Tel 33/4-74-714000; in the U.S., 800-735-2478; www.chateaudebagnols.co.uk. *Cost:* from $335 (off-peak), $680 (peak). **Georges Blanc:** Tel 33/4-74-509090; in the U.S., 800-735-2478; www.georgesblanc.com. *Cost:* from $255; dinner $235. **Pic:** Tel 33/4-75-441532; in the U.S., 800-735-2478; www.pic-valence.fr. *Cost:* rooms from $415; restaurant prix-fixe dinner $130, bistro dinner $40. **Maison Troisgros:** Tel 33/4-77-716697; www.troisgros.fr. *Cost:* dinner $255. **Best time:** Sep for grape harvest.

Year-Round Playground and Top-of-the-World Views

THE FRENCH ALPS

Chamonix, Megève, and Courchevel, Rhône-Alpes, France

Dominated by 15,761-foot Mont Blanc, the highest mountain in Western Europe, the French Alps and their legendary ski resorts are unsurpassed in Europe. Chamonix is nestled in the center of a 14-mile-long valley at the juncture of France, Italy, and Switzerland, and was the site of the first Winter Olympic Games in 1924. Skiing here can be a challenge even for the best with dramatic vertical drops and Vallée Blanche, at 14 miles the longest and most rugged off-piste ski run in Europe. In the center of town, stay at Auberge du Manoir, a friendly family-run hotel with a spare, country décor, or just outside of town at the refined Hotel Hameau Albert I, where you can choose between the century-old main house and the cluster of rustic guesthouses.

Cable car rides to Aiguille du Midi, part of the Mont Blanc massif, climb to heights of over 12,000 feet.

For unmatched panoramic views, take the cable car to Aiguille du Midi or in summer months the drive along the 460-mile Route des Grandes Alpes from Evian to Nice (see p. 133). Or strap on your boots—two of Europe's most popular hikes leave from here: the Haute Route, a 2-week, 100-mile trek to Zermatt, Switzerland (see p. 281), and the Tour de Mont Blanc, a spectacular 8-day round-trip through France, Italy, and Switzerland.

Chic Megève is perhaps the most romantic and charming of the resorts with its storybook village and horse-drawn carriages. It attracts royalty, old money, and celebrities with one of Europe's best ski schools, 47 miles of cross-country trails, and access to nearly 300 miles of skiable terrain. Snowfall at this lower-altitude resort can be unreliable, but many come simply to shop or take in the well-known dining and social scene. They check into the Hotel Les Fermes de Marie, a charming enclave of small Alpine buildings, tastefully reconstructed as guest chalets, or its sister property Hotel au Coin du Feu. Linger over lunch next to the slopes with the mink-clad set at L'Alpette, a Megève institution since 1935, or enjoy one of the most praise-worthy meals in town at the Flocons de Sel restaurant.

Courchevel is the most exclusive and expensive of the resorts, host to some events of the 1992 Winter Olympics and one of the highest, best-equipped, and most immaculately groomed ski locations in the French Alps. The four villages making up Courchevel sit at different altitudes at the confluence of three Alpine valleys, Les Trois Vallées. The varied terrain, hundreds of trails, and extensive network of lifts is great for all levels and one of the best ski establishments anywhere. For comfort in high style, stay at La Sivolière, a chalet-style hotel built in the '70s, tastefully renovated and tucked away near a small forest close to the slopes.

Where: Chamonix is 293 miles/417 km southeast of Paris. **Auberge du Manoir:** Tel 33/4-50-53-10-77; www.absolument-montblanc.com. *Cost:* from $165. **Hotel Hameau Albert I:** Tel 33/4-50-53-05-09; www.hameaualbert.fr. *Cost:* from $210. **How:** U.S.-based Wilderness Travel offers a 13-day hike of the Haute Route and an 8-day Tour du Mont Blanc. Tel 800-368-2794 or 510-558-2488; www.wildernesstravel.com. *Cost:* Haute Route from $4,995; Tour du Mont Blanc from $3,695. *When:* Jun–Sep. **Fermes de Marie:** Tel 33/4-57-747474; www.fermesdemarie.com. *Cost:* from $195 (off-peak), $670 (peak). **Hotel au Coin du Feu:** Tel 33/4-50-210495; www.coindufeu.com. *Cost:* from $275. **L'Alpette:** Tel 33/4-50-210369; www.alpette-megeve.com. *Cost:* lunch $50. **Flocons de Sel:** Tel 33/4-50-214999; www.floconsdesel.com. *Cost:* dinner $140. **La Sivolière:** Tel 33/4-79-080833; www.hotel-la-sivoliere.com. *Cost:* from $560.

A Jewel in the French Alps

Lac d'Annecy

Rhône-Alpes, France

On the north shore of the pristine Lac d'Annecy sits the picturesque Alpine resort of Annecy, an unspoiled medieval and Renaissance treasure in a region that led Impressionist painter Paul Cézanne to exclaim: "What a superb vestige of times past!"

Today the town is lovingly preserved and welcomes tourists who come to see this "Venice of the Alps." Snow-capped mountains and forests stand in the distance, while handsome churches, flower-bedecked quayside town houses, and arched pedestrian bridges are reflected in the crystal-clean canals fed by the Thiou River. Wander the streets in Vielle Ville (Old City), lined with half-timbered houses, restaurants, and shops, and visit the hulking 12th-century fort and palace, the Palais de l'Isle, sitting in the middle of a canal—this visual symbol of Annecy has been a mint, law courts, and a prison over the years. Nearby the small Hotel du Palais de l'Isle has a contemporary feel just steps away from the canal.

Ten square miles in area, Lake Annecy is known as a playground for wind-surfing, kayaking, and swimming; a boat tour or a drive along its shores, lined with pretty villages and towns, is a must. Stop at the charming port of Talloires south of Annecy, where you'll find a beacon in the French gastronomic world, the Auberge du Père Bise. A hotel-restaurant in a 1901 chalet decorated in an Art Deco style, it has been family-run for generations, and today is headed by Sophie Bise, one of France's most esteemed female chefs. The nearby grand Hotel de l'Abbaye de Talloires, once a Benedictine abbey, has been welcoming visitors since the French Revolution and is decorated in Empire style, with rich tapestries and high beamed ceilings.

Where: 20 miles/34 km west of Geneva. **Hotel du Palais:** Tel 33/4-50-458687. www.palaisannecy.com. *Cost:* from $150. **Père Bise:** Tel 33/4-50-607201; in the U.S., tel 800-735-2478; www.perebise.com. *Cost:* from $375; dinner $160. *When:* mid-Feb–mid-Dec. **L'Abbaye de Talloires:** Tel 33/4-50-607733; www.abbaye-talloires.com. *Cost:* from $275. **Best times:** antiques market on last Sat of every month; early Aug for fireworks display celebrating the lake; mid-Aug for classical music festival.

Bouchons, Brasseries, and Bocuse

Lyon's Food Scene

Lyon, Rhône-Alpes, France

Lyon sits between Paris and the Mediterranean near the Burgundy and Beaujolais regions with the Alps and Italy not far away—a location that helps explain why it has more restaurants per square mile (more than 2,000 in all) than any other European city except Paris.

Lyon's markets burst with fresh produce.

The silk trade flourished here in the 15th and 16th centuries and left behind Europe's largest collection of Renaissance architecture in the historic quarter called Vieux Lyon (Old Lyons), where covered passageways (*traboules*) linked buildings and courtyards and were used as shortcuts by tradesmen carrying valuable fabrics. Today it is a passion for food, not textiles, that defines France's third largest city, and dozens of bustling food markets fill the city, none greater than Les Halles de Lyon.

A peninsula between the Saône and Rhône rivers, the Presqu'ile is the city's more modern core, filled with 19th-century architecture, museums, fashionable shops, the city opera house, and a handful of small *bouchons*—traditional, homey brasseries that once dished up hearty fare for tradesmen and workers. The archetypal Café des Fédérations offers good charcuterie dishes and sawdust on the floor. Paying homage to the bouchon tradition, renowned chef Jean-Paul Lacombe transformed his award-winning Léon de Lyon restaurant into the more relaxed Brasserie Léon de Lyon.

The heavy-handed approach to cooking in France was given a makeover in the mid-1970s by native son Paul Bocuse, who changed the culinary tradition forever with his *nouvelle cuisine*. You'll find a timeless menu featuring this lighter, fresher fare at his Restaurant Paul Bocuse on the outskirts of Lyon, still a point of pilgrimage for those happy to pay handsomely for a stroll down memory lane. Now in his 80s, the superstar chef remains at the heart of the local scene, having opened a number of casual eating spots in the city, including the Brasseries le Nord, le Sud, de l'Est, and de l'Ouest.

Stay within strolling distance of everything at the Cours des Loges hotel in the heart of Vieux Lyon, built around an elegantly restored *traboule*. Or save your euros for fabulous dining and unpack at the cleverly furnished College Hotel on the edge of the quarter. In the hills outside of town, the Villa Florentine promises romance and beautiful views of the city.

Where: 288 miles/463 km south of Paris. **Café des Fédérations:** Tel 33/4-78-282600; www.lesfedeslyon.com. *Cost:* dinner $25. **Brasserie Léon de Lyon:** Tel 33/4-72-10-11-12; www.bistrotdescuisiniers.com. *Cost:* dinner $50. **Restaurant Paul Bocuse:** Tel 33/4-72-42-90-90; www.bocuse.fr. *Cost:* dinner $170. **Cours des Loges:** Tel 33/4-72-774444; www.courdesloges.com *Cost:* from $340. **College Hotel:** Tel 33/4-72-100505; www.college-hotel.com. *Cost:* from $175. **Villa Florentine:** Tel 33/4-72-565656; www.villaflorentine.com. *Cost:* from $365. **Best times:** Jun–Aug for the Nuits de Fourvière music festival; early Dec for the Festival of Lights.

A Belle Époque Spa and Picture-Book Woodland

Baden-Baden and the Black Forest

Baden-Württemberg, Germany

"I fully believe I left my rheumatism in Baden-Baden," wrote Mark Twain. "Baden-Baden is welcome to it." This town at the northern edge of the dense Black Forest has been the "summer capital of Europe" since the mid-19th century, when Queen Victoria and Napoleon III basked in its curative springs. Dignified old-world glory still abounds in the elegant gilt-and-stucco casino, in the pastel houses where high society resided, and in the shaded Lichtentaler Allee, a lushly landscaped promenade along the Oos River. An outstanding newcomer to the Allee is Museum Frieder Burda, a snow-white Richard Meier–designed showcase for modern and contemporary art. But "taking the waters" is still the primary draw, whether you soak in the palatial (suits-on) Caracalla baths or the unisex (suits-off) Friedrichsbad.

Overlooking the Oos River is one of Europe's few remaining grand spa hotels, the storied Brenners Park, built in 1872. The columns and Pompeiian-style frescoed walls of its glass-enclosed *Schwimmbad* (swimming pool) call to mind the ancient Roman general Caracalla, whose legionnaires first discovered the thermal springs in the 3rd century. For an elegant, relaxed alternative, the family-run Der Kleine Prinz (The Little Prince) offers luxuriously appointed guest rooms in the heart of town.

Leaving your aches and pains behind, go deeper into this fabled corner of Germany along the classic Schwartzwald Hochstrasse (Black Forest Crest Road), a 40-mile meander through natural beauty from Baden-Baden southeast to Freudenstadt. Despite its dense, lofty fir trees, the nearly 3,000-square-mile Black Forest boasts sunny charm at every turn and more than 14,000 miles of posted hike-and-bike trails.

Beautifully situated in Baiersbronn, in a lush green valley 31 miles southeast of Baden-Baden, is the grand dame Hotel Traube Tonbach, featuring a first-class spa and sporting facilities. The French-influenced menu at its famous Die Schwarzwaldstube reflects the refined style of long-time head chef Harald Wohlfahrt. South of Titisee, in Häusern, the delightful Schwarzwald Adler, in the same family for six generations, offers bright, tasteful rooms and an excellent restaurant serving such delicious regional specialties as grilled Black Forest trout and homemade spätzle. In warm weather, dine in the charming garden.

Where: 112 miles/180 km south of Frankfurt. **Visitor info:** www.baden-baden.de. **Museum Frieder Burda:** Tel 49/7221-398-980; www.museum-frieder-burda.de. **Brenners Park-Hotel:** Tel 49/7221-9000; in the U.S., 800-223-6800; www.brenners.com. *Cost:* from $480. **Der Kleine Prinz:** Tel 49/7221-346-600; www.derkleineprinz.de. *Cost:* from $280. **Hotel Traube Tonbach:** Tel 49/7442-4920; www.traube-tonbach.com. *Cost:* from $250; prix-fixe 5-course dinner at Die Schwarzwaldstube $174. **Schwarzwald Adler:** Tel 49/7672-4170; www.adler-schwarzwald.de. *Cost:* from $175; dinner $60. **Best times:** Apr–Oct for fine weather; May–Jun for Whitsun Festival in Baden-Baden.

Time Travel in the Neckar Valley

Heidelberg's Castle

Heidelberg, Baden-Württemberg, Germany

In a glorious hilltop setting of woodland and terraced gardens stands Heidelberg's magnificent, crumbling Schloss, possibly the country's most famous castle. Built over three centuries beginning in 1400, the red sandstone castle was sacked by Louis XIV's troops in 1689. Ever since, painters and poets have fallen under the romantic ruin's spell.

For a vision of the castle to cherish, stroll along the Philosophenweg (Philosopher's Walk), a hillside wooded path on the north bank of the Neckar River, where Goethe and Hegel wandered. Nestled on a historic side street off the Philosopher's Walk is Die Hirschgasse. Dating back to 1472, the hotel originated as a tavern for local university students (a tipsy Otto von Bismarck carved his name into one of the tables). The elite University of Heidelberg was founded in 1386, making it Germany's oldest, and since 1703 its students and many travelers have been lured to Zum Roten Ochsen tavern for beer, bratwurst, and singing. A fresh option for design-conscious travelers is the centrally located Heidelberg Suites, a 19th-century villa-residence reinterpreted as a Neoclassical-inspired sanctuary.

Heidelberg at Christmas is especially magical, when one of Germany's best holiday markets enchants the old quarter. Aromas of almond and cinnamon waft around more than 100 stands.

East of Heidelberg, the Neckar River forms a scenic, steep-sided valley that meanders past some of Germany's most famous vineyards. Follow the river upstream by bike or boat, or along the winding Castle Road, which unfolds for 620 miles from Mannheim to Prague.

Where: 55 miles/88 km south of Frankfurt. **Visitor info:** www.heidelberg-marketing.de. **Schloss Heidelberg:** Tel 49/6221-538-431; www.schloss-heidelberg.de. **Die Hirschgasse:** Tel 49/6221-4540; www.hirschgasse.de. *Cost:* from $230 (off-peak), from $295 (peak). **Heidelberg Suites:** Tel 49/6221-655-650; www.heidelbergsuites.de. *Cost:* from $280. **Castle Road:** www.burgenstrasse.de. **Best times:** late Mar–Apr for Spring Festival; 1st Sat of Jun and Sep and 2nd Sat of Jul for fireworks during Castle Illuminations; late Jun–Aug for Castle Festival; late Nov–Dec for Christmas markets.

A Beer Drinkers' Eden amid Architectural Treasures

Bamberg

Bavaria, Germany

Set like Rome on seven hills and justly known as one of the most beautiful small towns in all of Europe, this Franconian jewel is inextricably linked to a rich history as capital of the Holy Roman Empire under Heinrich II, the town's most famous son. More than 2,000 well-preserved buildings showcase architecture of all periods within a city that is by no means a static museum piece. Bamberg exudes a lively student vibe and is a joy to visit for its history, antiques stores, and breweries: Nine *Brauereien* produce close to 50 varieties of beer—even Munich can't match that—and each has its own personality. Schlenkerla Tavern is a must for the famous smoky Rauchbier, which pairs perfectly with the regional classic dish, *Schäufele* (crispy pork shoulder with dumplings and sauerkraut).

The four-towered Kaiserdom cathedral, built under Heinrich II and the site of his coronation in 1012, bears testimony to Bamberg's affluence and ecclesiastical power and is famous for its interior's elaborate sculptural decoration. The wonderfully half-timbered, frescoed Altes Rathaus (Old Town Hall), surely one of Europe's most photographed, occupies its own little island in the middle of the Regnitz River. Across the river is picturesque Kleine Venedig (Little Venice), where red geraniums spill from flower boxes on half-timbered cottages.

The spacious, sloping Domplatz square is a textbook illustration of the town's architectural evolution from Romanesque to Gothic, and Renaissance to Baroque. For pure atmosphere and an unmatched location by the dam's murmuring falls, the Hotel St. Nepomuk wins out. Built as a mill in 1410, it has cozy rooms overlooking the river and the Rathaus. The most romantic choice in the Old Town might be Hotel-Weinhaus Messerschmitt, dating from 1422 and owned by the same family since 1832. A charming restaurant serves regional specialties, and a recent addition complements the antiques-filled original with 50 modern guest rooms.

Altes Rathaus sits in the middle of the Regnitz River, between the city's former religious and secular sections.

WHERE: 143 miles/230 km northwest of Munich. **VISITOR INFO:** www.bamberg.info. **SCHLENKERLA TAVERN:** 49/951-56050; www.schlenkerla.de. **HOTEL ST. NEPOMUK:** Tel 49/951-98420; www.hotel-nepomuk.de. *Cost:* from $200. **HOTEL-WEINHAUS MESSERSCHMITT:** Tel 49/951-297-800; www.hotel-messerschmitt.de. *Cost:* from $225. **BEST TIMES:** May–Sep for beer cellars; late Nov–Dec for Christmas markets and the Nativity Trail.

A Charmed Time of Year

CHRISTKINDLMARKT

Bavaria, Germany

During Advent season, towns all over Germany turn into three-dimensional Christmas cards evoking the spirit of Christmas past. Originating at least 600 years ago in Germany and Austria, Christmas markets today are most prevalent in Bavaria and number more than 2,500 around the country, each showcasing regional specialties and traditions. With carolers and revelers strolling around snow-dusted squares, the scent of *glühwein* (hot mulled wine; literally, "glow wine") and baked apples fortifying crisp air, even the coldest Scrooge's heart would melt. The best markets feature the mouth-blown glass ornaments, hand-carved crèche figures, painted wooden nutcrackers, and candle-powered merry-go-rounds called Weihnachtspyramiden (Christmas pyramids) found in every German home. The challenge is deciding which will come home with you.

Perhaps most famous of all is Nuremberg's picturesque market (which competes with Dresden's for status as Germany's oldest), where 180 candlelit wooden stalls clustered around the Hauptmarkt (Central Market) vie for the gold Plum Person, first prize for most gorgeous display. Look for gingerbread houses, spice-infused ornaments, and *Zwetschgenmännle*, figurines made from dried plums, for which Nuremberg is justly famed. Convenient to the market and always decked out for the holidays is Hotel Elch, the oldest hotel in the city.

The Christkindlmarkt on Marienplatz in Munich is one of Germany's largest and most enjoyable, with hundreds of brightly garlanded stalls sprawled across the central square in the Old Town. Decked with twinkling lights, an enormous fir tree stands proudly before the Rathaus, the neo-Gothic town hall with a 43-bell carillon. Board the Christkindl Tram for a tour of some of the city's highlights. A short walk from Marienplatz is the historic, four-star Hotel Torbräu, which has been graciously run by the Kirchlechner family for more than a century.

Visitor info: *Nuremberg:* www.christkindlesmarkt.de; *Munich:* www.christkindlmarkt-muenchen.de. **When:** late Nov–Dec 24 for Christmas markets throughout Germany. **Hotel Elch:** Tel 49/911-249-2980; www.hotel-elch.com. *Cost:* from $135. **Hotel Torbräu:** Tel 49/89-24-2340; www.torbraeu.de. *Cost:* from $270.

Where Oktoberfest Happens All Year Long

Germany's Beer Culture

Bavaria, Germany

To many, Germany plus beer equals Oktoberfest. But that's only part of the equation, and those who arrive outside of festival time won't go thirsty or bored. Bavaria boasts more than one-sixth of the world's breweries, including Erdinger (in Erding) and Paulaner (in Munich), where you can tour the facilities and sample wheat beers at the source. Festivals, such as Fasching (Germany's version of Carnival) and Starkbierzeit (celebrating Bavarian culture and the potent doppelbock brew), warm up the winter months. Come April, brew flows at Munich's Volksfest, a mini-carnival, and the city's outdoor beer gardens spring to life. Since 1589, the Hofbräuhaus am Platzl has been Munich's biggest and most beloved beerhouse—a tourist destination that is eternal Oktoberfest.

Small accordions called melodeons help keep the spirits high.

The real Oktoberfest is Munich's annual last hurrah to *biergarten* season—a 16-day, quintessentially Bavarian festival celebrated in the company of boisterous hard-partying strangers from around the world. Oktoberfest central is the Theresienwiese (the meadow named after Princess Theresa, whose betrothal to Crown

Prince Ludwig in 1810 provided the reason for the first-ever October celebration), where 12 massive tents—some holding up to 6,000 stein-hoisting drinkers—are erected months in advance. The 2-week festival opens with a colorful, 7,000-strong parade of steed-drawn beer wagons followed by 13 big brass bands and hundreds of Oktoberfest waitresses in traditional dirndls. The fairgrounds are so huge they become a city of their own, filled with refreshment stands, sideshows, gut-churning thrill rides, and merry-go-rounds. To the sound of unending oompah music, some 6 million people consume 5 million liters of "Wies'n" beer brewed especially for the annual festival, along with 400,000 sausages and 600,000 chickens.

No visit to Munich is complete without a stop at two gastronomic institutions for provisions to go with all that brew: Dallmayr, the seriously grand purveyor of gourmet food since 1700, and 200-year-old Viktualienmarkt, the Old Town's 150-stall farmers market and beer garden. Overlooking the bustling open-air market is the new Louis Hotel, where 72 alpine-chic guest rooms are cozy but cool.

Visitor info: www.muenchen-tourist.de. **Erdinger Brewery:** Tel 49/81-224-09421; www.erdinger.de. **Paulaner Brewery:** Tel 49/89-480-05871; www.paulaner.de. **Hofbräuhaus am Platzl:** Tel 49/89-2901-3610; www.hofbraeuhaus.de. **Louis Hotel:** Tel 49/89-411-19080; www.louis-hotel.com. *Cost:* from $280 (off-peak), from $400 (peak). **Best times:** late Feb or early Mar for Fasching; mid-Mar for Starkbierzeit; late Apr for Volksfest; mid-Sep–early Oct for Oktoberfest.

Bavarian Beauties

Lake Constance and the Alpine Road

Bavaria, Germany

The northern shore of the Bodensee (Lake Constance), Bavaria's largest lake, is lined with a string of pretty resorts. But to truly appreciate the lake's beauty, board any of the countless ferries that crisscross the waters to Austria and Switzerland on the opposite shore and to islands in between. The belle of the Bodensee is tiny Mainau, an island paradise of riotous flowers (including more than 1,000 varieties of roses) and exotic vegetation that evoke balmy images of the Mediterranean. The island's Baroque castle was taken over in 1853 by the Grand Duke of Baden, who began introducing rare plants from his travels abroad.

The medieval core of Konstanz, the lake's largest and liveliest town, is a sheer delight. A 13th-century cloistered monastery is now the Steigenberger Inselhotel, set on its own island tethered to town by a causeway.

From the eastern shore, the ancient Alpenstrasse (Alpine Road) winds for 300 view-filled miles along the Bavarian Alps, a spectacular natural border between Germany and Austria. It meanders past ancient castles, quaint chalet-inns, and mountaintop villages with houses painted in a decorative style the Bavarians call Lüftlmalerei.

The Alpenstrasse leads to the peaceful town of Oberammergau, which comes alive every 10 years to honor a vow made in 1633.

The church of St. Bartholomä can only be reached by sailing Lake Königssee or by trekking the surrounding Watzmann Mountain.

After the townspeople were spared from a plague that devastated much of Europe, they promised to reenact the life of Christ once every decade, forever. (Start planning now for the 2020 performance.) Bavaria's other major cultural event, the Wagner Festival, is yearly (and some of the principal performances have years-long waiting lists). It's held every summer in Bayreuth, the composer's hometown.

The Alpine Road continues south through Garmisch, host of the 1936 Winter Olympics and home to the Zugspitze, Germany's highest mountain at 9,731 feet.

Bavaria has no shortage of castles, and fairy tales come to life in King Ludwig II's spectacular creations. His sumptuous Schloss Herrenchiemsee stands fantastically on its own island, one of three in the middle of the beautiful Chiemsee. After a trip to France, the young king created the castle in 1885 to mimic Versailles, and its Hall of Mirrors is reproduced to scale here, overlooking Ludwig's gardens. There's magic of another kind in nearby Aschau, an hour southeast of Munich, where one of Germany's finest chefs presides in his namesake restaurant, Residenz Heinz Winkler, housed in a charming 600-year-old coach inn.

There could be no greater finale at the end of the Alpine Road than the beautiful Königssee (King's Lake) at the Austrian border—and the best way to see it is by quiet electric boat. Don't miss the pint-size pilgrimage church of St. Bartholomä, which is wedged into a small cove. It was originally constructed in the 11th century and rebuilt some 600 years later. This gorgeous little corner of Germany is also the centerpiece of the stunning Berchtesgaden National Park, site of Hitler's infamous Eagle's Nest lodge.

WHERE: Konstanz is 141 miles/227 km southwest of Munich. **STEIGENBERGER INSELHOTEL:** Tel 49/7531-1250; www.konstanz.steigenberger.de. *Cost:* from $250 (off-peak), from $350 (peak). **WAGNER FESTIVAL:** Tel 49/921-78780; www.bayreuther-festspiele.de. *When:* 4 weeks in late Jul–Aug. **RESIDENZ HEINZ WINKLER:** Tel 49/8052-17990; www.residenz-heinz-winkler.de. *Cost:* from $340; prix-fixe dinner $130. **BEST TIMES:** late Apr–Jun for Konstanz's flower displays; May–Jun or Sep for hiking.

Treasures Abound, Innovations Astound

MUNICH'S PINAKOTHEKS AND THE DEUTSCHES MUSEUM

Munich, Bavaria, Germany

Munich's status as Germany's "secret capital" is largely due to its world-class museums, many of them clustered around the Kunstareal (Art District). There are very few cities that can boast so much art of the highest quality in such a small area.

Rivaling the Louvre (see p. 114) for high-style display, the Alte Pinakothek (Old Picture Gallery) features Old Masters and early northern European Renaissance masterworks in a collection that ranges from the 14th to the 18th centuries. You can marvel at young Leonardo da Vinci's *Virgin and Child* or Titian's *Crowning with Thorns,* as well as works by Memling, Brueghel, Hals, and Dürer (*The Four Apostles,* his final work, is a museum highlight). It has one of the world's largest concentrations (62 works) of the 17th-century Flemish painter Rubens: Van Dyck, his most distinguished student, is also extensively represented.

Across the street, the Neue Pinakothek (New Picture Gallery) picks up in the 18th century where its sister museum leaves off. From Rococo and Classicism to Art Nouveau, the gallery features major works by Van Gogh, Cézanne, and Klimt, among others. Opened in 2002 to house 20th- and 21st-century art, the Pinakothek der Moderne (Modern Picture Gallery) showcases modern and contemporary works as well as sculpture, design, and architecture by such modern masters as Klee, Picasso, Warhol, and Twombly.

Built on an island in the middle of the Isar River, the Deutsches Museum is the world's oldest and most complete science and technology museum. Throughout 55 different departments—including musical instruments, aeronautics, photography, physics, and textiles—it's a hands-on extravaganza of do-it-yourself chemistry experiments, gears, and levers that make it as absorbing for kids as for adults. A full day can easily be spent taking in Germany's first submarine (built in 1906), the laboratory bench at which the atom was first split, dozens of automobiles, including the first Benz of 1886, and an eerily convincing replica of Spain's Altamira caves (see p. 254). Aeronautics is also a favorite department; its hangar-sized halls house pioneering planes, from the Wright Brothers' Type-A Standard to military aircraft from the 1940s.

Pinakotheks: www.pinakothek.de. **Alte Pinakothek:** Tel 49/89-23805-216. **Neue Pinakothek:** Tel 49/89-23805-195. **Pinakothek der Moderne:** Tel 49/89-23805-360. **Deutsches Museum:** Tel 49/89-21791; www.deutsches-museum.de.

Medieval Masterpiece on the Danube

Regensburg

Bavaria, Germany

Capital of Bavaria before Munich and one of the most beautiful medieval cities in Germany, Regensburg and much of eastern Bavaria has remained an insider's secret even for Germans. During the years of Communist control, this area near the Czech border was considered a veritable dead end, leaving the city stuck in the past. Much of the surviving architecture dating to its glory days between the 13th and 16th centuries (which moved Emperor Maximilian to say in 1517 that "Regensburg surpasses every German city with its outstanding and vast buildings") remains unchanged.

Regensburg's architecture is all original, unlike many German towns damaged by World War II air raids and reconstructed. Tourism authorities exaggerate little in listing no fewer than 1,300 buildings as being of historical interest. Regensburg is known as "the city of churches" for good reason, and the Dom St. Peter (housing what is likely to be the only extant statue of the Devil's grandmother) is held by many to be Germany's crowning example of the Gothic. It is famous for both its 14th-century stained-glass windows and its internationally renowned boys' choir, the Domspatzen (Cathedral Sparrows).

Situated at the northernmost navigable point of the Danube, the best sunset view of the river is from one of Regensburg's earliest existing structures, the 12th-century Steinerne Brücke (Old Stone Bridge), built with 16 graceful arches. At Historische Wurstküchl, the town's oldest restaurant, outdoor tables on the Danube provide communal seating-with-a-view for a simple meal of grilled sausages and locally brewed beer. Seek out the Rosenpalais for a culinary surprise: You can go casual at the bistro or head upstairs for a more sophisticated experience. For understated charm, choose from three Orphée hotels: Grand Hotel Orphée and restaurant, nearby Petit Hotel Orphée, or the Country Manor Orphée just across the stone bridge.

From Regensburg hop a boat on the Danube to Walhalla, the Parthenon-inspired marble temple built by King Ludwig I in 1842. Beethoven, Luther, and Einstein are among nearly 200 busts and tablets here, commemorating Germany's most illustrious men and women throughout 2,000 years of history.

WHERE: 76 miles/122 km northeast of Munich. **VISITOR INFO:** www.regensburg.de. **HISTORISCHE WURSTKÜCHL:** Tel 49/941-466-210; www.wurstkuchl.de. *Cost:* lunch $10. **ROSENPALAIS:** Tel 49/941-599-7579; www.rosenpalais.de. *Cost:* dinner $55. **HOTEL ORPHÉE:** Tel 49/941-596-020; www.hotel-orphee.de. *Cost:* from $150. **BEST TIMES:** May–Sep for weather; late Nov–Dec for Christmas market; Sun for the Domspatzen singing mass in the cathedral (when not touring).

A Historic Road and a Fairy-Tale Castle

THE ROMANTIC ROAD AND NEUSCHWANSTEIN CASTLE

Bavaria, Germany

Stretching nearly 200 miles from Würzburg southeast to Füssen, the Romantic Road (Romantische Strasse) is as enjoyable for the dozens of medieval towns, villages, and castles it links as for the landscape of rivers, lakes, and dense forests in between.

Begin your journey in Würzburg, the hub of Franconia's wine region. The lovely Baroque city on the Main River is most visited for its 18th-century Residenz, one of Europe's most sumptuous palaces. Adorning the ceilings over the monumental vaulted staircase (the largest in the country) and in the already elaborate Throne Room are Giovanni Tiepolo's colorful frescoes, enhancing a space that is airy, opulent, and magical.

Sample local white wines in the Residenz's cozy cellar-tavern, then continue south to Rothenburg ob der Tauber (Red Castle on the Tauber), one of the best-preserved medieval towns in Europe. The crowds that flock here testify to the popularity of this walled town, where flowers spill from the window boxes of half-timbered houses leaning over cobblestone alleyways. The history and charm of Rothenburg are echoed in the world-renowned Hotel Eisenhut, where remnants of a 12th-century chapel can be found in the front lobby.

The next day, head to Dinkelsbühl, a less touristy version of Rothenburg surrounded by 10th-century walls. Be in Nördlingen in time to hear its town crier from high in the church tower, then continue on to Germany's best example of Rococo architecture, the gemlike Wieskirche, a petite church, standing in its own alpine meadow.

Begin or end your trip by touring Mad King Ludwig's two royal castles, Hohenschwangau and Neuschwanstein, which cap the southern end of the Romantic Road. Neuschwanstein is by far his most theatrical, created by the royal court's set designer rather than an architect. Set on an isolated rock ledge amid heart-stopping scenery, it is the turreted prototype that inspired the castle in Disney's *Sleeping Beauty*. Nearby Hohenschwangau was Ludwig's boyhood summer home, where he stayed while overseeing the work of Neuschwanstein. At the base of the road to Neuschwanstein, the luxurious Jägerhaus and modest Schlosshotel Lisl offer guest rooms with unobstructed views of the castles. At night, head to the terrace bar to see them spectacularly illuminated.

Soon after Neuschwanstein's costly completion, Mad King Ludwig was forced to abdicate his throne and mysteriously died.

WHERE: Würzburg is 74 miles/119 km southeast of Frankfurt; Füssen is 82 miles/132 km southwest of Munich. **VISITOR INFO:** www.romantischestrasse.de. **RESIDENZ:** Tel 49/9313-551712; www.wuerzburg.de. **HOTEL EISENHUT:** Tel 49/9861-7050; www.eisenhut.com. *Cost:* from $150; dinner $60. **NEUSCHWANSTEIN:** Tel 49/8362-93988; www.neuschwanstein.de. **SCHLOSSHOTEL LISL** and **JÄGERHAUS:** Tel 49/8362-887147; www.hohenschwangau.de. *Cost:* Schlosshotel Lisl from $150; Jägerhaus from $190. **BEST TIMES:** Apr–May, Sep–Nov to avoid traffic; late Nov–Dec for Christmas markets in most towns.

Wall Falls, Art Thrives

BERLIN'S MUSEUM SCENE

Berlin, Germany

The turn of the 21st century saw Berlin's inexhaustibly rich art collections shuffled, reorganized, and regrouped. Today, the city is once again firmly established as one of the world's premier cultural capitals. Of Berlin's array of more than 170 museums, the Gemäldegalerie's (Picture Gallery) unrivaled compilation is in a class all its own for the breadth and depth of its collection of European masterpieces from the 13th to the 18th centuries. No fewer than 20 Rembrandts make up one gallery alone.

Lovers of antiquities could spend days

on the Museumsinsel (Museum Island) in the middle of the River Spree, a cache of five museums whose lodestone is the Pergamonmuseum, built exclusively to house the colossal 2nd-century B.C. Pergamon Altar, a 40-foot-high colonnaded Greek temple, discovered in Turkey in 1864 and brought here in 1902. Reopened in 2009 with soaring new spaces and classical frescoes marked with bullets from World War II, the Neues Museum houses the Egyptian collection and the Museum of Prehistory and Early History. Its star attraction is the sublime bust of Nefertiti, created well over 3,000 years ago.

Berliners insist that their dynamic city is no longer all about die Mauer (the Wall), but its fragments reveal just how far the once-divided metropolis has come. Erected in 1961 and torn down in 1989, the Wall once measured 29 miles long and 13 feet high. Some protected sections have been left standing and designated as historic landmarks. Nearly a mile long, the East Side Gallery is the longest remaining stretch of the wall and the world's largest open-air gallery. Covering the dull concrete slabs are striking reminders of the former regime in more than 100 murals and graffiti, including images of Trabant cars, a symbol of the failed East Germany. The cluttered Mauer Museum (Museum of the Wall), a touristy mock-up of the former Checkpoint Charlie, is still fascinating for its tales of spectacular escapes and tragically failed attempts. Visit the more poignant Berlin Wall Memorial for the Chapel of Reconciliation, which commemorates the men and women shot while trying to escape into West Berlin; climb into the museum's watchtower to view the former "death strip." The adventurous can hike or bike the 100-mile-long Berlin Wall Trail, which traces the former East German border.

Ever since the Wall's dramatic fall, artists have been flocking to Berlin from all over the world and recharging the city's contemporary art scene. Though pop-up galleries and artistic hot spots shift regularly, the Mitte district (see p. 149) has an established presence. Add the exciting Hamburger Bahnhof contemporary art museum, housed in a brilliantly converted 19th-century railway station, and you will have barely scratched the surface of one of the world's most remarkable surveys of art in this 21st-century showcase city.

Gemäldegalerie am Kulturforum; Pergamonmuseum and **Neues Museum; Hamburger Bahnhof:** Tel 49/30-266-424242; www.smb.spk-berlin.de. **East Side Gallery:** www.eastsidegallery.com. **Museum of the Wall:** Tel 49/30-253-7250; www.mauermuseum.de. **Berlin Wall Memorial:** Tel 49/30-467-986666; www.berliner-mauer-gedenkstaette.de. **Best times:** Jun–early Aug for contemporary art Biennale; late Aug for Museums Night.

A Cityscape Transformed

Berlin's (Re)defining Architecture

Berlin, Germany

A vibrant, fascinating city more than eight centuries old, Berlin has been famous since the early 1900s for its experimental arts and architecture. World War II and the Cold War took their toll on the city (the capital of

Germany since 1991) and reminders of this past persist in several iconic structures. Erected in 1969, the 1,207-foot TV Turm (Tower) on Alexanderplatz is still Berlin's highest building. The Kulturforum complex includes the Gemäldegalerie (Picture Gallery) and Mies van der Rohe's only museum design, the 1968 Neue Nationalgalerie, but it's perhaps best known for the Philharmonie. Hans Scharoun's 1963 masterpiece of acoustic design seats 2,440 patrons of the world-renowned Berlin Philharmonic Orchestra, led by conductor Sir Simon Rattle, under tentlike golden roofs. Surely one of the most famous monuments to the futility of war is Kaiser-Wilhelm-Gedächtnis-Kirche (Kaiser Wilhelm Memorial Church). The remains of the original 1895 tower, damaged in World War II, have been adapted into a memorial chapel to go with the new 1961 church and bell tower.

With the fall of the Berlin Wall in 1989, an unprecedented period of restoration and unifying design has swept through this storied capital. No other building is a more potent symbol of Germany's history than the Reichstag, the seat of the German parliament. Redesigned in 1997–99 by Norman Foster, it features light, airy, environmentally efficient spaces that replaced the intimidating, dark interiors of the original 1894 shell. The glass-walled debating chamber allows the public unprecedented access, while battered stone walls covered in Cyrillic graffiti left by Red Army soldiers in 1945 provide a reminder of the past. The new glass-and-steel cupola, 130 feet in diameter, offers spectacular views; to avoid lines, make a reservation and head straight for Restaurant Käfer on the roof's terrace. The Jüdisches Museum (Jewish Museum), opened in 1998, is housed in a spectacular zinc-clad structure designed by Daniel Libeskind. Its jagged ground plan represents a brutally torn-apart Star of David, and its windows resemble vicious slashes in the walls.

Hans Scharoun's design replaced the previous Philharmonic Hall, which was destroyed in World War II.

In keeping with the city's transformation, architect and star hotelier Rocco Forte revamped a former 1889 bank building into the swanky, 146-room Hotel de Rome. Signature details include high ceilings, generous space, and mosaic marble baths. Highlighting the city's modern-design trend is chic Lux 11, where 72 apartment-style hotel rooms pair pastel walls with minimalist design in three connected 19th-century buildings. At Luchs, its stylish restaurant, Italian cuisine merges with a touch of South Tyrol in dishes such as ravioli stuffed with venison, plums, and ricotta in a red wine sauce.

Look for picturesque courtyards throughout Berlin, the most popular of which are Hackesche Höfe. The nine interlinked squares, some decorated in Art-Nouveau style, serve as one of Berlin's most popular hot spots, with trendy boutiques, cafés, and the ingenious Chamäleon Musik Theater Varieté.

TV TOWER: www.berlinerfernsehturm.de. **PHILHARMONIE AM KULTURFORUM:** Tel 49/30-254-88999; www.berlin-philharmonic.com. *When:* Aug–Jun. **KAISER-WILHELM-GEDÄCHTNIS-KIRCHE:** Tel 49/30-218-5023; www.gedaechtniskirche.com. **REICHSTAG:** Tel 49/30-2273-2152; www.bundestag.de. **RESTAURANT KÄFER:** Tel 49/30-2262-9900; www.feincost-kaefer.com. *Cost:* lunch $40. **JÜDISCHES MUSEUM:** Tel 49/30-2599-3300; www.jmberlin.de. **HOTEL DE ROME:** Tel 49/30-460-6090; www.hotelderome.com. *Cost:* from $570. **HOTEL LUX 11:** Tel 49/30-936-2800; www.lux-eleven.com. *Cost:* from $235; dinner $65. **BEST TIMES:** Sep for Musikfest; late Oct for Festival of Lights; early Nov for JazzFest.

A Neighborhood Reunites in Grand Style

MITTE

Berlin, Germany

After 4 decades as the grim no-man's-land of East Berlin, the Mitte district has reclaimed its place at the heart of the city. With the Berlin Wall now a historic relic, this former 18th-century showpiece of Hohenzollern Berlin has evolved into a stately yet very hip district with newfound polish and round-the-clock energy. The reunified city's most imposing historical monuments stand proudly among avant-garde galleries and edgy boutiques that showcase emerging talent (Auguststrasse is nicknamed "The Art Mile"), while masterpieces from across the ages grace Museum Island (see p. 146).

A symbolic portal to the Mitte district is the majestic Brandenburg Gate. Conceived in 1791 as a triumphal arch to celebrate a Prussian victory, the "Gate of Peace" was, ironically, incorporated into the Berlin Wall in 1961. East of the gate rolls the grand boulevard Unter den Linden (Under the Linden Trees), once the main east-west axis and today the site of many embassies and the revitalized pulse point of the restored capital. Opened in 1844, the templelike Staatsoper is the most famous of Berlin's three opera houses, and in 2013, after a 3-year renovation, it is scheduled to resume world-class productions under the direction of Daniel Barenboim. Quietly plush and superbly located, the Hotel Adlon was destroyed in 1945 and rebuilt in 1997, to reflect its prewar glory. It feels like a scene from the 1932 film classic *Grand Hotel,* whose setting was modeled after the hotel.

Lights and vendors fill Mitte's Gendarmenmarkt every year at Christmastime.

Filling an entire block between the Brandenburg Gate and Potsdamer Platz is the Memorial to the Murdered Jews of Europe, or Holocaust Memorial, designed by Peter Eisenmann and unveiled in 2005. The undulating field of 2,711 dark-gray concrete slabs, one for each page of the Talmud, serves as a stark reminder of that horrific period in history. Evoking the grace of a gentler era is Gendarmenmarkt, Berlin's prettiest plaza. At dusk, the glow of street lanterns casts a flattering light upon the Neoclassical Konzerthaus, home to the Berlin Symphony Orchestra, and the 18th-century Deutscher (German) and Französischer (French) cathedrals. Those in the know reserve well in advance for a niche table and likely celebrity spotting at Borchardt, an upscale brasserie serving French-German fare under a spectacular vaulted ceiling in a 1920s setting.

STAATSOPER: Tel 49/30-2035-4555; www.staatsoper-berlin.de. *When:* opera season is Sep–Jul. **HOTEL ADLON:** Tel 49/30-22610; in the U.S., 800-426-3135; www.hotel-adlon.de. *Cost:* from $315. **HOLOCAUST MEMORIAL:** Tel 49/30-2639-4336; www.holocaust-mahnmal.de. **BORCHARDT:** Tel 49/30-8188-6262. *Cost:* dinner $75. **BEST TIMES:** early Feb for International Film Festival; late Nov–Dec for Christmas markets and New Year's Eve.

Carefree and Rococo

SANS SOUCI

Potsdam, Brandenburg, Germany

Just outside his flourishing capital, Berlin, the enlightened Prussian ruler King Friedrich II—aka Frederick the Great—constructed a royal palace in 1745 that would be held as the finest example of Rococo architecture in Europe. There, amid the superb lakeland scenery, he was free to indulge in a flurry of cultural pursuits *sans souci*—without care (and preferably *sans* his queen, Elizabeth Christine)—with such visiting guests as the French writer and philosopher Voltaire.

Based on the king's own impeccable designs, Sans Souci was meant to rival Versailles (see p. 118) in detail and extravagance, although it is intimate by comparison. The long, one-story building, crowned by a dome and flanked by two round pavilions, is surrounded by tiered terraces and landscaped gardens. Other buildings, most notably the Neue Palais (the largest, with 638 rooms) and Schlosshotel Cecilienhof, were added over the following 150 years. The latter is a rambling, mock-Elizabethan country manor that was begun in 1913 for Crown Prince Wilhelm and his wife, Cecilie. It would go down in history as the site of the Potsdam Conference, July 17 to August 2, 1945, where the Allied statesmen Churchill (replaced mid-conference by Clement Attlee), Truman, and Stalin hammered out the division of postwar Germany.

Few of today's visitors traipsing through the conference rooms of the 175-room house realize that part of the manor has been quietly functioning as a hotel and restaurant since 1960. For those checking into any of the 41 guest rooms, the sense of *sans souci* is tangible once the day's visitors taper off. If they hand you the key to the luxury Hohenzollern Suite, you'll be staying in the onetime lodging for the family of the last emperor.

WHERE: 15 miles/24 km southwest of Berlin. **VISITOR INFO:** www.potsdam-tourism.com. **SCHLOSSHOTEL CECILIENHOF:** Tel 49/331-37050; www.relexa-hotel.de. *Cost:* from $160. **BEST TIME:** May–Jun for gardens at their best.

European Art: Then and Now

COLOGNE'S CATHEDRAL

Cologne, Rhineland, Germany

The 14th-century poet Petrarch thought Cologne's twin-towered Dom one of the finest cathedrals in the world. It took more than 600 years to complete; construction was begun on top of Roman ruins after Holy Roman Emperor Frederick Barbarossa donated the relics of the Three Magi to Cologne (Köln), establishing the city on the banks of the Rhine as an important pilgrimage destination. The relics

A stained-glass panel in the cathedral's St. Stephen window, assembled in 1848, depicts St. Apollinaris.

are still on display in their original 12th-century gilded reliquary behind the high altar, which itself dates back to the early 14th century. In 2007, the south transept received a burst of color from a massive new window designed by Cologne-based artist Gerhard Richter. The 11,500 hand-blown glass squares span 72 colors for an abstract echo of the surrounding figurative stained-glass windows. Take a 509-step hike up to the windswept gallery high in the 515-foot south tower and you will have climbed the highest church tower in the world. Petersglocke, the world's largest church bell, tips the scales at 24 tons; when it rings out the hour, you'll know.

You can view 2,000 years of Western art and architecture without leaving the shadow of the cathedral. Workers building an underground air-raid shelter in 1941 unearthed ancient Roman foundations, including a perfectly preserved mosaic floor from a Roman trader's villa; they are now the highlights of the Romano-Germanic Museum just south of the Dom. On its other side, the Wallraf-Richartz Museum, housed in a huge art complex, contains paintings from the 14th to the 20th centuries, while the Museum Ludwig, devoted exclusively to 20th-century art, has one of the largest modern collections outside the U.S.

At the end of the day, put your feet up at the Dom Hotel, which delivers old-fashioned, yet friendly service on a level that few hotels even aspire to these days. Nearby, the Früh am Dom is a lively century-old institution, where amiable waiters serve tourists and locals alike the popular Kölsch, a light, clear hometown brew.

Cathedral: Tel 49/221-17940-100; www.koelner-dom.de. **Romano-Germanic Museum:** Tel 49/221-24438; www.museenkoeln.de. **Wallraf-Richartz Museum** and **Museum Ludwig:** Tel 49/221-21119; 49/221-26165; www.museenkoeln.de. **Dom Hotel:** Tel 49/221-20240; www.starwoodhotels.com. *Cost:* from $225. **Früh am Dom:** Tel 49/221-2613-211; www.frueh.de. **Best times:** early Mar for Karneval; mid-Apr for Art Cologne; late Nov–Dec for Christmas market.

Rivers, Rieslings, and Ruins

The Rhine Valley

Rhineland, Germany

Cutting through 820 miles of European heartland from Switzerland to the North Sea, the Rhine River does not belong to Germany alone—but don't tell the Germans that. The span that runs through Germany, particularly the 50-mile Middle Rhine or Rhine Gorge, from Mainz to Koblenz, is where the river gained its historic importance and exhibits its greatest beauty, flanked by vineyard-clad hillsides, wooded forests, castle-topped crags, and tiny wine villages. The 433-foot Lorelei Rock that juts over the river's narrowest point is named for a mythic siren who sang sailors to their doom in her treacherous currents. Experience the Rhine by river cruise, train, or car—or by taking more than one option. Scenic roads and rails hug the riverbanks, while river-cruise lines specialize in tours ranging from a few hours to several days. During summer and early autumn, the Rhine in Flames festival lights up the river near Rudesheim, Koblenz, and St. Goar with fireworks, floodlit castles, and a fleet of illuminated boats.

Katz Castle faces neighboring Lorelei Rock.

A side trip along the winding Mosel River, which meets the Rhine at Koblenz, offers a magic all its own, with tranquil scenery, especially along the 85-mile stretch between Koblenz and the charming city of Trier. Dating from 2000 B.C., this ancient town boasts well-preserved Roman and medieval ruins standing amid today's lively street life. Farther up the Mosel, nestled in an enchanted setting, sits Burg Eltz, a 12th-century castle cared for by the same aristocratic family for the past 850 years.

Mülheim's Weinromantik Hotel Richtershof is a welcoming 17th-century manor house on a former wine-growing estate. It's conveniently close to one of Germany's finest restaurants, Waldhotel Sonnora, acclaimed for its excellent wine list and culinary magic using locally farmed ingredients. Both the Rhine and Mosel regions are noted for their light white wines. Come during the autumn grape harvest—centered along the Rheingau and the Mosel's Cochem and Bernkastel-Kues—to sample Germany's noblest grape, riesling, at its most famous vineyards.

WHERE: Mainz is 87 miles/140 km south of Cologne. **VISITOR INFO:** www.romantic-germany.info. **HOW:** Viking River Cruises offers trips from Paris to Prague. In the U.S., tel 800-304-9616; www.vikingrivercruises.com. *Cost:* 12-day cruises from $2,750, all-inclusive. *When:* departures May–Nov. **WEINROMANTIK HOTEL RICHTERSHOF:** Tel 49/6534-9480; in the U.S., 800-735-2478; www.weinromantikhotel.com. *Cost:* from $225. **WALDHOTEL SONNORA:** Tel 49/6578-406; www.hotel-sonnora.de. *Cost:* dinner $115. **BEST TIMES:** late Feb or early Mar for Karneval; Apr–May for smaller crowds; Jul–Sep for Rhine in Flames; Sep–Oct for wine harvest and fall foliage.

Cultural Capital on the Elbe, Reborn

DRESDEN'S ALTSTADT

Saxony, Germany

On a graceful bend of the Elbe River, one of Europe's most cherished cultural centers is experiencing a rebirth. In 1945, despite having no military targets, roughly 80 percent of Dresden's medieval inner city was destroyed in one of World War II's most savage air raids. Among the Aldstadt's (Old Town's) architectural casualties was the Frauenkirche (Church of Our Lady). Reconsecrated in 2005, the star of rebuilt Dresden stands strong once again behind a checkerboard façade of black (from the original structure) and tan stones.

One of Germany's most famous Baroque buildings, the 18th-century Zwinger palace, stands nearby, meticulously re-created in the late 1950s. The Zwinger complex is also home to the Rustkammer (arms room), containing stunning ornamental armor and weaponry, and the famous Porcelain Museum, showcasing the world's most significant Meissen collection. August the Strong (1694–1733), elector of Saxony, created this voluptuous pleasure palace and filled his showpiece, the Old Masters Picture Gallery, with such gems as Raphael's *Sistine Madonna*, Giorgione's *Sleeping Venus*, and Titian's *Tribute Money*. Revive yourself next door at the pretty Alte Meister Café, then head to the recently renovated Albertinum in the Royal Palace, where 19th- and 20th-century works reside. The hottest ticket in town may be the Green Vault, where the world's largest green diamond (41 carats) highlights a breathtaking collection of Saxon treasures.

Before August the Strong began to collect artwork, he collected women. Perhaps the most famous was Countess Cosel, for whom, in 1706, he commissioned the Taschenbergpalais. This great Baroque love nest, demolished in the 1945 raids, has risen phoenixlike again as the Kempinski Hotel Taschenbergpalais. With an ice rink in winter, opulent guest rooms, and an enviable location on the Theaterplatz, this is the most romantic and luxe hostelry in the area. A short stroll away is the world-famous Semper Opera, where Wagner and Strauss premiered most of their large-scale works. The new Hotel Suitess offers style and tranquility in Biedermeier-inspired rooms and a rooftop spa with views of the nearby Frauenkirche.

WHERE: 123 miles/198 km south of Berlin. **VISITOR INFO:** www.dresden-tourist.de. **ZWINGER COMPLEX, ALBERTINUM,** and **GREEN VAULT:** Tel 49/351-4914-2000; www.skd.museum. **ALTE MEISTER CAFÉ:** Tel 49/351-4810-426; www.altemeister.net. *Cost:* dinner $50. **KEMPINSKI HOTEL TASCHENBERGPALAIS:** Tel 49/351-4912-636; in the U.S., 800-426-3135; www.kempinski.com. *Cost:* from $205 (off-peak), from $320 (peak). **SEMPER OPERA:** Tel 49/351-4911-740; www.semperoper.de. **HOTEL SUITESS:** Tel 49/351-417270; in the U.S., 800-525-4800; www.suitess-hotel.com. *Cost:* from $225 (off-peak), from $275 (peak). **BEST TIMES:** May–Jun for Dresden Music Festival; late Aug for City Festival; late Nov–Dec for Christmas market.

A Wealth of Half-Timbered History

QUEDLINBURG

Saxony-Anhalt, Germany

On the edge of the Harz, Germany's northernmost mountain range, lies the finest—and some of the oldest—timber-framed townscape in the country and perhaps in all Europe. Besides holding this distinction, Quedlinburg also boasts a treasure trove of medieval religious art, which is displayed in Stiftskirche St. Servatius, the town's hilltop Saxon-Romanesque cathedral. The church's former abbey was transformed in the 17th century into a pocket-size Renaissance castle that houses a small museum containing priceless artifacts.

Boasting more than 1,000 years of history, Quedlinburg was the cradle of the Ottonian dynasty, the first line of Saxon kings in what later became the Holy Roman Empire. (Heinrich I, the first German king, died in 936 and is buried in the cathedral.) The town miraculously escaped both Allied bombing in World War II and the redevelopment plans of the former East German government.

Its historic wealth is still visible everywhere: in the gold and bejeweled sacred objects it exhibits and in its 1,300 half-timbered houses—the earliest, dating back to 1310, is the oldest in Germany. Architectural styles range from Gothic to Baroque to Quedlinburg's own idiom: façades accented with bright blues, reds, yellows, and greens.

On the main market square is the lovely Hotel Theophano, a half-timbered landmark created from five 17th-century buildings. Its restaurant offers memorable meals under candlelit vaulted ceilings. Hotel Am Brühl is a delightfully sunny hotel in a converted 350-year-old timbered farmhouse and 1920s stucco home, where some rooms open to castle views. The best place for regional fare and a local Braunbier, a centuries-old traditional brew, is the restored 1807 brewery Brauhaus Lüdde.

Where: 107 miles/172 km southwest of Berlin. **Visitor info:** www.quedlinburg.de. **Hotel Theophano:** Tel 49/3946-96300; www.hoteltheophano.de. *Cost:* from $125; dinner $40. **Hotel am Brühl:** Tel 49/3946-96180; www.hotelambruehl.de. *Cost:* from $145. **Brauhaus Lüdde:** Tel 49/3946-705206; www.hotel-brauhaus-luedde.de. *Cost:* dinner $35. **Best times:** Jun–Sep for Summer of Music; Dec for Advent in the Courtyards.

Belle of the Baltic

Lübeck

Schleswig-Holstein, Germany

This Baltic river port has a glorious past. In the Middle Ages, it was the capital of the important Hanseatic League, a loose-knit association of independent merchant towns in northern Europe. Enclosed within walls of fortifications, gates, and a moat, Lübeck's redbrick Altstadt (Old Town) is steeped in the history of the city's rich medieval days, when it dominated the highly lucrative trading routes along the Baltic. One would never guess that a quarter of the city's center was demolished by World War II bombings: Much of it has been painstakingly rebuilt. Serving as a memorial, the bells of the Gothic Marienkirche (St. Mary Church) lie shattered where they fell during an air raid. A boat ride along the Trave River reveals the true nature of this port city, offering unrivaled views of the treasured 15th-century Holsten Gate, imposing brick salt warehouses, and copper spires of the many Gothic churches.

The imposing medieval architecture of Holsten Gate is representative of Lübeck's role in the powerful Hanseatic League.

Come July, classical-music fans flock here for Germany's largest summer cultural event: the Schleswig-Holstein Music Festival. Ever since Leonard Bernstein launched the festival in 1986, world-class artists have marked it on their summer schedules. Some 125 performances are given in 50 venues throughout the province, including many in Lübeck.

At the graciously restored Hotel Kaiserhof, the union of two stately 19th-century homes recalls the comfort and civility of old Lübeck.

Stop in at Haus der Schiffergesellschaft, a tavern built in 1535 as headquarters for the sea captains' guild, or travel farther back in time to Brauberger's, a Romanesque cellar where beer has been brewed and served since 1225. Though marzipan's origins still spark a centuries-old debate, Lübeck's superiority with the almond confection is indisputable—and Café Niederegger is said to make the best in the world. Its famous cream-filled Nusstorte also begs to be sampled.

WHERE: 40 miles/65 km north of Hamburg. **VISITOR INFO:** www.luebeck.de. **SCHLESWIG-HOLSTEIN MUSIC FESTIVAL:** Tel 49/451-389570; www.shmf.de. *When:* Jul–late Aug. **HOTEL KAISERHOF:** Tel 49/451-703301; www.kaiserhof-luebeck.de. *Cost:* from $150. **HAUS DER SCHIFFERGESELLSCHAFT:** Tel 49/451-76776; www.schiffergesellschaft.com. **BRAUBERGER:** Tel 49/451-71444; www.brauberger.com. **CAFÉ NIEDEREGGER:** Tel 49/451-5301127; www.niederegger.de. **BEST TIMES:** summer for music festival; late Nov–Dec for Christmas market.

Glamorous and Fragile, an Island Beauty

SYLT

Schleswig-Holstein, Germany

This windswept barrier island off the northern tip of Germany is the status destination for the fashionable and chic of Hamburg. Stylish boutiques, excellent restaurants, and a tiny casino bestow a cosmopolitan flair on the skinny isle that otherwise cherishes its traditions and fragile beauty. The largest island in the Friesian Archipelago stretching from Denmark to the Netherlands, Sylt is just 1,148 feet wide at its narrowest point. Its ever-shifting landscape of soft dunes and 40 miles of sandy coastline is in danger of eroding off the face of the map someday. It has a sizable gay and lesbian population, a famous nude beach (said to have begun the craze in the 1800s), and a relaxed lifestyle centered around just-caught seafood dinners in small fishing villages. The invigorating air and bracing wind off the North Sea makes yellow oilskin windbreakers a common sight even on summer days. Sloping straw roofs and dollhouse-like brick cottages illustrate the islanders' desire to keep the modern world on the mainland; biking, horseback riding, and walking are the preferred means of transportation.

With just 12 villages on the 38-square-mile island, quaint Keitum is its "green heart," while the largest establishment is Westerland. The latter is where you'll find the elegant, 19th-century Hotel Stadt Hamburg, evocative of a dignified country estate and home to an excellent restaurant. For a refreshing antidote to the island's high-end hotels, the Long Island House boasts airy modern design and warm and welcoming hosts. There are homey oyster and shrimp joints around the island where everyone knows your name, but if you're looking for a fancier alternative, Restaurant Jörg Müller is among the country's finest eateries.

WHERE: 143 miles/230 km northwest of Hamburg. **VISITOR INFO:** www.sylt.de. **HOTEL STADT HAMBURG:** Tel 49/4651-8580; www.hotelstadthamburg.com. *Cost:* from $300; dinner $60. **LONG ISLAND HOUSE:** Tel 49/4651-9959550; www.sylthotel.de. *Cost:* from $195. **RESTAURANT JÖRG MÜLLER:** Tel 49/4651-27788; www.hotel-joerg-mueller.de. *Cost:* dinner $55. **BEST TIMES:** Jul–Aug for summer activities; end Sep–early Oct for windsurfing's World Cup Sylt.

German Classicism Meets Revolutionary Architecture

Weimar

Thuringia, Germany

The much-revered writer Johann Wolfgang von Goethe lived in Weimar for nearly 60 years while penning most of his major works, including the epic drama *Faust.* The town of Johann Sebastian Bach, Franz Liszt, Richard Strauss, Friedrich von Schiller, and Cranach the Elder and the Younger, Weimar was also home to Nietzsche in his last years and to Walter Gropius's revolutionary Bauhaus movement in architecture. Long protected as a cultural treasure, the Baroque town has remained intact, despite World War II and decades of Communist rule. Still, a somber reminder of the Nazi years remains, 6 miles north of town, at the Buchenwald Memorial and museum. Certainly the city has seen the very best and the very worst of German history. In 1999, Weimar was honored as a European Capital of Culture, inspiring a cultural and intellectual revival kept alive by small museums, institutes, theaters, and festivals. The Goethe-Nationalmuseum is housed above the home in which the poet lived from 1775 until his death in 1832. Furnished just as it was in Goethe's time, the 1709 building contains his art and scientific collections, library, and the modest room in which he died.

At day's end, return to the historic Deco- and Bauhaus-decorated Elephant Hotel, its 1696 façade still intact, ideally situated on the stage-set Marktplatz. Repair to the hotel's terrace bar overlooking life on the square, or savor Thuringian specialties at the popular Elephantenkeller. For a more elegant meal, try the Mediterranean-influenced menu at the hotel's highly acclaimed Anna Amalia. From Weimar, wrote Goethe (who celebrated his 80th birthday at the Elephant), "the gates and streets lead to every faraway place on earth."

Where: 190 miles/300 km southwest of Berlin. **Visitor info:** www.weimar.de. **Gedenkstätte Buchenwald:** Tel 49/3643-4300; www.buchenwald.de. **Goethe-Nationalmuseum:** Tel 49/3643-545400; www.klassik-stiftung.de. **Hotel Elephant:** Tel 49/3643-8020; www.hotelelephantweimar.com. *Cost:* from $140. *Cost:* dinner at Anna Amalia $70. *When:* closed mid-Jan–mid-Mar. **Best times:** Aug 28 for Goethe's birthday; mid-Oct for Onion Market.

The Most Important Ancient Monument in the Western World

The Acropolis

Athens, Greece

The Parthenon, the greatest achievement of Greek civilization's golden age, has crowned the loftiest point of the Athens horizon (acropolis means "upper town") since the 5th century B.C. The timeless Doric temple is dedicated to the patron goddess of the city, Athena, and was originally painted so vividly—like all the other buildings on the Acropolis—that an alarmed Plutarch complained, "We are gilding and adorning our city like a wanton woman." Today the temple shimmers golden white in the sunlight, visible through the glass walls of the ultramodern new Acropolis Museum in the Archaeological Park, a walkway that skirts the base of the 8-acre Acropolis plateau from Hadrian's Arch to the Agora.

The museum opened in 2009 with stunning light and airy galleries that house prized artifacts such as four of the original Caryatids, or maidens, that served as the Parthenon's columns, and the fragments from the Parthenon frieze left behind by Lord Elgin, who, as British Ambassador to the Ottomans, had permission to cart off the rest to London in 1801. Hopes are high that Britain may return the contested Elgin Marbles to Athens now that such a state-of-the-art home awaits them. During the summertime Athens and Epidaurus Festival, ancient dramas, operas, music, and ballet are performed in the 2nd-century Odeon of Herod Atticus (for drama at the sister festival in Epidaurus, see p. 171).

You can catch a glimpse of the gleaming Acropolis from a number of hotels, such as the elegant Grande Bretagne, an 1842 palace in the very heart of things on Syntagma (Constitution) Square. Upper-floor rooms enjoy bird's-eye views of the Acropolis, as do the open-air rooftop pool, bar, and excellent Mediterranean-cuisine restaurant. The nearby Electra Palace Hotel enjoys the same postcard-worthy views

Pericles oversaw construction of the Parthenon, one of the largest projects undertaken in ancient Greece.

and a location in the jumble of taverna-lined streets of the Plaka, touristy but still charming. Sometimes a great sight is even better appreciated from afar, and the popular boutique hotel St. George Lycabettus looks across the white sprawl of the city to the Acropolis from the old-money neighborhood of Kolonaki.

Acropolis Museum: Tel 30/210-900-0900; www.theacropolismuseum.gr. **Athens and Epidaurus Festival:** Tel 30/210-928-2900; www.greekfestival.gr. *When:* mid-Jun–Sep. **Grande Bretagne:** Tel 30/210-333-0000; in the U.S., 800-325-3589; www.grandebretagne.gr. *Cost:* from $415. **Electra Palace:** Tel 30/210-337-0000; www.electrahotels.gr. *Cost:* from $210 (off-peak), from $290 (peak). **St. George Lycabettus:** Tel 30/210-729-0711; www.sglycabettus.gr. *Cost:* from $200. **Best times:** Once a month, during the full moon, the Acropolis opens at night; May–Jun and Sep–Oct for coolest weather.

Preserving Greek Heritage

Athens's Museums

Athens, Greece

While the sparkling new Acropolis Museum (see above) tends to grab the spotlight these days, Athens is also home to several other world-class collections of ancient artifacts, an unmatched patrimony from the country's long-ago past.

On the short list of must-see sights in Greece is the National Archaeological Museum, housing more masterpieces of art and sculpture from ancient Greece than any other museum in the world and providing an essential introduction to classical civilization. The Artemision Bronze, possibly representing Poseidon (or Zeus) circa 5th century B.C.—the perfectly balanced body of an athlete about to throw a weapon or thunderbolt—is the star of the ground-floor sculpture rooms. A funerary mask of a bearded king, among the stunning treasures from the royal tombs of Mycenae, is now believed to be from the 15th century B.C. Artifacts from Thíra (Santorini) include beautiful frescoes from the Minoan settlement of Akrotiri, preserved Pompeii-like in a 1600 B.C. volcanic eruption (see p. 163).

The Benaki Museum, founded in 1931 by wealthy art collector Antoni Benaki and housed in his family's Neoclassical mansion, shows off 20,000 items from throughout Greek history, beginning with ancient bronzes and moving on to Byzantine icons, folk costumes, and reassembled 18th-century interiors. Two other museums are known for their more specialized collections. Elegantly elongated stone figures sculpted 5,000 years ago fill the galleries of the Museum of Cycladic Art. These ancient, slender shapes, the creations of one of Greece's earliest civilizations, from the island group that includes Mykonos, Delos, and Santorini, influenced such modern artists as Picasso and Modigliani. The Ilias Lalaounis Jewelry Museum showcases more than 3,000 pieces by the internationally renowned designer, including many based on or inspired by classical and Byzantine motifs. Exquisite copies are sold in the gift shop.

NATIONAL ARCHAEOLOGICAL MUSEUM: Tel 30/210-821-7724; www.culture.gr. **BENAKI MUSEUM:** Tel 30/210-367-1000; www.benaki.gr. **MUSEUM OF CYCLADIC ART:** Tel 30/210-722-8321; www.cycladic.gr. **ILIAS LALAOUNIS JEWELRY MUSEUM:** Tel 30/210-922-1004; www.lalaounis-jewelrymuseum.gr.

Island Style, Without Cars

HYDRA AND SPETSES

Saronic Gulf Islands, Attica, Greece

The islands of the Saronic Gulf hug the coast of the Peloponnese and, depending on your point of view, are blessed or cursed by their proximity to Athens. Aegina is so close to Athens that some islanders commute to work in the capital, and Athenians in turn flood the island for a day at the beach or a visit to the graceful hilltop Temple of Aphaia, surrounded by 25 of its original Doric columns from the 5th century B.C. Poros is separated from the mainland only by a narrow channel, meaning it's a good base to explore Nafplion and its nearby classical sites (see p. 170).

Hydra and Spetses, in the south of the archipelago, not only remain relatively unspoiled but are especially pleasant due to the banning of cars. As you approach Hydra by boat, the barren, mountainous island seems to be deserted. Then the quasicircular harbor comes into view, and old stone and red tile–roofed houses fan out into the rocky hills. Hydra once made its livelihood from the sea, but since the 1960s the 20-square-mile island has been popular with artists, writers, and the glitterati, who value the island's distinctive character. The quietly chic Bratsera Hotel blends into the austere environment, tastefully created within the shell of an 1860 sponge factory. The six-room Hotel Phaedra, named after the 1962 Melina Mercouri classic that was filmed on the island, is homey and unassuming but widely popular thanks to the energetic, hands-on owner.

Spetses is the most verdant of the Saronic Gulf Islands, and old stone mansions that are weekend homes for wealthy Athenians are tucked into fragrant stands of Aleppo pines and olive groves. Among the many seafarers who have lived on the island is Laskarina Bouboulina, the female hero of the 1821 Greek War of Independence; her home is a quirky museum filled with her letters and other personal belongings. The palatial Poseidonion Grand Hotel, a glamorous Côte-d'Azur–style 1914 landmark, reopened in 2010 on the harbor in the Dapia square. A fraction of the size but just as accommodating is the nearby Armata, an elegant family-run hotel that has an inviting pool, and is impressive for the proud owners' keen attention to detail and design.

WHERE: Aegina is 17 miles/30 km from Athens; Spetses is 53 miles/98 km from Athens. **HOTEL BRATSERA:** Tel 30/22980-53971; www.bratserahotel.com. *Cost:* from $215. *When:* closed Nov–mid-Mar. **PHAEDRA HOTEL:** Tel 30/22980-53330; www.phaedrahotel.com. *Cost:* from $195. **POSEIDONION GRAND HOTEL:** Tel 30/22980-74553; www.poseidonion.com. *Cost:* from $225 (off-peak), from $410 (peak). **ARMATA HOTEL:** Tel 30/22980-72683; www.armatahotel.gr. *Cost:* from $170. **BEST TIMES:** on Hydra: around Jun 21 when Miaoulia honors its local War of Independence hero. On Spetses: early–mid-Sep for similar festivities.

Famous Oracle of Antiquity at the Navel of the Earth

DELPHI

Central Greece

For more than 1,000 years, Delphi was home to the most powerful and important oracle of ancient Greece, believed to be the mouthpiece of Apollo himself. Hordes of pilgrims arrived from throughout the Mediterranean world with questions inscribed on stone tablets (many of which have survived) to be presented to a priestess, known as the Pythia, seated deep in a cave within the Temple of Apollo. She would utter cryptic and incoherent prophecies—her trance possibly the result of inhaling vapors escaping from a fissure in the earth—to priests who interpreted them as enigmatic riddles.

Spectacularly set against the craggy peak of Mount Parnassus, Delphi still resonates with mystery. The ancients believed that this was the center (or navel) of the world, as was determined by Zeus, who released two eagles from opposite ends of the earth who met here. The 4th-century B.C. ruins of the Temple of Apollo (built on an earlier structure) stand at the center of the site, though the most elegant remains are those of the Tholos, a round, column-encircled temple erected to Athena, the goddess of wisdom. The well-preserved 4th-century B.C. theater and stadium, with a capacity to seat 5,000, were built for the Pythian Games, forerunners of the Olympics and held every 4 years. A bronze statue of a charioteer, one of the great works to come down from ancient Greece, is but one gem of the small but important Delphi Museum.

You can take in sweeping views of the verdant slopes that cradle the ruins while enjoying wild boar and other specialties on the open terrace at Epikouros. The more recent past comes alive at the nearby 10th-century Ossios Loukas (Monastery of St. Luke), clinging to the side of Mount Helicon amid glorious countryside. Greek Orthodox visitors consider the lavishly decorated monastery to be a sacred spot. Its dazzling mosaics are held to be some of the finest in Greece.

WHERE: 110 miles/178 km northwest of Athens. **EPIKOURUS:** Tel 30/22650-83251; www.fedriades.com. *Cost:* lunch $20. **BEST TIMES:** early Jul for Festival of Delphi, when ancient Greek drama is staged.

Traces of an Early Civilization amid Spectacular Scenery

CRETE

Greece

Nationlike in its size and diversity, Crete is the largest of the Greek islands and also one of the most fascinating and beautiful. History buffs know it as the birthplace of the Minoans, Europe's first advanced civilization and culture. The reconstructed Palace of Knossos—dating to 1700 B.C. and discovered only in 1900—was their cultural and administrative center. The palace evokes a remarkably advanced and peaceful society, as do the sophisticated Minoan treasures and vibrant frescoes now housed in Heraklion's work-in-progress Archaeological Museum.

Crete is also an island of enormous natural beauty, with isolated coastlines and snow-capped mountains laced with deep gorges, none more dramatic than the 11-mile-long Samariá Gorge. The popular but strenuous downhill hike through this deep gash in the White Mountains begins with a drop via the steep, zigzagging wooden stairs, continues for 5 to 7 exhilarating hours along a well-trodden 11-mile trail, and ends with a cool dip in the Libyan Sea.

The Palace of Knossos contained over 1,000 rooms and was central to the Minoan civilization.

Chania, a character-filled Venetian town on the north coast and once the capital of Crete, is the common jumping-off place for gorge excursions and is a delight in itself. Narrow lanes curve around a beautiful harbor overlooked by a lighthouse and a mosque and a fine archaeological museum. A remnant of the Venetians who once held sway here for centuries is a handsome palazzo that now houses the Casa Delfino, where 24 distinctive guest rooms surround a flowered courtyard. About 45 miles to the east lies the university town of Rethymnon. Top off a visit here with a meal in the bougainvillea-filled garden of Avli, known for its innovative take on Cretan country cooking and for having one of the island's largest wine cellars. Settle into any of the seven adjoining suites, each awash in antiques and beautiful textiles.

Farther east, the shores of turquoise blue Mirabello Bay, outside the pretty town of Agios Nikolaos, are the setting for two of

Greece's most luxurious getaways: Elounda Mare, where half the suites come with their own wall-enclosed gardens and small plunge pools, and the larger Elounda Beach, whose accommodations run from sleek waterfront villas to cozy stone-walled suites hanging above the deep blue sea.

WHERE: 109 miles/175 km south of Athens. **SAMARIÁ GORGE:** Xylóskalo entrance is 42 miles/70 km south of Chania. *When:* closed mid-Oct–Apr. **CASA DELFINO:** Tel 30/28210-96500; www.casadelfino.com. *Cost:* from $245. **AVLI:** Tel 30/28310-58250; www.avli.gr. *Cost:* suites from $250; dinner $40. **ELOUNDA MARE:** Tel 30/28410-41512; in the U.S., 800-735-2478; www.eloundamare.gr. *Cost:* from $350 (off-peak), from $550 (peak). *When:* closed Nov–Mar. **ELOUNDA BEACH:** Tel 30/28410-63000; in the U.S., 866-435-9277; www.eloundabeach.gr. *Cost:* from $315 (off-peak), from $700 (peak). *When:* closed Nov–Mar. **BEST TIMES:** Apr or early May for Crete's renowned Orthodox Easter; Apr–May for wildflowers; May–Jun and Sep for fewer tourists.

Cycladic Chic and Magnificent Ruins

MYKONOS AND DELOS

Cyclades, Greece

Dry, scrub-strewn Mykonos is one of the smallest Greek islands and one of the most popular. Discovered by Jackie O. and other celebrity yachters in the '60s, the 34-square-mile island has long been a favorite with young dance-till-dawn partyers, jumbo cruise–ship passengers, well-tanned poseurs of both sexes, and, more and more these days, worldly travelers who come for the handsomely stylish hotels and the sophisticated restaurant scene. All are charmed by the many fine beaches, the centuries-old trademark windmills that line the ridges above the sea, the 400-some churches and chapels, and Chora, the main town.

It's a pleasure to get lost among the labyrinth-like streets filled with white sugar-cube houses—typical of Cycladic architecture—with splashes of sky blue doors and domes and brilliant red and pink bougainvillea. Upscale boutiques, tavernas, and welcoming bars spill out onto the cobblestones in the Little Venice quarter. An evening stroll along Chora's waterfront promenade can end at the family-owned To Maereio, where meze appetizers of meatballs, tomato fritters, and local cheeses are a meal in themselves.

Once used for wheat-grinding, thatch-roofed windmills are a Mykonos landmark.

Bars line the sands at Paradise Beach and elsewhere, but it is easy to escape the crowds. At Agios Sostis, you can swim along beaches of fine-grained sand, then enjoy a lunch of grilled fish-of-the-day at waterside Kiki's—there's no sign, so just follow the smell of barbecue. Enjoy the intimacy of Kivotos, an elegant villalike hotel on a secluded beach 2 miles out of Chora.

At the in-town retreat of Apanema, fresh, white rooms surround a beautiful terrace and pool, whereas the elegant Semeli is tucked into hillside gardens, with great sea views.

A short boat trip takes you to the tiny, windswept island of Delos, the mythical birthplace of Apollo, god of truth and light, and his twin sister, the moon goddess Artemis. Delos was abandoned around 70 B.C. and is still uninhabited. Most of the 1.5-square-mile island is an open-air archaeology museum, covered with the ruins of temples, theaters, markets, and villas decorated with mosaics, all unearthed in 1872.

WHERE: 96 miles/177 km south of Athens. **TO MAEREIO:** Tel 30/22890-28825. *Cost:* dinner $15. **KIVOTOS:** Tel 30/22890-24094; www.kivotosclubhotel.com. *Cost:* from $420 (off-peak), from $650 (peak). *When:* closed Nov–Mar. **APANEMA:** Tel 30/22890-28590; www.apanemaresort.com. *Cost:* from $230 (off-peak), from $430 (peak). **SEMELI:** Tel 30/22890-27466; www.semelihotel.gr. *Cost:* from $180 (off-peak), from $500 (peak). **BEST TIMES:** May, Sep–Oct for nice weather and fewer crowds. The small town of Ano Mera celebrates Easter with a lamb feast in the main square (Apr or May).

Green Valleys and Ancient Marbles

NAXOS AND PÁROS

Cyclades, Greece

Part of the 220-island Cycaldic archipelago and a short boat trip from each other, Naxos and Páros are rich in tradition, and natural and man-made wonders. They don't attract the crowds of tourists who flock to neighboring Mykonos (see previous page) and Santorini (see next page), but they lure those looking for a taste of authentic island life, with some exceptional beaches thrown in for good measure.

Naxos is the greenest and largest of the Cyclades, with a population of just 18,000. The highest peaks in the archipelago come into view as you pull into port. A small, 13th-century Venetian chapel dominates an islet just offshore, while the Portara, a massive marble doorway crowning a hilltop, is Naxos's other landmark: It is all that remains of an unfinished 6th-century B.C. temple to Apollo. Within the shadow of the hilltop citadel, the Venetians—in power from 1207–1566—built an imposing cathedral and mansions (one houses the interesting Archaeological Museum). The mazelike Kastro neighborhood is where you'll find the antiques-filled Château Zevgoli, an atmospheric family-run inn with views of the harbor. Use this as your base to explore the island and its beautifully frescoed Byzantine chapels, which date back to the 7th

About 500 churches can be found on Naxos, many of them rustic and centuries-old.

century. Farming is still important here, and the marble Temple of Demeter, goddess of fertility, stands amid tended fields.

Páros's celebrated quarries of translucent white marble gave the world the *Venus de Milo* and great monuments such as the Temple of Poseidon at Sounion on the mainland and Napoleon's tomb in Paris. The local stone appears in the walls of the seaside Venetian fortress in the charming main town of Parikia, and in a fragment of the Parian Chronicle, a marble tablet that records Greek events from 1500 B.C. to 264 B.C., displayed in the nearby Archaeological Museum.

Many consider Páros's highlight to be Parikia's Ekatontapyliani (Church of a Hundred Doors). The existing structure dates to the 10th century and is the oldest church in Greece in continuous use. Dedicated to the Virgin, it is the site of a special August 15 holy day celebration. Don't miss the postcard-perfect fishing village of Naoussa, where cafés line the quay next to a half-submerged Venetian castle, or mountainside Lefkes, the capital under Ottoman rule and Páros's highest and most charming inland town. The pool at the attractive Lefkes Village Hotel makes up for the lack of a beach, with views that stretch across the surrounding hillsides and out to the open sea.

WHERE: 103 miles/190 km southeast of Athens. **CHÂTEAU ZEVGOLI:** Tel 30/22850-25201; www.naxostownhotels.com. *Cost:* from $155. *When:* closed Nov–mid-Mar. **LEFKES VILLAGE:** Tel 30/22840-41827; www.lefkesvillage.gr. *Cost:* from $120. *When:* closed Oct–Apr. **BEST TIMES:** in Naxos: Jul 14 for feast day of patron saint. In Paros: Aug 15, for services at Ekatontapyliani church.

The Most Spectacular Greek Island of Them All

SANTORINI

Cyclades, Greece

Santorini provides one of the Aegean's most spectacular natural settings. The slim 12-mile crescent of land, also known as Thíra, is the rim of an ancient volcano. Villages of dazzling white houses and blue-domed churches cling to cliffs 1,000 feet above the indigo sea that now floods the sunken caldera (a "drinkable blue volcano," wrote Greece's Nobel Prize–winning poet Odysseus Elytis). The island is still jolted occasionally by intense volcanic activity (two smoldering cones rise out of the flooded caldera), and speculation is rife that Santorini is the mythical lost kingdom of Atlantis. Thirty-six varieties of grape are grown in the rich volcanic soil, and Santorini produces delightful white wine. Other island pleasures include beaches of red and black volcanic sand and two splendid ancient sites: Akrotiri, a Minoan village preserved in Pompeii-like ash during the massive volcanic eruption around 1600 B.C. that created the caldera, and Ancient Thera, a 9th-century jumble of Egyptian, Greek, Roman, and Byzantine ruins atop precipitous seaside cliffs.

Cruise-ship passengers and visitors all but take over the small island in the summer months, but it is easy to escape the fray in one of Greece's most distinctive retreats. Perivolas is high above the sea and just a 2-minute stroll from the heart of clifftop Oia, one of the most beautiful settlements in the Mediterranean. The small hotel's whitewashed, elegantly pared-down accommodations have curved ceilings and walls and showstopping views. Each room's terrace is the roof of the dwelling below, all fashioned from abandoned, 300-year-old, cavelike homes purchased by the owner and ingeniously cobbled together. The infinity pool is the same Aegean blue as the real thing beyond. On the horizon, you can make out the Perivolas Hideaway, the hotel's super-exclusive private villa built from 19th-century ruins on the tiny island of Thirassia, a 5-minute speedboat ride across the caldera.

Astra Apartments & Suites, in Imerovigli, another beautifully situated village above the caldera's rim, has airy, high-ceilinged, whitewashed accommodations that are highlighted with original artwork and contemporary furnishings, though the views are the real attraction.

In the evening, the tourist razzmatazz in the island's main town, Fira, slows down after day-trippers leave, and the main pastime is a stroll along the shop-lined streets. Take a seat at the no-frills decades-old Nikolas for such classic taverna favorites as lamb in lemon sauce and the flavorful eggplant and tomatoes for which the island is known. Selene, a fixture of Fira since 1986, has moved 10 minutes away from the bustle to the beautifully preserved and quiet town of Pyrgos. Its innovative and refined take on traditional island cuisine has not changed, and local bounty appears in such innovative creations as fava balls in caper sauce and octopus with smoked eggplant, now served with inspiring views from high above the sea.

Where: 126 miles/202 km southeast of Athens. **Perivolas:** Tel 30/22860-71308; www.perivolassuites.gr. *Cost:* from $600 (off-peak), from $740 (peak). *When:* closed Nov–Mar. **Astra Apartments:** Tel 30/22860-23641; www.astra.gr. *Cost:* from $270 (off-peak), from $400 (peak). *When:* closed Nov–Mar. **Nikolas:** Tel 30/22860-24550. *Cost:* dinner $20. **Selene:** Tel 30/22860-22249; www.selene.gr. *Cost:* dinner $60. *When:* closed Nov–Mar. **Best times:** Apr–Jul and Sep–Oct for nice weather and avoiding Aug's crowds; late Jul–early Sep for Fira's International Music Festival.

A Quiet, Unspoiled Getaway

Sifnos

Cyclades, Greece

This is what Sifnos doesn't have: famous antiquities, lively nightlife, spectacular beaches, nor the shoulder-to-shoulder crowds they attract. It is a favorite getaway of discerning Athenians, who take over the place in August but like to keep quiet about their find.

Town life is clustered in several adjoining villages that march up and down a ridge in the center of the island, an enticing cluster of whitewashed, bougainvillea-covered houses and blue-domed churches that are connected by scenic pathways, making this a hiker's delight. From Apollonia, the small-town capital, stone paths rise and drop to its twin sister Artemonas, where the multidomed Kochi church is built on the site of an ancient temple to the goddess Artemis. From Apollonia, it's an easy 1-mile walk to the old capital of Kastro, a medieval town huddled on a seaside cliff. Built on the dramatic site of an ancient acropolis, it is an architectural gem, with a small but impressive archaeological museum that comes as an added surprise.

Much of the island is ringed by tall cliffs, but here and there the coast drops down to pleasant coves, prime real estate that over the centuries was snapped up by monastic communities looking for remote natural settings that inspired contemplation. The sandy crescent of Apokofto beach stretches beneath the dramatically picturesque Panagia Chrysopigi, dedicated to the island's patron saint since 1650 and a popular point of pilgrimage. At Vathy, on a bay at the end of a green valley, another beautiful stretch of sand is overlooked by the seaside Taxiarchis Monastery, whose white walls and twin domes seem to rise out of the blue sea.

The island's highest monastery is the 12th-century walled Profitis Elias O Pilos (O Pilos means "the High One"), topping a 2,200-foot summit in the center of the island. It is accessible only by a fairly easy 2-hour climb from Apollonia, well worth it for the serenity of the chapel and Aegean views. Magnificent views are also part of the package at the Petali Hotel, on a hilltop above Apollonia. Terraces off the large, comfortable rooms and the pretty swimming pool all overlook white-roofed houses, terraced hillsides, and the shimmering sea. In addition to ceramics, Sifnos is well known for its olive oil and island cuisine, and any number of the island's small, unpretentious restaurants will illustrate why.

WHERE: 80 miles/130 km south of Athens. **PETALI HOTEL:** Tel 30/22840-33024; www.hotelpetali.gr. *Cost:* from $135 (off-peak), from $280 (peak). **BEST TIME:** Jul 20, when a torch-lit procession climbs to the monastery of Profitis Elias.

Religious Fervor Coupled with Worldly Sophistication

PATMOS

Dodecanese, Greece

It has been said that St. John the Divine, one of the 12 disciples of Jesus, was inspired to write the Book of Revelation (or the Apocalypse) during a 2-year banishment to Patmos in A.D. 95 for preaching Christianity at Ephesus (see p. 576). Find your own inspiration as you explore isolated coves and untrammeled beaches, or bask in the simple, quiet sophistication that infuses Skala, the attractive main port, and the hilltop town of Chora, where quiet lanes lined with old aristocratic mansions surround one of Greece's most important monastic complexes.

The small cave now known as the Sacred Grotto, where St. John composed the Book of Revelation, is at the core of the Monastery of the Apocalypse, on a hillside midway between Skala and Chora. Niches in the rock wall served as the saint's desk and pillow, and a large crack was supposedly opened by the voice of God, whose words John recorded for the last book of the Christian Bible.

Since its 11th-century founding, the Monastery of St. John the Theologian, which includes several chapels, has emphasized education.

The tall, brooding Monastery of St. John the Theologian dominates the island, an 11th-century complex of churches and courtyards fortified to protect a trove of religious treasures that includes paintings, carvings, sculpture, and an extensive library and archives, second only to the collection of Mount Athos (see next page). The monastery remains a focal point of the Orthodox and Western Christian faiths alike, and pilgrims from all parts of the world make their way to "the Jerusalem of the Aegean."

Other visitors come to enjoy Psili Ammos, Lambi, and other beautiful beaches, and hike on the donkey paths that crisscross the hilly interior. Despite its deep religious affiliation, the island also exudes an inherent elegance. The rooms and huge terraces of Petra, a small hotel above the beach at Grikos, have bay views and are tastefully furnished. Nearby, the seaside Benetos restaurant, run by a Greek-American couple, has created a stir with the chef's modern take on Mediterranean cuisine. On their atmospheric veranda, diners enjoy just-caught seafood and other dishes enhanced with fresh herbs and vegetables from the owners' small seaside farm.

WHERE: 160 miles/256 km from Athens. **PETRA:** Tel 30/22470-34020; www.petrahotel-patmos.com. *Cost:* from $280 (off-peak), from $460 (peak). *When:* closed Nov–Mar. **BENETOS:** Tel 30/22470-33089; www.benetosrestaurant.com. *Cost:* dinner $30. *When:* closed Nov–May. **BEST TIMES:** Apr–Sep for weather; Holy Week and Greek Orthodox Easter (Apr or early May); late Aug–Sep for Sacred Music Festival.

Medieval Might and Neoclassical Splendor

RHODES AND SÍMI

Dodecanese, Greece

Little remains of Rhodes's ancient past—an acropolis still rises above the seaside town of Lindos, but the most famous antiquity, the 100-foot-tall bronze Colossus of Rhodes, one of the Seven Wonders of the Ancient World, was toppled by an earthquake in 226 B.C. and long ago disappeared. The Middle Ages, however, remain very much in evidence in the Old Town, the largest inhabited medieval enclave in Europe. It's enclosed within wonderfully preserved walls, 3 miles long and up to 40 feet thick with remnants of a double moat still visible.

Medieval walls surround the Old Town of Rhodes, site of sieges and skirmishes over the centuries.

Rhodes was the stronghold of the powerful Knights of St. John of Jerusalem, who laid claim to the island on their return from the Crusades in the 14th century. You'll feel their spirit on the cobbled Street of the Knights, in their hospital, now housing the Archaeological Museum, and in their vast Palace of the Grand Masters. You can overnight in a medieval complex that houses the atmospheric, family-run San Nikolis hotel, whose rooftop garden offers a fine breakfast with fantastic views. As the easternmost island in Greece, Rhodes lies just 11 miles off the coast of Turkey—in 1522, Turks arrived with a 100,000-strong army and stayed for 4 centuries. One of their houses is now the romantic Marco Polo Mansion, with deep-hued guest rooms and a pleasant summertime courtyard where wonderful dinners of Greek-Italian fusion cuisine are served.

Excursions around the island will take you to whitewashed, seaside Lindos, where an ancient hilltop acropolis is enclosed by a medieval fortress. The breezy villalike Melenos Hotel enjoys views of both the acropolis and the water. Its 12 stylish rooms and suites overlook the sea, as does an outdoor tented restaurant that gives the place an exotic, timeless ambience.

The peaceful island of Sími is 45 minutes away by ferry. Its small harbor is considered by many to be the most beautiful in Greece, rimmed with tiers of pastel-colored 19th-century Neoclassical mansions from the days when shipbuilders and merchants prospered. Strike off on a hike that follows a coastline etched with small bays or turn inland for an easy 6-mile trek that takes you across the scenic interior to the monastery of the Archangel Michael at Panormitis, where overnight guests are welcome. Or book at Hotel Aliki, housed in a sea captain's elegant home on the unspoiled harbor, which can be viewed from most of the rooms and from the rooftop garden. A leisurely dinner at the Mylopetra, a 200-year-old flour mill, caps off the day—try the lamb or a homemade pasta flavored with Simiot herbs and spices.

Where: 150 miles/250 km southeast of Athens. **San Nikolis Hotel:** Tel 30/22410-34561; www.s-nikolis.gr. *Cost:* from $170. **Marco Polo Mansion:** Tel 30/22410-25562; www.marcopolomansion.gr. *Cost:* from $150 (off-peak), from $220 (peak); dinner $40. *When:* closed Nov–Feb. **Melenos Hotel:** Tel 30/22440-32222; www.melenoslindos.com. *Cost:* from $175 (off-peak), from $450 (peak); dinner $70. *When:* closed Nov–Mar. **Hotel Aliki:** Tel 30/22460-71665; www.simi-hotel-aliki.gr. *Cost:* from $100 (off-peak), from $195 (peak). *When:* closed mid-Oct–Mar. **Mylopetra:** Tel 30/22460-72333; www.mylopetra.com. *Cost:* dinner $65. *When:* closed Nov–Apr. **Best times:** May and Sep–Oct for pleasant weather and fewer crowds; late May for Medieval Rose Festival in Rhodes Town; Jul–Aug for Sími Festival with dance and music.

Spiritual Focus for the Eastern Orthodox World

Mount Athos

Macedonia, Greece

The Byzantine Empire may have ended with the fall of Constantinople in 1453, but tell that to the 1,400 or so monks of Mount Athos (the Holy Mountain), who carry on an unbroken 1,000-year tradition of study and liturgy. Women and children have not been allowed to set foot in this 140-square-mile semiautonomous state of the Greek Orthodox Church since the 11th century, but male visitors with the appropriate permit can step back 500 years to the time of the theocracy's heyday, when more than 40 monasteries housing 40,000 monks flourished.

Most of the 20 Eastern Orthodox monasteries that remain are on the rugged, pine-clad peninsula and resemble fortified castles, reminders that the monks once had to fend off pirates, European crusaders, and the Ottoman Turks. The monks have amassed priceless artwork and manuscripts over the years—the chance to see the sacred trove of relics, mosaics, and icons is one of the rewards for getting in rhythm with monastic routines that begin with prayer at 4:00 A.M. Visitors are welcome to dine in the refectory with the monks (meals are vegetarian) and stay in modest accommodations. Hikers can crisscross the peninsula on paths that climb forested mountainsides and plunge through unspoiled valleys ablaze with wildflowers. Rising above the pristine landscapes is 6,700-foot-tall Mount Athos, alleged to be the home of Zeus and Apollo before they made the move to nearby Mount Olympus.

Monks continue to live in the 11th-century Esphigmenou monastery, one of 20 on the peninsula.

Only 100 Orthodox and ten non-Orthodox men are welcomed onto the peninsula each day. Some monks are gregarious and welcoming, others oblivious to the almost constant stream of guests during summer months, when it is most difficult to procure a permit. Access is by 2½-hour boat ride from the nearby town of Ouranoupolis, and from there visitors can walk from one monastery to the next. Women (and men) can view the peninsula and seaside monasteries on one of many boat tours that cruise along the mountainous, forested shore. For visitors to the region not overnighting with the monks, the Eagles Palace in Ouranoupolis offers comfortably nonmonastic accommodations set amid tree-shaded grounds on its own beach.

WHERE: 80 miles/130 km southeast of Thessaloniki. **VISITOR INFO:** www.inathos.gr. **HOW:** Pilgrims must make requests for visits in writing to Mt. Athos Pilgrims' Bureau, 109 Egnatia, 54622 Thessaloniki, tel 30/2310-252578, fax 30/2310-222424. **EAGLES PALACE:** Tel 30/23770-31101; www.eaglespalace.gr. *Cost:* from $190. **BEST TIME:** May, when summertime pilgrims have not yet arrived and the countryside is in bloom.

Haunting Landscapes and Austere Towers

THE MANI PENINSULA

Peloponnese, Greece

For centuries, the Mani was inhospitable, a stark, rugged land where families engaged in banditry and bloody feuds and few outsiders dared to enter. The landscapes of the narrow peninsula, the middle of three prongs that extend from the southern Peloponnese, are no less haunting these days. Long, empty stretches of rockbound coast—lapped by the Aegean Sea in the east and the Ionian on the west—and craggy mountainsides are one of Greece's most unspoiled getaways.

The austere tower houses of Vathia and other nearby Maniot villages were built to protect against warring neighbors. The 800 still standing are now romantic sentinels rising above the rocky terrain. Some, such as the 19th-century Kapetanakou Tower Hotel, in the market town of Areopolis, are atmospheric guesthouses. The neighboring town of Limeni has been put on the culinary map thanks to its Fish Taverna Takis To, known for serving the peninsula's freshest catch.

Tower homes were designed to protect Vathia, at the southernmost point of the peninsula, from invading pirates or Turks.

Throughout the Mani, hiking paths follow mountain ravines past Byzantine chapels shaded by cypress trees and past broad bays. The Pirgos Dirou Caves, the Mani's one big attraction, extend for miles and are explored by boat along subterranean waterways canopied by fantastic stalactites. The humble beach town of Kardamyli is the gateway to the Outer Mani, the greener northern reaches of the region. The cypress-scented town was home to acclaimed travel writer Patrick Leigh Fermor, whose engaging 1958 classic *Mani* is considered the definitive book about this little-visited region. At Lela's Taverna, named after Fermor's former housekeeper and run by her son, old-fashioned dishes are served on a shady terrace perched just above the surf. Upstairs, five simple rooms overlook the sea.

Gerolimenas is the largest town in the Inner Mani, as the stark southern reaches of the region are known. Stone warehouses near the entrance to the harbor now house the comfortable and character-filled Kyrimai Hotel, where timbered, stone-walled guest rooms and poolside terraces edge the sea. Ancients believed that Cape Tenaro, at the southernmost tip of the Mani, was the entrance to the Underworld; looking at the forlorn, wind-shaped rock formations rising from the sea, it's easy to believe that is indeed the case.

WHERE: 185 miles/300 km southwest of Athens. **KAPETANAKOU TOWER HOTEL:** Tel 30/27330-51233; www.mani-hotel.com. *Cost:* from $100. *When:* closed Nov–Apr. **FISH TAVERNA TAKIS TO:** Tel 30/27330-51327. *Cost:* $40. **LELA'S TAVERNA:** Tel 30/27210-73541. *Cost:* $70; dinner $30. *When:* closed Nov–Mar. **KYRIMAI HOTEL:** Tel 30/27330-54288; www.kyrimai.gr. *Cost:* from $150. **BEST TIMES:** May–Jun and Sep–Oct for beautiful weather without intense heat; summer for plays staged at the Mani Theater in Platsa, south of Kardamyli.

Medieval Splendor on a Seaside Rock

MONEMVASSIA

Peloponnese, Greece

Monemvassia's nickname, "the Greek Mont St-Michel," conveys the charm of this walled medieval town that clings to the side of an islandlike rock jutting out of the southern Peloponnesian coast. As you approach along a causeway from the mainland, the rock seems to be uninhabited; then a lone Venetian gate, wide enough only for pedestrians and donkeys to pass through, appears in the side of the cliff. The name *moni emvassia,* the locals will tell you, means "single entrance."

Like Gibraltar, Monemvassia was once powerful thanks to its control of the sea lines between medieval Western Europe and the Levant during the time of the Byzantine, Venetian, and Ottoman empires. The number of beautiful Byzantine churches (40!) and façades adorned with elaborate stonework and marble attest to the town's onetime prosperity, with the octagonal 12th-century Agia Sofia (Holy Wisdom) perhaps its most beloved. Venetians took control of the town in 1464 and built the jagged line of (now ruined) fortifications high on the mountaintop. Making it to the top during your stay to experience the views is an obligatory rite, especially for sunset over the Mirtoon Sea.

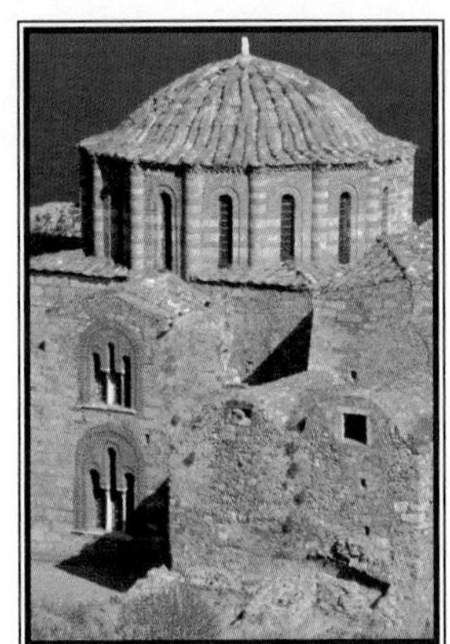

Agia Sofia is one of dozens of this peninsula's churches.

In recent years second-home owners have been renovating once-crumbling ruins, but off-season, Monemvassia is nearly deserted. A collection of three centuries-old buildings has been converted into the comfortable and atmospheric Hotel Malvasia, one of the Peloponnese's first boutique hotels. An unprecedented air of sophistication has recently arrived at the beautifully converted 13th-century mansion in the nearby hills above the sea—it is now the surpremely comfortable Kinsterna Hotel, where an opulent swimming pool is fed by an underground stream, and Ottoman-inspired lavender and rose scrubs are offered in the stylish spa.

WHERE: 217 miles/350 km south of Athens. **HOTEL MALVASIA:** Tel 30/27320-63007; www.malvasia-hotel.gr. *Cost:* from $125. **KINSTERNA HOTEL:** Tel 30/27320-66300; www.kinsternahotel.gr. *Cost:* from $260 (off-peak), from $370 (peak). **BEST TIMES:** Apr–Jun and Sep–Oct for fine weather and fewer crowds; 5 days around Jul 23 to celebrate liberation from the Turks.

Ancient Wonders Surround the Prettiest Town in the Peloponnese

NAFPLION AND NEARBY CLASSICAL SITES

Peloponnese, Greece

Nafplion is tucked onto a peninsula jutting into the Bay of Argos and backed by a range of imposing mountains on the mainland Peloponnese. This beautiful and well-preserved city offers such simple pleasures as long walks along a seaside promenade where the miniature 15th-century Bourtzi island fortress looms offshore, and lingering in any of the cafés lining Syntagma (Constitution) Square. Allot at least a morning at the Peloponnesian Folklore museum and its rich collection of traditional Greek costumes. But it is the town's proximity to some of the most evocative remains of ancient Greece that sets it apart.

The perfectly preserved theater at Epidaurus, 25 miles east, retains the original stage of beaten earth and 54 tiers of seats that accommodate 14,000, just as when the theater was built in the 4th century B.C. The theater is an architectural wonder famous for its near-perfect acoustics and the perfect venue for the classics of Sophocles and Euripides and musical concerts held here during the summertime Athens and Epidaurus Festival.

The oldest city on the Greek mainland (Knossos in Crete is older; see p. 160), Mycenae is located on a rocky hillside 12 miles north of Nafplion. It was the center of the Mycenaean civilization, which dominated the Mediterranean world from 1500 to 1100 B.C., and was the realm of the powerful King Agamemnon. Gold death masks and other treasures unearthed since the mid-19th century can be seen in the National Archaeological Museum in Athens (see p. 158), though there are copies on view in the new Mycenae Archaeological Museum. You can continue 35 miles north of Nafplion to ancient Corinth, which once rivaled Athens in wealth and power. The landmark Temple of Apollo was constructed at the city's height, in 550 B.C.; seven of the original 38 Doric columns still stand.

Make your home the family-run Aetoma boutique hotel, an 18th-century mansion full of family heirlooms on one of Nafplion's quiet squares. The same warm atmosphere envelops

The Mycenae Archaeological Museum holds frescoes and other artifacts that illustrate daily life in ancient times.

Paleo Archontika, serving traditional cooking in a stone-walled room and at tables on a narrow Old Town street. The Nafplia Palace, built in the 1970s on a cliff high above the Old Town, provides the most luxurious lodgings in town—its newer, handsome villas have private terraces and pools that look out on astounding views. At the Amphitryon, a sister property just below, chic rooms overlook the sea from contemporary teak-floored decks.

WHERE: 85 miles/136 km southwest of Athens. **FESTIVAL INFO:** Contact Hellenic Festivals, tel 30/210-928-2900; www.greekfestival.gr. *When:* weekends Jun–Aug. **HOTEL AETOMA:** Tel 30/27250-27373; www.nafplionhotel.com. *Cost:* from $160. **PALEO ARCHONTIKA:** Tel 30/27520-22449. *Cost:* lunch $20. **NAFPLIA PALACE AND AMPHITRYON:** Tel 30/27520-70700; www.helioshotels.gr. *Cost:* from $315; villas from $600. **BEST TIMES:** May–Jun and Sep–Oct to explore ruins but avoid summer heat; Jun for Nafplion Music Festival.

Monasteries Suspended Between Heaven and Earth

METÉORA

Thessaly, Greece

Perched on seemingly inaccessible pinnacles of rock 1,000 feet above the flat Piniós Valley, the six remaining monasteries of Metéora are as removed from earthly distractions as possible. *Metéora* means, literally, "in midair," and there are more than 60 pinnacles, looking like chimney-top storks' nests. The spikes, cones, and cliffs of this rock-forest landscape were created by thrusts of the seafloor and were then etched by the elements over the ages into curious and otherworldly shapes.

Hermit monks began living in caves in the rocks in the 9th century. As Turks took over the mainland, the monks discovered that the inaccessible pinnacles were safe refuges and by the 16th century had built 24 monasteries and hermitages, every stone or piece of lumber being hoisted up by ropes and pulleys. Until the 1920s, the only way for monks or visitors to reach them was by retractable ladders or nets. Since then steps to the monasteries have been hewn into the rocks, and some are now accessible by paths and roads as well.

Unlike the male-only domain of Mount Athos (see p. 167), the Metéora monasteries are open to all visitors for daytime (but not overnight) visits. On an energetic day you can visit all six, though most pilgrims settle for two or three. Within their hallowed walls are spartan living quarters, contrasted by churches decorated with frescoes and icons and libraries filled with ancient books and manuscripts. Megálou Meteórou is the grandest and the highest and possibly the oldest, having held sway over the area since it was built of massive rocks on the highest peak (1,360 feet) in the 14th century. Agia Triada may hold claim to the most spectacular position. All the monasteries are worth visiting for the religious artworks collected over the centuries, the views, and the chance to experience some of the most peculiar real estate on the planet. You are also likely to enjoy pleasant encounters with the few monks and nuns who continue to live in these unique surroundings.

Roussanou Monastery is surrounded by rocks of ever-higher elevations.

WHERE: 220 miles/356 km northwest of Athens. **WHERE TO STAY:** The new and stylish Dellas Hotel is near Kalambaka on the way to Metéora. Tel 30/24320-78260; www.dellasboutiquehotel.com. *Cost:* from $90. **BEST TIMES:** The feast days of the patron saints of the various monasteries: Agia Triada, Jun 2; Agios Stefanos, last Sun of Aug; Agia Varvara, Dec 4; Agios Nikolaos, Dec 6.

Byzantine Wonders on Aphrodite's Island

Cyprus's Painted Churches

Troodos Mountains, Cyprus

Cyprus is a land divided, historically between Greece and Turkey and these days also between crowded beach resorts and quieter, off-the-beaten-path places in its interior. Get away to the pine-scented Troodos mountain range, stretching across the Greek-controlled southwest corner of the island and largely preserved as a national park. Above seaside Lemosos and on the eastern flank of 6,500-foot Mt. Olympus, you'll also find ten magnificent medieval churches and monasteries, whose modest exteriors stand in contrast to their rich interiors, embellished with some of the finest Byzantine frescoes and icons in the Mediterranean.

At the ornate 11th-century Kykkos Monastery, even the cloisters are richly frescoed and a golden icon of the Virgin ascribed to St. Luke is said to work miracles. Agios Nikolaos tis Stegis (St. Nicholas of the Roof) is covered entirely in wall paintings.

The monks who lived here were not only gifted artists but also master vintners, following a 5,500-year-old wine-making tradition in Cyprus. Stop at Chrysorrogiatissa Monastery for a visit to the region's oldest wine-making site. The dark amber–colored Commandaria, a sweet wine that was a favorite elixir of medieval crusaders, is thought to be the world's oldest appellation and is made from centuries-old vines in the Troodos foothills. For something with a little more kick, stop in any village bar for a glass of *zivania,* a centuries-old Cypriot beverage produced from the residue of grapes. With a 45 percent (and up) alcohol content, it is also used to treat wounds and sore throats.

It is only fitting that Cyprus is so well entrenched in the sensual arts, being the birthplace of Aphrodite, goddess of love and beauty and protectress of the island. She allegedly arose from sea foam at Paphos, on the southwestern coast where the massive Rock of Aphrodite marks the spot and where a temple was built in her honor. Among the many antiquities in and around Paphos connected with the goddess and her cult is a wealth of colorful mosaics—including a rich cycle from the villa of a Roman nobleman, depicting the wine god Dionysus.

Where: Most of the monasteries and churches are within a 25 mile/40 km radius of Lemosos, in southwest Cyrpus. **Best times:** Apr–Jun, when heat is not yet intense and wildflowers are in bloom; Jul–Aug for International Festival of Ancient Greek Drama in Paphos.

Whimsical Trulli and Golden Beaches

Alberobello and the Salento Peninsula

Apulia, Italy

In Alberobello, a town with a peculiar charm, the *zona monumentale* of whitewashed, conical roofed houses known as *trulli* takes visitors inside a child's storybook—imagine Snow White and the Seven Dwarfs as interpreted by Tolkien. There are as many as 1,500 of these unique beehive structures in Alberobello and the surrounding Valle d'Itria, where they crop up in clusters like mushrooms.

The unique, rather eerie trulli have primitive shapes and mysterious rooftop decorations that give the impression that they are ancient, when in fact most date to the 18th century. Today the trulli are used as homes, stores, storage space—even the church of Sant'Antonio is in the form of a trullo. If you fancy eating in an 18th-century barn, the region's most elegant restaurant is Il Poeta Contadino, offering one of the area's best renditions of the simple *cucina pugliese.* Among the other charms of Apulia, on the heel of the Italian "boot," are unspoiled sunny landscapes, golden sands, and lavish Baroque monuments.

The cone-shaped trulli, *still inhabited today, are found nowhere else in the world.*

Fortified farmhouses called *masseri* are also unique to the region. Just east of Alberobello, two have been converted to comfortable hotels: Whitewashed Masseria San Domenico is one of the south's finest resorts, with a golf course, private beach, spa, and highly acclaimed restaurant, while Masseria Il Frantoio provides a more rustic charm, with rooms overlooking olive groves and meals made from the bounty of the working farm enjoyed alfresco.

In the heart of the Salento Peninsula, Lecce is a whimsical place: A sun-drenched theater set, it is known as the Florence of the South, where Baroque palazzos and churches are ornately carved in golden stone. Every inch of the façade of the Basilica di Santa Croce swirls with saints, demons, and imaginary creatures. If you stay at the Patria Palace Hotel, the basilica will be just out the front door. You'll also be close to Trattoria Cucina Casereccia (aka Le Zie, "the aunts"), which serves homemade pastas and other dishes deceptively known as *cucina povera,* poor man's cooking, in a no-frills, old-fashioned setting.

Where: 37 miles/60 km southeast of Bari. **Il Poeta Contadino:** Tel 39/080-432-1917; www.ilpoetacontadino.it. *Cost:* dinner $50. **Masseria San Domenico:** Tel 39/080-482-7769; www.masseriasandomenico.com. *Cost:* from $500 (off-peak), from $700 (peak). *When:* closed mid-Jan–Mar. **Masseria Il Frantoio:** Tel 39/0831-330276; www.masseriailfrantoio.it. *Cost:* $200 (off-peak), $315 (peak). **Hotel Patria Palace:** Tel 39/0832-245111; www.patriapalacelecce.com. *Cost:* $190. **Trattoria Cucina Casereccia:** Tel 39/0832-245-178; www.lezie.it. *Cost:* dinner $25. **Best times:** Apr–Jun and Sep–early Oct for nicest weather; in Lecce: mid-Jul for Jazz in Puglia festival; late Aug for Fiera di Sant' Oronzo, celebrating the city's patron saint.

A City Carved Out of Stone

The Sassi of Matera

Matera, Basilicata, Italy

Walking through Matera, one of the oldest inhabited cities on earth, is like stepping back into the primitive past. Some of the cave houses (or *sassi,* Italian for "stones") etched out of the soft tufa walls of a ravine have been inhabited for the past 9,000 years. The jumble of houses and churches are so evocative of biblical times that the town has served as a backdrop for dozens of movies including Pier Paolo Pasolini's 1964 classic *The Gospel According to St. Matthew* and Mel Gibson's *The Passion of the Christ.*

Families and their livestock once lived in the single-room caverns, while other caves were churches where the rock walls have been covered with frescoes. Some of these *chiese rupestri* (rock churches), such as the Crypt of Original Sin, are found outside the city center. Here, the crypt is so elaborately covered with images of colorful saints that it is known as the Sistine Chapel of cave churches.

In the 1950s, the Italian government moved some 20,000 impoverished cave dwellers to accommodations in the modern town. Since the 1970s, the *sassi* have slowly been reclaimed, used as homes, hotels, and restaurants.

Travelers can now bed down in stylishly refurbished caves at the Locanda di San Martino, where amenities include a swimming pool and thermal baths fashioned out of subterranean cisterns. At the Sassi di Matera Albergo Diffuso, caves are much the same way entrepreneur Daniele Kihlgren found them, with rough stone flooring and pitted walls chiseled by shepherds millennia ago; the sparse, simple furnishings are authentic and include vintage wrought-iron beds. Le Botteghe is one of many Matera restaurants that focus on the simple, distinctive flavors of the hilly, sparsely populated Basilicata region. Great antipasti, pasta with fried peppers and bread crumbs, delicious full-flavored cheeses, and crusty bread make for simple meals you won't forget.

WHERE: 124 miles/199 km southeast of Naples. **LOCANDA DI SAN MARTINO:** Tel 39/0835-256600; www.locandadisanmartino.it. *Cost:* from $135. **SASSI DI MATERA ALBERGO DIFFUSO:** Tel 39/0835-332744; www.sassidimatera.com. *Cost:* from $295. **LE BOTTEGHE:** Tel 39/0835-344072; www.hotelamatera.it. *Cost:* dinner $45. **BEST TIME:** Jul 2 for Festa per la Madonna della Bruna (Festival of the Brown Madonna), when an elaborately decorated cart is paraded through the streets, then torn to shreds, representing destroying the old to usher in the new.

La Dolce Vita and Italy's Dream Drive

THE AMALFI COAST

Campania, Italy

The vertiginous Amalfi Drive is a 30-mile stretch of hairpin curves that unfurls between Amalfi and Sorrento. Cliffs plunge into an impossibly blue Mediterranean, as a coastline of seaside towns and some of Italy's most precipitously-sited and glamorous retreats unfold among terraced olive and lemon groves and umbrella pines.

Tiny, picturesque Amalfi was the heart of a powerful maritime republic as early as the 9th century. A hint of the east shows up in its Duomo di Sant'Andrea: Mosaics adorn the cathedral's façade and the Moorish cloister suggests an Arabian courtyard. Some of that magic permeates the informally luxurious and character-filled Hotel Santa Caterina, tucked high above the coast in lemon-scented gardens; an elevator descends to a seaside swimming platform and the thatch-roofed Ristorante al Mare.

Ravello, perched 1,100 feet above Amalfi, is aptly described as "the place where poets go to die." Two romantic gardens—the Villa Rufolo and the Villa Cimbrone—are a stroll away from the 12th-century Moorish-inspired Palazzo Sasso hotel. You can get lost in the limitless views of the cerulean sea and sky from the balconies and floor-to-ceiling windows of the beautifully appointed guest rooms. The wrap-around views from the infinity pool of the nearby Hotel Caruso make it appear to float above the sea from the highest point in town and are reason enough to make this your home. For the best trattoria fare in town, follow the aroma of simmering tomato sauce and roast lamb to Cumpà Cosimo for delicious, full-flavored Neapolitan cooking and local white wines.

Cliffside Positano is a jumble of converted whitewashed and colored fishermen's houses that spill down a maze of narrow alleyways to the pebbly umbrella-lined beach. The Hotel le Sirenuse, a Pompeiian-red 18th-century villa draped in bougainvillea and honeysuckle, is operated by the same aristocratic family whose summer retreat this once was. Floors are paved in cool, hand-painted tiles, and a mingling of precious antiques enhances the hotel's personal elegance. Or travel just minutes out of town to the Hotel San Pietro, carved dramatically into a precipitous cliff. An elevator cut into solid rock descends to the airy lobby, terraced guest rooms, and the vest-pocket-size beach for guests. For a more affordable stay, few places have the views and charms of the family-run Casa Albertina.

Hop onto the motorboat for a 10-minute ride to the outdoor Da Adolfo for lunch of fresh grilled *mozzarella di bufala* and spaghetti with plump baby clams, then pull up a beach chair on the tiny beach and sleep it off.

The hazy outline of Mount Vesuvius dominates the view from cliff-top Sorrento, favored among 19th-century British travelers for its mild winters. At the Grand Hotel Excelsior Vittoria, marble staircases, elaborate Art Nouveau frescoes, and white-gloved service ensure that guests feel as enveloped in luxury as in that golden age. Save one evening for the 15-minute drive to Sant'Agata, where Alfonso and Livia Iaccarino's acclaimed hillside restaurant, Don Alfonso 1890, promises a magical evening.

WHERE: Amalfi is 38 miles/61 km southeast of Naples. **HOTEL SANTA CATERINA:** Tel 39/089-871-012; www.hotelsantacaterina.it. *Cost:* from $415 (off-peak), from $610 (peak). **PALAZZO SASSO:** Tel 39/089-818181; in the U.S., 800-323-7500; www.palazzosasso.com. *Cost:* from $330 (off-peak), from $460 (peak). *When:* Apr–mid-Oct. **HOTEL CARUSO:** Tel 39/089-858801; in the U.S., 800-237-1236; www.hotelcaruso.com. *Cost:* from $700 (off-peak), from $1,085 (peak). *When:* closed Nov–Mar. **CUMPÀ COSIMO:** Tel 39/089-857156. *Cost:* dinner $40. **HOTEL LE SIRENUSE:** Tel 39/089-875066; www.sirenuse.it. *Cost:* from $500 (off-peak), from $725 (peak). *When:* Nov–Mar. **SAN PIETRO:** Tel 39/089-875455; in the U.S., 800-735-2478; www.ilsanpietro.it. *Cost:* from $600 (off-peak), from $770 (peak). *When:* closed Nov–Mar. **HOTEL CASA ALBERTINA:** Tel 39/089-875143; www.hotelcasaalbertina.com. *Cost:* from $170 (off-peak), from $260 (peak). **DA ADOLFO:** Tel 39/089-875022; www.daadolfo.com. *Cost:* lunch $35. **GRAND HOTEL EXCELSIOR VITTORIA:** Tel 39/081-877-7111; in the U.S., 800-223-6800; www.exvitt.it. *Cost:* from $330 (off-peak), from $500 (peak). **DON ALFONSO 1890:** Tel 39/081-878-0026; www.donalfonso.com. *Cost:* from $400 (off-peak), from $640 (peak); dinner $200. *When:* Nov–Mar. **BEST TIMES:** May and Sep for mild weather and fewer crowds; Apr–Oct for Wagner Festival in Ravello; Jun 27 and Nov 30 for celebrating Amalfi's patron Sant'Andrea.

The view of the Amalfi coast from Ravello, one of the most exquisite in Italy, has inspired artists from Turner to Miró.

Playground of Roman Emperors and Modern-Day Sybarites

Capri and Ischia

Campania, Italy

Capri has been a favored summer playground since the Roman emperor Tiberius made the Villa Jovis—now an evocative cliff-top ruin with breathtaking views—his ruling seat in A.D. 26. Today, artists, designers, movie stars, divas, politicians, writers, royals, and financiers make regular appearances in the Piazzetta, described by Noël Coward as "the most beautiful operetta stage in the world." The hallmarks of this 5-square-mile getaway surrounded by emerald waters are the Faraglioni, three needlelike rocks towering just off the rugged coast. A boat trip into the azure light of the Grotta Azzurra (Blue Grotto) is justifiably one of the world's most written-about tourist experiences, while up in the town of Anacapri, the lush Mediterranean garden of the Villa San Michele offers a chance to escape the day-tripping crowds.

Despite the glitterati, Capri is not a fancy place. Pretensions are kept in check at the Hotel La Scalinatella, Capri's hideaway in excelsis, high above the sea. Providing relaxed luxury in a breezy villa, its 30 bright rooms all have open sea views. The bigger, more extravagant Hotel Quisisana, from the same owners, is one of the few accommodations in the heart of town. At the more modest Hotel Luna, there are views of the Faraglioni from the gardens, pool, and most of the 30 rooms.

The sun, the sea, good wine, and great food come together simply but gloriously on a sun-dappled, seaside terrace of La Fontelina, with the Faraglioni in sight. Diners can sunbathe and swim before and after a lunch that's likely to include the restaurant's signature fruit-filled sangria and a simple *insalata caprese,* the island specialty of super-fresh mozzarella and just-picked tomatoes. Dinner at Da Paolino is served in a lemon grove above the main port, where lantern-size fruits drip from the branches above your table, garnish your grilled fish, and flavor the homemade sorbet.

Larger, more laid-back Ischia, floating nearby in the Bay of Naples, is ringed with sandy beaches and so forested with fragrant pines that it's known as the Emerald Island. Although Ischia's Monte Epomeo has not erupted in more than 700 years, the dormant volcano still keeps the island's many thermal pools bubbling; its volcanic mud treatments have been known since antiquity. The seaside Grande Albergo Mezzatorre, built around a 16th-century villa and tower once used as a lookout for pirates, now has 59 contemporary rooms and a chic thermal spa.

Where: Capri is 22 miles/36 km south of Naples. **La Scalinatella:** Tel 39/081-837-0633; www.scalinatella.com. *Cost:* from $425 (off-peak), from $640 (peak). *When:* closed Nov–Mar. **Hotel Quisisana:** Tel 39/081-837-0788; www.quisisana.com. *Cost:* from $475. *When:* Mar or Apr–Oct. **Hotel Luna:** Tel 39/081-837-0433; www.lunahotel.com. *Cost:* from $300 (off-peak), from $420 (peak). *When:* closed mid-Oct–mid-Apr. **La Fontelina:** Tel 39/081-837-0845. *Cost:* lunch $35. *When:* closed Nov–mid-Apr. **Da Paolino:** Tel 39/081-837-6102; www.paolinocapri.com. *Cost:* dinner $65. *When:* closed Nov–Feb or Mar. **Grande Albergo Mezzatorre:** Tel 39/081-986111; www.mezzatorre.it. *Cost:* from $460 (off-peak), from $660 (peak). *When:* closed mid-Oct–late Apr. **Best times:** May and Sep for mild weather and fewer crowds.

Twenty-Five Centuries of Culture, Neapolitan Style

Naples

Campania, Italy

More than two millennia of history stokes the vitality and energy of this modern-day port city famous for its high-spirited, chaotic everyday life. Naples was the seat of a powerful, independent kingdom for more than 500 years, and drew Europe's finest architects and artists.

Explore its many historic overlays in the colorful Spaccanapoli, at the heart of the old city. Once an enclave of monumental palazzos and magnificent churches, Spaccanapoli now bustles against a backdrop of time-battered tenements and workshops; laundry hangs across narrow alleys; and Vespa-filled streets thrum with local vendors who hawk everything from contraband DVDs to gelato.

Food is a top priority in this city on the bay—said to be the birthplace of pizza—where small family-owned food shops line the backstreets.

Stroll to the massive, brooding Duomo, the Cathedral of San Gennaro, whose richly filigreed interior invites you to linger, or visit the National Museum of Archaeology, which holds priceless antiquities from nearby Pompeii (see next page). A veritable oasis in the city's center is Costantinopoli 104, the former home of a 19th-century marchesa, transformed into an elegant boutique hotel. The palm-shaded terrace surrounds a small pool, and the rooms reflect a classic yet contemporary aesthetic.

The bay-fronting Castel Nuovo, a massive fortification with ominous towers, moats, and dungeons that dates from the 13th century, is now home to Naples's civic museum. It's not far to the Palazzo Reale, the art-jammed 17th-century palace that was home to Naples's monarchs, and the famed Teatro di San Carlo opera house, one of Europe's largest and most splendid. Music courses through the veins of the *napoletani*: Enrico Caruso was born here and kept an apartment in the historic waterfront Grand Hotel Vesuvio, still one of the city's best addresses for old-world luxury and breathtaking views from the rooftop Ristorante Caruso. Not far from the Teatro San Carlo, the Chiaja Hotel de Charme has an elegant atmosphere and an interesting past as a high-end brothel.

Neapolitans insist that they invented pizza—it certainly was perfected here. The no-frills Da Michele, established in 1870, is considered by many the "sacred temple of pizza." Pizzeria Brandi, 100 years older, claims to have originated the Margherita pizza, first made for Italy's Queen Margherita with plump tomatoes, local *mozzarella di bufala*, and fresh basil—its colors echoing the Italian flag.

Where: 117 miles/189 km south of Rome. **Costantinopoli 104:** Tel 39/081-557-1035; www.costantinopoli104.com. *Cost:* from $200 (off-peak), from $315 (peak). **Grand Hotel Vesuvio:** Tel 39/081-764-0044; in the U.S., 800-223-6800; www.vesuvio.it. *Cost:* from $350. **Chiaja Hotel de Charme:** Tel

39/081-415555; www.hotelchiaia.it. *Cost:* from $145. **Da Michele:** Tel 39/081-553-9204; www.damichele.net. *Cost:* pizza $13. **Pizzeria Brandi:** Tel 39/081-416-928; www.brandi.it. *Cost:* pizza $13. **Best times:** Apr–Jun and Sep–Nov for fairest weather; 1st Sun in May and Sep 19 for celebrations of the city's patron, San Gennaro.

Treasures of Vanished Civilizations

Naples's Antiquities

Campania, Italy

Looming over the storied Gulf of Naples is Mount Vesuvius, the still-active 4,193-foot volcano that on Aug 24, A.D. 79, erupted with incredible force, spewing volcanic ash and mud over nearby cities and preserving them almost intact. Pompeii was the largest of the buried cities: It slumbered under 20 feet of ash for more than 1,500 years before its discovery and excavation, which continues today.

The Pompeiian homes, wine shops, public baths, and bordellos are windows on the life that flourished in this thriving port city during the days of the Caesars. The villas of the Casa del Fauno (House of the Faun), the elegant Casa dei Vettii, and the Villa dei Misteri (House of Mysteries) are worth visiting for their mosaics and frescoes. Once the center of daily life, the Stabian Baths survived—with rather explicit frescoes suggesting that something more than bathing went on here. Though the visible ruins of Pompeii are extensive, about two thirds (some 60 acres) remain buried. More than 2.5 million tourists visit yearly, but Pompeii is large enough to provide quiet corners and elusive enough to require a guide.

The town of Herculaneum (Ercolano) was also destroyed by Vesuvius, whose fast-moving waves of volcanic ash and mud served to preserve wooden structures, textiles, and, at the Villa dei Papiri, some 1,800 papyrus scrolls. Herculaneum is less thronged than Pompeii and gives fascinating insights into the lifestyles of the Roman elite, particularly at the House of the Stags and at the public baths of the House of Neptune and Amphitrite.

Most of the precious sculpture, murals, and mosaics excavated from Pompeii and Herculaneum can be found at Naples's National Museum of Archaeology, one of the world's richest treasure troves of Greco-Roman antiquities. The Gabinetto Segreto (Secret Gallery) contains more than 200 sexually explicit artworks on view only since 2000.

Not all of Naples's ruins date from Roman times: The Greek temple complex at Paestum, on the Sorrentine Peninsula, is one of the best preserved and the oldest; the so-called Basilica is the 6th-century B.C. Doric temple to Hera. Guests of the nearby Tenuta Seliano can enjoy warm hospitality at the *agriturismo* farm and inn of the Baronessa Cecilia Bellelli Baratta, whose herd of water buffalo supplies Italy with some of its finest *mozzarella di bufala.*

Where: Pompeii is 15 miles/24 km southeast of Naples. **Pompeii and Herculaneum:** Tel 390/81-857-5347; www.pompeiisites.org. **National Museum of Archaeology:** Tel 39/081-292823; http://museoarcheologiconazionale.campaniabeniculturali.it. **Paestum:** Tel 39/082-881-1016; www.infopaestum.it. **Tenuta Seliano:** Tel 39/082-872-3634; www.agriturismoseliano.it. *Cost:* from $130. *When:* closed Nov–mid-Mar. **Best times:** May–Jun and Sep–Oct for fine weather.

Where Food Is a Magnificent Obsession

The Quadrilatero

Bologna, Emilia-Romagna, Italy

Being the preeminent culinary center of a food-conscious country is an imposing role that "Bologna la Grassa" (Bologna the Fat One) has shouldered proudly and insouciantly for centuries. Those who come to this handsome medieval city solely for gastronomic pleasures never leave disappointed.

The Quadrilatero, the city's well-known food district, is just east of Piazza Maggiore, where sturdy brick palazzos and the massive Basilica di San Petronio surround an enormous fountain of Neptune. Step into this medieval labyrinth, the city's oldest and best-preserved quarter, and follow narrow streets named for guilds and lined with family-run shops and the stalls of the food markets. Window displays are piled high with fish, cheeses, wild mushrooms, cured meats, and Bologna's own inventions: mortadella sausage (the distant granddaddy of American bologna), tortellini hand-stuffed with meat and cheese, and the exquisitely chunky ragú alla bolognese. Everyone winds up at the legendary Tamburini, Italy's most lavish food emporium. A visit here is more about cultural enhancement than shopping, but no one leaves the store empty-handed. If you come at lunchtime, you can sample from the mouth-watering array of dishes at VeloCibò, the store's self-service bistro.

The city's chefs transform fresh market offerings into seasonal-based favorites at such eateries as Drogheria della Rosa, northeast of the Quadrilatero near the 11th-century university, the oldest in the Western world. A meal here and at other atmospheric trattorias lends credence to the old Italian saying that the two best places to eat are your mother's house and Bologna. You can also sleep well in Bologna, amid the plush luxury of the Grand Hotel Majestic or beneath medieval beams at the Corona d'Oro 1890, a chic inn occupying an aristocratic 14th-century palace in the shadow of the Due Torri, the city's famously leaning twin towers.

Where: 66 miles/106 km north of Florence. **Tamburini:** Tel 39/051-234726; www.tamburini.com. **Drogheria della Rosa:** Tel 39/051-222529; www.drogheriadellarosa.it. *Cost:* dinner $35. **Grand Hotel Majestic:** Tel 39/051-225445; http://grandhotelmajestic.duetorrihotels.com/en. *Cost:* from $275. **Hotel Corona d'Oro 1890:** Tel 39/051-236456; www.bolognarthotels.it. *Cost:* from $285.

A City of Great Art and Refinement

Piazza del Duomo

Parma, Emilia-Romagna, Italy

Parma is known as the home of Arturo Toscanini and Giuseppe Verdi and for such culinary delights as parmigiano cheese and prosciutto. This elegant little city offers much more, as you'll determine the moment you set foot in the Piazza del Duomo, one of the loveliest in Italy. The octagonal Battistero (Baptistery), perhaps the finest example of Romanesque architecture in northern Italy, is clad in pink Verona marble and festooned with reliefs by the local sculptor and architect Benedetto Antelami. A high point, quite literally, of the 12th-century Duomo next door is looking up toward the restored cupola at Antonio Correggio's famous *Assumption of the Virgin* (1522–1530). The "divine" Correggio was a great master of the High Renaissance, although the concentric circles of figures were described as a "mess of frogs' legs" by the bishop who commissioned the piece. You can get your fill of the Piazza del Duomo views from one of the large, antiques-filled guest rooms at the family-run Palazzo Dalla Rosa Prati.

Work on the Battistero began in 1196 and took over 100 years to complete.

Parma exudes a sense of well-being that harks back to its days of splendor as capital of the Farnese dukes from the mid-16th to the early 18th century and later as the duchy of Marie-Louise, widow of Napoleon. Marie-Louise filled the ducal palace, now the Galleria Nazionale, with art and left the city the Teatro Reggio, one of the world's finest opera houses. A meal based on the city's legendary ham and hard, pungent cheese at any number of excellent trattorias is usually a memorable performance as well. Sample the regional specialties at the acclaimed La Greppia, helmed by artistic chef Paola Cavazzini. Explore Parma's culinary traditions of cheese, prosciutto, and tomatoes in museums that are located in and around the city and together comprise the Musei del Cibo (Food Museums).

Where: 60 miles/97 km northwest of Bologna. **Palazzo Dalla Rosa Prati:** Tel 39/0521-386429; www.palazzodallarosaprati.it. *Cost:* from $195. **La Greppia:** Tel 39/0521-233686; www.ristoranteparmalagreppia.com. *Cost:* dinner $80. **Musei del Cibo:** www.museidelcibo.it. **How:** Food Valley Travel offers food and culture tours. Tel 39/0521-798515; www.foodvalleytravel.com. **Best times:** mid-Sep for Festival del Prosciutto di Parma; last weekend in Sep for medieval races of Palio di Parma; Oct for Verdi festival.

Dazzling Mosaics in a Former Capital of the Byzantine Empire

Ravenna

Emilia-Romagna, Italy

Ravenna's mosaics—among the most important in Western art—evoke the city's storied past as the last capital of the Western Roman Empire after the fall of Rome in the 5th century. Today Ravenna is sleepy, unpretentious, and—a blessing for art lovers—rarely crowded. The city's solid redbrick buildings contrast with the brilliance and refinement of the mosaics that cover the interiors of churches and mausoleums with designs of epic proportion and detail. There are six places to see these tapestries of mosaics, commissioned by the Byzantine rulers in their attempt to have Ravenna outdo rival cities. Most visited are the 6th-century Tomb of Gallia Placidia, who ran the Western Empire for 20 years as regent to her son, and the adjacent, octagonal Basilica di San

Vitale, a tribute to the Emperor Justinian and held by many to be the crowning achievement of Byzantine art in the world.

Among Ravenna's other monuments is the simple tomb of Dante Alighieri. The early Renaissance thinker and author of the *Divine Comedy* was banished from his hometown of Florence and died in Ravenna in 1321.

Where: 46 miles/74 km east of Bologna. **Visitor info:** www.ravennamosaici.it. **Where to stay:** Albergo Cappello offers contemporary style in a frescoed, 14th-century palazzo. Tel 39/0544-219813; www.albergocappello.it. *Cost:* from $185 (off-peak), from $260 (peak). **Best time:** Jun–Jul for Ravenna Festival of opera and classical music.

Crossroads of the North

Friuli

Friuli–Venezia Giulia, Italy

Tucked away into Italy's northeast corner, just south of Austria and snug against the border of Slovenia, Friuli is where Italians escape on gastronomic holidays. From the Adriatic coast and the regional capital of Trieste northward to the Julian Alps, Friuli is a landscape rich with mountain meadows, rolling hillsides, and fertile plains. It is a small region with a big reputation for sweet prosciutto hams from the village of San Daniele, robust artisanal cheeses, and what many consider Italy's best white wines from the Friulano grape. As befits the crossroads of Latin, Germanic, and Slavic cultures, the *cucina friulana* features hearty sausages, goulash, and polenta alongside *cjalsons* (sweet-and-savory ravioli), wafers of fried Montasio cheese called *frico,* and delicate herb sauces on pasta.

The stately medieval city of Udine, with its handsome Renaissance buildings by Andrea Palladio and wealth of luminous paintings by Tiepolo, stands at the center of it all. Chef Emanuele Scarello runs Agli Amici, his family's trattoria, which dates from 1887. His inventive cooking calls on the region's Austrian, Slovenian, and Italian traditions. Keepers of the flame of local cuisine, the Del Fabbro family operates Trattorìa Al Grop, a venerable inn in Tavagnacco, famed for its vast repertoire of recipes featuring the celebrated local asparagus. A few minutes' drive east of Udine, the medieval village of Cividale del Friuli is the hub of the wine trade in the Colli Orientali growing district. Locanda al Castello offers 16 atmospheric rooms in a vine-covered brick castle, originally a Jesuit monastery. Its dining room is noted for the local recipes made famous in the U.S. by chef, author, and TV personality Lidia Bastianich. She and son Joseph operate the nearby winery Azienda Agricola Bastianich, in Gagliano. The crowning glory of their operation is the single-vineyard selection of Friulano, the local grape that makes an intense, complex white wine.

Where: Udine is 79 miles/127 km northeast of Venice. **Trattoria Agli Amici:** Tel 39/0432-565411; www.agliamici.it. *Cost:* dinner $75. **Al Grop:** Tel 39/0432-660240; www.algrop.net. *Cost:* $160; dinner $60. **Locanda al Castello:** Tel 39/0432-733242; www.alcastello.net. *Cost:* $215; dinner $60. **Azienda Agricola Bastianich:** Tel 39/0462-700943; www.bastianich.com. **Best times:** Mar–Apr for asparagus season; late Jun for San Daniele prosciutto festival; and Sep–Oct for wine harvest.

"If there was no Rome, I would dream of her."
—SIR LAURENCE OLIVIER IN *SPARTACUS*

ROME

Lazio, Italy

Take in the swirling traffic and exuberance of life in the Italian capital and it's easy to believe that all roads lead to Rome. The city can overwhelm its visitors with millennia of history, unrivaled art collections, neighborhoods that feel like small villages, and an enviable marriage of *carpe diem* and *la dolce vita.* See the sights, embrace the vitality, and do as the Romans do: Linger awhile with an espresso or *aperitivo* while watching unfold the amazing spectacle that is Rome, *caput mundi.*

TOP ATTRACTIONS

BASILICA OF SANTA MARIA MAGGIORE—One of the city's four major basilicas was built in the 5th century on a site said to have been chosen by the Virgin Mary, then restored and extended between the 12th and 18th centuries. The original mosaics are among the oldest and most beautiful in the city; the 15th-century ceiling is said to have been gilded with some of the first gold brought from the New World; and rare marbles in the Cappella Sistina were plundered from a tower erected by Septimius Severus in A.D. 203. **INFO:** Tel 39/06-488-1094.

Eighty entrance arches run along the perimeter of the Coliseum, including four grand entrances.

BORGHESE GALLERY—The luxury-loving Cardinal Scipione Borghese amassed much of this rich collection through his patronage of the finest artists of his day. Marble sculptures such as Bernini's *Apollo and Daphne* and Casanova's *Pauline Bonaparte* join Caravaggio's *David with the Head of Goliath* and other treasures to fill several rooms in this wonderful 17th-century villa. **INFO:** Tel 39/06-32810; www.galleriaborghese.it.

THE COLISEUM—Once able to seat 50,000, the Coliseum was begun in A.D. 72 by Vespasian at a site just east of the Roman Forum (see next page). Neglected over the centuries, its stones quarried for other monuments and churches, the largest Roman amphitheater in the world is the enduring symbol of the Eternal City and the grandeur that was Rome. The mighty shell is forever associated with gory combat—between men, between animals, between men and animals, and even between ships, as the whole thing could once be flooded for mock sea battles. **INFO:** Tel 39/06-700-4261.

THE PANTHEON—Built in 27 B.C. by Marcus Agrippa and reconstructed by Hadrian in the early 2nd century, the most complete building to come down to us from ancient Rome—a temple for pagan gods until it was consecrated as a Catholic church in the 7th century—is a remarkable architectural wonder that is exactly as wide as it is high. The world's largest unreinforced concrete dome is supported by pillars hidden in the walls, providing a lesson in engineering to Michelangelo and others throughout the ages. One of them, Raphael, is entombed in a side chapel, as are Italian royalty and other luminaries. **INFO:** Tel 39/06-6830-0230.

The uncovered oculus is the Pantheon's only source of light.

PIAZZA DEL CAMPIDOGLIO AND THE CAPITOLINE MUSEUMS—Designed by Michelangelo in the 16th century, the Piazza del Campidoglio is one of Rome's most elegant spaces, with views over the Roman Forum. Three palazzos framing the piazza house the Capitoline Museums, home to a treasure trove of ancient Roman sculpture that includes bronzes of the she-wolf suckling Romulus and Remus and Marcus Aurelius astride a horse. Among the Renaissance paintings are numerous works by Tintoretto and Guido Reni. Some of the Campidoglio collection is housed in a former electrical plant, the Centrale Montemartini, where ancient pieces are placed, with magical effect, among the disused machinery. **CAPITOLINE MUSEUMS:** Tel 39/06-0608; www.museicapitolini.org. **CENTRALE MONTEMARTINI:** Tel 39/06-574-8030; http://en.centralemontemartini.org.

THE ROMAN AND IMPERIAL FORUMS—The busy and crowded center of Roman political, judicial, and commercial life in the days of the Republic, the Roman Forum is an evocative jumble of ruins. You'll need a map and guide to pick out the numerous temples; the Umbilicus Urbus, the designated center of Rome and ground zero from which all distances in the Empire were measured; the Curia, the main seat of the Roman Senate; and the House of the Vestal Virgins, home of the young women who minded the Temple of Vesta's sacred fire. The Imperial Forums were begun by Julius Caesar and include the Forums of Caesar, Augustus, and Trajan. Determined to leave his mark on Rome, Trajan also commissioned Trajan's Column, with bas-reliefs depicting his campaign against the Dacians, and Trajan's Market, with space for 150 shops and offices. **INFO:** Tel 39/06-3996-7700; www.capitolium.org.

SPANISH STEPS—This sweeping staircase, built in 1725, ascends in three majestic tiers from the busy Piazza di Spagna to the French Trinità dei Monti church. The boat-shaped fountain at the foot of the steps was designed in the late 16th century by Bernini or his father (the jury is still out); the poet John Keats died in a house overlooking the steps that is now a small museum; and the top is the place to be at sunset, for a view of Rome's seven hills. The steps take their name from the Spanish Embassy, which occupied a nearby palazzo in the 19th century. Via Condotti and its pedestrian grid of cobbled offshoots at the foot of the Spanish Steps offers ultrasmart shopping and the ideal venue for an early evening *passeggiata,* or stroll. Stop in at Caffè Greco, Rome's oldest watering hole, where Casanova, Goethe, and Lord Byron all stopped to linger.

TREVI FOUNTAIN—Neptune rides a chariot drawn by winged sea horses across this wildly fanciful Baroque assemblage of white marble and cascading water, completed in 1762. The piazza and fountain are especially enchanting and festive when floodlit at night, and at any time evoke the legend that a backward toss of a coin over the left shoulder into the basin ensures a return to Rome. The surprisingly small piazza was catapulted to international fame in the 1954 classic film *Three Coins in the Fountain,* and forever secured a few years later when Anita Ekberg and Marcello Mastroianni frolicked in its waters in *La Dolce Vita.*

VATICAN CITY—The world's smallest independent state is the epicenter of Roman Catholicism as well as the home of one of the world's greatest assemblages of art and architecture. La Basilica di San Pietro, begun in 324 on the site where St. Peter was crucified, rises above an elliptical colonnade by Bernini, and was lavishly rebuilt and embellished by the greatest talents of the 16th and 17th centuries. Michelangelo designed the dome of the basilica, and his *Pietà* is the finest of the hundreds of statues found in the chapels surrounding the 700-foot-long nave. Through a separate entrance to the Vatican Museums are the Renaissance master's magnificent ceiling frescoes of the Sistine Chapel, depicting the Creation and other biblical tales, and a terrifying scene of the Last Judgment behind the main altar. Michelangelo's startling use of light and bright colors and overall mastery of the human body brought his papal patrons to their knees. Inarguably the headliner, the chapel is but one element of the museum's labyrinth of palaces, apartments, and galleries that are gloriously lined with the greatest masterpieces of the ancient and Renaissance worlds: the Stanze di Raffaelo (Raphael Rooms), decorated with the frescoes the artist painted for Pope Julius II; the *Laocoön* and the *Belvedere Torso,* two of the most famous sculptures to come down to us from antiquity; frescoes by Fra Angelico, paintings by Caravaggio and Leonardo da Vinci, and modern ceramics by Picasso. **Info:** Tel 39/06-6988-3731 (basilica), 39/06-6988-3333 (museums); www.vatican.va.

Other Must-Dos

Etruscan Museum at the Villa Giulia—Often overlooked, Italy's largest and best collection of ancient Etruscan sculptures, terra-cotta vases, sarcophagi, and jewelry fills 35 rooms of an elegant 16th-century country villa built for Pope Julius III. The collection of sophisticated artistry sheds light on this little-known pre-Roman civilization that thrived on the Italian peninsula from the 8th through 3rd centuries B.C. **Info:** Tel 39/06-332-6571; http://villagiulia.beniculturali.it.

House of Augustus—The great-nephew and adopted son of Julius Caesar preferred to live modestly in this small house (opened to the public in 2008) of just four exquisitely frescoed rooms on Palantine Hill overlooking the Forum. As Rome's first emperor, he took up residence in the sprawling, more imperial Domus Augustana higher up the hill and lived there until his death in A.D.14.

Market at Campo dei Fiori—Rome's oldest and best outdoor marketplace, where the city's chefs snatch up the freshest produce available, also provides great theater as shoppers banter with vendors over the day's bounty. The glimpse into daily Roman life at its most authentic continues after the last stall closes—in the bars, cafés, and restaurants that line the piazza. Patrons of the popular hole-in-the-wall La Vineria wine bar spill out onto the piazza, wineglasses in hand, to discuss the day's soccer score. Or follow the heady aroma to the Forno (bakery) for a slice of fresh-from-the-oven *pizza bianca*: Made without tomato sauce, it is drizzled with extra-virgin olive oil and sprinkled with salt. **Forno Campo de Fiori:** Tel 39/06-6880-6662; www.fornocampodefiori.com.

The Eternal City, whose architecture goes back 25 centuries, welcomed the dramatic spectacle created by MAXXI, where the art collection is not always the center of attention.

MAXXI—The Museo Nazionale della Arte XXI Secolo, Rome's newest landmark, is a daring and striking assemblage of glass and concrete, slopes and angles. Italy's first national museum of contemporary art and architecture opened in 2010 in Rome's residential Flaminio neighborhood, so boldly designed by Anglo-Iraqi architect Zaha Hadid that it almost steals the scene from a young but impressive collection that includes Francesco Clemente and Anish Kapoor. **Info:** Tel 39/06-321-0181; www.fondazionemaxxi.it/en.

Ostia Antica—As evocative as Pompeii (see p. 179), twice as well preserved, and much easier to visit (it can be reached in 20 minutes by subway), this archaeological site is an excellent window into a once-thriving port town of 60,000 residents. Founded about 620 B.C., it flourished for 8 centuries. **Info:** Tel 39/06-5635-8099; www.ostia-antica.org. *How:* U.S.-based Context Travel leads walking tours. Tel 39/06-9762-5204; in the U.S., 800-691-6036; www.contexttravel.com.

Piazza Navona—In warm weather, take a front-row seat at any of the outdoor cafés or restaurants that line the ancient oval piazza once used for chariot races. At the Tre Scalini café, skip the food but linger over their rich chocolate *tartufo* ice-cream concoction. Against the background of Bernini's Baroque *Fontana dei Quattro Fiumi (Fountain of the Four Rivers),* a host of Felliniesque characters mingle with German students, musicians, retired American couples, and a parade of those out for a constitutional *passeggiata.* **Info:** Tel 39/06-687-9148; www.3-scalini.com.

Where to Stay

Albergo del Senato—So-close-you-can-touch-it views of the Pantheon have enshrined this venerable hotel in the hearts of generations. Rooms are small but comfortable, and the rooftop terrace is a picturesque perch high above the animated swirl of the old city. **Info:** Tel 39/06-678-4343; www.albergodelsenato.it. *Cost:* from $290 (off-peak), from $590 (peak).

Albergo Santa Chiara—In the same family for generations, this old-style hotel provides modest comforts and is most appreciated for its location: a short stroll from the Pantheon and overlooking the charming Piazza della Minerva. **Info:** Tel 39/06-687-2979; www.albergosantachiara.com. *Cost:* from $340.

Casa Howard—This chic accommodation in two nearby locations not far from the Trevi Fountain comes with such pampering touches as fresh flowers and a Turkish bath; there's no front desk, and guests come and go with their own set of keys. **Info:** Tel 39/06-6992-4555; www.casahoward.com. *Cost:* from $250.

Hotel Hassler—One of the world's most fabled hotels glories in its one-of-a-kind location at the top of the Spanish Steps. Dozens of the stylish and supremely comfortable rooms are blessed with terraces and awe-inspiring panoramas of the Eternal City (as is its rooftop Imago restaurant), plus superlative service. At least stop in for an *aperitivo* at the Hassler Bar. Il Palazzetto, the hotel's new and more intimate annex across the narrow street, offers a fine restaurant, wine academy, popular wine bar, and four handsome rooms—three with a view of the Spanish Steps. **Hotel Hassler:** Tel 39/06-699340; in the U.S., 800-233-6800; www.hotelhasslerroma.com. *Cost:* from $600 (off-peak), from $950 (peak); tasting menu at Imago $145. **Il Palazzetto:** Tel 39/06-699-34-1000; www.ilpalazzettoroma.com. *Cost:* from $390 (off-peak), from $570 (peak).

Inn at the Roman Forum—Housed in a 17th-century palazzo on a quiet picturesque street near the Forum, this stylish newcomer offers canopied beds and fireplaces in some of the 12 rooms, and a quiet garden that is the place to recharge with a Negroni after a day seeing the sights. **Info:** Tel 39/06-691-90970; www.theinnattheromanforum.com. *Cost:* from $275 (off-peak), from $590 (peak).

Inn at the Spanish Steps and View at the Spanish Steps—These two stylish hotels are located on Via Condotti, Rome's most fashionable shopping street. Rooms at the Inn are full of antiques and frescoes; those at the View are swathed in neutral tones and contemporary furnishings. **Info:** Tel 39/06-6992-5657; www.theviewatthespanishsteps.com. *Cost:* Inn from $290 (off-peak), from $515 (peak); View from $635 (off-peak), from $1,000 (peak).

Portrait Suites—The Ferragamo dynasty leaves its tailored imprint on this stylish town house just off Via Condotti, where black-and-white contemporary surroundings are offset with splashes of color, and amenities include kitchenettes and a rooftop terrace. **Info:** Tel 39/06-693-80742; www.lungarnocollection.com. *Cost:* from $600.

La Posta Vecchia—You'll feel like a coddled guest of J. Paul Getty at La Posta Vecchia, his 1640 seaside villa built on ancient Roman foundations, 20 miles north of Rome. The billionaire oil baron and art collector spent millions amassing an enormous collection of antiques and antiquities (Maria de' Medici's dowry chest and Gobelin tapestries among them) that still appoint this amazing 19-guest-room getaway removed from the city's chaos. **Info:** Tel 39/06-994-9501; in the U.S., 800-735-2478; www.lapostavecchia.com. *Cost:* from $460 (off-peak), from $575 (peak). *When:* closed early Jan–mid-Mar.

Eating & Drinking

Da Fortunato al Pantheon—At this simple but attractive local favorite, jacketed, bow-tied waiters serve classic Roman favorites to well-heeled crowds who linger for hours over some of the best meals in town. You'll pay for the location, so make sure to take your after-dinner stroll around the illuminated Pantheon, just a few steps away. **Info:** Tel 39/06-679-2788; www.ristorantefortunato.it. *Cost:* dinner $60.

La Pergola—Legions of food critics have long rated this elegant restaurant as the city's finest. It's located far from the historic center, in the large Rome Cavalieri hotel, but its perch on Monte Mario means gorgeous views to accompany the exceptional Italian-Mediterranean creations of German chef Heinz Beck, who has wowed a demanding clientele since the day he arrived in 1994. **Info:** Tel 39/06-3509-2152; www.romecavalieri.it. *Cost:* dinner $150.

La Rosetta—Much of the reliably fresh seafood is flown in daily from Sicily, where talented chef Massimo Riccioli has roots. Small and expensive but worth it, this beloved seafood-only institution near the Pantheon has had a strong following of locals and in-the-know out-of-towners since opening in 1966. Simple and delicate preparations with subtle Asian flourishes hint of his global meanderings. **Info:** Tel 39/06-686-1002; www.larosetta.com. *Cost:* dinner $100.

Taverna dei Fori Imperiali—This is the classic family-run neighborhood favorite with red-and-white checked tablecloths you expect to find everywhere but don't. A comfortable taverna in the area of the Roman Forum and Coliseum, it serves up Roman and southern Italian recipes with pride (follow the locals who always go with the day's special). **Info:** Tel 39/06-679-8643; www.latavernadeiforiimperiali.com. *Cost:* dinner $40.

Gelaterie—To find Rome's best gelato, try as many as possible, then cast your vote! Start with Giolitti, the city's oldest gelateria and in the same family since 1900—you won't be the only one standing in line to sample their 50-some homemade flavors. If Giolitti has a serious contender, it would be the no-cones Il Gelato di San Crispino, on a side street near the Trevi Fountain, where Armagnac, balsamic, and other amazingly intense ingredients find their way into countless creamy offerings. (The honey-and-hazelnut combo also deserves a taste.) Wander the cobbled backstreets around the Piazza Navona until you find Gelateria del Teatro, where dense Belgian chocolate, pistachios from Sicily, white peaches in season, or more curious ingredients like fennel and lavender make this a foodie's favorite. **Giolitti:**

Tel 39/06-699-1243; www.giolitti.it. **Il Gelato di San Crispino:** Tel 39/06-679-3924. **Gelateria del Teatro:** Tel 39/06-4547-4880.

Primo caffès—Cafés in Rome are a dime a dozen, but ask the caffeine-savvy locals who makes the finest coffee in town and two names will keep popping up—and they're both in the Pantheon neighborhood, whose water, they say, may be the secret. Caffè Sant'Eustachio is always packed with locals who stream in for superb espresso and the city's most delicious cappuccino (the latter never ever ordered after 11 A.M. except by innocents abroad). Since 1946, the powerful aroma of roasting coffee has lured visitors to the no-frills, stand-up-only Tazza d'Oro. **Caffè Sant'Eustachio:** Tel 39/06-6880-2084; www.santeustachioil caffe.it. **Tazza d'Oro:** Tel 39/06-678-9792; www.tazzadorocoffeeshop.com.

A Coastline Hike with Inspiring Seascapes

Cinque Terre

Liguria, Italy

Five villages collectively known as the Five Lands, hidden in tiny coves along the craggy southern stretch of the Ligurian Riviera (see next page), offer a glimpse of an elusive, pristine Mediterranean—Italy as it must have been a century ago. One of the country's most dramatic coastlines, the Cinque Terre was once virtually unknown to outsiders, with cliffs so unyielding that for centuries the fishing hamlets were isolated from the rest of the country, accessible only by boat or a network of mule paths strung along the precipices.

The half-hour hike from Riomaggiore to Manarola, known as the Via dell'Amore *or "The Lovers' Walk," affords easy access to swimming.*

Today hikers traverse these *sentieri*, enjoying some of the most gorgeously scenic and not-too-difficult trails in Europe. These panoramic footpaths pass through slowly disappearing scrublands, as well as agaves, prickly pears, palms, olives, and daringly carved stepped vineyards that produce wine renowned since Boccaccio praised it in the 14th century.

Monterosso, the busiest, northernmost town, is the only one with a notable selection of small hotels and restaurants and a good stretch of beach where you can enjoy the more leisurely luxuries of the Riviera. The bright, airy rooms of the Hotel Porto Roca are built into a cliff above the sea, while those of the Villa Steno are set amid lemon and olive trees. Ligurian seafood is served at Miky in uncomplicated age-old preparations (try the linguini with lobster). From here you can follow the Sentiero Azzurro (Blue Trail) and reach the southernmost village, Riomaggiore, by foot in 5 or 6 hours. Along the way, stop at Il Gambero Rosso, serving fresh fish on the loggia-lined waterfront in picturesque Vernazza. If you can't walk another step, continue by train or boat service that links the towns. Consider spending a night or two at Ca' d'Andrean, a former olive mill in Manarola whose cozy sea-facing rooms surround a garden.

If you're up for a challenge, follow the steep Sentiero Rosso (Red Path) through the mountains for 26 miles between Levanto, north of the Cinque Terre, and Portovenere, a beautiful village of brightly colored houses on a fishing harbor (more easily reached by boat).

WHERE: Monterosso is 57 miles/90 km east of Genoa. **HOTEL PORTO ROCA:** Tel 39/0187-817502; www.portoroca.it. *Cost:* from $250. *When:* closed Nov–mid-Apr. **VILLA STENO:** Tel 39/0187-817028; www.villasteno.com. *Cost:* $200 (off-peak), $300 (peak). **MIKY:** Tel 39/0187-817401. *Cost:* dinner $50. **IL GAMBERO ROSSO:** Tel 39/0187-812265; www.ristorantegamberorosso.net. *Cost:* dinner $60. *When:* closed Nov–Feb. **CA' D'ANDREAN:** Tel 39/0187-920040; www.cadandrean.it. *Cost:* from $120. **BEST TIMES:** May–Jun and Sep for nicest hiking weather (avoid weekends); late May for Sagra del Limone (Lemon Festival) in Monterosso.

Idyllic Harbors and Famous Retreats

THE ITALIAN RIVIERA

Liguria, Italy

The glorious arc of the Italian Riviera unfolds from the French border against a glittering panorama of turquoise sea and dense, rugged mountains. The narrow, 220-mile Ligurian coastline—which some say is far more stunning than the French Riviera—is made up of palm-fringed resort towns, with their historical centers and charming trompe l'oeil–painted façades. The steep, terraced hills produce extra-virgin olive oil, which flavors the region's seafood-based *cucina ligure.* Though the area is now mostly developed, you can still hire a local fisherman to transport you to wild, craggy coves with surprisingly unspoiled views along the way—not unlike ones native son Christopher Columbus might have seen.

At the pretty and popular little town of Portofino, former fishermen's dwellings painted in rich Ligurian hues—faded yellow, ocher, pink—crowd around a snug harbor full of bobbing yachts. Follow the heady perfume of pesto-flavored *trenette* pasta and grilled scampi to the chic waterside Ristorante Puny. The perfect address for close-up views of the sea and the *bella gente* is the stylish Hotel Splendido Mare, in the center of town. Or make the steep, 10-minute climb (or take the shuttle) to its big sister, the Hotel Splendido, a Benedictine-monastery-turned-villa-hotel tucked into luxuriant, semitropical gardens. The 12 contemporary-style rooms at Domina Home Piccolo are less grand but overlook terraced gardens and a private rocky beach. Make time to cross the pine-scented peninsula and follow remote coastlines on a network of well-marked paths (it's about 2 hours on foot or 20 minutes by summertime-only boat) to the seaside Abbey of San Fruttuoso, founded in the 10th century by Benedictine monks and today a favorite destination for a waterfront lunch.

Once a fishing village, today Portofino lures Italy's bella gente.

If traffic is light, Santa Margherita Ligure can be reached in 15 minutes from

Portofino. Although a bit subdued since its early 20th-century heyday, it is still elegant, with long stretches of pebbly beach backed by a palm-shaded promenade. From there, a 10-minute train ride delivers you to Camogli, an unspoiled fishing village, where you can take in the view from the terrace of the Cenobio dei Dogi hotel, onetime summer retreat of the rulers of Genoa, the historic port city just 12 miles west.

WHERE: Portofino is 23 miles/38 km southeast of Genoa. **HOTEL SPLENDIDO MARE** and **HOTEL SPLENDIDO:** Tel 39/0185-267801; in the U.S., 800-237-1236; www.hotelsplendido.com. *Cost:* Splendido Mare, from $900; Splendido, from $1,300. *When:* closed Nov–Mar. **DOMINA HOME PICCOLO:** Tel 39/0185-269015; www.dominahome.it. *Cost:* from $175 (off-peak), from $375 (peak). *When:* Nov–Mar. **CENOBIO DEI DOGI:** Tel 39/0185-7241; www.cenobio.it. *Cost:* from $225 (off-peak), from $325 (peak). **BEST TIMES:** mid-May for the Sagra del Pesce in Camogli, when a ton of fish is fried in a 12-foot-wide skillet; congestion on the road leading to Portofino can make visiting in Jul and Aug a test of patience.

Shimmering Beauties at the Foot of the Alps

THE ITALIAN LAKES

Lombardy, Italy

Italy's three major lakes—Maggiore, Como, and Garda—and a string of smaller beauties have long inspired music, poetry, and no end of appreciation from those who have witnessed their Alpine-framed spectacle. They hint of Switzerland just to the north, yet with their profusion of elegant villas, stylish lakeside villages, lush gardens, and simple pleasures, they are inherently Italian too.

Of the five islands that comprise the Borromean Islands, Isola dei Pescatori is the only one inhabited.

Lago Maggiore, just an hour's drive from Milan, has always been a summer retreat for the city's residents. The aristocratic Borromeo family built Baroque palaces and lavish gardens on the lake's two tiny islands. Ernest Hemingway set *A Farewell to Arms* on the lake's shores, in the 19th-century Grand Hotel des Iles Borromées in Stresa, which is still as romantic and princely as in its early days; linger with a Hemingway Martini in the elegant lobby bar. Lake Orta, just across a spur of mountains to the west, is smaller and much less worldly; its peaceful town of Orta San Giulio looks across the waters to the islet where the thousand-year-old Basilica di San Giulio appears to float.

Lago di Como, where mountainsides drop right into the deep, mirror-still waters, is surrounded by elegant villas and grand hotels. Bellagio, one of the prettiest towns anywhere, hugs a sylvan promontory on the lake, carpeted in part with the parklands of the waterfront Grand Hotel Villa Serbelloni. The Belle Époque hotel offers glorious views and a palpable sense of the past. The incomparable Villa d'Este, majestically positioned on the lakeshore south of Bellagio, was originally a cardinal's private pleasure palace and is now the gold standard from which all others take their inspiration. Grand but never overpowering, it has 10 acres of gardens and the exceptional Veranda Restaurant, whose retracting glass walls bring the lake to your dining table.

Million-dollar views; a fine restaurant; welcoming, hands-on hosts; and gentle prices make Albergo Milano the nicest choice in pretty lakefront Varenna.

Garda, the largest lake in Italy, is 90 miles east of here and was once the cool summertime destination for ancient Rome's VIPs: The ruins of the Grotte di Catullo are said to be the lakeside villa that the poet Catullus built outside Sirmione, where a 13th-century castello stands almost entirely surrounded by the deep blue waters of the lake. By comparison, the palatial 19th-century Villa Cortine Palace Hotel seems downright modern. Colonnaded, formidably decorative, and just this side of over-the-top, it is Sirmione's finest hotel, with impeccable gardens lapped by the lake's edge. Across the lake, a short walk from the pretty unspoiled town of Gargano, an aristocratic 1892 family manor (and temporary hideout for Mussolini) is now the glamorously old-world Grand Hotel Villa Feltrinelli, and may just be the most splendid of them all.

WHERE: Como is 25 miles/40 km north of Milan. **HOTEL DES ILES BORROMÉES:** Tel 39/0323-938938; www.borromees.it. *Cost:* from $245 (off-peak), from $385 (peak). **VILLA SERBELLONI:** Tel 39/031-950216; www.villaserbelloni.it. *Cost:* from $540 (off-peak), from $680 (peak). *When:* closed Nov–Mar. **VILLA D'ESTE:** Tel 39/031-3481; www.villadeste.it. *Cost:* from $580 (off-peak), from $900 (peak); dinner at Veranda $120. *When:* closed mid-Nov–Feb. **ALBERGO MILANO:** Tel 39/0341-830298; www.varenna.net. *Cost:* from $125. *When:* closed mid-Nov–mid-Mar. **VILLA CORTINE PALACE:** Tel 39/030-99-05890; www.hotelvillacortine.com. *Cost:* from $435 (off-peak), from $630 (peak). *When:* closed Oct–Mar. **VILLA FELTRINELLI:** Tel 39/0365-798001; www.villafeltrinelli.com. *Cost:* from $1,175 (off-peak), from $1,600 (peak). **BEST TIMES:** Jul–Aug is the busiest, preferred by some; mid-Aug–mid-Sep for the international festival, Settimane Musicali di Stresa.

A Celebration of Renaissance Splendor

PALAZZO DUCALE AND PALAZZO TE

Mantua, Lombardy, Italy

Located on the slow-moving River Mincio, Mantua (Montova) is locked in the rich past of the powerful Gonzaga family, who were to this city what the Medicis were to Florence (see p. 203). Under their influence, the city flourished for 400 years, and their sumptuously decorated 500-room, 15-courtyard Palazzo Ducale was built between the 13th and 18th centuries. Vast, gilded halls and huge galleries are filled with vibrant canvases by Renaissance masters, most notably Andrea Mantegna, whose fanciful *Camera degli Sposi (Bridal Chamber,* 1472–1474) is but one highlight of the palazzo.

One Gonzaga duke, Federico II, created his own retreat, Palazzo Te, where 16th-century architect and painter Giulio Romano covered every inch of ceilings and walls with rich frescoes, from equine portraits to pornographic mythological scenes. These wonderfully whimsical works are among the world's greatest masterpieces of Mannerist art.

You can dine like the dukes of Mantua on Gonzaga delicacies beneath the frescoed ceilings of Trattoria Il Cigno dei Martini. The elegant Ristorante Aquila Nigra is known for delicate pastas and regional specialties served with a light, creative touch in the stone-walled rooms of a medieval palazzo. The ambience is more casual at the informal Osteria La Porta Accanto next door.

Where: 95 miles/153 km southeast of Milan. **Trattoria Il Cigno:** Tel 39/0376-327101. *Cost:* dinner $75. **Aquila Nigra:** Tel 39/0376-327180; www.aquilanigra.it. *Cost:* dinner $100; dinner at La Porta Accanto $45. **Where to stay:** Casa Poli has bright, contemporary rooms in a 19th-century palazzo in the center of town. Tel 39/0376-288170; www.hotelcasapoli.it. *Cost:* from $200. **Best times:** On Good Friday, a vial allegedly containing Preziossimo Sangue di Cristo (Most Precious Blood of Christ) is paraded through the streets; mid-Sep for Festivaletteratura, a series of concerts, plays, and other events.

Genius of a Renaissance Man

The Last Supper and Other Works of Leonardo da Vinci

Milan, Lombardy, Italy

Completed for the convent of Santa Maria delle Grazie in 1498, Leonardo da Vinci's *Il Cenacolo* (*The Last Supper*) still captivates viewers with its power, depth, and humanity. Leonardo searched for years among the city's criminals for Judas's face, and the result, 16th-century art historian Giorgio Vasari declared, was "the very embodiment of treachery and inhumanity." Study the 28-foot-long mural and you begin to notice Leonardo's many other masterful touches: the apostles, arranged in groups of three (a sign of the Holy Trinity), are clearly distressed, whereas Christ is calm, almost beatific; Judas is cast in shadows.

Much to our loss, Leonardo did not use the typical fresco technique of applying oil paint to wet plaster to create a bond; instead he experimented by mixing his paints with tempera (egg yolk and vinegar) and working on dry plaster. The painting began to deteriorate almost immediately—even so, and despite some clumsy restorations over the centuries (with a successful 21-year restoration completed in 1999), exposure to the elements, and damage incurred when Napoleon's troops used the figures for target practice, one of the world's most famous paintings still evokes all the drama of this fateful moment.

The Last Supper was one of many projects Leonardo undertook during the 17 years he spent in Milan under the patronage of Duke Ludivico "Il Moro" Sforza. He engineered canals and dikes in the plains surrounding the city (some are still in use today), designed a dome for the Duomo (never undertaken), and painted a lovely fresco that transforms one of the duke's royal apartments in Castello

Nearly destroyed in World War II and subject to several ill-fated restoration attempts, The Last Supper *can now be viewed only by reservation.*

Sforzesco into an arbor. The *Rondanini Pietà*, the last work of Michelangelo (at age 90), is also here.

Another work attributed to Leonardo, a *Portrait of a Musician* (believed by some scholars to be a self-portrait), is in the Pinacoteca Ambrosiana. His *Codex Atlanticus,* a 1,100-page notebook of writings and drawings on subjects ranging from weaponry to flight, is on display in the adjacent Biblioteca Ambriosana; sections of the book are rotated every 3 months until 2015. Many of these designs see the light of day at the Museo Nazionale della Scienza e Tecnica (National Museum of Science and Technology), where replicas of Leonardo's airplanes, helicopters, submarines, and other machines show off the imagination of one of the greatest geniuses of all ages.

Info: Tel 39/02-8942-1146; www.cenacolo vinciano.org. **How:** Purchase tickets in advance through www.tickitaly.com. Or join a Skip the Line tour that guarantees a no-line entry with guided visit. Tel in Rome 39/06-8336-0561; www.lastsuppertickets.com. *Cost:* $45. **Castello Sforzesco:** Tel 39/02-8846-3700; www.milanocastello.it. **Pinacoteca Ambrosiana:** Tel 39/02-806921; www.ambro siana.it. **Museo Nazionale della Scienza e Tecnica:** Tel 39/02-485551; www.museo scienza.org.

The Epicenter of Fashion, Design, and Good Living

On and Around Piazza del Duomo

Milan, Lombardy, Italy

Milan appeals to those who enjoy the finer things in life—as a stroll across its Piazza del Duomo and along the surrounding streets will confirm. The Duomo, Milan's most famous landmark, captures the city's creative energy with its size and ornamentation. Five centuries in the making, one of the world's largest cathedrals has an exterior topped with 135 marble spires and adorned with 2,245 marble statues; the interior, meanwhile, is spartan, and so vast that it can seat 40,000. An elevator to the roof offers the chance to stroll amid the forest of white marble pinnacles and to study the flying buttresses up close. There are stunning views over Italy's most frenetic city and, on a clear day, a glimpse of the Swiss Alps 50 miles away.

As befits a city synonymous with style, the Galleria Vittorio Emanuele II was the world's first enclosed, pedestrian-only shopping mall, a 19th-century extravaganza that is often called the "living room" of Milan; fine shops and cafés line the mosaic-floored arcades beneath a soaring leaded-glass roof. The galleria leads to Teatro alla Scala, the world's most famous opera house, where Verdi's *Otello* and *Falstaff* premiered as well as Puccini's *Turandot* and Bellini's *Norma.* Maria Callas sang at La Scala more often than anywhere else.

Milan's tireless preoccupation with design is showcased a few blocks away, on the incomparable Via Montenapoleone and its offshoots, the single most fashionable retail acre in the world. Shopping this exclusive "golden triangle" that is home to the sleek boutiques of the high priests and priestesses of *la moda italiana* is heaven for those with deep pockets and purgatory for those reduced to window-shopping. Order a cappuccino and people-watch at Cova, an elegant café that's been a fixture here since 1822. Settle into the Four Seasons Hotel, a former convent that's been transformed into a unique 21st-century urban oasis enhanced with fragments of exposed frescoes and vaulted ceilings. A stay at the smart Hotel Spadari in the shadow of the Duomo puts you at the doorstep of the legendary Peck, Milan's magnificent food-as-art emporium. For something charmingly unpretentious, the nearby Trattoria Milanese serves perfectly prepared osso bucco and other classics to a well-heeled clientele in no-frills brick-walled surroundings.

"Not . . . commandingly beautiful but grandly curious," Henry James said of the Duomo, Milan's most enduring landmark.

Duomo: Tel 39/02-8646-3456; www.duomomilano.it. **Teatro alla Scala:** Tel 39/02-7200-3744; www.teatroallascala.org. *When:* Opera season runs Dec–Jul; ballet and concerts other months. **Cova:** Tel 39/02-7600-5599. **Four Seasons Hotel Milano:** Tel 39/02-77088; www.fourseasons.com/milan. *Cost:* from $860. **Hotel Spadari:** Tel 39/02-7200-2371; www.spadarihotel.com. *Cost:* from $330. **Peck:** Tel 39/02-802-3161; www.peck.it. **Trattoria Milanese:** Tel 39/02-8645-1991. *Cost:* dinner $60. **Best times:** Apr–May and Sep–Oct, when the city is buzzing with the arrival of new fashions.

Grand Palazzo Ducale and Bel Canto Opera

Urbino and Pesaro

Le Marche, Italy

Atop a steep hill in the region of Le Marche, Urbino could easily share the spotlight with better-known Italian cities for its history, art, architecture, and gastronomy if not for its location off the well-traveled path. During the second half of the 15th century, it was the seat of one of Europe's most prestigious courts, under the visionary direction of Federico da Montefeltro. The duke commissioned the finest artists and architects to build and embellish his immense Palazzo Ducale, considered the perfect expression of the Early Renaissance.

Today the palace houses the Galleria Nazionale (National Gallery) delle Marche, filled with a prodigious art collection that includes works by native son Raphael *(La Muta, The Silent One)*, Piero della Francesca (*Madonna di Senigallia* and *The Flagellation of Christ*; the latter considered by the artist his finest work), Paolo Uccello, and Luca Signorelli. Visitors to this underrated destination will often have the many rooms to themselves—as they will the steep lanes and airy piazzas of this small, proud town of 15,000 residents and the students of the 500-year-old university. The pleasant Hotel Bonconte, in a villa near the city walls, overlooks the undulating green countryside. If you venture just minutes outside town, you'll find the stylish stone-and-wood Locanda della Valle Nuova set beneath oak trees on 185 bucolic acres. Guests are immersed in the simple pleasures of *agriturismo*—fresh air, amiable hosts, and fresh cheeses, meats, and wine made on this organic farm.

A worldly atmosphere prevails down on the coast at Pesaro, an attractive resort and the hometown of Gioacchino Rossini. The great composer of *The Barber of Seville* is honored with the annual Rossini Opera Festival, devoted exclusively to the composer's work and a favorite among opera purists. Even if you don't come for the festival, enjoy the quintessential Pesaro experience with a stroll down the animated Via Rossini and settle into the handsomely refurbished, old-world Hotel Vittoria.

WHERE: 109 miles/176 km east of Florence. **GALLERIA NAZIONALE DELLE MARCHE:** Tel 39/0722-2760; www.palazzoducaleurbino.it. **HOTEL BONCONTE:** Tel 39/0722-2463; www.viphotels.it. *Cost:* $125 (off-peak), $200 (peak). **LOCANDA DELLA VALLE NUOVA:** Tel 39/0722-330303; www.vallenuova.it. *Cost:* from $80. *When:* closed Nov–May. **HOTEL VITTORIA:** Tel 39/0721-34343; www.viphotels.it. *Cost:* $185. **BEST TIMES:** late Jul for Urbino's Festival Internazionale di Musica Antica, Italy's most important Renaissance and Baroque music festival; Aug for Pesaro's Rossini Opera Festival.

Europe's Most Southerly Island

PANTELLERIA

Italy

Wind-tossed, stark, even forlorn, the remote Italian island of Pantelleria (the "daughter of the wind") is not for everyone. A craggy upthrust of lava, Pantelleria is an ancient crossroads of culture, lying between Sicily and Tunisia, just 43 miles from the African coast. The island's volcanic birthright is apparent, with abundant hot springs (some pouring directly into the sea to form natural baths), sauna caves, fumaroles, and crater lakes, including the Specchio di Venere (Mirror of Venus), where, according to myth, the goddess Venus sought her reflection in the emerald green waters. The rich black soil sustains olive groves, caper bushes (salted Pantelleria capers are renowned), and Zibibbo grapes, which are crafted into unusual wines, most notably the golden, honeylike passito. Pantelleria's cuisine is remarkable for its simple, full-flavored gusto, perhaps best savored at Al Tramonto Restaurant, with a beautiful stone patio high above the sea, where sunset (*tramonto*) views rival local seafood specialties.

Traditional *dammusi*, ancient stone homes and structures with domed roofs and arched, Moorish-style interiors, are an integral element of the windswept island's austere beauty. When Milan's creative set began to use Pantelleria for fashion shoots in the 1980s, the island quickly caught on as the ultimate getaway, and rustic-but-refined lodgings and restaurants quickly sprang up. Chic and intimate,

Monastero is the island's most noted lodging; it's the creation of fashion photographer Fabrizio Ferri, who transformed an abandoned dammusi village into a private retreat of timeless charm. Le Case di Gloria is a more casual collection of old dammusi converted to comfortable lodgings, with footpaths leading down to the rocky shore. More modern lodgings exist, such as the Mursia Hotel, whose rooms are designed with the arched dammusi style in mind.

The Arco dell'Elefante, formed of gray lava, resembles an elephant drinking from the sea and is the island's unofficial symbol.

WHERE: 118 miles/190 km southwest of Palermo, Sicily. **AL TRAMONTO:** Tel 39/0349-537-2065. *Cost:* dinner $55. **MONASTERO:** Tel 39/0349-559-5580; in the U.S., 917-370-7995; www.monasteropantelleria.com. *Cost:* from $550 per night (1-week minimum). **LE CASE DI GLORIA:** Tel 39/0328-277-0934; www.dammusidigloria.it. *Cost:* from $100 (off-peak), from $270 (peak). *When:* closed mid-Nov–Mar. **MURSIA HOTEL:** Tel 39/0923-911217; www.mursiahotel.it. *Cost:* from $200. *When:* closed Nov–Mar. **BEST TIMES:** Apr–Jun and Sep–Oct for nicest weather; late Jun for the Feast of the Madonna della Margana, with processions, feasting, and fireworks.

Where Truffles and Wine Take Center Stage

LE LANGHE

Piedmont, Italy

The vine-covered hills and proud old towns of Le Langhe are as mellow as the famous Barolo, nebbiolo, and Barbaresco wines they produce. Hot summers and misty autumns are also hospitable to the *tartufo bianco* (white truffle). With this and a number of other culinary pleasures near at hand, it's not surprising that the now-global Slow Food movement had its origins here. Asti is famous around the world for its sparkling (*spumante*) whites, as well as for its Palio, an ages-old bareback horse race around the Piazza Alfieri in late September. Explore nearby Alba on a Saturday morning, when a lively food market winds along Via Vittorio Emanuele.

Just outside Alba, the Hotel Castello di Sinio is a restored medieval castle set amid the Barolo vineyards; a stay in one of the stone-walled rooms can include wine tastings and cooking lessons. Villa Beccaris is a delightful 18th-century nobleman's domain just outside Monforte d'Alba. The Langhe Hotel is a more modest choice, on the outskirts of Alba, within easy reach of one of the region's finest restaurants, Lalibera. This contemporary osteria serves new takes on traditional favorites, such as zucchini flowers stuffed with trout mousse. At Il Convivio, in Asti, local wines from the huge cellar accompany a small menu of daily specials that often include gnocchi in a sweet pepper sauce, and *cardo gobo,* artichokelike cardoons dipped in *bagna cauda,* the region's favorite sauce of olive oil, garlic, and anchovies.

In many ways, the scenic and culinary pleasures of the Langhe are reminiscent of Tuscany, but, for now at least, this quiet little corner of Italy is a well-kept secret.

Where: Asti is 36 miles/60 km southeast of Turin; Alba is 42 miles/70 km southeast of Turin. **How:** Tour Piedmont leads food and culture tours. Tel 39/0333-390-8947; www.tourpiedmont.com. **Castello di Sinio:** Tel 39/0173-263889; www.hotelcastellodisinio.com. *Cost:* from $250. **Villa Beccaris:** Tel 39/0173-78158; www.villabeccaris.it. *Cost:* from $225 (off-peak), from $300 (peak). **Langhe Hotel:** Tel 39/0173-366933; www.hotellanghe.it. *Cost:* from $135. **Lalibera:** Tel 39/0173-293155. *Cost:* dinner $35. **Il Convivio:** Tel 39/0141-594188. *Cost:* dinner $35. **Best times:** Sat market in Alba; late Sep for the Palio race in Asti; early Oct for Palio degli Asini (Race of the Asses) in Alba; late Oct–early Nov for international Tartufo Bianco d'Alba fair.

Coastal Glamour and the Interior's Mystique

Sardinia

Italy

An ancient crossroads between East and West, coveted by every major maritime power in the Mediterranean over the millennia, Sardinia (Sardegna) is Italy's second largest island, both a glamorous playground and a rugged holdout of traditional life. More than 1,000 miles of soft-sand beaches (Europe's best, according to many) and clear waters ring the coast. In the interior a unique Sardo dialect (not far removed from Latin) is still spoken in medieval stone towns, and natives tend sheep and vineyards that produce rich cheeses and flavorful wines like red cannonau (grenache) and white vermentino.

Costa Smeralda, a 34-mile tract of boulder-strewn coast in the northeast, attracts the super-rich and world famous, many of whom arrive on private yachts to partake of la dolce vita. In the 1960s, Prince Karim, the Aga Khan, created the exclusive playgrounds of the fashionable Cala di Volpe hotel, which resembles a Sardinian fishing village with an exotic flourish of turrets and porticoes. The nearby Capo d'Orso is more down to earth; it's furnished in Sardinian style, with lovely rooms that overlook the sea.

Blue-green waters encircle Sardinia's "Emerald Coast."

Much of Sardinia seems light-years removed from cosmopolitan Costa Smeralda, and many places have changed little since D. H. Lawrence described the island as "lost between Europe and Africa and belonging to nowhere." A castaway ambience prevails on the seven uninhabited islands of Maddalena Archipelago National Park, an easy sail from the north coast.

The walled port of Alghero, tucked among pines and palms above the northwest coast, is the island's prettiest town, with narrow streets that wind past old churches and palaces. At its edge, Villa Las Tronas, once a holiday villa for Italian nobility, is now an exclusive enclave set amid lush gardens. Descend 650 steps into the Grotta di Nettuno (Neptune's Grotto), a spectacular cavern where boat tours ply a string of underground lakes. The Nuraghe Palmavera, where 50 conical stone huts (*nuraghe*) from around 1500 B.C. surround a beehive-shaped tower, is an island highlight. The rough, mountainous interior is dotted with more than 7,000 of these nuraghe, and the largest cluster comprises the walled city of Barumini, in the center of the island. Along the bay at Chia, on the southwest coast, towering sand dunes and centuries-old junipers evoke the timelessness of this enchanted isle.

WHERE: 112 miles/180 km west of mainland Italy. **CALA DI VOLPE:** Tel 39/0789-976111; in the U.S., 800-325-3589; www.caladivolpe.com. *Cost:* from $600 (off-peak), from $900 (peak). *When:* closed Nov–Mar. **CAPO D'ORSO:** www.delphina.it. *Cost:* from $330 (off-peak), from $600 (peak), inclusive. *When:* closed Oct–Apr. **VILLA LAS TRONAS:** Tel 39/079-981818; hotelvillalastronas.it. *Cost:* from $285 (off-peak), $520 (peak). **BEST TIME:** Jun–Aug for beach weather and people-watching.

Volcanic Drama and Barefoot Chic

AEOLIAN ISLANDS

Sicily, Italy

Named for Æolus, god of the winds, the seven Aeolian Islands (Isole Eolie) float off Sicily's northeastern flank. Washed by Italy's clearest waters and blessed with grottoes, bays, hidden coves, black sand beaches, and still-active volcanoes, the islands are a world unto themselves. Lipari, the attractive capital island, has an animated old town dominated by a 17th-century castello that houses a noted archaeological museum. Vulcano is laced with thermal springs and steaming fumaroles, though its volcano is dormant; Iddu, the volcano on Stromboli, most definitely is not, spewing hot lava into the sizzling sea. Panarea is surrounded by a dazzling seafloor that delights divers and snorkelers, many of whom are Italian fashionistas who enjoy the island's barefoot lifestyle and nightlife scene.

Stromboli is nicknamed "the lighthouse of the Mediterranean" for its regular, easily visible volcanic eruptions.

The only place to find glamorous digs is Panarea's Hotel Raya, where breezy open terraces, a fine restaurant, and a popular nightclub overlook Stromboli's volcano. The Quartara is stylish, though unpretentious, with airy, tile- and stone-floored guest rooms. On more remote and less developed Filicudi, La Canna's homey rooms surround flowered terraces and overlook the cerulean sea, while on Salina, the greenest of the islands, a group of beautifully restored old houses comprise the Hotel Signum, where amenities include an infinity pool and a thermal spa. The best hotel on Stromboli, put on the map in 1950 when Roberto Rossellini and Ingrid Bergman began an illicit love affair here, is La Sirenetta Park, facing Ficogrande beach and a good base for the 5-to-6-hour round-trip climb up the volcano.

Where: Vulcano, the island closest to Sicily, is 22 miles/35 km off the north shore. **Hotel Raya:** Tel 39/090-983013; www.hotelraya.it. *Cost:* from $250 (off-peak), from $420 (peak). *When:* closed Nov–Mar. **Hotel Quartara:** Tel 39/090-983027; www.quartarahotel.com. *Cost:* from $285 (off-peak), from $500 (peak). *When:* closed Nov–late Mar. **La Canna Hotel:** Tel 39/090-988-9956; www.lacannahotel.it. *Cost:* from $100 (off-peak), from $205 (peak). *When:* closed Nov–Mar. **Hotel Signum:** Tel 39/090-984-4422; www.hotelsignum.it. *Cost:* from $180 (off-peak), from $390 (peak). *When:* closed mid-Nov–mid-Mar. **La Sirenetta Park Hotel:** Tel 39/090-986025; www.lasirenetta.it. *Cost:* from $180 (off-peak), from $340 (peak). *When:* closed Nov–Mar. **Best times:** May–Jun and Sep for fewest crowds; Jul–Aug for scene-y season.

From Sacred and Serene to Modern-Day Chaos

The Gems of Palermo

Palermo, Sicily, Italy

No other city in Europe has hosted such a variety of civilizations and waves of conquerors as Palermo, shaped by 25 centuries of tumultuous history. Examples of this rich and eclectic heritage begin with the Palazzo dei Normanni, home to the island's 9th-century Arab rulers and transformed into a sumptuous palace (now the seat of Sicilian government) by the Normans in the 12th century but retaining its Islamic aesthetic. The palace's Cappella Palatina is completely encrusted with Byzantine mosaics, a blending of western and eastern traditions depicting harems, wild animals, and scenes from the Bible. Built in the same period, the Duomo melds similar influences with domes, towers, and elaborately tiled arches as does the evocative Chiesa di San Giovanni degli Eremiti (Church of St. John of the Hermits), topped with five red domes and surrounded by exotic gardens and the narrow streets of the Albergheria district, which centers on the busy Ballarò street market.

For the most breathtaking window on this unique heritage, travel 5 miles from the city center to Monreale, with its magnificent 12th-century Cattedrale di Santa Maria la Nuova. Built of golden Sicilian stone by the Norman king William II on a mountaintop overlooking his capital, the cathedral is an extravagant marriage of Moorish and Norman styles, with multicolored mosaics glorifying every centimeter of wall space. Enjoy a quiet moment in the adjacent cloisters, where no two of the 216 slender pillars are alike.

La Vucciria is Sicily's greatest market, a vibrant spectacle of merchants singing about their wares: piles of briny octopus and

The cathedral and cloister of Monreale represent the largest concentration of Arab, Byzantine, and Norman art in one place.

anchovies, mountains of fresh herbs, plump tomatoes, and glistening olives. Or take a seat overlooking the sprawling market at Shanghai, a bare-bones trattoria where fresh fish and greens are hauled up in baskets from the stalls below. Forgo the chaos for Piccolo Napoli, where the freshest seafood is simply grilled amid more formal surroundings.

The rambling 17th-century palazzo that was home to Prince Giuseppe Tomasi Lampadusa, author of *The Leopard*, is now the inviting Butera 28. The prince's adoptive son and daughter-in-law, the Duke and Duchess of Palma, house guests in nine spacious and comfortable apartments, host dinners, and arrange city tours and cooking lessons. In the heart of the old town, the six-room BB22 infuses an old palazzo with modern flair. The graceful Villa Igiea, an Art Nouveau doyenne-turned-hotel, on the bay 2 miles north of the city center, soothes guests with lush seaside gardens and old-world guest rooms awash in Sicilian charm.

Visitor info: www.palermotourism.com. **Palazzo dei Normanni** and **Cappella Palatina:** Tel 39/091-705-1111. **Trattoria Shanghai:** Tel 39/091-589-7025. *Cost:* dinner $30. **Piccolo Napoli:** Tel 39/091-320-431. *Cost:* dinner $50. **Butera 28:** Tel 39/0333-316-5432; www.butera28.com. *Cost:* double occupancy apartments from $70. **BB22:** Tel 39/091-611-1610; www.bb22.it. *Cost:* from $165. **Villa Igiea:** Tel 39/091-631-2111; in the U.S., 888-414-2018; www.hotelvillaigiea palermo.com. *Cost:* from $200 (off-peak), from $330 (peak). **Best times:** Holy Week (week before Easter); around Jul 15 for processions and celebrations honoring patron St. Rosalia.

Splendid Monuments of the Ancient World

Sicily's Greek Temples

Sicily, Italy

The Greek colonists who began arriving on the coastal areas of the southern Italian peninsula and the island of Sicily in the 8th century B.C. brought with them their Hellenic politics and culture and expanded their civilization to include what became known as Magna Graecia. At the southeastern tip of Sicily, in Siracusa, which once rivaled Athens in power and splendor, a Greek presence remains in the amazingly well-preserved Teatro Greco, which stages classic plays each summer. Other important landmarks are preserved in the nearby Parco Archeologico.

On the small island of Ortigia, in Siracusa's harbor, the Baroque Duomo incorporates the thick columns of an ancient temple of Athena. Checking into the nearby elegant, century-old Grand Hotel Ortigia puts guests amid waterside promenades, medieval lanes, and palazzo-rimmed piazzas—and close to Don Camillo, serving some of Sicily's most delicious seafood.

In Agrigento, the Greeks erected a string of golden-stone Doric temples along a ridge above the Valle dei Templi (Valley of Temples), one of the best-preserved concentrations of early Greek architecture outside Greece. Thirty-four exterior columns still surround the Tempio della Concordia (Temple of Concord), built around 430 B.C. The gargantuan, and entirely ruined, Tempio di Giove is one of the largest Greek temples ever built. In the summer months, evening tours are conducted of the illuminated temples, or you can view them in comfort from many of the rooms of the

Agrigento's Temple of Concord served as a church dedicated to Saints Peter and Paul in the Middle Ages.

18th-century Hotel Villa Athena. Top off your day with a dinner of homemade pasta and fresh grilled fish at Trattoria dei Templi, just outside the archaeological zone.

From Agrigento, it's an hour's drive west to Selinunte, the site of a thriving Greek colony settled in 650 B.C., where five temples and an acropolis were erected over the centuries and now lie in various states of preservation. Much of the south coast can be explored from the glamorous Verdura, which brought unprecedented stylish accommodations to Sicily. Guests enjoy two 18-hole golf courses, a luxurious spa, and a mile-long strip of white, sandy beach.

Segesta lies closest to Palermo (50 miles northwest of the city). There, a lone, perfectly proportioned temple and beautifully preserved theater command a windswept hill, surrounded by meadows of wild herbs and overlooking vineyards and olive groves.

WHERE: Siracusa is 155 miles/257 km southeast of Palermo; Agrigento is 76 miles/127 km south of Palermo. **VISITOR INFO:** www.regione.sicilia.it. **GRAND HOTEL ORTIGIA:** Tel 39/0931-464600; www.grandhotelsr.it. *Cost:* from $350. **DON CAMILLO:** Tel 39/0931-67133; www.ristorantedoncamillosiracusa.it. *Cost:* dinner $50. **HOTEL VILLA ATHENA:** Tel 39/0922-596288; www.hotelvillaathena.it. *Cost:* from $275 (off-peak), from $400 (peak). **TRATTORIA DEI TEMPLI:** Tel 39/0922-403110; www.trattoriadeitempli.com. *Cost:* dinner $35. **VERDURA RESORT:** Tel 39/0925-998001; in the U.S., 212-515-5776; www.verduraresort.com. *Cost:* from $675. **BEST TIMES:** Mar–May and Sep–Oct for fairest weather; early Feb for Agrigento's Almond Blossom Festival with floats, fireworks, and marzipan sweets; May–late Jun for ancient classics at Teatro Greco in Agrigento; Jul–Aug for ancient dramas at Segesta.

A Fashionable Resort and a Fiery Volcano

TAORMINA AND MT. ETNA

Sicily, Italy

This airy, mountainside town 650 feet above the Mediterranean Sea has been enticing travelers since the days of ancient Greece. Soak in Taormina's charm on a leisurely *passeggiata* along its bougainvillea-swathed strip of boutiques and ceramic shops, then linger for a lemon granita (shaved ice) or fruit-studded cannoli in an outdoor pasticceria or café while 11,000-foot-high Mount Etna stands bold against the blue Sicilian sky.

Sweeping views are among the many attractions at the Hotel San Domenico, a 15th-century monastery whose friars' cells have been enlarged and enhanced with wrought-iron chandeliers and richly carved wooden furnishings; the largest rooms in a new wing have high ceilings and sea-facing terraces.

The Grand Hotel Timeo, pampering guests since the 19th century, reopened in 2010 after a lavish renovation. Balconied rooms look over terraced gardens and down to the sea, where you'll find its sister hotel, the Villa Sant'Andrea. The Hotel Villa Ducale was once the ancestral home of the Quartuccis, who warmly welcome guests today in the 15 attractive seaview rooms. The hotel's tile floors, stone walls, and flowering terraces hold second place to the attentive service and familial ambience.

Dining in Sicily can be simple and sublime, as Vecchia Taormina proves with its pizza alla Norma, topped with roasted eggplant and ricotta. The charmingly modest La Piazzetta claims to serve the freshest fish in town in its cozy dining room and alfresco courtyard.

Sicily's most dramatic venue for summertime performances is Taormina's ancient Greek amphitheater, hewn into a rock face above the town. The acoustics are perfect, and stage columns frame the scene-stealer, Mount Etna. An hour's drive from Taormina brings you face-to-face with this volatile volcano, which has erupted 300 times since the first records were made 3,000 years ago. Jeep tours bounce toward the 10,922-foot summit, through groves of lemon, orange, and almond trees, and vineyards. The olive trees that flourish on the fertile lower slopes give way to a toasted, barren landscape—brooding, dark, and fascinating. The final ascent is via cable car over pinnacles of frozen lava, minor craters, and belching smoke holes—proof that this is Europe's most active volcano.

Where: 33 miles/53 km north of Catania. **Hotel San Domenico:** Tel 39/0942-613111; in the U.S., 212-515-5500; www.sandomenicopalace.hotelsinsicily.it. *Cost:* from $415 (off-peak), from $560 (peak). *When:* closed mid-Jan–mid-Mar. **Grand Hotel Timeo:** Tel 39/0942-627-0200; in the U.S., 800-237-1236; www.grandhoteltimeo.com. *Cost:* from $590. *When:* closed mid-Nov–mid-Mar. **Hotel Villa Ducale:** Tel 39/0942-28153; www.villaducale.com. *Cost:* from $145 (off-peak), from $290 (peak). *When:* closed Dec–Feb. **Vecchia Taormina:** Tel 39/0942-625589. *Cost:* lunch $20. **La Piazzetta:** Tel 39/0942-626317. *Cost:* dinner $35. **Best times:** Apr–May and Sep–Oct to avoid heat and crowds; mid-Jun for film festival; Jul–mid-Aug for arts festival of music, ballet, and opera with performances in Teatro Greco.

Italy's High Haven

The Dolomite Drive and Cortina d'Ampezzo

Trentino-Alto Adige, Italy

An engineering feat, the Dolomite Drive rises and falls for 68 miles through the majestic beauty of the saw-toothed peaks of the Dolomite Mountains in the northern reaches of Alpine Italy. From Bolzano, a Tyrolean city of onion-domed churches, the road climbs the 7,500-foot-high Passo del Pordoi before descending to 4,000-foot-high Cortina, Italy's number one ski resort and scene of the 1956 Winter Olympics. Today more than 95 miles of ski runs challenge intermediate and advanced skiers while trails beckon summertime trekkers, and the *via ferrata* (iron path), a network of cables, ladders, and rungs put in place during World War I, provides hikers with an extra challenge.

Cortina is also well suited to relaxing, people-watching, and witnessing the spectacle of the sunset enveloping the limestone peaks in a rosy glow. An excellent base for exploring is the celebrated 100-year-old Miramonti Majestic Grand Hotel, a former Austro-Hungarian hunting lodge on the outskirts of town. Most of the 105 rooms have balconies and captivating views, and inside are a blazing hearth and cozy bar offering 18 kinds of hot chocolate. Rosa Alpina Hotel and Spa is a delightful hideaway outside San Cassiano, ten miles west of Cortina and ten times more low-key; guests enjoy luxurious quarters and an acclaimed gourmet restaurant, St. Hubertus. The environmentally friendly Lagació Mountain Residence offers one of the most refreshing mountain retreats on earth; one- and two-bedroom apartments warmly paneled in local woods and facing the mountains, plus organic food and a Finnish sauna and steam bath.

The dramatic peaks and green valleys of the Dolomites bring a little piece of Austria to Northern Italy.

More than 50 refuges where shepherds and hikers once sought shelter in the mountains above Cortina have been converted to restaurants where you can ski or hike in for a hearty lunch or dinner. At Rifugio Averau, you can even spend the night in rustic accommodations and greet the mountain dawn without leaving the slopes.

WHERE: Cortina is 100 miles/161 km north of Venice. **HOW:** Dolomite Mountains offers several hiking, biking, and skiing tours. Tel 39/0436-7320, in the U.S., 303-898-3376; www.dolomitemountains.com. *Cost:* 7-day trips from $2,065, inclusive. **MIRAMONTI MAJESTIC:** Tel 39/0436-4201; www.miramonti majestic.it. *Cost:* from $550 (off-peak), from $840 (peak). *When:* closed late Mar–May, Sep–mid-Dec. **ROSA ALPINA:** Tel 39/0471-849500; www.rosalpina.it. *Cost:* from $485 (off-peak), from $940 (peak); dinner at St. Hubertus $70. **LAGACIÓ MOUNTAIN RESIDENCE:** Tel 39/0471-849503; www.lagacio .com. *Cost:* 1-bedroom apartments from $210 (off-peak), from $390 (peak). **RIFUGIO AVERAU:** Tel 39/0436-4660. *Cost:* from $70 per person, inclusive. *When:* mid-Apr–May, mid-Oct–Nov. **BEST TIMES:** Jan–Mar for skiing; Jul–Aug for hiking.

"The god who created the hills around Florence was an artist. No! He was a jeweler, engraver, sculptor, bronze founder and painter: He was a Florentine."
—*ANATOLE FRANCE*

FLORENCE

Tuscany, Italy

The capital of Tuscany, Firenze (Florence) is, most famously, the cradle of the Renaissance, epitomized by the cupola that Filippo Brunelleschi designed for the Duomo more than 600 years ago. Michelangelo's *David* and countless other treasures fill the city's museums and churches. The Florentine lifestyle is a work of art in itself, to be savored in historic cafés, welcoming trattorias, trendy boutiques, and the city's medieval streets and piazzas rimmed with fortresslike palazzos.

Top Attractions

Museo Nazionale del Bargello—The Bargello National Museum is to Renaissance sculpture what the Uffizi (see p. 206) is to painting. A Gothic fortress from 1255, once a prison and place of execution, it houses Florence's—and arguably Italy's—greatest collection of Renaissance sculpture. Galleries surrounding a vast courtyard are filled with such masterpieces as Michelangelo's slightly tipsy-looking Bacchus, a bronze of David by Donatello, and Brunelleschi's losing designs for the doors of the Baptistery (the award went to Ghiberti, but Brunelleschi proved his genius with the cathedral dome). **Info:** Tel 39/055-238-8606; www.polomuseale.firenze.it.

Basilica of Santa Croce—The church built by the Franciscans between 1294 and 1442 is the final resting place of some of the most famous Florentines of the Renaissance and also houses magnificent art treasures. The tombs of Michelangelo, Machiavelli, Galileo, Ghiberti, and others, along with a memorial to Dante, who died in exile in Ravenna (see p. 181), are surrounded by Giotto's masterful frescoes depicting scenes from the life and death of Saint Francis and Donatello's famous crucifix. Taddeo Gaddi's frescoes in the Cappella Baroncelli depict scenes from the life of the Virgin. **Info:** Tel 39/055-244619; www.santacroce.firenze.it.

The church's marble façade was added in 1863.

Basilica of Santa Maria Novella—Built for the Dominican order in the late 13th and early 14th centuries, Santa Maria Novella is the only major church in Florence that retains its original façade, a Gothic and Renaissance mélange of multicolored marble, friezes, and niches. Behind the massive doorways are some of Florence's greatest treasures: frescoes by Domenico Ghirlandaio, Filippino Lippi, and Nardo di Cione; two famous crosses, one by Giotto and one by Brunelleschi in the Cappella Gondi; Masaccio's *Trinità,* the first painting to ever use perspective; and the pulpit from which Galileo was denounced for saying the earth orbits the sun. Since 1221, the monks have formulated balms and ointments from herbs they cultivated, and some of the same recipes still find their way into scents and soaps available at the well-known 17th-century Officina-Profumo Farmaceutica di Santa Maria, just around the corner on Via della Scala. **Info:** Church: Tel 39/055-215918. Pharmacy: Tel 39/055-216276.

Galleria dell'Accademia—Michelangelo's colossal *David* has been acclaimed ever since the Florentine artist unveiled it in 1504, and for several centuries the imposing, dignified figure of the youth who slew Goliath commanded pride of place as the centerpiece of the Piazza della Signoria (see next page). Since 1873, *David* has stood inside the Accademia built to house him (a lifesize copy replaced him in the piazza), together with Michelangelo's four powerful, unfinished *Prisoners,* their forms struggling to break free from the raw marble that encases them. **Info:** Tel 39/055-238-8612; www.polomuseale.firenze.it.

Il Duomo (Cattedrale di Santa Maria dei Fiori)—Several architects overcame enormous technical challenges to design what is probably the central achievement of Renaissance architecture. The cathedral, finally consecrated in 1436, is topped by Filippo Brunelleschi's enormous octagonal dome (the largest in the world when it was built and now the very symbol of Florence) and houses an enormous Last Judgment fresco by Vasari and Federico Zuccari. The red, white, and green marble façade is a 19th-century addition. Other landmarks on the Piazza del Duomo are the freestanding baptistery, with its famous bronze Doors of Paradise by Ghiberti, and Giotto's slender bell tower. The Duomo Museum, behind the cathedral, houses much of the sculpture removed for protection. **INFO:** Tel 39/055-230-2885; www.operaduomo.firenze.it.

MEDICI CHAPELS—The Sagrestia Nuova (New Sacristy) of the Cappelle Medicee (Medici Chapels) was Michelangelo's first architectural project, begun in the 1520s to house the remains of Lorenzo the Magnificent and three other members of the ruling clan. Reclining, allegorical statues of female Dawn and male Dusk adorn the tomb of Lorenzo II, Duke of Urbino, and figures of male Day and female Night grace the tomb of Giuliano, Duke of Memours. Ironically, Michelangelo didn't complete the two most important tombs—those of Lorenzo Il Magnifico and his brother, Giuliano, who lie in a plain selpuchre opposite the altar. **INFO:** Tel 39/055-238-8602; www.polomuseale.firenze.it.

MUSEO SAN MARCO—The most celebrated friar of this 13th-century Dominican monastery was the mystical Fra Angelico. His masterworks, *The Annunciation*, *The Crucifixion*, and *The Last Judgement*, are found here, as are a number of painted panels, altarpieces, and a series of frescoes that grace many of the plain cells where the monks lived and prayed. Savonarola, the fire-and-brimstone fundamentalist who won and then lost favor with the Medicis, was prior of the monastery and resided in cell 11. Of a half dozen beautiful Last Supper frescoes found in Florence's various monasteries, the one in San Marco's refectory, by Domenico Ghirlandaio, is one of the most important. Ghirlandaio taught a young Michelangelo the art of fresco painting, something that would serve him well decades later in the Sistine Chapel in Rome (see p. 185). **INFO:** Tel 39/055-238-8608; www.museumsinflorence.com.

The Neptune fountain in the Piazza della Signoria was initially ridiculed as "the White Giant" and used as a basin for laundry.

PIAZZA DELLA SIGNORIA—The piazza that was the civic center of Florence for more than 700 years is now a popular outdoor sculpture gallery and site of round-the-clock street life. Giambologna's bronze of Grand Duke Cosimo I on horseback and other sculptures are originals, whereas others (notably Michelangelo's *David* and Donatello's *Marzocco*) are replicas of originals that now reside in the city's various museums. A plaque in front of Bartolomeo Ammannati's Neptune fountain marks the spot where Savonarola held his Bonfire of the Vanities in the 1490s and, a year later, was hanged and burned. You can enjoy some of these views from In Piazza della Signoria, a small welcoming inn with rooms overlooking the square. **IN PIAZZA DELLA SIGNORIA:** Tel 39/055-239-9546; www.inpiazzadellasignoria.com. *Cost:* from $230 (off-peak), from $315 (peak).

PALAZZO VECCHIO—The Gothic palace in the Piazza della Signoria was completed in 1302 to house the Republic's 500-man congress and later served as home to the Medicis, including Duke Cosimo I, until they moved into the Palazzo Pitti. You can now find Michelangelo's statue *Victory*; Vasari's

Quartiere degli Elementi; and Donatello's original *Judith and Holofernes* statue here. **INFO:** Tel 39/055-276-8465; www.museums inflorence.com.

PALAZZO PITTI AND THE GALLERIA PALATINA—Built by wealthy Florentine merchant and banker Luca Pitti in the late 15th century across the Arno from the Palazzo Vecchio, the Pitti Palace was bought by the Medicis in 1550 and substantially enlarged, becoming the official residence of the ruling dukes. Today it houses the Palatine Gallery (Galleria Palatina), whose 26 rooms display High Renaissance and later-era art, including works by Titian, a large number by Raphael, Rubens, Murillo, and Caravaggio, and a number of smaller museums. Climb the hill behind the palazzo and enjoy a picnic in the 16th-century Boboli Gardens, with sweeping views of Florence's historic center across the river. **INFO:** Tel 39/055-238-8616; www.polomuseale.firenze.it.

UFFIZI GALLERIES (GALLERIA DEGLI UFFIZI)—A palace designed in 1560 by architect Giorgio Vasari for Grand Duke Cosimo de' Medici houses many of the masterworks of Western civilization, collected by the Medicis themselves and bequeathed to the people of Florence. Botticelli (his *Allegory of Springtime* and *Birth of Venus* are among the attention-getters), Michelangelo (represented here by his only painting in Florence, the *Doni Tondo*), Cimabue, Raphael, Giotto, Leonardo da Vinci, Piero della Francesca, Filippo Lippi . . . the list amazes. **INFO:** Tel 39/055-294883; www.polomuseale.firenze.it. Advance tickets online: www.firenzemusei.it.

OTHER MUST-DOS

IL PONTE VECCHIO—The oldest and most famous bridge across the Arno River was built by Taddeo Gaddi in 1345. Butchers occupied the bridge's over-water shops until Medici dukes objected to the stench and installed the goldsmiths and jewelers who still occupy the premises today, selling everything from museum-quality hand-crafted heirlooms to more affordable mementos. So popular is the bridge that Germans retreating from Florence at the end of World War II did not blow it up, making the Ponte Vecchio the only Arno bridge to be spared.

The medieval Ponte Vecchio, spanning the Arno at its narrowest, replaced a bridge of wood and stone dating to Roman times.

MERCATO DI SAN LORENZO AND THE MERCATO CENTRALE—Italy's largest open-air market comprises hundreds of white canvas-topped stalls filling the streets around the Church of San Lorenzo. Amid the purveyors of leather goods and kitsch souvenirs rises the glass and cast-iron 19th-century Mercato Centrale, where butchers, fishmongers, cheese merchants, and other vendors supply Florentines, including many chefs, with their daily staples. If hunger strikes, hit Nerbone, a popular no-lingering lunch counter within the mercato. Or make your way across the piazza to Zà Zà, a boisterous and ever-popular trattoria where steak and other Florentine staples are served at crowded tables. **NERBONE:** Tel 39/055-219949. **ZÀ ZÀ:** Tel 39/055-215411; www.trattoriazaza.it. *Cost:* lunch $30.

PIAZZALE MICHELANGIOLO AND SAN MINIATO AL MONTE—The postcard-worthy views from the piazzale's hilltop square, centered around a copy of Michelangelo's *David,* have inspired Renaissance masters and countless modern-day shutterbugs. The nearby Chiesa di San Miniato al Monte—Florence's oldest church—dominates the city's highest hill. A daily program of Gregorian chant in this 11th-century Romanesque landmark transports you back to the Middle Ages. **Info:** Tel 39/055-234-2731; www.san-miniato-al-monte.com.

Where to Stay

Beacci Tornabuoni—Haven for travelers since the days of the Grand Tour, this newly refurbished hotel has retained its old-fashioned air of gentility amid amiable sitting rooms, a flowery terrace overlooking tile rooftops, and 28 large, airy guest rooms. One of its biggest assets may be the chic shops of the Via Tornabuoni just outside the door. **Info:** Tel 39/055-212645; www.tornabuonihotels.com. **Cost:** from $200 (off-peak), from $350 (peak).

Hotel Casci—A conveniently situated 14th-century palazzo that was once home to composer Gioacchino Rossini provides comfortable accommodations and a warm welcome from the Lombardi family. The euros you save you can spend on dinner. **Info:** Tel 39/055-211686; www.hotelcasci.com. *Cost:* from $115 (off-peak), from $215 (peak).

Four Seasons—Guests live better than the Medicis in a Renaissance convent and palazzo that have been meticulously restored and are awash in museum-quality frescoes, inlaid marble, and tapestries. The Duomo and other sights are a leisurely 20-minute walk away, but the pampering of a clairvoyant staff, a spa, the largest private garden in Florence, and the acclaimed il Palagio restaurant make it nearly impossible to leave. **Info:** Tel 39/055-26261; in the U.S., 800-819-5053; www.fourseasons.com. *Cost:* from $420 (off-peak), from $800 (peak); dinner at il Palagio $110.

Hotel Helvetia and Bristol—Travelers from Igor Stravinsky to the Danish royal family have lodged in this grandly revamped 19th-century palazzo, a plush mix of British-style comfort and old-world Italian elegance. It's nestled on a side street between the tony, shop-lined Via Tornabuoni and the Duomo, the very heart of Florence, and an enjoyable stroll away from all the major sights. **Info:** Tel 39/055-26651; in the U.S., 800-223-6800; www.royaldemeure.com. *Cost:* from $550.

Stylish quarters—Florentines have always been trendsetters, and several fashion-forward hotels occupying centuries-old buildings bespeak the latest word in Italian style. J. K. Place sports an exquisitely refined Neoclassical look, and a roof terrace looks across red tile roofs to the Duomo. The Continentale infuses a 14th-century riverside palazzo with a clean 1950s Italian style, with the Ponte Vecchio only an arm's length away; the hotel is part of a group run by the style-infallible Ferragamo clan that also includes the nearby and equally chic Gallery Hotel Art and Hotel Lungarno. The aura of a private home permeates Casa Howard, where antiques are scattered among contemporary pieces and amenities include a Turkish bath. **J. K. Place:** Tel 39/055-264-5181; www.jkplace.com. *Cost:* from $450. **Continentale:** Tel 39/055-2726-4000; www.lungarnohotels.com. *Cost:* from $240 (off-peak), from $375 (peak). **Gallery Hotel Art:** Tel 39/055-27263; www.galleryhotelart.com. *Cost:* from $440. **Hotel Lungarno:** Tel 39/055-27261; www.lungarnocollection.com. *Cost:* from $470. **Casa Howard:** Tel 39/0669-924555; www.casahoward.com. *Cost:* from $150 (off-peak), from $300 (peak).

Villa retreats—Villas in the countryside surrounding Florence have been favored retreats for centuries, and three that continue the tradition today—each about 5 miles from the historic center—provide an inviting level of luxury. Tucked into the cool hills of Fiesole, with a façade believed to be the design of Michelangelo, the Villa San Michele is a former monastery now devoted to worldly pleasures. Especially welcome are the distant views of Brunelleschi's Duomo and grassy terrace with one of the world's most beautifully situated pools. Housed in a handsomely restored 15th-century villa with 11 acres of gardens, Il Salviatino offers similarly inspiring views, but with less formality and with a boutique-hotel ambiance and less stratospheric rates. Villa La Massa, a luxuriously updated 16th-century villa on the banks of the Arno, is a sister property of Lake Como's Villa d'Este (see p. 190) and here provides another slice of Tuscan life, aristocracy style. **Villa San Michele:** Tel 39/055-567-8200; in the U.S., 800-237-1236; www.villasanmichele.orient-express.com. *Cost:* from $1,350. *When:* closed mid-Nov–Mar. **Villa Il Salviatino:** Tel 39/055-904-1111; www.salviatino.com. *Cost:* from $560 (off-peak), from $850 (peak). **Villa La Massa:** Tel 39/055-62611; in the U.S., 800-745-8883; www.villalamassa.com. *Cost:* from $565 (off-peak), from $700 (peak). *When:* closed mid-Nov–mid-Mar.

Eating & Drinking

Caffè Rivoire—Outdoor tables of this 19th-century fixture on Piazza della Signoria are the command post of choice for idling away the hours over a cappuccino, panino, or one of their signature sweets. When cold weather dictates a move indoors, order the house specialty, dense bittersweet hot chocolate with a de rigueur dollop of fresh whipped *panna*. **Info:** Tel 39/055-214412; www.rivoire.it. **Cost:** lunch $25.

Cibrèo—Florentines don't mind sharing their famous trattoria with visiting travelers, and all share an enthusiasm for some of the best Tuscan cooking anywhere. Just don't expect any pasta on the menu. Waiters pull up a chair to explain classic recipes that mix delightfully with innovation, such as the velvety yellow bell-pepper soup or roasted duck stuffed with minced beef and raisins. Many of the kitchen's acclaimed dishes are available at the less expensive Cibrèo Trattoria (better known as Cibreino) with a shorter menu, just around the corner while the cozy but refined Caffè Cibrèo is fun for lunch. Fabbio Picchi is the mastermind behind the Cibrèo name. **Cibrèo:** Tel 39/055-234-1100; website for all 3: www.edizioniteatrodelsalecibreofirenze.it. *Cost:* dinner $70. **Cibrèo Trattoria:** Tel 39/055-234-1100. *Cost:* dinner $40. **Caffè Cibrèo:** Tel 39/055-234-5853. *Cost:* lunch $65.

Coco Lezzone—Some places are best never tampered with. Basic fare, including a hearty *ribollita* (bread and vegetable soup), grilled steaks, and fresh fish on Fridays, is served here in a simple, white-tiled room jammed with tables. With no menu and barely a hint of pretension, the emphasis is clearly on enjoying a simple but memorable meal on a backstreet off the tony Via Tornabuoni. **Info:** Tel 39/055-287178. *Cost:* dinner $40.

Omero—This atmospheric, century-old trattoria is definitely worth the 15-minute taxi ride to Acetri, on the outskirts of town. Take in the beautiful view of the countryside from the outdoor terrace, then head inside for a traditional Tuscan feast. Everyone is here for the pasta, plus just about the best and most tender *bistecca alla fiorentina* around and, in artichoke season, the deep-fried *carciofini* wedges. Portions of the perfectly executed *cucina toscana* are abundant, but save room for the homemade dessert. **Info:** Tel 39/055-220053; www.ristoranteomero.it. *Cost:* dinner $50.

Ristorante la Giostra—A Hapsburg prince and his handsome twin sons serve treasured family dishes in an arched, 16th-century room that is always full and festive. Carpaccio of sturgeon, thin slices of baby artichokes topped with aged Parmigiano and other offerings reflect the best of simple Tuscan cooking. If it is mushroom and truffle season, you're in for a treat. **Info:** Tel 39/055-241341; www.ristorantelagiostra.com. *Cost:* dinner $60.

Gelaterie—Ice-cream purists may insist that Vivoli is no longer the city's best, but don't tell that to the crowds always loitering outside, sampling flavors that run the gamut from familiar-but-delicious vanilla to whiskey, rice, and fig. Gelateria Michelangiolo enjoys the best location in town, overlooking the city from the Piazzale Michelangiolo, whereas Gelateria Carabè serves Sicilian-style gelato, dense with the season's best fruits (its homemade cannolis are also a treat) on the street linking the Accademia and the Duomo. **Vivoli:** Tel 39/055-292334; www.vivoli.it. **Gelateria Michelangiolo:** Tel 39/055-234-2705. **Gelateria Carabè:** Tel 39/055-289476; www.gelatocarabe.com.

Wine bars—The handsome Osteria del Caffè Italiano, housed in a landmark early-Renaissance palazzo near Piazza Santa Croce, is the best place in town for a self-styled *degustazione* by the glass, accompanied by artisanal salami and cheeses and simple meals of seasonal ingredients. There's also a pizzeria and a softly lit tablecloth restaurant attached. At Pitti Gola, an excellent selection of wines by the glass is served by the incredibly knowledgeable and friendly owners. A few daily simple pastas are available in casual and intimate surroundings across from the Pitti Palace. Frescobaldi pours 40-plus wines from the proprietor's 700-year-old vineyards, along with other Tuscan vintages, and accompanies them with simple but excellent Tuscan fare. **Osteria del Caffè Italiano:** Tel 39/055-289368; www.caffeitaliano.it. **Pitti Gola:** Tel 39/055-212704. **Frescobaldi:** Tel 39/055-284724; www.frescobaldi.it.

Connecting the Dots in a Postcard-Perfect Landscape

The Hill Towns of Tuscany

Tuscany, Italy

Few travel experiences in Italy are more exhilarating than winding along a country road and coming upon the silhouette of yet another Tuscan hilltown on a cypress-lined crest. You will discover countless enchanting vignettes when you drive south for about 120 miles from Florence (see p. 203) to the wine town of Montepulciano.

The Chianti region unfolds just beyond Florence, by many accounts the most beautiful wine region in Italy. For a lazy vineyard-hopping drive with serendipitous wine-tasting stops, follow the old Via Chiantigiana (Chianti Road) from Florence to Siena (see p. 212) through a landscape of rolling hills, medieval castles, and stone farmhouses. Spend the night at the family-owned Castello di Volpaia wine estate, where guests stay in a restored centuries-old hamlet.

The busy wine hub of Greve in Chianti is surrounded by vineyards that produce some of the finest Tuscan reds. Outlying Villa Le Barone is a former 16th-century wine estate, with 30 lovely rooms, that retains the feel of a private manor. Plan a day trip to San Gimignano, called a "Medieval Manhattan" for its distinctive skyline bristling with towers that date back to the 12th century. Linger over lunch at the

From Pienza you can see the cultivated hills and charming farmhouses of Val d'Orcia, a classic Tuscan landscape.

rustic dining room of the Bel Soggiorno, where a delicious meal of wild game shares the spotlight with the glorious views.

The small, sleepy, but well-to-do hill town of Montalcino overlooks vineyards yielding the sangiovese grosso grapes used for brunello wine, and its lighter-weight cousin rosso di Montalcino. Hike up to the 14th-century Fortezza that moonlights as the town enoteca for a wine tasting or sit for hours in the Piazza del Popolo's 19th-century Caffè Fiaschetteria Italiana. Dinner at the very respected Osteria Leccio just outside town, in Sant'Angelo in Colle, puts you in the company of in-the-know local wine-industry folks.

Pienza, just 15 miles east of Montalcino, is the fulfillment of the dream of 15th-century Pope Pius II to create an ideal High Renaissance city as a papal retreat—today's "Pearl of the Renaissance." Walk behind the cathedral for views of the Val d'Orcia, where green, cypress-clad hills rise and fall below Monte Amiata. The countryside will probably look familiar—it was the inspiration of Renaissance masters and appears as background in countless religious paintings. Set amid the same hills is La Bandita, a stylishly restored farmhouse where eight bright suites overlook the picture-perfect valley.

Nearby Montepulciano is the loftiest hill town of them all, set 2,000 feet above the Val di Chiana and famous for its hearty *vino nobile*. Views from Montepulciano extend east across the valley to medieval Cortona, another hill town appearing like a floating mirage. But you might want to unpack here in one of the six antiques-filled rooms at Follonico, which enjoy views of the countryside and the beautiful Tempio di San Bagio church, a gem of High Renaissance architecture.

WHERE: San Gimignano is 35 miles/56 km southwest of Florence. **CASTELLO DI VOLPAIA:** Tel 39/0577-738066; www.volpaia.com. *Cost:* double-occupancy villas from $525 (off-peak), from $850 (peak). **VILLA LE BARONE:** Tel 39/055-852621; www.villalebarone.com. *Cost:* from $265 (off-peak), from $350 (peak). *When:* closed Nov–mid-Apr. **BEL SOGGIORNO:** Tel 39/0577-943149. *Cost:* dinner $40. **OSTERIA LECCIO:** Tel 39/0577-844175. *Cost:* dinner $40. **LA BANDITA:** Tel 39/333-404-6704; www.la-bandita.com. *Cost:* from $340 (off-peak), from $425 (peak). *When:* closed Jan–Feb. **FOLLONICO:** Tel 39/0577-669773; www.follonico.com. *Cost:* from $175. **BEST TIMES:** May for wildflowers; Jul for sunflowers; Oct for grape and olive harvests.

Puccini's Hometown and a Leaning Tower

LUCCA AND PISA

Tuscany, Italy

Blessedly bypassed by mass tourism and protected within its perfectly preserved Renaissance walls, Lucca is a quiet though refined town where you can rent a bike to explore its timeless cobblestone streets. Visit the ancient palazzos that today house handsome antiques shops and food stores or any of its medieval churches, such as the elaborate San Michele in Foro, begun in 1143, and the even older Duomo, both masterpieces of intricate Romanesque stone carving. Follow the 3-mile oak-shaded path atop the city's ramparts for a bird's-eye view of the ancient olive groves that unfold beyond the town: The Lucchesia area gives the world its finest *olio di oliva*.

Enjoy a gelato in the atmospheric Antico Caffè Simo, a favored respite for Giacomo

Puccini, Lucca's most famous son. For lunch, join locals at the unpretentious Da Giulio in Pelleria, an airy trattoria beloved for its time-honored Tuscan specialties. Or up the ante at Buca di Sant'Antonio, near Piazza San Michele, a fixture in the Lucca dining scene since the 18th century whose fine cuisine refines and updates ancient tradition.

Almost 300 steps lead to the top of Pisa's leaning tower.

Stay within the city walls at the restored 12th-century Palazzo Alexander, a palace that's now a regal small hotel filled with marble, brocade, timbered ceilings, and the kind of old-world décor that seems operatic—in fact, many of the rooms are named after the works of Puccini. But if you've always dreamed of renting a Tuscan villa, this is the place to do it—the Lucca-based company Salogi is a specialist in quality rentals throughout the region (and beyond) and can help you find the perfect spot.

The workaday neighboring city of Pisa deserves to be seen for its Leaning Tower alone. The tilt of the tower is the result of unstable foundations—after completion, it leaned a fraction of an inch more each year, until a 1990s restoration arrested the tilt at a (hopefully) permanent 14 feet off the perpendicular. Begun in 1174, the tower was designed as a free-standing bell tower for the Duomo, the spectacular cathedral begun even earlier, in 1063, and offset by the baptistery, with its filigree exterior and astonishing acoustics (be sure to sing a few notes inside).

Where: Lucca is 45 miles/72 km west of Florence. **Da Giulio in Pelleria:** Tel 39/0583-55948. *Cost:* dinner $35. **Buca di Sant'Antonio:** Tel 39/0583-55881; www.bucadisantantonio.it. *Cost:* dinner $55. **Hotel Palazzo Alexander:** Tel 39/0583-583571; www.hotelpalazzoalexander.it. *Cost:* from $145 (off-peak), from $210 (peak). **Salogi:** Tel 39/0583-48717; www.salogi.com. *Cost:* 2-bedroom villas from $1,735 per week (off-peak), from $2,220 per week (peak). **Best times:** May–Jun and Sep–Oct for nicest weather; mid-Jul–mid-Aug for Puccini Opera Festival in Torre del Lago; Sep 13 for Luminara di Santa Croce candlelight procession in Lucca; 3rd Sun of every month for outdoor antiques market.

Etruscans and Cowboys in the Far Reaches of Tuscany

Maremma

Tuscany, Italy

The southwest stretches of Tuscany are far removed, in distance and landscape, from the rolling vineyards and art-filled cities travelers usually associate with the region. Here, sun-burnt hills and wide open space are covered in golden wheat and grazing lands where a dying breed of *butteri* (cowboys) tend the region's white, long-horned *maremmano* cattle. Maremma's acclaimed beaches extend along Italy's longest stretch of unspoiled coastline, much of it protected by the Parco Nazionale della Maremma. Enjoy grilled *bistecca* and wild boar in simple trattorias, accompanied by excellent local wines such as sassicaia, a hearty red.

The Etruscans, who settled in this region as early as 700 B.C., left behind elaborate tombs and *vie cave* (sunken passageways linking necropoli and sanctuaries) in and around the village of Sovana. Their Roman successors built elaborate baths at Saturnia, where sulfurous, 98°F springs bubble into naturally terraced pools. Modern-day bathers luxuriate at the stylish Terme di Saturnia, with seven thermal pools, spa treatments based on the mineral-rich waters, and an 18-hole golf course.

On a peninsula in the southernmost reaches of the region, the craggy cliffs of Monte Argentario drop into the sea near the pretty little resort town of Porto Ercole. The secluded cottages of Il Pelicano Hotel are scattered among centuries-old pine and olive groves on the mountain's flank, high above a tiny private cove. The atmosphere is relaxing and laid back but service is refined, and alfresco candlelit dinners with panoramic views of the sea and fresh grilled fish are superb. The amenities of gentle breezes and sea vistas can also be enjoyed at the nearby family-run Don Pedro, a simple hotel with a terrace high above Porto Ercole's harbor with access to a private beach below.

WHERE: Porto Ercole is 74 miles/119 km north of Rome. **TERME DI SATURNIA:** Tel 39/0564-60011; in the U.S., 800-745-8883; www.termedisaturnia.com. *Cost:* from $600 (off-peak), from $800 (peak). **IL PELICANO:** Tel 39/0564-858111; in the U.S., 800-735-2478; www.pelicanohotel.com. *Cost:* from $600 (off-peak), from $845 (peak). *When:* closed mid-Oct–mid-Apr. **DON PEDRO:** Tel 39/0564-833914; www.hoteldonpedro.it. *Cost:* from $145 (off-peak), from $215 (peak). **BEST TIMES:** May–Sep to enjoy the seaside; Jan 5 for celebration the eve of Epiphany with costumed processions in Sovana and nearby towns.

Horse Races amid Medieval Monuments

SIENA

Tuscany, Italy

Built on a series of hilltops, Siena reached its zenith in the 13th century with an explosion of art and architecture (and a university founded in 1240)—then the Black Death struck in 1348. The High Renaissance largely bypassed the city, leaving its medieval monuments intact. The Duomo of Santa Maria Asunta is the city's magnificent Gothic cathedral, with an intricate façade and interior that's striped with black and white marble. At Siena's heart is the scallop-shaped Piazza del Campo (il Campo), ringed with 13th- and 14th-century palazzos. Climb the 505 steps of the Palazzo Pubblico bell tower for an unforgettable view of the idyllic Tuscan countryside. Il Campo also serves as the track for the raucous Palio bareback horse race that takes place each year on July 2 and August 16. Following a procession of drummers and banner bearers comes the race: 90 seconds and three hair-raising laps around the earth-covered piazza. Obtaining tickets to the Palio is nearly impossible (ask your hotel to help way in advance). Or you can stand in the packed campo with 50,000 new best friends.

Stay at the historic Palazzo Ravizza Hotel for its homelike atmosphere, or unpack just outside the city walls at the family-owned Hotel Santa Caterina, which has comfortable rooms and a lovely garden where guests gather for breakfast.

Tuscany is noted for rustic cuisine and world-class wines, both splendidly presented at Osteria le Logge, a classic trattoria with an ample list of brunello wines. Set within 2,000-year-old Etruscan walls, Antica Osteria da Divo offers dining areas chiseled from bedrock beneath ancient arches, a highly romantic setting for such Tuscan classics as *bistecca alla fiorentina*. Wine lovers should not bypass the vaulted cellars of the Enoteca Italiana, housed in the 15th-century Medici fortress with vintages from surrounding Chianti vintners. For an immersion in the vineyards north of town, book a room in the Borgo Argenina, medieval stone farmhouses transformed into a movie-set bed-and-breakfast: Beyond its riot of gardens, Merchant Ivory views unfold. More elaborate is the magically converted 13th-century hamlet at Locanda dell'Amorosa, replete with stables transformed into a well-regarded restaurant and a pool with views of vineyards and olive groves as far as the eye can see.

WHERE: 21 miles/34 km south of Florence. **HOW:** Canada-based Spyns offers 7-day tours for Palio races including coveted balcony seats and more. Tel 36/0566-2412; in Canada, 888-825-4720; www.spyns.com. *Cost:* $3,500, inclusive. Originate in Florence. *When:* Jul and Aug. **PALAZZO RAVIZZA:** Tel 39/0577-280462; www.palazzoravizza.com. *Cost:* from $170 (off-peak), from $240 (peak). **HOTEL SANTA CATERINA:** Tel 39/0577-221105; www.hscsiena.it. *Cost:* from $95 (off-peak), from $175 (peak). **OSTERIA LE LOGGE:** Tel 39/0577-48013; www.giannibrunelli.it. *Cost:* dinner $55. **ANTICA OSTERIA DA DIVO:** Tel 39/0577-286054; www.osteriadadivo.it. *Cost:* dinner $65. **ENOTECA ITALIANA:** Tel 39/0577-228811; www.enoteca-italiana.it. **BORGO ARGENINA:** Tel 39/0577-747117; www.borgoargenina.it. *Cost:* from $240. *When:* closed Nov–Feb. **LOCANDA DELL'AMOROSA:** Tel 39/0577-677211; www.amorosa.it. *Cost:* from $270 (off-peak), from $375 (peak). **BEST TIMES:** May–Jun and Sep–Oct for best weather; Jul and Aug for pre-Palio excitement.

Il Campo's soaring bell tower was built exactly as tall as Siena's Duomo to indicate equality between church and state.

In the Footsteps of St. Francis

ASSISI AND GUBBIO

Umbria, Italy

The humanity, humility, and love for nature of one man, St. Francis, infuse Assisi, a small, pink-hued Umbrian hill town. An enormous basilica was built in honor of the barefoot friar who is buried in the crypt (its size would most likely have mortified him). In the early 13th century, Giotto, whose work was the first to break with the static icons of the Byzantine school, covered much of the upper and lower basilica with remarkable frescoes depicting the life of St. Francis (1182–1226), Italy's patron saint. More in keeping with the spirit of *il poverello* is Ermeo delle Carceri (Hermitage of Prisoners), a primitive monastery in the surrounding hills where he and his followers "imprisoned" themselves in prayer. The Basilica di Santa Chiara is dedicated to

St. Clare, one of Francis's most ardent followers, who is buried here. She founded the sister order to the Franciscans, the Poor Clares, who still serve the poor.

An overnight at the family-run Hotel Umbra allows you to enjoy the stillness and beauty of Assisi after the crowds leave. Housed in a 15th-century building, the Umbra affords panoramic views of the serene valley below from its roof terrace. Of the city's many religious guesthouses welcoming pilgrims from around the world, St. Anthony's is a central oasis run by the hospitable Franciscan Sisters of the Atonement.

St. Francis is also associated with taming a wolf that was menacing the nearby austere hamlet of Gubbio. Its nickname, City of Silence, still lingers. The town's roots as a Roman settlement are in evidence at its ancient Roman amphitheater.

From 1387 to 1508, the Montefeltro counts of nearby Urbino (see p. 194) ruled Gubbio, putting up emissaries at their aristocratic guest quarters on the Piazza della Signoria. The premises have been reborn as the Hotel Relais Ducale, offering the same vistas of Gubbio and the Umbrian plains that must have dazzled the dukes' guests. Reconnect with nature and the countryside that St. Frances so loved with an *agriturismo* stay at Casa Branca, a lovingly restored farmhouse 10 minutes outside of town.

Where: 110 miles/177 km northeast of Rome. **Hotel Umbra:** Tel 39/075-812240; www.hotelumbra.it. *Cost:* from $125. *When:* closed Jan–mid-Mar. **St. Anthony's Guesthouse:** Tel 39/075-812-542; atoneassisi@tiscalinet.it. *Cost:* $80. *When:* closed Nov–Feb. **Relais Ducale:** Tel 39/075-922-0157; www.relaisducale.com. *Cost:* from $150. **Casa Branca:** Tel 39/075-927-0016; www.casabranca.it. *Cost:* $115. **Best times:** in Assisi: Easter Week for processions and music performances; early May for medieval festival of Calendaggio. In Gubbio: May 15 for Corsa dei Ceri, a raucous race of huge wooden "candles" celebrating patron Sant' Ubaldo.

Frescoes by Giotto, including this one depicting the pope blessing St. Francis, fill much of the interior of the Basilica of San Francesco d'Assisi.

High in the Sky, a Romanesque Jewel

Il Duomo

Orvieto, Umbria, Italy

The dramatically situated hill town of Orvieto commands a position atop a high, flat column of tufa stone more than 1,000 feet above sea level. The Duomo, the centerpiece of this ancient town, can be seen from far across the plains below when the sunlight catches the ornate Gothic façade, covered with carved marble and glistening mosaics. For almost 300 years, beginning in the late 13th century, artists and architects from all over Italy labored to complete this fascinating hybrid of Romanesque,

Gothic, and High Renaissance styles. The supreme achievement was the cycle of frescoes that portray the end of the world and cover almost 10,000 square feet of the walls and ceiling of its San Brizio chapel. They were begun by Fra Angelico in 1447 and completed in 1499–1503 by Luca Signorelli and were probably the inspiration for Michelangelo's *Last Judgment* in the Vatican's Sistine Chapel nearly half a century later (see p. 185). (An unimpressed Leonardo da Vinci said the figures reminded him of sacks "stuffed full of nuts.") Orvieto is also justly famous for its dry white wine, which can be sampled at local wine cellars and restaurants.

Golden mosaics and bas-reliefs adorn the cathedral's gabled façade.

I Sette Consoli, behind the cathedral, is one of the finest dining experiences in Umbria for perfect presentations of regional specialties and excellent local wines. La Badia, a beautifully preserved 12th-century abbey at the base of the rock, is now a charming hotel where stone-walled, vaulted guest rooms surround former cloisters and overlook outlying vineyards and olive groves. A few miles outside Orvieto, in San Giorgio, Inncasa provides a perfect country respite. Its old stone manor house and cottages are comfortably decorated with contemporary flair, and the garden-surrounded pool looks out over vineyards to Orvieto in the distance.

Where: 60 miles/97 km northwest of Rome. **I Sette Consoli:** Tel 39/0763-343911; www.isetteconsoli.it. *Cost:* dinner $70. **Hotel La Badia:** Tel 39/0763-301959; www.labadiahotel.it. *Cost:* from $225. *When:* closed early Jan–mid-Mar. **Inncasa:** Tel 39/0763-393692; www.inncasa.eu. *Cost:* from $125 (off-peak), from $175 (peak). **Best time:** late Aug for Orvieto's Umbria Folk Festival with local food and crafts.

History and the Arts in the Umbrian Hills

Perugia

Umbria, Italy

One of Italy's most beloved hill towns, Perugia is also one of the most ancient, dating back to the days of the pre-Roman Etruscans. Trade and the arts flourished here in the Middle Ages, when much of the city's fortresslike backdrop was built. The 13th-century Fontana Maggiore, in the *centro storico* (Old Town) was the terminus of the city's ancient aqueducts; the nearby Collegio del Cambio, built for money changers and traders, is covered with early Renaissance frescoes; and the Palazzo dei Priori now holds the Galleria Nazionale dell'Umbria, a comprehensive collection of regional sculpture and paintings highlighted by works of native son Pietro Perugino, one of the most important painters of the High Renaissance. Next to chocolate, he may be the city's best-known export.

Maybe because it's the only flat strip of land in an exceptionally hilly town or maybe because a vibrant international student population keeps this prosperous city humming (Perugia has been a university center since 1270), but when it's time for the late-afternoon stroll, or *passeggiata,* "il Corso" is the place to be. *Perugini* turn out to shop, chat, and argue soccer scores or political scandals.

Within the ancient city walls, you'll find the dignified Hotel Brufani Palace, standing atop Perugia's highest hill for over 120 years. Travelers can also immerse themselves in the nearby Umbrian countryside at the 18th-century Palazzo Terranova, a country hotel of rustic sophistication.

Summer finds Umbria alive with music: In July, one of Italy's premier jazz festivals, Umbria Jazz takes place; during September, Umbria Music Fest presents a series of regionwide concerts, here and in Spoleto, Assisi, Pescara, and Todi. The famed Spoleto Festival of Two Worlds was established in 1957 by composer Gian Carlo Menotti (and spawned a sister festival in Charleston, S.C.; see p. 867). It presents world-class dance, music, cinema, art, and drama. During the festival, rooms are scarce in Spoleto, so book early to stay at Hotel Gattapone, one of the city's finest small hotels, with a parklike setting popular with performers and festival-goers.

Where: 96 miles/154 km southeast of Florence. **Galleria Nazionale dell'Umbria:** Tel 39/075-5866-8410; www.gallerianazionaleumbria.it. **Hotel Brufani Palace:** Tel 39/075-573-2541; www.brufanipalace.com. *Cost:* from $150 (off-peak), from $465 (peak). **Palazzo Terranova:** Tel 39/075-857-0083; www.palazzoterranova.com. *Cost:* from $350 (off-peak), from $630 (peak). *When:* closed mid-Nov–Feb. **Umbria Jazz:** www.umbriajazz.com. **Umbria Music Fest:** www.umbriamusicfest.it. **Spoleto Festival:** www.festivaldispoleto.com. **Hotel Gattapone:** Tel 39/0743-223447; www.hotelgattapone.it. *Cost:* from $175 (off-peak), from $245 (peak). **Best times:** Apr–Jun and Sep–Oct for nicest weather; mid-Jun, Jul, and Sep for various music festivals.

High Life in the Alps

Courmayeur and Mont Blanc

Valle d'Aosta, Italy

Stylish yet old-fashioned Courmayeur is one of the most popular ski resorts in Europe, nestled at the base of Monte Bianco (Mont Blanc, Europe's highest mountain), which it shares with France, and surrounded by a dozen other peaks higher than 13,000 feet. Courmayeur's slopes are geared to beginners as well as die-hard enthusiasts who can enjoy the long ski season from November to April. Some visitors may never strap on a pair of skis, but pass the time strolling the cobblestone streets and enjoying the chic bars, boutiques, and numerous restaurants.

Stunning mountain scenery and cool temperatures make Courmayeur a favorite summer retreat as well. Hikers can follow hundreds of miles of trails, including those of the nearby Parco Nazionale del Gran Paradiso, the former hunting grounds of Vittorio Emanuele, the first king of Italy. Steel-nerved adventurers travel by cable car from nearby La Palud up and over the Mont Blanc Massif, one of the most breathtaking rides in the world (the winter route extends as far as the ski station at Punta Hebronner). Aptly called "Riding the Glaciers," the trip reaches a dramatic climax when the cable car dangles more than 2,000 feet above a sea of glacial snowfields before arriving at the viewing station high above Chamonix, France (see p. 135). There a mountaintop bar's sunbathing terrace offers more sensational views.

In the tiny hamlet of Entreves, just outside of Courmayeur, is one of the most famous restaurants in the Italian Alps, La Maison de Filippo. An avalanche of regional selections makes up the bulk of a seemingly endless meal in a festive all-you-can-eat atmosphere. One of the region's most comfortable retreats is the Mont Blanc Hotel Village, laid out like a small mountain hamlet 5 miles southwest of Courmayeur, in La Salle. All of the rooms are nicely appointed and have big windows and balconies or terraces overlooking scene-stealing Mont Blanc.

Where: 22 miles/35 km northwest of Aosta. **La Maison de Filippo:** Tel 39/0165-869797; www.lamaison.com. *Cost:* dinner $65. *When:* mid-May–mid-Jul and Nov–Dec. **Mont Blanc Hotel Village:** Tel 39/0165-864111; www.hotelmontblanc.it. *Cost:* from $400 (off-peak), from $540 (peak). *When:* closed Oct–Nov. **Best times:** Feb–Mar for skiing, Jun–Aug for hiking.

Bikers can ride the famed Tour du Mont Blanc route, which lets you circumnavigate the mountain in 4 days.

"Your visit to Venice becomes a perpetual love affair."
—Henry James

Venice

Veneto, Italy

Venice confuses and enchants, so toss the map and let yourself wander. Give in to this fragile, watery world built on 118 small islands and lose yourself among Byzantine domes and palazzos. Step back in time to when Venezia, the queen of the Adriatic, ruled much of the Mediterranean world. Meander through neighborhoods where not much has changed since native son Marco Polo set sail for the distant corners of the world, courtesans and doges passed as shadows in the narrow alleyways, and Casanova glided down the Grand Canal on his way to a nocturnal assignation.

Top Attractions

Gallerie dell'Accademia—The most extensive collection of Venetian masters in the world fills a former church and guild hall with works by Titian, Giorgione, Bellini, Carpaccio, and others. Venice is the colorful backdrop for Tinteretto's St. Mark Cycle and many other works that reveal how little the city has changed over the centuries. **Info:** Tel 39/041-522-2247; www.gallerieaccademia.org.

Ca' d'Oro and the Galleria Giorgio Franchetti—A beautiful 15th-century palazzo on the Grand Canal where Titian's *Venus at the Mirror* vies with Mantegna's *St. Sebastian* for your attention. These and other paintings, sculptures, and furniture were donated to the Italian government by philanthropist Baron Giorgio Franchetti. **Info:** Tel 39/041-520-0345; www.cadoro.org.

CHIESA DEI FRARI (CHURCH OF THE FRIARS)—In a city filled with churches, this immense Franciscan bastion, built in the 13th and 14th centuries in San Polo, stands out as a showcase for Titian, including an *Assumption* depicting the ascension of the Virgin Mary into heaven surrounded by swirling putti (cherubs). **INFO:** Tel 39/041-522-2637; www.basilicadeifrari.it.

CHIESA DEI SANTI GIOVANNI E PAOLO (CHURCH OF SAINTS JOHN AND PAUL)—The largest church in Venice after St. Mark's contains the tombs of 25 doges, plus works by Bellini and Veronese, and ceilings that depict New Testament scenes. Andrea del Verrocchio's famous 15th-century bronze equestrian statue of the mercenary Bartolomeo Colleoni, one of the great masterworks of early Renaissance sculpture, commands the surrounding *campo*. You can take it all in from the outdoor tables of Rosa Salva, a centuries-old coffeehouse and pastry shop. **CAMPO SS. GIOVANNI E PAOLO:** Tel 39/041-523-5913.

A centuries-old sumptuary law required that gondolas be painted black, a tradition that continues to this day.

THE GRAND CANAL—Venice's Main Street is a 2-mile-long, S-shaped aquatic thoroughfare lined with hundreds of weather-worn Byzantine and Gothic palazzos and abuzz with canal life. Jump aboard the number 1 vaporetto (water bus) and float through 1,000 years of Venetian history, dodging gondolas and delivery boats. Start at either Piazza San Marco or the Santa Lucia train station, and savor the ride at least twice: once by day for rush-hour stimulus and once at night for the quiet, unmatched romance of it all. A cruise by gondola brings you through an enchanting web of more than 150 sleepy back canals—seeing the hidden corners of this unique city built on water.

PEGGY GUGGENHEIM COLLECTION—An unfinished 18th-century palazzo on the Grand Canal that was once the home of art collector Peggy Guggenheim is filled with works by Pollock, Brancusi, Picasso, Klee, Rothko, Chagall, and (her husband) Max Ernst—and many other 20th-century artists to whom the American heiress was a patron. Some of the rooms at DD724, an intimate, contemporary hotel next door, overlook the Guggenheim's sculpture-filled garden. **GUGGENHEIM COLLECTION:** Tel 39/041-520-6288; www.guggenheim-venice.it. **DD724:** Tel 39/041-277-0262; www.dd724.it. *Cost:* from $225 (off-peak), from $575 (peak).

PUNTA DELLA DOGANA MUSEUM OF CONTEMPORARY ART—Overlooking the sea lanes of the lagoon and Piazza San Marco across the Grand Canal, the 17th-century Customs Hall was recently transformed by architect Tadao Ando into a luminous gallery of contemporary art housing the collection of French magnate François Pinault. (Its neighbor, the spectacular Santa Maria della Salute Church, deserves a peek as well.) More of the collector's masterpieces by Jeff Koons, Cy Twombly, and other luminaries of today's art world are housed a bit up the Grand Canal in the grand 18th-century Palazzo Grassi. **INFO:** Tel 39/0445-230313; www.palazzograssi.it.

PIAZZA SAN MARCO AND BASILICA DI SAN MARCO—Napoleon was inspired to call the elegant, colonnaded heart of Venice "the finest drawing room in Europe." Two bronze Moors atop the 15th-century Torre dell'Orologio (Clock Tower) strike the hour, and the Campanile—a 20th-century re-creation of the 8th-century original, the

The city's emblem and mascot, the statue of a winged lion near the Palazzo Ducale was looted by Napoleon's troops in 1797, but was returned in 1815.

tallest structure on the Venice skyline—provides a miraculous view over the city. Byzantine and almost mosquelike, the Basilica di San Marco was built as the final resting place of St. Mark, the city's patron. Reproductions of four bronze horses looted from Constantinople in 1204 preside over the ornate façade (the originals are in St. Mark's Museum, inside the basilica), and magnificent glittering mosaics cover the dimly lit ceilings and columns. The Pala d'Oro altar screen, one of the basilica's greatest treasures, is composed of more than 2,000 precious stones and enameled panels. **INFO:** Tel 39/041-522-5205; www.basilicasanmarco.it.

PALAZZO DUCALE (DOGE'S PALACE)—The pink-and-white marble palace that flanks the basilica and faces St. Mark's Basin was meant to impress Venice's wealth and power upon visitors arriving by ship. Doges ruled *La Serenissima* (the Most Serene Republic) and much of the eastern Mediterranean for 1,000 years from assembly rooms and private apartments here, filled with paintings by Veronese, Tintoretto, and the other Venetian masters. The so-called Bridge of Sighs (Ponte dei Sospiri) links the palace with the Palazzo delle Prigioni, where prisoners were held after being judged by the council. **INFO:** Tel 39/041-522-4951; www.museiciviciveneziani.it.

SCUOLA GRANDE DI SAN ROCCO—The most renowned of the influential religious and social confraternities that once proliferated in Venice was built in 1515. Some 50 works that Tintoretto painted for the *scuola* from 1564 to 1594 constitute the largest collection of his dark and dramatic work anywhere. Gaze upon scenes from the New and Old Testaments, including the enormous *Crucifixion,* considered Tintoretto's masterpiece. **INFO:** Tel 39/041-523-4864; scuolagrandesanrocco.it.

OTHER MUST-DOS

TORCELLO—The green, quasideserted island of Torcello is the idyllic setting for a picnic, far from the crowds of tourists and pigeons in the Piazza San Marco. The terrace tables of Trattoria al Ponte del Diavolo also promise a perfect lunch. Let dessert be a viewing of Torcello's cathedral and its breathtaking 12th- and 13th-century Byzantine mosaics, some of the most important in Europe. Should you want to spend a night, the stylishly simple Locanda Cipriani (founded by the owner of Harry's Bar) offers six delightful rooms, fine dining in a casual setting, and romantic ambience. **TRATTORIA AL PONTE DEL DIAVOLO:** Tel 39/041-730401; www.osteriapontedeldiavolo.com. *Cost:* lunch $40. **LOCANDA CIPRIANI:** Tel 39/041-730150; www.locandacipriani.com. *Cost:* from $280; lunch $50.

CHIESA DELLA PIETÀ (VIVALDI'S CHURCH)—Baroque maestro and native son Antonio Vivaldi worked as choirmaster for the church's orphanage and conservatory from 1703 to 1741, while composing some of his greatest masterworks. These and other works by contemporaries of the Red Priest are often performed here by candlelight. Hearing a performance of *The Four Seasons* beneath Tiepolo's luminous ceiling fresco is magical. **INFO:** Tel 39/041-522-2171; www.vivaldi.it.

CARNEVALE AND OTHER FESTIVALS—Venice's hedonistic Carnevale, a season of unbridled and licentious festivities, expired along with the rest of the Republic with the arrival of Napoleon in 1797. It was enthusiastically resuscitated in 1980, complete with rich damasks, cascades of lace, and powdered wigs, elaborate costumes, and everywhere the characters and masks from Italy's Commedia dell'Arte. Carnevale lasts 2 weeks prior to Ash Wednesday, but Venice remains in a celebratory mood year-round. The Voga Lunga, a kind of aquatic marathon, is a 20-mile race among almost 1,500 boats of all shapes and sizes in late May or early June. The Biennale d'Arte Contemporanea e Architettura, a prestigious exhibition of art (in odd years) and architecture (in even years), runs from June through October. The Biennale's Venice Film Festival, every August, brings celebs and filmmakers from around the world. The Festa del Redentore, in late July, celebrates the end of the 1578 plague with a pilgrimage across a makeshift temporary bridge over the Giudecca Canal to Andrea Palladio's church of Il Redentore and with fireworks filling the sky. During the Regata Storica, in early September, gaily decorated gondolas and historic craft of all types glide down the Grand Canal, carrying passengers in historical costume. **Biennale d'Arte:** Tel 39/041-521-8711; www.labiennale.org. **Regata Storica:** Tel 39/041-241-2988; www.veneziamarketingeventi.it.

Carnevale's "Best Mask" contest is judged by a panel of international costume and fashion designers.

Where to Stay

Historic palazzo hotels—The legendary Hotel Danieli occupies the 14th-century canal-front home of a former doge and surrounds a courtyard now enclosed as the spectacular lobby. Take a seat at the Bar Dandolo, a retreat favored by hotel guests and curious drop-ins alike. Many rooms look out onto the Grand Canal. Similar theater prevails at the dignified Gritti Palace, former home of Doge Andrea Gritti built on the Grand Canal in 1525; a candlelit dinner or sunset *aperitivo* on the open-air terrace comes with views of the magnificent Baroque Chiesa della Salute (Church of Good Health), directly across the Grand Canal. Set on the tip of the peaceful island of Giudecca, a ten-minute ride by private launch from Piazza San Marco, the Cipriani is like a private estate in the middle of Venice. Guests revel in acres of flowering gardens, an Olympic-size saltwater pool, the swank Fortuny restaurant, and silk drapes and wall coverings in the discreetly gorgeous guest rooms. Exquisite apartments are tucked away in adjacent palazzos. **Hotel Danieli:** Tel 39/041-522-6480; in the U.S., 800-325-3589; www.danielihotelvenice.com. *Cost:* from $425 (off-peak), from $725 (peak). **Gritti Palace:** Tel 39/041-794611; in the U.S., 800-325-3589; www.hotelgrittipalacevenice.com. *Note:* Closed for renovation till early 2013. **Hotel Cipriani:** Tel 39/041-520-7744; in the U.S., 800-237-1236; www.hotelcipriani.it. *Cost:* from $1,200; dinner $110. *When:* closed mid-Nov–Mar.

Small hotels with gardens—The atmospheric Hotel Flora, not far from Piazza San Marco, surrounds a flowering courtyard, an oasis of thick climbing vines and flowering plants where breakfast, tea, or an *aperitivo* can be enjoyed in warmer months. Katharine Hepburn's character in the film *Summertime* stayed at the charming Pensione Accademia/Villa Maravege, and the antiques-filled lounges and guest rooms facing two gardens continue to provide a magical retreat not far from the Accademia. The delightful canalside Oltre Il Giardino is like a bucolic country retreat, with stylish rooms overlooking a verdant garden with olive and magnolia trees where breakfast is served in the summer. **Hotel Flora:** Tel 39/041-520-5844; www.hotelflora.it. *Cost:* from $200 (off-peak), from $415 (peak). **Pensione Accademia/ Villa Maravege:** Tel 39/041-521-0188; www.pensioneaccademia.it. *Cost:* from $200 (off-peak), from $340 (peak). **Oltre Il Giardino:** Tel 39/041-275-0015; www.oltre ilgiardino-venezia.com. *Cost:* from $215 (off-peak), from $360 (peak).

High character without high prices—The friendly Hotel Ai Do Mori enjoys a five-star address, with modest, upper-story rooms within poking distance of the onion-shaped Byzantine cupolas of St. Mark's Basilica and the bronze Moors of the Piazza San Marco's clock tower. (Be prepared for early-morning bells and make sure your knees are up to the climb: The hotel has no elevator.) Practically in the shadow of the Doge's Palace, the Ca' dei Dogi is a small, stylish oasis of calm. **Hotel Ai Do Mori:** Tel 39/041-520-4817; www.hotelaidomori.com. *Cost:* from $75 (off-peak), from $185 (peak). **Ca' dei Dogi:** Tel 39/041-241-3759; www.cadeidogi.it. *Cost:* from $180.

Eating & Drinking

Al Covo—Summertime meals are served at a few outdoor tables and year-round in a small brick-walled, art-filled dining room that exudes a special warmth. Sharing the helm is the talented and amiable Italo-American duo: Charming Cesare meets and greets while overseeing the kitchen's simple but deft preparations of just-caught seafood while *simpatica* Diane shares the floor (she's also responsible for the scrumptious desserts). **Info:** Tel 39/041-522-3812; www.ristorantealcovo.com. *Cost:* dinner $75.

Da Fiore—In a city where fine dining is associated with seafood, Da Fiore is generally regarded as the best. The formal but welcoming dining room is renowned for the all-around excellence of the refined Adriatic delicacies, prepared to perfection. **Info:** Tel 39/041-721308; www.dafiore.net. *Cost:* set dinner menu $125.

Alle Testiere—This tiny, informal trattoria near Campo Santa Maria Formosa is forever full with a convivial mix of Venetians and tourists. The young owners are serious about food as a sampling of their gnocchi stuffed with octopus and other sophisticated seafood preparations will prove (meat lovers should book elsewhere). **Info:** Tel 39/041-522-7220; www.osterialletestiere.it. *Cost:* dinner $65.

The Cafés of Piazza San Marco—During the cold months, the elegant 18th-century interior makes the Caffè Florian the command post of choice in the magnificent Piazza San Marco. But in warm weather, when tables are moved outdoors and the orchestras are playing their timeless tunes into the moonlit hours, Caffè Quadri or any of the outdoor cafés will do just fine. You might even set up camp in the lesser-known Caffè Chioggia around the corner, which faces the lacy pink-and-white marble façade of the Doge's Palace and a flotilla of gondolas bobbing in the fabled lagoon. **Caffè Florian:** Tel 39/041-520-5641; www.caffeflorian.com. **Caffè Quadri:** Tel 39/041-528-9299; www.caffequadri.it. **Caffè Chioggia:** Tel 39/041-528-5011.

Wine bars—The atmospheric Cantina do Mori is Venice's most beloved *bacaro*, serving aristocrats and fishmongers alike regional wines and a variety of *cichetti* (finger foods in the style of Spanish tapas) in a high-spirited, timeless setting so authentic you expect Casanova to tap you on the shoulder. Just across from Dorsoduro's San Trovaso gondola boatyard, the Cantinone Gia Schiavi has a huge selection of house wines to accompany a mouthwatering assortment of crostini—toasted bread topped with cheese, salamis, smoked fish, and other delectables. **Cantina do Mori:** Tel 39/041-522-5401. **Cantinone Gia Schiavi:** Tel 39/041-523-0034.

And Beyond

Asolo—Robert Browning pronounced this Renaissance town nestled in the gentle green hills of the Veneto "the most beautiful spot I ever was privileged to see." This enchanting hilltop retreat still lures foreign writers, artists, and intellectuals with its lush countryside of fruit orchards, cypresses, and vineyards. Many lodge at Browning's Palladian-style villa, now the perfectly faded Hotel Villa Cipriani. One of Europe's most seductive country hotels, it is known for top-notch dining and a fragrant garden full of roses, pomegranates, and birdsong. A 4-mile drive takes you to Maser and to Andrea Palladio's 16th-century masterpiece, the elegant Villa Barbaro, abounding with trompe l'oeil frescoes by Paolo Veronese. **Where:** 40 miles/64 km northwest of Venice. **Visitor Info:** www.asolo.it. **Hotel Villa Cipriani:** Tel 39/0423-523411; www.villaciprianiasolo.com. *Cost:* from $300 (off-peak), from $570 (peak).

Vicenza—The great Andrea Palladio, who helped define Western architecture, bestowed his native city with what is possibly his greatest work, the Teatro Olimpico. Inspired by the theaters of antiquity, with a backdrop representing ancient Thebes, the theater uses cunningly designed trompe l'oeil to make the stage appear far deeper than its actual 14 feet—an effect enjoyed by audiences since 1585. Palladio also designed numerous villas along the Brenta Canal and elsewhere in the Veneto; his most famous country estate is Villa Capra, aka Villa la Rotonda, a substantial but enjoyable walk from Vicenza's center. **Where:** 46 miles/74 km west of Venice. **Visitor Info:** www.vicenza.org. **Teatro Olimpico:** www.teatroolimpico.org.

Padua—Lively market squares, a beautiful 13th-century basilica honoring St. Anthony, and the world's second oldest university (founded in 1222) are among Padova's many charms, but most remarkable is the 13th-century Scrovegni Chapel. Here Giotto and his students labored from 1303 to 1306 to create 38 biblical scenes that transform late-medieval and early Renaissance painting with their realism and emotion and the power of the colors—especially the famous cobalt blue. **Where:** 26 miles/42 km west of Venice. **Scrovengi Chapel:** Tel 39/049-201-0020; www.cappelladegliscrovegni.it.

Venice Simplon-Orient-Express—On the world's most celebrated train ride—a 32-hour trek across the continent from Venice to London (or the reverse; a selection of other overnight routes within Europe, including Florence and Rome, are also available)—much of the 1920s glamour and mystique of Agatha Christie still lingers. The dining and white-glove service are faultless in this grand hotel on wheels—all that's missing are the spies, silent-film stars, and royalty of yesteryear. **Info:** In the U.S., 800-524-2420 or 843-937-9068; www.orient-expresstrains.com. *Cost:* $3,200, inclusive (shorter segments can also be booked). *When:* mid-Mar–late Nov.

Home of Romeo, Juliet, and Aïda

Verona

Veneto, Italy

Suspend all disbelief and immerse yourself in the romance of Verona. Millions of the curious and lovelorn come here to breathe the air that Shakespeare's Romeo and Juliet once inhaled, and local officials, determined to keep the allure of the star-crossed lovers alive (though there is no real proof they ever existed), have designated a 14th-century palazzo—complete with requisite balcony—as the residence of the Capulets. Love notes left behind, scribbled in every language, are innocent, humorous, and bittersweet. Few visit the courtyard without rubbing the right breast of a nubile bronze Juliet—said to ensure luck in affairs of the heart. Romantics will love the Sogno di Giulietta (Juliet's Dream), the only hotel with rooms—in rich fabrics with ornate headboards and beamed ceilings—that overlook Juliet's balcony. To savor local Veneto specialties in an inimitable ambience, dine at the 12 Apostoli, Verona's oldest restaurant and one of its finest. Ask to see the wine cellar built around ancient Roman ruins.

The bronze statue's right breast is shiny from good-luck rubs.

If it's summertime, join your fellow romantics for a night of opera in the impeccably preserved Roman amphitheater whose perfect acoustics have survived 2,000 years. *Aïda,* first performed here in 1913 to commemorate the 100th anniversary of Verdi's birth, has been the constant in each year's changing schedule, and even the opera-challenged will take home the memory of a lifetime when hundreds of cast members fill the stage during the Triumphal March. Performers may seem an inch tall from the highest and cheapest seats in the house (which you'll be lucky to get, as all 20,000 regularly sell out), but their voices will be as crystal clear as the cool night air, and the view of the surrounding hills of the Veneto is thrown in at no extra cost.

Postopera, head to the historic Caffè Dante to sit outdoors in Verona's most beautiful square, the Piazza dei Signori, and enjoy a glass of Valpolicella wine from Veneto's celebrated vineyards. In fact, a wine-tasting tour of the world-class vineyards of the Veneto makes a perfect day trip from Verona. The palace-flanked Piazza delle Erbe, site of the Roman forum and these days a weekday market, is reached from the Piazza dei Signori through the Arco della Costa—it is said that a whalebone hanging over the passageway will fall only when someone who has never told a lie walks beneath; the artifact has remained in place for centuries.

WHERE: 71 miles/114 km west of Venice. **ARENA DI VERONA:** box office tel 39/045-800-5151; www.arena.it. *When:* late Jun–early Sep. **SOGNO DI GIULIETTA:** Tel 39/045-800-9932; www.sognodigiulietta.it. *Cost:* from $280 (off-peak), from $470 (peak). **12 APOSTOLI:** Tel 39/045-596-999; www.12apostoli.it. *Cost:* dinner $60. **CAFFÈ DANTE:** Tel 39/045-800-0083; www.caffedante.it. *Cost:* dinner $40. **BEST TIMES:** summer months for opera; Jul for Shakespearean Festival, with plays (some in English) and music.

A Hidden Fortress

LUXEMBOURG CITY

Luxembourg

Upon a sandstone plateau bordered with ravines cut by the Alzette and Petrusse rivers sits the Grand Duchy of Luxembourg. For a capital, it's lilliputian—just 80,000 residents—but it's the undisputed heart of the country. Strategically located at the crossroads of Belgium, France, and Germany, the city was built around a 10th-century castle. Each time invaders passed through, fortifications were added; by 1867, it was so daunting that the Treaty of London ordered it dismantled. Just 10 percent of the fortifications remain in the Old Town, but the medieval ambience is still palpable, albeit mixed with a contemporary vibe.

I. M. Pei's MUDAM stands just behind Fort Thüngen, which was once part of the ancient walls that protected the city.

Tour the city on foot, starting in the tree-lined Place d'Armes, home to trendy eateries and accommodations. The lauded gourmet patisserie Wenge has a très chic upstairs restaurant, and the Hotel Le Place d'Armes is handsomely ensconced in an ornate 18th-century building. A few blocks away, past the flagship store for the country's ubiquitous Villeroy & Boch porcelain, is the Grand Ducal Palace, the official residence of the royal family and erstwhile town hall.

Art lovers will want to stay at the charming Hotel Parc Beaux Arts, where the ten suites are decorated with contemporary paintings. The Chemin de la Corniche, "Europe's most beautiful balcony," offers the finest views of the Alzette River and the gentrified neighborhood of Grund, home to Mosconi, a restaurant loved by discerning Luxembourgers who come for some of the best Italian fare north of the Alps.

The city is more than just the Old Town. I. M. Pei designed the Museum of Modern Art (MUDAM), a striking glass structure that opened in 2006, and the city's philharmonic orchestra performs at the brand-new Grand-Duchesse Josephine-Charlotte Concert Hall, a teardrop-shaped masterpiece from French architect Christian de Portzamparc. This flurry of construction speaks to the prosperity of Luxembourg's citizens, a mixture of French, German, and Lëtzebuergesch (the native tongue) speakers, who have one of the world's highest gross national incomes per capita.

Attractions beyond the city can all be reached in an hour or less. Sample the crémants and rieslings of the Moselle Valley in the southeast, or travel to the Ardennes Mountains in the north to visit the brewery town of Diekirch, home to the National Museum of Military History, and the restored medieval castle of Vianden.

WHERE: 135 miles/218 km southeast of Brussels; 232 miles/373 km northeast of Paris. **VISITOR INFO:** www.lcto.lu. **WENGE:** Tel 352/26-20-10; www.wenge.lu. *Cost:* lunch $40. **HOTEL LE PLACE D'ARMES:** Tel 352/27-47-37; www.hotel-leplacedarmes.com. *Cost:* from $410. **GRAND DUCAL PALACE:** Tel 352/47-96-27-09. *When:* tours mid-Jul–early Sep, when royal family is vacationing. **HOTEL PARC BEAUX ARTS:** Tel 352/26-86-761; www.parcbeauxarts.lu. *Cost:* from $300. **MOSCONI:** Tel 352/54-69-94; www.mosconi.lu. *Cost:* dinner $160. **MUDAM:** Tel 352/45-37-85-1; www.mudam.lu. **LUXEMBOURG PHILHARMONIC:** Tel 352/26-02-271; www.philharmonie.lu. **NATIONAL MUSEUM OF MILITARY HISTORY:** Tel 352/80-89-08; www.mnhm.lu. **BEST TIMES:** Mar–Jun for pleasant weather; Jun 23 for Luxembourg National Day with parades, fireworks, and revelry.

Historic Headquarters of the Knights of St. John

VALLETTA

Malta

The tiny island of Malta, today a stop for cruise ships, yachts, beach lovers, and history buffs, long enjoyed a strategic importance out of all proportion to its size. Located at the crossroads of the Mediterranean, this speck of limestone south of Sicily was vital to the control of busy sea lanes from the 16th century until 1945. With four sister islands, it is now an independent nation, with its capital the lovely city of Valletta, its streets lined with Baroque palaces, gardens, and churches.

Malta was presented as a gift to the Knights of St. John, or Hospitallers, by the Holy Roman Emperor Charles V in 1530, after they had been driven from Rhodes (see p. 166) by the Ottoman sultan. After repelling Ottoman invaders in the Great Siege of Malta in 1565, the knights fortified their island and built Valletta, overlooking the Grand Harbour. One of Europe's first planned cities, Valletta was designed and constructed from scratch, hewn from the island's honey-colored limestone, a city "built by gentlemen, for gentlemen" in the assessment of Benjamin Disraeli.

The Grand Harbour separates Valletta from the town of Kalkara, across the water.

The knights gave pride of place to St. John's Co-Cathedral. Its plain exterior conceals a riot of Baroque extravagance inside, with polychrome marble floors and ornate side chapels, and its museum holds Caravaggio's *The Beheading of St. John the Baptist,* considered by some to be the artist's masterpiece. The elaborate decoration of the nearby Grand Masters' Palace includes colorful frescoes depicting the Great Siege and priceless Gobelin tapestries. The Armory, despite having been looted by Napoleon, houses 5,000 suits of armor.

But the knights' most impressive legacy is the fortifications that surround the city. Take a walk around the massive walls, bastions, and batteries and pause at the Upper Barrakka Gardens for a superb view over the Grand Harbour and, if your timing is right, the firing of the noonday cannon.

Just outside Valletta's city gate stands the lovingly restored Hotel Phoenicia, an Art Deco grand hotel surrounded by shaded gardens and with views of Valletta's second natural harbor, Marsamxett. In 1949, Princess Elizabeth (now Queen Elizabeth) and Prince Philip, then a naval officer stationed in Malta, made several visits to the Phoenicia, dancing as newlyweds in its Grand Ballroom.

VISITOR INFO: www.visitmalta.com. **GRAND MASTERS' PALACE:** Tel 356/2124-9349; www.heritagemalta.com. **HOTEL PHOENICIA:** Tel 356/2122-5241; www.phoeniciamalta.com. *Cost:* from $180 (off-peak), from $250 (peak). **BEST TIMES:** Sep for perfect weather; Feb or Mar for Carnival; Dec for Christmas festivities.

World Famous Enclave of Royalty and the Jet Set

Monaco

Monaco

Bordered by France on three sides, the tiny principality of Monaco has been a playground for Europe's elite for more than a century—they come for its sandy beaches, luxury yachts, and hilltop Mediterranean panoramas, while the nation's tax-free status and renowned Grand Casino in the capital, Monte Carlo, sweeten the deal. The ornate and elegant Belle Époque casino on Place du Casino was designed in 1863 by Charles Garnier, architect of the Paris Opéra; he also designed the Opera House in the casino complex. Slot machines in the casino's lobby are free of charge if you dress nicely and carry a passport; there's a fee to enter the front gambling rooms and those leading to the Salons Privés, the high rollers' inner sanctum. A de rigueur stop next door is the Garnier-designed Café de Paris, where the crêpe Suzette was invented in the early 1900s.

This 76-square-mile city-state is the world's most densely populated country.

The Grimaldi family has ruled Monaco since the 13th century from a fortified palace on a dramatic promontory of Le Rocher, the historic core of the city also known as Monaco-Ville. Prince Albert, son of Prince Rainier III and former film star Grace Kelly, lives in the palace compound with his bride, Charlene, and visitors may tour parts of the palace and watch the daily changing of the guard. Rainier III and Kelly are buried in the grand Monaco Cathedral where they married in 1956. Nearby is the crowd-pleasing Oceanographic Museum with one of Europe's best aquariums.

Place du Casino is also home to the palatial Hôtel de Paris, the regal stopping place of emirs and archdukes since 1864. Its marquee restaurant is the dazzling Le Louis XV, domain of world-famous chef Alain Ducasse. Refined dishes composed of local ingredients by chef Franck Cerutti are served amid opulent Louis XV décor brimming with Baccarat crystal, damask linens, and gold-rimmed china. Across the square, the Hôtel Métropole is no less palatial albeit in a modern style, and showcases legendary chef Joël Robuchon's first gourmet Japanese restaurant, Yoshi. Its terrace is ideal for watching the annual Formula One Grand Prix of Monaco.

Where: 15 miles/24 km east of Nice. **Visitor info:** www.visitmonaco.com. **Casino de Monte Carlo:** Tel 377/98-062121; www.montecarlocasinos.com. **Café de Paris:** Tel 377/98-067623. *Cost:* dinner $68. **Oceanographic Museum:** Tel 377/93-153600; www.oceano.mc. **Hôtel de Paris:** Tel 377/98-063000; www.hoteldeparismontecarlo.com. *Cost:* from $550 (off-peak), from $840 (peak); dinner at Le Louis XV $255. **Hôtel Métropole:** Tel 377/98-151515; in the U.S., 800-745-8883; www.metropole.com. *Cost:* from $525 (off-peak), from $680 (peak). *Cost:* dinner at Yoshi $150. **Best times:** late May for Formula One Grand Prix; Jul–Aug for International Fireworks Festival.

"I like Amsterdam more than Venice because, in Amsterdam, one has water without being deprived of land. . . ."—CHARLES DE MONTESQUIEU

AMSTERDAM

Netherlands

Amsterdam is spread out across a web-shaped network of canals, lined with five centuries' worth of gabled buildings. It is charmingly low-rise—those decorative façades are seldom more than four or five stories high—but it's high impact. World-class art museums, the heritage of a glorious golden age, and a vibrant contemporary culture await you at every turn. Amsterdam has all the advantages of a metropolis with hardly any of the drawbacks. The city is small enough to walk or cycle almost anywhere, but its rich cultural fare is world class, served up against a backdrop of unassuming brick houses, pretty bridges, and quiet canals that give the city a villagelike charm.

TOP ATTRACTIONS

RIJKSMUSEUM—The Netherlands' greatest museum—and one of the world's prime repositories of fine art—is a treasure trove of the country's most notable works from the 17th-century golden age. Rembrandt's magnificent *The Night Watch* (1642) is the pivotal point around which this turreted neo-Gothic museum was designed in 1885 by P.J.H. Cuypers. The enormous canvas is still the centerpiece of the largest collection of Dutch paintings in the world, including 20 other works by Rembrandt—such as his sensitive *Jewish Bride* (1662) and *Self-Portrait as the Apostle Paul* (1661)—as well as paintings by Jan Vermeer, Frans Hals, Jacob van Ruisdael, and other Old Masters. **INFO:** Tel 31/20-674-7000; www.rijksmuseum.nl.

Although the highlight of the Rijksmuseum Amsterdam's one-million-piece collection is the Dutch golden age, its Asian art also impresses.

VAN GOGH MUSEUM—With a main building based on a design by Gerrit Rietveld (perhaps Holland's most famous architect) and a dramatic annex designed by Japanese architect Kisho Kurokawa in 1999, the Van Gogh Museum is a fitting tribute to the 19th century's most important Dutch artist. The museum provides an outstanding home to some 200 of Vincent van Gogh's paintings, 500 drawings, and 700 letters as well as Japanese prints (many from his own collection) and other 19th-century works that influenced him. The collection—the largest of his work anywhere in the world—ranges from his earliest paintings, done in 1881 in the Netherlands, to those done just days before his suicide in France at the age of 37. Among the images painted by this anguished, visionary genius: *The Potato Eaters, Sunflowers,* and *Wheatfield with Crows.* **INFO:** Tel 31/20-570-5200; www.vangoghmuseum.nl.

ANNE FRANK HOUSE—Anne Frank, the second daughter of German-Jewish immigrants to Amsterdam, was given a diary for her 13th birthday on June 12, 1942. Just weeks later, she and her family were in hiding from Nazi occupying forces. They took refuge in a small group of rooms above her father's business, on the Prinsengracht canal in the city center. The family, joined by a few others, stayed in this "Annex" for two years. In August 1944, German police raided it; all of its occupants, except Anne's father, died in concentration camps. Anne's diary, left behind in the tumult, went on to become one of the bestselling books of all time. Today, the Annex is stripped bare of furniture, though some of the magazine cuttings Anne pasted on her bedroom wall remain. It is an almost unbearably poignant monument to her memory. Downstairs, a large new wing adjacent to the building holds exhibitions on tolerance and oppression. **INFO:** Tel 31/20-556-7100; www.annefrank.org.

RED LIGHT DISTRICT—Amsterdam's red light district, known locally as De Wallen (The Walls), occupies the oldest part of town, near the former city wall. At its heart is the Oude Kerk (Old Church), dating from about 1300; connoisseurs rate the church's carillon as one of the best in the world, and the joyful sound of the bell music cascading down cobblestoned streets and across the canals and squares is one of Amsterdam's delights. Nearby, the Catholic church of Ons' Lieve Heer op Solder (Our Dear Lord in the Attic) is up a narrow stairway at the top of a canal house. It dates from 1663, at a time when Protestant Holland allowed Catholic worship only if churches were not visible from the street. This ancient quarter is also home to the world's oldest profession. But in this historically tolerant city, the women who sit on display in the rose-tinted windows are registered, regulated, taxed, and represented by a union since 1984. Patiently they await their next assignation while showing off their wares to sailors, foreign businessmen, and assorted innocents abroad. **OUDE KERK:** Tel 31/20-625-8284; www.oudekerk.nl/infoeng.htm. **ONS' LIEVE HEER OP SOLDER:** Tel 31/20-624-6604; www.opsolder.nl.

ON THE CANALS—If you think it's too touristy to see Amsterdam by boat, then you'll miss seeing this City of Canals the way it was meant to be seen. The waterfront town houses and warehouses built by merchants in the 17th century were high (four or five stories) and narrow (property taxes were based on the width of frontages), each distinguished by its fanciful gables. Of the five concentric semicircles of elm-lined canals and the 160 smaller canals connecting them, Herengracht (the "Gentlemen's Canal") is lined with the largest and most stately houses, while the trim brick homes on the smaller canals (especially in the Jordaan neighborhood) can be more engaging architecturally. Many façades are illuminated at night, and so are many of the city's 1,281 characteristic arched bridges. Add that to the reflections of old-fashioned streetlamps in the glimmering canals and a cruise by candlelight makes for a very romantic evening. **HOW:** Canal Company (transport/cruises); tel 31/20-623-9886; www.canal.nl.

The "Venice of the North," Amsterdam consists of 90 islands, connected by more than a thousand bridges.

BEGIJNHOF—To one side of the busy city square called the Spui is a nondescript wooden door. Open it and a dark passageway will lead you to a tranquil spot of green lawn and gardens, edged by little cottages. This is the Begijnhof, once home to the Beguines, an order of lay nuns founded in the early Middle Ages. The last of the order, Sister Antonia, died here in 1971, but the court is still home to single or widowed Catholic women over the age of 30. Most of the houses were rebuilt in the 17th and 18th centuries, but at No. 34 stands one of only two remaining medieval wooden houses in Amsterdam. The small church at the center of the court is the original Begijnkerk, consecrated in 1419, and now known as the English Church, as it is here that a group of Protestant dissenters fleeing England in 1607 met for worship. They formed the core of the Pilgrim Fathers who sailed for America 13 years later. **INFO:** www.begijnhofamsterdam.nl.

AMSTERDAM MUSEUM—Amsterdam has had a long and eventful history, from its muddy medieval beginnings as a settlement around a dam on the river Amstel, through the glories (and considerable riches) of the 17th-century golden age. It endured the terrors of World War II, partied through the 1960s and 1970s as a countercultural center, and became the gay capital of Europe in the '80s. The Amsterdam Museum brings this all together in a series of richly imaginative displays and exhibitions. You'll find a medieval child's shoe, an extraordinary bird's-eye view of Amsterdam painted in 1538, precious objects, and thought-provoking photographs. The museum is housed in a former orphanage dating back to 1520—in one courtyard the boys' wooden lockers are still visible in the wall. **INFO:** Tel 31/20-523-1822; www.ahm.nl.

MARKET CITY—Amsterdam is speckled with intriguing markets, all within an easy walk of one another. The famous Flower Market, with its banks of bright blooms and buckets of tulips, also sells sealed bags of bulbs with the requisite export health certificate so you can take them back home. The sprawling Fleamarket is just the spot to pick up vintage clothing, handcrafts from all over the world, even the odd bicycle part. Stretching for over half a mile, merchants in the Albert Cuyp Market sometimes boast that it is Europe's longest; it is where Amsterdammers buy their fruit, spices, and fresh fish still flapping on ice. Across town, tucked in between the charming canals of the Jordaan, the indoor De Looier Antiques Market is the place to find old delftware tile. And over weekends, squares like Nieuwmarkt, the Spui, and Thorbeckeplein host a rotation of book, art, and collectibles markets.

WHERE TO STAY

THE DYLAN—For nearly 250 years, this 18th-century canalside building was the head office of a church charity. In 1998 it received a makeover under the guidance of hotel-design queen Anouska Hempel, emerging as a luxury boutique hotel with classy, contemporary décor. Rooms are arranged gracefully around a courtyard and come in a variety of styles, with clean lines, warm fabrics, and the occasional Eastern touch. Vinkeles restaurant keeps consistently high standards, and you can also get brasserie-style meals in the secluded courtyard. The Dylan lies in the heart of Amsterdam's Canal Belt, with museums, shops, restaurants, and the pulse of Amsterdam life all within easy reach. **INFO:** Tel 31/20-530-2010; www.dylanamsterdam.com. *Cost:* from $500; dinner $96.

HOTEL DE L'EUROPE—Built in 1896, de l'Europe is one of the oldest hotels in Amsterdam. It was renovated in 2011, but old favorites remain, such as the clubby Freddy's Bar, once the regular socializing spot of Alfred "Freddy" Heineken (the brewery now owns the hotel). The Bord'Eau restaurant, which occupies a coveted spot beside the Amstel River, received a new lease on life under chef Richard van Oostenbrugge, who prepares unfussy yet inspired French cuisine. Genuine Old Master paintings donated by Freddy Heineken decorate public spaces. Rooms in the old part of the building retain a classic ambience, whereas a new wing of individually decorated suites is quirkier and more contemporary, with unrivaled river views. **INFO:** Tel 31/20-531-1777; www.leurope.nl. *Cost:* from $450; dinner at Bord'Eau $105.

THE GRAND—This building, dating from 1578, was once a guesthouse for royal visitors, then an Admiralty Building, and for many years Amsterdam's City Hall. A recent makeover of rich colors and witty detail gives warmth to the monumental public areas and an elegant coziness to the 177 rooms. Bridges Restaurant, which features the famed 1949 mural *Questioning Children,* by Dutch artist Karel Appel, is one of the best spots in town for fish and seafood, with a first-rate raw bar. Beautiful canal views and a calming spa with a large pool all add to the special charm. **INFO:** Tel 31/20-555-3111; www.sofitel-legend-thegrand.com. *Cost:* from $350 (off-peak), $420 (peak); dinner at Bridges $90.

HOTEL ORLANDO—Occupying an elegant golden-age canal house, Hotel Orlando's seven rooms are decorated with refined taste and quiet charm. In 2011, it expanded to occupy the *achterhuis* ("back house"), traditionally part of the main house, and reached across a garden courtyard. Breakfast is served in the 17th-century kitchen, with an old hearth and the original tiles. **INFO:** Tel 31/20-638-6915; www.hotelorlando.nl. *Cost:* $170.

SEVEN ONE SEVEN—Revel in the experience of living in a stately Amsterdam canal house without the bother of actually owning one. The rear section of Seven One Seven dates from the 17th century, its grand canal frontage being added in 1810. Eight spacious rooms brim with period décor yet have a homey touch. Complimentary afternoon tea is laid out on a table in the library, and in the evenings wine is offered. The two executive suites at the front of the house have enormous windows, with prime views of the Prinsengracht canal; the others overlook a charming courtyard garden. **INFO:** Tel 31/20-427-0717; www.717hotel.nl. *Cost:* from $415 (off-peak), from $515 (peak).

SUNHEAD OF 1617—The odd name of this cozy guesthouse derives from the sun image on the gable stone above the door and the year the house was built. The friendly owners have traveled extensively, so they know that little touches matter: burnished wood, rich fabrics, antique furniture, and bright modern frescoes. Just two rooms and an apartment-suite lead off a perilously steep staircase typical of many old Amsterdam houses; those at the front of the house enjoy magnificent views of the Herengracht canal. **INFO:** Tel 31/20-626-1809; www.sunhead.com. *Cost:* from $170.

EATING & DRINKING

CIEL BLEU—Ciel Bleu (Blue Sky) derives its name from its location on the 23rd floor of one of the tallest buildings in town, and its cuisine is appropriately haute. Star of the show is young Dutch chef Onno Kokmeijer, who made a name for himself as one of the Netherlands' trailblazers for new and inventive cooking, with his self-proclaimed "wayward French cuisine." A country boy with a healthy obsession with fresh ingredients and a daring turn of imagination: For example, breast of pigeon comes with pistachio cream and smoked beetroot—all with a panoramic view over Amsterdam. **INFO:** Tel 31/20-678-7450; www.cielbleu.nl. *Cost:* dinner $150.

DE KAS—A former greenhouse dating from 1926, De Kas (the Greenhouse) is still partly given over to the cultivation of herbs, fruit, and salad greens, but nowadays these find their way directly onto diners' plates in the designer-cool restaurant that occupies the rest of the space. De Kas also has its own private vegetable gardens nearby, and deals only with local farmers and fishermen. The menu is minimal—what's ripe and in season shows up in dishes exquisitely prepared by chefs Ronald Kunis and Martijn Kajuiter. **Info:** Tel 31/20-462-4562; www.restaurantdekas.nl. *Cost:* dinner $70.

The Rijsttafel—Holland's colonial heritage finds delicious culinary expression in the *rijsttafel* ("rice table")—a spicy feast of small Indonesian dishes served with rice. This dining tradition goes back to the days when hungry Dutch settlers found Indonesian portions unsatisfying, so cooks came up with mini-banquets to keep their employers satisfied. Today, the *rijsttafel* is such a fundamental Dutch dining experience that people regard it as local rather than exotic. The best place to try the feast is in one of the many little family-run establishments around town. It is hard to beat Tujuh Maret, with its plain tables, simple atmosphere, and customer care. **Tujuh Maret:** Tel 31/20-427-9865; www.tujuhmaret.nl. *Cost:* $40.

D'Vijff Vlieghen—The insalubriously named D'Vijff Vlieghen (the Five Flies) is housed in five 17th-century buildings. The restaurant dates back to 1939, when eccentric raconteur and inveterate self-publicist Nicolaas Kroese set up a bar and began selling food here. In the 1950s he became a darling of the American media, after oddball appearances in New York carrying a musical cage containing five copper flies. Intrigued by this engaging character, Walt Disney, Gary Cooper, Elvis Presley, and many more dropped in on visits to Amsterdam. The stream of the rich and famous dried up after Kroese's death in the 1970s, but you can still get a good meal here, with favorite Dutch fare such as cod and North Sea prawns given a contemporary twist. **Info:** Tel 31/20-530-4060; www.thefiveflies.com. *Cost:* $80.

Café Society—Amsterdammers are very attached to the concept of *gezelligheid*—an amalgam of "coziness" and "conviviality"—and nowhere is more *gezellig* than a "brown café," its walls and ceiling burnished by time (and, until recently, tobacco smoke). There are said to be more than 1,000 of these social sanctuaries in Amsterdam. Check out barrel-lined Café 't Smalle, a favored watering hole since it first opened in 1786, and partake in the local habit of a glass of beer followed by a *genever* (Dutch gin) chaser. If you're looking for old-world glamour, try the decidedly unbrown Café Americain, built as part of a grand hotel in 1880. Mata Hari would still recognize its ornate, albeit faded, Art Deco interior as the location of her wedding reception. If your taste is more contemporary, head to De Jaren—spacious and light-soaked, with a modern minimalist interior and two of the best waterside terraces in town. Cafés are not to be confused with coffee shops, a ubiquitous part of the Amsterdam scene since the 1970s, where mind-altering substances are legally sold in small quantities. **Café 't Smalle:** Tel 31/20-623-9617. **Café Americain:** Tel 31/20-556-3000; www.edenamsterdamamericanhotel.com. **De Jaren:** Tel 31/20-625-5771; www.cafedejaren.nl.

Day Trips

Flowers in the Spring—Visit Holland in springtime and you'll find the entire region west of Amsterdam a bright patchwork of brilliant hues as bulbs come into bloom. The season lasts from late March to early May, a wonderful time to visit parks and gardens in the area. Supreme above all else is the magnificent Keukenhof Gardens, near Lisse (open late March to late May). The facts and figures just hint at what's in store for you at this 15th-century

Keukenhof is the largest bulb garden in the world.

hunting ground turned spectacular public garden: 79 acres containing over 7 million flowers, including 4.5 million tulips of 100 varieties. For a lower-key experience, visit the ancient Hortus Botanicus (Botanical Garden) attached to Leiden University, where the botanist Carolus Clusius planted the first tulips in Holland, imported from Turkey, in 1593. Or simply cycle the Bulb Route, a 19-mile course through gorgeous flower fields between Haarlem and Sassenheim (near Leiden). Alternatively, take a barge cruise on the Dutch waterways, stopping off at picturesque towns en route, including (in springtime) Keukenhof and other flower-filled sights. Get up early enough and you can visit the Aalsmeer Flower Auction, 16 miles south of Amsterdam (sales start at 6:30 A.M.). It's one of the busiest in the world, with around 20 million flowers from all over the globe auctioned every day. **WHERE:** Keukenhof is 22 miles/35 km southwest of Amsterdam. Tel 31/252-465-555; www.keukenhof.nl. **HORTUS BOTANICUS:** Tel 31/71-527-7249; www.hortus.leidenuniv.nl. **TULIP CRUISES:** contact Barge Lady, in the U.S., 800-880-0071 or 312-245-0900; www.bargelady.com. *Cost:* $4,500 for a 7-day cruise. **AALSMEER FLOWER AUCTION:** Tel 31/297-39-3939; www.flora.nl.

ZAANSE SCHANS—See working windmills up close and experience historical Holland firsthand at this open-air museum near the town of Zaandam. Twelve windmills churn away beside a little cluster of green wooden houses dating largely from the 17th and 18th centuries, transported here in the 1950s to reconstruct a traditional village. The windmills—just a hint of what life here must have been like when more than 1,000 were at work in the area—are still engaged in their original activities. One grinds mustard seeds, another produces cooking oil, and a third grinds pigments for paint. There's also a working dairy, pewterer, and clog maker—and the first-ever Albert Heijn grocery store, now the name you see above almost every supermarket in the country. **WHERE:** 13 miles/20 km northeast of Amsterdam. **INFO:** Tel 31/75-681-0000; www.zaanseschans.nl.

Splendid Marriage of Art and Nature

DE HOGE VELUWE NATIONAL PARK

Apeldoorn, Netherlands

The industrialist Anton Kröller loved nature; his wife, Helene (née Müller), loved art. He bought tracts of wild land; she was one of the first-ever collectors of Vincent van Gogh. Together they left the nation a treasure—13,000 acres of duneland and meadows, fens and forests that became De Hoge Veluwe, Holland's largest national park, with the Kröller-Müller Museum at its heart, home to 278 of Van Gogh's works. Jump on one of the free white bicycles left about for public use and explore the property (keeping an eye open for deer and wild boar). Drop in Jachthuis St. Hubertus, the hunting lodge designed for the couple by the father of modern Dutch architecture, H. P. Berlage. The home's early-20th-century features and fittings, from furniture to decorative tiling, remain beautifully intact.

The Kröller-Müller Museum will be your

visit's highlight. Together with the collection in Amsterdam's Van Gogh Museum (see p. 227), the works here constitute nearly the entire oeuvre of the 19th-century Dutch artist, including one of the *Sunflowers* paintings, *The Bridge at Arles*, and *L'Arlesienne*, with some superb sketches and works on paper too. Kröller-Müller went on to collect work by other major artists, predominantly of the 19th and 20th centuries: Courbet, Seurat, Picasso, and Mondrian, to name a few. Surrounding the museum is one of Europe's largest outdoor sculpture gardens, 47 acres of works by 20th-century sculptors such as Henry Moore, Richard Serra, and Claes Oldenburg.

Trade your white bike in for a car for the short drive to Het Loo, an exquisitely restored royal palace. It was built in the late 17th century by the prince and princess of Orange, who would thereafter take over the throne of England as William and Mary. A small-scale Versailles, the palace houses a museum celebrating the history of the House of Orange, but the formal Baroque gardens are the jewel in this royal crown.

WHERE: 56 miles/89 km southeast of Amsterdam. Tel 31/55-378-8119; www.hogeveluwe.nl. **KRÖLLER-MÜLLER MUSEUM:** Tel 31/318-591241; www.kmm.nl. **HET LOO:** Tel 31/55-577-2400; www.paleishetloo.nl. **BEST TIME:** Helene Kröller-Müller loved autumn colors and purposefully planted trees to display a spectrum of shades of foliage throughout the park; spring for tulips.

Blue Porcelain and the House of Orange

DELFT

Netherlands

Delft's delicate gables, tree-lined canals, bridges, and ancient spires transport you straight back to the world so exquisitely captured in the canvases of Jan Vermeer and Pieter de Hoogh. Perhaps more so than in any other city in the country, the 16th and 17th centuries are preserved in this town whose name is known worldwide for its characteristic blue-and-white china. Still made and hand painted here, delftware's timeless patterns and color scheme have survived the passage of centuries and collectors' trends. When the sea of day-trippers heads back to Amsterdam or The Hague and the town returns to serenity, or as the morning sun touches church steeples and takes on a soft, focused quality, you can imagine yourself in Vermeer's time. Not a prolific artist, none of his original work hangs in Delft now—for that you need to make a pilgrimage to Amsterdam's Rijksmuseum (see p. 227) or The Hague's Mauritshuis (see p. 235)—but a brand-new Vermeer Center not only displays his paintings but also has exhibits that reveal how he dealt with light and color.

Delftware got its start in the 16th century.

Located on the attractive market square is the 14th-century Gothic Nieuwe Kerk (New Church), where William I, founder of the royal House of Orange and a kind of Dutch George Washington, lies in a magnificent marble and alabaster mausoleum surrounded by

22 columns; most Dutch monarchs and members of the royal house since him have been brought here for burial as well. A marvelous panoramic view from the church tower provides a glimpse of The Hague on a clear day. The nearby Oude Kerk (Old Church), founded around 1200, is the final resting place of Vermeer.

A stroll along the tree-lined Oude Delft, possibly the first city canal (and arguably the prettiest) in the Netherlands, brings you to the town's most famous site: the Prinsenhof, a former 15th-century royal residence where William lived and was assassinated in 1584 (the bullet hole is still visible). Today it houses a museum dedicated to the history of the Dutch Republic, along with some prime pieces of delftware and other prized objects from the 17th-century golden age of Delft. In the former storerooms of the Prinsenhof, with an entrance on a small alleyway off the Oude Delft canal, is an atmospheric restaurant, De Prinsenkelder, promising the end to a perfect day in the town that inspired some of Holland's greatest artists.

Where: 9 miles/14 km southeast of The Hague. **Vermeer Center:** Tel 31/15-213-8588; www.vermeerdelft.nl. **Prinsenhof Museum:** Tel 31/15-260-2358; www.prinsenhof-delft.nl. **De Prinsenkelder:** Tel 31/15-212-1860; www.de-prinsenkelder.nl. *Cost:* dinner $75. **Best times:** Thurs for market day in the central square, with a flower market along the canal at Brabantse Turfmarkt; Apr–Sep for Sat flea market along canals.

Southern Style and Charisma

The European Fine Arts Fair

Maastricht, Netherlands

The ancient Roman town of Maastricht is known for its bon vivant ambience and excellent food, all to be enjoyed amid rich cultural offerings and venerable history—along with the city's charm, sophistication, and high-end shopping. Here at Holland's southernmost point, wedged in between Belgium and Germany, languages, customs, and trends flow freely across borders. Lively eateries—from the sublime Beluga restaurant and its food-as-art to the more casual wood-paneled De Bóbbel café—are at their most vivacious during the late-winter Carnival celebration with parades of elaborate floats, parties, and fancy dress.

The city barely has time to catch its breath before connoisseurs roll into town every March to pick up an extra Rembrandt etching or add to their collection of Gobelin tapestries, at the prestigious European Fine Art Fair (TEFAF)—billed as the world's leading art and antiques fair. More than 250 dealers from over a dozen countries arrive to show works of art to aficionados, collectors, and curators. Major museums from around the globe are regularly represented among the expert buyers at the fair, assured by the team of international experts who examine all objects for authenticity, provenance, and condition.

But Maastricht packs a year-round cultural punch too. The Bonnefantenmuseum, housed in a spectacular new building with a bullet-shaped dome designed by Italian architect Also Rossi, houses a collection of medieval religious carvings unequalled anywhere in the country. Take in such glories as Basiliek van Onze Lieve Vrouw (Basilica of Our Beloved Lady), a Romanesque church that dates to before the year 1000 and is a pilgrimage church even today, then spend the night in a former 15th-century monastery, the Kruisherenhotel, where the Gothic building has been given a sleek contemporary redesign. Alternatively, check into an elegant boutique hotel, such as Hotel Les Charmes, or head out of town to one of Holland's most luxurious country hotels, Château St. Gerlach. The exceptional estate has been reborn with hand-loomed Venetian fabrics and precious antiques, all surrounded by Baroque gardens that blend into a natural preserve.

Where: 130 miles/207 km southeast of Amsterdam. **Beluga:** Tel 31/43-321-3364; www.rest-beluga.com. *Cost:* dinner $125. **De Bóbbel:** Tel 31/43-321-7413; www.debobbel.com. *Cost:* lunch $30. **TEFAF:** Tel 31/411-64-5090; www.tefaf.com. *When:* 1 week mid-Mar. **Bonnefantenmuseum:** Tel 31/43-329-0190; www.bonnefanten.nl. **Kruisherenhotel:** Tel 31/43-329-2020; www.chateauhotels.nl. *Cost:* from $290. **Hotel Les Charmes:** Tel 31/43-321-7400; www.hotellescharmes.nl. *Cost:* from $210. **Château St. Gerlach:** Tel 31/43-608-8888; www.chateauhotels.nl. *Cost:* from $220. **Best times:** Feb or Mar for Maastricht's famous Carnival; late Aug for prominent Preuvenemint food fair.

A Feast of Fine Art

Het Mauritshuis

The Hague, Netherlands

Vermeer's signature painting, *Girl with a Pearl Earring*, together with other gems such as Rembrandt's graphic *Anatomy Lesson of Dr. Nicolaes Tulp* (the first canvas to bring him recognition), form the core of a small collection of the great 17th-century Dutch masters in the Mauritshuis museum. Long acknowledged as one of the world's finest small museums, it occupies the beautiful, Palladian-inspired mansion of Maurits van Nassau-Siegen, the 17th-century Dutch governor-general of Brazil. Inside, it's almost like viewing a private collection, while outside a small, tree-shaded pond is crisscrossed by resident swans. Tour groups are uncommon, and most art lovers linger on the upper floor, home to other works by Vermeer (including his *View of Delft*, which moved the French writer Marcel Proust to call it the most beautiful painting in the world), Rembrandt, and Jan Steen. The heart of the Mauritshuis collection comes from the private art horde of Prince William V of Orange, who in 1773 built a gallery in his palace (just across the pond from the Mauritshuis) and allowed the public in 3 days a week. In 2010, the Galerij Prins Willem V reopened to the public after a magnificent restoration. The cream of the collection's crop had been transferred to the

Vermeer's masterpiece Girl with a Pearl Earring *remained unknown until 1882, when it was sold for nearly nothing.*

Mauritshuis decades ago, and remains there, but the Galerij has the edge when it comes to grandeur, with its high, Louis XVI stucco ceilings.

As the seat of government for the Netherlands and home to the monarch, The Hague is a prosperous and dignified city. Some of this stateliness is captured at high tea in the magnificent lounge of the city's Hotel des Indes, built in 1856 for the private adviser to King William III. It was in this lavish former baronial town house that Mata Hari practiced her subtle subterfuge during the dark days of World War I, when the hotel was used as Allied headquarters.

WHERE: 31 miles/50 km southwest of Amsterdam. **HET MAURITSHUIS:** Tel 31/70-302-3456; www.mauritshuis.nl. **GALERIJ PRINS WILLEM V:** Tel 31/70-302-3435; www.mauritshuis.nl. **HOTEL DES INDES:** Tel 31/70-361-2345; in the U.S., 888-625-5144; www.hoteldesindesthehague.com. *Cost:* from $250 (off-peak), from $340 (peak); high tea $50. **BEST TIME:** late May–early Jun for Tong Tong Fair, a popular festival of Euro-Indonesian food and culture.

The Essence of the Low Countries

ZEELAND

Netherlands

Travelers to Amsterdam who leave the Netherlands without a foray into the Low Country for a glimpse of this gentle farmland, the waterland teeming with birds, the long beaches and pretty towns—and most especially for a taste of just-caught culinary offerings from the North Sea—are missing out on a real Dutch treat. This patchwork of land and water forms the appropriately named province of Zeeland ("Sea-Land"). The complex system of dams, dikes, and levies that comprises the Delta Works storm-surge barrier, built following a disastrous flood in 1953 to protect Zeeland from another such inundation, is itself an impressive sight—the longest barrier stretching 5.6 miles across the water.

Visit pretty medieval towns like Zierikzee, Veere, and Middelburg, which date back to the time when the wide rivers that run into Zeeland were busy channels of trade. Take a bicycle ride across table-flat farmland dotted with windmills amid apple and pear orchards. Then stop off in the waterside village of Yerseke, famed for its mussels and oysters. Though you frequently hear that much of the Netherlands is below sea level, it is rarely as evident as here. At the cozy bistro Nolet's, you can tuck into great bowls of mussels and, a few minutes' walk away, climb the bank of a dike and see where they grow. There's even finer dining just a few miles away at Inter Scaldes. People find their way from all parts to the dramatic thatch-roofed farmhouse now an inn-restaurant and English-style gardens created by a local husband-and-wife team. They come not only for some of Europe's tastiest shellfish, but for conversation-stopping preparations of lobster and langoustine and for lamb raised in seaside pastures down the road.

WHERE: 75 miles/120 km south of The Hague. **NOLET'S VISTRO:** Tel 31/113-572-101; www.vistro.nl. *Cost:* lunch $55. **INTER SCALDES:** Tel 31/113-381-753; www.interscaldes.eu. *Cost:* from $300; 4-course dinner $135. **BEST TIMES:** early spring for the orchard blossoms; late Aug for Yerseke's Mussel Festival.

Hilltop Castles in Ancient Border Towns

Estremoz and Marvão

Alentejo, Portugal

East of Lisbon, rolling red-earth plains bear miles of vineyards and great swaths of wheat, giving the Alentejo a tranquil look that belies its stormy history. Moors and Christians, Portuguese and Spaniards fought over this enchanting countryside, and there is a medieval fort or castle on every hilltop to prove it. By far the grandest structure in Estremoz is the 13th-century castle constructed by King Dinis for his child queen—the sainted Isabel—and rebuilt after an 18th-century fire. It is now the Rainha Santa Isabel, probably the most gracious of the 45 government-owned pousadas (inns) scattered across Portugal. The views still entrance and the castle-inn retains its regal mien, with museum-quality antiques and tapestries and grand public areas with 22-foot ceilings, monumental staircases, and plenty of marble from the famed Alentejo quarries. An attentive staff brings warmth to the banquet hall where the restaurant serves Alentejano specialties—such as pork stewed with vegetables and potatoes, and rabbit braised with turnips—and boasts a cellar of superb local Borba wines. Rugs from nearby Arraiolos and canopied four-poster beds lavishly decorate the 30 guest rooms. The room where Saint Isabel died in 1336 escaped the fire and is now a small chapel open to the public.

Marvão Castle's turrets afford magnificent views of the Serra de Ossa and Serra de São Mamede Mountains, and to Spain just beyond.

Almost within shouting distance of the Spanish border, tiny Marvão (population 300) is one of Portugal's most charming and dramatic border towns. Built around a 13th-century castle that offers 360-degree views, the town's small white buildings crouch on its hilltop, reminiscent of the flocks of white birds that can be found nesting in the surrounding Natural Park of Serra de São Mamede. Marvão's Pousada de Santa Maria has a winning modesty. Converted from adjoining 18th-century houses, the inn has handsome beamed ceilings and stone fireplaces decorated with *azulejo* tiles, but it's the views over the ridges to Spain that will take your breath away. A panorama of countryside spreads out beneath the 3,000-foot-high hill town—the perfect spot to be alone with your thoughts and "look down on the eagles," as one Portuguese poet wrote.

Where: Estremoz is 90 miles/145 km east of Lisbon; Marvão is 140 miles/224 km northeast of Lisbon. **Pousada Rainha Santa Isabel** and **Pousada de Santa Maria:** Tel 351/258-82-1751; in the U.S., 800-223-1356; www.pousadasofportugal.com. *Cost:* from $250; dinner at Rainha Santa Isabel $50. **Best times:** Apr–May and Sep–Oct; Sat in Estremoz for the market on the central plaza.

An Open-Air Museum of Portuguese Architecture

Évora

Alentejo, Portugal

Every age has left its trace on Évora. Protected as a national treasure, its mansions and palaces are especially evocative when floodlit at night. Although the area has been settled for nearly 7,000 years, most of the architecture left standing after the great Lisbon earthquake of 1755 is Manueline, an exuberant Portuguese style that combines the rock-solid proportions of Gothic with the harmonious scale of the Renaissance. Often likened to Florence and Seville (see pp. 203 and 250) for its lyrical grace, Évora is far more intimate and wonderfully Portuguese, with Moorish overtones in its pierced balconies, attractive whitewashed homes, and cool tiled patios.

When the Moors were ousted in the 12th century after 450 fruitful years in residence, Évora became a favored destination of Portuguese kings and flourished as a center of learning and the arts in the 15th and 16th centuries. Most places of interest can be found in the core of the Old City, within medieval walls, including the Gothic cathedral and the 16th-century Church of dos Lóios, dedicated to São João (St. John) and famous for its *azulejos,* the traditional hand-painted blue-and-white tiles of Portugal. Adjacent to the church, and next to the well-preserved ruins of a 2nd-century Roman temple dedicated to Diana, is a former 15th-century baronial mansion (later a convent) that is now the Pousada dos Lóios and one of Portugal's more gracious inns. The former refectory serves as the dining room, but in good weather, meals are enjoyed in the open courtyard of the vaulted cloister.

Another 15th-century convent turned luxury hotel, the Convento do Espinheiro Hotel & Spa offers a countryside setting and an opulence unusual for Alentejo (its spa is the area's finest). The convent sprawls on luxuriously landscaped grounds with a panoramic view of the city; its Divinus Restaurant is especially noted for its centuries-old wine cellar. No visit to Évora is complete without seeing the Almendres Cromlech, a mysterious, megalithic site of 96 standing stones on the hill above the city. Dating to circa 5000 B.C., it is the Portuguese counterpart to Stonehenge.

WHERE: 86 miles/138 km southeast of Lisbon. **POUSADA DOS LÓIOS:** Tel 351/258-82-1751; in the U.S., 800-223-1356; www.pousadasofportugal.com. *Cost:* from $290 (off-peak), from $430 (peak); dinner $60. **CONVENTO DO ESPINHEIRO HOTEL:** Tel 351/266-788-200; www.conventodoespinheiro.com. *Cost:* from $200 (off-peak), from $300 (peak); dinner at Divinus $80. **BEST TIMES:** Apr–May and Sep–Oct for nice weather and fewer crowds; last 10 days of Jun for the Feira de São João, a fair dedicated to the city's patron saint.

Each corner of the Cathedral of Évora's Gothic cloisters houses a marble statue of one of the four evangelists.

Sylvan Setting for a Pleasure Palace

Bussaco Forest

Beiras, Portugal

The secluded Bussaco Forest (Floresta do Bussaco) isn't a natural forest but an enormous walled arboretum planted by Carmelite monks in the 17th century. It grew with the Portuguese empire, as exotic trees were brought in from all corners of the globe; in fact, such was its botanical splendor that a 17th-century Papal bull threatened to excommunicate anyone who tampered with the plantings. After religious orders were suppressed in the 19th century, King Carlos I commissioned a summer pleasure palace to be built in the midst of the 250-acre wood. The result is an extravagant pastiche of pinnacles, turrets, and arched windows, with stained-glass windows, hand-painted murals and tiles, and suits of armor inside. It was the Portuguese monarch's last hurrah: Carlos was assassinated a year after it was finished in 1907. His son used the palace before fleeing to England after his 1910 abdication. Today it is the 64-room Palace Hotel do Bussaco, one of Europe's most special hotels, a turn-of-the-century jewel of romance in the neo-Manueline style. It is also a good base for exploring the romantic city of Coimbra nearby.

Seat of Portugal's oldest university, established in 1290, the streets of Coimbra are filled with students wearing their traditional ceremonial black capes. The city is renowned for its own strain of fado (Portugal's often plaintive popular folk music) sung by men (unlike in Lisbon, where it is sung by women; see next page). It is best heard at club àCapella, housed in an old chapel in the Jewish Quarter. Coimbra's own luxury hotel, the late Gothic-Renaissance Quinta das Lágrimas (Estate of Tears), occupies a sylvan enclave just outside the city walls. Long a retreat of kings and generals, it is a sumptuous historic country palace with a state-of-the-art spa, well-known restaurant, and lovingly landscaped gardens.

Where: 137 miles/220 km north of Lisbon. **Palace Hotel do Bussaco:** Tel 351/231-937-970; www.almeidahotels.com. *Cost:* from $180 (off-peak), from $245 (peak). **àCapella:** Tel 351/239-833-985; www.acapella.com.pt. **Quinta das Lágrimas:** Tel 351/239-802-380; www.quintadaslagrimas.pt. *Cost:* from $160 (off-peak), from $300 (peak). **Best times:** May–Sep for the gardens; Sep during Festa das Latas when the university opens.

A Town That Belonged to the Queens of Portugal

Óbidos

Estremadura, Portugal

Enveloped by a Moorish wall, the tiny whitewashed village of Óbidos was deemed so lovely that it became a queen's dowry. In 1282 King Dinis presented Queen Isabel with the fief as a wedding present, and for the next 600 years, every Portuguese monarch would do the same, perpetuating its name, Casa das Rainhas (the House of Queens), until 1834. Visitors enter this museum of a town through massive gateway arches characteristic of a medieval fortress. Cars are allowed inside the walls only to pick up or drop off hotel guests and their luggage. Cobbled steps help walkers negotiate the steep inclines between whitewashed houses framed in ancient bougainvillea vines. The ramparts of Óbidos, almost a mile of crenellated battlements, have wide walkways at the top that yield spectacular views of the town and the surrounding green countryside punctuated by large outcrops of weathered limestone.

Óbidos's imposing 15th-century castle was built as a fortress and converted into a royal palace in the 16th century. Now one wing has been transformed into the nine-room Pousada do Castelo, where you can be a knight for a night in one of Portugal's most atmospheric hotels. The baronial hall is filled with suits of armor, seemingly still awaiting long-ago queens and their royal retinues. The restaurant's simple food often includes a catch of the day from the picturesque nearby fishing village of Peniche. But you can feast on the views alone, and best of all, overnight guests have the town to themselves before the tour buses arrive and long after they depart.

Where: 50 miles/80 km north of Lisbon. **Pousada do Castelo:** Tel 351/258-82-1751; in the U.S., 800-223-1356; www.pousadasofportugal.com. *Cost:* from $350 (off-peak), from $490 (peak); dinner $50. **Best times:** May–Jun and Sep–Oct for best weather and fewer crowds; Jul for the Medieval Market.

An Ancient Neighborhood Where History and Fado Live

Bairro Alfama

Lisbon, Portugal

The Alfama is Lisbon's most moody and evocative neighborhood. The steep streets and twisting alleyways still bear witness to the Moors who, imposing their rule on much of the Iberian Peninsula, invaded Portugal from North Africa in 711. They built a fortress on the city's eastern hill (believed to have been occupied in pre-Roman times) where a lively settlement, now the *bairro* (neighborhood) of the Alfama, grew in its protective shadow. Visitors can follow the ancient paths to the Castelo de São Jorge (Castle of St. George), where King Alfonso Henriques erected a royal castle on the site of the Moorish citadel after the city was recaptured in 1147. The castle's glory days as a royal residence lasted until 1511, when King Manuel I moved the court to the Palacio Ribeira, on the waterfront. Castelo de São Jorge was severely damaged in the 1755 earthquake, but city views from the towers and ramparts, largely rebuilt in the 1930s, are as stupendous as ever. Housed within the formidable walls of the Alfama castle and reachable only by foot, the hotel Solar do Castelo occupies an intimate 18th-century mansion with an inner courtyard and garden. The secluded, romantic lodging melds medieval with contemporary style.

When threat of earthquakes prompted wealthy families to leave the Alfama for safer ground, it became the home of fishermen, sailors, and other hard-working families despite its distance from the waterfront. It was this tight-knit community that spawned and nurtured fado, the city's signature "urban song."

The ancient but restored towers of Castelo de São Jorge stand on a hilltop above the city of Lisbon.

Literally meaning "fate," fado is Portugal's most vivid art form, an expression of deep longing, usually sung with great emotion in a minor key in soaring octaves and accompanied by simple folk instruments like the Spanish guitar, mandolin, and the 12-string *guittara portuguesa.* Fado is most beautiful when performed live, especially at the legendary venue Parreirinha de Alfama, where top female performers pour out their hearts in an intimate tiled room full of rapt listeners. With both displays and audio recordings, the Museu do Fado traces fado's ascent from the streets and wharves in the 19th century to its emergence as the Portuguese soul music of the 20th century, dispelling the commonplace myth that this music has Moorish roots or is akin to Spanish flamenco.

Castelo de São Jorge: Tel 351/218-800-620; www.castelodesaojorge.pt. **Solar do Castelo:** Tel 351/218-806-050; www.solardocastelo.com. *Cost:* from $190 (off-peak), from $390 (peak). **Parreirinha de Alfama:** Tel 351/218-868-209. **Museu do Fado:** Tel 351/218-823-470; www.museudo fado.egeac.pt. **Best times:** Tues or Sat for Feira da Ladra (Thieves Market), a famed flea market on the edge of the Alfama.

Awe-Inspiring Gifts

Great Museums of Three Collectors

Lisbon, Portugal

Spread across seven hills overlooking the Tagus River, Lisbon is Europe's smallest capital city. It's also one of the most alluring, with gracious architecture, broad plazas, and mesmerizing black-and-white mosaic sidewalks.

Three astute collectors have further enriched the city with magnificent museums. Armenian oil tycoon Calouste Gulbenkian, who lived in Portugal after World War II, was the city's first and most generous benefactor. When he died in 1955, he bequeathed one of the world's greatest private art collections to his adopted country. With works ranging from sculpture, pottery, and stone carving of ancient Egypt and Mesopotamia to medieval illuminated manuscripts and early-20th-century Impressionists and Post-Impressionists, Gulbenkian's treasure trove is the result of 50 years of passionate collecting. The Museu Calouste Gulbenkian includes many masterpieces of European painting—such as those by Rembrandt, Renoir, Monet, Manet, Turner, and Fragonard—many purchased from the Hermitage between the world wars, when the Soviet Union needed hard currency.

With the Berardo Collection Museum,

Portuguese businessman José Manuel Rodrigues Berardo has assembled a representative collection of the most significant artistic movements from early Modernism to the present day. About 250 paintings, sculptures, and photographs include pieces by Picasso, Dalí, Duchamp, Magritte, and Pollock. The museum opened in 2007 at the Belém Cultural Center, the largest cultural complex in the country, built in the early 1990s.

Covering a similar time frame but with a narrower focus, the Museu do Design e da Moda (Design and Fashion Museum, aka the MuDe) revels in the glories of 20th-century innovative product design and fashion. Since 2009, the museum, created by local Portuguese businessman Francisco Capelo, has occupied the stripped-down interior of a Beaux Arts former bank headquarters. It provides a striking setting for innovative furniture by Philippe Starck and the team of Charles and Ray Eames and couture masterpieces by Balenciaga and Yves Saint Laurent.

MUSEUM CALOUSTE GULBENKIAN: Tel 351/217-823-000; www.museu.gulbenkian.pt. **BERARDO COLLECTION MUSEUM:** Tel 351/213-612-878; www.berardocollection.com. **MUDE:** Tel 351/218-886-117; www.mude.pt. **BEST TIMES:** late May–early Jun for Festas de Lisboa; Jun for Festas dos Santos Populares.

Summer Resort of Palaces and Castles

SINTRA

Lisbon, Portugal

Lord Byron had seen his fair share of the Continent when he wrote to his mother from Sintra, calling it "perhaps the most delightful [village] in Europe." Portuguese royalty certainly agreed: Sintra was a favorite summer residence for more than 500 years. Today the same cool climate and garden setting provide an idyllic respite from the heat and bustle of Lisbon for city dwellers and visitors alike. The dramatic 8th-century ruins of a Moorish citadel, the Castelo dos Mouros, sits atop a 1,350-foot peak, offering visitors a heavenly view to the sea.

On a hillside surrounded by a lush park, the Palácio Nacional de Pena offers the most revealing look at the vanished lifestyle of Portugese nobility. The glorious 19th-century draw-bridged Pena Palace is a pink-and-yellow fantasy of varied architectural styles. The interior has been preserved much as the royal family left it in 1910 after the declaration of the Portuguese Republic—complete with trompe l'oeil painted walls, neo-Gothic chandeliers, and 19th-century furniture.

Built in the 1840s by a Prussian architect, the lavish Pena Palace ranks among the most famous castles in Europe.

Within the old town, the Palácio Nacional de Sintra (Sintra Palace) is a treasured landmark. Built in the 14th century on a site once favored by Moorish rulers, this royal palace has been largely rebuilt with echoes of Moorish architecture. It's particularly known for the magnificent glazed tiles on the walls and for the fanciful ceiling of swans in the banquet room.

Stay in a castle of your own at the Palácio de Seteais, on the crest of a hill just outside town. Built in the 18th century by the Dutch consul to Portugal, it looks down across vineyards and orange groves to the sea mist. The name Seteais refers to the seven sighs elicited by the peace treaty signed here in 1807 that ended Napoleon's campaign in Portugal.

Once the site of a 16th- and 17th-century royal retreat, the Penha Longa Hotel is in a nature reserve about 3 miles south of Sintra. The 14th-century monastery and royal fountains and gardens on the grounds lend an air of history to this elegant 194-room resort, which features an 18-hole Robert Trent Jones Jr. championship-level golf course and a less demanding 9-hole course. From here it's just 20 minutes along the coast to windswept Cabo da Roca and its lone lighthouse marking continental Europe's westernmost point.

Where: 18 miles/29 km northwest of Lisbon. **Castelo dos Mouros** and **Palácio Nacional de Pena:** Tel 351/219-237-300; www.parquesdesintra.pt. **Palácio Nacional de Sintra:** Tel 351/219-106-840; www.pnsintra.imc-ip.pt. **Hotel Tivoli Palácio de Seteais:** Tel 351/219-233-200; www.tivolihotels.com. *Cost:* from $240 (off-peak), from $440 (peak). **Penha Longa Hotel:** Tel 351/219-249-011; www.penhalonga.com. *Cost:* from $220 (off-peak), from $290 (peak). **Best times:** Apr–May and Aug–Sep for nicest weather; late May–early Jul for Sintra Festival of Music and Dance.

Pearl of the Atlantic

Madeira

Portugal

With a subtropical climate warmed by the Gulf Stream, this volcanic island—which lies 323 miles off the coast of Africa—is Portugal's own floating garden. The early 15th-century discovery of Madeira by Prince Henry the Navigator launched Portugal's golden age. It was "discovered" again in the 19th century by winter-weary British vacationers who were taken by the lush, vertical landscapes; the wild terrain that had been terraced and farmed; the dark, sweet wine—and "days of perpetual June."

Dramatic peaks and an extensive network of signposted walking paths encourage forays into the verdant countryside. A longtime favorite hike follows the old *levadas*—the manmade irrigation channels that carried water from the mountaintops to the farms, fields, and villages below. The 36- by 14-mile island (70 percent of which is national park) packs more into its chaotic terrain than most areas five times its size. A serpentine drive from Ribeira Brava in the south to São Vicente in the north takes you up into the dramatic interior and over its razorback spine, and rewards you with views of Pico Ruivo—at 6,109 feet, Madeira's highest mountain.

More relaxing is a stroll through the rose gardens and grottoes at Quinta Palmeira, a lush landscape punctuated with tiled fountains and benches to enjoy the mesmerizing view. Madeira developed a significant wine industry in the 18th century, when it was discovered that the fortified wine improved in the hot holds of ships bound for the New World. Madeira vintners soon figured out how to get the same effect without the wines leaving home. The best introduction to Madeira's signature wine is a tour of the Old Blandy Wine Lodge, in the center of town, where the 17th-century St. Francis monastery was converted to a wine-aging building in 1852. Tours illuminate the unique *canteiro* aging system and end with a tasting of the local elixir.

The exploration of Madeira helped launch Portugal's Age of Discovery.

The distinguished Reid's Palace hotel has been the undisputed queen of Funchal since opening in 1891. High on a promontory with sweeping views, Reid's is enveloped in a fragrant riot of flowers, palms, and birds-of-paradise. The hotel's Les Faunes restaurant is considered the best on the island, and late-afternoon high tea is an institution. Less dramatic, but full of charm, Quinta do Monte Hotel and Panoramic Gardens is nestled in the old hill town of Monte. Sitting 1,804 feet above sea level, the area provides a welcomed retreat from the busy city. The salmon-pink 19th-century manor house is decorated in the elegant traditional Madeiran style of gleaming wood floors and Persian carpets. Although connected to Funchal by the sleek *teleferico* cable car, Monte village boasts a famous alternate mode of transportation: a two-seat wicker toboggan guided by two men, or *carreiros*, down a staggeringly steep 1-mile descent.

WHERE: 400 miles/644 km south of Lisbon. **THE OLD BLANDY WINE LODGE:** Tel 351/291-740-110; www.theoldblandywinelodge.com. **REID'S PALACE:** Tel 351/291-717-171; in the U.S., 800-237-1236; www.reidspalace.com. *Cost:* from $330; dinner at Les Faunes $75, afternoon tea $35. *When:* Les Faunes closed Jun–Sep. **QUINTA DO MONTE:** Tel 351/291-724-236; www.quintadomontemadeira.com. *Cost:* from $125 (off-peak), from $200 (peak). **BEST TIMES:** Apr or May for the Flower Festival; Sep for Madeira Wine Festival; New Year's Eve for Funchal's Feast of St. Sylvester celebration, featuring stunning fireworks.

Storied History on the Golden River of Wine

PORTO AND THE DOURO VALLEY

Porto, Portugal

There's magic in the air—or the rocks—in the upper Douro River Valley, where vintners conjure wine from the stony riverbanks. The vineyards that cling to towering cliffs above the golden river that snakes along a deep gorge are tended by hand because tractors can't negotiate the steep incline. Yet out of this unlikely landscape comes one of the world's sweetest and richest wines—port. The area's 350-year-old tradition of making port is portrayed at Sandeman's modern Quinta do

Seixo Wine Center in the upper Douro. At the Aquapura Douro Valley, a graceful 19th-century port-producer's manor transformed into a high-design hotel and spa, guests relax on the terraces above the river, sipping local vintages and musing on the Douro's journey to the sea. In nearby Folgosa, homegrown chef Rui Paula's D.O.C. restaurant offers modern twists on the Douro's rich traditional cuisine.

The port wine grown in the upper Douro comes downriver to Porto, the country's second largest city, to mature. The port lodges—where the wines are blended, fortified, stored, and aged—have lined the banks of Vila Nova de Gaia, just across the river from Porto, since the 1700s. Today, Cruzeiros Via d'Ouro offers river tours with panoramic views of the Douro bridge—designed by Gustave Eiffel in 1877—and of the old houses with red-tiled roofs rising like terraced vineyards up the city slopes.

The same striking view can be enjoyed with a glass of wine from the terraces at Taylor Fladgate Port Lodge, where tours and tastings are offered. The venerable company is also behind the Yeatman, a sumptuous 82-room hotel and wine-lover's refuge whose cellar boasts the largest collection of Portuguese wines in the world. Across the river, in central Porto, the luxurious Teatro Hotel, located on the site of a gilded 1859 theater, exudes opulence and originality, in a distinctive theatrical mode. For dining, chef/owner Marco Gomes, of the esteemed Foz Velha restaurant, wins international plaudits for his contemporary reinterpretations of classical Portuguese cuisine.

Where: 197 miles/317 km north of Lisbon. **Quinta do Seixo Wine Center:** Tel 351/254-732-800; www.sandeman.eu. **Aquapura Douro Valley:** Tel 351/254-660-600; www.aquapurahotels.com. *Cost:* from $325 (off-peak), from $450 (peak). **D.O.C.:** Tel 351/254-858-123; www.ruipaula.com. *Cost:* dinner $40. **Cruzeiros Via d'Ouro:** Tel 351/222-081-935; www.viadouro-cruzeiros.com. **Taylor Fladgate Port Lodge:** Tel: 351/223-742-800; www.taylorsportwinelodges.wordpress.com. **The Yeatman:** Tel 351/220-133-100; www.the-yeatman-hotel.com. *Cost:* from $260 (off-peak), from $345 (peak). **Hotel Teatro:** Tel 351/220-409-620; http://hotelteatro.pt. *Cost:* from $150. **Foz Velha:** Tel 351/226-154-178; www.fozvelha.com. *Cost:* tasting menu $55. **Best times:** Jun 24 for Festa do São João; late Sep–early Oct for grape harvest.

The landscape surrounding the river Douro is filled with vineyards famous for producing port wine.

The Flower of al-Andalus

La Mezquita

Córdoba, Andalusia, Spain

Of the Mezquita's original 1,293 columns, 856 still stand today, creating a forest of onyx, jasper, marble, and granite, topped by horseshoe arches of candy-striped red-and-white marble. Add decorative mosaics and plasterwork and you have one of Europe's—and the world's—most breathtaking examples of Muslim architecture.

Constructed between 784 and 987 on the site of a razed Visigoth church (itself originally a Roman temple), La Mezquita, the Great Mosque of Córdoba, has managed to transcend numerous Roman Catholic modifications made in the 5 centuries after Córdoba fell to Christian forces in 1236—including the ill-conceived Cathedral of the Assumption of the Virgin erected in the middle of the structure. After exploring the interior of the Mezquita, step outside and enjoy the cool sounds of running water in the Courtyard of the Oranges, where the faithful once performed the ritual of washing before prayer.

The Omayyad rulers of Damascus (see p. 469) established themselves in Córdoba in 716. By the 10th and 11th centuries, Córdoba had become the bright light in Europe's Dark Ages and the most important city west of Constantinople. Muslims, Jews, and Christians jointly created the most cultured and learned city on the continent, and with nearly 500,000 inhabitants, it was also the largest.

Remnants of this culture can be explored just steps from the Mezquita in the Barrio de la Judería, a twisting warren of cobbled thousand-year-old streets that was the old Jewish and Arabic quarter (a small synagogue dating to 1315 still stands on Calle de los Judíos) until the monarchs Ferdinand and Isabel expelled the Jews from Spain in 1492. Distinctive for their flower-bedecked patios, private homes are open to visitors during the annual Courtyard Festival in early to mid-May. A charming complex of five homes reopened in 2010 as the stylish Casas de la Judería hotel, with 64 guest rooms around an open courtyard.

Just outside the district, Arabic-influenced classic Córdoban cuisine is the specialty of the historic Restaurante Almudaina, fronting the Guadalquivir River and adjacent to the Alcázar, the 14th-century fortress-cum-royal-residence where statues in the beautiful gardens commemorate the fateful meeting between Columbus and Ferdinand and Isabel. Enjoy a luxurious stay in the exquisitely restored Hospes Palacio del Bailío. It's housed within a number of Renaissance/Baroque mansions that date to the 16th–18th centuries, but the ancient Roman ruins that support the hotel's foundations are also on display through the glass floor in its noted Senzone Restaurant.

WHERE: 86 miles/138 km northeast of Seville. **LA MEZQUITA:** Tel 34/95-747-0512. **LAS CASAS DE LA JUDERÍA HOTEL:** Tel 34/95-720-2095; www.casasypalacios.com. *Cost:* from $250 (off-peak), from $360 (peak). **RESTAURANTE ALMUDAINA:** Tel 34/95-747-4342; www.restaurantealmudaina.com. *Cost:* dinner $60. **HOSPES PALACIO DEL BAILÍO:** Tel 34/95-749-8993; www.hospes.com. *Cost:* from $215. **BEST TIMES:** Apr–Jun and Sep–Oct for nicest weather; Semana Santa (week before Easter) and Easter Week; May for lots of festivals, including the Courtyard Festival; mid-Jul for Guitar Festival.

What Wonders Lie Within

THE ALHAMBRA

Granada, Andalusia, Spain

With the white peaks of the Sierra Nevada rising behind it, the breathtaking complex of the Alhambra represents the final flowering of European Islamic art and architecture when Granada flourished as

One of Alhambra's most impressive sites is its Court of the Lions, whose centerpiece is a fountain held up by 12 marble lions.

Spain's last Muslim state. Although austere and unassuming on the outside, nearly every surface of its interior is covered with ornate geometric and flowing arabesque patterns.

For almost 250 years this "Red Fortress" served the Moorish rulers of Granada as palace, harem, and residence for court officials. As one city after another of the kingdom of al-Andalus fell to Christian Spain, the Moors of Granada struck a deal with the kings of Castile and became a refuge for Muslim artists, scholars, and intellectuals, effectively concentrating Spanish Muslim high art and culture to a degree not seen since 10th-century Córdoba (see p. 245).

With the Christians' ultimate victory on January 2, 1492, the "boy-king" Boabdil (Mohammed XII) surrendered the Alhambra and left Spain forever. Catholic monarchs Ferdinand and Isabel moved into the palace and, tradition holds, signed the final exploration papers with Christopher Columbus on April 17 in its Hall of Ambassadors. Separated from the Alhambra by a patch of woodlands, the smaller but equally sumptuous Generalife summer palace is set among fountains and tiered gardens.

The most famous of Spain's government-run inns, the Parador de Granada San Francisco lodges guests within the Alhambra's enchanted walls where they enjoy the thrill of meandering the patios and grounds after closing hours. Rooms in the richly appointed original building are most notable for the privileged views of the complex and of Granada below. A contemporary option is the boutique Gar-Anat Hotel, in the historic city center; each of its 15 imaginative rooms showcases a famous poet, philosopher, or literary luminary associated with Granada.

After the Reconquest, the Moors lived in the medieval Albaicín quarter that rises on the slope facing the Alhambra. Follow the warren of narrow, cobbled streets past flower-draped walls enclosing ancient houses and their gardens to the Mirador de San Nicolás for the finest views of this enchanting city. Enjoy dinner at San Nicolás Restaurante, where it's worth the splurge for their contemporary Andalusian cuisine. Also in the Albaicín, the well-known Peña de Arte Flamenco "La Platería" hosts rising stars of flamenco in an authentic, no-frills setting. To enjoy some of Spain's best and most generous tapas, head to the adjoining plazas of Pescadería and Bib-Rambla.

WHERE: 160 miles/256 km east of Seville. **ALHAMBRA:** Tel 34/902-888001; www.alhambra-tickets.es. **PARADOR DE GRANADA SAN FRANCISCO:** Tel 34/958-221440; www.parador.es; in the U.S., Marketing Ahead, 800-223-1356; www.marketingahead.com. *Cost:* from $460. **GAR-ANAT HOTEL:** Tel 34/958-225528; www.gar-anat.es. *Cost:* from $125 (off-peak), from $175 (peak). **SAN NICOLÁS RESTAURANTE:** Tel 34/958-804262. *Cost:* dinner $45. **PEÑA DE ARTE FLAMENCO "LA PLATERÍA":** Tel 34/958-210650. *When:* Thurs, Feb–Jul. **BEST TIMES:** Apr–Jun and Sep–Oct for nicest weather; Semana Santa (week before Easter); late Jun–mid-Jul for 17-day International Music and Dance Festival; early Nov for International Jazz Festival.

Raise a Glass to the Dancing Horses

Jerez de la Frontera

Andalusia, Spain

You only have to watch the Andalusian horses rear back and dance in perfect synchronicity to fully understand the Spanish love affair with all things equine. The compact, muscular breed known locally as the *pura raza española* (pure Spanish breed) was bred by Carthusian monks in the late Middle Ages and became the darling of the sherry aristocracy in and around Jerez in the 19th century. Horse mania arrives every year during the Feria de Caballo in early May, but weekly year-round performances go on at the Fundación Real Escuela Andaluza del Arte Ecuestre (Royal Andalusian School of Equestrian Art).

Jerez is best known as the world headquarters of sherry, an English corruption of the city's name. Winemaking began in the region under the Phoenicians around 1000 B.C., but the current system of making oak-aged, oxidized wine fortified with brandy didn't begin until the 19th century, when a collaboration of Spanish and English companies led to sherry's becoming one of the world's most famous wines. Twenty sherry bodegas are still located in the city, and González Byass (makers of Tio Pepe)—in the shade of the 12th-century Alcazar Castle—provides the best tour. To appreciate a more intimate and deluxe operation, make an appointment to visit Bodegas Tradición.

At the School of Equestrian Art you can take in a show as well as visit the school's stables, tack room, and museums.

Despite Franco's attempt to exterminate the gypsies of Jerez, the city's heritage as the birthplace of a distinctive flamenco style has been preserved. Visit the Centro Andaluz de Flamenco for suggestions on where to see a number of performances on any given night in venues that are generally less touristy than those in nearby Seville (see p. 250).

Stay as a guest of the local Garvey family in their grand Neoclassical home that has been transformed into the contemporary 16-room Palacio Garvey hotel. The tapas bars around Plaza Arenal are world famous for Jerez specialties—the good bars each stick loyally to a single sherry brand.

Summers in southernmost Spain can be brutal. Escape to the country retreat of Casa la Siesta, an hour's drive from town in Vejer de la Frontera, and enjoy the keen style and amiable attention of the young British owners. From there, day trips into Jerez are easy, or spend your stay exploring Andalusia's stunning Pueblos Blancos (see next page).

Where: 49 miles/79 km south of Seville. **Fundación Real Escuela Andaluza del Arte Ecuestre:** Tel 34/956-318015; www.realescuela.org. *When:* performances Tues and Thurs. **González Byass:** Tel 34/956-357046; www.bodegastiopepe.com. **Bodegas Tradición:** Tel 34/956-168628; www.bodegastradicion.es. **Centro Andaluz de Flamenco:** Tel 34/956-814132; www.centroandaluzdeflamenco.es. **Hotel Palacio Garvey:** Tel 34/956-326700; www.sferahoteles.com. *Cost:* from $215 (off-peak), from $430 (peak). **Casa la Siesta:** Tel 34/699-619430; www.casalasiesta.com. *Cost:* from $260. **Best times:** late Feb–early Mar for Flamenco Festival; Semana Santa (week before Easter); May for Feria de Caballo; Sep for grape harvest festival.

A Scenic Drive Through History

Ruta de los Pueblos Blancos

Andalusia, Spain

The beauty of the Sierra de Grazalema region is unmatched in Spain. Its combination of dramatic mountain scenery and splendid, whitewashed villages makes you half expect to see medieval Berber farmers and Christian knights. Follow the scenic Ruta de los Pueblos Blancos (Route of the White Towns) connecting Arcos de la Frontera on the west to the high redoubt of Ronda on the east.

Arcos rises steeply on the wedge of a sandstone ridge crowned by a ruined Moorish castle and the spectacular Parador Arcos de la Frontera, the 18th-century palace of the king's magistrate (*corregidor*) and now an atmospheric inn. Historic rooms overlook the town square, but many guests prefer the suites with cliff-hanging terraces overlooking the Guadalete River. The town's narrow streets are lined with buildings that date to the 18th-century Enlightenment, built after an earlier earthquake left the town in shambles.

The land east of Arcos rises swiftly into mountains contested by Arab and Christian armies for 700 years, leaving "de la Frontera," or "on the border," as an appendage to the names of many towns. The villages wear history on their sleeves—from the distinctly North African Berber look of Grazalema, gateway to mountain hikes and Europe's southernmost trout streams, to the mountaintop Moorish-then-Christian fortress at Zahara de la Sierra that commands three strategic mountain passes. In between, don't miss high-flying Algodonales, Spain's hang-gliding capital, and Ubrique, long famed for its leather crafts.

Acclaimed for 2,000 years by everyone from Pliny the Elder to Hemingway, Ronda (43 miles east of Arcos) is an incredible sight. It stands perched on a dramatic limestone escarpment that is sliced in two by the El Tajo gorge, where the Guadalevín River flows 393 feet below. Streets of the Arabic old city twist like vines around the escarpment; across the gorge, the new city seems to emanate from Spain's oldest (1785) and most beautiful bullring, where, every September, corridas are held with matadors in full Goyaesque costumes. For a country retreat just 10 minutes outside town, a late-18th-century olive mill has been magically transformed into the Hotel La Fuente de la Higuera, a small, stylish hotel that is luxurious without any pretense.

Standing more than 300 feet above El Tajo gorge, Ronda's New Bridge is a misnomer for this 18th-century structure.

Where: Arcos is 45 miles /73 km south of Seville. **Parador Arcos de la Frontera:** Tel 34/95-670-0500; www.parador.es; in the U.S., Marketing Ahead, tel 800-223-1356; www.marketingahead.com. *Cost:* from $230. **Hotel La Fuente de la Higuera:** Tel 34/95-211-4355; www.hotellafuente.com. *Cost:* from $260. **Best times:** Apr–Jun and Sep–Oct for nicest weather; 1st week of Sep for Ronda's Feria Goyesca de Pedro Romero.

The City of Don Juan and Carmen

SEVILLE

Andalusia, Spain

Seville is a storied city that has been Andalusia's seat of power and glory for nearly 1,000 years. The Alcázar (royal residence) and Cathedral, built over the Moorish palace and mosque, lie at its heart. In fact, the Giralda bell tower of the Cathedral (the world's largest Gothic church) is the old Moorish minaret.

Flamenco dancing originated in this region.

This is a city that celebrates excess, from the encrusted Baroque decoration of its churches to a nightly devotion to flamenco and tapas. Even religious observances can be extreme: During Semana Santa (the week before Easter), members of the city's 60 *cofradías* (brotherhoods)—many of them in long, hooded robes, barefoot, and dragging chains—slowly parade through the darkened streets to haunting, deeply devotional music. Two weeks later, the city does an about-face with the exuberant Feria d'Abril (April Fair)—a heady week of drinking, dancing till the small hours, and daily bullfights, topped off by Sunday night's fireworks.

Andalusia is the birthplace of flamenco, and weekend performances at the new Museo del Baile Flamenco, founded by legendary dancer Cristina Hoyos in the central neighborhood of Santa Cruz, are some of the purest examples of this authentic music and dance. Also in Santa Cruz, you can find impromptu guitar and dancing on the back patio at La Carbonería. Located nearby is the historic hotel Casas de la Judería; arrayed around a number of leafy patios, it is an oasis in Seville's former Jewish quarter and most colorful neighborhood.

Seville is the mother church of tapas, and *tapeo* (tapas-hopping) is a way of life here—just follow the *sevillanos* from bar to bar. Be sure to visit El Rinconcillo, the city's oldest (established in 1670) and quintessential bar, with vintage posters of the April Fair on the walls, hams hanging overhead, and tabs chalked up on the massive wooden bar.

No in-town hotel surpasses the grand Alfonso XIII for its history and glamour. Built to accommodate visiting royalty during Seville's 1929 World's Fair, its design borrowed freely from the Moorish influence of the palace of the Alcázar, with beautiful tiles and inlaid columns and archways. But also consider the romantic countryside retreat of Hacienda de San Rafael, about an hour south, in Las Cabezas de San Juan. In an 18th-century farmhouse on a 350-acre olive estate, the Anglo-Spanish owners have created a sophisticated getaway where every detail is spot on.

WHERE: 90 miles/144 km southwest of Córdoba. **MUSEO DEL BAILE FLAMENCO:** Tel 34/954-340311; www.museoflamenco.com. **LA CARBONERÍA:** Tel 34/954-229945. **LAS CASAS DE LA JUDERÍA:** Tel 34/954-415150; www.casasypalacios.com. *Cost:* from $180 (off-peak), from $315 (peak). **EL RINCONCILLO:** Tel 34/954-223183. *Cost:* tapas "meal" $12. **ALFONSO XIII:** Tel 34/954-917000; www.starwoodhotels.com. *Cost:* from $415 (off-peak), from $920 (peak). **HACIENDA DE SAN RAFAEL:** Tel 34/954-227116; www.haciendadesanrafael.com. *Cost:* from $350.

Best times: Mar–May and Sep–Nov for nicest weather; Semana Santa (week before Easter); 2 weeks after Easter for Feria de Abril; Sep–Oct in even years for the Bienal Flamenco.

Mediterranean Idylls

Balearic Islands

Spain

With their long, sandy strands and lush, green interiors, the Balearic Islands are the jewels of the western Mediterranean. And like so much else in this region, they were bitterly contested first by the Carthaginians and Romans, then a millennium later by the Moors and Christians. As a result, on the largest island of Mallorca (Majorca), the foundation of a grand mosque supports the lavish Gothic Catedral de Santa María de Palma. The church, in the capital city of Palma, has astounding stained-glass rose windows, *modernista* iron canopies designed by Antoni Gaudí (see p. 261) above the altar, and local artist Miguel Barceló's avant-garde ceramic mural. But then Mallorca is no stranger to artists. Lyrically abstract painter and sculptor Joan Miró worked on the outskirts of Palma, where his studio and some late works are displayed in the Fundació Pilar i Joan Miró.

Stay about 8 miles west of town at Hospes Maricel; high ceilings and glass walls minimize the visual divide between indoors and out. The beach is a 5-minute walk, but between the gourmet restaurant and the inviting spa, it could be hard to leave for a swim.

Don't miss a drive clockwise around the island on the Costa Rocosa, the unspoiled coastline of craggy cliffs. Visit beautiful Valldemossa, famed for the Carthusian monastery where Frédéric Chopin and his lover, novelist George Sand, spent the personally miserable but creatively productive winter of 1838–39. You, however, can find happiness at the Valldemossa Hotel, on the same property. The poet Robert Graves found his paradise in the village of Deià. Enjoy it from the flower-filled patio at La Residencia; then nourish your palate at the hotel's famed El Olivo restaurant. Continue on to the wild scenery of the Peninsula de Formentor, where a rocky cape seems to strike out to sea like a serpent.

Ibiza is the Mediterranean's party island. Much of the club scene is centered on the Porto Deportivo, in Eivissa (Ibiza City). Outside the city, Ibiza boasts some of the finest beaches and amusing remnants of the backpacking infusion of the 1960s. Sample the hippie market on Saturdays in the village of Sant Carlos, especially if you've chosen to stay in the farmhouse retreat of Can Curreu. Or hop a boat to tiny Formentera, where spectacular, largely undeveloped beaches are popular with nudists and divers.

Where: Mallorca is 345 miles/555 km southeast of Madrid. **Visitor info:** www.illesbalears.es. **Fundació Pilar i Joan Miró:** Tel 34/971-701420; miro.palmademallorca.es. **Hospes Maricel:** Tel 34/971-707744; www.hospes.com. *Cost:* from $260 (off-peak), from $550 (peak). **Valldemossa Hotel:** Tel 34/971-612626; www.valldemossahotel.com. *Cost:* from $500. **La Residencia:** Tel 34/971-639011; www.hotel-laresidencia.com. *Cost:* from $300 (off-peak), from $790 (peak). **Can Curreu:** Tel 34/971-335280; www.cancurreu.com. *Cost:* from $325. **Best times:** Apr–May and Sep–Oct for hiking, walking, and cycling; Jun–Aug for beach activities.

A Masterwork of Architectural Sculpture

Guggenheim Museum Bilbao

Bilbao, Basque Country, Spain

Looking like a hybrid of giant bird, great ship, and armored dinosaur, the titanium- and stone-covered Guggenheim Museum Bilbao (a satellite of the New York–based Guggenheim Museum; see p. 843) has become this Basque port city's signature building, transforming the once gritty shores of the Nervión River. Cross the river on a glass-floored pedestrian bridge by star architect Santiago Calatrava for the best views of the Guggenheim building, designed in 1997 by Canadian-American architect Frank Gehry. The flamboyant exterior forms translate inside into 18 similarly idiosyncratic galleries.

In the much vaunted "Guggenheim effect," Gehry's audacious masterpiece jump-started the economic and architectural revival of the city, with striking contemporary sculptures and structures by many of the world's top talents, and a lively café scene. The riverside walking path leads to Bilbao's Casco Viejo, or old city, where some of Spain's finest *pintxos* (peent-SHOS, Basque tapas) are found in the bars under the Neoclassical arches of Plaza Nueva (also the site of a lively Sunday-morning market). The city has emerged as one of the important centers for new Basque cuisine, best enjoyed at Gure Kide, where chef Aitor Elola fuses Basque tradition, respect for ingredients, and the Spanish penchant for whimsy. Both the bistrot and the restaurant-in-residence of the Guggenheim Museum also highlight Basque cuisine. Two excellent hotels across the street from the Guggenheim echo Gehry's design sensibility—the minimalist and more modest Hotel Miró, by Spanish fashion designer Antonio Miró, and the avant-garde–chic Silken Gran Hotel Domine, where diners on the rooftop terrace enjoy Guggenheim views.

Where: 249 miles/395 km north of Madrid. **Guggenheim:** Tel 34/944-359059 (museum), 34/944-239333 (restaurant); www.guggenheim-bilbao.es. *Cost:* dinner at Bistrot $25; at Restaurant $90. **Gure Kide:** Tel 34/944-415004. *Cost:* dinner $60. **Hotel Miró:** Tel 34/946-611880; www.mirohotelbilbao.com. *Cost:* from $135. **Silken Gran Hotel Domine:** Tel 34/944-253300; www.hoteles-silken.com. *Cost:* from $150. **Best time:** late Aug for Semana Grande festival.

A Newly Stylish Wine Region Emerges

Rioja

La Rioja and Basque Country, Spain

The "Guggenheim effect" that took root in Bilbao (see above) quickly spread to neighboring Rioja, Spain's most celebrated wine country. In 2006, architect Frank Gehry redesigned the facilities of the Marqués de Riscal winery, in the tiny Basque village of Eltziego (Elciego in Spanish). Marqués de Riscal pioneered Rioja winemaking here, releasing its first vintage in 1862 and making a name for Rioja's elegant reds when disease was ravaging the vineyards north of the region, in Bordeaux. Just as the company jump-started the wine business then, it has revolutionized Rioja wine tourism today by commissioning Gehry to integrate its 19th-century warehouses with visionary 21st-century structures known as the City of Wine. You need to reserve ahead for a tour, but casual tastings are available at the new shop. To cap the experience, spend the night at the Hotel Marqués de Riscal, Gehry's sweeping 43-room architectural fantasy of undulating titanium that squats like a great bird on a hill above the winery. The Marqués de Riscal Gastronomic Restaurant lives up to its grand name with cutting-edge contemporary Basque cuisine and one of the finest wine cellars in Spain.

Gehry's inspiration for Hotel Marqués de Riscal: the pink hue of Rioja, the gold adorning the bottles, the silver foil around the cork.

Other world-class architects have also put their stamp on La Rioja. Zaha Hadid designed a postmodern cathedral-like tasting pavilion for Bodegas López de Heredia, in Haro, whereas Santiago Calatrava created low-lying, undulating buildings for Bodegas Ysios, in Laguardia. In Logroño, the regional capital, take your pick of several casual bars or restaurants on Calle Laurel to sip and snack on tapas or to dine on lamb chops, salt cod–stuffed peppers, or potatoes in a smoky paprika sauce. The city's starkly minimalist modern Hotel Marqués de Vallejo makes a good home when touring the region.

WHERE: 60 miles/97 km south of Bilbao. **CITY OF WINE TOUR:** Tel 34/945-180880; www.marquesderiscal.com. **HOTEL MARQUÉS DE RISCAL:** Tel 34/945-180880; www.luxury collection.com. *Cost:* from $390; dinner $140. **HOTEL MARQUÉS DE VALLEJO:** Tel 34/941-248333; www.hotelmarquesdevallejo.com. *Cost:* from $80 (off-peak), from $150 (peak). **BEST TIMES:** May–Oct for nicest weather; Jun 29 for Haro's "Wine Battle," when participants dressed all in white squirt each other with red wine; late Aug–early Oct for harvest season.

Culinary Mecca in a Coastal Belle Époque Setting

SAN SEBASTIÁN AND BASQUE COUNTRY

Spain

Along with France's Biarritz (see p. 100), San Sebastián is the great Belle Époque resort of the Basque coast. Crescent-shaped La Concha beach is punctuated on either end by misty mountains and lined with 19th-century resort buildings—perhaps the most beautiful urban beach in Europe. The setting lured Spanish queen-regent María Cristina to make the city the royal court's summer home.

Today San Sebastián is less Spanish than Basque, which is most visible in the use of street signs in Euskara, the Basque language. San Sebastián goes locally by its Basque name, Donastia, and functions as the cultural capital of the Basque coast from Bilbao to Bayonne, France. (Basque nationalists see the Spanish Basque region, the Basque-speaking parts of Spanish Navarre and La Rioja, and the three Basque provinces of France as the single nation of Euskadi.)

The Basques have political autonomy within Spain but have yet to get their own country. Nonetheless, they conquered the tables of Spain (and of some of France) in the 1980s with the explosion of *nueva cocina vasca* (New Basque cuisine) and have maintained their role as Spain's great culinary mecca. The godfather of the movement is Juan Mari Arzak, who applied the light principles of French nouvelle cuisine to traditional Basque flavors and invented a new, fresh ingredient–driven approach to cooking. His Arzak restaurant, where daughter Elena shares the kitchen, attracts food lovers from around the world. Inventive New Basque cuisine is also available in the tapas bars of the newly gentrified Gros district. The legendary Bar Bergara sets out a mind-boggling spread, and the front bar at Kursaal MB lets you sample chef Martín Berasategui's savory creations.

San Sebastián's signature Kursaal cultural center, designed by Rafael Moneo, is home to esteemed jazz and film festivals. The aristocratic Hotel María Cristina, which sits like a queen on the west bank of the Urumea River, serves as unofficial headquarters for the annual film festival. The 1912 landmark still dazzles with its opulent lobby of ormolu, onyx columns, and Carrara marble floors. A good alternative at (but not on) La Concha beach is the gently weathered Hotel Londres y de Inglaterra, a dignified grande dame from the Belle Époque. From either hotel it's an easy jaunt to visit the Basque fishing ports of Lekeitio, Getaria, and Ondárroa, or the artist-haunted resorts of Zumaia and Zarautz.

Where: San Sebastián is 57 miles/92 km east from Bilbao, 12 miles/21 km west of the French border. **Arzak:** Tel 34/943-285593; www.arzak.info. *Cost:* prix fixe menu $72. **Bar Bergara:** Tel 34/943-275026. *Cost: pintxo* "meal" $15. **Kursaal MB:** Tel 34/943-003162. *Cost: pintxo* "meal" $15. **Hotel María Cristina:** Tel 34/943-437600; www.starwoodhotels.com. *Cost:* from $295 (off-peak), from $500 (peak). **Hotel Londres y de Inglaterra:** Tel 34/943-440770; www.hlondres.com. *Cost:* from $230 (off-peak), from $350 (peak). **Best times:** Jan 20 for St. Sebastian's Day; late Jul for Jazz Festival; mid-Aug for Semana Grande; mid-Sep for International Film Festival.

Fragile and Invaluable Link to the Ice Age

The Caves of Altamira and Santillana del Mar

Cantabria, Spain

Forbidden to all but a chosen few, the Caves of Altamira (las Cuevas de Altamira) are often described as the Sistine Chapel of prehistoric art. Together with the Lascaux caves (see p. 102) in southern France, they contain the best Upper Paleolithic cave paintings in Europe. Discovered in perfect condition by a local hunter in 1879, the red-and-black bison, bulls, horses, and boars demonstrate Neolithic man's love of beauty and astonishing artistic skill. The cave paintings range from 4 to 8 feet high and are estimated to be 14,000 to 20,000 years old. Unfortunately, a century's worth of heat and moisture from throngs of tourists caused serious deterioration, and public admissions were suspended in 2002; but there is continual speculation that the caves may be reopened under a plan of tightly limited visitation. The adjacent Museo de Altamira re-creates the setting and paintings (including before-and-after photos that show the damage) with superb exhibits on anthropology and archaeology, but perhaps minus the goosebumps of the real thing.

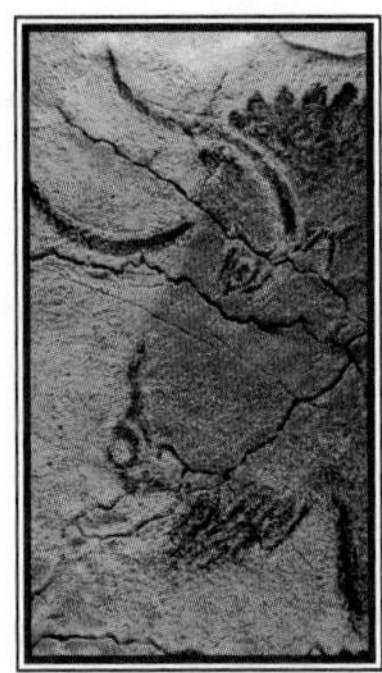

The caves were painted in the Paleolithic period.

The caves are 2 miles outside the small town of Santillana del Mar, a cluster of perfectly preserved mansions and palaces with a palpable medieval spirit. Jean-Paul Sartre called it "the prettiest little village in Spain." Despite its name, the town actually lies 3 miles from the sea. Stroll through town to the 12th-century church of St. Juliana, the burial place of the 3rd-century martyred saint. (Over time, her name was corrupted and evolved into Santillana.) At the other end of the main street is the 400-year-old Convent of the Poor Clares (Convento de Regina Coeli), whose museum contains a surprisingly rich assemblage of religious paintings and statues.

If you've fallen under the spell of this tiny town, end your stroll at the Plaza de Ramón Pelayo, where the Parador Santillana Gil Blas occupies the 17th-century manor of local nobility. Across the small plaza, an annex built recently in the same style absorbs the guest overflow. Call ahead: A visit to Santillana is incomplete if there's no room at this inn.

WHERE: 21 miles/34 km west of Santander. **MUSEO DE ALTAMIRA:** Tel 34/942-818005; www.museodealtamira.es. **PARADOR SANTILLANA GIL BLAS:** Tel 34/942-028028; www.parador.es; in the U.S., Marketing Ahead, 800-223-1356; www.marketingahead.com. *Cost:* from $250. **BEST TIME:** May–Oct for pleasant weather.

Spain's Greenest Heights

PICOS DE EUROPA

Cantabria and Asturias, Spain

An unspoiled enchantment envelops these soaring mountains that wall off the wet northern coast of Spain from the arid high plateau of Castile and León. Rising to nearly 9,000 feet, they hold a thousand secrets of earlier times. The remote forests and deep gorges of the 250-square-mile Parque Natural de Picos de Europa (Peaks of Europe) are stomping grounds of the Iberian brown bear and shaggy wild Asturcón horse. Human habitations in the limestone caves go back 140,000 years. Covadonga National Park, outside Cangas de Onís on the western edge of the Picos, is where the near-legendary Pelayo led his revolt against the advancing Moors in 722 and began the reconquest of Spain that was completed by his distant descendant, Isabel of Castile, in 1492. Don Pelayo made Cangas de Onís his first capital of Christian Spain, and the picturesque mountain village makes a good starting point for touring the historic sites (including Pelayo's tomb, high above a waterfall in adjacent Covadonga) and for hiking, canoeing, and spelunking.

The limestone peak of Naranjo de Bulnes rises over 8,000 feet above the park.

On the banks of the Sella River, the Parador de Cangas de Onís, housed in an atmospheric 12th-century monastery, provides lodging on the west end of the mountains, in the town of Villanueva. There is great middle-of-nowhere dining just outside Arriondas, where master chef Nacho Manzano has turned his farmhouse birthplace into one of northern Spain's most exciting restaurants, Casa Marcial. On the east end of the Picos park, over the line in Cantabria, the modern mountain lodge of the Parador Fuente Dé sits at the base of a gondola—one of the longest single-span cable cars in Europe—that ferries trekkers to alpine hiking trails. Narrow river gorges make the twisting roads of the Picos one of the most exciting road trips in Spain. Stop off in the village of Las Arenas de Cabrales to buy some of the locally made Cabrales blue cheese and a loaf of bread for your road trip.

Where: 45 miles/72 km east of Oviedo. **Parador de Cangas de Onís:** Tel 34/985-849402; www.parador.es; in the U.S., Marketing Ahead, 800-223-1356; www.marketingahead.com. Cost: $210. *When:* closed Jan–Feb. **Casa Marcial:** Tel 34/985-840991; www.casamarcial.com. *Cost:* dinner $60. **Parador Fuente Dé:** Tel 34/942-736651; www.parador.es; in the U.S., Marketing Ahead, 800-223-1356; www.marketingahead.com. *Cost:* $150 (off-peak), from $190 (peak). *When:* closed Jan–Feb. **How:** U.S.-based Mountain Travel Sobek offers 8-day hikes through the Picos. Tel 888-831-7526 or 510-594-6000; www.mtsobek.com. *Cost:* $3,395, inclusive. Originate in Oviedo. *When:* Jul, Sep. **Best time:** May–Oct for snow-free hiking, wildflower blooms, and least rain.

A Gravity-Defying Aerie That Is Home to Abstract Art

Cuenca

Castilla-La Mancha, Spain

Of Spain's many hilltop cities, none seems quite as vertical or gravity-defying as Cuenca, perched high above the gorges and confluence of the Júcar and Huécar rivers. The Castilians wrenched the city from the Moors in 1177, and within a century they ran out of space and began to cantilever their *casas colgadas,* or hanging houses, over the gorges. So steep is the hill that the back doors of some buildings fronting the main street of Calle Alfonso VIII are three stories below, making the city feel like a three-dimensional puzzle.

No wonder the abstract artists known as El Grupo Paso fell in love with Cuenca in the 1950s and made it the epicenter of a new artistic movement. Their legacy is three fine museums, one of which, the small but wonderful Museo de Arte Abstracto Español, occupies one of the city's most famous casas colgadas. The handful of remaining hanging houses are also still very much part of the local scene. The town's most prestigious address is the Parador de Cuenca, located in a 16th-century monastery on a nearby crag. It stands across a vertigo-inducing footbridge from the hanging houses in the town's center, while the town's best eatery (and a great spot to linger with a drink) is the Mesón Casas Colgadas, oft photographed for its precarious perch and located next to the museum. The town specialty, *zarajos,* roasted lamb intestines, is usually on the menu.

In the Old Town, check into the atmospheric Posada de San José, just around the corner from the Anglo-Norman cathedral. It is said that the painter Diego Velázquez frequently stayed here and may have used local inspiration while painting *Las Meninas,* one of the Prado's most famous artworks (see p. 267).

WHERE: 105 miles/169 km east of Madrid. **MUSEO DE ARTE ABSTRACTO ESPAÑOL:** Tel 34/969-212983; www.march.es/cuenca. **PARADOR DE CUENCA:** Tel 34/969-232320; www.parador.es; in the U.S., Marketing Ahead, 800-223-1356; www.marketingahead.com. *Cost:* from $225. **MESÓN CASAS COLGADAS:** Tel 34/969-223509; www.mesoncolgadas.com. *Cost:* dinner $55. **POSADA DE SAN JOSÉ:** Tel 34/969-211300; www.posadasanjose.com. *Cost:* from $115. **BEST TIME:** Apr–Oct for nicest weather. Nights are cool in Cuenca, even in Aug.

To reach the famed hanging houses, visitors must navigate the town's steep and narrow cobbled streets.

A Saint's Birthplace Conveys a Vivid Sense of the Past

ÁVILA

Castilla y León, Spain

The nearly perfect 11th-century walls of Ávila are a protected national treasure. Ten feet thick and 40 feet high, they took more than 2,000 workers 10 years to build. They wend a mile and a half around this much-photographed hilltop town and include 90 semicircular guard towers, 9 narrow arched gates, and more than 2,300 embattlements, which still look astonishingly new. A walkway along the top allows you to envision an approaching army of Moors—or get a good view of the storks that nest in the town's bell towers. Even the city's rugged 12th-century cathedral was built into the walls to serve partly as a military fortress.

Ávila has long been central to Spain's religious history as the hometown of St. Teresa, born here in 1515. A frail, witty Carmelite nun from a family of Jewish descent, she was a key figure of the Spanish Counterreformation, who became the first female Doctor of the Church and the female patron saint of Spain. The treasured souvenirs called *yemas de Santa Teresa,* the candied egg yolks named in her honor, are sold all over town.

Reputedly built by Moorish prisoners, the walls of Ávila become the world's largest illuminated monument at night.

A stay at the Hotel Palacio de los Velada, next to the bishop's palace and cathedral, puts you in the spiritual and geographic heart of Ávila. The modernized Renaissance palace exudes contemporary opulence. You can lounge with a drink in the glamorous, glass-covered cloister courtyard unless it's been taken over by a local wedding party—who will probably invite you to join in.

WHERE: 68 miles/110 km northwest of Madrid. **VISITOR INFO:** www.avilaturismo.com. **HOTEL PALACIO DE LOS VELADA:** Tel 34/920-215100; www.veladahoteles.com. *Cost:* from $100 (off-peak), $200 (peak). **BEST TIMES:** Mar–Oct for nicest weather; Oct 15 for feast day of St. Teresa, which also launches a weeklong festival of flamenco.

An Architectural Wonder and a Shelter for Knights

León

Castilla y León, Spain

Begun in 1205, the walls of León's Gothic cathedral are more glass than stone: One hundred and twenty-five stained-glass windows, three giant rose windows, and 57 oculi fill the lofty interior with bejeweled shafts of light. In the cathedral-building mania of the Middle Ages, European cities strove to outdo one another with the highest steeples and biggest rose windows. Because the kingdom of León was leading the battle against Islam in Spain, artisans from across Europe made León's cathedral the boldest in Christendom, creating a building that amazes even modern-day architects with its illusion of weightlessness and profusion of light. Some windows soar as high as 110 feet, and altogether they cover more than 18,000 square feet. Some of Spain's most important sacred art can be found in the adjacent Cathedral Museum.

Designated the capital of Christian Spain in 914, León is now a charming provincial city that retains the aura of its regal past. Eleven kings, 14 queens, and many nobles are buried in the Royal Pantheon, located in the convent of the beautiful Romanesque church Colegiata de San Isidro where fanciful 12th-century ceiling frescoes look down on their sepulchres.

The Parador San Marcos deserves a prize for its sumptuous entrance in the plateresque style (so-called because of its resemblance to lacy plate work in silver, or *plata,*) and the elaborate, coffered ceiling of the entry hall. A landmark of Spanish Renaissance architecture, it has become Spain's largest parador since the addition of a modern annex. Its original wing was completed in 1549, upon the orders of King Ferdinand, as the mother house of the Order of Santiago and a hospice for visiting pilgrims. Thirty of the 250 rooms are housed in the historic wing, as is the celebrated restaurant with views of the Río Bernesga.

León is also one of two departure points for a special weeklong train excursion across historic northern Spain on El Transcantábrico Classico. Stops include Bilbao (see p. 252), Santillana del Mar (see p. 254), a coach excursion through the Picos de Europa (see p. 255), Oviedo, the north coast of Galicia, and ends in Santiago de Compostela (see p. 265). A new Transcantábrico luxury train with additional creature comforts (el Gran Lujo) introduced in 2011 travels between Santiago and San Sebastían (see p. 253).

WHERE: 200 miles/320 km north of Madrid. **CATEDRAL DE LEÓN:** Tel 34/987-875770; www.catedraldeleon.org. **PARADOR SAN MARCOS:** Tel 34/987-237300; www.parador.es; in the U.S., Marketing Ahead, 800-223-1356; www.marketingahead.com. *Cost:* $175 (new wing), $290 (historic wing); dinner $55. **EL TRANSCANTÁBRICO:** Tel 34/902-555902; www.eltranscantabricoclasico.com. *Cost:* 8 days from $3,385. *When:* May–Oct. **HOW:** U.S.-based Palace Tours arranges train travel. Tel 800-724-5120; www.spaintraintours.com. **BEST TIMES:** Apr–Oct for nice weather; late Jun for Fiesta de San Juan, featuring concerts, bullfights, and fireworks.

The best time to admire the stained-glass windows of León's cathedral is on a sunny afternoon.

Spain's Most Beautiful Square

SALAMANCA'S PLAZA MAYOR

Salamanca, Castilla y León, Spain

Visitors to Spain's leading city of wit and wisdom—wit in the architectural adornments, wisdom in one of Europe's oldest universities—inevitably gravitate to the heart of the town, the lovely 18th-century Baroque Plaza Mayor (Main Square), often called the most beautiful in all of Spain. The ancient city's other attractions are within walking distance of the plaza, but linger awhile to take in the spirit of Salamanca. What was once Spain's most important university was founded here in 1218 by Alfonso IX, and you can still visit the buildings of the original school. (Join students searching for the tiny good-luck frog among the elaborate carvings on the entryway's façade.) As one of Europe's oldest universities, Salamanca was considered an equal to Oxford, Bologna, and Paris. Today, its 30,000 students keep the city young and fuel its stimulating arts scene. They fill the café tables that pour out from the plaza's shaded arcades, where roving groups of *tunas* (caped student minstrels in Renaissance garb) often serenade visitors and *salamantinos* in the late afternoon. A few blocks south, the "new" 16th-century cathedral, with its extraordinary carved façades, shares a wall with its older Romanesque sibling. Both are important sites, especially for their main altars. So is the Hotel Rector, formerly the private mansion of a family that now lives upstairs, leaving 14 faultlessly decorated rooms for in-the-know travelers.

Where: 127 miles/204 km northwest of Madrid. **Hotel Rector:** Tel 34/923-218482; www.hotelrector.com. *Cost:* $220. **Best times:** Mar–Jun and Sep–Nov for nicest weather; mid-Sep for Feria de Salamanca.

Ancient Heartbeat of a Modern City

Ciutat Vella

Barcelona, Catalonia, Spain

While the fantasy excesses of *modernista* architecture (see next page) define the stately grid of Barcelona's L'Eixample neighborhood, the Ciutat Vella (Old City) is filled with the atmospheric twisting alleys of the Barri Gótic (Gothic Quarter). Bounded on the west by the carnival-like promenade of La Rambla, the Barri Gótic is dominated by the Cathedral of Barcelona (begun in 1298, completed circa 1450), whose plaza becomes especially festive on Sunday afternoons when it swells with people performing the Catalan circle dance known as the *sardana.* You can watch the action from many of the rooms at the nearby Hotel Colón, a graciously old-fashioned lodging that was a favorite choice of Joan Miró. A few blocks away, the Neri Hotel and Restaurant delivers contemporary style with neo-Gothic flourishes in the seclusion of an 18th-century palace.

Five medieval town houses east of the cathedral are linked together as the Museu Picasso, which houses 3,800 of his works and is second only to the Picasso Museum in Paris (see p. 114). Many are early examples, including boyhood sketchbooks, showing how a talented youth from Málaga evolved into a master artist during his years in cosmopolitan Barcelona (1895–1904).

He spent part of that transition hanging out at Els Quatre Gats (The Four Cats), a Barri Gótic bar-restaurant that was designed by Modernist architect Josep Puig i Cadafalch in 1897 and has catered to bohemia ever since. The streets around Els Quatre Gats northwest of the cathedral are especially good for evening tapas hopping. But even in Barcelona, little can compete with the long tree-lined avenue called La Rambla—"the very spirit of the city," wrote Federico García Lorca. Amid the sensory overload created by this swath of florists, buskers, caricaturists, and café waiters inviting you in, there appears the Mercat de la Boqueria, the city's temple of fresh food. The Boqueria market is a gastronome's idea of heaven, with more than 300 stalls purveying everything from wild mushrooms to squirming eels. Just inside the entrance on the right, the always packed Bar Pintxo is a perfect spot to grab some tapas or a sandwich to curb your appetite before shopping. La Rambla isn't all street theater; at its midpoint stands the Gran Teatre del Liceu, one of the world's grandest opera houses, rebuilt in 1994 after a devastating fire.

Bisbe Irurita Street in the Barri Gótic was an ancient Roman thoroughfare.

Hotel Colón: Tel 34/933-011404; www.hotelcolon.es. Cost: from $105 (off-peak), from $165 (peak). **Neri Hotel:** Tel 34/933-040655; www.hotelneri.com. *Cost:* from $260 (off-peak), from $400 (peak). **Museu Picasso:** Tel 34/932-563000; www.museupicasso.bcn.es. **Els Quatre Gats:** Tel 34/933-024140; www.4gats.com. *Cost:* lunch $35. **Mercat de la Boqueria:** Tel 34/933-182584. **Bar Pintxo:** Tel 34/933-171731; www.boqueria.info. *Cost: pintxo* "meal" $18. **Gran Teatre del Liceu:** Tel 34/934-859913; www.liceubarcelona.com. **Best times:** Thurs for Mercat Gótic de Antiguitats flea market on Plaça Nova; Christmas season for Fira de Santa Llúcia.

A Visionary Architect Defines Barcelona

Gaudí and La Sagrada Familia

Barcelona, Catalonia, Spain

Rising to the heavens with eight candle-wax spires, the enormous Sagrada Familia church remains a masterpiece in the making. Eccentric genius and Catalan architect Antoni Gaudí was run over and killed by a tram before he could complete his strangest, most controversial creation. It is finally slated for completion in 2026 to mark the centenary of his death. Gaudí, a national hero, is buried in the church's crypt, but his spirit persists throughout the city. The most famous proponent of *modernisme* (the Catalan Art Nouveau style of 1890 to 1920), Gaudí put Barcelona on the architectural map with a design approach that was rooted in a playful Catalan sensibility later expressed by Picasso, Miró, and Dalí. His flowing, organic forms remain landmarks, especially the Casa Milà apartment block (often called "the rock pile," or La Pedrera), where the chimneys are shaped like surrealistic warriors. It is one of seven secular buildings by Gaudí. His designs for Parc Güell delight with tile-encrusted benches and undulating ramparts. Inside the park, his home, the Casa-Museu Gaudí, contains a small exhibit about his work and life.

It's called "House of Bones" for its skeletal quality, but Gaudí actually drew inspiration for Casa Batlló from marine life.

To see Modernist buildings built by other masters, stroll through the neighborhood of L'Eixample; be sure to pass by the fairy-tale mansion called Casa de les Punxes (House of Spikes), designed by Josep Puig i Cadafalch in 1905. Try to attend a concert in the Palau de la Música Catalana, designed by Lluís Domènech i Montaner. Almost sedate on the outside, the interior is a hallucinogenic riot of stained glass, ceramic sculpture, and stone carvings capped by a grand stained-glass dome. Top off the *modernisme* experience by staying either at Hotel Casa Fuster, a landmark hotel that has retained features of the original 1908 urban palace designed by Domènech i Montaner, or at the Mandarin Oriental Barcelona, which opened in 2010 in a mid-20th-century structure with great views of Gaudí's Casa Batlló, a marvel of sinuous curves and colorful glass and ceramic details.

La Sagrada Familia: www.sagradafamilia.org. **Casa-Museu Gaudí:** Tel 34/932-93811; www.casamuseugaudi.org. **Palau de la Música Catalana:** Tel 34/932-957200; www.palaumusica.org. **How:** The city has published a pamphlet for a self-guided walking tour of 115 Modernist landmarks, the "Ruta del Modernisme de Barcelona." Tel 34/933-177652; www.rutadelmodernisme.com. **Hotel Casa Fuster:** Tel 34/932-553000; www.hotelcasafuster.com. *Cost:* from $250 (off-peak), from $460 (peak). **Mandarin Oriental Barcelona:** Tel 34/931-518888; in the U.S., 800-526-6566; www.mandarinoriental.com. *Cost:* from $460 (off-peak), from $725 (peak).

Gardens and Culture on Barcelona's Green Crown

Parc de Montjuïc

Barcelona, Catalonia, Spain

Modern *barceloneses* take their ease where ancient Romans once held their ceremonies—in a park high atop the gentle hill of Montjuïc that rises behind the city. The most exciting way to get there is to soar from the port on the aerial tram, the Transbordador Aeri. You'll arrive amid the cactus gardens, where some species stand more than 20 feet tall. Walk on toward the sleek Fundació Joan Miró and the landscape shifts to rolling greenery and formal gardens. Several hundred paintings and sculptures by the 20th-century Catalan surrealist are arrayed throughout minimalist galleries, perfectly illuminated by indirect skylights; the views of Barcelona from the sculpture-dotted roof deck are unsurpassed. Nearby is the 1929 replica of a Greek theater, Teatre Grec de Montjuïc, which hosts concerts and dance performances all year but comes into its own as the main stage of the summertime Festival Grec.

Fundació Joan Miró holds over 14,000 of the artist's works, including Lovers Playing with Almond Blossom *(above).*

Catalans view their region as a distinct country, and the park's Museu Nacional d'Art de Catalunya

(MNAC) would do any nation proud. Housed in the imposing Palau Nacional (National Palace), the museum is home to the world's finest treasure trove of Romanesque and Gothic paintings, sculpture, and metalwork. The masterful altarpieces, frescoes, and polychrome icons, mostly salvaged from Catalan churches and monasteries, are displayed as they were originally installed in country churches. They chronicle the evolution of Romanesque style from its crude beginnings to its zenith between the 11th and 13th centuries. A highlight is the Pantocrator from the main apse of the Iglesia de San Clemente de Taüll, dating from 1123. Built for the 1929 World's Fair and reopened in 1995 after a major renovation, the Renaissance-Baroque–style Palau Nacional is often called the Prado of Romanesque art. At the foot of the steps to the palace, enjoy the spectacle of the Font (fountain) Màgica, where great shoots of water are floodlit at night and choreographed to popular music.

Fundació Joan Miró: Tel 34/934-439470; www.fundaciomiro-bcn.com. **Teatre Grec de Montjuïc:** Tel 34/934-132400. **MNAC:** Tel 34/936-220360; www.mnac.es. **Best time:** late Jul for Festival Grec.

Surreal Art and Cuisine on the Wild Coast

Costa Brava

Catalonia, Spain

Cadaqués, the northernmost resort on the Catalan coast, reachable only by sea or a precipitous switchback road, is often called the world's most painted village. Picasso, Utrillo, Miró, Max Ernst, Man Ray, and filmmaker Luis Buñuel all took inspiration from its simplicity, but Salvador Dalí, who had a studio (now a museum) in adjoining Portlligat for many decades, is the most enduring presence.

A quiet point in the swirling world of the madcap coast, the whitewashed village wraps around a rocky harbor at the eastern tip of the Empordà peninsula. Little has changed since Dalí played chess with Marcel Duchamp at Bar Meliton in the 1920s. The indolent pace continues as bars and cafés fill after siesta and stay open till dawn. The lack of sandy beaches sends the hedonists elsewhere, making Cadaqués a town of artists and fishermen. Outdoor portside restaurants serve simple dinners of grilled sardines and dorado, and no-frills hangouts like Casa Anita (one of Dalí's favorites) serve locally caught seafood to a new generation of artists.

Art and sublime food also collude in Dalí's nearby hometown of Figueres. Late in life, he transformed a 19th-century theater (where his first exhibition was shown in 1919) into an installation work, the Teatre-Museu Dalí. From the plastic store mannequins to the pile of rubber tires out front, the entire display is as phantasmagoric as any of the artist's "landscapes." Dalí called it "a gigantic surrealist object in which everything is coherent, nothing is beyond my understanding." His private art collection resides here—and he is buried beneath the central dome.

At the Restaurant Empordà (in a hotel of the same name), long acclaimed for its Catalan game and seafood specialties, patrons come less for the Dalí sketches than for the artistry of chef Jaume Subirós. Indeed, chefs are the new artists of the Costa Brava, inspired in part by local son and chef extraordinaire Ferran

Adriá's wildly experimental cuisine at El Bulli outside the town of Roses. Closed for transformation, El Bulli is scheduled to re-open as a think tank for creative cuisine and gastronomy in 2014, and Adriá plans to serve a limited number of diners.

In the meantime, travelers in search of culinary genius drive farther south along the coast—pausing for the medieval marvels of San Feliu de Guixols and the castle-topped headlands of Tossa del Mar. South of Blanes and close to Barcelona, Carme Ruscalleda marries Catalan traditions with Adriá-like inspiration at a neighboring gastro-destination, the Restaurante Sant Pau, in Sant Pol de Mar.

Where: 107 miles/172 km north of Barcelona. **Visitor info:** www.costabrava.org. **Portlligat Casa-Museu Salvador Dalí:** Tel 34/972-251015; www.salvador-dali.org. **Casa Anita:** Tel 34/972-258471. *Cost:* dinner $45. **Teatre-Museu Dalí:** Tel 34/972-677505; www.salvador-dali.org. **Empordà:** Tel 34/972-500562; www.hotelemporda.com. *Cost:* from $90; prix fixe dinner $90. **Restaurante Sant Pau:** Tel 34/937-600662; www.ruscalleda.com. *Cost:* prix fixe dinner $190.

City of Conquerors and Warriors

Cáceres

Extremadura, Spain

Judging from its architecture, Cáceres must have been the most embattled city in western Spain. When the Christian kings of northern Spain beat the Moorish armies in 1212, Alfonso VIII of Castile presented parcels of land in Cáceres to his knights. Often building around the original Arab towers (30 are still standing), the warriors constructed fortified houses and launched a virtual arms race among Castilian clans. The noble toughs of Cáceres proved especially useful to the Spanish crown in the conquest of the New World, and plunder from Mexico and Peru allowed many to convert their medieval fortresses into Renaissance palaces—making Cáceres unique in Spain for the variety of monumental architecture it squeezed into a medieval street plan. Today, Spanish film crews regularly use the city as a backdrop in historical films, which are made all the more atmospheric by the hundreds of storks that return regularly to nest on the towers and ramparts between February and August.

The crenellated Bujaco tower is the most famous of Cáceres's 30 towers dating to the Moorish era.

Offering big-hotel service for down-to-earth prices, the Casa Don Fernando is perfectly situated on the central Plaza Mayor. But the Atrio hotel has stolen the spotlight with its 14 sleek, luxurious rooms set in the medieval shell of two adjoining buildings, also in the heart of the historic district. Whether or not you sleep here, you'll want to dine at its acclaimed restaurant. Well-known chef Toño Perez's interpretation of the traditional

Extremaduran cuisine verges on modern alchemy, and it's complemented by an exceptional wine cellar. The local cooking owes a lot to New World peppers, which were naturalized here and provide the famous smoked paprika that's prized all over Spain. A good place to try those traditional dishes is at the Restaurante Pizarro, on the historic main plaza in the nearby town of Trujillo, the birthplace of Francisco Pizarro, conqueror of Peru and the Incas. Before you dine, head up the hill to see the house where he spent much of his childhood.

WHERE: 157 miles/253 km east of Lisbon. **HOTEL CASA DON FERNANDO:** Tel 34/927-214279; www.casadonfernando.com. *Cost:* from $100 (off-peak), from $150 (peak). **HOTEL AND RESTAURANTE ATRIO:** Tel 34/927-242928; in the U.S., 800-735-2478; www.restauranteatrio.com. *Cost:* from $350; dinner $130. **RESTAURANTE PIZARRO:** Tel 34/927-320255. *Cost:* dinner $40. **BEST TIMES:** early May for Cáceres stork festival and World of Music, Arts and Dance (WOMAD) Festival; weekend nearest May 1 for National Cheese Festival in Trujillo.

The Road to Heaven

El Camino de Santiago and Santiago de Compostela

Galicia, Spain

It's a long walk to Santiago de Compostela on the Camino de Santiago (Way of St. James), but the Christian faithful have made the pilgrimage since the bones of St. James the Apostle were unearthed here in the 9th century, spreading the cultural rebirth of Europe. The apparition of St. James was said to aid Christian armies in battles with the Moors, so Spaniards adopted Santiago Matamoros (aka St. James, the Moor-slayer) as their patron saint.

Hikers travel the trail across the Castilian plateau.

Modern hikers follow in the footsteps of El Cid, Louis VII of France, and St. Francis of Assisi to this pilgrimage destination that's on a par with Rome and Jerusalem. Whether their motives are spiritual or not, the experience of the walk lingers. Most travelers follow a variant of the French Route, which begins in the Basque village of Roncesvalles, in the Pyrenees at the French-Spanish border, and trek 500 miles through the Rioja wine country (see p. 252) and the former kingdoms of northern Spain. Hostels, inns, and restaurants along the entire stretch cater to the pilgrims. Those who lack time or stamina for the 4-plus-week journey by foot walk only the final 62 miles, through rugged but green inland Galicia. At Monte de Gozo, 2 miles from Santiago de Compostela, tired but elated travelers typically get their first glimpse of the twin towers of Santiago's cathedral.

Construction of the majestic Cathedral of Santiago de Compostela began in 1078, on the site of a 9th-century basilica destroyed by the

Moors, and Maestro Mateo's original designs rank among Europe's finest Romanesque art. The cathedral's elaborate, two-towered Baroque façade, added in the 18th century, protects the now restored original Porta de Gloria from weathering. The impact of the cavernous interior—as simple as the façade is ornate—is heightened by the golden-cloaked, bejeweled statue of St. James above the main altar, embraced by arriving pilgrims.

The cathedral shares the vast Plaza del Obradoiro ("work of gold") with the Hotel Reyes Católicos (Catholic Kings), built by King Ferdinand and Queen Isabel in 1499 as a hospice for pilgrims. Now one of the most renowned paradors in Spain, it has rooms overlooking the square and the cathedral and many more overlooking four courtyard cloisters. Only a short walk away, the Palacio del Carmen has transformed an 18th-century convent into comfortable if less majestic lodging.

WHERE: Santiago de Compostela is 375 miles/603 km northwest of Madrid. The most popular route of the Camino de Santiago starts in Roncesvalle and runs 500 miles/800 km across the northern regions of Spain, from east to west. **HOW:** U.S.-based Saranjan, Inc., offers 1- to 2-week tours by minibus, on foot, or on bicycle. Tel 800-858-9594 or 206-720-0623; www.saranjan.com. *Cost:* 9-day tours from $3,300; all-inclusive. Originate in León. **HOTEL REYES CATÓLICOS:** Tel 34/981-582200; www.parador.es; in the U.S., Marketing Ahead, 800-223-1356; www.marketingahead.com. *Cost:* from $200 (off-peak), from $390 (peak). **PALACIO DEL CARMEN:** Tel 34/981-552444; www.palaciodelcarmen.com. *Cost:* from $145 (off-peak), from $250 (peak). **BEST TIMES:** late Feb or early Mar for Antroido (carnival); last 2 weeks of Jul for succession of fiestas; Jul 25 for feast day of Santiago, celebrated with fireworks, music, and processions.

"It has none of the look that you expect of Spain. . . . Yet when you get to know it, it is the most Spanish of all cities, the best to live in, the finest people, month in, month out the finest climate."
—*ERNEST HEMINGWAY*

MADRID

Spain

An elegantly formal, even decorous city by day, Madrid is transformed after dark into one of Europe's liveliest capitals. Your first thought, and your parting one, may be that no one ever sleeps in this town—just visit any neighborhood *bar-restaurante* or *taberna* around midnight for a vibrant confirmation. Madrid lets down its guard and shows its private face in the *madrugada*—the hours between midnight and cock's crow.

TOP ATTRACTIONS

CENTRO DE ARTE REINA SOFÍA—Home of Picasso's *Guernica*, Spain's modern and contemporary arts museum is just a few blocks from the Prado, in an 18th-century former hospital building and a Post-Modern minimalist extension designed by Jean Nouvel. Its collection includes works by Spanish artists such as Miró, Dalí, Juan Gris, and Antoni Tàpies, as well as Alexander

Calder, Man Ray, and Jean Dubuffet, and it deconstructs the *isms* of the 20th century with fascinating juxtapositions. Enjoy contemporary bar fare at fashionable Café Arola. **INFO:** Tel 34/91-774-1000; www.museoreinasofia.es.

FLAMENCO—Flamenco was born in Andalusia, but it came out of the shadows and onto the main stage in Madrid in the 1980s. Although it caters mostly to tourists, Corral de la Morería is drenched in tradition, and every night is filled with foot-stomping passion. Hardcore aficionados prefer the more casual environs and contemporary artists of Casa Patas. **CORRAL DE LA MORERÍA:** Tel 34/91-365-8446; www.corraldelamoreria.com. **CASA PATAS:** Tel 34/91-369-0496; www.casapatas.com.

MUSEO SOROLLA—Avoid the Prado crowds and visit the restored, elegant 1910–11 home of artist Joaquín Sorolla, Spain's foremost painter of light. It maintains a lived-in feel and showcases portraits of aristocrats and paintings of Spain's common folk on the sun-drenched coast of his native Valencia. **INFO:** Tel 34/91-310-1584; museosorolla.mcu.es.

PALACIO REAL—Begun in 1738 on the site of the old Moorish Alcázar fortress, the Palacio Real was the royal residence from 1764 until King Alfonso XIII abdicated the throne in 1931. Today it functions as the official residence of King Juan Carlos I and his wife, Queen Sofía, though they live in the Palacio de la Zarzuela. State business takes up much of the palace, but rooms once occupied by Alfonso and his family are open to the public, as are the Throne Room, the Reception Room, the Royal Pharmacy, the Painting Gallery (with works by Caravaggio, Velázquez, and Goya), and the Royal Armory. **INFO:** Tel 34/91-454-8700; www.patrimonionacional.es.

THE PRADO—The keystone of the "Golden Triangle of Museums" (with Reina Sofía and Thyssen-Bornemisza), the Prado is a treasure-house that could keep Madrid on the cultural map all by itself. The museum is primarily known for its collection of more than 8,600 paintings by El Greco, Goya, Murillo, Rubens, Titian, Bosch, Raphael, Botticelli, Fra Angelico, and many others. Eighty percent of Velázquez's paintings are here, including his *Las Meninas,* as are the proto-Surrealist "Dark Paintings" of Goya. Rafael Moneo's extension behind the original building cleverly encapsulates the Jerónimos monastery cloister within a glass cube. **INFO:** Tel 34/91-330-2800; www.museodelprado.es.

At the Prado, viewers admire the paintings of Francisco Goya, the quintessential Spanish Romantic master.

THE TAPAS CRAWL—Embrace the Madrileño style and wander from watering hole to watering hole, nibbling as you go, leading up to dinner around 11:00 P.M. (or simply replacing it). Grazing possibilities are endless, from *albondigas* (meatballs) to *zamburiñas* (small scallops). The streets around Plaza Santa Ana remain the premier tapas district for locals: Don't leave without trying smoked trout on toast at La Trucha. Likewise, there's always a lively scene of locals and tourists on Cava Baja (south of Plaza Mayor), where the best food is the Basque fare (especially grilled octopus) at Taberna Txakoli, and the best sherry-bar atmosphere is at Taberna Alamendro. From the neighborhood around Ópera, work your way uphill toward Plaza Mayor after starting at the bar of Taberna del Alabardero. In

Chueca, begin in the century-old, lavishly tiled vermouth bar Antigua Casa Ángel Sierra before wandering to your next stop.

THYSSEN-BORNEMISZA MUSEUM—Two of the most extraordinary private art collections amassed in the 20th century—both assembled by Baron Hans Heinrich Thyssen-Bornemisza of Switzerland and his Spanish-born fifth wife, Carmen Cervera—fill artistic gaps in the Prado and Reina Sofía with superb Italian and German 13th-century Gothic art through 19th-century Impressionists (notably Monet) and 20th-century works of American Abstract Expressionists. **INFO:** Tel 34/91-369-0151; www.museothyssen.org.

Juan Gómez de Mora laid out the Plaza Mayor in 1619, and it continues to be an important hub of urban life.

THE PLAZA MAYOR—The huge cobblestone square, completed in 1619 in the Baroque style, has seen its share of bullfights, hangings, riots, wild carnivals, and the nasty doings of the Inquisition. Today it's the heartbeat of Viejo (Old) Madrid, and it's the gateway between the Centro and La Latina neighborhoods. Its nine arched exits lead into streets crowded with *tabernas* and tapas bars. For a wide variety of tapas, a full meal, or prepared food to go, duck into the historic and recently revitalized Mercado San Miguel, just outside the plaza's west entrance.

OTHER MUST-DOS

BULLFIGHTS AT LA PLAZA DE LAS VENTAS—Bullfighting is a controversial sport (Queen Sofía detests it), but it is an inextricable part of Spanish history, culture, and national identity. During the March to October season, aficionados and the merely curious can experience a Sunday-afternoon corrida at the extremely beautiful Plaza de las Ventas. **INFO:** Tel 34/91-356-2200; www.las-ventas.com.

MONASTERIO DE LAS DESCALZAS REALES—This Franciscan convent was founded by the sister of King Felipe II in 1559. For the next 250 years, it was the retreat of choice for noblewomen taking the veil, many of whom brought their family riches (and staff) with them. The building is replete with great art, such as the Rubens tapestries that warmed a former dormitory. **INFO:** Tel 34/91-454-8700; www.patrimonionacional.es.

REAL ACADEMIA DE BELLAS ARTES DE SAN FERNANDO—Goya's presence is still palpable in the Museum of the Royal Academy of Fine Arts. As director, he designed the lower galleries to illustrate his theory that all Spanish painting climaxes with . . . Goya. His programmatic itinerary, the highlight of the museum, concludes with 13 of his paintings and his last color-smeared palette under glass. **INFO:** Tel 34/91-524-0864; rabasf.insde.es.

RETIRO PARK—A stroll through Retiro Park is a Sunday morning ritual for many a *madrileño* family. Laid out in the 1630s and once reserved for royals and their guests, the 300-acre park is full of fountains and statues, plus there's a lake (with rowboats to rent) and elegant 19th-century exhibition halls. The luxurious Palacio del Retiro hotel stands just across from the park, in an early 20th-century landmark building; about half its 50 rooms have park views. **PALACIO DEL RETIRO:** Tel 34/91-523-7460; www.marriot.com. *Cost:* from $360 (off-peak), from $475 (peak).

EL RASTRO FLEA MARKET—Come early or you'll miss the bargains at this famous, sprawling, 5-century-old flea market (at Plaza Cascorro and Ribera de Curtidores), teeming with gawkers and hawkers selling everything imaginable. Everyone eventually winds up at the market's most famous bar, Los Caracoles, for a *copa* (a "glassful") and the specialty of spicey stewed snails.

Where to Stay

Hotel Ópera—Wedged between the Teatro Real and the gardens of the Palacio Real, this modern hotel has a plain façade but wins points for rooms with sleek style and fine appointments. Some upper-level rooms have slanted ceilings with large skylights; the best have glassed-in Jacuzzis and spacious outdoor terraces with great city views. **Info:** Tel 34/91-541-2800; www.hotelopera.com. *Cost:* from $150.

Ritz Hotel and Palace Madrid—Embarrassed by the lack of proper accommodations for guests at his 1906 wedding, King Alfonso XIII commissioned these two Belle Époque gems where guests are still treated like royalty. The Ritz, which opened in 1919 and was built under the supervision of legendary hotelier César Ritz, is set in beautiful gardens on the Paseo del Prado. Its acclaimed Goya Restaurant features classic cuisine in ceremoniously formal surroundings. Three times larger, the 468-room Palace, which opened in 1912, is only a block from the Prado. Its grand public spaces include a stunning stained-glass dome above the hotel's main restaurant, La Rotunda, a Madrid favorite for Sunday brunch. **Ritz Hotel:** Tel 34/91-701-6767; in the U.S., 800-237-1236; www.ritzmadrid.com. *Cost:* from $335 (off-peak), from $450 (peak); dinner at Goya Restaurant $100. **Westin Palace Madrid:** Tel 34/91-360-8000; in the U.S., 888-625-5144; www.westinpalacemadrid.com. *Cost:* from $300 (off-peak), from $390 (peak); dinner at La Rotunda $65, brunch $110.

Room Mate Alicia—The international Room Mate chain specializes in chic budget boutique hotels, and the Alicia, located at a corner of the lively Plaza Santa Ana, is one of four in Madrid (the others are named Mario, Oscar, and Laura). Ask for the highest floor available if you're inclined to retire early. Breakfast is served until noon, a highlight if you've been up all night enjoying the city. **Info:** Tel 34/91-389-6095; www.room-matehotels.com. *Cost:* from $145.

Santo Mauro—This exquisite 50-room hotel in a leafy neighborhood near the Sorolla Museum (see p. 267) was built in the 19th century as a ducal palace. With pretty gardens and an indoor pool, it is the hotel of choice for celebrities who treasure their privacy. **Info:** Tel 34/91-319-6900; www.marriot.com. *Cost:* from $330 (off-peak), from $475 (peak).

Hotel Urban—The first 21st-century hotel built in central Madrid, the Urban makes a powerful Post-Modern design statement with its massive glass curtain wall facing the busy avenue east of Puerta del Sol. Light floods the rooms, which are decorated with dense earth-toned fabrics, wood paneling, and padded leather furniture. Location is ideal for touring the three main museums or strolling up to Plaza Santa Ana for tapas. **Info:** Tel 34/91-787-7770; www.derbyhotels.com. *Cost:* from $250.

Madrid is one of Spain's premier tapas grounds, with dozens of bars serving everything from bite-size pinchos *to half-meal* raciones.

Eating & Drinking

Café Gijón—Amid the busy rush of Madrid, Café Gijón oozes Belle Époque decorum and seems little changed since it opened in 1888, although the literary crowd left when Franco came to power. The bar is a stand-up affair, while the dining room is reserved for meals, and the summer outdoor patio is a perfect stop for afternoon tea. **Info:** Tel 34/91-521-5425; www.cafegijon.com. *Cost:* tea $20.

Casa Botín—Possibly Spain's oldest restaurant, this folkloric tavern in the shadow of Plaza Mayor has been an obligatory stop for passing luminaries since it opened in 1725. It looks like a tourist trap—and it is—but discerning locals still love it for its atmosphere and its *cochinillo asado* (roast suckling pig). If Botín is full, try the ever-reliable Casa Lucio nearby. **Info:** Tel 34/91-366-4217; www.botin.es. *Cost:* $60. **Casa Lucio:** Tel 34/91-365-3252; www.casalucio.es. *Cost:* dinner $55.

Chocolatería San Ginés—Just off Puerta del Sol, this tiny beloved institution fuels the *madrileño* addiction to hot chocolate and sugar-dusted churros (fried doughnut sticks) at all times of day and night (except briefly between 6:00 and 9:00 a.m.). **Info:** Tel 34/91-365-6546.

El Ñeru—Push through the tapas crowd at street level just east of Plaza Mayor to go into the old-fashioned Asturian dining room down a flight of stairs. The *merluza* (hake) dishes are always delicious, especially braised in Asturian cider. On a cold night, consider a *fabada*—a stew of white beans, sausage, and ham. **Info:** Tel 34/91-541-1140; www.restauranteelneru.com. *Cost:* dinner $40.

Pedro Larumbe—This award-winning chef's restaurant includes one of the city's most interesting venues for fine dining. The library and the main restaurant are studies in old-world elegance, but the rooftop terrace (summer only) sits high above the elegant Salamanca district, eye to eye with great architectural details. Larumbe reinvents the classics with panache with dishes like roasted hake topped with shaved black truffle, or a napoleon of layered foie gras and caramelized mango. **Info:** Tel 34/91-575-1112; www.larumbe.com. *Cost:* dinner $70.

Sergi Arola Gastro—Located near the Museo Sorolla (see p. 267), the flagship of rocker-turned-star-chef Sergi Arola is Madrid's ultimate destination for foodies from around the globe. Arola deftly combines just a few intense flavors per dish, cooking with great imagination but never over-the-top. The contemporary minimalist décor lets the artistically prepared plates take center stage. There's a choice of three menus at dinner with no à la carte ordering. **Info:** Tel 34/91-310-2169; www.sergiarola.es. *Cost:* dinner $150.

Day Trips

Toledo—Let the painter El Greco guide you through his adopted hometown, an ancient treasure house of Moorish, Jewish, and Christian history. About 30 of his paintings hang in the sacristy of the 13th-century cathedral, and his most famous work, *The Burial of Count Orgaz,* is mounted in the entry to nearby Iglesia (Church) de Santo Tomé. The Museo de Santa Cruz, housed in a magnificent 16th-century building, features a dozen El Grecos, and you can stand close enough to see the brushwork. Recharge at Toledo's best-known restaurant, Hostal del Cardenal, housed in an elegant 18th-century cardinal's palace. Visit in June to catch the celebration of Corpus Christi, when a 500-pound gold reliquary made in 1595 from New World gold is paraded through the streets. **Where:** 43 miles/69 km south of Madrid. Tel 34/92-522-0862; www.hostaldelcardenal.com. *Cost:* dinner $50.

Segovia—Segovia is bookended by its two main attractions: the soaring arches of the Roman Aqueduct and its Alcázar Palace, rebuilt in the 19th century as a fantasy version of a medieval castle (it's said to have inspired the castle in Disney's *Snow White*). Gastronomes come to Segovia to eat *cochinillo asado* (roast suckling pig) at Mesón de Cándido, possibly the best in Spain. It is rivaled only by the *cordero lechero asado* (roast baby lamb), another regional delicacy.

Where: 48 miles/68 km northwest of Madrid. Tel 34/92-142-5911; www.mesondecandido.es. *Cost:* dinner $55.

Architecture, Paella, and Big Bangs

Valencia

Spain

With architecture that rivals Bilbao's (see p. 252), dining that rivals Barcelona's (see p. 260), and a penchant for Europe's most extreme celebrations, Valencia ranks among the world's most dynamic small cities.

You quickly grasp Valencia's wit at L'Hemisfèric, the 1995 planetarium building of the 86-acre City of Arts and Sciences, where native son Santiago Calatrava constructed the glass-and-metal shell of the building to open and close like the blinking of an eyelid. Set into a dry riverbed, the complex's monumentally scaled buildings have biomorphic forms: the fish-shaped performance halls of the 2005 Palace of Arts, the underwater coral-reef organization of the 2002 L'Oceanogràfic Aquarium, even the rib-cage entrance walkway and gardens of the 1995 L'Umbracle. So striking are the pools, walkways, and abstract views of shapes and forms that you could easily spend hours walking around without ever entering a building.

Before there was the vision of Valencia, there was the taste. The Mercado Central is a temple of food in a vast 1928 *modernista* building. Valencia is the birthplace of paella—not surprising, since it is also where rice was first cultivated in Spain in the 8th century. If you prefer the seafood paella served in the U.S., order *arroces con mariscos*; purists will prefer the *paella valenciana*, filled with fresh vegetables, rabbit, and chicken and dotted with snails. Try it at informal La Pepica, still as good as when Ernest Hemingway ate here in the 1950s. For a cutting-edge contemporary take on classic Valencian dishes, visit Ca' Sento, where El Bulli (see p. 264) alumnus Raúl Aleixandre has revolutionized his parents' seafood restaurant with deftly contemporary touches.

Valencia becomes a madhouse during Las Fallas, which takes place on the days leading up to the feast of St. Joseph (March 19), as huge statues and scenes are erected in every square in the city, long processions of people in 18th-century costumes bring flowers to a six-story-high effigy of the Virgin Mary, and every child and childlike adult sets off endless piles of firecrackers and Roman candles. On March 19, the *ninots* (the huge figures), constructed of colored papier-mâché over elaborate wooden frames—some 20 feet tall—are set afire in a pyromaniac's equivalent of Mardi Gras.

Where: 188 miles/302 km east of Madrid. **City of Arts and Sciences:** Tel 34/902-100031; www.cac.es. **Mercado Central:** Tel 34/963-829101; www.mercadocentralvalencia.es. **La Pepica:** Tel 34/963-710366. *Cost:* dinner $35. **Ca' Sento:** Tel 34/963-301775. *Cost:* dinner $50. **Where to stay:** The luxurious beachfront Hotel Santos Las Arenas, has a seaside spa. Tel 34/963-120600; www.hotel-lasarenas.com. *Cost:* from $190 (off-peak), from $270 (peak). **Best times:** week leading up to Mar 19 for parades and fireworks of Las Fallas; 3rd week of Jul for Festival Eclèctic, when free outdoor performances fill the City of Arts and Sciences.

Riding the Rails

The Alps' Most Scenic Train Trips

Switzerland

The Swiss have taken train travel to new heights. Over the past century, Swiss engineering expertise has created an elaborate system of narrow passes, viaducts, and tunnels that make even the most dramatic Alpine scenery accessible to all. You can ride the rails between Zermatt and St. Moritz on the ever-popular Glacier Express, touted as the slowest express train in the world (it averages 25 miles an hour). This red little-engine-that-could passes through the heart of the Swiss Alps and offers an up-close look at riveting scenery on its roller-coaster journey. It passes over 291 bridges, many trestled high above dramatic gorges, through 91 tunnels, and crosses the Oberalp Pass at 6,706 feet—the 7.5-hour, 180-mile trip's highest point.

The 213-foot-high Landwasser Viaduct, stretching nearly 500 feet, is a highlight of any trip on the Glacier Express.

Quintessentially Swiss, chocolate and cheese are both served onboard the Chocolate Train, a day-long journey that runs in summer and fall. Climb aboard in Montreux (see p. 282), overlooking Lake Geneva on the Swiss Riviera, for the nearly 10-hour roundtrip journey to Broc. As you roll northeast in a Belle Époque Pullman car, feast your eyes on the Lavaux vineyards, especially vibrant just before October's harvest. In medieval, car-free Gruyère, you can visit the enchanting turreted castle and tuck into fondue at the cheese dairy before continuing on to Broc's world-famous Cailler-Nestlé chocolate factory for a tour and a sampling of the 65 tons of chocolate produced on-site each day.

Completed in 1910, the Bernina line is the highest railway crossing in the Alps. From St. Moritz to the charming northern Italian town of Tirano, the vertigo-inducing Bernina Express goes past the Morteratsch Glacier, with its jaw-dropping views and the highest peak in the Eastern Alps, the Piz Bernina (13,284 feet), before arriving in Italy on a famous corkscrew viaduct. The 90-mile, 4-hour trip reaches an apex of 7,391 feet then descends 5,905 feet before coming to the end of the train line in Tirano. In summer, you can continue by bus along the banks of Lake Como to Lugano (see p. 279).

How: Book online at www.raileurope.com or locally upon your arrival at any Swiss rail station. In the U.S., contact Rail Europe, tel 800-622-8600 or 914-682-2999; in Canada, tel 800-361-7245. **Glacier Express:** between St. Moritz and Zermatt. *Cost:* one-way $195. **Swiss Chocolate Train:** between Montreux and Broc. *Cost:* one-way $115, first class only. *When:* May–Oct. **Bernina Express:** between St. Moritz (via Tirano, Italy) and Lugano. *Cost:* one-way $35. **Best times:** May–Jun and Sep–Oct for most colorful scenery from the Chocolate Train; Jun for ideal weather for the Bernina Express; Sep–Oct for lighter crowds on the Glacier Express.

Crossroads of Creativity

Basel: Art City

Switzerland

On the banks of the Rhine, where the Swiss, French, and German borders meet, Basel shines as a world-class capital of art. Among its 30-plus museums are the impressive Kunstmuseum of fine art, the Museum Tinguely with its playful mechanized sculptures, and the Fondation Beyeler's superb 20th-century art collection in a Renzo Piano–designed building.

Every June, this pocket-size city hosts Art Basel, the world's leading international art show for modern and contemporary works. Bringing together painting and drawing, sculptures, installations, photography, videos, and multimedia works, nearly 300 galleries display works by more than 2,500 artists—from the great masters of modern art to the latest emerging stars. Beyond the main event, culture vultures canvas the town for smaller exhibitions, film screenings, concerts, and parties during this art-rich week. Book your hotel well in advance or consider finding lodging an hour away by train in Zürich, whose own cultural delights make the option an appealing one (see p. 283).

Art lovers are naturally drawn to Der Teufelhof Basel, whose minimalist guest rooms (nine in the Art Hotel, 24 in the adjoining Gallery Hotel) are regularly redecorated by different Swiss artists, and exhibitions feature contemporary artists in the wine cellar and medieval finds in the archaeological cellar. The gracious, riverside Hotel Krafft has the medieval Old Town at its doorstep and 45 spacious and simply furnished rooms, many with river views.

Epicureans have long revered Restaurant Stucki Bruderholz, whose erstwhile master chef, Hans Stucki, was one of Switzerland's culinary giants until his premature death in

The great 20th-century Swiss artist Jean Tinguely's kinetic sculptures are on permanent display at the museum bearing his name.

1998. Today, the trailblazing restaurant continues to hit new heights under chef/owner Tanja Grandits—a rising star in the culinary world. The décor, mood, and menu have lightened up, but the culinary style remains assertive: Grandits applies a hint of the exotic to regional ingredients, earning her food the label "Filigree Art." For a great simple meal—fondue, sliced veal with *rösti* (hash browns)—the Löwenzorn's snug, wood-paneled rooms and airy courtyard feel part bistro and part beer hall, and all wonderfully convivial.

Where: 53 miles/86 km northwest of Zürich. **Art Basel:** Tel 41/58-200-2020; www.artbasel.com. *Cost:* tickets $45–$100. *When:* mid-Jun. **Der Teufelhof Basel:** Tel 41/61-261-1010; www.teufelhof.com. *Cost:* from $265 (off-peak), from $550 (peak); dinner $70. **Hotel Krafft:** Tel 41/61-690-9130; www.krafftbasel.ch. Cost: from $300 (off-peak), from $430 (peak). **Restaurant Stucki Bruderholz:** Tel 41/61-361-8222;

www.stuckibasel.ch. *Cost:* dinner $130. **Löwenzorn:** Tel 41/61-261-4213; www.loewenzorn.ch. *Cost:* dinner $55. **Best times:** late Feb or early Mar for Fasnacht carnival-like festival (begins Mon after Ash Wednesday); mid-Jun for Art Basel.

Magnificent Mountain Playground

Gstaad

Bernese Oberland, Switzerland

At the confluence of four Alpine valleys and dubbed the Aspen of the Bernese Oberland, Gstaad reigns as one of the world's best winter playgrounds. With its 155 miles of downhill runs, 60 miles of cross-country trails, and a host of year-round activities, this is where royalty and the world's celebs ski, yet an unspoiled and unpretentious air prevails.

Gstaad can be enjoyed on skis and snowshoes.

Gstaad is so low-key and quiet you might even find it a tad boring, unless you're staying at the Gstaad Palace Hotel, one of the most sought-after hideaways in Europe. Towering over tiny Gstaad like a neomedieval castle, this 104-room hotel, built in 1913, bills itself as Switzerland's largest family pension (meals are included), but don't let the classic but cozy rooms fool you: This hotel is the epicenter of the local social scene. The pace is more subdued at the family-owned Hotel Alphorn, a traditional chalet that offers 30 Alpine-style guest rooms with balconies overlooking the slopes. For local wintertime *gemütlichkeit* (homeyness) and a view you'll never forget, take the cable car to the mountaintop terraced Berghaus Eggli restaurant or gravitate to the fireside charm and the best fondue in the village, at Saagi Stübli, the cozy eatery of the Hotel Gstaaderhof.

Come January, the nearby village of Château d'Oex takes on a carnival ambience during the annual Winter Alpine Balloon Festival, when as many as 80 colorful balloons from more than 18 countries fly over the rugged mountain peaks, drifting above the snow-covered valleys. Summertime flights take in the softer rolling hills of the Emmental valley, over picture-perfect farmland and flower-decked rural wooden chalets.

Where: 42 miles/67 km southwest of Interlaken. **Gstaad Palace Hotel:** Tel 41/33-748-5000; www.palace.ch. *Cost:* from $695 (off-peak), from $775 (peak), inclusive. *When:* closed mid-Sep–mid-Dec, Apr–mid-Jun. **Hotel Alphorn:** Tel 41/33-748-4545; www.gstaad-alphorn.ch. *Cost:* from $185 (off-peak), from $245 (peak). **Berghaus Eggli:** Tel 41/33-748-9612. *Cost:* dinner $38. **Saagi Stübli:** Tel 41/33-748-6363; www.gstaaderhof.ch. *Cost:* dinner $40. **How:** Contact the U.S.-based Bombard Society for Balloon Festival and nonfestival trips, tel 800-862-8537 or 561-837-6610; www.bombardsociety.com. *Cost:* 8-night festival trip $17,988, land only, all-inclusive. Originates in Geneva. *When:* mid-Jan. **Best times:** Jan–mid-Mar for skiing; mid-Jul–early Sep for Gstaad's annual Musiksommer, founded by Yehudi Menuhin.

Walking on Top of the World

High-Country Hiking

Bernese Oberland, Switzerland

Early-19th-century visitors put Switzerland on the map as a summer destination prescribed for its invigorating and bracing Alpine air. The Bernese Oberland, or Highlands, with its 1,553 miles of trails, is Switzerland's most popular choice for hiking, thanks to idyllic mountain villages, dramatic peaks, and deep, verdant valleys, offering plenty to rejuvenate both body and soul.

The steep-sided ravines of charming Kandersteg are a rambler's paradise. Head for the cable car that lifts walkers to the historic Gemmi Pass, or to Lake Oeschinen, one of Switzerland's most striking natural wonders. Color-coded signposts throughout town point hikers on their way, indicating the time needed round-trip. The handsome Royal Park Hotel, Kandersteg's finest lodging, has been in the same family since 1893. Its popular restaurant and spa await weary hikers at the end of the day.

Facing the dramatic Jungfrau massif from its perch on a ledge above the Lauterbrunnen Valley, Mürren is the highest year-round inhabited village in the canton and is accessible only by cog railway or cable car. Even if you don't stay at the homey Hotel Bellevue, whose 17 balconied rooms have breathtaking views, stop in for hearty Swiss fare by the fireplace in its cozy Jägerstübli restaurant. Outside, choose from hundreds of hiking trails or ride the cable car to the Schilthorn's 9,742-foot summit, Piz Gloria; enjoy the panorama of some 200 peaks from the summit's revolving restaurant, made world famous by the 1969 James Bond thriller *On Her Majesty's Secret Service.* Descend by cable car one stop and exit at Birg to take a high-country hike, serenaded by cowbells and waterfalls, down to the storybook-quaint village Gimmelwald.

For staggering mountain scenery and views of the Mönch and Jungfrau peaks and 14-mile-wide Aletsch Glacier, put your boots up and ride the rails to the 11,400-foot Jungfraujoch terminus, the world's highest railroad station. Visit the chilled depths of the famed Eispalast (Ice Palace), then vary your return trip by taking the route to the picturesque mountain town of Grindelwald, dramatically set beneath the towering Eiger peak and especially favored for high-terrain hiking. Top off your adventure in Interlaken, at the refined

Rising more than 13,000 feet, Mönch (monk) Mountain forms part of the great north wall of the Bernese Oberland.

Victoria-Jungfrau Grand Hotel & Spa, a faultless monument to luxury built in 1865.

Where: Kandersteg is 28 miles/45 km southwest of Interlaken; Mürren is 9 miles/31 km south of Interlaken; Interlaken is 90 miles/145 km southwest of Zürich. **Visitor info:** Kandersteg: www.kandersteg.ch. Mürren: www.muerren.ch. Interlaken: www.interlaken tourism.ch. **Royal Park Hotel:** Tel 41/33-675-8888; www.royalkandersteg.com. *Cost:* from $430 (off-peak), from $580 (peak). **Hotel Bellevue:** Tel 41/33-855-1401; www.muerren.ch/bellevue. *Cost:* from $185 (off-peak), from $225 (peak); dinner at Jägerstübli $50. **Piz Gloria:** Round-trip from Mürren via cable car, $125. **Jungfraujoch rail trip:** full-day round-trips offered daily from Interlaken and Grindelwald. *Cost:* $245 round-trip from Interlaken. *When:* Jun–Sep. **Victoria-Jungfrau Grand Hotel:** Tel 41/33-828-2828; www.victoria-jungfrau.ch. *Cost:* from $590 (off-peak), from $660 (peak). **Best times:** mid-Jun–Aug for alpine flowers; Sep–Oct for cooler weather.

A Pair of Peak Performers

Davos-Klosters

Graubünden, Switzerland

Offering top-of-the-line skiing for all levels, Davos is Europe's largest ski resort. At 5,120 feet, it is also its highest city, great for cold-weather sports even in warm winters. Long, scenic valley trails make it second only to the neighboring Engadine region for cross-country skiing (see next page).

Davos shares a sweeping network of lifts and slopes with its (barely) lower twin city Klosters, whose more attractive Alpine village is where you want to unpack your bags (Swedish and British royalty return here faithfully). Almost intimate compared to Davos, Klosters still nurtures its sobriquet of "Hollywood on the Rocks" because of the international movie set it attracts. VIP or not, they all come for the exemplary Parsenn-Weissfluh ski area, which many experts agree is one of the finest in Europe. Its famous descent from Weissfluhgipfel (9,331 feet) to Küblis (2,658 feet), a magnificent 8-mile piste over vast, open snowfields, is a thrill for even the accomplished skier.

You won't need royal connections to be treated as such at the atmospheric Chesa Grischuna. Housed in a handsome wooden chalet in the very center of town, Klosters's preferred inn offers traditionally furnished rooms with ornately carved ceilings and the area's finest restaurant, where specialties include rack of lamb and shrimp-stuffed crêpes. The aptly named Rustico Hotel, a mountain retreat near the Gotschnabahn ski lift, has simple but spacious guest rooms with duvet-plumped beds and Alpine warmth; the timber-ceilinged loft rooms are a special treat. In a 226-year-old chalet next door is the hotel's Prättiger Huschi, serving up bubbling fondue to the après-ski crowd that fills the cowhide benches.

Where: Klosters is 100 miles/161 km southeast of Zürich; Davos is 7 miles/11 km south of Klosters. **Hotel Chesa Grischuna:** Tel 41/81-422-2222; www.chesagrischuna.ch. *Cost:* from $170 (off-peak), from $340 (peak); dinner $60. *When:* closed mid-Apr–late Jun and mid-Oct–mid-Dec. **Rustico Hotel:** Tel 41/81-410-2288; www.rustico.klosters.com. *Cost:* from $190; dinner $45. **Best times:** Mar for skiing; Jul for alpine flowers; Aug–Sep for hiking.

Top-Notch Skiing and an Untrammeled Valley

St. Moritz and the Engadine Valley

Graubünden, Switzerland

Despite its celebrated glamour and who's who cachet, St. Moritz is not as ultraexclusive as its popular image leads one to expect. The world-class (and, yes, pricey) resort can be a generally sporty place with superb downhill skiing on all levels and ideal cross-country skiing. Intermediate skiers will enjoy hopping the cable car to Piz Corvatsch—almost 11,000 feet above sea level, its annual snowfalls are dependable.

Today's discreet set gravitates to the glitz-free Suvretta House and its Christmas-card views of the mountains. This triumph of subdued luxury behind a grand Edwardian façade impresses with vaulted arches, oak paneling, and 210 understatedly elegant guest rooms. The family-owned Hotel Languard is a smaller delight, some of whose well-kept rooms have balconies and carved wood paneling. Follow the locals to Engiadina for Champagne-infused fondue and *steak frites* in a simple, rustic setting. For a creative menu and possibly one of the country's best eating experiences, head to Jöhri's Talvo, delightfully set in a charming 17th-century Engadine farmhouse.

One of eastern Switzerland's most beautiful and least trammeled corners, the nearby Engadine Valley supplies countless hiking paths and high-mountain trails through woodlands, Alpine meadows, and old Romansch-speaking villages. Lovely Pontresina has become one of Europe's best hiking bases and mountaineering centers. In Scuol, taste pure mineral water bubbling from a village fountain before going to the first Roman-Irish baths in Switzerland. Wander the ancient cobbled streets of Guarda, one of the country's most photogenic hamlets. And explore the country's only national park, Parc Naziunal Svizzer (Swiss National Park), a pristine 65-square-mile sanctuary with 16 hiking circuits.

The Engadine Valley is rich with meadows, mineral springs, and a national park.

A 10-minute drive east of Guarda brings you to the flower-decked Schlosshotel Chastè, a place where old traditions flourish and hospitality is reflected in the heartfelt local greeting "Allegra!" Run by the Pazeller family since 1500, this lovely sgraffito-covered (decorative stucco) inn commands the center of tiny Tarasp, named for the fantasylike feudal castle that looms on a nearby hilltop. Host and chef Rudy Pazeller's talents shine in the kitchen and throughout the inn's impeccable guest rooms.

Where: St. Moritz is 125 miles/201 km southeast of Zürich. **Suvretta House:** Tel 41/81-836-3636; www.suvrettahouse.ch. *Cost:* from $600 (off-peak), from $880 (peak), inclusive. *When:* closed mid-Apr–late Jun, mid-Sep–Nov. **Hotel Languard:** Tel 41/81-833-3137; www.languard-stmoritz.ch. *Cost:* from $250. **Engiadina:** Tel 41/81-833-3265; www.restaurant-engiadina.ch. *Cost:* dinner $50. **Jöhri's Talvo:** Tel 41/81-833-4455; www.talvo.ch. *Cost:* prix-fixe 4-course dinner $245. **Swiss National Park:** www.nationalpark.ch. **Schlosshotel Chastè:** Tel 41/81-861-3060; www.schlosshotelchaste.com. *Cost:* from $400 (off-peak), breakfast only; from $550 (peak), inclusive. *When:* closed late Mar–May and mid-Oct–mid-Dec. **Best times:** Jan–late Mar for skiing; late Jan for St. Moritz Polo World Cup on Snow; late Jun–early Oct for hiking; forests are most colorful late Sep–early Oct.

Lakeside Music Mecca

Lucerne Riviera

Switzerland

Surrounded by mountains, Lucerne's fairy-tale turrets and covered wooden bridges—including the much photographed Chapel Bridge and Water Tower—make this lakeside medieval town a longtime tourist favorite. Every summer, music lovers descend here for the Lucerne Festival, one of Europe's oldest, most eclectic and appealing major music events (complemented by an Easter and fall piano program). Inaugurated by Toscanini in 1938, it's a veritable who's who of big-name conductors, orchestras (sometimes more than a dozen), soloists, and chamber ensembles that perform at a variety of locations, including the ultramodern KKL Culture and Convention Center. Positioned on the banks of Lake Lucerne, the Jean Nouvel–designed venue makes for a dramatic departure from the city's storybook setting.

Originally built in the 14th century and later reconstructed after a fire, Lucerne's pedestrian Chapel Bridge spans the Reuss River alongside the Water Tower.

"I do not know of a more beautiful spot in this world!" wrote Richard Wagner, who stayed at the large 19th-century Schweizerhof Hotel. In the same family for five generations, this modernized classic never disappoints with its sweeping views of the lake and mountains. Experience old Lucerne at the gracious Hotel Wilden Mann, where stone, brass, and burnished wood accent 50 guest rooms across seven delightful town houses in the Old Town. The inn's Burgerstube is a cozy and popular spot for such traditional fare as pan-fried perch or farmer's sausage with *rösti.*

Across gorgeous Lake Lucerne, the elegant Park Hotel Vitznau is scheduled to reopen in 2012, after a top-to-toe renovation turns it into an all-suite year-round property. Since opening in 1903, the hotel has been the stronghold of tiny Vitznau, with immaculately tended, flower-filled grounds reaching right down to the water's edge. Its towering neighbor Mount Rigi is mirrored in the calm waters of the lake, and the climax of many a traveler's visit to the area is watching the sun rise over the Alps from the mountain's 5,896-foot summit. Built in 1871, the cog railway to Rigi-Kulm is Europe's oldest, one of many railways and aerial tramways to the surrounding mountains, permitting spectacular views.

Where: 36 miles/57 km southwest of Zürich. **Lucerne Festival in Summer:** Tel 41/41-226-4400; www.lucernefestival.ch. For tickets tel 41/41-226-4480. *Cost:* tickets $35–$375. *When:* 6 weeks, Aug–Sep. **Hotel Schweizerhof Luzern**: Tel 41/41-410-0410; www.schweizerhof-luzern.ch. *Cost:* from $340 (off-peak), from $460 (peak). **Hotel Wilden Mann:** Tel 41/41-210-1666; www.wildenmann.ch. *Cost:* from $295 (off-peak), from $365 (peak); dinner $65. **Park Hotel Vitznau:** Tel 41/41-399-6060; www.parkhotel-vitznau.ch. **Best times:** May–Sep for best weather; Mar or Apr for Lucerne Festival at Easter; late Nov for Lucerne Festival at the Piano and for Lucerne Blues Festival.

Swiss Living, Italian Style

Lugano

Ticino, Switzerland

A land of palm trees and magnolia blossoms, sinuous lakes, and some of Europe's most elegant towns, Switzerland's southernmost corner is a blend of Italian charm and Swiss efficiency. The Italian-speaking canton of Ticino is closer to Rome in temperament than it is to Zürich, 143 miles away. Sun-drenched Lugano, its main town, seduces with ancient churches and piazzas connected by a tangled maze of steep cobblestone streets that spill down to its namesake lake.

One of Lugano's special pleasures is a walk along the shady lakefront promenade past magnificent private villas and their meticulously tended gardens. When you're ready for your own liberal dose of la dolce vita, head just outside of town to the Collina d'Oro and check into the Italianate Villa Principe Leopoldo. Built by the aristocratic Prussian von Hohenzollern family in 1868, the 75-room property still speaks of princely grandeur inside and out. Its unique hilltop setting offers spectacular views of the mountain-fringed Lake Lugano and one of the area's most stylish dining rooms and outdoor terraces. A quiet, more modest option right in town is the gracious Hotel Federale. Many of the simply furnished and immaculately kept guest rooms have balconies and lovely lake views—especially delightful from the top floor.

For a taste of old Lugano, follow Italian-speaking locals down an Old Town alley to La Tinera. The intimate taverna draws loyal fans for its authentic fare, both regional and from across the border—cumin-specked Luganighe

Lake Lugano's Mediterranean climate means palm and bamboo trees flourish and magnolias bloom in the spring.

sausage and risotto parmigiana are house specialties—and Ticinese wines (think robust merlot) served in small ceramic vessels. The next day, take a pleasant hour-long *passeggiata* to the picturesque lakeside town of Gandria, built up the wooded flank of Monte Brè.

WHERE: 143 miles/230 km south of Zürich, 45 miles/72 km north of Milan. **VILLA PRINCIPE LEOPOLDO:** Tel 41/91-985-8855; www.leopoldohotel.com. *Cost:* from $440 (off-peak), from $645 (peak); dinner $100. **HOTEL FEDERALE:** Tel 41/91-910-0808; www.hotel-federale.ch. *Cost:* from $215. **LA TINERA:** Tel 41/91-923-5219. *Cost:* dinner $35. **BEST TIMES:** Apr when the magnolia trees blossom; Apr–May for Lugano Festival of classical music; late Aug–early Sep for Blues-to-Bop Music Festival.

Thrill Seeking On and Off the Slopes

VERBIER

Valais, Switzerland

With some of Europe's steepest and best off-piste skiing and a lively nightlife, Verbier, in the French-speaking region of Valais, is a magnet for young, adventurous ski buffs who consider this stylish but relaxed town nothing short of heaven. Advanced (and aspiring expert) skiers will have their field day at this nexus of more than 250 miles of pistes connecting four valleys, where they can enjoy wonderful top-to-bottom off-piste runs in the company of a guide.

The slopes aren't the only thing in town that are steep: Hotel and restaurant rates are consistently high. In the heart of this remote but *très chic* town is the modest Hotel Farinet, overlooking the main square and the slopes beyond, and just a few minutes' walk from the chair lifts. You don't need to be a hotel guest to enjoy its vibrant après-ski scene at the bar or at the Casbah lounge, abuzz with a healthy-looking and fashionable crowd, many of them young professionals from nearby Geneva.

Off-piste "runs"—including Stairway to Heaven and the Backside of Mont Fort—are best tackled with a guide.

Conveniently located near the main lift station of Médran is the welcoming Hôtel Les 4 Vallées. The contemporary, chalet-style inn offers spacious, often sun-drenched, pine-clad guest rooms with balconies. For traditional Swiss fare—and a terrace popular with skiers fresh off the slopes—try the nearby Au Vieux Verbier, where brightly polished brass, stone, and candlelight serve as the jazzy backdrop for hearty and filling house specialties such as grilled steak flambéed at your table in red-wine sauce.

Where: 100 miles/161 km east of Geneva. **Hotel Farinet:** Tel 41/27-771-6626; www.hotelfarinet.com. *Cost:* from $250 (off-peak), from $320 (peak). *When:* closed late Apr–Jun, late Sep–Nov. **Hotel Les 4 Vallées:** Tel 41/27-775-3344; www.les4vallees.com. *Cost:* from $300. **Au Vieux Verbier:** Tel 41/27-771-1668. *Cost:* dinner $70. **Best times:** Jan, Jul, and Sep are least crowded; mid-Jul for classical music Verbier Festival.

In the Matterhorn's Shadow

Zermatt and Saas-Fee

Valais, Switzerland

The granite profile that launched a million postcards, the Matterhorn rises above the music-box chalets and car-free streets of the popular resort town of Zermatt. Zermatt's three ski areas rise to well over 9,600 feet and draw an international mix of intermediate and advanced skiers who flock here for wonderful ski runs. The famous Kleine Matterhorn cable car takes you to Europe's highest piste skiing plus one of Zermatt's tastiest adventures: skiing across the border into Italy for lunch. Zermatt is also the Alps' biggest heli-skiing center: The most epic run is from Monte Rosa, at almost 14,000 feet, through remarkable glacier scenery.

In 1865, English explorer and mountaineer Edward Whymper struck out from Zermatt and became the first to scale the 14,691-foot Matterhorn. You may not feel inclined to follow in his footsteps, but you can lodge in the same hotel where he did—the 46-room Hotel Monte Rosa (considerably more luxurious today than when it opened in 1839). Hotels accommodate skiers of all budgets and most promise great views, such as the Hotel Admiral, along the river promenade. When the views fade, the nightlife picks up.

Saas-Fee, 11 miles east of Zermatt, delivers equally spectacular views of the awesome Matterhorn as well as 12 other peaks that tower over 13,120 feet. While the steep terrain and extensive glaciers have limited runs, Saas-Fee offers some of the best snow conditions and the longest season in Europe. Its Felskinn-Mittelallalin ski area is one of Switzerland's premier ski destinations, and when the snow melts, its high-terrain walking paths draw amblers of all ages.

The charm of this car-free Alpine village makes it a year-round destination, as does the other big draw in town: chef Markus Neff, the king of the Waldhotel Fletschhorn. High on a forested hill, in a chaletlike hotel-restaurant, Neff's French-based seasonal cuisine blends local flavors with smatterings of the exotic. Head back to town for a stay at the unpretentious Hotel Europa, with spacious, comfortable rooms and an excellent spa for relaxing after a day outdoors.

Where: 150 miles/241 km east of Geneva. **Hotel Monte Rosa:** Tel 41/27-966-0333; www.monterosazermatt.ch. *Cost:* from $360 (off-peak), from $515 (peak). *When:* closed mid-Sep–mid-Dec and mid-Apr–mid-Jul. **Hotel Admiral:** Tel 41/27-966-9000; www.hotel-admiral.ch. *Cost:* from $220. **Waldhotel Fletschhorn:** Tel 41/27-957-2131; www.fletschhorn.ch. *Cost:* from $355; dinner $135. *When:* closed May, Nov. **Hotel Europa:** Tel 41/27-958-9600; www.europa-saasfee.ch. *Cost:* from $155. **Best times:** Jan–Apr for best ski conditions; late Feb–Mar for shorter lift lines; Jul–Sep for glacier skiing.

Music Takes Center Stage

Montreux Jazz Festival

Vaud, Switzerland

Europe's leading jazz event since 1967, the Montreux Jazz Festival has blossomed into an international celebration of music that showcases blues, reggae, soul, rap, rock, and pop as well as its namesake style.

Always ahead of the curve, it features the finest sound stages, with big-time acts dominating the two main halls, while lesser-knowns perform more intimate sets at the Montreux Jazz Café and small open-air venues. A strong musical tradition only heightens the allure of this ever-popular town that hugs the banks of lovely Lake Geneva.

Château de Chillon, which seems to rise out of Lake Léman, claims to be Switzerland's most-visited historic monument.

Since the 19th century, artists, writers, and musicians have been attracted to the city's French ways and worldly atmosphere, which are sometimes compared to those of Cannes (see p. 127). Idle at any of the waterside cafés amid the palms, cypresses, and magnolias that flourish here (thanks to mountains that protect the city from harsh winter winds) and you'll understand why Lake Geneva is called the Swiss Riviera. What Cannes lacks is the Château de Chillon, Switzerland's most important and most photographed castle, parts of which date back 1,000 years. From Montreux, a postcard-worthy 2.5-mile walk along the shore to Chillon wows with a kaleidoscope of flowers and Alpine views.

You'll feel like an honored guest at the Hôtel Masson, built in 1829 as a winemaker's mansion overlooking the lake and now offering 35 high-ceilinged guest rooms with balconies. Popular with Jazz Festival–goers and performers is the opulent Le Montreux Palace, a jewel of Belle Époque architecture that features 236 elegant and spacious guest rooms, a top-flight spa, and impeccable service.

Of the plethora of lakeside eateries, La Rouvenaz's heartwarming Italian fare and casual ambience make it a perennial favorite. But serious gastronomes flock to the village of Crissier (18 miles northwest of town) for the magic performed at Restaurant de l'Hôtel de Ville, where patrons book at least two months in advance. Culinary maestro Philippe Rochat comfortably balances the German and the French, combining the simple and the sublime.

Where: 62 miles/100 km east of Geneva. **Montreux Jazz Festival:** Tel 41/21-963-8282; www.montreuxjazz.com. *When:* 16 days that include the first 3 full weekends of Jul. **How:** U.S.-based Ciao! Travel offers a 6-night package with tickets to 5 concerts. Tel 800-942-2426 or 619-297-8112; www.ciaotravel.com. *Cost:* from $3,950, includes air from New York, hotel, tickets. **Hôtel Masson:** Tel 41/21-966-0044; www.hotelmasson.ch. *Cost:* from $210. *When:* closed Nov–mid-Apr. **Fairmont Le Montreux Palace:** Tel 41/21-962-1200; www.fairmont.com. *Cost:* from $450. **La Rouvenaz:** Tel 41/21-963-2736;

www.rouvenaz.ch. *Cost:* dinner $60. **Restaurant de l'Hôtel de Ville:** Tel 41/21-634-05-05; www.philippe-rochat.ch. *Cost:* 10-course tasting dinner $360. **Best times:** May–Sep for nicest weather; Jul for Jazz Festival; Dec for Christmas market.

A Wealth of Culture

Zürich's Artbeat

Switzerland

Straddling the Limmat River and graced with a mountainous backdrop, Switzerland's most financially powerful city capitalizes on natural beauty and cultural riches. Coupled with Basel (see p. 273), Zürich pumps the country's artistic heart. The birthplace of the Dada movement (1916) has long nurtured creativity and today boasts not only a top-ranked orchestra and superb theater company but a 19th-century opera house acclaimed for its lavish 1,100-seat intimacy and stellar acoustics. Even the delicate-spired Fraumünster and twin-towered Grossmünster churches are testaments to Zürich's creative leanings, with stained-glass windows by Marc Chagall and Augusto Giacometti. The largest collection of works by Alberto Giacometti (Augusto's cousin) are displayed along other 19th- and early-20th-century art at the revered Kunsthaus. Recent years have seen the Zürich West neighborhood reinvented, with former factories and an old train viaduct now home to the Kunsthalle contemporary art museum, edgy art galleries, and a bustling nightlife. Popular with the stylish art crowd is the cozy Hotel Helvetia, with a lobby and lively restaurant that showcase contemporary Swiss artists.

Looking down on it all from an extravagant 125-acre park high above town is the castle-like Dolder Grand Hotel, reached by funicular. The Norman Foster–led renovation completed in 2008 refurbished the original 1899 main building of understatedly elegant guest rooms and added two new wings. From the hotel's acclaimed Mediterranean restaurant to the gorgeous nine-hole golf course and pool with a wave-making machine, everything at the Dolder shares remarkable city views.

Tradition reigns supreme at the well-loved classic Kronenhalle, where every inch of the restaurant's burnished wood paneling is covered with original works by Klee, Picasso, Kandinsky, and other modern masters. The animated scene here is best enjoyed over delicious standards like steak or sausage and *rösti* potatoes. Just 6 miles south of town, Rico's Kunststuben wows its clientele with a market-based cuisine that is almost compulsively inventive, every mouthful a revelation.

Visitor info: www.zuerich.com. **Kunsthaus:** Tel 41/44-253-8484; www.kunsthaus.ch. **Kunsthalle:** Tel 41/44-272-1515; www.kunsthallezurich.ch. **Hotel Helvetia:** Tel 41/44-297-9999; www.hotel-helvetia.ch. *Cost:* from $250; dinner $80. **Dolder Grand Hotel:** Tel 41/44-456-6000; www.thedoldergrand.com. *Cost:* from $630; dinner $160. **Kronenhalle:** Tel 41/44-262-9900; www.kronenhalle.com. *Cost:* dinner $100. **Rico's Kunststuben:** Tel 41/44-910-0715; www.kunststuben.com. *Cost:* dinner $145. **Best times:** Apr–Oct for nicest weather; Apr for Sechseläuten spring festival; late Jun–mid-Jul for Zürich Festival of performing arts; mid-Aug for dancing at the Street Parade; early Sep for Long Night of Museums.

EASTERN EUROPE

Playground on the Adriatic

Dubrovnik and the Dalmatian Coast

Croatia

A rugged shoreline and more than 1,000 islands in the warm, turquoise waters of the Adriatic Sea make the Dalmatian Coast one of Europe's most beautiful seaside playgrounds. Dubrovnik, "the Pearl of the Adriatic," is the most magical of Croatia's many coastal towns. Rising directly from a wave-lapped limestone promontory, the Stari Grad, or Old Town, is ringed with 15th-century stone walls as much as 80 feet high and 20 feet thick. In its glory days, Dubrovnik was an independent republic vying for influence with Venice. Stroll atop the 1.3 miles of city walls and look down at terracotta roofs and an ancient urban grid. The Placa (aka Stradun), a wide, marble-paved main thoroughfare, is lined with boutiques, cafés, and galleries. Narrow side streets and alleys lead to a monastery with Romanesque cloisters, a tiny 15th-century synagogue (Europe's second oldest), and Gundulic Square, which fills most mornings with a lively food market. The cathedral and Rector's Palace lie just beyond. There aren't many options for spending the night within the old walls, but one is the small, cozy Hotel Stari Grad, a former aristocratic home. For grander lodging, the Excelsior Hotel and Spa blends timeless style and nonchalant luxury just steps from the beach and a ten-minute stroll from the Old Town.

Split, north of Dubrovnik, has a birthright shared by few other cities: It was the retirement estate of a Roman emperor. In the 3rd century, Diocletian built a walled enclave covering nearly 10 acres, and it is still the heart of this pretty coastal city. History has recycled the imposing Roman structures; the cathedral was once Diocletian's mausoleum. The emperor's boudoir is now part of Vestibul Palace, a boutique hotel blending high-design modern luxury and ancient Roman stonecraft.

Split is the hub for a ferry system serving the coastal islands and their exclusive resorts. Brač is known for its wine, marble (used for Diocletian's palace, America's White House, and Berlin's Reichstag), and beaches that are favorites with windsurfers. Hvar is famous for being famous, with lavender fields and superb beaches that draw tycoons and rock stars. At its most stylish hotel, Adriana, a rooftop terrace overlooks the yacht-filled harbor. Korčula is noted for its golden wine called Grk and its

Dubrovnik's walls fortified the city against pirate attacks.

claim to be the birthplace of Marco Polo. Adjacent to the house known as his home is the small and exclusive Lešić Dimitri Palace Hotel, once an 18th-century bishop's palace. The island of Vis has marvelous antiquities and vineyards and offers diving, miles of sandy beaches, and a low-key, relaxed vibe.

From Split, it's 70 miles north to Zadar, which was the island capital of Dalmatia for over a millennium. Within its old walled town are two cathedrals, the remains of a Roman forum, and a lively mix of cafés and shops. At the Riva, a seafront promenade, listen to the Sea Organ, tubes installed beneath large marble steps to let the wind and waves make music. Sign up for a boat trip to visit Kornati National Park, 89 stark white limestone islands busy with divers and sailboats.

Hotel Stari Grad: Tel: 385/98-534-819; www.hotelstarigrad.com. *Cost:* from $190 (off-peak), from $330 (peak). **Excelsior Hotel:** Tel 385/20-353-353; www.hotel-excelsior.hr. *Cost:* from $185 (off-peak), from $330 (peak). **Vestibul Palace:** Tel 385/21-329-329; www.vestibulpalace.com. *Cost:* from $300 (off-peak), from $450 (peak). **Adriana:** Tel 385/21-750-200; www.suncanihvar.com/adriana. *Cost:* from $225 (off-peak), from $425 (peak). **Lešić Dimitri Palace:** Tel 385/20-715-560; www.lesic-dimitri.com. *Cost:* from $500 (off-peak), from $650 (peak). *When:* closed Nov–Mar. **Kornati National Park:** www.kornati.hr. **Best times:** Apr–Jun and Sep–Nov for pleasant weather; Jul–Aug for Dubrovnik Summer Festival and Split Festival.

The Tuscany of Croatia

Istria

Croatia

In Croatia's northwest corner, just south of Trieste, Italy, the peninsula of Istria juts into the Adriatic Sea. With rolling vineyards, olive groves, and ancient, walled hill towns, it resembles Tuscany in both looks and spirit as well as boasting a gleaming, beach-lined coast. The Romans colonized Istria in the 2nd century B.C., and the arena they left behind at Pula, near its southern tip, testifies to the peninsula's importance in ancient times. Designed for gladiatorial combat, with seating for 22,000 spectators, the amphitheater is one of Europe's largest and best preserved and is used today for rock concerts, operas, and film festivals.

You'll find authentic medieval charm farther north. Rovinj, a coastal town thrusting thumblike into the sea, is a tangle of steep, narrow streets and centuries-old stone houses, crowned by the imposing 18th-century Church of St. Euphemia. The saint's 6th-century marble sarcophagus is said to have floated here from Constantinople in about A.D. 800. It's not far to the inviting Hotel Monte Mulini, set in a forested park overlooking the beach. It has large rooms, a three-story spa, and the Wine Vault Restaurant, which serves contemporary French and Mediterranean cuisine.

Poreč invites exploration with an ancient town center and the magnificent 6th-century St. Euphrasius Basilica, whose intricate mosaics are considered among the finest examples of Byzantine art. Surrounded by beach resorts, the newly restored Grand Hotel Palazzo, built above the harbor in 1910, is Poreč's top choice, combining period charm and up-to-date luxury.

Leave the coast and journey into Istria's verdant heartland, a rolling patchwork where oak forests yield pungent truffles and excellent wines from traditional Malvasia and Teran grapes. The fortified town of Motovun is a medieval time capsule of winding cobblestone streets, bell towers, and a hilltop 17th-century Venetian palazzo. The last is now the family-run Hotel Kaštel, complete with a spa and charming historical quirks. If you don't have time for a wine tour, savor local specialties in Palladio, the hotel's restaurant.

WHERE: Pula is 73 miles/118 km south of Trieste. **HOTEL MONTE MULINI:** Tel 385/52-636-000; www.montemulinihotel.com. *Cost:* from $375 (off-peak), from $730 (peak); dinner $60. **GRAND HOTEL PALAZZO:** Tel 385/52-858-800; www.hotel-palazzo.hr. *Cost:* $125 (off-peak), from $300 (peak). *When:* closed late Oct–Feb. **HOTEL KAŠTEL:** Tel 385/52-681-607; www.hotel-kastel-motovun.hr. *Cost:* from $120; dinner $20. **BEST TIMES:** Apr–Jun and Sep–Oct for nicest weather; Jun–Aug for Pula's Histria Festival with concerts at the amphitheater; late Jul or Aug for Motovun Film Festival; Sep–Nov for truffles.

Wonderland of Water

PLITVICE LAKES NATIONAL PARK

Croatia

High in the Dinaric Mountains, on the road between Zagreb and coastal Split (see p. 284), the nascent Korana River drops through a verdant valley of stair-stepped lakes and hundreds of waterfalls that was long known as the Vržji Vrt (Devil's Garden), so rich in mystery and beauty that locals felt it was enchanted. One of Europe's premier natural wonders, the terraced and interconnected Plitvice Lakes extend over 5 miles. The water pools in one and then flows to the next via waterfalls, springs, caves, and chutes. The Veliki Slap (Big Waterfall), which drops 230 feet into a steep canyon, separates the lakes into two clusters: 12 in the upper valley and four below.

Interlinked pools and surrounding forests make up Plitvice Lakes, Croatia's first national park.

The terraces are travertine, a mineral created when limestone dissolved in water gradually collects and petrifies into ridges and ledges. Jewel-like in color, the lakes vary from deep blue to turquoise as sunlight refracts at different angles off minerals in the water. Elevated wooden footpaths and bridges allow visitors to explore the lakes without disturbing this extremely fragile environment.

The lakes are beautiful year-round. Spring brings runoff from snowmelt that makes the waterfalls even more numerous and dramatic.

In summer, the valley is a cool escape from the heat, and in autumn the forests are a kaleidoscope of multihued foliage. When snow blankets the peaks, the lower lakes trail remains open, allowing visitors to see waterfalls and cascades transformed into icy stalactites.

WHERE: 80 miles/129 km southwest of Zagreb. **VISITOR INFO:** www.np-plitvicka-jezera.hr. **WHERE TO STAY:** Hotel Jazero is closest to the lakes and the only game in town. Tel 385/53-751-400; www.np-plitvicka-jezera.hr. *Cost:* from $120 (off-peak), from $160 (peak).

A Medieval Town on the Meandering Vltava

ČESKÝ KRUMLOV

Bohemia, Czech Republic

Český Krumlov is a fairy-tale river town that opens a lively window on genuine Bohemian life. It's a popular destination for day-trippers from Prague (Praha in Czech), but plan to stay a night to enjoy a meal in a traditional riverside restaurant, then rise early before the crowds arrive: You'll have the twisting alleyways and numerous nooks and crannies of the town almost to yourself.

The town of Český Krumlov grew around the castle of the same name.

Most notable among the town's fascinating architectural collage of medieval, Renaissance, Baroque, and Rococo buildings is the splendid Český Krumlov *hrad,* also called the Schwarzenberg Castle. With 300 rooms, this is the Czech Republic's second largest castle after Prague's (see p. 291), and for three centuries it was the official residence of the Rosenberg dynasty, the noble family that ruled southern Bohemia from the 13th to the 16th century. Cross from the soaring Round Tower through the grandiose stone arches of the Most na Plášti bridge to the expansive castle gardens, where, during the summer months, ballet, opera, and theater are performed alfresco in the Revolving Theater.

The Czech Republic is famous for its beer (see p. 289), and Český Krumlov's local Eggenberg brewery conjures up a tasty dark lager best sampled at the Hospoda Na Louži pub. One of the town's most atmospheric dining experiences is the riverside U Dwau Maryí (the Two Marys) with medieval recipes such as roast pheasant and excellent *medovina* (mead). On the main square, Krčma v Šatlavské offers sizzling platters of grilled meat served in a candlelit 16th-century stone-lined cellar illuminated by candles or outdoor terrace.

The meandering Vltava river is a defining feature of Český Krumlov, and several local companies offer rafting and canoeing trips through the forests of south Bohemia. At sunset, as shadows bounce off the town's haphazard angles, flat-bottomed wooden boats carry visitors slowly along the river as it twists and turns through the old town.

WHERE: 112 miles/180 km south of Prague. **VISITOR INFO:** www.ckrumlov.info. **ČESKÝ KRUMLOV CASTLE:** www.castle.ckrumlov.cz. *When:* closed Nov–Mar. **HOSPODA NA LOUŽI:** Tel 420/380-711-280; www.nalouzi.cz. **U DWAU MARYÍ:** Tel 420/380-717-228.

Cost: dinner $15. **Krčma v Šatlavské:** Tel 420/380-713-344; www.satlava.cz. *Cost:* dinner $40. **Where to stay:** The historic Hotel Konvice has castle views and is located just off the central square. Tel 420/380-711-611; www.en.stadthotel-krummau.de. *Cost:* from $90. **Best times:** Apr and Oct for fewer visitors; Jun for Five-Petalled Rose Festival with street performers and medieval pageantry; Jul–Aug for International Music Festival.

Trio of Bohemian Spas

Karlovy Vary

Bohemia, Czech Republic

"I feel as if I'm in some paradise of innocence and spontaneity," wrote Goethe, who spent 16 summers in Karlovy Vary, also known by its German name, Karlsbad. Beethoven, Brahms, Bach, and Liszt also found inspiration here. Of the Czech Republic's 30-plus spa towns, Karlovy Vary and its centuries-old competitor Mariánské Lázně (Marienbad) are the largest and most renowned.

For more than 400 years, the world's rich and famous have come to "take the waters" of Karlovy Vary's 12 natural thermal springs. Located in a meandering wooded valley, the town retains an elegant and important air, enlivened by impromptu classical music concerts held amid graceful 19th-century architecture.

Dating from 1701, the Grand Hotel Pupp was one of Europe's most famous hotels, with countless celebrities, including Goethe, Paganini, and Freud, filling its guest register. Drenched in old-world ambience, it deserves a peek, but consider unpacking at the Hotel Ontario, a more modest affair, within a minute's walk from everything. Either is a perfect base for exploring the best of west Bohemia's spa country. Just 20 minutes away, Loket may not feature springs, but this compact medieval village is on a scenic bend of the Ohře River and has a brooding castle. On summer evenings, the Hotel Cisar Ferdinand holds alfresco barbecues, with robust local food accompanied by one of Bohemia's best lagers.

Forty-five minutes' drive south of Karlovy Vary is the much smaller Mariánské Lázně, whose 40 mineral springs were a favorite choice of Kafka, Chopin, and England's King Edward VII (the latter frequented the Hotel Nové Lázně, still a town landmark). Chopin's legacy is celebrated in August with the annual Chopin Music Festival. Stop by the Chodovar Beer Spa in nearby Chodová Planá, where bathing in restorative tubs of warm, specially brewed beer is on offer. Continue to sleepy Františkovy Lázně (Franzenbad), near the German border. This is the smallest and most unspoiled town in the country's spa triangle, despite the allure of its 26 curative springs.

Where: Karlovy Vary is 88 miles/142 km west of Prague, and Mariánské Lázně is 106 miles/172 km west of Prague. **Grand Hotel Pupp:** Tel 420/353-109-111; www.pupp.cz. *Cost:* from $270. **Hotel Ontario:** Tel 420/353-222-091; www.hotelontario.cz. *Cost:* from $135. **Hotel Cisar Ferdinand:** Tel 420/352-327-130. *Cost:* $95. **Hotel Nové Lázně:** Tel 420/354-644-111; www.danubiushotels.com. *Cost:* from $150. **Chodovar Beer Spa:** Tel 420/374-611-653; www.chodovar.cz. **Best times:** Jun–Sep for nicest weather; Jul for Karlovy Vary International Film Festival; Sep for Dvořák autumn music festival.

A Cathedral to Rival Prague's, and a Macabre but Compelling Display

KUTNÁ HORA

Bohemia, Czech Republic

This quiet town was once a serious rival to the might and glory of Prague. Kutná Hora's wealth was drawn from the silver ore enriching the surrounding hills, and in 1308, during the reign of Wenceslas II, the town became the royal mint. The silver coins minted here were the monetary lingua franca of central Europe, and Prague and Kutná Hora became fierce economic, cultural, and political rivals. By the 16th century, the silver reserves were expiring, but the town was left with a fascinating legacy of significant architecture. The town's interesting Silver Museum is housed in a building that was originally part of its fortifications.

Dedicated to the patron saint of miners, the superb Gothic Cathedral of St. Barbara stands proudly on a ridge above Kutná Hora's compact old town. With a soaring nave and an elegant ribbed ceiling, the scale and magnificence of the structure reinforce the town's historic influence. Intermittent construction lasted from 1380 to the late 19th century. It was worth the wait—the cathedral is one of the country's most grandiose.

Kutná Hora's other treasure is the macabre Bone Church (Sedlec Ossuary), in the town's suburbs where a Cistercian monastery has stood since the 12th century. When the Black Plague devastated Europe in the mid-1300s, the monastery's graveyard overflowed, and this church was built to house the volume of human bones. For 5 centuries the bones of some 40,000 people were stored randomly, but when the aristocratic Schwarzenberg family purchased the chapel in 1870, they enlisted a local woodcarver to organize the mountains of skulls, femurs, and ribs into creative arrangements. The result is a highly artistic display of bones transformed into chandeliers, pyramids, and crosses. Look closely and you'll see the Schwarzenberg coat of arms and the signature of the artist, František Rint, at the bottom of the steps.

WHERE: 45 miles/73 km east of Prague. **VISITOR INFO:** www.kutnahora.cz. **CZECH SILVER MUSEUM:** Tel 420/327-512-159; www.cms-kh.cz. **SEDLEC OSSUARY:** Tel 420/326-551-049; www.kostnice.cz. **BEST TIMES:** Jun–Sep for nicest weather; Jun for International Classical Music Festival.

A Country's Proud Heritage

CZECH BEER

Prague and Plzeň, Bohemia, Czech Republic

"Wherever beer is brewed, all is well. Whenever beer is drunk, life is good" goes an old proverb in a country whose per capita beer consumption is the world's highest. And many decades after pilsner beer was first perfected in the west Bohemian city of Plzeň (Pilsen in German) in 1842, there's never been a better time to be a *pivo* (beer) aficionado in the Czech Republic. Of the country's 125 breweries, many are located in the capital, Prague. Sampling them is easy—plenty of the city's *hospody* (pubs) offer an eveningful of brews on tap.

A leisurely sampling from Prague's abundance of choice might begin at the Pivovarsky Dum (Brewery House), where you can try "beer champagne" or coffee- or banana-flavored beer. Or amble across town to the associated Pivovarsky Klub (Brewery Club), which showcases the best of regional Czech brewers. It gets busy with loyal regulars in the evening, so come for a long lunch combining traditional Czech food with up to six different beers on tap. Not enough? Several refrigerators are packed with bottled brews from around the country. Names to look for include Primátor, Svijany, Kout na Šumavě, and Lobkowicz.

In the city's castle district, the Klášterní Pivovar is set in the 12th-century Strahov Monastery, and the adjacent beer garden is perfect for sampling some of Prague's best microbrewed beer (a special Christmas ale is released in December). Diligent monks carry on the centuries-old tradition of making light and dark Czech lagers as well as local spins on German *hefeweizen* (wheat beer) and American pale ale. There's good goulash, and a brass combo pumps out central European tunes to sustain the all-around bonhomie.

Across the river, in the Old Town, the Prague Beer Museum (Pražské Muzeum Piva) has a regular selection of as many as 30 beers on tap. The museum display is lightweight, but with so many hops-laden options on offer, no one seems to care. For a worthwhile peek into brewing history, take a day trip 60 miles west to Plzeň, the spiritual home of modern brewing. Combine a pilgrimage to the Pilsner Urquell Brewery with a visit to Plzeň's interesting brewery museum nearby. The *nefiltrované pivo* (unfiltered beer) alone, served in the museum's Na Parkanu pub, is worth the scenic train journey. For over-the-top indulgence, beer lovers should consider the Chodovar Beer Spa (see p. 288) near Karlovy Vary.

Pivovarsky Dum: Tel 420/296-216-666; www.gastroinfo.cz. **Pivovarsky Klub:** Tel 420/222-315-777; www.gastroinfo.cz. **Klášterní Pivovar:** Tel 420/233-353-155; www.klasterni-pivovar.cz. **Prague Beer Museum:** Tel 420/732-330-912; www.praguebeermuseum.com. **Pilsner Urquell Brewery and Brewing Museum:** Tel 420/222-710-159; www.prazdroj.cz. **Best time:** mid-May for Prague's Czech Beer Festival and Czech Food Festival.

Center Stage in the City of Spires

Old Town Square

Prague, Bohemia, Czech Republic

Old Town Square is Prague's energetic hub. Once the haunted neighborhood of Franz Kafka, today it overflows with bright café umbrellas, busking musicians, and legions of tourists watching the hourly procession of apostles and allegorical figures on the Orloj, Prague's famous 600-year-old astronomical clock. Ascend the 200-foot tower of the former Town Hall to see a dazzling panorama of this "City of One Hundred Spires." The wedding-cake Baroque confection of St. Nicholas Church is one architectural gem to look for, and another is the 14th-century Church of Our

Lady Before Tyn, its magnificent Gothic façade and elegant twin gables one of Prague's most recognizable silhouettes.

From Old Town Square, narrow and winding lanes lead to the hidden squares and plazas of Staré Město (the Old Town). Seek out the elegant Savic Hotel, originally a 14th-century convent, or experience a multicourse exploration of classical Bohemian cuisine at La Degustation. Refined and light dishes taken from an obscure 1880s cookbook create an inspiring 3-hour gastronomic experience.

A few minutes' walk brings you to the cherub-filled Estates Theater. Mozart loved Prague and chose this theater for the premier performance of his *Don Giovanni.* Restored to its Neoclassical elegance, and reopened in 1991 on the 200th anniversary of the composer's death, this jewel case of tiered boxes is spectacular inside and out and continues its Mozart performances.

From the central square, Karlova Street meanders west to Charles Bridge, a beloved icon of the city constructed in 1357 by Charles IV. Fourteen other bridges span the swirling Vltava River, but the view from this pedestrian bridge is special, encompassing the west bank's Malá Strana (Lesser Quarter) and Prague Castle high atop the opposite bank (see below). Thirty-six Baroque saints, most added in the 17th century, line the bridge's graceful 16-arched crossing. The riverside Four Seasons has suites that deliver beautiful castle views and the exceptional Allegro restaurant. Rise early to have the bridge largely to yourself while the guardian statues hover like ghosts shrouded in the lifting mist.

Savic Hotel: Tel 420/224-248-555; www.savichotelprague.com. *Cost:* from $175. **La Degustation:** Tel 420/222-311-234; www.ladegustation.cz. *Cost:* 7-course tasting menu $120. **Estates Theater:** Tel 420/224-902-231; www.narodni-divadlo.cz. **Four Seasons:** Tel 420/221-427-000; in the U.S., 800-819-5053; www.fourseasons.com. *Cost:* from $450 (off-peak), from $575 (peak); dinner at Allegro $100. **Best times:** late Apr–Mar for Prague Spring music festival; late Sep–Oct for Prague's autumn classical music festival; late Nov–Dec for Christmas markets in Old Town and Wenceslas Squares.

Religious and Political Symbol of Might and Glory

Prague's Castle District

Bohemia, Czech Republic

High atop the hilly west bank of this "Golden City" is one of the most beautiful sights in Europe: Prague Castle (Pražský hrad), perched above the curving Vltava River, which flows below it, with the Gothic masterpiece of St. Vitus Cathedral soaring behind it. This was the site of early Prague, and everything that evolved from it lay in its proverbial shadow. An amble through this hilltop town-within-a-town provides views of the river and the Charles Bridge. The skyline of spires and turrets of the lower Old Town rises above the ancient rooftops of the east bank (see previous page). Prague Castle is a monumental fortress-like collection of buildings and courtyards spanning the millennium from the 10th to the 20th centuries. Its spiritual core is St. Vitus Cathedral, begun in the 14th century and not completed until 1929. Of its 21 chapels, the most lavish is dedicated to "Good King" Wenceslas, patron saint of Bohemia. Adjacent is the Royal Palace, residence for the lords of Bohemia from the 11th to the 16th centuries.

Prague's two most important art galleries are the highlight for many visitors: The deconsecrated Convent of St. George houses a stellar collection of 19th-century Bohemian art, and six centuries of European art is found in the Sternberg Palace. At the eastern edge of the sprawling complex, the Lobkowicz Palace showcases the private collection of the Lobkowicz family, including paintings by Canaletto and handwritten scores by Mozart and Beethoven.

St. Vitus Cathedral took 6 centuries to complete.

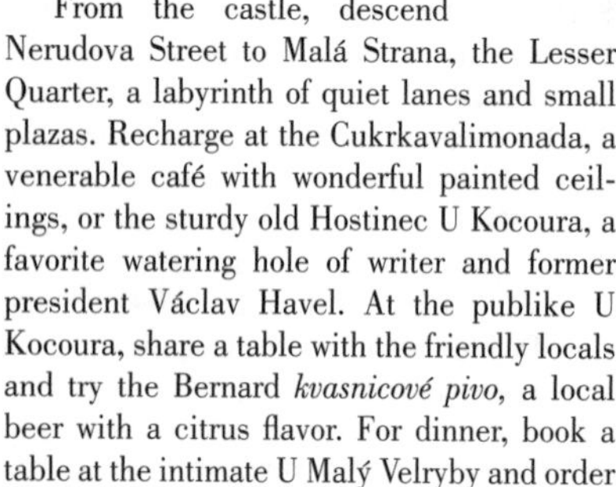

From the castle, descend Nerudova Street to Malá Strana, the Lesser Quarter, a labyrinth of quiet lanes and small plazas. Recharge at the Cukrkavalimonada, a venerable café with wonderful painted ceilings, or the sturdy old Hostinec U Kocoura, a favorite watering hole of writer and former president Václav Havel. At the publike U Kocoura, share a table with the friendly locals and try the Bernard *kvasnicové pivo,* a local beer with a citrus flavor. For dinner, book a table at the intimate U Malý Velryby and order up a feast of seafood tapas and a bottle of Moravian white wine.

Malá Strana is a delightful area to stay in. The Augustine, located in a restored 13th-century monastery, is one of the city's finest hotels, with 100 rooms arranged around quiet, leafy courtyards and a minimalist spa with a treatment based on dark lager brewed by the resident monks. Almost next door, behind a medieval façade, the 22 brightly colored rooms at the hip Hotel Sax are a funky alternative combining retro 1960s design with a convenient location in a small, peaceful square.

Prague Castle: Tel 420/224-373-368; www.hrad.cz. **Convent of St. George:** Tel 420/257-531-644; www.ngprague.cz. **Sternberg Palace:** Tel 420/233-090-570; www.ngprague.cz. **Lobkowicz Palace:** Tel 420/233-312-925; www.lobkowicz.cz. **Cukrkavalimonada:** Tel 420/257-225-396. *Cost:* lunch $15. **U Malý Velryby:** Tel 420/257-214-703; www.umalevelryby.cz. *Cost:* dinner $35. **The Augustine:** Tel 420/266-112-233; in the U.S., tel 888-667-9477; www.theaugustine.com. *Cost:* from $350. **Hotel Sax:** Tel 420/257-531-268; www.hotelsax.cz. *Cost:* from $130. **Best time:** May for Prague Spring classical music festival and quirky Prague Fringe Festival.

Châteaux, Wine, and a Little Slice of Italy

Borderlands of Southern Moravia

Moravia, Czech Republic

Described by Czech poet Jan Skácel as "a piece of Italy moved to Moravia by God's hand," the quiet castle-topped town of Mikulov is perched on a rocky hillside a few scenic miles north of the Austrian border. The surrounding Pálava landscape—perfect for gentle bicycling and hiking—does retain an unmistakable aura of Tuscany; it's an area of rolling hills and sleepy towns that is also the hub of the country's rapidly improving wine scene. Its aromatic white—notable labels are Tanzberg and Mikrosvín—are now making their mark internationally. In September, Mikulov's population of 8,000 swells with the advent of the Pálava Wine Harvest.

A synagogue built in 1550 still stands in Mikulov's well-preserved Jewish quarter, established in 1421. The neighborhood is the location of the stylish and art-filled Hotel Templ, a Baroque building that once housed a small synagogue.

Use Mikulov as your base to explore the countryside called Europe's Garden, once favored by the aristocratic Liechtenstein family. Now based in their minuscule Alpine principality, the family used to hold significant estates throughout central Europe, including the twin residences of Lednice and Valtice Castles. Part of the Liechtenstein dynasty for five centuries until World War II, they are now centerpieces of a bucolic 124-square-mile parkland of landscaped gardens, lakes, and pavilions that make up the Lednice-Valtice Cultural Landscape. The Valtice Castle is one of the Czech Republic's finest Baroque buildings, while neighboring Lednice is known for its neo-Gothic château, which was the Liechtensteins' summer residence from 1582 to 1945. Today the châteaux and environs are owned by the Czech government, and the gardens are full of summertime visitors enjoying pleasure-boat rides, bike paths, and "Birds of Prey" shows where trained eagles, falcons, and hawks patrol the skies above Lednice in a thrilling spectacle.

Where: Mikulov is 182 miles/293 km southeast of Prague. **Visitor info:** www.mikulov.cz. **Hotel Templ:** Tel 420/519-323-095; www.templ.cz. *Cost:* from $90. **Valtice Castle:** Tel 420/519-352-423; www.zamek-valtice.cz. **Lednice Château:** Tel 420/519-340-128; www.zamek-lednice.info. *When:* Lednice and Valtice closed Nov–Mar. **Best times:** Jun–Sep for nicest weather; Aug for Baroque Music Festival in Valtice; mid-Sep for Pálava Wine Harvest in Mikulov.

The Liechtensteins settled in the Lednice-Valtice area in the mid-13th century.

Moravia's Underrated Gem

Olomouc

Moravia, Czech Republic

"They say we are going to Olomouc, and Olomouc is a very decent town," wrote Leo Tolstoy in *War and Peace.* Although the story was fiction, the town is real, and the line rings true more than 140 years after it was first published. Like Prague and Český Krumlov (see pp. 290 and 287), Olomouc is centered on a gorgeous Old Town, but in this easygoing city of 100,000, visitors share the pristine collage of Renaissance, Baroque, and Gothic buildings with few other tourists. You're more likely to find a relaxed combination of students from across Europe and locals who know instinctively that they're living in one of the Czech Republic's underrated gems.

About 3 hours east of Prague, Olomouc pulls off the trick of being both provincial and cosmopolitan. In the Upper Square, the larger of two town squares, is the 100-foot-high Holy Trinity Column, an exceptional example of the Baroque style popular in central Europe. It was erected in the early 18th century by grateful townsfolk to commemorate the end of a period of plague. Also here are six of Olomouc's famous fountains, including the Hercules Fountain depicting the muscleman warding off the attack of the nine-headed Hydra.

The Holy Trinity Column is adorned with statues of saints.

Olomouc also has a proud ecclesiastical history, and along bustling May 1st Street is peaceful Wenceslas Square. The brooding St. Wenceslas Cathedral was originally consecrated as a Romanesque basilica in 1131. The nearby Přemysl Palace complex hosts the Olomouc Archdiocesan Museum, with a dazzling collection of treasures from the 12th to the 18th centuries, when Olomouc was the capital of Moravia.

Visit the Vila Primavesi for both its fine architecture and food. The Primavesi family were supporters of the Viennese Art Nouveau movement—Gustav Klimt was a regular recipient of their friendship and patronage. Now the rambling, restored villa is the city's finest restaurant. Look forward to innovative preparations of fish and seafood and to lighter versions of traditional Czech food—try the roast veal with cream sauce, cranberry dip, and plump homemade dumplings.

Where: 155 miles/250 km east of Prague. **Visitor info:** www.olomouc-tourism.cz. **Olomouc Archdiocesan Museum:** Tel 420/585-514-190; www.olmuart.cz. **Vila Primavesi:** Tel 420/777-749-288; www.primavesi.cz. *Cost:* dinner $30. **Where to stay:** In a thoroughly modernized historic building, the Penzion Na Hrade is just steps from the main square. Tel 420/585-203-231; www.penzionnahrade.cz. *Cost:* from $110. **Best times:** Jun–Sep for pleasant weather; Apr or May for Flora Festival; May for Spring Music Festival; Jun for the Festival of Songs and City Festival.

The Epitome of Baltic Beauty

Saaremaa Island

Estonia

Estonia may be the smallest of the Baltic nations, but it has the lion's share of coastline, with hundreds of islands sprinkled in the Baltic Sea. One of its most captivating coastal settings is Saaremaa, a largely forest-covered island with old-fashioned seaside villages, desolate beaches, and a picturesque town with spa resorts and an imposing castle. Saaremaa has always had an independent streak, and its people have their own customs, song traditions, and costumes. Attending a local festival—like the Castle Days fest in early July or midsummer night on June 23—is a great way to experience the rich island heritage.

The biggest community on Saaremaa is Kuressaare (population 16,000), which harbors the Baltic's best-preserved castle, a 14th-century dolomite fortress with drawbridge over a water-filled moat. The warren of vestibules, narrow passageways, defensive tower chambers, and dungeonlike basement rooms make for a fascinating wander.

Beyond Kuressaare, the Estonian countryside in all its quiet beauty unfolds. The Sõrve Peninsula, on the southwestern reaches of the island, has a rugged landscape of jagged cliffs and fine sea views; the ruins of an old Soviet military base and various gravesites attest to the heavy fighting here in World War II. The Viidumäe Nature Reserve Saaremaa is located on the island's highest point and is home to unusual orchid and bird species (including black storks) and rare plants like the Saaremaa yellow rattle found nowhere else, as well as 600 species of butterflies and moths. A 72-foot-high watchtower provides a scenic vantage point over the forest and meadows.

The George Ots Spa Hotel in Kuressaare is one of the island's best accommodations, with handsome rooms, a good restaurant, and a full range of spa treatments. Take to the countryside for something more romantic and lavish, and book a room in the Pädaste Manor, on Muhu Island (which is connected to Saaremaa by bridge). With roots dating back to the 16th century, this aristocratic waterfront manor has 14 beautifully appointed rooms. At the award-winning Alexander Restaurant, you can sample Nordic island cuisine composed of fresh local ingredients in a sophisticated culinary interpretation, served in a serene, light-filled space.

WHERE: 125 miles/201 km southwest of Tallinn. **VISITOR INFO:** www.saaremaa.ee. **GEORGE OTS SPA HOTEL:** Tel 372/455-0000; www.gospa.ee. *Cost:* from $70 (off-peak), from $155 (peak). **PÄDASTE MANOR:** Tel 372/454-8800; www.padaste.ee. *Cost:* from $275; dinner at Alexander $90. *When:* closed Nov–Feb. **BEST TIMES:** May–Sep for pleasant weather; Jun 23 for Jaanipaev, the midsummer night's festival; early Jul for Castle Days Festival.

A Perfectly Preserved Medieval City

OLD TALLINN

Tallinn, Estonia

The best way to arrive in the capital city of Tallinn is by ferry from Helsinki (see p. 347), 53 miles across the Gulf of Finland. The soaring spires of the capital rise into view, with 600-year-old ramparts, red-tiled roofs, and glistening church domes soaring over the approaching hilltops. Above it looms the ancient stronghold of the Toompea quarter. Once on land, it's an easy stroll to the narrow cobblestone streets of Vanalinn, or the Old Town of Tallinn.

Since the nation regained its independence in 1991, tourism has flourished in this proud and vibrant city. Despite centuries of living under the foreign rule of Danes, Swedes, Germans, and Russians, Estonians kept their language, customs, and culture intact.

The heart of Old Town is Raekoja Plats, a magnificent square that has been the center of Tallinn life since the 13th century. Today it's a remarkably lively place, with outdoor cafés ringed by a handsome assortment of historic pastel-painted buildings with the 14th-century gothic Raekoda, one of Europe's oldest town halls, at its center.

Wandering through the old quarter is the best way to peer back in time, losing yourself amid 500-year-old merchant houses and tiny lanes that open onto striking Gothic churches. A short walk east of the Raekoja Plats, on Müürivahe Street, you'll find an outdoor market where vendors sell their handmade crafts beneath the shadow of Old Town's imposing defensive wall, studded with 26 watchtowers, each topped by a pointy red roof. Don't bypass adjoining Katariina Passage; browse its medieval-style workshops where ceramics, glasswork, quilts, and jewelry are made and sold.

Tallinn's Old Town has excellent accommodations. The Three Sisters is a boutique hotel set in three gabled 1362 merchant houses close to St. Olav's church. Rooms have old-world architectural details that mix with contemporary furnishings, and there's a wine cellar bar, library, lounge with fireplace, and the new Bordoo restaurant that is regarded as one of the city's most innovative. The Schloessle Hotel is another historic charmer, in a 17th-century baronial building with a garden-fringed courtyard, steps from Raekoja Plats. Also in Old Town is the Merchant House, a handsome 37-room boutique hotel done up with great style.

Visitor info: www.tourism.tallinn.ee. **Three Sisters:** Tel 372/630-6300; www.threesisters.com. *Cost:* from $260 (off-peak), from $360 (peak); dinner at Bordoo $50. **Schloessle Hotel:** Tel 372/699-7700; www.schloesslehotel.com. *Cost:* from $200 (off-peak), from $250 (peak). **Merchant House:** Tel 372/697-7500; www.merchanthousehotel.com. *Cost:* from $125 (off-peak), from $190 (peak). **Best times:** Jun–Aug for warmest weather; late Apr for Jazzkaar fest; late May–early Jun for Old Town Days with dancing, concerts, and events; Dec for the Christmas market.

Cave City and Cradle of Culture

Vardzia

Samtskhe-Javakheti, Georgia

Tucked away in a remote valley close to the Turkish border lies one of Georgia's greatest cultural treasures, the 800-year-old cave town of Vardzia. A vast monastery complex hewn into the rock of a mountainside, Vardzia was created during the reigns of King George III (1156–84) and his daughter Queen Tamar (1184–1213), Georgia's first female ruler. Tamar's reign was a cultural golden age when distinctively Georgian church architecture flourished and the country's greatest poet, Shota Rustaveli, composed his epic tale of chivalry and courtly love, *The Knight in the Panther's Skin.*

An entire city, hidden from the view of possible invaders, was carved into the mountainside, a maze of houses, monks' cells, workshops, water cisterns, and wine cellars, all linked by tunnels, staircases, and irrigation channels hewn from the rock. Within 100 years an earthquake shook away the outer walls of some of the cave rooms, opening them to view. Another quake, in the 15th century, caused the outer face of the mountain to collapse, exposing no fewer than 600 chambers spread over 13 levels, creating the honeycomb view that visitors see today.

At the center of the cave city, now supported by an arch of modern concrete, is the Church of the Assumption. This remarkable structure, entirely hollowed out of the rock, is decorated with colorful frescoes from the 12th century that include lifelike portraits of Queen Tamar and other members of the royal family.

Twelve smaller churches are scattered through the complex, but no less fascinating are the remnants of everyday life in medieval times. Living quarters are equipped with rock-cut sleeping platforms, stone tables and seats, and niches that once held oil lamps. There are 25 wine cellars, complete with the remains of grape presses and stone basins for collecting and fermenting the juices. Vardzia was abandoned in the 1550s, but now the complex, which operates mostly as a museum, is once again occupied by a handful of monks.

Vardzia lies at the head of a remote valley with not even a village nearby, so you'll need to bring food and water, and the guides on hand to lead you through the cave city are not likely to speak English. It's 2 hours by taxi from the closest town, Akhaltsikhe, where the new Hotel Rio is a good place to spend the night.

WHERE: 160 miles/257 km southwest of Tbilisi. **VISITOR INFO:** www.georgia.travel. **HOTEL RIO:** Tel 995/32-319-101; www.riohotelakhaltsikhe.com. *Cost:* $45. **HOW:** U.S.-based MIR includes Vardzia as part of a 10-day "Essential Georgia" tour. Tel 800-424-7289 or 206-624-7289; www.mircorp.com. *Cost:* from $3,295. Originates in Tbilisi. **BEST TIME:** May–Sep for good weather.

The Heart and Soul of Georgia

OLD TBILISI

Tbilisi, Georgia

Named for its sulfurous hot springs (*tbili* is Georgian for "warm"), Tbilisi is an ancient river town set against a mountain backdrop. It has been the capital of Georgia since the 5th century, and today, with a population of 1.2 million, it is the liveliest and most cosmopolitan of the Caucasus cities and home to more than a quarter of Georgia's people.

Nestled beneath the ancient walls of Narikala Fortress, which commands the narrows of the Mtkvari (or Kura) River valley, Old Town is a delightful maze of cobbled alleys and old houses with carved wooden balconies and stained-glass windows. Stroll among early Armenian and Georgian churches, mosques, synagogues, and inns, or wander into a café to sample the spicy meat dumplings called *khinkali.* Wash them down with one of the well-regarded local wines; Georgians, thought by some to be the world's original vintners, were making wine by 5000 B.C.

At the north end of Old Town is the Anchiskhati Basilica, erected in the 6th century. To the south is Sioni Cathedral, dating from the 7th century but rebuilt many times. Inside is Georgia's holiest relic, a cross made of braided grape vines entwined with

The 6th-century Jvari Monastery, near Mtskheta, played an important role in early Christianity in Georgia.

the hair of Saint Nino, the woman who brought Christianity here in the 4th century.

In Abanotubani, the bath district, warm sulfur baths steam under domed brick roofs dating back to the 17th century. The colorful tile of the Orbeliani baths, the most ornate, is reminiscent of a central Asian mosque. A soak and massage here are a relaxing way to end a day of sightseeing. The small and welcoming Hotel Villa Mtiebi, in the heart of Old Town, is a comfortable place to stay.

To the northwest are the broad, stately streets and squares of New Town, lined with government buildings, theaters, concert halls, gleaming glass-and-steel shopping malls, and modern hotels, including the luxurious Radisson Blu Iveria. It puts you close to the Janashia Museum and its priceless collection of pre-Christian gold objects and jewelry.

In Mtskheta, 15 miles west of Tbilisi, the religious capital of Georgia until the 5th century, stands the Svetitskhoveli Cathedral, dating from 1020 and the country's most important church. From here, a 1-hour hike or short taxi ride leads to the Jvari Monastery, which was built in the 6th century. From its commanding hilltop site, take in spectacular views of the town and the Mtkvari River valley.

VISITOR INFO: www.info-tbilisi.com. **HOW:** Explore Georgia offers 1-day tours of Old Tbilisi and Mtskheta. Tel 995/32-921-911; www.exploregeorgia.com. *Cost:* from $50. **HOTEL VILLA MTIEBI:** Tel 995/32-920-340; www.hotelmtiebi.ge. *Cost:* from $100. **RADISSON BLU IVERIA:** Tel 995/32-402-200; www.radissonblu.com/hotel-tbilisi. *Cost:* from $190. **JANASHIA MUSEUM:** Tel 995/32-998-022; www.museum.ge. **BEST TIMES:** May–Jun and Sep for nicest weather; late Oct for the Tbilisoba cultural festival.

Spa City

Budapest's Traditional Thermal Baths

Budapest, Hungary

Deep below Budapest, more than 120 thermal springs gush from 14 sources, with temperatures ranging from warm-as-toast 70°F to a hard-boiled 169°. The world's only capital city with such natural attractions within town, Budapest has taken advantage of this mineral-water wealth since the times of the Romans, and the tradition of "taking the waters" continues. The city counts about a dozen traditional thermal baths, some of them a legacy of the Turks, who popularized public bathing during their century-and-a-half occupation that began in 1541. Other baths are splendors of Art Nouveau, and still others spic-and-span modern establishments. Some baths have sections devoted exclusively to men and to women; others reserve certain hours for each. Most of the city's fine hotels have sanctuary-like, state-of-the-art spas, from the painstakingly restored Royal Spa at the Corinthia Grand Hotel Royal to the small but sublime spa at the landmark Four Seasons Gresham Palace Hotel.

The most Turkish of all the historic baths is the Rudas, along the Danube in Buda below the sleek Elizabeth Bridge. Built just 25 years after the arrival of the Turks, it was recently given a major facelift that shows off its octagonal main pool, domed cupola set with colored glass, and massive columns that are straight out of a *1,001 Nights* film set. The Széchenyi Baths, built in 1913 in Pest's enormous City Park, will have you thinking less of the Ottomans than of some 19th-century neo-Baroque sanatorium. Unusual for its immense size (a dozen thermal baths and three outdoor swimming pools) it has a bright, clean (some might say antiseptic) look. Don't leave without catching one of the chess matches being played on floating boards in the pools.

The extravagant Gellért Baths are built over 18 hot springs, with pools said to be modeled after the baths of Caracalla in ancient Rome. Beneath the Gellért's spectacular arched glass dome and alongside gushing Zsolnay ceramic fountains, locals socialize in hushed tones or paddle about in the elaborately tiled pools. Taking a soak in this Art Nouveau palace has been compared to taking a bath in a cathedral. The adjacent Danubius Gellért Hotel, which opened its doors in 1918, has been undergoing a protracted renovation but has loads of character and remains the city's much-loved grande dame.

Corinthia Grand Hotel Royal: Tel 36/1-479-4000; www.corinthia.hu. *Cost:* from $180 (off-peak), from $335 (peak). **Four Seasons Gresham Palace:** Tel 36/1-268-6000; www.fourseasons.com/budapest. *Cost:* from $350 (off-peak), from $450 (peak). **Bath info:** www.spasbudapest.com. **Rudas Baths:** Tel 36/1-356-1322. **Széchenyi Baths:** Tel 36/1-363-3210. **Gellért Baths:** Tel 36/1-466-6166. **Danubius Gellért Hotel:** Tel 36/1-889-5500; www.danubiusgroup.com/gellert. *Cost:* from $180 (off-peak), from $280 (peak), includes admission to baths.

Where History and Scenery Vie for Attention

Castle Hill

Budapest, Hungary

Budapest was formed by combining the two distinct cities of Buda and Pest (pronounced pesht) in 1873. Much of Pest, on the left bank of the Danube River, is flat and most of it dates back to the 19th century. It is the city's sprawling commercial, entertainment, and shopping district. Buda, on the right bank, is hilly, leafy, and a whole lot older, dominated by Castle Hill, which looms 558 feet above the Danube River. It is the site of Old Town, full of colorful, medieval houses where commoners once lived, and of Buda Castle (Budai Vár), constructed in the 13th century and home to Hungarian kings for almost 7 centuries. Immense and lovingly reconstructed, the castle commands stunning views of the Danube and Pest's monumental buildings.

Buda's Castle Hill towers over the Danube.

Reaching the castle is half the fun. From Pest, stroll across the Danube on the Chain Bridge—the most graceful of Budapest's nine crossings—and board the steep-climbing funicular that will whisk you up to Castle Hill in minutes. At the top you'll find a complex that today contains a national library and museums, including the

Hungarian National Gallery, and part of a 17-mile-long network of caves and medieval tunnels used during World War II. Within them is the Buda Castle Labyrinth and, with its tacky waxworks, the Hospital in the Rock, which opened in 1944 as a military hospital. On the edge of the Old Town and flanking the monumental Matthias Church, the seven-turreted Fishermen's Bastion, a viewing platform offering wonderful views was built in 1905 and named after the guild responsible for defending this stretch of the castle wall in the Middle Ages. For a slice of something sweet, hope for a table at Ruszwurm, a diminutive *cukrászda* (patisserie) that has lured patrons since 1827 with wood-inlay counters, glass-and-mahogany display cases, and delicious baked goods.

Castle Hill is not short of elegant lodgings. The Hilton Budapest incorporates the ruins of a 14th-century church and maintains the Baroque façade of a 17th-century Jesuit college as the main entrance of its contemporary 322-room hotel. The newer, boutique Buda Castle Fashion Hotel has a stylish interior in a 15th-century building on a quiet street.

Visitor info: www.tourinform.hu. **Hungarian National Gallery:** Tel 36/1-201-9082; www.mng.hu. **Buda Castle Labyrinth:** Tel 36/1-212-0207; www.labirintus.com. **Hospital in the Rock:** Tel 36/70-701-0101; www.hospitalintherock.com. **Ruszwurm:** Tel 36/1-375-5284; www.ruszwurm.hu. **Budapest Hilton:** Tel 36/1-889-6600; in the U.S., tel 800-445-8667; www.budapest.hilton.com. *Cost:* from $170 (off-peak), from $335 (peak). **Buda Castle Fashion Hotel:** Tel 36/1-224-7900; www.budacastlehotelbudapest.com. *Cost:* from $130 (off-peak), from $300 (peak). **Best times:** May–Oct for pleasant weather; late Mar–early Apr for Budapest Spring Festival; Sep for International Wine Festival on Castle Hill.

Two High Notes of Hungarian Gastronomy

Gundel and Gerbeaud

Budapest, Hungary

Budapest's reputation as a gastronomic capital suffered greatly during the chilly days of Communism in the 1950s, when restaurants were put under state control and the best chefs, including the renowned Károly Gundel, fled the country. But 1989 brought new aromas with the winds of change, and in 1992, Gundel's restaurant in City Park reopened.

Budapest's (and Hungary's) fanciest and most famous place to eat, Gundel retains the aristocratic air that it had on opening day in 1894, when Budapest was considered the "Paris of Central Europe." The menu is filled with delightfully old-fashioned classics—goose liver and game predominate. Some of Hungary's best wines can be found on the extensive wine list, including bottles produced under Gundel's own label and "the wine of kings and the king of wines," as France's Louis XIV called the noble Tokaj (or Tokay) dessert wine. Just next door is Bagolyvár (Owl's Castle), Gundel's popular sister restaurant, staffed entirely by women. The menu here is less extensive and less expensive and offers a more home-style dining experience (goulash is a favorite).

As much as Hungarians like their paprika, they love their sweets, especially rich pastries like *dobos torta,* a layered chocolate-and-cream cake with a caramelized brown sugar top, or strudel filled with poppy seeds, cherry preserves or *túró* (curd or cottage cheese). These are usually enjoyed not after a meal but mid-afternoon in a *cukrászda,* or patisserie. Budapest's most famous is Gerbeaud, a neo-Baroque throwback to imperial times and an oasis of relaxation just off the main shopping street. The "café as castle" concept goes back to the late 19th century, when Budapest was one of the fastest-growing cities in the world, and the city's coffeehouses became second homes for writers, artists, and journalists. Opened in 1858 and at its current site since 1870, Gerbeaud survived the bleak period of Communism and is as popular with locals as it is with visitors, making it nearly impossible to find a late-afternoon table in the vast, mansionlike interior. If you do, be sure to sit back and linger amid the silk wallpaper, crystal chandeliers, and marble-topped tables.

Gundel: Tel 36/1-468-4040; www.gundel.hu. *Cost:* dinner $85. **Bagolyvár:** Tel 36/1-468-3110; www.bagolyvar.com. *Cost:* dinner $30. **Gerbeaud:** Tel 36/1-429-9000; www.gerbeaud.hu.

The Most Beautiful Section of Hungary's Revered River

The Danube Bend

Hungary

The Danube ("blond" and not "blue" to Hungarians) begins in the Black Forest in southwest Germany and flows east until it reaches a point about 25 miles north of Budapest. Here low-rising hills on both banks force it to bend sharply southward through Budapest and the rest of Hungary. The "Danube Bend" (Dunakanyar) is the name given to the region of scenic peaks, resorts, and historic towns to the north and northwest of Budapest. It is the most beautiful stretch of the Danube along its entire course of almost 1,865 miles and a classic (and easy) day trip from the capital by boat, bus, car, or train. The most popular of the riverside towns is Szentendre, settled in medieval times by Serbs escaping the Turkish invasion to the south and a charming artist colony since the 1920s. It still harbors a number of Orthodox churches as well as galleries and museums, one dedicated to the work of celebrated Hungarian ceramicist Margit Kovács (1902–77). If you're ready for a change from heavy, traditional Hungarian fare, book at Promenade. With vaulted ceilings and a wonderful terrace overlooking the Danube it is one of the town's best restaurants, offering meat and fish dishes simply grilled on lava stones.

The riverside town of Visegrád gets its name from the Slovak word for "high castle."

A bit farther west along the river is tiny Visegrád, home to Renaissance palace ruins and a forbidding hilltop castle. Carry on to Esztergom, seat of the Magyar kingdom until the 13th century, when the capital was moved to Buda. As the center of the Hungarian Catholic Church for a millennium, Esztergom remains the nation's most sacred city and is dominated by Hungary's largest basilica, built in the mid-19th century. If time allows, visit the Christian Museum, below the cathedral, which houses a fine collection of Hungarian medieval religious art. Enjoy lunch at nearby Padlizsán, with its view of a sheer rock face topped by a castle bastion and modern Hungarian dishes. For a more traditional experience, head for the tried-and-true Csülök Csárda (Pork Knuckle Inn), which specializes in—guess what?—smoked trotters as well as *bableves* (hearty bean soup). Pack an appetite.

WHERE: Szentendre is 16 miles/25 km north of Budapest; Esztergom is 33 miles/53 km north of Budapest. **MARGIT KOVÁCS CERAMIC COLLECTION:** Tel 36/26-310-244. **PROMENADE:** Tel 36/26-312-626; www.promenade-szentendre.hu. *Cost:* dinner $25. **CHRISTIAN MUSEUM:** Tel 36/33-413-880; www.christianmuseum.hu. **PADLIZSÁN:** Tel 36/33-311-212; www.padlizsanetterem.hu. *Cost:* dinner $25. **CSÜLÖK CSÁRDA:** Tel 36/33-412-420; www.csulokcsarda.hu. Cost: dinner $20. **BEST TIMES:** May–Jun and Sep–Oct for nicest weather.

Hungary's Inland Sea

LAKE BALATON

Central Transdanubia, Hungary

Hungary may not have a coastline, but it does have Balaton, the largest freshwater lake in Europe outside Scandinavia. This inland sea, 48 miles long and 5.6 miles across at its widest point, is bounded by hills to the north and gentle slopes to the south. Its mirror-smooth surface seems to change color according to the seasons and time of day.

Balaton has something of a split personality. On the southern shore are grassy beaches and the razzle-dazzle of a "seaside" resort. It's ideal for families with children and those who like to paddle rather than swim (the lake is relatively shallow; you'll need to wade for half a mile before the water reaches your waist). On the north shore are lush hills, vineyards, and historical towns and spas.

Balatonfüred is the oldest and most atmospheric resort on the north shore. It has none of the frenzy or brashness of Siófok, "Hungary's Ibiza," on the southern shore, partly because of its aristocratic origins and partly because its thermal waters attract an older crowd. While you can't visit the baths themselves (they are reserved for heart patients), you can take a "drinking cure" at the Kossuth Pump House, which dispenses slightly sulfuric (but potable) thermal water, which reputedly does wonders for the circulation. The well-located and recently renovated Anna Grand Hotel, once the town's sanatorium, is now the nicest of the lake's basic overnight options.

Tihany, a thumb-shaped peninsula jutting into the Balaton, is the most historic spot on the lake, with a celebrated Benedictine Abbey Church featuring fantastically carved altars, pulpits, and screens that date to the late 18th century. The peninsula itself is a nature reserve (Hungary's first, set aside in 1952) of hills and marshy meadows; several color-coded walking trails lead past ancient castle and church ruins to geyser cones and quiet lakeshore. Wind up your stroll at Ferenc Pince Csárda, about a mile south of the Abbey Church. As its name ("Frank's Cellar") implies, wine gets equal billing with the food here, and this is your chance to sample some of Tihany's best vintages.

At the western end of Balaton, you'll find the spa town of Hévíz, on the shores of a 10-acre thermal lake (Europe's largest) of the same name. The water surface temperature averages 91°F and never drops below 72°, even in winter, allowing bathers to enjoy it when ice and snow cover the surrounding fir trees. The attraction for many may be the indoor spa in the adjoining park, where you can sign up for therapies and beauty treatments.

WHERE: 80 miles/135 km southwest of Budapest. **VISITOR INFO:** Balatonfüred, www.balatonfured.hu; Tihany, www.tihany.hu. **ANNA GRAND HOTEL:** Tel 36/87-581-200; www.annagrandhotel.eu. *Cost:* from $110 (off-peak), from $180 (peak). **FERENC PINCE CSÁRDA:** Tel 36/87-448-575; www.ferenc pince.hu. *Cost:* dinner $20. **HÉVÍZ SPA:** Tel 36/83-501-700; www.spaheviz.hu. **BEST TIMES:** liveliest in Jul–Aug; Sep–Oct for smaller crowds and nicest weather.

A Town Full of Mediterranean and Turkish Delights

PÉCS

Southern Transdanubia, Hungary

Pécs, the capital of the Hungarian region called Southern Transdanubia, is one of those small, perfectly formed Central European cities that seems to have it all: fine museums, fabulous architecture in the form of Moorish-style buildings left behind by the Turkish occupiers, a mild, almost Mediterranean climate in which almonds and apricots thrive, and café tables fighting for space along charming pedestrian streets. What's more, Hungary's premier region for red wine, Villány, is close by.

The imprint of the Ottomans is everywhere, and the greatest reminder of their former reign is the Inner Town Parish Church, aka the Mosque Church. The largest Ottoman structure left standing in Hungary, it is known for its striking windows framed with Moorish arches, its *mihrab,* or prayer niche, and the faded Koranic verses found on its walls.

The Mosque Church stands in central Szechenyi Square.

Of the wealth of world-class museums—one of many reasons Pécs was chosen as a European Capital of Culture in 2010—the Vasarely Museum is most worthy of a visit. It contains a number of works by local son Victor Vasarely (1906–97), called by some the father of Op Art. You'll also want to stop at the Csontváry Museum for the paintings by Tivadar Kosztka Csontváry (1853–1919), whose tragic life is sometimes compared with that of Vincent van Gogh.

For an old-world ambience, choose the Palatinus Hotel, located on the city's central pedestrian street. It features plenty of marble, red carpet, and Moorish flourishes. For cozier accommodations, drive 27 miles south to Villány, where several wine producers have opened smart little hotels with excellent restaurants, such as the family-owned Crocus Gere Bor Hotel. Its Mandula Restaurant & Wine Bar is the place to sample refined versions of regional dishes, like duck breast with forest mushroom risotto and pike-perch fillet with nutmeg-seasoned pumpkin. The Gere family's own red wines, including cabernet sauvignon and cabernet franc, are also on offer. Stroll the town's main street and stop at one of the many cellars offering tastings for more local vintages.

Where: 142 miles/238 km southwest of Budapest. **Visitor info:** en.pecs.hu. **Vasarely Museum:** Tel 36/72-514-044. **Csontváry Museum:** Tel 36/72-310-544. **Palatinus Hotel:** Tel 36/72-889-400; www.danubius hotels.com/palatinus. *Cost:* from $90 (off-peak), from $130 (peak). **Crocus Gere Bor Hotel:** Tel 36/72-492-195; www.gere.hu. *Cost:* from $115; dinner $25. **Best times:** late Mar for Spring Festival of the arts; late Sep for Heritage Days Festival of dance, music, and wine.

From the Medieval to the Art Nouveau

Old Riga

Latvia

Set on the banks of the serene Daugava (Dvina) River, Riga looms large over the Baltics, with a stunningly preserved Old Town full of medieval treasures. But it is the concentrated enclave of gorgeous Art Nouveau (aka Jugendstil) buildings that sets this capital city apart: It ranks as the finest, most extensive collection in Europe and is the reason Riga is called "the Paris of the Baltics."

A wander through the cobblestones of Old Town reveals surprises at every turn, from the enormous Dome Cathedral (founded in 1211) to the House of Blackheads, a beautiful 14th-century guild hall with an elaborate Dutch Renaissance façade. Destroyed during World War II, it was painstakingly rebuilt after Latvia regained its independence in 1991. Next door is the stark and moving Latvian Museum of the Occupation, which provides a one-of-a-kind, eye-opening account of Latvian life under Nazi and Soviet rule.

A few blocks north of Old Town, you'll encounter Riga's Art Nouveau/Jugendstil neighborhood. On Alberta Street and nearby Elizabetes Street, dozens of gloriously decorated buildings bear the stylized motifs and bold geometry of Riga's reigning design aesthetic during an enormously creative period at the turn of the 20th century. After strolling the area, stop in the Riga Art Nouveau Museum, housed in a 1903 building.

Two blocks from the museum you'll find Vincents, one of Latvia's finest restaurants, where local ingredients are used in Baltic creations that incorporate Scandinavian and subtle French accents. Vincents Martins Ritins is the chef and mastermind behind the cool, minimalist, and highly celebrated space.

In Old Town, the Grand Palace Hotel, built as the State Bank in 1877, has 56 rooms with classical furnishings and handsome details. Impeccable service also reigns at the boutique Bergs Hotel, refurbished in a decidedly more contemporary style, with 38 spacious rooms. At the onsite Restaurant Bergs enjoy an alfresco dinner of rack of Welsh lamb or roast Barbary duck on the covered veranda during the warmer weather months. Sample a shot of Riga Black Balsam, a strong traditional liqueur, if you dare.

Visitor info: www.liveriga.com. **Museum of the Occupation:** Tel 371/6721-2715; www.occupationmuseum.lv. **Riga Art Nouveau Museum:** Tel 371/6718-1464; www.jugendstils.riga.lv. **Vincents:** Tel 371/6733-2830; www.restorans.lv. *Cost:* dinner $90. **Grand Palace Hotel:** Tel 371/6704-4000; www.grandpalaceriga.com. *Cost:* from $250. **Bergs Hotel:** Tel 371/6777-0900; www.hotelbergs.lv. *Cost:* from $195 (off-peak), from $250 (peak); dinner $65. **Best times:** Jun–Aug for nicest weather; mid-Jun for Opera Festival; Jul for Riga Rhythm international music festival; Aug–Sep for Sacred Music Festival in the Dome Cathedral.

Old Town's reconstructed House of Blackheads was a medieval home for unmarried guild members.

Storied Castles and Bucolic Scenery

Gauja Valley

Vidzeme, Latvia

Although just 35 miles northeast of Riga, the enchanting landscapes of the Gauja Valley seem like they're right out of a fairy tale. Amid pine-scented forests and lush, rolling countryside lie medieval castles, frozen-in-time villages, and archaeological sites dating back to the Bronze Age.

Several charming towns make good bases for exploring the valley. In the east, Sigulda has long captivated visitors, with an idyllic location on a steep, wooded hillside overlooking the Gauja River. The area was first settled before 2000 B.C. by Finno-Ugric tribes, who built strategic fortifications along the hilltops. Sigulda's oldest standing citadels date back to the 13th century and make for fascinating exploring.

On the opposite side of the river lie the ruins of Krimulda Castle and the grand 19th-century Krimulda Manor. The best way to get there is to take the aerial cable car, which provides panoramic views over the river and countryside. From the castle, there are lovely walking trails and the chance to observe the rich flora and fauna of the Gauja Valley—some 150 bird and 50 mammal species inhabit this protected region.

The most impressive stronghold is the red-brick Turaida Castle, which houses a museum covering medieval life under the Livonian state (1300s to 1500s). Take a walk along its impressive ramparts to see the surrounding pristine forest, which is but one reason why the ancient inhabitants called this Turaida, meaning "God's Garden." There's also a 1750 wooden church and a sculpture garden dedicated to Latvia's rich folkloric traditions.

Sigulda offers a range of adventures, from hot-air balloon trips to an action-packed ride down a 4,000-foot-long bobsled track, open year-round. Ski slopes attract snow lovers come wintertime, and hikers come for the bucolic scenery in spring, summer, and autumn.

The romantic town of Cēsis, which is 20 miles northeast of Sigulda, is another highlight of the Gauja. Its medieval center is lined with old stone buildings, and an imposing castle is surrounded by landscaped parks. You can sample local beer from the Cēsu Alus, one of the oldest breweries in the Baltics. Pristine wilderness lies just outside town, with access to the steep sandstone cliffs along the Gauja River some 3 miles to the north.

WHERE: Sigulda is 33 miles/53 km northeast of Riga. **VISITOR INFO:** www.sigulda.lv. **BEST TIMES:** Apr–May for wildflowers; Jun–Aug for warm weather.

Fragile Seascape of Beaches, Dunes, and Forests

THE CURONIAN SPIT

Lithuania

Crisp, wildlife-filled pine forests, alluring beaches, and enormous dunes sweeping down to the sea set the stage for one of the most dramatic landscapes in the Baltic countries. Sometimes described as "the Sahara of Lithuania" because of its wildly shifting sands, the Curonian Spit has lush forests where deer, elk, and wild boar roam, plus traditional villages where fishermen still smoke their catch using age-old Curonian recipes. With its fragile ecology and unique ecosystems, the entire spit, which stretches for 60 miles (divided equally between Lithuania and Russia), is protected as national parks. It's a major site for bird-watchers, with millions of migratory birds passing over in spring and autumn. You may spot gray herons, cormorants, and cranes, or brown kites, pink starlings, and peregrine falcons. The spit itself is narrow—less than a mile wide in parts—with gentle surf from the Baltic on one side and the peaceful Curonian Lagoon on the other.

Owing to its unique surroundings of dunes and forests, and to its Germanic roots, the charming fishing village of Nida feels a world away from mainland Lithuania. In the early 20th century, the town, located about 30 miles south of mainland Klaipėda, became a colony for German Expressionist artists and intellectuals, and in the 1930s, it was a summer home for celebrated writer Thomas Mann. You can visit the cottage where the Nobel laureate lived and about which he penned, "It is truly impossible to write about the uniqueness and beauty of the nature of these environs."

From the town, it's a short stroll to the scenic waterfront overlooking the Curonian Lagoon, where you can sign up for a memorable boat ride—local outfits offer everything from 2-hour sails to all-day fishing jaunts. The white sand beaches of the Baltic are less than a mile's walk through pine forest. South of town lies the 170-foot-high Parnidis Dune, one of the highest in Europe. You can climb steps to the top, where you'll find windswept views over the vast, rippling sands stretching to the south. There's also an 18-mile cycling path through forest and along the seaside to the tiny village of Juodkrantė.

WHERE: 191 miles/307 km west of Vilnius. **VISITOR INFO:** www.nerija.lt/en. **THOMAS MANN MEMORIAL MUSEUM:** Tel 370/4695-2260; www.mann.lt. **WHERE TO STAY:** In Nida, Misko Namas is a B&B in a historic wooden house with spacious rooms overlooking a garden. Tel 370/4695-2290; www.miskonamas.com. *Cost:* from $50 (off-peak), from $100 (peak). **BEST TIMES:** Jun–Aug for warmest weather; Mar–May and Sep–Oct for bird-watching.

A Great Baroque Beauty

OLD VILNIUS

Vilnius, Lithuania

The Old Town of Vilnius—one of the largest historic districts in Europe—is a magnificent canvas of Gothic, Renaissance, and Baroque architecture. Don't miss the dramatic Vilnius Cathedral, which dates back to the 14th century. Above it looms Gediminas Castle, with sunset views over the city.

Vilnius lacks some of the sophistication and glamour of its sister Baltic capitals of Riga and Tallinn (see pp. 304 and 295), whose German and Scandinavian influences are more apparent. The only inland Baltic capital, Vilnius is closer in feel to Poland and Russia. The cobblestone Pilies Gatvė is the buzzing main thoroughfare through the old quarter, with shops and cafés, buskers, and folk artists selling their wares. More than 40 centuries-old churches can be found along the narrow streets; 15th-century St. Anne's is one of its most photogenic. Napoleon, visiting in 1812, said that he'd like to take the whole building back to Paris in the palm of his hand.

Vilnius was once home to a thriving Jewish community. Visit the 1903 Moorish-inspired Choral Synagogue, just outside Old Town—it is one of the few prewar prayer houses still functioning. In the former headquarters of the KGB, the Museum of Genocide Victims is a quiet tribute to those imprisoned, tortured, or executed here and to the countless who were shipped off to Siberia.

The city's most sumptuous digs are the Stikliai Hotel, occupying a stately 17th-century Baroque residence. Or check into the 20-room Grotthuss boutique hotel whose common areas and elegant rooms are decorated with Italian-made furniture and the owner's art collection. Its restaurant, La Pergola, serves beautifully prepared international cuisine—and in the summer, you can dine in the courtyard in the back.

VISITOR INFO: http://lietuva.lt/en. **MUSEUM OF GENOCIDE VICTIMS:** Tel 370/5249-7427; www.genocid.lt/muziejus/en. **STIKLIAI HOTEL:** Tel 370/5264-9595; www.stikliaihotel.lt. *Cost:* from $275. **GROTTHUSS HOTEL:** Tel 370/5266-0322; www.grotthusshotel.com. *Cost:* from $155; dinner $50. **BEST TIMES:** Jun–Aug for pleasant weather; late May–early Jul for Vilnius Music Festival.

Fjordlike Wonder

BAY OF KOTOR

Montenegro

Lord Byron described it as "the most beautiful encounter between land and the sea." Limestone cliffs plunge into the deep blue, fjordlike Boka Kotorska (Bay of Kotor), where the waters of the Adriatic thrust deep into coastal highlands and steep mountains. Of this small country's natural attractions, the Bay of Kotor takes best in show.

At the head of the bay is the secluded, walled town of Kotor, one of the best-preserved medieval ports in Europe. Narrow, marbled streets and open squares are lined with medieval houses abutting grand Venetian-style palazzos, all dominated by the spires of six Romanesque churches, including the magnificent St. Tryphon Cathedral, dating back to 1166. Open-air markets proffer fresh figs, olives, and local cheeses, and the squares bustle with cafés. It is 1,300 steps up to St. John's Fortress for unforgettable views.

Kotor's 3 miles of defensive stone walls are especially beautiful when illuminated at night. Built to repel foreigners, they now attract them, and Kotor has quickly adjusted to Montenegro's sudden rise as a tourist hot spot. Cruise-ship passengers on their way to and from Venice (see p. 217) disembark for an afternoon; day-trippers from Dubrovnik (see p. 284), an hour's drive away, fill the squares. Spend the night and you'll have your pick of small Old Town restaurants, such as the family-owned Cesarica, with ancient, vaulted stone walls and excellent seafood dishes. With its lively street life, the area can be noisy at night, so consider sleeping in one of the neighboring seaside villages. A beautifully restored 18th-century villa, Palazzo Radomiri, stands on the bay front of Dobrota, a 5-minute drive or half-hour walk from Old Town. The stone villa's original character has been carefully preserved, and it features a patio and pool, café, and ten elegant rooms with sea views. Also on the Dobrota waterfront, Forza Mare is a thoroughly modern small luxury hotel, with a restaurant and high-design suites. Once you've had your fill of Kotor, you can explore ancient towns like bay-front Perast or try some of Europe's best whitewater rafting in the nearby Tara River Canyon.

Perast reached its peak in the 18th century under the Republic of Venice.

WHERE: 37 miles/60 km southeast of Dubrovnik, Croatia. **CESARICA:** Tel 382/32-336-093. *Cost:* dinner $50. **PALAZZO RADOMIRI:** Tel 382/32-333-172; www.palazzoradomiri.com. *Cost:* from $125. *When:* closed Nov–Mar. **FORZA MARE:** Tel 382/32-333-500; www.forzamare.com. *Cost:* from $250. *When:* closed Dec–Mar. **BEST TIMES:** Mar–Jun and Sep–Oct for nice weather and fewer crowds; Jul and early Aug for Kotor Art festival.

Highlights of the Adriatic Coast

The Budva Riviera and Sveti Stefan

Montenegro

Montenegro's most stunning beaches stretch along the 62-mile expanse of mountainous coastline between Budva and the Albanian border, where only a few years ago, fishing villages snoozed in isolated beauty.

This rugged coastline with fine, pink-tinged sand beaches has vaulted into international popularity since Montenegro gained its independence from Serbia in 2006. Today, big, flashy destination resorts rub shoulders there, yet you don't have to look long to recapture the charming, old-world Montenegro.

Budva is a major center for new beach resorts, but its pedestrian-only Stari Grad, or Old Town, is a lively, boutique- and café-filled vestige of medieval architecture. The most atmospheric place to stay in the quarter is at the Hotel Astoria, which mixes ancient stone walls and a clean modern style. Beaches are just a few strides away. Farther east, along Budva Bay, is the village of Rafailoviči, where the area's best seafood restaurant, Tri Ribara (Three Fishermen), serves delicious, freshly caught grilled fish on its beachfront terrace.

The coast's showpiece can be found 5 minutes south of Budva: the hotel-village of Sveti Stefan, a cluster of 15th-century fishermen's cottages built on a rocky outcrop in the emerald waters of the Adriatic. A partly walled islet sometimes called a Mediterranean Mont St-Michel, Sveti Stefan rises just one hundred yards from the mainland and is tethered to it by a narrow isthmus. In the 1950s, Yugoslav President Tito converted it into a jet-set resort that attracted a stream of celebrities like Elizabeth Taylor, Richard Burton, and Sophia Loren. Today, the revitalized hotel is operated by the exclusive Amanresorts and is a car-free showcase of ancient stone homes and exquisite modern luxury. Among its various restaurants, the most coveted table is at the open-air La Piazza, which serves refined interpretations of traditional Montenegrin cuisine and welcomes nonguests. Even more exclusive is the sister Villa Miločer on the mainland, a former royal residence transformed into eight sumptuous suites.

An enjoyable, more wallet-friendly alternative is the family-owned Vila Drago, whose simple balconied rooms have perfect views of the island. You'll have to look hard to find better seafood and roasted meats than those served at its grapevine-shaded restaurant.

WHERE: Budva is 19 miles/33 km southeast of the international airport at Tivat. **HOTEL ASTORIA:** Tel 382/33-451-110; www.budva.astoriamontenegro.com. *Cost:* from $155 (off-peak), from $260 (peak). **TRI RIBARA:** Tel 382/33-471-050; www.triribara.com. *Cost:* dinner $25. **AMAN SVETI STEFAN** and **THE VILLA MILOČER:** Tel 382/33-420-000; in the U.S., 800-477-9180; www.amanresorts.com. *Cost:* from $850 (off-peak), $990 (peak); dinner $95. **VILA DRAGO:** Tel 382/33-468-457; www.viladrago.com. *Cost:* from $65; dinner $20. **BEST TIMES:** Apr–Jun and Sep–Oct for nicest weather and fewer crowds; early Jun for Budva Music Festival.

Killing Fields in the Center of Europe

AUSCHWITZ

Poland

The industrial city of Oświęcim would not be given a second look had the Nazis not chosen it in 1940 as the site of the most notorious extermination camp the world has ever known. Oświęcim is the town known as Auschwitz in German, where workers at the camp of the same name and the nearby Brzeziny (Birkenau) camp organized the systematic murder of an estimated 1.6 million people. The majority of the victims were Jews, transported here from all over Nazi-occupied

Europe. It is a harrowing place to visit, beginning with the infamous motto above the camp's entrance (*Arbeit Macht Frei*, or "Work Brings Freedom") and continuing on to the "barracks"—built for 52 horses but later housing up to 300 people—and the haunting exhibits of confiscated shoes, suitcases, and other personal effects. Auschwitz and Birkenau are just over a mile apart, and you can either walk between the two, taking time to meditate in the quiet surroundings, or board one of the hourly buses. Built to alleviate congestion at Auschwitz, Birkenau was the largest and most lethal of the camps intended to be the "final solution to the Jewish Question."

Accommodation is limited in Oświęcim, as most visitors come on organized day trips from nearby Kraków (see below), where they can visit the former Jewish district of Kazimierz, currently undergoing a cultural renaissance, and the impressive Galicia Museum, which commemorates Jewish victims of the Holocaust and celebrates Jewish culture in the Galicia region of southeastern Poland and western Ukraine. The neighboring district of Podgórze (Podgorica), site of the wartime ghetto, is where Oskar Schindler had his enamelware factory and the lesser-known pharmacist Tadeusz Pankiewicz dispensed medicine and sheltered Jews on the premises of his Eagle Pharmacy throughout World War II. Both sites are now open to the public.

Where: 25 miles/40 km west of Kraków. **State Museum Auschwitz-Birkenau:** Tel 48/33-844-8100; www.auschwitz.org.pl. **Galicia Museum:** Tel 48/12-421-6842; www.galiciajewishmuseum.org. **Schindler's Factory:** Tel 48/12-257-1017; www.krakow-info.com/schindler.htm. **Eagle Pharmacy:** Tel 48/12-656-5625; www.mhk.pl.

Europe's Largest Medieval Market Square

Rynek Główny

Kraków, Poland

All of Kraków sooner or later passes through Rynek Główny, Europe's largest and most authentic medieval market square. Ringed by Gothic, Renaissance, and Baroque buildings, this massive plaza is dominated by the 15th-century Sukiennice (Cloth Hall), whose vaulted ground-floor passages are filled with souvenir stalls.

But it's the mismatched towers of St. Mary's Church, looming above the square to the northeast, that really catch the eye. The taller of the two was once the city's watchtower, and every Polish child knows the story of its heroic trumpeter, killed by an arrow that hit his throat mid-note while he was warning of a Tatar invasion. Today the incident is reenacted every hour by a handful of firemen in costume. Inside the church's 14th-century Gothic basilica is Kraków's most prized possession, a wooden altarpiece carved by renowned Gothic sculptor Wit Stwosz in 1489.

The Rynek Główny (Main Market Square) is the very heart of Kraków's Stare Miasto (Old Town), about 4 square miles of preserved streets and centuries-old buildings and monuments. Laid out in the mid-13th century, it has survived in more or less its original form. On its narrow streets are a dozen museums and some 20 of the city's 120 churches. Bars and cafés are filled with the students of Jagiellonian University, Poland's oldest and finest, keeping alive the former capital's legacy as an academic, cultural, and artistic center.

Just off the square is the Stary Hotel, housed in a charming 18th-century residence. Many of the 53 guest rooms are a seamless blend of centuries-old frescoes and contemporary design; there's a pool and spa, and from the open rooftop terrace you can almost touch the towers of St. Mary's.

Overlooking the Rynek Główny to the south is the historic restaurant Wierzynek, the perfect place to enjoy traditional Polish specialties and courtly service since King Casimir the Great hosted his daughter's wedding banquet here in 1364. Enjoy seasonal game, trout, and other specialties in the elegant ground-floor café or any of the eight atmospheric salons in the upstairs restaurant. A few doors west on the main market is the Hotel Wentzl, opened in 1792. It is particularly known for its restaurant, whose beamed ceilings, Oriental carpets, fine oil paintings, and views of the square take a backseat to its menu: Try the duck marinated in Żubrówka (the national herb-flavored vodka).

Every hour, a trumpet signal rings out from St. Mary's Church.

WHERE: 186 miles/299 km southwest of Warsaw. **VISITOR INFO:** www.krakow-info.com. **HOTEL STARY:** Tel 48/12-424-3400; www.hotelstary.com. *Cost:* from $190 (off-peak), from $295 (peak). **WIERZYNEK:** Tel 48/12-424-9600; www.wierzynek.com.pl. *Cost:* dinner (restaurant) $65, (café) $40. **WENTZL:** Tel 48/12-431-9220; www.wentzl.pl. *Cost:* from $245; dinner $45. **BEST TIMES:** May–Oct for nicest weather; May for Juwenalia, a student festival; Jun for the Jewish Culture Festival; Aug for International Music Festival; Christmas and Easter for markets in the square.

Symbol of the Nation's Identity

WAWEL HILL

Kraków, Poland

Kraków's centerpiece is the Royal Castle and Cathedral, a majestic complex of Gothic and Renaissance buildings that presides over the city from a rocky hill high above the Vistula River. The Royal Castle was the seat of Polish kings for more than 500 years until 1596, when the center of power moved to Warsaw. It is the silent guardian of a millennium of Polish history and is the most visited site in the country. Among the treasures in the historic interior of the royal chambers (or state rooms) are 16th-century Flemish tapestries, Italian and Dutch paintings, royal portraits, elaborate ceiling frescoes, and ornate Baroque furnishings. Other sections open to the public include the crown treasury and the armory.

Wawel Cathedral, consecrated in 1364 and dubbed "the sanctuary of the nation," was led by Archbishop (later Cardinal) Karol Wojtyla from 1964 until his election as Pope John Paul II in 1978. For centuries, Polish kings were crowned and buried here; the royal crypts below the nave also contain the tombs of statesmen and heroes, including Tadeusz Kościuszko, who fought in the American Revolutionary War as a colonel in the Continental Army. From the bell tower you can see much of Old Town (see p. 310) and its wealth of impressive buildings. (Unlike Warsaw, Kraków wasn't bombed during World War II, and as a result it is the only major Polish city to have retained its remarkable concentration of prewar architecture.)

For lunch or dinner, head ten minutes south of Wawel Hill to Chłopskie Jadło. The food here is traditional Polish "peasant grub" (which is what the name means) including roast goose and *żurek*, a soup made with beef or chicken stock, bacon, onion, mushrooms, and sour cream, flavored with *kwas* (a fermented beverage made with rye flour), and served in a carved-out loaf of bread. From Wawel, it's also just a few minutes' walk to the venerable Hotel Copernicus, situated on the oldest (and most picturesque) street in Kraków. The 29-room inn handsomely blends 16th-century features and modern comforts, with elegant, dark furniture upholstered in luxurious fabrics and set against reproductions of period frescoes on the walls. Pope John Paul II, who lived just across the street as a young priest, considered it one of the finest addresses in town.

Wawel Royal Castle: Tel 48/12-422-5155; www.wawel.krakow.pl. **Chłopskie Jadło:** Tel 48/12-421-8520; www.chlopskiejadlo.pl. *Cost:* dinner $25. **Hotel Copernicus:** Tel 48/12-424-3400; www.copernicus.hotel.com.pl. *Cost:* from $225 (off-peak), from $315 (peak).

Tributes to Poland's Poet of the Piano

Showcases on Chopin

Warsaw and Żelazowa Wola, Poland

Frédéric Chopin, who took well-loved Polish folk tunes and dances such as the *polonez* (polonaise) and the *mazurek* (mazurka) and turned them into virtuoso concert pieces, lived in Poland for his first 20 years—more than half his short life. Here he acquired a reputation mostly as a pianist before leaving for Paris and international fame. He is Poland's greatest cultural export.

A statue in Lazienki Park honors Chopin.

Chopin aficionados in Warsaw will make a beeline southwest of the Stare Grad (Old Town) for the Ostrogski Palace, the headquarters of the Chopin Society and a wonderfully intimate venue for chamber music concerts. Stop at the small Chopin Museum here, which contains some interesting items, including the composer's last piano and his death mask, before taking a bus from just outside the museum to the tiny village of Żelazowa Wola, 33 miles west, where the great composer was born in 1810.

Although Chopin is buried in Paris's Père-Lachaise Cemetery (see p. 113), music lovers find the journey to his Polish birthplace (now a museum) and the shady park that surrounds it a poignant pilgrimage. Schedule your trip to coincide with one of the Sunday concerts (from May to September) performed by noted pianists in the modest home's parlor. (Warsaw also has a schedule of summer Chopin concerts that take place in the city's pretty Royal Lazienki Park, near the Frédéric Chopin Memorial, on Sundays from mid-May to September.) Afterward, consider a trip to Kampinos National Park, which includes Europe's largest area of inland sand dunes.

The well-marked green trail originates in Żelazowa Wola and makes its way through thick forests and flower-strewn meadows—a setting that would have fueled Chopin's creative fires.

For an après-concert meal, head to Gessler Restauracja U Kucharzy, in Warsaw, and sample its peerless pierogi—Polish "ravioli" stuffed with either savory or sweet fillings—or one of a host of other traditional dishes. Run by the well-known Gessler family, the busy restaurant is set within the kitchen of a former hotel, affording you the opportunity to watch the chefs prepare your meal.

Chopin Museum: Warsaw, tel 48/22-441-6251; Żelazowa Wola, tel 48/46-863-3300; www.chopin.museum/en. **Gessler Restauracja U Kucharzy:** Tel 48/22-826-7936; www.gessler.pl. *Cost:* dinner $65. **Where to stay:** The elegant boutique hotel Le Regina is housed in an 18th-century palace in Old Town. Tel 48/22-531-6000; www.leregina.com. *Cost:* from $150 (off-peak), from $350 (peak). **Best time:** Chopin International Piano Competition held in Warsaw every 5 years (2015, etc.) with concerts scheduled at various venues and a gala concert on Oct 17, the anniversary of Chopin's death.

Mountain Resort Town with Its Own Architectural Style

Zakopane

Poland

Poland's very own St. Moritz, Zakopane is the nation's top center for winter sports and its highest town. It transforms in warmer months to a verdant base for hiking and trekking in the Tatra Mountains, the highest range of the Polish Carpathians. Zakopane's popularity goes back to the 1870s, when its clean air, idyllic surroundings, and folkloric past began to attract writers, artists, and craftsmen in search of inspiration.

Among them was the architect Stanisław Witkiewicz, father of the more famous writer, playwright, and painter known as Witkacy. He designed a house for a client that was inspired by the farmhouses and outbuildings of the Podhale, the highland region north of Zakopane and it launched the Zakopane style, which dominated the look of housing throughout Poland until World War I. Some of the buildings Witkiewicz designed still stand and can be visited; among the best examples is Villa Koliba, completed in 1893 and now housing the Museum of Zakopane Style.

When he was known as Karol Wojtyla, the late Pope John Paul II (who hailed from these parts) liked to take a good schuss on these trails. The ski slopes of the Zakopane region, the highest of which grace Mount Kasprowy Wierch (6,520 feet), are suitable for skiers of all levels. Don't expect Aspen, but you'll find that the town has good equipment and

Hotels and homes sit in the shadow of the Tatras.

facilities, including a cable car, chair lifts, and decent runs, plus a season that can extend as late as April. Hikers and trekkers will appreciate the 186 miles of trails that crisscross Tatra National Park, just south of Zakopane.

The massive gingerbread house containing the 54-room Grand Hotel Stamary opened in 1905 and now, after a total makeover, holds Poland's best spa. You'll find traditional touches at the more intimate chaletlike Hotel Lipowy Dwor, with 15 small, well-maintained rooms on a quiet street near the center of town.

On Krupowki Street, the long, pedestrian main street, where horse-drawn sleds make their way, several restaurants offer traditional Carpathian cuisine and live alpine music. The best is Staro Izba; its menu includes excellent lamb dishes, kielbasa, and *kwaśnica,* a hearty mutton and sauerkraut soup.

Where: 65 miles/105 km south of Kraków. **Visitor info:** www.promocja.zakopane.pl. **Museum of Zakopane Style:** Tel 48/18-201-5205; www.muzeumtatrzanskie.pl. **Grand Hotel Stamary:** Tel 48/18-202-4510; www.stamary.pl. *Cost:* from $150 (off-peak), from $210 (peak). **Hotel Lipowy Dwor:** Tel 48/18-206-6796; www.gat.pl. *Cost:* from $75. **Best times:** Dec–Mar for skiing; Jun–Sep for trekking; mid-Aug for International Festival of Mountain Folklore.

The Last Thriving Peasant Culture in Europe

Maramureş

Romania

Folded into the Mara and Izei valleys in northern Romania is time-warped Maramureş, a rural region where a medieval way of life persists largely untouched by the intense transformations that the rest of Romania has weathered over the past 25, 80, even 200 years. Peasants continue to live off the land, traditional villages are improbably preserved, and centuries-old customs are still dutifully followed: Hitchhikers along the single-lane back roads are just as likely to get a ride in a horse-drawn cart as in a car.

Maramureş's PAUSE button is stuck largely because of poor economic conditions and an exodus of skilled workers. But the glimpse of the past it offers—amid a hypnotic, undulating landscape—has generated unexpected appeal. Travelers who spend some time in this green landscape of haystacks, ancient farmsteads, and fields plowed with teams of oxen will find a warm welcome, often punctuated with a shot of homemade *ţuică,* a plum brandy that's prized locally and popular in all of Romania.

This has always been a forested region, and its builders and carvers made lavish use of wood in intricately carved wooden gates, traditional houses with steeply pitched roofs, and even wooden grave markers. At the Cimitirul Vesel (Merry Cemetery) in the town of Săpânta, 13 miles northwest of Sighetu Marmaţiei, the unofficial tourism hub of Maramureş, a local wood-carver created blue-painted markers starting in 1935, each including a portrait and a warm, often humorous epitaph. The markers have appeared in art exhibits across Europe, but most are still in the cemetery, ready to be visited.

Wood construction reached a kind of apogee in tall, wooden, Orthodox churches built of logs and thick beams without the use of a single metal nail. One in Surdeşti, built in 1724, is 236 feet tall. Other notable examples are two

17th-century churches in Călineşti and the region's oldest church, built in 1365, in Ieud.

WHERE: Sighetu Marmaţiei is 344 miles/ 554 km northwest of Bucharest. **VISITOR INFO:** www.romaniatourism.com/maramures.html. **WHERE TO STAY:** The Casa Iurca, in Sighetu Marmaţiei, is a family-run inn whose popular restaurant is a plus. Tel 40/262-318-890; www.casaiurca.ro. *Cost:* from $50. **HOW:** Staying in the villages is highly recommended. The website www.pensiuni.info.ro is an excellent source for finding guesthouses. *Cost:* from $35. **BEST TIMES:** May–Sep for nicest weather; Jul for Maramusical Festival in Botiza; early Aug for Hora de la Prislop folk music festival, held on the Prislop Pass; Dec 27 for Winter Festival, featuring food, music, costumes, and a parade in Sighetu Marmaţiei.

The Sistine Chapels of the East

THE PAINTED MONASTERIES OF SOUTHERN BUCOVINA

Moldavia, Romania

In the 15th and 16th centuries, painters working for local princes and powerful families in what is now northeastern Romania took entire buildings as their canvases, covering a cluster of small monasteries from top to bottom, often inside and out, with brightly colored frescoes. Their purpose was to record the good fortune bestowed on their patrons, especially in regional warfare, and to tell stories of redemption and damnation to a largely illiterate populace. What they left to modern Romania was a unique and surprisingly enduring cultural gift.

Spread over an area 45 miles west of Suceava, in the dramatically unspoiled region of the Carpathian foothills called Southern Bucovina, the painted monasteries remain remarkably vivid in color and detail despite 500 years of exposure to harsh weather, assorted vandals, and the whims of successive rulers. Acclaimed as brilliant examples of a Byzantine aesthetic infused with the vitality of local folk art, mythology, and historical references, they were a kind of poor man's Bible—late-medieval billboards of Orthodox Christianity in a time when this part of Europe was under the threat of Turkish invaders.

Perhaps the most striking is the 15th-century monastery of Voronet, known to Romanians as the "Sistine Chapel of the East." Its unique cerulean blue, particularly resistant to the elements and popularly known as

Sucevita Monastery's exterior walls depict biblical scenes in colors that are still bright despite centuries of exposure.

"Voronet blue," is obtained from lapis lazuli. Nearby are the painted monasteries of Humor, Moldovita, and Sucevita, all inhabited by small communities of nuns who keep their brand of faith fervently alive in this remote and ruggedly beautiful outpost where life has resisted the passing of the last few centuries.

Where: Suceava is 270 miles/434 km north of Bucharest. **Visitor info:** www.romaniatourism.com/painted-monasteries.html. **Where to stay:** The new and surprisingly good Gerald's Hotel is in the market town of Radauti. Tel 40/330-100-650; www.geraldshotel.com. *Cost:* from $110. **How:** U.S.-based MIR offers 16-day tours that include the monasteries. Tel 800-424-7289 or 206-624-7289; www.mircorp.com. *Cost:* from $5,495. Originates in Bucharest. *When:* May and Sep. **Best time:** Jun–Sep for nicest weather and numerous local festivals.

Mountains, Saxon Villages, and Folklore of the Undead

Southern Transylvania

Romania

Thrill seekers, wine lovers, photography enthusiasts, and travelers wanting total immersion in a gorgeous, untrammeled corner of Europe are drawn to Transylvania—the land "beyond the forest" in Latin—one of the last great European wildernesses. Cradled by the Carpathian Mountains, it is replete with ancient towns, fortified churches, Gothic castles, and legends about a certain nocturnal humanoid with prominent canines.

Though 21st-century influences are spreading—you may encounter sights like a rural farmer armed with a pitchfork and a mobile phone—centuries-old peasant lifestyles and traditions endure in Southern Transylvania's villages. The cities too speak of the past. The walled Saxon towns of Braşov, Sibiu, and Sighişoara offer equal parts medieval architecture, traditional and modern culture, and thriving dining and café scenes. Hiking, biking, and skiing opportunities abound in the nearby Bucegi and Fagărăs Mountains. Tour-bus gridlock notwithstanding, guided trips to the area's castles are also appealing, especially Bran Castle, inaccurately but fondly known to vampire fans around the world as Dracula's Castle.

Saxons built Bran Castle in the 14th century.

Bram Stoker's 1897 novel *Dracula* was inspired by Vlad Dracula, a 15th-century Transylvanian prince known for his bloody habit of impaling his enemies on stakes. It's been established that Vlad spent at most a few nights in Bran Castle, but that hasn't stopped the steady flow of Dracula buffs, who come from all corners of the world. Rising dramatically out of a rocky bluff, the castle looks the part of a vampire's den and is worth a visit.

A night or two spent in the surrounding villages allows a glimpse of the traditional ways that still dominate the lives of over 40 percent of Romanians. There are dozens of inviting possibilities, including the carefully restored Saxon villages of Biertan, Viscri, and Malancrav, all within an hour of Sighişoara. They have maintained their traditional appearance and are building a modest tourist infrastructure with the help of the United Kingdom–based Mihai Eminescu Trust, whose benefactors include Prince Charles.

WHERE: 130 miles/209 km northwest of Bucharest. **VISITOR INFO:** www.romaniatourism.com/transylvania.html. **WHERE TO STAY:** The aristocratic Mikes family welcomes guests at Zabola Estate's Machine House. Tel 40/724-003-658; www.zabola.com. *Cost:* from $100. **MIHAI EMINESCU TRUST:** arranges guesthouse stays in villages around Sighişoara. Tel 40/723-150-819; www.mihaieminescutrust.org. *Cost:* from $80. **HOW:** California-based Wilderness Travel leads a 12-day walking/cultural tour through Southern Transylvania. Tel 800-368-2794 or 510-558-2488; www.wildernesstravel.com. *Cost:* from $3,695, all-inclusive. Originates in Bucharest. **BEST TIMES:** May–Jun and Sep–Oct for nice weather and fewer crowds; 1st week after Easter for the Days of Braşov festival; Jul for Sighişoara's Festival of Medieval Arts and Crafts; Jul–early Aug for Sibiu's folk crafts and music festivals.

Otherworldly Wilderness in Russia's Far East

KAMCHATKA PENINSULA

Kamchatka Krai, Russia

Often dubbed "the land of fire and ice," the dramatic Kamchatka Peninsula is one of the most beautiful regions in Russia. Jutting between the Sea of Okhotsk and the Bering Sea, the 770-mile-long peninsula—roughly the size of California—is a land of verdant forests, awe-inspiring mountains, and more than 150 volcanoes, 29 of them active. Lava fields, crystal clear rivers, towering glaciers, and mist-covered lakes all add to the feeling that you've stepped back into the Pleistocene era. The area is also incredibly remote—an 8.5-hour flight east of Moscow and some 1,000 miles west of Alaska.

Kamchatka is home to herds of reindeer and bighorn sheep, the world's largest population of brown bears, moose, wolves, and half the world's population of the magnificent Steller's eagle. Off the coast, a variety of aquatic mammals—seals, sea lions, whales, dolphins, walruses—frequent the nutrient-rich waters. Among them is the massive blue whale: Earth's largest living animal, it grows up to 90 feet long and can weigh up to 200 tons.

Roads are often badly rutted or nonexistent here. Travel is by four- or six-wheel drive, light plane, or, more often, helicopter, with experienced guides a necessity. Petropavlovsk-Kamchatsky (usually called simply PK), founded by a Danish-born naval captain in 1741, is the main town and the ideal base for expeditions. The town itself (population around 200,000) consists of decrepit Soviet-era apartment blocks but enjoys a majestic setting overlooking Avacha Bay and surrounding snow-covered peaks. Don't leave without taking a tour of the bay, where fascinating rock formations rise like curved pillars from the water.

Around 120 miles north of the city is the spectacular, 4-mile-long Valley of the Geysers. Carved by the Geysernaya River, it has 90 geysers (second only to Yellowstone, in the U.S., see p. 909), along with gurgling mud pits, sulfur pools, and hot springs, all of which help to create a scene straight out of Middle Earth. Nearby is the massive 7-mile-wide Uzon Caldera, remnant of an ancient volcano. You can visit both on a day trip by helicopter from the city. Visits to meet the indigenous Koryak and Even people, seminomadic reindeer herders, can be arranged by overland or helicopter tours to their remote summer camps. You can also sign on for 2-day trips down the Bystraya River (little matches it for king salmon and wild rainbow trout fishing), which include horseback-riding excursions and ascents up the spectacular peaks for which Kamchatka is famed.

Where: 1,410 miles/2,269 km northeast of Vladivostok. **Where to stay:** The small, modest Explore Kamchatka B&B and travel agency (it also arranges custom tours) in Petropavlovsk-Kamchatsky is owned by an American expat. Tel 7/41531-66-601; www.explorekamchatka.com. *Cost:* rooms from $85; 10-day excursions from $3,100, all-inclusive. **Best time:** Jun–Sep for warmest weather.

Russia's Most Famous Temple of Culture

The Bolshoi Theater

Moscow, Russia

One of the world's most magnificent performance halls, the Bolshoi ("Grand") Theater is looking more dazzling than ever following its top-to-toe renovation begun in 2005 and scheduled for completion in 2013.

(Until then, performances take place in the adjacent, more intimate New Stage Theater.) Located near the heart of Moscow, a short stroll from Red Square (see next page), this is one of Europe's largest venues—seating over 2,000 spectators—and the place where some of the greatest musical works ever to emerge from Russia premiered. The historic pink-and-white theater was founded in 1824 and debuted Tchaikovsky's *Swan Lake* in 1877 (still a standard on the program, as is *The Nutcracker* at Christmastime). For much of the 20th century, it continued to serve as a launch pad for some of Russia's best-known operas and ballets, including works by Prokofiev and Shostakovich, among many others, while star dancers like Galina Ulanova, Rudolf Nureyev, and Nadezhda Pavlova helped bring world renown to the Bolshoi Ballet.

For decades, the Bolshoi was a sacred artistic institution, flourishing under czars and, later, free from the oppression of the Soviets. After the fall of Communism, Russia's perilous economy gave rise to the rumor that the Bolshoi had exhausted itself and was now simply resting on its laurels. But the excitement is back, and the opera and ballet companies are once again deserving of their majestic, gilded theater. Although tradition remains sacrosanct—the repertoire still consists primarily of the Russian classics—innovation, reform, and new blood have brought the Bolshoi into the 21st century.

Be sure to visit the venerable landmark across the street, the grand Hotel Metropol, an enclave of early-20th-century Russian opulence. Stop by for tea, a preballet drink, or an extravagant dinner in the cavernous, glass-domed Art Nouveau restaurant, where scenes in *Doctor Zhivago* were filmed and where Lenin once delivered impassioned speeches.

The century-old Hotel Savoy, a short stroll from the Bolshoi, offers pre-Revolutionary Russian romance; its 67 classic-style rooms are outfitted with Italian furniture and marble-filled bathrooms. For those who think bigger is better, the nearby Marriott Royal Aurora Hotel, on historic Petrovka Street, has a more contemporary look, with 231 handsomely appointed rooms and a towering, sunlit atrium.

INFO: Tel 7/499-250-7317; www.bolshoi.ru. *When:* closed mid-Jul–Aug. **HOTEL METROPOL:** Tel 7/499-501-7800; www.metropol-moscow.ru. *Cost:* dinner $150. **HOTEL SAVOY:** Tel 7/495-620-8555; www.savoy.ru. *Cost:* from $300 (off-peak), from $585 (peak). **MOSCOW MARRIOTT ROYAL AURORA HOTEL:** Tel 7/495-937-1000; in the U.S., 888-236-2427; www.marriott.com. *Cost:* from $475 (off-peak), from $775 (peak). **BEST TIME:** May–Oct for nicest weather.

Inside—and Outside—the Fortress Walls

THE KREMLIN AND RED SQUARE

Moscow, Russia

The historic seat of power for fabulously wealthy czars and despots, and a prized conquest for the odd foreign invader (Napoleon holed up here in 1812), the Kremlin, meaning "citadel" or "fortress," has seen dramatic upheaval since it was a mere wooden stronghold that arose beside the Moscow River in the 12th century. Today, its role is to serve as the official residence of the president of Russia, though it is perhaps better known for its magnificent architecture and for the dazzling treasures it houses.

Enclosed by high, 15th-century brick walls that run for more than a mile with 19 watchtowers, the sprawling 68-acre complex served for decades as the epicenter of the Soviet Union, beginning when power was transferred here from St. Petersburg in 1918, and it still exudes an air of mystery. The Armory Museum, its most visited site, offers a dizzying crash course on the lifestyles of the rich and famous czars: Its 4,000 objects, dating back to the 12th century, include exquisite Fabergé eggs, the jewel-studded helmet of the first czar, Mikhail Fyodorovich Romanov, and the ivory throne of Ivan the Terrible. View the baubles and regalia of the Romanovs in the Almazny Fond (Diamond Fund), where you'll find the scepter of Catherine the Great—topped by the 190-carat Orlov Diamond, a gift from her lover Count Orlov—and her diamond-encrusted coronation crown.

Three cathedrals are among the Kremlin's star attractions. The 15th-century Assumption Cathedral (aka Cathedral of the Dormition), with five glittering gold domes and a marvelous collection of icons, is where reigning princes swore fealty and czars were crowned. The majestic Archangel Cathedral was a burial site for princes and czars. Lording over them, the Cathedral of the Annunciation claims the tallest structure in the Kremlin—the octagonal, 266-foot-high Ivan the Great Bell Tower.

The vast, magnificent Red Square, the Krasnaya Ploshchad, stands just outside the Kremlin's east wall. In old Russian, *krasnaya* (red) also meant "beautiful," but for years to come, Red Square will be associated with Communism and the choreographed military parades that regularly took place here. Also in the shadow of the Kremlin is the Lenin Mausoleum, where the first Soviet leader's embalmed body has been eerily lying in state since his death in 1924. At the far end of the cobblestoned square stand the exuberant, candy-colored pinnacles and onion domes of St. Basil's Cathedral, commissioned by Ivan the Terrible in the mid-1500s.

Overlooking it all is the Hotel National in its original Art Nouveau splendor. Spacious rooms are decorated with Italian furnishings, and most suites afford enviable Kremlin and Red Square views. Ask for Suite 107, where Lenin lived for a time in 1918. In the capital, things are done on a grand scale, including the newly built Ritz-Carlton Moscow. It enjoys an imperial vantage point from its location on Tverskaya Boulevard, known for its upscale shopping. The best place to drink in the views is from the sleek, penthouse O2 Lounge, especially when the square is illuminated at night. Sunday brunch is the draw at the hotel's intimate Caviarterra restaurant, famous for a buffet of more than 60 dishes. A surprisingly inexpensive alternative (this, after all, is one of the priciest areas in Moscow) is the Melody Hotel, a reliable and well-located option a 15-minute walk away.

A prominent feature of Red Square, St. Basil Cathedral commemorates Ivan the Terrible's conquest of the city of Kazan.

The Kremlin: www.kreml.ru. **Hotel National:** Tel 7/495-258-7000; in the U.S., 800-543-4300; www.national.ru. *Cost:* from $330. **Ritz-Carlton Moscow:** Tel 7/495-225-8888; in the U.S., 800-542-8680; www.ritzcarlton.com. *Cost:* from $680; brunch $100. **Melody Hotel:** Tel 7/495-660-7178; www.melody-hotel.com. *Cost:* from $175. **Best times:** May–Sep for nice weather; early Sep for Den Goroda (City Day), which features a parade, live music, and fireworks.

A World of Art Above and Below Ground

The Tretyakov and the Moscow Metro

Moscow, Russia

Among the many museums and architectural splendors of Moscow is the Tretyakov Gallery, which houses one of the country's finest collections of Russian art—over 150,000 works from the 11th to the 20th centuries.

Wander through Russia's first public museum, started in 1856 by the wealthy banker Pavel Tretyakov, and come face-to-face with some of the world's great masterpieces, both well known and obscure. You'll find evocative works by medieval icon painter Andrey Rublev (including his celebrated *Holy Trinity*), and brilliant portraits by 19th-century master Ilya Repin (such as his disturbing portrait *Ivan the Terrible and His Son Ivan* and a gentler one of the celebrated composer M. P. Mussorgsky). The museum complex also contains the adjacent 17th-century Church of St. Nicholas in Tolmachi, whose exquisite, five-tiered iconostasis dates back to the same period. Nearby, a new branch of the Tretyakov showcases Russian avant-garde artists of the 20th and 21st centuries—including Kandinsky, Chagall, and Malevich—and also displays more curious works of Socialist Realism created in the 1930s, when idealized portraits of peasants and factory workers were all the rage.

For more art from the Soviet period, head underground, to the Moscow metro, where you'll marvel at the repository of elegant marbles, bas-reliefs, and mosaics—sometimes illuminated by glittering chandeliers. The first stage of the 180-plus stations was completed in 1935 and was quickly hailed as one of Stalin's shining triumphs. Much of the artwork found in the stations pays tribute to historical events—portrayed through a pro-Soviet lens. The palatial Komsomolskaya station features an enormous hall with Baroque details and ceiling mosaics depicting Russian military triumphs. The Mayakovskaya station may be the metro's crown jewel, with its stainless-steel columns and white-and-pink marble floors. The ceiling mosaics depict scenes from "24 Hours in the Land of the Soviets," a poem by Soviet playwright Vladimir Mayakovsky. Novosloboskaya station boasts 32 backlit stained-glass panels portraying joyful farmers and workers in the Socialist Realist style. Brass borders frame each panel, with pink Ural marble and conical chandeliers adding to the grandeur.

State Tretyakov Gallery: Tel 7/495-953-1051; www.tretyakovgallery.ru. **Where to stay:** The famously quirky but well-located Golden Apple is one of the city's newer boutique choices. Tel 7/495-980-7000; www.goldenapple.ru. *Cost:* from $190 (off-peak), from $270 (peak). **Best time:** Jun–Aug for nicest weather.

Cruising the Volga and Beyond

Waterways of the Czars

Moscow, Russia

Although Moscow and St. Petersburg are featured on many sailing itineraries, neither is actually on the Volga. The river is, however, part of a network of interconnected canals, locks, and lakes that makes a journey by boat possible from either city. On your way, you'll pass medieval towns with Orthodox monasteries and cathedrals standing silently on the banks, towns that make up what's known as Moscow's "Golden Ring" for their wealth of artistic and architectural treasures. The charming city of Uglich, dating back to 937, is known for striking examples of Russian architecture built over the centuries, including the famed 17th-century Church of St. Dmitry on the Blood, erected in memory of Ivan the Terrible's son, who died on this spot in 1591.

In Lake Onega, the second largest lake in Europe, you'll find the island of Kizhi, covered with an extraordinary array of centuries-old wooden buildings that were transported here from various parts of the region, creating an open-air museum of more than 80 structures. The 17th-century St. Lazarus church is one of the country's oldest wooden chapels, while the 22-domed Church of the Transfiguration was built in 1714 without a single nail.

From Moscow, river journeys also head south along the largely unexplored Lower Volga, with a stop at Kazan. The proud center of Tatar culture, it is home to an ancient kremlin (fortress) that dates back to 1005 and holds an impressive array of historic treasures. The spires of mosques and the onion-shaped domes of cathedrals rise around the town, which also has a sprawling market that's ripe for exploring. Farther along is Volgograd, formerly Stalingrad, the site of World War II's bloodiest battle (over a million Soviet and Nazi soldiers died over 200 days). The event is memorialized today by the 280-foot-high statue *Motherland Calls.* The final stop on a Lower Volga cruise is Astrakhan, the world capital of caviar, where the river—Europe's longest—meets the Caspian Sea. Set amid the wetlands of the Volga Delta, Europe's largest estuary, this pretty town and its environs are a wondrous habitat for flamingos and pelicans, as well as for the beluga sturgeon that have made it famous.

The newly refurbished *Volga Dream,* a 314-foot luxury liner, feels more akin to a private yacht than to a cruise ship, with just 56 cabins—all with river views—and 60 crew members. Guests can enjoy private recitals of Rachmaninoff and Chopin in the Neva lounge, rejuvenate in the sauna after history-filled days on shore, or sample the vodka collection in the handsome Ladoga Bar while a first-rate kitchen prepares dinners of local cuisine interpreted with a European flourish.

WHERE: departures from Moscow and St. Petersburg. **HOW:** U.S.-based Exeter International offers *Volga Dream* cruises between Moscow and St. Petersburg and between Moscow and Astrakhan. Tel 800-633-1008 or 813-251-5355. *Cost:* 10-day tours (with 6-night cruise) from Moscow to St. Petersburg or reverse, from $2,900, all-inclusive. *When:* Jun–Oct. **BEST TIME:** May–Oct for nicest weather.

The Birthplace of Russia

NOVGOROD

Novgorod Oblast, Russia

Veliky Novgorod, which means "Great New City," is the misleading name for a place where Russian history began over a thousand years ago. Led by the Viking warrior prince Rurik of Jutland, Norsemen made the strategic town overlooking the Volkov River their capital in the 9th century. Rurik's successor, Oleg of Novgorod, then used the fortified town as a base from which to conquer surrounding territories, and by 880, the budding empire of Kievan Rus—the early progenitor to modern-day Russia—was born.

Novgorod continued to flourish, and by the 12th century it was Russia's biggest center for trade, education, and the arts. An early form of democracy took root here, with government by a people's assembly, which elected an archbishop and commissioned a ruler or prince to provide defense. One of Russia's oldest buildings from that time, the Cathedral of St. Sophia, built in 1052, still stands in the town center. The imposing white stone church was built to withstand attack, though perhaps

Muscovites rebuilt Novgorod's kremlin in brick in the 15th century.

it wasn't the walls alone that defended it. According to legend, a 12th-century icon of the Virgin Mary saved Novgorod from destruction when the town was under siege. As the story goes, an enemy arrow pierced the icon, causing tears to flow from it and darkness to descend. In the confusion, the offending army attacked itself and the town was saved. The icon still hangs inside the church today, and up close, you can see a notch over the saint's left eye, where the arrow is said to have struck.

St. Sophia and the town's other historic sites are protected within the walls of Novgorod's beautifully preserved kremlin, one of the oldest in Russia. Overlooking the river, the fort was originally constructed in the 9th century and later rebuilt of brick.

Where: 120 miles/193 km south of St. Petersburg. **Visitor info:** www.novgorod.ru/english. **Where to stay:** The modern, 132-room Hotel Volkhov is 2 blocks from the kremlin. Tel 7/8162-225-500; www.hotel-volkhov.ru/en. *Cost:* from $100. **Best time:** May–Sep for nicest weather.

Twilight Magic in the City of the Arts

The White Nights Festival

St. Petersburg, Russia

St. Petersburg may not be the country's economic or administrative capital, but when it comes to the arts, this glorious city on the Neva River is Russia's brightest star. Boasting renowned ballet and opera companies and a world-class symphony, it is also the former home of Stravinsky, Shostakovich, Prokofiev, and Rachmaninoff; the place where Diaghilev, Nijinsky, and Balanchine made their names; and where Pushkin, Gogol, and Dostoevsky penned some of Russia's best-loved works.

The calendar is always awash with cultural offerings, but the city is especially vibrant in summer, during the performance-packed White Nights Festival. Founded in 1993 by Valery Gergiev, the world-renowned director of the Kirov Opera, the festival began as a two-week event centered around the solstice, when the sun disappears for only a few hours and residents celebrate the season's long, white nights of summer. It has grown to an eight-week spectacle that lasts from May to July and attracts more than a million visitors.

Especially coveted are tickets to the prestigious Stars of the White Nights concerts, held at the dazzling, five-tiered Mariinsky Theater, which has premiered some of Russia's greatest works—including Mussorgsky's *Boris Godunov* in 1874 and Prokofiev's *Romeo and Juliet* in 1940. The state-of-the-art Mariinsky Concert Hall, opened in 2006, has flawless acoustics, and the 2,000-seat New Mariinsky Theater is under construction.

One of the many highlights of the White Nights Festival is the Scarlet Sails celebration, in late June, which presents mock pirate battles, rowing competitions, outdoor concerts, and a fireworks display over the Neva. Late-night river and canal cruises to witness the raising of the bridges are a fun tradition in this "Venice of the North."

The Grand Hotel Europe, a refurbished landmark built in 1877, upholds its tradition with beautifully furnished guest rooms and unrivaled service; Tchaikovsky chose to spend his honeymoon here. Its elegant restaurant L'Europe, with an exquisite Art Nouveau stained-glass ceiling, occasionally hosts *Swan Lake* duets while guests dine. The simple, pleasantly furnished Northern Lights Hotel, in a 19th-century building, is another option, near St. Isaac's Square and just a 15-minute walk from the Mariinsky.

Mariinsky Theater: Tel 7/812-326-4141; www.mariinsky.ru. **Grand Hotel Europe:** 7/812-329-6000; in the U.S., tel 800-237-1236; www.grandhoteleurope.com. *Cost:* from $400 (off-peak), from $680 (peak); 3-course dinner at L'Europe $105, jazz brunch $160. **Northern Lights Hotel:** Tel 7/812-571-9199; www.nlightsrussia.com. *Cost:* from $120 (off-peak), from $160 (peak). **How:** U.S.-based Exeter International offers a 6-night White Nights trip filled with performances. Tel 800-633-1008 or 813-251-5355; www.exeterinternational.com. *Cost:* $7,175, inclusive. Originates in St. Petersburg. *When:* early Jun.

Splendors of Another Age

The Winter Palace and the Hermitage

St. Petersburg, Russia

Looming majestically over the Neva River, the mint-green and white-and-gold Winter Palace was designed by court architect Bartolomeo Rastrelli in 1754, during Empress Elizabeth I's reign, and served as the official residence of every subsequent czar and czarina until the 1917 Revolution that took place just outside. With over 1,000 rooms and 117 staircases, it is an unmissable showcase of Russian Baroque magnificence, from the Malachite Hall—filled with rich green columns, vases, and decorative details made of the gemstone—to the elaborate Hall of St. George, featuring twin rows of crystal chandeliers and a parquet floor fashioned from 16 kinds of rare woods. The Armorial Hall boasts a blinding display of gilded columns and bronze chandeliers. Lavish winter balls were hosted in the elaborate Great Hall.

But the Winter Palace is best known as the home of the Hermitage Museum, Russia's Louvre, and one of the world's richest repositories of art. Scattered throughout the Winter Palace and five other buildings on the vast Palace Square are 150,000 works that make up only a fraction of the museum's 3-million–piece collection. Many were gathered by Catherine the Great, one of history's great art collectors. The bounty includes more than 40 works by Rembrandt, 40 by Rubens, 8 Titians, masterpieces by Michelangelo and Leonardo da Vinci, and a collection of Impressionist and post-Impressionist art that has few rivals. The antiquities collection includes over 100,000 items from ancient Greece and Rome; 50 rooms of relics from ancient Egypt, Mesopotamia, and Byzantium; and a Treasury Gallery laden with gold and jewelry dating back to the 7th century B.C.

The 18th-century Yusupov Palace, a pleasant 20-minute stroll away, is a monument to conspicuous consumption that was home to five generations of a wealthy landowning family. Its sumptuously decorated rooms and precious Rococo theater, where Chopin and Liszt once played, hint at what life was like in the decades before the Revolution. The palace is also the famed site where Grigory Rasputin ("the mad monk" and advisor to the throne) was assassinated in 1917.

The domed St. Isaac's cathedral stands

nearby, completed in 1848 and decorated inside with frescoes, mosaics, and 14 kinds of precious stones. There's also a beautifully crafted cupola and a three-tiered iconostasis. For poster-perfect views of the cathedral, check into the Art Nouveau Hotel Astoria, with updated, handsomely furnished rooms. Next door (and under the same management), the Angleterre Hotel was a favorite of artists and poets in the 1920s, and its attractive, contemporary rooms cost a few rubles less. For sheer czarist grandeur, opt for the inimitable Taleon Imperial Hotel, within the once-private 18th-century Eliseev Palace and brimming with oil paintings, antique furnishings, and intricate parquet floors. The elegant, reasonably priced Tradition Hotel, located on the north bank of the Malaya Neva, near the early-18th-century Peter and Paul Fortress, is a 20-minute walk from the Hermitage.

STATE HERMITAGE MUSEUM: Tel 7/812-710-9625; www.hermitagemuseum.org. **HOTEL ASTORIA:** Tel 7/812-494-5757; www.thehotelastoria.com. *Cost:* from $375 (off-peak), $500 (peak). **ANGLETERRE HOTEL:** Tel 7/812-494-5666; www.angleterrehotel.com. *Cost:* from $300 (off-peak), from $410 (peak). **TALEON IMPERIAL HOTEL:** Tel 7/812-324-9911; www.eliseevpalacehotel.com. *Cost:* from $375 (off-peak), from $475 (peak). **TRADITION HOTEL:** Tel 7/812-405-8855; www.traditionhotel.ru. *Cost:* from $200 (off-peak), from $310 (peak). **BEST TIME:** May–Sep for pleasant weather.

Imperial Grandeur in Two of Russia's Greatest Homes

CATHERINE PALACE AND PAVLOVSK PALACE

Pushkin and Pavlovsk, Leningrad Oblast, Russia

A short journey outside of St. Petersburg, you'll find two of Russia's most magnificent imperial estates: Tsarskoe Selo (Czar's Village, now part of the town of Pushkin) and Pavlovsk. (The Peterhof Palace completes the trio; see p. 326.) Tsarskoe Selo dates back to the early 18th century, when Peter the Great gave the land to his wife, the future Empress Catherine I, who had a modest summer residence built there in 1717. Their daughter Empress Elizabeth replaced it with a grand palace, named for her mother and designed in part by Bartolomeo Rastrelli (who would seal his fame with the Winter Palace; see previous page). The Catherine Palace was completed in 1756 and immediately set a new standard for royal excess.

The tastes of Catherine I and II are reflected in Catherine Palace.

The flamboyant Rococo structure stretches over 1,000 feet, and at one time the gilded electric-blue façade alone contained over 200 pounds of gold. Inside lie dozens of grand rooms with lavish ceiling murals, inlaid wood floors, sumptuous oil portraits, and dazzling gilt work. Catherine II (aka "the Great") later commissioned Scottish architect Charles Cameron to add a new wing that includes the spectacular Agate Rooms, covered in semiprecious stones.

Most awe-inspiring of all, however, is the Amber Room, a staggering $11 million reconstruction of the early-18th-century room that, along with much of the rest of the palace, was looted and almost completely destroyed during World War II. Its reconstruction—25 years in the making—recaptures the original magic with its exquisite inlaid amber panels, mosaics, and wall-mounted mirrors.

A few miles away stands Pavlovsk, the gold-and-white palace that Catherine the Great gave to her son, Paul (in Russian, Pavel; hence its name), in 1777. Conceived as a summer home, it was built in a neo-Palladian style that is more restrained than that of Catherine's own over-the-top confection. By palace standards, its 45 rooms are intimate (though exquisite). Although Pavlovsk seems miraculously untouched by the ravages of history, it is, like the Catherine Palace, an extraordinary replica. Hitler's troops burned the original in 1944, and it took a virtual army of Russia's finest artisans 25 years to successfully recreate it, then fill it with many of the original furnishings and artwork that a loyal palace staff somehow managed to hide. The surrounding 1,500-acre estate is now a lovely park of ponds, lime tree–lined allées, rolling lawns, pavilions, and woodlands.

Where: 16 miles/26 km south of St. Petersburg. **Catherine Palace:** Tel 7/812-465-2024; www.tzar.ru. **Pavlovsk:** Tel 7/812-470-2155; www.pavlovskart.spb.ru. **Best times:** May and Sep for nice weather and fewer crowds.

A Czar's Palace to Rival Versailles

Peterhof

Leningrad Oblast, Russia

Russia has no shortage of grand and gilded palaces that stagger the imagination, but one of the most splendid of them all is the summer palace of Peterhof (Petrodvorets), just outside St. Petersburg. Peter the Great took his inspiration from Versailles (see p. 118), introducing European grandeur to Russia. Like the city of St. Petersburg itself, which he founded when he moved the imperial seat of power here from Moscow in 1712, the palace would be his "window to Europe."

Although he had help from the French architect Jean-Baptiste LeBlond, the chief designer of St. Petersburg, Peter drew up his own plans for the palace and sprawling estate on the shores of the Gulf of Finland. It was completed by 1721, and plans for expansion were under way when the great czar died unexpectedly in 1725, and the project came to a halt.

In fact, the entire project was nearly abandoned until Peter's daughter Empress Elizabeth took the throne in 1741 and set her sights on building the grand palace that Peter had always imagined. She commissioned the celebrated court architect Bartolomeo Rastrelli to work his magic, transforming the structure into a long, narrow, 30-room palace with a lavish interior. Highlights include the photogenic Chesma Hall, adorned with oversize paintings depicting the victory of the Russian navy over the Turkish fleet in 1770. Notable among the original rooms is Peter's simple but beautiful study—one of the few rooms to survive the destruction of World War II.

The most outstanding feature of the rich yellow palace, however, lies outside. It is the Grand Cascade—a monumental series of more than 170 fountains and canals that were partly designed by Peter himself. The gilded, spouting figures and oversize deities are truly magnificent—particularly the statute of Samson tearing open the jaws of a lion, a symbol meant to commemorate Russia's victory over the Swedes in 1709. All the fountains are powered by a 13-mile-long system of gravity-fed pumps. The 300 acres of gardens are a fine place to take in the grandeur and contemplate the narrowly avoided destruction of this extraordinary place. Petrodvorets and nearby St. Petersburg experienced near-annihilation during the 900-day German siege in World War II, but the Cascade was painstakingly rebuilt.

Musical fountains and golden statues mark Peterhof's entrance.

Where: 20 miles/32 km southwest of St. Petersburg. **Visitor info:** Tel 7/812-450-5287; www.saint-petersburg.com/peterhof. **Best times:** May and Sep for pleasant weather and fewer crowds.

Exploring the Divide between Europe and Asia

Yekaterinburg and the Ural Mountains

Sverdlovsk Oblast, Russia

The majestic and little-visited Ural Mountains stretch for over 1,200 miles, from the arctic ice of the Kara Sea to the Central Asian Steppe of Kazakhstan in the south. Modest by Himalayan or Andean standards (the highest peaks reach about 6,500 feet), the Urals are one of the world's oldest mountain chains and have long served as both the geographic and symbolic demarcation between Europe and Asia. They harbor rich biodiversity, with lynx, elk, sables, wolves, otters, brown bears, and more than 200 bird species inhabiting virgin boreal forests.

The gateway to the Urals is burgeoning Yekaterinburg, Russia's third largest city and infamous as the site of the Romanov family's execution during the bloody Russian Revolution of 1918. The massive Byzantine-style Church of the Blood stands on the site of the former house (since destroyed) where they were held captive. But there is more to see here than this somber memorial. Yekaterinburg is chock-full of theaters, cinemas, museums, and houses of culture, and the Baroque 1912 Opera House hosts a stellar lineup of opera and ballet performances each season.

Yekaterinburg is also one of the best places to arrange a journey into the wilderness of the Urals. Reputable outfitters can organize a wide range of adventurous outings, lasting anywhere from one to 17 days, that may include everything from hiking, rafting, and mountain climbing to horseback riding; may even offer winter trips, featuring dogsledding, ski tours, ice fishing, and snowmobiling.

If you choose, you can also delve into some of Russia's darkest history in this region. Perm-36, about 200 miles northwest of Yekaterinburg, was one of the most infamous gulags in the repressive Soviet system. Political prisoners—artists, intellectuals, writers, and dissidents—languished here in cold, windowless, concrete cells, surviving on meager portions of bread and watery gruel. The reconstructed prison camp is a moving museum and memorial to the victims.

WHERE: 880 miles/1,416 km southeast of Moscow. **WHERE TO STAY:** The modern Hyatt Regency Ekaterinburg is the city's finest hotel. Tel 7/343-253-1234; http://ekaterinburg.regency.hyatt.com. *Cost:* from $350. **HOW:** Ural Expeditions & Tours offers geologist-led tours lasting 1–17 days, including as many activities as you can handle. Tel 7/343-356-5282; www.welcome-ural.ru. *Cost:* 2-day rafting trip, $520; 2-day trek, $460. **BEST TIME:** Jun–Aug for warmest weather.

An Epic Train Ride Across Mother Russia

The Trans-Siberian Express and Lake Baikal

Russia

The world's longest continuous rail line, the Trans-Siberian Railway stretches over 6,000 miles—one-third of the distance around the globe—and crosses eight time zones between Moscow, in the west, and Vladivostok, on the Pacific coast. The network of routes is one of the truly heroic engineering marvels of the last century, crossing taiga, steppe, desert, and mountains. An arduous trip of several months before the rails were laid, this epic journey can now take just 7 days.

Various routes and options connect Moscow with Russia's far east and beyond. The most luxurious option by far is the recently introduced *Golden Eagle* Trans-Siberian Express, a private train offering 13- to 15-day tours between Moscow and either Vladivostok or Ulaan Baatar, Mongolia, including stops and excursions en route. The less upscale but eminently comfortable *Tsar's Gold* train travels from Moscow to Beijing via Mongolia.

Accessible from any of the three routes, Lake Baikal is one of the most interesting off-rail excursions. Disembark at Irkutsk, once called the "Paris of Siberia," just 30 miles from Baikal—the world's oldest freshwater lake and also its deepest, plunging a mile below the surface in parts and containing as much water as all of North America's five Great Lakes combined. Ringed by rocky, tree-covered shores, with mountains rising in the distance, the crystal-clear blue Baikal and its environs are home to an extraordinary variety of flora and fauna. Some 1,800 species—many found nowhere else—have earned the lake the moniker "Galápagos of Russia." Siberian brown bears, moose, elk, sables, and deer roam the forests, while the Baikal seal flourishes in the lake. The area is also home to Buryat tribes, who live along the eastern shore, raising sheep, goats, and camels. Some tours include a night or more aboard lake cruisers, exploring pristine islands, bays, and rivers, while others strike off on one- or multiday hiking tours.

Other stops include Kazan, the Tatar capital, on the Volga River (see p. 321); Yekaterinburg (see previous page); and the charming university town of Tomsk—one of Siberia's highlights thanks to its lovely wooden mansions and vibrant arts scene.

WHERE: departures eastbound from Moscow and St. Petersburg; westbound from Vladivostok or from Beijing or Ulaan Baatar, Mongolia. **HOW:** Both GW Travel Limited in the U.K. (tel 44/161-928-9410; www.gwtravel.co.uk) and MIR Corporation in the U.S. (tel 800-424-7289 or 206-624-7389; www.mircorp.com) offer guided 15-day trips on the *Golden Eagle*. *Cost:* from $12,795, all-inclusive (land only). Real Russia sells tickets for basic trans-Siberian train service. In Moscow, tel 7/495-616-8086; in London, tel 44/207-100-7370; www.realrussia.co.uk. *Cost:* Moscow to Beijing from $1,175. **BEST TIME:** late May–mid-Sep for nicest weather.

Central Europe's Unsung Capital City

BRATISLAVA'S OLD TOWN

Bratislava, Slovakia

The mighty Danube flows through more national capitals—Vienna, Budapest, Belgrade, and Bratislava—than any other river. Of these four modern cities, Bratislava is the most intimate. Since the peaceful dissolution of Czechoslovakia in 1993's "Velvet Divorce," the capital of Slovakia is quietly becoming an essential central European detour just a 4-hour train journey from glamorous and more visited Prague (see p. 290). From Vienna, boat travel to Bratislava takes just 75 minutes along the Danube.

The area encompassing Bratislava Castle (Bratislavský Hrad), the labyrinthine Old Town (Starý Mesto), and the banks of the Danube makes up the center of one of Europe's most relaxed and easygoing capital cities.

Sip a coffee and people-watch in Kaffee Mayer, established in 1873 and still famous for its luscious cakes and sweets. For a traditional dinner, Old Town's Prašná Bastá restaurant serves Slovak specialties, including venison ragout with mushrooms and homemade dumplings. A few winding lanes nearer the slow-moving Danube, Marrol's Hotel channels the retro elegance of the 1920s and 1930s in a 21st-century luxury accommodation.

The Blue Church is the city's architectural gem, blue on the outside and richly decorated within. While other capitals dazzle with buildings of scale, gravity, and might, Bratislava surprises with more compact, playful, and personal structures. The 1911 Church of St. Elizabeth is a pristine Art Nouveau confection of sparkling blue inside as well.

Bratislava Castle stands on a rocky outcrop and was used as a fortress during Celtic and Roman times. From atop the castle, distinctively shaped like a four-poster bed, look out along the meandering Danube toward Austria to the southwest and Hungary to the south. Crouched in the castle's lower ramparts is the Museum of Jewish Culture, one of a handful of small but excellent museums in the city.

VISITOR INFO: www.visit.bratislava.sk. **KAFFEE MAYER:** Tel 421/254-41-1741; www.kaffeemayer.sk. **PRAŠNÁ BASTÁ:** Tel 421/254-434-957; www.prasnabasta.sk. *Cost:* dinner $30. **MARROL'S HOTEL:** Tel 421/257-784-600; www.hotelmarrols.sk. *Cost:* from $165. **MUSEUM OF JEWISH CULTURE:** Tel 421/220-490-101; www.snm.sk. **BEST TIMES:** Jun–Aug for the nicest weather; Jun–Sep for Cultural Summer Festival; Oct for Bratislava Music Festival; Dec for Christmas markets.

A Lake and Fairy-Tale Castle

Bled and the Julian Alps

Gorenjska Province, Slovenia

For such a diminutive country (barely the size of New Jersey), Slovenia boasts incredible natural diversity. The old spa town of Bled is the attention-getter. To enjoy the emerald-green glacial lake surrounded by the snow-dusted Julian Alps, jump aboard a gondola-like *pletna* for a visit to the tiny island at its center, and ring the 16th-century "wishing bell" in the church belfry. Or climb to the 11th-century cliffside Bled Castle for a visit to its museum followed by lunch at the silver-service Bled Castle Restaurant, with million-dollar views topped off by Bled's culinary specialty, the *kremma rezina* (cream cake).

Hotel Vila Bled, once a residence of Yugoslav President Tito and surrounded by 12 acres of lakeside parkland, has 1950s décor and one of the best restaurants in town. Directly on the lake, the Grand Hotel Toplice is charmingly mid-19th century, while the newly restored Hotel Triglav Bled first opened in 1906 and has long been favored for its delightful terrace restaurant and its perchlike location slightly removed from town.

If you climb to the top of 9,396-foot Mt. Triglav, the country's highest peak, by tradition you will become an honorary Slovene. For a closer look at the Julian Alps without getting your boots dirty, take the scenic 25-mile drive northwest to Kranjska Gora, Slovenia's top ski-resort town and the gateway to Triglav National Park. A winding road leads through the park, up into the Alps, over the awesome 5,285-foot Vršič Pass, and down to sunny Primorska Province in 1 hair-raising hour.

A small white church stands on Bled Island, in the middle of the lake of the same name.

Follow the cobalt-blue Soča River through unspoiled countryside to Kobarid, a pretty market town, with a small but fine World War I museum. This is also where you'll find one of the greatest concentrations of fine dining establishments in provincial Slovenia. One of the best is Topli Val, a superb seafood restaurant in the stylish Hotel Hvala. The family-owned Hiša Franko is a Slow-Food phenomenon in a converted farmhouse with delightful themed guest rooms. From here it's just a 10-minute drive southeast to Paradise. That's the translation of "Nebesa," an exquisite enclave of modern Alpine chalets in Livek, 2,952 feet up in the mountains; you'll understand the reason for its name upon arrival.

Where: 55 miles/89 km northwest of Ljubljana. **Visitor info:** www.bled.si. **Bled Castle Restaurant:** Tel 386/4-579-4424; www.blejski-grad.si. *Cost:* dinner $40. **Hotel Vila Bled:** Tel 386/4-575-3710; www.vila-bled.com. *Cost:* from $300 (off-peak), from $330 (peak); dinner $80. **Grand Hotel Toplice:** Tel 386/4-579-1000; www.hotel-toplice.com. *Cost:* from $230 (off-peak), from $315 (peak). **Hotel Triglav Bled:** Tel

386/4-575-2610; www.hoteltriglavbled.si. *Cost:* from $140 (off-peak), from $215 (peak); dinner $40. **Hotel Hvala and Topli Val:** Tel 386/5-389-9300; www.hotelhvala.si. *Cost:* from $145; dinner $45. **Hiša Franko:** Tel 386/5-389-4120; www.hisafranko.com. *Cost:* from $105 (off-peak), from $180 (peak); dinner $65. **Nebesa:** Tel 386/5-384-4620; www.nebesa.si. *Cost:* from $320. **Best times:** Apr–Oct for nicest weather; late Jul for Bled Days, a multimedia festival; Aug for Okarina Etno Festival of folk and world music.

Medieval Core Overlooked by a Hilltop Fortress

Ljubljana's Old Town and Castle

Ljubljana, Slovenia

The old quarter of Ljubljana, Slovenia's small capital, is a treasure trove of varied architecture. Medieval and Baroque stand companionably side by side, while the early 20th century is represented by the unique and eclectic design of local architect Jože Plečnik.

Begin a walking tour of Staro Mesto (Old Town) in the colorful Central Market area at the foot of the early 18th-century cathedral. Head south, taking in delightful courtyards and passageways, old doorways, and centuries-old churches. The half dozen or so bridges, most of them for pedestrians, over the Ljubljanica River, include the landmark Dragon Bridge, Plečnik's unique Triple Bridge, and the new Butchers' Bridge, with sculptures by Jakov Brdar and minute padlocks left behind by lovers, symbolic of the longevity of their devotion.

Standing guard over Old Town from atop a wooded hill is Ljubljana Castle, one of five open to the public. Its architecture mirrors the city's history, with a medieval chapel, fortified walls dating from the early 16th century, and some uninspired buildings from the socialist 1970s. Museums within the castle will guide you through the history of the city and the nation, and an inviting terrace café serves regional specialties such as *jelenov golaž* (venison goulash). For dazzling views, ascend to the castle via the glass-bubble funicular.

At the Grand Hotel Union, make sure you stay in the Art Nouveau "executive" wing dating to 1905—its public areas are glorious. One of the new boutique hotels in the heart of Old Town is the family-run Antiq Hotel, cobbled together from a series of 18th-century town houses. Just across the road, the Allegro Hotel has a charming courtyard and a cozy, parlorlike lobby.

Cross the Ljubljanica to find the Antiq Palace, a suites-only hotel surrounding two courtyards of a 16th-century palace. Nearby is the city's finest restaurant, Pri Vitezu. For more relaxed dining and a taste of the best local dishes and wines, head back into Old Town for Špajza, a beautifully decorated romantic warren with rough-hewn tables and chairs and an outdoor courtyard. Slovenia is justifiably proud of its thousand-year-old wine history, and here you can choose from a dozen different producers in Goriška Brda, Slovenia's premier area for full-bodied reds.

Visitor info: www.visitljubljana.si. **Grand Hotel Union:** Tel 386/1-308-1270; www.gh-union.si. *Cost:* from $345. **Antiq Hotel:** Tel 386/1-421-3560; www.antiqhotel.si. *Cost:* $110. **Allegro Hotel:** Tel

386/59-119-620; www.allegrohotel.si. *Cost:* from $150. **Antiq Palace:** Tel 386/8-389-6700; www.antiqpalace.com. *Cost:* from $345. **Pri Vitezu:** Tel 386/1-426-6058; www.privitezu.si. *Cost:* dinner $40. **Špajza:** Tel 386/1-425-3094; www.spajza-restaurant.si. *Cost:* dinner $40. **Best times:** May–Sep for nicest weather; May for Druga Godba festival of alternative music; Jul–Aug for the Ljubljana Festival, the nation's premier cultural event.

Land of Underground Caverns and Snow-White Horses

The Caves of the Karst Plateau

Notranjska and Primorska provinces, Slovenia

Slovenia's Karst region, with the Alps hovering above and the Adriatic at its feet, is commonly associated with *pršut* (air-dried ham like Italian prosciutto) and the ruby-red Kraski Teran wine. But visitors are more inclined to head underground: Some of the world's largest and most astonishing caves have been sculpted by underground rivers cutting through the porous limestone to create massive caverns like the ones at Postojna and the village of Škocjan.

A footbridge leads over the deep chasm in the Škocjan caves.

At 67,487 feet long and 377 feet deep, the Postojna is Europe's most expansive cave. Thirty million visitors have marveled at its weird and wonderful stalactite and stalagmite formations. A 90-minute guided tour, most of it via miniature electric open-topped train, takes you through a wonderland of what looks like frozen spaghetti, drapes, cauliflower, and sand castles. The best accommodation in the area is at the landmark Hotel Kras, a modern 27-room hotel in the center of Postojna town. Ten minutes northwest of town is Predjama Castle, built in the mouth of a cavern with what must be among the most dramatic fortress settings anywhere. It was the stronghold of Erazem Lueger, a 15th-century robber baron who, like Robin Hood, waylaid wagons in the deep forest and handed the goods over to the poor.

The Škocjan caves are smaller—a mere 1,903 feet long—but possibly even more captivating, a page right out of Jules Verne's *Journey to the Center of the Earth.* There are plenty of otherworldly formations, but the attraction is the sheer depth of the underground chasm, crossed by a dizzying footbridge 148 feet above the Reka River that flows through the caves. A welcome addition to the rather limited list of places to stay in the vicinity is the new and very comfortable Hotel Malovec in nearby Divača, just minutes from the Italian border. Nearby is the small town of Lipica, where the Habsburgs founded a stud farm in the 16th century to breed graceful Lipizzaner horses for the acclaimed Spanish Riding School in

Vienna (see p. 85). The snow-white beauties are still raised at the farm here, which offers tours, lessons, and carriage rides.

Where: 34 miles/54 km southwest of Ljubljana. **Postojna Cave:** Tel 386/5-700-0100; www.postojnska-jama.si. **Hotel Kras:** Tel 386/5-700-2300; www.hotel-kras.si. *Cost:* from $120 (off-peak), $145 (peak). **Škocjan Caves:** Tel 386/5-708-2110; www.park-skocjanske-jame.si. **Hotel Malovec:** Tel 386/5-763-3333; www.hotel-malovec.si. *Cost:* from $110. **Lipica Stud Farm:** Tel 386/5-739-1580; www.lipica.org. **Best times:** May–Sep for nicest weather; Dec for Christmas concerts and the Live Christmas Crib, a reenactment of the Nativity.

A Timeless Byzantine Wonder

Kiev Caves Monastery

Kiev, Ukraine

In 988, Vladimir the Great, grand prince of the fledgling Kievan Rus state, married a Byzantine princess and converted his subjects to Christianity, laying the foundation of a unified Russia. Over the next 2 centuries, Kievan Rus would take over much of modern-day Ukraine, Belarus, and European Russia. Its capital, Kiev, emerged as a grand center of Eastern Orthodoxy on the banks of the Dnieper River, and scores of Byzantine cathedrals and monasteries sprang up in and around it. Many of the grandest occupied a long, leafy hill along the Dnieper's right bank. One can only imagine the awe with which first-time visitors, usually arriving by boat, regarded the display of onion domes stacked dramatically up the hillside.

Kiev's first great church was St. Sophia's Cathedral (Sofiyski Sobor in Ukrainian), modeled after the Hagia Sofia in Constantinople (see p. 578); it is still standing, its original 11th-century frescoes intact. But the city's most splendid attraction is Kievo-Pechers'ka Lavra, the Kiev Caves Monastery. It was founded in 1051 by St. Anthony, an influential Greek intellectual, who tunneled out an elaborate network of caves beneath the monastery buildings to serve as study and meditation rooms for reclusive monks. When the monks died, their bodies were left in place and naturally mummified in the cool, dry atmosphere. Today the monastery, which remains Ukraine's most important religious center, occupies 70 acres of majestic real estate overlooking the Dnieper. Tourists and pilgrims come to visit the caves carrying candles as they walk quietly amid the narrow, eerie crypts, where the monks' desiccated hands and feet protrude from their robes.

Above ground, the sprawling Lavra complex is a feast for the eyes. A great Baroque bell tower, soaring more than 300 feet and topped by a radiant gold cupola, dominates the skyline, providing those who climb its interior stairs with a bird's-eye view of the monastery's churches, towers, and dormitories. The centerpiece, the Dormition Cathedral, was Kiev's second great church (after St. Sophia), built in the 11th century and last reconstructed in the early 2000s (after being destroyed in the Soviet era). One of the Lavra's many museums is the Historical Treasures Museum, with a trove of ancient Scythian gold jewelry among its vast hoard of precious gemstones and antiques. Another is the quirky Museum of Microminiatures, where visitors look through microscopes to view tiny artistic creations, including a chess set on the head of a pin and a flea fitted with golden shoes.

Visitor info: www.lavra.ua. **Where to**

STAY: The Hyatt Regency is the city's most luxurious choice, with views of St. Sophia. Tel 380/44-581-1234; www.kiev.regency.hyatt.com. *Cost:* $375. **BEST TIMES:** Apr–May and Sep–Oct for pleasant weather; Jan 18–19 for Epiphany, when the Orthodox faithful honor Vladimir's mass baptism of Kiev by jumping into the freezing Dnieper.

Ukrainian Beauty Finally Flourishing

THE HISTORIC CENTER OF LVIV

Lviv, Ukraine

When you stand on Castle Hill and take in the sweeping view of the historic city center, you will understand why the Western Ukrainian city of Lviv was once known as the Florence of the East. A sea of green, silver, and copper spires greets the eye, representing different architectural styles and topped by crosses denoting the city's main Roman Catholic and Orthodox religions.

Lviv bounced between Polish and Austrian rule for centuries, was terrorized by the Nazis in World War II, and then fell under Soviet rule. When the Soviet Union collapsed in 1991, the city seamlessly settled into the role of newly independent Ukraine's cultural and spiritual center, an unabashedly patriotic, Ukrainian-speaking, Western-leaning antidote to the country's Russophile East.

Compared to Kiev (see previous page), Lviv suffered limited World War II damage, yet years of Soviet neglect had left it a crumbling and faded beauty when independence arrived. It took more than a decade to spruce it up and resuscitate its spirit. Today the Florence of the East (also dubbed the New Prague) has recaptured its grandeur, yet remains one of Europe's least visited major cities, a delightfully uncrowded, culture-packed destination.

The Old Town revolves around Ploshcha Rynok (Market Square), a cobbled plaza surrounding a 19th-century town hall. The square is fringed by a solid row of splendid 16th-century town houses festooned with decorative renditions of everything from gargoyles to patron saints to the likenesses of former merchant owners. Shoulder-to-shoulder buildings in Renaissance, Baroque, Rococo, and Neoclassical styles make the city an architectural treasure. Get a panoramic view from the town hall's 210-foot tower, or enjoy it all from a café over a cold Livske beer.

The alleys that branch off from Ploshcha Rynok offer up small museums, a memorial to Lviv's lost Jewish population, and quaint courtyards. A café beckons on every corner, and Vienna-style pastry and coffee shops hark back to the days of the Austro-Hungarian Empire.

Lviv's splendid churches all have their own personalities: The Armenian Cathedral from 1363 is the elegant grande dame; Dormition Church oozes Florentine style; Bernadine Church is a picture of Baroque opulence. Just off Ploshcha Rynok, the Dominican Church has a riotous Baroque interior under a famous Rococo dome. Join those who try to find an old cannonball lodged in the side of the Roman Catholic Cathedral.

WHERE: 50 miles/80 km east of the Polish border; 336 miles/541 km west of Kiev. **VISITOR INFO:** www.tourism.lviv.ua. **WHERE TO STAY:** The stylish newly opened Hotel Leopolis, behind the main market square, puts you in the middle of everything. Tel 380/32-295-9500; www.leopolishotel.com. *Cost:* from $315. **BEST TIME:** May–Sep for nicest weather.

SCANDINAVIA

The Sunniest Spot in the Baltic

Bornholm

Hovedstaden, Denmark

This wave-lashed island in the middle of the sea is the sunniest spot in the Baltic. It is a perennially popular summer retreat for Danes and visitors from nearby Germany, and an acquired taste for others. Denmark is the birthplace of the fiery Vikings and their legacy is everywhere—herring smokehouses trace their roots to the first Viking inhabitants who made landfall here a millennium ago and Viking runic stones lie in the tangled Almindingen forest. It's also a country defined by a national word, *hyggelig* ("cozy and warm"). The sleepy island of Bornholm offers the chance to experience both.

Bornholm's medieval past is memorably revealed through its whitewashed 12th-century *rundkirkem,* or round churches. Capped with ink-black conical roofs, they lend a stylized splendor to the rolling countryside. One of the more impressive examples is in Østerlars. Looming over northern Bornholm are the remains of the 13th-century clifftop castle Hammershus Slot, the largest such ruins in Northern Europe.

With its flat terrain and mild weather, 230-square-mile Bornholm is tailor-made for two wheels. So do as the Danes do—hop on a bicycle and ride south to explore the island's longest beach, Dueodde. Make time to visit Bornholm's best-preserved fishing village Gudhjem (God's Home), with its winding cobblestone streets, yellow half-timbered houses, and spinning windmill. The town is known for smoked fish and features a traditional *rogeri* (smokehouse), where you can see the silvery herring hung over alderwood embers, then enjoy eating them at long wooden tables outside. The nearby island of Christiansø makes an even more renowned smoked herring.

Sample the local specialty of "Sun over Gudjhem," smoked herring on dark bread, topped with an egg and raw onions. Perpetuating the Viking tradition of free-flowing mead, it is generally accompanied by plenty of chilled Tuborg and strong shots of *snaps* (aquavit).

Where: 95 miles/153 km east of Copenhagen. **Visitor info:** www.bornholm.info. **Best times:** May–Sep for warmest weather (and greatest number of visitors); off-season is quieter, though much is closed.

The thick walls and round shape of Østerlars—the most recognized of the island's 12th-century rundkirkem*—may have protected it from invasions.*

Timeless Appeal of Impeccable Style

Danish Design

Copenhagen, Hovedstaden, Denmark

What do the Lily and the Egg have in common? They're both chairs designed by Arne Jacobsen. His modern furniture, along with designs from other Danes, including Hans J. Wegner and Finn Juhl, bring style and elegance to living rooms and hotels around the world. The timeless appeal of Danish design—which has long followed the philosophy of "form follows function"—has ensured its enduring success, and it defines the country's aesthetic, from the famous silver work by Georg Jensen (browse the well-known Danish Silver shop for the largest collection of antique Jensen—just part of the remarkable selection) to the simple efficient lines of Lego blocks. Danish architects have also made their stamp on the world, including Jørn Utzon, who designed the Sydney Opera House (see p. 648). Copenhagen's own Opera House, an eye-catching glass-and-steel structure by Henning Larsen that opened in 2005, is a prime example of the city's progressive style. So is the cubist København Koncerthuset (Copenhagen Concert Hall) by Frenchman Jean Nouvel, which is swaddled in blue fabric "skin" that projects dancing images of performers.

To peruse the best of Danish design under one roof, visit the sleek, glass-paneled Dansk Design Center, with changing exhibits that feature everything from the legendary artichoke lamps by Poul Henningsen to stylized housewares.

Copenhagen's hotels also offer an excellent overview of the Danish aesthetic. The Hotel D'Angleterre, which has been accommodating guests since 1775, displays old-world elegance and hospitality. Sumptuous surroundings are marked by sparkling chandeliers, marble floors, and an aristocratic air that reflect the hotel's origin as a 1594 manor house. Its excellent location adds to its appeal—steps from the Strøget, the capital's famous miles-long pedestrian shopping boulevard, and at the top of the Nyhavn harbor area with its café- and restaurant-lined canal. The Copenhagen Admiral Hotel introduces another angle on old-meets-new: Originally an 18th-century grain warehouse, the building has been smartly renovated and has inspiring views of the Opera House.

Copenhagen's new waterside Opera House is clad in glass, steel, and limestone.

At the other end of the hotel spectrum is the Radisson Blu Royal, designed by Arne Jacobsen in 1960 and replete with his furniture. Even the heavy door handles were created by him. The most famous room is 606, which looks just like it did when it opened, with all the original furnishings. For the price of a cocktail, you can bask in Jacobsen's aura in the elegant hotel bar. Another apex of chic is the First Hotel Skt. Petri, a revamped Modernist hotel with minimalist décor—and a hopping bar.

Danish Silver: Tel 45/3311-5252; www.danishsilver.com. **Opera House:** Tel 45/3369-6969; www.kglteater.dk. **Concert Hall:** Tel 45/3520-3040; www.dr.dk/Koncerthuset. **Dansk Design Center:** Tel 45/3369-3369;

www.ddc.dk. **Hotel D'Angleterre:** Tel 45/3312-0095; www.remmen.dk. *Note:* The hotel is under renovation until mid-2012. **Copenhagen Admiral Hotel:** Tel 45/3374-1414; www.admiralhotel.dk. *Cost:* from $250. **Radisson Blu Royal Hotel:** Tel 45/3342-6000; www.radissonblu.com. *Cost:* from $265. **First Hotel Skt. Petri:** Tel 45/3345-9100; www.hotelsktpetri.com. *Cost:* from $225. **Best time:** May–Sep for nicest weather.

New Nordic Cuisine: Paying Homage to the Soil and the Sea

Denmark's Culinary Revolution

Copenhagen, Hovedstaden, Denmark

Denmark is consistently voted one of the happiest nations in the world. Perhaps it's the strong bonds between family and friends; the top-notch infrastructure, including efficient public transport; or the fact that the nation's icon is a winsome mermaid gazing out to sea. But for many, it's the cuisine—fresh, sea-sourced, delectable. For a taste of old and new Nordic cuisine, Copenhagen, featuring a rich array of both, is the place to start.

Those who think a sandwich by any other name is still a sandwich should lunch at Ida Davidsen, a century-old institution and showcase of the national open-faced buttered treat called smørrebrød. The menu of 250-plus variations, said to be the largest in Scandinavia, is nearly book length. The choices range from haute to homey: tongue with fried egg; shrimp and caviar; *frikadeller* (meatballs); liver paté; roast beef; and, of course, Denmark's famous herring. Even the queen arranges for the occasional takeout and has had royal occasions catered by Ida Davidsen at her residence, Amalienborg Palace.

Copenhagen also features beautiful, old-world dining palaces like Kong Hans Kaelder, which was a vineyard and wine cellar more than five centuries ago and now offers classic Danish cuisine with modern flourishes, served in an unpretentious ambience.

There's no escaping the neo-Nordic culinary movement that is redefining Danish cuisine, and Noma is at the helm. It consistently tops the world's short list of best restaurants and is headed up by young and visionary chef René Redzepi. Noma pays homage to the "soil and sea," with a rarefied menu that hopscotches across the region, and includes Faroe Islands horse mussels, Baltic wild salmon, fresh asparagus, and little known wild herbs.

Noma has blazed the trail for a cadre of pioneering restaurants turning Copenhagen into a culinary destination (see Herman and The Paul, next page). Two others sharing the spotlight have roots in classic French cuisine: Formel B, a high-class bistro serving impeccable fresh local ingredients and the less expensive Les Trois Cochons, a former butcher shop reborn as a stylish and hugely successful eatery.

Ida Davidsen: Tel 45/3391-3655; www.idadavidsen.dk. *Cost:* lunch $20. **Kong Hans Kaelder:** Tel 45/3311-6868; www.konghans.dk. *Cost:* dinner $170. **Noma:** Tel 45/3296-3297; www.noma.dk. *Cost:* 7-course prix-fixe dinner $175. **Formel B:** Tel 45/3325-1066; www.formel-b.dk. *Cost:* dinner $100. **Les Trois Cochons:** Tel 45/3331-7055; www.cofoco.dk. *Cost:* dinner $45. **Best time:** late Aug for Nordic Food Festival.

A Theme Park that Inspired Disney

TIVOLI GARDENS

Copenhagen, Hovedstaden, Denmark

Located in the very center of town, Copenhagen's fabled Tivoli Gardens is one of the world's oldest theme parks—and Denmark's most popular attraction. It is said to have inspired Walt Disney to create Disneyland.

Since the day this classic amusement park opened in 1843, a visit here has been a much-loved summertime tradition for Danes. More than 2,000,000 twinkling Christmas-style lights, fragrant flowers—from tulips and roses to chrysanthemums—and a small lake with ducks and swans set the fun-filled (and come evening, romantic) scene. The leafy park features carnival games and old-world amusement rides (the creaky 1914 roller coaster is the same vintage as the merry-go-round of tiny Viking ships) as well as Denmark's biggest roller coaster. Beer gardens, a full schedule of mostly free, open-air stage performances, and the parade of the red-uniformed Tivoli Boys Guard keep young and old entertained and coming back.

True Tivoli fans can also opt to stay overnight on the grounds: On the western edge of the park is the new and much heralded 13-room Nimb Hotel, housed in a fanciful 1909 Moorish-inspired palace that is splendidly illuminated at night. Antiques and oil paintings are balanced by sleek, Scandinavian furnishings and splashes of color. Traditional Danish cuisine undergoes a makeover at the hotel's acclaimed restaurant, Herman: A dish like the classic *leverpostej* (liver paté) is reinterpreted as a delicate seared foie gras and pickled cherries. Tivoli features dozens of restaurants, but the other culinary temple is The Paul, which serves inspired Nordic fare in the Glassalen, a greenhouse-style building created by legendary Danish designer Poul Henningsen. You'll also find delicious street food throughout the park, including *rød pølse* (hot dogs with fried onions), a favorite among Danes, and an old-fashioned *vaffelbageriet* (ice cream in a waffle cone).

INFO: Tel 45/3315-1001; www.tivoligardens.com. *When:* closed Jan–Mar. **NIMB HOTEL:** Tel 45/8870-0000; www.nimb.dk. *Cost:* from $475; dinner at Herman $90. **THE PAUL:** Tel 45/3375-0775; www.thepaul.dk. *Cost:* dinner $165. **BEST TIME:** Tivoli is most magical at night.

To Be or Not to Be at Hamlet's Elsinore

KRONBORG SLOT

Helsingør, Hovedstaden, Denmark

Elsinore Castle's real name is Kronborg Slot ("slot" means castle in Danish), and it was built centuries after the time of the Danish prince on whom Shakespeare based his tormented, brooding Hamlet. But this fortified

Nordic icon of secret passages, with its gloomy dungeon and cannon-studded battlements, could not have been a better backdrop for Shakespeare's dark tragedy. The great moat-encircled castle rises grandly above the town of Helsingør, which sits next to the strait separating Denmark from Sweden. Its vast coffers were filled by 400 years of legal piracy—tolls paid to the Danish crown from passing ships—until the taxes were abolished in 1857.

Built in 1420 and expanded in 1574, Kronborg has all the trappings of a great regal Renaissance residence. Its starkly furnished Knights Hall is one of the largest and oldest in northern Europe, and the sumptuous castle chapel is still the dream wedding location for lucky Danish couples. Occasional summertime performances of *Hamlet* are staged in the torch-lit courtyard where audiences can envision the prince agonizing over the "slings and arrows of outrageous fortune." Somewhere off in a dark and dank chamber reposes the spirit of Viking chief Holger Danske, a mythic Charlemagne-era hero; legend has it that as long as he sleeps, the kingdom of Denmark will be safe.

Another easy day trip from Copenhagen is Frederiksborg Slot, the largest and most sumptuous Renaissance castle in Scandinavia. It was built in the early 1600s on three small islands as the royal residence of King Christian IV.

Where: 28 miles/45 km north of Copenhagen. Tel 45/4921-3078; www.kronborg.dk. **Best time:** first half of Aug for theater performances of *Hamlet.*

A Memorable Marriage of Art and Nature

Louisiana Museum of Modern Art

Humlebaek, Hovedstaden, Denmark

Follow one of Zealand's scenic drives north of Copenhagen to this exceptional museum situated at a beautiful site on the "Danish Riviera." Since opening in 1958, the Louisiana Museum has brought together art, nature, and architecture in perfect harmony. Its highly regarded exhibitions of modern classics of the post–World War II era as well as the (sometimes controversial) vanguard of contemporary art are displayed in spacious, light-flooded halls that embody the very essence of Danish modernism. No less impressive are its permanent holdings, including an extensive collection of the spindly sculptures of Alberto Giacometti and works by Pablo Picasso, Francis Bacon, and Henry Moore. The sparkling water of the Øresund that separates Denmark from Sweden vies for your attention from every window, and the open-air sculpture garden invites you to stroll among works by such artists as Alexander Calder and Jean Arp. Linger for the chamber music concerts that are often set here or enjoy a respite on the terrace café. The origin of the museum's name is a curious one: The original landowner had a succession of three wives, all named Louise.

A Calder sculpture stands in the museum's park.

Where: 22 miles/33 km north of Copenhagen. Tel 45/4919-0719; www.louisiana.dk.

Where the Ancient and Avant-Garde Merge

ÅRHUS

Midtjylland, Denmark

The Danish royals summer in lively Århus, and when you stroll its leafy, historical streets, you'll understand why. Even though it has an easygoing small-town vibe, Århus is actually Denmark's second largest city (with a population of about 300,000); its art and architecture rival Copenhagen's, from headliner jazz shows to the longest cathedral in the country. At heart, Århus is a university town, with all the requisite student-friendly features: progressive art museums, indie bands, and outdoor bars and cafés flowing with Danish beer and high spirits.

Founded in the 10th century as a Viking settlement, Århus is one of the oldest cities in Scandinavia. The Århus Domkirke, which dates to the 12th century, is dedicated to St. Clemens, the patron saint of sailors. Look closely at the unique painted (not stained) glass window, by Norwegian artist Emanuel Vigeland, behind the altar. Steps from the cathedral, a whiff of old-time luxury permeates the Hotel Royal, the city's class-act historic hotel with stained-glass windows and a filigreed vintage elevator. For a touch of nature, head to Århus's fragrant botanical gardens, established in 1873. Then visit nearby Den Gamle By (the Old Town), an open-air museum of 75 traditional half-timbered houses. Dating from the 17th to 19th centuries—with the exception of the 1595 Mayor's Residence—they were brought here from around the country and painstakingly re-created as a provincial town. In the summer, concerts are held on the bandstand, while at Christmastime, the place is alive with twinkling lights and carols.

Among the Old Town's reconstructed treasures are a candlemaker's workshop, a house containing a bicycle museum, and a windmill.

Århus's avant-garde art scene rivals its history. The towering Cubist ARoS art museum showcases works by great Danes, like Golden Age landscape painter P. C. Skovgaard and contemporary artist Olafur Eliasson. In the evening, enjoy new Nordic cuisine at the very chic Malling & Schmidt restaurant, groove to everything from soul to classical at the modern glass-walled Musikhuset concert hall, or stroll along the Århus River, where open-air beer bars are busy until the wee hours.

WHERE: 109 miles/175 km west of Copenhagen. **VISITOR INFO:** www.visitaarhus.com. **HOTEL ROYAL:** Tel 45/8612-0011; www.hotelroyal.dk. *Cost:* from $325. **DEN GAMLE BY:** Tel 45/8612-3188; www.dengamleby.dk. **AROS ART MUSEUM:** Tel 45/8730-6600; www.aros.dk. **MALLING & SCHMIDT:** Tel 45/8617-7088; www.mallingschmidt.dk *Cost:* dinner $65. **MUSIKHUSET:** Tel 45/8940-4040; www.musikhusetaarhus.dk. **BEST TIMES:** mid-Jul for Århus Jazz Festival; late Aug or early Sep for the Århus Festival Week of music, dance, films, and sports events.

Remote and Romantic, the "Land's End" of Denmark

SKAGEN

Nordjylland, Denmark

The Danes consider the Skagen headland something of a Riviera, while Americans liken it to Cape Cod. At the Jutland peninsula's northernmost tip, the small, weather-hardened fishing communities that for centuries inhabited these heathered moors and sea-swept coastline have been joined by a thriving artists colony—and the tourists who followed. All are lured by Skagen's simple life, the character-filled town, the unspoiled dunes, and luminous skies.

The small but noteworthy Skagens Museum showcases works of the local, late-19th-century Danish Impressionist movement that was inspired by the land- and seascapes and the shifting colors and quality of the light here—which pours through the nicely designed building's many skylights and windows. At Grenen, the country's northernmost point, you can saunter along a pale finger of sand and plant your feet in the frothy coupling of two seas, the Skagerrak and the Kattegat.

Danish writer Isak Dinesen wrote much of *Out of Africa* while a guest at the gabled, wonderfully charming Brøndums Hotel. Creaking floors and antiques-furnished sitting rooms make this feel like a private home, one distinguished by a number of old paintings given in exchange for lodging. The 150-year-old inn's intimate dining room produces exceptionally fresh and delicious meals, with a predictable accent on seafood. Every morning at dawn, the townsfolk and restaurant owners have the pick of the best at the wharf's barnlike fish-auction house before the day's catch is shipped off to markets all over northern Europe. The harbor-side Skagen Fiskerestaurant is an excellent spot at which to feast on the water's bounty, from lobster and filets of sole drizzled with lemon to the ubiquitous herring.

WHERE: 300 miles/482 km northwest of Copenhagen. **VISITOR INFO:** www.skagen.dk. **SKAGENS MUSEUM:** 45/9844-6444; www.skagens museum.dk. **BRØNDUMS HOTEL:** Tel 45/9844-1555; www.broendums-hotel.dk. *Cost:* from $185. **SKAGEN FISKERESTAURANT:** Tel 45/9844-3544; www.skagen-fiskerestaurant.dk. *Cost:* dinner $50. **BEST TIMES:** Jun–Aug for warmest weather; Jun for Skagen Festival of music.

A Stroll Through Danish History in a Former Royal Capital

ROSKILDE

Sjælland, Denmark

The fjordside Roskilde was until 1455 the ecclesiastical seat and royal capital of Denmark. The city's hallmark building is its twin-spired 13th-century Gothic cathedral, a kind of Westminster Abbey of Denmark—

38 Danish kings are buried here in royal marble and alabaster tombs. For something a bit more lively, head into the midst of this centuries-old trading town, where you'll find a dynamic student population and, on Wednesdays and Saturdays, a colorful, bustling market with 350 stalls and live entertainment.

Vikingeskibsmuseet Roskilde, the nation's best Viking Ship Museum, displays five perfectly preserved longships discovered and painstakingly reconstructed in 1957. Dating from approximately A.D. 1000, they were presumably sunk in the Roskilde Fjord to stop the entry of enemy ships. It's worth jumping on the old wooden steamer that sails out of Roskilde to cruise this lovely fjord, one of the longest and largest in Denmark. In late June or early July, an international crowd descends on Roskilde for what vies with England's Glastonbury (see p. 28) as Europe's largest open-air rock festival; more than 100 bands from the world over gather to play at outdoor venues around the ancient town.

WHERE: 20 miles/32 km west of Copenhagen. **VIKING SHIP MUSEUM:** Tel 45/46-300-200; www.vikingeskibsmuseet.dk. **ROSKILDE ROCK FESTIVAL:** Tel 45/4636-6613; www.roskilde-festival.dk. *Cost:* 1-day ticket $175, includes camping; 8-day ticket $325. *When:* late Jun or early Jul.

A Taste of Herring and History on a Windswept Isle

ÆRØ

Syddanmark, Denmark

Folks from Copenhagen go to Funen, or Fyn, to relax (see next page); to really get away from it all, they head south to Ærø, its little-sister island with quiet marinas, quintessentially Danish villages, and a patchwork of farms. It's a popular sailing center, ringed by about 90 smaller neighboring islands, some of which are privately owned, in the Danish Baltic Sea.

Life in low-key Ærø centers on salty, perfectly preserved Ærøskøbing, a 14th-century market town that reached prosperity in the late 1600s, when it was home to more than 100 windjammers. Today, visitors browse in the shops and stroll along cobblestone streets lined with winsome, sometimes gently listing, half-timbered houses decorated with red geraniums and lace curtains. (Particularly charming is the post office, built in 1749, the oldest in Denmark.) Ease into the evening at the Ærøskøbing Røgeri and enjoy freshly smoked herring and a Danish Tuborg beer while overlooking the harbor lined with bobbing boats. Denmark is a nation of bicycle riders, and touring by bike is understandably popular on both Ærø and Funen, where more than 580 miles of marked bike paths crisscross the gentle curves of the islands' topography. Ærø's empty country roads, sometimes single-laned, meander past old windmills, a 12th-century Gothic church, and thatched houses whose painted, decorative doors are unique to the island. Well-tended farms cover much of the 5-by-19-mile island, and produce is left alongside the roadway for sale on the honor system. Ærø is also proudly one of the greenest islands in Denmark, with wind turbines producing more than 50 percent of the energy for its 7,000 residents.

WHERE: 46 miles/74 km south of Odense, Funen's principal town. **VISITOR INFO:** www.aeroeisland.com. **ÆRØSKØBING RØGERI:** Tel 45/6252-4007. *Cost:* lunch $20. **BEST TIMES:** Jun–Aug for the warmest weather; late Jul for a lively music festival.

Fairy Tales in the Garden of Denmark

FUNEN

Syddanmark, Denmark

The island of Funen is best known to the world as the birthplace of Hans Christian Andersen. He is possibly the world's most esteemed storyteller, and his work—including beloved classics like "Thumbelina" and "The Ugly Duckling"—is more widely translated and read than anything except the Bible and the writings of Karl Marx. A bronze statue of his Little Mermaid is Copenhagen's world-recognized icon. His hometown of Odense on Funen is Denmark's third largest city, and it attracts fairy-tale lovers from all over. Born in 1805 to a local shoemaker and washerwoman, both illiterate, Andersen was an inveterate traveler, whose battered suitcases are on display at the museum adjoining his childhood home. Visitors can view original manuscripts and letters to his close friend Charles Dickens, then explore Odense, with its charming medieval core, boutiques, and outdoor cafés.

Seventeen miles south of Odense looms the regal Egeskov Castle, widely held to be Europe's best-preserved Renaissance island castle. Constructed in 1554, it passed into the hands of the current owners' ancestors in 1784. A Victorian-era suspension drawbridge links the castle to a grand forecourt where white peacocks roam; beyond lies working farmland. Among the highlights are the 30 manicured acres that feature Denmark's most important private gardens (including a large collection of fuchsias).

Funen is home to a number of beautiful, historic inns, including the aristocratic Steensgaard Herregårdspension, whose main house dates from 1310. Set in its own shady 25-acre park and surrounded by well-tended English gardens, this half-timbered country manor lies beyond a swan-filled pond, at the end of a tree-lined entryway. In the candlelit dining room, you may feast on seasonal game specialties such as pheasant or wild boar.

Known as the Garden of Denmark for its tapestry of farmlands and meadows, Funen is ideal for exploring by bike, thanks to both the relatively short distances between sights and to Denmark's signature flat terrain. The island's bucolic countryside is dotted with farmhouses, orchards, manor houses, and inns called *kros*. Falsled Kro is undoubtedly the finest of these, a complex of elegant, rustic buildings with thatched roofs and large, open fireplaces and set in a lovely farming village on Funen's southern coast. Falsled Kro's stellar restaurant is the real draw: Together with suppliers and

Egeskov Castle is surrounded by a moat, which provided protection in uncertain political times.

gatherers from neighboring castles and manor houses, chef and co-owner Jean-Louis Lieffroy breeds, fishes, grows, hunts, and smokes much of what winds up on your plate.

Where: Odense is 97 miles/156 km west of Copenhagen. An 11-mile suspension bridge connects Copenhagen to Funen. **Hans Christian Andersen Museum:** Tel 45/6551-4601; www.hcandersen-homepage.dk. **Egeskov Castle:** Tel 45/6227-1016; www.egeskov.com. **Steensgaard Herregårdspension:** Tel 45/6261-9490; www.herregaardspension.dk. *Cost:* from \$280; dinner \$75. **Falsled Kro:** Tel 45/6268-1111; www.falsledkro.dk. *Cost:* from \$370; dinner \$150. **Best time:** May–Aug for warmest weather.

Denmark's Oldest and Best-Preserved Medieval Town

Ribe

Syddanmark, Denmark

Ribe was a bustling Viking trading center starting in the 9th century, and is Denmark's oldest town. Its medieval cathedral, the Ribe Domkirke, was one of the first Christian houses of worship in the country (before that, the Danes worshipped the Nordic gods). It is well worth climbing the cathedral's 248 steps to the top for panoramic views of the Danish countryside. Then take a step back into Ribe's history by strolling its ancient core, Gamle Stan, one of whose historic streets leads to the town's 16th-century schoolhouse.

Ribe Domkirke is Denmark's oldest—and only five-aisled—cathedral.

The postcard-perfect Torvet, the old market square, is the charming location of the country's oldest inn, the Hotel Dagmar, named after a medieval Danish queen. Dating back to 1581, the 50-room hotel sits across from the cathedral and has been beautifully renovated, its sloping floors and low ceilings left intact. It also houses one of the finest restaurants in town.

The most popular residents in Ribe aren't people. They're white storks, which migrate yearly at the end of March to settle comfortably at the top of the town hall and atop chimneys throughout town—much to the delight of locals and visitors. Ribe's surrounding marshland is alive with far more than just storks, drawing birders from around the country.

Ribe is well situated for taking a day trip to one of Denmark's most kid-friendly spots: Legoland. Everything is constructed from the iconic building bricks at this colorful theme park, from miniature trains to kid-size cars. Their name comes from the Danish *leg godt* ("play well"), and they achieved a long-lasting, worldwide success after their launch in the late 1940s.

Where: 151 miles/244 km west of Copenhagen. **Visitor info:** www.visitribe.dk. **Ribe Domkirke:** Tel 45/7542-0619; www.ribe-domkirke.dk. **Hotel Dagmar:** Tel 45/7542-0033; www.hoteldagmar.dk. *Cost:* from \$235; prix-fixe dinner \$75. **Legoland:** Tel 45/7533-1333; www.legoland.dk. *When:* closed Nov–Mar. **Best times:** May–Aug for nicest weather; late Mar–Aug for the town's famous storks; May–Sep at 8 and 10 P.M. to follow the night watchmen.

Moody and Humbling Nature in the North Atlantic

Faroe Islands

Autonomous Region of Denmark

Amid the foamy waves of the North Atlantic, midway between Scotland and Iceland, lie the 22 Faroe Islands, an autonomous region of Denmark. They form an archipelago that is achingly beautiful, in which rugged mountains are cleaved by deep fjords.

What strikes you upon arrival is how resolutely proud the Faroese—some 50,000 in all—are of their unique history, culture, and, especially, language, which descends from Old Norse. It's taught and spoken throughout the islands, and many villages have their own dialects.

The archipelago's rich history is revealed at every turn: ancient Viking settlements that date back to the 9th century, medieval churches, colorful fishing boats, and the distinctive turf-roofed houses. The small capital, Torshavn, on the principal island of Streymoy, features an atmospheric old quarter and a 15th-century *munkastovan* (monk's house) built by Irish friars.

Throughout the islands, the backdrop is breathtaking: craggy mountains, bright-green valleys with tumbling waterfalls, and treeless expanses. No matter where you are, the sea is never more than a few miles away.

And then there's the astonishing array of seabirds: Peer up at any cliff ledge and you'll see puffins. These red-billed birds—along with other species, like fulmars and guillemots—flourish in the Faroes, from the Vestmanna Bird Cliffs to the tiny, remote island of Mykines. They carpet the islands in guano, which keeps them surprisingly green, as do the warm currents of the Gulf Stream.

Few visitors come during the colder months, missing out on nature's ultimate show: the magnificent aurora borealis (northern lights) that transforms the sky into a giant, swirling painting of greens and blues.

Where: 495 miles/797 km southeast of Reykjavik, Iceland. **Visitor info:** www.visitfaroeislands.com. **Where to stay:** The contemporary Hotel Føroyar overlooks Torshavn. Tel 45/298-31-75-00; www.hotelforoyar.com. *Cost:* from $175. **Best times:** Jun–Aug for warmest weather and midnight sun; Oct–Apr for the northern lights.

Glorious Corner of the Largest Island in the World

Disko Bay

Greenland, Autonomous Territory of Denmark

For many adventure travelers, Greenland is the ultimate frontier. About 85 percent of the island is covered in ice, and adrenaline-spiking activities abound, from sea kayaking ("kayak" is from the Greenlandic word *qajaq*) and rock-climbing to musk ox safaris and biplane flights over mountain-size icebergs.

Though Greenland, a self-governing territory of Denmark, has the lowest population density in the world and is decidedly remote—it claims the world's northernmost point of permanent land—visitor numbers are climbing. There are still only two stoplights on the entire island, and both are in the petite capital of Nuuk.

Cruise among the icebergs in Disko Bay via kayak or tour boat.

For prime exploring, head west to Ilulissat ("icebergs" in the local Inuit)—with a population of just 4,500, it is the country's third largest city—and Disko Bay, where you can board a tour boat that noses its way past massive blue-streaked icebergs floating in the fjord. Time your visit for early summer, when the drift ice takes on a warm, luminous glow under the 24-hour sun.

Greenland is alive with arctic creatures, including sleek seals, reindeer, the majestic Greenlandic eagle, and even the narwhal whale, distinct for its impressive, 9-foot tusk. Popular whale-watching safaris take off from Nuuk, where it is common to spy minke and humpback varieties. Your best chance to see the elusive and endangered polar bears is on a trip to the vast Northeast Greenland National Park.

Global warming is no longer just an abstraction, and Greenland is on the front line. The island has been heating up every year and now claims the fastest-retreating ice cap in the Northern Hemisphere. Flying over the massive inland ice reveals how this phenomenon has affected the landscape as ice gives way to aquamarine rivers and deep pools of beautiful, bright blue meltwater. Southern Greenland is indeed greener than in the past, with summer highs in the balmy mid-50s Fahrenheit.

VISITOR INFO: www.greenland.com. **HOW:** Hurtigruten Cruises offers 9-day trips; in the U.S., tel 866-552-0371 or 212-319-1300; www.hurtigruten.us. *Cost:* from $5,915. Originates in Copenhagen, round-trip flight to Greenland included. *When:* Jun. **WHERE TO STAY:** The modern Hotel Arctic, on Disko Bay, offers views of the icebergs. Tel 299/944-153; www.hotelarctic.com. *Cost:* from $315. **BEST TIMES:** May–Jul for 24-hour daylight; Aug–Sep for hiking, camping, and sea kayaking.

Islands of Enchanting Beauty

THE ÅLAND ARCHIPELAGO

Finland

The extraordinary Åland Archipelago is among Finland's most unusual regions. Jutting into the Gulf of Bothnia, the province consists of more than 6,500 small islands and is home to a people with their own distinctive culture and folk traditions. In fact, most residents here—citizens of Finland—speak Swedish and take pride in their high degree of autonomy: Åland has its own parliament, flag, and license plates and issues its own stamps. It even has its own Internet domain, ending with "dot ax" (as in www.aland.ax).

The islands themselves offer a vision of tranquility, with lush oak and elm forests backdropped by the emerald hues of the placid waters of the Baltic. Interspersed among the dense woods are fields and meadows and red granite outcrops, with nature trails winding through the rugged scenery. Ruins of old fortresses attest to the strategic importance of the archipelago. This was a vital trading center during the Viking era, which flourished in the 8th or 9th century. Åland was part of Sweden until 1809, when the Russian Empire swallowed it up (along with the rest of Finland). When Finland gained its independence in 1917, it took Åland with it—despite the wish of many Ålanders' to reunite with Sweden.

Some 65 of the islands are inhabited, and the slow pace of life and sublime natural beauty of the landscape make the islands a popular destination for Finns, Swedes, and Danes, both in summer (for walking, bicycling, and boating) and in winter (for long-distance ice-skating, ice fishing, and iceboating around the smaller islands and skerries).

Mariehamn (population 12,000) is the principal town on Fasta Åland, the largest island in the archipelago, and makes a good base for exploring the region. From here, you can hire a car or rent a bicycle and set out into picturesque countryside, taking in centuries-old stone churches like the fascinating, 12th-century Sankt Michaels Kyrka in Finström, with its wealth of medieval frescoes and wooden sculptures. East of there in Sund stands the Kastelholms Slott, a beautifully sited citadel founded in the 14th century. During the Gustav Vasa-Dagarna festival, medieval-style revelry rules the day as locals enjoy feasting, jousting, and dancing. For a glimpse of Åland's serene beauty, head west to Eckerö, a picturesque island with sandy beaches and a harbor lined with photogenic red boathouses.

WHERE: Mariehamn is 200 miles/320 km west of Helsinki, 100 miles/160 km northeast of Stockholm. **VISITOR INFO:** www.visitaland.com. **WHERE TO STAY:** Hotell Arkipelag is situated along the harbor in Mariehamn. Tel 358/18-24020; www.hotellarkipelag.com. *Cost:* from $230. **BEST TIMES:** Jun–Aug for warmest weather; early Jul for Gustav Vasa-Dagarna festival at Kastelholms Slott.

Grand Finnish

THE DESIGN DISTRICT

Helsinki, Finland

Considering the country's small size (its population is just over 5 million), Finland has a formidable reputation in the design world. This is the country that nurtured the talents of textile design house Marimekko, the award-winning houseware designers behind Iittala, and architectural superstars like Eliel and Eero Saarinen and Alvar Aalto (see next page). Today, companies like Arabia, Hackman, and Artek continue to turn everyday objects—tableware, cookware, and furniture—into timeless works of art found in every Finnish home.

Helsinki is the epicenter of Finnish creativity, and the downtown is awash in cutting-edge galleries, stores, hotels, and restaurants eager to herald their design smarts. In 2005, Helsinki even christened a huge swath of the capital as its Design District, with repositories such as the Design Forum Finland, a great place to see the works of both celebrated and up-and-coming Finns. A small, temporary exhibition space showcases new talents, while a store sells works by over 200 Finnish designers and manufacturers. For a crash course on modern Finnish design, visit the stellar Design Museum, set in a 19th-century Beaux Arts building. The permanent collection focuses on the 20th century, with everything from blown glass and ceramics to chairs illustrating the evolution of the Finnish aesthetic over the years.

To stay with the theme, book a room at Klaus K. The 137-room boutique hotel takes its design seriously, with an ethereal lobby of white modular furniture, a mural of painted glass columns, and an ice-crystal-like sculpture floating over the reception desk. Guests can even stay in one of two special "design suites" amid lush original paintings by important Finnish artists.

Within the shell of a converted 1920s bank building, the stylish Hotel GLO created an interior of beautiful contemporary rooms and thoughtful extras—including in-room spa treatments and delivery of musical instruments, painting supplies, and gym equipment to your door. Around the corner is GLO's venerable big sister, the Hotel Kämp, a fin de siècle beauty with a stately marble lobby and rooms furnished with both antiques and contemporary touches. Steps from the hotel, you'll find superb shopping, including a Marimekko store with a wide array of colorful fashion and housewares.

The Design District is a hotbed of innovation. See how that translates in the world of gastronomy at Kuurna, whose delectable Nordic dishes are served with a creative twist. The menu changes weekly and features the likes of fried whitefish with saffron potatoes and braised lamb belly with Jerusalem artichoke puree.

Visitor info: www.designdistrict.fi. **Design Forum:** Tel 358/9-622-0810; www.designforum.fi. **Design Museum:** Tel 358/9-622-0540; www.designmuseum.fi. **Klaus K:** Tel 358/20-770-4700; www.klauskhotel.com. *Cost:* from $180. **Hotel GLO:** Tel 358/9-5840-9540; www.hotelglohelsinki.com. *Cost:* from $200. **Hotel Kämp:** Tel 358/9-576-111; www.hotelkamp.com. *Cost:* from $225. **Kuurna:** Tel 358/9-670-849; www.kuurna.fi. *Cost:* dinner $60. **Best times:** Jun–Aug for warm weather; late Aug–early Sep for Helsinki Design Week.

The Father of Modern Scandinavian Design

The World of Alvar Aalto

Helsinki and Jyväskylä, Finland

Among the greatest 20th-century architects, Alvar Aalto (1898–1976) made seminal contributions to the world of art and design. He was firmly rooted in "organic architecture"—buildings that suited their environment—and often designed not just a building but its interior surfaces, furnishings, and sometimes even lamps, glassware, and other items. Aalto was also one of the first to make good design affordable, and his flowing vases and curved wood chairs became international design collectibles that are still sought after today for their timeless appeal.

Visitors to Helsinki don't have to travel far to find iconic works by the great Finnish master. One of the city's most famous buildings, Aalto's Finlandia Hall (completed in 1971) looms majestically over the shimmering waters of Töölönlahti Bay; Aalto designed both the interior and exterior. The striking white marble building looks particularly dazzling against a snowy backdrop.

For a look at another one of Aalto's visionary interiors, visit the elegant Savoy restaurant. The classic 1937 design is untouched by time: Aalto designed everything here, from the service stations to the lighting fixtures to the undulating flower vases that have become an Aalto trademark. After a decadent meal with sweeping views of the city, head to the flagship store of Artek, which was founded by Alvar, his wife, Aino (also an architect and designer), and two partners in 1935. The now legendary furniture company still carries Aalto's signature pieces—including the curved wood "Paimio" armchair, elegant brass pendant lamps, and classic birch nesting tables.

The Aalto pilgrimage continues in the charming university town of Jyväskylä, 3 hours north of Helsinki, where Aalto studied and opened his first offices. Here he produced such structures as the Palladian-inspired Workers Club Building (one of his earliest designs), the Muurame Church with its Italianate influences, and eight buildings of the University of Jyväskylä, which embody Athenian ideals in minimalist fashion.

Aalto also designed the building that now houses the museum that bears his name. Through furniture and glassware exhibits, video footage and building designs, the museum does a fine job of conveying the great Finn's philosophy.

In Jyväskylä, the boutique Hotel Yöpuu has simple but elegant rooms, the best of which has a private sauna. The hotel's Restaurant Pöllöwaari is among the region's finest—you might dine on Nordic delicacies such as roe of whitefish with crispy blini or fillet of reindeer with peppered carrots, creamed winter apples, and rosemary sauce.

WHERE: Jyväskylä is 168 miles/270 km north of Helsinki. **FINLANDIA HALL:** Tel 358/9-402-4400; www.finlandiatalo.fi. **SAVOY:** Tel 358/9-6128-5300; www.royalravintolat.com/savoy/en. *Cost:* dinner $90. **ARTEK:** Tel 358/10-617-3480; www.artek.fi. **ALVAR AALTO MUSEUM:** Tel 358/14-266-7113; www.alvaraalto.fi. **HOTEL YÖPUU:** Tel 358/14-333-900; www.hotelliyopuu.fi. *Cost:* from $190; dinner $75. **BEST TIME:** Jun–Aug for warm weather.

Santa's Busy Workshop, an Exhilarating Icebreaker Cruise, and a Real-Life Snow Castle

FINNISH LAPLAND

Lapland, Finland

One of the world's wildest landscapes, Lapland is a region of vast coniferous forests and frozen tundra. It's home to herds of roaming reindeer as well as the indigenous, formerly nomadic Sami people, who occupy the northern regions of Finland and neighboring Sweden, Norway, and Russia. Despite the subzero temperatures and long, dark nights, winter can be a magical time to be here, when you can head out onto the frozen sea on an otherworldly icebreaker cruise with the aurora borealis lighting up the night sky.

The village of Rovaniemi is considered the gateway to Finnish Lapland (Sweden also has its own Lapland province; see p. 365) and to Finland's Arctic Circle. It's also Santa's home turf, which is just as every child imagines it: a snowy winter wonderland with a jovial Santa in attendance every day. The post office displays some of the 700,000 letters he receives every year from over 150 countries, and an old-fashioned gift shop stocks a myriad of Yuletide presents that can be shipped back home with a Santa Claus Village postmark. A nearby reindeer farm offers Magic Sleighrides (albeit ones that never leave the ground) drawn by Rudolph and Dasher lookalikes. Rovaniemi was nearly razed by the Germans in 1944 and was largely rebuilt following plans that Finnish architect Alvar Aalto (see p. 348) laid out in the shape of reindeer antlers. Its excellent Arktikum Science Center depicts life above the Arctic Circle.

During the Christmas season, Santa Claus Village, including the Elves' Toy Factory, hosts up to 4,000 visitors a day.

To immerse yourself in the shimmering world of white, head half an hour north of Rovaniemi. Overlooking a small lake, the Lapland Hotel Bear's Lodge is set amid picturesque pine forest and has simple but attractive wood-paneled rooms. Winter days with limited light are spent riding skimobiles, snowshoeing, or taking a reindeer safari through the dazzling white surroundings. In summer, you can hike, mountain bike, boat, or fish under the midnight sun.

South of Rovaniemi, catch a 4-hour ride on the MV *Sampo* from the town of Kemi. The former Arctic icebreaker ventures onto Europe's largest continuous ice field on the frozen Gulf of Bothnia, the northernmost tip of the Baltic Sea. Once out at sea, passengers are invited to don bright-orange watertight survival suits and float amid the newly broken ice, which is sometimes 3 feet thick. They can alight from the vessel onto the rock-hard sea for ice fishing or be whisked away by snowmobiles or husky-hauled sleds. Either way, it is an exhilarating ride through splendid solitude as the midwinter half-light reflects off the white solid surface of the sea.

You can overnight on land at the "World's Largest Snow Castle"—preferably in the Honeymoon Suite. The 18-room hotel is part of Kemi's fantastic SnowCastle, the LumiLinna, created every winter since 1996. The three story–tall wintry stronghold includes everything from a café to a chapel, all made of ice, and grows larger and more inventive every year.

WHERE: Rovaniemi is 516 miles/830 km north of Helsinki. **VISITOR INFO:** www.laplandfinland.com. **SANTA CLAUS VILLAGE:** Tel 358/16-356-2096; www.santaclausvillage.info. **ARKTIKUM:** Tel 358/16-322-3260; www.arktikum.fi. **LAPLAND HOTEL BEAR'S LODGE:** Tel 358/16-530-0400; www.laplandhotels.com. *Cost:* from $205. **SAMPO TOURS:** Tel 358/16-258-878; www.sampotours.com. *Cost:* from $365. *When:* late Dec–mid-Apr. **SNOWCASTLE:** Tel 358/16-258-878; www.snowcastle.net. *Cost:* from $300 (off-peak), fom $415 (peak). *When:* Feb–early Apr. **BEST TIME:** Oct–Mar for the northern lights; in Jan–Feb the average temperature is around –25°F.

Wondrous World of Water and a Classic Smoke Sauna

LAKELAND

Northern and Southern Savonia, Finland

Finland is a land of lakes (it has close to 188,000 of them), and with myriad coastal islets and rivers as well, it claims more water by proportion than any other country. From the Saimaa Lake District, near the Russian border, to the Gulf of Bothnia, in the west, it is also one of the most heavily wooded regions on earth—the interlocking network of lakes, surrounded by dense forests of pine and birch trees, creates a vision of pristine nature rarely seen anywhere. Lakeland, or Järve-Suomi, is the heart of Finland's watery kingdom, home to the biggest lake system in Europe and to Saimaa, the largest lake in Finland, with more than 13,000 islands spread across some 1,700 square miles.

On three of these lies the town of Savonlinna. Long a spa destination for the Russian czars and their retinues, it is home to one of Northern Europe's most spectacular citadels, the 15th-century Olavinlinna Castle which stands majestically in the middle of the lake. It's the evocative setting for one of Finland's most famous music festivals, the Savonlinna Opera Festival, held in July in the main covered courtyard, inside the castle walls.

There are many ways to take in the idyllic landscape, from bike rides along country lanes to canoe trips out on the lake. Boat rides provide some of the most memorable journeys including the 11-hour summertime cruise on the MS *Puijo* between Savonlinna and Kuopio, passing through picturesque waterways, canals, and locks with stops at small lakeside villages along the way. Once you're in easy-going Kuopio, you can take strolls through spruce forest and sample the famous *muikku* lakefish at waterfront restaurants. The real reason to come here, though, is to experience the traditional log-hewn, wood-fired Jätkänkämppä smoke sauna on Lake Kallavesi. Finns invented the sauna, and this is the largest of its kind in the world, and in one of Finland's most gorgeous settings. You can sweat it out, then cool off in the lake—even in winter, when an opening is cut into the ice.

Back in Savonlinna, the tiny five-room Lossiranta Lodge has small but charming rooms with terraces and a splendid location facing the castle. The best room has its own wood-burning sauna and a Jacuzzi. And you can swim in the lake off the lodge's dock.

WHERE: Savonlinna is 214 miles/344 km northeast of Helsinki. **VISITOR INFO:** www.visitfinland.com. **SAVONLINNA OPERA FESTIVAL:** Tel 358/15-476-750; www.operafestival.fi. **MS *PUIJO*:** Tel 358/15-250-250; www.mspuijo.fi. *Cost:* $125. *When:* late Jun–mid-Aug. **LOSSIRANTA LODGE:** Tel 358/44-511-2323; www.lossiranta.net. *Cost:* from $135. **BEST TIME:** Jun–Aug for nicest weather.

The island castle of Olavinlinna was originally built to repel attacks from Russian forces.

Cultural Riches and a Historic Road

Turku and the King's Road

Finland

Finland's oldest city and its original capital entered the spotlight in 2011, when it was named a European Capital of Culture. Such a designation seemed apt for the historic, free-spirited, and artistically inclined city of Turku. After all, the town has produced some of Finland's leading artists, many of whom studied at the venerable Turku Arts Academy. It's also home to the superb Sibelius Museum, where you can gaze at the 300 musical instruments and memorabilia on display and then listen to the moving compositions of Finland's most famous composer. Wednesday night concerts (September to May) showcase classical, jazz, and folk artists from across the country.

Turku has a lively festival calendar, and one of its biggest events, Medieval Market, brings the Middle Ages to life in the atmospheric setting of Turku Castle. Strategically set near the mouth of Aurajoki (the Aura River), this imposing citadel dates back to the 13th century and is one of the largest surviving medieval buildings in Scandinavia.

Near the heart of old Turku looms another landmark, the iconic Tuomiokirkko, called "the mother church" of Finland's Lutheran faith. Founded in the 1300s, the cathedral was badly damaged in the catastrophic fire of 1827; its soaring Neoclassical tower and the dazzling frescoes of famed Finnish artist Robert Wilhelm Ekman were added in the 19th century. The 18th- and 19th-century houses of Luostarinmäki, an open-air museum, are among the few survivors of the great fire. The period furnishings and craftsmen's workshops give a sense of what life was like in Turku 2 centuries ago, when the city boasted a flourishing port and served as the national capital.

Turku is the gateway to an archipelago of 20,000 islands linked by the 118-mile Archipelago Trail for cars and bikes. It is also the beginning of the centuries-old King's Road, a 293-mile route that travels east to Vyborg, Russia, and continues on through St. Petersburg to Moscow. The route, which has been around since at least the 13th century, was rarely traveled by kings, although it was built and maintained by the king's royal decree—instead it was used by diplomats, couriers, and everyday travelers. Most of the route winds along idyllic roadways, through pine and birch forests, past old stone churches and sleepy villages, hugging the coast for much of the way. An excellent place to stop is Porvoo, Finland's best-preserved medieval town. The route bypasses Helsinki (see p. 347), though if time allows, the capital is an easy 13-mile detour that should not be missed.

Where: 102 miles/164 km west of Helsinki. **Sibelius Museum:** Tel 358/02-215-4494; www.sibeliusmuseum.abo.fi. **Turku Castle:** Tel 358/02-262-0300. **Luostarinmäki Handicrafts Museum:** Tel 358/02-262-0350; www.museumcentreturku.fi. **Where to stay:** The Art Nouveau Park Hotel is close to everything. Tel 358/2273-2555; www.parkhotelturku.fi. *Cost:* from $195. **Best times:** Jun–Aug for nicest weather; late Jun–early Jul for Medieval Market Festival; early Jul for Ruisrock, Finland's oldest and biggest rock festival; Aug for Handicraft Days in Luostarinmäki; late Nov–Dec for Turku's Christmas Fair.

Waterfalls, Lava Fields, and Canyons

LAKE MÝVATN AND ICELAND'S GRAND CANYON

Iceland

Iceland's northeast is the gateway to grand adventure and breathtaking scenery. Its centerpiece is the photogenic Mývatn, a shallow lake that's ringed by extensive lava fields, sulfur springs, craters, and otherworldly rock formations and is home to prolific birdlife. Indeed, in May and September and October, the lake harbors one of the greatest varieties of ducks, geese, swans, and waders found at a single location anywhere on the planet.

A road loops around the 14-square-mile lake, with several villages that offer pleasant but modest accommodations scattered along the shore. A popular base for exploring the region is tiny Reynihlíd. Not-to-be-missed sights include the wild "black castles" of Dimmuborgir—lava-formed caves, pillars, and arches that resemble the ruins of an ancient citadel. A hike up Hverfjall, a volcano with a massive crater that lies at an elevation of nearly 1,400 feet, provides a fine vantage point. Nearby are several giant fissures in the volcanic rock, including Grjótagjá, a clear, steaming pool with temperatures around 120°F—too hot for soaking, but the scenic Mývatn Nature Baths, outlets of geothermal waters, are much more tolerable at 100°F.

A short drive northeast of the lake brings you to Jökulsárgljúfur (glacial river canyon) in the northern section of the vast Vatnajökull National Park. At over 4,600 square miles, it is Europe's largest. Jökulsárgljúfur is often described as Iceland's Grand Canyon, and it offers superb vistas of the winding river Jökulsá á Fjöllum and the rugged landscape all around it. At the southern end of the canyon are several spectacular waterfalls, including thundering 144-foot Dettifoss, Europe's most powerful. The horseshoe-shaped Ásbyrgi Gorge is the most stunning area, with cliff walls descending 300 feet to birch-filled woodlands. The hiking here is excellent, encouraging one to contemplate the region's mythical origins: Early Norse settlers attributed this unusual formation to the god Odinn's eight-legged airborne horse, Sleipnir, who allegedly alighted here one night and left behind his hoofprint.

The force of Dettifoss is so great that the bedrock beneath it trembles as the water hits the ground below.

WHERE: Mývatn is 292 miles/470 km northeast of Reykjavik. **VATNAJÖKULL NATIONAL PARK:** www.vatnajokulsthjodgardur.is. **WHERE TO STAY:** The simple Hótel Reynihlíd is a solid choice. Tel 354/4-64-4170; www.reynihlid.is. *Cost:* from $200 (off-peak), from $275 (peak). *When:* closed Nov–Jan. **BEST TIMES:** Jun–Aug for warmest weather and maximum sunlight; May and Sep–Oct for best bird-watching.

Fabled Island of Fire and Ice

The Ring Road

Iceland

Just below the Arctic Circle lies a volcanic and otherworldly nation that is sadly misnamed. Iceland is in fact about 90 percent ice-free, and it boasts one of the planet's most varied and incredible landscapes, with a mix of lunarlike deserts, windswept tundra, extraordinarily green grassland, and glacier-carved valleys and canyons. Medieval Europeans believed it to be the threshold of the underworld, and Jules Verne chose an Icelandic volcano as the entranceway for his *Journey to the Center of the Earth.* The word "geyser" was coined here, named after Geysir, the largest of the island's many spouting hot springs. There are also lava fields, bubbling mud pools, and steam vents here. And, yes, ice. The dramatic glacial lagoon at Jökulsárlón, in the southeast, is famous for icebergs that break off from the glacier face and form an ever-changing maze that challenges chugging tour boats.

The coastal township of Vik is situated on the Ring Road.

The two-lane Ring Road (or Route 1—the only motorway circling the island) runs a roughly 830-mile loop. Along the way, you can stop and explore dramatic canyons, thundering waterfalls, and lava formations like those near Mývatn, a detour in the northeast corner (see p. 353); plan to spend about 8 days to complete the circuit around the island.

Reykjavik is your likely arrival point in Iceland. The world's northernmost capital is perched on a scenic peninsula and boasts a vibrant music scene, cutting-edge galleries, a sprawling market, and first-rate dining. Weekend nights can be rowdy here (particularly during the summer), when locals and visitors alike take part in the late-night *runtur* (pub crawl), which tends to get more animated as the evening progresses. Reykjavik has a handful of excellent hotels, including the Hótel Holt, with its praised Gallery Restaurant serving Icelandic-French fusion, a cozy bar with fireplace, and 41 classically decorated guest rooms filled with Icelandic artwork: It houses the largest private art collection in the country.

The island's fabled Blue Lagoon, just 35 minutes outside town, is one of a dozen public thermal pools that are said to be Iceland's health and beauty secret. The swimming area is filled with silica-rich water whose milky turquoise color comes from blue-green algae. With temperatures near 102°F sending up billowing white steam, and a geothermal power plant just next door, the scene seems almost surreal—much like the entire island.

Visitor info: www.icelandtouristboard.com. **Hótel Holt:** Tel 354/5-52-5700; www.holt.is. *Cost:* from $160 (off-peak), from $335 (peak); dinner $55. **Best time:** Jun–Aug when average temperature in Reykjavik is 50°F. Jul sunset is about 1 A.M., and the sky never completely darkens.

Historic "Wooden City" in a Spectacular Setting

BERGEN

Norway

Founded in 1070, Bergen was the capital of the Kingdom of Norway during the Middle Ages and an outpost of the powerful Hanseatic League of Baltic merchant communities organized in the 12th century. At that time the wharfside district of Bryggen (the Quay) was a bustling trading center. Today it is the only neighborhood where you'll find the city's much-photographed gabled wooden buildings with their distinctive rust red and ocher façades. The remarkable collection of timbered warehouses and hostelries—responsible for the town's nickname, the Wooden City—now house artisan workshops, cafés, and the Hanseatic Museum, in one of the city's best-preserved buildings.

Enjoy spectacular views of the sunlit harbor, fish market, and mountains from the sleek, colorful rooms of the elegant Clarion Collection Hotel Havnekontoret. The Augustin Hotel is Bergen's oldest family-run hotel. Perched on the harbor and housed in a 1909 building, it is thoroughly contemporary on the inside. More historic digs can be found at the cozy Steens Hotel, with just 18 rooms set in a beautifully maintained 1890 house.

Finnegaardsstuene, one of the finest restaurants in western Norway, is housed in a former Hanseatic League warehouse (parts of which date to the 17th century) and serves seasonal cuisine from roast pigeon to grilled monkfish. During the summer months, pack a picnic and head just south of town to Troldhaugen (Troll's Hill), the 19th-century summer villa of Norway's greatest composer, Edvard Grieg, where summertime concerts are held.

The funicular to Fløyen climbs 1,000 feet to the steepest of Bergen's seven surrounding mountains for breathtaking views of the fjords. Bergen is the ideal jumping-off point for the unique Norway in a Nutshell tour, a 12-hour day trip that features the best of this stunningly beautiful corner of the country. Start with a bus trip through steep switchback roads to Gudvangen, where you can board a boat to sail through the Nærøyfjord (the narrowest in Norway) and the Aurlandsfjord, both branches of the highly dramatic Sognefjord (see p. 362). After that, board the train from the town of Flåm traveling up and over the side of a gorge to Myrrdal where, for 12 white-knuckle miles, you'll pass in and out of more than 20 tunnels maneuvering 21 hairpin turns past waterfalls and steep overhangs, with occasional glimpses of the resplendent fjords far beyond.

WHERE: 347 miles/558 km west of Oslo (one of the country's most scenic drives). **VISITOR INFO:** www.visitbergen.com. **HANSEATIC MUSEUM:** Tel 47/55-54-4690. **HOTEL HAVNEKONTORET:** Tel 47/55-60-1100; www.choicehotels.no. *Cost:* $250 (off-peak), $385 (peak). **AUGUSTIN HOTEL:** Tel 47/55-30-4000; www.augustin.no. *Cost:* $200 (off-peak), $280 (peak). **STEENS HOTEL:** Tel 47/55-30-8888; www.steenshotel.no. *Cost:* $190 (off-peak), $240 (peak). **FINNEGAARDSSTUENE:** Tel 47/55-55-0300. *Cost:* prix-fixe dinner $100. **TROLDHAUGEN:** Tel 47/55-92-2992; www.troldhaugen.com. **NORWAY IN A NUTSHELL:** Tel 47/81-56-8222; www.norwaynutshell.com. *Cost:* $180. **BEST TIMES:** Jun–Aug for the most pleasant weather; late May for NattJazz Festival; Jun 15 for Grieg's birthday; mid-Jun–end Sep for concerts at Troldhaugen.

Norway at Its Most Majestic

GEIRANGERFJORD

Norway

The vertical cliff–walled, 10-mile-long Geirangerfjord was—and still is—the ne plus ultra of the country's fjords. View it from the remarkable Ørnevegen (Eagles' Road)—with its 11 hairpin, hair-raising turns—that snakes from Åndalsnes to Geiranger. Completed in 1952, it remains an astounding feat of engineering. Stop at the last bend, known as Eagle's Turn, to take in the unforgettable view of the fjord winding through the verdant valley. From Åndalsnes to Valldal is another of Norway's audacious serpentine roadways, the Trollstigen (Trolls' Path), which follows the fjord and crosses one of Norway's most desolate regions.

Visitors to the fjord can choose from numerous attractions—half-day cruises, salmon fishing, hiking, bicycling, visits to deserted hilltop farming hamlets, and excursions to Jostedalsbreen, Europe's largest glacier, as well as to spectacular waterfalls with names like Seven Sisters and Bridal Veil. Naerøyfjord, said to be Norway's narrowest (at one point it is less than 820 feet wide), lies just 75 miles south of Geirangerfjord and shares the same stunning landscape of sheer cliffs beyond its crystalline waters.

One of the world's deepest fjords, Geirangerfjord formed during the Ice Age.

The lovely, waterfront town of Øye is a great base for enjoying the Geirangerfjord area and neighboring Norangsfjord. Check in at the Union Hotel, one of the traditional "fjord castles" so popular at the end of the 19th century and now thoroughly modernized. Norway's King Harald and Queen Sonja chose to celebrate their silver wedding anniversary here in 1993, and visitors continue to delight in its historical ambience.

The gorgeous coastal fishing town of Ålesund lies west of Åndalsnes and is spread out over three islands. When two-thirds of the town's wooden houses were destroyed in a fire in 1904, Germany's Kaiser Wilhelm II, who favored Ålesund as a vacation spot, led the swift rebuilding efforts. The town was reconstructed in a German Art Nouveau style with Nordic touches, evident in the flourishes on everything from turrets and towers to spires and gables. Pay a visit to the well-curated Ålesunds Museum for an in-depth look at the town's unique history and architecture. The superb Radisson SAS, a modern hotel built in the Art Nouveau style, offers panoramic views. From your window you can see the Hurtigruten cruise ships (see p. 359) come and go.

WHERE: Ålesund is 147 miles/236 km northeast of Bergen. **HOTEL UNION ØYE:** Tel 47/70-06-2100; www.unionoye.no. *Cost:* from $345. *When:* late Apr–mid-Oct. **ÅLESUNDS MUSEUM:** Tel 47/70-12-3170; www.aalesunds.museum.no. **RADISSON SAS:** Tel 47/70-16-0000; www.alesund.radissonsas.com. *Cost:* $215 (off-peak), $300 (peak). **BEST TIMES:** May–Sep for nice weather; Jul for Molde Jazz Festival; Jul or Aug for Norwegian Food Festival in Ålesund.

The Soul of Northern Norway

LOFOTEN ISLANDS

Norway

Norway's natural landscape is astonishingly beautiful, so it says a lot when the Lofoten Islands are regularly cited as one of the country's standout attractions. Explore the Lofotens and you're reminded of nature's power and splendor at every turn: jagged, snow-capped peaks and a sea that may be the stormiest in Europe during the winter but in summer months is bathed in a mystical Arctic light.

Rorbus, *the traditional wooden fishermen's huts that frequently are rented for vacation use today, are built on stilts above the Norwegian Sea.*

Although the 118-mile-long archipelago with six principal islands lies 122 miles north of the Arctic Circle, the climate is surprisingly mild. The islands are dotted by small fishing communities and ringed by towering peaks that date back several billion years. The traditional *rorbus* (fishing cottages) were built on docks extending over the water; today they are popular as rentals and inns for their cozy, traditional simplicity.

Ferries arrive here from mainland Bodø, where Edgar Allan Poe spent a number of years writing "A Descent into the Maelstrom." (The word *maelstrom* is derived from the Dutch, meaning "grinding stream.") His inspiration was the 2-mile-long Saltstraumen Eddy, a furious, natural whirlpool that creates a goose bump–inducing howl and is worth a visit before embarking on the boat to the Islands.

Svolvær (population 4,000) is the islands' capital and has a thriving summer art colony. The inviting Anker Brygge inn is on a tiny island in the small harbor, overlooking red-painted cottages and the craggy Lofoten Mountains. Svinøya, just across the bridge, was Svolvær's first settlement. There you will find accommodation at Svinøya Rorbuer, a collection of comfortable, 19th-century fishermen's cabins, as well as one of the area's most distinctive restaurants: the Børson Spiseri, housed in an atmospheric warehouse dating back to 1828. Diners can enjoy the simple but superb Arctic cod (cod tongues are a specialty) and other fresh seafood that is always on the menu.

WHERE: Bodø is 466 miles/750 km north of Trondheim. Ferries from Bodø to the

Lofoten take 4–6 hours; 30–45 min flights. **Anker Brygge:** Tel 47/76-06-6480; www.anker-brygge.no. *Cost:* from $275. **Svinøya Rorbuer:** Tel 47/76-06-9930; www.svinoya.no. *Cost:* from $190; dinner $50. **Best times:** Midnight sun shines Jun–Jul; Feb and Jul for the Lofoten International Chamber Music Festival.

Polar Bears and Ice at the Top of the World

The North Pole and Svalbard

Norway

Few places in the world conjure up the mystical isolation of the North Pole, where the summer sees no darkness, and the winter no light. Just a century ago, no person had ever stood at latitude 90 degrees north. Today the North Pole, a remote spot that fascinated generations of explorers, has become a tourist destination, albeit a rarefied one. Unlike the South Pole, a continent surrounded by oceans, the North Pole is pack ice surrounded by continents. And that pack ice may be melting—so come and see it now.

Sailing from Spitsbergen, the main island of the Norwegian archipelago of Svalbard, and Murmansk, Russia's northernmost port, special nuclear-powered icebreaker ships navigate the Arctic Basin at speeds of up to 20 knots. Passengers enjoy lectures and presentations by on-board specialists, from naturalists to undersea experts, and stay on the lookout for sightings of polar bears, walruses, and Arctic birds. Inflatable expedition boats and helicopters provide the chance to experience the area up close.

When the ship reaches 90 degrees north it finds a suitable parking space, lowers the gangway (ice conditions permitting), and allows passengers to descend for a walkabout, and, for the truly hardy, a plunge into the Arctic Sea. Champagne flows and celebrating begins, as everyone pays homage to the great names who first reached this fabled place after so much adversity.

The gateway to Arctic adventure lies some 600 miles south of the North Pole and 350 miles north of Norway's mainland: the Arctic archipelago of Svalbard ("Cold Coast" in Norwegian), Europe's most northerly landmass. This wilderness is filled with vast, creaking icebergs, snow-topped mountains, and deep fjords, and is considered the wildlife capital of the Arctic. Cruise expeditions allow you to kayak past icebergs and massive walruses, bearded seals, arctic foxes, and reindeer, as well as polar bears. Svalbard is considered the best place in the Arctic—if not on the earth—to observe them in their natural habitat.

The comfortable, 16-room Basecamp Trapper's Hotel, constructed of driftwood, slate stone, and furs, is located in Longyearbyen, the capital of the region and the only town on the island of Spitsbergen.

Where: Departures to the North Pole are from Murmansk, Russia, or Spitsbergen, 1,250 miles/2,012 km north of Oslo and 600 miles/966 km south of the North Pole. **How:** U.S.-based Quark Expeditions offers 14-night expeditions to the North Pole. Tel 888-892-0334 or 802-735-1536; www.quarkexpeditions.com. *Cost:* $22,760, all-inclusive, with all flights in Scandinavia and the Arctic. Originate in Helsinki. *When:* Jun. National Geographic/Lindblad Expeditions organizes 11-night expeditions to Svalbard only. Tel 800-397-3348 or 212-765-7740; www.expeditions.com. *Cost:* $8,240, all-inclusive. Originates in Belgium. *When:* Jun–Jul.

Basecamp Trapper's Hotel: Tel 47/79-02-4600; www.basecampexplorer.com. *Cost:* from $250 (off-peak), $400 (peak). **Best times:** Jun–Aug for 24-hr daylight; Jan for Polar Jazz on Spitsbergen, the world's northernmost jazz festival.

Cruising to—and Beyond—the Arctic Circle

Norway's Coast and the North Cape

Norway

One of the most alluring ways to penetrate the northern reaches of the globe is aboard Norway's legendary Hurtigruten cruise steamers, which have been making the grand coastal journey from Bergen (see p. 355) to deep within the Arctic Circle for over a century. Hurtigruten (which means "fast route") hugs the filigreed coastline, a region of shimmering fjords, creaking glaciers, and sky-piercing mountains. The lifeline for the remote towns of northern Norway—some still accessible only by sea—this fleet of coastal steamers carries passengers, mail, and cargo to some 35 ports over the 3,200-mile, 12-day round trip (one-ways are possible too).

Shore excursions are many and include a day in historic Trondheim, Norway's third largest city and its capital until the early 1200s, or a stop in Bodø, gateway to the Lofoten Islands (see p. 357). Tromsø, the largest city inside the Arctic Circle in the Nordic countries, is home to the world's northernmost university, brewery, and cathedral, earning it the title of "Paris of the North." It is also among the finest spots to view the famous aurora borealis ("dawning of the north"), or northern lights. Tromsø's Northern Lights Planetarium is the perfect place to learn the science behind the famous swirling light show. For a lesson in the wonders of Nordic cuisine, book ahead at the restaurant Emma's Drømmekjøkken (Emma's Dream Kitchen). You'll experience the magic produced by Anne Brit, a culinary personality in Norway's north: Her grilled Arctic char with chanterelles is a revelation.

The boat journey continues to Hammerfest, one of the world's northernmost towns, and the ethereal Nordkapp (North Cape), a sheer, granite cliff rising 1,000 feet out of the frigid Norwegian Sea. The cape's plateau is a largely uninhabited place of wild and romantic moonscape—nothing grows on this tundra. Visitors either love it or not, but most adventurers join the celebration in the clifftop observatory's Champagne bar, where you feel as if you're about to fall off "the World's very end," as one Italian pilgrim wrote in 1664. The final port of call is Kirkenes, 240 miles above the Arctic Circle, at the border with Russia, where the boat turns around and heads back home.

Unapologetically lacking a casino or spa, a no-fuss Hurtigruten ship is not a luxury cruiser—and that is precisely its charm. The cabins are more modest than luxe, but once the voyage begins, everything is eclipsed by Mother Nature—deep-blue fjords, pounding ocean, eye-smarting skies—and, above all, the palpable sense of wind-in-your-hair adventure in the northernmost part of the globe.

Where: Tromsø is 758 miles/1,220 km north of Bergen. **Northern Lights Planetarium:** Tel 47/77-62-0945; nordnorsk .vitensenter.no. **Emma's Drømmekjøkken:** Tel 47/77-63-7730; www.emmasdrommekjokken.no. *Cost:* $100. **Hurtigruten:** Tel 47/81-00-3030; in the U.S., tel 866-522-0371; www.hurtigruten.us. 4- to 12-day cruises offered. *Cost:* 7-day cruise from $1,185. Originates in Bergen. **Best times:** Jun–Aug for midnight sun; Nov–early Apr for northern lights; late Jan for Tromsø's Northern Lights Festival of classical and contemporary music.

Remarkable Nordic Art and Architecture

Munch Museum and National Gallery

Oslo, Norway

Oslo has emerged as one of Scandinavia's most artistically diverse cities, with an enticing blend of old and new, from the famous Munch Museum and National Gallery, which together feature Norway's greatest collection of art, to the soaring architecture of the recently opened waterfront Opera House.

No one is as synonymous with Nordic art as Edvard Munch (1863–1944), one of Scandinavia's most famous artists. Hailed as the father of Expressionism, Munch bequeathed to Oslo 22,000 pieces of his work, which became the foundation of the collection at the Munch-museet (Munch Museum). The museum, which opened in 1963, now houses paintings (including his most recognizable works, *The Scream* and *Night*), drawings, prints, sculptures, and personal possessions such as books and letters—all of which will move to a new location on the Oslo waterfront in 2014 as part of a large-scale art center near the celebrated Opera House. Designed by the Norwegian architectural firm Snøhetta and unveiled in 2007, the futuristic Opera House—white marble with a delicate glass façade—holds the distinction of being the largest cultural building constructed in Norway since 1300.

An 1893 version of *The Scream* (of which Munch painted four) and some 50 other notable pieces by the painter, such as *The Dance of Life*, are on view at the Nasjonalgalleriet (National Gallery) and are part of Norway's most extensive collection of art. Work by Nordic landscape painter Johan Christian Dahl (1788–1857) is also featured here along with a broad overview of European art from Picasso to Van Gogh.

A fine collection of Munch lithographs accents some of the common areas of the Hotel Continental, one of the capital's finest accommodations and still run by the Brochmann family since its opening in 1900. Right across the street from the National Theater (and in the privileged shadow of the Royal Palace), the hotel has hosted performers and playgoers for over a century, and its Viennese-style Theatercaféen is legendary. Lively and always full, it is eclipsed only by its more formal younger sister establishment, the stylish Eik Annen Etage, which serves French-influenced seasonal cuisine, from fresh Arctic seafood to grilled lamb.

Munch Museum: Tel 47/23-49-3500; www.munch.museum.no. **Opera House:** 47/21-42-2121; www.operaen.no. **National Gallery:** Tel 47/21-98-2000; www.nasjonalmuseet.no. **Hotel Continental:** Tel 47/22-82-4000; www.hotelcontinental.no. *Cost:* from $275; dinner at Theatercaféen $65, at Eik Annen Etage $90. **Best times:** Jul–Aug for warmest weather; Jul or Aug for Mela World Music Festival; Oslo Jazz Festival in Aug.

Maritime Masterpieces

Viking Ship Museum

Oslo, Norway

The Age of the Vikings, when Norsemen terrorized the coasts of Europe, lasted approximately from 800 to 1050. (Perhaps the most famous among them was Leif Ericsson, the bold explorer and son of Erik the Red from western Norway; he is said to have "discovered" America in 1001.)

Few of their vivid sagas and legends were written down, but plenty of heritage is nevertheless preserved at the cathedral-like Vikingskiphuset, the Viking Ship Museum. Built in 1936, it houses three remarkably intact 9th-century Viking burial ships discovered at the turn of the last century in the nearby Oslo Fjord. Considered the country's most important archaeological cache, the three long, low-slung wooden vessels contained the bodies of Viking chieftains and one queen (believed to be the grandmother of Harald Hårfagre, the first king of Norway), all entombed with weapons, horses, jewelry, tools, and artifacts meant to serve them in the afterlife. Although partially plundered by grave robbers, they nevertheless represent the largest Viking find ever recorded and have shaped the understanding of Norway's distant maritime past.

The Oseberg, *one of the museum's three showpieces, was built around 820* A.D.

For a more recent example of the Nordic fascination with the sea, fast-forward to the late 1940s, when a young, adventurous Norwegian scientist, Thor Heyerdahl, and his five-man crew sailed a fragile balsa-log raft from Peru to Polynesia, to prove Heyerdahl's belief that people from South America could have settled the South Sea islands in pre-Columbian times. The *Kon-Tiki,* as the raft was christened, sailed for 101 days over 4,300 miles across the Pacific Ocean before smashing into a reef in the Tuamotu Islands of Polynesia (see p. 691). The crew was rescued, and today the vessel is proudly displayed in the Kon-Tiki Museum, where you'll also find striking exhibits of Heyerdahl's explorations of Easter Island (see p. 1021).

Viking Ship Museum: Tel 47/22-13-5283; www.khm.uio.no. **Kon-Tiki Museum:** Tel 47/23-08-6767; www.kon-tiki.no.

Exploring the Deepest Fjord in the World

SOGNEFJORD

Norway

Norway's wild, breathtaking beauty is rooted in its fjords, and the Sognefjord is not only the longest and deepest but also one of the most dramatic. It is wonderfully diverse, awash in fertile parkland, glassy lakes, thundering waterfalls, and blindingly white glaciers—all of it bathed in the clear northern light. It's also one of the most popular fjords, particularly among time-strapped visitors, owing to its accessibility from Bergen (see p. 355).

The Flåm Railway passes by narrow, scenic fjords.

The petite harbor town of Balestrand, which lies about a four-hour sail northwest of Bergen along a spectacular coastal landscape, is the best base for exploring Sognefjord. A walk through town takes you past romantic 18th-century villas as well as the wooden St. Olaf's church, built in 1897. The finest place to stay is the rambling Kviknes Hotel, which stands on a small peninsula jutting into the 127-mile-long fjord. Dating back to 1752, the hotel has been a favorite destination of everyone from poets to monarchs. Today, the fourth-generation owners maintain a casual base-camp ambience, encouraging treks and bike rides into the extravagantly beautiful countryside. Ask for a room in the original house, which takes you back in time while promising stunning water and mountain views. The hotel restaurant features a smorgasbord buffet in an elegant, historic dining room.

Well worth a day trip from Balestrand is a breezy sail up the gorgeous little Fjærlandfjord north of Sognefjord, to see the Jostedalsbreen (Jostedal Glacier). The melting ice from this plateau is what gives the local rivers, lakes, and fjords their distinct blue-green cast. The pretty town of Fjærland, lined with rustic clapboard houses and small shops, lies near the southern end of the glacier, and from here you can strike off on organized hikes in the area. Or visit the small scenic town of Flåm, which is perched on Aurlandsfjord, one of the many arms of Sognefjord. You can arrive on a Norway in a Nutshell trip from Bergen as part of an action-packed day that includes a thrilling train ride on the line connecting Myrdal and Flåm. It's considered one of Scandinavia's—if not the world's—most scenic railways.

WHERE: Balestrand is 121 miles/195 km north of Bergen. **KVIKNES HOTEL:** Tel 47/57-69-4200; www.kviknes.no. *Cost:* from $230; dinner $90. *When:* closed Oct–Apr. **BEST TIMES:** Jun–Sep for the warmest weather; 1st week of May for Balejazz festival in Balestrand.

The Garden Fjord Banked by Blossoms and Fruit

HARDANGERFJORD

Utne, Norway

Fjords have become synonymous with Arctic nature and craggy peaks, but Hardangerfjord offers a rural departure, with lush, terraced fruit orchards tumbling down its fertile banks. Hardanger, called the Garden Fjord, is generally considered Norway's most beautiful fjord, particularly in the late spring when the apple and cherry trees are in bloom.

At the foot of the steep banks is the petite town of Utne. One of most charming accommodations in the country and Norway's oldest inn, the small, modernized Utne Hotel has hosted guests from all over the world since 1722. Its 25 rooms feature beautiful historic furnishings and textiles, and you'll find warm hospitality and charm here too, thanks to the amiable innkeepers. The traditional painted-wood Norwegian interior provides a backdrop for antiques, photos, and works left behind by the artists who have favored this spot since the late 1800s. Nearby is the excellent open-air Hardanger Folk Museum, featuring a cluster farm made up of 19th-century buildings.

Just east lies another striking destination: the small resort town of Ulvik, which is ringed by the characteristic looming mountains of the fjords but also acres of fragrant fruit farms. Hiking trails fan out into the surrounding countryside, which is especially beautiful during the spring, when the fruit trees burst into blossom, and summer, when they're laden with juicy pears and plums. Stay at either the light-filled Rica Brakanes Hotel, a large and well-known resort proud of its panoramic views of Hardangerfjord, or the welcoming Ulvik Fjord Pensjonat, managed by a friendly family and featuring rural Norwegian design and heavy wood furnishings. The small hotel's cozy Café Bar is perfect for nursing a beer or mulled wine after a day of hiking.

WHERE: 87 miles/140 km southeast of Bergen. **UTNE HOTEL:** Tel 47/53-66-6400; www.utnehotel.no. *Cost:* $240. *When:* closed Jan–Mar. **FOLK MUSEUM:** Tel 47/53-67-0040; www.hardanger.museum.no. **RICA BRAKANES HOTEL:** Tel 47/56-52-6105; www.brakanes-hotel.no. *Cost:* $310. **ULVIK FJORD PENSJONAT:** Tel 47/56-52-6170; www.ulvikfjordpensjonat.no. *Cost:* $170. *When:* closed Oct–Mar. **BEST TIME:** May–Jun for blooming fruit trees; Jun–Sep for warmest weather.

Sweden's Engineering Masterpiece

GÖTA CANAL

Götaland, Sweden

The Göta Canal, the "Blue Ribbon," is the backbone of an extensive waterway network connecting Sweden's two largest cities, Göteborg in the west and Stockholm in the east. One of the country's engineering masterpieces, the 45-foot-wide canal was hand dug between 1810 and 1832, by close to 60,000 soldiers, who removed more than 200 million cubic feet of earth and rock in order to create 58 locks. The best way to appreciate the 118-mile-long canal is by boat, and a variety of companies offer trips, ranging from 1 to 6 days, or even longer cruises that include the canal as part of their Swedish or Scandinavian itinerary.

Both small, private boats and large, commercial vessels travel the canal.

Among the shorter tours are those aboard century-old ships that brim with character and traverse parts of the 382-mile waterway, including the canal as well as lovely Lake Vänern, Sweden's largest, and even a stretch of inland sea. You'll glide past well-tended farms, castles, monasteries, and medieval churches, along with leafy canal-side towpaths (you can get off and walk or bike along these). Land excursions to a number of small towns alternate on east- and westbound trips, encouraging round-trip journeys. The rambling 18th-century manor house Ronnums Herrgård, near the southern tip of Lake Vänern and 5 miles from the town of Vänersborg, is a prime example of the charmingly rustic accommodations in this region. The beautifully restored hotel is surrounded by rolling hills, and the comfortable restaurant takes its inspiration from the Swedish countryside, featuring robust dishes like venison, lamb, and butter-fried trout.

WHERE: From Stockholm to Göteborg and the reverse; shorter cruises available. **HOW:** Rederi AB Göta Kanal offers 2- to 6-day cruises on historic ships. Tel 46/318-06315; www.stromma.se/en/Gota-Canal. *Cost:* from $965, inclusive. *When:* Apr–Sep. U.S.-based Nordic Saga Tours offers 3- to 8-day escorted and independent cruises. Tel 800-848-6449 or 425-673-4800; www.nordicsaga.com. *Cost:* from $945. *When:* May–Sep. **RONNUMS HERRGÅRD:** Tel 46/521-260-000; www.ronnums.com. *Cost:* from $165; dinner $55. **BEST TIME:** Jun–Aug for nicest weather and long days.

Viking and Medieval History on a Sea-Swept Island

GOTLAND

Sweden

It takes very little time to fall in love with Gotland, a sea-swept island just off the coast of Sweden in the middle of the stony-gray Baltic Sea. When Stockholmers want to escape, they head here. Once a strategic hub of Hanseatic trade and, at 78 miles long, the Baltic's largest island, Gotland—the ancient home of the Goths—still exudes an alluring, medieval atmosphere. Stone walls, country churches, and pristine farmlands date back to the 6th-century Vikings (nowhere else in Sweden have so many Viking and medieval treasures been discovered). Along the island's eastern shore, dramatic limestone pillars called *raukar* have been eroded by the wind and waves. They dot a coastline marked by long, empty beaches, tiny fishing villages, and steep cliffs.

Gotland's highlight is the once-prominent Hanseatic town of Visby, known as the "city of ruins and roses." You'll get a glimpse of the island's 14th-century heyday, when it was a country all its own (it was not incorporated into Sweden until 1679) and Visby boasted 16 churches. The town's defensive walls—more than 2 miles long with 44 lookout towers—are some of the best preserved in Europe, often compared to those in Ávila, Spain (see p. 257) and Carcassonne, France (see p. 120).

Inland you'll find thick forests and meadows that are tapestries of poppies, wildflowers, and 35 species of wild orchids, while Tofta Strand, unfolding on the west coast, is one of the island's most inviting beaches. Rent a bike and head to the northern end for quiet relaxation (the southern strip sees its share of partying and people-watching). Stop along the way at a café to eat saffron pancakes with jam and cream. Gotland also features inviting farmhouse restaurants, like the historic Konstnärsgården, 20 miles southeast of Visby, where you can enjoy fresh salmon and seafood in either the airy dining room, hung with colorful art, or in the small garden.

During the summer, festivals come thick and fast, and Gotland finds itself at the forefront of Sweden's artistic and cultural life (legendary director Ingmar Bergman lived and filmed here, on Gotland's ancillary island of Fårö in the north). Stay at the restored 19th-century Clarion Wisby Hotel, located in the historic center within the walls, in August for annual Medieval Week. You'll see townspeople going about their business in colorful gowns and velvet doublets and minstrels and street performers bringing the city back to when it was as vibrant, rich, and powerful as London or Paris.

Where: 60 miles/97 km off the southeast Swedish mainland. **Konstnärsgården:** Tel 46/498-55063; www.konstnarsgarden.se. *Cost:* lunch $50. **Clarion Wisby Hotel:** Tel 46/498-257-500; www.wisbyhotell.se. *Cost:* from $235. **Best times:** Jun–Aug for warm weather; May and Sep offer sunshine but cooler weather; Jun 23 for Midsummer Eve; early Aug for Medieval Week.

Ephemeral Igloo in the Arctic Circle

The Ice Hotel

Jukkasjärvi, Norrland, Sweden

A towering paean to winter, the Ice Hotel sits 125 miles north of the Arctic Circle. This is the vast reindeer-herding tundra called Lapland, one of the 24 provinces that make up the massive region of Norrland, which spreads across the entire north of Sweden. The hotel is crafted entirely from snow and ice, including guest rooms, galleries, a futuristic-looking reception hall with pure ice chandeliers lit by fiber optics, and a long vodka bar replete with drinking glasses made from ice.

Built every November since 1990 out of more than 4,000 tons of frozen water and densely packed snow, the hotel disappears each spring when it melts into the River Torne on whose banks it is constructed. The surreal ice creation is a marvel in itself, but the interior trappings can be even more amazing: The furniture, art, and sculptures in the public rooms are the work of skilled engineers and well-known ice carvers. Your ice-block bed is lavishly draped with layers of reindeer hide and topped with Arctic-survival sleeping bags. You'll be awoken with hot lingonberry juice in the morning and can revel in the sauna before indulging in a hearty breakfast.

Then it's off for a day full of fun (though not in the sun—remember, this is the Arctic Circle, and it's dark or nearly dark for 6 weeks from December to January). Choose among snowmobile (or reindeer) safaris, dogsledding, ice fishing, cross-country skiing, and experiencing the breathtaking spectacle of the northern lights. The hotel also arranges visits to villages populated by Sami, the once-nomadic reindeer-herding people formerly called Laplanders who have lived here since ancient times. You can join them for lunch prepared over a campfire. For those who have had their share of the deep freeze after just one night at the Ice Hotel (internal temperature hovers around 20–25°F), nearby chalet-style "warm rooms" (featuring creature comforts such as toilets and central heating) offer alternative accommodations, some with skylights through which to watch the northern lights. The restaurant is impressive, taking far northern cuisine very seriously, from hearty dishes like elk stew to fresh-caught Arctic salmon, and homemade cloudberry tarts for dessert.

The small community of Jokkmokk is the cultural heart of the Sami people. Visit in early February, when they hold their Great Winter market, drawing Sami from as far away as Norway and Finland (see p. 349). To warm up, head inside to the Museum Ájtte, which is dedicated to the native people.

WHERE: 770 miles/1,240 km north of Stockholm. **HOW:** U.S.-based Mountain Travel Sobek offers a 10-day reindeer- and dog-sledding trip that includes a stay at the Ice Hotel. Tel 888-831-7526 or 510-594-6000; www.mtsobek.com. *Cost:* $5,795, inclusive. Originates in Stockholm. *When:* Mar. **ICE HOTEL:** Tel 46/980-66800; www.icehotel.com. *Cost:* from $345. *When:* mid-Dec–late Apr. **MUSEUM ÁJTTE:** Tel 46/971-17070; www.ajtte.com. **BEST TIMES:** Oct–Mar for northern lights; early Feb for Sami festival and market in Jokkmokk.

Norrland's latitude makes it a prime place to take in the northern lights during the dark winter months.

A Capital City's Greatest Natural Asset

STOCKHOLM ARCHIPELAGO

Sweden

Sweden's summer is brief but glorious, and the Stockholm Archipelago is one of the best places to celebrate it—by kayaking, biking, or simply walking the unpaved island roads and taking in the magnificent scenery.

The archipelago is a latticework of some 24,000 islands and smooth, glacier-polished outcroppings that dot a 150-mile stretch off of Sweden's eastern coast. You can explore the area by ferry, vintage steamer, three-mast schooner, sailboat, or yacht. It is one of the country's most important natural attractions as well as its wild frontier: Only about 6,000 people live on 1,000 of the islands; the rest are free of humans save for those who come for a picnic and a swim.

The islands feature a number of restaurants that range from rustic to daring, and it's possible to sail from one delicious meal to the next. Take a 30-minute ferryboat ride from Stockholm to the well-known Fjäderholmarnas Krog in Fjäderholmarna (the four Feather Islands), accessible only by boat, for a leisurely lunch of scallops and mussels, grilled char, or roasted salmon. Or board a steamer for a tour of the scenery: flower-bedecked fishing cottages, meadows, farms, beaches, and, depending on when you set sail, a late-evening sky of changing pastels.

Artists and writers have always been drawn to the small seaside town of Vaxholm, gateway to the islands, while the boating crowd firmly favors Sandhamn, site of the prestigious annual Royal Regatta as well as plenty of shops and restaurants. This area also features some lovely country hotels, such as Häringe Slott (Häringe Castle), which is set on a peninsula close by the archipelago 21 miles south of Stockholm. The castle-turned-hotel dates back to 1657, and everyone from Greta Garbo to Elizabeth Taylor has slept in its sumptuous beds. Enjoy views of the bay and the ferries from Waxholms Hotell, which was built in 1902 and is painted a can't-miss sunflower yellow. Its second-floor restaurant is the reason to come, with outstanding seafood culled from the region, including Norwegian lobster and the perennial favorite of fried Baltic herring and mashed potatoes. Carnivores can tuck into a juicy burger topped with locally picked lingonberries.

Where:. Vaxholm is 10 miles/16 km northwest of Stockholm. **How:** Strömma Kanalbolaget offers 8-hour cruises. Tel 46/8-5871-4000; www.stromma.se. *Cost:* from $200, includes lunch and dinner. *When:* Jul–Aug. **Fjäderholmarnas Krog:** Tel 46/8-718-3355; www.fjaderholmarnaskrog.se. *Cost:* lunch $40. *When:* May–Aug. **Häringe Castle:** Tel 46/8-504-2040; www.haringeslott.se. *Cost:* from $275 (off-peak), $425 (peak). **Waxholms Hotell:** Tel 46/8-541-30150; www.waxholmshotell.se. *Cost:* from $175; dinner $50. **Best times:** Jun–Aug for the warmest weather; Jul for the Around Gotland regatta, which begins and ends in Sandhamn; Aug for crayfish season.

The Historic Heart of Stockholm

Gamla Stan

Stockholm, Sweden

Filled with ancient squares, medieval buildings, and cobblestone lanes, Gamla Stan (Old Town) is one of the 14 islands that make up Stockholm and is the site of the original city. Its heart is the main square of Stortorget, and surrounding it, on the narrow streets of Västerånggatan and Österlånggatan, you'll find dozens of popular restaurants, galleries, and boutiques. Stockholm's history is revealed through Gamla Stan's impressive variety of architecture, culminating with the Kungliga

Slottet, or Royal Palace, one of the largest in Europe. Built in the 16th century atop the ruins of a 13th-century fortress, the 608-room structure features a lavish interior, from state apartments dripping in 18th- and 19th-century décor and paintings to a royal chapel and a museum exhibiting the castle's original defense walls. It is used today mainly for ceremonial occasions, as the royal family now lives in Drottningholm, just outside the city (see p. 370).

The cast-iron steeple of Riddarholm Church is one of Stockholm's most distinctive landmarks.

For an interesting overview of the history of the Nobel Prize, which is presented each year in Stockholm (with the exception of the Peace Prize, which is awarded in Oslo), and its inspiring array of recipients, from Gabriel García Márquez to Martin Luther King, visit the well-curated Nobel Museum in the old Börsen (Stock Exchange) building.

Gamla Stan's hotel choices may be limited, but a handful that marry the historic with the new are the most inviting. The refurbished waterfront First Hotel Reisen features 144 contemporary rooms, a sleek bar, and a basement pool crowned by a 16th-century arched ceiling. The past and present also commingle at the handsome, nautical-themed Victory Hotel, originally built in 1642 on 14th-century foundations and named after Lord Nelson's ship (it is also the flagship of a mini-chain of privately owned hotels in the Old Town that includes the nearby Lady Hamilton and the Lord Nelson).

Round out your Gamla Stan night with a meal at the unabashedly luxurious restaurant Operakällaren, which is housed within the Royal Opera House and faces the royal palace. Dress up and expect to pay for a night out at one of Scandinavia's most famous eateries, an instant landmark since it opened in 1787 by decree of King Gustav III. It has since evolved into a complex of many dining rooms that vary in formality and price, but the main one, Belle Époque, is the draw, a handsome space with carved oak walls and ceiling panels, murals once considered risqué, extravagant crystal chandeliers, and service as impeccably polished as the silverware. A tender fillet of reindeer and other seasonal dishes are highlights. So is Stenborgare, the restaurant's own schnapps.

If you can splurge on only one dinner, consider Mathias Dahlgren, the namesake of one of the country's most forward-thinking chefs. It is housed in the Grand Hôtel, a bastion of Scandinavian refinement (see next page) just beyond the Old Town, in the Norrmalm neighborhood. In both the dining room (Matsalen) and food bar (Matbaren), the chef puts forth a "natural cuisine" that wows diners with such pairings as scallops with cucumber foam and foie gras with licorice.

Royal Palace: Tel 46/8-402-6123; www.kungahuset.se. **Nobel Museum:** Tel 46/8-5348-1800; www.nobelmuseum.se. **First Hotel Reisen:** Tel 46/8-223-260; www.firsthotels.com/reisen. *Cost:* from $250. **Victory Hotel:** Tel 46/8-5064-0000; www.victoryhotel.se. *Cost:* from $250. **Operakällaren:** Tel 46/8-676-5801; www.operakallaren.se. *Cost:* dinner $90. **Mathias Dahlgren:** Tel 46/8-679-3584; www.mathiasdahlgren.com. *Cost:* dinner $120. **Best time:** May–Sep for nicest weather.

A Meal Fit for a King

SMÖRGÅSBORD

Solna and Stockholm, Sweden

Sweden is famous throughout the world for its superb buffet-style smörgåsbord, the nation's great culinary art form. And while some of it may not be for everyone (the preponderace of herring may raise eyebrows), much will delight even the unadventurous palate.

According to unofficial smörgåsbord etiquette, one never mixes hot with cold nor sweet with sour, and multiple visits to the food-laden table are expected, the first for herring (there are often over a dozen varieties) and the last for desserts. In between are a panoply of Nordic specialties such as smoked eel, gravlax, sweet Baltic shrimp, reindeer, those famous Swedish meatballs or pork chops with lingonberry sauce, and the much-loved national specialty, *Janssons frestelse* (Jannson's Temptation)—a delectable quiche of anchovies, potatoes, onions, and heavy cream. And then there is the cornucopia of sweets, the final undoing for many. The typical beverage to accompany such indulgence is beer or Swedish aquavit with a beer chaser. For a true Swedish experience, time your splurge for Christmas and the traditional *Julbord* (Christmas table), an even more lavish affair.

Families generally reserve smörgåsbords for weddings and special occasions. And because it is expensive and difficult for restaurants to prepare, the smörgåsbord is not as ubiquitous as visitors may think. But there is one place long known for the feast: Ulriksdals Wärdshus, 5 miles from downtown Stockholm. An elegant country inn built in 1868 within its own parkland upon request of the Swedish crown, it serves what is arguably the nation's finest layout. Expect to find tables elaborately laden with more than 75 different offerings that have drawn everyone from royalty (including the present-day king and queen) to local regulars. The inn also has one of the finest wine cellars in the country, and all except the most expensive are available by the glass. If you visit at sunset (which is not until 9 P.M. in July), watch as the country's blue-and-yellow flag is ceremonially lowered out on the lawn and everyone stands to sing the national anthem. It's one of the inn's more delightful traditions.

Enjoy similarly extravagent dining without leaving Stockholm at the Grand Hôtel, an 1874 showcase of old-world charm. Here, the smörgåsbord is proudly rolled out every day at lunchtime and dinner in the glass-walled Grand Veranda, with its magnificent views of the harbor and the royal palace (a simple à la carte menu is also available). The quayside hotel also offers the city's top accommodations. During the second week in December, it hosts Nobel Prize winners and their entourages, but less distinguished guests enjoy the same elite hospitality year-round. Even if you aren't staying overnight, stop for a drink at the classic Cadier Bar or for a memorable meal by celebrity chef Mathias Dahlgren (see previous page) at the stylish restaurant of the same name.

ULRIKSDALS WÄRDSHUS: Tel 46/8-850815; www.ulriksdalswardshus.se. *Cost:* lunch smörgåsbord $40; dinner smörgåsbord $70. **GRAND HÔTEL:** Tel 46/8-6793500; www.grandhotel.se. *Cost:* from $325 (off-peak), from $440 (peak); smörgåsboard at the Grand Veranda $75. **BEST TIME:** mid-Nov–Dec for Christmas smörgåsbord at Ulriksdals Wärdshus.

Sweden's Most Powerful Battleship

Vasa Museum

Stockholm, Sweden

The magnificent royal warship *Vasa*—a 226-foot, 64-cannon man-of-war—was built to be the largest and most powerful battleship ever constructed. It took two years to complete on the site where Stockholm's Grand Hôtel now stands. But on August 10, 1628, the pride of the Swedish war fleet sank before she even left the harbor on her maiden voyage (sudden gusts of wind and not enough ballast are the most popular explanations).

Salvaged 333 years after her demise and since then painstakingly restored, the warship can now be viewed at the Vasa Museum, the only maritime museum of its kind in the world and the most visited museum in Scandinavia. Large enough to nearly fill the wondrous structure specially built around her at enormous cost in 1990, the *Vasa* is the oldest fully preserved warship in the world. Elaborate wooden carvings cover the exterior, and the ship's salvaged cargo includes 4,000 coins, medical equipment, and a backgammon set.

After your visit, stroll through more history at nearby Skansen, an outdoor museum—it's said to be the world's first and is often called "Old Sweden in a Nutshell." More than 150 reconstructed dwellings were brought here from all parts of the country to re-create a 19th-century town on 74 acres of parkland. In the summertime, you can enjoy folk dancing and free concerts, and in December there's a Christmas market, best appreciated with a glass of glögg, the traditional Swedish mulled wine.

Vasa Museum: Tel 46/8-519-54800; www.vasamuseet.se. **Skansen:** Tel 46/8-442-8000; www.skansen.se. **Best times:** in Skansen, the weekend closest to Jun 24 for Midsummer festivities and late Nov–Dec for Christmas market.

The Versailles of the North

Drottningholm Palace and Court Theater

Lake Mälaren, Svealand, Sweden

The official year-round home of Sweden's present-day monarchs, King Carl XVI and Queen Silvia, Drottningholm is widely held to be the finest northern European royal palace and one of the most delightful on the continent. The many-windowed Rococo structure, set in Lake Mälaren, on its own tree-covered island (Drottningholm means "queen's island") is open to the public even when the royal family is in residence. The palace was built in 1622 for Sweden's Queen Eleonora, and the interior still dazzles with its collection of opulent 17th- to 19th-century art and furniture, gilt ceilings, and magnificent chandeliers. Fountains and Baroque gardens further encourage comparisons to Versailles. To enjoy an afternoon on the grounds, bring a picnic meal or stroll the gardens in the direction of the Chinese Pavilion, built in 1753 and now open to the public as a café.

The Drottningholm Court Theater is the palace's highlight, the world's most perfectly preserved 18th-century theater, where performances are still given using original sets and stage machinery. Originally lit by 400 candles, today it is illuminated by as many flickering, flame-shaped electric bulbs. The wooden, chocolate-box structure was built in 1766 by Queen Louisa Ulrika for her son King Gustav III. This was the golden age of the palace, when it was a veritable beehive of activity, and the 18th-century operas and ballets performed today during the summer season by some of Europe's premier talents (accompanied by musicians playing original period instruments) transport audiences back to that golden age.

Where: 7 miles/11 km west of Stockholm. **Court Theater:** Tel 46/40-635-6200; www.dtm.se. **Best time:** late May–Aug, when the theater holds performances during the Drottningholm Festival.

A Royal Castle in a Lakeside Village

Gripsholm Castle

Mariefred, Svealand, Sweden

The endearing lakeside village of Mariefred (Marie's Place), with its impressive redbrick Gripsholm Castle, is the perfect jaunt from Stockholm—arrive on a century-old, coal-fired steamboat, the SS *Mariefred,* then return by vintage narrow-gauge steam train. The castle, a 16th-century, onion-towered structure on Lake Mälaren, was occupied until 1864 and is one of the royal palaces of Sweden. But it's principally known as the national portrait gallery, with a superb collection of paintings and one of Europe's largest collections of displayed portraits. The castle also houses the lovely Gripsholm Theater, which dates to 1781 and the reign of Gustav III, the "actor-king." Although not as spectacular as the Drottningholm Court Theater, built by his mother (see previous page), it is nevertheless beautifully preserved.

Mariefred invites wandering, followed by a few hours spent over a wonderful lunch in the glassed-in veranda of the lakeside Gripsholms Värdshus & Hotel, the oldest inn in Sweden and a ten-minute walk from the castle. It first welcomed guests in 1609, when it was just a hospice built on the site of a monastery that was first occupied in 1493. The restaurant features traditional Swedish cooking, including roast lamb and game when in season, and the romantic guest rooms and lakeview suites are beautifully decorated in a country style. It all makes for a wonderful and easy getaway, and day-trippers often regret not planning an overnight stay: Bring your toothbrush and check in.

Where: 40 miles/64 km southwest of Stockholm. **Gripsholms Värdshus:** Tel 46/159-34750; www.gripsholms-vardshus.se. *Cost:* from $265; dinner $65. **Best time:** Jun–Aug for nicest weather.

Celebration in the Spiritual Home of the Swedes

Midsummer Eve in Dalarna

Tällberg, Svealand, Sweden

All Scandinavia celebrates the Nordic festival of *Midsommar* (Midsummer), but perhaps nowhere is it heralded with as much enthusiasm as in Sweden. This ancient Germanic ritual honoring life itself has pagan roots—originally a fertility rite, it was held at the exact time the sun and earth were considered at the peak of their reproductive powers. These days Swedes take to the countryside, often dressing in colorful local costumes, to engage in singing and maypole dancing, eat favorite foods, and imbibe substantial amounts of aquavit. Young girls believe they will dream of their future husbands if they sleep with a freshly picked bouquet of nine different wildflowers under their pillows.

Maypoles and Swedish flags accompany the start of Dalarna's Midsommar *festivities.*

One of the best places to celebrate Midsommar is in Sweden's central, rural province of Dalarna. With the beautiful Lake Siljan at its center, this hilly area is often referred to as Sweden's "folklore district." Traditions and customs still flourish here, and are on display at the Dalarnas Museum in Falun. Sweden's most famous painter, Carl Larsson, found great inspiration here, and his garden-surrounded lakeside cottage outside of Talun is a popular pilgrimage site. To explore the lake further, head to either Leksand or Tällberg, the charming waterfront towns that are the gateways to Lake Siljan. Tällberg is less built up and more authentic and is home to one of the region's great historic country inns, the family-owned Åkerblads Hotel, a 15th-century, red-framed farmstead that was converted to an inn in 1910 and expanded upon in the century since. The old-fashioned rooms are furnished with canopied beds and grandfather clocks and decorated with paintings and carvings, while the restaurant is known for hearty, home-style cooking and a weekend smörgåsbord.

Where: 155 miles/250 km northwest of Stockholm. **Dalarnas Museum:** 46/23-765-500; www.dalarnasmuseum.se. **Åkerblads Hotel:** Tel 46/247-50800; www.akerblads.se. *Cost:* $175; dinner $30. **Best time:** Midsummer is celebrated on the Fri closest to St. John the Baptist's feast day (Jun 24).

AFRICA

NORTH AFRICA

WEST AFRICA

EAST AFRICA AND SOUTHERN AFRICA

ISLANDS OF THE INDIAN OCEAN

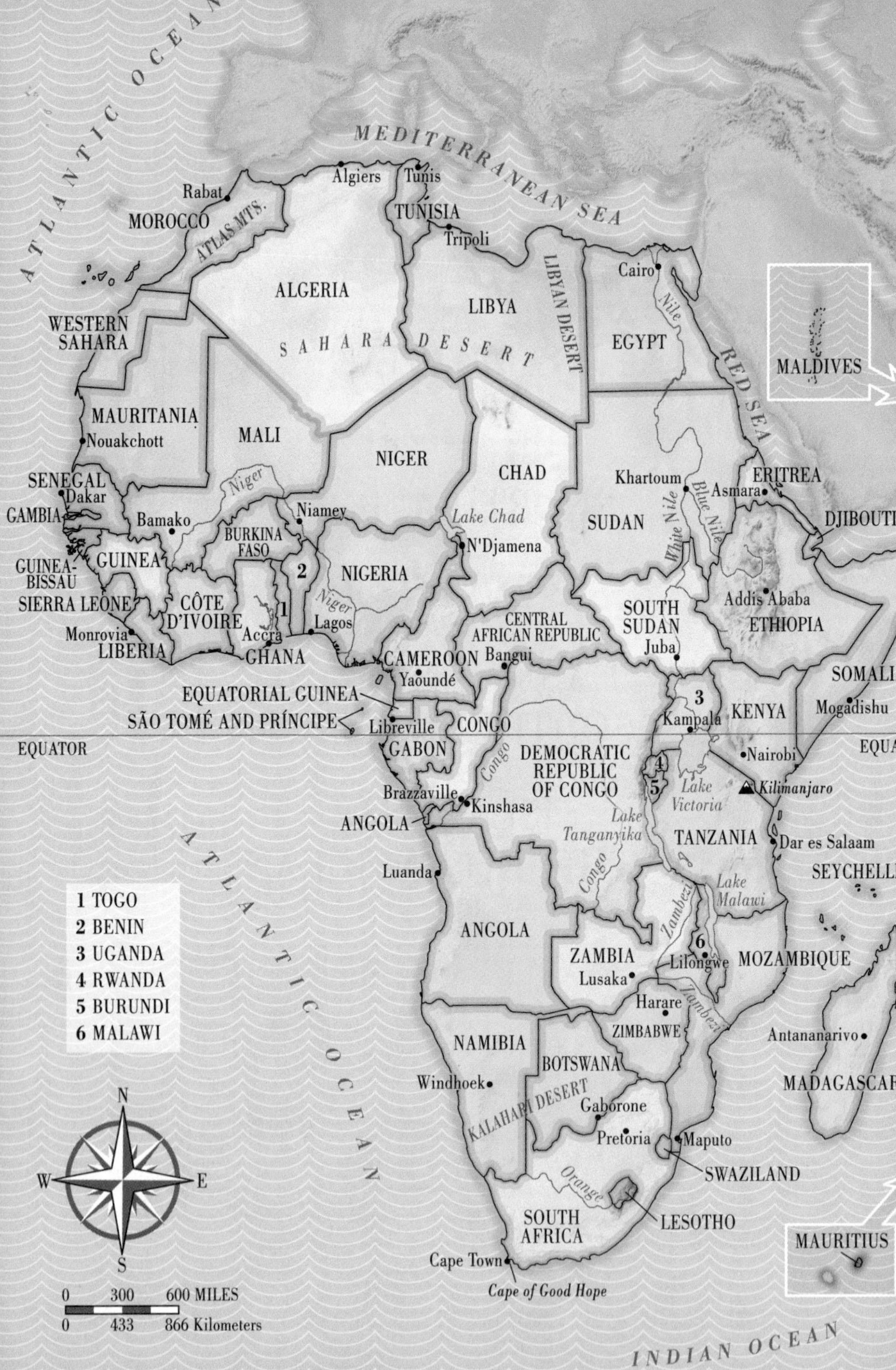
ATLANTIC OCEAN
MEDITERRANEAN SEA
Rabat
MOROCCO
ATLAS MTS.
Algiers
Tunis
TUNISIA
Tripoli
ALGERIA
LIBYA
LIBYAN DESERT
Cairo
EGYPT
Nile
RED SEA
MALDIVES
WESTERN SAHARA
SAHARA DESERT
MAURITANIA
Nouakchott
MALI
NIGER
CHAD
SUDAN
Khartoum
Blue Nile
White Nile
Asmara
ERITREA
DJIBOUTI
SENEGAL
Dakar
GAMBIA
Bamako
Niger
Niamey
BURKINA FASO
Lake Chad
N'Djamena
GUINEA
GUINEA-BISSAU
SIERRA LEONE
NIGERIA
CÔTE D'IVOIRE
Monrovia
LIBERIA
Accra
GHANA
Lagos
CENTRAL AFRICAN REPUBLIC
Bangui
SOUTH SUDAN
Juba
Addis Ababa
ETHIOPIA
CAMEROON
Yaoundé
SOMALI
Mogadishu
EQUATORIAL GUINEA
SÃO TOMÉ AND PRÍNCIPE
Libreville
CONGO
Kampala
KENYA
EQUATOR
EQUA
GABON
Congo
DEMOCRATIC REPUBLIC OF CONGO
Nairobi
Lake Victoria
Kilimanjaro
Brazzaville
Kinshasa
ANGOLA
Lake Tanganyika
TANZANIA
Dar es Salaam
Luanda
SEYCHELLI
Lake Malawi
Zambezi
ANGOLA
ZAMBIA
Lusaka
Lilongwe
MOZAMBIQUE
Harare
ZIMBABWE
Antananarivo
NAMIBIA
BOTSWANA
Windhoek
KALAHARI DESERT
Gaborone
Pretoria
Maputo
MADAGASCAR
SWAZILAND
Orange
LESOTHO
SOUTH AFRICA
Cape Town
Cape of Good Hope
MAURITIUS
INDIAN OCEAN
1 TOGO
2 BENIN
3 UGANDA
4 RWANDA
5 BURUNDI
6 MALAWI
N
S
E
W
0 300 600 MILES
0 433 866 Kilometers

NORTH AFRICA

A City By—and Beneath—the Sea

ALEXANDRIA

Egypt

Founded by Alexander the Great, captured by Julius Caesar, and home to Cleopatra and Antony, Alexandria was a leading city of the ancient world, known for its Pharos lighthouse and its library. The ruins of the lighthouse, lost to earthquakes in the 14th century, were recently discovered underwater. Debate still rages over whether the library was burned during Caesar's invasion or simply deteriorated over time, but the city replaced it in 2002 with the Bibliotheca Alexandrina, which stands on the same site and houses museums, galleries, a planetarium, and a manuscript restoration center. Its main building is a marvel of hypermodern architecture, a giant cylindrical slice of stone, steel, and glass, rising diagonally from the coastline. Inside, 11 sun-drenched levels cascade into a vast reading hall.

Most of the modern-day city is along or near the Corniche, its waterfront boulevard, while most of ancient Alexandria lies beneath the water just offshore. It's here that archaeologist-divers discovered Cleopatra's palace and a treasure trove of thousands of ancient objects, including 26 sphinxes, statues bearing gifts to gods, and Roman and Greek shipwrecks.

While plans are under way to open the world's first underwater museum, there's still lots to see above water. The famed Roman catacombs are not far from the 88-foot-tall Pompey's Pillar, built in A.D. 297; and the hulking Quaitbey Fort, erected in 1480 on the site of the Pharos lighthouse, is also well worth a visit. Long a home to artists, intellectuals, and literary giants (including Lawrence Durrell and E. M. Forster), the city is also renowned for a vibrant café society. The ornate Trianon Café, in Saad Zaghloul Square, is perhaps the most famous place to linger with an aperitif. Dinner at Fish Market involves choosing from the fresh catches bathed in ice near the entrance, then settling in for moonlit views of the harbor and the fort. The pinnacle of contemporary opulence in the city is the Four Seasons Hotel at San Stefano Beach, where most rooms have balconies overlooking the ocean. Back on the Corniche, the venerable Windsor Palace Hotel showcases Edwardian architecture and furnishings in 70 comfortable nostalgia-filled rooms.

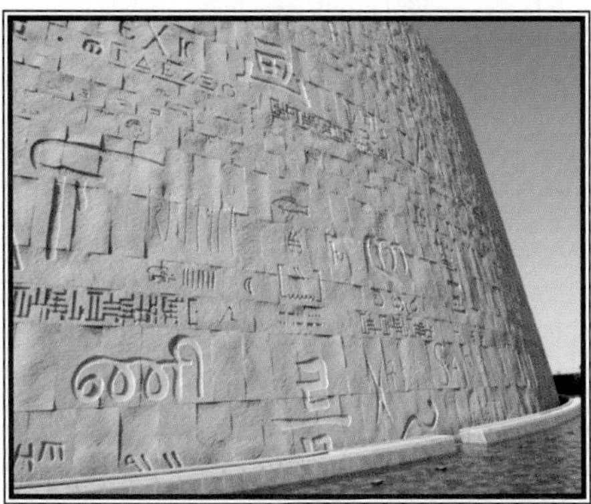

Made of granite, the Bibliotheca Alexandrina's exterior features carvings of characters from more than 100 different languages, both living and dead.

WHERE: 136 miles/200 km northwest of

Cairo. **Bibliotheca Alexandrina:** www.bibalex.org. **Trianon Café:** Tel 20/3-483-5881. **Fish Market:** Tel 20/3-480-5119. *Cost:* dinner $35. **Four Seasons Hotel:** Tel 20/3-581-8000; in the U.S., 800-819-5053; www.fourseasons.com. *Cost:* from $530 (off-peak), from $650 (peak). **Windsor Palace Hotel:** Tel 20/3-480-8700; www.paradiseinnegypt.com. *Cost:* from $100. **Best times:** Oct–Apr for cooler weather; Oct of even years for Alexandria Biennial.

A Maze of Bazaars and Medieval Monuments

Islamic Cairo

Cairo, Egypt

An amble through this ancient quarter of Cairo assails the senses and confounds the mind. Chickens, horses, and sheep walk the narrow, potholed streets, which are further congested by donkey carts, itinerant street vendors, and people going about their daily lives. Dust and rubble often obscure the faded architectural grandeur of what is still the intellectual and cultural center of the Arab world.

There are a daunting number of sites to see here, but start at the spectacular 12th-century Citadel of Saladin, a heavily fortified bastion that was founded by the chivalrous foe of the Crusaders and offers a matchless panorama of Cairo's minaret-punctuated skyline. Amid the sprawl rise the marvelous carved stone dome of the 15th-century Mosque of Qaitbey and the spiral minaret of the 9th-century Mosque of Ibn Tūlūn, one of the grandest and oldest places of worship in Egypt. Adjacent to the mosque are two joined Ottoman-era homes containing the Gayer-Anderson Museum's vast collection of pharaonic artifacts and Islamic art. An even more extensive collection, spanning the 7th to 19th centuries, is found to the north at the Museum of Islamic Art. Still farther north is the richly ornamented Qalawun complex, built by three important Mamluk sultans; it contains a madrassa, a hospital, and elaborate mausoleums.

Cairo's wonderful and chaotic centerpiece is Khan el-Khalili, one of the world's great bazaars, started as a caravansary in 1382. Lose yourself in the bewildering warren of back alleys, awash with the smells of spices, incense, and leather. This is where Cairenes still shop for their dowries, cotton galabiyas, fezzes, and *shishas* (hookahs or water pipes). You can practice your haggling with merchants specializing in everything from carpets, gold, and fabrics to perfume and cosmetics (including pots of kohl with which to line your eyes, Cleopatra-style).

Take a break from it all at El Fishawy, the Khan's most famous coffee- and teahouse (it's been open around the clock since 1772). You can bask in its 19th-century European décor of gilded mirrors, hammered brass, and marble-topped tables, puff on a water pipe, have your fortune told, and order some of the city's best coffee. Later, you'll want to lunch at the Oberoi-managed Naguib Mahfouz Café, named for the Nobel Prize–winning author of *The Cairo Trilogy* and famed for its excellent Middle Eastern dishes. Locals flood the recently opened Taj al Sultan at Al Azhar Square for dinner; the fusion of Egyptian and Indian cuisine is echoed in the dazzling glasswork, antiques, decorated pillars, and woven rugs.

As Africa's largest city, with a metropolitan population nearing 20 million, Cairo faces serious infrastructure issues and intense poverty. Yet the Egyptians' legendary hospitality remains. Living up to its name is Le Riad Hotel de Charme, a short walk from the Khan on the pedestrian-only street of Al Muizz li Din-Allah. It features an inviting collection of 17 suites and a peaceful rooftop garden. Sophisticated solitude also awaits at the Four Seasons at Nile Plaza, where you can gaze at the citadel from your room or board a private *felucca* just steps from the hotel and enjoy a cruise along the river.

Gayer-Anderson Museum: Tel 20/2-364-7822. **Museum of Islamic Art:** Tel 20/2-390-9330. **Naguib Mahfouz Café:** Tel 20/2-590-3788. *Cost:* lunch $15. **Taj al Sultan:** Tel 20/2-2787-7273; www.tajalsultan.com. *Cost:* dinner $40. **Le Riad:** Tel 20/2-2787-6074; www.leriad-hoteldecharme.com. *Cost:* suites from $345. **Four Seasons at Nile Plaza:** Tel 20/2-2791-7000; in the U.S., 800-819-5053; www.fourseasons.com. *Cost:* from $550. **Best times:** Nov–Mar for pleasant weather; Feb or Mar for Al-Nitaq Festival celebrating Cairo's vibrant theater, poetry, and art scene; Nov for Arabic Music Festival.

Storehouse of a Great Civilization

Museum of Egyptian Antiquities

Cairo, Egypt

Exploring Ancient Egypt's empty tombs and monuments will leave just about anyone hungry to gaze upon the relics that were found inside. Which is why a visit to the Museum of Egyptian Antiquities (aka the Egyptian Museum) is a must. Housing an unparalleled collection of treasures that are arranged chronologically from the Old to the Middle to the New Kingdoms (which date from 2700–2200 B.C., 2100–1800 B.C., and 1600–1200 B.C., respectively), it is so vast that if you allowed just one minute to examine each of its 136,000 pharaonic artifacts, it would take 9 months to see it all. Many visitors focus on the breathtaking mummified remains of 27 pharaohs and their queens, along with the 1,700 objects unearthed in 1922 from the small tomb of the relatively insignificant (but now iconic) Pharaoh Tutankhamun (King Tut). An astounding 40,000 other items remain crated in the basement, evidence of the chronic space shortage that has plagued Egypt's greatest museum since its 1858 founding. A visit here is overwhelming, to say the least. Catch your breath with a stroll to nearby Tahrir Square, where thousands of Egyptians gathered peacefully during the 2011 revolution.

The Egyptian Museum houses the coffin of the priest Petosiris.

The Ministry of Culture broke ground in 2002 on the $500 million, 120-acre Grand Egyptian Museum (GEM for short) in Giza, barely a mile from the pyramids (see p. 378). The complex, designed by Heneghan Peng Architects, will include restoration laboratories and a giant, sloping alabaster wall that glimmers in the desert sunlight. The 3,200-year-old, 36-foot-high Statue of Ramses II was moved to the site in 2006. The museum will also be a new home to many of the King Tut objects. Sections of the GEM may open as early as 2013.

Museum of Egyptian Antiquities: Tel 20/2-579-6974; www.egyptianmuseum.gov.eg. **Grand Egyptian Museum:** www.gem.gov.eg.

Eternal Wonders of the Ancient World

The Pyramids of Egypt

Giza, Saqqara, and Dahshur, Egypt

The only wonder of the ancient world to have survived nearly intact, the Pyramids at Giza embody antiquity and mystery—and their logic-defying construction continues to inspire plenty of speculation. The funerary Great Pyramid of Cheops (or Khufu) is the oldest, and it is also the largest in the world, built circa 2500 B.C. with some 2.3 million limestone blocks, weighing an average 2.75 tons each and moved by a force of 20,000 men. Two smaller pyramids nearby belonged to Cheops's son and grandson. Lording it over them all is the famed Sphinx (Abu al-Hol or "Father of Terror"), which you can learn more about—along with something about pharaonic history—during the booming, melodramatic, but surprisingly entertaining nightly sound-and-light show. Still, the pyramids are most magical at dawn and dusk, or when bathed in moonlight and silence, after the last tourists have gone.

The Sphinx has the head of a human and the body of a lion.

As greater Cairo's population approaches 20 million, growing suburbs infringe on Giza's former isolation, but 20 miles south by car, less visited and even older pyramids pierce the sky. The most famous is the Step Pyramid designed for Pharaoh Djoser by Imhotep, Egypt's most beloved architect, priest, and healer. Archaeologists are still uncovering intact tombs around the Step in the complex of Saqqara, the cemetery of Memphis, which was the capital of the Old Kingdom from 2575 to 2130 B.C. Farther south, the Dahshur pyramid field attracts still fewer visitors. Ticket lines won't be long to visit this site's steeply sloped Bent Pyramid and to descend the thrilling—though tight—staircase into the Red Pyramid, Egypt's first "true" pyramid with smooth sides. Both predate the Giza pyramids by 50 to 100 years.

The elegant and recently restored 19th-century Mena House is set within 40 acres of manicured parkland less than half a mile from the Giza Pyramids. The wondrous monuments loom in full, unobstructed view from many rooms, the breakfast terrace, the nine-hole golf course, and the garden-enveloped swimming pool. The hotel's original wing was where Churchill and Roosevelt initiated the plans for D-day and where Begin and Sadat signed the 1978 peace treaty between Israel and Egypt. Back in Cairo, many of the palatial rooms in the Four Seasons at the First Residence have more distant pyramid views.

WHERE: Giza Pyramids are 11 miles/18 km southwest of central Cairo; it's another 20 miles/32 km to Saqqara and Dahshur. **OBEROI MENA HOUSE:** Tel 20/2-3377-3222; in the U.S., 800-562-3764; www.oberoimenahouse.com. *Cost:* pyramid-view rooms from $320 (off-peak), from $465 (peak). **FOUR SEASONS AT THE FIRST RESIDENCE:** Tel 20/2-3567-1600; in the U.S., 800-819-5053. *Cost:* pyramid-view rooms from $600. **BEST TIME:** Nov–Mar to avoid scorching summer weather.

Heavenly Pursuits

MOUNT SINAI AND THE RED SEA

Sinai, Egypt

According to the book of Exodus, Moses spent 40 days and nights on the rocky slopes of Mount Sinai before he was given the Ten Commandments. For today's pilgrims, the challenging "Path of Moses" up Mount Sinai takes just a few hot daytime hours—or part of a dark night if you're seeking a magnificent sunrise: It's 3,750 rock steps up to the 7,500-foot summit for expansive views. Or ride a camel along the gentler "Camel Path" (even if you choose the latter, you'll still have to tackle the final 750 steps on foot).

At the mountain's base, built around what was believed to be the site of the "burning bush," is Saint Catherine's, the world's oldest functioning monastery. Continuously inhabited since completion in A.D. 550, it's said to have been home to the Byzantine monk who constructed the stepped path up the mountain. Today, about a dozen Greek Orthodox monks live here, overseeing the largest collection of codices outside of the Vatican, a 6th-century mosaic of the Transfiguration of Christ, and some of the world's finest illuminated manuscripts and oldest Christian icons.

Many visitors choose to pair their heavenly climb with rapturous scuba dives off the southern tip of the Sinai Peninsula. The waters of the Red Sea were praised by Jacques Cousteau as "a corridor of marvels—the happiest hours of my diving experience." They are famed for their diverse marine life (10 percent of the species are endemic) and spectacular visibility (often in excess of 150 feet). While Israel and Jordan (see p. 456) have their own Red Sea resorts, those in Egypt grant the best access to the finest dive and snorkeling sites. From Sharm al-Sheikh and its smaller, bohemian neighbor to the north, Dahab, a range of day boats service the Straits of Tiran and Ras Mohammed, Egypt's first national marine park, replete with dramatic rock overhangs, sheer underwater cliffs, and deep pools full of barracudas and hammerheads. Sites like Shark Reef and Yolanda Reef feature innumerable starfish, sea urchins, mollusks, and crustaceans, while farther offshore, divers can explore the ghost hull of the *Thistlegorm,* a British Merchant Navy ship that sank in 1941.

Sharm's recently opened Four Seasons has gorgeous rooms tucked into the coastal hillside, while the nearby Savoy Sharm El Sheikh offers lodging options from standard rooms to supremely luxurious ocean-view villas. Bypass the crowds at Sharm altogether on one of

Tornado Fleet's live-aboard boats and enjoy even more pristine reefs, steep drop-offs, seamounts, and shipwrecks.

WHERE: Sharm al-Sheikh is 357 miles/575 km southeast of Cairo; Saint Catherine's is 137 miles/220 km north of Sharm al-Sheikh. **FOUR SEASONS RESORT:** Tel 20/69-360-3555; in the U.S., 800-819-5053; www.fourseasons.com. *Cost:* from $360 (off-peak), from $470 (peak). **SAVOY HOTEL:** Tel 20/69-360-2500; www.savoy-sharm.com. *Cost:* from $115 (off-peak), from $325 (peak). **TORNADO FLEET:** Tel 20/22-331-213; www.tornadomarinefleet.com. *Cost:* 6-night dive trips from $1,000. Originates in Sharm al-Sheikh. **BEST TIMES:** Apr and Nov for pleasant weather; May–Aug for optimal diving conditions and fewest divers, though days are hot.

Irreplaceable Monuments Where Egypt Ends

ABU SIMBEL AND ASWAN

Lake Nasser, Upper Egypt, Eygpt

On the 34th anniversary of his reign, the never-modest Pharaoh Ramses II ordered the colossal Sun Temple of Abu Simbel to be carved into the side of a cliff—with four 65-foot-high statues of himself, seated, to grace the exterior. The immense monument took 36 years to complete. More than 3,000 years later, an ingenious UNESCO operation saved it and 22 other monuments (including the Temple of Isis on Philae) from being submerged forever when the dam was built at Aswan. From 1964 to 1968, the $40 million rescue plan worked to move Abu Simbel to higher ground before the Aswan High Dam created the 300-mile-long Lake Nasser, or "Nubian Sea." Tourists didn't discover the lake till 1993, when its waters were first cruised by the 52-cabin M.S. *Eugénie,* a faux steamboat named after a French empress and decorated to evoke fin de siècle Egypt. Guests aboard it—and its slightly larger, Art Deco–style sister ship *Kasr Ibrim*—gaze at the temple-dotted shores and beyond to the empty desert, with its wind-hewn natural pyramids and bluffs.

The figures of Pharaoh Ramses II wear the double crown of Upper and Lower Egypt.

Journeys begin or end in Aswan, on the banks of the Nile, where palm-studded islands and elephantine granite boulders lend a wild beauty to Egypt's southernmost town. Aswan's position at the crossroads of caravan routes once meant a flourishing trade in gold, slaves, and ivory; the souk—almost as lively as Cairo's (see p. 376)—still brims with spices, perfumes, and produce. Thousands of items rescued before the creation of Lake Nasser are in the city's Nubia Museum, but the best way to soak in the region's history is aboard the small, traditional wooden sailboats known as *feluccas*. Check in at Aswan's Old Cataract Hotel, set on a picturesque bend in the river that inspired Agatha Christie to write *Death on the Nile*. Completely restored in 2011, the hotel preserves its marriage of Edwardian and Oriental elegance.

WHERE: Aswan is 133 miles/214 km south of Luxor; Abu Simbel is 176 miles/283 km south of Aswan. **HOW:** U.S.-based Travcoa leads an 8-day journey including Aswan and Abu Simbel. Tel 800-992-2003 or 310-649-7104; www.travcoa.com. *Cost:* from $3,495, all-inclusive. Originates in Cairo. **M.S. *EUGÉNIE* AND M.S. *KASR IBRIM*:** In Cairo, tel 20/2-516-9656; www.eugenie.com.eg. *Cost:* 3- to 7-night cruises from $240 per person per night, all-inclusive. Departures from Aswan or Abu Simbel. **OLD CATARACT:** Tel 20/97-231-6000; in the U.S., 800-221-4542; www.sofitel.com. *Cost:* from $370 (off-peak), from $440 (peak). **BEST TIMES:** Nov–Mar to avoid the heat of summer; Feb 22 and Oct 22 for semiannual Abu Simbel Festivals, when the day's first rays of sunlight illuminate the Sun Temple's murals of Ramses II and Egyptian deities.

The Watery Lifeline to the New Kingdom

LUXOR AND A NILE CRUISE

Upper Egypt, Egypt

Herodotus described Egypt as "the gift of the Nile," and to sail along the river's ageless green shores is to understand why ancient Egyptians worshipped it and why it remains the lifeblood of the country. It retains a timeless quality: Pajamaed children run from mud-brick settlements to wave at your boat, men waist deep in water wash their oxen, lateen-sailed *feluccas* glide by—the same scenes that inspired Plato and Flaubert. In earlier days, cruises began in Cairo, but now more than 300 ships ply the calm waters between Aswan (see previous page) and Luxor, where a matchless concentration of ancient ruins includes the Temple of Horus at Edfu, Egypt's best preserved, and the Temple of Sobek and Horus at Kom Ombo, with its mummified crocodiles. One of the finest of the larger ships is the all-suite Sonesta *Star Goddess,* featuring 33 elegant cabins, each with a private terrace. For a completely different experience, book a cruise on one of the restored 19th-century wooden sailboats called *dahabeahs*, such as Nour El Nil's 120-foot *Assouan,* which offers six airy and gleaming white cabins and two suites. Relatively new to the tourist market, these vessels introduce small groups to the leisurely, Victorian style of travel, taking time to fit in swims, desert walks, and village visits.

Larger dahabeahs *coexist with traditional* feluccas *and modern craft on the timeless waters of the Nile.*

The city of Luxor lies on the site of ancient Thebes, the capital of Egypt's New Kingdom; its population at one point numbered 1 million.

On the north end, along the Nile's east bank, stands the most astounding religious shrine of antiquity, the Temple of Karnak, part of a complex that was constructed over a period of 1,500 years and sprawls across 100 acres. The awe-inspiring 60,000-square-foot Hypostyle Hall contains 134 hieroglyphic-clad columns 70 feet high and 33 feet around. A 2-mile Nile-side promenade, once lined with sphinxes, leads south to the Temple of Luxor. Across the river, in the sandy hillside, is ancient Egypt's most famous necropolis, the Valley of the Kings. After the female pharaoh Hatshepsut built a mortuary temple and was the first royal to be buried here, more than 60 male pharaohs followed suit. Centuries of plundering emptied all the tombs except Tutankhamun's (whose treasures are now in Cairo; see p. 376), but the decorated subterranean vaults are still a wonder to behold. Among the burial places of royal wives and children in the nearby Valley of the Queens is the seven-chambered tomb of Ramses II's consort Nefertari, an intricately painted labor of love for the favorite of the pharaoh's 40 wives.

After a long, dusty day spent exploring the tombs, repair to the Sofitel Winter Palace, a 19th-century hotel on the river promenade. In the original wing, high ceilings, giant armoires, Oriental carpets, and ornate crystal chandeliers welcome you. The garden is the largest and most beautiful in town, and a cool haven for tea. Alternately, get away from the Luxor crowds and closer to the Valley of the Kings with a stay at Al Moudira, built in 2002 using material salvaged from old Egyptian villas. Its 54 palatial rooms are decorated with antique Egyptian furnishings, and meals in its domed, Ottoman-inspired Great Room mix Mediterranean and Eastern influences.

WHERE: Luxor is 133 miles/214 km north of Aswan and 415 miles/668 km south of Cairo. **SONESTA *STAR GODDESS*:** In the U.S., tel 800-766-3782 or 617-315-9100; www.sonesta.com. *Cost:* 3- to 7-night cruises, suites from $540 (off-peak), from $675 (peak) per night, all-inclusive. ***ASSOUAN*:** Tel 20/65-78322; www.nourelnil.com. *Cost:* 5-night cruises from $1,500, all-inclusive. **WINTER PALACE:** Tel 20/95-238-0425; in the U.S., 800-221-4542; www.sofitel.com. *Cost:* from $215 (off-peak), from $540 (peak). **AL MOUDIRA:** Tel 20/12-325-1307; www.moudira.com. *Cost:* from $250 (off-peak), from $380 (peak). **BEST TIMES:** Nov–Mar to avoid the heat; 2 weeks before Ramadan for the music, parades, and horse races of Luxor's Festival of Moulid of Abu al-Haggag.

Better Than a Mirage

SIWA OASIS

Western Desert, Egypt

Covering two-thirds of Egypt and the antithesis of the green Nile Valley, the Western Desert (an extension of the Sahara) is punctuated by a handful of exotic oases. Picturesque Siwa, 30 miles from the Libyan border on a centuries-old caravan route, is the most remote, with dates and olives long known as some of the finest in the world. Despite the recent arrival of television and a steady but growing trickle of adventure tourists (more than a dozen modest hotels now welcome guests), it remains an intriguing desert outpost. Siwan culture and customs continue much as they did when Alexander the Great visited in 331 B.C. to consult the legendary

Oracle of Amun (the discovery of Alexander's alleged tomb here made headlines in 1995).

Siwi, a Berber tongue, is spoken here instead of Arabic. Siwan women, while not often seen in public, are almost always veiled in black, and many still wear their hair in numerous braids, as their Berber ancestors did, and cover themselves with large, ornate silver jewelry. Houses are made of *kershef* (mud, salt, and straw), and the more than 300,000 palms and 70,000 olive trees attract a robust bird population, including harriers, owls, wagtails, and warblers. All of it is sustained by 300 springs and freshwater streams. The most famous is near the Temple of Amun ruins, a bubbling pool called Cleopatra's Bath—first described by Herodotus in the 5th century B.C. and still used for fully clothed bathing (though rarely by women). Day trips on horseback take riders to more springs on the outskirts of town, then into the Great Sand Sea, where jeeps climb the dunes and thrill seekers surf the sand on modified snowboards.

Within a lush grove of date palms lies the magical Adrère Amellal, a 40-room lodge bent on proving that luxury and nature are not mutually exclusive. There is no electricity, no phones, and no nightlife; instead, you'll find *kershef* houses, candlelit alleys, exquisite dinners made from whatever is growing in the hotel's organic garden, and excursions into the desert. The owner's dedication to environmental and cultural conservation is similarly reflected in Shali Lodge, his humbler hotel in the nearby 13th-century Siwa village.

WHERE: 461 miles/762 km southwest of Cairo. **ADRÈRE AMELLAL:** Tel 20/2-736-7879; www.adrereamellal.net. *Cost:* from $660, all-inclusive. **SHALI LODGE:** Tel 20/2-738-1327; www.siwa.com/shalilodge. *Cost:* from $65. **BEST TIMES:** Nov–Mar to avoid scorching days and mosquitoes; 3 days surrounding Oct full moon for the Siwa Festival.

A Windsurfer's Paradise

ESSAOUIRA

Morocco

The walled port of Essaouira is perched above some of Morocco's finest beaches, with dunes that unfurl for miles to the south. The city's relaxed atmosphere—along with its exotic medina and stalwart stone ramparts—first attracted backpackers and hippies here in the 1960s (Jimi Hendrix and Cat Stevens each came to drop out). Today's young visitors come for some of Africa's best wind- and kite surfing. Along with excellent shopping for local crafts and the arty ambience, these sports make Essaouira one of Morocco's favorite destinations—particularly in June, when thousands arrive for the 5-day Gnaoua and World Music Festival to hear the hypnotically rhythmic and joyful music of the Gnaoua, descendants of black slaves.

The medina and fortifications were designed in the 18th century by Théodore Cornut, a French architect held prisoner here by Sultan Sidi Mohammed Ben Abdellah; the sultan liked the orderly city plan and rewarded Cornut with freedom. The car-free medina is a delight to explore, and many galleries feature the work of local artists (particularly marquetry made of indigenous thuya wood and lush, colorful canvases created by Gnaoua painters during mystical trances). You'll also find local products like rich argan nut oil, used in all manner of beauty products. The busy fishing port is where you come eye-to-eye with lunch: Pick your fresh-caught favorite (sardines, sea bass, and squid are delicious choices) and the fishmonger grills it right in front of you.

Many of Essaouira's historic *riads* (multistory mansions built around central courtyards) have been converted to small inns and hotels. The simple and stylish Villa Maroc has 21 rooms with blue-painted balconies and gardens filled with jasmine and bougainvillea; the spa offers massages that use local argan oil and has a private hammam. The best part just might be breakfast on the open-air roof terrace. The nearby Ryad Watier began a century ago as a school. Master craftsmen recently transformed the classrooms into ten very spacious guestrooms, some with fireplaces and private terraces. The rooms surround a four-story courtyard resplendent with fountains, Berber carpets, and palms. Essaouira's best Moroccan cooking is found at Restaurant Ferdaous, a rather plain, unpretentious space in the medina that's always packed with locals and in-the-know travelers who come for the tagine, couscous, and fresh seafood.

WHERE: 100 miles/161 km west of Marrakech. **VILLA MAROC:** Tel 212/524-47-61-47; www.villa-maroc.com. *Cost:* from $118; dinner $24. **RYAD WATIER:** Tel 212/524-47-62-04; www.ryad-watier-maroc.com. *Cost:* from $115. **RESTAURANT FERDAOUS:** Tel 212/524-47-36-55. *Cost:* dinner $15. **BEST TIMES:** Mar–May and Sep–Dec for nicest weather; late Jun for Gnaoua and World Music Festival.

Symbolic and Spiritual Heart of Morocco

FÈS EL BALI

Fès, Morocco

The intellectual, cultural, and religious center of Morocco for 1,200 years, Fès (or Fez) is Morocco's oldest imperial capital and is known for the Fès el Bali, its large, sprawling, walled medina. With 9,500 streets and by some accounts over 180 miles of alleys, it is crammed with every conceivable sort of workshop, market, and restaurant. Fès el Bali is a delirious assault of sights, sounds, and smells, with dye pits, tanneries, butcher shops, tiled fountains, mosques, palaces, spice markets, madrassas, and a legion of persistent rug merchants. It will all seem overwhelming, so consider hiring an official Fassi guide.

Fès el Bali's medina is one of the largest and best conserved historic towns of the Arab-Muslim world.

Apart from electricity, everything in Fès el Bali seems to belong to another century. Medersa Bou Inania, built in the 1350s, is a masterpiece of extravagance, highlighted by a grand courtyard decorated with intricate geometric motifs, dazzling wood carvings, and plasterwork. The Fondouk el-Nejjarin, opened in the 14th century, served for hundreds of years as home to Fès's itinerant woodcrafters, who carved elaborate friezes (it's now a museum of woodworking). The medina's centerpiece is the Kairaouine Mosque, founded in 857 and with room for 20,000 worshippers.

Just steps from the mosque is an exquisite small guesthouse, Dar Seffarine—with magnificent tilework, a column-flanked courtyard, large, enchantingly furnished rooms, and warm hospitality. You'll find ambience on a grander scale at the Sofitel Fès Palais Jamaï, a princely, 140-room former palace built in 1879, with lush gardens and opulent, tiled décor. The beautifully restored hotel La Maison Bleue is a top choice for its restaurant. Enjoy flaky pigeon *pastilla,* a specialty of Fès, in a candlelit salon after cocktails beside the courtyard fountain.

At the weeklong Fez Festival of World Sacred Music in early June, performances may include Berber music, Turkish whirling dervishes of Konya, a Harlem choir singing gospel music, female musicians from France performing Gregorian chants, or ancient Judeo-Spanish lullabies.

Music festival events are sometimes staged 40 miles west of Fès among the remains of Volubilis, the largest and best-preserved Roman ruins in North Africa. The city flourished in the first century A.D. as the place where the Romans and Berbers met to trade. Wander the ancient streets and squares to see the grand triumphal arch and forum, humble homes and olive presses, and dozens of exquisite, well-preserved mosaics.

WHERE: 155 miles/249 km east of Casablanca. **DAR SEFFARINE:** Tel 212/671-11-35-28; www.darseffarine.com. *Cost:* from $92. **FÈS PALAIS JAMAÏ:** Tel 212/535-63-43-31; www.sofitel.com. *Cost:* from $225. **LA MAISON BLEUE:** Tel 212/535-636-052; www.maisonbleue.com. *Cost:* from $225; dinner $65. **HOW:** U.S.-based Morocco Tours offers 10-day music festival packages. Tel 800-799-3080 or 646-643-1420; www.fesmusicfestival.com. *Cost:* from $1,890, meals and concert passes extra. Originates in Casablanca. *When:* Jun. **BEST TIMES:** Sep–Nov and Apr–Jun for pleasant weather; early Jun for Sacred Music Festival; late Oct for Fès Culinary Festival.

Romancing the Palate

DINING IN MARRAKECH

Marrakech, Morocco

The great chef Paul Bocuse once said, "There are only three cuisines in the world: French, Chinese, and Moroccan." And not necessarily in that order, one is inclined to believe after spending time in Marrakech. The food of Morocco owes much of its distinct character to the ancient trade caravans, which brought in rare spices and other ingredients. The Berbers also shared their traditions and their foods (like dates, lamb, honey, and almonds), while French, Portuguese, Arab, and Spanish influences made their way here too, thanks to Marrakech's position as gateway between Europe and Africa.

For sheer variety and atmosphere, the first stop in which to explore it all must be the evening food market at the Djemaa el-Fna square (see p. 386). Amid exotic aromas and sounds, vendors at more than 100 open-kitchen food stalls prepare such traditional foods as sizzling lamb *merguez* sausages, slabs of cumin-scented bread, bean-and-vegetable *harira* soup cooked in 50-gallon pots, escargots simmered in broth and garlic, and, for the daring, sheep's head stewed with chickpeas.

In the narrow lanes of the medina, you'll find dozens of fine restaurants. Behind the massive, unmarked door of a sumptuous 200-year-old palace, Yacout (which means "sapphire" in Arabic) is *One Thousand and One Nights* romantic, with hundreds of flickering candles, ornate mosaics, the scent of jasmine in the air, and the hypnotic strumming of Gnaoua music. Try the traditional *pastilla,* a sweet-and-savory pastry made with almonds and pigeon or chicken. Le Tobsil, another glittering Scheherazade's jewel box of a restaurant, is more intimate but also serves a dizzying sequence of courses in the style of a traditional Marrakech feast.

Le Foundouk's style is more chic and contemporary, as evidenced by its elegant, understated décor and its innovative cooking combining Moroccan and French flavors. Enjoy an aperitif on the rooftop terrace, then retreat to one of the private candlelit salons that ring the courtyard.

In the modern Guéliz district is the delightfully atypical Al Fassia, staffed entirely by women and offering an extensive à la carte menu. The cooking here is lighter and more varied, and some of the specialties, such as *méchoui* (roast lamb shoulder), require a day's notice, so order ahead when you reserve your table.

Learning to prepare Moroccan dishes at one of the city's cooking schools is a great way to absorb even more of the culture. One is run by La Maison Arabe, an elegant *riad* hotel with a pool, spa, and acclaimed restaurant.

Yacout: Tel 212/44-38-29-29; www.yacout.net. *Cost:* prix-fixe dinner $85. **Le Tobsil:** Tel 212/524-44-40-52. *Cost:* prix-fixe dinner $70. **Le Foundouk:** Tel 212/524-37-81-90; www.foundouk.com. *Cost:* dinner $33. **Al Fassia:** Tel 212/524-43-40-60; www.alfassia.com. *Cost:* dinner $35. **La Maison Arabe:** Tel 212/524-38-70-10; www.lamaisonarabe.com. *Cost:* rooms from $190 (off-peak), from $240 (peak); half-day cookery workshops $70.

Everyday Carnival at the City's Center

Place Djemaa el-Fna and the Medina

Marrakech, Morocco

According to Paul Bowles, a Moroccan at heart, Marrakech without the huge Djemaa el-Fna, the teeming central plaza at the heart of the medina, would be just another Moroccan city. This is where it all happens, an impromptu medieval circus enacted around the clock. During the day, snake charmers, performing monkeys, and souvenir sellers lure the tourists, while dentists, barbers, and scribes serve the locals. Later, the square fills with food vendors selling everything from lamb couscous to orange juice, and the air is filled with the smoke and sizzle of grilled kebabs. When Djemaa el-Fna echoes with the muezzin call to evening prayer and lights flood the towering minaret of the Koutoubia Mosque, the impact is magical. The square is lined—at street level and above—with cafés and restaurants. Take in the mayhem from the "Grand Balcon" of the Café Glaciers.

To the north is the souk, the mazelike marketplace of narrow streets and alleys lined with street merchants and overflowing stores and stalls. Here, while dodging motorbikes and donkey carts, you'll find silk babouche slippers, bags of spice, leather goods, ethnic silver jewelry, carpets, and objets d'art.

Escape to an oasis of comfort and serenity behind the thick walls of newly restored *riads*, historic homes built around courtyards and now transformed into restaurants and guesthouses that range from modest to sumptuous. Created from five smaller riads in the medina's core, Riad Farnatchi is a nine-suite masterwork of tasteful renovation, blending contemporary European and traditional Moroccan design in a rambling series of rooms, courtyards, and terraces. At the handsome Riad Malika the vibe is relaxed, the style eclectic, and the welcome friendly. The owner's collection of 20th-century art and furniture is displayed throughout and the pool and terrace are a riot of potted palms and bougainvillea.

When Truman Capote advised, "Before you go to Marrakech, make sure you say goodbye to all your friends and draw your savings from the bank," he must have been booked at the lavish La Mamounia, a grand and glamorous hotel built in the 1920s outside the Medina's walls. Recently refurbished, it combines classic Moroccan and Art Deco influences, and juxtaposes a sultan's original 16th-century gardens with a fabulous new spa and hammam. Its rooms and suites have entertained Winston Churchill, the Rolling Stones, and Nelson Mandela.

WHERE: 149 miles/240 km south of Casablanca. **RIAD FARNATCHI:** Tel 212/524-38-27-40; www.riadfarnatchi.com. *Cost:* from $390. **RIAD MALIKA:** 212/524-38-54-51; www.riadmalika.com. *Cost:* from $120 (off-peak), from $185 (peak). **LA MAMOUNIA:** Tel 212/524-38-86-00; www.mamounia.com. *Cost:* from $700. **BEST TIMES:** Mar–May and Sep–Nov for most clement weather; mid-Jul for the Popular Arts Festival.

Desert Beauty and Mystique

THE GREAT SAHARA

Morocco

The Sahara desert is easy to reach in Morocco, and once you're there, you'll find mountains of sand, vibrant green oases, miles of barren scrub and stone that the Berbers call *hammada,* turbaned nomads astride camels, ancient mud-walled casbahs, and, at night, an ocean of stars, uncannily clear and bright.

The road trip from Marrakech into the Sahara brings you across the Atlas Mountains (see p. 390) and into barren desert basins where underground rivers sustain oases of date palms and almond, citrus, and olive trees. For millennia, camel caravans traversed this seemingly empty landscape carrying spices, jewels, and gold. The gateway is Ouarzazate, where two routes diverge, both leading toward the great dunes of the central Sahara. South from Ouarzazate, the road follows the palm-fringed Drâa Valley to Zagora, where a sign at the edge of town reads "Timbuktu: 52 Days by Camel." Leave that trail to the nomads, and instead continue south to M'hamid. From here, only jeeps or camels can penetrate the massive Erg Chigaga dunes, enormous mounds of sand stretching for 25 miles and nearing heights of 1,000 feet. Dar Azawad, an elegant lodging where you'll find a talented chef who trained in France, comes as a surprise in this remote wilderness. Set in a palm-shaded oasis, its fit-for-a-sultan rooms, heated swimming pool, and spa with hammam create a splendid base for overnight trips to luxury tent camps deep in the dunes.

The route east from Ouarzazate, following the Road of the Thousand Kasbahs, leads toward the lush oasis of Skoura, where two of the desert's finest hotels await. Dar Ahlam is a meticulously restored 1920s casbah with plush suites and villas, superlative food, and an expansive garden-surrounded pool and spa, though the real highlight is the personalized tours and services offered by the friendly staff. Kasbah Ait Ben Moro is a landmark 18th-century fortress transformed into a hotel offering simply decorated rooms and impressive Moroccan dining. From Skoura, continue past the mighty Dadès and Todra gorges and then to Merzouga, where the soaring dunes of Erg Chebbi rise 450 feet above the verdant oasis.

Whichever route you choose, don't miss an overnight excursion to camp among the dunes. By jeep or camel, you will travel deep into the shifting and undulating hills of towering sand to your tented campsite. Dune walks are arranged for the cool, early hours of the morning; jeeps convey you to desert towns, fortresses, ruins, and lush oases where foreigners rarely venture.

Ergs, which are fields of wild-blown sand, cover about 20 percent of the desert.

WHERE: Ouarzazate is 125 miles/200 km southeast of Marrakech. **DAR AZAWAD:** Tel 212/524-84-87-30; www.darazawad.com. *Cost:* from $175, inclusive. **DAR AHLAM:** Tel: 212/524-85-22-39; www.maisonsdesreves.com. *Cost:* from $1,155 (off-peak), from $1,565 (peak), all-inclusive. **KASBAH AIT BEN MORO:** Tel 212/524-85-21-16; www.aitbenmoro.com. *Cost:* from $80, inclusive. **HOW:** U.S.-based Overseas Adventure Travel offers a 16-day Morocco Sahara Odyssey that includes 2 nights camping in the Sahara. Tel 800-221-0814 or 617-350-7500; www.oattravel.com. *Cost:* from $2,895, all-inclusive. **BEST TIMES:** Jan–Apr and Sep–Dec for nicest weather; Oct for Erfoud Festival of Dates.

An Ancient Port and Artist's Playground

TANGIER'S MEDINA

Tangier, Morocco

This ancient port and trading center was considered such a vital gateway between Europe and Africa (it lies directly across the Strait of Gibraltar from Spain, just 8 miles distant) that throughout much of its history it was an independent city-state. It only became part of Morocco in 1957. Largely unconstrained by the social mores of either Europe or Muslim Africa, Tangier became known for its decadent ways and attracted such artists and writers as Henri Matisse, Oscar Wilde, André Gide, and, later, Paul Bowles, Allen Ginsberg, and William Burroughs, who would find his inspiration here for *Naked Lunch*.

Tangier has cleaned up considerably since its lawless days, though the city's medina—the ancient, walled city center—still maintains its slightly seedy and intriguing authenticity. From the Grand Socco, the largest market square, follow Rue es Siaghin past colorful stalls and cavelike souks to the Petit Socco, the "small market" ringed with busy street cafés. Climb the winding Rue des Chrétiens toward the casbah, the highest point in the medina, a former Roman fortification that is now home to the Dar El Makhzen museum.

Amid the casbah's 14th-century ramparts, Dar Nour (House of Light) is a small, charming hotel consisting of a group of ancient houses and featuring ten unique rooms filled with objets d'art as well as a rooftop terrace with views over the old city and harbor. At the casbah's summit, you'll find the elegant, eclectic Hotel Nord-Pinus Tanger (a sister property to the Grand Hotel Nord-Pinus in Arles, France; see p. 125), whose colorful tilework, bold contemporary art, and striking modern furnishings, all in a former pasha's palace, set a new standard for Tangier hotels. The restaurant's tagines and updated Moroccan classics are among Tangier's best (as are the unrestricted views across the strait to Spain). Be sure to stroll along the Avenue Mohammed Tazi to the shaded terrace at Café Hafa for mint tea and phenomenal cliff-top views.

An hour south of Tangier, in a deep fold of the Rif Mountains, is Chefchaouen, a remote town with a medina that glows with blue-washed mud houses. Founded by Moors and Jews expelled from 15th-century Spain, Chefchaouen became a pilgrimage site for devout Muslims, and Christians were strictly forbidden to enter. The town now welcomes all visitors, and the lucky ones find their way to either of two small sibling hotels. Casa Hassan is a rambling, 350-year-old home converted into a lovely guesthouse filled with local art and handmade furnishings; the rooftop restaurant-with-a-view is the best in town. Nearby, two late-19th-century mansions have been transformed into Dar Baibou, where sumptuous guestrooms face onto courtyards filled with arches and colonnades; weary travelers can relax at the adjoining hammam.

WHERE: 185 miles/298 km north of Casablanca. **DAR NOUR:** Tel 212/662-11-27-24; www.darnour.com. *Cost:* from $86. **HOTEL NORD-PINUS TANGER:** Tel 212/661-22-81-40; www.nord-pinus-tanger.com. *Cost:* from $292. **CASA HASSAN** and **DAR BAIBOU:** Tel 212/539-98-61-53; www.casahassan.com. *Cost:* from $95, inclusive. **BEST TIMES:** Mar–May and Sep–Nov for pleasant weather; Jun for the Tangier Jazz Festival.

Morocco's Little-Changed, Little-Known Walled City

TAROUDANNT

Morocco

Relatively few travelers journey to southern Morocco's wide and fertile Souss Valley, ringed by the Atlas and Anti-Atlas Mountains, but wonderfully picturesque Taroudannt, a 4-hour drive from Marrakech along the exquisitely scenic Tizi n'Test road, is the reward for those who do. Set amid almond and date plantations, Taroudannt is an authentic Berber market town little changed for centuries. It is enclosed within castellated mud walls and centers on two vibrant souks offering good-quality, traditional crafts and foodstuffs. Often called "little Marrakech" because of its ramparts and bustling medina, Taroudannt offers an opportunity to experience the edge-of-the-desert daily life of local Berbers, who are welcoming if mostly oblivious to the travelers in their midst.

A horse-drawn caleche will make a 3-mile sightseeing circuit of the tawny-brown medina walls before dropping you off at the heart of the city, its markets. Souk Assarag, also called the Arab Souk, features locally made leather goods, rugs, and silver jewelry, while at the Marché Berbère, local farmers gather to sell produce and spices (saffron is one of the valley's major crops). Once you've explored the markets, you can enjoy any number of activities offered by the British responsible-travel tour company Naturally Morocco, including wildlife tours, craft tours, trekking, and cooking and language classes. You can unpack inside the medina in their small, comfortable guesthouse known for its home-cooked meals.

Just steps from the markets and souks and hidden behind thick walls is the jewel-like Palais Oumensour hotel. Its capacious, palm-shaded patio, with fountains and a swimming pool, and its rooftop terrace invite guests to linger during the afternoon's hottest hours until it's time for a dinner of French-influenced Moroccan cuisine. Taroudannt's highlight is one of North Africa's most luxurious retreats: the Gazelle d'Or, a former hunting lodge (once owned by a French baron), situated a mile outside the medina walls and surrounded by its own oasis. Amid the jasmine, roses, and towering lilies and hibiscus are 30 flower-covered stone cottages set on as many acres. There is a riding stable on the grounds for sunset forays, plus clay tennis courts and a croquet lawn, but many guests are happy to simply luxuriate by the pool or to relax in the spa. Meals are served on the terrace or in the opulent, tented dining room, with white-robed waiters carrying trays laden with exquisite Moroccan and international fare.

WHERE: 138 miles/223 km southwest of Marrakech. **NATURALLY MOROCCO:** In the U.K., tel 44/12-39-710-814; www.naturallymorocco.co.uk. *Cost:* from $65. **PALAIS OUMENSOUR:** Tel 212/528-55-02-15; www.palaisoumensour.com. *Cost:* from $80. **GAZELLE D'OR:** Tel 212/528-85-20-39; www.gazelledor.com. *Cost:* from $440, inclusive. *When:* closed mid-Jul–mid-Sep. **BEST TIMES:** Mar–Jun and Sep–Dec for nicest weather; Jul for Festival du Dakka Roudania, a celebration of regional music.

Cultures and Vistas Untouched by Time

TREKKING AND ROMANCE IN THE ATLAS MOUNTAINS

Morocco

The Moroccans believe that the High Atlas Mountains are as close as you can get to heaven without leaving earth. You can glimpse these majestic, snow-capped mountains from as far away as Marrakech (see p. 386), and they lure an increasing number of hikers who wish to experience the fascinating culture and friendly hospitality of Berber villagers while staying in restored casbahs, or walled fortresses. One of these is Kasbah du Toubkal, a feudal chieftain's summer palace that is now an eco-lodge. Its magnificent setting above the Imlil Valley is at the base of 13,665-foot Mount Toubkal, the highest point in North Africa. Comfortable rather than luxurious, the casbah is closely integrated with the local village, and everything from the meals to the simply decorated rooms reflects the rich Berber heritage. Just outside the front door are hiking trails leading up into the mountains; the best trek is the guided, two-day odyssey by foot and mule up towering Mount Toubkal, a climb that, while stunning, isn't overly strenuous.

For young Berber women, the Betrothal Festival can be a life-changing event.

For a high-end bohemian experience, check into Kasbah Tamadot, a former Berber chief's fortress, in the Atlas foothills, now owned by Sir Richard Branson. At this exclusive enclave—it has 18 rooms and suites and six handsome Berber tents with private plunge pools—you would be tempted to pass the days relaxing in the spa if the Atlas backcountry didn't beckon. The hotel can arrange horseback riding, mule treks, and mountain biking excursions.

Farther north, in the Middle Atlas Mountains, Berber sheep herders return from the high country in September, gathering at the village of Imilchil for a 3-day marriage *moussem* (festival). Here the scattered clans trade livestock, buy winter provisions, socialize, and engage in the ancient rituals of the Betrothal Festival, in which singles, dressed in their finest, come to meet and marry. It's the girls who do the browsing: If a young woman decides a young man is a kindred soul, she asks him to walk with her to the scribes' tent, where their two families negotiate, and by that evening the couple may be wed. The festival has become increasingly popular with tourists, though accommodations nearby remain few to none.

WHERE: The Imlil Valley is 40 miles/65 km south of Marrakech. **KASBAH DU TOUBKAL:** Tel 212/524-48-56-11; in France, 33/05-49-05-01-35 (reservations); www.kasbahdutoubkal.com. *Cost:* from $215. **KASBAH TAMADOT:** In the U.K., tel 44/208-600-0430; www.virginlimitededition.com. *Cost:* from $550. **IMILCHIL BETROTHAL FESTIVAL:** www.imilchil.adrar.org. *When:* early Sep. **BEST TIMES:** Apr–May for warm spring weather and snow on the peaks; Jun and Sep–Oct for ideal trekking.

Clifftop Charm and an Ancient Empire

SIDI BOU SAID AND CARTHAGE

Tunisia

Its very name makes you smile. Sidi Bou Said is a vision in Wedgwood blue and white, an utterly charming collection of whitewashed stone houses and cobbled lanes jumbled together on a hill overlooking the Gulf of Tunis.

The village began as a series of watchtowers built nearly 1,000 years ago to spot invaders. But it soon became a community of Sufi Muslims, and it has enchanted tourists and artists for two-and-a-half centuries, ever since well-to-do families from Tunis started building summer homes here. The indigo Mediterranean below blends with an immaculate azure sky and is accented by a multitude of brass-studded wooden doors painted in a similar color. All that blue is almost too intense against the dazzling whitewashed, domed houses smothered in bougainvillea.

Discovered by wealthy French and other European expats at the turn of the 20th century, Sidi could have been overbuilt had not the government issued orders in 1915 to preserve its character. The irony is that non-Muslims were not permitted to roam these streets until 1820, when followers of Abu Said lifted a centuries-old ban. Abu Said ibn Khalef (who died here in 1231 and is buried in the local mosque) was a teacher of Sufism, adopted by the anti-Christian Corsair pirates as their protector against the European infidels—the very ones who now flock here for the obligatory mint-tea-with-a-view on the open terrace of the much vaunted Café des Nattes overlooking the main square. For even better views, linger with a freshly squeezed fruit juice at the pretty Café Sidi Chabanne. Spend the night at the Maison de Charme's Dar Saïd, built in the mid-19th century as a family home and renovated in 1998 to incorporate 24 stylishly decorated guest rooms, a small pool, and a restaurant. It's situated in the heart of Sidi Bou Said, overlooking the village, the sea, and Carthage.

Any trip from nearby Tunis should include a stop in Carthage, site of one of the largest and most enduring of the ancient empires. Founded in 814 B.C. by Phoenician traders, this once-thriving coastal city is where many of the ancient mosaics and statues now housed in the Bardo Museum (see below) were found. Only a handful of ruins remain, including Roman baths, but history buffs will thrill at the opportunity to walk the ground trod by the great Carthiginian general Hannibal and the legendary Queen Dido, sister of Pygmalion. Louis IX of France (St. Louis) died here in 1270 while on crusade. A late 19th-century cathedral dedicated to him (and now used for concerts) stands on the site of an ancient citadel, near the fine National Museum of Carthage.

Sidi Bou Said is known for its blue-and-white motif.

WHERE: Sidi Bou Said is 13 miles/21 km east of Tunis; Carthage is 9 miles/15 km east of Tunis. **DAR SAÏD HOTEL:** Tel 216/71-729-666; www.darsaid.com.tn. *Cost:* from $250. **BEST TIMES:** Sep–Nov or Mar–May for pleasant, warm days and evenings; Jul–Aug for International Festival of Carthage.

Africa's Priceless Mosaics

BARDO MUSEUM

Tunis, Tunisia

Tunisia's national museum, a complex of 13th- to 19th-century buildings that includes the former royal palace, houses the continent's largest assemblage of ancient mosaics, arguably the finest in the world.

The collection is so extensive—covering the floors and walls—that visitors run the risk of overload (and that's to say nothing of the magnificent statuary and artifacts also scattered throughout the museum).

Tunisia was the heart of Roman Africa, and the Bardo's offerings come primarily from the 2nd–4th centuries A.D., during the height of Roman influence. It is worth noting that the world's earliest true mosaics (dating to the 5th or 4th century B.C.) were discovered in nearby Carthage (see p. 391), indicating that the Carthaginians, not the Romans, may have invented the art form. But the Romans adopted and refined the Carthaginian techniques, combining small pieces of marble, limestone, and glass to create "tapestries" of richly colored landscapes and portraits, where visual depth was conveyed through gradation of colors in much the same way painters employ shades and tints of paint. All aspects of rural and urban life are represented in these elaborate works, which seem to illustrate an inscription on a piece found at an archaeological site in Algeria: "To hunt, to bathe, to gamble, to laugh, that is to live."

WHERE: 3 miles/5 km west of central Tunis. Tel 216/71-513-650.

Festivals of Tunisia

EL DJEM AND THE SAHARA DOUZ

Tunis, Tunisia

The Tunisian joie de vivre bursts forth in a multitude of annual festivals; even the smallest village sets aside a time for celebration, whether for the summer harvest, the fishing season, or the arrival of spring. The International Festival of Symphonic Music is one of the biggest and the best, offering magnificent performances in El Djem, the world's best-preserved and largest Roman amphitheater after the Coliseum in Rome (see p. 183). In the 3rd century, chariots raced and gladiators battled in this grand arena, to the cheers of tens of thousands. Events are more sedate these days, but the setting is no less stunning. For three weeks or more in July and August, world-renowned artists take to the stage in these majestic, often candlelit ruins. European and North African orchestral music make up the majority of the performances, but it's not unusual for Italian opera, American blues and gospel, and other musical genres to appear on the program. Combine the music festival with a visit to the seaside resort of Sousse, an hour's drive away and the summer destination of choice for many Tunisian families, who know to check out the medina for local finds.

At the Douz Festival, Arabian stallions flaunt their speed and stamina.

Perhaps the liveliest of the many Tunisian festivals can be found in Douz, gateway to the Sahara Desert. Decades ago, residents began gathering outdoors to welcome the cooler weather, celebrating with dance and music. Nearby Tunisian towns started participating, foreigners eventually joined in, and now the Douz Festival attracts more than 50,000 visitors, who spend 4 days amid the sand dunes, delving into joyous desert traditions. These include an authentic, lively mix of North African folk music (incorporating strings, flutes, and drums), dancing, races in which *sloughi* (a breed of desert hunting dog) chase rabbits, camel fights and races, and galloping Arabian horse races. Even Bedouin marriages take place in the organized chaos. Cultural lectures, folkloric theater shows, and poetry readings also play an important part. If you're looking for more to do, Tozeur, the closest city of note and a popular gateway to desert tourism, is a 2-hour drive away. Be sure to stroll through its atmospheric, 14th-century medina before you leave town.

How: U.S.-based Hedfi Consulting Partners offers custom trips within Tunisia. Tel 877-220-9357 or 201-765-0208; www.authentictunisia.com. **El Djem Music Festival:** Tel 216/73-630-714; www.festivaleljem.com. *Where:* Roman amphitheater, 125 miles/201 km south of Tunis. *When:* 3–5 weeks in Jul–Aug. **Douz Festival:** www.festivaldouz.org.tn. *Where:* 80 miles/129 km southeast of Tozeur. *When:* 4 days in Dec.

WEST AFRICA

Celebrations of Life and Death

Akwasidae Festival

Kumasi, Ghana

Kumasi, the ancient and traditional capital of the Ashanti tribe of the Akan-speaking people, is still the heart of Ghana, home to 2.5 million people. One Sunday out of every six in the traditional 42-day Akan month, Kumasi throws a colorful celebration capping off a 3-day religious festival. This is when the Ashanti pay homage to their ancestors and present their chiefs with greetings, songs, dances, and gifts, drawing on all the vibrancy of their culture.

On the first 2 days of the Akwasidae festival, the celebrations are private. On the third day, visitors are welcome to join in, and the revelers pull out all the stops. Akwasidae finds many Ghanaians clad in kente cloth: woven garments with hundreds of designs and colors that communicate symbolic meanings. The Ashanti bring out their sacred objects, among them the golden stool that is the royal throne. They display them and follow their king (called Asantehene) in a procession that includes ritual sword bearers, guards, and subordinates carrying huge umbrellas and ostrich-feather fans.

Stop by Kumasi's Manhyia Palace Museum and check out the royal regalia, including massive gold ornaments similar to those worn by the king and his court.

Ashanti funerals, while not rigidly scheduled like Akwasidae, can be almost as spectacular. They are often held on Saturdays, when people are not working, and are major social events, more elaborate than weddings. Depending on the status of the deceased, they can be held anywhere from homes to soccer stadiums, often taking place years after the death and going on for 3 days.

Members of the deceased's family wear bright-red garments and stand in a line to receive gifts from the attendees, who are clothed in black. Far from somber, it's a bon-voyage party for the spirit, filled with drumming, drinking, and dancing. Attending an Ashanti funeral, even for a few hours, is an unforgettable glimpse into the deeply religious, exuberantly artistic, and irrepressibly festive Ashanti culture.

Where: 168 miles/270 km northwest of the capital city, Accra. **When:** every 42 days. **How:** U.S.-based Wilderness Travel offers two 15-day trips to Ghana, Benin, and Togo, with one departure coinciding with Akwasidae.

Tel 800-368-2794 or 510-558-2488; www.wildernesstravel.com. *Cost:* from $5,995. Originate in Accra. *When:* Mar and Dec. **Best time:** Nov–Feb to avoid the rainy season.

The Door of No Return

Elmina Castle

Elmina, Ghana

Perched on the water's edge about 3 hours west of Accra stands Elmina Castle, the first European slave-trading post in all of sub-Saharan Africa. Originally built in 1482 by the Portuguese to protect the gold traffic, the castle was captured by the Dutch in 1637 and used primarily to trade, house, and dispatch slaves. While European merchants were lodged in luxury accommodations in the upper levels, slaves captured in the African interior were jammed into appallingly filthy quarters, sometimes as many as 200 or 300 to a cell, without enough space to move or sit. It is estimated that by the 18th century, 30,000 slaves a year passed through the "Door of No Return," a small, metal-gated exit from the white stone fortress. From there, they were loaded onto ships for the brutal, months-long journey known as the Middle Passage, bound for a life of slavery, usually in the Portuguese colony of Brazil or the Carribean. Elmina Castle eventually fell to the British, who outlawed the slave trade in 1833. The building was restored in 1957 by the Ghanaian government after its people gained total independence, and a plaque now hangs at the entrance, imploring, "May humanity never again perpetrate such injustice against humanity. We the living vow to uphold this."

Elmina Castle has become an important destination for African Americans looking to explore their heritage.

Despite its grim past, the town of Elmina now has its lighter distractions. The harbor is the site of a lively market, along with a collection of colorful pirogue fishing boats. Climb St. Jago hill for views of the "old town," which has been undergoing restoration since 2003; it is due to be completed in 2015. And while passing through small fishing villages on the road to Accra, look for the coffin-carpentry shops. The Ga tribe in this area celebrate death by creating brightly colored "fantasy coffins," whose shapes represent some facet or love of the deceased's life: a fish for a fisherman, a hammer, a car, even a beer bottle for someone who loved to drink.

Where: 100 miles/167 km west of Accra. **How:** U.S.-based Wilderness Travel offers 15-day trips to Ghana, Benin, and Togo. Tel 800-368-2794 or 510-558-2488; www.wildernesstravel.com. *Cost:* from $5,995. Originates in Accra. *When:* Mar and Dec. **Best time:** Nov–Feb to avoid the rainy season.

Magnificent Mud

The Great Mosque of Djenné and Dogon Country

Djenné, Mali

Mopti, an energetic river port and trading center built on three islands at the confluence of the Niger and Bani rivers, is a melting pot. It is also the gateway to the centuries-old city of Djenné, 60 miles to the southwest, a once affluent and powerful market center in the trans-Saharan gold trade, located on the river route to Timbuktu (see next page). It fell under the influence of Muslim merchants in the 13th century, and within 200 years it was a center of Islamic learning, a place where children from all West Africa were sent to be educated. Magnificent buildings were constructed from the main material at hand—mud—and half a millennium later, Djenné has survived as one of the world's largest and most beautiful mud-brick towns, with some 2,000 traditional houses. Its superb Great Mosque was built in 1907 after a 13th-century model and is touched up every spring after the heavy rains by thousands of volunteers amid a festive atmosphere. It is the largest and most elaborate mud structure in the world.

Three minarets stand above the mosque's main face, one of the most recognized landmarks in Africa.

Try to schedule your visit for Monday, when Mali's most vibrant market spreads out in front of the mosque. Keep an eye out for *bogolan*, handwoven mud-cloth that incorporates the colors of the Malian bush, and ball-shaped soap made from shea butter harvested from a local tree. To quench shoppers' thirst, vendors sell plastic bags of fresh ginger juice and bright-red *bissap* juice brewed from hibiscus petals, then chilled.

South of here is the geographically isolated Dogon country, home to a civilization that has so far resisted both Christianity and Islam, preserving the traditions of its animist ancestors, who came here 700 years ago. More than 700 Dogon villages, most with fewer than 500 inhabitants, are built entirely of mud around a central *toguna*, the traditional men's meeting place.

The villages blend so harmoniously with the rocky, monochromatic surroundings that you can find yourself looking straight at one without realizing it's there. The Dogon are highly artistic, as shown by their beautifully molded mud granaries, mosques, and churches and by their intricately carved wooden masks, whose meanings remain unknown to outsiders. They are used in fantastic *damas* (traditional dances honoring their ancestors) including those performed during the most important Dogon festival of the year, the Fête des Masques, held every spring.

Where: 395 miles/635 km northeast of the capital city of Bamako; 220 miles/354 km southwest of Timbuktu. **How:** U.S.-based Geographic Expeditions offers 9-day tours of Mali. Tel 800-777-8183 or 415-922-0448; www.geoex.com. *Cost:* from $4,800, all-inclusive. Originates in Bamako. *When:* Nov and Dec. **Best times:** Nov–Jan for coolest weather; Apr–May for the Fête des Masques.

Doorway to the End of the World

Timbuktu

Mali

Settled by Tuaregs—the nomadic Berbers known as the "Blue Men of the Sahara"—sometime in the 11th or 12th century, Timbuktu bears one of those fabled names that conjures up a far-off corner of the world that is impossible to reach, a *cité mystérieuse et mystique*, as the French called it. It thrived in the 13th century as a key location just north of the Niger River on the ancient trans-Saharan caravan routes, which transported ivory gold, salt, and slaves. It was known in Europe for its material and intellectual wealth and for its dissemination of Islam throughout Africa. In the 15th century as many as 25,000 scholars may have studied here. Many historical documents were hidden in chests and buried in the sand, and are now being unearthed. In 2009, Timbuktu opened a library dedicated to preserving this ancient town's treasure trove of books and manuscripts.

Tuaregs are called the "Blue Men of the Sahara."

Today the city, with a population of approximately 35,000, is little visited in spite of its great mosques—Djingareyber, Sankoré, and Sidi Yahia—built between the 14th and 16th centuries and still standing amid the city's adobe buildings and the desert's shifting sands. They evoke Mali's former glory as one of the most powerful nations in Africa, while much that surrounds them points to its current status as one of the world's poorest.

Nevertheless, the government has made an effort to attract more tourism, most notably with Le Festival au Désert, a 3-day world music festival and celebration of Tuareg culture that takes place in January in the oasis town of Essakane, about two hours north of Timbuktu. The event harks back to the annual gatherings the Blue Men of the Desert have hosted for centuries to settle disputes, race camels, exchange ideas about the issues of the day, and then show off their swordsmanship and play music. The range of music today goes beyond Tuareg tunes—you might catch anything from an impromptu reunion of the famed Malian group Super Rail Band de Bamako to a duet by Jimmy Buffett and Oumou Sangaré, the "songbird" of West African Wassoulou music.

Where: 625 miles/1,006 km northeast of Bamako. **How:** U.S.-based Wilderness Travel offers a 15-day tour of Mali that features Le Festival au Désert. Tel 800-368-2794 or 510-558-2488; www.wildernesstravel.com. *Cost:* from $5,995, all-inclusive. Originates in Bamako. **Le Festival au Désert:** www.festival-au-desert.org. *Cost:* admission $190. **Best time:** Nov–Jan for coolest weather.

EAST AFRICA AND SOUTHERN AFRICA

The Four Corners of Southern Africa

CHOBE NATIONAL PARK

Botswana

At Chobe National Park, in a corner of Africa that evokes the game-rich continent of old, four countries come together: Botswana, Zambia, Namibia, and Zimbabwe. The 4,200-square-mile park teems with all kinds of wildlife but is best known for its incredible birds and also for its huge elephant population—in the dry season, it holds Africa's highest concentration of them. Sunset boat rides along the Chobe River float you past herds of the creatures, along with yawning hippos, giant storks, and flocks of myriad waterfowl lining the banks. The floodplains are full of grazing buffalo and big game, while the skies and trees are dotted with raptors, including the lappet-faced vulture and the bright-beaked bateleur eagle.

Overnight boat tours of the park are now possible as well, thanks to the 2009 launch of the *Zambezi Queen*, a sleek, three-decked riverboat that docks in Kasane and ferries 28 passengers (in 14 roomy suites) up and down the river. The park is also a perfect day trip from Victoria Falls (see p. 435), but for maximum impact, stay at the Sanctuary Chobe Chilwero. Secluded and sitting high on a hill, its 15 luxurious, thatch-roofed bungalows, each with its own garden, afford the best lookout over the park and the river. (The name of the lodge translates to "riveting view.") Each has a spacious bathroom with a freestanding window-side tub. If those don't provide enough relaxation, the lodge's full-service spa is surely up to the task.

WHERE: Kasane Airport is 63 miles/100 km west of Livingstone, Zambia. **HOW:** U.S.-based Abercrombie & Kent offers scheduled safaris and customized itineraries that include Chobe. Tel 800-323-7308 or 630-725-3400; www.abercrombiekent.com. *Cost:* 12-day trip from $8,495. Originates in Johannesberg. *When:* Apr–May, Jul–Sep, and Nov. **ZAMBEZI QUEEN:** In South Africa, tel 27/21-438-0032; www.zambeziqueen.com. *Cost:* 2-night cruises from $925 (off-peak), from $1,275 (peak), all-inclusive. **CHOBE CHILWERO LODGE:** Tel 44/20-7190-7728; www.sanctuarylodges.com. *Cost:* $655 (off-peak), $995 (peak) per person, all-inclusive. **BEST TIME:** Jun–Sep for cooler, drier weather.

Land of the Bushmen

JACK'S CAMP

Kalahari Desert, Botswana

Ostrich Jack—hunter, explorer, bush hero—fell in love with the magic of this remote corner of Botswana in the 1960s, pitched camp, and never left. Today an old-fashioned, permanent safari camp run by Jack's son,

Ralph Bousfield, stands on the edge of the Makgadikgadi salt pans in the middle of the Kalahari, a desert bigger than the state of Texas. This is the home of the much romanticized San Bushmen (aka Basarwa), hunter-gatherers who anthropologists believe represent the most ancient race on earth. Ralph has inherited his father's passion for this moonlike landscape, and he and his partner, Catherine, arrange for such exhilarating activities as ATV treks across the pans, or sleeping under the star-studded black skies. You can join a traditional hunt with the Bushmen or simply accompany one on a walk as he points out the camp's wildlife and unique and delicate ecosystem, including the ever-present meerkats. Even for the jaded traveler, the light, silence, solitude, and sheer vastness of the space here guarantee a unique safari experience.

Gemsbok are a kind of antelope commonly found in the Kalahari Desert.

Jack's Camp has a double life. When the rains come, the salt pans—once the bed of a lake the size of Lake Victoria—sprout green and create an abundant water source for enormous flocks of flamingos. It becomes one of the last open migration routes in Africa and wildebeest and zebra arrive by the thousands, with lions, cheetahs, and hyenas fast on their heels. This is an unblemished, wild Africa evocative of other times. So are the ten classic 1940s canvas tents set up in a palm oasis and furnished with the iron beds and worn Persian carpets that once belonged to Ralph's grandparents. The outdoor showers—featuring the Southern Cross as your ceiling—clouds of mosquito netting, chambray sheets, and a silver tea service only enhance the irresistible romanticism.

If you want something more affordable, try the nearby, funky-but-stylish Planet Baobab, owned by the same people and community-run. Here they eschew colonial trappings and offer comfortable, contemporary versions of the locals' grass-and-mud huts. Guests gather at the colorful, open-sided bar, lounge on cowhide-covered chairs (under a surprisingly beautiful chandelier made from empty green beer bottles), sip a local brew, and exchange adventures of the day.

WHERE: 124 miles/200 km southeast of Maun. **HOW:** Uncharted Africa books trips to both Jack's Camp and Planet Baobab. Tel 267/241-2277; www.unchartedafrica.com. *Cost:* Jack's Camp from $1,020 (off-peak), from $1,275 (peak) per person, all-inclusive. Planet Baobab from $165 for double huts. **BEST TIMES:** Apr–Oct for dry weather; Nov–Mar for wildebeest and zebra migration in the wet season.

Big-Game Hunting—for Lions Only

NEW SELINDA RESERVE

Botswana

Lions, large herds of elephants, and packs of wild dogs are just part of what distinguishes the Selinda Reserve, a 320,000-acre private wildlife sanctuary in northern Botswana that links the outer reaches of the

Okavango Delta (see below) in the west with the Linyanti marshes in the east. There's much more that makes this place spectacular, however, and the husband-and-wife team of Dereck and Beverly Joubert have captured nearly all of it over the past 25 years in their award-winning National Geographic documentaries. But it's only since 2007 that the two have truly been able to share this gem with the outside world. That's when they and a small group of equally passionate conservationist friends purchased the Selinda Reserve, in the northeast corner of the park, with an eye to ecotourism. After imposing a moratorium on hunting, they rebuilt the camps, keeping them small and intimate. Today, Selinda Camp's nine canvas tents have attractive wooden floors and verandas, and each is appointed with deep stone baths and beds that encourage siestas. You'll see more elephants than you will other guests. Located to the south and powered entirely by solar energy, Zafara Camp ("the beloved one") is even smaller, with just four open-air tents. But what grand tents they are. Each measures 1,000 square feet, and includes an outdoor shower, private plunge pool, leather sofas, and its own bar.

While the fondness of Selinda's lions for hunting large animals is legendary, this is also a place to glimpse spotted predators—cheetahs on the open plains and leopards in the dense woodlands. Or you can track elephants, hippos, and giraffes; quietly observe packs of wild dogs; or wait in a secret hide to see what comes along—perhaps the rare slaty egrets and wattled cranes coming to fish, or a herd of buffalo in search of a drink. Lodge guests may also follow the trails through riparian forests and open plains, arriving at a remote clearing to find that an overnight bush camp has been set up for them and dinner awaits under the stars.

WHERE: In northern Botswana, 30 minutes by air charter from Maun. **SELINDA** and **ZAFARA:** www.greatplainsconservation.com. *Cost:* Selinda from $650 per person, all-inclusive (off-peak), from $995 (peak); Zafara from $1,095 per person, all-inclusive (off-peak), from $1,630 (peak). **HOW:** U.S.-based The Wild Source provides customized itineraries featuring Selinda. Tel 720-497-1250; www.thewildsource.com. **BEST TIME:** Jul–Sep when weather is drier and game is most abundant.

An Incomparable Wildlife Oasis

OKAVANGO DELTA

Botswana

The inland delta where the Okavango River meets the Kalahari Desert has been called the world's largest oasis. The Okavango, a tributary of the mighty Zambezi, creates a unique "water in the desert" ecosystem the size of Switzerland, forming floodplains, lagoons, channels, and islands that all act as a magnet for wildlife. As a local brochure puts it, "If you see 10 percent of what sees you, it's an exceptional day." The birdlife is second to none, and there are legions of elephants, zebras, buffaloes, giraffes, and hippos. As you glide through a labyrinth of papyrus-fringed, lily-covered waterways in the traditional *mokoro* dugout canoe or explore islands and islets on foot, you're immersed in a lush environment of otherworldly colors and sounds. Climb atop an elephant for an even better view of the wildlife. At Wilderness Safari's Abu Camp, consisting of six canvas tents on elevated wooden decks, the stars are a motley crew of elephants that owner Randall Moore adopted from zoos. The smell from these sure-footed beasts masks your own, so the mahout (trainer) who straddles the neck of your mount can approach animals that would normally run from humans.

Mokoro *dugout canoes carry travelers through the endless waterways of the Okavango Delta.*

The camp is one of several excellent private safari concessions that surround the Okavango Delta's Moremi Wildlife Reserve. Also owned by Wilderness Safari is Mombo Camps, a group of perched, tented suites on Chief's Island, in the northeast, and the spare and beautiful, wood-decked Vumbura Plains Camps overlooking a waterhole on the edge of a large floodplain in the extreme north. Or you can choose to stay at either Xudum or Xaranna, two new properties opened by the luxury travel firm &Beyond in the southern part of the delta. There's nothing rough about these camps' huge billowing tents, contemporary lines, indoor-outdoor showers, and, in some cases, private plunge pools.

WHERE: 62 miles/100 km north of Maun; 30 minutes by scheduled air charter. **ABU, MOMBO, AND VUMBURA CAMPS:** www.wilderness-safaris.com. *Cost:* Abu from $2,625, Mombo $1,570 (off-peak) and $1,995 (peak), Vumbura $1,095 (off-peak) and $1,630 (peak), all per person, all-inclusive. *How:* U.S.-based Natural Migrations offers customized safari itineraries, including to the Wilderness Safaris camps. Tel 866-988-7575 or 541-988-7575; www.naturalmigrations.com. **XUDUM** and **XARANNA:** Contact &Beyond in South Africa, tel 27/11-809-4314; in the U.S., 888-882-3742; www.andbeyondafrica.com. *Cost:* from $600 (off-peak), from $1,500 (peak) per person per night, all-inclusive. **BEST TIME:** May–Sep for coolest, driest weather.

Palaces, Castles, and Churches in an Ancient Capital

GONDER

Amhara Region, Ethiopia

Strategically positioned at the foothills of the Simien Mountains, one of the highest ranges in Africa, the fortress city of Gonder became in the 17th century the first capital of the Ethiopian empire, under Emperor Fasilides.

The city flourished for more than 200 years, thanks to its location at the meeting point of three caravan routes, until Emperor Tewodros II (aka Theodore) relocated the capital to Magdala, a mountain stronghold that fell to the British less than 13 years later.

Surrounded by towering stone walls and filled with juniper and wild olive trees, the Royal Enclosure lies at the heart of Gonder and contains the country's most important imperial buildings. The oldest of the five castles is attributed to Fasilides; the most recent dates to the mid-18th century. But Gonder was also the empire's religious center. The city's rulers claimed biblical lineage, tracing their roots to King Solomon and the Queen of Sheba, and many of the buildings they erected were dedicated to Orthodox Christianity. Of the dozens of churches that once stood here, seven were built during Fasilides's reign. The most important one that remains today is Debre Birhan Selassie (Trinity at the Mountain of Light), famous for its walls covered with biblical scenes and its 17th-century ceiling fresco of 80 cherubic faces. Hindu and Arab influences are seen throughout, blended with the Baroque style brought to Gonder by the Jesuit missionaries in the 16th and 17th centuries.

WHERE: 471 miles/758 km north of Addis Ababa. **HOW:** Addis Ababa–based Ethiopian Quadrants includes Gonder in many itineraries. Tel 251/11-515-7990; www.ethiopianquadrants.com. *Cost:* 7-day trips from $1,250, all-inclusive. Originate in Addis Ababa. U.S.-based Safari Experts offers customized trips in Ethiopia. Tel 435-649-4655; www.safariexperts.com. *When:* Oct–May. **BEST TIMES:** Sep–Nov for nicest weather; Jan 7 for Ethiopian Christmas; Jan 19 for Timkat (Epiphany).

The Mystery of the Subterranean, Rock-Hewn Churches

LALIBELA

Amhara Region, Ethiopia

The subterranean rock-hewn churches of Lalibela are Ethiopia's most popular—and mysterious—attraction. They have been in continuous use by Orthodox priests since the 12th century, when this remote mountain town was the capital of the Zagwe dynasty. Lalibela, a Zagwe king, commissioned the one called Beta Golgotha, the first of the extraordinary structures to be built and his burial place. Lalibela wanted his church to be made from a single piece of stone, and so it and subsequent ones were excavated rather than erected, some carved 30 to 40 feet below the surface. Their roofs are at ground level, and stairs lead down to the entrances. Some have interconnecting courtyards and trenches that form tunnels and passages between them.

St. George's church and Lalibela remain an important pilgrimage site for members of the Ethiopian Orthodox church.

Each of the 11 churches is unique in size, shape, and execution, precisely and painstakingly carved out of solid bedrock, some say by tens of thousands of workers. Unique for the technical expertise used in their construction, they are also remarkable for their refinement and are decorated with handwoven rugs, colorful paintings, carvings depicting saints and Christian symbols, and cross-shaped windows. The oft-photographed flat roof of St. George's church (Beta Giyorgis) is carved with concentric Greek crosses.

One legend has it that at least one of the churches was built by angels in a single day; another holds that the churches came to the Zagwe king in a dream about creating a new Jerusalem for those unable to make the pilgrimage to the Holy Land. The real reasons for building the churches, as well as the secrets of how, exactly, it was done, remain a mystery.

They are as treasured in Ethiopia as the Great Pyramids are in Egypt (see p. 378) and even today are a place of pilgrimage and devotion; on holy days, this dusty rural town is taken over by tens of thousands of worshippers.

Small and undeveloped, the town of Lalibela is set amid craggy, dramatic escarpments more than 8,000 feet high and looks down on the famed churches below. It is distinguished by a lively market and a collection of round, two-storied homes made of mud bricks and roofed with thatch.

WHERE: 454 miles/730 km north of Addis Ababa. **HOW:** U.S.-based Adventures in Africa has scheduled tours featuring Lalibela. Tel 866-778-1089 or 303-778-1089; www.adventuresinafrica.com. *Cost:* 12-day tour from $3,325. U.S.-based Safari Experts offers customized itineraries in Ethiopia. Tel 435-649-4655; www.safariexperts.com. **BEST TIMES:** Sep–Nov for pleasant weather; Jan 7 for Ethiopian Christmas; Jan 19 for Epiphany; Apr or May for Fasika (Easter), corresponding to the Gregorian calendar.

Disappearing Tribes

OMO RIVER VALLEY

Ethiopia

A trip to the South Omo River Valley, much of it accessible only by boat, takes you back thousands of years through a kaleidoscope of vanishing, nomadic cultures. Because Ethiopia is the only African nation never to have been colonized by Europeans, the tribes here have remained nearly intact. The few thousand people who live in these green hills have preserved their culture to a remarkable degree, even as their numbers dwindle. Those who come to glimpse their distinct way of life before it disappears make one of a few tented camps or basic lodges their base, hiring guides to take them on trips to the communities nearby.

Not far from some of the camps is the bankside home of the Muguji (aka Kwegu), a tribe of just a few hundred fishermen, hippo hunters, and gatherers. They coexist in a harsh land with the larger Karo tribe, agriculturists who prepare for ceremonial dances by painting their faces and decorating their bodies with charcoal, chalk, and other minerals.

Farther upriver, you'll find the remote Mursi and Suri tribes, whose women wear huge lip plates and whose men engage in ritualistic stick duels in order to determine who can marry. Even more intriguing is the rite of passage undertaken by young men in the nearby Hamar tribe. To prove their worth as initiated men, they must perform *bullah,* a challenging feat that is essentially a game of hopscotch across the backs of dozens of castrated bulls. Falling is the most shameful failure; success results in acquiring a bride. The Hamar women, among the most adorned in Africa (their decorative scars are a symbol of strength), roll their hair in animal fat and red ochre and wear metal ornaments to indicate marital status.

The Omo River ends at Lake Turkana, which lies primarily in Kenya, though its northern shores are in Ethiopia. It is here that you will find the Dassanech and the Nyangatom; the latter are warriors and hunters who harpoon crocodiles from dugout canoes and wear ostrich feathers in their hair, caked with blue and ochre clay, to indicate bravery. Elders are distinguished by their lower lip plug—ivory for men, copper for women. Their culture stretches back to a time lost to the rest of humanity, revealed only to those lucky enough to travel here and discover their hidden world.

WHERE: The riverside town of Omurate is 457 miles/736 km southwest of Addis Ababa and is accessible via private air charter. **HOW:** U.S.-based Africa Adventure Company offers a 10-day Omo River safari. Tel 800-882-9453 or 954-491-8877; www.africa-adventure.com. *Cost:* from $7,995. Originates in Nairobi. *When:* Jul. **BEST TIME:** Jul–Oct for nicest weather.

A Trek Over the Roof of Africa

SIMIEN MOUNTAINS NATIONAL PARK

Ethiopia

The Simien Mountains, known as the "Roof of Africa," offer some of the continent's most dramatic scenery: great volcanic plugs, formed 40 million years ago and eroded over the eons into fantastic crags, pinnacles, and flat-topped peaks stretching from Ethiopia's northern highlands to Eritrea. Simien Mountains National Park was established in 1969 to protect the land and wildlife, but the task is not an easy one. Development of farming villages in the park has hindered conservation efforts and placed the region on UNESCO's list of World Heritage Sites in Danger.

Human settlement poses a threat to the rare species that are endemic to the Simien Mountains region.

The park has just one dirt road and sees relatively few international visitors, so exploring by foot offers a rare experience. An organized trek employs the services of a guide, a mandatory armed scout, and mules that carry food and camping supplies. The journey starts out following trails through terraced fields used by locals to walk from village to village. It continues past tree heather, giant lobelias, and other unique flora, stopping at campsites every night. This is the only place in the world to see many animal species, including the endangered walia ibex and troops of gelada, commonly known as the bleeding-heart baboon for the red patch on its chest. The entertaining gelada is the last surviving species of grazing monkey in the world and has more types of vocalization and behavior patterns than any animal but humans. Keep your eyes peeled too, for raptors, including lammergeiers (bearded vulture-eagles, with 9-foot wingspans), Auger buzzards, Verreaux's eagles, kestrels, and falcons.

An optional ascent to Africa's fourth highest peak, Ras Dashen (15,158 feet), takes about 9 hours. It's not a technical climb; the only equipment required is a pair of strong legs. For those not fond of camping, the new, basic-but-comfortable, eco-friendly Simien Lodge ("the highest hotel in Africa") has a

16-bed dormitory, along with 20 rooms that resemble traditional Ethiopian thatch-roofed *tukuls* on the outside and modest hotel rooms on the inside. The lodge can be used as a base for both trekking and biking. Guests will appreciate its hearty meals and radiant heating on chilly mountain nights.

Where: Trek begins in Debark 75 miles/120 km from Gonder. **How:** Ethiopian Quadrants organizes treks of various lengths. Tel 251/11-515-7990; www.ethiopianquadrants.com. *Cost:* from $100 per night, all-inclusive. Originates in Addis Ababa. **Simien Lodge:** Tel 251/11-55-24758; www.simiens.com. *Cost:* from $155; transfer from Gonder $135. **Best time:** Sep–Apr to avoid the rainy season.

In the Shadow of Mount Kenya

Private Wildlife Reserves

Isiolo, Central Highlands, Kenya

In the foothills of Mount Kenya, on the edge of the Laikipia Plateau, a few fortunate guests can revel in spellbinding views of ridge after mountain ridge and enjoy the freedom to see wild game—great herds of everything from elephants and giraffes to zebras and antelopes—on vast private properties. Borana Lodge and Lewa Wilderness, neighboring cattle ranches comprising more than 100,000 acres in northern Kenya, offer game drives led by top-notch trackers and guides. You'll rarely see another vehicle on these safaris, an almost unheard-of luxury in East Africa's comparatively crowded national parks. Both offer horseback expeditions that allow for close wildlife encounters, as well as exhilarating nighttime game drives to spot predators and shy nocturnal creatures.

The lodges are small—eight cottages at Borana and nine hill and garden rooms at Lewa—but offer an intimate experience and personal service. Both are family affairs, passed down over generations. The Dyers at Borana and the Craigs at Lewa have been living on the land for nearly a century. Borana became the first eco-lodge in the region more than 20 years ago. Earlier, the Craigs had converted a parcel of their 60,000-acre ranch, along with some adjacent government land, into the Ngare Sergoi Rhino Sanctuary, now called Lewa Wildlife Conservancy. Fifty-eight black rhinos and 42 white rhinos are now protected from poachers by walkie-talkie–armed guards, who prowl the sanctuary, where guests at Borana are also welcome. While many African lodges discourage the presence of children, the Dyers and Craigs are happy to share their families' experiences with yours. They have perfected the art of entertaining kids of all ages while simultaneously providing quiet, romantic settings fit for a king—or at least a prince. It was at Lewa that Prince William asked Kate Middleton to marry him.

Where: 150 miles/241 km north of Nairobi. **Borana Lodge:** Tel 254/2-567-251; www.borana.co.ke. *Cost:* from $560 (off-peak), from $640 (peak) per person, all-inclusive. *How:* Nairobi-based Safari and Conservation Company. Tel 254/20-211-5453; www.thesafariandconservationcompany.com. **Lewa Wilderness:** Tel 254/721-970-340; www.lewawilderness.com. *Cost:* $510 (off-peak), $740 (peak) per person, all-inclusive. *How:* Book through Nairobi-based Bush and Beyond. Tel 254/20-600-0457; www.bush-and-beyond.com. **Best times:** mid-Jul–Oct and mid-Dec–Mar to avoid the rainy season.

A Corner of Kenya's Vanishing Wilderness

OL DONYO WUAS

Chyulu Hills, Kenya

Ol Donyo Wuas sits at the foot of the dramatic Chyulu Hills amid a quarter of a million acres on the open plains of Masai land. One of East Africa's most beloved bush lodges, it is a partnership between local tribes and an old safari hand named Richard Bonham, who first touched down here in a Cessna in the 1980s. When he saw the rolling, wooded grassland and the snow-capped peak of Mount Kilimanjaro (see p. 425) looming across the Tanzanian border, he knew he needed to stay awhile and built Ol Donyo Wuas, whose name means "Spotted Hills" in the local Masai language.

Amboseli National Park, with its cavalcade of minibuses and Land Rovers, is a mere 50 miles away, but it might as well be on the other side of Kenya. Guests at Ol Donyo Wuas are granted exclusive access to the Mbirikani Group Ranch, one of Kenya's few remaining wilderness areas that harken back to the Africa of old, where you'll never encounter a traffic jam of safari jeeps. Rebuilt in 2008, the lodge itself is perched high on a ridge (the Chyulu Hills are really volcanic mountains), and its two stand-alone suites and seven villas have uninterrupted views of Mount Kilimanjaro. The villas all have private pools, and every room has two beds to choose from: an indoor one and a romantic rooftop "star-bed" where guests can opt to sleep with the constellations as their ceiling. When he's not occupied by his work with the Maasailand Preservation Trust, the organization that protects the ranch and its inhabitants, Richard Bonham may pop in to lead a game drive, bushwalk, or horseback ride. Hear him share his years of wisdom as you set out into the vast land where young Masai herders and their cattle live among giraffes, cheetahs, and the Big Five (the lion, African elephant, Cape Buffalo, leopard, and rhinoceros).

WHERE: 135 miles/218 km southeast of Nairobi; www.oldonyowuas.com. **COST:** from $500 (off-peak), from $720 (peak) per person, all-inclusive. **HOW:** Nairobi-based Bush and Beyond organize trips to the lodge. Tel 254/20-600-0457; www.bush-and-beyond.com. **BEST TIMES:** Jul–Sep and Dec–Jan to avoid the rainy seasons.

Seat of the Gods

CLIMBING MOUNT KENYA

Kenya

Africa's second highest peak rises 17,058 feet above the equator, its ragged, snow-dusted summits looking down on glacier-sculpted valleys and alpine moorland. Mount Kenya, a former volcano, is graced with more than 20 clear mountain lakes and trout-filled streams. Elephants, buffaloes, and the rare striped antelopes known as mountain bongos roam its lower slopes, where moss-covered cedars and giant lobelias vie for space amid the ferns, wildflowers, and orchids. Small wonder it is considered sacred by the local Kikuyu, Kenya's most populous tribe: They build their homes so the doors face the mountain, believed to be the home of the god Ngai.

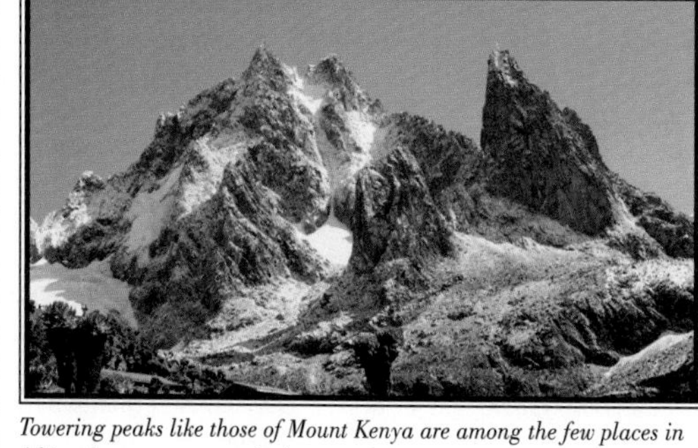

Towering peaks like those of Mount Kenya are among the few places in Africa that see snow regularly.

Although the highest peaks are reserved for experienced climbers, Point Lenana, a 16,000-foot peak, is open to serious trekkers, who can complete a guided ascent in four or five nights. This is considered the hidden gem of East Africa treks—you won't see the legions of climbers who flock each year to the slopes of Kilimanjaro (see p. 425), whose summit is sometimes visible 200 miles away. Accommodations are in mountain tents that porters set up in spectacular valleys with views of the peaks and down across the vast central Laikipia Plateau district.

Start and end your trek at Ol Pejeta Bush Camp, a traditional riverside tented camp that allows an insider's view of a modern, 94,000-acre private wildlife conservancy with the highest game-to-area ratio of any park or reserve in Kenya. It's a 1- to 2-hour drive from the point of ascent. Once here, you'll have the chance to visit the conservancy's chimpanzee sanctuary, meet its tame black rhino, Baraka, and maybe even see the four northern white rhino, which constitute half the population of the world's rarest large mammal.

WHERE: Mount Kenya is 100 miles/161 km north of Nairobi. **HOW:** Nairobi-based Insiders Africa offers guided climbs and accommodations at Ol Pejeta. Tel 254/734-445-283; www.insidersafrica.com. *Cost:* 7 nights, including 4-night ascent, from $2,800. *When:* Ol Pejeta closed Apr–May and Nov. **BEST TIMES:** Jan–mid-Mar and Aug–mid-Oct for pleasant weather.

Locked in Time on the Swahili Coast

ISLAND OF LAMU

Kenya

Not quite undiscovered, but still relatively unspoiled, the tiny island of Lamu is where you'll find Kenya's oldest living city and a fascinating glimpse of the country's ancient Swahili and Islamic cultures. There are just a handful of cars on Lamu—its streets are generally too narrow to accommodate any conveyance bigger than a donkey. And though it lies just one mile off the mainland, in the Indian Ocean, it is more reminiscent of the Middle East than it is of Africa.

Like Mombasa and Malindi farther south, Lamu is one of a string of Swahili port towns founded by Arab traders who dealt in ivory, spices, and slaves; it is the oldest and the best preserved. Men wear full-length white robes and caps, veiled women are clothed in black, and travel is by the traditional wooden sailing vessels called dhows. You can rent one (be sure to negotiate) for a romantic day trip around the Lamu archipelago, with a lunch of grilled fresh fish prepared on board. If you stay in Lamu town, choose among one of the old merchants' homes converted into boutique hotels. At Baytil Ajaib ("House of Wonder"), a painstakingly restored 17th-century town house, all four suites have two views: into a palm-filled courtyard and into the bustling city.

Most of the hippies who arrived on the island in the '70s have gone, replaced by younger European backpackers and a growing mix of the curious and the beautiful, along with a tight-knit group of return visitors. The latter stay at any of the dozens of private homes for rent or check into the Peponi Hotel, located on a 12-mile strip of virgin beach in Shela, a 20-minute walk or a dhow ride north of Lamu town. Full of international eccentrics, villagers, and Nairobi expats, the hotel's restaurant and bar—the island's social nerve center since 1967—hum with life and color. On Lamu's sister island, Manda, the exclusive, 16-cottage Manda Bay Resort caters to guests who fish justly famed Manda Bay for its marlins, tunas, and other sport fish.

Dhows, with their classic triangular sails, navigate the Indian Ocean.

Back on Lamu, kick off your shoes at the Kizingo resort on the other end of bone-white Lamu Beach. Sedate and rustic, its eight spacious *bandas,* or cottages, are constructed from palm, bamboo, and other local materials and provide cool respite from the African sun.

WHERE: 255 miles/410 km east of Nairobi. **HOW:** Nairobi-based Safari Company creates custom itineraries featuring Lamu. Tel 254/723-914094; www.thesafarico.ltd.com. **BAYTIL AJAIB:** Tel 254/121-32033; www.baytilajaib.com. *Cost:* from $195. **PEPONI HOTEL:** Tel 254/20-802-3655; www.peponi-lamu.com. *Cost:* from $275. **MANDA BAY RESORT:** Tel 254/20-600-6769; www.mandabay.com. *Cost:* from $860 (off-peak), from $1,270 (peak), inclusive. **KIZINGO:** Tel 254/733-954-770; www.kizingo.com. *Cost:* from $390, inclusive. **BEST TIMES:** Dec–Mar for hot and dry weather, good sport fishing, and snorkeling; in Lamu Town, May–Jun for Maulidi Festival celebrating the birth of Mohammed.

The World's Greatest Animal Migration

THE MASAI MARA

Kenya

The Masai Mara is nature's stage for the most spectacular wildlife pageant on earth. Every May, hundreds of thousands of wildebeests mass in Tanzania's Serengeti (Masai for "endless plains"; see p. 429), moving north in search

Always in search of food and water, blue wildebeests take part in the largest moving animal migration anywhere in the world.

of sustenance to the wide-open grasslands of Kenya's Masai Mara, where they arrive in July and August. The wildebeests, as well as migrating herds of zebras, antelopes, and gazelles, make up the more than one million animals on the move in the 583-square-mile game reserve. The Mara is also one of the best places for seeing all the big cats.

You can find yourself in the middle of the action via four-wheel drive or above it all in a hot-air balloon. Stay at one of four tented camps owned by Governors' Camp Collection in the northwestern corner of the reserve, a legendary spot on the Mara River. The group is made up of Main Governors', located on what is reputed to have been one of Teddy Roosevelt's favorite campsites; Little Governors', which offers a more intimate setting next to an active watering hole; the luxurious Il Moran; and the exclusive Governors' Private Camp (bookable only by a family or group of 16 or fewer). For another perspective, the seasonal Rekero Camp has eight tents in the heart of the reserve along the Talek River near the confluence of the Mara. Or try Richard's Camp, just north of the reserve. Its six private tents sit within riverine forest in a less-trafficked conservation area.

A horseback safari takes you out of the reserve and toward the forested Loita Hills. You'll pass the dung-walled huts that make up the *manyattas* (villages) of the Masai, perhaps Africa's most famous tribe. Often clad in their distinctive red *shukas* (plaid fabric derived from Scottish tartan kilts) and rubber sandals fashioned from tire treads, these herders view the migrating game as "God's cattle," and they protect them as such.

WHERE: About 150 miles/241 km southwest of Nairobi. **HOW:** U.S.-based Micato Safaris offers customized safaris that can incorporate a variety of luxury camps in the Mara. Tel 800-642-2861 or 212-545-7111; www.micato.com. **GOVERNORS' CAMP COLLECTION:** Tel 254/20-273-4000; www.governorscamp.com. *Cost:* from $250 per person, all-inclusive (off-peak), from $440 (peak); balloon trips from $450 per person. *When:* closed Apr–May. **REKERO:** Contact Asilia Africa in Cape Town, South Africa, tel 27/21-418-0468; www.asiliaafrica.com. *Cost:* from $510 per person, all-inclusive (off-peak), from $730 (peak). *When:* closed Apr–May and Nov. **RICHARD'S CAMP:** Contact the Nairobi-based Safari and Conservation Company, tel 254/20-211-5453; www.thesafariandconservationcompany.com. *Cost:* from $610 per person, all-inclusive (off-peak), from $700 (peak). *When:* closed May and Nov. **RIDING TOURS:** U.S.-based Equitour hosts horseback safaris outside the reserve. Tel 800-545-0019 or 307-455-3363; www.ridingtours.com. *Cost:* 7-nights from $5,435 all-inclusive; with air transfer from Nairobi. *When:* year-round except for May and Nov. **BEST TIMES:** May–Oct for cooler weather; Jul–Sep for best chance at seeing the migration.

God's Aquarium

Lake Malawi

Malawi

Famed explorer David Livingstone called Lake Malawi the Lake of Stars; the Malawians call it Lake Malawi; and Tanzanians and Mozambicans (who share its border) call it Lake Nyasa. It also has a nickname: the Calendar Lake. It's 365 miles long and 52 miles wide, making it the third largest lake in Africa, not to mention the second deepest (at 2,300 feet). The clear, warm water teems with more species of tropical fish than any other lake on earth, including over 800 species of neon-colored, freshwater cichlid fish, some of which you may recognize from pet store tanks and the majority of them endemic to the lake.

On the eastern shore, overlooking the mountains of Mozambique, lies the beautiful, blissfully remote Likoma Island. Just 10 square miles, the island is home to approximately 9,000 people, a handful of cars, a few ATVs and motorcycles, a forest reserve, and an Anglican church built in 1903 to rival in size England's colossal Winchester Cathedral. The island is also known for its hospitality. In a nation that many refer to as the "warm heart of Africa," these are among the friendliest people you'll meet, ready to teach you to snorkel and sail or to guide you to nearby villages, markets, and local community projects. You'll be greeted with the same warmth at a gemlike resort on the island's southern end called Kaya Mawa (Maybe Tomorrow). Its ten romantic waterfront cottages are built from local materials in the traditional style, and its 11 rooms and guesthouses are named after nearby fishing villages. South of Likoma, on the western shores of the Nankumba Peninsula, is the casually luxurious Pumulani (Place of Rest), with ten exquisitely designed villas spread along a verdant hillside overlooking the crystal-clear waters of the lake and a white sandy beach. Come here for relaxation. The Pumulani is commonly used as a postsafari destination for kaleidoscopic dives and lazy sunset dhow cruises, but many visitors are content simply to relax on their hillside decks and reflect on their African adventures.

The lake is famous for its hundreds of varieties of brightly colored cichlids, many of which are found only here.

Where: Pumulani is 144 miles/232 km east of Lilongwe. **Kaya Mawa:** Tel 265/9993-18360; www.kayamawa.com. *Cost:* from $335 (off-peak), from $375 (peak) per person, all-inclusive. **Pumulani:** Tel 265/177-0540/60; www.pumulani.com or www.robinpopesafaris.net. *Cost:* from $340 (off-peak), from $450 (peak) per person, all-inclusive. **Best time:** Jun–Oct for nicest weather.

Azure Waters and White Beaches

Archipelagos of Mozambique

Mozambique

Unspoiled, uncrowded specks of land with china-white beaches of sand so fine it squeaks and turquoise waters dotted with some of the world's most pristine unbleached reefs—this is the magic of Mozambique.

After two decades of war and instability, the mainland is still struggling to restore its image as a safe place to experience the safari days of old. But spectacular lodges have been appearing in the northern Quirimbas Archipelago (32 undeveloped coral islands) and the five more-accessible islands of the southern Bazaruto Archipelago. They lend the surroundings a seductive ambience that's part tropics and part Mediterranean, with a whiff of the country's days as a Portuguese colony.

The waters surrounding tiny Pansy Island and Bazaruto Island are perfect for diving and fishing.

Both Quirimbas and Bazaruto offer a marvelous variety of marine beauty, and the snorkeling and diving are spectacular. Shallow reefs protect schools of brightly colored fish, including moorish idols and lionfish; sharks, rays, and turtles find safe harbor among reefs farther out; and deep channels serve as a playground for whales, whale sharks, dolphins, and dugongs (pale, voluptuous rare sea mammals that are related to the manatee and fabled to have made bygone mariners believe in mermaids). Both archipelagos also boast some of the world's most diverse flora and fauna, with samango monkeys, nesting turtles, and over 100 species of tropical birds.

Protecting all this is the mission of the Maluane Project, which recently opened Vamizi Island Lodge in the Quirimbas. Each of its 13 exceedingly private, open-air villas of wood, wicker, and thatch features its own secluded stretch of perfect beach backed by dense bush. Dive, kayak, or lounge the day away, and dine on fresh seafood under tiki torches at night.

Benguerra Island, a national park and the second largest island in the Bazaruto Archipelago, is home to the Benguerra Lodge, set in a thick, shady forest and featuring two beachside cabanas and ten larger casitas. In addition to dives, you can enjoy leisurely dhow cruises, nature hikes, and visits to villages. Also located on the 21-square-mile island is the newer, eco-vigilant Azura, the most elegant lodging in the archipelago. Amenities include a private infinity swimming pool for each of its 15 villas, which resemble modern boutique hotel suites fused with traditional Mozambican design: The structures have old-style thatch roofs but are missing a wall, the better to let in cool ocean breezes.

Where: Quirimbas Archipelago is 300 miles/500 km southeast of Dar es Salaam, Tanzania. Benguerra Island is 454 miles/730 km northeast of Maputo. **How:** U.K.-based Bushbuck Safaris offers customized trips. Tel 44/1669-630386; www.bushbucksafaris.com. *Cost:* from $400 per person, per night. **Vamizi Island Lodge:** Tel in the U.K. 44/1285-762218; www.vamizi.com. *Cost:* from $590 per person, all-inclusive (off-peak), from $890 (peak). **Benguerra Lodge:** Tel 27/11-452-0641; www.benguerra.co.za. *Cost:* from $430 per person, inclusive (off-peak), from $525 (peak). **Azura:** Tel 27/767-050599; www.azura-retreats.com. *Cost:* from $525 per person, inclusive (off-peak), from $750 (peak). **Best times:** Beautiful year-round but especially in Apr–Oct; Jul–Sep for humpback whales; Sep–Oct for exceptional diving.

Southern Africa's Big Wild

Etosha National Park

Namibia

Despite its harsh climate, Namibia has some of the world's most compelling scenery, with diverse and plentiful wildlife that has adapted to the rigors of the desertlike conditions. Etosha National Park, in the north, a semiarid savanna grassland ten times the size of Luxembourg, is the third largest game reserve in the world and the country's premier national park. Etosha roughly translates as "great white place" or "land of dry water," a reference to the Etosha Pan, the vast, shimmering salt pan in the heart of the park, where the variety and profusion of creatures found at the spring-fed water holes at any one time—including some of the 144 species of mammals and well over 300 species of birds who live here—make for a veritable arkful. You may see great numbers of elephants, zebras, giraffes, blue wildebeests, and springboks. The endangered black rhino, leopards, and cheetah also inhabit the park. And for a few days every year after the rains, when the pan fills with water, flamingos and pelicans descend by the tens of thousands.

The giraffes found in Etosha may constitute their own subspecies.

Of the number of comfortable lodges nearby, only four are located within the park, and all are operated by Namibia Wildlife Resorts. The newest is the luxurious Onkoshi Camp, offering superb vistas from its 15 chalets over the Etosha Pan. In the mornings and evenings, guests can take guided drives and walks within the northeastern sand veldt area and on the pan; then, once the sun sets, there is unbeatable stargazing and the unusual opportunity for a night game drive. The government only recently began to allow night game-watching drives within park grounds, and Namibia Wildlife Resorts offers them exclusively here.

Where: Andersson's Gate entrance is 262 miles/421 km north of Windhoek, the capital city. **How:** U.S.-based Africa Adventure Co. offers a 7-day "Best of Namibia" flying safari. Tel 800-882-9453 or 954-491-8877; www.africa-adventure.com. *Cost:* from $3,950 (off-peak), $4,750 (peak) all-inclusive. Originates in Windhoek. **Namibia Wildlife Resorts:** Tel 264/61-285-7200; www.nwr.com.na. *Cost:* Onkoshi Camp from $600 per person, all-inclusive. **Best times:** Jun–Oct for dry, mild weather and optimum game viewing; pans flood in Jan–Mar.

Haunting Beauty and Unconfined Space

Skeleton Coast

Namibia

When the world is too much with you, this is the safari to consider—not to view game (which is a bonus) but to experience the strange solitude of one of the world's most unusual and scenic areas.

Namibia's Skeleton Coast is a little-explored desert paradise of wide-open spaces—undeveloped, unpeopled, and far from civilization. Its name refers to the treacherous, barren shoreline, where shipwrecks and whale bones litter the fog-shrouded beaches. The area's Cape Cross Seal Reserve is a breeding ground for tens of thousands of Cape fur seals; they lounge on the rocks and sand, and their blue-eyed pups arrive in late November or early December. Light aircraft is the only way to visit much of this desolate land, which at times resembles a vast sea—of shifting sand dunes, twisted veins of schist, and shelves of granite—and is inhabited only by the occasional herd of springbok or a massive flock of brilliant pink flamingos. You may even spot a rare desert elephant.

The Skeleton Coast includes the entire Namibian coastline and continues north to the Kunene River, about 100 miles inside Angola. It stretches approximately 1,000 miles in total, with nearly 75 percent protected within parks and reserves. A small Cessna plane will be your safari vehicle should you choose to travel with the Schoeman brothers, natural-born pilots and teachers who inherited Skeleton Coast Safaris from their father, one of the pioneers of ecotourism in the region. Flying nearly at sea or dune level, you'll land wherever the fog allows, then continue by four-wheel drive, boat, or your own two feet to see geologic formations, wildlife, or ancient Bushman paintings little known to the outside world.

Skeleton Coast Safaris: Tel 264/61-224-248; www.skeletoncoastsafaris.com. *Cost:* 4-day safaris $5,995, all-inclusive, with accommodation in tented desert camps. Originates in Windhoek. **Best time:** Jun–Oct is mildest and the ideal choice if you want to pair your trip with a Namibian safari.

Waves of Sand and a Sea of Stars

Sossusvlei Dunes and NamibRand Private Reserve

Namibia

The Namib Desert, from which Namibia takes its name, is known for its apricot-red Sossusvlei Dunes. Shaped and driven like waves by the sea winds, at 1,000 feet these dunes are some of the highest in the world.

They are at their most magnificent at sunrise and sunset, when the colors and shadows shift like a living painting. Attempt to appreciate something of the scale and silence of this empty region by climbing them. After an hour of two steps up and one step back, the feeling of accomplishment is as awe-inspiring as the view of vivid blue skies and seemingly endless undulations of golden-orange sand. A wondrous spectacle appears during rare years of extreme rainfall, when the valleylike depression fills with water, reflecting a vast mirror image of the dunes and gnarled trees shimmering like a desert mirage.

Just south of the dunes is Sossusvlei Desert Lodge, whose ten villas are built of stone and glass. The lodge is located in the northern part of the 444,800-acre NamibRand Reserve, one of the largest private reserves in Africa. Spend the morning on a quad bike tour of the desert, stopping to check out the more elusive wildlife living in this 55-million-year-old ecosystem, including the long-nosed elephant shrew, the spotted leopard tortoise, the sturdy buffalo weaver, the fuzzy antlion, and the horned rhino beetle—Namibia's "Little Five."

Nighttime in Namibia brings a dazzling show as the skies seem to fill with diamonds. The Southern Cross, the Milky Way, and almost all the constellations of the zodiac are visible to the naked eye; plus, Sossusvlei Desert Lodge houses a state-of-the-art observatory. Farther south in NamibRand are the Wolwedans Lodges, established by the reserve's original founder, environmentalist Albi Brueckner. They offer a range of accommodations, from the not-so-basic Dune Camp to the exclusive Boulders Camp with four magnificent tents where you may never feel the need to put down the flaps: the entire desert is your bedroom.

WHERE: 224 miles/360 km southwest of the capital city of Windhoek. **SOSSUSVLEI DESERT LODGE:** Contact &Beyond in South Africa. Tel 27/11-809-4314; in the U.S., 888-882-3742; www.andbeyond.com. *Cost:* from $415 (off-peak), from $775 (peak) per person, all-inclusive. **WOLWEDANS LODGES:** In Windhoek, tel 264/61–230-616; www.wolwedans.com. *Cost:* from $450 per person at Dune Camp; from $750 per person at Boulders; all-inclusive. **BEST TIME:** Jun–Oct for dry, mild weather and top game viewing.

"This cape is the most stately thing and the fairest cape we saw in the whole circumference of the earth."
—*SIR FRANCIS DRAKE*

CAPE TOWN

South Africa

The cosmopolitan city of Cape Town, where Africa and Europe culturally collide at the tip of the continent, is one of the most beautifully sited coastal cities in the world. Overlooking it is the iconic Table Mountain and its rolling "tablecloth" cover of clouds; at its summit, take in the breathtaking panorama of blue skies and blue oceans and the modern expanse of South Africa's oldest and favorite city. Cape Town enthralls visitors with its eclectic mix of Dutch, English, Malay, and African culture, encroaching wilderness, and nearby world-class vineyards. A safari may be your main meal, but Cape Town will be your dessert.

Top Attractions

Bo-Kaap (formerly Malay Quarter)—The Bo-Kaap, on the slopes of Signal Hill and above the city center, is a historic suburb of Cape Town rich in Cape Malay culture. Cape Malays are descended from slaves first brought here from Indonesia and Malaysia as farm workers by the Dutch East India Company in 1657. Cobbled streets are lined with brightly painted houses, mosques, and restaurants. No cause for alarm when the Signal Hill cannon goes off each day at noon; sailors set their watches by this. Pop in to the Noon Gun Tea Room (273 Longmarket Street) or Biesmiellah (2 Upper Wales Street) for an inexpensive, authentic Cape Malay meal, which might include curries, samoosas, or bobotie, a minced beef dish not unlike a spicy moussaka. On New Year's Day Bo-Kaap hosts a colorful Minstrel Carnival.

Boulders Beach and Cape of Good Hope—More than 3,000 penguins rule the relatively warm waters of Boulders Beach and neighboring Foxy Beach, which are among the few places on earth where they occupy the mainland rather than an island. The distinctive black-and-white African penguins whoop and surf the waves, waddling comically ashore to nest or to sun themselves. They obliviously share their space with locals toting picnic baskets and with curious out-of-towners, and as long as you don't get too close, you can observe their behavior from a number of wooden walkways. February to May is the breeding season, when they lay and cover their eggs on the beach. Continue south along the Cape Peninsula to its southernmost point, the Cape of Good Hope. The rugged and windswept Cape Point has great hiking paths, exotic wildlife, deserted beaches, and a bottom-of-the-world feeling in knowing there is nothing between you and Antarctica. **Boulders Beach:** 26 miles/42 km south of Cape Town. **Cape Point:** 65 miles/105 km south of Cape Town.

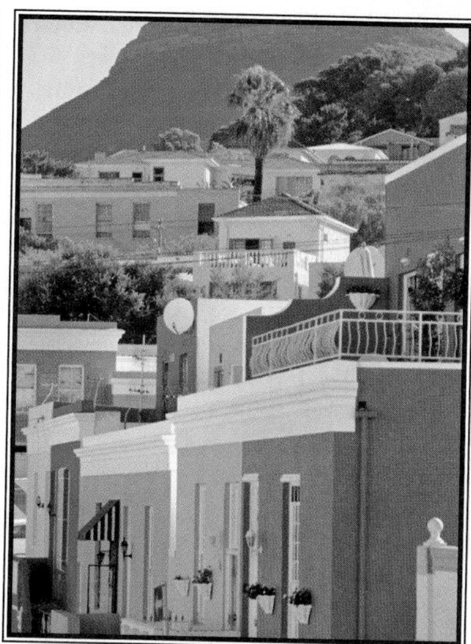

Colorful Bo-Kaap is a prime destination for an authentic Cape Malay meal.

District Six Museum—This "living memorial" tells the disturbing story of the forced displacement of 60,000 nonwhites living in a multicultural inner-city neighborhood from the late '60s through the early '80s. The Sixth Municipal District of Cape Town in 1867 began as a mixed community of freed slaves, merchants, artisans, laborers, and immigrants of all races—something not tolerated by the apartheid government. The museum presents residents' personal experiences from the time when the area was declared a White Group Area until all of it had been razed and everyone relocated to remote "townships" in what is now known as the Cape Flats (see Khayelitsha; p. 416). Opened in 1994, this compelling museum is also a meeting place and community center for those who were part of this very recent history. **Info:** Tel 27/21-466-7200; www.districtsix.co.za.

Gold of Africa Museum—Most of South Africa's gold originates from the gold mines near Johannesburg, 1,000 miles away. Yet here in the Gold of Africa Museum is where you'll find the world's finest assemblage of African gold art, craft, and jewelry, many pieces dating to the 19th century. It is housed in the painstakingly restored 18th-century Martin Melck house. The Gold Restaurant serves a wonderful fusion of African and Cape Malay–style foods, and at the Goldsmith's Studio workshop, it's fun to take your own precious stones, or even start from scratch, to create your instant heirloom at a jewelry-making course. **Info:** Tel 27/21-405-1540; www.goldofafrica.com.

Khayelitsha—Visitors generally see this sprawling shantytown, with close to 1 million residents and unending shacks lining miles and miles of open road lit by floodlights, from the outside. A first impression gives no clue to the vibrant culture within. The entrepreneurial energy among residents (relocated here from nonwhite suburbs) is inspiring; a knowledgeable local guide is a must and can introduce you to the small businesses, craft centers, schools, shebeens (local bars), and eateries, where most visitors are greeted with a smile. The sense of community in this maze of shacks (where, by some miracle, the postman actually knows the addresses) is palpable. Despite the poverty, you'll leave feeling a sense of hope for the future generation. **Where:** N2 Highway on the Cape Flats, outskirts of Cape Town. **How:** Go2Africa is a reputable company offering township tours. Tel 27/21-481-4900; in the U.S., 888-818-8821; www.go2africa.com. *Cost:* from $65.

Kirstenbosch National Botanical Gardens—Kirstenbosch, on the eastern slope of Table Mountain, was one of the first botanical gardens ever founded to preserve a country's flora. Miles of walking trails wind through 89 acres of rolling lawns and streams, with gorgeous displays of South Africa's indigenous plants, such as fynbos, proteas, and cycads. On summer Sunday evenings from November to April, Capetonians unpack their picnic baskets on the carpets of green lawn and settle in for wonderful outdoor concerts. **Info:** Tel 27/21-799-8783; www.sanbi.org.

Robben Island—Cape Town is best viewed from the 30-minute ferry on the way to Robben Island, known today as the maximum-security prison where former president Nelson Mandela spent 18 of his 27 years of incarceration (1964–1982) and where he secretly wrote his book *Long Walk to Freedom.* The last prisoner left in 1996, and the small island is now a museum. Some of the guides are former political prisoners from the troubled apartheid years and contemporaries of Mandela, and they bring to life the three centuries that the island has stood as a place of isolation and banishment. A boardwalk leads to a beach full of African penguins. **Info:** Tel 27/21-413-4220; www.robben-island.org.za.

Table Mountain—The sweeping panorama from Table Mountain (more than 3,500 feet high and visible from 40 miles out at sea) captures the mountains, city, ocean, and stretches of unspoiled wilderness. A cable car takes just five minutes to reach the flat summit that gave the landmark mountain its name. You can also make the journey

The cable car to Table Mountain's summit offers great views of Lion's Head, another mountain.

via a 2- to 3-hour hike, nicest between September and March when the slopes are ablaze with blooms, including more than 100 species of iris. Most of the year sees the mountain covered by a "tablecloth" of clouds at some point during the day. **Info:** Tel 27/21-424-8181; www.tablemountain.net.

Victoria and Alfred Waterfront—Cape Town's commercial heart beats at the historic V&A Waterfront (or just "the Waterfront" to Capetonians), set on the shores of a bustling harbor. It's lined with dozens of shops, eateries of all kinds, an aquarium, and a few choice hotels. It buzzes with buskers, musicians, and lots of boat traffic, including the water taxis ferrying folks from one bar to another in the summer months and boats going to Robben Island (see previous page). New Year's Eve in Cape Town is a gala affair, and the Waterfront hosts the biggest of all the parties with fireworks, music, international DJs, dancing, and general revelry. **Info:** Tel 27/21-408-7600; www.waterfront.co.za.

Where to Stay

Cape Grace Hotel—On its own private quay tucked between the working harbor of the V&A Waterfront and the serenity of an international yacht marina, the Cape Grace is a small-scale hotel that consistently wins recognition as one of the best in Africa. Not only are the service and attention to detail impeccable, but its 120 spacious and bright rooms enjoy views of the harbor, Table Mountain, or both. The Bascule Whisky, Wine and Cocktail Bar offers the largest collection of whiskey in the Southern Hemisphere. The luxury *Spirit of the Cape* yacht is available for the exclusive use of Cape Grace guests. **Info:** Tel 27/21-410-7100; www.capegrace.com. *Cost:* from $650 (off-peak), from $775 (peak).

Ellerman House—South Africa's finest boutique hotel sits high on a hill in Bantry Bay, a 10-minute drive from the Waterfront. Built in 1912 as the private home of a British shipping magnate, its ambience is akin to that of a French Riviera hideaway. It has nine rooms in the House and an additional five in the Villa, all decorated with paintings by a who's who of prominent South African artists. Exceptional hospitality is delivered in a dramatic setting, which offers awe-inspiring views of Robben Island and the South Atlantic. **Info:** Tel 27/21-430-3200; in the U.S., 800-735-2478; www.ellerman.co.za. *Cost:* from $850 (off-peak), from $1,000 (peak).

Mandela Rhodes Place—In the central business district, opposite the legendary St. George's Cathedral on Wale Street, is the modern Mandela Rhodes Place, an all-suite hotel offering apartments ranging from studios to two-bedrooms. Request rooms on the higher floors for magnificent views of the Waterfront and Table Mountain. The Azura Restaurant offers poolside or inside dining with expansive views of the city and South African specialties that range from the traditional *braai* (barbecue) to queen prawns and crayfish. **Info:** Tel 27/31-310-6900 or 27/21-481-4000; www.mandelarhodesplace.co.za. *Cost:* studio apartments from $175 (off-peak), from $375 (peak); dinner $40.

Mount Nelson Hotel—Ever since it opened its doors in 1899, this pink stucco grande dame has been welcoming Cape Town's most illustrious and colorful visitors, ranging from Arthur Conan Doyle and Winston Churchill to Oprah Winfrey and the Dalai Lama. Mount Nelson is the hub around which the city's social life traditionally revolves, and if you partake of only one afternoon tea in the country, have it here. Served indoors or on the flower-filled veranda, tea is a bacchanalia of pastries, cakes, and dainty nibbles. The English ambience remains delightfully intact. Even though the hotel isn't oceanfront, it makes up for it with 6 acres of luxuriant gardens full of rose beds and hibiscus trees in the shadow of

Table Mountain. **Info:** Tel 27/21-231-000; www.mountnelson.co.za. *Cost:* "superior" doubles from $425 (off-peak), from $550 (peak); tea $30.

One&Only Cape Town—In the heart of the V&A Waterfront, this urban chic resort boasts some of the largest rooms and suites in the city, all with views of Table Mountain, the harbor, or waterways, and accented with ethnic textiles and contemporary South African art. Nobu, the legendary Nobuyuki Matsuhisa's first restaurant in Africa, is here, making this an epicure's delight as well. You won't find corned beef sandwiches at Reuben's, but you will get excellent bistro dishes and regional interpretations from local celebrity chef Reuben Riffel. **Info:** Tel 27/21-431-5888; www.oneandonlycapetown.com. *Cost:* from $625 (off-peak), from $725 (peak) in the Marina Rise tower; dinner at Nobu $70, Reuben's $55.

African penguins have called Boulders Beach home since they established a colony here in 1982.

Eating and Drinking

Aubergine—Once the fashionable 19th-century home of South Africa's first chief justice of the Cape, Sir John Wylde, Aubergine extends his legacy. Wylde's flamboyant lifestyle was the talk of the town, as were his elegant parties. Aubergine's interior has been renovated with flair (from bamboo ceilings to mismatched yellowwood tables) in a contemporary style that complements the old building's elegance. Just minutes from the V&A Waterfront and a couple of blocks from the Mount Nelson Hotel, the lush terrace is the perfect setting for aperitifs before dinner, which features chef Harald Bresselschmidt's innovative cuisine. Specializing in seafood, meat, and game, he also offers excellent vegetarian dishes. **Info:** Tel 27/21-465-4909; www.aubergine.co.za. *Cost:* dinner $60.

Caveau—A favorite choice of Capetonians, Caveau offers several hundred South African wines by the glass, paired with local tapas-style small plates. Regulars come back for the cheese and meat platter, served on a wooden board with biltong (South African jerky), prosciutto, artisanal cheeses, and a melon or fig preserve. Dinner is a heartier and sometimes exotic affair with a chalkboard menu that changes frequently—you might find Eland (a type of antelope) Wellington or ostrich rubbed with *dukkah* (an Egyptian blend of nuts and spices). Caveau readily shares its recipes, and if you love the local wine you tasted and can't find a bottle to take home with you, the staff is happy to source it for you. **Info:** Tel 27/21-422-1367; www.caveau.co.za. *Cost:* dinner $60.

La Colombe—Fifteen minutes from Cape Town's city center, Constantia Uitsig Farm and Winery is home to three fine restaurants with La Colombe consistently voted the city's best. The property was once a portion of governor Simon van der Stel's original land grant, Groot Constantia (see p. 423). In this beautiful valley of vines, chef Luke Dale-Roberts has made his mark: Provence-inspired South African cuisine with an exciting Asian influence. Choose from the à la carte blackboard menu or spoil yourself with a six-course seasonal "gourmand menu." A lighter lunch or dinner is the draw at the more casual River Café, whose array of tapas keeps it a perennial favorite. **INFO:** Tel 27/21-794-2390; www.constantia-uitsig.com. *Cost:* gourmand menu $90; lunch at River Café $25.

DIAS TAVERN—Named after the 17th-century Portuguese explorer Bartholomeu Dias, the informal tavern (picture plastic chairs and vintage beer posters) is an old-time favorite. Seafood lovers come for the daily catch and prawns peri-peri (prepared with a hot chili that South Africans love); the carnivorous come for the charcoal-grilled steak, or *espetada,* traditionally *braaied* (barbecued) rump steak on a skewer. Everyone comes for the perfectly done chips (fries). Friday and Saturday nights feature loud, live, golden-oldie music; lunchtime and weeknights offer a less frenetic atmosphere. You'll get stunning views of Table Mountain no matter when you come. **INFO:** Tel 27/21-465-7547. *Cost:* $25.

A Confluence of Habitats

PHINDA PRIVATE GAME RESERVE

KwaZulu-Natal, South Africa

This relatively new private reserve in northern Zululand is exceptional not only for the seven African ecosystems that meet within its 56,800 acres, but for its diverse approach to safaris. Morning and night game drives that take you to elephants, leopards, and cheetahs are just the beginning. Boat and canoe trips provide close-up looks at the birdlife, crocs, and hippos. Bushwalks allow you to track the elusive black rhino by foot. Then there is the nearby Indian Ocean, offering big-game fishing, diving in the world's southernmost reefs (off the deserted coast of Maputaland), and, on the coast, the highest vegetated sand dunes in the world.

The astounding biodiversity is the big draw here, but the accommodations are equally impressive. The Mountain Lodge and its 25 split-level suites with private plunge pools sit atop a hill with endless views, taking in the Lebombo Mountains and Maputaland coastal range. Another option, the contemporary Forest Lodge, is a masterpiece of 16 glass-walled cabins built around twisted trees and set on stilts in a rare sand forest. The Zen-like design is deliberately spare, allowing the outdoors in. You can relax in bed while birds sing and butterflies flutter outside your floor-to-ceiling windows.

Lions and other big cats are part of the menagerie at Phinda, meaning "the return" in Zulu.

WHERE: 185 miles/300 km north of Durban on the Indian Ocean. **HOW:** Johannesburg-based &Beyond can make arrangements. Tel 27/11-809-4314; in the U.S., 888-882-3742; www.phinda.com. **COST:** Mountain Lodge and Forest Lodge from $480 per person, all-inclusive (off-peak), from $830 (peak). **BEST TIME:** Oct–Feb to combine a safari with a warm weather beach vacation.

A Journey to Middle Earth

The Drakensberg Mountains

KwaZulu-Natal and Mpumalanga, South Africa

Few places in the world match the Drakensberg ("Dragon's Mountain" in Afrikaans) for physical beauty; the range is believed to have inspired the phantasmagorical setting for the Lord of the Rings cycle, written by South African–born J.R.R. Tolkien. The Zulu call it uKhahlamba, "Barrier of Spears." These are South Africa's highest mountains, and their narrow passes, grassy valleys connecting 11,000-foot peaks, rivers, forests, and waterfalls (the Tugela Fall is the second highest on the planet) make up a dramatic landscape. The region also offers opportunities for hiking, horseback riding, bird-watching, golfing, fishing, and exploring hundreds of sites where ancient rock art dates back 3,000 years.

The Drakensbergs form a massive barrier separating the KwaZulu-Natal region in the east from Lesotho to the southwest. The only road linking them is a former donkey trail through the Sani Pass, which is the third-highest pass in the world (at more than 9,000 feet) and is accessible only by four-wheel drive vehicle.

Just outside of the small town of Winterton in central Drakensberg is the Drakensberg Boys Choir School, where on most Wednesday afternoons the boys perform for visitors. Their singing of classical pieces rivals that of the Vienna Boys Choir, but they also perform jazz, pop, and traditional African folk songs, all enthusiastically infused with tribal rhythms.

It's hard to imagine the tranquil mountains that surround Winterton as bloody battlefields, but in the late 19th century they were the scene of a brutal war between the British, Voortrekkers (Boers), and Zulus. The spectacular Fugitives' Drift property, a Natural Heritage Site in KwaZulu-Natal, overlooks the Isandlwana and Rorke's Drift (sites of two battles in 1879), and is named after a river crossing where British forces were defeated. Fugitives' Drift Lodge, a collection of eight luxurious suites and a private guesthouse, was built by local storyteller David Rattray and his wife, Nicky, who share the region's conflict-filled history through thought-provoking tours led by some of the finest guides in Zululand.

On the Mpumalanga side of the mountains lies the magnificent Blyde River Canyon, or Motlatse Canyon, a 15-mile-long gorge as deep as 2,630 feet; it is, by some measures, the third largest in the world. The Blyde River meets the Treur River at Bourke's Luck Potholes, cylindrical, cliff-side holes up to 20 feet deep formed by river erosion. You can take in the spellbinding vistas from God's Window, the canyon's unsurpassed lookout point, though nothing beats the bird's-eye view offered by a chartered, jet-powered helicopter that swoops over the dramatic rock formations of the canyon and through valleys bursting with vegetation and color. After hovering over river rapids and cascading waterfalls, it lands on a remote mountaintop in an otherwise unreachable grassy clearing where lunch with a view is served.

Afterward, you'll want to check into Cybele Forest Lodge and Health Spa and relax in one of its exquisite private suites or cottages. Each boasts cozy fireplaces and a garden, and some feature private swimming pools.

Where: Fugitives' Drift, in the KwaZulu-Natal, is 161 miles/259 km north of Durban.

Cybele Forest Lodge, in Mpumalanga, is 261 miles/420 km east of Johannesburg. **How:** Passage to Africa specializes in custom itineraries. Tel 27/15-793-0811; www.passagetoafrica.com. **Fugitives' Drift:** Tel 27/34-642-1843; www.fugitivesdrift.com. *Cost:* from $290 per person, inclusive (off-peak), from $420 (peak). **Cybele Forest Lodge:** Tel 27/13-764-9500; www.cybele.co.za. *Cost:* from $200 (off-peak), from $275 (peak) per person. **Drakensberg Boys Choir:** Tel 27/36-468-1012; www.dbchoir.info. **Best times:** Sep–Oct and Mar–Apr to avoid rainy summers and chilly winter nights.

Beauty and the Beasts

Greater Kruger Park Area

Mpumalanga, South Africa

Some of South Africa's best game-viewing can be found in the expanse of land west of Kruger National Park. Sharing an unfenced border with the enormous park, these collectively owned and managed private reserves and concessions are home to a remarkable variety of wildlife but don't get the human traffic that typically follows it, so you'll very likely never share the surrounding terrain with more than one or two other jeeps in the course of each exhilarating drive. The animals are not tame, but they are accustomed to the sight of vehicles and let them approach fairly close. Rangers and trackers are educated and entertaining, with a wealth of experience and a passion for the bush. They will drive you through various habitats and ecosystems, from rolling hills to open grasslands and thick forests. Around every turn in the dirt road a surprise awaits: slinking leopards, cheetahs, endangered African wild dogs, and magnificent black and white rhinos, not to mention 500 species of birds, thriving prides of lions, and scores of zebras, buffalo, hippos, giraffes, and elephants (13,000 of them!).

Nearly as staggering is the unabashed luxury of the splendor-in-the-bush accommodations at the exalted trio of lodges here, the Londolozi, Royal Malewane, and Singita. Of Londolozi's five camps, the finest are the three Granite Private Suites, directly on the banks of the Sand River and accommodating just six privileged guests altogether. Royal Malewane, with its eight thatched suites, each with a private infinity swimming pool, boasts a Chaîne des Rôtisseurs Blazon, a plaque given by the legendary Parisian gastronomic society to recognize an exemplary level of cuisine. Singita's four luxurious lodges, each with its own distinctive identity, have reinterpreted the concept of the permanent safari

All the Big Five game animals can be found at Kruger, with elephants being the easiest to spot.

camp—they all feature a spa and stylish suites with private pools. Down-to-earth budgets will be just as happy at the privately owned Kapama Karula, a riverside lodge hosting just 14 guests in tents and chalets with excellent guides and under-the-stars dinners.

WHERE: Nelspruit and nearby Kruger Mpumalanga International Airport service the Kruger National Park area, 221 miles/346 km east of Johannesburg; small airstrips at some properties receive scheduled flights and charters from Johannesburg. **LONDOLOZI:** Tel 27/11-280-6655; www.londolozi.com. *Cost:* from $1,000 per person, all-inclusive. **ROYAL MALEWANE:** Tel 27/15-793-0150; www.royalmalewane.com. *Cost:* from $1,550 per person, all-inclusive. **SINGITA:** Tel 27/21-683-3424; www.singita.com. *Cost:* from $1,700 per person, all-inclusive. **KAPAMA KARULA:** Tel 27/12-368-0600; www.kapama.co.za. *Cost:* $320 per person, all-inclusive. **BEST TIME:** Mar–Oct for cooler, drier weather.

The Golden Age of Train Travel, Past and Present

ROVOS RAIL AND THE BLUE TRAIN

South Africa

Tiny planes transport safarigoers from park to park bestowing bird's-eye views of the vast landscapes in between. For those with time to slow down, a rail journey permits entry to a world not many see, and in South Africa, you have two exemplary choices. The Rovos Rail, which features some cars that date to the late 1800s, is a throwback to the glory days of steam travel, when sleeper coaches and carriages were built with ornately carved embellishments and serviced by tuxedoed porters. The Blue Train is all contemporary luxury and efficiency, like a slender and sleek hotel kitted out with lacquer, leather, and African prints. Both roll along from Cape Town northeast to Johannesburg and Pretoria, a journey of nearly 1,000 miles across the starkly beautiful plains of the Great Karoo and the canyons of the Highveld in the center of South Africa.

Rovos Rail offers a number of itineraries that can be mixed and matched according to time and budget. The 25-hour Cape Town to Knysna round-trip, for example, chuffs through the fabled Hottentots Holland Mountains, taking in the lake district and the dramatic coastline. Three times a year, Rovos offers a 14-day odyssey from Cape Town to Dar es Salaam, Tanzania, with stops at Victoria Falls (see p. 435), Kruger Park (see p. 421), and Zambia's Chishimba Falls. Exceptionally large suites are outfitted with queen-size beds and private bathrooms. Dressing for dinner on the aptly named *Pride of Africa* is only fitting when a meal of Cape rock lobster, paired with any of South Africa's finest wines, awaits.

The Blue Train first took to the rails in 1946. As stylish and comfortable as the original trains were, passengers will appreciate their new generation of sophisticated railcars, introduced in the late 1990s. Private bathrooms are decked out with marble vanities and walls; suites include full entertainment centers, while meals feature local wines in crystal glassware and dishes that will satisfy the most discriminating palates. The journeys on Blue Train are faster than those on Rovos and are limited to overnight jaunts between

Cape Town and Pretoria, just north of Johannesburg (and with transfers available to Durban and Kruger).

WHERE: Board in either Cape Town or Pretoria. **ROVOS RAIL:** Tel 27/12-315-8242; www.rovos.com. *Cost:* 3-day journey between Cape Town and Pretoria from $2,600. **BLUE TRAIN:** Tel 27/12-334-8459; www.bluetrain.co.za. *Cost:* 2-day journey between Cape Town and Pretoria from $1,600. **BEST TIMES:** Oct–Mar if paired with a winelands tour; Apr–Sep if paired with a safari.

An Oenophile's Odyssey

THE CAPE WINELANDS

Western Cape, South Africa

A wine safari combines two of South Africa's greatest treasures: the bounty of the spectacular Cape wine region and its excellent regional cuisine—an exotic mix of Dutch, French, British, Portuguese, German, and Malay influences. Within easy reach of Cape Town (see p. 414), both major wine estates and the small, sophisticated towns of Stellenbosch, Paarl, and Franschhoek (and to a lesser degree Robertson and McGregor) have roots dating back to Dutch and French Huguenot settlement in the mid-1600s. Gracious Cape Dutch homesteads are set against the granite-peaked Drakenstein mountains, forests, and rolling vineyards that produce a range of varietals, most notably cabernet sauvignon and pinotage among the reds and sauvignon blanc and chenin blanc among the whites.

Franschhoek ("French corner" in Afrikaans) is the gourmet capital of South Africa, and it alone boasts more than 40 wineries as well as two memorable boutique hotels. Le Quartier Français, a charming, self-contained minivillage tucked away in the quaint downtown is celebrated for its dining. La Residence boasts a 30-acre farm and vineyard, along with 11 extravagant suites opening onto wide verandas and views of the nearby mountain range. If you're staying elsewhere, treat yourself to lunch or dinner, a theatrical, candlelit event. North of Franschhoek, in Paarl, Grande Roche is a restored 18th-century homestead renowned for its service, its sophisticated suites, and Bosman's, its casually elegant dining room, whose wine list is often lauded as one of the best in South Africa.

In the 19th century, Groot Constantia supplied wines to Napoleon and the king of the Netherlands.

The country's first vineyards were planted in Constantia, the smart suburb just 20 minutes south of Cape Town. Groot Constantia, the oldest wine estate in the country, was originally owned by the first governor of the Dutch Colony here in the 17th century. Buitenverwachting, whose tongue-twisting name is Old Dutch for "beyond expectations," is another well-known Constantia wine estate and restaurant. Cellars-Hohenort, a historic country hotel and restaurant nestled against the forested eastern slopes of Table Mountain, occupies the 18th-century cellars of the former Cape governor's wine estate as well as a triple-gabled manor house.

Where: Franschhoek is 50 miles/80 km east of Cape Town. **Visitor info:** www.wine.co.za. **Le Quartier Français:** Tel 27/21-876-2151; www.lequartier.co.za. *Cost:* rooms from $420 (off-peak), from $680 (peak); dinner with fixed menu at the Tasting Room $90. **La Residence:** Tel 27/21-876-4100; www.laresidence.co.za. *Cost:* from $635 per person. **Grande Roche:** Tel 27/41-407-1000; www.granderoche.com. *Cost:* from $310 (off-peak), from $440 (peak); dinner with tasting menu at Bosman's $90. **Groot Constantia:** Tel 27/21-794-5128; www.grootconstantia.co.za. **Buitenverwachting:** Tel 27/21-794-3522; www.buitenverwachting.co.za. *Cost:* dinner $60. **Cellars-Hohenort:** Tel 27/21-794-2137; www.cellars-hohenort.com. *Cost:* from $340 (off-peak), from $600 (peak). **Best times:** Sep–May for warmer, drier weather; the weekend closest to Jul 14 for Bastille Day celebrations in Franschhoek.

Africa's Southernmost Coast

The Garden Route

Western Cape, South Africa

This 130-mile stretch that begins east of Cape Town and runs along Africa's southernmost tip is a coastal terrain of lakes, mountains, forests, and golden beaches. Indian Ocean waters just offshore are full too—of penguins, dolphins, and migrating whales that have traveled here to breed and calve. Beautiful year-round, the area is positively glorious between July and October, when an unequaled diversity of wildflowers, supported by a unique combination of soil and climate, bursts into bloom and gives full meaning to the drive's name: "The Garden Route." See it by hiking any of the hundreds of miles of trails or on leisurely drives through forests and parkland.

The charming town of Knysna has a cliff-fringed harbor replete with sailboats, a colorful community of artists, and plenty of well-heeled vacationers. Sample the area's renowned oysters during its event-packed July oyster festival, when you can stop by the Knysna Oyster Company's alfresco tasting tavern, one of dozens of participating restaurants, to slurp down some of the bivalves with garnishes from caviar to mango and a chaser of a cold Mitchell's, the local ale. Follow walking trails out along the coast to view the Heads, rock sentinels at the mouth of the lagoon. On a gorgeous sweep of beach lies the Plettenberg, the coastline's most exclusive hotel, with a box-seat view of the wild and rugged headland and a half-moon bay. Come at least for lunch on the open terrace, and whale-watch while you dine.

Although not officially part of the Garden Route, visit the coastal city of Hermanus for more whale-spotting. Or head out in the direction of nearby Dyer Island (a breeding colony for African penguins and Cape fur seals), where shark diving (safely ensconced within specially made cages) provides unparalleled thrills. On the south end of whale-rich Walker Bay, check into the hilltop Grootbos Lodge set amid a multitude of flowering shrubs in a private nature reserve; or, on the north end, the smartly styled Birkenhead House; perched on the rocky Hermanus Cliffs. The famous Otter Trail in Tsitsikamma National Park is a 5-day trek through jaw-dropping scenery; half-mile trails descend from the park's visitor's center for those with less time or stamina.

WHERE: The Garden Route runs from Mossel Bay, 237 miles/382 km east of Cape Town, to Storms River mouth, 359 miles/578 km east of Cape Town. **KNYSNA OYSTER COMPANY:** Tel 27/44-382-6941. *Cost:* lunch $15. **PLETTENBERG HOTEL:** Tel 27/44-533-2030; www.plettenberg.com. *Cost:* from $340 (off-peak), from $610 (peak); lunch $25. **GROOTBOS LODGE:** Tel 27/28-384-8053; www.grootbos.com. *Cost:* from $215 (off-peak), from $550 (peak) per person, all-inclusive. **BIRKENHEAD HOUSE:** Tel 27/15-793-0150; www.birkenheadhouse.com. *Cost:* from $375 (off-peak), from $410 (peak) per person, inclusive. **BEST TIMES:** Jun–Oct for wildflowers and whales; early Jul for Knysna Oyster Festival; late Sep for Hermanus Whale Festival.

The Continent's Highest Peak

MOUNT KILIMANJARO

Kilimanjaro National Park, Tanzania

"Wide as all the world, great, high, and unbelievably white in the sun," wrote Ernest Hemingway in his famous short story "The Snows of Kilimanjaro." As global warming has caused temperatures to creep up, those snows have been melting, but even now, few mountains rival Kilimanjaro—Swahili for "mountain of greatness"; at 19,340 feet, it dwarfs all of Africa's other peaks. The 9-day, 25-mile round-trip trek to the dormant volcano's oddly flat top, ascending by way of the remote, seldom-used Shira Plateau, has several advantages over the more popular, five-day Marangu Trail, or "tourist route." Besides avoiding hordes of trekkers, the longer route allows a few days to get acclimated to the altitude. Elevation is the biggest and most underestimated obstacle; one-third of Marangu trekkers never make it past Gillman's Point, 600 feet below the summit, unable to adjust to the low level of oxygen—approximately half of what humans normally breathe at sea level. Other than this ability to cope with the altitude, no technical skills, equipment, or previous experience is needed, though the grade is gentle but deceptive: going *pole pole* ("slowly slowly" in Swahili) is the key, and the ascent must be undertaken with an organized group. A battalion of porters bolts ahead to pitch tents at spectacular sites and set up camp by the time everyone straggles in. At the summit, your lightheadedness

About 25,000 people set out to climb Mount Kilimanjaro each year, but it is estimated that only about half of them make it to the top.

might be the altitude, or it might simply be a response to the satisfaction of accomplishing an epic climb and the thrill of seeing the sun rise over the plains of Tanzania and Kenya more than 3 miles below you.

Where: Arusha is 168 miles/270 km south of Nairobi. **How:** U.S.-based Mountain Madness offers 12-day Shira route trips. Tel 800-328-5925 or 206-937-8389; www.mountainmadness.com. *Cost:* from $4,975 all-inclusive. Originates in Arusha. **Best times:** Sep–Oct and Dec–Jan for clearer, warmer, and drier days on the mountain, but also biggest crowds.

Life Among the Chimpanzees

Greystoke Camp

Mahale Mountains National Park, Tanzania

Just 60 miles south of where Stanley uttered his famous greeting, "Doctor Livingstone, I presume?" on the remote eastern shores of Lake Tanganyika, lies Mahale Mountains National Park, home to the world's largest known population of wild chimpanzees, mankind's closest relatives. The 600-square-mile, road-free park remains almost untouched by the outside world, yet on the lake's sandy shores at the foot of the mountains lies Greystoke Camp, the embodiment of all safari fantasies and a strong candidate for the most beautiful in all of Africa. Six wooden *bandas* (traditional thatched huts) open onto a soft sand beach, their interiors fashioned from reclaimed dhow timber and decorated with billowing fabric. They are nestled against the forest and surround the imposing dining pavilion that rises two stories high with soaring prowlike wings.

Guides know the name and history of all of the camp's chimps.

Within hiking distance is the Mimikire clan of about 60 chimps that became habituated to humans when a group of Japanese researchers began monitoring them in the mid-1960s. Every morning, trackers from the lodge go out early to find the chimps. Then, after breakfast, guides will lead you along the forest paths until you're surrounded by their calls. You can sit quietly, watching them groom, wrestle, bicker, forage, eat, and nurture their young. Guides explain the well-defined hierarchy in this extended family, marked by complex relationships and histories. You have only one hour to watch them each day. Other guided walks give you a chance to spot colobus monkeys and leopards, as well as the countless birds and butterflies that also call this area home. When you return to the lodge, you might choose to relax until dinner, or perhaps you'd prefer to snorkel, fish, or kayak the impossibly clear waters populated by more than 1,000 species of fish.

Where: on the shores of Lake Tanganyika, in western Tanzania; accessible via charter from Arusha, plus a boat transfer to camp; www.greystoke-mahale.com. **Cost:** from $1,075 per person per night, all-inclusive, with round-trip charter from Arusha (off-peak), from $1,225 (peak). **How:** U.S.-based Africa Adventure Company offers custom itineraries. Tel 800-882-9453 or 954-491-8877; www.africa-adventure.com. **Best time:** Trekking can be easier Aug–Oct when chimpanzees are often closer to the bottom of the mountains.

Africa's Garden of Eden

Ngorongoro Crater

Tanzania

The volcanic Ngorongoro Crater, the world's largest unflooded, intact caldera is considered one of the natural wonders of the world, both for its unique beauty and for the staggering concentration of animals that live there.

This natural amphitheater is the Serengeti (see p. 429) in miniature, with wildebeests, zebras, and gazelles roaming from one side of the 12-mile-wide, vegetation-dense crater to the other. Elephants, buffalo, hippos, and dark-maned lions are also plentiful, and Ngorongoro is possibly the best place on earth to see the rare black rhino. In the middle of the crater is the mirror-like Lake Magadi, a year-round supply of fresh water that makes this one big spectacular wildlife oasis. Masses of flamingos are not uncommon, while in the marshes and grasslands surrounding the lake, storks, ostriches, and hornbills come and go. And at night, the piercing call of a thick-tailed bush baby will remind you that smaller, more timid creatures make this place their home too.

The human species is beginning to outnumber the wildlife, but accommodations along the rim of the crater are still limited. Lemala Tented Camp, a seasonal collection of nine luxury tents, is the closest to the crater floor and has a staff with encyclopedic knowledge and a knack for avoiding herds of fellow gazers (they're always first out in the morning).

The world's black rhinos declined severely in the 20th century due to poaching, but here they live safely, slowly increasing in population.

At an elevation of 7,500 feet, the crater has its share of chilly nights, so many visitors take a pass on Lemala's canvas tents and instead stay at Ngorongoro Crater Lodge, one of East Africa's most luxurious hotels. Check into any of the 30 thatched, stilted suites with floor-to-ceiling windows perched at the crater's edge, ask your butler to draw your bath, and watch from your tub as the sunset's magic unfolds. Afterward, enjoy a leisurely firelit dinner of pan-African cuisine and Cape wines.

Where: 120 miles/190 km west of Arusha. **Lemala Tented Camp:** Tel 255/27-254-8966; www.lemalacamp.com. *Cost:* from $495 per person, all-inclusive (off-peak), from $595 (peak). *When:* closed rainy season Apr–May. **Ngorongoro Crater Lodge:** Contact &Beyond in South Africa, tel 27/11-809-4314; in the U.S., 888-882-3742; www.andbeyondafrica.com. *Cost:* from $685 per person, all-inclusive (off-peak), from $1,500 (peak). **Best times:** Animal numbers are high year-round, but expect rain in Apr–May; Jul–Aug for cooler, drier weather.

Safaris Like They Used to Be

Selous Game Reserve

Tanzania

When Teddy Roosevelt needed help outfitting his legendary 1909 safari, he turned to Frederick Courteney Selous, a British explorer he later called "the most fearless yet the gentlest and straightest of men." Selous was a soldier, a hunter, and a naturalist, and when he died here his name was given to Africa's second largest game reserve (the largest is the central Kalahari Desert Game Reserve; see p. 398). More than three times the size of South Africa's Kruger Park and twice the size of the Serengeti (see p. 421 and next page), the lesser-known, 21,000-square-mile Selous Game Reserve is home to Tanzania's greatest elephant population, along with over a million other animals, the Great Rufiji River, and Stiegler's Gorge, a canyon more than 300 feet deep and 300 feet wide.

Portered walking safaris (with just a few porters, not like those of Roosevelt's day) are still possible here. You can book one for a few days, or you can spend two weeks venturing deep into the reserve's remote corners, either on foot or by boat. Porters carry your lightweight fly-camps (little more than mosquito-net cubes that serve as tents), allowing you to sleep safely under the stars while still enjoying the luxury of fine linen sheets, a hot shower, and meals prepared by a traveling chef.

If you prefer an utterly luxurious lodge that still captures some of that open-skies feeling, settle in along the banks of the Rufiji at the Sand Rivers Selous (seven rooms and suites, and a private honeymoon cottage) or its sister lodge, Kiba Point (with four open-fronted cottages). Even more remote is Lukula Camp (four magnificent tents in 300,000 acres of privately owned wilderness), which overlooks the Luwegu River.

Where: 94 miles/150 km southwest of Dar es Salaam. **How:** U.S.-based Africa Adventure Company arranges custom trips. Tel 800-882-9453 or 954-491-8877; www.africa-adventure.com. **Sand Rivers Selous and Kiba Point:** www.sand-rivers-selous.com. *Cost:* Sand Rivers Selous, from $750 per person, all-inclusive, 4-night minimum (off-peak), from $950 (peak). Kiba Point, from $525 per person, all-inclusive, 4-night minimum (off-peak), from $700 (peak). **Lukula Camp:** Tel 255/767-755-537; www.greatplainsconservation.com. *Cost:* from $615 per person all-inclusive, 3-night minimum (off-peak), from $1,450 (peak). All three lodging options offer 1- to 14-day portered walking safaris. **Best times:** Jan–Apr for bird-watching; Jun–Nov for best weather and greatest opportunity for wildlife viewing.

Magnificent Migration in the Cradle of Mankind

The Serengeti

Tanzania and Kenya

The Serengeti, one of the oldest ecosystems on earth, is Africa's No. 1 World Heritage site. It has barely changed since early humans first appeared about 2 million years ago, a fact that remained unknown until Louis and Mary Leakey began excavation work in the Olduvai Gorge in the 1950s. It remains an important region for the study of human origins, but what brings in the Land Rovers packed with wide-eyed nature lovers and shutterbugs is the grandest of all wildlife shows: the great migration.

In Tanzania, the Serengeti region encompasses Serengeti National Park, most of the Ngorongoro Conservation Area (see p. 427), Maswa Game Reserve, and the Loliondo, Grumeti, and Ikorongo Controlled Areas as well as the Masai Mara National Reserve in Kenya (see p. 408). Every year, more than 1.5 million wildebeests circle these vast grasslands in order to graze and calve, starting in the northern hills of the Mara in November, then chasing the rains south and lingering for months in the Serengeti until heading back north in the summer. Zebras, Thompson's gazelles, and other ungulates join in, creating endless, teeming vistas of animals.

The Serengeti—Masai for "flat endless plains"—is home to a number of beautiful wilderness properties scattered over its 10,000 square miles. Among the very best of these is Singita's Grumeti Reserves, which is made up of three handsomely designed lodges: The nine stunning contemporary suites at the Faru Faru Lodge are the picture of laid-back rustic elegance; while Sabora Tented Camp, with nine luxury tents, evokes the golden age of safaris with antique chests and Persian rugs; Sasakwa Lodge's nine breathtaking cottages and villa were built in the style of an Edwardian manor.

Since the path and timing of the migration are not entirely predictable, Nomad Tanzania offers two luxurious mobile lodges: the Serengeti Safari Camp, with six tents, and Nduara Loliondo, with six yurts. Both move to follow the migrating animals and either one can give you the chance to be right there where the action is.

Where: Northwestern Tanzania. **How:** U.S.-based Africa Adventure Company arranges custom trips. Tel 800-882-9453 or 954-491-8877; www.africanadventure.com. **Singita's Grumeti Reserves:** Tel 27/21-683-3424; www.singita.com. *Cost:* from $1,000 per person, all-inclusive. **Serengeti Safari Camp** and **Nduara Loliondo:** www.nomad-tanzania.com. *Cost:* from $850 per person, all-inclusive, 4-night minimum. **Best time:** Wildlife abounds throughout the Serengeti year-round. Jun–Jul are typically good months for the migration in the Grumeti Reserves.

Blue wildebeests have been following the rains to the Serengeti for millennia.

Island Outpost of Old Araby in the Indian Ocean

Zanzibar

Tanzania

The very name Zanzibar conjures up images of romantic spice islands, and—like legendary Timbuktu or Kathmandu—the name alone is almost reason enough to make the trip. The historic center of its capital city is known as Stone Town, a maze of narrow streets, crooked passages, and crumbling houses once owned by Arab traders, with enclosed balconies and carved, brass-studded doors. The merchants built homes here after amassing their wealth by trafficking in gold, ivory, cloves, and—most lucratively—slaves destined for Arabia and Persia.

Zanzibar was once the largest slave market on Africa's east coast. Today an Anglican church, erected to celebrate the end of the slave trade in 1873, stands on the grounds of the old slave market, the main altar built where the whipping post once stood. More clues to the island's history can be found everywhere, from the Arab mosques and forts to the British and Portuguese Colonial architecture to the pulsing Swahili market, with its colorful fruits and spices (in particular, nutmeg, cardamom, cinnamon, and cloves), grains, and fish from the surrounding waters. At the center of it all is the Zanzibar Palace Hotel boutique in a renovated Arabic town house with nine rooms (three on each floor) wrapped around a bright atrium. Persian rugs, hanging lamps, tile work, beaded pillows, wood carvings, and silk drapes transport guests to the early days of the spice trade.

Traditional carvings frame a wooden door in Stone Town.

The two main islands of Zanzibar—Zanzibar Island (or Unguja), where Stone Town is located, and Pemba—have become popular beach getaways to tack onto the end of mainland safaris. While their coasts are thick with hotels, the finest retreats are on smaller satellite islands, like Chumbe where a stone lighthouse and thatched eco-bungalows are the only landmarks you'll see. With its pristine coral garden, it is the place to drop off the map and enjoy snorkeling.

Tiny Mnemba, not even 1 mile in circumference, peeks out from a perfect coral atoll and beckons honeymooners, divers, and all lovers of barefoot indulgence. Ten romantic and understated *bandas* line the white sandy coast lapped by clear waters. Dinner on the beach follows lazy days of kayaking, sailing, and scuba diving.

Where: 22 miles/35 km off eastern coast of Tanzania. **Zanzibar Palace Hotel:** Tel 255/24-223-2230; www.zanzibarpalacehotel.com. *Cost:* from $170. **Chumbe Island:** Tel 255/24-223-1040; www.chumbeisland.com. *Cost:* from $260 per person, all-inclusive. *When:* closed mid-Apr–mid-Jun. **Mnemba Island:** Contact &Beyond in South Africa, tel 27/11-809-4314; in the U.S., 888-882-3742; www.mnemba-island.com. *Cost:* from $1,150 per person, all-inclusive (off-peak), from $1,500 (peak). *When:* closed Apr–May. **Best times:** Dec–Feb and Jun–Oct for dry season; early Feb for Sauti Za Busara African music celebration; Jul for Stone Town's Festival of the Dhow Countries, with film, art, and cultural events.

The Last Great Apes

TRACKING THE MOUNTAIN GORILLA

Bwindi Impenetrable National Park, Uganda

The narrow valleys and lush, steep slopes of Uganda's Bwindi Impenetrable Forest offer the chance for an encounter of the closest kind with a rare mountain gorilla in its last remaining habitat. It is only here, and just across the border in Rwanda and the Democratic Republic of Congo, that these powerful but gentle creatures are still found. Poaching has gravely diminished their numbers to barely 700, half of which live in Bwindi, while political unrest has curtailed the efforts at preservation made by the late Dian Fossey at Rwanda's Karisoke Research Center.

Despite their fierce reputation, mountain gorillas are gentle and peaceful by nature.

Today, Uganda and Rwanda are courting tourism to help protect these magnificent beasts. Bwindi Impenetrable National Park, on the edge of the western Rift Valley, allows a limited number of visitors accompanied by authorized guides to track the gorillas. The trail through the tropical rain forest, while not exactly impenetrable, is challenging. It is punctuated throughout with a legendary variety of birdlife (23 species are endemic to the western slopes of the Rift Valley) and primates, such as baboons, chimpanzees, vervets, and colobus monkeys. There is no guarantee of a gorilla sighting, but local guides are experts at interpreting every broken twig and second-guessing the daily routines of the four family groups that have been partially habituated to human presence. Gorilla families are ruled by a dominant male silverback, who acquires a harem of females loyal to him until he dies or is ousted by a rival. The guides, many of whom are affiliated with the Dian Fossey Gorilla Fund, are primate specialists and enhance these trips by explaining gorilla behavior and speaking about the history and ecology of the region. If you are staying at Clouds Mountain Gorilla Lodge, the trek back will end at the door of one of the lodge's ten stone cottages, which are situated on a ridge with views of the verdant forest canopy below and the silhouettes of the Virunga volcanoes in the distance.

WHERE: 330 miles/530 km southwest of the capital city, Kampala. **CLOUDS MOUNTAIN GORILLA LODGE:** Tel 256/41-425-1182; www.wildplacesafrica.com. *Cost:* $470 per person, all-inclusive; gorilla permits an extra $500 per person, per trek. **HOW:** U.S.-based Natural Habitat Adventures offers a 10-day safari. Tel 800-543-8917 or 303-449-3711; www.nathab.com. *Cost:* $9,795. Originates in Entebbe. *When:* Jan, Jun, and Aug. **BEST TIMES:** May–Aug and Dec–Feb to avoid the rainy season, when roads are often impassible and the forest is hot, humid, and muddy.

Through the Eye of a Needle

Murchison Falls

Uganda

Winston Churchill wasn't the first to describe Uganda as "the pearl of Africa," and in a country on the mend from past political upheaval, visitors may sometimes feel they have the bevy of natural wonders he had in mind all to themselves. Murchison Falls has been called the most exciting thing to happen to the Nile in its 4,200-mile stretch. It is a fitting East African counterpoint to the massive 5,600-foot expanse of cataracts at Victoria Falls (see p. 435) along southern Africa's Zambezi. Here, in Uganda's largest national park, the mighty Nile explodes through a rock cleft 23 feet wide before plunging 131 feet with unimaginable force. It is a mesmerizing sight, whether approached on foot or by boat. If you choose the latter, you'll slip past massive animals along the way—sometimes 100 grunting hippos appearing around a bend, and everywhere some of Africa's largest crocodiles, immobile, watching. Keep an eye out for the distinctive-looking shoebill, a very rare cousin of storks and pelicans, with its almost cartoonishly large beak—Uganda is one of the few places outside Sudan where they can be spotted. If the landscape looks familiar, it may be because it was used as a location for the 1951 Hollywood classic *The African Queen*.

There are few concessions to the 21st century here (or even the 20th), and it takes little to imagine yourself a Victorian explorer on a quest to find the source of the Nile. Choose among three fine accommodation options: At the ten-room Nile Safari Lodge, riverside chalets and tents incorporate natural, local materials and blend seamlessly with the surrounding papyrus forest. The hillside 54-room Paraa Safari Lodge is more traditional, decorated in a Colonial style and featuring a swimming pool and rooms overlooking the river. The refurbished Chobe Safari Lodge is the largest and most opulent (though farthest from the falls), with 36 guest rooms and 21 luxury tents, each with modern furnishings and a balcony facing the river, where dozens of hippos and buffalo gather.

Where: 186 miles/299 km north of Kampala. **How:** Kampala-based Let's Go Travel arranges trips throughout Uganda. Tel 256/41-434-6667; www.ugandaletsgotravel.com. **Nile Safari Lodge:** Tel 256/41-4258273; www.geolodgesafrica.com. *Cost:* from $150 per person, all-inclusive. **Paraa Safari Lodge:** Tel 256/31-226-0260; www

The falls are named after Roderick Murchison, a Scottish geologist who presided over the Royal Geographic Society.

.paraalodge.com. *Cost:* from $160 per person, all-inclusive. **Chobe Safari Lodge:** Tel 256/31-226-0260; www.chobelodgeuganda.com. *Cost:* from $160 (rooms), from $175 (tents) per person, inclusive. **Best time:** Dec–Mar for cooler, drier weather.

An Eccentric Brit's African Utopia

Shiwa Ng'andu

Zambia

In one of the remotest areas of Zambia, visitors can not only delve into the country's natural wonders by foot, boat, or bush vehicle, but can lodge in an intriguing monument to the historical British obsession with taming earth's wildest places. Shiwa Ng'andu is an extraordinary manor house that has inspired writers for years. Christina Lamb, in her 1999 book *The Africa House,* describes arriving for the first time: "We drove through and up a long steep drive bordered by Italian cypress trees, of all things to find in Africa, passing terraced gardens ablaze with colours. . . . And then there it was . . . . In all my travels in ten years as a foreign correspondent in Africa, Asia and South America, I had never seen anything like it."

Shiwa was built by Sir Stewart Gore Brown, born to wealth in London in 1881 and sent off to join the Boer War in southern Africa at the age of 19. In 1914, he visited Shiwa Ng'andu, the "lake of the royal crocodiles," an uninhabitable place in what was then Northern Rhodesia. Immediately enchanted, the eccentric Gore Brown began building his African utopia in 1920, not stopping until the late 1950s. There were no roads, and the nearest railroad was 400 miles away, but hundreds of laborers and teams of oxen hauling materials produced a brick house with a tower, a gatehouse, porticoes, and courtyards surrounded by nurseries, walled gardens, and tennis courts. In true English aristocratic style, the property became an extended community and included two schools, a hospital, shops, playing fields, a post office, and 80 houses for the workers who serviced the estate and its 60,000 acres of wilderness and farms.

Upon Gore Brown's death in 1967, the house and estate were left to crumble, and the surrounding community slowly lost its access to jobs, health care, and education. Gore Brown's eldest grandson, Charlie Harvey, and his wife, Jo, couldn't bear to see it all fall apart. So they undertook the herculean task of restoring the estate in 2002, including bringing the schools and hospital back to serve the 11,000 villagers. They also opened Shiwa Ng'andu's doors to guests, filling eight bedrooms (divided equally between the main manor house and a nearby farmhouse) with original furnishings to provide a taste of life from the estate's heyday. They arrange boating on the lake, soaking in hot springs, horseback rides, and game walks and drives to spot lesser-known birds and beasts, such as the palm nut vulture and two reclusive antelopes: the marsh-dwelling sitatunga and the diminutive blue duiker. On a rainy day, you can sift through history in the extensive Gore Brown family archives.

Where: 497 miles/800 km northeast of the capital city of Lusaka. Tel 260/97-666-4090; www.shiwangandu.com. *Cost:* farmhouse rooms $220 per person, all-inclusive (off-peak), $270 (peak). **Best time:** May–Oct for cooler, drier weather.

Hippos, Bee-Eaters, Leopards, and Much More

SOUTH LUANGWA

Zambia

Every moment in Zambia's South Luangwa National Park has its highlights, from the lush "emerald season" following the January to March rains, when the best mode of transportation is boat, to the dry months from July to October, when massive herds of big game gather around the shrinking Luangwa River and waterholes. This is also when spectacularly colorful carmine bee-eaters use their beaks to dig thousands of nest burrows in the vertical river banks of the river. It's not uncommon to drive around an oxbow bend of the river and encounter red-faced yellow-bills and other storks mingling with startlingly white egrets fishing from giant green lily pads as buffalo, pukus, impalas, and waterbucks look on. A raft of semisubmerged hippos (Zambia is thought to have more hippos than any other nation) can often be seen as well, resembling stepping-stones along the riverbanks. And South Luangwa is celebrated as being Zambia's big-cat country, so you are almost guaranteed to see a leopard during its twilight hunt, along with one or two lion kills in one day during the hot summer months.

Hippos are the third-largest land mammals, and among the most dangerous animals you'll find in South Luangwa.

The late Norman Carr pioneered walking safaris in Zambia and set guide standards in South Luangwa that are now respected by all of Africa. His remarkable fostering, teaching, and freeing of two orphaned lion cubs in 1958 is the stuff of legend (and of literature with Carr's 1962 memoir *Return to the Wild*). Carr died in 1997, but the safari company he founded runs Kapani Lodge, a well-appointed riverside retreat with eight suites and two lagoon houses. For multiday safaris you can stay put in the lodge or start there and move on into luxury bush camps in remote areas. Staying outside the lodge allows you the luxury of walking from camp to camp and surprising (or being surprised by) herds of up to 1,000 buffalo or as many as 100 elephants making their way to the water. If the entire family is in tow, Flatdogs Camp, just outside the park on the other side of the river, may be your best choice. With six en suite safari tents, six two-storied stone chalets, and the stilt-supported Jackal-Berry tree house, it offers friendly surroundings to a few dozen guests (and to the elephants, which are known to come and sip from the freshwater swimming pool in the evenings).

WHERE: 400 miles/644 km northeast of Lusaka. **NORMAN CARR SAFARIS:** Tel 260/216-24-6025; www.normancarrsafaris.com. *Cost:* 7-night safaris from $2,650 all-inclusive (off-peak, which is during emerald season), $3,360 (peak). **FLATDOGS CAMP:** Tel 260/216-24-6038; www.flatdogscamp.com. *Cost:* from $190 per person, all-inclusive (off-peak), $235 (peak). *When:* closed mid-Jan–mid-Mar. **BEST TIMES:** Dec–Mar (emerald season) for birding; Jun–Sep (dry season) for walking.

So Close and Yet So Far

Tongabezi Safari Lodge

Livingstone, Victoria Falls, Zambia

Just 10 miles or so downstream from the Tongabezi Safari Lodge is the thundering Victoria Falls (see below); although you cannot hear its roar, you somehow feel its power. Tongabezi itself is a place of tranquility, built along the banks of the Zambezi River, where the gentle waters offer no hint of the violent dive ahead. This is no average bush camp: There's a riverside swimming pool, four-poster beds, and bathtubs set upon verandas for luscious sunset views. Tasteful natural furnishings one could describe as "high bush" decorate the 11 thatch-roofed houses and cottages. The Tree House is just that—tree trunks literally burst through its floor. The open-air Honeymoon House and its forest-hugged patios make couples feel as if this is their own private Africa, while the Dog House is hardly worthy of the metaphorical name, featuring both a sunken bath and stone fireplace. It all adds up to the perfect romantic base, enhanced by invigorating morning bush and bird walks, gentle canoe trips, and sundowners on a dhow. To explore the Zambezi further, take a wild, whitewater rafting trip through the ancient gorges, or stay at one of the five chalets on Tongabezi's private Sindabezi Island, a small patch of trees and sand just a short boat ride away. You can also soar over the falls in a helicopter or, if you're particularly courageous, in a microlight, a gliderlike conveyance equipped with seats and a propeller.

Where: 10 miles/16 km upriver from Victoria Falls. Tel 260/213-327-468; www.tongabezi.com. *Cost:* cottages, $470 per person, all-inclusive (off-peak), $565 (peak). **Best times:** during the end of the rainy season in Mar–Jun, the falls are at their greatest flow, but the weather can be hot and wet; Jul–Sep offers mild temperatures and the most opportunities for game viewing and activities on and in the water.

The Smoke That Thunders

Victoria Falls

Zambia and Zimbabwe

Victoria Falls is every bit as monumental and magnificent as you imagine, its noise greater than a million migrating wildebeests, its mists visible from 40 miles away. Europeans first set eyes on it in 1855 during an expedition led by Dr. David Livingstone, the Scotsman who came to Africa in 1840 as a medical missionary but who earned his fame when he led quixotic journeys in search of the Nile's source. The natives call the falls Mosioa-tunya, which translates as "the smoke that thunders," but Livingstone thought it deserved something more regal (and British), so he named it in honor of his queen, who, sadly, would never see it.

The falls are a mile wide, spanning the breadth of the Zambezi River. As they crash from a height of 360 feet—twice that of Niagara (see p. 929)—they create a delicate, endless shower of rain and rainbows, or (if the moon is bright and full enough) lunar rainbows that drift in and out of view. At dawn and dusk the sky, water, and mist take on hues of pink and orange, especially during the wet season from March to May, when the cascades are at their greatest capacity and the spray vaults 1,000 feet into the sky and is visible from miles away. It is easy to imagine Dr. Livingstone's awe as he wrote: "On sights as beautiful as this, Angels, in their flight must have gazed." Today's heart-stopping "Flight of the Angels" refers to jaunts over the falls by helicopter, single-engine plane, or microlight aircraft (basically a hang glider with seats and propellers). Just as thrilling is the whitewater rafting at the foot of the falls: The white-knuckle rapids are some of the most exciting in the world, with plenty of Class IVs and Vs. You can also sign up for a visit to Livingstone Island (where Dr. Livingstone first set up camp), traveling by boat to this big chunk of land that splits the falls in two. Once you've arrived, you'll stop for a three-course meal that comes with a view and sound effects you won't soon forget.

The Zambezi serves as the natural barrier between Zimbabwe and Zambia, with a bridge connecting the two countries that is also a stage for bungee jumping. On the Zimbabwe side is the venerable Victoria Falls Hotel, open since 1904, an elegant grande dame redolent of the Edwardian era and within walking distance of the falls. On the Zambia side is the newer Royal Livingstone Hotel, whose graceful Colonial architecture and furnishings evoke an earlier, romantic age of exploration. Vervet monkeys and zebras roam the broad lawns that reach down to the river while, inside, guests dine and lounge beneath chandeliers in an open-air bar-lounge.

Where: 443 miles/713 km west of the Zimbabwean capital of Harare. **Victoria Falls Hotel:** Tel 263/13-44751; in the U.S., 800-745-8883; www.lhw.com/victoria. *Cost:* from $265. **Royal Livingstone Hotel:** Tel 206/21-332-1122; www.royal-livingstone-hotel.com. *Cost:* from $700. **Best times:** Falls are heaviest Mar–Jun; Jul–Sep also considered optimal.

A Landscape Wild and Weird

Matobo National Park

Matobo Hills, Zimbabwe

Huge granite masses—seamed, split, shaped, and sculpted by time and the elements—form an array of giant whalebacks, fanciful castles, knobby outcrops, and precariously balanced boulders that extend for thousands of square miles through the Matobo Hills (or the Matopos). This bizarre landscape so bewitched British financier and statesman Cecil J. Rhodes (after whom the republics of Zimbabwe and Zambia took their former name of Rhodesia) that he arranged to be buried here. No one leaves the 170-square-mile Matobo National Park—Zimbabwe's first—without spending an awe-inspiring moment at the site of his hillside grave, which Rhodes named "View of the World."

Believed to have been formed some 2

billion years ago, the otherworldly formations have been considered a center of spiritual power since the first hunters and gatherers created rock art here some 30,000 years ago. This is one of Africa's largest concentrations of cave paintings, their quality and quantity as impressive today as the area's wildlife. Many depict the rhinos, both white and black, that still live here in great numbers. Also found living here are leopards, cheetahs, and some 200 species of birds, including the world's largest number of raptors, among them black eagles, hawks, and owls.

Hidden away in this vast, natural rock garden is the Big Cave Camp, which accommodates just 16 guests in a 2,000-acre wilderness right outside the national park. Anything your hosts don't know about the area's geography, art, and wildlife isn't worth learning. The rooms they offer are A-frame huts of granite and thatch, built to stay cool during the sweltering summers. Drinks and tales are served around an open fire pit that stays lit well into the night, and if you're lucky enough to be there when a full moon illuminates the rock configurations, you'll understand why Rhodes could never leave.

WHERE: 30 miles/48 km south of Bulawayo. **BIG CAVE CAMP:** Tel 272/1-914-0966; www.bigcave.co.za. *Cost:* $120 per person, all-inclusive. **BEST TIME:** Apr–Sep, after the rains, when large numbers of animals collect at waterholes and temperatures are cooler.

ISLANDS OF THE INDIAN OCEAN

Rain Forest Sanctuary That Meets the Sea

MASOALA NATIONAL PARK

Madagascar

Accessible only by boat or multiday trek, Masoala National Park is Madagascar's best-kept secret, even though, at 840 square miles, it is the largest of the country's national parks. Established in 1997, Masoala is located on an incisor-shaped peninsula in the northeast corner of the island and is home to 10 of the island's 30 species of lemurs, which range widely in color and appearance; the most beautiful, the red-ruffed lemur, is not found anywhere else. But perhaps the strangest lemur, which can also be spied here, is the nocturnal aye-aye, an enchanting little creature with bony fingers, batlike ears, and the long, bushy tail of a squirrel. The small island of Nosy Mangabe, now part of the park, was designated a reserve in the 1960s specifically to protect the aye-aye; it is also home to a large collection of leaf-tailed geckos, pygmy chameleons barely an inch long, ancient Malagasy burial sites, and rock carvings left behind by Dutch sailors who visited in the 16th century.

Native to Madagascar, the endangered red-ruffed lemur is found only in Masoala.

Some of the world's healthiest coral reefs are found in Tampolo Marine Park, off the west coast of the peninsula, while farther offshore, in Antongil Bay, thousands of humpback whales congregate to breed from June to September. Watch them breech and spray, listen for the males' eerie song, and, in August, look for calves accompanying their mothers. Although Masoala National Park makes up only 2 percent of Madagascar's landmass, approximately 20 percent of its plants exist here, including many little-known varieties: Four out of five of all plant and animal species that live in Madagascar are found nowhere else on the planet. Despite its protected status, Masoala Park still suffers encroachment from loggers (especially those looking to harvest ebony and rosewood) and lemur hunters. Sustainable tourism, as practiced by the lodges within the park, helps combat these illegal practices.

WHERE: Maroantsetra, at the northeastern tip of Madagascar. **HOW:** Morondava-based Remote River Expeditions offers customized itineraries. Tel 261/20-95-52347; www.remoterivers.com. U.S.-based Wilderness Travel offers 15-day trips that include the Masoala. Tel 800-368-2794; www.wildernesstravel.com. *Cost:* from $4,695. Originate in Antananarivo. *When:* May, Sep, and Nov. **BEST TIMES:** Aug–Sep for drier weather and whales calving and orchids blooming; Sep–Nov for birding.

Expedition into the Eighth Continent

RAFTING THE MANGOKY RIVER

Madagascar

One of the best ways to experience Madagascar, with its limited and primitive roads and lack of tourist facilities, is by paddling the calm waters of the Mangoky River to the island's remote and seldom visited southwest corner. A beautiful and wild region, it also reveals that the mini continent of Madagascar is a veritable laboratory for evolution. More than 30 species of lemurs and 8,000 species of plants are found only on this island, which is also home to 3,000 species of butterflies, seven species of baobab trees, and half the world's chameleons. You'll get plenty of chances to disembark and explore the diverse ecosystems here—from misty rain forests to dry, deciduous woodlands to harsh and beautiful spiny forests, where massive baobabs mingle with cacti and strange, barbed plants. Knowledgeable, passionate guides will point it all out and get you some face time with the lemurs, including the tall (and very vocal) Indri indri, the rubriventer (red-bellied) lemur, and the nocturnal bush baby. Visits to markets provide a glimpse of day-to-day life and the chance to meet the Malagasy people who inhabit the riverside settlements.

At the end of each of the wonder-packed days of rafting along the river, sandbar camps are set up under the evening sky and dinners are cooked over an open fire. After all the paddling is done, those wishing to extend their visit with a beachside retreat will find a warm welcome at Chez Maggie in Morondova, where a charming collection of bungalows and chalets is set within gardens and sand. Being so close to the Tropic of Capricorn ensures that the spectacular sunsets will linger through the whole length of your first rum-and-lime.

HOW: Remote River Expeditions offers 13- and 21-day trips, of which 7 days are spent rafting on the Mangoky River. Tel 261/20-95-52347; www.remoterivers.com. *Cost:* from $2,560. Originate in Antananarivo. *When:* departures May and Jun. **CHEZ MAGGIE:** Tel 261/20-95-52347; www.chezmaggie.com. *Cost:* from $50.

Delicate Masterpieces of the Indian Ocean

The Maldive Islands

Maldives

Made up of 26 atolls scattered across the Indian Ocean from north to south in a shape that resembles an exclamation point, Maldives is a fragile wonderland of white sand, palms, lagoons, reefs, and Hockney-blue seas. Of the 36,000 square miles it covers, less than 1 percent is land. If the sea level were to rise just a few feet, its nearly 1,200 tiny, flat-as-a-tabletop islands would be gone; don't underestimate the urgency when those who have been there suggest that you see the world's lowest-lying nation before it's too late.

Each resort—there are almost 100—occupies a private island and is dedicated to showing off its own jewel of the sea. Divers and snorkelers revel in the easy access to miles of coral gardens in shallow, crystal-clear waters. They come in search of small, colorful creatures like unicornfish, harlequin sweetlips, and glassfish, as well as hulking reef sharks and manta rays. Above the water, visitors enjoy everything from deep-sea fishing to kayaking, or simply reading, snoozing, and contemplating one's enormous good fortune in a hammock with a view.

The Maldive Islands consist of a series of atolls, each one ideal for sunbathing or exploring the surrounding waters.

Native Maldivians inhabit not even one-fifth of the islands, and it is rare to meet a local aside from those employed by resorts. Tourism is vital to the Maldivian future, and many of the resorts are environmentally and socially responsible. The Banyan Tree Vabbinfaru—where 48 villas (each with an ocean view, four-poster bed, and private garden) stand just steps from the aquamarine water—prides itself on stewardship of the ocean and has established a marine lab that, among other efforts, protects sea turtles that nest on its beaches. The award-winning Soneva Gili by Six Senses, with its 45 over-water bungalows (some reachable only by boat) built from natural materials and open to sea breezes, blissfully operates under the oft-borrowed "No News No Shoes" mantra. It strives to achieve complete sustainability through ambitious preservation policies and educational programs with local communities. Both resorts are nothing short of island heaven; for confirmation, spend an afternoon being pampered at their world-class spas and open-air waterside dining venues. Unlike the majority of resorts accessible only by seaplane from the airport at Malé, the capital city and island, each is a 20-minute boat ride away.

Where: 250 miles/400 km southwest of India, spreading more than 500 miles north to south. **Banyan Tree Vabbinfaru:** Tel 960/664-3147; in the U.S., 800-591-0439; www.banyantree.com. *Cost:* from $900 (off-peak), from $1,600 (peak), inclusive. **Soneva Gili by Six Senses:** Tel 960/664-0304; www.sixsenses.com. *Cost:* from $1,000 (off-peak), from $1,600 (peak), inclusive. **Best time:** Dec–Apr for driest days and clearest waters.

Heaven's Prototype

MAURITIUS

Mascarene Islands

Thanks to an enlightened policy of ecotourism and preservation, this tiny, pear-shaped, volcanic speck of an island in the middle of the Indian Ocean remains unspoiled and intriguing. Independent since 1968, Mauritius is a 28-mile-wide microcosm of cultural diversity, an exotic mosaic of Indian, African, British, Continental, and Chinese influences. It's a long way from anywhere, but people flock here, including European sun seekers, honeymooners, and those who unwind après safari at the island's exquisite resort hotels.

With 200 miles of coastline, Mauritius is full of snorkel-perfect lagoons.

Mauritius can easily be separated into quadrants. In the north, you'll find St. Louis, the capital. Congested on weekdays, it's the place to be on weekends from May through November to catch Thoroughbred racing, the island's most popular sport. A day at the Champ de Mars racecourse in Port Louis, one of the world's oldest, borders on mandatory.

In the east, along the Flacq coastline, luxury hotels line the gorgeous white sand beach. Even if you don't stay at the One&Only Le Saint Géran, make reservations at the Spoon des Îles (Alain Ducasse's first restaurant outside Europe) or chef Vineet Bhatia's excellent Rasoi by Vineet. Both showcase the intricate flavors of the Indian Ocean. Golfers flock to the course here designed by Ernie Els at the Four Seasons at Anahita as well as to Le Touessrok's Bernhard Langer–designed course across the water on Île aux Cerfs.

Most visitors to Mauritius don't make it farther south than the airport. Buck the trend. Take a road trip through the picturesque village of Mahébourg with its colorful old houses, then visit Vieux Grand Port. Its ruins and monuments date back to the first landings of the Dutch in 1598 and hint at Mauritius's dramatic past.

The west, the most "African" part of the island, comes alive with sega music and dancing and is world renowned for deep-sea fishing. The best beaches are the public ones, especially on weekends, when Mauritian families turn up for boisterous reunions and feasts where all are welcome.

WHERE: 1,120 miles/1,770 km off the east coast of Africa. **ONE&ONLY LE SAINT GÉRAN:** Tel 230/401-1688; in the U.S., 866-552-0001; www.lesaintgeran.oneandonlyresorts.com. *Cost:* rooms from $775 (off-peak), from $1,150 (peak); tasting menu at Spoon $145, dinner at Rasoi $100. **FOUR SEASONS:** Tel 230/401-3131; in the U.S., 800-819-5053; www.fourseasons.com/mauritius. *Cost:* from $600 (off-peak), from $950 (peak), includes golf; greens fees for nonguests from $250. **LE TOUESSROK RESORT:** Tel 230/402-7400; www.letouessrokresort.com. *Cost:* from $600 (off-peak), from $1,300 (peak), inclusive; greens fees from $250 for guests. **BEST TIMES:** year-round for good weather, but particularly Sep–Dec; Oct–Apr for deep-sea fishing; Dec for Derby Day.

Fearless and Protected Wildlife

BIRD ISLAND

Seychelles

Bird Island belongs to beautiful tropical birds so isolated they know no fear of man, freely nesting, courting, and preening within arm's length of curious visitors. The opportunity to observe birds at such close range in their natural habitat sets Bird Island in a class of its own. The most northerly of the Seychelles islands, a tiny 170-acre coral cay, it hosts more than 100 endemic and migratory bird species. At any one time, you should be able to spot 20 different species, including—from May to October—2 million sooty terns. Each year, the terns drop seawater on the island's grass, causing it to go dry over the course of a few weeks. Then the nest building begins. Some birders consider Bird Island one of the best wildlife experiences in the world. The moment you touch down on the island, the pace of life stops and natural simplicity takes over.

The island is also home to the endangered green and hawksbill turtles, as well as Esmeralda, a giant tortoise who is more than 200 years old. Monitoring the fascinating turtles' movements while they nest or lay their eggs can constitute a busy day, but there are also plenty of opportunities to snorkel or just take a dip in the gin-clear waters. The east and south sides of the island are protected by a reef that harbors many varieties of colorful tropical fish; the rest is wide swaths of white sand beaches and turquoise sea. A simple family-owned lodge with 24 chalets is the sole place to stay on the island, and its friendly Seychellois staffers are the only inhabitants. They prepare some of the freshest and most flavorful meals imaginable. There are no televisions, no air-conditioning, no telephones, no swimming pool, and no pretensions. Only the birds' lively chatter interrupts the quiet.

WHERE: 60 miles/97 km north of Mahé. **BIRD ISLAND LODGE:** Tel 248/22-49-25; www.birdislandseychelles.com. *Cost:* from $600, all-inclusive. **BEST TIMES:** Oct–Apr for best snorkeling; Oct–Nov and Apr–May, winds bring in a greater variety of migrant seabirds; lodge website shows what to expect month-to-month, including the nesting and hatching schedules of terns and hawksbill turtles.

Crystalline Water, Talcum Sand, and Swaying Palms

MAHÉ

Seychelles

An archipelago of 115 coral and granite islands (only about 20 of them inhabited) in the middle of the Indian Ocean, the Seychelles islands are the idyllic destination for a honeymoon or post-safari R&R. Travelers come to relax (and for the most part, pay handsomely to do so) on the blindingly white beaches and enjoy the lush tropical flora. Most head to the resorts on Mahé, the country's biggest island and home to 90 percent of its population and some of its loveliest shoreline.

Uberluxury prevails on the south end of the island, where the Maia Luxury Resort offers 30 butler-serviced pavilion villas, each with its own infinity pool; an open-air spa hidden in dense jungle; and sophisticated Creole-Mediterranean-French cuisine. It vies with the recently opened Four Seasons Seychelles for belle of the ball (the latter might win for its slightly less stratospheric prices). Nestled among boulders on a lush hillside, it has an indulgent spa and top-notch restaurant, 67 villas with wooden decks and plunge pools, and unbeatable views of palm-lined cliffs and the incredibly blue Indian Ocean.

Anse Source d'Argent's seclusion and sculpturelike boulders make it one of the world's most alluring and picturesque beaches.

Those who aren't ready for such opulence gravitate toward the accommodations on the north end of the island. It's a minute's walk from the most popular (and still rarely crowded) beach, the palm-tree studded Beau Vallon, to the newly built Hanneman Holiday Residence. The Clef des Îles also beckons, with glorified beach huts overlooking the water, right next to an excellent dive center.

Break away from resort life for a visit to the energetic, colorful market in the capital city of Victoria. Enjoy a family-style feast (fish fritters, chicken curry, fried eggplant) at the Colonial house now turned restaurant Marie Antoinette, where you'll soak in the still-vibrant culture of local Creoles, descendants of European colonists and African and Malagasy slaves. Victoria's National Botanical Gardens protect endemic species, including the coco de mer, the famous national tree. You'll see it everywhere, beginning with the stamp in your passport: Its massive seed takes the form of a woman's buttocks. It's a short boat ride to the six tiny islands that make up Sainte Anne Marine National Park, the Indian Ocean's first, and arguably most beautiful, underwater park. To the delight of landlubbers, the abundant fish and corals can be viewed from a semisubmersible "sub-sea viewer"; snorkelers and divers will be thrilled by the warm, clear water.

It's an easy island-hop to neighboring La Digue, where you'll find one of the world's most photographed (yet still blissfully empty) beaches, Anse Source d'Argent. Huge, artfully weathered pink and rust-colored granite boulders and pale pink sand are all that's left of the peaks of the supercontinent Gondwanaland, submerged millions of years ago. Jump on an oxcart and have a guide take you into the forest in search of 12 endemic bird species, including the Seychelles paradise flycatcher, whose male has a long trailing tail.

Visitor info: www.seychelles.travel. **Maia Luxury Resort:** Tel 248/390-000; www.maia.com.sc. *Cost:* villas from $2,200. **Four Seasons Resort Seychelles:** Tel 248/393-000; www.fourseasons.com/seychelles. *Cost:* villas from $980 (off-peak), from $1,200 (peak). **Hanneman Holiday Residence:** Tel 248/425-000; www.hanneman-seychelles.com. *Cost:* from $180. **Clef des Îles:** Tel 248/527-100; www.clefdesiles.com. *Cost:* from $350. **Marie Antoinette:** Tel 248/266-222. *Cost:* dinner $20. **Best times:** Mar–May and Sep–Nov for clear waters and less rain; late Oct for food, art, and music at Victoria's Festival Kreol.

THE
MIDDLE
EAST

CASPIAN SEA
MEDITERRANEAN SEA
SYRIA
Euphrates
Tigris
LEBANON
Beirut
Damascus
West Bank
Tel Aviv
Jerusalem
Amman
Dead Sea
ISRAEL
JORDAN
Sinai
Gulf of Suez
IRAQ
Baghdad
KUWAIT
PERSIAN GULF
BAHRAIN
QATAR
OMAN
Strait of Hormuz
Dubai
Abu Dhabi
GULF OF OMAN
Muscat
UNITED ARAB EMIRATES
SAUDI ARABIA
HEJAZ
Medina
Riyadh
Jeddah
Mecca
ASIR
RED SEA
OMAN
YEMEN
Sanaa
ARABIAN SEA
Socotra Islands
GULF OF ADEN
INDIAN OCEA
N
S
E
W
0 100 200 MILES
0 161 322 Kilometers

Crusader Stronghold on the Sea

Acre

Israel

Surrounded by Ottoman-era walls, Acre (also known as Akko) has been visited by everyone from Marco Polo to St. Francis during its more than 4,000 years of existence. As with Caesarea (see next page), the Crusaders left their imprint, establishing this ancient port as the maritime center and largest city of their Christian empire. They built a citadel and monumental fortifications, seawalls, and the Knights' Hall, a subterranean network of vaulted corridors that held 50,000 soldiers during their 12th-century heyday.

Greatly overlooked in recent centuries, Acre is a well-preserved historic city, still displaying its Ottoman and Crusader influences in its mosaic-adorned mosques with towering minarets and churches with similarly soaring steeples. There's a teeming souk (be sure to sample the hummus at Said's, said to be the best), Turkish baths, traditional coffeehouses, and charming seafood restaurants on the streets leading to the port.

With its Ottoman-era setting and views of the waterfront, the cozy Uri Buri restaurant is easily one of the most atmospheric in town, featuring imaginative cuisine and wines exclusively from Israel. Owner Uri Yirmias's mango-spiked creole shrimp and calamari with kumquats are inventive takes on Israeli classics. The menu at Abu Christo hasn't changed much in 6 decades, where just-caught fish is simply prepared, either grilled or deep fried, and served on a waterfront patio where guests enjoy the sunset free of charge.

Acre's population is proud to be the country's greatest ethnic mix, with Christian, Muslim, Druze, and Baha'i minorities. The Baha'i, whose little-known monotheistic religion was established in 19th-century Persia, revere Acre as the sacred burial place of a prophet of their faith, Bahā' Allāh. The faith's headquarters is in nearby Haifa, which delights with its own unique charm. The magical gardens at the Baha'i World Centre are the city's centerpiece, spanning the face of Mount Carmel and cascading down it in a profusion of manicured lawns, reflecting pools, statues, and marble temples.

The area surrounding the base of Mount Carmel has been transformed into a casual, car-free promenade lined with outdoor restaurants and cafés. This is also where you'll find the Villa Carmel, a 16-room hotel housed in a restored Bauhaus-era building and featuring a Mediterranean garden restaurant.

Crusaders used the Knights' Hall for resting and eating.

Where: 70 miles/112 km north of Tel Aviv. **Uri Buri:** Tel 972/4-955-2212. *Cost:* lunch $45. **Abu Christo:** Tel: 972/4-991-0065; www.abu-christo.co.il. *Cost:* lunch $30. **Baha'i Gardens:** Tel 972/4-835-8358. **Villa Carmel:** Tel 972/4-835-7777; www.villacarmel.co.il. *Cost:* from $200 (off-peak), from $350 (peak). **Best times:** early Oct for Akko Fringe Theater Festival; Sats in Dec for Holiday of Holidays Festival in Haifa.

Roman Fortress by the Mediterranean

Caesarea

Israel

Caesarea is the kind of multilayered historic site that results from conquests and reconquests over millennia, and is the location of some of the Levant's most important Roman ruins. Built some 2,000 years ago by emperor Herod the Great, who dedicated it to Caesar Augustus, Caesarea was once a thriving metropolis with a population over 125,000, the largest in the eastern Mediterranean.

The city's ruins survived periods of Roman, Byzantine, and Muslim rule.

Caesarea's archaeological gems, now expertly excavated, serve to evoke daily life during the time of Jesus. A double aqueduct and one of the largest and best-preserved hippodromes in the classical world, as well as Herod's palace and columned pool, have all survived the ages. An easily navigable trail passes among restored Roman arches, roads, baths, and granaries. But the grand Roman theater with the Mediterranean as a backdrop is perhaps Caesarea's greatest highlight, a mostly re-created venue that seats 3,600 and is popular for summertime concerts and performances.

Well over a millennium after it was founded, Caesarea began its second incarnation: as an important Crusader stronghold. These medieval Christians built important fortifications in their quest to rescue the Holy Land from the armies of Saladin. Eight hundred years later, the remnants of these 12th-century citadels loom just steps from the Mediterranean, most of them surrounded by a stone wall and moat.

Today, Caesarea is an important tourist destination, home to Israel's only golf course, and—just minutes outside of Tel Aviv (see p. 454)—one of its wealthiest residential communities. The city has redeveloped its Mediterranean waterfront, which features sandy beaches within sight of the ruins, and has built what bills itself as the world's first underwater archaeological museum. Intended for divers of all skill levels using waterproof maps and spread over nearly 165 square miles of the sea floor, the site offers four trails to view sunken anchors, statues, and Roman shipwrecks.

Considering its impressive natural and historical setting, Caesarea would seem like a logical resort location. Although an inviting café and restaurant scene has emerged along the beachfront, there is only one hotel of note, the Dan Caesarea, a modern, 114-room 1980s property spread across 15 manicured acres of gardens and lush landscaping.

WHERE: 36 miles/58 km north of Tel Aviv. **OLD CAESAREA DIVING CLUB:** Tel 972/4-626-5898; www.caesarea-diving.com/en/. **DAN CAESAREA HOTEL:** Tel 972/3-520-2552; www.danhotels.com. *Cost:* from $240 (off-peak), from $370 (peak). **BEST TIMES:** Mar–May for balmy yet bearable temperatures; early Jun for Caesarea Jazz Festival.

Rolling Hills, Wildflowers, a Freshwater Sea, and a Holy Town

THE GALILEE

Israel

A fertile region blanketed in spring by seas of wildflowers and blossoming trees, few places have as much resonance for Christians and Jews as the Galilee. With constant appearances in ancient scriptures, it is home to some of Israel's most important pilgrimage sites, from the holy town of Nazareth to the shores of the harp-shaped Sea of Galilee. This rich earth is also where Jewish pioneers set up the country's first kibbutz and where Israelis today come for beaches and outdoor fun.

The Sea of Galilee is actually a 62-square-mile freshwater lake that is almost completely ringed by cliffs and high hills. For millennia the main city on its shores has been Tiberias, built by the son of Herod the Great in A.D. 20. No hotel in the region outshines the shorefront Scots Hotel, a former 19th-century church hospital that opened as a resort in 2004 with 69 spacious guest rooms. Owned by the Church of Scotland, the stylish hotel claims one of the Galilee's only private beaches and is conveniently close to Decks, an elegant restaurant set on piles jutting out over the water.

Nazareth, a short drive north, is the home of Israel's largest Arab community, which makes up two-thirds of the city's population of 65,000; the rest is a multicultural mix of Jews, Druze, Muslims, and Christians. In this hilltop town hewn from marblelike stone and anchored by its teaming souk, the Basilica of the Annunciation—the largest church in the Middle East—was built on the site where the Bible claims Jesus's birth was heralded by the angel Gabriel. Make time to stroll along Paul VI Street to snack on Israel's best Arab sweets, but save room for lunch at Diana, where simple yet exquisite local dishes—kebabs, grilled meats, and Middle Eastern mezze (small-dish) salads—are prepared right before your eyes.

Nazareth was also the boyhood home of Jesus, who returned here to teach; a newly organized Jesus Trail begins here and follows the 40-mile terrain that he would have walked during his ministry. It connects such spots as Canaan, the Sea of Galilee, Tabgha (and its Byzantine-style Church of the Multiplication of the Loaves and Fishes), and the Mount of Beatitudes, where the Sermon on the Mount took place. You'll shift from the Biblical era to the early Middle Ages with a trek up to Safed (Zefat), Israel's highest town and the historic home of Jewish mysticism known as Kabbala. A stroll through the 1,000-year-old city's mazelike Synagogue Quarter remains one of Judaism's most enchanting experiences, while the art galleries that fill the old Arab Quarter lend a slightly bohemian air. If you're spending the night, you have two very different options: the exclusive hilltop Mizpe-Hayamim (Sea View) outside town, known for its spa and its farm-to-table restaurant, or the family-run Vered HaGalil, which affords a dose of the American West at a hillside horse ranch with modest rooms and sweeping views.

Where: Tiberias is 81 miles/131 km northeast of Tel Aviv. **Visitor info:** www.gogalilee.org. **Scots Hotel:** Tel 972/4-671-0710; www.scotshotels.co.il. *Cost:* from $285. **Decks:** Tel 972/4-672-1538. *Cost:* dinner $35. **Diana:** Tel 972/4-657-2919. *Cost:* lunch $25. **Jesus Trail:** www.jesustrail.com. **Mizpe-Hayamim:** Tel 972/4-699-4555; www.mizpe-hayamim.com. *Cost:* from $390 (off-peak), from $550 (peak). **Vered HaGalil:** Tel 972/4-693-5785; www.veredhagalil.com. *Cost:* from $135 (off-peak), from $210 (peak). **Best times:** Feb–Mar for wildflowers; May and Dec for Jacob's Ladder Festival in Ginosar; early Jul for folk dancing festival in Karmiel; Jul or Aug for Klezmer Festival in Safed; Christmastime in Nazareth.

Remote and Nature-Filled: Israel's Wild North

The Golan Heights

Israel

This mountainous and sparsely populated outcrop is unexpected in a land of the unexpected—where snow falls in the winter and nights remain cool in the summer even as the rest of Israel bakes. Rising over 3,500 feet, the Golan Heights is known to outsiders more for being captured from Syria by Israel following the 1967 Six-Day War than as the recreational destination Israelis have come to treasure.

Surrounded by lush volcanic hills and bordering much of the Sea of Galilee (see previous page), the Golan is Israel at its "frontier" best: a land of cattle ranches, ski resorts, and boutique wineries; olive groves and orchards; nature reserves; organic restaurants and Druze villages. Most of all, the Golan is Israel untouched—a quiet corner that has for the most part avoided being overrun by tourists.

While the Golan may lack the archaeological richness of the neighboring Galilee, history buffs will not be disappointed. The settlement of Gamla, which dates back 5,000 years, is known as the "Masada of the North" (see p. 452); it is where some 9,000 Jews revolted against Roman rule in A.D. 67 and ultimately chose to end their lives rather than be conquered by the empire (Masada would fall to the Romans 6 years later). Today, the ruins of much of their original settlement remain, lorded over by a colony of rare and majestic griffon vultures that breed in the surrounding hills.

Farther on is the deer reserve in the dense Odem forest, whose name means "red" in Hebrew and refers to the rust-colored soil of the surrounding countryside. Here, trickling streams and cooling cascades run along Mount Bental, while the torrents of the nearby Banyas River are mighty enough for whitewater rafting.

All are close to Katzrin, the Golan's de facto capital, known for its small-scale inns and Israel's top microbrewery, the German-style Golan Brewery, founded in 2006. Pop in for a tour and a pint, or sample what many consider Israel's best wine at the Golan Heights Winery, a short drive away.

Where: Katzrin is 135 miles/200 km north of Tel Aviv. **Golan Brewery:** Tel 972/4-696-3625; www.golanbeer.co.il. **Golan Heights Winery:** Tel 972/4-696-8420; www.golanwines.co.il. **Best time:** May for cooler temperatures.

Spiritual Enclave of Ancient Sites and Sacred Places

Historic Jerusalem

Jerusalem, Israel

Within the 16th-century walls built by Suleiman the Magnificent and accessed via eight fortified gates, ancient Jerusalem is a place that transcends time, place, and faith. It's here that you'll find the capital city's spiritual heart, where more than 200 historic sites—the most sacred of Judaism, Christianity, and Islam—commingle. View it all from the Tower of David before strolling through the Jewish Quarter en route to the Western Wall. It is Judaism's holiest site, where worshippers come to pray and leave handwritten notes in its stone crevices.

In the city's ancient Muslim Quarter, merchant stalls are heavy with sweets and embroidered tunics, while the smells of sizzling shashlik (shish kebab) waft through the air. It's all a prelude to the gold-topped Dome of the Rock (Qubbat as-Sakhrah in Arabic), the oldest existing Islamic shrine and the third holiest site in Islam after Mecca and Medina (see p. 467). Built in A.D. 690, the resplendent mosque rests upon the location where the prophet Mohammed is said to have ascended to heaven. Jews revere it as the site of the altar where Abraham was called upon by God to sacrifice his son Isaac. You'll also find the holiest place in Christianity here. The Church of the Holy Sepulchre was completed in A.D. 335 on the site, known as Calvary, where Jesus is believed to have been crucified, buried, and resurrected. Pilgrims approach the church by the mile-long Via Dolorosa (the Way of the Cross; literally, the Road of Pain), whose 14 stations mark the path Jesus took as he carried his cross to his execution.

You can find respite in the Old City at the cloistered Austrian Hospice, one of many modest European-run guest houses welcoming visitors of all faiths (this one distinguished by a Viennese café serving great Wiener schnitzel and strudel) right on the Via Dolorosa. The hostelry is just a minute's walk from the always busy Abu Shukri, the town's best hummus takeout.

For more elegant accommodations, head north of the Damascus Gate, where you'll find the American Colony, built around a 19th-century Ottoman pasha's mansion. This Levantine-style hotel lures foreign correspondents, Israeli artists, intellectuals, diplomats, and a who's who of the Palestinian elite to gather beside the fragrant lemon trees and burbling fountains in the courtyards or in its legendary Cellar Bar. Come hungry on Saturday for the feastlike Middle Eastern luncheon, a Jerusalem tradition.

The King David is a more formal affair, the equivalent of Raffles in Singapore (see p. 618). Built in 1931 during the British Mandate, this hotel features a mix of Art Deco and Levantine details, with modern flourishes courtesy of Adam Tihany. Linger at the veranda café and enjoy its panoramic Old City views.

Where: 36 miles/58 km east of Tel Aviv. **Austrian Hospice:** Tel 972/2-626-5800;

www.austrianhospice.com. *Cost:* from $140; lunch $12. **Abu Shukri:** Tel 972/2-627-1538. **American Colony Hotel:** Tel 972/2-627-9777; www.americancolony.com. *Cost:* from $380. **King David Hotel:** Tel 972/2-620-8888; www.danhotels.com. *Cost:* from $440 (off-peak), from $530 (peak). **Best times:** Mar–May and Sep–Nov for pleasant weather; all major Christian, Muslim, and Jewish holidays, including the period around Passover, when thousands come for the blessing at the Western Wall.

Millennia-Old Capital Gets a Contemporary Makeover

West Jerusalem

Jerusalem, Israel

The ancient City of David has quietly developed a surprisingly modern edge in its predominantly Jewish western quarters. While the area still abounds with treasures millennia old, it's now also filled with world-class contemporary architecture, culture, and cuisine. Long perceived as the sleepy alternative to ubercool Tel Aviv an hour away (see p. 454), Jerusalem is getting a makeover.

Spanish architect and master bridge-builder Santiago Calatrava helped launch Jerusalem's new image with the completion of his towering, swooping Chords Bridge in 2008, which welcomes visitors with a flourish and will serve as the anchor for Jerusalem's mass transit system, now under development. Rising to over 400 feet, the bridge's name honors the 66 steel cables that hold it in place—a massive support lattice evocative of a harp, the favored instrument of King David, Jerusalem's biblical-era founder.

But Jerusalem's march into modernism really began in 2005, with the opening of the Historical Museum at the Yad Vashem Holocaust Memorial, designed by Israeli-Canadian architect Moshe Safdie. Overlooking the tranquil village of Ein Kerem, the museum is shaped like a triangular column and dramatically cuts through more than 600 feet of mountainside. An unsettling structure, it sets an apt tone for the journey that awaits inside.

The Chords Bridge was designed by Santiago Calatrava and built to accommodate both trains and pedestrians.

Safdie lent this same cool aesthetic to the Mamilla Hotel, the first important "design" hotel in Jerusalem if not all of Israel. Located minutes from the King David Hotel (see p. 449), the 194-room Mamilla is clad in creamy Jerusalem stone, with contemporary interiors by Italian design master Pierro Lissoni. Even if you're staying elsewhere, the rooftop brasserie deserves a visit for its Old City views and wide choice of Israeli wines. Safdie was also behind the adjacent Alrov Mamilla Avenue's shop-lined walkway; like a stylish open-air bazaar, it links downtown Jerusalem with the Old City's iconic Jaffa Gate.

On the opposite side of town, the venerable Israel Museum—home of the Dead Sea Scrolls—has emerged from a massive, 2-year renovation by American architect James Carpenter. Adding to its existing 1965 footprint, Carpenter created a set of glass-walled hillside pavilions that nearly double the museum's display space. There are important new site-specific works by sculptor Anish Kapoor and artist Olafur Eliasson as well as an 18th-century synagogue from Surinam, painstakingly restored and rebuilt.

YAD VASHEM: Tel 972/2-644-3565; www.yadvashem.org. **MAMILLA HOTEL:** Tel 972/2-548-2222; www.mamillahotel.com. *Cost:* from $350 (off-peak), from $500 (peak). **ISRAEL MUSEUM:** Tel 972/2-670-8811; www.english.imjnet.org.il. **BEST TIMES:** May or Jun for the arts-filled Israel Festival; Jul for Israel Film Festival; Aug for Jerusalem Wine Festival.

The Site of Jesus's Birth

WEST BANK

Palestinian Authority

Technically located beyond Israel's borders, the West Bank is mere miles from Jerusalem, but it feels like another world entirely. Conflict-fraught and Israeli-occupied since 1967, it remains one of the most hotly disputed and spiritually rich places on earth. Getting there requires a bit of advance planning (Israeli-registered cars and Israelis themselves are not allowed in), but for intrepid visitors not put off by the checkpoints, roadblocks, and controversial Israeli security wall, a quick passport check will put you swiftly on the road to Bethlehem for a glimpse of life in this land sacred to Arabs, Jews, and Christians.

Although the West Bank is revered by Jews as the birthplace and hometown of David, King of Israel, most modern-day pilgrims are Christians, following in the footsteps of the Holy Family to Bethlehem—today a busy and modern city of 25,000—to visit the place of Jesus's birth. Manger Square is the site of the fortresslike Church of the Nativity, built around A.D. 330 (later destroyed and rebuilt) and one of the world's oldest continually operating churches. Custody is shared by the Greek Orthodox Church, the Franciscan Order of the Roman Catholic Church, and the Armenian Orthodox Church. Within its Grotto of the Nativity, a 14-point star marks what is thought to be the place where the infant Jesus was born. Near Manger Square, Jews, Christians, and Muslims all flock to the tomb of Rachel, second and favorite wife of Jacob. It is the third holiest site in Judaism.

Tourist facilities are limited and most visitors come for the day from Jerusalem, but overnighters can stay at the 250-room Jacir Palace InterContinental Hotel, whose original wing was built in 1910 as the home of the wealthy Jacir mercantile family. It's a short drive—or atmospheric stroll—from here to the city's most important landmarks.

Outside Bethlehem—where the scenery quickly shifts from olive and pine forests to stark desert valleys—lesser-known (but no less important) religious sites abound. The ancient town of Jericho, where Joshua led the Israelites from bondage in Egypt, is surprisingly green. Despite being one of the lowest cities on earth, it is the breadbasket of the West Bank and, having been inhabited for some 11,000 years, vies with Damascus (see p. 469) as the world's oldest city. The 12th-century Greek Orthodox Monastery of Deir Quruntal atop the Mount of Temptation was built where Jesus fasted for 40 days while tempted by the devil. Ascend via a scenic cable car that provides views of the Dead Sea and Jordan to the east. Also outside Jericho is Nabi Musa, an Islamic shrine to Moses said to be his burial site (a designation also given to Mount Nebo, in Jordan; see p. 458), and Mar Saba, a beautiful 5th-century Greek Orthodox monastery open to men only.

WHERE: Bethlehem is 7 miles/10 km southeast of Jerusalem; Jericho is 13 miles/20 km southeast of Jerusalem. **JACIR PALACE INTERCONTINENTAL:** Tel 972/2-276-6777; www.ichhotelsgroup.com. *Cost:* from $150 (off-peak), from $250 (peak). **BEST TIMES:** Christmas and Easter for processions in and near Manger Square in Bethlehem.

A Legendary Fortress Near the Dead Sea

MASADA

Israel

"Masada will not fall again" is a phrase known by every Israeli youth and countless numbers of their Jewish brethren around the world—a declaration of invincibility commemorating the 967 Jewish men, women, and children who died atop this stark plateau defending themselves from Roman forces in A.D. 73.

At that time, Palestine was a Roman colony, and Masada was built and ruled—with an iron fist—by Herod the Great. His 18-acre palace stood on a sheer-sided plateau, 1,440 feet above the shores of the Dead Sea and surrounded by a desolate desert. Abandoned by Roman forces after Herod's death, Masada became the ultimate refuge for a tenacious band of Jewish patriots who repelled an invasion by 15,000 heavily armed Roman troops for three long years.

Ultimately, the Jews opted for mass suicide over defeat—a tragic act that has come to symbolize Israel's ongoing struggle for survival since its 1948 independence. The fortress itself is remarkably well preserved: a complex of ancient homes, cisterns, thermal baths, a church, synagogues, and Herod's three-tiered villa, all ringed by citadel-like walls.

The best time to experience Masada is early, with a predawn climb to witness sunrise over the Dead Sea and the Judean Desert (for citizens, scaling these heights at least once is a matter of national pride). Although a 5-minute cable-car ride is available, many visitors brave one of Masada's two hiking paths. The steep Snake Path is the most challenging, wending its way up the plateau's eastern flank. After descending, the nearby Dead

Archaeologists excavated Masada in the 1960s.

Sea and its main beaches are a welcome relief, easily reached via a waterside highway.

The Dead Sea—at 1,300 feet below sea level, the lowest land point in the world—is a landlocked salt lake that creates a natural border with Jordan, whose waterfront is less commercially developed (see p. 456). On the Israeli (western) side, it is an hour's drive from Jerusalem to the stretch of coastal towns that lure with mineral-rich muds, sulfuric baths, and easy floating in water nine times saltier than the ocean. The stretch around Ein Gedi and Ein Bokek offers hotels, spas, and restaurants, whereas the sea's northern tip, near Kalya, is less developed. Stop along the way for a hike and take a soak in the springs at the oasislike En Gedi Nature Reserve. Escape the heat in the cool Qumran Caves, where the Dead Sea Scrolls were found in 1947.

WHERE: 5 miles/8 km southeast of Jerusalem. **EN GEDI NATURE RESERVE:** Tel 972/8-658-4285; www.parks.org.il. **BEST TIMES:** Mar–May and Sep–Nov to avoid the crowds and heat.

Tel Aviv's Sister City Shines with a Charm All Its Own

OLD JAFFA

Tel Aviv–Jaffa, Israel

Long before Jerusalem welcomed King David through its stone gates, there was Jaffa (Yafo in Hebrew, Yafa in Arabic)—the Bible-era port town that some believed to be named after Noah's son and that can rightfully claim to be one of the oldest cities in the world. Dating back to 7500 B.C., Jaffa, now technically part of the city of Tel Aviv, is one of Israel's rare mixed Arab-Jewish urban enclaves. It's home to the Bronze Age–era harbor from which Jonah reputedly set sail for his fateful date with a whale. The once run-down Old Jaffa Port area has been restored and offers incredible views of Tel Aviv.

Start by visiting the Ilana Goor Museum, located in a stunning century-old mansion built by a wealthy Turkish merchant. The museum displays a collection of works by its namesake and owner, a noted Israeli-born sculptor, artist, and furniture maker, and features a rooftop café with sweeping views. Just past Jaffa's iconic Ottoman-era Clock Tower awaits the ramshackle flea market, a casbah-like warren of merchants and mongers who offer everything from Levantine antiques to Middle Eastern–styled textiles and crafts, plus the occasional live chicken. In the heart of the market is Puah, a small café offering legendary baked goods, tomato salad topped with tahini, and homemade couscous. Locals display an intense loyalty to nearby Abu Hasan, a second-generation hummus purveyor where the creamy chickpea-based dish is prepared every morning and is almost always sold out by early afternoon. To experience a more upscale part of Old Jaffa, stop by the elegant Yoezer Wine Bar near the Old Clock Tower. Set in a Crusader-era building, it offers one of the country's best wine lists—including many Israeli wines—and very inspired dining as well.

Jaffa's southern edge remains predominantly Arab, nowhere more so than in Ajami, a 200-year-old neighborhood founded by Maronite Christians. Named after one of Mohammed's Koranic companions and full of arched, Ottoman-styled homes, Ajami is the site of the new Peres Center for Peace. Ten years in the making, this dramatic concrete-and-glass building by Italian architect Massimiliano Fuksas is one of the most impressive pieces of contemporary architecture in all of Israel, and the gardens, which front the Mediterranean, are open to all.

WHERE: 5 miles/8 km south of central Tel Aviv. **ILANA GOOR MUSEUM:** Tel 972/3-683-7676; www.ilanagoor.com. **PUAH:** Tel 972/3-682-3821. **ABU HASAN:** Tel 972/3-682-0387. **YOEZER WINE BAR:** Tel 972/3-683-9115. *Cost:* dinner $70. **PERES CENTER FOR PEACE:** Tel 972/3-568-0860; www.peres-center.org. **BEST TIME:** early May for Fresh Paint Art Fair at Old Jaffa Port.

European Bauhaus on Mediterranean Shores

THE WHITE CITY OF TEL AVIV

Tel Aviv, Israel

Tel Aviv—dubbed the "Miami of the Middle East"—has long enjoyed its image as a city with chutzpah, one that, while embracing its past, is always moving brashly into the future. For a sense of this country's millennia-old history, go to Jerusalem (see p. 449), but for a glimpse of its more recent past, look no further than the White City, as Tel Aviv's historic heart is called. It's here you'll find roughly 4,000 sleek examples of Bauhaus architecture—the world's largest trove of buildings from this seminal design movement. Originating in Dessau, Germany, in 1919 and banned by the Nazis a mere 14 years later, the style found an unlikely home along Israel's hot and humid Mediterranean shores in the period just before the nation's 1948 independence. It was a surprisingly successful fit. The Bauhaus signature—unadorned pale white façades and curved balconies—turned out to be an inexpensive and efficient way to house the thousands of immigrants pouring in from Russia and Europe.

Over the subsequent decades, many of Tel Aviv's Bauhaus buildings fell into disrepair as affluent locals abandoned the city center for luxury towers to the north. But today, vast swaths of the area are being cleaned up, particularly along Bauhaus-rich arteries such as Rothschild Boulevard and Ahad Ha'Am Street. There, you'll find pristine architectural beauties: not only private homes, but elegant restaurants and cutting-edge galleries as well. Founded in 2000, the dynamic Bauhaus Center Tel Aviv serves as a repository for all things Bauhaus and organizes walking tours of the city's most important landmarks from this period. And at the jewel-like Bauhaus Foundation Museum, housed in a meticulously renovated 1934 building, you'll find important furniture and design pieces by the likes of Marcel Breuer and Mies van der Rohe.

Experience yet another Bauhaus wonder, the Gordon Hotel, a 12-room retreat across from the beach. It's the city's first luxury boutique hotel, set in a modernist marvel.

BAUHAUS CENTER: Tel 972/3-522-0249; www.bauhaus-center.com. **BAUHAUS FOUNDATION MUSEUM:** Tel 972/3-620-4664. **THE GORDON HOTEL:** Tel 972/3-520-6100; www.gordontlv.com. *Cost:* $215 (off-peak), $350 (peak). **BEST TIMES:** early May for mild spring weather and Houses from Within architecture fair; early Jun for White Night festival of fashion, food, and art.

Nature's Largest Spa

THE DEAD SEA

Israel and Jordan

The Dead Sea is actually a landlocked lake in the middle of the desert, lying 1,305 feet below sea level. It is the lowest spot on earth, a high point of any Middle Eastern itinerary, and the sooner visited the better: Due to evaporation and industrial exploitation, the Dead Sea is rapidly shrinking, having lost a third of its surface area in the past half-century alone.

Boasting one of the highest concentrations of sea salt in the world—it's about nine times saltier than the nearby Mediterranean—the Dead Sea is a buoyant wonderland where bathers float effortlessly upon the glass-smooth surface. Its mineral-packed waters (called "dead" because they kill virtually all marine life) are believed to heal skin problems and arthritis, while the concentrated oxygen in the surrounding air has been shown to ease asthma and other respiratory ailments. Indeed, the Dead Sea's restorative and therapeutic powers and beauty regimens have been a not-so-well-kept secret since the days of Cleopatra and the Queen of Sheba.

Today, it's the luxury spas on both the Israeli and Jordanian sides of the sea as much as it is the water itself that lure cure seekers. While the Israeli side is more visited (see Masada, p. 452), Jordan's resorts—an hour's drive from Amman—are busy playing catch-up. One of the originals, the Mövenpick Resort and Spa, staked out what might be the best waterfront location when it opened in 1999. Laid out in the style of a traditional desert village, it has 358 simple but elegant rooms; it is not small, but it feels personal. Its architecturally striking and ultrachic Zara Spa is one of the finest in the country. Although not on the Dead Sea, the Six Senses Spa at the nearby Evason Ma'In Hot Springs Resort near Ma'daba also revolves around water-based treatments. Located in the limestone canyon of Wadi Zarqa, it features a series of rocky pools filled with soothing hot water that cascades from towering cliffs, creating a veritable oasis below. Guests can laze amid the hot pools or under the steamy waterfall and then enjoy a bite on the terraced restaurant with panoramic views of the Dead Sea, which is just a 20-minute drive away.

It's a half-hour drive east from the Dead Sea to the Mujib Nature Reserve. Owned by the Royal Society for the Conservation of Nature (RSCN), this newly popular ecotourist destination is made for adventure lovers: Its five river and dry trails deliver some of the most dramatic hiking in the country. Guides are necessary for all except the Siq Trail and should be booked in advance through the RSCN headquarters in Amman.

Saltier than Utah's Great Salt Lake or any ocean, the Dead Sea's salinity makes it difficult to swim, but easy to float.

WHERE: 60 miles/90 km southwest of Amman. **MÖVENPICK DEAD SEA:** Tel 962/5-356-1111; www.movenpick-hotels.com. *Cost:* from $140 (off-peak), from $220 (peak). **EVASON MA'IN HOT SPRINGS:** Tel 962/5-324-5500; www.sixsenses.com/evason-ma-in/. *Cost:* from $175. **MUJIB NATURE RESERVE (RSCN):** +Tel 962/6-535-0456; www.rscn.org.jo. *When:* Apr–Oct. **BEST TIMES:** Mar–May and Sep–Nov for mildest weather.

Red Sea Diving and Desert Canyons

AQABA AND WADI RUM

Jordan

For years, Aqaba, Jordan's only beach resort, languished in the shadow of its better-known neighbors: Eliat, in Israel, and Egypt's Sharm al-Sheikh (see p. 379), across the Gulf of Aqaba, both of whose coral-lined shores have lured divers and other vacationers for decades. Now this ancient, sunny port, which has some of the region's most pristine dive sites, is being developed and groomed as serious competition to those more established beach towns, with brand-new, upscale resorts to tempt potential visitors. For the moment, at least, Aqaba still delivers authentic small-town Arabian culture, while the best of southern Jordan, including Petra (see p. 459) and Wadi Rum, are an easy day trip away.

So important is Aqaba's new incarnation that its development is being overseen by King Abdullah himself. Economic incentives have resulted in a flurry of luxe new hotels, like the curvy, Miami-esque Kempinski, set on its own sandy beach and featuring 200 rooms with sea views. But the real reason to come is for Aqaba's snorkeling and diving options: Along 15 miles of coastline are wide fields of technicolor coral reefs (with more than 300 varieties of coral), considered among the most dazzling and least damaged in all of the Red Sea.

Aqaba is the gateway to the nearby Wadi Rum, a majestic desert moonscape and the largest valley in Jordan. It is mentioned in the Koran for its beauty and is full of massive canyons, nature-sculpted rock formations, granite ridges, and sandstone mountains that reach 2,625 feet above the desert floor, plus the villages of the seminomadic Bedouin. Those who choose to camp out with local outfitters can enjoy the spectacle of light and color on display at dawn and dusk.

Lawrence of Arabia used Wadi Rum, which he described as "vast, echoing and godlike," as a base camp during the Arab Revolt of 1917–18. Almost 50 years later, David Lean chose the area as the real-life location for his 1962 Oscar-winning film *Lawrence of Arabia*. Today, you can enjoy an early morning trek (or explore by camel, horse, jeep, or hot-air balloon) and be back in Aqaba by lunchtime at a café overlooking the sea.

WHERE: Aqaba is 200 miles/365 km south of Amman. **KEMPINSKI AQABA:** Tel 962/3-209-0888; www.kempinski.com. *Cost:* $215 (off-peak), $425 (peak). **HOW:** U.S.-based Cultural Crossroads offers a 7-day "Explore Jordan" trip that includes visits to Wadi Rum (but not Aqaba). Tel 877-479-7040 or 802-479-7040; www.culturalcrossroads.com. *Cost:* from $3,286, all-inclusive. Originates in Amman. *When:* May, Sep. **BEST TIMES:** Feb–May and Sep–Dec for mild weather.

Monument to the Power and Brilliance of the Roman Empire

JARASH

Jordan

Jarash is to Jordan what Baalbek is to Lebanon (see p. 460), Leptis Magna to Libya, or Volubilis to Morocco—a sprawling, dazzling, provincial Roman city in the heart of the modern Arab world. It is widely considered one of the largest and best-preserved outside Italy.

Located just beyond the capital city of Amman, in the region known in biblical times as Gilead, the city dates to the 4th century B.C., when it was founded by soldiers serving Alexander the Great. Within 5 centuries, Jarash had become a flourishing part of Rome's eastern nexus. Known as Gerasa at that time, it was a crucial component of the Decapolis League, a network of ten affluent and cosmopolitan cities that was formed during the 1st century B.C. and anchored the Romans' regional rule in the Levant.

Jarash was wealthy thanks to agriculture, mining, and its prime location along key caravan routes, allowing for easy trade with the nearby Nabataeans, who built legendary Petra (see p. 459). Lavish edifices were splendidly realized in Jarash's Oriental Baroque style. Many of those buildings, which were ecclesiastic in purpose, were completed just centuries after the dawn of Christianity.

Some 15 impressive churches remain, along with a triumphant arch built to welcome the emperor Hadrian in A.D. 129, a massive column-ringed oval forum, a hippodrome large enough for 15,000 spectators (where chariot races are frequently reenacted today), and hot and cold baths. Most splendid of all, however, is the Temple of Artemis, which honors the patron goddess of Jarash and is accessed via a grand, column-lined avenue. The temple and surrounding complex form a magnificent backdrop for Jarash's annual three-week-long festival that was inaugurated by Queen Noor al Hussein in 1981 and still draws world-class dancers, musicians, and actors from the Middle East and beyond. They all perform in the original Roman-era theater, which provides 32 ascending rows of seats and, even today, pitch-perfect acoustics.

WHERE: 30 miles/48 km north of Amman. **HOW:** U.S.-based Wilderness Travel offers a 7-day trip that includes Jarash. Tel 800-368-2794 or 510-558-2488; www.wildernesstravel.com. *Cost:* from $3,095, inclusive. Originates in Amman. *When:* Oct–Apr. **BEST TIMES:** Mar–Jun and Sep–Nov for cool, dry weather; Jul–Aug for Jarash Festival.

Corinthian columns remain standing at the ruins of the 2nd-century Temple of Artemis, patron goddess of Jarash.

Connecting the Dots in an Ancient Land

KING'S HIGHWAY

Jordan

The King's Highway is a 5,000-year-old route first mentioned in the Old Testament. All kinds of travelers have followed this 200-mile trail: Israelites to the Promised Land, Muslims to Mecca, Crusaders on their way to retake the Holy Land. Today's well-paved road twists and winds through deep ravines, fertile farmland, and red-rock desert, beginning just outside the capital city of Amman and ending at Aqaba, on the Red Sea (see p. 456).

At the head of the highway is Ma'daba, home to a 6th-century map of the Holy Land. The oldest-known map in the world, it is laid in mosaic form on the floor of the 19th-century Greek Orthodox basilica of St. George. Barely 8 miles west of Ma'daba is Mount Nebo (known as Pisgah in the Bible), perched 2,600 feet above sea level. From here, it is said, God gave Moses his fleeting glimpse of the Promised Land that he would never enter. On a clear day you can see the Dead Sea, the West Bank, Bethlehem, and Jerusalem. According to biblical legend, this is also the site of Moses's death at 120 years of age.

Beyond Ma'daba and Mount Nebo is Kerak, the largest Crusader Castle in the Levant outside of Syria (see Krak des Chevaliers, p. 470). Completed in 1142 by Paganus the Butler under orders from King Baldwin II of Jerusalem, the castle looms over the modern city of Kerak and includes impressive Romanesque vaults and porticoes.

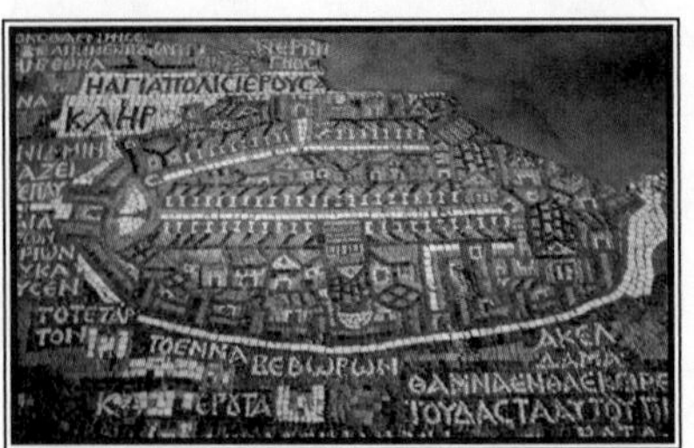

Ancient Jerusalem is the focal point of the Ma'daba Map.

History and nature come together at the 124-square-mile Dana Biosphere Reserve, Jordan's largest and most important. Set in a deep and isolated valley, it stretches from peaks that rise as high as 4,900 feet to the Wadi Araba some 150 feet below sea level. It is home to a rich, diverse, and unique ecosystem made up of 800 plant varieties, 215 bird species, and 449 different animals, including the sand cat, red fox, and Syrian wolf. Living in the reserve are members of the hospitable Ata'ta tribe, who have made the region their home since 4000 B.C. Traveling through ridged canyons, towering sand dunes, and oasis-like wadis (valleys), hikers can head to ruins that date back more than 12,000 years (there are more than 100 archaeological sites in the area).

Accommodations include camping under the star-studded desert sky, modest guesthouses, and the most romantic option: the Feynan Ecolodge. The ultimate desert retreat, featuring 26 rooms that are solar-powered and candlelit at night, the lodge was designed in traditional mud-brick style and includes cozy courtyards with relaxing hammocks, hiking trails that crisscross the reserve, and staff and guides from the local Bedouin community. Arrange in advance for one of the latter to lead you on a 3- to 5-day trek to Petra (see next page), the fabled Pink City 35 miles south of the Dana Biosphere.

Where: Ma'daba is 20 miles/32 km south of Amman. **How:** U.S.-based R. Crusoe & Son offers 10-day "All Roads Lead to Jordan" tours that include the King's Highway. Tel 800-585-8555 or 312-980-8000; www.rcrusoe.com. *Cost:* from $3,980, all-inclusive. Originates in Amman. **Dana Biosphere Reserve:** www.rscn.org.jo/rscn. **Feynan Ecolodge:** Tel 962/6-464-5580; www.feynan.com. *Cost:* from $120. **Best time:** Oct–Mar for cooler weather.

Pink Palaces Half as Old as Time

Petra

Jordan

Petra is lovingly known as the "Pink City" because of the red-hued sandstone used by the ancient Nabataeans to create its splendid palaces, tombs, and treasury. One of the unofficial wonders of the ancient world, Petra was declared one of the New Seven Wonders in 2007, an acknowledgment of its enduring allure.

Although it dates back to 1200 B.C.—and was built in an area first inhabited nearly 6 millennia earlier—Petra has only been known to the Western world since 1812, when it was "discovered" by Swiss explorer Johann Ludwig Burckhardt, who unearthed a complex, ancient settlement. Poet John William Burgon later described it as "a rose-red city half as old as time." Petra is reached via the narrow, mile-long Siq gorge, a winding footpath at times barely 10 feet wide and flanked by towering rock face up to four stories high. It's the only way in and out of the city, and during peak season it is crowded with tourists, guides, vendors, and donkeys.

At the end of this slim passageway is Petra's iconic Khaznah, which is known as the Treasury, though it may actually have been used as either a temple or a tomb. Elaborately and symmetrically columned, this elegant Greek-style building is hewn from the face of a sheer 130-foot cliff and dates to 56 B.C., the time of the Nabataean heyday. Sheltered from wind-blown sand, it is Petra's best-preserved monument, one immortalized for modern-day visitors by its appearance in the 1989 film classic *Indiana Jones and the Last Crusade.*

Unlike its decorative façade, the interior of the Khaznah (Treasury) is very plain.

Beyond the Khaznah, Petra opens up to reveal a once-thriving city and trading center that, until the mid–first century A.D., controlled the ancient trade routes linking Arabia to Northern Africa and the Mediterranean. The Nabataeans' wealth and power can be seen in the hundreds of homes, temples, storerooms, and tombs carved into the canyon walls. It's an 800-step climb along a winding path (donkey rides are available) to El Deir, Petra's grand monastery high atop a plateau with views over the entire Petra basin.

A smooth 3-hour drive on good roads from Amman, Jordan's star attraction can be (superficially) conquered in a day. But book a hotel in order to be there at sunrise or at dusk, when visitors arrive to candlelight, Bedouin music, and mint tea. The Mövenpick Resort is located directly across from Petra's entrance gates; with a blend of contemporary and traditional Middle Eastern décor, it is the best option in town. Another good choice is the clifftop Taybet Zaman, 5 miles from town. The tasteful transformation of this 19th-century Bedouin village was the brainchild of Queen Noor. Its 105 rustic yet modernized stone-walled rooms line bougainvillea-filled alleyways that lead to a pool, hammam spa, and a street souk reborn as a gift shop.

Where: 140 miles/225 km south of Amman. **Mövenpick Petra:** Tel 962/3-215-7111; www.movenpick-hotels.com. *Cost:* $220 (off-peak), $550 (peak). **Hotel Taybet Zaman:** Tel 962/3-215-0111; www.jordantourismresorts.com. *Cost:* from $100 (off-peak), from $210 (peak). **How:** U.S.-based Caravan Serai offers a 7-day "Historic Jordan" tour that includes Petra. Tel 800-451-8097 or 206-545-1735; www.caravan-serai.com. *Cost:* from $1,070. Originates in Amman. **Best times:** Mar–May and Sep–Nov for best weather; late afternoon when the sun turns the city a deep pink.

One of Rome's Greatest Achievements

Baalbek

Lebanon

The ancient city of Baalbek—aka Heliopolis, "City of the Sun"—is where the Romans displayed the power of the Empire, a place where even hyperbole fails. It's the largest Roman temple complex ever constructed—supported by the tallest columns attempted by ancient builders and hewn from the biggest stones quarried by human hands. Throw in a stunning setting on a high plateau in the verdant Bekáa Valley, with a backdrop of low, snow-capped mountains, and Baalbek can easily lay claim to being the Middle East's most impressive ancient ruins. As Mark Twain wrote, "Such grandeur of design, and such grace of execution, as one sees in the temples of Baalbek, have not been equaled . . . in any work of men's hands."

Baalbek dates back at least to the Greek empire in the 3rd century B.C., and it reached its true zenith under the Roman emperor Julius Caesar. Temples built to the Roman triad of Heliopolis—Bacchus, Jupiter, and Venus—helped maintain the town's prominence until the establishment of Christianity in the 4th century spelled the end of its importance. Some 17 centuries later, the Temple of Bacchus remains Baalbek's unrivaled highlight, a majestic site (named the best-preserved Roman temple in the world) surrounded by 42 Corinthian columns each rising 62 feet high. They're smaller than the 65.5-foot tall columns at the nearby Temple of Jupiter, the largest Roman temple ever built, but a mere 6 of Jupiter's original 54 remain intact.

The temples' longevity lies in their expert craftsmanship and sturdy construction from

Egyptian rose-pink granite—also used to build the 128 columns lining the Great Court, most of which no longer stand. Massive stones appear throughout the Baalbek complex, some weighing 1,200 tons, including the massive foundation stones and blocks supporting the Temple of Jupiter. Scholars are still unsure how stones of such immense size and weight reached Baalbek and were hoisted into place.

Touring the complex can take hours: Recharge from the day's heat with a post-visit drink from the rooftop bar at the Hotel Palmyra, a shabby-genteel relic of another era with views of the ruins, one of the few untouched old-time hotels left in the Middle East.

Where: 52 miles/85 km northeast of Beirut. **Hotel Palmyra:** Tel 961/8-370-230. **Best times:** Nov–Feb for cooler weather; Jun–Aug for Baalbek International Festival, which features opera, classical, and jazz performances against the backdrop of the ruins.

Born-Again Glamour in the Land of the Cedars

Beirut's Corniche

Beirut, Lebanon

Beirut was once known as the "Paris of the Middle East"—a Levantine Left Bank with the warm Mediterranean as its Seine. Then came Lebanon's 20-year civil war, which divided the nation and destroyed its thriving tourism scene. With the war long past, Lebanon is enjoying a period of (relative) calm and the Beurutis are once again giving Parisians a run for their money.

Like the cosmopolitan cities of Tel Aviv and Alexandria (see pp. 454 and 375), Beirut lies directly on the shores of the eastern Mediterranean—an azure backdrop that informs nearly every element of its low-key and generally alfresco lifestyle. Fronting the sea is the Corniche, a palm-fringed promenade stretching for 2.5 miles with the striking Pigeon Rocks in front and towering Mount Lebanon visible to the east. The Corniche could rightly be considered Beirut's backyard: rich and poor, pious and secular, Christian and Muslim come every evening to enjoy the cool breeze and picture-perfect sunsets. Some of the most enjoyable views are from the many open-air restaurants, such as Casablanca, popular for its East-West menu featuring fish, lobster, and organic vegetables from the owner's farm, and the Palace Café, a mainstay of local writers who come to linger over an arak, the potent local anise-flavored liqueur.

Lebanon's famed cuisine, like its people, is a surprisingly refined cultural hodgepodge. Arab, Armenian, and Turkish influences show up in dishes that are often served in mezze (small-dish) style during long, languorous meals. Classic restaurants such as the stylish Abd el Wahab are perennial favorites, serving feasts of Lebanese specialties, including hummus, tabouleh, and *moutabala* (a spicy eggplant dip), followed by fiery kebabs and minced-meat kibbeh. For decades, the old-school, home-style Le Chef has been serving hearty portions of traditional Lebanese fare such as the spinach-rich stew called *moulakhiyeh,* succulent roasted lamb, and rose-water-doused rice pudding for dessert. Regional specialties from all over Lebanon prevail at Tawlet ("kitchen table" in Arabic), a casual and popular lunch spot in the vibrant Souk el-Tayeb farmers market.

Beirut's hotel scene is also flourishing with unprecedented vigor. The Hotel Le Gray, opened in 2009 by British hotelier Gordon Campbell Gray, flaunts a rooftop infinity pool and bar with 360-degree views, as well as art-filled rooms, some facing the Al Amin Mosque. The rooms in the more classic Hotel Albergo, a former 1930s home, are designed with either Ottoman-era or classic French décor, and there's a chic rooftop lounge. One of the more modest and welcoming hotels for everyday budgets is the Orient Queen Homes, which features contemporary décor.

Casablanca: Tel 961/1-369-334. *Cost:* dinner $30. **Palace Café:** Tel 961/1-364-949. *Cost:* lunch $15. **Abd el Wahab:** Tel 961/1-200-550. *Cost:* dinner $65. **Le Chef:** Tel 961/1-445-373. *Cost:* dinner $20. **Tawlet:** Tel 961/1-448-129; www.tawlet.com. *Cost:* lunch $15. **Hotel Le Gray:** Tel 961/1-971-111; www.campbellgrayhotels.com. *Cost:* $375 (off-peak), $660 (peak). **Hotel Albergo:** Tel 961/1-339-797; www.hotelalbergobeirut.com. *Cost:* $375 (off-peak), $430 (peak). **Orient Queen Homes:** Tel 961/1-361-140; www.orientqueenhomes.com. *Cost:* from $150. **Best times:** Mar–May for pleasant weather; Oct for the Beirut International Film Festival.

Fjords on the Strait of Hormuz

Musandam Peninsula

Oman

One of Oman's most stunning destinations is actually far removed from the rest of the country. Jutting into the Strait of Hormuz, the 695-square-mile Musandam Peninsula is surrounded by the United Arab Emirates at its base and is some 5 hours away from the rest of Oman. This unusual geographic arrangement puts Musandam within 90 minutes of Dubai (see p. 472) by car—a dose of strategic good fortune that has allowed it to emerge as one of the most vibrant ecotourism destinations in the region.

Musandam's allure is as clear as the crystalline waters of its Persian Gulf shores: Its pristine coastline is set against a striking tableau of rocky cliffs hewn by water and wind. The most dramatic are called *khors*, deep fjords that are the reason this land is known as the Norway of the Middle East. Romantic afternoon or twilight rides on *dhows*, traditional Arabian wooden vessels, are often trailed by dolphins, and you may also catch a glimpse of what may be the world's only population of nonmigratory humpback whales.

The tourism scene in this stark corner of Oman has always been small-scale, luring visitors with otherworldly scenery rather than luxury accommodations. Visitors traditionally trekked, scuba dived, or kayaked during the day and then camped out at night. But Musandam's resort scene shifted into overdrive with the 2008 opening of the Six Senses Zighy Bay, an exclusive waterfront resort that blends perfectly with its dramatic environment and takes its "Old Arabia" design motifs from the nearby traditional fishing village.

Each of the 82 enormous villas includes a private plunge pool, and the resort's dreamy spa set alongside a burbling brook is often lauded as the finest in the Arabian Peninsula. It has a traditional hammam, or Turkish bath, and treatments that use native organic ingredients, such as gold, clay, mint, and frankincense. The clifftop bar and restaurant provide breathtaking views, along with an inspired menu accented by regional ingredients.

Less posh but still pleasingly tucked into the natural setting is the Golden Tulip Resort, Khasab, with excellent Persian Gulf views and that most crucial of Musandam necessities: an on-site dive center. The modern, 60-room hotel is the only one in Khasab—Cape Musandam's de facto capital—with sea-front views and a liquor license.

WHERE: 360 miles/500 km northwest of Muscat, 100 miles/160 km northeast of Dubai. **SIX SENSES ZIGHY BAY:** Tel 968/2673-5555; www.sixsenses.com. *Cost:* from $1,050 (off-peak), from $1,235 (peak). **GOLDEN TULIP KHASAB:** Tel 968/2673-0777; www.goldentulipkhasab.com. *Cost:* from $210. **BEST TIME:** Sep–Nov to avoid summer heat and winter rains.

Old-World Arabia and a Capital City

NIZWA AND MUSCAT

Oman

At the height of its imperial-era glory, coastal Oman prospered from sea trade with Zanzibar, India, and China. But inland Oman was anchored around the city of Nizwa, where instead of trade, learning and cultural achievement were the chief endeavors, overseen by the imams who ruled Oman's interior for centuries. Nizwa was also strategically important in defending the area against foreign marauders, and its 17th-century fort—one of more than 500 found scattered throughout this country at the southeast end of the Arabian Peninsula—still stands. The solid, circular edifice is Oman's most visited national monument.

Oman is famous for its forts.

At the fort's base, Nizwa's famed souk is a showcase of unique crafts mixed in with the necessities of everyday life. In a scene plucked from ancient times, marketgoers stock up on everything from frankincense and tiny bottles of perfume to sheep, fresh dates, and *khanjars*, the intricate silver daggers that are a symbol of Omani manhood. A corner of the market is given over to silver jewelry, considered to be the best in the country; the entrance to this section is at the foot of Nizwa's large, blue-domed mosque.

The souks are at their liveliest on Friday mornings, when the loud livestock market is in full swing. Overnighting at Nizwa's contemporary Golden Tulip Hotel gives you a head start, though alternatively you can opt for a full-day tour of the city that leaves from the capital of Muscat.

Muscat is an adventure in itself: Fronting the Arabian Sea, it is home to an impressive array of royal and Islamic wonders. Chief among them is the Sultan Qaboos Grand Mosque. Named after Oman's current leader, it was completed in 2001 and is an enormous, dazzling affair, decorated with intricate tilework and calligraphy. The nearby Sultan's Palace is clad in glittering turquoise and gold, guarded on both sides by a pair of 16th-century forts built by the Portuguese, who ruled here for 150 years. And after a stroll along the Corniche and Muscat's seafront historic port in the Old Town, make sure to visit the warrenlike Muttrah Souk, which overflows with gold, silver, fragrances, and rich textiles.

Make your base at the beachfront Al Bustan Hotel, built by Oman's sultan himself in 1985 and renovated in 2009. *Bustan* means "garden" in Arabic, and the golden-domed hotel, in a secluded mountain-backed bay, is surrounded by 200 lush green acres, with an infinity pool nestled within. Inside, there are massive chandeliers, elaborately carved wall coverings, and ample views of the Gulf. Closer to town (and the average budget), the Crowne Plaza Muscat promises similar Gulf views.

WHERE: Nizwa is 100 miles/160 km northwest of Muscat. **HOW:** Zahara Tours in Muscat can organize personalized tours to Nizwa and throughout Oman. Tel 968/2440-0844; www.zaharatours.com. **GOLDEN TULIP NIZWA HOTEL:** Tel 968/2543-1616; www.goldentulipnizwa.com. *Cost:* from $190. **AL BUSTAN PALACE INTERCONTINENTAL MUSCAT:** Tel 968/2479-9666; www.al-bustan.intercontinental.com. *Cost:* from $445. **CROWNE PLAZA MUSCAT:** Tel 968/2466-0660; www.ichotelsgroup.com. *Cost:* $185. **BEST TIMES:** Oct–Mar for nicest weather; Jan–Feb for Muscat Festival, which celebrates traditional Omani culture.

An Architectural Treasure Box

MUSEUM OF ISLAMIC ART

Doha, Qatar

Over the past decade, the sheikhdom of Qatar has emerged as a smaller-scale (though no less ambitious) rival to its gulf neighbor Dubai (see p. 472). Fabulously rich from oil and natural gas profits, Qatar's Sheikh Hamad bin Khalifa al-Thani is fashioning his homeland into a dynamic cultural destination—the arts hub of the Arab world—that will flourish even after the petroleum disappears.

Qatar's most spectacular achievement in this regard is its Museum of Islamic Art, designed by legendary architect I. M. Pei. The building is located on a tiny artificial island off the Corniche promenade in the capitali city of Doha, and Pei says he drew his inspiration for its powerful white Cubist design from Islamic architecture ranging from a 9th-century Egyptian mosque to Spain's famed Alhambra (see p. 246). Inside, Qatar's royal family has filled the soaring space with the largest collection of Islamic art in the world: more than 700 priceless works from the 7th through the 19th centuries, including sacred calligraphic scrolls, silk tapestries, Ottoman swords, and textiles and tiles from Morocco to China.

Architect I. M. Pei studied Muslim history and culture to better inform his design.

Like the Islamic Museum, most of Qatar's other cultural attractions are newly built but imbued with history and tradition. Along the seafront Corniche, the palm grove Rumeila is home to a working model of a traditional Qatari village, complete with weavers, goldsmiths, carpenters, and shipbuilders. The Rumeila also houses Souq Waqif, a refurbished, century-old bazaar that still feels like the real deal, filled with daggers, carpets, jewels, and textiles. There's also a Birds Center that stocks all things related to falconry, a favorite Qatari pastime. Hotel Souq Waqif, a 13-room boutique-style lodging done up in chic Arab décor, puts you in the middle of it all.

In the evening, the 5-mile, crescent-shaped Corniche fills with local families who stroll along the sea, taking in the views of the Persian Gulf, the city's ever-morphing skyline, and the museum. At the southern tip of the Corniche, the Ritz-Carlton Sharq Village and Spa is laid out like a traditional Qatari village, with verdant courtyards and gardens, and is the ideal place to absorb the flavor of a country that sees itself as a bridge between East and West.

Museum of Islamic Art: Tel 974/4422-4444; www.mia.org.qa. **Hotel Souq Waqif:** Tel 974/4443-3030; www.hotelsouqwaqif.com. *Cost:* from $210. **The Ritz-Carlton Sharq Village and Spa:** Tel 974/4425-6666; www.sharqvillage.com. *Cost:* from $260. **Best times:** Mar for Doha Cultural Festival; Apr for Emir GCC Camels Race Finals; Oct or Nov for Doha Tribeca Film Festival; Nov–Mar for clement weather.

The Gateway to Mecca—Where History and Modernity Meet

Old Jeddah

Jeddah, Saudi Arabia

Jeddah has always been known primarily as the gateway to Mecca (see p. 467), the endpoint of devout Muslims' annual pilgrimage called the Hajj. But this coastal city—often referred to as the Bride of the Red Sea—is a surprisingly cosmopolitan and commercial metropolis. Indeed, in a country known for religious observance and conservatism, Jeddah is where Saudis let loose, relatively speaking.

Jeddah's cityscape is like no other in the country. Rather than raze and rebuild on top of its rich archaeological patrimony, Jeddah's municipal planners have built around it, leaving the city's original core mostly intact. The best of what remains is located in Al-Balad, Old Jeddah's heart, which is legally protected from further destruction or development. The homes are traditional Arabian in style, many made from coral harvested from nearby reefs, with those owned by the merchant elite featuring ornate decorative details hand-carved from local hardwoods.

Many of these houses are now museums, including the oldest and most impressive, the Naseef House, built in 1872 and containing more than 100 rooms, with delicate latticework windows gracing its façade. Equally grand are the Al-Tayibat City Museum for International Civilization, a sprawling 300-room former palace known as "Jeddah's Louvre," and the Shallaby Museum with its vast trove of silver antiques, coins, and traditional Bedouin clothing.

You would be excused for thinking that the days of the Silk Route linger on after a visit to Souq al-Alawi, Jeddah's main market and the largest souk in all of Saudi Arabia. Surrounded by towering, traditionally styled buildings, the market is a warren of stalls selling coffee, jewelry, fabrics, and incense.

Beyond Al-Balad, follow the locals at sunset out to the seafront Corniche, which unfurls along the Red Sea for more than 20 miles. Four mosques are built along the Corniche, including one that appears to float during high tide, while hundreds of sculptures by international artists adorn the well-lit promenade, part of a city beautification program that began in the 1960s. Stop for dinner at Al-Nakheel restaurant, directly on the Corniche, where Saudi families linger over long meals of freshly caught fish. Designed like a traditional tent, the restaurant is open to the sea, prompting a few veiled women to let their hair down in the cool sea breeze.

WHERE: 44 miles/71 km west of Mecca. **NASEEF HOUSE:** Tel 962/2-647-2280. **AL-TAYIBAT CITY MUSEUM:** Tel 966/2-693-0049. **SHALLABY MUSEUM:** Tel 962/2-697-7442. **AL NAKHEEL:** Tel 966/2-606-6644. *Cost:* dinner $15. **WHERE TO STAY:** Many rooms at the modern Rosewood Corniche have sea views. Tel 962/2-257-8888; www.hotelcorniche.com. *Cost:* $265 (off-peak), $365 (peak). **BEST TIME:** Nov–Feb to avoid the heat and humidity.

A Magnificent Secret City

MADA'IN SALEH

Saudi Arabia

Some 450 miles south of Jordan's city of Petra (see p. 459), the ancient Nabataeans carved another, less known city from the stone of the stark, silent desert. This is Mada'in Saleh, the second most important city in the Nabataean kingdom and a midway stop between Mecca (see next page) and Petra on the biblical-era caravan routes. Merchants transporting precious cargo of frankincense and other aromatics and spices between the Arabian interior and bustling Mediterranean ports in Syria were heavily taxed here, allowing the city to grow fabulously wealthy.

Mada'in Saleh's moment in the sun was short-lived: The city had declined by the 1st century as its Roman ruler began to ship the region's goods via the Red Sea rather than over land. But as Saudi Arabia begins to open itself up to tourism, Mada'in Saleh is emerging as one of the country's historical crown jewels, a legitimate rival to famed Petra.

Hewn from a form of stone sturdier than Petra's iconic red rocks, Mada'in Saleh's structures lack Petra's extraordinary elegance, but they retain a similar mix of classical elements, including rows of columned tombs capped with cornices. In fact, there are some 111 tombs (94 of which have decorated

The Nabataeans who lived here were those who built Petra.

façades) spread throughout the 8-square-mile site, the last completed in A.D. 76 and many far better preserved than those in Petra.

But the relatively intact archaeological structures are only one reason to visit. Millions of years of erosion have resulted in a wealth of unusual rock formations and mineral strata that shift in color with the sunlight. And unlike Petra, which is secreted within towering ravines, Mada'in Saleh is spread out, a vast compound in the desert.

WHERE: 208 miles/330 km north of Medina. **HOW:** U.S.-based Caravan Serai Tours leads a 16-day trip through Saudi Arabia that includes Mada'in Saleh. Tel 800-451-8097 or 206-545-1735; www.caravan-serai.com. *Cost:* $6,445, all-inclusive. Originates in Riyadh. *When:* mid-Feb. **WHERE TO STAY:** Modern and modest, the Mada'in Saleh Hotel is a solid choice. Tel 966/4-884-2888; www.mshotel.com.sa *Cost:* $75. **BEST TIME:** Oct–Apr for cooler weather.

Islam's Holiest of Holies

MECCA

Saudi Arabia

Like Jerusalem or Vatican City, Mecca is a city defined by its religious relevance. It is the destination point of the Hajj, a pilgrimage of the Islamic faithful that compels more than 2 million people a year, the largest annual migration of humankind anywhere in the world. The Hajj is the fifth pillar, or core belief, of Islam: that a once-in-a-lifetime journey to Mecca is incumbent upon all of the world's 1.7 billion Muslims who are physically and financially able to do so. Considered the most significant manifestation of Islamic faith, it takes place over a 5-day period in the twelfth month of the Muslim lunar calendar.

Muslims have revered Mecca, the birthplace of both the Prophet Mohammed and the religion he founded, as their holiest site since the 7th century. Over the following centuries, Mecca flourished thanks to its proximity to coastal Jeddah (see p. 465) and its status as an oasis on the old caravan route. Today, it is one of the most visited sites on earth, though only Muslims will glimpse the wondrous attractions of the Holy Mosque Al-Masjid al-Haram and its focal point, the cuboid shrine of Kaaba. This holy place is strictly *haraam*—forbidden—to non-Muslims, a rule enforced at checkpoints just outside the city. The mosque is the largest in the world, accommodating up to 820,000 worshippers during Hajj.

From Mecca it is 250 miles to Medina, the second holiest site in Islam and an integral (though not required) part of the journey. The Prophet Mohammed was given sanctuary here after he left Mecca in A.D. 622, and the town served as the capital of the Islamic world for the next 40 years. Medina houses the remains of the world's first mosque, the Masjid al-Quba. But it is the al-Nabawi Mosque (the prophet's mosque) that is the second most important site in Islam after the Great Mosque in Mecca: It stands over the site of Mohammed's home and tomb, first built at the time of his death in A.D. 632.

WHERE: 44 miles/71 km east of Jeddah. **VISITOR INFO:** www.sct.gov.sa. **BEST TIMES:** for Muslims, during the Hajj, which takes place each fall during the 8th–12th days of the final month of the Islamic calendar (Oct 24–27, 2012; Oct 13–16, 2013; Oct 2–5, 2014); Nov–Apr for milder weather.

Where the Ancient World Came to Shop

THE COVERED SOUKS OF ALEPPO

Aleppo, Syria

Aleppo has been the major center of trade between Asia and the Levant since Roman times, and to see how commerce and culture collide here, you need go no farther than the fascinating labyrinth that is the city's covered souks. Dating back to the 13th century and mostly built by the Ottomans, these market passageways are a veritable Aladdin's cave, with shops and stalls selling mounds of cinnamon, saffron, cumin, coffee, Berber jewelry, olive oil soap, textiles, freshly slaughtered goats and lambs, and sacks of local pistachios. The markets extend some 5 miles, with an unending cast of traders—Arabs, Kurds, Armenians, Turks, and Iranians—along with shoppers, donkeys, and the errant minivan. Bargaining is expected and respected, with final prices settled only after a hearty session of back-and-forth haggling and a glass of tea.

Anchoring the souks is the Great Mosque of Aleppo. Younger sibling of Damascus's Omayyad Mosque (see next page), it was built on the site of a Roman temple and completed in the 13th century. Said to house the remains of Zachariah, the father of John the Baptist, the restored mosque features vast courtyards and grand colonnaded arcades. Looming above it all is Aleppo's most famous landmark, a massive stone-walled citadel built by the Crusaders in the 12th century on a site that has been fortified since the 10th century B.C.

Syria's cuisine is as flavorful as it is finely executed, and Aleppo is the nation's culinary capital. Delicately spiced minced-meat kebabs are a signature; they are often studded with tart cherries. Aleppo is known as the king of kibbeh, a mixture of ground bulgur, lamb, onion, and spices fried to crispy perfection. Try at least one of the 40 varieties, a favorite component of mezze appetizers offered at Beit Sissi, housed in an elegant 17th-century home in El Jedeide, or Christian Quarter, part of the largest Christian community in the Middle East outside Beirut.

The congested, ancient alleyways of the Christian Quarter are where Aleppo's most interesting eateries and architecturally rich boutique hotels are concentrated. The lavish nine-room Mansouriya Palace was one of the first to arrive on the scene, though the more discreetly decorated Yasmeen d'Alep is also appealing and offers a sumptuous Syrian breakfast. Both are a welcome addition to Aleppo's hotel scene, which has long been characterized by impersonal modern options and the faded, eccentric Baron Hotel. Built in 1919, the Baron features an alfresco terrace that's perfect for a cool drink, but only true nostalgia buffs should stay overnight. It was a favorite of Lawrence of Arabia (his unpaid bill is on display in the lobby) and Agatha Christie: It was here that she wrote the first part of *Murder on the Orient Express.*

WHERE: 220 miles/360 km north of Damascus. **BEIT SISSI:** Tel 963/21-221-9411. *Cost:* dinner $25. **MANSOURIYA:** Tel 963/21-363-2000; www.mansouriya.com. *Cost:* $360. **YASMEEN D'ALEP:** Tel 963/21-212-6366; www.yasmeenalep.com. *Cost:* $135 (off-peak), $240 (peak). **BARON HOTEL:** Tel 963/21-211-0880. **BEST TIMES:** Mar–May after the winter snows; Sep–Nov following the summer heat.

Islamic Gem at the Heart of a Historic City

Omayyad Mosque

Damascus, Syria

Although Damascus can trace its roots back to the 3rd millennium B.C., the city's golden age was during the period immediately following the founding of Islam in A.D. 610. It was at this time that the revered Omayyad Mosque was built, named for the 7th-century caliphate responsible for spreading Islam from the Middle East across North Africa and eventually as far as Spain. It was the largest contiguous empire the world has ever seen, and its capital was Damascus.

The mosque, also known as the Great Mosque of Damascus, anchors the Old City and today is one of the most important sites in all Islam—second in spiritual significance only to the mosques of Mecca and Medina (see p. 467). Built in A.D. 705 on the remains of a Byzantine cathedral (itself built on the site of earlier temples), its design influenced Islamic art and architecture around the world. Unlike Jerusalem's Dome of the Rock or Istanbul's Blue Mosque (see pp. 449 and 580), the Damascus Omayyad's most eye-catching features are within, where detailed golden mosaics cover the façades of its enclosed central courtyard. A sacred site that is open to non-Muslims, the mosque complex houses the remains of three legendary figures: the 7th-century martyr Hussein (Mohammed's grandson); John the Baptist, who is revered as a prophet in Islam and for whom there is a small shrine believed to contain his head; and the Crusade-era warrior Saladin.

Just west of the Mosque is the Souq al-Hamidiyeh, the Old City's main market. It's actually a clutch of mini souks clustered according to the goods they sell: spices, sweets, handicrafts, and textiles such as damask, named after the city where it was first made.

Damascus's dining scene has become increasingly sophisticated. Naranj—"orange" in Arabic—across from the Roman Arch on the wrongly named Straight Street—is always busy with those who come for its traditional, regional menu. Enjoy lamb cooked with okra and a sublime *sayadieh* (fish with rice) in a lively inner courtyard or on the roof terrace.

The Dome of the Treasury has eight mosaic-covered sides.

Outside the Old City, near the National Museum, the Four Seasons is a classic Western retreat that distinguishes itself by its Syrian hospitality. For those who crave Oriental charm, the eight-room Beit Al Mamlouka, set in a 17th-century Damascene home, was the first in the city's burgeoning boutique-hotel scene.

Naranj: Tel 963/11-541-3443. *Cost:* dinner $35. **Four Seasons:** Tel 963/11-339-1000; www.fourseasons.com/damascus. *Cost:* from $340. **Beit Al Mamlouka:** Tel 963/11-543-04-456; www.almamlouka.com. *Cost:* from $180. **Best times:** Mar–May for nice weather; Nov for Eid al-Fitr, at the end of Ramadan.

"The Finest Castle in the World"

Krak des Chevaliers

Syria

Castles are the stuff of knights and legends, but no fanciful tale could ever live up to the reality that is the Krak des Chevaliers (Castle of the Knights). Indeed, back in 1909—long before becoming known as Lawrence of Arabia—a 20-year-old T. E. Lawrence declared that Krak des Chevaliers was "the finest castle in the world. Certainly the most picturesque I have ever seen—quite marvelous."

Bleak and brooding, the impregnable castle sits alone like a vast battleship on an impenetrable spur above an endless green plain in western Syria and remains one of the world's best-preserved medieval castles. Most of it was superbly constructed and expanded, from 1144 on, by the Knights of St. John. Under their care, the castle became the largest Crusader fortress in the Holy Land.

The Krak is ideally located on an age-old caravan route between Damascus and Beirut, at the only significant break in the mountain range between Syria and Lebanon. As for its construction, so mighty was this moated bastion, with 13 watchtowers studding its fortified walls and the capacity to hold 5,000 soldiers, that it was impenetrable. Even the fearsome Arab sultan Saladin forebore to attack the Krak, taking one look at its thick walls and retreating without a fight. Ultimately, the castle did fall, taken in 1271 by folly rather than force when a forged letter convinced the knights of their commander's order to surrender.

For the next several centuries, the Krak maintained its military usefulness, though by the early 1800s European travelers were beginning to appreciate its form as much as its function. It is one of the few places displaying frescoes from the time of the Crusades. Swiss explorer Johann Ludwig Burckhardt—who would ultimately rediscover Petra and Abu Simbel (see pp. 459 and 380)—described Krak as "one of the finest buildings of the Middle East I ever saw." Today, it remains just as fine, thanks to light restoration work carried out in 1936 by the French, who ruled the country (along with Lebanon) in the period between the two World Wars.

Where: 93 miles/150 km north of Damascus; 111 miles/180 km south of Aleppo.

Grandeur in the Desert

Palmyra

Syria

"It is lovely and fantastic and unbelievable," enthused Agatha Christie of Palmyra, which she visited while living in Syria and writing *Come, Tell Me How You Live.* Palmyra (City of Palms) dates back to the 19th century B.C., when it was known as Tadmo; it emerged as an important oasis centuries later, a stop on the fabled Silk Road, a vital link between feudal China and the Crusader-era Mediterranean. Palmyra's coffers brimmed as it levied heavy tolls on caravans transporting precious cargo; because of its wealth and prestige it became known as the "Bride of the Desert."

What remains today of Palmyra are its incomparable ruins—elegant arches and pillars crafted from pink stone that rise from the desert across a 100-acre site and date to the town's zenith during the 2nd century, when it was an annex of Rome. At that time some 200,000 people inhabited the city, which was so prosperous it mimicked Rome itself in its elaborate architecture. The half-Greek half-Arab Queen Zenobia mounted a successful rebellion against Rome in A.D. 269—an act that made her a heroine in both the ancient and modern worlds. But Palmyra's decline followed a few centuries after, beginning with a conquest by the Muslims in 634 and ending with a massive earthquake in 1089.

Almost 9 centuries later, in 1924, excavation began on Palmyra, most notably of its magnificent Temple of Bel (circa A.D. 32) and its amphitheater, both of which have been partially reconstructed. The Great Colonnade, Palmyra's main street, is almost a mile long and is lined with more than 300 standing columns. An unusual series of more than 150 tower tombs serve as vertical repositories for the dead. Looming over the site are the nearby mountaintop ruins of a 17th-century Arab citadel, an atmospheric perch from which to view the sunset and to see the ruins bathed in pink and orange light at the day's end.

Romans called the ancient oasis city Palmyra, which meant "city of palms."

WHERE: 135 miles/217 km northeast of Damascus. **HOW:** U.S.-based Travcoa's 9-day "Essence of Syria" tour includes Palmyra. Tel 800-992-2003 or 310-649-7104; www.travcoa.com. *Cost:* from $4,285, all-inclusive. Originates in Damascus. *When:* Oct. **BEST TIMES:** Oct–Jan to avoid the scorching heat; 1st week of May for Palmyra Music Festival.

Oasis in a Sea of Sand

THE EMPTY QUARTER

Abu Dhabi, United Arab Emirates

Despite its unpromising name, there's much to see in the Empty Quarter, a massive 250,000-square-mile desert expanse encompassing parts of Saudi Arabia, Yemen, Oman, and the United Arab Emirates. It is earth's largest uninterrupted desert, a no-man's-land bigger than Holland, France, and Belgium combined.

The Quarter, as it is known, is characterized by an ocean of sand dunes reaching up to 820 feet in height. There is little plant or animal life and lots of extreme heat, along with some of the largest oil fields on the entire planet. Explorers, geographers, geologists, and other scientists have traversed this forbidding space since the 16th century; biologists have recently discovered new plants and birds whose ability to survive in such conditions continues to confound them.

As for tourists, they have begun to explore the area close to Abu Dhabi's Liwa Desert, near the Saudi border. This is where you'll find the new Qasr al Sarab Resort, a mirage-come-true modeled after an ancient Emirati fort. Built on a vast scale, its rooms, suites, and villas are sumptuous, decorated with hand-woven textiles and carpets. At night its crenellated towers and turrets are lit with torches straight out of Ali Baba. It's a carefully staged production that gets all the details right, from the palm-lined pool to the Asian/Arabian Anantara Spa offering coconut body wraps and sand exfoliation. Dinner is served in a Bedouin tent under a star-studded desert sky.

All across the Liwa are those mythic, massive red dunes, home to both desert villages and the oasis of Al Ain, where fresh waters sustained the ancient caravans of traders. Today Liwa offers some of the most adrenaline-pumping off-road adventures. Dune bashing is a roller coaster ride for 4WD buggies that blaze vertical trails up and over the towering dunes. There is plenty for the serenity seeker here, as well, including early-morning rides to watch the sunrise and silent desert walks in the late afternoon. The resort can also arrange camel treks with the local Bedouins and lessons in the traditional Arab pastimes of archery and falconry.

WHERE: Al Ain is 90 miles/144 km south of Abu Dhabi. **QASR AL SARAB DESERT RESORT:** Tel 971/2-886-2088; www.anantara.com. *Cost:* from $490. **BEST TIME:** Jan–Apr, when the desert heat is less.

A Desert Town's Meteoric Transformation

DUBAI

United Arab Emirates

A gleaming, towering, skyscraping, Persian Gulf–front metropolis, the pint-size emirate of Dubai has risen from the desert floor in a never-ending quest for the world's biggest, brightest, and costliest urban amenities. Under the leadership of its prime minister, the visionary Sheikh Mohammed bin Rashid al-Maktoum, it has become the region's leading cultural, commercial, and leisure destination seemingly overnight. But beyond the sleek towers and *Jetsons*-like modernity, Dubai's historic core still resonates with surprising Arabian authenticity. Experience it firsthand at the Dubai Museum, housed in the 1787 Al-Fahidi Fort, one of the city's oldest buildings. The museum's interactive installations explain in fascinating detail the story behind the city's meteoric transformation.

Another glimpse into pre-petrodollar Dubai can be had next door in the historic enclave of Bastakiya, where coral- and gypsum-walled buildings are capped by the traditional wind towers that kept Emiratis cool in an era before electric power. Bastakiya has been transformed into a cultural district, with cutting-edge galleries, boutique hotels, and restaurants. Basta Art Café offers lunch in the leafy courtyard of a traditional home; order from a menu of simple, regional dishes, such as grilled haloumi cheese and a lemony asparagus salad. Things turn romantic at Bastakiya Nights, where Emirati and Arabian cuisine is served in either a candlelit courtyard or on the rooftop, with views of Old Dubai.

Dubai Creek is the city's original thoroughfare, and the best way to experience it is with an evening cruise aboard a traditional dhow. Hop on an *abra* (a water taxi) to reach Dubai's celebrated souks in the old Deira district: Follow the smell of saffron, chiles, and frankincense to the Spice Souk, but save your money for the Gold Souk, Dubai's—and one of the gulf's—largest and most famous. The long promenade lined with hundreds of tiny gold shops, offering finished pieces as well as raw metal, is a regulated market and an international center of gold trade.

The Burj Khalifa rises over the city.

At Dubai's opposite extreme is a spectrum of man-made wonders. Although its brand-new appeal is mellowing (it was completed in 1999), the city's most recognizable structure remains the Burj al-Arab, an elegant sail-shaped hotel perched on its own private island in the emerald Persian Gulf. The seven-star resort may be beyond most budgets, but come for a look (though visits for nonguests aren't free, and even a table for tea in the hotel's 27th floor Sky Bar will cost you).

New architectural arrivals include the eye-popping Burj Khalifa, which opened to much fanfare (and with a price tag of over $1.5 billion) in 2010 as the world's tallest building at 2,717 feet. On 30 of its lower floors is the Armani Hotel: Each of the 160 rooms and suites is a showcase of design from high priest of fashion Giorgio Armani. Both the tower and the hotel are part of Dubai's downtown development, where you'll find The Address, a 63-floor hotel-and-apartment hybrid whose guest rooms offer perhaps the best Burj Khalifa views in town.

With barely a third of its residents actual Emirati citizens, Dubai is powered by the labor of millions of foreign workers. Many are Muslims, for whom the stunning Jumeirah Mosque was built in 1998. Crafted from smooth white stone and capped by a pair of elegant minarets, the mosque is one of the few in the UAE open to non-Muslims, with frequent informative tours.

VISITOR INFO: www.definitelydubai.com. **DUBAI MUSEUM:** Tel 971/4-353-1862; www.dubaitourism.ae. **BASTA ART CAFÉ:** Tel 971/4-353-5071. *Cost:* lunch $20. **BASTAKIYA NIGHTS:** Tel 971/4-353-7772; www.bastakiya.com. *Cost:* dinner $40. **BURJ AL-ARAB:** Tel 971/4-301-7000; www.jumeirah.com. *Cost:* from $1,500; afternoon tea $110. **ARMANI HOTEL DUBAI:** Tel 971/4-888-3888; www.dubai.armanihotels.com. *Cost:* from $450 (off-peak), from $1,000 (peak). **THE ADDRESS:** Tel 971/4-436-8888; www.theaddress.com. *Cost:* from $350. **JUMEIRAH MOSQUE:** Tel 971/4-344-7755. **BEST TIMES:** Nov–Mar for mildest weather; last Sat in Mar for Dubai World Cup.

The Unique Architecture of Arabia Felix

OLD SANAA

Sanaa, Yemen

Sanaa, located in a deep mountain valley some 7,200 feet above sea level, was supposedly founded by one of Noah's sons and claims to be the oldest inhabited city on earth. Its ancient medina quarter, Old Sanaa, is a miragelike confection of extraordinarily ornate mud-brick houses that form an intoxicating architectural tableau—some 6,000 of them are 400 or more years old.

Most of the flat-roofed homes rise four to six stories along the narrow streets and are decorated with delicate *moucharabies* (the projecting windows and balconies enclosed with elaborate wooden filigreed screens that are ubiquitous throughout Arabia). Mud-brick walls are embellished with brilliant white gypsum that lends the façades a wedding-cake-like appearance. Blue doors and slim window panes made of delicate alabaster serve as final accents on this unique form of medieval architecture.

The structural wonders continue. A thicket of minarets rise from more than 100 mosques. Sanaa's Great Mosque is among the most striking in the Islamic world. Dating back to A.D. 630, the time of the Prophet Mohammed himself, it is also among the oldest. More than 40 markets make up the labyrinthine Suq al-Milh, each with its own specialty. Frankincense and myrrh are sold here, together with roasted locusts, sticky dates, sequined fabrics, and handwoven carpets. There are endless spices, some used to spike fiery kebabs, which can be sampled along with flat breads, honey cakes, and dried fruits at hole-in-the-wall eateries.

While there are numerous modern hotels in the new city, staying in the old quarter is a great way to get lost in its endless charms. The Burj al Salam (Tower of Peace) is the best of the lot. Located in the heart of the old city, it is a modest but atmospheric hotel with 47 comfortable rooms in a traditional building. It provides both Old Yemeni hospitality and modern conveniences, along with a rooftop terrace where you can experience the sunset, when Sanaa is at its most magical.

Rounded minarets are frequently seen in Old Sanaa's ornate mud-brick architecture.

How: U.S.-based Caravan Serai offers a 13-day tour that includes Old Sanaa. Tel 800-451-8097 or 206-545-1735; www.caravan-serai.com. *Cost:* $3,480 all-inclusive. Orginates in Sanaa. *When:* late Jan–early Feb. **Burj al Salam:** Tel 976/1-483-333; www.burjalsalam.com. *Cost:* $85. **Best time:** Oct–Mar for good weather.

The Manhattan of the Middle East

SHIBAM

Yemen

Eight stories may not seem particularly tall by modern city standards, but in Shibam—an ancient walled city in eastern Yemen's Wadi Hadhramawt oasis—it's high enough to have once earned the town the title "Manhattan of the Desert," bestowed by British explorer Freya Stark, who first came here in the 1930s. A *wadi* is a verdant valley during the rainy season, and Hadhramawt is the largest in the Arabian Peninsula, owing its wealth to both its fertile soil and its prime position on Yemen's historic Incense Route. For 500 years, from roughly the 3rd century B.C. onward, caravans laden with frankincense—then the region's most valuable commodity—plied these ancient corridors. The trade of frankincense, along with dates, textiles, and myrrh, fueled and funded a building boom that resulted in a wealth of unique, multistoried, cube-formed architecture.

Today, some 500 of these "tower" houses are crammed into Shibam's walled core, a car-free quadrangle barely half a mile long. Most were completed in the 16th century, crafted from straw-reinforced mud bricks and painted at their tops and bases with white lime plaster. Delicate-yet-angular wooden screened windows festoon their façades, which average five to ten floors in height. Strict building codes mean that newer homes are virtually indistinguishable from Shibam's originals. And a new, joint Yemeni-German preservation program is helping ensure that Shibam's distinctive design is not lost to modernity.

It can feel like time travel to stroll through the narrow streets and high-walled alleys of Shibam, a city of 7,000 where women are covered head to ankle in black and wear conical straw hats nearly two feet tall when working in the fields outside of town. Shibam's Jami Mosque is a 10th-century marvel, whitewashed in crushed gypsum and standing near the town's fortified 17th-century walls, while the Fort of Shibam has guarded the town since the 13th century, surviving numerous destructive floods.

Accommodations in Shibam are limited; most travelers make for Say'un (Seiyoun), the valley's largest town, a short drive away. Along with some of the most beautiful mosques and minarets in Yemen and an evocative market, Say'un is home to the Al-Hawta Palace, a traditional whitewashed mud-brick hotel set in a lovely garden with a tiny yet refreshing pool.

WHERE: 350 miles/500 km east of Sanaa. **HOW:** Universal Touring Company in Sanaa specializes in customized itineraries, including those to Wadi Hadhramawt. Tel 967/1-272-861; www.utcyemen.com. *Cost:* 7-day tours from $830. **AL-HAWTA PALACE:** Tel 967/1-440-305. *Cost:* $120. **BEST TIMES:** Apr–May and Sep–Oct for dry, cool weather.

Shibam's use of vertical space was innovative for its time.

An Otherworldly Botanical Treasure Trove

SOCOTRA ISLANDS

Yemen

Utterly remote and virtually untouched, this tiny, four-island archipelago in the Indian Ocean—far off Yemen's southern coast and halfway to the Horn of Africa—is one part Galápagos, one part Jurassic Park.

The Socotras' biodiversity (particularly on the eponymous main island) reflects their extreme isolation from both Arabia and Africa. Indeed, some 700 species of plants and animals found here exist nowhere else on earth: Only Hawaii and the Galápagos have greater numbers. The flora and fauna are protected by the annual monsoons, which keep predators at bay, and by the natural barrier of the islands' geological formations. There are towering granite mountains, sheer limestone cliffs, and endless red stone ridges—all sheltering verdant valleys filled with oddly shaped trees, strange-looking insects, and the ubiquitous frankincense-producing trees, nine species of which are unique to Socotra.

There are locals too—some 40,000 residents live on Socotra Island, many of whom speak their own non-Arabic tongue, follow a unique 23-month calendar, and subsist mostly as goatherds or fishermen. Legend has it that they're descended from subjects of the Queen of Sheba, who ruled the mainland 3 millennia ago. Increasingly, they dabble in tourism, guiding Socotra's barely 3,000 annual visitors to its powdery white beaches that stretch unspoiled for miles, to the world-class deep-water diving offshore, or on treks to view the islands' unique red-sapped dragon's blood trees. Increasingly rare, the trees can live for more than 300 years, with their unusual inside-out-umbrella shape and their cinnamon-spiked nectar.

The peculiar dragon's blood trees are unique to the islands.

Despite outside pressures, the Yemeni government has kept Socotra's development well under control, permitting shorefront tent camps instead of massive hotels, small-scale guesthouses in place of sprawling resorts. And getting to Socotra is difficult: Just a pair of flights depart each week from the Yemeni mainland. But the isolation and small number of accommodations mean that you can enjoy the sandy shores, colorful coral reefs, and groves of those otherworldly dragon's blood trees without fear of fighting the crowds.

WHERE: 320 miles/500 km south of the Yemeni mainland; flights from Sanaa, Aden, or Mukalla. **VISITOR INFO:** www.socotraisland.org. **HOW:** Universal Touring Company specializes in customized itineraries. Tel 967/1-272861; www.utcyemen.com. *Cost:* 5-day trip, $455. **BEST TIME:** Oct–Apr to avoid monsoon season.

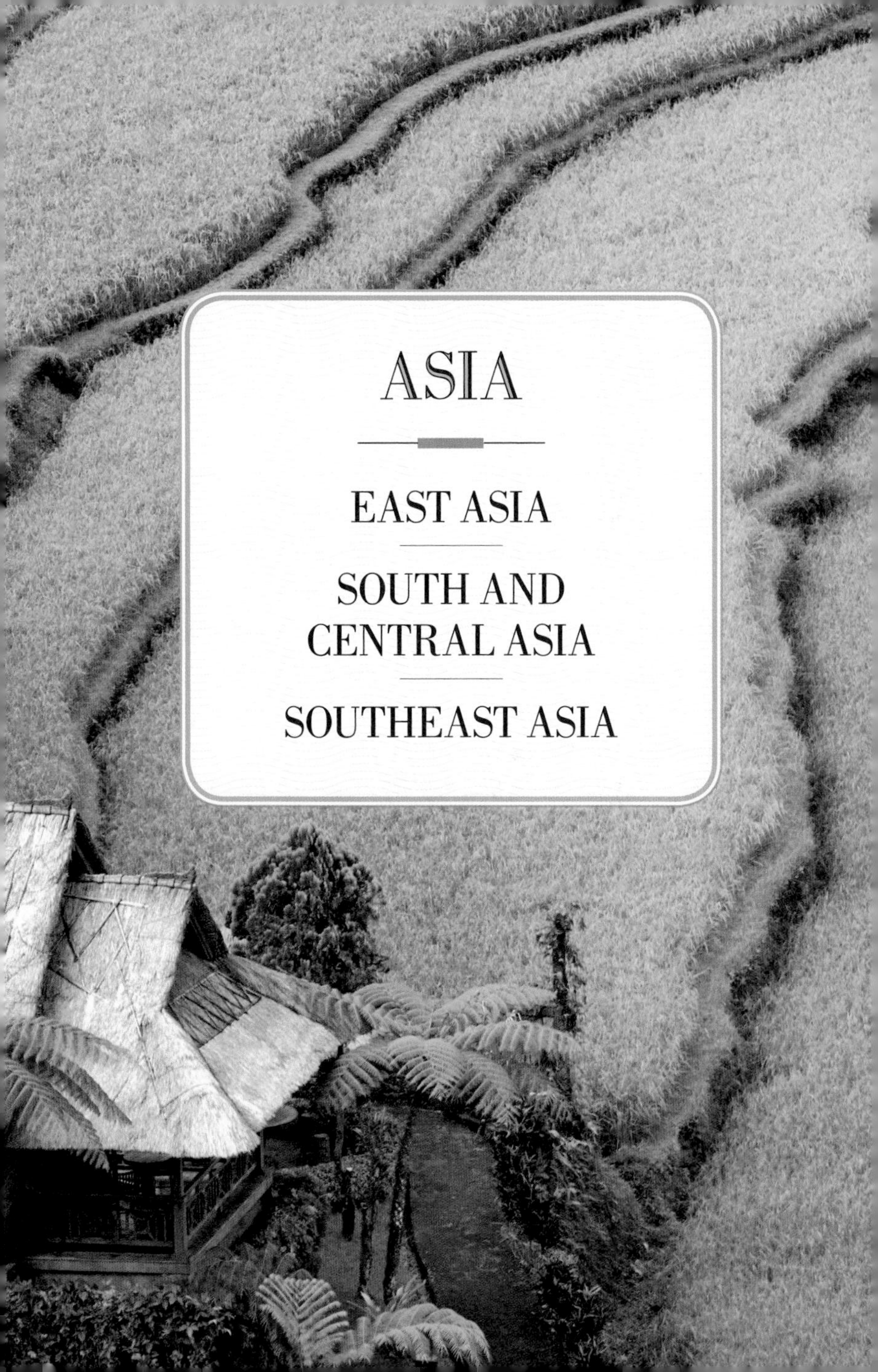

ASIA

EAST ASIA

SOUTH AND CENTRAL ASIA

SOUTHEAST ASIA

1 GEORGIA
2 ARMENIA
3 AZERBAIJAN
4 TURKMENISTAN
5 KYRGYZSTAN
6 TAJIKISTAN
7 BHUTAN
8 CAMBODIA
9 NORTH KOREA
Istanbul
BLACK SEA
Ankara
TURKEY
CAUCASUS
CASPIAN SEA
Tehran
IRAN
Ural
Aral Sea
Astana
KAZAKHSTAN
UZBEKISTAN
AFGHANISTAN
Kabul
Islamabad
PAKISTAN
New Delhi
INDIA
ARABIAN SEA
Ulaanbaatar
Gobi Desert
MONGOLIA
Manchurian Plain
Beijing
Huang He
CHINA
PLATEAU OF TIBET
HIMALAYAS
Mekong
Yangtze
NEPAL
Mt. Everest
Kathmandu
Thimphu
Ganges
Bay of Bengal
BANGLADESH
MYANMAR
Naypyidaw
Yangon
LAOS
Vientiane
THAILAND
Bangkok
Phnom Penh
Hanoi
VIETNAM
Ho Chi Minh City
SEA OF JAPAN
JAPAN
Tokyo
Pyongyang
Seoul
SOUTH KOREA
Shanghai
Taipei
TAIWAN
Hong Kong
SOUTH CHINA SEA
Manila
PHILIPPINES
PACIFIC OCEAN
PHILIPPINE SEA
SRI LANKA
Colombo
MALDIVES
INDIAN OCEAN
EQUATOR
MALAYSIA
Kuala Lumpur
SINGAPORE
BRUNEI
Borneo
Sulawesi
West Papua
Sumatra
Jakarta
Java
Bali
Moyo
INDONESIA
N
S
E
W
0 300 600 MILES
0 433 866 Kilometers

EAST ASIA

A Walk in the Clouds

HUANGSHAN

Anhui, China

Huangshan (Yellow Mountain) in eastern China's Anhui Province is the perfect blend of natural beauty and human ingenuity. Emperors and poets have lauded the mountain range's misty landscapes, scroll painters have sought to capture its ethereal beauty, and a thousand years of labor have gone into creating its dizzying pathways and staircases. The mountain has no religious associations: It's as if the power of nature alone has been enough to inspire centuries of admirers.

The Huangshan mountain range is known for its jutting granite peaks and pine trees shaped by time and the elements.

The range is comprised of over 70 peaks characterized by gnarled pine trees, teetering rock formations, bubbling hot springs, and a shifting sea of clouds. A cable car can transport you up (you can also travel by sedan chair), but hiking is traditional. The eastern steps will take 3 to 4 hours, the western steps 4 to 6 hours, but the longer trek is compensated by even more spectacular scenery. The going is tough and steep and is unsuitable for those with no head for heights, but the scenery is among the most amazing in the world. While the extremely fit could hike up and return down on the same day (taxis and minibuses are also available), staying at the top means the chance to experience sunrise piercing the sea of mist, surely one of China's most awesome natural sights.

Even though Huangshan's hotels aren't going to win any prizes, they should be booked well in advance. The Shilin Hotel provides compact but cozy rooms and basic services; the Xihai Hotel is a Swiss-designed establishment popular with foreign visitors.

On the southwest slopes of the mountain, Hongcun is a venerable village of 1,000 or so residents. Founded 900 years ago, it was laid out by a feng shui master in the auspicious shape of a buffalo. One of China's most beautiful historic villages, it is comprised of some 150 buildings, including a farmhouse and clan halls that date back to the Ming and Qing dynasties and are among the best preserved in China. Scenes in the movie *Crouching Tiger, Hidden Dragon* were filmed here in 2000.

WHERE: 315 miles/500 km southwest of Shanghai. Nearest airport is Tunxi, 40 miles/65 km away. **SHILIN HOTEL:** Tel 86/559-558-4040; www.shilin.com. *Cost:* from $190. **XIHAI HOTEL:** Tel 86/559-558-8888. *Cost:* from $165. **BEST TIMES:** Mist and fog shroud Huangshan at any time; May–Oct is busiest.

"The city was bigger, noisier, brighter, more prosperous—it amazed me . . ."
—Paul Theroux, Riding the Iron Rooster

Beijing

China

China's political and cultural capital—and the center of imperial and Communist power alike for half a millennium—Beijing, home to over 15 million people, is a city in the throes of a vast transformation.

Its world-famous historic sights are staggering, and the last remaining ancient *hutong*s (residential alleyways) are now being carefully preserved. But Beijing is also about futuristic buildings, architectural experimentation, a modern can-do spirit, and a striking optimism. It's forward-looking and fast-paced—at least when traffic doesn't grind it all to a standstill.

The daunting, maze-like interior of the Forbidden City humbles the seven million visitors it receives annually.

Top Attractions

The Forbidden City—Off-limits to commoners for 500 years, this is the largest, most complete, and best-preserved cluster of ancient buildings in China. Also known as the Imperial Palace or Palace Museum, it was the court for 24 emperors—from the 15th-century days of the Ming Dynasty until the fall of the Qing Dynasty in 1911. Fires and lootings over the years have left a largely post-18th-century shell that mimics its original layout, and much of its storied wealth and opulent furnishings are long gone. Nonetheless, this vast complex of halls, pavilions, and courtyards is a masterwork of architectural balance—monumental, but never oppressive. An audio guide helps bring it alive, with tales of eunuchs, concubines, ministers, priests, court intrigues, and fabulous excesses. It was not unusual for emperors and servants alike never to venture beyond the moat-surrounded 35-foot walls and formidable gates—the fantasy that they were at the cosmic center of the universe can readily be appreciated today. **Info:** www.dpm.org.cn.

The Hutongs of Beijing—The bustling, frenetic Chinese capital of traffic jams, American fast food, and oft-spectacular modern architecture does have another side—that of its labyrinthine *hutong*s (residential alleyways), so narrow that only pedicabs, pedestrians, and bicycles can fit through. While many of the hutongs have disappeared in the rush for development, those that remain are now being carefully preserved. They are atmospheric remnants of imperial Beijing, where honking horns give way to the occasional ding of bicycle bells and the squawks of chickens and quacks of ducks from inside walled courtyards. The chief sight in the area—sometimes referred to as the Back Lakes District—is Prince Gong's Mansion, built in 1777 by a favorite at the court of Emperor Qianlong. But wandering about and getting lost is the best way to enjoy it—along with dining by the lakeshores and dropping into any of the tiny but lively alleyway bars.

SUMMER PALACE—In the suburbs of Beijing, away from the hectic hustle and bustle of downtown, lies China's largest ancient garden. Spread over 726 acres on the shores of Kunming Lake, the Summer Palace was the summertime playground for royal families, beginning with the Qing Dynasty in 1749. Its most famous resident was the Empress Dowager Cixi, who diverted navy funds to finance what would become her permanent residence. The collection of more than 2,000 beautifully landscaped gardens, temples, and pavilions had been ravaged by war and fire many times before being reconstructed to its current beauty in 1902. You can spend half a day visiting the park's most famous sites: the half-mile Long Corridor, with painted scenes of Chinese history on every beam, pillar, and wall; the 490-foot Seventeen Arch Bridge, the longest in any Imperial Chinese garden; and the Hall of Benevolence and Longevity, where the empress managed her Court—and where tales of her many excesses abound. **WHERE:** 7 miles/11 km northwest of downtown Beijing.

TEMPLE OF HEAVEN—Considered one of the finest examples of Ming Dynasty architecture, the Yongle Emperor began construction of this temple in 1406 while simultaneously overseeing the creation of the Forbidden City: Both took 14 years to complete. Like many of Beijing's historical monuments, the Temple of Heaven (Tian Tan) has seen numerous renovations: The wooden Hall of Prayer for Good Harvests, after being ravaged by fire in 1889, was rebuilt completely—without a single nail, an exact copy of the original. In the early mornings, locals flock to the huge surrounding park to perform traditional activities: tai chi, sword fencing, and amateur Peking Opera performances among them. **INFO:** Tel 86/10-6702-8866; www.tiantanpark.com.

LAMA TEMPLE—Visitors often overlook this 300-year-old temple (officially called Yonghe Temple) in northeast Beijing. The Yongzheng Emperor's former home became a Buddhist monastery that was patronized by the imperial family throughout the Qing Dynasty; it is China's largest (16 acres) and best-preserved lamasery, with Tibetan-influenced architecture. A series of five halls and courtyards is crammed with decorative stonework, sweeping red and gold eaves, and Buddhist art. The details are delightful: Decorative steles are carved with calligraphy and stone lions smile against red walls. Visitors come and go, spinning prayer wheels and burning incense and visiting the 59-foot-tall Buddha sculpted from the trunk of a single sandalwood tree. **INFO:** Tel 86/10-6404-4499.

OLYMPIC GREEN—Beijing may be rightly famous for its imperial architecture, but some of its contemporary buildings are just as awe-inspiring. A walk around Olympic Green, site of the 2008 Summer Olympic Games, is an eye-opening lesson in the architectural swagger and scale of modern-day Beijing. The green is presided over

Built for the 2008 Summer Olympics, the National Stadium is the world's largest steel structure.

by an ultramodern tower known as Ling Long Pagoda. The National Stadium has a spectacular and challenging roof that resembles a bird's nest, whereas the National Aquatics Center is nicknamed the Water Cube for its translucent, avant-garde design. The latter reopened in 2010 as a water park, where slides and wave pools offer a refreshing pastime for kids and kids at heart. **Info:** Tel 86/10-8836-2233; http://en.beijing2008.cn/venues.

798 Arts Area—If you want to see the capital at its most cutting-edge, head northeast to the Dashanzi Art District. Originally the vast Communist-era compound of the 798 Electronics Factory (built in the 1950s in the Bauhaus style), it has slowly been taken over by artists and now thrives as an edgy enclave of exhibit spaces, galleries, studios, design companies, and video screening rooms. Exhibitions change all the time, and activities include everything from fashion shows to of-the-moment product launches. Dozens of nightclubs and bars have sprung up in the surrounding streets, lending the area a new moniker: the Soho of Beijing. **Info:** Tel 86/10-6438-4862; www.798space.com.

Where to Stay

Aman at Summer Palace—As a guest of the wonderful Aman at Summer Palace, you'll gain access to the imperial complex (see p. 481) through a secret door. Set within painstakingly restored Qing and Ming dynasty pavilions and a maze of courtyards, the 51 rooms are simple, elegant, and redolent of the past. Naoki, famed chef Okumara's French-influenced Japanese *kaiseki* restaurant, is just one of four excellent eateries. The hotel can arrange master demonstrations in Chinese arts like calligraphy and *jianzhi* (Chinese paper cutting) and private visits to artists' studios or the Chinese Dance Academy. Or just put your feet up in the hotel's small, leather-chaired theater for a private showing of *The Last Emperor.* **Info:** Tel 86/10-5987-9999; in the U.S., 800-477-9180; www.amanresorts.com. *Cost:* from $550 (off-peak), from $650 (peak); 10-course dinner at Naoki $150.

Hotel G—Located in the buzzy Sanlitun neighborhood, Hotel G's design was inspired by the retro-chic Hollywood era of the '60s, then infused with a Chinese accent. All three levels of rooms (from "good" to "greatest") are elegant, loft style, and understated, and all should please the fussy. The artwork, provided by artists of the 798 Dashanzi Art District, has an avant-garde edge. A fun choice for those looking for Beijing's glam side. **Info:** Tel 86/10-6552-3600; www.hotel-g.com. *Cost:* "good" rooms from $165, "greatest" from $255.

The Opposite House—The theme is hip and minimalist at this 99-room hotel designed by prominent Japanese architect Kengo Kuma. Situated in the trendy nightlife area of Sanlitun, Zen-like rooms are light and luxe, with floor-to-ceiling windows and brushed-oak floors, and amenities include a walking tour through Beijing's *hutong*s and a ground-floor art gallery showcasing contemporary Chinese works. Splurge on the hotel's airport transfers—choose between a Maserati Quattroporte or an Audi Q7—then work out your jet lag with laps in the hotel's 22-meter stainless-steel swimming pool. Its acclaimed restaurant, Bei, offers pan-Asian flavors in a sophisticated space. **Info:** Tel 86/10-6417-6688; www.theoppositehouse.com. *Cost:* from $250; dinner at Bei $35.

Park Hyatt Beijing—Located in the prestigious Beijing Yintai Center, with its lobby on the 63rd floor, the Park Hyatt Beijing overlooks the CCTV towers, the World Trade Center, and the Forbidden City—an incredible vista when illuminated at night. The China Grill, on the 66th floor (and a fitness center on the 60th featuring sunlit pools), is equipped with similarly inspiring panoramas—enjoy the unique 360-degree view from the floor-to-ceiling windows. Guest rooms are the size of small apartments, with glass-walled bathrooms, light-wood fittings, and subtle lighting. **Info:** Tel 86/10-8567-1234; in the U.S., 800-633-7313; www.beijing.park.hyatt.com. *Cost:* from $250; dinner at China Grill $90.

Red Capital Residence—It's back to the future at this unique boutique hotel—a retro shrine to Maoist chic inside an old *hutong* residence. Staff in Red Guard uniforms man the red-lacquer front doors, helping to capture the essence of long-vanished revolutionary optimism with unabashed Communist kitsch and Mao memorabilia (you can even take a tour of Beijing in Madame Mao's limousine). There are only five rooms centered around a tiny courtyard, each named for such revolutionary writers as Han Suyin and Edgar Snow, all with a contemporary and well-run polish. **Info:** Tel 86/10-8403-5308; www.redcapitalclub.com.cn. *Cost:* from $135.

Meat kebabs and deep-fried insects are sold at the night markets.

Sofitel Wanda Beijing—To get an idea of how far the modern Chinese miracle has come, stay at one of the most recently arrived hotels. The Tang Dynasty meets contemporary France in the Sofitel Wanda's stunning lobby, and its suave guest rooms have luxurious bathrooms and the latest in high-tech amenities. And in Le Pré Lenôtre restaurant, enjoy the city's best French cuisine in surroundings that rival a room in Versailles. The hotel's M Bar, with retro velvet couches and glistening crystal curtains, is perhaps the city's best upscale watering hole. **Info:** Tel 86/10-8599-6666; www.sofitel.com. *Cost:* from $160; 7-course tasting dinner at Le Pré Lenôtre $135.

Eating & Drinking

Blu Lobster—Beijing's international offerings have improved in recent years, and Blu Lobster's Irish-born Brian McKenna is one of the chefs leading the way. One of the city's more inventive tasting menus showcases his acclaimed mastery of molecular gastronomy while uniting flavors of Asia and Europe. The foie gras and lobster dishes (the lobster bisque is a signature) are a culinary adventure, but desserts—such as a dark-chocolate, coriander, and hazelnut tart—are also a favorite of the chef's. The Shangri-La Hotel's flagship restaurant has a chic, contemporary décor and a superb selection of Bordeaux wines. **Info:** Tel 86/10-6841-2211; www.shangri-la.com. *Cost:* tasting menu $100.

Da Dong Kaoya—Beijing's preponderance of restaurants serving the local specialty of Peking duck can make the choice impossible. Of the handful of established institutions bandied about by those in the know, the new and stylish Da Dong is a winner, according to locals. After experiencing the dish elsewhere, you'll appreciate Da Dong's special method of reducing the amount of fat in their succulent birds while enhancing the taste. The foreigner-friendly menu (with photos) is long on nonduck options, but order half a bird and get a lesson in various cuts and condiments from the waitstaff. Even the delicate duck soup that comes with your meal is delectable. **Info:** Tel 86/10-6582-2892. *Cost:* $25.

Dali Courtyard—This delightful dining experience can be found off Nanluo Guxiang, one of the Back Lakes district's best-preserved alleyways. Set in a pretty *hutong* courtyard that catches the summer breezes and resounds to quiet jazz music, the friendly open-air restaurant specializes in the light, Vietnamese-influenced Yunnan cuisine of southwest China. Set menus save you the worry of knowing what to order; just relax and enjoy the romantic, slightly bohemian vibe and let the food come to you. Expect chili fish, dumplings, vegetables, papaya salad, and stir-fried chicken, among other light and delicious dishes. **Info:** Tel 86/10-8404-1430. *Cost:* dinner $45.

Family Li Restaurant—This unusual dining spot serves just a dozen extremely lucky diners at a time. Here, six family members work 'round the clock to duplicate royal recipes from the Qing Dynasty, handed down by a grandparent who worked at the imperial court. Visiting diplomats, local expats, and ardent food lovers from around the world all make their way to this tiny restaurant, where the parade of subtly-flavored multiple courses is different for each of the three prix-fixe menus. Each is a revelation. **Info:** Tel 86/10-6618-0107. *Cost:* dinner $65.

Fangshan Restaurant—If your visit to the Forbidden City has fostered a fascination with all things imperial, spend an evening at this prestigious restaurant, preserving the extravagant cuisine of the Qing Dynasty (1644–1911) since 1925, using the favored recipes of the 19th-century imperial court. In a lavish, theatrical setting, the staff (in vintage imperial garb) shows guests what it might have been like to dine with the last Dowager Empress, who employed 128 cooks. The kitchen produces over-the-top banquets and traditional delicacies such as shark's fin or bird's nest soup that are fit for a royal palate. Fangshan's setting—an ancient pavilion on an island in the middle of Beihai Lake, just past the Bridge of Perfect Wisdom—couldn't be more appropriate. **Info:** Tel 86/10-6401-1879; www.fangshanfanzhuang.com.cn. *Cost:* dinner $45.

Bricks, stones, wood, rammed earth, and tile make up the Great Wall.

Beijing street food—For the non-Chinese-speaking first-time visitor, Beijing can be frustrating—even more so for a food enthusiast hoping to sample local fare at the Wangfujing or Donghuamen night markets. Hias Gourmet Culinary Excursions offers private or small-group tours of market and street food, plus a tea-tasting safari through the Maliandao District. Go one step further with American-born author Jen Lin-Liu's Black Sesame Kitchen, which hosts basic Chinese cooking classes in local *hutong* kitchens, as well as gourmet 10-course dinners with free-flowing wine. **Hias Gourmet:** Tel 86/10-6400-9199; www.hiasgourmet.com. *Cost:* 2-hour scheduled tour $55. **Black Sesame Kitchen:** Tel 86/1369-147-4408; www.blacksesamekitchen.com. *Cost:* communal dinner and cooking classes, each $40.

Day Trips

The Great Wall—Long a symbol of the country's strength, the Great Wall of China has long captured the world's imagination. It was built piecemeal over a period of 2,000 years as a defense against marauding nomadic tribes from the north, and in 221 B.C., various sections were connected to span some 3,750 miles. More than a million workers—peasants, soldiers, and prisoners—took part in the construction, building it wide enough to allow ten soldiers (or five horses) to travel abreast between the 10,000 battlements and watchtowers. Only one-third of the original wall remains, and on the average day its restored viewing points, near Beijing, are barely able to accommodate the hordes of tourists and souvenir hawkers. Still, a viewing of the Wall—following the contours of the serene mountains and valleys like an imperial ridge-backed dragon—is enormously impressive. A less touristy alternative is the section at Mutianyu or, better yet, at Simatai, where a half-hour hike will find you alone among soaring hawks and pine trees. Consider overnighting at the new Commune by the Great Wall, near the Shuiguan section; it's an award-winning collection of contemporary villas by famous architects and designers, with private access to the Wall. **WHERE:** The restored mile-long section at Badaling is 50 miles/80 km northwest of downtown Beijing. Mutianyu and Simatai are 57 miles/91 km, 69 miles/111 km northeast of Beijing, respectively. **THE COMMUNE BY THE GREAT WALL:** Tel 86/10-8118-1888; www.commune.com.cn/en. *Cost:* from $290.

The Peace of the Thousand Buddhas

MOGAO CAVES

Dunhuang, Gansu, China

For centuries, the busy Silk Road connected China's western-desert oasis towns with Central Asia and beyond. Silk, cotton, jade, and wool traveled as far as Persia and Rome, while foreign goods and influences such as Buddhism and Islam were absorbed in return. Dunhuang, a remote garrison town on the southern Silk Route, boasts an incredible repository of Buddhist culture in a series of 492 man-made caves hidden in the desert just outside town. They were rediscovered by Taoist monk Wang Yuan Lu in 1900, who subsequently devoted 30 years to preserving the find, now recognized as the most significant Buddhist site in China. National tourism powers have rightfully positioned the Mogao Caves with the Great Wall (see previous page), Forbidden City (see p. 480), and Xi'an Warriors (see p. 495) as China's peerless cultural attractions.

Carved into the face of the valley wall between the 4th and 10th centuries and ultimately numbering more than 1,000, the cave temples housed sculptures, friezes, and frescoes; handwritten account books, court records, and embroidery were also unearthed. Visitors can trace Greek, Persian, and Hindu influences in the thousands of sculpted and intricately painted artworks. Giant stone Buddhas have maintained a millennium of serene smiles, while Tang Dynasty courtiers flaunt their costumes and mythical beasts roam. Among the highlights are the 116-foot brightly painted seated Buddha of Cave 96 and the peaceful, sleeping Buddha of Cave 148. An alternating selection of about 30 caves is open to the public at any one time. Guided tours last about 2 hours, with several routes offered simultaneously. If the ten caves you've seen are not enough, you can ask to view another ten.

South of Dunhuang you'll find yourself deep in the desert, surrounded by vast, sculpted sand dunes. The Minsha, or Singing Sand Mountain, is named for the curious sound the sand makes as the wind blows across its grains. The Silk Road Dunhuang Hotel offers tours to the caves and desert, and is impressive itself with mud walls that evoke a desert fortress. A rooftop patio provides a perfect vantage to watch the late-afternoon light play off the desert dunes. Or experience the sunrise aboard a camel—the hotel concierge can arrange it.

WHERE: 1,146 miles/1,845 km west of Beijing. **SILK ROAD DUNHUANG HOTEL:** Tel 86/937-888-2088; www.dunhuangresort.com. *Cost:* from $60 (off-peak), from $120 (peak). **BEST TIME:** May–Oct for clear skies and cool evenings, though expect hot days Jul–Aug.

The Magical China of Poets and Painters

THE LI RIVER

Guilin, Guangxi, China

Guangxi Province, with its beautiful mountains and rivers, has been eulogized for 13 centuries by painters and writers who have tried to capture its unearthly landscape on paper. A cruise down the Li River is like floating through a classic Chinese scroll painting of mist, mountains, and rivers. From Guilin, the jade green Li winds through spectacular, almost surreal scenery of humpbacked and eroded karst formations with whimsical names like Bat Hill, Five Tigers Catch a Goat, and Painting Brush Peak. Tour boats ply past picturesque villages where young boys bathe the family water buffalo, women wash clothes, and farmers plow rice fields. A dwindling number of fishermen on bamboo rafts still train cormorants (mostly for the benefit of camera-wielding tourists) to dive and trap fish in their beaks.

The Li River winds through some of China's most prized scenery.

Some 50 miles downriver, the small town of Yangshuo is the southern terminus of these river cruises, and though it may not be the "real China"—cybercafés, B&Bs, and cafés offering "American Brunch" cater to foreign tourists—prices are low, the locals are friendly, and many people speak English. From here, day trips by bike over the surrounding green plains and the forest-covered limestone peaks allow you to see some of China's most remarkable scenery. Some of the peaks can even be climbed: From the summit at Moon Rock, a dramatic army of jagged peaks goes marching off into the distance.

During the evenings, the spectacular *Impression: Third Sister (Sanjie) Liu* is performed on the River Li with the dark mountain profile as the backdrop. Directed by the acclaimed Zhang Yimou (art director for the opening and closing ceremonies of the 2008 Beijing Olympic Games), this famous Chinese love story is enacted on a grand scale by a cast of more than 600 locals on hundreds of bamboo rafts.

Peacefully removed some 20 miles from both Guilin and Yangshuo, the HOMA (Hotel of Modern Art) sits surrounded by lakes, rice paddies, and misty karst formations. The hotel's innovative contemporary design extends to its 46 rooms and highlights its collection of more than 200 sculptures by international artists. In town, the fully renovated Sheraton Guilin Hotel is set right on the Li River.

WHERE: Cruises begin in Guilin, 323 miles/520 km northwest of Hong Kong. ***IMPRESSION: THIRD SISTER LIU:*** Tickets can be arranged by any hotel or travel agency in Yangshuo. *Cost:* $30. **HOMA:** Tel 86/773-386-5555; www.guilinhoma.com. *Cost:* $365 (off-peak), $660 (peak). **SHERATON GUILIN HOTEL:** Tel 86/773-282-5588; www.sheraton.com. *Cost:* $120. **BEST TIMES:** Apr and Sep–Oct for nicest weather.

"A city-state like no other, spectacularly unique . . . a boast, a marvel and a show, whirling away night and day in the South China Sea."—JAN MORRIS

HONG KONG

China

The lure of Hong Kong is immediate: Flashing neon lights, a dazzling harbor skyline, and crowded sidewalks surging with humanity highlight the fast-paced, exciting side of this classic East-meets-West city. But Hong Kong is also full of alternative activities and hidden surprises, with traditional ways of life, tranquil green spaces, and offshore islands, revealing a more contemplative side to the former colonial territory. Visitors who know where to look will find both.

TOP ATTRACTIONS

VICTORIA HARBOUR—The busy Victoria Harbour, China's most important after Shanghai, is the soul and centerpiece of this dynamic port city, and the place for which Hong Kong (Fragrant Harbour) was named. At any given hour, its crowded waters host a round of bumper boats, as the Star Ferry threads its way through a melee of tugs, barges, commuter boats, and the occasional junk, sampan, and gleaming cruise ship. The two-tiered green-and-white ferries transport visitors and commuters from Kowloon to Hong Kong Island and back. It is one of the world's most unforgettable 10-minute ferry rides—not only for the drama of the round-the-clock aquatic rush hour, but to view Hong Kong's granite forest of skyscraping banks and trading companies that stand as expressionless monoliths by day, illuminated towers of energy by night. (Nightly at 8:00 P.M., weather permitting, the Symphony of Lights laser show is cast on the skyscrapers' façades; it is best viewed from a harbor cruise.) Go first class for pennies more—the upper deck guarantees a better perspective. Then again, second class promises better people-watching. **INFO:** Tel 852/2118-6208; www.starferry.com.hk.

VICTORIA PEAK—Spectacular views are to be had via one of the world's steepest funicular railways, which makes the climb to the 1,811-foot Victoria Peak. Up top you can marvel at the indefatigably busy harbor, some of the 200-plus outer islands dotting the South China Sea, and, when the weather is clear, the distant coast of mainland China. Landscaped gardens and paved paths such as Governor's Walk provide quiet, solitude, and greenery. Peak Tower boasts 360-degree views at its multilevel Sky Terrace (shaped like an upside-down wok), which houses a variety of restaurants—from fast food to the stylish Tien Yi Restaurant, whose dim sum is best savored at a harbor-view table. While every time of day has its own magic, dusk may be the most special, when an orgy of neon begins to grip the "Manhattan of Asia." **INFO:** Tel 852/2522-0922; www.thepeak.com.hk/en. **TIEN YI RESTAURANT:** Tel 852/2907-3888; www.rcgastronomic.com. *Cost:* lunch $40.

CHI LIN NUNNERY—In the middle of the organized chaos that is Hong Kong, Chi Lin Nunnery is a garden of utter peace and tranquility. This timeless Buddhist complex is an impeccable 1998 re-creation of ancient

Tang Dynasty architecture. Comprising 16 halls made of timber without the use of nails, it's surrounded by meditative gardens filled with lotus ponds, artful rockeries, and carefully tended bonsai plants and frangipani flowers. Venture away from the nunnery on a pathway leading to the Nan Lian Garden for an even more serene oasis—a great place to relax and enjoy a cup of tea in the mini-gazebo before stepping back into the maelstrom of the city. **Info:** Tel 852/2354-1888.

Happy Valley Racecourse—On Wednesday evenings from September to early July, there's one be-there destination: Happy Valley Racecourse, one of the city's very few legal gambling options and where winnings are tax-free. Win or lose, the exuberance of the crowd and the brightly lit night racing makes the experience a winner. Introduced by the British more than 150 years ago, horse racing is the most popular sporting event in Hong Kong, with Wednesday nights topping the bill. There are weekend races at the larger and more modern Sha Tin, in the New Territories suburbs. Major corporations do their entertaining in private boxes here, while the general public gets standing room only. Tourists with a passport can avoid the latter by purchasing a temporary Jockey Club Membership badge to enter the exclusive club area. **Info:** Tel 852/2966-8111; happyvalleyracecourse.com. **Sha Tin:** Tel 852/2966-6520; www.hkjc.com.

Hong Kong Museum of History—Start your Hong Kong exploration here and your stay will be twice as rich. This new museum magically re-creates historical city streets, providing an in-depth feel of Hong Kong from its beginnings up to its 1997 reunification with China. Thousands of exhibits, with audiovisual and lighting effects, multimedia programs, and a re-created arcaded street from 1881—complete with an authentic, relocated herbal medicine shop—also cover the region's natural history and ethnography, beginning 6,000 years ago. **Info:** Tel 852/2724-9042; http://hk.history.museum.

Ten Thousand Buddhas—The impressive name for this surprising monastery is actually an understatement, as its 20 acres of grounds hold between 12,000 and 13,000 Buddhas.

Some 400 steps up a steep incline lead to the monastery of Ten Thousand Buddhas.

The winding entrance path, followed by the 400-plus steps up to the main temple, is lined with life-size Buddhas in various poses. Founded by Yuet Kai when he arrived in Hong Kong in 1933 to preach Buddhism and establish a Buddhist college, the monastery was built starting in 1949. It took Yuet Kai and his disciples 8 years to carry the building materials from the foot of the mountain and to complete construction—and another 10 years to install the thousands of Buddhas. At the top, reward yourself with a delicious *do fu fa* (tofu custard), sold in the temple courtyard. **Info:** Tel 852/2691-1067.

The New Territories—Despite rapidly becoming the "suburbs" of Hong Kong, the New Territories (NT) offer miles of treks through surprisingly lush countryside—some to pristine beaches and others on trails that have been used for 400 years, wending through ancient villages and farmland. Sitting alongside Hong Kong Island and Kowloon, the NT are the third main region of Hong Kong, with 75 percent of its outer stretches of terrain (including 200 outlying islands) remaining wild—too steep to be cultivated or developed. Almost 40 percent of the countryside is committed to conservation and recreation, offering perfect hiking trails just minutes from the 24/7 congestion of the city. **How:** Hansens Hikes leads treks and private tours. Tel 852/9552-0987; www.hansens-hikes.com.

Festivals

Chinese New Year—The Chinese love their festivals, and Chinese New Year's Eve in Hong Kong may just rate as the most joyous annual revelry on earth alongside Carnaval in Rio (see p. 1012) or Mardi Gras in New Orleans (see p. 797). Celebrated over a nearly three-week period, with the New Year itself falling on any date between January 21 and February 20, Hong Kong turns into a huge, vibrant flower market, with decorated floats, performers, and dancers parading through the Tsim Sha Tsui district. Sporting events, lantern carnivals, and much more all lead up to a final, fantastic fireworks display launched off barges in Victoria Harbour (see p. 487), with buildings lit up to complement the show. **Info:** www.discoverhongkong.com.

Dragon Boat Festival—According to legend, a young, beloved scholar, Tuen Ng, drowned himself in a bid to expose corrupt rulers more than 2,000 years ago. When locals heard, they set off in boats to find him, banged on drums, and threw rice in the water while beating the water with their paddles to stop the fish from eating him. He could not be saved, but since 1976 the legend is honored in Hong Kong on the fifth day of the fifth month on the Chinese calendar (early June), when hundreds of teams in ornately decorated boats compete fiercely in one of the most exciting events of the year—likened to an adrenaline-charged version of the Oxford and Cambridge boat races. **Info:** www.discover hongkong.com; for racing schedules, www .dragonboat.org.hk.

Mid-Autumn Festival—Sometimes known as the Lantern (or Moon Cake) Festival, this is Hong Kong's biggest except for Chinese New Year. For three nights in September, straddling the harvest moon (when it is at its brightest and biggest), families gather in parks and on peaks to light lanterns in all colors, shapes, and sizes and to eat moon cakes, pastries filled with a sweet lotus-seed paste. Many legends are associated with this festival, including an uprising against the Mongols in the 14th century, when a rebel movement hid notes in moon cakes instructing readers to "rise against the Tartars on the 15th day of the eighth moon." The rebellion was a success, and is commemorated on just that day. **Info:** www.discoverhongkong.com.

Shopping

Night markets—Hong Kong is known the world over as a shopper's nirvana. Competition in the city is steep and furious, and reproductions and fakes are ubiquitous. This doesn't detract from the fun of bargaining at the variety of Hong Kong's night markets (those who don't like to haggle should stay away) that often thrum with shoppers till midnight. The best in town are the Ladies' Market, for inexpensive women's clothing, bags, and accessories, and the Temple Street Night Market, for an astonishing selection of everything from clothes and CDs to luggage and shoes—even fortune tellers—at the Yau Ma Tei end of the street.

Antiques—Hollywood Road is a world-renowned antiques-buying and -selling center brimming with Tang, Song, and Han Dynasty treasures, including figurines, books, chests, and popular ancestor portraits. Counterfeits are rampant (and some vendors might forget to remind you that it's against the law to take pre-1795 artifacts out of China), but reputable shops give a certificate of authenticity. Trustworthy dealers include Lam & Co., specializing in ceramics and pottery figurines; Dragon Culture, owned by Victor Choi, a well-known antiques collector and book author (with a second gallery in New York); Honeychurch, with a huge selection of handwoven carpets, as well as a superb collection of opium pipes and antique books; and Chak's for all things Buddha-related. Near the western end of Hollywood Road is Upper Lascar Row, commonly known as Cat Street, where more antiques shops and contemporary art can be found. **LAM & CO.:** www.lamantiquities.com. **DRAGON CULTURE:** www.dragonculture.com.hk. **HONEYCHURCH:** www.honeychurch.com/hongkong. **CHAK'S:** www.chaks.com.hk.

Antiques connoisseurs head to Hollywood Road for the best selection.

TAILORED SUITS—Nothing fits or feels better than a custom-made suit, and the world's top tailors can be found in Hong Kong, rivaling those on London's Savile Row for a fraction of the price. Most of the better hotels have tailors on-site, and if not, the concierge will have one on speed dial. It usually takes a few days and two or three fittings before a suit is completed, so make an appointment for your first day in town. Some of the more famous options: Sam the Tailor, who has been making shirts for royalty, U.S. presidents, and celebrities for decades; Punjab House, with more than 100 years experience and a reputation for friendly service; W. W. Chan, who also makes women's clothing; Jim's Tailor Workshop, a favorite with Hong Kong expats and locals alike; and Mode Elegante, with a shop in the historic Peninsula Hotel (see p. 492). **SAM THE TAILOR:** www.samstailor.biz. **PUNJAB HOUSE:** www.punjabhouse.com.hk. **W. W. CHAN:** www.wwchan.com. **JIM'S TAILOR WORKSHOP:** www.jimstailor.com. **MODE ELEGANTE:** www.modeelegante.com.

WHERE TO STAY

FOUR SEASONS HOTEL—Wall-to-wall windows and fantastic views of Victoria Harbour, Kowloon, or the Peak are the highlights at this cool urban stunner, in either the traditional Chinese–inspired or Western-style rooms, both of which are enormous. An outdoor infinity pool on the sixth floor is outfitted with underwater speakers. Of its two outstanding restaurants, Caprice (see next page) serves contemporary French cuisine, while Lun King Heen—one of the most renowned restaurants in Hong Kong—focuses on Cantonese seafood and dim sum lunches, both with views of the harbor. **INFO:** Tel 852/3196-8888; in the U.S., 800-819-5053; www.fourseasons.com/hongkong. *Cost:* from $540; lunch at Lun King Heen $100.

HOTEL INTERCONTINENTAL—Perched at the tip of Kowloon Peninsula and actually built out over the harbor's edge, the InterContinental isn't just the city's haute hotel, it's the social center, and the ultimate see-and-be-seen scene. The heart-stopping views from its 40-foot windows make its lobby one of the most visually stunning in the world (with many of the guest rooms—as well as the Presidential Suite's infinity pool—sharing the same stupendous vista). Take in an uninterrupted 180 degrees of Hong Kong's skyline and unceasing water traffic in its buzzy Lobby Lounge. Its refined Chinese restaurant, Yan Toh Heen, is lauded as one of Asia's—and the world's—finest, for traditional Cantonese cuisine, here served on exquisite table settings of hand-carved jade and ivory. Switch cuisines at NOBU, where master chef Matsuhisa showcases his world-famous Japanese fusion fare. **INFO:** Tel 852/2721-1211; in the U.S., 800-424-6835; www.hongkong-ic.intercontinental.com. *Cost:* from $300; prix-fixe dinner at Yan Toh Heen $130, at NOBU $115.

JW MARRIOTT HONG KONG—Sitting atop the Pacific Place shopping and dining complex, this 27-story hotel is right in the middle of the action. Angled windows offer views over the harbor or Victoria Peak, and rooms come stocked with of-the-moment comforts, from BOSE sound systems to the finest of linens. Talented chefs work wonders with the freshest of lobster and fish at the fifth-floor sushi bar, adjacent to the hotel's signature JW's California grill, loved by locals. A whole roster of facilities—including a heated outdoor pool and round-the-clock top-grade gym—will sweeten your stay. **Info:** Tel 852/2810-8366; in the U.S., 888-236-2427; www.jwmarriotthk.com. *Cost:* from $385; dinner at JW's California $120.

Novotel Citygate Hong Kong—Novotel is raising the bar considerably for airport hotels. Just a complimentary 10-minute shuttle ride away from the runways in the thriving new Tung Chung district, it provides an affordable, alternative look at Hong Kong, especially if you're only in town for a quick stopover. The hotel offers easy access to Lantau Island and Hong Kong Disneyland, and it sits beside the city's best brand outlet mall—plus an adjacent MRT (train) station makes getting into the city center fast and easy. Perfect soundproofing, sleek interior design, a stylish outdoor pool area, and several excellent restaurants make for a very pleasant stay. **Info:** Tel 852/3602-8888; www.novotel.com. *Cost:* from $140.

The Upper House—Opened in 2009, this contemporary hotel is located above the swanky Pacific Place shopping center in Admiralty. Andrew Fu designed it as a tranquil retreat, using natural woods and bamboo in each of the 117 apartment-size rooms. Contemporary paintings and sculptures are displayed throughout the hotel; meanwhile Café Gray, on the 49th floor, marks the return of celebrated Chef Gray Kunz to Hong Kong. The restaurant features a 46-foot-long open kitchen and bar and serves dressed-up American comfort fare before spectacular panoramic views. **Info:** Tel 852/2918-1838; www.theupperhouse.com. *Cost:* from $425; dinner at Café Gray $80.

Eating & Drinking

Bo Innovation—Tantalize your tastebuds at the novel restaurant of tattooed chef Alvin Leung. Born in London, raised in Toronto, he now baffles and thrills Hong Kong with his "extreme Chinese" molecular cuisine. Foodies should come for the traditional dishes that have been given a radical twist with Japanese and French influences: egg-tart martinis, smoked quail eggs with caviar, or stir-fried Wagyu beef, the likes of which you won't likely taste anywhere else. In a city of superlative food, competition is ferocious, but nowhere else will you find a chef so humorously daring and resolutely determined to catapult classic Chinese cuisine into the 21st century. **Info:** Tel 852/2850-8371; www.boinnovation.com. *Cost:* tasting menu $100.

Caprice—Book before you arrive in Hong Kong for this splash-out dinner—one of the city's great dining experiences. Within the rarified environs of the Four Seasons hotel (see previous page), Caprice's sleek and spectacular dining room combines Chinese and Art Nouveau décor with views over Victoria Harbour or into the open kitchen. Providing a departure from the city's local cuisine (it's a good choice for when you can't look another dumpling in the face), here the meals are French provincial, offering the likes of lobster bisque, beef and lamb fillets, duck with foie gras and Savoy cabbage, generous sprinklings of truffles, and superb cheese selections. The prolific wine list is international but focuses on Bordeaux and Burgundy. **Info:** Tel 852/3196-8888; www.fourseasons.com/hongkong. *Cost:* dinner $140.

Da Ping Huo—Hong Kong has one of the most vibrant food scenes on the planet, and the recent rise of hugely popular "speakeasies," aka private kitchens—unlicensed restaurants, often located in private homes—has only added to the variety. One of the best of these unusual venues is Da Ping Huo, where a 12-course tasting menu takes you through all the many (and very spicy) delights of Sichuan cuisine and may include fresh crab, braised beef, or delicate melon soup. The intimate, contemporary restaurant has a laid-back and friendly vibe and is decorated with the owner's artworks; the chef and co-owner sometimes emerges from the kitchen to serenade the guests with an aria of Chinese or Western opera. **INFO:** Tel 852/2559-1317. *Cost:* dinner $40.

LUK TEA HOUSE—Having opened its doors in 1933, the most famous teahouse in Hong Kong—with ceiling fans, marble-topped tables, and a days-gone-by Art Deco ambience—is probably the oldest too. Try a variety of Chinese teas and Cantonese dim sum, all made tourist-friendly with English photo menus. Since this is one of the few establishments where dim sum is served late (until 5:30 P.M.), it's easy to avoid the breakfast and lunch rush. Just don't expect your waiter to smile. **INFO:** Tel 852/2523-5464. *Cost:* dim sum "meal" $35.

TEA—AND DINNER—AT THE PENINSULA—If it's late afternoon in Hong Kong, what better way to absorb the city's colonial past than beneath the gilded, coffered ceiling of the Peninsula's exquisite lobby? A virtual shrine to past empires, it has been the white-glove venue of choice for afternoon tea (and for an overnight stay among discerning guests) since its doors opened in 1928. Everyone is here: international businessmen, frazzled shoppers, impeccably groomed *tai tai*s from Hong Kong's old-moneyed families, the wide-eyed and curious. Tea consists of trimmed finger sandwiches, delicate French pastries, and scones with clotted cream, all delivered on three-tiered silver servers by waiters in starched uniforms. If you're looking for something trendier, the hotel's top-floor Felix Bar and restaurant has an interior designed by Philippe Starck, dazzling views, a chic, champagne-quaffing crowd, and a Pacific Rim fusion menu. **INFO:** Tel 852/2920-2888 (hotel); in the U.S., 866-382-8388 and 852/2315-3188 (Felix); www.peninsula.com. *Cost:* afternoon tea $25, dinner $80.

YUNG KEE RESTAURANT—For over 30 years, Chef Ho Tung Fung has been cooking in the restaurant started as a modest food stall by his grandfather in 1942. Now a Hong Kong institution, everyone (from both Presidents Bush to Angelina Jolie) flocks here for its specialty goose menu. It runs many pages, but the consistent favorite is the Roasted Goose in Five Delightful Varieties. The restaurant occupies four floors in its own Yung Kee Building, efficiently serving 2,000 people a day with 300 to 500 Black Crest geese delivered here daily. And note: You needn't like goose to love the experience. **INFO:** Tel 852/2522-1624; www.yungkee.com.hk. *Cost:* dinner $45.

DAY TRIP

MACAU—Before reverting back to Chinese sovereignty in 1999, the 11-square-mile peninsula of Macau had been under Portuguese rule for 442 years. Its curious

Neoclassical buildings line Macau's tiled, pedestrian-only Senado Square, a hub since colonial times.

mix of Portuguese history, Chinese traditions, and Las Vegas casinos is a 1-hour ferry ride (or adrenaline-pumping 15-minute helicopter jaunt) away from Hong Kong. Soak up the Portuguese vestiges at Macau's namesake: the A-Ma Temple, parts of which are more than 500 years old. Or head to the 17th-century Guia fortress and chapel of St. Paul's atop Macau's highest hill, and the Moorish Barracks, a military barracks named for its architectural style. Fisherman's Wharf, opened in 2004 on reclaimed land, is alive with performances, shops, and restaurants—and round-the-clock casinos, including the Sands Macao, Wynn Macau, and Venetian Macao, each with a roster of designer restaurants. Before hopping the return ferry, dine at the pink 1870 Clube Militar de Macau, once the officer's club for the Portuguese army, now serving both Portuguese and Macanese dishes in a time-worn colonial atmosphere. **Where:** 40 miles/64 km southwest of Hong Kong. **Visitor Info:** www.macautourism.gov.mo. **Clube Militar:** Tel 853/2871-4009; www .clubemilitardemacau.net. *Cost:* dinner $25.

The Yangtze River: A Gallery of Natural Art

The Three Gorges

Hubei and Chongqing, China

The mighty Yangtze River cuts right across the geographical and imaginative heartland of China, and its most famous stretch through the Three Gorges ranks among the world's most beautiful places. The gorges offer unparalled scenery and are renowned in Chinese poetry and painting for their history and lore.

The Three Gorges—Qutang, Wu, and Xiling—encompass 126 miles of the almost 4,000-mile-long river, the third longest in the world. River cruising is popular here, with some trips from Shanghai to Chongqing taking a leisurely week or longer, while other, shorter itineraries concentrate on the Three Gorges alone. At Wushan, most cruise ships stop to shift passengers to smaller, more maneuverable boats for a detour to the Three Little Gorges along the narrow and even more dramatic Daning River.

The Three Gorges made headlines in 1995 when work began on the world's largest dam and hydroelectric project, a multibillion-dollar effort that resulted in the relocation of more than a million people. Completed in 2009, it has partially submerged the gorges' vertical cliffs, rapids, and dozens of cultural sites and ancient temples, not to mention hundreds of villages and cities. The sheer scale and beauty of the gorges remains impressive, though it is true that the peaks are not as high nor is the bottom of the ravine as narrow. Visitors often find a shore excursion to view the immense hydroelectric project an unexpected highlight of the cruise.

The new Viking River Cruises' *Viking Emerald* carries 256 passengers in rooms and suites that all have private balconies, while Abercrombie & Kent's MS *Yangzi Explorer* accommodates just 124 passengers, in cabins and suites that feature private balconies and elegant imperial style.

Where: Chongqing, 895 miles/1,440 km west of Shanghai, is usually the start or end point for the especially scenic Chongqing-Yichang section of Yangtze cruises. Tours generally originate in Beijing and end in Shanghai (or reverse). **Viking River Cruises:** 12-day "Imperial Jewels of China" itinerary includes a 6-day cruise. In the U.S., tel 800-304-9616; www.vikingrivercruises.com. *Cost:* from $2,445 (off-peak), from $5,000 (peak). **ABERCROMBIE & KENT:** 12-day "Highlights of China" trip includes a 3- or 4-night cruise. In the U.S., tel 888-785-5379; www.abercrombiekent.com. *Cost:* from $5,475 (off-peak), from $7,180 (peak). **WHEN:** both companies Apr–Oct. **BEST TIMES:** Apr–May and Sep–Oct for warm weather and generally blue skies.

Landscape Art That Still Casts a Spell

THE GARDENS OF SUZHOU

Suzhou, Jiangsu, China

An ancient Chinese proverb remains true today: "In Heaven there is paradise; on Earth, Suzhou." Founded 2,500 years ago and known as the Venice of the East for its many lakes and canals, the picture-book city of Suzhou was one of the oldest and wealthiest cities in the empire during the Ming Dynasty and was praised by Marco Polo when he wrote about far away Cathay. Today, it's a thriving city, with more than 100 gardens, as many silk factories, and a bustling central shopping district.

Suzhou's historic gardens are the very embodiment of Chinese landscape design, with every rock, plant, path, stone lantern, and pond carefully placed so that each step frames another impeccable vista. The Garden of the Humble Administrator is the largest, built in the early 16th century on 10 acres of lakes and pools connected by graceful arched bridges and stepping-stone pathways, and giving the impression that the entire middle section of the garden is floating on water. Look for the city's smallest garden, Master of the Nets—first laid out in 1140, it is considered to be Suzhou's most perfect.

Situated just south of the Garden of the Humble Administrator, across an artificial lake, the Suzhou Museum was designed by I. M. Pei (whose ancestors came from the city) and opened in 2006. It illustrates the Chinese-American architect's goal of bridging ancient and modern China, blending East and West, and mingling tradition with innovation. Resembling an ancient structure of whitewashed walls and dark gray clay roofing, the low-rise museum showcases over 30,000 cultural pieces, including many excavated relics and other local works spanning three dynasties.

Liuyuan, the Lingering Garden, was built in 1593, and is considered one of China's four most important gardens.

WHERE: 52 miles/84 km northwest of Shanghai. **GARDEN OF THE HUMBLE ADMINISTRATOR:** Tel 86/512-6751-0286; www.szzzy.cn. **MASTER OF THE NETS GARDEN:** Tel 86/512-6529-3190; www.szwsy.com. **SUZHOU MUSEUM:** Tel 86/512-6757-5666; www.szmuseum.com. **WHERE TO STAY:** In the new, western area of the city, the Shangri-La Hotel is located in a high-rise with great views. Tel 86/512-6808-0168; www.shangri-la.com. *Cost:* $105 (off-peak), $400 (peak). **BEST TIMES:** Apr and Sep–Oct for gardens at their best; Sep for Suzhou's famous crab season.

What's Black and White and Loved All Over?

GIANT PANDA TRACKING

Foping, Shaanxi, China

It's estimated that less than 1,600 giant pandas remain on earth, and despite aggressive programs creating reserves for these gentle giants, they are limited in number, and the never-ending threat of poaching leaves their future in question. High in central China's Shaanxi province, the biologically rich forests of the rugged Qinling Mountains are home to the Foping National Nature Reserve, the only place in the world where the public is able to track giant pandas in the wild.

The mountains provide abundant cane and bamboo, pandas' preferred diet, and local trackers and porters guide small groups of wildlife enthusiasts in search of the animals as they forage for food. Summers find the pandas at very high altitudes, making them difficult to follow, but in autumn and early winter, they gravitate to lower stretches and, with the likely presence of soft snow, tracking becomes easier.

The giant panda, a national treasure in China, is related to the bear family and born so small (weighing about 4 ounces) that it is totally dependent on its mother for the first two years. It eventually grows to 5 feet in height and can weigh more than 330 pounds. Sightings of wild giant pandas are never guaranteed at Foping, but it is likely that you will encounter at least one over the course of a few days. While most visitors are here for the pandas, there are also 37 other species of mammals to spot, including the rare and beautiful clouded leopard, the Asiatic brown bear, golden monkey, crested ibis, and golden eagle.

There is basic, comfortable lodging in the reserve at the Sanguanmiao Research Station, with hot and cold solar-powered showers and "green" electricity.

WHERE: 98 miles/158 km north of Hanzhong, 130 miles/210 km southwest of Xi'an. **HOW:** U.S.-based Terra Incognita Ecotours offers a 12-day guided expedition including 4 days tracking giant pandas. Tel 855-326-8687 or 813-476-2810; www.ecotours.com. *Cost:* from $6,000, inclusive. Originates in Xi'an and finishes in Beijing. *When:* May.

Silent Guardians of Ancient History

XI'AN AND THE TERRA-COTTA WARRIORS

Shaanxi, China

The magnificent walled city of Xi'an was home to 11 dynasties, including the Qin Dynasty, first to rule over all eastern China (under the powerful Emperor Qin Shi Huang, who died in 210 B.C.). Today the life-size honor guard of terra-cotta warriors that stand near his tomb are one of China's supreme cultural treasures and surely the most sensational archaeological discovery of the 20th century. Left in situ beneath a protective hangar that now comprises the Museum of the Terra-Cotta Warriors, the soldiers were discovered in 1974 by a well-digging peasant. Since then, three pits have been excavated, the first containing more than 6,000 soldiers and horses in an imposing formation of 38 columns, 16 feet deep. A second pit contains 1,000 more soldiers and 500 horses, while the highlight of the third is an elaborate war chariot. Every soldier differs in facial features, hair, and expressions, and some carry weapons of the day.

Xi'an was the easternmost city on the fabled Silk Road, providing a route for merchant caravans since the 2nd century B.C. The resulting exchange of precious cargo, philosophy, religions, and technology transformed every culture along its route to the doorstep of Europe and beyond. To explore the city's legacy, allot at least a full afternoon for the Shaanxi History Museum, one of the country's largest and most enlightening, then search out the 8th-century Great Mosque (China's oldest) in the Old City, with its marvelous combination of Ming Dynasty and Islamic architecture. The mosque is two blocks from Xi'an's Bell Tower, which offers citywide views from its third-floor balcony.

Enjoy dinner at Defachang Restaurant, serving dumplings for over 70 years just north of the Bell Tower. À la carte dumplings are served downstairs in a large space where you'll rub elbows with local patrons, while a more refined restaurant upstairs is calmer and offers a preset multicourse menu of mouthwatering, artistically styled dumplings. For evening entertainment, look no further than the well-known Tang Dynasty Theater and Restaurant, whose lavishly produced theatrical show of music and dance, while admittedly touristy (voiceovers are in English), will take your breath away.

Where: 568 miles/914 km southwest of Beijing. **Museum of the Terra-Cotta Warriors:** Tel 86/29-8139-9170; bj.bmy.com.cn. **Shaanxi History Museum:** Tel 86/29-8525-4727; www.sxhm.com. **Defachang Restaurant:** Tel 86/29-8721-4060. *Cost:* dumpling meal $20. **Tang Dynasty Theater and Restaurant:** Tel 86/29-8782-2222; www.xiantangdynasty.com. *Cost:* $30. **Where to stay:** Shangri-La Hotel, on the edge of the Old City (not to be confused with a second Shangri-La called the Golden Flower) is the best choice in Xi'an. Tel 86/29-8875-8888; in the U.S., 866-565-5050; www.shangri-la.com. *Cost:* from $170. **Best times:** Apr–May and Sep–Nov for nicest weather; Sep for weeklong Xi'an Art Festival of ancient folk and street culture.

A Spectacular City's Marriage of Past and Future

The Bund

Shanghai, China

Visitors to China's economic, financial, and commercial center head for Shanghai's waterfront boulevard, known as The Bund (or to locals, Waitan). Stretching along the west bank of the Huangpu River, it's the perfect place to experience the juxtaposition of old and new Shanghai. An elevated walkway is backed by Colonial architecture that dates mostly to the prosperous 1920s and 1930s.

On quiet mornings on The Bund, the Pudong district skyline rises in the distance.

Pedestrians can stroll the promenade, and ferries offer a relaxing parallel alternative. Either way, it's an awe-inspiring picture, with old Shanghai on one bank and the futuristic skyscrapers in Pudong—the face of new Shanghai—on the other. The Pudong Shangri-La Hotel, one of the first buildings to grace Shanghai's modern skyline, holds its own against the extremely luxurious Park Hyatt Shanghai. Occupying the 79th to the 93rd floors of the Shanghai World Financial Center, the Park Hyatt is one of the world's highest hotels, with a 100th-floor observation deck that is also the world's loftiest. The entire urban profile, presided over by the famous silhouette of the Oriental Pearl TV Tower, is spectacular when illuminated at night.

The Bund comes alive at sunrise as locals practice ballroom dancing, aerobics, and tai chi; the rest of the day bustles with busy pedestrians and sightseeing tourists. Many of the historic buildings along the Bund are enjoying new life: The tony shopping center Three on the Bund is housed in an elegant seven-story landmark building built in 1916 by the Union Assurance Company, while the trailblazing M on the Bund restaurant is perched atop the 1921 Nissin Shipping Building. The famous Old Peace Hotel reopened in 2010, after an extensive renovation, as the Fairmont Peace Hotel; much of the original charm and ambience remains, including its world-renowned Jazz Bar, a Shanghai institution since 1929. The Art Deco–inspired Peninsula Shanghai is the only new structure built on the Bund in the last 60 years and is the classiest address in town. Like its sister hotel in Hong Kong (see p. 492), it boasts a famous afternoon tea; even if you are staying elsewhere, stop by and linger.

PUDONG SHANGRI-LA: Tel 86/21-6882-8888; in the U.S., 866-565-5050; www.shangri-la.com. *Cost:* from $350. **PARK HYATT:** Tel 86/21-6888-1234; in the U.S., 800-633-7313; www.shanghai.park.hyatt.com. *Cost:* from $500 (off-peak), from $610 (peak). **THREE ON THE BUND:** Tel 86/21-6323-3355; www.threeonthebund.com. **M ON THE BUND:** Tel 86/21-6350-9988; www.m-restaurantgroup.com. *Cost:* dinner $60. **FAIRMONT PEACE:** Tel 86/21-6321-6888; in the U.S., 866-940-4914; www.fairmont.com. *Cost:* from $265 (off-peak), from $365 (peak). **PENINSULA SHANGHAI:** Tel 86/21-2327-2888; in the U.S., 866-382-8388; www.peninsula.com/shanghai. *Cost:* from $320 (off-peak), from $530 (peak). **BEST TIMES:** Apr and especially Sep–Nov for nicest weather.

Unique Pageant of Chinese Antiquities

SHANGHAI MUSEUM

Shanghai, China

The spectacular Shanghai Museum was designed by well-known local architect Xing Tonghe, in a shape resembling a three-legged cooking vessel from the Western Zhou Dynasty (1100–771 B.C.), one of which is on display inside. The beautifully configured, high-tech, and user-friendly space is spread across four floors surrounding an oval atrium that allows plenty of light into the building. There are 11 galleries in all, as well as three areas for special exhibitions that change throughout the year.

The museum is a fine showcase of Chinese art and antiquities, with more than 120,000 cultural relics that trace 5,000 years of China's history, from the Neolithic Age through the Ming (1368–1644) and Qing (1644–1911) Dynasties to modern times. Display items are arranged not by dynasty or chronology but by theme, with galleries devoted to bronzes, ceramics, calligraphy, jade, coins, furniture, and other art forms. Ancient scroll paintings, elaborate Qing Dynasty four-poster beds, calligraphy penned by emperors a thousand years ago, imperial seals, bronzes in the shapes of animals, and porcelain figures from the Tang Dynasty are among the highlights. Handicrafts, costumes, and jewelry from China's many ethnic minorities are also on show. If you have limited time, the Bronze Gallery and Stone Sculpture Gallery are widely considered to have the most impressive collections. As a capper, the museum shop, featuring quality reproduction antiques and ceramics and smaller gift items, is definitely worth a browse. It's the nicest you'll find in any of China's museums.

INFO: Tel 86/21-6372-3500; www.shanghaimuseum.net.

Fortress Home of the Dalai Lamas

POTALA PALACE

Lhasa, Tibet, China

Lhasa, which in Tibetan means "Place of the Gods," is the epicenter of Tibetan spirituality, a city that mystifies and intoxicates, despite the ubiquitous Chinese presence. The vast hilltop Potala, the empty 13-story fortress that was once the winter palace and seat of the revered leader, the Dalai Lama, is the most recognizable of the city's landmarks. Its white-and-red walls and golden roofs rise above the holy city as if it had grown out of the hill on which it has stood since the 17th century. Although today a museum and an empty shell, the words of 20th-century Chinese-born novelist Han Suyin ring true: "No one can remain unmoved by the sheer power and beauty of the structure, with its thousand windows like a thousand eyes."

Tibetan monks pray at the Potala Palace, whose name comes from a Sanskrit word meaning "abode of the Buddha of mercy."

The Dalai Lamas, each of whom is believed to be the reincarnation of Avalokiteshvara, the Buddhist embodiment of compassion, have ruled Tibet as spiritual and temporal leaders since 1644; the current Dalai Lama, the 14th reincarnation, was just 16 when China's occupation of Tibet forced him to flee to India in 1959, where he continues to live. His private apartments have been left untouched and the palace is undergoing restoration by the Chinese, with future tourism in mind.

All Tibetan Buddhists aim to get to Lhasa at least once in their lives to visit the Jokhang Temple, the spiritual heart of Lhasa city and hub of the main market district, known as the Barkhor. Founded more than 1,300 years ago, the golden-roofed Jokhang is a mixture of Tibetan, Indian, Nepalese, and Chinese architecture and is Tibet's holiest shrine. Tibetan Buddhists express devotion to a holy site by walking clockwise around it. At the temple's entrance, devout worshippers repeatedly prostrate themselves to gain religious merit, while inside, a million butter candles softly illuminate the most important statue of Buddha, one of more than 200 in the temple.

For Tibetan hospitality, stay at the welcoming, family-run Kyichu Hotel, centered around a traditional Tibetan inner courtyard in the old quarter of Lhasa. Demonstrating sheer ambition as well as the changes Lhasa is undergoing to encourage tourism, the impressive St. Regis Lhasa Resort opened in 2010 replete with all the latest in Western amenities, soaring views of the Potala, and a level of service heretofore nonexistent in Lhasa. Sitting 11,808 feet above sea level, the hotel has a doctor on call for guests who suffer from the altitude.

WHERE: 594 miles/955 km northeast of Kathmandu, Nepal. Getting there via the "Friendship Highway" from Kathmandu takes roughly 2 days but offers spectacular vistas. **KYICHU HOTEL:** Tel 86/891-633-5728; www.hotelkyichu.com. *Cost:* from $40. **THE ST. REGIS LHASA RESORT:** Tel 86/891-680-8888; in the U.S., 877-787-3441; www.starwoodhotels.com/stregis/. *Cost:* from $300 (off-peak), from $410 (peak). **BEST TIME:** May–Oct for nicest weather.

Climbing Your Way to Enlightenment

MOUNT KAILASH

Tibet, China

Though at 22,028 feet it's not among the highest peaks of the Himalayas, Kailash ("crystal" in Sanskrit; Gang Rinpoche in Tibetan) is one of the most beautiful. More important, it's the most sacred mountain in Asia, revered by Hindus as the abode of Lord Shiva, as well as by Jains, Buddhists, and indigenous Tibetans who follow the ancient Bon religion. The devout of all four religions associate the mountain with eternal bliss and spiritual power. For more than 1,000 years, they have come here on pilgrimages to perform a *kora,* a 32-mile circumambulation of the mountain, ideally completed in a single day. Hindus and Buddhists travel clockwise, Jains and Bon Tibetans counterclockwise, and some can be seen prostrating their way along the trail. For Buddhists, one circuit is said to erase the sins of a lifetime, and 108 assure Nirvana, the ultimate spiritual enlightenment.

Intrepid trekkers can join the pilgrims in their circuit, en route experiencing the austere beauty of the landscape, visiting far-flung monasteries, and encountering the occasional nomad family or yak herder.

Trekking begins and ends at Darchen, on the mountain's southern flank, where there is very modest infrastructure and accommodations. Most recreational visitors aim to complete the circumambulation in 3 days. Reaching Darchen entails a rough 4-day journey by four-wheel drive across the Tibetan Plateau from Lhasa or Kathmandu (see previous page and p. 562). However, the isolation is all part of the mountain's mystic appeal. There is no mistaking the holiness of Mount Kailash, one of the world's very few major peaks that, out of respect for its religious significance, has never been climbed.

WHERE: in western Tibet, approx 1,250 miles/2,000 km west of Lhasa. **HOW:** Lhasa-based Tibet Wind Horse Adventures, which is affiliated with Geographic Expeditions in the U.S., has 22-day expeditions to Mount Kailash and customized trips upon request. Tel 86/891-683-3009; www.windhorsetibet.com; in the U.S., 800-777-8183; www.geoex.com. *Cost:* from $8,000. Originate in Lhasa and end in Kathmandu. **BEST TIMES:** May–Oct for cool to warm weather; late May–early Jun for the colorful pilgrims' Saka Dawa Festival.

The Crossroads of the Silk Road

SUNDAY MARKET

Kashgar, Xinjiang, China

At the foot of the Pamir Mountains—where it's hard to remember you're still in China, much less the 21st century—the remote city of Kashgar hosts a mind-boggling market that is any photographer's dream. By most accounts, it is Asia's (and arguably the world's) largest market, with an estimated attendance of over 100,000 per day.

These days, the impact of the numbers of visitors is slightly diminished, as the market has been split between two sites. The original Sunday Bazaar, which has been going strong for more than 1,000 years, has been covered and renamed the International Grand Bazaar. It's open for business every day, selling clothing, household items, fur hats, daggers, dowry chests, and carpets. While it has taken on a touristy air with pashminas and embroidered dolls, the locals still frequent its deeper passages. The livestock market, known as the Ivan Bazaar, has been relocated to the outskirts of town; it also operates daily but is particularly worth visiting on Sunday. Muslim Uighurs are the majority population in China's Alaska-size Xinjiang Autonomous Region, and bearded Uighur men in traditional blue-and-white garb and women hidden behind veils of brown gauze come to trade, sell, and haggle over sheep, cattle, and horses. It is a scene not unlike what Marco Polo must have witnessed when he passed through in the 13th century, heading east.

Kashgar is just east of the Kyrgyzstan and Tajikistan borders (see pp. 559 and 571), and its culture has more in common with the Central Asian republics than with Beijing, 2,500 miles east. It is the last stop in China on the Karakoram Highway (KKH), the highest paved international road in the world, which winds along the very same paths the ancient Silk Road once traversed and links Kashgar with Islamabad, Pakistan, over the Khunjerab Pass. Completed in 1986, the Karakoram Highway has become a prized destination for adventure travelers, and is also used by expeditions en route to scaling some of the world's tallest mountains.

WHERE: 913 miles/1,469 km southwest of Urümqi, the provincial capital. **WHERE TO STAY:** Seman Hotel is a timeworn but decent and characterful hotel in the former Russian consulate. Tel 86/0998-258-2129. *Cost:* suite $110 (off-peak), $195 (peak). **BEST TIMES:** Apr–Oct for warm, sunny weather; Aug–Sep especially pleasant.

Remote, Rural, and Rich with Diversity

The Road to Shangri-La

Yunnan, China

The remote agricultural Yunnan Province lies deep in China's southwest. With its beautiful eastern Himalayan scenery, its ancient trading towns, and the vibrant cultures of many ethnic minorities (members of almost half of China's ethnic groups live here), it is one of China's most unique destinations.

Bright colors and embroidery accent the traditional clothing of the Bai people, who are concentrated in the Yunnan province.

Northern Yunnan was once part of the powerful 8th- and 9th-century Nanzhao, or Southern Kingdom. Its ancient capital Dali is perfectly situated between lovely Lake Erhai and the towering Cang Mountains; some of its city gates and pagodas date back over 1,000 years. Wooden houses are still built in traditional style, with gables and painted eaves, and the town's Bai minority wear bright costumes and bonnets in pink and scarlet. Twelve miles along the lake, the small town of Xizhou has been trading horses and tea since the Tang Dynasty and is the location of the Linden Centre—an inn and cultural retreat of sorts, offering painting, photography, and writing programs. From here, visit Shaxi, with its Old Town of beautiful Bai architecture and a Friday market that harks back to the days of caravans on the trade route to Tibet.

Some 90 miles northwest, 2,000-year-old Lijiang was once the end of Tibet's trading route between India and China. The delightful market village is the cultural center for the ancient Naxi people, a matriarchal tribe whose women run the markets and inherit all personal property while the men raise the children. At the center of a strikingly beautiful rural area, the canals and cobbled lanes of ancient Lijiang have become a charming home base from which to explore Yunnan's ethnic and cultural diversity, especially if you can score a room at the newly inaugurated Banyan Tree Resort, the region's most stylish eco-friendly lodge. Outside town, Black Dragon Pool Park boasts a lakeside tea pavilion, just the spot for viewing the Jade Dragon Snow Mountains.

Beyond Lijiang, the Yangtze River turns sharply to form the 18-mile-long Tiger Leaping Gorge—one of the deepest in the world—offering a challenging trek and extraordinary scenery. Beyond, the newly anointed Shangri-La County (formerly Zhongdian County) is believed to have been the inspiration for James Hilton's *Lost Horizon.* Sunlight gleams on golden temple rooftops at Ganden Sumtseling Gompa monastery, snow-capped mountains loom, and a sense of ageless tranquility greets visitors.

Many visitors to Yunnan start at the provincial capital, Kunming, nicknamed the "City of Spring." It's a laid-back town with pleasant weather and is known for its popular day trip to Stone Forest, a dramatic landscape of limestone rocks sculpted by wind and rain. Xishuangbanna, tucked between Myanmar and Laos in southwest Yunnan. It is home to another two dozen ethnic minorities and is a tropical holiday destination often compared to northern Thailand. It is characterized by forested hills dotted with Buddhist temples and is home to China's last remaining elephants and tigers.

Where: Kunming is 744 miles/1,200 km northwest of Hong Kong; Dali is 874 miles/1,407 km northwest of Kunming. **How:** U.S.-based Myths and Mountains offers custom trips and 17-day scheduled departures. Tel 775-832-5454; www.mythsandmountains.com. *Cost:* from $5,695. Originate in Kunming. *When:* Feb, Apr, and Oct. **Linden Centre:** Tel 86/872-245-2988; www.lindencentre.com. *Cost:* from $120. **Banyan Tree Lijiang:** Tel 86/888-533-1111; in the U.S., 800-591-0439; www.banyantree.com/lijiang. *Cost:* from $270. **Best times:** Climate is mild year-round; rainy season Jun–Aug; Jun for Gyalthang Horse Festival in Shangri-La.

China's Most Famous Beauty Spot

West Lake

Hangzhou, Zhejiang, China

Described by Marco Polo as "the finest and most beautiful city in the world," Hangzhou still offers a glimpse of old China, notwithstanding the hordes of modern-day tourists. During off-season or a quiet moment at sunrise, the city's West Lake remains one of the loveliest sights in China. Its mist-shrouded shores are lined with landscaped gardens, pagodas, teahouses, shaded walkways, and classic pavilions. The lake may be at its most beautiful (and crowded) in July and August, when it's covered with a mantle of lotus flowers. Ubiquitous willows create the perfect Chinese vignette, joined by groves of peach blossoms in spring, orange-scented acacia in autumn, and plum in winter. By hired boat, row to the Three Pools Mirroring the Moon, the stone pagodas on the Island in the Little Ocean, or, opposite this, the Island of the Hill of Solitude, whose excellent Louwailou Restaurant, established in 1838, is one of many reasons to come ashore for traditional beggar's chicken or lake carp.

Impression West Lake is a spectacular show that dramatizes Hangzhou folklore created by famous movie (and Beijing Olympic ceremony) director Zhang Yimou. Hundreds of actors participate in this sound-and-light extravaganza on a stage slightly submerged under the water of Yue Lake, making for a surreal floating drama effect.

Hangzhou has been a favored tourist destination for centuries, especially now that the train from Shanghai takes just 90 minutes. You can avoid the crowds of day-trippers and still absorb the beauty of the lake along the less frequented south or east shore, where surrounding hills have meandering pathways through old tea plantations. For an overnight stay, Shangri-La Hotel Hangzhou is the lovely grande dame of lakeshore hotels on the leafy (but busier) northwest shore, while Sofitel Westlake Hangzhou is a more contemporary option close to the city on the developed east shore. Or splash out at the secluded and exquisitely designed Four Seasons, which melds traditional with contemporary in a serene lakeside village setting.

WHERE: 115 miles/185 km southwest of Shanghai. **LOUWAILOU RESTAURANT:** Tel 86/571-8796-9023; www.louwailou.com.cn. *Cost:* lunch $25. ***IMPRESSION WEST LAKE:*** tickets available through your hotel concierge. *Cost:* from $36. **SHANGRI-LA HOTEL HANGZHOU:** Tel 86/571-8797-7951; in the U.S., 866-565-5050; www.shangri-la.com. *Cost:* from $200. **SOFITEL WESTLAKE HANGZHOU:** Tel 86/571-8707-5858; in the U.S., 800-221-4542; www.sofitelhangzhou.com.cn.net. *Cost:* from $145. **FOUR SEASONS:** Tel 86/571-8829-8888; in the U.S., 800-819-5053; www.fourseasons.com/hangzhou. *Cost:* from $400. **BEST TIMES:** Apr and especially Sep–Nov for nicest weather; Jul for West Lake Lotus Festival.

More than 8,000 Years of Art History

The National Palace Museum

Taipei, Taiwan

The world's largest and most valuable collection of Chinese art—nearly 700,000 pieces—is housed at the National Palace Museum in Taipei, one of the most visited museums on the planet. Only a small fraction—about 15,000 pieces, rotated every three months—is exhibited at any one time. It would take 12 years to see the entire treasure trove.

A Ming Dynasty Buddha exudes serenity.

Displays are vastly improved following renovations completed in 2006. The works are jaw-dropping, with artifacts spanning eight millennia from prehistory to the early 20th century. Many of the paintings, calligraphy, bronzes, ceramics, rare books, sumptuous jade carvings, curios, and coins come from Beijing's Forbidden City (see p. 480) and were once part of the private collections of Chinese emperors. Some of the most significant items remain on permanent display. A ruffled Chinese cabbage with a delicate carved grasshopper hidden among the leaves made of a single piece of white/green jadeite was nominated by the public as the museum's most outstanding treasure. Another superb artwork is the Qingming Scroll, a great masterpiece of Chinese painting depicting a Song Dynasty festival. Also a crowd-pleaser for its blend of western and Chinese influences is a 1728 study of horses by Jesuit missionary Giuseppe Castiglione.

Almost as interesting as the collection is the story of how it came to Taipei. Some 13,000 crates of these treasures were hauled around mainland China as the Japanese advanced during World War II. The nationalists, led by Chiang Kai-shek, shipped the best pieces to Taiwan as they fled 1949's Communist takeover. They were stored in a railway warehouse, then a sugarcane factory until a new museum building opened in 1965.

After he established a new Taiwanese government, Chiang Kai-shek had the Grand Hotel built near the museum to house foreign ambassadors and VIP guests; in the 1960s, the Grand was considered one of the world's finest hotels. It's not quite as majestic as it used to be, but old-hotel buffs still love it. For an experience of more contemporary chic, Shangri-La's Far Eastern Plaza Hotel soars 43 stories above Taipei's business district and has rooms and suites overlooking the city skyline.

Info: Tel 88/62-2881-2021; www.npm.gov.tw. **The Grand Hotel:** Tel 88/62-2886-8888; www.grand-hotel.org. *Cost:* from $195. **Shangri-La Far Eastern Plaza:** Tel 88/62-2378-8888; in the U.S., tel 866-565-5050; www.shangri-la.com. *Cost:* from $240. **Best time:** Sep–Nov for autumn weather.

Ski Hokkaido's Prince of Powder

Niseko

Hokkaido, Japan

Three major bodies of water surround Japan's main northern island of Hokkaido—the Sea of Japan, the Sea of Okhotsk, and the Pacific Ocean—and when the freezing winter winds blow in from Siberia, they dump as much as 40 feet of dry powder snow (with a downy 4 percent moisture content). Niseko, a resort area that sits at the same latitude as Portland, Oregon, gets more of this perfect snow than Whistler or Vail could ever dream of, creating some of the world's greatest ski runs.

Due to its relatively close proximity and the mere 1-hour time difference, Australian ski-hounds are no strangers to Niseko's slopes. On the western side of the island and just a 2-hour drive from Hokkaido's capital, Sapporo (see next page), the reigning prince of powder is marketed as Niseko United, a mountain comprised of four separate ski areas: Grand Hirafu, Niseko Village, Annupuri, and Hanazono. Buy a single electronic lift pass and you can ski across all four, all day, and hardly cover a run twice. Backcountry skiing is possible, as is night skiing, and when you're done, the resort has plenty of *onsen* (hot springs) in which to soothe slope-weary limbs.

Recent injections of capital from Australia and Asia have seen a boom in new properties in Niseko, particularly in and around the main village of Hirafu, with aspirations of becoming the Aspen of the East. Among several seriously chic lodges, Souiboku stands out. The apartment-size accommodations have a stripped-down décor that is softened by cashmere throws, antiques, and contemporary art, and all have spectacular views of Fuji-like Mt. Yotei. In the same league are the apartments at J-Sekka, a complex that includes Niseko's most impressive deli café, a gourmet restaurant, and a chic bar with roaring log fire.

If you prefer your resorts on a grander scale, there's also the Windsor Hotel Toya Resort & Spa, less than an hour's drive south. Overlooking deep Lake Toya, this five-star property with spacious, comfortable rooms hosted the 2008 G8 Summit meeting.

Come summer, there's just as much to do in the area, from hiking and biking to river rafting and enjoying fireworks over Lake Toya.

Where: 160 miles/257 km southwest of Sapporo. **Visitor and skiing info:** www.niseko.ne.jp/en/. **Souiboku:** Tel 81/136-21-5020; www.suibokuhirafu.com. *Cost:* $510 (off-peak), $730 (peak). **J-Sekka:** Tel 81/136-21-6133; www.j-sekka.com. *Cost:* from $200. **Windsor Hotel Toya:** Tel 81/142-73-1111; in the U.S., 800-745-8883; www.lhw.com/hotel/the-windsor-hotel-toya-resort-spa-hokkaido-japan.com. *Cost:* from $390 (off-peak), from $730 (peak). **Best times:** Dec–Mar for skiing; May–Oct for fireworks at Lake Toya.

A Winter Extravaganza

Sapporo Snow Festival

Sapporo, Hokkaido, Japan

The Japanese talent for reshaping nature is unmatched. The country that raised ikebana (flower arranging) and garden design to high art also transformed the weeklong Sapporo Snow Festival (Yuki Matsuri) into a world-famous show where mammoth snow and ice sculptures depict universal icons ranging from Michelangelo's *Pietà* to Hello Kitty. Ice palaces and a host of other fantasy shapes are created from more than 38,000 tons of snow that must be trucked in from the nearby mountains by Japan's armed forces. Some sculptures that reach more than 130 feet in height and 80 feet in width are begun weeks before the festival's early-February opening. The highlight is the Snow Sculpting Contest, where teams compete from around the world, often from unlikely destinations such as Hawaii and Singapore.

The festival was established in the 1950s, after the dismal years following World War II, when local students built six snow sculptures in Odori Park in downtown Sapporo, still the main venue for today's festival. It really caught on in 1972 when Sapporo, Japan's newest major city, gained global attention as the site for the Winter Olympics. The city serves as an excellent base for exploring ski resorts within a 2-hour drive, such as Niseko (see previous page), or Hokkaido's wild national parks, including Daisetsuzan and the Shikotsu-Toya.

Don't leave town without heading to the 19th-century brick brewery that still produces the liquid gold Sapporo beer for which the city is famous. Flagons of ale go perfectly with the barbecued lamb dish known as Ghengis Khan served at the beer hall next door. During the Sapporo Summer Festival, Odori Park is transformed into a beer garden under the trees. There's live music and a chance to sample food from across the island. Big bowls of miso-based ramen (soup noodles) with a variety of toppings are the local specialty.

Where: 594 miles/955 km northeast of Tokyo. **Visitor info:** www.snowfes.com/english. **Where to stay:** The classy Sapporo Grand Hotel is still one of the city's best Western-style hotels. Tel 81/11-261-3311; www.grand1934.com. *Cost:* from $245. **Best times:** Jun–Sep for the clearest weather; early Feb for the Snow Festival; late Jul–Aug for the Summer Festival.

Japan's Last Frontier

Shiretoko Peninsula

Hokkaido, Japan

Hokkaido is Japan's most untamed island, with ragged peaks, surf-beaten shorelines, thick forests, and gorgeous lakes. While its capital city, Sapporo (see above), and the ski resort of Niseko are well known, huge areas of the island see few visitors. Off the beaten track in Hokkaido's far northeast is the Shiretoko Peninsula, an extraordinary mountainous and forested landscape protected within a national park.

Shiretoko means "the end of the earth" in the language of the Ainu, the original people of Hokkaido, and it is the southernmost area in the world where ocean drift ice reaches the shore. The standout natural features of Shiretoko include the Five Lakes (Shiretoko Goko) and the more remote Lake Rausu, the largest lake on the peninsula, where alpine flora carpets the adjoining land in June and July.

Shiretoko is home to 2,000 Steller's sea eagles (half of the world's population) as well as 10,000 Yezo deer, the endangered Blakiston's fish owls, Steller sea lions, and the biggest concentration of brown bears in the world; offshore, minke whales and orcas are frequently spotted, with sightseeing cruises leaving from the small town of Rausu on the peninsula's east coast. According to experts, Shiretoko is among the first of the world's great ecosystems to feel the full force of climate change. The rise in temperatures and melting of ice is already affecting local fishermen accustomed to catching crab, salmon, and scallops, who are now encountering bonito, sunfish, and other species normally found in warmer waters.

There are no roads or paths in the northern part of Shiretoko, and the only way to appreciate the breathtaking views of the rugged shoreline is by boat in the Sea of Okhotsk. There's basic accommodation in Rausu, but the best places to stay are in the west coast town of Utoro, where you'll find the fairly opulent Shiretoko Grand Hotel beside the harbor. It has spacious Western- and Japanese-style rooms, some of the latter with their own outdoor hot tubs. In the depths of winter, short day cruises from Utoro on an icebreaker through the drift ice can be arranged.

Where: 733 miles/1,189 km northeast of Toyko. **How:** Michi Travel Japan offers 3-day trips, staying at a local inn with its own *onsen* (hot springs). Tel 81/352-13-5040; www.michitravel.com. *Cost:* from $1,200, includes most meals, boat, and English-speaking guide. Originate in Shiretoko. **Shiretoko Grand Hotel:** Tel 81/152-24-2021; www.shiretoko.co.jp/english. *Cost:* from $250, inclusive. **Best times:** Jan–Apr for migratory eagles; Apr–Oct for whales; Jun–Aug for hiking.

A Traditional Touch in the Alps of Japan

Takayama

Gifu, Honshu, Japan

After centuries of peaceful isolation on the Miyagawa River in the mountainous region of Hida, Takayama has retained a traditional touch like few other Japanese towns, particularly in Sanmachi Suji, its beautifully preserved downtown area. Surrounded by dense forests, Takayama was well known for its skilled carpenters who helped to build imperial palaces and temples as far away as Tokyo, Kyoto, and Nara. As you'll see, they saved their finest talents for their hometown.

Founded in the 16th century, Takayama's charm lies in its old merchant houses, good small museums, serene temples (the city's oldest dates to 1588), inns with traditional wood-lattice windows, and six small sake breweries (distinguished by a cedar ball suspended at the entrance), all clustered into a compact grid of streets immediately east of the river. A 5-minute taxi ride west of town brings you to the Hida Folk Village, a fascinating outdoor museum made up of over 20 traditional farmhouses and workshops, from 100 to 500 years old, relocated from the outlying area. Some display local folk artifacts and others house artisans and artists who demonstrate the town's well-known woodcarving craft. The A-shaped structures with thatched roofs prevent snow from piling up and are called *gassho-zukuri* (meaning "praying hands"). They were built without nails; strips of hazel branches hold the beams together, allowing them flexibility to sway with the wind. You can see similar homes in the picturesque hamlet of Ogimachi, 50 miles northwest of Takayama, the most popular of the three areas that make up the Shirakawa-go and Gokayama heritage districts.

Many of the farmhouses of Hida Folk Village are centuries old.

Always bustling with tourists, Takayama becomes most crowded during its famous semiannual *matsuri* (festivals), one of which takes place in spring (*sanno*) when the cherry blossoms are in bloom, the other in autumn (*hachi-man*) when foliage peaks. Tens of thousands of spectators gather for parades of large 11th-, 17th-, and 18th-century *yatai* (floats), each elaborately decorated and beautifully preserved, showcasing Takayama's legendary craftsmanship. Each yatai carries a sophisticated *karakuri ningyo* (marionette show) controlled by puppeteers who balance atop the floats. Four of these floats can be viewed year-round at the Takayama Festival Float Exhibition Hall.

There are plenty of small traditional inns in Takayama, and the modern Takayama Green Hotel, close to the train station, offers very spacious Japanese- and Western-style rooms. There's a good range of restaurants here too and excellent *onsen* (natural hot springs), some with landscaped outdoor pools.

WHERE: 331 miles/533 km northwest of Tokyo, 100 miles/161 km northeast of Nagoya. **VISITOR INFO:** www.hida.jp/english. **TAKAYAMA GREEN HOTEL:** Tel 81/577-333-5500; www.takayama-gh.com. *Cost:* from $230, inclusive. **BEST TIMES:** May–Aug for nicest weather; Apr 14–15 for Spring Festival; Oct 9–10 for Autumn Festival.

Peace and Tranquility

HIROSHIMA AND MIYAJIMA

Honshu, Japan

It's hard to imagine that the Hiroshima so devastated on August 6, 1945, is now a vibrant forward-looking city visited by millions every year who come from all over the world to pay their respects. The most prominent reminder of that fateful day is the twisted and charred shell of the old Industrial Promotion Hall, now known as the A-Bomb Dome (Genkaku Domu), left in its distressed state as a symbol of humankind's self-destructiveness. Across the Motoyasu River is the Peace Memorial Park (Heiwa Kinen Koen), dotted with monuments to the victims of the world's first atomic-bomb attack, and a sobering museum with displays that relive one of the worst days in history, beginning with a watch forever stopped at 8:15 A.M.

The most touching memorial is the Children's Peace Monument, an elongated dome featuring a statue of a girl holding a giant origami crane, the symbol of happiness and longevity in Japan. The base of the monument is always covered with garlands and origami cranes made by Japanese schoolchildren in honor of Sadako Sasaki, a girl exposed to radiation as a toddler who succumbed to leukemia at age 12. The Flame of Peace under the Memorial Cenotaph will burn until the last nuclear weapon on earth has been banished.

When visiting the tiny, picturesque island of Miyajima in the Seto Inland Sea, make sure you take the half-hour ferry ride from Hiroshima during high tide to view the majestic orange gate (*torii*) in the bay, when it appears to be floating on water. One of Japan's most recognizable symbols, the current version of the gate (which was originally erected in 1168) dates to 1875. It stands at the entrance to the wooden Itsukushima Shrine, dedicated to the Shinto god of the moon, and is the main attraction on this 12-square-mile island rich with natural beauty and romance.

After the day-trippers return to the mainland, stay at the well-known 150-year-old Iwaso Ryokan to see the gate and shrine illuminated at night. Guests receive the same treatment as the Japanese royal family, who head up a long list of illustrious visitors. A few separate, exquisitely decorated private cottages are worth the splurge, and if there's no room at the inn, at least stay for their rightly praised 10-course dinner.

WHERE: 537 miles/864 km southwest of Tokyo on the Seto Inland Sea. **VISITOR INFO:** www.hcvb.city.hiroshima.jp. **IWASO RYOKAN:** Tel 81/829-44-2233; www.iwaso.com. *Cost:* from $425, inclusive; dinner $80. **BEST TIMES:** Aug 6 for bombing anniversary, when white doves are released; late Mar–Apr for cherry blossoms; Oct–early Nov for autumn foliage on Miyajima island.

Gorgeous Gardens, Geisha, and the Arts in a Castle Town

KANAZAWA

Ishikawa, Honshu, Japan

Facing the Sea of Japan coast, with the lofty peaks of the Japanese Alps behind it, Kanazawa was once a great castle town, the heart of a prime rice-growing area ruled by the powerful Maeda family. One of the few major Japanese cities that escaped the World War II air raids, its historic center is rich with the culture and architecture of Old Japan.

Kanazawa's unchallenged main attraction is Kenroku-en, Japan's largest garden, considered to be one of its three most beautiful: 25 acres of trees, ponds, footpaths, waterfalls, and flowers, plus a teahouse and a 19th-century villa. The gardens were begun in 1676 by the feudal lord living in the adjacent Kanazawa Palace (you can visit a replica of the earlier castle destroyed by fire). Pick up a *bento* (box lunch) at the 100-year-old Miyoshian or stay for tea and sweets.

The 21st Century Museum of Contemporary Art catapults you back into the present. Designed by SANAA, the Tokyo-based architectural firm that also designed the New Museum of Contemporary Art in New York City, the low-slung circular building of glass walls showcases permanent exhibits, including James Turrell's *Blue Planet Sky* and Leandro Erlich's *Swimming Pool*.

Kenroku-en garden has been open to the public since 1871.

The Higashi-Chaya district of wooden-latticed teahouses is one of several areas in the city where geisha are trained in the performing arts; the city's tourist offices will tell you when public performances are scheduled. The former samurai quarter of Nagamachi reveals flowing canals, twisted cobblestone lanes, and old houses of mud walls and tiled roofs.

Kanazawa means "Marsh of Gold," and the town produces about 90 percent of Japan's gold leaf (it supplied the gold leaf that covers Kyoto's Golden Pavilion; see p. 510)—it is found on local crafts and even as flakes in the local tea (said to help rheumatism). The Yasue Gold Leaf Museum houses fine examples of Buddhist altars, ceramics, and screens. Other local arts and crafts, perfected over the last 500 years, include handmade silks, potteries, and lacquerware: These are showcased in the Museum for Traditional Products and Crafts and fill gift stores across the city.

Food is a key part of the Kanazawa experience. The principal component of the local cuisine, *kaga ryori,* is fresh fish, found in small sushi bars in and around the lively fish market, Omicho Ichiba, a mini-version of the one you'll find in Tokyo.

WHERE: 268 miles/431 km north of Kyoto. **VISITOR INFO:** www.kanazawa-tourism.com. **WHERE TO STAY:** Hotel Nikko Kanazawa is a modern high-rise that still manages to feel personal. Tel 81/76-234-1111; in the U.S., 800-645-5687; www.jalhotels.com. *Cost:* from $150. **BEST TIMES:** Apr for cherry blossoms; Aug–Sep for clearest weather.

"Tokyo may be the capital of Japan but Kyoto is its heart and soul."—JULIET WINTERS CARPENTER

KYOTO

Honshu, Japan

To stroll through Kyoto is to travel through 11 centuries of Japan's history. Once the home of the imperial court, the city was also a center of Japanese religion, aesthetics, music, theater, and dance, reaching its height as a center for crafts during the Muromachi Period (1334–1568). Spared by Allied bombing during World War II, the city is said to hold 20 percent of all Japan's national treasures, including more than 1,700 Buddhist temples and 300 Shinto shrines, all dispersed (often hidden) amid its modern cityscape. Kyoto's beauty can sometimes be elusive, but thoughtful visitors can still glimpse the Japan of the past in its temples and gardens, while its modern side offers a sophisticated mix of tradition and contemporary innovation.

Temples and Top Attractions

Fushimi Inari—One of Kyoto's greatest sights is the 10,000 reddish orange *torii* (gates) of the *taisha* (shrine) of Inari, in the Fushimi area of Kyoto. Forming a 2.5-mile tunnel up the wooded mountainside, the lacquered torii are donated by Japanese businesses, their names written in black lettering on each gate, asking Inari—the god of rice, sake, and prosperity—for a blessing. This is the largest and most famous shrine dedicated to Inari and the head shrine of more than 40,000 found nationwide. A 2- to 3-hour walk up to Mount Inari rewards you with magnificent views of Kyoto, and there are plenty of stops along the way for *inarizushi* (sushi rice in a pocket of fried tofu) and a cup of tea. **Info:** Tel 81/75-641-7331; www.inari.jp.

Torii (gates) line the Fushimi Inari shrine, which dates to the 8th century, when worshippers were more likely to pray for a good rice harvest than business prosperity.

Kinkaku-ji and Ginkaku-ji—Shogun Ashikaga Yoshimasa commissioned the 14th-century Kinkaku-ji (Temple of the Golden Pavilion) as his retirement home, intending its two top floors to be sheathed in gold leaf, though he got no farther than the ceiling of the third floor in his lifetime. After his death, his son converted the building into a Zen temple in accordance with his father's wishes. The temple was torched by a disgruntled monk in 1950 and rebuilt to its original specifications by 1955; by 1987, the gold-leaf coating finally extended to the top two floors. Kinkaku-ji is highly revered as a *shariden*, a site housing relics of the Buddha, and is probably the most photographed structure in Kyoto.

On the opposite side of town, the shogun's grandson, also named Ashikaga Yoshimasa, commissioned the two-story, pagoda-roofed Ginkaku-ji (Temple of the Silver Pavilion) in the 1470s in homage to his grandfather's Kinkaku-ji, with plans to cover it in silver leaf. He too died before his plan could be realized, and Ginkaku-ji took over 30 years to complete. Formerly part of a much larger villa, it stands surrounded by a reflecting pool and gardens designed by a master landscape architect for meditative strolling. The mile-long Philosopher's Path outside its gate follows a narrow canal that is particularly beautiful when the cherry trees that line its banks are in full bloom. **Kinkaku-ji:** Tel 81/75-461-0013; www.shokoku-ji.or.jp/english/. **Ginkaku-ji:** Tel 81/75-771-5725; www.shokoku-ji.or.jp/english/.

Kiyomizu-dera—One of the most celebrated temples of Japan, Kiyomizu-dera, the Pure Water Temple, was founded in 780 and was associated with the Hosso sect of Buddhism, one of the oldest in Japan. Its present buildings were constructed in 1633 without a single nail; the main hall's large, wooden terrace juts out over the valley, offering beautiful views of the city. Below, three streams tumble into a pond, creating the Otowa (Sound of Feathers) waterfall, where you can drink the springwater, said to have wish-granting powers. The complex houses several shrines; the Jishu Shrine is dedicated to the deity of love and attracts young men and women who make offerings and buy lucky charms to help find their life partners. **Info:** Tel 81/75-551-1234; www.kiyomizudera.or.jp.

Nijo-jo—Completed in 1626 by Ieyasu, the first Tokugawa shogun of a united Japan, Nijo Castle is a perfect example of the paranoia of the era. The castle is surrounded by a moat and stone walls, and has secret rooms and corridors where hidden samurai guards could keep watch. The castle, built almost entirely of Japanese cypress, was built with ingenious "nightingale" floors that "sing" when walked upon. Extensive gardens designed by the renowned gardener Kobori Enshu originally had no trees, as falling leaves symbolized the transience of life to the shogun and his samurai. **Info:** Tel 81/75-841-0096.

Ryoan-ji—A lovely half-hour walk from Kinkaku-ji leads to the Ryoan Temple, whose small, simple, 500-year-old garden of raked white gravel and 15 rocks arranged in three groupings has become a world-recognized symbol of Zen wisdom. In Buddhism, the number 15 denotes "completeness" or "enlightenment." At Ryoan-ji, regardless of where you stand, only 14 of the 15 rocks can be seen at any given time—interpreted by some to mean that true completion is never possible. The garden's designer remains a mystery, the rock arrangement's meaning a riddle. It is one of Japan's most famous gardens, attracting large crowds daily; best to visit very early in the morning for a moment of quiet contemplation. **Info:** Tel 81/75-463-2216; www.ryoanji.jp.

Saiho-ji—Also referred to as Kokedera (Moss Temple), the Zen Buddhist Temple of Saiho was re-created in 1339 by priest Muso Soseki on the site of an earlier temple and is now known for its more than 120 varieties of moss. Soseki designed the two-tiered dry gardens around a pond in the shape of the Chinese character for heart or mind; then Mother Nature took over and draped the gardens in a soft moss blanket in hues of gold and green. Visitors must write to the temple in advance to gain admission; once permission is granted, an entrance fee of $37 (the highest in Kyoto) is expected on arrival. Visitors take part in a 2-hour Buddhist ceremony, chanting sutras with the monks and practicing Japanese characters (calligraphy), before enjoying the dark, soothing Zen gardens. **Info:** Tel 81/75-391-3631. *Mailing address:* 56 Matsuo-Jingatani-cho, Nishikyo-ku, Kyoto-shi, Kyoto.

Sanjusangendo—Behind a simple and austere exterior, Sanjusangendo (known locally as Rengeo-in) is a 400-foot-long hall (the longest wooden structure in Japan), the remarkable repository of 1,001 standing statues of Bodhisattva Kannon, the Buddhist Goddess of Mercy. View row upon row of life-size statues beautifully carved from Japanese cypress and covered in gold leaf: Each statue has 40 arms and the power to save 25 worlds. They surround one seated Kannon, joining the 28 deities who protect the universe. Many of the statues date back to the 12th century, and the structure dates from 1266. **Info:** Tel 81/75-525-0033; http://sanjusangendo.jp.

Tenryu-ji—The 14th-century Tenryu-ji (Temple of the Heavenly Dragon) is the first ranked of the Kyoto Gozan or Five Great Zen Temples of Kyoto (the others are Shokoku-ji, Kennin-ji, Tofuku-ji, and Manju-ji), dedicated to the Rinzai school of Zen Buddhism. Rinzai focuses on riddles that lack a rational answer, forcing the mind to ponder insoluble problems. Nestled in tranquil surroundings on the western edge of the suburb of Arashiyama, Tenryu-ji offers fine Zen gardens, including a strolling garden and Japan's oldest example of *shakkei*, or borrowed scenery, which incorporates distant landmarks into the garden's design. Don't miss the dragon painting on the ceiling of the lecture hall where monks meditate. A simple but artful lunch of Zen cuisine is served for visitors at Shigetsu, within the temple grounds, but must be reserved in advance. **Info:** Tel 81/75-881-1235; www.tenryuji.org.

Other Must-Dos

Gion District—Traditional Kyoto town houses, with their red-and-white paper lanterns, are iconic within the entertainment quarter of Gion, where the geisha (*gei*, "art," plus *sha*, "person") live and work. Geisha (or *Geiko*, as they are called locally) are women who are trained in traditional music and dance and entertain at private, usually all-male, parties. Gion was originally developed to accommodate travelers and visitors to the Yasaka Shrine, then evolved into the most famous geisha district in all Japan; it remains very exclusive but is more welcoming to visitors than in the past. Geisha and young apprentices called *maiko* dressed in exquisite kimonos can still be seen in the evenings as they travel between their various engagements at exclusive *ochaya* (teahouses and restaurants), particularly those on Hanami-koji Street. Another integral part of Gion's entertainment culture is the Minami-za Kabuki Theater, which was established in the 17th century, making it Japan's oldest theater. The current structure, which dates from 1929, hosts regular performances as well as the yearly December Kaomise festival, a showcase of Kabuki's most celebrated performers. **INFO:** Tel 81/75-561-1155.

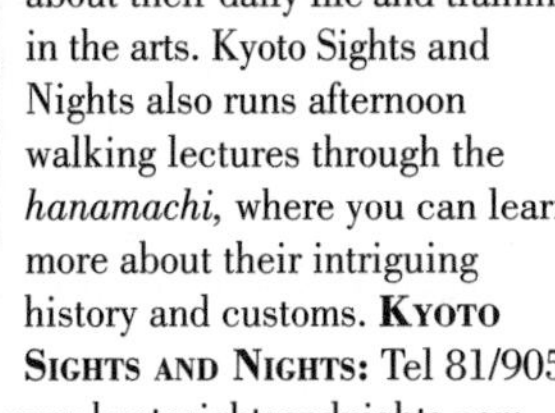

Gion's apprentice geisha are known as maiko.

NISHIKI-KOJI—Steeped in culture and history, Nishiki Market (known as "Kyoto's kitchen") is a narrow, covered street lined with more than 100 shops. Some of the fishmongers, fresh-produce grocers, and pickle purveyors have been here for generations (and often live directly over their shops) and are joined by newer tofu doughnut sellers and green-tea ice-cream vendors. You can eat on the run or savor samples along the way, enjoying a wonderful glimpse into Kyoto's food culture. **HOW:** For customized Kyoto food tours, contact Michi Travel. Tel 81/352-13-5040; www.michitravel.com.

VISIT WITH A GEISHA—Thanks to the development of international tourism in Kyoto, it is now far easier than it used to be to experience the traditional entertainment of a geisha party in one of Kyoto's five *hanamachi* (geisha entertainment districts). Kyoto Sights and Nights organizes private engagements with geisha and *maiko*, including dinner and musical entertainment. This is an unusual and enlightening chance to speak directly with these traditional entertainers about their daily life and training in the arts. Kyoto Sights and Nights also runs afternoon walking lectures through the *hanamachi*, where you can learn more about their intriguing history and customs. **KYOTO SIGHTS AND NIGHTS:** Tel 81/905-169-1654; www.kyotosightsandnights.com.

FESTIVALS (*MATSURI*)

CHERRY BLOSSOMS—From late March until early April, tens of millions of Japanese flock to the parks and temple gardens across the country in pursuit of *hanami*, or cherry blossom viewing (see p. 517). Maruyama Park, in eastern Kyoto, the Gosho (Imperial Palace), in the center, and Arashiyama, in the west, are three of the city's main viewing areas, but the perennial favorite is the cherry tree-lined canalside Philosopher's Path that begins near Ginkaku-ji (see p. 510). Visit early on weekdays for a relatively crowd-free mile-long stroll beneath a gentle flurry of pink and white petals.

JIDAI FESTIVAL—Proud Kyotoites by the thousands participate in the Jidai Matsuri, or Festival of the Ages, one of the city's newest events (it started just over a century ago and is held annually on October 22), to commemorate the founding of Kyoto. A theatrical procession in costumes from the dynasties of the 8th through the 19th centuries snakes its way through town, beginning at the Imperial Palace and ending at the Heian Shrine.

Aoi Festival—The cherry blossoms are gone when the Aoi Matsuri, or Hollyhock Festival, floats through town on May 15, but spring will still be at its loveliest as hundreds of participants wearing the costumes of imperial courtiers parade to the Shimogamo and Kamigamo shrines to pray for the city's prosperity. The annual Aoi dates back to the 6th century and is believed to be the world's oldest surviving festival.

Gion Festival—On July 17, make way for 32 huge wooden floats that are part of the grand parade of the popular Gion Matsuri, a procession that asks for the protection of Kyoto. First held in the 9th century as a ritual purification to ward off plague in the humid summer months, it has grown into one of the most famous festivals in Japan. The three nights leading up to the grand parade are especially exciting; the streets of central Kyoto are lined with food stalls and packed with wandering locals wearing *yukata* (summer kimonos) and fanning themselves with traditional *uchiwa* (paper fans).

Where to Stay

Granvia—If traveling to and from Kyoto by train, the Granvia is conveniently located—as well as exceptionally comfortable. Its location high above the futuristic JR station means that most of the stylishly equipped 535 rooms offer excellent city views, and despite its size, service is personal and attentive. The spacious rooms and public areas are all adorned with the work of Kyoto artists. There are over a dozen in-house restaurants and bars to choose from, including a small branch of the highly esteemed Kitcho (see next page). **Info:** Tel 81/75-344-8888; www.granvia-kyoto.co.jp. *Cost:* from $280.

Hyatt Regency Kyoto—Located in the Higashiyama Shichijo district, just steps away from the Sanjusangendo Temple and the Kyoto National Museum, this is one of the finest of the city's Western-style modern hotels. The elegant lobby leads to 189 comfortable rooms that are stylishly decorated using natural colors, white oak, and kimono fabrics. The spacious bathrooms offer separate deep soaking bathtubs and excellent Japanese-style showers, and the Riraku Spa has an extensive menu of traditional Japanese and Asian therapies. Touzan Restaurant, modeled after a traditional-style Kyoto house with views of the hotel's rock garden, is popular with both locals and visitors and serves charcoal-grilled specials as well as a large selection of sushi and sake. **Info:** Tel 81/75-541-1234; in the U.S., 800-233-1234; www.kyoto.regency.hyatt.com. *Cost:* from $450 (off-peak), from $560 (peak); dinner at Touzan, fixed menu $65.

Hotel Mume—Small and precious, Mume is located behind a big red door on a quiet street lined with antiques galleries in the geisha entertainment district of Gion. Seven rooms are tastefully decorated with antique Asian furniture and accented with Kyoto artifacts and French and Italian fabrics. Mume provides a delightfully tranquil experience, with an exceptional staff who are charmingly attentive and sensitive to guests' needs. The hotel's salon faces the Shirakawa canal and has a gorgeous view of cherry blossoms in the spring. Enjoy the view with a complimentary cappuccino or over cocktails during the nightly happy hour. **Info:** Tel 81/75-525-8787; www.hotelmume.jp. *Cost:* from $240.

The Screen—Kyoto's first high-design boutique hotel opened in 2008 with 13 chic and glamorous rooms, all spacious and uniquely decorated by different designers; some have sofas covered with locally woven brocade and hand-painted shoji screens, while others are more like loft-style apartments with traditional-style earthen walls (depending on availability, guests can choose their room at check-in). Because of its central location, great food and drink is close by, but many guests gravitate to the hotel's French restaurant, Bron Ronnery, which serves sophisticated meals made with locally sourced ingredients. The fifth-floor bar and champagne garden, Shoki, looks down on the surrounding temple rooftops and ancient trees of the nearby Imperial Palace. **Info:** Tel 81/75-252-1113; www.screen-hotel.jp. *Cost:* from $386; dinner at Bron Ronnery $90.

Tawaraya Ryokan—Of the country's many traditional inns, Tawaraya, a 300-year-old family-run ryokan now in its 11th generation, is one of the most famous and luxurious. Elegance and refinement pervade its every aspect, from the subdued, almost spartan accommodations to the small, private gardens off most of the 18 rooms, each a harmonious blend of red maple, bamboo, ferns, stone lanterns, moss-covered rocks, and water. A restorative soak in the steaming water of a perfumed cedar tub is followed by dinner, an elaborate, multicourse, *kaiseki*-style meal served in your room by a kimonoed attendant. After that the shojis (paper screens) are drawn and a plump futon is brought out and made up with starched, fine linen. **Info:** Tel 81/75-211-5566. *Cost:* from $1,000, inclusive.

Eating & Drinking

Giro Giro Hitoshina—The chefs may sport Mohawks or pink hair, but don't be fooled: They know what they're doing in this contemporary *kaiseki*. Artfully presented morsels of traditional dishes arrive on antique lacquer plates or funky ceramics; expect to be surprised and entertained and to eat very, very well. Giro Giro Hitoshina is surprisingly small but conveniently located on the Takase-gawa canal south of Shijo-dori, with counter seating downstairs and table seating on the second floor. It is open only in the evening, and its growing popularity means reservations are necessary well in advance. **Info:** Tel 81/75-343-7070; www.guiloguilo.com. *Cost:* set dinner $45.

Ippodo Kaboku Tearoom—Ippodo has been in the business of selling tea across Japan since 1717, and the original main store, with its walls of antique ceramic tea jars and the wood-beamed ceiling, is worth a visit for a glimpse of old Kyoto. The adjacent Kaboku tearoom is a newer addition and the perfect place to sample various grades of green tea grown in nearby Uji. From the green frothy *matcha* (the fine powdered green tea of the tea ceremony) to the lighter *hojicha* (a roasted blend of coarser tea leaves), you can make your own or have the staff do it for you, plus you can stock up on gifts for those back home. All teas are served with a traditional seasonal sweet—usually red or white bean jam encased in fresh *mocha* (pounded rice). **Info:** Tel 81/75-211-3421; www.ippodo-tea.co.jp.

Izusen—Izusen is tucked into the peaceful garden of Daiji-in, a sub-temple of the large Daitokuji complex in northern Kyoto. It specializes in *shojin-ryori,* Buddhist vegetarian cuisine, which mostly consists of soybean ingredients, such as tofu and miso, and ofu (wheat-gluten), alongside delicious seasonal vegetables. It is both nutritious and flavorsome, with sesame seed, citrus, and seaweed used to accent many dishes. A beautifully presented seasonal lunch is served outdoors in the temple garden, with dishes presented in exquisite red-and-black lacquerware bowls. Izusen is perfect for lunch either before or after visiting Kinkaku-ji and Ryoan-ji temples (see pp. 510 and 511). **Info:** Tel 81/75-491-6665; www.kyoto-izusen.com. *Cost:* set lunch $38.

Kitcho—Kitcho enjoys a storied reputation for offering the country's unquestioned finest in Japanese *kaiseki* (traditional multicourse) dining. It was described by science fiction writer Arthur C. Clarke as "frighteningly expensive," but if your purse can afford it, you'll savor the gourmet meal of a lifetime—specifically designed to include impeccable regional produce of the season and the unique preferences of each guest (you'll be interviewed when making a reservation), all in a quasi-ethereal environment. Preparations begin days in advance, and the most infinite care is taken in producing multiple courses of too-beautiful-to-eat artistry. The main restaurant is in Arashiyama, western Kyoto, but there is also a small branch in the Granvia Hotel at Kyoto station (see p. 513). **INFO:** Tel 81/75-881-1101; www.kitcho.com. *Cost:* set lunch $520, set dinner $810.

Himeji, said to resemble a bird taking flight, is called "White Heron Castle."

OMEN—Located on the Philosopher's Path (and the perfect destination after a visit to Ginkaku-ji temple, see p. 510), Omen promises the best *udon* (thick wheat) noodles in Kyoto. Omen's noodles are renowned for being served with a delicious combination of fresh ginger, roasted sesame seeds, pickled daikon radish, and a lightly flavored *shoyu* (soy) dipping sauce. The menu also features some excellent side dishes such as tempura vegetables, fresh silken tofu, grilled *hamo* (conger eel), and other seasonal dishes. There are two other branches of Omen located downtown on Shijo-dori. **INFO:** Tel 81/75-771-8994; www.omen.co.jp. *Cost:* lunch $18.

DAY TRIPS

NARA KOEN—The highlight of the ancient parkland of Nara Koen is a colossal bronze image of a sitting Buddha that has drawn Buddhist pilgrims and foreign visitors for centuries. Nara's most visited site, it is housed in Todai-ji, the Great Eastern Temple, the world's largest wooden structure. The 53-foot Daibutsu (Great Buddha), the largest in Japan, was commissioned in 743, not long after Nara was founded as the capital of a newly united Japan. Buddhism flourished, and so did Nara as a center of politics and culture. Nara is on a smaller scale than Kyoto, but it too has a fascinating array of ancient buildings and temples. Nara Koen's 1,300 acres of ponds, grassy lawns, trees, and temples are home to more than 1,000 deer, believed to be sacred emissaries of the temples' gods. **WHERE:** 26 miles/42 km south of Kyoto.

MIHO MUSEUM—A mountain literally had to be moved—and then put back again to allow the completion of I. M. Pei's masterpiece. Finished in 1997, it features some of the same design elements and materials he used at the Louvre (see p. 114). Two wings sit harmoniously in a natural setting, connected to the main entrance by a tunnel and suspension bridge. The Miho Museum houses the magnificent private collection of Asian art and antiquities belonging to the Koyama family, the founders of a new-age sect called the Shinji Shumeikai, which claims that spiritual fulfillment lies in the beauty of art and nature. Among the Miho's treasures are classical Chinese, Egyptian, and Assyrian artifacts, but they are on display for only a few months every year, so check exhibition dates well in advance. **WHERE:** Shigaraki is 40 miles/65 km southeast of Kyoto. Tel 81/748-82-3411; www.miho.or.jp/english.

HIMEJI—The 16th-century Himeji Castle (White Heron Castle) is Japan's oldest UNESCO World Heritage Site and one of its grandest. A fortress built in the days of the samurai, it offers an enlightening glimpse into Japan's feudal past. Himeji Castle is one of only four remaining castles built before the Edo Period (1603–1867), and it never saw battle (its confusing maze of paths leading to the main "keep," meant to repel attackers, was never tested); it thus retained its present shape for over 300 years (and is currently undergoing restoration through 2016, though all areas remain accessible). Himeji has frequently appeared in Hollywood productions, including the miniseries *Shogun,* the James Bond movie *You Only Live Twice,* and *The Last Samurai.* The adjacent Koko-en gardens are nine connected Edo Period–style gardens built on the former site of the castle's samurai residences. **WHERE:** Hyogo is 111 miles/180 km west of Kyoto. Tel 81/79-285-1146; www.himeji-castle.gr.jp.

In the Footsteps of Samurai

WALKING THE NAKASENDO

Narai, Tsumago, and Magome, Nagano, Honshu, Japan

In the 17th century the 330-mile Nakasendo—literally "the road through the central mountains"—was the principal inland route between the Imperial capital, Kyoto (see p. 509), and Edo, the Shogun's seat of power (better known these days as Tokyo; see p. 519). The 74-mile-long Kiso-ji section of the Nakasendo, winding its way through the Kiso Valley, is one of the most scenic and best-preserved parts of the route. Three of the 11 post towns (places where travelers would rest and take refreshments) that originally lined the Kiso-ji are particularly worth visiting for their efforts to preserve the look and feel of feudal Japan.

Traveling south by train from the central Japan castle town of Matsumoto, you'll first come to Narai, which has a painstakingly preserved main street of wooden houses, inns, craft shops, temples, and a sake brewery. Cars running through Narai shatter the illusion that you've slipped back several centuries, but farther south in Tsumago the time travel effect is complete: The picturesque village surrounded by steeply raked forests is a pedestrian-only zone. Tsumago also marks one end of the most popular hiking stretch of the Kiso-ji, a 5-mile route along the original Nakasendo path that winds over a mountain pass to the equally well-preserved village of Magome.

The Japan-based travel operator Walk Japan covers Narai, Tsumago, Magome, and other post towns along the route in an organized tour that starts in Kyoto and finishes in Tokyo. Luggage goes by car while walkers put in a moderate 14 to 16 miles a day, staying in family-run *ryokans* (inns), many of which date from the early 1600s. These inns are a highlight of the trip, providing home-cooked meals, the ambience of Hiroshige feudal woodblock prints, and the occasional soak in *onsen* (hot springs). Japanese-speaking American or British academic specialists accompany you and provide running commentaries on both the Edo Period (1603–1867), when the road traffic of feudal lords, itinerant merchants, and pilgrims was at its height, and contemporary issues in Japan. For a luxurious stay at the beginning of your trip, consider a splurge at the venerable Tawaraya, a 300-year-old family-run ryokan now in its 11th generation (see p. 514).

WHERE: Tsumago is 50 miles/80 km south of Matsumoto. **HOW:** Walk Japan organizes

12-day tours of the region. Tel 81/90-5026-3638; www.walkjapan.com. *Cost:* $3,980, includes most meals. *When:* Mar–Nov. Originate in Kyoto. **Best times:** Apr for cherry blossoms; May for azaleas; late Oct–Nov for fall foliage.

A Venerated National Pastime

Cherry Blossom Viewing

Yoshino and beyond, Nara, Honshu, Japan

Witnessing the exquisite yet fleeting beauty of countless cherry trees exploding into bloom is a quintessential Japanese experience not to be missed. Come spring, *sakura* (cherry blossom) devotees check daily TV weather reports for advice on when each area of Japan can expect these short-lived blooms to peak. The pale pink flowers' ephemeral nature—they last no more than a week or two—draws crowds to wander beneath the heavily laden boughs and picnic and drink sake with family, friends, and work colleagues at *hanami,* or flower viewing parties, amid flurries of gently falling petals.

The cherry tree was imported into Japan from the Himalayas, and the custom of hanami is said to date back to 8th-century Nara (see p. 515), the capital that predates Kyoto. The courtly Chinese tradition of flower viewing was adopted and given the Japanese twist of *mono-no-aware,* the melancholy appreciation of the transient. A half hour's train ride from Nara, visitors can witness one of the most beautiful natural wonders of the season: the blooming of tens of thousands of wild sakura across the slopes of Mount Yoshino.

Thousands of sakura *trees make Mount Yoshino Japan's top spot for cherry blossom appreciation.*

The mountain is covered with centuries-old white mountain cherry trees divided into groves (called Hitome-Sembon, or One Thousand Trees at a Glance) that, according to their altitude, bloom at different times, usually beginning in early April. Marked pathways, scattered temples, a predominantly Japanese blossom-viewing crowd, and the shops and teahouses in the pleasant town of Yoshino promise an unforgettable experience.

You don't need to venture into the countryside to take part in hanami. In Tokyo, cherry blossom hot spots include Ueno Park; Shinjuku Gyoen; the Chidori-ga-fuchi moat, at the northwest corner of the Imperial Palace grounds; and the stretch of the Meguro river flowing through Naka-Meguro, which becomes a tunnel of fluffy blossoms. Kyoto's key blossom-viewing locations include the Kyoto Imperial Palace Park; the mile-long Philosopher's Path, a sakura-lined walkway beside a canal that begins at the Ginkaku-ji Temple (see p. 510); and Maruyama-koen, a park that's home to the famous Gion no Yozakura (Night-time Cherry of Gion), a spectacular weeping cherry tree that is illuminated at night.

Where: Yoshino is 21 miles/34 km south of Nara, 42 miles/68 km south of Kyoto. **When:** usually in Apr, with lowest grove blossoming in early Apr. **Best time:** Apr 11–12 for Hanakueshiki, the annual cherry-blossom festival at Kinpusen-ji Temple in Yoshino, although in some years this can be on the early side for peak viewing.

Pilgrimage to Japan's Sacred Mountain

Mount Fuji

Shizuoka and Yamanashi, Honshu, Japan

Revered in the Shinto religion as a sacred mountain, 12,388-foot Mount Fuji is Japan's highest peak and its national symbol. Elegant, snow-capped, symmetrical—and spellbinding when not shrouded in clouds—Fuji-san (as it is affectionately called by the Japanese people) is particularly beautiful when reflected on the mirror-calm surface of Lake Ashi.

The Japanese say that *goraiko* (sunrise) on Fuji's summit is a spiritual experience. Prepare yourself for a lot of company and camaraderie on what is reputedly the world's most climbed mountain: Huge numbers of trekkers show up every summer (an impressive percentage of senior citizens among them).

The various mountain paths that lead to the summit all have ten stations, and most climbers begin the 4- to 8-hour trek to the top from the fifth station (reachable by paved road) at either Gogome, on the north side, or Shin-Gogome, on the south. Many climbers hike at night with flashlights, arriving at the summit by dawn to catch sunrise, avoiding the packed dormitory-style accommodations along the way. The descent is a (3-hour) breeze.

Fuji last erupted in 1707, but in the nearby resort area of Hakone, within the Fuji-Hakone-Izu National Park (Japan's most visited park), intense volcanic activity can be observed daily from the funicular that passes above the Valley of Great Boiling and its steaming, sulfurous gorge. For centuries, public baths have tapped into searing-hot, mineral-rich *onsen* (hot springs) that promise to cure everything from stress to rheumatism to sore muscles. On weekends, wonderfully scenic Hakone fills with Tokyoites who come for a long, hot soak.

Of the handful of traditional *ryokan* inns with their own indoor and outdoor onsen, Gora Kadan, the former summer residence of the Kan-In-No-Miya imperial family, is one of the most acclaimed in the country. Enjoy their exquisite spa followed by a traditional 10-course *kaiseki* meal served in your tatami room.

Those with a less imperial budget should check into the old-fashioned Fujiya Hotel, the sprawling grande dame that has welcomed guests since 1878. The renowned Hakone Open-Air Museum is an escape from the summer weekend crowds and is home to sculptures by Henry Moore, Rodin, Giacometti, and Takeshi Shimizu. An indoor pavilion is filled with Picasso pieces from his later years.

Where: 44 miles/71 km south of Tokyo. **Visitor info:** www.city.fujiyoshidayamanashi.jp. **Gora Kadan:** Tel 81/460-23331; in the U.S., 800-735-2478; www.gorakadan.com. *Cost:* rooms with private open-air onsen $1,000 (off-peak), $1,445 (peak), inclusive. **Fujiya Hotel:** Tel 81/460-82-2211; www.fujiyahotel.jp/english. *Cost:* from $185. **Best times:** Mar–Apr during cherry blossom season; May when azaleas are in bloom; Jul–Aug for climbing Mt. Fuji, but you won't be alone.

"More than any other city, Tokyo demonstrates that 'city' is a verb, not a noun."—Mori Toshiko

Tokyo

Honshu, Japan

Japan's frenetic capital is a trip in more ways than one. By turns reassuringly familiar and unsettlingly strange, Tokyo offers up neon-bright canyons of consumerism, contemporary pop cultural escapades, outstanding dining, and blissful, Zen-calm gardens and shrines. The effects of the catastrophic 2011 earthquake and its aftermath will be felt for years to come. But to the unsuspecting eye, life in Tokyo continues without a blip at high speed and around the clock. An astonishing architectural mishmash, its densely packed neighborhoods include everything from the remnants of a 17th-century castle to high-tech towers wrapped in giant LED displays. With perpetual change hardwired into its DNA, it is the ultimate urban adventure.

Top Attractions

Imperial Palace and Gardens—In the center of Tokyo, surrounded by a massive moat, lies the residence of the Japanese royal family. While the Imperial Palace building itself is off-limits, part of the royal compound is open to official tours (advance booking essential). No reservation is needed, however, to access the palace's 50-acre Higashi Gyoen (East Garden). Wooded paths, bridges, and impeccably manicured gardens lead you to the stone foundations of the Honmaru (inner citadel), one of the few remaining original structures dating from 1640, when the first imperial palace (at the time, the largest castle in the world) was completed. From Kokyo Gaien, the large public plaza on the southeast side of the Imperial Palace, visitors can view the serene Nijubashi, the double layer bridge forming an entrance to the inner palace grounds, with the picturesque turret Fushimi Yagura behind. **Info:** Tel 81/3-3213-1111; www.kunaicho.go.jp/eindex.html.

The Hozo Mon gate leads toward Senso-ji's main hall.

Senso-ji—This Buddhist temple, also known as Asakusa Kannon, is dedicated to the goddess Kannon. It is Tokyo's oldest temple and one of the country's most visited. According to legend, around the year 628 two brothers fishing in the nearby Sumida River netted a tiny golden statue of Kannon, the Buddhist goddess of mercy. They presented it to their village chief, who was inspired to become a Buddhist priest and remodel his home into a temple dedicated to her so the villagers could come and worship. According to rumor, the statue is still here, although it is never shown to the public. Rebuilt after being damaged in World War II, the temple complex is home to the Sanja Festival, held the third weekend in May and said to be the biggest and loudest party in town, with over 100 *mikoshi* (portable shrines) paraded through the surrounding streets. Walk the colorful Nakamise Dori, a historic pedestrian lane leading to the shrine lined with shops selling beautiful, traditional Japanese souvenirs, or search out the nearby Demboin Garden. **Info:** Tel 81/3-3842-0181; www.senso-ji.jp.

Tokyo National Museum—Since its opening in 1872, the Tokyo National Museum has been through many address and name changes, a closing during World War II, and even earthquake damage, to emerge today as the oldest and largest museum in Japan. Four main buildings collectively house over 110,000 objects, with more than 3,000 on display at any one time. The main gallery, the Honkan, is devoted to Japanese art chronologically organized from 10,000 B.C. to the late 19th century, while the Toyokan houses Asian art and archaeological artifacts from outside Japan, including China, Korea, Cambodia, India, Iran, and Turkey, even a mummy from Egypt. The Heiseikan is home to Japanese archaeological relics, including pottery and Haniwa clay burial figurines of the Jomon Period (10,000–1000 B.C.); the Horyu-ji Homotsukan displays priceless Buddhist treasures from Nara's Horyu Temple. **Info:** Tel 81/3-3822-1111; www.tnm.go.jp/en/.

Cruising Tokyo—During the Edo period almost all of Tokyo's rivers and canals were busy thoroughfares of commerce, but when wheeled transport grew more popular, many slipped into decay or were built over. In recent years, however, water traffic along the city's main river, the Sumida, has increased, and taking one of its regular boat services provides a fascinating alternative view of Tokyo. Starting from Hinode Pier, the boat sails up the river, passing first between Tsukiji Fish Market (see next page) and Tsukuda Island, which escaped the worst of the World War II bombing and remains a center of old Edo culture. The boat passes under 12 bridges, each painted a different color and lit up at night. Depart the boat at Asakusa, a perfect spot from where you can walk to the Senso-ji (see previous page). If heading in the opposite direction, get off at Tsukiji and walk just 5 minutes to the beautiful bayside garden Hama Rikyu Teien. **How:** Tokyo Cruise Ship Company operates a variety of routes. Tel 81/120-977311; www.suijobus.co.jp.

Sumo wrestling—The rules of the game are simple: Pit two extremely large *rikishi* (wrestlers, generally over 300 pounds) wearing silk loincloths and elaborate hairdos in a ring against each other, and the one who goes over the boundaries or touches the ground with his body (aside from the soles of his feet) is the loser. Tournaments (called *basho*) lasting 15 days are held six times a year—three of them in Tokyo (January, May, and September), with matches between newcomers beginning in early afternoon and top-ranked *ozeki* and *yokozuna* (grand champions) competing later in the day. Tokyo tournaments are held in the National Sumo Stadium (Kokugikan) in Ryogoku. Some of the training stables (*heya*) are situated near the Kokugikan, and visits can be arranged via the Tokyo Tourist Information Center (TIC). **Nihon Sumo Kyokai Ticket Sales Office:** Tel 81/3-3622-1100; www.sumo.or.jp/eng/. **TIC Tokyo:** Tel 81/3-5321-3077; www.tictokyo.jp/en.

Sumo wrestlers dress in ceremonial kesho-mawashi.

Shopping—The Japanese love to shop and Tokyo is the jackpot. There are areas devoted to certain items, such as kitchenware (Kappabashi, near Asakusa), electronic goods and computers (Akihabara), and food (Tsukiji; see below). Ginza and neighboring Nihombashi have long been the domain of high-end boutiques and venerable department stores such as Mitsukoshi and Takashimaya. Stiff competition comes from the tree-lined avenue Omotesando in Aoyama, home to some of Tokyo's classiest fashion labels (including the dazzling Prada building). Younger shoppers will appreciate the funky emporiums of "Cat" Street and Takeshita-dori in Harajuku, and the buzz of Shibuya. Marunouchi, between the Imperial Palace and Tokyo Station, has also undergone a major retail revamp, morphing from an area of nondescript office buildings into a glitzy shopping corridor, particularly along Naka-dori.

Tsukiji Fish Market—Jet lag can be a wonderful thing. If you find yourself wide awake at 5:00 A.M. and in the mood for some predawn action, the cavernous wholesale Tsukiji Fish Market seethes with activity, as you would expect at the place that supplies 90 percent of the fish consumed in Tokyo (over 2,000 tons per day). Wander this staggering market's aisles; you won't believe some of the things considered edible, much less prized delicacies. In a country where fresh seafood reigns supreme, *maguro* (tuna) is king: Frozen, torpedo-size tunas (one fish alone can weigh more than 1,000 pounds) are hauled in from the fishing boats alongside the market's riverside piers or flown in from as far away as Africa. No one guarantees fresher fish nor a wider variety than the market's no-frills sushi bars, such as Sushi Dai. **Info:** Tel 81/3-3547-8011; www.tsukiji-market.or.jp. **Sushi Dai:** Tel 81/3-3547-6797. *Cost:* 10-piece sushi meal $45.

Roppongi Art Triangle—For decades Roppongi has been one of Tokyo's liveliest and most foreigner-friendly nightlife districts, and in recent years, the area has taken on a more sophisticated tone. At the summit of the 54-story Mori Tower, in Roppongi Hills, is the impressive Mori Art Museum, one point of the so-called Roppongi Art Triangle. Another is Suntory Museum of Art (known for its collection of exquisite traditional ceramics, lacquerware, textiles, and art) in Tokyo Midtown. The last point is the National Art Center Tokyo, set in a stunning building designed by Kisho Kurokawa, the architect who founded the Metabolist movement. Spend a day exploring these institutions as well as the 21_21 Design Sight, a cutting-edge, design-dedicated facility that is the brainchild of fashion designer Issey Miyake and architect Tadao Ando. **Mori Art Museum:** Tel 81/3-6406-6100; www.mori.art.museum. **Suntory Museum of Art:** Tel 81/3-3479-8600; www.suntory.com/culture-sports/sma. **National Art Center Tokyo:** Tel 81/3-6812-9900; www.nact.jp. **21_21 Design Sight:** Tel 81/3-3475-2121; www.2121designsight.jp.

Yanaka—Natural and man-made disasters plus a seemingly insatiable need for change have conspired to destroy and rebuild Tokyo to the point that it is practically impossible to find anything of old Edo (the name of the capital prior to 1868). This is what makes Yanaka, a charming district north of the rail hub of Ueno, so miraculous. Accessed from Nippori Station, it is a short walk to Yanaka Cemetery, a leafy enclave that is the resting place of the last Tokugawa Shogun, Yoshinobu, and to the pedestrian street of Yanaka Ginza, lined with small neighborhood shops selling handcrafted slippers, chopsticks, baskets, fine teas, and rice crackers. Meander around the residential area and you'll find small temples and shrines, picturesque wooden houses, and sturdy traditional storehouses turned into galleries, such as Oguraya, once a mid-19th-century pawnbroker's shop, as well as the venerable traditional paper shop Isetatsu. **Oguraya:** Tel 81/3-3828-0562; www.oguraya.gr.jp. **Isetatsu:** Tel 81/3-3823-1453.

Where to Stay

Claska—As super chic as an Issey Miyake outfit, Claska is one of the few bona fide boutique hotels in Tokyo, a fabulous mix of traditional and contemporary Japanese design. The choice destination for Tokyo's hipsters, Claska features a stylish lobby café/bar, a dog grooming salon, and the gift shop, Do, which stocks a must-have array of modern Japanese designer wares. There are just nine guest rooms: some with modern Japanese furnishings, some with more traditional *tatami* (mat flooring) style, and three "DIY" rooms individually conceptualized by different local artists. Although not based in the most convenient area for sightseeing, Claska, on a busy shopping street in a residential neighborhood, is just a short taxi ride to Meguro Station. **Info:** Tel 81/3-3719-8121; www.claska.com. *Cost:* from $240.

Park Hotel Tokyo—The elegantly designed Park Hotel Tokyo is a more affordable alternative to the Park Hyatt Hotel (with which it is sometimes confused—both opened in 2003). The lobby of the hotel is on the 25th floor, with 273 guest rooms on the 26th to 34th floors, and it's a short walk to Shiodome Station. The rooms may be smaller, but the facilities are ultramodern and the Tokyo views just as sweeping—on a clear day you can see Mt. Fuji. A helpful staff offers to arrange sightseeing or tickets to a sumo wrestling show, and you can catch a flower-arranging class at the on-site, well-known Constance Spry Flower School. **Info:** Tel 81/3-6252-1100; www.parkhotel tokyo.com. *Cost:* from $320.

Park Hyatt—This chic and sophisticated hotel (immortalized in the 2003 film *Lost in Translation*) occupies the top floors of a futuristic 52-story skyscraper, one of the city's most dramatic. The largest guest rooms in Tokyo come equipped with every gadget and top line amenity (including huge bathrooms) and offer superlative views of the surrounding Shinjuku district and distant Mount Fuji (see p. 518). The Hyatt's brace of restaurants were some of the first to bring an unprecedented level of sophistication to Tokyo. Reserve a window-front table at the starkly beautiful Japanese restaurant Kozue; or opt for the stylish, super-trendy top-floor New York Grill, with two-story windows, an amazing 1,600-bottle wine cellar, gallery-quality original art, and a Sunday brunch that is legendary. **Info:** Tel 81/3-5322-1234; in the U.S., 800-233-1234; www.tokyo.park .hyatt.com. *Cost:* from $500; dinner at Kozue $150, at New York Grill $100.

Peninsula Tokyo Hotel—Overlooking the Imperial Palace and Hibiya Park, the 24-story Peninsula Hotel occupies an entire block adjacent to the upscale Ginza and Marunouchi shopping districts (see previous page). Designed to look like a giant Japanese lantern, the Peninsula exudes elegance and class like its sister hotel in Hong Kong (see p. 492), and taking afternoon tea in the lobby is a decadent treat. The luxurious guest rooms are international in design, but Japanese by inspiration, blending rich earth tones with lacquered wood and marble bathrooms. The award-winning restaurant Peter, on the 24th floor, offers a modern interior that is sensual, playful, and theatrical, and chef Patrice Martineau creates internationally inspired cuisine and signature dishes, including Hokkaido zuwaigani crab. **Info:** Tel 81/3-6270-2888; www.peninsula.com. *Cost:* from $725; prix-fixe dinner at Peter $95.

Sukeroku-no-Yado Sadachiyo—Tokyo isn't known for its *ryokans* (traditional Japanese lodgings more commonly found in Kyoto; see p. 514). However, if you're in search of somewhere to stay that harks back to the Edo era, then a fine option is Sukeroku-no-Yado Sadachiyo, a delightful inn just steps away from Senso-ji temple in the heart of Asakusa (see p. 519). The 20 spacious, traditionally decorated tatami rooms have the advantage of private bathrooms (not common among ryokans), with guests also having access to the communal wood-and-stone Japanese-style baths. A stay at a ryokan is as much about the delicious and beautifully presented *kaiseki*-style meals that are offered (upon advance request), and the Sukeroku-no-Yado Sadachiyo doesn't disappoint. The accommodating management can arrange performances of traditional arts, including geisha dances—another rarity in Tokyo. **Info:** Tel 81/3-3842-6431; www.sadachiyo.co.jp. *Cost:* from $230.

Eating & Drinking

Hantei—A short walk from Nezu subway station and easily combined with a stroll around Yanaka (see p. 521) is a visit to this fine, inexpensive restaurant specializing in *kushiage*—deep-fried pieces of meat, fish, and vegetables skewered on sticks. These tasty morsels are served six sticks at a time with a few appetizers, and you keep ordering until you're full. Part of the pleasure is dining inside a beautiful old three-story wooden house built around a stonewalled *kura* (storehouse). **Info:** Tel 81/3-3828-1440. *Cost:* dinner $35.

Inakaya—The first Tokyo location of this *robatayaki* (a restaurant specialized in Japanese-style grilling) opened over 30 years ago in Roppongi and has two more outlets in the city today. Although it is tourist oriented, it is also a fun, delicious place for dinner, frequented by locals too. Customers sit around long U-shaped counters, and kneeling male chefs in traditional garb offer a selection of fresh vegetables, meat, fish, and seafood. You point to what you want (scallops, steak, eggplant), your waiter yells it out, the chef shouts back his confirmation and then grills it. In minutes your sizzling meal is served to you on an 8-foot wooden paddle. **Info:** Tel 81/3-5775-1012; www.roppongiinakaya.jp. *Cost:* dinner $75.

Kurosawa—Named after the illustrious movie director Akira Kurosawa, this atmospheric restaurant specializes in freshly made soba (buckwheat noodles) and dishes such as *shabu shabu* (a kind of DIY hot-pot meal) made with cuts of the finest quality pork and beef. Favored by politicians from the nearby Diet Building, Japan's parliament building, the two-story restaurant is styled like a set from one of the director's samurai dramas. Downstairs is the section for noodles; the more formal upstairs is for pork-based banquets. Three other Kurosawas in town specialize in other Japanese cuisines. **Info:** Tel 81/3-3580-9638; http://9638.net/eng. *Cost:* noodles $10, pork-based meal $60.

Maisen—*Tonkatsu* is a meal of tender deep-fried breaded pork cutlets, traditionally served on a bed of shredded cabbage with a spicy, dark brown sauce, along with a steaming bowl of rice, pickles, and miso soup. When done right, it is delicious, satisfying, and easy on the pocketbook. One exemplary Tokyo tonkatsu restaurant is Maisen, housed in a cleverly converted pre-World War I public bathhouse a short stroll from the trendy shopping boulevard of Omotesando into the backstreets of Harajuku. Various cuts of breaded pork are their specialty, but there are a few tasty alternatives such as deep-fried fish or giant prawns. **Info:** Tel 81/3-3470-0071; http://mai-sen.com. *Cost:* dinner $30.

Shunju—Drinking is seldom done without eating in Japan, and *izakaya* are publike places serving alcohol—principally sake (rice wine), *shochu* (a grain spirit like vodka), or beer—alongside a tasty menu of food. Among the most stylish of Tokyo's many izakaya is a small chain called Shunju. The Tameiki-Sanno branch, atop the Sanno Park Tower, is more restaurant than bar, offering panoramic views from its double-story windows, a chic interior, and dishes showcasing the freshest seasonal ingredients. The Tsugihagi branch, opposite the Imperial Hotel, is in a basement, but the décor is very imaginative and the dining space intimate; choose from sushi, premium grilled seafood, and tofu made at your table. **Info:** Tameiki-Sanno, tel 81/3-3592-5288; Tsugihagi, tel 81/3-3595-0511; www.shunju.com/ja. *Cost:* dinner $80.

Tokyo food—Dining in Tokyo is incredibly exciting; the level of food preparation is exceptional and can be highly specialized. Some sushi restaurants serve only certain types of sushi like *oshizushi* (pressed sushi) or *inarizushi* (deep-fried tofu), while others may specialize in a particular type of noodle or regional cuisine. All Tokyoites know that department-store basements (*depachika*) are where you'll find the finest groceries, or where to find the best restaurants for *kaiseki*—meticulously prepared, traditional meals built around seasonal ingredients. Sign up for one of the food-themed "safaris" organized by Bespoke Tokyo, a company that specializes in connecting visitors to the pulse of modern Japan through tailor-made programs. **Bespoke Tokyo:** www.bespoketokyo.jp.

Day Trips

Kamakura—Minamoto no Yoritomo, Japan's first shogun, chose this natural seaside fortress as his capital in the late 12th century. In this beautiful setting are 65 Buddhist temples and 19 Shinto shrines, including Kotoku-in temple, location of the bronze Great Buddha (Daibutsu). Cast in 1292, sitting 37 feet high, and weighing 93 tons, the Daibutsu was originally housed in a wooden temple that was washed away by a tsunami in 1495. Since then, the loving Buddha has remained exposed to the elements. Nearby is one of the most beautiful temples in Kamakura, Hase-dera. Leading up the stone steps to the temple grounds are hundreds of small stone images of Jizo, the savior of children. Its Kannon Hall is home to the largest carved wooden statue in Japan, the 8th-century figure of Juichimen Kannon, an 11-headed goddess of mercy, standing 30 feet tall and bearing a crown of 10 smaller heads, allowing her to see in all directions for those in need of her compassion. **Where:** Kanagawa Prefecture, 25 miles/40 km southwest of Tokyo; www.kanagawa-kankou.or.jp/.

One of the largest bronzes in Japan, the Great Buddha at Kamakura sits peacefully, with no cover to protect it from the elements.

Nikko—Surrounded by a mountainous national park with miles of outstanding walking trails and a breathtaking waterfall, the small town of Nikko, really just one street about 1 mile long, is home to one of Japan's best-known and most opulent shrines, the fabulously decorated Tosho-gu Shrine. Built in the 17th century, Tosho-gu is the burial place of Tokugawa Ieyasu, famous as the founder of the Tokugawa shogunate. A mixture of Shinto and Buddhist elements and elaborate carvings decorated with vibrant colors and gold leaf give the shrine complex a distinctly Chinese style. Thousands of tourists visit this shrine, especially on May 17 and 18, when a procession of hundreds of men in authentic samurai costume re-create the moving of Shogun Ieyasu's body from the Shizuoka prefecture to Nikko. Surrounding temples include the Futarasan-jinja shrine and the Buddhist Temple of Rinno-ji. **Where:** Tochigi Prefecture, 74 miles/119 km north of Tokyo. **Visitor info:** www.nikko-jp.org/english/.

The Smallest Island with the Biggest Heart

Shikoku Island

Japan

Exquisite scenery, including craggy mountains, dramatic sea cliffs, historical castles, and villages with 300-year-old craft shops, along with excellent river rafting, and easy cycling are just a few of the delights that make Shikoku extraordinary. But most of all, Shikoku, the smallest (at 7,260 square miles) and least visited of Japan's four main islands, is loved for its friendliness.

Every year thousands of pilgrims *(henro-san)* pay their respects at the island's 88 temples, following in the footsteps of Kobo Daishi, founder of the Shingon Buddhist sect in the 9th century. It is one of only two UNESCO World Heritage pilgrimage routes in the world (the other being the road to Santiago de Compostela in Spain; see p. 265) and takes over 2 months if done on foot. For those without the time or stamina for the full trek, the highlights of Shikoku's four prefectures—Kagawa, Tokushima, Kochi, and Ehime—can be enjoyed in a "circuit" lasting around a week.

Start in Kagawa in the northeast, where the capital city, Takamatsu, is the first major train stop across the Seto Ohashi Bridge, and be sure to visit the traditional garden Ritsurin-koen. Moving east brings you to Tokushima prefecture. Its main city is also called Tokushima, and in August, over a million tourists converge here to enjoy the Awa Odori, when groups of thousands of choreographed dancers spill onto the streets accompanied by musicians as part of the Obon, a festival celebrating the spirits of the dead.

Kochi, capital of the southern prefecture of the same name, has a splendid castle, as does Matsuyama, the capital of Ehime, in the west. Here, you'll also find the venerable Dogo Onsen (hot springs) resort, the oldest in Japan, mentioned in the 1,300-year-old history book *Nihon-shoki.* There are several luxurious ryokan in Dogo, all with their own *onsen*, but don't miss sampling the waters at the public facility Dogo Onsen Honkan, housed in a handsome wooden structure dating to 1894. Treat yourself to a private room on the third floor, where you'll be served tea and sweet rice dough balls after a restorative soak in the mineral-laden waters.

Where: Matsuyama, Shikoku's largest city, is 332 miles/534 km southwest of Osaka. **How:** U.S.-based Wilderness Travel offers 13-day trips. Tel 800-368-2794 or 510-558-2488; www.wildernesstravel.com. *Cost:* $6,995. Originate in Osaka. *When:* late Oct. **Best times:** late Mar–Apr for cherry blossoms; Aug 9–12 for Yosakoi dance festivals in Kochi; Aug 12–15 for Awa Odori in Tokushima; Oct for autumn foliage.

One of Japan's largest gardens, Ritsurin-koen is known for its pine trees as well as its teahouse.

Remote, Vast, and Hauntingly Beautiful

THE GOBI DESERT

Mongolia

Lying between Siberia to the north and the Tibetan Plateau to the south—and covering a landmass of 500,000 square miles—the Gobi is one of the most remote and least trodden deserts in the world. The third largest in the world after the Sahara and Arabian Deserts, it covers nearly one-third of Mongolia. It's also one of the world's most beautiful, with mountain peaks, gravel plains, grasslands, desert steppes, sand dunes, and oases.

Dinosaur fossils, including the first eggs ever unearthed, were discovered near the Flaming Cliffs.

But there's a reason this is also one of the world's least inhabited deserts: The Gobi ("desert" in Mongolian) can be inhospitable, with extreme temperatures (ranging from –20°F in winter to 100°F in summer), near-continuous winds, and little rain. The best way to explore is by four-wheel drive or organized camel trips, during which you might spot herds of wild horses or encounter nomadic herdsmen living in the round, tentlike huts known as *gers*, into which you'll likely be invited for food and drink.

Only about 3 percent of the Gobi is covered by sand—including the Singing Sands dunes, so named for the peculiar sound made by the winds blowing over the smooth, round grains—the rest is mostly gravel plains and exposed rock. One of the most famous rock formations is the Flaming Cliffs, named by American explorer and paleontologist Roy Chapman Andrews for its vivid red sandstone cliffs. In 1923, Andrews and his team made the world's first discovery of dinosaur eggs here. Since then thousands of bones and footprints have been found in the area, including the remains of a velociraptor; organized tours are sometimes invited to help excavate. Trekking along the Jargalant mountain range or within the Gobi Gurvansaikhan National Park is also unparalleled.

Not far from the Flaming Cliffs, the Three Camel Lodge—a sophisticated, eco-efficient ger camp—appears like a mirage. It's a stylish refuge lodge of Mongolian traditional design, with wood stoves, solar-powered electricity, and hand-painted furniture. Its biggest perk may be the remarkable stargazing in this remote and incomparably beautiful place.

WHERE: Dalandzagrad is the gateway to the Gobi, 344 miles/553 km northeast of Ulaanbaatar, the capital. **HOW:** U.S.- and Mongolia-based Nomadic Expeditions offers organized group tours and customized guided individual tours. In Ulaanbaatar, tel 976/11-313396; in the U.S., 800-998-6634; www.nomadicexpeditions.com. *Cost:* 12-day trips from $2,885, all-inclusive. Originate in Ulaanbaatar. **THREE CAMEL LODGE:** Tels same as Nomadic Expeditions;

www.threecamellodge.com. *Cost:* from $250, inclusive. **Best times:** May–Sep for pleasant temperatures; late Jan–late Feb for camel races and polo matches at the 1,000 Camel Festival.

An Ancient Tradition in the Altai Mountains

The Golden Eagle Festival

Mongolia

For centuries, the nomadic people of Mongolia's Altai Mountains have hunted with the aid of the magnificent golden eagle—one of the world's most powerful raptors and a symbol of military might—to capture small mammals for pelts and food. To honor and preserve this ancient tradition, the Golden Eagle Festival has been held each October since 2000 in Mongolia's Bayan-Ölgii Province, home to the Kazakhs, a Turkic minority group who number about 80,000 in this region (many have emigrated to nearby Kazakhstan since the fall of Communism in Russia). Eagle hunters and festivalgoers arrive from miles around on horseback for a competition held in an open valley surrounded by the snow-capped Altai Mountains. Wearing traditional clothing, competitors partake in events that measure the speed, agility, and accuracy of their magnificent hunting eagles. Eagles are released from peaks, and then race to land on the galloping rider's arms. Those with the fastest speeds and best techniques get the highest scores—and so the competition unfolds.

The best-known bird of prey in the Northern Hemisphere, the golden eagle enjoys an almost mystical reverence in Central Asia. With its powerful legs, talons, and a wingspan of 6 to 7 feet, it can snatch up animals as large as young deer. For centuries they've been trained in western Mongolia to attack foxes and wolves. The festival promotes both the conservation of the golden eagle and the traditional culture of the Kazakh people. Visitors can ride on horseback with the hunters or visit an eagle hunter's family to see how the birds are trained.

These magnificent "gold mountains" stand on the edge of Siberia where Mongolia, China, Russia, and Kazakhstan meet and are an important habitat for endangered animals, including the snow leopard. It's an increasingly popular destination even outside the time of the festival, when small groups come to hike through untracked terrain, their gear carried ahead by horses and camels. Such a trek offers the unbeatable chance to meet nomadic Kazakh families, camp along alpine lakes at 9,800 feet (in the shadow of 14,350-foot Tavan Bogd Uul, Mongolia's highest mountain peak), and encounter sites rich with centuries-old Neolithic petroglyphs.

Where: 780 miles/1,250 km west of Ulaanbaatar. **How:** U.S.- and Mongolia-based Nomadic Expeditions offers an 11-day tour including the Golden Eagle Festival and 4 days of staying in nomadic gers and riding with local eagle hunters. Tel in Ulaanbaatar, 976/11-313396; in the U.S., 800-998-6634; www.nomadicexpeditions.com. *Cost:* from $2,275. *When:* Sep–Oct (other departures Aug–Sep). U.S.-based Wilderness Travel leads a 15-day tour that includes hiking in the Altai Mountains. Tel 800-368-2794 or 510-558-2488; www.wildernesstravel.com. *Cost:* $5,395. Originates in Ulaanbaatar. *When:* Jun, Aug. **Best times:** Jun–Sep for hiking in the Altai Mountains; early Oct for the Golden Eagle Festival.

In the Wake of Genghis Khan

The Steppes and Forests of Mongolia

Mongolia

Ever since Genghis Khan encouraged his people to live by the sword, not the plow, Mongolians have been nomadic herders, holding to their horse-based culture and leaving vast tracks of ruggedly beautiful countryside virtually untouched over the centuries. To experience the land and spirit of this traditionally hospitable nation that's half the size of Europe (and fiercely independent since breaking free in 1990 from the Communist rule that began in the '20s), get on a horse or jump in a jeep to ride through a largely undisturbed landscape—one of Asia's last wild places.

Women wear traditional silk robes for the Nadaam festival.

Small, organized groups head out from Lake Hovsgol, known as the "dark blue pearl" and one of the deepest freshwater lakes in the world. Ride through forests of Siberian larch trees and magenta fireweed before descending to the grassy steppe of the Darhat Valley, a huge basin edged on three sides by mountains. You might encounter isolated campsites made up of *gers* (known elsewhere by the Turkic word "yurts"), the traditional felt-covered homes of nomadic herders who customarily invite visitors in for a bowl of mutton soup or a cup of *airag*, fermented mare's milk. You may also meet the Tsaatan, an ethnic minority that raises, rides, and herds reindeer and lives in the taiga forest.

The region of Arhangay is known for its beautiful scenery of forests, rivers, and mountains, and in its small towns, races among the stout and sturdy Mongolian horses take place during colorful Naadam, a 3-day national holiday held each July. Headlining the festival are the Three Manly Games (Eriin Gurvan Naadam) that epitomize the culture of Mongolia: archery, wrestling, and horseback-riding, with participants in traditional dress. More than 1,000 years old, and with its roots in the hunting expeditions of the Mongolian army, this Olympics-like sporting competition is a timeless test of strength and endurance held throughout the country. It's experienced most genuinely in smaller towns with fewer tourists—though it's a heart-stopping sensation to witness the horse race just outside the capital of Ulaanbaatar, a more professional (and crowded) affair during which more than 600 horses charge across the open steppe in a headlong gallop on a 10-mile course.

How: U.S.-based Boojum Expeditions offers a 13-day horse trek that includes Naadam. Tel 800-287-0125 or 406-587-0125; www.boojum.com. *Cost:* from $2,150, all inclusive. Originates in Ulaanbaatar. *When:* Jul (other departures available). U.S.- and Ulaanbaatar-based Nomadic Expeditions leads a variety of trips to Mongolia. In the U.S., tel 800-998-6634 or 609-860-9008; in Mongolia, 976/11-313396; www.nomadicexpeditions.com. *Cost:* 14-day trip $3,650, all-inclusive. **Best times:** May–Oct to avoid cold weather; early Jul for Naadam festival.

An Ancient Capital Embraces Modernity

SEOUL'S DESIGN BOOM

Seoul, South Korea

Until recently, Seoul's cityscape has been dominated by the unremarkable gray buildings erected after the Korean War in the 1950s; today, residents sometimes have trouble orienting themselves, due to round-the-clock construction. It's thanks to a vibrant economy—fueled by the likes of electronics leaders Samsung and LG Electronics—and sweeping plans to transform Seoul into an international design destination. And its time may have already come: The International Council of Industrial Design named the city "World Design Capital" in 2010.

Visitors will find ambitious design and urban renewal plans throughout the city—in the harmonized street graphics, bus shelters, and public benches, and in massive new construction projects, some associated with celebrity architects like Rem Koolhaas, Daniel Libeskind, and Jean Nouvel. You'll have to wait until 2014 to see the new opera house, being built on an island in the cleaned-up Han River, but for now you can wander through the new design district, or Dogndaemun History and Culture Park, created by architect Zaha Hadid. While away some time in the cafés along the banks of the Han, or investigate the art scene flourishing in the pleasant Samcheong-dong neighborhood. You'll not be alone, as local competitions like the Design Olympiad are nurturing a grassroots interest in culture, style, and design.

Continue gazing at all that's new and stunning in the Cheongdam-dong district near Dosan Park, where Belgian fashion designer Ann Demeulemeester's dramatic flagship store represents the new design spirit with its curved lines and vegetation-covered outer walls. The same goes for the Leeum Samsung Museum of Art, featuring art by Korean and international artists and designed in part by Koolhaas and Nouvel. Adding an almost Vegas feel to it all is the Moonlit Rainbow Fountain on the Banpo Bridge; it's the world's longest bridge fountain, shooting 190 tons of water a minute from 10,000 nozzles and illuminated with colored lights.

Glimpse Seoul's high-tech future at the Digital Media City complex—a wired "city" of electronics manufacturers, researchers and developers, universities, apartments, and exhibition spaces that have been under construction for the past decade. When the new sleek 133-story skyscraper is completed in 2015, it will be the second-tallest building in the world.

Explore the new direction of nouvelle Korean food at stylish Jung Sik Dang, where creative dishes like kimchi consommé or green salad with grasshopper are on the menu. You can check into a cutting-edge new room at the IP Boutique Hotel, which has a playful design approach through its colorful Lego-like exterior and bold contemporary furnishings. The luxury W Hotel, meanwhile, perched on a hillside outside the city center, has sleek lines and soothing views of the Han River.

LEEUM SAMSUNG MUSEUM OF ART: Tel 82/2-2014-6900; www.leeum.samsungfoundation.org. **DIGITAL MEDIA CITY:** www.dmc.seoul.go.kr. **JUNG SIK DANG:** Tel 82/2-517-4654; www.jungsikdang.com. *Cost:* dinner $98. **IP BOUTIQUE HOTEL:** Tel 82/2-3702-8000; www.ipboutiquehotel.com. *Cost:* from $180. **W HOTEL:** Tel 82/2-465-2222; www.wseoul.com. *Cost:* from $230.

Splendors from the Past

The Palaces of the Joseon Dynasty

Seoul, South Korea

The capital of the nation for centuries, today's Seoul is one of the densest places in the world, with more than 24 million people crammed in a sprawling metropolis of high-rises and neon-lit streets. But Seoul is also home to some of the country's most historic and beautiful buildings, including the elaborate Five Grand Palaces, sitting behind imposing walls and gates in the heart of bustling downtown. The palaces are a testament to Korea's feudal past, all built during the Joseon Dynasty (the last royal and imperial dynasty), which reigned for almost 500 years, from the 14th to the 19th centuries.

Changdeokgung Palace's Secret Garden contains trees that are centuries old.

Two of the five are exceptional: the Gyeongbokgung Palace (Palace of Shining Happiness) and the nearby Chandeokgung Palace (Palace of Prospering Virtue), both in the Jongno-gu district. The Gyeongbokgung is the city's oldest and largest palace—first constructed in 1392 and the country's main seat of power through the centuries—and its scale is staggering. With fairy-tale views and a backdrop of the Bukansan mountain range, the palace was the traditional home to kings for 200 years until the Japanese invasion of 1592. Five hundred buildings stood on its property when it was first built, making it a city unto itself. Visit the beautiful lotus pond, then exit through the back gate and stroll past Blue House, South Korea's presidential residence.

The Jongmyo Royal Shrine, perched on the eastern edge of the Gyeongbokgung Palace grounds and surrounded by dense woodland, is believed to hold the spirits of deceased kings and queens of the Joseon Dynasty. Built in 1385, it's also the country's oldest preserved royal Confucian shrine, and each May it is the site of a ceremony in honor of deceased monarchs.

More than 13 of Korea's kings have lingered in the beautiful wooded Secret Garden of the Changdeokgung Palace. Despite its central location in busy Seoul, wandering its pathways and crossing the elegant stone bridges spanning ponds (the Arch of Longevity was carved from a single piece of stone) feels like a walk in the countryside. It was constructed in 1405 and rebuilt in the 17th century, and today, in the summer months, the palace provides a glorious backdrop for music, dance, and opera.

Visitor info: www.visitseoul.net. **Gyeongbokgung Palace:** www.royalpalace.go.kr. **Jongmyo Royal Shrine:** www.jongmyo.net. **Changdeokgung Palace:** http://eng.cdg.go.kr/. **Where to stay:** A long-time favorite, the elegant Shilla Seoul is set in a 23-acre private park. Tel 88/2-2233-3131; www.shilla.net. *Cost:* from $350. **Best times:** late Mar–May for spring weather, late Aug–Oct for pleasant and cool weather.

SOUTH AND CENTRAL ASIA

A Whirling Spectacle of Tradition

The Festivals of Bhutan

Bhutan

The sacred festivals of Bhutan—or *tsechus*—are the perfect way to take in the rich Buddhist heritage of the country known as the "Land of the Thunder Dragon." Filled with the sounds of flutes, cymbals, and trumpets and the sight of people dancing in magnificent, brightly colored traditional dress, the festivals take place around the country throughout the year. The largest are usually held in the courtyards of the great *dzongs*—fortified monasteries that are the centers of religion, education, and government in each district of the small Himalayan kingdom.

Of the nearly two dozen annual festivals in Bhutan, the most famous is the Paro Festival. Taking place in mid-March in the city of Paro, it's a celebration held in honor of Guru Padmasambhava (aka Guru Rinpoche), who introduced Tantric Buddhism to the Himalayan region in the 8th century. The event draws throngs of joyful Bhutanese from all over the valley, while monks or trained laymen wear magnificent masks and costumes, taking on aspects of deities, demons, and animals, dancing and reenacting Himalayan Buddhist legends and visions seen by Buddhist saints. The performances are meant to bring blessings and protection to onlookers.

Another of the country's major festivals, created in 1670 to celebrate the birth of Guru Rinpoche, is held in the capital city of Thimphu at the beginning of October. It takes place in the courtyard of the Tashichho dzong, drawing crowds from miles around. Later that month, as part of the celebrations during the Bumthang Fire Dance Festival, participants gather behind a procession of monks who lead them to a field where a huge arch is set on fire. It is believed that this will purify the souls of those who dare dance through the flames. The festival, held in Punakha in late February, reenacts the 17th-century Bhutanese victory over the Tibetan army.

Where: Paro is 40 miles/65 km west of the capital city of Thimphu. **Visitor info:** www.tourism.gov.bt. **How:** U.S.-based Geographic Expeditions offers 7–14-day tours to all the major festivals. Tel 800-777-8183 or 415-922-0448; www.geoex.com. *Cost:* 7-day trip from $3,150, all-inclusive. Originates in Paro. **When:** Feb or Mar for Punakha; Mar or Apr for Paro; Sep or Oct for Thimphu; Oct or Nov for Jambay; Dec or Jan for Trongsa.

The Dance of the Eight Kinds of Spirits is performed during Paro's tsechu, *Bhutan's most important festival.*

Untrammeled Terrain in a Himalayan Kingdom

Chomo Lhari Trek and the Tiger's Nest

Paro Valley, Bhutan

Tucked along the southern slope of the Himalayas below Tibetan China and bordered by India on three sides, the little-visited nation of Bhutan is one of the most remote and protected places in the world, tantalizing for its pristine natural beauty and rich cultural heritage. Slightly larger than Switzerland and 70 percent covered by forest—practically a third of the country is designated as national parks—this primarily Buddhist country has a deeply spiritual population of fewer than a million people, nearly all connected to the land through agriculture (hunting is against both federal and religious law).

The "Tiger's Nest" monastery is one of Bhutan's holiest sites.

Tourism is a carefully monitored industry (Bhutan opened its doors to the world in 1974), but the intrepid visitor will be rewarded with glorious landscapes and ancient temples, monasteries, and villages, all while encountering few fellow travelers.

A trek to the base of Mount Chomo Lhari ("Mountain of the Goddess"), which at 23,997 feet is Bhutan's highest and most sacred mountain, is a perfect way to experience the country's unspoiled wilderness. Climbers hike through villages and low forests; alongside terraced farms, verdant rice paddies, and rushing streams; and beyond the treeline into a world of glaciers and rock, where the legendary snow leopard prowls. Campsites are set up high in alpine pastures, where herdsmen graze yaks and the Himalayan blue sheep, or *bharals*, roam in lush meadows. Bird-watching in Bhutan is among the best in the world, with more than 700 species recorded.

The trek from the capital city of Thimphu to Chomo Lhari, or a day or overnight hike from the Paro Valley, leads to the greatest of all Bhutanese monuments: the famed monastic retreat of Taktsang, the "Tiger's Nest." It was founded in A.D. 747 by a Tibetan missionary who, according to legend, landed here astride a flying tiger. The stone and wood monastery—built in 1692 on the spot where he meditated—clings to a sheer cliff face 2,700 feet above Paro valley, accessible only by a bridge and steep, winding track (horses are available for a portion of the trail). Since its near-destruction by fire in 1998, the structure has been painstakingly restored.

Where: Paro is 40 miles/65 km west of the capital of Thimphu. **How:** Bridge to Bhutan offers 8–16-day customized treks including Chomo Lhari, along with day treks to the Tiger's Nest. Tel 975/2-331766; in the U.S., 434-390-5763; www.bridgetobhutan.com. *Cost:* 8-day trek from $1,750, all-inclusive. Originates in Thimphu. **Best times:** Mar–May and Sep–Dec to avoid extreme temperatures; Apr and early May for rhododendrons in bloom.

Indian Cuisine at Its Finest

Top Tables

New Delhi, Delhi, India

When it comes to India's cuisine, you'll find many of New Delhi's long-reigning favorites housed in its finest hotels. The ITC Maurya Sheraton boasts two: Dumpukht and Bukhara. Dumpukht is an airy and elegant dining room that serves refined court food with roots that go back to the 18th century: Slow steam-cooking produces meat and vegetables tender enough to melt in your mouth. Bukhara is radically different, offering robust north-western cuisine in a hunting-camp-like space of stone walls, wooden tables, and a glassed-in kitchen that's always good for a show. It is acclaimed for its perfectly prepared tandoori that's fit for a king (or a former president—Bill Clinton is known to dine here when he's in town).

There are also a number of small and innovative restaurants bringing a whiff of change to the dining scene in the city, including Indian Accent, in the newly refurbished Manor Hotel. Although Chef Manish Mehrotra's stellar reputation in both India and London is long established, there's nothing "establishment" about this award-winning restaurant's inventive Indian cuisine, deft pairings of global favorites, and regional specialties.

A classic landmark and the city's most impressive heritage hotel, the Imperial is famous for its Raj-era, Art Deco interiors, cool, lush green gardens, and an excellent contemporary restaurant, the Spice Route. Painters from Kerala took 7 years to complete the murals depicting the famed passage for which the restaurant is named, and the cuisine is a mélange inspired by that journey: stir-fried Kerala-style prawns, classic Thai soups, and distinctive Sri Lankan curries.

ITC Maurya Sheraton: Tel 91/11-2611-2233; www.starwoodhotels.com. *Cost:* dinner at Dumpukht $65, at Bukhara $70. **Indian Accent:** Tel 91/11-2692-5151; www.themanordelhi.com. *Cost:* dinner $40. **The Imperial:** Tel 91/11-2334-1234; www.theimperialindia.com. *Cost:* dinner at the Spice Route $40.

Sensory Overload in the City's Beating Heart

Red Fort and Chandni Chowk

Old Delhi, Delhi, India

A city teeming with close to 17 million people, Delhi is the capital of a rapidly changing India and can seem utterly daunting to the casual visitor. To get your bearings and reinvigorate your senses, find your way to its beating heart, Shahjahanabad, the ancient walled city of Shah Jahan (builder of Agra's Taj Mahal, see p. 552), also known as Old Delhi.

The Mughal emperor moved the capital from Agra to Delhi in the mid-17th century, creating the same magnificent architecture in the latter as he had in the former. Masterworks include the tomb of the 16th-century Mughal emperor Humayun and the Jama Masjid, the country's largest mosque. Perhaps the most visited site is the hulking Lal Quila, the Red Fort, named for the color of its 1.5 miles of turreted sandstone walls and the former seat of Mughal power. Armies, servants, and ladies of the court once filled the various mosques, lush gardens, royal quarters, richly decorated halls, and marble-floored *hammams* or bath chambers. That all ended with the Mutiny of 1857, when the British expelled the last Mughal ruler. For close to one hundred years they used it as barracks, until Jawaharlal Nehru first unfurled the flag of newly independent India from this very spot on August 15, 1947. On Independence Day, the prime minister traditionally hoists the flag and delivers his nationally televised speech here.

The Indian flag flies above the three-story Lahore Gate, the main entrance to Lal Quila, the Red Fort.

But there's more to see here than the fort. Branching off of the half-mile-long Chandni Chowk (Moonlight Alley) is a network of ancient lanes and timeless bazaars selling everything imaginable, in chaotic operation since the 17th century. Flag down a cycle-rickshaw at Lahore Gate, the entrance to the Red Fort, negotiate fiercely, then let your *wallah* (driver) navigate the winding backstreets teeming with traffic and people. Pop into a hole-in-the-wall food stall for savory samosas, or stop at a *halwai,* or candy store, sampling sweets made from recipes that have been passed down over generations. Pick up a Kashmiri carpet or a stack of skinny bangles. The smells of dust and incense mingle with the headier ones that emanate from Khari Bioli, one of Asia's largest spice markets. In nearby Kinari Bazaar, watch local Hindu families shopping for wedding festivities that usually go on for days.

No one with an appetite leaves this part of town without searching out Karim's, an unassuming landmark restaurant in an alleyway not far from the Jama Masjid. Packing them in for a hundred years is the authentic Mughlai cuisine: Karim's fourth-generation owner traces his heritage to the chefs who once prepared these royal recipes for Mughal emperors.

KARIM'S: Tel 91/11-2326-4981. *Cost:* lunch $13. **BEST TIMES:** Feb–Apr and Aug–Nov for nicest weather; Aug 15 for National Independence Day.

The Good Life with More than a Touch of Portugal

THE BEACHES OF GOA

Goa, India

Nowhere else in India will you find the laid-back atmosphere of the tiny, Portuguese-influenced state of Goa, known to many as "India lite." Transformed from the hippie nirvana of yesteryear, Goa is now the place where young Indian urbanites and well-traveled Europeans come to shed their inhibitions and enjoy the languid pace. That's thanks in part to the stylish upscale hotels and beachside villas that have recently popped up and sit cheek-by-jowl with modest hostelries on the Arabian Sea coast, with its 66-mile strip of palm-fringed beaches.

Goa was the first state of India colonized by Europeans and the last to be liberated (after a protracted battle with the Portuguese, who had ruled since 1510 and didn't leave until 1961). Portuguese influence is everywhere, including in the architecture and religion: Goa is 30 percent Catholic and contains a cluster of magnificent cathedrals, monasteries, and convents. The centerpiece of the former capital of the Portuguese Indies is the huge Baroque basilica of Bom Jesus, which houses the remains of St. Francis Xavier, co-founder of the Jesuit order and Goa's patron saint.

South Goa's peace and quiet make it a lovely oasis, but North Goa is where the buzz is. You'll find lively towns lining its pristine beaches, as well as weekly markets that let you shop for both food and information about where to find the week's best trance music and full moon parties. Wednesday's sprawling flea market is in the popular beach town of Anjuna (a throwback to hippie days), whereas Mapusa's colorful showcase is the Friday farmers market, where vendors hawk fresh-cooked local food. Saturday it's over to Baga for its nighttime market, which brims with stalls selling Goan cuisine, a unique, spicy mix of southern Indian and Portuguese influences. (Sample the curry-charged pork vindaloo, which originated here.)

Check in at the chic, Portuguese-inspired Pousada Tauma in North Goa. It is within walking distance of the popular 4-mile-long Calangute beach and a leafy and secluded home from which to explore Old Goa and Panaji, the capital city. Enjoy a glass of the local *feni*, the double-distilled spirit made from coconut or cashew nuts, followed by a dinner of lobster masala in the open-air poolside restaurant, one of the best in the area. There's more of a house-party ambience at the seven-suite Vivenda dos Palhacos, an old Portuguese mansion in South Goa impeccably restored and run by the charming India-born brother-and-sister team of the Haywards. Or stay at the secluded Elsewhere, a coconut plantation that has been in the owner's family since 1886. Four colorful colonial-era beach houses afford front-row views of multihued sunsets over the Arabian Sea and three candy-colored tents sit at the wooded edge of a narrow, saltwater creek.

So where have all the hippies gone? About 150 miles south to Om Beach, in Karnataka, every bit as beautiful as the shores of Goa.

Where: 360 miles/582 km south of Mumbai. **Pousada Tauma:** Tel 91/832-227-9061; www.pousada-tauma.com. *Cost:* from $195 (off-peak), from $340 (peak), inclusive. **Vivenda dos Palhacos:** Tel 91/832-322-1119; www.vivendagoa.com. *Cost:* from $75 (off-peak), from $150 (peak). **Elsewhere:** Tel 91/98-2003-7387; www.aseascape.com. *Cost:* 2- and 3-bedroom houses from $1,530 per week (off-peak), from $4,520 (peak); tents from $485 per week (off-peak), from $1,340 (peak). *When:* Nov–Apr. **Best times:** Oct–Mar for nicest weather; Feb or Mar in Panaji for Carnival; Dec 3 for feast of St. Francis Xavier and the Old Goa Fair; Dec–Jan 6 for Christmas decorations and festivities.

North Goa's bohemian feel and Catholic influences mix at Arambol Beach.

In a Former Summer Capital, a Relic of the Raj

SHIMLA

Himachal Pradesh, India

Kipling once called the heat "the central fact of India." No surprise, then, that to carry on business during the summer months, the British would head north to the Himalayas and the town of Shimla (then Simla), "Queen of the Hills." Here, melting snows kept the temperature tolerable, and Victorian architecture, gardens, and entertainment—including The Mall, Gaiety Theatre, and lawn tennis at the posh Viceregal Lodge—helped to create a simulacrum of the sceptered isle they'd left behind.

Chapslee harks back to those earlier times: a stately, decidedly British, ivory-colored manor-house-turned-hotel, built in 1835 at 7,000 feet and one of the last great homes of the Indian aristocracy. From the start, it offered the kind of princely living, cuisine, and hospitality that were the hallmark of the golden age of the Raj, and reminders of that era can still be found, including Gobelin tapestries, Venetian chandeliers, Persian carpets, and an imposing portrait of the present owner's great-grandfather, the former maharaja of Kapurthala in the Punjab.

Shimla remains one of India's most venerated British-built hill stations and provides an imperial starting point for visitors who wish to explore Himachal Pradesh, among India's loveliest states. Its rural landscape is dotted with Hindu and Buddhist temples and communities whose festivals enliven the summer months. Just a 45-minute drive from Shimla, through forested hills, is the lavish, newly built Wildflower Hall, an 85-room luxury hotel nestled within 22 acres of virgin pine, rhododendrons, and cedar, grounds where Lord Kitchener's summer home once stood, 8,250 feet above sea level. Here, nature lovers and adventurers can trek, mountain bike, river raft, and golf on one of the world's highest courses, the century-old Naldhera. After an Ayurvedic treatment, soak in the outdoor Jacuzzi and take in the breathtaking views of the Himalayas' snowy peaks.

Once a maharaja's summer residence, Chapslee now welcomes overnight guests to a world of Victorian charm.

You can arrive in Shimla as the British did: on the narrow-gauge railroad that departs from Kalka. This steam-powered "toy train" line, like the earlier railway built to service the hill station of Darjeeling (see p. 554), dates to 1903 and is considered an engineering marvel, passing through 102 tunnels, crossing 969 bridges, and delivering endless high-altitude beauty along its 63-mile, 6-hour run.

WHERE: 230 miles/375 km north of New Delhi. **CHAPSLEE:** Tel 91/177-280-2542; www.chapslee.com. *Cost:* from $350, inclusive. **WILDFLOWER HALL:** Tel 91/177-264-8585; www.wildflowerhall.com. *Cost:* from $270 (off-peak), from $400 (peak). **KALKA-SHIMLA TRAIN:** www.himachalpradesh.us. **BEST TIMES:** Mar–May and Oct–Nov for cool weather; late May–early Jun for Shimla's Summer Festival.

Altitude, Snow Leopards, and a Taste of Tibet

LADAKH

Jammu and Kashmir, India

Also known as Little Tibet and Moon Land (for its unearthly landscape), the awe-inspiring, high-altitude plateau of Ladakh sits between the world's two highest mountain ranges, the Karakoram and the Great Himalayas. While politically Indian, it is geographically and ethnically Tibetan and shares a religion and culture with Tibet that is fast disappearing elsewhere. As part of India, Ladakh was protected from the Chinese Cultural Revolution and today contains one of Asia's most intact Buddhist societies. Ladakh was closed to tourism until 1974, but since then has slowly been attracting visitors, despite the troubles in China's Tibet, to the north and east, and in the Kashmir Valley, to the west.

The flight to Leh, the region's principal city, is one of the most spectacular in the world, offering a magnificent perspective on this remote area. Such a trip can only be topped (literally) by a journey to the Nubra Valley, Ladakh's "Valley of Flowers," which requires you to cross Khardung La Pass (Ladakh translates as "land of high passes"). At 18,383 feet, it is believed to be the world's highest drivable road. The air is crisp, and the views are out of this world.

Immersion in the culture of this isolated region would not be likely without the help of an unusual Indian tour company called Shakti, which owns a network of traditional village houses in the Indus Valley, renovated to include en suite bathrooms and comfortable bedding, but still maintaining authenticity and great charm. Journey from village to unspoiled village by foot, boat, and 4WD vehicle, visiting schools, *gompas* (fortified monasteries), and other places of interest along the way.

Ladakh is also home to both the Hemis National Park and the Hemis Gompa; the latter is one of the state's most interesting and best-known Buddhist monasteries. Its festival of masked dances, music, and handicrafts in June and July draws villagers from all parts. Wildlife is the attraction at the national park, India's largest. It is home to the beautiful and elusive snow leopard and is one of the very few areas anyplace where they can be tracked on foot. Cold winter months are the best time to spot the creature, which means only true and seriously fit adventurers need apply.

The Hemis Gompa monastery, established in 1630, stands at an altitude of 12,000 feet.

WHERE: 380 miles/613 km north of New Delhi. **SHAKTI:** Tel 91/124-456-3899; in the U.S., 866-401-3705; www.shaktihimalaya.com. *Cost:* 7-night package from $3,889, all-inclusive. *When:* May–Sep. Originates in Dehli. **HOW:** U.K.-based Steppes Discovery leads snow leopard–tracking trips. Tel 44/1285-643-333; www.steppesdiscovery.co.uk. *Cost:* 14-day trip from $3,795, all-inclusive. Originates in New Delhi. *When:* Nov and Mar. **BEST TIMES:** late Jun or early Jul for the Hemis Festival; Sep 1–15 for the Ladakh Festival in Leh; Nov–Mar for tracking snow leopards.

Unique Waterworld of Canals and Lagoons

THE BACKWATERS OF KERALA

Kerala, India

Isolated, peaceful, and exotically beautiful, the southern coastal state of Kerala sits on the lush and tropical Malabar coast. An elaborate labyrinth of 44 rivers, twisting *kayals* (lakes), palm-fringed backwater canals, and lagoons meander past dazzlingly green rice fields and forests rich with wildlife. Once used to transport coconuts, rice, and spices, today this 600-mile watery maze links sleepy islands and villages inhabited by people famous for their religious tolerance, their flavorful cuisine, and their Ayurvedic traditions. Kerala is believed to be the birthplace of Ayurveda, the ancient practice of natural medicine and well-being. The region has a wealth of Ayurvedic clinics and spas (called *shalas*) offering millennia-old restorative treatments and massages using herbal oils made from the exotic spices that first drew Vasco da Gama to Kerala's shores in 1498.

Vallams, *propelled by standing polesmen, ply Kerala's network of canals.*

The kayals are the only way to reach secluded Coconut Lagoon Village, an enclave of 30 gracious *tarawads*—400-year-old carved wooden bungalows made without nails that were painstakingly dismantled and moved here—along the cool banks of the backwaters. Enjoy the fine spa or lazy poolside R&R in the shade of a nutmeg tree.

Many of Kerala's old Colonial houses have been converted into guest accommodations as well, including the five charming, traditional waterfront cottages found at Philipkutty's organic farm. The 45-acre island plantation also serves as an abundant pantry to the amiable Aniamma and her daughter-in-law Anu, from whose kitchen three marvelous feasts appear daily and who happily invite you to join in the preparation or at their table. They'll then send you off on a canoe-type boat called a *vallam* to float through the silent backwaters and observe the calmness of everyday life—you'll witness fishermen in their traditional longboats, children splashing, fishing birds of every kind, and the occasional houseboat, or *kettu vallam*. Ranging from rustic to exquisite, these refurbished floating guest quarters have become a popular overnight accommodation alternative in recent years.

Most visits to Kerala begin in Kochi (formerly known as Cochin), the state's fascinating capital. A busy port for more than 1,000 years, it was once the hub of India's spice trade and is still considered the pepper capital of the world. It is home to a unique people, whose Chinese, Dutch, Portuguese, and British roots and Jewish and Syrian Christian religions are evident in the town's melting pot of culture, architecture, and cuisine.

The old quarter of Fort Cochin is where you'll find St. Francis Church, the first European church to be built in India. Vasco Da Gama died and was buried here in 1524, though his remains were eventually returned to

Portugal. South of here is the ancient district called Jew Town and the Pardesi Synagogue. Housed in a building that dates back to 1664, it is the oldest synagogue in the Commonwealth of Nations (the congregation, which still has a handful of members, was founded in 1568).

Kochi is a city deservedly proud of its cuisine; to sample it, choose from the day's catch at the Fort Cochin Restaurant in the Casino Hotel, famed for its great seafood. Its sister hotel, the historic, harborfront Brunton Boatyard, was one of the first of the boutique hotels to open in Fort Cochin and is still the gold standard to which others aspire.

WHERE: 658 miles/1,059 km south of Mumbai. **COCONUT LAGOON:** Tel 91/484-301-1711; www.cghearth.com. *Cost:* from $150 (off-peak), from $320 (peak). **PHILIPKUTTY'S FARM:** Tel 91/482-927-6529; www.philipkuttysfarm.com. *Cost:* from $175 (off-peak), from $240 (peak). **CASINO HOTEL:** Tel 91/484-301-1711; www.cghearth.com. *Cost:* from $130; dinner $30. **BRUNTON BOATYARD:** Tel 91/484-301-1711; www.cghearth.com. *Cost:* from $175 (off-peak), from $410 (peak). **BEST TIMES:** Oct–Mar for cool and dry weather; mid-Aug–Sep for the Snake Boat (Chundan Vallam) races, part of the harvest festival of Onam.

On the Trail of India's 2,500-Year-Old Emblem

Bandhavgarh and Kanha National Parks

Madhya Pradesh, India

African safaris have the Big Five must-see animals, but India has these same five (elephant, rhino, buffalo, lion, and leopard) plus one—the tiger. Although they are the largest members of the cat family, India's tigers have not been able to defend themselves against shrinking habitats and poaching, and the tiger population has dwindled from an estimated 45,000 at the turn of the century to less than 1,500 today. All the remaining six subspecies are endangered, and India is especially struggling to save the Bengal—its national animal.

India's iconic tiger is severely endangered.

If you want to glimpse one of these rare beasts, Bandhavgarh National Park, although a relatively small reserve (278 square miles), has one of the subcontinent's highest densities of tigers per square mile. With a 2,000-year-old fort, a 10th-century statue of Lord Vishnu, and a dense sal-tree jungle, it's one of India's most scenic national parks as well. And it gets better: Just 20 minutes from the entrance is a new luxury bush lodge, Mahua Kothi, which offers an unprecedented level of service and amenities in the park. Just 12 guest suites are housed in *kutiyas* (jungle village huts), decorated in safari style. Set off by foot, jeep, or elephant in search of the Big One, and spot some of the park's other prolific wildlife along the way: leopards, chitals (spotted deer), guar (Indian bison), nilgai antelope (also known as the blue bull), hyenas, wild dogs, rich birdlife, and 111 species of butterflies.

If time allows for a twofer, it's a 6-hour drive south of Bandhavgarh to Kanha National Park, where, it is said, Rudyard Kipling found his inspiration for *The Jungle Book*. One of India's largest parks, it is one of the nine founding reserves of Project Tiger (launched in 1973 to save the species). You'll find here beautiful areas of bamboo trees and sal forests, and lush green meadows, which are home to swamp deer, leopards, mongooses, wild boars, and over 200 bird species in addition to tigers. Banjaar Tola offers simple luxury with two elegant, tented camps (of just nine suites each) set on a 90-acre private concession overlooking the park. On the park's edge, the conservation-minded Wright family have since 1982 owned and run Kipling Camp, a complex of cottages with 15 comfortable double rooms.

Where: Bandhavgarh National Park is 103 miles/165 km northeast of Jabalpur Airport; Kanha National Park is 99 miles/160 km southeast of Jabalpur Airport. *When:* parks are closed Jul–Oct. **Mahua Kothi** and **Banjaar Tola:** Tel 91/22-660-11825; in the U.S., 866-969-1825; www.tajsafaris.com. *Cost:* from $450 per person, all-inclusive (off-peak), from $750 (peak). **Kipling Camp:** Tel 91/11-6519-6377; www.kiplingcamp.com. *Cost:* from $380, all-inclusive. **Best time:** Nov–May for pleasant weather.

Erotic Tableaux in the Middle of Nowhere

The Temples of Khajuraho

Madhya Pradesh, India

In this sleepy little town in central India, a long way from anywhere, a century-long burst of creativity happened during the dynasty of the Chandela kings, a clan of Rajput warriors who ruled between the 10th and 13th centuries and who claimed descent from Chandra, the Moon God. More than 85 temples were built, of which 22 remain. They are decorated with long friezes, which intersperse scenes of daily life with military processions. But the most renowned are highly erotic: Celestial maidens pout and pose while other figures engage in every imaginable position of the Kama Sutra, the ancient Sanskrit treatise on the art of lovemaking. Their extraordinary sexual explicitness makes them as remarkable today as they must have been when they were first unveiled.

The British officer who rediscovered the friezes of the Khajuraho temples in 1838 found himself shocked by their erotic imagery.

The temples, both Hindu and Jain, are divided into three distinct groups—western, eastern, and southern—that are spread over 8 square miles. The western group includes the best-known, oldest, and largest temples and is the site of the Archaeological Museum. Since 2002, the western temple grounds have also served as the dramatic background for some of the country's best classical dancers, who come together for an annual, weeklong festival of classical (and more recently a bit of modern) dance. They celebrate the marriage of the Hindu gods Shiva and Parvati, to whom some of the temples are dedicated.

Where: 385 miles/620 km southeast of Delhi. **Where to stay:** Hotel Chandela is about half a mile from the temples. Tel 91/7686-272355-64; www.tajhotels.com. *Cost:* $125. Hotel Lalit Temple View is more expensive, but is closer to the temples. Tel 91/7686-272111; www.thelalit.com. *Cost:* from $220. **Best times:** Oct–Mar, at sunset when the temples turn a deep shade of red; last week of Feb–early Mar for the Khajuraho Dance Festival.

Architectural Achievements of Mysterious Power

The Cave Temples of Ajanta and Ellora

Maharashtra, India

Mumbai may be the pulsating, commercial heart of India, but the country's soul lies far off in the interior, around Aurangabad and its astonishing hand-hewn cave temples. Of the two cave complexes found here, Ajanta is by far the older, with dozens of *chaityas* (temples) and *viharas* (monasteries) carved from solid rock faces and known for their lavishly painted frescoes. The 30 Buddhist cave temples date from around 200 B.C. to A.D. 650 but were virtually forgotten until the 19th century, which probably accounts for their excellent state of preservation.

Whereas the Ajanta caves dazzle with their paintings, the 34 rock-cut temples of Ellora, 62 miles southwest, are sculptural masterpieces. Their creation was a feat equivalent to carving an entire cathedral—interior and exterior, roof to floor—out of solid rock, using handheld tools only. Unlike Ajanta, Ellora was located on a major trade route and was used for worship until the 1800s. It is believed that the Buddhist creators of Ajanta moved here after their work was finished there: Of Ellora's 34 caves, the 12 earliest are Buddhist and were begun in A.D. 600 at approximately the time that work in Ajanta stopped. Work continued until the 11th century, producing 17 Hindu and 5 Jain temples and grottoes. Ellora's tour de force is the Kailash Temple, whose dimensions and complexity astound; at almost 10,000 square feet, it covers twice the area of the Parthenon in Athens (see p. 156) and is half again as tall. It has been estimated that it took 150 years for

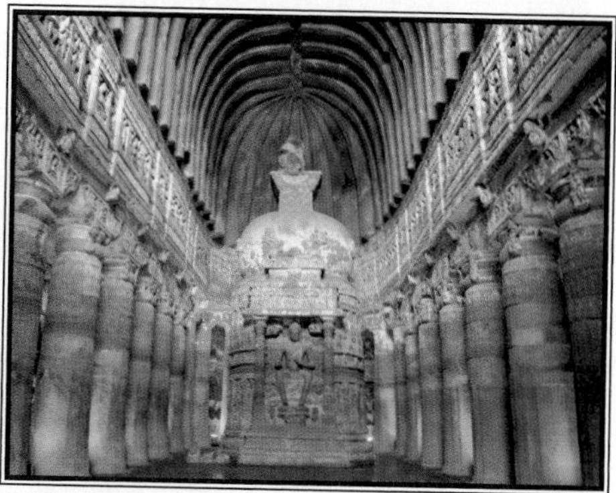

Buddhist monks carved the elaborate chaityas *and* viharas *of the Ajanta caves using only basic tools.*

approximately 200,000 tons of rock to be removed by some 800 artisans in order to make this single cave temple, the largest known rock-cut temple in the world.

WHERE: Aurangabad is 241 miles/388 km northeast of Mumbai. **VISITOR INFO:** www.maharashtratourism.gov.in. **WHERE TO STAY:** The palace-style Taj Residency in Aurangabad offers a pool, good restaurant, and full-day excursions to the caves. Tel 91/24-6613737; in the U.S., 866-969-1825; www.tajhotels.com. *Cost:* from $170. **BEST TIMES:** Oct–Mar for nice weather; Nov for Ellora Festival, featuring classical Indian music and dance.

Beloved Landmark

THE TAJ MAHAL PALACE HOTEL

Mumbai, Maharashtra, India

The Taj Mahal Palace, a Mumbai landmark since 1903, is India's most famous hotel and the very embodiment of opulence. A Victorian extravaganza that is an exotic mix of Moorish and Renaissance style, it gazes serenely over the Arabian Sea and has welcomed a host of luminaries, from maharajas to Mick Jagger.

Rock stars, maharajas, and heads of state have stayed at the landmark hotel that overlooks the Arabian Sea.

Splendidly uniformed doormen usher locals and guests into the deliciously cool, gleaming, white-marbled interior of the elegant Palace Wing; the high floors of the 30-story Tower wing, built in 1972, offer views of the sea and the stately Gateway of India. The arched, harborside monument was built by the British to welcome King George V and Queen Mary in 1911 (the only visit to the Raj by a reigning monarch). It was also the point of departure when the last British colonialists left in 1948. From here, catch a breezy ferry ride for the 6-mile trip to Elephanta Island, where a complex of 6th- to 8th-century cave temples honoring the Hindu god Shiva are carved into the rocks. It is an excellent, leafy vantage point for a view of Mumbai's skyscraper-studded skyline.

Decompress at the hotel's Jiva Spa, with yoga, meditation, or any of the time-honored Indian holistic healing treatments that rejuvenate after a frenzied day of sightseeing. Join the stylish Mumbaikars (Mumbai residents) who come for high tea and desserts, like masala tea crème brûlée at the contemporary Sea Lounge or at the open-air Aquarius café overlooking the hotel's legendary swimming pool. Or book dinner at one of the many fine restaurants, including Masala Kraft for all-time Mumbai favorites created at various cooking stations.

The Taj Mahal Palace was built by J. N. Tata after, it is said, he was refused lodging at one of the city's hotels because he was Indian. The Taj Group—a sliver of the massive Tata Group, in its fifth generation of stewardship—now owns more than 60 hotels in India and abroad. The Taj was the target of a devastating terrorist attack in November 2008, during which 31 guests and staff were killed and hundreds injured. Heavily damaged by fire, the hotel was repaired within the year. A simple plaque serves as a memorial to an event that succeeded in bringing the people of Mumbai closer together while securing the hotel a place of honor in their hearts.

Info: Tel 91/22-6665-3366; in the U.S., 866-969-1825; www.tajhotels.com. *Cost:* from $220 (off-peak), from $550 (peak); dinner at Masala Kraft $40. **Best times:** Oct–Mar for most pleasant weather; Feb for dance festival on Elephanta Island; Aug for Ganesh Chaturthi festival; Oct–Nov for Diwali (Festival of Lights) on Chowpatty Beach.

A Place of Extraordinary Peace Where Everyone Is Welcome

The Golden Temple

Amritsar, Punjab, India

In the bustling city of Amritsar, India's dazzling Harmandir Sahib, also called the Golden Temple, seems to float on an island in the middle of a serene lake whose name means "pool of nectar." One of the country's most beautiful buildings, the temple is the Sikh religion's holiest shrine and one that welcomes everyone, irrespective of religion, race, or caste.

Construction of Harmandir Sahib began in 1574 on the site of the lake, which was believed to have healing powers, in order to house the book of holy scriptures. Since then, the three-story temple, connected by a man-made causeway, has seen many restorations and embellishments, including the addition of over 220 pounds of gold to cover the upper stories and an inverted, lotus-shaped dome in the 19th century. Signifying the importance of acceptance, the temple has open doors and balconies on all four sides, and the interiors are decorated with inlaid marble, carved woodwork embossed with gold and silver, and intricate mosaics. The atmosphere is both festive and serene. As with Muslims and Mecca, every Sikh hopes to visit the Golden Temple at least once in his life.

There is no organized worship, but during the day, the scriptures are chanted and hymns are sung from the Adi Granth (the Sikh Holy Book) beneath a jeweled canopy, while a small group of musicians plays an accompaniment. At night, thousands of worshippers line up for the Palki Sahib ceremony, when the holy book is returned on a palanquin to its resting spot.

No pilgrimage for Sikhs would be considered complete without a visit to the Langar, a giant communal dining hall run by volunteers, who feed more than 30,000 people daily for free—twice that during holidays. Stop by to experience the spirit of hospitality and equality that are central to Sikhism and that make a visit to Amritsar so special.

Where: 254 miles/410 km northwest of Delhi and 40 miles/64 km east of Lahore, Pakistan. **Golden Temple:** www.darbarsaheb.com. **Where to stay:** Ranjit's Svaasa is a family-run boutique hotel in a 19th-century building. Tel 91/183-256-6618; www.svaasa.com. *Cost:* from $100. **How:** U.S.-based Asia Transpacific Journeys leads a 17-day trip through the Himalayas that includes Amritsar. Tel 800-642-2742 or 303-443-6789; www.asiatranspacific.com. *Cost:* $8,295. Originates in Delhi. *When:* Sep. **Best times:** Sunrise or late afternoon, when the golden domes are illuminated and reflected in the waters; Sep–Nov and Feb–Mar for pleasant weather; mid-Apr for the Sikh holy days, such as Vaisakhi.

Strictly for the Birds

KEOLADEO NATIONAL PARK

Bharatpur, Rajasthan, India

Between the historic cities of Agra and Jaipur (see p. 552 and below) lies the diminutive Keoladeo Ghana National Park, aka the Bharatpur Bird Sanctuary. It has the reputation of being India's (and perhaps all of Asia's) best avian sanctuary, especially during the winter months, when its marshland attracts staggering numbers of birds arriving from Afghanistan, Turkmenistan, China, Siberia, and Europe. More than 400 resident and migrant species, including egrets, storks, herons, and cormorants, build over 10,000 nests annually, with the highly endangered Siberian crane occasionally making an appearance. Previously the private duck-hunting grounds of the maharaja, the park includes a plaque giving testament to successful hunts from the recent past, including a day in 1938 when a British viceroy bagged 4,273 birds.

White-throated kingfishers find sanctuary in Keoladeo.

The 18-square-mile park is car-free, navigable only by bicycle, horse cart, or rickshaw. The latter is the best mode for the novice ornithologist, as the rickshaw pullers have been trained by park management and are quick to spot birds. Remember to look down as well; pythons, porcupines, mongooses, jackals, civets, wild boars, nilgais (Asia's largest antelope), and the endangered jungle cat reside here too.

The nearby Bagh Hotel is set on 12 acres of 200-year-old gardens and has resident naturalists who delight birders with their knowledgeable presentations and who lead guided tours of the park.

WHERE: 34 miles/55 km west of Agra. **VISITOR INFO:** Tel 91/11-279-48870; www.keoladeonationalpark.co.in. **THE BAGH:** Tel 91/564-422-5415; www.thebagh.com. *Cost:* from $145. **BEST TIMES:** Oct–Feb (after monsoons) for migratory birds and Aug–Nov for resident birds; early mornings and evenings at sunset for greatest bird activity.

Where Royal Concubines Watched the World Go By

PALACE OF WINDS

Jaipur, Rajasthan, India

Pink is the Rajput color of hospitality, and Jaipur, capital of the desert state of Rajasthan, is known as the "Pink City." It is a worthy home for Hawa Mahal, the five-story, salmon-hued "palace of winds," built in 1799 and adorned with delicate floral motifs and fronted with honeycomb windows. The upper two stories (of five in all) are really an elegant façade, just one room deep but pierced by 953 windows from which the Hindu ladies of the royal household in *purdah* (concealment from men) could enjoy the breeze while viewing state processions or the parade of everyday life in the Old City below. In the late-afternoon light, the sandstone palace takes on a special glow. The building is just around the corner from the rambling City Palace complex, an exotic blend of Rajasthani and Mughal architecture that still houses the former maharaja and his family on a high floor.

To escape the teeming carnival of street life, repair to the exquisite Oberoi Rajvilas hotel, just a few miles outside of town, where the fantasy of Rajasthan's princely life lives on. This 32-acre oasis of exotic pavilions, pools, open courtyards, and fountains, with a pink fortress at its heart, looks like a royal village that has always been here, although it was actually built in 1997, the first of India's new luxury hotels. Relax in one of the teak-floored, ultraluxe royal tents, and visit the spa for an Ayurvedic shirodhara treatment. For Jaipur's real-deal princely homes—historic digs redolent of the days of the maharajas,

The architect of the palace, with its many perforated balconies and crown-like shape, also planned Jaipur city.

where overnight guests are welcomed—stay at the Samode Palace Hotel, the Samode Haveli, the Taj Rambagh Palace (for information on these see p. 547), or any of Udaipur's opulent contenders such as the inimitable Taj Lake Palace (see p. 549).

WHERE: 162 miles/260 km from New Delhi. **OBEROI RAJVILAS:** Tel 91/141-268-0101; in the U.S., 800-562-3764; www.oberoihotels.com. *Cost:* from $775. **BEST TIMES:** Sep–Mar for pleasant weather; sunrise and late afternoon, when the palace glows; late Feb or Mar for the festival of Holi; Jul–Aug for premonsoon Teej Festival, dedicated to the goddess Parvati.

A Giant Sand Castle in the Heart of the Great Indian Desert

JAISALMER

Rajasthan, India

Known as the "Golden City," this once-important caravan stop on the route to the Khyber Pass is famed for its 12th-century sandstone fortress that rises from the desert floor, its crenellated walls, 99 bastions, and medieval silhouette soaring into the sapphire sky as if it were a mirage. Jaisalmer is the only functioning fortress city in India—one of the few left in the world—with one quarter of its population living within the Sonar Killa, or Golden Fort. Just 40 miles from the Pakistani border, it languished for years as a little-visited backwater, but now even the luxury *Palace on Wheels* train (see p. 550) makes a stop in Rajasthan's most beguiling desert town.

The city's wealth originally came from the heavy levies it placed on camel caravans that passed through. Noblemen and merchants used that income to build handsome *haveli*s (ornate town houses and mansions), which are distinguished by façades and balconies elaborately carved from the local golden stone. A number of them have been reborn as hotels, such as the 300-year-old Nachana Haveli, which is outside the fort and owned and run by the royal family of Jaisalmer. Twelve guest rooms are eclectically decorated with family portraits and memorabilia. Saffron, its rooftop restaurant, offers dishes made from family recipes and superb sunset views of the fort.

The bright saris of Jaisalmer women offset the drab colors of the Thar Desert.

For nomadic glamour in the middle of nowhere, head 45 minutes outside town to The Serai, whose elegantly spare, campaign-style tents (some with plunge pools) and small spa have brought a new level of luxury to the Thar Desert (aka Great Indian Desert). Sign up for a jeep or camel jaunt onto the shifting sands of the surrounding dunes and enjoy sundowners while local musicians serenade you. The canopy of stars is breathtaking at night, when the encampment is all movie-set romance, lit with candles and lanterns.

During the full moon in January or February, the exotic Desert Festival of Jaisalmer is held over three days, featuring music, dancing, and camel polo and races. The highlights are the fire dancers and the moustache competition, though it's really all about the people in brilliant saris and turbans, who come from distant corners of the desert to celebrate.

Where: 177 miles/285 km from Jodhpur. **Nachana Haveli:** Tel 91/29-9225-5565; www.nachanahaveli.com. *Cost:* from $65. **The Serai:** Tel 91/11-4606-7608; www.the-serai.com. *Cost:* double tents from $650. *When:* Sep–Mar. **Best times:** Oct–Feb for weather and camel safaris; Jan or Feb for the Desert Festival.

Luxury Accommodations Fit for a King

Maharaja Palace Hotels

Jodhpur and Jaipur, Rajasthan, India

India's most colorful state, Rajasthan, isn't called the Land of Kings for nothing. The fabulously wealthy maharajas built hundreds of rambling palaces and hilltop forts, many of them restored and converted into one-of-a-kind hotels after the once-powerful rulers were stripped of their regal stipends following independence in 1947 but allowed to keep their real estate. And what real estate it is; the cleverest opened their palace doors in their newfound roles as hoteliers, offering an all-out *Passage to India* fantasy for overnight guests who were willing to pay.

The most imposing hotel of them all is the Anglo-Indian Umaid Bhawan Palace, perched high above the "Blue City" of Jodhpur. One of the largest private residences and the last royal palace ever built in Rajasthan, it was commissioned in 1929 and its construction employed 3,000 artisans and laborers as a famine-relief project organized by Maharaja Umaid Singh for his subjects; it took 15 years to complete. The building, extravagant even by maharaja standards, is unique for its Art Deco details. Fifty-five of the palace's 347 grandest rooms now serve as a deluxe hotel; the rest is a museum of glorious paintings and armor along with a private wing where the current maharaja and his family reside. Dine in the pavilion for views of Jodhpur's outstanding 15th-century Mehrangarh Fort—"the work of angels and giants," according to Rudyard Kipling.

Jaipur (see p. 544) is the heart of Rajasthan and the location of the Samode Haveli, a 22-room jewel-box hotel originally built as a city residence for a prime minister of the royal court. A sumptuous oasis amid the hectic city—with courtyards, original colored windows, mirror inlay, archways, and frescoes of flowers and court life scenes—it brims with the spirit of old Jaipur. For a look at a royal country idyll, head just outside town to the exquisite Samode Palace Hotel, a luxurious 18th-century retreat that was used for holidays and special events. Both hotels are privately owned and run by the Samode royal family.

Jaipur's grandest estate, however, is the Rambagh Palace, built in 1835 on a modest scale for the queen's favorite handmaidens and later refurbished as a royal guesthouse and hunting lodge. It was transformed in 1925 into the royal residence of the Maharaja of Jaipur and became India's first heritage palace hotel in 1957. Sumptuous accommodations at the "Jewel of Jaipur" include the Maharani Suite, which was built as a surprise gift from Maharaja Jai to his third and favorite bride, Maharani Gayatri Devi.

UMAID BHAWAN PALACE: Tel 91/291-510-101; in the U.S., 866-969-1825; www.tajhotels.com. *Cost:* from $320 (off-peak), from $965 (peak). **SAMODE HAVELI AND SAMODE PALACE:** Tel 91/141-263-2370; www.samode.com. *Cost:* Haveli from $175, Palace from $220 (off-peak), from $400 (peak). **TAJ RAMBAGH PALACE:** Tel 91/141-221-1919; in the U.S., 866-969-1825; www.tajhotels.com. *Cost:* from $320 (off-peak), from $945 (peak). **HOW:** U.S.-based Ker & Downey offers a 13-day Royal India trip that includes most of these properties. Tel 800-423-4236 or 281-371-2500; www.kerdowney.com. *Cost:* from $7,115. Originates in Delhi. **BEST TIMES:** Oct–Mar for nicest weather; Oct for the Jodhpur Folk Festival in Mehrangarh Fort.

Hand-painted accents and glasswork contribute to the opulence of Samode Palace Hotel.

A Tribal Gathering Unlike Any Other

THE PUSHKAR CAMEL FAIR

Pushkar, Rajasthan, India

In Rajasthan, livestock breeding flourished under the maharajas, who maintained legions of camels for warfare, while commoners relied upon them for the tasks of daily life. The arrival of the automobile largely sidelined this beast of burden, but you can still see the legacy of those times at the annual Pushkar Camel Fair. It's not the only animal market in Rajasthan's Thar Desert; however, it is certainly the largest and is unequaled for music, costumes, and festivities.

Rajasthan has the largest concentration of tribal people in India, and they converge by the tens of thousands on the tiny lakeside town of Pushkar every November shortly before the full moon. They parade, race, trade, and sell their prized dromedaries, some 50,000 in number, which have been groomed and festooned for the occasion. Rajasthanis are known for their love of brilliant clothing colors, so the human participants can outshine the steeds with their jewelry, saris, and turbans, which helps explain the festival's popularity with foreign tourists, filmmakers, and photographers. A nonstop carnival, with marriage arranging, camel polo, bazaars, and dancing under the stars, it is one of the most important annual fairs in this desert state.

For Hindus, Pushkar is also an important pilgrimage center; the lake is said to have sprung from the spot where the creator god, Brahma, dropped a lotus from the sky, and hundreds of temples now line its banks. For 2 days around the full moon, particularly at dawn, pilgrims gather to bathe in Pushkar Lake and to celebrate Kartik Purnima, the holy day of the full moon.

Thousands of camels, some decked out in jewelry, come to the fair from across the desert state of Rajasthan.

Where: 220 miles/354 km southwest of New Delhi. **When:** 2 weeks in late Oct–early Nov. **How:** U.S.-based Equitours offers an 18-night equestrian safari in the Thar Desert to coincide with the Pushkar Camel Fair. Tel 800-545-0019 or 307-455-3363; www.ridingtours.com. *Cost:* $6,895. Originates in Delhi. U.S.-based Geographic Expeditions offers 15-day luxury jeep safaris through Rajasthan, with a 2-day stay at Pushkar during the festival. Tel 415-922-0448; www.geoex.com. *Cost:* from $9,450. Originates in Delhi.

Opulence and Romance in the City of Lakes

The City Palace and Royal Hotels

Udaipur, Rajasthan, India

Nowhere are the power, pride, and wealth of the local maharanas (outside Udaipur called maharajas) more evident than at the immense City Palace in Udaipur. Onetime home of Udaipur's princely ruler amd the largest palace complex in Rajasthan, this massive group of elaborately decorated buildings now serves mostly as a museum. The exceptions are the private wing, where the present maharana still resides, and the royal guesthouse, which has been reincarnated as the deluxe Shiv Niwas Hotel, offering spacious accommodations that are rich with character as well as dreamy views of Lake Pichola.

The man-made Lake Pichola was the setting for another pleasure palace of the maharana's, built in the 18th century on a 4-acre island. It now welcomes guests as the legendary, white-marble Taj Lake Palace, converted (so rumors say) at the suggestion of Jacqueline Kennedy. Set against the backdrop of the majestic Aravalli Mountains on one side and the lofty palace complex on the other, it boasts white-glove butlers, descendants of the original palace retainers; the excellent Jiva spa; an open-air restaurant; gardens; and sunset cruises—helping prove why Udaipur is considered the most romantic city in India.

Back on the mainland—but removed by a 45-minute drive from the congested heart of Udaipur—the impeccably restored and beautifully located 18th-century fort-palace Devi Garh stands high atop a hill overlooking the small village of Delwara. It took 15 years and a team of India's finest young designers to transform this crumbling ruin into a unique, 39-suite boutique hotel that strikes a perfect balance between storied history and modern, minimalist chic. Helpful staff can organize treks with experts to nearby ancient temples, set up camel or horse safaris, or arrange an appointment with the in-house astrologer on the roof at sunrise.

Built in 2002 on 30 acres along the shores of Lake Pichola, the Oberoi Udaivilas was inspired by the palaces of Rajasthan, with its pavilions and decorative domes, hand-painted frescoes, and masterfully crafted artifacts. Its setting, however, is timeless, a series of elegant courtyards, rippling fountains, reflecting pools, and verdant gardens, and with amenities that are strictly 21st-century. Don't miss the property's 20-acre wildlife conservatory, where peacocks and spotted deer roam free. If the maharanas were looking for real estate today, they'd need look no further.

Shiv Niwas Hotel: Tel 91/294-252-8016; www.heritagehotelsofindia.com. *Cost:* from $150 (off-peak), from $265 (peak). **Taj Lake Palace:** Tel 91/294-242-8800; in the U.S., 866-969-1825; www.tajhotels.com. *Cost:* from $320 (off-peak), from $810 (peak). **Devi Garh:** Tel 91/29-5330-4211; www.deviresorts.in. *Cost:* from $225 (off-peak), from $550 (peak). **Oberoi Udaivilas:** Tel 91/294-243-3300; in the U.S., 800-562-3764; www.oberoihotels.com. *Cost:* from $320 (off-peak), from $825 (peak). **How:** U.S.-based Ker & Downey offers a 13-day Royal India trip that includes most of these properties. Tel 800-423-4236 or 281-371-2500; www.kerdowney.com. *Cost:* from $7,115. Originates in Delhi. **Best time:** Sep–Mar for nicest weather.

Once the Private Trains of Maharajas

Royal Wheels of India

India

With over 67,900 miles of track, 7,000 passenger trains, and a workforce of 1.5 million, India's railway is one of the greatest transportation networks in the world. Its 6,853 stations serve almost every corner of the country, and the general chaos caused by crowded cars and inevitably missed connections can all be part of the adventure.

Many visitors do little more than ride the rails from New Delhi to Agra for a too brief day trip to the Taj Mahal (p. 552). But for those who prefer a longer, more luxurious trip, there are a handful of trains that treat passengers like royalty, with musicians and richly caparisoned elephants greeting each arrival. Luncheons are arranged at lavish former palaces, camel treks and tiger photo safaris fill out the days, and nights are spent back onboard enjoying the attention of a staff outfitted in crisp tunics and brilliant turbans straight out of *The Jewel in the Crown.*

Both the *Palace on Wheels* and the *Royal Rajasthan on Wheels* travel mostly at night, allowing full days of sightseeing in the north's magical cities of Jaipur (see p. 544), Udaipur (see p. 548), Jaisalmer (see p. 545), and Jodhpur (see p. 546) and culminating in a visit to the Taj Mahal before heading back to New Delhi. The *Deccan Odyssey* journeys from Mumbai southward to Tarkarli, through Maharashtra, on the western coast, and on to Goa (see p. 534); then inland to Pune (the "Oxford of the East") and the ancient sites at Ajanta and Ellora (see p. 541). Its new sister train, *The Indian Maharaja,* operates from Mumbai north to Delhi, crossing through the desert state of Rajasthan. The main route of the purple-hued *Golden Chariot* starts in Bangalore and winds through ancient Karnataka, in southern India, visiting magnificent palaces and historic sites and stopping at Nagarhole National Park, where you can disembark for a wildlife safari. It moves on to the 14th-century ruins at Hampi, and then to Goa before returning to Bangalore. An alternate route encompasses Tamil Nadu and Kerala (see p. 538).

The Palace on Wheels *lives up to its name with luxurious compartments for eating, drinking, and sleeping.*

The newest addition to these lavish options is the *Maharajas' Express,* the first pan-India luxury train, with three different one-week themed tours—princely, royal, and classical—covering different regions of India. Hours between stops are filled with sampling food prepared by on-board celebrity chefs, listening to lectures by Indian luminaries, and watching the scenery go by.

How: All trains can be booked through Palace Trains, with offices worldwide. In the U.S., tel 800-724-5120 or 609-683-5018; www.palacetrains.com. ***Palace on Wheels:*** In the U.S., tel 888-463-4299 or 609-683-5018; www.palaceonwheels.net. *Cost:* 8-day trips from $2,460. ***Royal Rajasthan on Wheels:*** Tel 91/11-2338-3837; www.royalpalaceonwheels.com. *Cost:* 8-day trips from $4,340. ***Deccan Odyssey:*** Tel 91/22-2283-6690; www.mtdcdeccanodyssey.com. *Cost:* 8-day trips from $3,055. **Golden Chariot:** Tel 91/80-434-6340; www.goldenchariot.org. *Cost:* 8-day trips from $3,055. **Maharajas' Express:** Tel 91/22-6690-4747; in the U.S., tel 212-292-5712; www.rirtl.com. *Cost:* 7-day trips from $6,265, all-inclusive.

Isolated Splendor No Longer Out of Bounds

Hiking in Sikkim

Gangtok, Sikkim, India

One of the smallest and least visited of India's 22 states, Sikkim is bordered by Nepal, Tibet, and Bhutan in the heart of spectacular mountain scenery. It was an independent Buddhist kingdom before joining India in 1975 and is still regarded as one of the last Himalayan Shangri-las, a place apart. Ancient Buddhist *gompas* (monasteries) are perched on almost every outcrop of the awesome landscape, often wrapped in mist. The local Sikkimese believe their mountains—which aren't even named unless they're over 20,000 feet tall—are the "altar of the gods," and who could disagree? Straddling the border of Nepal and Sikkim is the sacred Mount Kanchenjunga (its Tibetan name, which means "Five Treasure-Houses of the Great Snow Mountain," refers to its five peaks). At 28,169 feet, it is the third highest mountain in the world and is worshipped as a guardian deity.

About 200 Buddhist monasteries can be found in Sikkim.

By far the most meaningful and exhilarating way to experience Sikkim's dramatic beauty and serene culture is by hiking to Sikkimese villages and sharing their daily life. Organized treks take visitors along verdant footpaths from village to village, following unspoiled routes along lush ridgelines and past sacred lakes. Guests stay in small, family-run lodges and homes and visit Buddhist temples and monasteries. The land that surrounds them is a botanist's fantasy: During a typical trip you can pass from subtropical jungle to alpine meadow within hours and glimpse some of the more than 550 species of birds, 500 kinds of orchids, and 35 varieties of rhododendrons, all the while enjoying the abundant and luxuriant pine forests.

WHERE: northeast corner of India; Bagdogra airport is 70 miles/113 km from the capital, Gangtok. **HOW:** U.S.-based Geographic Expeditions offers a 13-day touring and walking trip in Sikkim. Tel 800-777-8183 or 415-922-0448; www.geoex.com. *Cost:* $4,950, all-inclusive. Originates in Kolkata. *When:* Feb–Apr and Oct–Nov. **BEST TIMES:** Mar for wildflowers; Nov for most spectacular mountain views.

Nirvana in the Himalayas

ANANDA SPA AND RISHIKESH

Uttarakhand, India

It's hard to imagine a better setting in which to restore and rejuvenate your body and soul. The Ananda Spa, built around a former maharaja's palace, lies amid 100 acres of virgin forest in the foothills of the Himalayas and overlooks the sacred Ganges River. You begin your experience at Ananda (Sanskrit for "happiness and contentment") by consulting with an Ayurvedic expert, who will personalize a program that includes treatments in the spa—there are some 80 regimens to choose from—as well as yoga and meditation in an open pavilion with views that amaze.

While the gardens and grounds themselves offer miles of walking trails, treks up into the Himalayas or a half-hour car ride down through verdant sal forests to the Hindu pilgrimage town of Rishikesh can also be arranged. Known as the gateway to the Himalayas and the birthplace of yoga (dozens of yoga centers can be found throughout town),

Rishikesh is where the Beatles holed up in the 1960s at the now closed Maharishi Mahesh Yogi ashram, seeking enlightenment and finding inspiration for their *White Album.* Here, every evening at sunset, the Hindu ritual of *aarti* is performed on the banks of the Ganges, during which small lamps are lit and *bhajans* (hymns) are sung to the deities. Simple hotels like the Great Ganga let you tap into the town's love-and-peace vibe; its inspiring views and a good restaurant encourage you to stay awhile. The proximity to Rishikesh is no doubt responsible for Ananda's emphasis on spiritual reawakening despite the ample options of Western treatments and spa therapies that help fill out the menu.

The 24,000-square-foot Ananda Spa focuses on yoga and meditation, but also offers more modern services.

Ananda hosts visiting masters from all over the world who teach everything from stress reduction to advanced meditation and will even lead you on an exhilarating morning of river rafting down the Ganges. Confirmation that Ananda indulges on all levels can be found in its 75 deluxe rooms and suites and three private villas. The luxurious facilities include a Turkish steam bath, Finnish sauna, hydromassaging facilities, a heated swimming pool, and even a challenging six-hole golf course.

WHERE: 161 miles/260 km north of New Delhi. Tel 91/137-822-7500; www.anandaspa.com. *Cost:* from $540 per person, all-inclusive. **GREAT GANJA:** Tel 91/135-244-2119; www.thegreatganja.com. *Cost:* $75. **BEST TIMES:** Mar–Apr and Sep–Oct; Mar for International Yoga Festival in Rishikesh; Oct–Nov for Diwali festival of lights.

The World's Greatest Monument to Love

THE TAJ MAHAL

Agra, Uttar Pradesh, India

Nothing can adequately prepare the visitor for his or her first glimpse of the Taj Mahal. It may be a visual cliché, the Niagara Falls of architecture, but it's also the embodiment of grace and romance, of balance and symmetry, an architectural icon revered for three and a half centuries as one of the most beautiful and dazzlingly constructed buildings in the world.

The fifth Mughal emperor, Shah Jahan, built the Taj as a tomb to honor his third and favorite wife, Mumtaz Mahal (Chosen One of the Palace), who died giving birth to their 14th child in 19 years. It took 22 years and 20,000 laborers to build the white-marble mausoleum, completed in 1653, and costing the equivalent in today's currency of $340 million. It was an extravagance that moved one of Jahan's sons to eventually depose and imprison him in the nearby Agra Fort.

Long considered the "architect" of the powerful Mughal dynasty, Shah Jahan had renovated the red sandstone fortified palace that now served as his jail. It had been built by his grandfather Akbar—the third and greatest of the Mughal emperors—over 8 years and completed in 1573. From his chambers, Shah Jahan would gaze at the Taj Mahal downriver, mourning the loss of his wife and his empire, until his death in 1658.

Akbar's other landmark fort, Fatehpur Sikri (City of Victory), is worth a visit to understand the legacy of the Mughal dynasty, as is the elegant Tomb of Itmad-ud-Daulah. A transition from the older architectural style, which incorporated heavy red sandstone architecture, to that of translucent marble, it was a precursor to—and likely inspiration for—the Taj Mahal.

Although many people visit Agra as a day trip from Delhi, thanks to the Oberoi Amarvilas (Sanskrit for "eternal haven"), there's now an irresistible reason to linger overnight in this otherwise unlovely city. The Moorish- and Mughul-inspired palace hotel boasts terraced gardens, bubbling fountains, a marble pool, the fine Esphahan restaurant, and the Oberoi spa. It and every one of the hotel's 100-plus rooms afford an unobstructed view of India's most beloved national monument, a mere 650 yards away. A less extravagant interpretation of the Amarvilas is the new Orient Taj resort (no relation to the Taj hotels), where the welcome is no less grand. If you plan your visit to fall on the night of the full moon or within two nights before or after, you'll find the Taj Mahal grounds open for viewing.

Where: 118 miles/190 km southeast of New Delhi. **Taj Mahal:** Archaeological Survey of India, tel 91/562-222-7261; www.asi.nic.in. **Oberoi Amarvilas:** Tel 91/562-223-1515; in the U.S., tel 800-562-3764; www.oberoihotels.com. *Cost:* from $320 (off-peak), from $780 (peak); dinner at Esphahan $65. **Orient Taj:** Tel 91/172-3000-311; www.orienttajagra.com. *Cost:* $175. **Best times:** mid-Oct–Mar, sunrise and sunset, and during the full moon; Feb for Taj Mahotsav Festival.

Symmetrical gardens and reflecting pools, meant to invoke paradise, lead up to the unforgettable Taj Mahal.

An Eternal City on the Banks of the Sacred Ganges

The Ghats of Varanasi

Varanasi, Uttar Pradesh, India

Every Hindu yearns to visit Varanasi at least once. Originally called Kashi ("resplendent with divine light") and later Benares by Britain's empire builders, Varanasi is dedicated to Lord Shiva and has been the religious center of Hinduism throughout recorded time. Founded 3,000 years ago, it is one of the world's oldest continuously inhabited cities. Mark Twain wrote that Varanasi was "older than history, older than tradition, older even than legend, and looks twice as old as all of them put together."

The Ganges River is the city's lifeline, and Hindus believe it washes away their sins and holds salvation in every drop. Some 70 broad stone ghats (stepped areas leading down to the river) line a 4-mile stretch of its banks and teem with life: An estimated 1 million pilgrims flock here every year. Most are elderly, since devout Hindus believe that anyone who dies here achieves instant nirvana, their soul freed from the endless cycle of reincarnation known as samsara. If their wish is fulfilled, their bodies are burned on one of the ghats, where cremation pyres are fueled around the clock, and their ashes are then scattered on the Ganges. The birth of babies is also celebrated on the ghats by dipping the newborns in the water.

Bathers congregate and make offerings on the banks of the Ganges.

The dark, tangled streets of the Old Town are lined with shops selling colorful silk saris (for which the city is known), bangles, and food, and all roads seem to lead down to the river. Hire a cyclo driver to expertly weave his way through traffic, somehow avoiding collision with other rickshaws, cars, bikes, people, and wandering cows and dogs. The next day, pay a boatman to take you on the river at dawn, when the light and the scene are the most magical. You'll see Hindus bathing in the river, performing *puja,* a ritual of reverence, to the rising sun, and making offerings of food or flowers. Although puja is a solemn ritual, Hinduism is a joyous religion, and bathing is often accompanied by loud splashing and laughing, sounds that echo and mingle with the bells and gongs of the temples that line the Ganges's shores. Be there when the blowing of the conch shell welcomes the sun's first rays reflecting off the life-giving *Ganga Ma,* or Mother Ganges, and Varanasi becomes a transcendent place.

WHERE: 481 miles/774 km southeast of New Delhi. **WHERE TO STAY:** Nadesar Palace is an 18th-century maharaja's residence recently transformed into 10 large luxury suites. Tel 91/542-666-0002; in the U.S., 866-969-1825; www.tajhotels.com. *Cost:* from $330 (off-peak), from $565 (peak). Flowering gardens and pool make the Gateway Hotel Ganges Varanasi a true oasis. Tel 91/542-666-0001; www.thegatewayhotels.com. *Cost:* from $210. **BEST TIMES:** crack of dawn at the ghats and just before dark; Nov–Mar for nice weather; Oct–Nov for Diwali, the Festival of Lights.

Teatime and the Glory of the Raj

THE DARJEELING HIGHLANDS

West Bengal, India

Guarded by the awe-inspiring Himalayan peaks that rise out of the mist, the 7,000-foot summer retreat of Darjeeling was founded by the British as a sanatorium. It later became a scenic escape from the steamy heat of

Calcutta and the low-lying Bengali plains for socialites, diplomats, and other government workers (it also often served as the Indian seat of government during the summer). Explorers stopped here, bound for the Himalayas, just 30 miles to the north.

But before all the elbow-rubbing came the tea. The British established extensive plantations, and the tea produced here became known worldwide as "the champagne of teas." Of the 80 or so working tea estates in Darjeeling today, many offer tours and tastings. One of the few that now welcome overnight guests is the venerable 1,600-acre Glenburn Tea Estate, a scenic hour's drive outside town. Established in 1860 by the Scottish, it is owned and run by the gracious Prakash family. Visitors stay in stylishly refurbished bungalows surrounded by the workings of the tea-making process, which doesn't appear to have changed much since it began. The mountaintop estate is a great place for hiking, birding, fishing, and relaxing and affords direct views of Mount Kanchenjunga, the world's third highest mountain.

Watching sunrise over the snowy peak of Kanchenjunga is a Darjeeling tradition. Make the trek (or travel by car) to the top of 8,284-foot-high Tiger Hill, 5 miles outside town, and you might be able to see Mount Everest too. Darjeeling has a rich climbing heritage, having served as the launch point for the earliest expeditions to Everest. Treks today can last a few hours (to visit nearby monasteries or neighboring plantations) or a few weeks (into neighboring Sikkim and Bhutan; see pp. 550 and 532). The adventurous can also enjoy whitewater rafting, kayaking, and elephant-back safaris.

Or perhaps enjoying an authentically prepared English afternoon tea is exertion enough, served at the Windamere, the "colonial hotel of the Himalayas." A gem left over from the days of the visiting viceroys and other Raj dignitaries, it is loved for its profusely flowering gardens, mountain views, and its accommodations: a collection of heritage suites, bungalows, and cottages. The amiable staff tucks hot-water bottles between the sheets while guests enjoy an after-dinner brandy in front of the crackling fire.

The most scenic way of reaching the hill station is aboard one of the steam trains that have been in service since 1881 and are so diminutive that they are nicknamed "toy trains" (see Shimla; p. 536). Winding along a narrow-gauge line and gaining over 7,000 feet in elevation between New Jalpaiguri or Siliguri and Darjeeling, they puff away for approximately 50 miles through incredibly scenic countryside. In 8 hours, they cross 500 bridges and maneuver 909 hairpin curves, without a single tunnel to block the view.

Where: 60 miles/97 km from Bagdogra, the nearest airport. **The Glenburn Tea Estate:** Tel 91/98-300-70213; www.glenburnteaestate.com. *Cost:* $490, inclusive. **Windamere Hotel:** Tel 91/354-225-4041; www.windamerehotel.com. *Cost:* from $210, inclusive. **Darjeeling Himalayan Railway:** www.irctc.co.in. **Best times:** Mar–May and Sep–Nov for nicest weather; tea picking and processing takes place in Apr and Nov; Dec–Jan for tea festival.

One of several plantations established by the British, Happy Valley Tea Estate exports tea leaves around the world.

Museums in India's Cultural Nerve Center

PALACES OF KOLKATA

Kolkata, West Bengal, India

The Indian Museum, the country's biggest and the oldest in the Asia-Pacific region, is right where it should be: in a city known for its intelligentsia. Three of India's Nobel Prize winners hail from Kolkata (formerly Calcutta), and the city boasts nine universities. It has a vibrant intellectual life and is also the nerve center of the Bengali film industry. The museum began as a sort of rambling, Victorian palace; eventually it grew to over 60 galleries dedicated to archaeology, art, anthropology, zoology, and industry. Among the over 1 million items in what the locals call Jadu Ghar—House of Magic—is an ancient urn believed to contain the Buddha's ashes, an emerald goblet that once belonged to Shah Jahan, builder of the Taj Mahal (see p. 552), a 4,000-year-old mummy, and an extraordinary collection of other cultural artifacts.

The museum's many treasures come as no surprise. This port city (known as the "City of Palaces") amassed enormous wealth under the British, who were responsible for the rich mix of Raj-era architecture, one of Kolkata's brightest highlights, even though its monumental Colonial structures and royal homes are now crumbling. In its day, the 19th-century Marble Palace was an imposing Neoclassical mansion of the deep-pocketed trader Raja Rajendra Mullick Bahadur, who made lavish use of Italian marble to create his showcase, typical of the period's ostentation. Descendants of the original owners live in the upper quarters, leaving the lower floors—chockablock with what remains of its former glory—open to the public. One can only imagine the heirlooms that have been sold off, but look what remains: paintings by Reynolds, Rubens, and Titian; dust-covered crystal chandeliers the size of elephants; Uffizi-like corridors with marble statuary and inlaid-mosaic floors; and an empty throne room where an errant peacock roams.

Founded in 1814, the Indian Museum, or House of Magic, occupies a white palace in Kolkata.

Seek out your own lavish quarters at the landmark Oberoi Grand, a vast, block-long Colonial hotel that is part palace, part society bastion, and entirely old school. Locals come for afternoon tea and an *adda* (local parlance for a chat) over a plate of Bengali sweets, catching up on life in their "City of Joy."

THE INDIAN MUSEUM: Tel 91/33-2286-1699; www.indianmuseumkolkata.org. **MARBLE PALACE:** Tel 91/33-2269-3310. **HOW:** Calcutta Walks offers various accompanied routes as well as home stays. Tel 91/33-4005-2573; www.calcuttawalks.com. **OBEROI GRAND:** Tel 91/33-2249-2323; in the U.S., 800-562-3764; www.oberoihotels.com. *Cost:* from $200 (off-peak), from $455 (peak); tea $20. **BEST TIMES:** Nov–Feb for nicest weather; late Jan–Feb for world's largest public book fair; Sep–Oct for the city's biggest festival, Durga Puja, honoring the Hindu goddess Durga.

A Former Capital's Rich Legacy

Imam Square

Isfahan, Iran

In its heyday of the 16th and 17th centuries during the Safavid dynasty, Isfahan was the capital of the vast Persian Empire—as sophisticated as Paris or London, with some of the best schools, shops, and libraries and the most beautiful parks in the world. Half a million people lived among 163 mosques and 263 public baths in this lush oasis, surrounded by the arid deserts of the central Iranian plateau at the foot of the Zagros Mountains. Isfahan's decline began after Afghan raids in 1722, when the capital was moved to Tehran. Still, today this city of 1.6 million remains one of Iran's most cultured and striking, with sculpted gardens, wide avenues, historic bridges, and thrumming bazaars, plus the finest concentration of Islamic monuments in the country.

The most exquisite examples of architecture can be found in the city's showstopping Imam Square (known as Shah Square prior to 1979). One of the largest public spaces in the world, it's ringed by 17th-century buildings and a two-story galleried arcade that contains gardens, shops, and teahouses. You'll get the best view from the elevated terrace of the Alī Qapū palace, a formal royal residence that shows off the elegance of the Safavid Royal Court. To the south is the crown jewel of Isfahan, the stunning Masjid-i-Imam mosque. Built over a period of 18 years and completed in 1629, the structure features seven-colored arabesque tile work (dominated by pale blue and yellow, an Isfahan trademark) covering almost every inch of its vaulted halls. On the western side of the square is the Sheikh Lotf-Allah Mosque—an extraordinary showcase of Islamic architecture, with an elaborately decorated interior and a blue and yellow tiled dome that seems to change color in different light.

To the north is the entrance to Bazar-e-Bozorg, one of the largest and oldest markets in Asia. It's an explosion of color and aromas, packed with shops where you can watch craftsmen hammer copper pots or artists paint exquisite miniatures. Another bazaar, located on the eastern side of the square, is geared more to the national tourists who come here from all over the country. Shop for dazzling Persian carpets here or in the shops along the square or sip tea, chat with the locals, and soak up the atmosphere at the indoor Azadegan teahouse.

For a taste of Isfahan's glory days, book a room or sumptuous suite at the Abbasi Hotel, built on the site of a 300-year-old caravansary and now one of the most evocative hotels in the region. Rooms are restrained, but they surround a tranquil courtyard and gardens of persimmon trees and rose bushes that remind you of where you are. It's a lovely place to come for tea or to dine on eggplant-rich *khoresh*

Thousands of tiles adorn the entranceway to the Masjid-i-Imam mosque, Isfahan's most beautiful.

bademjan and an orange-crusted saffron rice called *tahdig*—just two delicate specialties of Iran's rich cuisine.

WHERE: 208 miles/335 km south of Tehran. **VISITOR INFO:** www.isfahan.ir. **ABBASI HOTEL:** Tel 98/311-222-6011; www.abbasihotel.ir. *Cost:* from $180. **HOW:** U.S.-based MIR leads small-group tours to Iran sites including Isfahan, Tehran, and Shiraz with a guest scholar. Tel 800-424-7289 or 206-624-7289; www.mircorp.com. *Cost:* 18-day trip, $5,495, includes internal flights, most meals. Originates in Tehran. *When:* Apr and Sep. **BEST TIMES:** Mar–May and Sep–Nov for nicest weather; sunset in Imam Square for the changing light and social buzz.

Ceremonial Center of an Ancient Empire

PERSEPOLIS

Iran

Perched on a giant, elevated, stone plateau in the dusty foothills of the Zagros Mountains, the massive and magnificent palace complex of Persepolis was the glory of the vast Persian Empire at its peak, when it reached from Greece to India. It was the showpiece of Darius I, who began building it in about 515 B.C. It was expanded by his successors, who erected massive pillars, an ornate treasury hall, and an audience hall with a capacity of 10,000. The hall was lavishly topped with a roof made of cedar carried here from Lebanon, and was supported by 36 stone columns, each 65 feet high. The king, inscriptions read, was empowered by God, and the royal tomb of each was elaborately cut into the mountainside on the scale of the Egyptian pharaohs'.

In Persepolis, one of the Persian Empire's greatest achievements, staircases feature reliefs of Persian soldiers.

Officials and dignitaries from far-flung provinces came to pay homage to the "king of kings," attending festivals and ceremonial events at this isolated location. They arrived by chariot or in royal processions bearing gifts—and taxes—and climbed a massive staircase to the audience hall with thousands of soldiers standing guard. Alexander the Great put an end to Persian dominance when he ransacked and destroyed Persepolis in 330 B.C., and over the centuries, the ruins disappeared into the sand.

Archaeologists from the University of Chicago uncovered Persepolis in the 1930s. Now, there are more than a dozen columns and re-created buildings on display as well as magnificently carved reliefs, the main staircase built by Darius (and another by his son Xerxes the Great), and a massive entryway flanked by giant carved bulls. For Iranians, the ruins stand as a testament of the glory of their land's rich history. The nearby university town of Shiraz is the most practical and delightful base—a cultural outpost brimming with structures either built or restored in the 18th century, when it was the Iranian capital.

Located in a fertile region an hour's drive from Persepolis, it is known as the "City of Roses," full of parks and trees, beautiful buildings, and wide, shady avenues.

Where: 36 miles/58 km northeast of Shiraz; 400 miles/640 km south of Tehran. **Where to stay:** Homa Hotel, with a modern wing, is the nicest in Shiraz. Tel 98/711-228-8000; www.homahotels.com. *Cost:* from $145. **How:** U.S.-based Distant Horizons specializes in customized travel to Iran; small-group tours include Tehran, Isfahan, and Persepolis with a guest scholar. Tel 800-333-1240 or 562-983-8828; www.distant-horizons.com. *Cost:* 19-day trip from $5,960, all-inclusive; includes airfare from New York. **Best times:** Mar–May and Sep–Nov for nicest weather; at sunset, when the stone grows rosy in the changing light.

Awaken Your Inner Nomad

Yurt Stay at Lake Song Köl

Kyrgyzstan

Lake Song Köl is cowboy country—Kyrgyz style. The blue, almost perfectly round body of water is ringed by prairie and mountains, located at an elevation of 9,953 feet, and is one of the world's biggest lakes. The golden grass that grows along its shores is ideal pastureland for herders to graze their sheep, goats, cows, and horses, plus the occasional yak or camel. For the visitor, it's an idyllic setting in which to escape civilization and one that is exceptionally welcoming to travelers.

Kyrgyz nomads live in portable yurts.

A peek inside the yurt of a nomad family is a highlight of any visit to Song Köl. Local tour operators can arrange visits to families, but independent travelers are likely to have an invitation extended. An age-old tradition of hospitality means that strangers are always welcome, with the understanding that the favor may one day be returned. Yurt homestays during the summer will almost inevitably include a round or two of *koumiss* (fermented mare's milk), usually brewed by the host family.

While visiting in the felt tent among new Kyrgyz friends, take careful note of the wonderful *shyrdak*s (carpets) the family will likely have decorating the walls and floor. These handmade mosaic felt rugs are a colorful splash of interlocking patterns based on the shapes of animal horns and cosmic symbols.

Lunch is likely to include a few chunks of *kazy* (horsemeat) or *kesme* (noodle soup with potato, meat, and vegetable). Another popular local dish is *besbarmak* (noodle and lamb cooked in broth); the name translates to "five fingers," indicating the required use of the hands rather than forks and knives.

Your Kyrgyz hosts can organize a number of activities around the lake. Horseback riding is the most popular, and rides can last from a couple of hours to several days. Hiking and wildlife- and bird-watching are also possible here; one can often spot wolves around the lake, as well as plenty of waterfowl, including whooper swans and mountain geese.

With good planning, it's possible to catch an annual horse games festival at Song Köl, which includes traditional games like *kok-boro,* a pololike sport that involves men on horseback fighting for control of a goat carcass. This is also a great time to see the Kyrgyz in traditional dress and listen to their lyrical music. Bring warm clothes (at this altitude, it can get chilly in the evenings, even in summer), small gifts for your hosts, and a healthy sense of adventure.

WHERE: 260 miles/418 km south of Bishkek. **VISITOR INFO:** www.cbtkyrgyzstan.kg. **HOW:** British-run Celestial Mountains in Bishkek offers custom tours to Song Köl. Tel 996/312-311814; www.tours.kg. **BEST TIMES:** late Jun–mid-Sep, when herders arrive with their flocks; Jul or Aug for the horse games.

A City Older than Rome

OSH

Kyrgyzstan

Osh is one of the oldest cities of Central Asia, and its residents claim it's even older than Rome. The assertion may not be far from the truth, as historical remains indicate human habitation since around the 5th century B.C.

It's unknown precisely how the city came to be, but there is no shortage of theories. Some say it was King Solomon who ordered its construction; others suggest Alexander the Great. There is no doubt that Osh was an important stop along the Silk Road. By the 8th century, it was considered one of the most important centers for silk production. The city was also an important location for Ferghana horses, mentioned by Marco Polo and prized by Chinese traders to the east.

Today the legacy of the Silk Road lives on in the great Jayma Bazaar, still one of the largest markets in all of Central Asia and most dynamic on Sunday morning. It's a great place to pick up anything from locally produced knives to a traditional *kalpak,* the tall black-and-white hat favored by Kyrgyz men. The market bursts with seasonal fruit plucked from the rich soil of the Fergana Valley, one of the world's oldest agricultural regions.

Wander through and you'll rub shoulders with a great many different Central Asian peoples, including Uzbeks, Kyrgyz, and Tajiks. Women don their most colorful dress for market days, while local men labor in smithies down side alleys. It's impossible to leave the bazaar without trying some sizzling mutton kebabs and fresh, tandoor-baked *nan* bread.

The most important historical site in Osh is Solomon's Throne, a towering rock that dominates the city skyline and is thought to be the site of King Solomon's burial. It is also an important place of pilgrimage for Muslims, as they believe the Prophet Mohammed prayed here. In 1497, Babur, the king of Fergana, constructed a mountainside mosque—and with a strong set of lungs and legs, it's possible to reach the top in 20 minutes and take in the spectacular views of the city.

Osh is one of the most scenic cities of Central Asia, and it's worth spending a day wandering its leafy streets and river promenade. During national holidays, you can watch traditional horse games and eagle hunting competitions. From here, take an overnight trip to the base of Lenin Peak (23,542 feet), a great area for hikers and mountain climbers.

WHERE: 384 miles/620 km south of the capital city of Bishkek. **HOW:** Kyrgyz Concept runs tours to Osh and the nearby Pamir-Alai mountains. Tel 996/312-903232; www.concept.kg. **BEST TIMES:** Apr–May and Sep–Oct for nicest weather.

Asia's Richest Wildlife Sanctuary, Home of the Royal Bengal Tiger

Chitwan National Park

Nepal

The 360-square-mile Chitwan National Park was once the private hunting grounds of the king of Nepal but is now one of the finest protected forests and grassland regions in Asia. Boat and jeep safaris and jungle walks, all led by naturalists and expert guides, allow you to explore this natural kingdom rich with wildlife; with more than 500 bird species, it is Nepal's finest birding destination. But the best safaris are a more traditional affair: A cadre of gentle elephants and their skilled mahouts are ready to take you in search of the great one-horned rhinoceros and—an uncontested highlight of any safari—the critically endangered royal Bengal tiger. There are fewer than 100 breeding adult royal Bengals left in Nepal, of which about 50 live in Chitwan and the adjacent Parsa Wildlife Reserve.

The Tiger Mountain Group has three properties located in the Chitwan area. Tiger Tops Jungle Lodge, a cluster of stilted, treetop-level thatched huts, was opened in the 1960s as the park's first safari lodge. In the early morning, guests set out in search of the elusive beasts; at night, they return to simple, candlelit dinners (there's no electricity aside from solar-powered fans and reading lights). The experience is reminiscent of the safaris of Nepalese aristocrats and the Raj's great white hunters. Elephant polo matches—once the sport of maharajas—are resurrected during Tiger Tops' annual international tournament in December.

Four miles east of Jungle Lodge is Tiger Tops Tented Camp, 12 en suite safari tents in the beautiful Surung Valley. And on the northern bank of the Narayani River is the newest addition to the Tiger Mountain Group, Tiger Tops Tharu Lodge, whose location just outside the park means wildlife safaris can be easily enjoyed along with visits to the villages of the Tharu, Bote, and Mushyar tribes, who have lived here for millennia.

Where: 75 miles/121 km southwest of Kathmandu. **Tiger Mountain Group:** Tel 977/1-4361500; www.tigermountain.com. *Cost:* from $430 (Jungle Lodge), from $310 (Tented Camp and Tharu Lodge) per person, all-inclusive. *When:* Sep–Jun. **Best times:** Oct–Nov and Mar–Apr for pleasant weather and best chance of tiger sightings.

Astounding Scenery (and Rhododendrons) Above the Clouds

Jaljale Himal

Nepal

Adventurers arriving en masse since the 1960s have indelibly altered Nepal's most popular treks, but unforgettable hill cultures and breathtaking scenery can still be found on less traveled routes.

Officially closed to the public until 1988, the Jaljale Himal High Ridge Trek in remote eastern Nepal remains a hidden jewel, offering some of the most pristine wilderness in the Himalayas and one of the area's best short treks. Trekkers find themselves among some of the highest peaks in the world, with frequent views of four of the world's grandest peaks—Everest, Kanchenjunga, Lhotse, and Makalu—and some of the friendliest people in Nepal. You'll see few non-Nepalese faces except for a handful of trekkers on the final three days—foreigners rarely visit most of the picturesque villages on this route.

The journey begins with some relatively easy ridge trekking on Milke Danda, the lower section of the Jaljale Himal Range, a biodiversity treasure-house with 16 types of rhododendrons and over 100 bird species. The trek culminates atop pyramid-shaped Patibhara, a dramatic 12,450-foot "hill" in front of the majestic 28,169-foot Kanchenjunga. Legend has it that shepherds used to bring sheep up here to graze, until one day when most of the sheep disappeared. A goddess named Patibhara Devi appeared in the shepherds' dreams and instructed them to pay homage to her by sacrificing some of the remaining sheep. They obeyed and the next day their sheep miraculously reappeared. Expect to share the incredibly scenic trail up to the Patibhara temple with local pilgrims passing dense rhododendron forests and taking in nonstop mountain views. But beware: This trip will spoil you. After Jaljale Himal, everything else will seem tame and commercialized by comparison.

WHERE: The trek begins at Biratnagar, 337 miles/541 km southeast of Kathmandu. **HOW:** U.S.-based Above the Clouds offers a 15-day trip (with 8-day moderate/strenuous trek). Tel 800-233-4499 or 802-482-4848; www.aboveclouds.com. *Cost:* from $3,650, all-inclusive, with domestic air. Originates in Kathmandu. *When:* Mar and Nov. **BEST TIMES:** Mar–Apr and Oct–Dec for nicest weather and flowers in full bloom.

Ancient Palaces Frozen in Time

KATHMANDU VALLEY

Nepal

At just over 15 miles long and 12 miles across, Kathmandu Valley is Nepal's political, cultural, and commercial hub; before development began 30 or so years ago, it held as many temples and shrines as it did houses. Since Nepal first opened to foreign tourism in 1951, legions of flower children and trekkers have come and lingered in the history-rich Durbar Square (*durbar* means "palace") in the capital city of Kathmandu and explored the astounding concentration of more than 50 temples, shrines, and old palaces nearby. Packed with tourist groups, touts, and bicycle rickshaws, Kathmandu can seem overwhelming when viewed from the platform steps of the triple-roofed Maju Deval temple, but the square still has its moments of magic. On the south side of the square is Kumari Ghar, the three-storied palace residence of the young girl who bears the royal title Kumari Devi and is worshipped as the bodily incarnation of the goddess Taleju. Around the square, modern consumerism has obliterated much of Kathmandu's medieval character, but it's still a great thrill to meander the tangle of alleyways a bit farther away, heady with incense and spices and full of hole-in-the-wall shops.

Traditional Nepalese architecture surrounds Kathmandu's Durbar Square, one of the valley's busiest places.

North of the square, just off the commercial stretch of the Durbar Marg (or King's Way), you'll find one of the best known and most historical of Kathmandu's hotels, the rambling Hotel Yak & Yeti, with 270 stylish and modern rooms and suites. The hotel's original wing is part of the Lal Durbar, the royal 19th-century home of a former *rana* (prime minister). The smaller Dwarika's Hotel is a newer arrival: The simple, Nepali-style brick building embellished with decorative woodcarvings opened as a hotel in 1977. For years, its owner, the late Dwarika Das Shrestha, who was also a visionary conservationist, rescued thousands of ancient carved wooden pieces, then employed traditionally trained Nepali craftsmen to integrate them into this atmospheric, ancient-looking haven, a virtual oasis in a very busy city.

For less action, head to the small town of Bhaktapur, also called Bhadgaon, the City of Devotees. This former capital of one of the other two independent kingdoms in the Kathmandu Valley is far less developed—it's evocative of Kathmandu in the days before trekkers arrived. There's plenty of impressive, medieval architecture, including more than 40 temples and the royal Palace of Fifty-Five Windows, which is entered through the Golden Gate, the heavily embellished, 18th-century doorway held to be the most important piece of art in the valley. A short walk in any direction from the square brings you into the twisting back alleyways where the town's craftsmen, for centuries a source of the city's renown, carry on their traditional handiwork. Unpack your bags at Krishna's House, where rooms are simple, clean, and sunny and the Prajapati family are the very embodiment of Nepalese kindness.

WHERE: Bhaktapur is 9 miles/14 km east of Kathmandu. **HOTEL YAK & YETI:** Tel 977/1-248999; www.yakandyeti.com. *Cost:* from $200. **DWARIKA'S HOTEL:** Tel 977/1-4479488; www.dwarikas.com. *Cost:* from $225. **KRISHNA'S HOUSE:** Tel 977/1-6610462; www.krishnashouse.com. *Cost:* $45. **BEST TIMES:** Mar–May and Sep–Nov for dry, pleasant weather; late Oct–early Nov for Tihar Festival throughout Nepal, a Hindu holiday honoring Lakshmi that fills the cities with the glow of countless candles.

Sagarmatha, "Mother Goddess of the Universe"

MOUNT EVEREST

Nepal

The history of the West's conquest of the world's tallest mountain is nearly as riveting as the views from its peak. After a number of failed attempts, New Zealander Edmund Hillary and Sherpa guide Tenzing Norgay were the first documented climbers to reach the top, in 1953, and thousands of adventurers have tried (often unsuccessfully) to repeat their feat ever since—the most famed in recent times being those documented in 1996 in Jon Krakauer's bestseller *Into Thin Air.* But trekkers don't need to scale the summit in order to experience the might of Sagarmatha, "Goddess of the Sky," as Everest is known to the Sherpas. Most who come here encounter the legendary mountain by way of a journey to the beautiful Khumbu Valley, with its timeless Sherpa villages, spectacular Buddhist monasteries, and unique wildlife.

Prayer flags are hung at a Mount Everest base camp to bless those preparing for the ascent.

One attainable highlight of such an Everest trek is the 17,600-foot-high Everest Base Camp, where climbers prepare for their summit attempts. Here at the foot of the notoriously treacherous Khumbu Icefall, amid the jumble of boulders, tents, and prayer flags, you can soak up the atmosphere and excitement as the expedition teams plan their ascent and Sherpa cooks and porters ready the supplies. Views of Everest are obscured from camp. For those, you'll need to take to the surrounding trails, where you'll enjoy breathtaking close-ups of the 29,035-foot peak and of Lhotse, Makalu, and Cho Oyu, all over 26,000 feet high. Balancing all this impossible grandeur is the friendliness of the Sherpa people, whose hospitality provides an experience as memorable as Everest itself.

WHERE: The trek begins in Lukla, near the Tibet border, approximately 85 miles/137 km northeast of Kathmandu. **HOW:** U.S.-based Mountain Travel Sobek offers 14- and 25-day trips. Tel 888-831-7526 or 510-594-6000; www.mtsobek.com. *Cost:* 19-day trip to Base Camp I from $4,435, all-inclusive. Originates in Kathmandu. *When:* Apr–May, Oct–Nov. **BEST TIMES:** Mar–May, which is before monsoon season, or Oct–Nov after it is over.

The Last Forbidden Buddhist Kingdom

MUSTANG

Nepal

Surrounded by Tibet on three sides and governed by a Tibetan royal family, Mustang—formerly a kingdom within a kingdom—survives as one of the last remnants of ancient Tibet. Although nominally integrated into what was once the kingdom of Nepal in the early 1950s, this district, slightly smaller in size than Rhode Island, remains largely autonomous, and much of its medieval culture flourishes still. In fact, Mustang is said to be more like Tibet before the Chinese occupation than Tibet itself, filled with walled fortress-villages and monasteries hewn from rock that ranges from muted grays to rusty reds.

The landscape here is rugged and austere, a dramatic high-desert terrain flanked by towering peaks, including the snowcapped

Buddhist monuments, called chortens or stupas, can be found throughout Lo Manthang.

Annapurnas to the south. Though Nepal opened to tourism in the 1950s, Mustang's sensitive position along the Tibetan border kept it off-limits until 1992, when the Nepali government began admitting a trickle of foreign tourists. Even today, travel to Mustang is restricted and visitors must arrange treks through a licensed trekking company. Ironically, Mustang was well traveled in the past—its ancient trade routes date back more than 1,000 years. Surely the treeless vistas along the way appeared extraordinary to European traders returning from China with their precious cargo—as they do to today's trekkers overwhelmed by the otherworldliness of it all.

Every spring, at the palace in the ancient, walled capital city of Lo Manthang, a colorful, 3-day Buddhist festival called Tiji is hosted by the crown prince. The highlight occurs when a thousand costumed men, women, and children participate in elaborate, age-old reenactments of the story of a deity named Dorje Jon, who battled his demon father to save the Mustang kingdom from destruction.

WHERE: Lo Manthang is along the Tibetan border, 130 miles/209 km northwest of Kathmandu. Treks begin in Jomsom, 45 miles/72 km south of Lo Manthang. **HOW:** U.S.-based Myths & Mountains offers 14- and 19-day trips (the latter includes 3 days in Lo Manthang at Tiji). Tel 800-670-6984 or 775-832-5454; www.mythsandmountains.com. Originates in Kathmandu. *Cost:* 14-day trip from $3,795, all-inclusive. *When:* Apr–May and Oct. **BEST TIMES:** Oct for nicest weather; May for the Tiji festival.

Rooms—and Treks—with a View

POKHARA AND THE ANNAPURNA SANCTUARY

Nepal

Pokhara's reputation as one of the most beautiful cities in the world is well deserved, particularly in early morning when the reflections of snow-capped mountains are mirrored in the calm waters of Phewa Tal. Nepal's third largest city is also known as the trekker's capital of the world. Most visitors here are gearing up for (or recovering from) treks on the Annapurna Circuit, which rival—and are less crowded than—those around Everest Base Camp (see p. 563). Like them, you'll want to set out for the glorious Annapurna Sanctuary, a glacial basin that serves up a 360-degree panorama in the heart of the Himalayas as well as the best views of Annapurna I. At 26,545 feet it's the world's tenth highest mountain and one of the most treacherous. Trekkers in the sanctuary may only go as far as Annapurna Base Camp at 13,340 feet, but even this constitutes an unforgettable odyssey into traditional Nepali villages, over thrilling suspension bridges, through forests filled with bamboo and rhododendron, and above the tree line to a rocky wonderland in the clouds.

Off the beaten track, in Old Pokhara, is where you'll find old Nepali charm and hospitality. The many Newari houses here, with their decorative brickwork and unique woodcarvings, make this quarter a joy to explore either on foot or bicycle. Avoid the main tourist scene on the eastern shores of Phewa Tal, along the strip known as Lakeside, and seek out the only hotel that sits on the calm southern shore: The Fish Tail Lodge is graced by heartstopping views of both the Annapurna massif and the 22,946-foot Machhapuchhare (Fish Tail Peak). The only way to reach the hotel is by rowboat or a manually operated rope ferry, as experienced by Prince Charles and the emperor of Japan.

A number of yoga retreats have opened in recent years, most of them basic operations.

The Annapurna mountain range is reflected in Lake Phewa Tal, Nepal's second largest lake.

There is the occasional exception, however, such as the comfortable Begnas Lake Resort, set on the lush shores of a lake of the same name and just 10 minutes from Pokhara. For the nicest lodging in the area, drive a half hour from Pokhara to the Tiger Mountain Pokhara Lodge, which perches 1,000 feet above the valley and offers panoramic views of the Himalayas. You'll feel a world away at this 19-room boutique hotel, part of the conservation-minded Tiger Mountain Group, which includes Tiger Tops in Chitwan National Park (see p. 561). It is the perfect base for short strolls and day hikes to Begnas Lake or nearby villages; other activities include golf, bird-watching, and fishing. Or spend the day sightseeing and shopping in Pokhara and be back at the lodge for a home-style dinner.

Where: 125 miles/201 km west of Kathmandu. **How:** U.S.-based REI Adventures offers a 15-day Annapurna Sanctuary trip (includes 11-day moderate/strenuous trek). Tel 800-622-2236 or 253-437-1100; www.rei.com/adventures. *Cost:* $2,930, all-inclusive. Originates in Kathmandu. *When:* Feb–Apr and Oct–Nov. **Fish Tail Lodge:** Tel 977/61-460248; www.fishtail-lodge.com. *Cost:* from $180. **Begnas Lake Resort:** Tel 977/61-560030; www.begnaslakeresort.com. *Cost:* from $170. **Tiger Mountain Pokhara Lodge:** Tel 977/1-4361500; www.tigermountain.com/pokhara. *Cost:* from $620, inclusive. **Best times:** Oct–Apr for clear, dry weather; Dec 28–Jan 1 for the Street Festival, when Lakeside is lined with food stalls, games, and competitions.

For a Spot of Ceylon Tea at the Source

The Galle Face Hotel

Colombo, Sri Lanka

Connoisseurs of Raj-era hotels seek out the Galle Face, one of the few remaining colonial hotels still rich in period detail and with a lingering air of pampered 19th-century luxury. Barefoot waiters serve tea or sundowners at the open-air, sea-breeze-swept Veranda Restaurant, a famed watering hole during British rule, when Ceylon—as Sri Lanka was called then—was synonymous with tea. To get even closer to the sultry waters of the Indian Ocean, savor your chilled Lion lager and spicy bar snacks on the Checkerboard, the large, paved, open-air patio. Many prefer the vintage suites in the Classic wing of the hotel that are a charming throwback to colonial times, seeming large enough to host a cricket match, with polished, creaking teak floors, ceiling fans, and ocean views; the more recent rooms in the Regency Wing have contemporary décor and offer modern comforts including air-conditioning. A butler delivers breakfast with a smile and a graciousness that the British must have been loath to leave behind.

The colonial hotel has always prided itself on its high standard of hospitality.

The hotel borders the Galle Face Green, a mile-long promenade between Galle Road and the ocean. Built in 1859 by the British governor, Sir Henry Ward, for the ladies and children of Colombo, then and now the country's capital, the green is a popular local gathering place where lovers stroll, families gather, children fly kites, and everyone comes for the excellent array of street food. With a little imagination, it's easy to picture it 100 years ago, when it was used as a golf course and even a race track.

Experience the city's contemporary spirit at the Paradise Road shopping enclave, a pleasant walk from the hotel. Recharge at the Gallery Café, formerly the offices of the renowned 20th-century Sri Lankan architect Geoffrey Bawa (his old workbench is now a table in the popular bar). The café displays contemporary Sri Lankan art and opens onto a patio and garden. It draws a stylish crowd who come to enjoy cocktails and dishes like lemongrass and ginger chicken and prawn curry with coconut risotto.

GALLE FACE HOTEL: Tel 94/11-254-1010; www.gallefacehotel.com. *Cost:* from $110. **GALLERY CAFÉ:** Tel 94/11-258-2162; www.paradiseroadsl.com/cafe. *Cost:* dinner $30. **BEST TIMES:** Dec–Mar is the driest season; Jan for the Duruthu Perahera procession: 3 days surrounding the full moon, celebrating Buddha's first visit to Sri Lanka; Feb for full-moon festival, Navam Perahera, when 100 elephants are paraded with music, dance, and celebration.

The Deep South

GALLE FORT

Galle, Sri Lanka

In the coastal city of Galle, in Sri Lanka's deep south, the old fortified city of Galle Fort stands protected by thick, 17th-century Dutch stone-and-coral ramparts. Asia's best preserved colonial sea fortress, Galle Fort was built by the Portuguese 400 years ago and expanded by 17th-century Dutch settlers, who used it as the Ceylonese headquarters of the Dutch East India Company. Walk around it to soak up the history embedded in its churches, mosques, temples, warehouses, and hundreds of Dutch houses, many with tiled roofs and shuttered Dutch-style doors and windows still intact. Diners sit at postage-stamp cafés, and the meandering streets are filled with auto rickshaws (three-wheeled cars), old bicycles, goats, cats, and street peddlers selling fish, lace, or even hand-cut gems.

Wander up Church Street to the intimate Galle Fort Hotel, a 17th-century Dutch merchant's home, where spacious rooms filled with antiques surround a colonnaded courtyard pool. Its restaurant draws a chic mixed crowd of local residents and travelers. For views of Galle Fort and the Indian Ocean, the perfect vantage point is the seven-room Sun House hotel, an 18th-century Scottish spice merchant's hilltop house a 5-minute walk from the center of town. The barman at the award-winning Dick's will be happy to mix up a Sun House Sour. Next door is the Dutch House, or Doornberg, built in 1712 for an admiral of the Dutch East India Company and now an inn with four magnificently restored rooms.

Just a couple of miles east of Galle, rocky outcrops break up the waves at the beautiful crescent-shaped beach of Unawatuna, creating ideal swimming and snorkeling conditions December through March (June through September bring monsoons). Farther east are the quieter beaches of Dalawella and Thalpe. Farther still is Mirissa, once known as Sri Lanka's most inviting deserted beach but now thoroughly discovered. Mirissa is also the place for whale-watching. Researchers have only recently begun monitoring the movements of the blue and sperm whales that pass 3 to 6 miles off Mirissa, mainly between November and April. Your whale-watching boat may be accompanied by curious groups of another sea creature: spinner dolphins.

Where: 66 miles/107 km south of Colombo. **How:** Sri Lanka In Style offers customized itineraries. Tel 94/11-239-6666; www.srilankainstyle.com. **Galle Fort Hotel:** Tel 94/91-223-2870; www.galleforthotel.com. *Cost:* from $160. **Sun House:** Tel 94/91-438-0275; www.thesunhouse.com. *Cost:* from $175 (off-peak), from $220 (peak). **Dutch House:** Tel 94/91-438-0275; www.thedutchhouse.com. *Cost:* from $320. **Whale-watching:** Mirissa Water Sports leads 3–4-hour whale-watching trips. Tel 94/77-359-7731; www.mirissawatersports.com. *Cost:* from $90. *When:* Nov–Apr. **Best times:** Nov–Apr for best weather and for whale-watching; Jan for the Galle Literary Festival.

A Treasure Trove at the Island's Heart

The Cultural Triangle

Kandy, Anuradhapura, Polonnaruwa, Sri Lanka

Three ancient capitals delineate Sri Lanka's Cultural (aka Golden) Triangle: Kandy, in the south (see next page); Anuradhapura, in the north; and Polonnaruwa, in the northeast. Anuradhapura, founded around 380 B.C., was ruled by 113 successive kings (and four queens) whose magnificent palaces stood alongside dozens of monasteries housing tens of thousands of Buddhist monks; the ancient monarchs presided over a culture of great creativity. Reclaimed by the jungle after falling to Tamil conquerors from India in the 11th century, Anuradhapura was gradually uncovered beginning in the 19th century, and preservation work continues today. The city

Between the lion's paws at Sigiriya Rock, a steep climb leads to fresco-filled monasteries and far-reaching views.

that has reemerged was a place of temples, sculptures, beautiful gardens, and massive *dagobas* (bell-shaped stupas, or Buddhist shrines, built to house sacred relics). The Jetavanaramaya Dagoba, over 300 feet high and made up of 90 million bricks, is the second largest man-made structure from the ancient world, after the Egyptian pyramids.

Polonnaruwa, the capital of Sri Lanka after the fall of Anuradhapura, was a fabulous garden city; amid its many well-preserved ruins are monuments built by the Indian invaders.

At Dambulla, in the center of the triangle, a steep climb leads to Buddhist cave temples carved out of rock in the 1st century B.C. and embellished by the kings of Kandy during the 17th and 18th centuries. At the top, visitors find stunning views of the entire Cultural Triangle and the archaeological site of Sigiriya (Lion Rock), a 1,214-foot, flat-topped volcanic pillar that served as an impregnable citadel in the 6th century. An entrance between the lion's paws leads to the monasteries where 20 frescoes depict 500 beautiful women with flowers in their hair; experts say there may once have been as many as 500 frescoes covering the entire western face of the rock.

An excellent refuge is the Heritance Kandalama, in Dambulla, designed in 1991 by famed Sri Lankan architect Geoffrey Bawa. Blending into the lush landscape overlooking the Sigiriya citadel, the hotel features luxury rooms with floor-to-ceiling windows and restaurants that serve Sri Lankan cuisine.

WHERE: Anuradhapura is 128 miles/205 km north of Colombo; Polonnaruwa is 162 miles/262 km northeast of Colombo; Kandy is 72 miles/116 km northeast of Colombo. **HERITANCE KANDALAMA:** Tel 94/665-55-5000; www.heritancehotels.com. *Cost:* from $185 (off-peak), from $245 (peak). **HOW:** U.S.-based Asia Transpacific Journeys offers a 16-day "Splendid Sri Lanka" tour that includes Cultural Triangle destinations. Tel 800-642-2742 or 303-443-6789; www.asiatranspacific.com. *Cost:* $7,995. Originates in Colombo. *When:* Aug. **BEST TIME:** Nov–Apr for cool weather.

A Sacred City and Its Glorious Festival

KANDY AND THE ESALA PERAHERA

Sri Lanka

Nestled in lush hill country, Kandy is Sri Lanka's cultural and religious stronghold, forming the southern tip of the nation's Cultural Triangle (see previous page). Although it is Sri Lanka's second largest city,

Kandy retains something of a small-town air. Temples and colonial-era houses blanket its hills, and everyone enjoys a stroll around its large artificial lake, created in 1807 by the last of the Sinhalese kings who made Kandy their capital.

Visitors who come in July or August during the centuries-old Esala Perahera festival will experience one of Asia's greatest spectacles. Sri Lanka's most revered relic is a sacred tooth of Buddha smuggled into the country in A.D. 310 and enshrined in the Dalada Maligawa, or Temple of the Tooth, in Kandy. In the elaborate *perahera* (pageant or procession) asking the gods for rain, a brilliantly costumed elephant carrying a replica of the tooth is preceded by a showstopping parade of dozens of other elephants and a frenzied cast of thousands of Kandyan dancers and drummers. The processions continue for several days, and the best display occurs on the final night.

From Kandy, it's an easy 30-mile trip to the Pinnawela Elephant Orphanage, home to dozens of elephants from adults to babies no more than a few weeks old. Visitors help bottle-feed the youngest ones and can watch the twice-a-day baths in the Ma Oya River, where the babies splash and wallow while *mahouts,* or elephant handlers, scrub the adults. Keep an eye out for a proud and patient elephant with only three feet, the victim of a land-mine accident in Sri Lanka's formerly war-town north. The refuge, operated by the Millennium Elephant Foundation, cares for elephants rescued from abuse or retired from temple work.

It's a 20-minute drive along a bumpy, winding road from Kandy to the village of Gunnepana and the Kandy House, a boutique hotel with eight elegant rooms, lush gardens, and an infinity pool surrounded by emerald-green rice paddies. Built in 1804 as the home for an aristocratic family, the hotel is the perfect base for exploring Kandy and the nearby Royal Botanical Gardens, which date back to the Kandyan kingdom. They cover close to 150 acres with a spectacular display of more than 400 species of indigenous tropical flora and exotic plants. A giant Javan fig tree, said to be the largest tree in the world, is a favorite point of rendezvous for local courting couples.

WHERE: 72 miles/115 km northeast of Colombo. **PINNAWELA ELEPHANT ORPHANAGE:** www.mysrilanka.com/travel/elephants. **MILLENNIUM ELEPHANT FOUNDATION:** www.millenniumelephantfoundation.com. **THE KANDY HOUSE:** Tel 94/81-492-1394; www.thekandyhouse.com. *Cost:* from $230. **BEST TIMES:** Climate is good year-round; Jul or Aug for Esala Perahera festival, which peaks at the full moon of Esala.

Tea Plantations and Adam's Peak

THE HILL COUNTRY

Nuwara Eliya, Sri Lanka

Although Sri Lanka is now known as the tea capital of the world, tea wasn't planted here until 1867. In 1880, Scottish-born Thomas Lipton began buying tea directly from estates in the hill country, bypassing London's wholesale markets to deliver, in his phrase, "direct from the tea garden to the teapot." Once a beverage for the rich, Lipton made tea a mass-market one.

Today the cool central hill country is blanketed with lush green plantations of *Camellia sinensis* (the botanical name of the tea plant). Vestiges of the British era linger in Nuwara

Eliya, Sri Lanka's highest town, which still boasts some fine old colonial hotels, an 18-hole golf course, and an 1875-vintage race course. A dinner at the Hill Club, a massive stone hotel that was once home to a British plantation owner, is a step back into other times with one difference: Ladies are now allowed in the bars. Celebrate with an arak sour, a local cocktail, before playing a round in the wood-lined billiard room.

Hill Country tea has long been a mainstay of Sri Lanka's economy.

For a wonderful immersion into the world of tea, stay at the Tea Factory just outside town, a 25-acre green-tea estate that dates back to the Raj era. Greater comfort is offered 30 miles from Nuwara Eliya, at Ceylon Tea Trails, four colonial tea planters' bungalows perched at 4,000 feet above sea level near Castlereagh Lake. Each of the cottages, which are 2 to 9 miles apart along marked scenic trails, comes with its own small staff and contains four to six luxurious suites; you can book a room or the entire bungalow.

Few miss a day trip to the hill country landmark, 7,362-foot Adam's Peak (Sripada). Buddhists, Hindus, Christians, and Muslims all make pilgrimages to this cone-shaped mountain with a footprint-shaped depression at the summit thought to be that of Adam—or perhaps Buddha or the Hindu lord Shiva—first stepping onto earth. Pilgrims begin their hikes around 2 A.M., following illuminated pathways lined with stalls offering white tea that grows atop the peak, in order to arrive at dawn, when the peak casts a spectacular shadow across the morning mist.

Another essential early-morning experience is hiking through the mountain-shaded serenity of Horton Plains National Park to World's End, an escarpment that drops dramatically half a mile to the plains below. Wildlife spotters here may see sambar deer, rare bear-faced (aka purple-faced) monkeys, and, if they are extremely lucky, an elusive leopard. This is also one of Sri Lanka's best areas for bird-watching.

WHERE: 112 miles/180 km east of Colombo. **VISITOR INFO:** www.nuwaraeliya.org. **HILL CLUB:** Tel 94/52-222-2653; www.hillclubsrilanka.net. *Cost:* dinner $15. **TEA FACTORY:** Tel 94/52-222-9600; www.heritancehotels.com. *Cost:* from $210. **CEYLON TEA TRAILS:** Tel 94/11-230-3888; www.teatrails.com. *Cost:* from $505 (off-peak), from $630 (peak), inclusive. **SRIPADA:** http://sripada.org. *When:* pilgrimage season Dec–Apr; Jan–Feb are the busiest months. **BEST TIME:** Dec–Apr for the drier months.

A Ride on the Roof of the World

PAMIR HIGHWAY

Tajikistan

To locals, it's known simply as the M41. To foreign travelers heading deep into Central Asia, it's the legendary Pamir Highway. This incredibly scenic road begins at Khorog, in southern Tajikistan, and loops its way north through the raw Pamir Mountains before dropping down into the lush Fergana Valley, completing the route at Osh, in Kyrgyzstan (see p. 560). Bring your camera—the photo ops will leave you breathless (as will the thin mountain air).

The Russian Red Army constructed the M41 Highway between 1931 and 1934. It is an engineering feat reaching a top elevation of 15,362 feet at the Ak-Baital Pass. The 450-mile journey will take a minimum of 3 days, and should be done in a 4WD vehicle with a local driver or by organized trip. With more time, there are endless opportunities for hikes and exploration of little-visited historic sites and villages. If the ride seems a bit too long and arduous, think of Marco Polo, who traversed this mountain range (and wrote, in awe, about its beauty) en route to China in far more primitive conditions.

A delightful place to start the journey is Khorog, a bustling mountain town slung along the fast-flowing Gunt River near the Afghanistan border. From here, the M41 climbs steadily in the Pamirs. Some of the highest mountains in the world, they are known locally as the Bam-i-Dunya ("Roof of the World"). Enormous, snowcapped peaks come into view, along with the occasional village, turquoise lake, or solitary yurt.

Murghak marks the halfway point. It lacks the charm of Khorog but has a good range of facilities, including a few welcoming guesthouses that serve hot, homemade meals. The town makes a great base for hikes and camel treks, with nights spent in a yurt. From here, one of the geographic highlights on the way to Kyrgyzstan is Kara-Kul, a lake formed by the impact of a meteor some 10 million years ago.

Traversing the only pass through the mountains, the Pamir Highway once formed part of the Silk Road.

Once you've reached Osh, across the border, take a breather, shake the dust from your boots, and plot the next stage of your trip—over the mountains to Bishkek, across the Chinese border to Kashgar (see p. 500), or west to Uzbekistan (see p. 587) and Tashkent.

WHERE: Khorog is located 170 miles/274 km southeast of the capital city of Dushanbe. **VISITOR INFO:** www.pamirs.org. **HOW:** Dushanbe-based Hamsafar Travel can make arrangements for jeep tours. Tel 992/37-228-0093; www.hamsafar-travel.com. U.S.-based MIR Corp organizes an 18-day trip through Kyrgyzstan and Tajikistan that travels a portion of the Pamir Highway. Tel 800-424-7289 or 206-624-7289; www.mircorp.com. *Cost:* $6,995. Originates in Bishkek, Kyrgyzstan. *When:* Aug. **BEST TIME:** mid-May–Sep is the only practical season to cross the high mountain passes.

A Byzantine Wonderland Created by Wind, Water, and Time

CAPPADOCIA

Anatolia, Turkey

Countless centuries of wind and water have sculpted Cappadocia's surrealistic landscape from the soft volcanic terrain: Minarets, cones, spires, "fairy chimneys," and rocky pinnacles in shades of pinks and russet brown soar as high as five-story buildings. Ancient inhabitants of Cappadocia (Kapadokya in Turkish) hollowed out the soft *tufa* (limestone) cones and cliffs to create cave dwellings that are still lived in today. Once a major trade route between East and West, Cappadocia was home to a dozen different civilizations. The early Christians arrived in the 4th century, sculpting from the rock domed churches, complete with vaulted ceilings, columns, and pews. The region is spread over about 50 square miles encompassing numerous towns and villages.

The open-air museum in Göreme is the site of an ancient monastic colony, once said to have had more than 400 churches, hermitages, and small monasteries, most sculpted from the rock face. Today 15 are open to the public. Some are covered with simple frescoes that date back to the 8th century, but it's the rich Byzantine ones from the 10th through the 13th centuries that are the most striking.

Few topographies are as thrilling to see from a hot-air balloon's vantage than that of Cappadocia. Float over the inhabited moonscape from April through October, when visibility is best. Then explore the other extreme: Dozens of subterranean towns, carved from the stone, extend as far as eight levels below ground. The most frequently visited are those entered at the village of Kaymakli, about 12 miles from Göreme. Some of these cave-cities date back to the Hittite times (1500 B.C.) and were expanded over the centuries as the dwellers welcomed the protection from marauding armies that the subterranean homes afforded them. Churches, wine presses, livestock pens, and intricate airshafts ensured that underground populations could last for months without surfacing.

The town of Göreme was originally a backpackers' hangout, but now can claim a wealth of accommodations, ranging from hostels to boutique cave hotels. Ürgüp, just ten minutes from Göreme, caters to those with a slightly higher budget. The ever popular ten-room Esbelli Evi located there maintains an inviting, personal atmosphere; most of its rooms are suites hewn from golden stone, with terraces that give way to views of the Cappadocian landscape. The utterly unique Yunak Evleri is a romantic beehive of 30 rooms carved out of six tastefully restored caves dating back as far as the 5th century. Warm hardwood floors, kilim carpets, Ottoman antiques, and a 19th-century Greek mansion façade give it a Mediterranean elegance.

WHERE: Ürgüp is 41 miles/66 km southwest of Kayseri, the closest city with an airport. **GÖREME OPEN-AIR MUSEUM:** Tel 90/384-271-2687; www.goreme.com. **BALLOON RIDES:** Royal Balloon offers 60- and 90-minute flights. Tel 90/384-271-3300; www.royalballoon.com. *Cost:* 60-minute flight from $180. **ESBELLI EVI:** Tel 90/384-341-3395; www.esbelli.com. *Cost:* from $200. *When:* closed Nov–Mar. **YUNAK EVLERI:** Tel 90/384-341-6920; www.yunak.com. *Cost:* from $175 (off-peak), from $245 (peak). **BEST TIMES:** Apr–Jun and Sep–Oct for nicest weather.

Dazzling Both Ancient Romans and Modern-Day Visitors

PAMUKKALE

Anatolia, Turkey

A beautiful freak of nature, Pamukkale (Cotton Castle) resembles a series of bleached rice terraces as you approach. The white travertine tiers, joined together like huge water lilies by petrified waterfalls and gleaming stalactites, are the result of hot mineral springs, whose calcium-rich deposits have been accumulating for millennia. A popular resort since Roman times, the springs draw gatherings of festive tourists. Pamukkale is especially mesmerizing at sunset, when the colors of the pools warm from dazzling white to the muted pinks and purples of the sky.

Nowadays very few pools are open to the public, with preservation codes dictating that anything more than a wallow in the 97°F shin-deep waters is prohibited. For a deeper plunge, visitors can enjoy relaxing mineral baths, just as the Romans did, at the nearby ancient spa town of Hierapolis. In the modernized Sacred Pool, constantly refreshed by thermal waters, bathers can swim among and over submerged ancient marble columns, plinths, and other architectural remains leveled by earthquakes over the ages. An entire day could be spent exploring Hierapolis, whose ruins include a spectacular amphitheater designed to hold 12,000 spectators.

Follow in the footsteps of the pilgrims who have been coming to nearby Aphrodisias, the city of Aphrodite (known as Venus to the Romans), to pay homage to the goddess of love, beauty, and sexuality since the 8th century B.C. Archaeological remains suggest a sacred site existed here 2 millennia before that, on the broad, fertile Meander River Valley, 80 miles southwest of Pamukkale.

Many visitors try to see it all in a rushed day trip from the hyperactive cruise-ship port of Kuşadasi or cosmopolitan Izmir. For a more relaxed visit and a chance to explore Pamukkale after the tour groups have left, stay at the simply furnished, family-run Hotel Hal-Tur. What the place lacks in superfluous amenities it makes up for in friendly service and tasty dinners served beside the floodlit pool. Most of the hotel's 11 rooms have balconies with panoramic views of the travertine formations that glow in the moonlight.

The terracelike appearance of Pamukkale is the natural result of petrified waterfalls.

WHERE: 116 miles/186 km east of Kuşadasi. **HOTEL HAL-TUR:** Tel 90/258-272-2723; www.haltur.net. *Cost:* from $95. **BEST TIMES:** May–Jun and Sep–Oct for cooler weather.

Sailing the Turquoise Coast

THE BLUE VOYAGE

Bodrum and Antalya, Turkey

A sailing odyssey along Turkey's Turquoise Coast unveils the glories of the region's ancient cultures. Whether chartered by a group or individually rented by the cabin, a fully crewed wooden *gület,* the two-masted diesel-propelled boat of traditional design, is the perfect way to explore the sinuous coast that stretches over 300 miles from Bodrum, on the Aegean, south and eastward to the

Mediterranean port city of Antalya. The waters here take on a luminous blue that can be found nowhere else in Europe, giving rise to the local phrase *mavi yolculuk*, or "blue voyage." Along the way, boats take in Greco-Roman and Lycian ruins, sun-drenched beaches, lazy lunches at dockside cafés, and even a small uninhabited island given to Cleopatra as a gift by Mark Antony.

Cruises usually cast off from Antalya, Fethiye, or Bodrum, a whitewashed seaside resort whose harbor is dominated by the striking Petronium, or St. Peter's Castle, built in 1402 by the Rhodes-based Knights Hospitaller. Surrounded on three sides by water, it is one of the finest examples of Crusader architecture in Turkey, and was built from the remains of one of the Seven Wonders of the Ancient World: the 4th-century B.C. marble tomb built for King Mausolus by his sister *and* wife, Artemesia. Inside St. Peter's Castle, the unusual Museum of Underwater Archaeology is a showcase of historic wrecks and treasures found off the Aegean coast.

These are supreme cruising waters, with scores of anchorages dotting the bays, inlets, and harbors between Bodrum and Antalya. Even a one-day sail from Bodrum to the gorgeous mountain-rimmed Gökova Körfezi (Gökova Gulf) is a joy for the secluded cove and a simple fish lunch prepared by your crew. Some cruises focus on natural beauty, while others explore the fascinating history and archaeology of the region, and standards vary from Spartan bunks to luxurious berths.

Bodrum has changed considerably in the past few decades and is widely known today as the fashionable and busy yachting center of the Aegean. Hotels range from small in-town inns such as the welcoming oasis-like 20-room El Vino Hotel with views of St. Peter's Castle, to large swank resorts like the stylish Kepinski Hotel Barbaros Bay, a 30-minute drive from town. They both offer pampering and privacy that are heaven after a week spent on a boat. Or consider a stay on the less developed stretch called the Lycian Coast (see p. 584), south of Bodrum and on the way to Antalya.

WHERE: Antalya is 452 miles/727 km south of Istanbul; Bodrum is 266 miles/429 km west of Antalya. **MUSEUM OF UNDERWATER ARCHAEOLOGY:** Tel 90/252-316-2516. **HOTEL EL VINO:** Tel 90/252-313-8770; www.elvinobodrum.com. *Cost:* from $75. **KEPINSKI HOTEL BARBAROS BAY:** Tel 90/252-311-0303; www.kempinski.com/en/bodrum. *Cost:* from $145 (off-peak), from $450 (peak). **HOW:** U.K.-based Peter Sommer Tours offers 1- and 2-week gület cruises. Tel 44/1600-888-220; www.petersommer.com. *Cost:* from $2,875, inclusive. Originates in Bodrum or Antalya. *When:* May–Jun, Sep–Oct. **BEST TIMES:** May–Jun and Sep–Oct to avoid the big tour groups that come in Jul–Aug.

Unspoiled Turkey on the Aegean

THE DATÇA PENINSULA

Turkey

The long, mountainous Datça Peninsula points its narrow finger into the sea for 60 miles west of Marmaris. Unlike that loud and brash resort town so popular with package tourists and visitors in search of all-day nightlife, this is Turkey at its wildest and most unspoiled. Boaters appreciate the pine-clad coasts and hundreds of secluded coves. Others come to explore sleepy fishing villages and isolated mountain hamlets or, at the end of the peninsula's single roadway, the ruins of Cnidus. This once prosperous port, dating back to 400 B.C. and including two amphitheaters, enjoys a spectacular location on hills giving directly onto the sea.

From Cnidus, retrace your steps to the delightful harbor town of Datça. A cluster of simple but excellent portside restaurants, the nearby picture-postcard town of Eski Datça (Old Datça), and three small beaches make it a favorite post-ruins stop.

Enjoying an isolated bluff-top location outside of town, the castlelike but newly built Villa Aşina has 17 themed rooms, some with carved wooden ceilings. The views of the sea are almost 360 degrees, and there's direct access to two sandy beaches. Villa Tokur, closer to town and just uphill from the town's best beach, commands a similar hilltop position. The airy rooms and public areas are stylishly done, with an emphasis on stone and wrought iron, and the swimming pool is the centerpiece of a pretty flower-bedecked garden.

Arguably the most beautiful palace hotel on the Turkish coast is the Mehmet Ali Ağa Konaği in Reşadiye, just north of Eski Datça. Home to a wealthy local family for centuries and recently restored, the *konak* (residence), dating from the early 19th century, and four small buildings set amid lush gardens and pool are a veritable museum of Ottoman art and craftsmanship. The family hammam has been converted into a modern spa, the artwork throughout is original, and the ceiling and wall engravings in the main house are masterpieces of restoration. Walk through the rose garden and citrus grove to reach the hotel's celebrated restaurant, Elaki, with exquisite meze and fish and meat dishes from Turkey's Aegean and Mediterranean regions.

WHERE: Marmaris is 290 miles/466 km southwest of Istanbul. **VILLA AŞINA:** Tel 90/252-712-2444; www.villaasina.com.tr. *Cost:* from $125. **VILLA TOKUR:** 90/252-712-8728; www.hoteltokur.com. *Cost:* from $90. **MEHMET ALI AĞA KONAĞI:** Tel 90/252-712-9257; www.kocaev.com. *Cost:* from $220 (off-peak), from $410 (peak); dinner $65. **BEST TIME:** May–Oct for pleasant weather.

Turkey's Most Spectacular Roman Ruins

EPHESUS

Turkey

One of the best-preserved ancient cities in the world, Ephesus is Turkey's showpiece of archaeology. Although it is now 3 miles away from the Aegean Sea, Ephesus was one of the wealthiest trading port cities of the Greco-Roman era, ideally situated between the Near East and the Mediterranean ports of the West. Its extensive and impressive ruins testify to its ancient role as capital of the Roman province of Asia—in the time of Augustus Caesar, it was the second largest city in the eastern Mediterranean after Alexandria (see p. 375).

Today, a mile-long marble-paved street grooved by chariot wheels leads past partially reconstructed buildings, such as the Great Theater, with a capacity of 25,000 spectators, and the beautiful two-story Celsus Library built in A.D. 135, one of the most graceful surviving buildings of antiquity. The Greek Temple of Artemis (known to the Romans as Diana) was considered one of the Seven Wonders of the Ancient World. Only the foundations remain, but during Ephesus's golden day in the mid-4th century B.C., it was four times the size of the Parthenon in Athens (see p. 156), with a forest of 127 marble columns 60 feet high supporting the roof. The recently opened terraced houses—a warren of villas belonging to the city's rich and famous—rival Pompeii (see p. 179) in their splendor. Ephesus continued to flourish until the 3rd century, when it was razed by Goth invaders from northern Europe. Hundreds of columns and statues disappeared from the site over the ensuing centuries; some showed up in Constantinople and were used to build and embellish its Byzantine cathedrals. Nevertheless, the Ephesus Museum has one of the best collections of Roman and Greek artifacts to be found in Turkey.

Just outside the sprawling archaeological site of Ephesus is Meryem Ana Evi, the House of the Virgin Mary. Rediscovered by a German nun in the 19th century, it has become an important pilgrimage site—it is believed to be the final home of the Virgin, who was brought to Ephesus in her later years by St. John the Evangelist.

The typical jumping-off point for this and a variety of other sights, including the nearby Greek island of Sámos, is Kuşadasi, a major Aegean resort and popular destination for cruise ships and pleasure craft just 10 miles away. Skip its international playground atmosphere and head instead 72 miles northwest of Ephesus to Alaçati, a lively and picturesque village of restored Greek stone houses. Join the well-heeled Turkish visitors who come for its small, fine restaurants, craft shops, and buzzy atmosphere, and water-lovers who are lured by the excellent windsurfing. An estimated 80 boutique inns line the cobbled, winding streets of what was until fairly recently a sleepy hamlet. The chic Taş Otel is a special choice: The 19th-century building features only seven rooms, each flaunting 15-foot ceilings, linen curtains trimmed with handmade lace, fluffy bedding, and a charming personal ambience. The breakfast spread served on the leafy open-air terrace is renowned.

With Ionic columns on the bottom level and Corinthian on the top, Celsus Library is known for its well-preserved façade.

WHERE: 42 miles/67 km south of Izmir. **EPHESUS MUSEUM AND HOUSE OF THE VIRGIN MARY:** Tel 90/232-892-6010; www.ephesus.us. **TAŞ OTEL:** Tel 90/232-716-7772; www.tasotel.com. *Cost:* from $130 (off-peak), from $240 (peak). **BEST TIMES:** Apr–Jun and Oct–Dec offer cooler weather for sightseeing; early May for Ephesus Festival of Culture and Art.

"If the earth were a single state, Istanbul would be its capital."—NAPOLEON BONAPARTE

ISTANBUL

Turkey

Straddling Europe and Asia, the pulsating metropolis of Istanbul has captured visitors' imaginations for centuries with its dazzling legacy of the Byzantine and Ottoman empires. Today's Istanbul offers the traveler a rich array of contemporary and historical museums, world-class restaurants, and glamorous hotels—a sensory overload where East meets West at every turn. Set against the backdrop of hills, water, and the delicate spires of minarets, this enchanting and complicated place radiates a unique energy.

Top Attractions

Hagia Sophia—The massive dome and four elegant minarets of the Hagia Sophia (Aya Sofya, Church of Holy Wisdom) elegantly rise above the chaos of downtown Istanbul. Constantinople was nearing its zenith as the religious, commercial, and artistic center of the Holy Roman Empire when, in the 6th century, Emperor Justinian began work on the greatest church in ancient Byzantium. Hagia Sophia was later converted to a mosque by the Ottoman Turks and then was stripped of all religious significance under the Turkish Republic. But it will always be a spiritual oasis and remains the single finest structure to have survived late antiquity. A decade-long restoration project has been completed, leaving Hagia Sophia's 30 million mosaic tiles to dazzle yet again. Step inside, into the mystical and haunting beauty of its dimly lit interior, one of the largest enclosed spaces in the world. **Info:** Tel 90/212-522-0989; www.hagiasophia.com.

Topkapi Palace—Over a period of nearly four centuries, 25 sultans ruled the vast Ottoman Empire from the sprawling 175-acre Topkapi Palace complex, built on a formidable bluff overlooking the Bosporus, with tiled rooms and exhibits that still impress. The Treasury's highlight is the famous Topkapi dagger, encrusted with enormous emeralds, but you'll also see the 6,666 cut diamonds that adorn two 105-pound gold candelabra and the 86-karat Spoonmaker's Diamond used in the coronation turban of Mehmet IV in 1648. For many visitors, the most exotic stop on the palace grounds is the 400-room Harem. The number of odalisques (female slaves) increased steadily with the decline of the Ottoman Empire, reaching more than 800 in the mid-19th century. **Info:** Tel 90/212-512-0480; www.topkapisarayi.gov.tr.

The Grand Bazaar—Everything imaginable can be purchased at Istanbul's great Kapali Çarşi (literally, "covered bazaar"), a warren sprawling across 65 streets that houses some 4,000 shops, tiny cafés, and restaurants. Originally constructed by Mehmet the Conqueror in the 1450s, it has been substantially rebuilt over the years due to fires, though its original style of arched passageways and tiled fountains remains. One of the largest and oldest shopping malls in the world, it offers a sea of local curios and souvenirs: carpets, textiles, gold and jewelry, icons, leather, bronze, and copperware. Follow the locals to the less touristy outer corners. **Info:** www.grandbazaaristanbul.org.

Completed in A.D. 537, Hagia Sophia was once the largest Christian church in the world.

Spice Market—Also called the Egyptian Market because many of its goods were once imported from there, this 17th-century sprawling complex is the place to buy *lokum* (Turkish delight), figs, spices, coffee, apricots stuffed with almonds, pistachios, and honey. The aroma will work up your appetite, so take lunch or tea at the century-old Pandeli restaurant, located upstairs just inside the main entrance to the bazaar. **Pandeli restaurant:** Tel 90/212-527-3909; www.pandeli.com.tr. *Cost:* lunch $30.

Operational since 1741, Cağaloğlu Hamam preserves the Turkish bath experience of the Ottoman Empire.

Cağaloğlu Hamam—To relax in this chaotic city, indulge in a traditional Turkish bath at Cağaloğlu Hamam. Close to the Hagia Sophia (see previous page), the Cağaloğlu was a gift to the city in 1741 from Sultan Mehmet I, and Kaiser Wilhelm II, Florence Nightingale, and Tony Curtis are all said to have visited its magnificent white marble–domed steam room. Public baths were founded by the Romans, who passed the tradition on to the Byzantines and they to the Turks. While the penalty for a man discovered in the women's section used to be death, these days, you can escape with your life . . . but expect to find the men's and women's baths still separately housed. **Info:** Tel 90/212-522-2424; www.cagalogluhamami.com.tr.

Kariye Museum—This *müzesi* (museum), commonly known as the Chora Church, awes visitors with its dazzling 14th-century mosaics and frescoes depicting biblical scenes as well as with some of the most extensive holdings of Byzantine paintings in the world. Also known as the Holy Savior Church, it is tucked away near the city walls, where it was erected in the 5th century (most of the present structure dates from the 11th). Virtually all the magnificent interior decoration was completed in 1321 by Theodore Metochites, leader of the artistic and intellectual renaissance that transformed late Byzantium. It served as a mosque for four centuries before being converted into a museum. A number of historic Ottoman houses nearby form an evocative pocket of "Old Stamboul" in the shadow of the city's ancient walls, which are several stories high and up to 20 feet thick. Continue to explore the past at airy Asitane, just steps away, whose unusual menu of ancient Ottoman dishes, once served at Topkapi Palace, reflects Greek, Persian, and North African influences. **Info:** Tel 90/212-631-9241; www.choramuseum.com. **Asitane:** Tel 90/212-635-7997; www.asitanerestaurant.com. *Cost:* lunch $30.

Mosque of Suleiman the Magnificent—Known for its graceful minarets and stained-glass windows, the Kanuni Sultan Süleymaniye Camii (Mosque of Sultan Suleiman the Lawgiver; Süleymaniye for short) is the largest and arguably most beautiful of all of the mosques in Istanbul. Crowning a hill with its looming, unmistakable silhouette, it is the city's most identifiable landmark. Süleyman I, the greatest, richest, and most powerful of the Ottoman sultans, created this monument to himself between 1550 and 1557 and was buried here with his favorite wife, known in the West as Roxelana, "the Russian." **Info:** Tel 90/212-513-0093.

A cruise up the Bosporus Strait—There are several options for boating along the 20-mile Bosporus, or Bogaziçi, the narrow divide linking the Black Sea with the Sea of Marmara and separating Europe from Asia. Special public ferries operate for locals and tourists, making fewer stops than the ordinary service; they depart from the Eminönü pier and take up to 6 hours for a round-trip. Frequent excursion boats run by the TurYol cooperative give a more limited glimpse of the shoreline and go only as far as Rumeli Hisari, a 15th-century fortress, with the round-trip lasting 1.5 hours. Private tour companies also offer boat trips, which often include lunch or snacks. Once aboard, sit back and enjoy the view; along the way you'll pass grand palaces (watch for the Çirağan—now a hotel; see next page), upscale communities where graceful wooden Ottoman houses called *yalis* still line the water, castles, modern bridges, and forests. **How:** Turista Tourism Travel Agency offers Bosporus cruises. Tel 90/212-527-7085; www.turistatravel.com.

Other Must-Dos

Istiklal Caddesi—To visit the heart of modern Istanbul head to this pedestrian-only thoroughfare in the buzzy Beyoğlu neighborhood. Jostle your way around shoppers, a vintage tram, and nightclubbers to enjoy the atmosphere of 19th-century European-style architecture, trendy shops, period arcades full of restaurants, and the ornate Çiçek Pasaji (Flower Passage), on the corner of Istiklal Caddesi and Galatasaray Square. Follow the young and beautiful to 360, an 8th-floor aerie with intoxicating city views; it is the city's most famous watering hole, open well into the wee hours. Skip the food and stick to the drinks and unmatched people-watching. **360:** Tel 90/212-251-1042; www.360istanbul.com.

The Blue Mosque—The 17th-century Mosque of Sultan Ahmet I is more commonly called the Blue Mosque, for the 20,000 shimmering handmade blue İznik tiles creating intricate patterns across the upper reaches of the interior. When viewed from the outside, its six slender minarets (more than any other mosque in Istanbul) and cascading layers of domes and half domes vie with nearby Hagia Sophia (see p. 578) for architectural splendor. Unlike its neighbor, the building is a functioning mosque, so visiting hours are restricted during the five daily prayer times, particularly on Fridays.

The Princes' Islands—For a trip back in time, take a 90-minute ferry ride to the Princes' Islands, some 13 miles from Istanbul in the Sea of Marmara. The 19th-century getaway for the city's wealthy Jews, Armenians, and Greeks provides a welcome break for today's Istanbul residents from the bustle of their packed metropolis. Cars are banned, the wooden Ottoman and Victorian homes are genteel, and the air is clean. Heybeliada and Büyükada are the most rewarding of the four inhabited islands in the group. Stroll up the hilly lanes to admire the preserved architecture or hire a *fayton,* a horse-drawn carriage, before enjoying a leisurely lunch along the water. **How:** Frequent ferries depart daily from the Adalar Iskelesi, the "Islands Ferry Pier" at Kabataş.

Three fine art museums—In recent years Istanbul has made great strides in establishing world-class privately funded art museums—complete with trendy eateries—among the scores of more established specialist institutions. You'll find the Istanbul Modern housed in a stylishly renovated warehouse overlooking the Bosporus. Its collection features mainly contemporary Turkish paintings, which are displayed in a vast, stark room. A few miles upriver, in the Emirgan district (also on the Bosporus), is the Sakip Sabanci Museum. Situated in a 1927 villa, the Sabanci houses the collection of one of Turkey's leading industrialists, who once lived here. A new wing displays its top-rate collection of Ottoman calligraphy and paintings from Turkish and foreign artists working in Turkey in the 19th and early 20th centuries. Recharge at the popular Müzedechanga restaurant, within the garden. The Pera Museum is housed in the 19th-century Bristol Hotel, just a stone's throw from the venerable Pera Palace Hotel (see p. 582). Its five floors include more than 300 Orientalist paintings, mainly by European artists of the 17th to 19th centuries. **Istanbul Modern:** Tel 90/212-334-7300; www.istanbulmodern.org. **Sakip Sabanci Museum:** Tel 90/212-277-2200; http://muze.sabanciuniv.edu. *Cost:*

lunch at Müzedechanga $30. **Pera Museum:** Tel 90/212-334-9900; www.peramuzesi.org.tr.

Where to Stay

Çirağan Palace Kempinksi—Built right on the Bosporus in the 19th century, the Çirağan Palace was home to some of the last Ottoman sultans and remains the summit of Turkish elegance. Opulent yet understated guest rooms and suites are located in a new wing; all have balconies and many have Bosporus views as does the dramatic pool at water's edge. The Tuğra restaurant serves fare from bygone Constantinople in an exquisite Ottoman dining room, with French doors opening onto an alfresco terrace for dinner with a view of Asia. **Info:** Tel 90/212-326-4646; www.kempinski.com/en/istanbul. *Cost:* from $485 (off-peak), from $675 (peak); dinner $90.

Hotel Empress Zoe—An expat American opened the first boutique hotel here in an attractive and charming locale right in the heart of the historic Sultanahmet district. Cobbled from several old Turkish houses, it centers around an enticing garden where breakfast is served, and there are views of the Blue Mosque, Hagia Sophia, and Topkapi Palace from the upper terrace lounge. The 25 rooms and suites are individually decorated with Turkish textiles and original paintings. Some have four-posters, while others feature private terraces and balconies. **Info:** Tel 90/212-518-2504; www.emzoe.com. *Cost:* from $175.

Four Seasons Hotels—A century-old former prison is now home to one of Istanbul's most exclusive hotels, the Four Seasons Hotel Istanbul at Sultanahmet. Watchtowers and cells have been remodeled into 65 supremely elegant rooms and suites, set around a tranquil courtyard garden. The buttercup-yellow hotel is situated in the very heart of the historic Sultanahmet district, with Hagia Sophia, Topkapi Palace, and the Blue Mosque (see p. 578 and previous page) just steps away. The hotel's refined Seasons restaurant is a perennial favorite with locals and expats, especially for its sumptuous Sunday brunch. A newer sister property, the Four Seasons Hotel at the Bosphorus, is located about 15 minutes away in a converted Ottoman Empire mansion with two modern wings on the waterfront, in the fashionable suburb of Beşiktaş. The sumptuous spa features a hammam, an outdoor pool close by the water's edge, and service fit for a pasha (sultan). **Four Seasons Hotel Istanbul at Sultanahmet:** Tel 90/212-402-3000; www.fourseasons.com/istanbul. *Cost:* from $480 (off-peak), from $695 (peak); dinner at Seasons $60. **Four Seasons Hotel at the Bosphorus:** Tel 90/212-381-4000; www.fourseasons.com/bosphorus. *Cost:* from $510 (off-peak), from $960 (peak).

Sultans occupied Topkapi Palace for almost 400 years.

The Marmara Taksim—Rising 20 stories above central Taksim Square in central Beyoğlu, the Marmara is a landmark with expansive views of the Bosporus. A large outdoor pool and spacious sunbathing terrace are rare finds in Istanbul, and the rooftop Panorama restaurant and always popular Tepe Lounge offer breathtaking vistas of the city. The location is perfect for enjoying Istanbul's busiest shopping street, pedestrianized Istiklal Caddesi (see previous page). **Info:** Tel 90/212-334-8300; www.themarmarahotels.com/the-marmara-taksim. *Cost*: from $220 (off-peak), from $385 (peak); dinner at Panorama $65.

Park Hyatt Maçka Palas—The Maçka, which occupies an Art Deco palace, is an impeccable fusion of old and new, surrounded by a wealth of upscale shopping and fine-dining options in Istanbul's fashionable Şişli district. Blessed with a lovely outdoor pool, a full spa, and a fitness center, it has 90 handsomely appointed rooms, many with views across the Bosporus to Asia and 25 of which have their own steam rooms and Turkish baths. The acclaimed restaurant, Prime, is Istanbul's first authentic steakhouse, specializing in delicious cuts of meat and seafood prepared on a charcoal grill. **Info:** Tel 90/212-315-1234; www.istanbul.park.hyatt.com. *Cost:* from $440 (off-peak), from $655 (peak); dinner at Prime $65.

Pera Palace—Founded in 1892, the grande dame of Istanbul's hotels welcomed its first guests—passengers arriving on the Orient Express from Europe—in 1895 and was the choice of Agatha Christie, Greta Garbo, Mata Hari, and Ernest Hemingway. Today's guests can visit Room 101, the favorite of Mustapha Kemal Ataturk, founder of modern-day Turkey, and now a museum, while Agatha Christie fans can book Room 411, where, it is believed, she wrote *Murder on the Orient Express.* The year 2010 saw the completion of a massive restoration of the 115 tastefully uncluttered rooms, most with balconies and many with views over the Golden Horn. The surrounding Beyoğlu area (known as Pera to 19th-century Europeans) is packed with shops, restaurants, and bars. **Info:** Tel 90/212-377-4000; www.perapalace.com. *Cost:* from $350 (off-peak), from $575 (peak).

Sumahan on the Water—On the Asian side of the Bosporus, in the fishing village of Çengelköy, this 19th-century distillery-turned-hotel takes first prize for its views. Floor-to-ceiling picture windows provide contemporary guest rooms with some of the most memorable panoramas of old Istanbul across the water. A complimentary launch transports guests to the opposite shore in 15 minutes. Diners at Kordon, one of Istanbul's best fish restaurants, can enjoy the spectacle of the city's well-heeled docking their private launches at the restaurant's own jetty as the sun sets over Topkapi Palace across the strait. **Info:** Tel 90/216-422-8000; www.sumahan.com. *Cost:* from $280 (off-peak), from $425 (peak); dinner $45.

Eating & Drinking

Balikçi Sabahattin—"Fisherman Sabahattin" has been at the helm of his acclaimed fish restaurant, a 5-minute downhill walk from Sultanahmet, for several decades now. *Istanbullu*s fight over the pavement tables, which are packed to the gills during warm-weather nights, while the old, timbered house itself is divided into several small rooms over three floors. Expect Turkish classics like rice-stuffed steamed mussels, shrimp and octopus *güveç* (a type of stew) or, of course, the day's catch. **Info:** Tel 90/212-458-1824; www.balikcisabahattin.com. *Cost:* dinner $40.

Feriye Lokantasi—A 19th-century civic building has been converted into a stylish waterside haven, where you can enjoy traditional old-Ottoman cuisine. Specialties include spiced *pastirma* (pastrami) wrapped in vine leaves or fish stuffed with pine nuts and spiced red peppers. The picturesque seaside village of Ortaköy, with its atmospheric streetside cafés and artisan markets, is just a 10-minute walk away. **Info:** Tel 90/212-227-2216; www.feriye.com. *Cost:* dinner $45.

Imroz—In the never-ending parade of nearly identical fish restaurants on Nevizade Sokak, in bustling Beyoğlu, Imroz stands out for its fresher-than-fresh offerings and its extensive selection of meze. Presided over by the Greek-Turkish owner and named after a formerly Greek island now called Gökçeada, off the coast of Gallipoli, Imroz is one of the few authentic tavernas left in Istanbul. Grab a street-side table, order an anise-flavored *raki*, and let the evening unfold. **Info:** Tel 90/212-249-9073. *Cost:* dinner $30.

Mikla—At Mikla, reckoned by many epicurean devotees to be Istanbul's premier restaurant, American-trained Turkish-

Finnish chef Mehmet Gürs has created a marriage of modern Mediterranean and Nordic flavors. Nurse a drink on the open terrace perched on the top two floors of the 18-story Marmara Pera Hotel, with wraparound city views, before proceeding inside to a sleek, Scandinavian-inspired space. It's a perfect setting for the minimalist menu, where you might find raw grouper with black olives or cherry-wood smoked lamb loin with walnut pistou on the menu. **INFO:** Tel 90/212-293-5656; www.miklarestaurant.com. *Cost:* dinner $75.

RAMI—This delightful restaurant has been serving Ottoman specialties such as *hünkar beğendi* (spiced, slow-cooked lamb on smoked eggplant puree) for more than 2 decades in historic Sultanahmet. Set in an old timber *konak* (residence) over four floors, including a top-floor roof terrace, it is the former home of 20th-century Istanbul artist Rami Uluer. **INFO:** Tel 90/212-517-6593; www.ramirestaurant.com. *Cost:* dinner $35.

SOFYALI 9—Occupying several floors of an old Istanbul house, Sofyali 9 is another great place to sample hot and cold meze plates paired with the anise-flavored drink *raki*. The restaurant is slightly more elegant than similar *meyhane* eateries in the neighborhood, offering an excellent array of small plates, some of which you probably won't find elsewhere in the city. Exposed brickwork and wood floors create a cozy atmosphere for cold nights, and tables spill onto the pavement in summer. **INFO:** Tel 90/212-245-0362; www.sofyali.com.tr. *Cost:* dinner $35.

Prayer in Motion in Turkey's Holiest City

THE WHIRLING DERVISHES OF KONYA

Konya, Turkey

Konya is Turkey's most important center of Sufism, a mystical sect of Islam, and for nearly 700 years has been home to the Whirling Dervishes of the Mevlevi order. Their Mevlana Tekke (Mevlana Monastery) was founded by the 13th-century poet and philosopher *Mevlânâ* (meaning "master") Celaleddin Rumi, who preached love, charity, humility, equality, and tolerance. He believed that an ecstatic, trance-like state of universal love could be induced by the practice of whirling around and around, in the manner of all things in the universe. Each year in mid-December, the Mevlana's ascetic followers, known as dervishes, mark his death (his *şeb-i arûs*, "wedding night" with God) in 1273 by performing the meditative *semâ*, the ritual dance, one of the world's most mesmerizing spectacles. An orchestra of traditional instruments accompanies the dancers who, with their right palms up to the sky as if to receive God's grace, their left palms down as if to distribute it to the earth, spin away their earthly ties.

Dervishes spin to attain a trance-like state.

Following Mustapha Kemal Atatürk's overthrow of the Ottoman Empire in 1924, the Mevlevi order was banned as an obstacle to Turkey's modernization. After an interruption of 25 years, a group of dervishes convinced the local Konya government to once again allow the performance of "the turn" as a cultural performance. The Mevlana Monastery is now a museum containing the elaborate tomb of Rumi, making it a pilgrimage site for Muslims who venerate the saint. Non-Muslim tourists are also welcome.

Konya, considered one of Turkey's most conservative cities, is also home to some of the country's most important medieval mosques and buildings. These monuments are legacies of the Seljuks, an enlightened Turkic tribe that ruled much of Anatolia for 300 years, beginning in the 11th century.

WHERE: 170 miles/274 km west of Cappodocia. **WHERE TO STAY:** The Dedeman Konya is a modern hotel just outside the center of town, with great views. Tel 90/332-221-6600; www.dedeman.com. *Cost:* from $75. **HOW:** Argeus Tourism & Travel can help secure accommodation or tickets to the Mevlana Festival. Tel 90/384-341-4688; www.argeus.com.tr. **WHEN:** 10 days mid-Dec, culminating on Dec 17, the day of the master's death.

Looking for St. Nick on the Lycian Coast

PATARA AND DEMRE

Turkey

Children around the world would be astonished to learn that Santa Claus hails not from the winter wonderland of the North Pole but from Turkey's sultry Mediterranean coast. St. Nicholas—to use his proper name—was born at Patara, now better known for its beautifully pristine, 11-mile stretch of dune-studded white sand beach on today's fashionable Lycian Coast. In the time of St. Nick, the 3rd century, Patara was waning as one of the Mediterranean's most important ports, developed over the centuries by the Lycians, Greeks, and Romans. In its heyday, however, St. Paul changed ships at Patara en route to Jerusalem, and gladiators fought at the amphitheater; it stands today, well preserved, in Patara National Park.

St. Nicholas eventually made his way to nearby Demre, where he was appointed regional bishop and served until his death in A.D. 343. The church built on the site where he is believed to have preached is now named in his honor and dates mainly from the 8th century. It was restored in 1043 by the Byzantines and again in 1862 by Tsar Nicholas I and has become a popular pilgrimage site for Russian tourists.

Today the rugged coastline between Patara and Demre abounds in excellent resort hotels and inns, nestled in the hills or in the picturesque Mediterranean villages that are now trendy holiday destinations. Perched atop a steep bluff outside the well-heeled village of Kalkan, secluded Villa Mahal is one of Turkey's finest coastal hotels. Chic, minimalist rooms all have inspiring views of Kalkan and the Mediterranean, some with their own infinity pools and a private beach club 181 steps below. In contrast, Hoyran Wedre Country House, on the coast 10 miles west of Demre, is an idyllic rural oasis of stone buildings spread over fields of aromatic plants. The hotel—actually a cluster of traditional-style houses—sits 1,640 feet up in the Taurus Mountains, with fantastic views of the sea. Antiques decorate the 16 rooms and public areas, and superb meals are prepared from products sourced or raised locally such as freshly made yogurt or lamb sautéed with oregano, green chile peppers, and homemade olive oil—all from the hotel's grounds.

WHERE: Patara is 60 miles/95 km west of Demre and 603 miles/970 km south of Istanbul. **VILLA MAHAL:** Tel 90/242-844-3268; www.villamahal.com. *Cost:* from $285 (off-peak), from $325 (peak). **HOYRAN WEDRE COUNTRY HOUSE:** Tel 90/242-875-1125; www.hoyran.com. *Cost:* from $145. **BEST TIMES:** May and Oct–Dec for visiting ruins in cooler weather; Jun–Sep for swimming; Dec 6 for the feast of St. Nicholas.

The 8th-century Church of St. Nicholas contains the saint's tomb as well as the original nave and altar.

Pilgrimage to a Solemn World War I Battleground

GALLIPOLI

Thrace, Turkey

It's not difficult to imagine that ghosts still haunt Gallipoli nearly a century after the greatest Allied disaster of World War I. Many visitors still come today to pay homage to the 130,000 men killed and 400,000 wounded during the 9-month battle in 1915 to gain control of the Dardanelles, the narrow and strategically important sea lane that connects the Black Sea with the Mediterranean.

For Australians and New Zealanders, whose soldiers were drawn into their first global conflict, the battlefield has assumed an almost holy stature. Turks too flock to Gallipoli (known in Turkish as Gelibolu) to honor the victory by Lieutenant Colonel Mustafa Kemal (later known as Atatürk, "Father of Turks") over the Western armies. His triumph paved the way, 8 years later, for the creation of modern Turkey from the ashes of the Ottoman Empire.

There are more than 50 Allied and Turkish war cemeteries and memorials scattered along the rugged 22-mile peninsula, which today is a peaceful national park covered in brush and pine forests. On April 25, thousands of Australians and New Zealanders come for the annual memorial service at Anzac Cove, the disastrous landing site of their troops.

Although Gallipoli can be seen on a long day trip from Istanbul, an overnight stay at one of the charming inns in the area allows one to feel the character of the place more fully. The amiable Belgian owner of Gallipoli Houses (Gelibolu Evleri), a history buff and Gallipoli expert, and his wife, a superb cook, make the ten tastefully furnished rooms a perfect base from which to explore the area. End the day by gazing at the stars from the hotel's rooftop terrace, with a glass of local wine and a newfound sense of history.

WHERE: 192 miles/309 km southwest of Istanbul. **VISITOR INFO:** www.gallipoli-association.org. **GALLIPOLI HOUSES:** Tel 90/286-814-2650; www.gallipoli.com.tr. *Cost:* from $110; dinner $20. **BEST TIMES:** Mar–May and Sep–Oct (the period around Apr 25, Anzac Day, is crowded).

Color and Chaos in the Desert

Tolkuchka Bazaar

Ashgabat, Turkmenistan

The Central Asian state of Turkmenistan is the home of one of the world's least known and most reclusive societies, ruled for 15 years by Saparmyrat Nyýazow, a president-for-life eccentric who renamed the months after family members. He dubbed himself Türkmenbaşy ("Father of All Turkmen") and erected a 40-foot-tall gold statue in his image that rotates to face the sun. Türkmenbaşy is now an uncomfortable memory (he passed away unexpectedly in 2006), and this former Soviet republic is slowly revealing itself as a fascinating, if enigmatic, country, largely trapped in time. Isolated and reticent toward foreigners (visitors are required to have a guide at all times), it offers serene desert landscapes and a fascinating history along the Silk Road, the ancient network of trade routes that ran from China to the Mediterranean Sea.

It also has the unparalleled Tolkuchka Bazaar, one of the largest markets in Central Asia, near the capital city of Ashgabat and a throwback to the marketplaces that have dotted this area for millennia. You can buy anything here—horses, camels, produce, and more—but the main draw for centuries has been carpets. Marco Polo wrote home about these beauties in the 13th century, commenting on their intricacy, workmanship, and rich colors; the quality of the craftsmanship is still unrivaled. Most are hand-woven locally in the age-old tradition and naturally dyed, but be on the lookout for factory-produced imitations. Although the prevailing style of carpet draws its name from the Uzbek city of Bukhara (where they have long been traditionally sold), these rugs have always been made in Turkmenistan. The best specimens, utilizing tribal designs, are used to cover the floors and walls of nomadic Turkmen's yurts.

Oriental rugs—the finest of which are handmade—have drawn shoppers to the bazaar since the 13th century.

Even if you aren't in the market for a rug, the bazaar is a feast for the senses. Rows of predominantly red carpets in all sizes contrast brilliantly with an invariably blue desert sky and the tawny tones of the surrounding landscape. Wizened old men smile through gold teeth and women stroll the aisles in colorful robes and silk headscarves. The smells of freshly cut melon, lamb kebabs, camel dung, wool, and *plov* (an Uzbek rice dish) waft through the air.

Customarily a Sunday market, these days the Tolkuchka Bazaar springs to life on Thursdays and Saturdays as well. In 2011, the Turkmen government opened a massive new bazaar, Altyn Asyr, nearby. Ashgabat is a jumping-off point for trips to the ancient ruins of Merv or for an exploration of neighboring Uzbekistan (see next page).

Where: 415 miles/669 km northeast of Tehran. **How:** U.S.-based Geographic Expeditions includes Ashgabat and the

Sunday market on many of its trips to Central Asia. Tel 800-777-8183 or 415-922-0448; www.geoex.com. *Cost:* 15-day trip from $5,250, all-inclusive. Originates in Ashgabat. **Best times:** Apr–Jun and Sep–Nov are sunny but not too hot.

Holy City Suspended in Time

Bukhara

Uzbekistan

As a key stop along the ancient trade route between China and the West, Bukhara became one of the holiest cities in the Muslim world by the 10th century. It declined, courtesy of Genghis Khan, then returned with a vengeance in the 16th century, eventually becoming—along with Kokand and Khiva (see next page)—one of Central Asia's three dominant khanates (kingdoms).

Blue domes flank the entrance of Mir-i-Arab, which was founded in the 16th century and continues to function as a madrassa today.

The most pious of the three, Bukhara was also the cruelest. A string of ruling emirs (1785–1920) terrorized neighboring states and their own subjects with equal rapacity. Enemies were tossed off of Bukhara's 155-foot-high Kalon Minaret (Tower of Death), built in 1127 and still standing—one of the few buildings not destroyed by Genghis Khan. The emirs were also voracious builders, erecting hundreds of mosques, madrassas (Islamic schools and colleges), caravansaries, and covered bazaars. Many of the madrassas are masterpieces, with towering, arched entrance portals splashed with blue tile work. The holiest and most spectacular of these is the Mir-i-Arab Madrassa, opposite the Kalon Minaret. Its luminous blue domes jump out against the pale brick that dominates the city's skyline.

Compared with nearby Samarkand (see p. 589), Bukhara's architecture is more subtle and austere. Remarkably, the Old Town remains as thoroughly lived-in as it was 500 years ago, providing the best insight on pre-Russian Uzbekistan: As you wander the residential area's maze of narrow, mud-brick alleys, you'll encounter hidden mosques, splendid 19th-century homes, and even old synagogues. Outside the protected center are more architectural gems, like the 1,000-year-old Ismail Samani Mausoleum and the opulent summer palace of the last Bukaran emir.

Bukhara B&Bs are characterful and wonderfully affordable. Many of them occupy 19th-century mansions bearing the hallmarks of "Bukhara style"—alabaster walls covered with intricate carvings, porticoes supported by handsome wood columns, and courtyards filled with pomegranate and other fruit trees. The Amulet Hotel is a preserved madrassa, where the students' rooms have been converted into welcoming quarters, complete with 21st-century amenities.

Where: 167 miles/269 km west of Samarkand. **Amulet Hotel:** Tel 998/65-224-5342; www.amulet-hotel.com. *Cost:* $60. **Best times:** Mar–Apr and Sep–Nov for cool weather; early May for Silk & Spices Festival, which celebrates local music and folk art.

Time Travel in a Silk Road Capital

Khiva

Uzbekistan

For over two millennia, the Silk Road linked the Mediterranean and China, allowing caravans laden with spices, perfumes, jewels, medicines, and precious textiles to traverse the forbidding deserts and mountain valleys of Central Asia. East of the Caspian Sea, in the midst of the Karakum desert, it passed through the oasislike valley of Khorezm and on to its resplendent capital, Khiva, a monumental city that was fabled for its extravagant wealth, haunting beauty, and often harsh despotism.

The mile-long walls of Ichan-Kala, Khiva's well-preserved inner city, evoke its medieval origins.

The finest showcase of medieval Islamic architecture in Central Asia and the best-preserved city on the old Silk Road, Khiva rises miragelike from the desert, an ancient, walled fortress built from the soil on which it stands. According to legend, the city was founded by Shem, the son of Noah, though archaeological excavations indicate that the first settlement here arose about 2,500 years ago. The city first flourished as a trade center around A.D. 1000. Its central location later propelled it to notoriety: From the 17th through the 19th century, Khiva was home to Central Asia's primary slave market.

Perhaps Khiva's most impressive feature is the fortified Ichan-Kala, its vast royal court surrounded by crenellated clay-brick walls that reach 33 feet high and extend for a protective mile. Embraced within are the city's maze of palaces, mosques, minarets, madrassas, and other ancient structures, many elaborately decorated with delicate majolica tiles in varying shades of blue. During the Soviet era, Khiva received a thorough restoration, and, though beautifully intact, many areas are as ghostly as a museum. The oldest structures date back over 1,000 years, including the Kuhna Ark, the Old Citadel, built as a palace for Khiva's rulers, with harems, stables, throne room, and a jail lined with manacles for holding slaves and prisoners. Established in the 10th century, the Djuma Mosque is supported by a forest of more than 200 wooden pillars, many carved with intricate, spiraling motifs. Another of Khiva's striking monuments is the Pahlavan Mahmoud Mausoleum, a series of royal burial tombs that are a masterpiece of graceful architecture and proverb-inscribed tiles, whose deep turquoise color matches the extraordinary blue of the desert sky.

Where: 635 miles/1,025 km west of the

capital city of Tashkent. **Where to stay:** Hotel Malika has comfortable modern rooms just outside the Ichan-Kala walls. Tel 998/ 6237-52665; www.malika-khiva.com. *Cost:* from $70. **Best times:** Mar–May and Sep–Nov to avoid the heat; early May for the Asrlar Sadosi (Echoes of Ages) Festival, a celebration of traditional Uzbek art and culture.

Crossroads of Culture in the "Rome of the East"

Samarkand

Uzbekistan

Like Athens or Jerusalem, the name Samarkand evokes images of medieval armies, ancient architectural wonders, and bygone splendor. It was a romantic destination even for the Greeks: "Everything I have heard about [Samarkand] is true, except that it is even more beautiful than I ever imagined," effused Alexander the Great in 329 B.C.

Part of the Registan, Tilla Kari Madrassa is adorned with intricate mosaics.

The city was once an important desert stop on the ancient Silk Road, despite the periodic attacks by foreign invaders. Unsurprisingly, Genghis Khan topped them all by reducing the city to rubble in 1220. Tamerlane the Great (Timur Lenk), born not far from here in 1330, bucked the trend of destruction by restoring the city and made it the capital of his vast empire.

Tamerlane's greatest architectural legacy is the mausoleum of the Timurid dynasty, the colossal Gūr-e Amīr. The dead have it good in Samarkand. Besides Tamerlane's magnificent mausoleum, the city is also home to the Sha-i-Zinda, a huge necropolis containing dozens of others, each one seemingly more detailed and intricate than the last. The cemetery is built around the tomb of Qussam Ibn Abbas, a cousin of Mohammed who is said to have brought Islam to the region in the 7th century. Nearby stands the Bibi Khanum mosque. Distinguished by a massive dome, it is dedicated to the memory of Tamerlane's favorite wife.

Samarkand's pièce de résistance, however, is the Registan, a glorious ensemble of three madrassas (Islamic colleges) that flank a vast, sun-drenched square. Every inch of these buildings is covered with mosaics and highly stylized arabesque designs, which, along with their turquoise domes, soaring minarets, and timeless sense of grandeur, have awed visitors for centuries. For a small fee the guards allow visitors to climb the twisting staircases to the top of a minaret, affording wonderful views of the Registan and square below and the adjacent bazaar. Here life and trade continue much as they did in the heyday of the Silk Road, when spices such as peppercorns and saffron were more valuable than gold.

Where: 170 miles/275 km southwest of Tashkent. **Where to stay:** Hotel Malika Samarkand is a comfortable choice and a 10-minute walk to most attractions. Tel 998/662-330197; www.malika-samarkand.com. *Cost:* from $65. **How:** U.S.-based MIR Corp., with an office in Tashkent, specializes in small-group tours and independent travel to Central Asia. Tel 800-424-7289 or 206-624-7289; www.mircorp.com. *Cost:* 15-day tours from $4,195. Originates in Tashkent. *When:* departures May and Sep. **Best times:** Apr–May and Sep for nicest weather.

SOUTHEAST ASIA

A Colonial Coastal Retreat

KEP

Cambodia

Unlike other getaway destinations enjoyed by the colonial French in Indochina, the Cambodian seaside town of Kep is not a cool-weather hill station. The French residents of old Saigon may have ventured to Da Lat for verdant valleys and bracing mountain air (see p. 632), but the appeal of Kep-sur-Mer (Kep by the Sea) has always been its wonderful beaches. From the 1900s to the 1960s, colonials journeyed to Kep from Phnom Penh, yet it's only in recent years that this sleepy resort on the Gulf of Thailand has truly awakened from its tropical slumber. The graceful arc of the island's main beach still seems transplanted from an early-20th-century French daydream. With its broad pedestrian corniche punctuated by graceful wrought-iron lamps, it is blissfully free of modern distractions. On public holidays, families crowd here and float contentedly on rubber tubes. But any French reverie is tempered with telling reminders that you're definitely in Asia: From bamboo shelters fringing the beach come freshly grilled platters of local seafood, while sheets of the region's prized peppercorns (revered by the top chefs of Paris) lie drying in the tropical sun. Troops of monkeys patrol the trees near the clifftop ruins of King Sihanouk's former summer villa.

Kep's low-key beaches are a local treasure.

A century on from Kep's beginnings as a *station climatique* for the French, it's now been rediscovered by Phnom Penh's expat smart set. Leading Kep's resurrection as a luxury destination is the gorgeous Knai Bang Chatt, a trio of restored 1960s Modernist villas just across from the beach. Housing 11 air-conditioned rooms and including a spa and a lovely infinity pool, it is one of Cambodia's finest, most relaxing boutique hotels. The adjacent Sailing Club restaurant and bar is the perfect ending to a day out on the water. Or, on a forested hill overlooking Kep, the Veranda Natural Resort has stylish bungalows and a palm tree–shaded pool.

There's still not a lot to do in Kep. You can check out the afternoon crab market, trek to the monkey-populated jungle of Kep National Park, sail in a local fishing boat to nearby Koh Tonsay (Rabbit Island) for immaculate beaches, snorkeling, and grilled fresh prawns—or just while away the hours poolside in a hammock, waiting for another perfect sunset.

WHERE: 105 miles/170 km south of Phnom Penh. **KNAI BANG CHATT:** Tel 855/12-349-742; www.knaibangchatt.com. *Cost:* from $135; dinner at the Sailing Club $20. **VERANDA NATURAL RESORT:** Tel 855/33-399-035; www.veranda-resort.com. *Cost:* from $50. **BEST TIMES:** Dec–Jan is the coolest period; the wet season is May–Oct.

Khmer Treasures in a City Rediscovering Itself

THE SILVER PAGODA

Phnom Penh, Cambodia

Once considered the loveliest of the French-built cities of Indochina, Phnom Penh still retains much of its charm despite the violence of Cambodia's late-20th-century history. A recent influx of foreign investors has brought change, but this city still moves at a relatively languid pace. French-Colonial buildings line the city's easygoing thoroughfares, many restored and housing restaurants, cafés, and hotels.

In the midst of the city is the sprawling Royal Palace. Some of the complex, still home to Cambodian royalty, is off-limits to visitors, but you can visit the grounds, a few buildings, and one of the country's most magnificent sites: the Silver Pagoda, a rare showcase for the brilliance of Khmer art and civilization. Pol Pot, the 1970s Communist prime minister, destroyed most of the art in the palace but not the life-size gold Buddha, weighing close to 200 pounds and adorned with more than 9,500 diamonds. More Cambodian treasures are displayed at the National Museum, a Khmer-style open-sided pavilion just a pleasant stroll away, including 15th-century Buddha statues from the period following the fall of Angkor, the seat of the Khmer Empire, to the start of the Thai kingdom in 1431, providing an interesting counterpoint to what you'll see at Angkor Wat (see next page).

Like Angkor's bustling tourist town of Siem Reap, Phnom Penh offers a growing range of excellent accommodations. Originally built in 1929 and reopened after significant restoration in 1997, Raffles Le Royal is the city's most gracious and elegant hotel—a drink in its Elephant Bar is infused with the glamour and romance of old Indochine. The Pavilion is a smaller, more intimate colonial property, with just 20 comfortable rooms a stone's throw from the Royal Palace.

Stop by the FCC (Foreign Correspondents Club), a Colonial-style bar-restaurant cooled by slowly spinning ceiling fans and tropical breezes from the Mekong River. Order a chilled Angkor beer or a dry martini and take in the views of bustling Sisowath Quay below. It's a good place to catch up on the local expat gossip, and there are often excellent documentary-style photo exhibits on view. The FCC has a few guest rooms, but a better option is its sister property The Quay. A stylish hotel just one block away in a modern riverside building, it features eco-friendly design touches and the sophisticated Chow restaurant, specializing in small-plate spins on regional southeast Asian flavors.

NATIONAL MUSEUM OF CAMBODIA: Tel 855/23-217-643; www.cambodiamuseum.info. **RAFFLES HOTEL LE ROYAL:** Tel 855/23-981-888; in the U.S., 800-768-9009; www.raffles.com. *Cost:* from $215 (off-peak), from $290 (peak). **THE PAVILION:** Tel 855/23-222-280;

Part of the Royal Palace complex, the Silver Pagoda contains silver floors and crystal and diamond-encrusted Buddhas.

www.thepavilion.asia. *Cost:* from $90. **FCC:** Tel 855/23-724-014; www.fcccambodia.com. **THE QUAY:** Tel 855/23-992-284; www.thequayhotel.com. *Cost:* suites with river views from $130; dinner at Chow $20. **BEST TIMES:** Nov–Feb for the cooler, dry season; mid-Apr for celebration of Khmer New Year; late Nov for Bon Om Tuk Water Festival.

A Temple City Reborn

ANGKOR WAT

Siem Reap, Cambodia

One of the world's premier architectural sites, Angkor's temples and monuments encompass an area of about 40 square miles in northwestern Cambodia. The capital of the powerful Khmer Empire from A.D. 800 to approximately 1200, the site was abandoned in 1431 following the conquest of the Khmer kingdom by the Thai kingdom. Today Angkor is enjoyed by more visitors than ever thanks to the extended peace following the dark days of the murderous Khmer Rouge regime (1975–1979).

Now notable for the tree roots that engulf it, Ta Prohm was built in 1156 and once held a priceless cache of pearls and precious stones.

Angkor's grand scale means it's still possible to experience your own private slice of centuries-old Khmer grandeur. The area's uncontested highlight is Angkor Wat, a vast temple complex built at the beginning of the 12th century. It took 25,000 workers more than 37 years to complete, but after the fall of the empire it was unknown to the outside world—and remained so until 1860, when French botanist Henri Mouhot stumbled upon it deep in the jungle. Cambodians revere the site, whose iconic profile is featured on the national flag, and it's especially important to Buddhists. Teenage monks are a common sight here, their vibrant saffron robes standing out from Angkor Wat's austere gray stonework and the shadowed waters of the moat surrounding the main temple.

At the heart of nearby Angkor Thom is the Bayon, the last great temple built at Angkor. Mimicking the sacred Mount Meru at the center of the Hindu-mythology universe, the Bayon rises through three imposing levels with numerous towers featuring multiple carvings of massive, serene faces at the top. About a mile east of the Bayon, the much photographed Ta Prohm temple complex is a labyrinth of porticoes and halls that is slowly being entombed by the massive roots of ancient trees.

Before the tragedies of the Khmer Rouge period, Angkor was a favored destination for colonial French travelers. Now the nearby town of Siem Reap is a travelers' hub with a growing number of new resorts and boutique hotels. But the restored 1930s colonial splendor of Raffles Grand Hotel d'Angkor—

featuring an inviting spa and a grand pool set within 14 acres of gardens—is still its greatest historical throwback. Though its 120 rooms make it one of the town's largest colonial hotels, the service is still personal.

The riverside La Résidence d'Angkor is built in traditional Khmer style, and it is one of the resorts nearest to the temples. With 62 balconied rooms and suites, a lush walled garden with a pool at its center, and a highly rated spa, it's an enticing oasis located right in town. A more intimate boutique option is the Pavillon d'Orient, with 18 tastefully furnished rooms in a French Colonial-style mansion with a pool and spa just 5 minutes from central Siem Reap.

Where: 196 miles/315 km northwest of Phnom Penh. **How:** U.S.-based Asia Transpacific Journeys offers custom and group trips to Cambodia. Tel 800-642-2742 or 303-443-678; www.asiatranspacific.com. *Cost:* land costs average $325 per person per day. **Raffles Grand Hotel d'Angkor:** Tel 855/63-963-888; in the U.S., 800-768-9009; www.raffles.com. *Cost:* from $240 (off-peak), from $300 (peak). **La Résidence d'Angkor:** Tel 855/63-963-390; www.residencedangkor.com. *Cost:* from $245 (off-peak), from $345 (peak). **Pavillon d'Orient:** Tel 855/63-760-646; www.pavillon-orient-hotel.com. *Cost:* from $100. **Best time:** Nov–May for dry season.

Oceanfront Escapes on the Island of the Gods

Beaches of Bali

Bali, Indonesia

Beautiful Bali is justly celebrated for its palm-fringed beaches. In the south, the graceful arc of Jimbaran Bay is an antidote to the nightclub-enhanced shopping mall that Kuta Beach is slowly becoming, and the best way to cap off a day spent there is with dinner at one of the simple alfresco seafood restaurants nearby. Choose from large tanks or among the offerings presented on mounds of ice—prawns, lobster, and squid are all popular—and wait for it to be cooked at a surfside table with your toes in the sand. On the bay's southern edge, Four Seasons Jimbaran Bay is a luxurious resort masquerading as a traditional Balinese village. Breezy, bougainvillea-covered guest villas cascade down its terraced hillside leading to a 4-mile white crescent beach. Arrange for a *lulur* treatment, and look forward to being exfoliated from head to toe with sandalwood and spices, splashed with yogurt, then taking a soak in a bath infused with flower petals. The drama—and rates—drop a few notches at the small and welcoming Jamahal Private Resort & Spa, where the spirit of Bali still prevails and where the pampering staff is unfailingly gracious.

On the island's northwest coast, Lovina Beach is a quieter alternative to the energetic south coast. Dolphin-watching is a highlight, easily arranged through any of a cluster of hotels, including Sunari Villas & Spa Resort, but be prepared to get up early—the creatures are most frequently sighted just after sunrise. The nearby town of Singaraja offers a glimpse into the days of Dutch colonial rule, with tree-lined streets, whitewashed architecture, and a charming old waterfront where nothing much happens—very, very slowly. An easy 2-hour drive west is Pulau Menjangan (Deer Island), renowned for scuba diving, but also a great place for snorkeling, with straight-off-the-beach access to an underwater wall teeming with tropical fish. East of Lovina are some of Bali's less discovered beaches. The Amed area is a series of compact coves dotted with fishing villages.

From Amed, it's possible to travel a beautiful coast road around Bali's eastern tip back to the south coast. As you drive between the imposing volcanic profile of Mount Seraya and the aquamarine waters of the Bali Sea, you realize you could only be on the Island of the Gods.

WHERE: Jimbaran Bay is 5 miles/8 km south of Denpasar. Singharaja is 62 miles/100 km north of Denpasar. **FOUR SEASONS JIMBARAN BAY:** Tel 62/361-701-010; in the U.S., 800-332-3442; www.fourseasons.com. *Cost:* villas from $680. **JAMAHAL PRIVATE RESORT & SPA:** Tel 62/361-704-394; www.jamahal.net. *Cost:* from $290. **SUNARI VILLAS:** Tel 62/362-41775; www.sunari.com. *Cost:* from $90. **BEST TIME:** Apr–Oct is dry season.

Bali's Capital of Art and Culture

UBUD

Bali, Indonesia

The island of Bali stands out in Indonesia not only for its beautiful landscapes but also for its sophisticated Hindu art and culture. The Balinese have always believed that the gods live in the mountains and this is as good a reason as any to leave the busy beach areas of Kuta and Sanur and head north into the hills.

For years, Ubud has been known as the capital of Bali's artistic heritage, a significant distinction on an island where art is everywhere and everyone lives to create and embellish as a way of honoring the gods. The town still possesses much of the allure that first drew European painters and sculptors in the 1920s. Jump onto a ramshackle *bemo* (minibus) packed with locals and chickens, and get off beyond Ubud's congested main strip to take in its fabled rice fields; the same farmers you see cultivating terraced rice paddies by hand may be the very performers or musicians you see in tonight's temple dance. Or journey by bicycle for a closer look at village life. And if you're after more excitement, join a river-rafting trip down Ubud's Ayung River, past towering cliffs and cascading waterfalls.

One of Ubud's unexpected attractions is its sophisticated restaurant scene. One of the front-runners, Mozaic, opened in 2001 and is well-known for its six-course Discovery Menu, an exotic introduction to the world of delicate Balinese flavors. It might even tempt you to sign up for cooking classes at Paon Bali in the nearby village of Laplapan—you'll start with a visit to a market to gather ingredients before repairing to the kitchen to prepare an elaborate feast.

Ubud's compelling mix of accommodations ranges from basic home stays to exquisite resorts that rank among the world's finest. The Amandari, an idealized adaptation of a walled Balinese village, is more retreat than hotel. The reception area, an open thatch-roofed building, recalls a *wantilan*, or traditional meeting hall, while its pool hugs the contours of the surrounding emerald green rice paddy terraces, overlooking the Ayung River and the valley beyond. Those same inspiring rice-field views are yours from Waka di Ume, while at the stylish Purist Villas, luxury is found in Ayurvedic massage, yoga, and meditation classes.

WHERE: 14 miles/23 km north of Denpasar. **HOW:** U.S.-based Back Roads offers 8-day tours including biking, river rafting, and snorkeling. Tel 800-462-2848 or 510-527-1555; www.backroads.com. *Cost:*

$3,800, all-inclusive. Originates in Ubud. **Mozaic:** Tel 62/361-975-768; www.mozaic-bali.com. *Cost:* 6-course dinner $70. **Paon Bali:** Tel 62/81-337-939095; www.paon-bali.com. *Cost:* half-day class from $45. **Amandari:** Tel 62/361-975-333; in the U.S., 800-477-9180; www.amanresorts.com. *Cost:* from $850. **Waka di Ume:** Tel 62/361-973-178; www.wakadiume.com. *Cost:* from $305. **Purist Villas:** Tel 62/361-974-454; www.thepuristvillas.com. *Cost:* from $240. **Best times:** Apr–Oct for the dry season; May–Jun for Rice Harvest Festival in rural villages; mid-Jun–mid-Jul for Bali Arts Festival.

Discovering Java's Hindu-Buddhist Past

Borobudur and Prambanan

Java, Indonesia

The hike to the top of the Buddhist monument of Borobudur, a 1-hour clockwise path from base to apex, takes pilgrims through the three levels of Buddhist cosmology: the worlds of desire, form, and formlessness. Ideally, the journey ends with complete detachment from the here and now—a concept that's not hard to grasp when you're hit with the powerful 360-degree panorama, including a quartet of active volcanos.

Construction probably began around 800, during the era of the devoutly Buddhist Sailendra dynasty; it is thought to have taken 75 years to complete. Mysteriously, Borobudur was abandoned only 200 years later, possibly as a result of its being partially buried in ash from the eruption of nearby Mount Merapi in 1006. It lay undisturbed in the overgrown jungle for centuries until the site was rediscovered by the British in 1814.

A massive UNESCO-directed restoration was completed in 1983, refurbishing more than 3 miles of hand-carved reliefs representing the Buddhist universe of worldly, spiritual, and heavenly spheres that wrap around the pyramidal structure's ten terraces. The higher levels are studded with 72 bell-shaped stupas and more than 400 Buddhas, which give Borobudur, the world's largest Buddhist monument, its prickly-porcupine silhouette. Five minutes by car from Borobudur, the Amanjiwo resort echoes the circular layout of the monument, which is visible from the lushly landscaped grounds. Amanjiwo translates to "peaceful soul," a state of mind effortlessly achieved after one of the resort's traditional Javanese massages. Another of Amanjiwo's draws is the chance it offers to visit Borobudur at dawn, but if you stay at the welcoming hotel Manohra, you are considerably closer—just steps from the temple entrance. Rise before the sun to watch the mist rise off the rice fields and densely packed coconut plantations, revealing the silhouettes of Borobudur and the volcanoes in the distance.

The 9th-century Borobudur features more than 500 statues of Buddha, all in the lotus position.

Around 37 miles southeast of Borobudur is another revered ancient monument: The Hindu site of Prambanan is a 9th-century complex of more than 200 temples and shrines, eight of which have been restored. In the dry season, during the full moon and the nights leading to it, Prambanan becomes the floodlit backdrop for a cast of hundreds that performs the Ramayana ballet before a transfixed audience.

WHERE: 26 miles/42 km northwest of Yogyakarta. **AMANJIWO:** Tel 62/293-788-333; in the U.S., 800-477-9180; www.amanresorts.com. *Cost:* from $750. **MANOHRA:** Tel 62/293-788-680; www.manohraborobudur.com. *Cost:* from $75. **BEST TIMES:** Apr–Oct for the dry season; during the full moon in May for Waisak festival, celebrating the Buddha's birthday; May–Oct for performances at Prambanan.

Keeper of Javanese Heritage

YOGYAKARTA

Java, Indonesia

In the lush central region of Java, under the smoldering glare of the Mount Merapi volcano, lies the flourishing art center and university city of Yogyakarta. Known to Indonesians simply as Yogya, this cultural hub and the nearby city of Solo are still ruled by sultans, whose sprawling *kratons* (palaces) are fascinating windows into 18th-century Islamic court life. Visits to the kratons often include performances of gamelan music, which has been described as "the sound of moonlight." Mesmerizing gamelan orchestras sometimes feature up to 80 performers on xylophones, gongs, and bamboo flutes. Exquisite classical dance productions, which originated in these very palaces, are still attended by members of the royal family and their batik-uniformed court retainers.

Royal patronage also helps keep alive Javanese decorative arts, and workshops are everywhere: Intricate silverware, leather *wayang* shadow puppets, and colorful batiks make shopping the city's many *pasar* (bazaars) a challenge for those with limited suitcase space. What doesn't tempt your eye will tantalize your palate—Yogya's street eats are ubiquitous and renowned. Flag down one of the passing *warungs*, the mobile street vendors who sizzle up noodles, satays, curries, and sweets. Try a hot *lumpia ayam* (chicken spring roll) and some fresh *kelepons* (sweet rice-flour rolls in shredded coconut).

The wandering traveler in Yogya is guaranteed to stumble upon poetry recitals, folk music, underground art galleries, and even ballet troupes in backstreet taverns. Just take a *jalan-jalan* (walk) around the old quarter and wind up at the Colonial-style Phoenix Hotel. The Raffles of Yogya, it was built in 1918 and is now a restored and relaxing haven from the busy streets. Or stay at Yogya's most intimate accommodation, Villa Hanis, a traditional wooden Javanese two-bedroom house with a private garden and small swimming pool. The well-known bakery and restaurant next door serves European-style breads and salads. Located about 3 miles from busy downtown, it's an ideal base for visiting Borobudur and Prambanan (see previous page).

WHERE: 370 miles/595 km southeast of Jakarta. **THE PHOENIX HOTEL:** Tel 62/274-566-617; www.mgallery.com. *Cost:* from $105. **VILLA HANIS:** Tel 62/274-867-567; www.villahanis.com. *Cost:* $110. **BEST TIMES:** Apr–Oct for the dry season; Jul for Gamelan Festival.

Into the Dragons' Den

KOMODO NATIONAL PARK

Komodo, Indonesia

Komodo Island, a mere 150 square miles and with a population of just 2,000, is the nearest thing to a 21st-century Jurassic Park. It was established as a national park in 1980 to protect *Varanus komodoensis,* better known as the Komodo dragon, the largest lizard in the world, which grows to between 6 and 10 feet long and weighs in at around 150 pounds.

The islands of the Komodo archipelago are among the most arid in Indonesia and are home to an extraordinary mix of Asian and Austronesian wildlife. (The nearby Wallace Line marks the maritime division between the two continents.) Besides the dragons, the park is home to Timor deer (the main prey of the dragons), wild horses, wild boar, long-tailed macaques, palm civets, and giant fruit bats. The latter, which have a wingspan of around 4 feet, make an unforgettable sight as they leave their roosts at twilight to feed. Komodo also has one of the world's richest marine environments, with dolphins, whales, dugongs, sea turtles, more than 1,000 species of fish, and 250 types of coral—and, not surprisingly, spectacular diving and snorkeling.

It is both obligatory and sensible to visit the park as part of a guided tour—Komodo dragons are very dangerous, as are the island's hooded cobras and Russell's pit vipers. The professional guides know the park intimately, and, armed with a sturdy forked staff, provide protection from them all.

Komodo dragons are also found on nearby Rinca, a smaller and less visited island, better known for its diving and snorkeling. If you're inclined to strap on a mask, head straight to the safe and clear waters off Pantai Merah, or Pink Beach.

WHERE: 340 miles/550 km east of Bali. **HOW:** U.S.-based Asia Transpacific Journeys includes Komodo and Rinca as part of their 17-day "Bali and Beyond" tour. Tel 800-642-2742 or 303-443-6789; www.asiatranspacific.com. *Cost:* $8,395, all-inclusive. Originates in Bali. Bali-based Perama Travel offers 5-day "Hunting Komodo by Camera" boat tours departing from Lombok and visiting other islands en route to Komodo and Rinca. Tel 62/361-750-808; www.peramatour.com. *Cost:* cabins from $470, inclusive. **BEST TIME:** Apr–Oct for the dry season.

An Evolving Alternative to Bali

LOMBOK AND THE GILI ISLANDS

Lombok, Indonesia

There is a saying: "You may find Bali in Lombok, but you'll never find Lombok in Bali." True, the island may not have Bali's Hindu temples, processions, and colorful festivals, but its welcome is just as warm, and its unhurried pace, unspoiled beauty, and relative lack of commercial tourism make it a compelling alternative.

Lombok is slightly smaller than Bali and markedly different in character. The local Sasak people are Muslim, and the climate is drier, with sparse vegetation. Just off the northwest coast, the three smaller Gili islands are evolving from being favorites of the beach-loving backpacker set to providing more sophisticated hotel and dining options for discerning travelers. Opportunities for excellent diving and snorkeling also abound. On Gili Trawangan's quieter and more rugged north coast, the Desa Dunia Beda eco-resort fronts a private beach and features three relocated and restored wooden Javanese bungalows outfitted with colonial-era furniture.

The 3-day trek to the top of volcanic 12,224-foot Mount Rinjani in the north of Lombok is considered one of the best climbs in the area. Less athletic visitors settle for a guided 4-hour hike along pathways that follow the contours of terraced rice paddies through farming villages to 150-foot waterfalls. On the northwest coast, private sailing and motor boat outings can be arranged on Medana Beach. Take a day trip around the island and stop in the coves on the southern coast, where surfers and kite boarders challenge the forces of nature.

Lombok's finer accommodations can be found in Senggigi Beach. The relatively new Quinci Villas, with their minimalist, modern design and perfect beachfront location, are among the most stylish.

Outrigger canoes set sail from Senggigi Beach.

A few more excellent hotels can be found on other parts of the island. The Oberoi Lombok is spread luxuriously across 24 beachside acres on Medana Beach, offering 20 thatch-roofed, Lombok-style villas with huge marble baths and private pools. Consider indulging in the spa's Mandi Lulur treatment, which combines relaxing steam heat with aromatherapy and the therapeutic effects of mud.

Where: 40 miles/64 km east of Bali. **Desa Dunia Beda:** Tel 62/370-641-575; www.desaduniabeda.com. *Cost:* from $95 (off-peak), from $130 (peak). **Quinci Villas:** Tel 62/370-693-800; www.quincivillas.com. *Cost:* pool villas from $140. **Oberoi Lombok:** Tel 62/370-6138-444; in the U.S., 800-562-3764; www.oberoihotels.com. *Cost:* from $360. **Best times:** Apr–Oct for the dry season; Jul for 1-week Senggigi Festival, showcasing the culture of the local Sasak people.

Bridging Cultures and the Centuries

Baliem Valley

Papua, Indonesia

Papua (formerly Irian Jaya) is Indonesia's most remote province, and not just in the geographical sense. Adjectives like "tribal," "primitive," and "primeval" best describe the "lost world" of the former Dutch West

New Guinea. Indonesia's largest province comprises the western side of the planet's second largest island, with the independent nation of Papua New Guinea to the east (see p. 693).

In Indonesian West Papua, trading paths link villages to the cool, green highlands and the vast lowland home of the Asmat people, famous for their wooden carvings and rituals. In the latter, you might happen upon a celebration with feasting and dancing around a roaring fire and meet the indigenous Dani tribesmen, known to the outside world as the "gentle warriors" of the Baliem Valley. In some villages they wear only ornamental headdresses, war paint, pig tusks through their noses, and penis sheaths known as *kotckas* fashioned from dried-out gourds, though much of this is staged for tourists or during special festivals. These materially poor but culturally rich people, not "discovered" until 1938 by the American explorer Richard Archbold, teeter between the Stone Age and the 21st century. Leave the valley's main town and commercial center of Wamena, accessible only by air, to strike out on foot for some of the remote Dani villages.

Traveling through the 40-mile-long Baliem Valley is a unique experience, but individual travel in Papua is not for the inexperienced, and a visit is best arranged through a specialist company. Alternatively, tours and treks, from half-day walks or longer, can be arranged right in Wamena.

WHERE: Papua's provincial capital of Jayapura is a 7-hour flight from Jakarta, with onward flights connecting to Wamena in the heart of the Baliem Valley. **HOW:** U.S.-based Asia Transpacific offers custom trips in Indonesia. Tel 800-642-2742 or 303-443-6789; www.asiatranspacific.com. *Cost:* averages $350 per person per day. Bali-based Alpes Travel offers 5-day and longer Baliem Valley adventure tours. Tel 62/361-802-6669; www.balialpes.com. Originate in Jayapura. **BEST TIMES:** May–Nov is the drier season, but Papua can get rain year-round; Aug for local festivals.

A Coral Cornucopia

RAJA AMPAT ARCHIPELAGO

Papua, Indonesia

Raja Ampat is a long way from anywhere, and that is a significant part of the pristine archipelago's appeal. So is the fact that it is one of the richest coral reef ecosystems on the planet. Located in the warm, shallow waters off the western Bird's Head Peninsula of Indonesia's Papua Province, Raja Ampat—or Four Kings—comprises more than 1,500 islands and islets clustered around the three main islands of Waigeo, Salawati, and Misool. The archipelago spans over 15,400 square miles of sea and is home to Cendarawasih Bay, the largest marine national park in the country. In geological terms, the islands form the northernmost tip of the Australian continent, though politically they are Indonesian.

The three largest islands have just a few hundred inhabitants scattered along the coasts, and many smaller islands are mostly uninhabited. But this paucity of humanity is more than made up for by the richness of surrounding marine life: It is believed that Raja Ampat has the greatest diversity of underwater life of anywhere on earth, making it a naturalist's dream and a diver's paradise.

Scientists report more than 1,300 species of fish, 700 species of mollusk, and a staggering 537 varieties of coral that are home to vast shoals of multicolored fish, sea turtles, manta rays, sharks, and dolphins. This high marine diversity is thought to be due to Raja Ampat's location between the Indian and Pacific oceans, where it attracts corals and fish from both. Raja Ampat is also fortunate that its extensive coral reefs are relatively resistant to global warming threats, such as bleaching and disease, which jeopardize so many coral ecosystems around the world.

Bali Diving organizes weekly round-trip cruises from Bali to Raja Ampat, with a side visit to the Komodo National Park (see p. 597), making it possible to take in two of Indonesia's most remote and spectacular marine national parks at the same time. For divers preferring to stay ashore, the Misool Eco Resort, located on the islet of Batbitim, off the southern island of Misool, is composed of eight beautiful overwater bungalows. They are largely constructed from driftwood and are equipped with solar- and wind-generated electricity.

WHERE: 995 miles/1,600 km northeast of Jakarta. **BALI DIVING:** Tel 62/361-282-664; www.divingbali.com. *Cost:* 7-day trips aboard the Raja Ampat Liveaboard $1,820, all-inclusive. Originate in Bali. **MISOOL ECO RESORT:** www.misooleco resort.com. *Cost:* 7-day stay from $2,400, inclusive. Dives extra. *When:* closed Jul–Sep. **BEST TIMES:** Drift diving is possible year-round, although seas may be rougher from Jul–Sep; Apr–Sep is the wet season.

Ancient Capital and Spiritual Heart

LUANG PRABANG

Laos

Most places in Laos are apt to take you back in time, but this is especially true in sleepy, temple-filled Luang Prabang (City of the Buddha of Peace), in the mountainous north. This small city sits on a peninsula at a confluence point between the Mekong and Khan rivers, lending it something of a remote, island feel, though in truth its regional airport connects it to many nearby cities.

Luang Prabang is Laos's second largest city, with a population of around 100,000. A former royal capital, it is today a center of Laotian Buddhism, with more than 600 saffron-clad monks inhabiting its 32 pagoda-like temples. The most exceptional of these is the 16th-century Wat Xieng Thong, the Golden City Temple, built by royalty who held court in Luang Prabang until 1975, when the monarchy was abolished. The temple compound's many Thai-influenced structures, containing impressive images of the Buddha, escaped an 18th-century invasion by Chinese pirates, making it the oldest in town.

A leisurely stroll takes you from temple to temple, along unpaved backstreets that exude a languid backwater calm, with roosters roaming and children at play. Main streets are lined with well-preserved French-Colonial architecture that melds seamlessly with traditional wooden houses, golden tiled temples, and newer Laotian structures.

Waterfalls, mountains, and caves for exploring are all within an easy day trip, and boats sail the Mekong for a few hours or a few days (see next page).

Some of the region's finest resorts are here, led by the exquisite Amantaka, occupying a

French-Colonial hospital. It's wonderfully tranquil despite its location in the center of town. Massive suites, most with their own pools, are understated and elegant. Breakfast on the terrace overlooking the Mekong is one of many treats at the Belle Rive, a 13-room boutique hotel done up in modern Lao style and central to everything. For a touch of the country, La Résidence Phou Vao stands on a hilltop just outside the city center, with 34 airy, minimalist rooms, verandas, plenty of windows, a gemlike spa, and inviting pool that lets guests take in the panorama of the surrounding gardens and mountains. Luang Prabang has grown into a fine destination for eating, with an array of good dining possibilities—don't miss dinner at Les 3 Nagas, served in a gorgeous modern setting that includes an outdoor garden and is connected to a charming hotel of the same name. It's not often you'll see betel-leaf soup on a menu, and the river fish marinated in lemongrass and chilies is just spicy enough.

WHERE: 134 miles/219 km north of Vientiane. **AMANTAKA:** Tel 856/71-860-333; in the U.S., 800-477-9180; www.amanresorts.com/amantaka. *Cost:* from $750. **BELLE RIVE:** Tel 856/71-260-733; www.thebellerive.com. *Cost:* $130. **LA RÉSIDENCE PHOU VAO:** Tel 856/71-212-194; in the U.S., 800-237-1236; www.residencephouvao.com. *Cost:* from $260 (off-peak), from $470 (peak). **LES 3 NAGAS:** Tel 856/71-253-888; www.3-nagas.com. *Cost:* $110 (off-peak), $240 (peak); dinner $35. **BEST TIMES:** Nov–Mar for cool, dry weather; Aug for boat racing festival.

Ornate Buddhist temples fill the former royal capital.

Indochina's Timeless Lifeline

SAILING THE MEKONG

Laos

Laos, Cambodia, and Vietnam share a history of war and French colonial influences. But it's the Mekong River that both links them and, in many places, separates them, running along much of Laos's western border with Myanmar (Burma) and Thailand, then through Cambodia and Vietnam, where it empties into the South China Sea at the Mekong Delta (see p. 639). The river was once the major artery of the Angkor Empire and remains a symbol and lifeline of Indochina, whose principal sites and cities flourished beside it. Today, glimmering Khmer temples, forgotten villages, and bustling markets line its timeless banks and dot the rich countryside.

Both commuter and tourist boats ply the Mekong as it wends through Laos, traveling various distances and offering passengers a number of levels of comfort. Even working fishing boats will take on intrepid travelers who want to cruise along the river for a few miles or a few days. In northern Laos, sail in comfort with the *Luang Say*, a handsomely restored river barge that travels from Luang Prabang north to Houie Say on an overnight cruise with a night at Pakbeng's comfortable Luang Say Lodge along the way. Spend 3 days aboard its sister ship, the *Vat Phou,* and tour the little-visited southern segment of the river, viewable from the vessel's varnished-wood deck that serves as a wide veranda. Of the various shore excursions—from the roaring waterfalls of Phapheng (the largest in Southeast Asia) to the untamed region of Si Phan Don (4,000 islands that sprinkle the lower Mekong near the Cambodian border)—it is the pre-Angkorian temple Wat Phou that is the journey's highlight.

Built in stages between the 6th and 14th centuries and thus predating Cambodia's Angkor Wat (see p. 592) by some 200 years, the hilltop temples of Wat Phou contain some of the best Khmer art in Southeast Asia. Even though centuries of abandonment have left little of the original temples intact, the scale and age of the complex is breathtaking—as is the hike up the massive stairs to the ruins of a 9th-century temple dedicated to the Hindu god Shiva. It's a fantastic site, set against the majestic mountain Linga Parvata. On a clear day you can see as far as Vietnam, 120 miles away.

WHERE: Pakse is 288 miles/464 km southeast of Vientiane. Luang Prabang is 134 miles/219 km north of Vientiane. **MEKONG CRUISES:** Tel 856/21-215-958; www.mekong-cruises.com. *Cost:* 2-day all-inclusive cruises on the *Luang Say* from Luang Prabang to Houie Say (or reverse) from $270 (off-peak), from $415 (peak); 3-day all-inclusive cruises on the *Vat Phou* from Pakse to Wat Phou (or reverse) from $505 (off-peak), from $630 (peak). **BEST TIME:** Nov–Mar for drier and cooler weather.

Sleepy Capital Rich with Pleasures

VIENTIANE

Laos

Although it reflects the laid-back, friendly nature of the country that surrounds it, it is hard to believe that tiny, drowsy Vientiane on the banks of the Mekong River is the capital city. Nearly all of Vientiane was razed in 1828 by the Siamese in response to Laos's failed attack on neighboring Siam. The oldest structure that remains today is Wat Sisaket, completed in 1824, which houses thousands of Buddhas in small niches carved into the temple's walls. One of its newest structures is the Australian-engineered "Friendship Bridge" connecting Laos to Thailand on the other side of the coffee-colored river, and bringing Southeast Asia–circuit tourists who come to slow down, chill out, and recharge.

Though it lacks the obvious charm of Luang Prabang (see p. 600) and there are no must-see sights in the city (although the Nam Phou Palace, the gold-gilded stupa Pha That Luang, and central market are well worth a few hours of your time), Vientiane is a joy to explore. It boasts a host of atmospheric hotels and restaurants serving excellent Laotian and French cuisine. Try the stylish and elegant French-managed Ansara Hotel, whose fresh breakfast croissants served on the outdoor terrace may be the best in town. The Settha Palace is big and rambling, with simple but luxurious Colonial-style rooms outfitted with four-poster beds, ceiling fans, and plenty of hardwood details. Its popular Belle Epoque restaurant is convenient for when you're homesick for good continental cuisine. Otherwise, head to the thatched bars along the Mekong for a meal of barbecued chicken and spicy green-papaya salad with a cold Beer Lao at sunset. For an authentic dinner with a refined touch, Kua Lao is a favorite among travelers and affluent locals. In addition to providing excellent service and intensely flavorful Lao specialties, the restaurant often features a performance of traditional music and dance.

The image of Pha That Luang is visible on Laos's national seal.

ANSARA HOTEL: Tel 856/21-213-514; www.ansarahotel.com. *Cost:* $120. **SETTHA PALACE:** Tel 856/21-217-581; www.setthapalace.com. *Cost:* $165; dinner at Belle Epoque $30. **KUA LAO:** Tel 856/21-215-777; www.kualao.laopdr.com. *Cost:* dinner $20. **BEST TIMES:** Nov–Mar for cooler and drier weather; mid-May for Bun Bang Fai (Rocket) Festival; Oct for Ok Phansa Boat Race Festival.

Epic Diving in the Celebes Sea

SIPADAN

Sabah, Borneo, Malaysia

"I have seen other places like Sipadan—forty-five years ago—but now, no more," said Jacques Cousteau. "Now we have found again an untouched piece of art." Part of the Semporna Archipelago, off the coast of Borneo, tiny mushroom-shaped Sipadan sits atop a submerged volcano in a protected conservation zone. With a cap of only 120 visitors a day and no overnight accommodations, this speck of an island in the Celebes Sea appears on every diver's dream list.

Walk 15 feet out from the soft white sandy beach, stick your head in the water, and be prepared for the treat of a lifetime. Incredibly clear and calm waters enable even novice snorkelers to enjoy the wonders of the underwater kingdom. Experienced scuba divers can choose from 12 dive locations with seawalls that plunge 2,000 feet into a deep blue abyss, all less than a few minutes from shore by boat.

Sightings of green and hawksbill turtles, various species of shark, barracuda, and manta are practically guaranteed. And that's on top of the thousands of other species of fish and hundreds of different multicolored corals, sea fans, and sponges that brighten these parts.

Borneo Divers, the outfitter that pioneered diving on Sipadan—and introduced Cousteau to the archipelago—relocated their dive center and resort from Sipadan to the nearby island of Mabul, 20 minutes to the north by speedboat. Guests stay in semidetached mahogany bungalows and enjoy a pool and beautiful palm-fringed private beach—plus, of course, great shore and boat diving.

More luxurious is the eco-conscious Sipadan-Kapalai Dive Resort, on a barely-above-water sandbar called Kapalai. Located a few minutes by boat southeast of Sipadan, its 50 stilted bungalows resemble those inhabited by the local Baja Laut (or Sea Gypsies).

While waiting for your Sipadan dive slot, you can explore sites around Kapalai and the islands of Mataking and Sibuan. And the snorkeling and kayaking are guaranteed to keep nondivers content.

Where: 22 miles/36 km off northeast coast of Borneo. **Borneo Divers:** Tel 60/88-222226; www.borneodivers.info. *Cost:* 1-night package from $765 per person, inclusive. **Sipadan-Kapalai Dive Resort:** Tel 60/89-765200; www.sipadan-kapalai.com. *Cost:* 3-night package from $800 per person, inclusive. Diving extra. **Best time:** May–Oct for nicest weather, but diving is good year-round.

Schools of redtail butterfly fish dazzle divers in the Celebes Sea.

Island of Incredibly Big Adventures

Borneo

Sarawak and Sabah, Borneo, Malaysia

Ginger-haired orangutans swinging through tropical rain forest and communal longhouses once home to legendary headhunters are the images commonly associated with Borneo. The world's third largest island, territorially shared by Malaysia, Indonesia, and Brunei, boasts a super-rich biodiversity—more than 15,000 varieties of flowering plants as well as 200 mammal and 420 bird species. It's also home to a fascinating tapestry of tribal and ethnic groups.

The Malaysian part of Borneo is comprised of two states, Sarawak and Sabah. Start your exploration in Kuching, Sarawak's historic capital and a picturesque spot from which to organize expeditions to the hinterland. Kuching-based Borneo Adventure is expert at getting visitors from chugging riverboats and puddle-jumper planes to remote areas, such the Danum Valley, the Kelabit Highlands, and Gunung Mulu National Park, where limestone pinnacles poke out of the steamy jungle and massive caves are the cathedral-like hangouts for armies of bats.

The river rides and primeval beauty of the encroaching jungle may make Borneo the adventure of a lifetime, but learning about local cultures and sharing gifts and *tuak* (hooch made from fermented rice) with the inhabitants of a longhouse isn't something you'll soon forget either. Many longhouses welcome overnight guests, including Nanga Sumpa, on a remote, vine-covered tributary flowing into the vast Batang Ai reservoir. Though most longhouses are communal, this one provides visitors with separate accommodations at the end of the evening. (Borneo Adventure will make arrangements.)

Over in Sabah, the Sepilok Orangutan Rehabilitation Centre (SORC) is one of only four such sanctuaries in the world. Homeless, orphaned, and injured primates are brought here and raised in a natural setting before being released into the forest. Stay at the Sepilok Nature Resort, within walking distance of the orangutan center, and learn about these shaggy tree dwellers found in the wild only on the islands of Borneo and Sumatra.

The 2-day climb up 13,435-foot Mount Kinabalu, Southeast Asia's third highest peak, is stamina-sapping but manageable if you are accompanied by a guide from Mountain Torq. They have constructed a *via ferrata*, a series of iron rungs and bridges anchored to the rock, to facilitate the climb.

Afterward, soothe aching muscles in the spa at the Gayana Eco Resort, with 52 villas perched over waves lapping gently on a coral reef. This luxurious tropical retreat on Gaya Island, in the Tunku Abdul Rahman Marine Park, is a short boat hop from the state's coastal capital, Kota Kinabalu.

WHERE: Sabah and Sarawak cover the northern side of Borneo. Kota Kinabalu is 1,009 miles/1,635 km east of Kuala Lumpur. **HOW:** U.S.-based International Expeditions offers a 20-day tour that covers Mount Kinabalu, Sepilok Forest Reserve, and the Danum Valley. Tel 800-234-9620 or 205-428-1700; www.ietravel.com. *Cost:* from $6,850. Originates in Kuching, Sarawak. *When:* Jun. **BORNEO ADVENTURE:** Tel 60/88-486800; www.borneoadventure.com. *Cost:* 2-day tour from $155. **SEPILOK NATURE RESORT:** Tel 60/89-535001; http://sepilok.com. *Cost:* from $90. **MOUNTAIN TORQ:** Tel 60/88-251730; www.mountaintorq.com. *Cost:* from $255 for a 2-day tour. **GAYANA ECO RESORT:** Tel 60/88-271098; www.gayana-eco-resort.com. *Cost:* from $310, all-inclusive. **BEST TIME:** Mar–Oct for dry season.

Jewel of Kedah

PULAU LANGKAWI

Langkawi, Kedah, Malaysia

Located where the Andaman Sea meets the Straits of Malacca, this picture-perfect archipelago of 99 islands is officially known as Langkawi the Jewel of Kedah, a title the Sultan of Kedah bestowed in celebration of his golden jubilee in 2008. Even though it has been heavily promoted for years as a travel destination, Langkawi is remarkable for remaining the genuine article: a tropical paradise of pure white sand, primary rain forest, magical sunsets, and sun-filled days.

Only two of the archipelago's islands are inhabited, the main one being mountainous Pulau Langkawi, approximately the size of Singapore. In its remote northwest corner is the Datai, one of Malaysia's most stylish and fabled resorts. Inspired by the local Malay kampong-style structures, and made from native balau wood and local white marble, the Datai snuggles unobtrusively between its own private white sand cove and an ancient rain forest that you can explore in the company of the hotel's resident naturalist.

Aesthetic influences are at times Thai and Indonesian, at times hinting of Japanese. The tasteful guest rooms, spacious lobbies, walkways, and elevated Thai restaurant are all open-sided, letting in the jungle and creating a cool, exotic cocoon that envelops guests who are generally happy to stay put—except, perhaps, for those who make it to the hotel's adjacent 18-hole championship golf course, not your average rain forest attraction.

Close to Pantai Cenang, the island's most commercial beach strip, is the delightful boutique Bon Ton Resort and Restaurant, which has relocated eight antique Malay wooden houses, some on stilts, to a lovely site amid swaying palms. Decorated with brilliant colors and interesting patterns and textures, this villagelike compound is irresistible, not least because of the fine cooking at its Nam Restaurant.

The Australian owner has recently upped the ante on intriguing hotel offerings by devising Temple Tree, a neighboring property of eight historic houses of Chinese, Malay, Indian, and Eurasian provenance. Salvaged from across Malaysia, these buildings proudly bear the patina of time but are equipped with contemporary fixtures, creating a charming architectural park.

WHERE: 19 miles/30 km off the northwest coast of Malaysia. **THE DATAI:** Tel 60/4-959-2500; www.langkawi-resorts.com. *Cost:* from $465 (off-peak), from $865 (peak). **BON TON RESORT AND TEMPLE TREE:** Tel 60/4-955-1688; www.bontonresort.com.my. *Cost:* from $220. **BEST TIME:** Nov–Apr for driest weather.

A Melting Pot of Cuisines

Feasting on KL's Streets

Kuala Lumpur, Malaysia

Don't let the dazzling, steel-clad Petronas Towers and slick shopping malls sidetrack you: It's the authentic array of edible delights that makes Kuala Lumpur such a great city to visit. Commonly known as KL, Malaysia's cosmopolitan capital offers a feast of dining options from streetside hawker stalls and brightly lit night markets to white-tablecloth restaurants with world-class chefs.

The range spans the globe, focusing principally on the many delicious permutations of Chinese, Indian, and Malay kitchens. Becoming acquainted with these myriad tastes is as simple as taking the elevator up to Seri Angkasa, the revolving restaurant atop the 1,380 foot KL Tower, where the tempting buffet competes with a bird's-eye view of the city.

Back on the street, the hawker stalls and outdoor restaurants lining the Jalan Alor, in the city's Golden Triangle district, are the star attraction. It's impossible to go wrong here. Among the choices: the famous barbecue chicken wings at Wong Ah Wah, spicy Thai grilled pork skewers, and crispy oyster omelets fried up in sizzling woks. Around the corner is Changat Bukit Bintang, a sophisticated buzzing strip of restaurants and bars. The pick of the bunch is Frangipani, where chef Chris Bauer concocts inventive contemporary French-fusion cuisine, served in a chic dining room centered around a small reflecting pool.

It was Chinese tin prospectors who literally carved KL out of the jungle in the mid-1800s, some of them becoming fabulously wealthy in the process. The culinary heritage that generations of these immigrants brought to the city can be sampled in KL's Chinatown. For breakfast, tuck into freshly made noodles or stuffed tofu from the stalls on Madras Lane, behind the lively wet market. At night, push through the jam-packed market stalls along Petaling Street to reach the Old China Café, where tasty Nyonya (the fusion of Chinese and Malaysian) dishes from Malacca and Penang are served in what was once the guildhall of the Selangor & Federal Territory Laundry Association.

For a real treat, sign up for one of the cooking courses offered by food writer and cook Rohani Jelani, who teaches out of her former house, which also serves as a charming bed-and-breakfast, Bayan Indah. Perched on the edge of a rain forest, it is just a halfhour's drive from the city center. But if you'd rather be more centrally located, the longtime accommodation of choice is Carcosa Seri Negara, a pair of Colonial mansions atop a hill in the lush Lake Gardens district. Afternoon teas on the veranda are a local tradition.

Seri Angkasa: Tel 60/3-2020-5055; www.serimelayu.com. *Cost:* buffet lunch $22, dinner $50. **Frangipani:** Tel 60/3-2144-3001; www.frangipani.com.my. *Cost:* dinner $65. **Old China Café:** Tel 60/3-2072-5915; www.oldchina.com.my. *Cost:* lunch $18. **Bayan Indah:** Tel 60/3-7729-0122; www.bayanindah.com. *Cost:* room plus cooking class $140; 1-day cooking class $74. **Carcosa Seri Negara:** Tel 60/3-2295-0888; www.shr.my. *Cost:* from $330; afternoon tea $25.

Malaysia's Historic Cradle

Melaka

Malaysia

Half a millennium before the Petronas Towers and other skyscrapers rose in Kuala Lumpur, Melaka (also known as Malacca) was the Malay Peninsula's greatest city. Located opposite the Indonesian island of Sumatra, in a pivotal spot on the lucrative spice route between China and Europe, the busy trading port was ruled by sultans who converted the population to Islam and developed a courtly culture. Such was Melaka's wealth that a succession of colonial powers fought for and won control over it.

Melaka's glory days may now only be a page in Malaysia's textbooks, but the town's stock of monuments and historic buildings attracts ever-growing numbers of visitors. The Catholic St. Paul's Church dates back to 1521 and the rule of the Portuguese, when St. Francis Xavier was a regular visitor. The most representative building of the ensuing 150 years of Dutch rule is the rosy pink Stadthuys, the former governor's residence and town hall. At its doorstep, trishaws festooned with tassels and fake flowers wait to take tourists to the lazy Melaka River where boats ferry them to neighboring Chinatown.

Florally decorated trishaws wheel passengers through the city.

Chinatown is a vibrant warren of narrow streets lined with colonial-era shop houses, some still home to ancient trades, such as cobblers who make the beautifully beaded shoes worn by Baba Nyonyas, the daughters of intermarriages between Chinese men and Malay women. You can visit a preserved shop house at 8 Heeren Street, a two-story building constructed in the 1700s. Other houses have been converted into boutique hotels such as Heeren House, a former warehouse. One of the most atmospheric places to stay, it features a café and craft shop on the ground floor and six traditionally furnished rooms, with river views.

For more luxury, have your trishaw driver head to the Majestic Malacca, whose public spaces are housed in a faithfully restored 1920s Colonial Chinese mansion. Behind it, sumptuously appointed guest rooms are found in a new annex; the pair of top-floor suites provides sweeping views of the river and charming Kampung Morten, a neighborhood of traditional wooden houses.

Make sure to return to Chinatown's Jalan Hang Jebat for the Jonker's Walk Night Market, held every Friday and Saturday. It's touristy, but a fun place to pick up souvenirs and sample local dishes from any of the countless hawker stalls—try chicken rice balls or the fonduelike *satay celup* and *Melaka cendol* (shaved ice desserts). And if you're wondering what's next on your horizon, you can have your fortune told as well.

WHERE: 90 miles/145 km southwest of Kuala Lumpur. **HEEREN HOUSE:** Tel 60/6-281-4241; www.melaka.net/heerenhouse. *Cost:* from $50. **MAJESTIC MALACCA:** Tel 60/6-289-8000; www.majesticmalacca.com. *Cost:* from $250. **BEST TIMES:** Fri and Sat for the Jonker's Walk Night Market; Jan–Feb for least rain.

A Sultan's Island Escape

PANGKOR LAUT RESORT

Pulau Pangkor Laut, Perak, Malaysia

Word has it that Luciano Pavarotti cried when he first took in the beauty of this 300-acre island. Covered by primary rain forest that's home to macaque monkeys and more than 100 species of exotic birds, Pangkor Laut was once the domain of the Sultan of Perak. Still privately owned, it has only one hotel, the Pangkor Laut Resort, fashioned after a *kampong* (Malay village), with dozens of bungalows built either on stilts over the sea or nestled in the hillside. One of Asia's most luxurious and beautifully situated hotels, it offers a host of enticements, including sandy white beaches, an award-winning spa, and a marina filled with sleek yachts and cruisers for visiting neighboring islands in the storied Straits of Malacca.

Most of the private island consists of pristine terrain.

Plenty of guests spend their entire vacation on their private balconies overlooking the water, or in villas lost amid the ancient treetops. And for those who crave complete exclusivity, there's the Estates, nine mini-homesteads with their own staff to take care of your every need, even helicopter connections to and from the mainland.

The resort's excellent restaurants serve everything from Chinese and Malaysian to East-meets-West cuisines in handsome open-air pavilions or under a canopy of stars.

Pangkor Laut's big brother island Pulau Pangkor may not be as high-end, but it is relatively low-key and crowd-free during the week. The best place to stay is at Tiger Rock.

The eco-friendly retreat is cocooned by the jungle and feels both friendly and very exclusive, offering just eight rooms spread across two houses, a studio, and a pool-house chalet. The staff is happy to drive guests to the best beaches, markets, and local places to eat, though it's the hotel's "nonhotel" vibe and amazing home cooking that account for the large number of return guests.

Where: 3 miles/5 km off the coast from the port of Lamut, which is 168 miles/270 km north of Kuala Lumpur. **Pangkor Laut Resort:** Tel 60/5-699-1100; www.pangkorlautresort.com. *Cost:* villas from $350, Pavarotti suite from $900. **Tiger Rock:** Tel 60/4-264-3580; www.tigerrock.info. *Cost:* from $430, inclusive. **Best times:** pleasant temperatures year-round; Jan–Feb are least rainy.

Pearl of the Orient

Penang

Malaysia

The island of Penang has been a vibrant cultural crossroads since it was leased to British adventurer Captain Francis Light by the Sultan of Kedah in 1786. As one of the key ports on the Straits of Malacca, Penang became a strategic way station on European traders' lucrative routes from Madras to Canton. Today it's one of the most colorful, multiethnic communities in Asia, home to Muslim Malays, Indians of various religions, and Buddhist and Taoist Chinese, all coexisting alongside a diverse Eurasian and expat population.

The island shows off its heritage in a more authentic manner than nearby Singapore (see p. 617) does. In the main city of Georgetown, a ride on a man-pedaled trishaw is the classic way to get around and take in the distinctive townscape of colonial-era shops, temples, and clan houses that make up Chinatown and Little India. Can't-miss stops include the outrageously ornate Khoo Kongsi clan house, the impressively restored Anglo-India Suffolk House, and Cheong Fatt Tze (aka the Blue Mansion), a brightly painted, atmospheric boutique hotel that was formerly the 1880s home of a fabulously wealthy merchant trader known as the Rockefeller of the East.

History buffs and entrepreneurs are busy restoring many of the long-neglected shops and houses of old Georgetown and turning them into small hotels, restaurants, and boutiques. The Straits Collection, a group of stylish accommodations and gift shops along Stewart Lane and nearby Armenian Street, captures the essence of old Penang with a modern twist; the Stewart Lane strip includes the excellent Kopi Cine Café & Bar.

Clove Hall, a boutique hotel in an impeccably restored Anglo-Malay mansion, has six antiques-decorated suites, tropical gardens, and a lap pool beside which stand giant Chinese pottery rice jars. The hotel was built in 1910 on land that was once a plantation belonging to the Sarkies brothers, owners of Penang's E&O, the Eastern & Oriental Hotel. Sister hotel to Singapore's Raffles (see p. 618) and the Strand in Yangon, Myanmar, it dates to 1884 and stands as a reminder of colonial days, when visitors like Noël Coward, Rudyard Kipling, and Somerset Maugham dallied over gin slings on the breezy veranda.

Swap the urban scene for nature by jumping on the funicular for a joyride up 2,720 feet through dense jungle and bamboo groves to the peak of Penang Hill, where you can enjoy a panoramic view across the 404-square-mile island. Back in town, join locals at the open-air hawker stalls and tuck into the best street food in Malaysia. Sample local specialties such as *char kway teow* (a noodle-based stir fry in a dark soy sauce) and *curry mee* (egg noodles in a spicy coconut-curry soup) along New Lane, in the heart of Georgetown, or at sunset on Gurney Drive, beside the sea.

WHERE: 250 miles/402 km northwest of Kuala Lumpur. **CHEONG FATT TZE MANSION:** Tel 60/4-262-0006; www.cheongfatttzemansion.com. *Cost:* from $125. **STRAITS COLLECTION:** Tel 60/4-263-7299; www.straitscollection.com.my. *Cost:* from $130. **CLOVE HALL:** Tel 60/4-229-0818; www.clovehall.com. *Cost:* from $185. **E&O HOTEL:** Tel 60/4-222-2000; www.e-o-hotel.com. *Cost:* from $195. **BEST TIMES:** Sep–Feb for driest weather; Jan-Feb for Chinese New Year; Mar for International Food Festival; May for Dragon Boat Festival; Jul for the Georgetown Festival.

Home to a Nomadic Seafaring People

MERGUI ARCHIPELAGO

Andaman Sea, Myanmar

The islands that make up the Mergui (Myeik) Archipelago in the Andaman Sea are mostly uninhabited. Some are made up of towerlike limestone formations pockmarked with caves and covered with tropical forests inland. The underwater topography, whether explored by snorkeling or diving, is equally striking, with alien-looking cuttlefish navigating around large, fragile corals. The people who do live here are known as Sea Gypsies to English speakers and as the Moken among themselves. They continue to live a traditional lifestyle, moving in flotillas to trade fish, mollusks, sea snails, and whatever other bounty can be foraged from the sea. The Mokens' boats, called *kabangs*, are made from a single tree and when lashed together, these houseboats often become something of a small floating village.

This archipelago of 14,000 square miles remains relatively unexplored—as evidenced, in part, by the fact that British surveyors have recorded a total of 200 to 800 islands here, while locals put the number closer to 4,000. The main islands are accessible from Kawthaung on the mainland but there's no regular transport to the outer islands.

Closed to travelers until 1997, the islands' accommodations remain limited. One of the only hotels is the beachfront, bungalow-style Myanmar Andaman Resort on Fork (Mcleod) Island, which can arrange for every imaginable land or water excursion in the area. Two of the more noteworthy islands are Lon Khuet, where bird's nests—a key ingredient in a soup considered a delicacy in Chinese cuisine—are farmed in huge caverns, and the large and rugged Lampi Kyun, which features a mountainous interior, home to a wide variety of wildlife, including flying lemurs, crocodiles, sea otters, countless bird species, and the rare tiger.

WHERE: 500 miles/800 km south of Yangon, 40 nautical miles from Kawthaung as well as from Ranong, Thailand. **HOW:** U.S.-based Asia Transpacific Journeys offers custom itineraries in Myanmar, including to Mergui. Tel 800-642-2742 or 303-443-6789; www.asiatranspacific.com. **MYANMAR ANDAMAN RESORT:** Tel 95/1-549-234; www.myanmarandamanresort.com. *Cost:* from $1,200, inclusive (4-night minimum). **BEST TIME:** Oct–Feb for coolest, most pleasant weather.

Drifting Down Myanmar's Watery Highway

Bagan and a Cruise on the Ayerwady River

Bagan and Mandalay, Myanmar

A cruise down the Ayerwady (Irrawaddy) River—the country's great natural highway and the focal point of Burmese life—is an opportunity to observe the languid and timeless rhythms of rural life as well as the area's 2,500 years of history. Choose your floating hotel: You can opt for the cushy *Road to Mandalay* owned and operated by Orient-Express, a microcosm of Burmese hospitality and European efficiency, or a more boutique-style ship, the RV *Pandaw,* a meticulously retrofitted 1947 Scottish paddle steamer, operated by Ayravata Cruises. They also operate two new and stylish ships, both called RV *Paukans.*

Buddhist pagodas fill the ancient city of Bagan.

The Ayerwady runs for over 1,300 miles, nearly the entire length of Myanmar. The most arresting of its riverside settlements is the ancient city of Bagan (formerly Pagan), where, along 8 dusty miles of riverbank, some 2,200 Buddhist pagodas resemble a forest of spires and pinnacles. Founded by a Burmese king in 849, Bagan reached its apogee in about 1000 as capital of the first Burmese Empire, and was abandoned in 1283 when Kublai Khan, in control of northern India, swept south with his soldiers. It was believed that building religious structures gained merit for a king and his people. So an army of skilled artisans embellished this spiritual center of what originally numbered more than 10,000 religious monuments and is now one of the world's greatest archaeological sites. Among the most impressive highlights is the ornate Ananda Temple, with its many-tiered roof and four golden, 30-foot statues of the Buddha, plus hundreds of murals from his life. Just as noteworthy is the Shwezigon, with its golden stupa, said to house the collarbone and a tooth of the Buddha. Scramble to the top terrace of the crumbling Shwe San Daw (Sunset Pagoda) for a near-sacred experience at day's end, when the sun is sinking below the horizon.

Ninety miles north of Bagan is Mandalay. Perhaps one of the most evocative names on the globe and also known as the Golden City, it was the royal capital of Burma (now Myanmar) before the British conquered the country in the 1880s. Slightly run-down today, it still evokes its royal past as the heartland of Burmese culture and remains an important religious destination with a huge, teeming market.

Farther upriver is the leafy village of Katha, easily explored by foot once you arrive. Populated by a mix of Bamar, Kachin, and Chin people, it's also the famous setting for George Orwell's novel *Burmese Days;* the writer was posted here as a colonial police officer in 1927. Some cruises travel as far north as Bhamo, where a visit to its bustling daily market lets you wander amidst the Lisu, Kachin, and Shan people, who come from the surrounding countryside to buy and sell.

Where: Bagan is 90 miles/145 km southwest of Mandalay. **Visitor info:** www.ancientbagan.com. **Where to stay:** The new and appropriately named Amazing Bagan Resort is built in the style of ancient Burmese architecture with all modern comforts. Tel 95/61-600-35; www.bagangolfresort.net. *Cost:* $55. **Orient-Express Trains and Cruises:** In the U.S., tel 800-524-2420 or 843-937-9068; www.orient-express.com. *Cost:* 3 nights and longer from $2,290, all-inclusive. Originates in Yangon. **Ayravata Cruises:** Tel 95/1-380-877; www.ayravatacruises.com. *Cost:* 1 night and longer from $300, inclusive. **Best times:** Oct–Mar for coolest weather; in Bagan, full moon in Dec–Jan for Pyatho festival, when monks chant day and night.

Floating Islands and Jumping Cats

Inle Lake

Myanmar

The quiet magic of Inle Lake in central Myanmar feels a world apart from the congested capital, Yangon, offering a time-warp setting of calm waters, gentle light, and warm smiles. Most of the tribal people who live on its shores subsist by fishing—and many still practice their unique method of propelling the boat forward by wrapping one leg around the oar and moving it in a circular motion, while leaving their hands free to manipulate the conical net they use to haul in their catch. Others farm their man-made floating islands, which are anchored to the lake's shallow bottom by bamboo poles that eventually become rooted. Settled centuries ago by the Intha, or "sons of the lake," Inle, the country's second largest lake, is roughly 48 square miles in size. Motorized boats are used for longer trips, but most journeys through its maze of canals, marsh paddies, and tangled hyacinths at the lake's edge are via flat-bottomed canoes.

Intha fishermen propel their boats forward using a unique "leg rowing" technique.

Around the lake about 70,000 people live in 20-some simple villages—some no more than a small cluster of fragile bungalows sitting gingerly on stilts. Ywama is the best known because of its floating market, which takes place every 5 days. The Intha pile their canoes high with leafy greens, rice, melons, bright flowers, and the plump, tasty tomatoes for which Inle is known. By 9 A.M., the market is winding down for the locals, and when the canoes show up bearing curious tourists, all attention swings to the animated sale of bamboo hats, bundles of Burmese cheroots, woven shoulder bags, traditional silk and cotton sarongs, and carved wooden Buddhas. If you miss the market in Ywama, make sure you go looking for it: It travels to other villages on other days of the week.

There are close to 1,000 stupas around the lake as well as 100 *kyaung* (monasteries), many on chopsticklike stilts. Perhaps the most curious (and visited) is Nga Phe Kyaung, known as the "Jumping Cat Monastery," where the monks have trained their cats to leap through small hoops and perform other tricks.

Where: 205 miles/330 km south of Mandalay. **Where to stay:** The lake's premier location is the attractive Inle Princess Resort. Tel 95/81-209-055; www.inleprincessresort.com. *Cost:* from $160. **Best times:** Sep–Mar, especially Sep–Oct for lake holidays; Nov for fairest weather.

The Soul of Burma

Shwedagon Pagoda

Yangon, Myanmar

Rising majestically above Yangon's tangled skyline, the enormous, glowing Shwedagon Pagoda can leave one grasping for superlatives (Rudyard Kipling referred to it as "a golden mystery . . . a beautiful winking wonder"). Rising 320 feet and sheathed in some 60 tons of gold leaf, the glowing bell-shaped stupa stands at the center of the 14-acre Shwedagon (Golden Victory Mound). Tradition dictates that devotees and visitors walk clockwise around the space, passing a profusion of mosaic-covered columns, spires, ornate prayer pavilions, images of Buddha, and 78 smaller filigreed pagodas. Bells tinkle. Incense burns. It's a serene and sensual mélange, all enhanced by the perfume of flower offerings, the deep saffron robes of the Buddhist monks, and the soothing sound of chanting and prayer.

The radiant 32-story stupa rises ever upward, dominating the city's skyline. It's topped by a golden orb that is studded with 5,448 diamonds, 2,317 rubies, sapphires, and other gems, 1,065 golden bells and—too high for the eye to see—a 76-carat diamond on its tip. To Buddhists, this is the most revered site in the country, said to house relics from the four Buddhas who so far have appeared on earth. Four covered walkways lead up Singuttara Hill to the platform on which the pagoda stands (before you take the first step, you're required to remove your shoes). All but one of the entranceways are lined with vendors selling everything a Buddhist visitor could want, from ceremonial paper umbrellas to incense sticks. The pagoda is most resplendent at the end of the day, when the sun's last rays create a dramatic orange glow and hundreds of sparrows take off from the grounds (to return the next morning).

After a day of battling tropical humidity and navigating the dilapidated, fume-belching buses in this city of more than 4 million people, the elegant accommodations at the Governor's Residence are nearly as Zen-like as the Shwedagon Pagoda, which is just a short walk away. Built in the 1920s as the guesthouse for key members of the Kayah state government, the hotel is a handsome showcase of teak Burmese architecture inside and out, restored to its height of colonial-era luxury. Tucked away in the leafy embassy district, its meticulously manicured grounds, lotus pond gardens, and Kipling Bar evoke the languid Rangoon (as Yangon used to be called) days of yore.

Visitor info: www.shwedagonpagoda.com. **Governor's Residence:** Tel 95/1-229-860; www.governorsresidence.com. *Cost:* from $175. **Best times:** Nov–Feb for coolest temperatures; during full moon in Feb–Mar for Tabaung or Shwedagon Pagoda Festival.

Millennia-Old Earth Art

The Ifugao Rice Terraces

Cordillera, Luzon, Philippines

Rising like massive emerald green staircases out of the Cordillera Central, the mountains in northern Luzon, the steep Ifugao rice terraces stretch as far as the eye can see. They were hand-hewn more than 2,000 years ago by the Ifugao people who populate the Cordillera's eastern flank around the town of Banaue and were flooded through a sophisticated and labor-intensive irrigation system that endures to this day. However, as younger tribespeople leave for less arduous work in the cities, the terraces' future is in question.

Some of the most picturesque rice terraces can be found in the village of Batad, about 10 miles from Banaue. Resembling a giant amphitheater, they slope down to a cluster of thatch-roofed huts that constitute the village. Once you get to the top of the manicured gallery the views of the intricate patchwork of square plots below are awe-inspiring. Entry to Batad is on foot only. Guides stand ready to help you navigate a hiking network and locate local craftspeople. A tricky climb that begins near the village leads to the base of the magnificent 100-foot-tall Tappia Waterfall, where you can enjoy a dip in a clear, chilly pool. A clutch of simple guesthouses serves up prime views of the terraces, good food, and rooms for a song.

From Batad you can hike several hours to more remote Ifugao settlements nestled in the high Cordillera, or head back to Banaue and plan a 4WD trip to any number of rice terraces that are the equal of those in Batad but lesser known, such as those in the villages of Asipulo, Kiangan, Mayoyao, and Maligcong.

Bring a sweater, camera, and good hiking boots. The clarity of the light, mountain air, excellent treks, and drama of the ancient earthworks explain why backpackers have long gravitated to these highlands. The utilitarian-looking Banaue Hotel on the outskirts of town is the best operation in the area—and much more attractive inside than out. Ask for a balconied room for magical views of Banaue's mud-walled terraces at sunrise. Staff can organize trips by car or foot into the surrounding country, known to the Ifugao as the "Stairway to Heaven."

Where: Banaue is 219 miles/353 km north of Manila. **Banaue Hotel:** Tel 63/74-356-4087; www.philtourism.gov.ph. *Cost:* from $55. **Best times:** in Banaue: Mar–Apr when least obscured by clouds or Jun–Jul before harvest. In Batad: greenest in Apr–May and Oct–Nov.

Passed down as an oral tradition, the agricultural methods of the rice terraces have changed little over the centuries.

Garboesque Isolation on a Private Isle

AMANPULO

Pamalican Island, Cuyo Islands, Palawan Province, Philippines

Of the 7,000-odd islands in the Philippines, the most exclusive is Pamalican, a minuscule speck in the Sulu Sea. It is occupied by a solitary luxury enclave, Amanpulo, and reachable only by private twin-engine charter from Manila, 1 hour away. Part of the Aman family of ultraluxurious resorts, Amanpulo, which means "peaceful island," is arguably the chain's most idyllic property, at least for lovers of tropical beaches and water sports.

Guests can fill their days with as much or as little activity as they want—there's windsurfing, sailing, sea kayaking, fishing, and some of the best diving in the Philippines, which is saying a lot, as the entire country is a diving mecca. A polychromatic coral reef encircles the 220-acre island only about 1,000 feet from shore, in some of the purest water imaginable. Sightings of small sharks, sea turtles, and entire schools of eagle rays are common.

Guests have their own golf carts to explore the tiny island via a web of dirt roads. But most people come here to relax, and there are few better places in the world to do so. Amanpulo's 40 exquisite casitas are arranged so that your neighbors remain practically invisible; from your private sun deck, you'll feel like you have the island to yourself. The large, airy villas are modeled after Philippine *bahay kubo* (traditional houses), but there's nothing old-fashioned about them on the inside. Spacious bathrooms, gargantuan beds swathed in the finest linens, and state-of-the-art music systems mean you won't be wanting for creature comforts. Gallery-quality local crafts heighten the spirit of place.

The beach casitas are just steps away from the footprint-free, talcum-powder beach, surely the most dazzling in the Philippines, while other accommodations are tucked into the hills overlooking the ocean. The hillside swimming pool commands spectacular views of the surrounding islands, all framed by the aquamarine, peacock, and turquoise blues of the Sulu Sea.

WHERE: 223 miles/360 km southwest of Manila. Tel 63/2-976-5200; in the U.S., 800-477-9180; www.amanresorts.com. *Cost:* casitas from $800 (off-peak), from $900 (peak). **BEST TIME:** Nov–May is the dry season.

A Last Frontier of Extraordinary Natural Beauty

PALAWAN

Philippines

At the heart of this 1,760-island archipelago is a 270-mile-long sliver of island known as Palawan. Stretching all the way to the tip of Borneo in the south, and bordered by the Sulu Sea to the east and the South China Sea to the west, it rightly promotes itself as the Philippines' Last Frontier.

The island's prized west coast, clad in rain forest, is virtually untouched save for a smattering of small coastal communities. Off the northwest tip lies Palawan's showpiece: the Bacuit Archipelago. Rivaling Guilin in China, and Vietnam's Ha Long Bay (see pp. 486 and 632) for sheer dramatic seascape, these 40 islands feature deserted white sand beaches surrounding jagged limestone outcroppings that soar hundreds of feet into the air. Idyllic days are spent island-hopping in a *bangka* (a traditional outrigger canoe), swimming, snorkeling, sea kayaking, and sunbathing.

The town of El Nido looks out onto the limestone cliffs of the Bacuit Archipelago.

The humble town of El Nido offers front-row access to Bacuit Bay's offshore wonders, and its cluster of small hotels makes a convenient base. Alternatives include one of a handful of exclusive resorts built on private islands. At conservation-minded Miniloc Island Resort, you can kayak into hidden lagoons ringed by cliffs on which swiftlets build nests using their own saliva. (El Nido is named after these nests, which are considered an aphrodisiac and are an ingredient in a soup delicacy found in much of Asia.) Get there early in the morning and you'll have the lagoons all to yourself. Nearby, the even more eco-chic sister property, the Lagen Island Resort, features romantic over-water bungalows.

On the east coast of Palawan, the provincial capital of Puerto Princesa is the jumping-off point for tours of Subterranean River National Park, home to one of the world's longest navigable underground rivers. Experienced divers can explore the uniquely rich Coral Triangle ecosystem in the Tubbataha Reefs, a protected marine reserve 12 hours southeast by boat. Live-aboard dive trips are the only way to experience these remote, world-class waters surrounding two atolls that teem with six varieties of sharks, as well as rays, endangered turtles, and iridescent schools of fish.

WHERE: El Nido is 148 miles/238 km northwest of Puerto Princesa, both serviced by ferries from Manila. **EL NIDO RESORTS:** Tel 63/2-894-5644; www.elnidoresorts.com. *Cost:* Miniloc from $350; Lagen from $550. **HOW:** ABC Diving offers live-aboard trips to the Tubbataha reefs. www.abcdive.com; info@abcdive.com. *Cost:* 6-night trip $825, all-inclusive. Originates in Puerto Princesa. **BEST TIME:** Feb–May for driest weather.

Heaven in a Former Backpacker Haven

BORACAY

Visayas, Philippines

They say the powdery soft sand here is so white that it glows at night and turns pink when it reflects the sunset. Though Boracay Island is no longer the drowsy backwater it used to be, its White Beach remains the crown jewel of Philippine tourism and the country's most famous image. The 4-square-mile-long island is also known for its kite surfing, windsurfing, and diving—there are over 20 dive sites all a short boat ride away. Today's international visitors come for family fun as well as nightlife that lasts well into the small hours.

Boracay's subtle metamorphosis from backpacker haven in the 1970s to one of Southeast Asia's trendy destinations was sealed with the arrival of resorts such as the Shangri-La Boracay Resort and Spa, set on 20 acres in a secluded cove. It's just minutes from White Beach and its round-the-clock offerings, but feels a world away. Or choose the stylish cliff-top accommodations with turquoise-water views at the Nami Resort, set high above Diniwid Beach.

Visitors rarely venture beyond Boracay to see the sprawling central chain of islands known as the Visayas (or to other parts of the country, for that matter). Southeast of here is the island of Panay, a microcosm of what is most alluring about the Philippines. Colonial-era churches with Baroque flourishes are dilapidated but still in use, dominating many of the small plazas along the rugged coastline. In vibrant Iloilo City, the Spanish empire's last capital in Asia, local families line up for dinner at the all-you-can-eat, open-air beachside buffet restaurants of Arevelo, just west of the city center. To the north is the rocky Bulabog Puti-An National Park, with plenty of routes for climbers and trekkers, and rough roads that lead to Panay's rural areas, where life still follows traditional rhythms.

WHERE: 215 miles/345 km south of Manila. **SHANGRI-LA RESORT AND SPA:** Tel 63/36-288-4988; www.shangri-la.com. *Cost:* from $400. **NAMI RESORT:** Tel 63/36-288-6753; www.namiresorts.com. *Cost:* from $175. **BEST TIMES:** Oct–Jun for nicest weather and best diving conditions; Jan for carnival-like Ati-Atihan Festival in Kalibo, on the north coast of Panay.

A City-State's Extreme Makeover

THE NEW FACE OF SINGAPORE

Singapore

The nation of Singapore, the second smallest in Asia, has seen more than its fair share of makeovers. Having evolved from an obscure, sparsely populated island crawling with tigers to a scruffy port city in the 19th century, it transformed itself again after declaring independence from Malaysia in 1965 into what it is today: the squeaky-clean economic heavyweight of Southeast Asia. Its recent bold plan: to create an equatorial Las Vegas, where glamorous casinos, trendy bars, late-night discos, and outdoor restaurants aim to appeal to both residents (the country boasts the world's highest percentage of millionaires) and visitors, who will hopefully feel enticed to linger longer.

Two new glamorous resorts, combining hotels, entertainment, and casinos, lure both families and high rollers looking to risk a few colorful Singapore dollars. Designed by U.S.-based Moshe Safdie, the spectacular Marina Bay Sands stands right on the edge of the city and within easy walking distance of the financial center. It was an instant landmark when it opened in 2010, sweeping into the air with three futuristic 57-story hotel towers joined at the top by the Sands Sky Park, a cantilevered platform as big as three football fields. The aerial perch is home to some of the city's trendiest restaurants, highlighted by Sky on 57, where native chef Justin Quek puts a modern twist on classic Singaporean dishes. You'll find breathtaking 360-degree vistas at floating nightclubs, an observation deck, and an infinity swimming pool that is three times Olympic length and the longest elevated swimming pool in the world.

Resorts World Sentosa sits closer to earth, blissfully isolated on a small, picturesque, and formerly sleepy island off southern Singapore, 10 minutes from downtown. With its massive aquarium, the region's only Universal Studios and a maritime museum in the works, it prides itself on being the more family friendly of the two resorts. Both have a raft of celebrity chefs from across the world (from Mario Batali and Guy Savoy to Tetsuya Wakuda and Joël Robuchon) and more than 1,800 hotel rooms each. Pint-size as it may be, this city-state is out to make a splash.

Survey the city from the infinity pool atop the Marina Bay Sands.

Marina Bay Sands: Tel 65/6688-8868; www.marinabaysands.com. *Cost:* from $275; dinner at Sky on 57 $75. **Resorts World Sentosa:** Tel 65/6577-8899; www.rwsentosa.com. *Cost:* from $275. **Best times:** Mar–Oct for nicest weather; May–Jun for Singapore Arts Festival; Aug 9 for National Day; Sep for Grand Prix; New Year's Eve.

Colonial Time Travel

Raffles Hotel and the E&O Express

Singapore

Despite Singapore's full-throttle thrust toward the future and determination to be the epitome of cool, visitors who have their fill of modernity can still glimpse prized vestiges of its colonial past amid the malls and cutting-edge hotels. Its dignified Singapore Cricket Club lies smack in the middle of the city. And Raffles, arguably the world's best-known hotel, is one of Singapore's most iconic sites. With its landscaped palm and frangipani trees, magnificent white façade, and antiques-filled rooms with 14-foot ceilings, the place "stands for all the fables of the exotic East," or so wrote Somerset Maugham. The impeccably renovated hotel was founded in 1887 and has only gotten better with age. Still a magnet for well-heeled travelers and the merely curious, it's become as much a tourist attraction as it is a place to stay.

Maugham liked his Million Dollar Cocktail in the hotel's Writers Bar (Joseph Conrad and Rudyard Kipling frequented this watering hole too), though most visitors today head for the Long Bar, where the Singapore Sling was invented in 1915; more than 2,000 of the sweet pink concoctions are made here daily and cost what you'd pay for a full meal at any of the city's hawker centers (see below).

Another remnant of more opulent times is the Eastern & Oriental Express train, evoking Asia's colonial age with its small but elegant compartments, stewarded tea service, formal meals, and evening cocktails in the piano bar. The luxurious hotel-on-wheels travels from Singapore up the Malay Peninsula through rubber and palm plantations to Bangkok (see p. 621), with stops along the way—to take a trishaw ride through old Penang (see p. 609) or a visit to the bridge over the River Kwai. Golden pagodas roll by your window as you travel through the dense, damp jungle. From the observation car, you'll catch glimpses of country life: rice paddies dotted with toiling farmers, plows drawn by water buffalo, waving children from thatch-roofed villages. After making the 1,200-mile, 2-night journey, you'll want to spend time in Bangkok, Thailand's City of Angels. Then hop back onboard to experience a journey along one of the Eastern & Oriental Express's other routes, such as the 7-day Epic Thailand run, which takes you from Bangkok through Thailand's rural northeast region then up to Chiang Mai (see p. 624) for temple touring and elephant rides.

RAFFLES HOTEL: Tel 65/6337-1886; in the U.S., 800-768-9009; www.raffles.com. *Cost:* from $475 (off-peak), from $695 (peak). **EASTERN & ORIENTAL EXPRESS:** Tel 65/6392-3500; in the U.S., 800-524-2420; www.orient-express.com. *Cost:* 3-day journeys from Singapore to Bangkok or reverse from $2,440, all-inclusive. **BEST TIME:** Mar–Oct for coolest and driest weather.

Where Dining Is King

SINGAPORE'S STREET FOOD

Singapore

It's no wonder that eating (even more than shopping) is Singapore's favorite pastime—the city may well be the best place on earth for sampling the astonishing variety of Asia's many cuisines, which you can do with pleasure at a plethora of food stalls. In fact, the wealth of street food isn't sold on the street at all these days. This being tidy and well-organized Singapore, sidewalk vendors have been relocated to government-regulated "hawker centers"; by some accounts, there are over 100 of these open-air food courts. Day and night, locals and visitors, dignitaries and cabdrivers gather at stalls (all subject to stringent health inspection) that offer a staggering array of dishes.

Here in the tropical heat, amid the din of clanging trays and the shouted orders and the smells of fermented fish paste, ginger, and curry is a gastronomic and cultural experience that can be had only in Singapore. Malay, Indonesian, Indian, and Chinese dishes—and the unique local Peranakan, a blend of Chinese and Malaysian traditions—bump up against each other. Enjoy Sri Lankan chili crab or simple, flavorful Hainanese chicken rice alongside your *nasi goring* (fried rice) or *roti martabak* (thin, crepelike flatbread stuffed with meat and rice and served with curry). If you're feeling adventurous, top it off with some notoriously smelly but delicious durian fruit for dessert.

Every Singaporean has his or her own favorite hawker center, many of which are located out of town in large housing developments. Reliably good, the centrally located Newton Circus is the most famous, most touristy, and most expensive; the Maxwell Road cluster is just as conveniently located but still attracts a fair share of loyal locals who consider it the best in the city. The renovated multistoried Chinatown Complex Food Center offers the chance to sample dozens of different (mostly southern Chinese) dishes, all ideally accompanied by a cold Tiger beer.

INFO: www.myhawkers.sg. **NEWTON CIRCUS:** Newton Circus at Clemenceau Rd., near the Newton MRT. **MAXWELL ROAD HAWKER CENTER:** Maxwell Rd. at South Bridge Rd., near the Outram Park MRT. **CHINATOWN COMPLEX FOOD CENTER:** near the Outram Park MRT. **HOW:** Makansutra offers a variety of 4-hour food tours. Tel 65/6438-4038; www.makansutra.com. *Cost:* $135. **BEST TIMES:** Mar–Oct for nicest weather; Jul for Singapore Food Festival.

The Ancient Capital of Siam

AYUTHAYA

Thailand

Once called the "Pearl of the East," Ayuthaya—the artistic, spiritual, and military center of Southeast Asia—was the capital of Thailand from 1350 until its destruction by marauding Burmese 4 centuries later.

Thirty-three kings of various dynasties built hundreds of temples and created thousands of images of Buddha in a city-state that archives claim was one of the richest in the entire region. The city's destruction in 1767 was so complete that rather than rebuild, the heartbroken king chose to relocate his court to Bangkok, 50 miles downriver, where he would soon build the Grand Palace (see p. 622). Today Ayuthaya's ruins hint at the city's former splendor, and visitors with a healthy imagination (and a good guide) will easily grasp its onetime grandeur and importance. While you're there, check out the former *kraal* (stockade), where wild elephants were once kept and which is now used to rehabilitate ones that are elderly, injured, or orphaned.

A row of silk-draped Buddhas surrounds Wat Yai Chai Mongkol, a meditation site that dates back to 1357.

Ayuthaya is easily and inexpensively reached by road or rail from Bangkok, but a popular day-trip option is to travel on the Chao Phraya River, then return by road. The river has been a vital trade and transport thoroughfare for centuries. Today it provides a fascinating journey between Thailand's current and former capitals. Various boats take from 1 to 3 days to complete the 100-mile round-trip, and overnight departures usually also include a visit to Bangkok's Royal Barges Museum. The ornately decorated vessels on display are used in infrequent river processions, such as the one in 2006 for the 60th anniversary of King Bhumibol's ascension to the Thai throne. The *Manohra Song*, a lovingly restored 100-year-old teak rice barge, captures a bit of the royal treatment with four beautiful staterooms, and is one of the most luxurious live-aboard boats on the river. Its sister boat, the *Manohra Dream*, is even more opulent, with just two spacious guest rooms accented with Thai silk pillows and bed coverings.

WHERE: 50 miles/80 km north of Bangkok. ***MANOHRA SONG:*** Tel 66/2-477-0770; www.manohracruises.com. *Cost: Manohra Song*'s 3-day "Voyage of Kings" from $1,985 (off-peak), from $2,320 (peak), all-inclusive. **BEST TIME:** Nov–Feb for the cooler dry season.

Food, Flowers, and a Shopping Frenzy

BANGKOK'S MARKETS

Bangkok, Thailand

You'll be able to explore only a small part of Chatuchak's 30 jam-packed, awning-covered acres before your head starts to swim from cultural and visual overload. One of the world's largest outdoor markets, with an estimated 5,000 merchants ready for business every Saturday and Sunday at 6 A.M., Chatuchak is the ultimate Bangkok shopping experience. It's a sprawling extravaganza where the rare, the costly, and the unusual are sold side by side with authentic street food, tribal crafts, and counterfeit everything. Heady spices, delicate orchids, and creatures ranging from Siamese kittens to Siamese fighting fish all reinforce being in one of southeast Asia's most vibrant and compelling cities.

Stop at one of Chatuchak's food stalls and you'll understand why Bangkok is considered one of the world's great destinations for street food. Sample a plate of pad thai (fried noodles) studded with fresh herbs and peanuts, or brave the zingier chile flavors of *som tam*, a traditional Northern Thai dish made with shredded green papaya. Those with a sweet tooth line up for the *khao tom ka thi:* coconut-infused sticky rice wrapped in a banana leaf.

If you're on the hunt for gifts to haul back home, this is your one-stop shopping destination. Traditional silk garments and hand-painted china sell alongside modern housewares, video games, and even computers. It's a crowded, sense-numbing carnival, teeming with old ladies with sharp elbows, saffron-robed monks, mothers shopping for toys with their children, and suited businessmen buying provisions for dinner.

Bangkok has another essential market experience: Pak Khlong Talat. Every night of the week around dusk, Pak Khlong's daytime

Dragonfruits and mangosteens are among the exotic offerings at Chatuchak, a Thai institution that sells everything under the sun.

role as a vegetable market is transformed, and the city's biggest flower market takes over. Flowers are very important in Thai culture, used to decorate homes and as offerings at neighborhood temples, which explains why growers from around the Thai kingdom converge nightly here to sell mounds of orchids, roses, lotuses, chrysanthemums, and several blooms you've probably never seen before. Getting to this riverside market is half the fun if you take one of Bangkok's buzzing water taxis along the Chao Phraya River. Exit at the Tha Saphan Phuts boat stop, and follow the fragrance of jasmine and crowds of locals through a floating teak pavilion to Pak Khlong's multihued blur. Negotiation and bartering continue until well after midnight.

WHERE: Chatuchak Park: Catch the Skytrain to Mo Chit or metro to Chatuchak Park. Pak Khlong Talat: by water taxi or ordinary taxi.

Royal Digs and Ancient Massage

THE GRAND PALACE AND WAT PHO

Bangkok, Thailand

Once the walled residence of the Thai monarch, the Grand Palace—a study in monumental excess—was created more than 2 centuries ago by the revered Chakri dynasty of the Kingdom of Siam. Today the sprawling palace complex is one of Thailand's most popular attractions (the current king, Bhumibol, is regally ensconced at nearby Chitralada Palace, which is closed to the public).

The Grand Palace's shimmering labyrinth of more than 100 buildings is a fantastically ornate maze, and the greatest single display of traditional Thai arts and architecture in the world. The gilded and inlaid compound includes the most famous of Bangkok's 400-odd temples: Wat Phra Kaeo, popularly known as the Temple of the Emerald Buddha and symbolically linking Thailand's spiritual heart with its former seat of temporal power. Here sits Thailand's most venerated religious object, a delicate 26-inch seated Buddha carved from semiprecious jade. The cherished figure, perched on a 34-foot-high golden throne guarded by ancient bronze lions, was lost and then rediscovered in the 15th century. As protector of the country, the Buddha presides over the only area of the Grand Palace where incense-burning Thai worshippers outnumber awestruck tourists.

Wat Pho, also known as the Temple of the Reclining Buddha, contains more than 1,000 depictions of the enlightened one.

To see the Buddha in repose, head to nearby Wat Pho, a 10-minute stroll south of the Grand Palace through

Bangkok's busy streets. The 17th-century building is Thailand's oldest and largest temple and is built around an impressive 150-foot-long, gold-leaf-covered reclining statue of the Buddha. It is also famous for its centuries-old university and as the center for the teaching and preservation of traditional Thai medicine and massage. The latter is traditionally viewed as a spiritual and healing art closely linked to Buddhist teachings, and was, for centuries, practiced exclusively at temples. If you decide to sign up for one, expect a thorough workout for all your body's pressure points, as a slim but strong therapist rigorously stretches you to a state of unexpected Nirvana (unlike with other forms of massage, you'll be worked on while fully clothed). Tropical breezes drifting through Wat Pho's open-sided pavilion enhance the bliss.

Visitor info: www.bangkokforvisitors.com. **Cost:** $13 for a 1-hour massage at Wat Pho.

The Epitome of Gracious Hospitality

A Trio of Bangkok Hotels

Bangkok, Thailand

Bangkok is a sprawling and fascinating city, composed of neighborhoods that embody all the different facets of the Thai capital. And in a country known for its gracious hospitality and impeccable service, Bangkok's hotels have won every award in the book. Three stand out: one more than a century old, one cutting-edge, and one Colonial-style, each encapsulating Bangkok at its finest.

The riverside Oriental Hotel is a legend, as venerable and visited as Bangkok's Grand Palace (see previous page). It first opened in 1879, on the banks of the Chao Phraya River, and since then it has hosted everyone from Joseph Conrad to Elizabeth Taylor to Neil Armstrong. Contemporary visitors can celebrate the history of this Bangkok landmark in the Authors Suites, housed in the only part of the original building still standing. Elaborate suites named after Somerset Maugham, Noël Coward, and James Michener are tributes to the Oriental's storied past. A riverboat shuttle whisks guests to the opposite bank, where Bangkok's best classical dance performances take place nightly in the Oriental's lavish Sala Rim Naam restaurant. This is also where you'll find the hotel's celebrated spa, a beautifully simple oasis concealed in a restored teakwood house. While other luxury hotels also enjoy box-seat locations on the banks of the Chao Phraya, the history-laden Oriental was the city's first, and it's unlikely the hotel's raffish past and stylish present will be eclipsed anytime soon.

A few blocks east of the river, amid the bustle of Bangkok's commercial district, sits the Sukhothai Hotel, perfect for guests seeking sleek, understated accommodations that combine hushed elegance with the timeless elements of Thai culture. A palm-lined drive and 6 acres of flower gardens and lily ponds recapture the tranquility of the 13th-century kingdom after which it was named. Despite its size (it holds 200 exquisite rooms, each with an oversize, teak-floored bathroom), the air of a Buddhist retreat prevails, with Sukhothai-style stupas reflected in illuminated pools of lotus blossoms. The hotel's Spa Botanica features signature treatments, like the 3-hour Thailand Flower Ritual, combining a petal-strewn bath with a jasmine-and-coriander body scrub. On the alfresco terrace of the Celadon restaurant, traditionally spicy Thai cuisine mingles effortlessly with more cosmopolitan flavors in one of the city's most romantic settings.

In the city's older streets around the Grand Palace and Wat Pho (see p. 622), two sister heritage properties lovingly resurrected by their architect owners channel the Bangkok of yesteryear. The Bhuthorn is located in a corner shop house with three guest rooms, individually furnished with Thai antiques collected over the years. Overflow guests find a warm welcome at the nearby Asadang, featuring nine bed-and-breakfast rooms in a restored Colonial mansion.

ORIENTAL: Tel 66/2-659-9000; in the U.S., 800-526-6566; www.mandarinoriental.com. *Cost:* from $295 (off-peak), from $420 (peak). **SUKHOTHAI:** Tel 66/2-344-8888; www.sukhothai.com. *Cost:* from $255; dinner at Celadon $50. **BHUTHORN:** Tel 66/2-622-2270; www.thebhuthorn.com. *Cost:* from $135. **ASADANG:** Tel 66/85-180-7100; www.theasadang.com. *Cost:* from $135. **BEST TIME:** Oct–Mar for dry season.

Markets and Mansions in the "Rose of the North"

CHIANG MAI

Thailand

Chiang Mai is Thailand's second largest city and the unofficial capital of the country's north. Previously the sleepy hub of a rural hinterland and gateway to treks to the outlying hill tribes, this cooler-climate city dubbed the "Rose of the North" has been developing a distinct urban buzz. Excellent boutique hotels are popping up, and the city offers some of Southeast Asia's best market shopping and delicious street food. Factor in the fascinating neighborhood of the Old City—combining ancient walls, moats, and beautiful *wats* (or Buddhist temples, the oldest dating to the late 13th century)—and travelers have plenty of reasons to take the 1-hour flight or 12-hour overnight train from Bangkok.

Chiang Mai has changed with the arrival of hotels that exude unmistakable character—such as the elegant Ping Nakara, a 100-year-old Colonial beauty with just 19 rooms. At the U Chiang Mai, Colonial style meets a 21st-century Zen aesthetic. Its lounge is housed in the 19th-century residence of a former Chiang Mai governor. It's also just a 5-minute walk to the biggest game in town, the weekly Sunday-night market along Ratchadamneon Road (Walking Street).

On weekends, locals sell handicrafts at Chiang Mai's Walking Street markets.

The Night Market kicks into action every day around 6 P.M., but it is a mere prelude to the Saturday and Sunday Walking Street markets, when the wats lining the thoroughfare become giant alfresco food centers. The scene draws as many locals as visitors, tucking into *laab gai* (spicy chicken salad) or *som tam* (green papaya salad), accompanied by coconut juice straight from the fruit. If you thrill to the local flavors, consider spending an insightful day at the Thai Cookery School, which has been offering classes since 1993.

In addition to serving up delicious Thai cuisine, the Walking Street markets are a great place to shop, with crafts brought into town by the hill peoples. Cheaper Chinese copies have infiltrated the stalls, so keep an eye out for the real thing. Workshops in town craft silver, celadon pottery, screen-printed silks, and woven textiles; meanwhile, contemporary design studios are creating their own scene, blending traditional with modern, and Thai with foreign aesthetics.

Beyond central Chiang Mai's enticing buzz, in the nearby Mae Rim Valley, is the incomparable Four Seasons Resort. Incorporating architectural traditions from neighboring Myanmar, Laos, and China, the gorgeously landscaped 20-acre resort resembles a northern Thai village, right down to the water buffalos that help plow and prepare the hotel's own rice paddies. Raft down a calm river on bamboo floats, or mountain bike through lush forests to hidden waterfalls. Afterward, give in to an aromatic Oriental massage with ginger- and lemongrass-infused oils at the resort's renowned spa.

WHERE: 400 miles/644 km north of Bangkok. **PING NAKARA:** Tel 66/53-252-999; www.pingnakara.com. *Cost:* from $165 (off-peak), from $240 (peak). **U CHIANG MAI:** Tel 66/53-327-000; www.uhotelsresorts.com. *Cost:* from $120. **THAI COOKERY SCHOOL:** Tel 66/53-206-388; www.thaicookeryschool.com. **FOUR SEASONS CHIANG MAI:** Tel 66/53-298-181; in the U.S., 800-819-5053; www.fourseasons.com/chiangmai. *Cost:* from $600 (off-peak), from $800 (peak). **BEST TIMES:** Nov–Mar for cooler, drier weather; Sat and Sun for Walking St. Night Market; Feb for Chiang Mai Flower Festival; Apr for Songkran Water Festival.

Elegance and Elephants

GOLDEN TRIANGLE

Thailand

In the rugged north where Thailand, Laos, and Myanmar meet and the Ruak and Mekong rivers converge, travelers encounter a lush, mountainous region with an abundance of opportunities for adventure. Treks to hill tribe communities—who were compromised in the Chiang Mai area by decades of insensitive exploitation—can still be arranged here by local socially conscious agencies for visits by foot, jeep, or boat.

Until recently, this remote area of bamboo jungles and misty hills was notorious for its warranted reputation of illicit opium manufacturing: The area's meandering rivers had been favored trade highways that supplied narcotics markets of the West since the 1920s. In the new century, the illegal action has shifted to Myanmar's Shan states to the west, and as if to prove the area's safety, a pair of exclusive resorts has joined the growing number that has set up camp in this northernmost point of the country.

With a secluded location on the Ruak River, the Four Seasons Tented Camp brings a romantic slice of African-safari style to Southeast Asia. Access is only by long-tail boat, and there are just 15 luxurious hillside "tents," offering one of Thailand's most exclusive and unusual overnight experiences. Each teak-floored canvas accommodation evokes the grand days of 19th-century expeditions, with period furnishings and river views from the spacious and private outdoor decks. Sit with a sundowner and take in the misty mountains of Laos and Myanmar, and the dense surrounding jungles. Luxury amenities include private yoga classes, aromatic spa treatments, and dining under the stars, but a key reason to come here is to interact with the resort's team of elephants. Guests are encouraged to take part in daily pachyderm-friendly activities, including working with the *mahout* trainers, riding the elephants, even helping with their daily baths. You can also adopt an elephant through a special program, supporting those that have been orphaned or rescued from a life working in the cities.

Experience elephants in a different way at the Anantara Golden Triangle Resort & Spa. Elephant polo was first played in India in the early 20th century but was not introduced to Thailand until 2004 at the Anantara sister resort in the southern coastal town of Hua Hin (see below). Now the annual King's Cup Tournament is shared between Anantara's Hua Hin and Golden Triangle properties. Players come from India, Sri Lanka, the United States, and Iceland—and high-profile sponsorship ensures that the event is one of Thailand's hottest social tickets. The leafy and luxurious Anantara resort also runs a year-round elephant camp on the grounds, allowing visitors, whether guests or not, to get up close and personal with these gentle giants.

Indian royalty originated elephant polo in the early 20th century, and the sport made its way to Thailand about a century later.

WHERE: 430 miles/690 km north of Bangkok. **FOUR SEASONS TENTED CAMP:** Tel 66/53-910-200; in the U.S., 800-819-5053; www.fourseasons.com. *Cost:* from $800. **ANANTARA GOLDEN TRIANGLE RESORT & SPA:** Tel 66/53-784-084; www.anantara.com. *Cost:* from $215. **HOW:** U.S.-based Smithsonian Journeys leads a 14-day trip to northern Thailand and Laos. Tel 202-349-0677 or 800-528-8147; www.smithsonianjourneys.org. *Cost:* $2,599 with most meals, air extra. Originates in Bangkok. *When:* Feb, Apr, Sep, Nov. **BEST TIMES:** Nov–Mar for cooler, drier weather; late Mar–early Apr for King's Cup elephant polo.

Thailand's Royal Resort

HUA HIN

Thailand

As the Thai royal family's favorite weekend escape from steamy Bangkok, Hua Hin was the country's first glamorous getaway. The transformation of this former fishing village south of Bangkok began in 1922, when King

Rama VII built his summer compound, Klai Kangwon ("Far from Worries") here. The current monarch, King Bhumibol (Rama IX), still takes advantage of the Spanish-influenced palace regularly, and almost a century of royal patronage has seen Hua Hin develop into a favorite beach resort for Thai and international visitors alike. On first impression, the town's humble fishing village roots are subdued under a cosmopolitan veneer, but a bit of exploration soon reveals reminders of a sleepier past. Small, open-walled seafood restaurants pepper the waterfront thoroughfare of Thanon Naresdamri and spill onto an improbably long teakwood jetty. Freshly cracked crab along Hua Hin's expansive beach pairs perfectly with an ice-cold Singha beer.

Hua Hin's vintage train station is adorned with twinkling lights.

An enjoyable way to reach Hua Hin from Bangkok is by train, with the 4-hour journey south concluding at the town's lovely 1920s-era terminus. The station's Royal Waiting Room is a red-painted teak confection combining Thai style with British whimsy. One of Hua Hin's best hotels also recalls the age of rail travel. Formerly the Railway Hotel, the Sofitel Centara Grand Resort & Villas is arrayed along Hua Hin's best expanse of beach. The gracious two-story hotel was originally built in 1923. Now fully restored and with the addition of 42 garden villas, it's an inviting seaside retreat from the congested capital.

The city's indisputable pièce de résistance, however, is the Chiva-Som International Health Resort, serenely set on a private lake just 2 miles south of town. The ancient Sanskrit name translates to "Haven of Life," and the exclusive getaway has built its reputation by promising travelers the ultimate in rest and renewal. All-inclusive stays fuse Eastern and Western approaches to health, nutrition, and exercise, and its expert staff of over 200 knows what it's doing. Just ask any of the celebrity guests from around the globe.

WHERE: 150 miles/240 km south of Bangkok. **SOFITEL CENTARA GRAND RESORT:** Tel 66/32-512-021; www.sofitel.com. *Cost:* from $160. **CHIVA-SOM HEALTH RESORT:** Tel 66/32-536-536; www.chivasom.com. *Cost:* from $500 per person, all-inclusive. **BEST TIME:** Nov–May for the cooler, drier season.

Floating Gems

KOH PHI PHI

Thailand

In an area of southern Thailand garlanded with beautiful islands, Koh Phi Phi (Phi Phi Island) is a standout. Against a backdrop of steep, jungled, limestone cliffs, bungalow resorts dot crescents of palm-shaded, bleached-white sand.

The tsunami of December 2004 hit Koh Phi Phi with full force, but the island has rebounded to again become one of Thailand's most popular destinations. Getting there is still possible only by ferry—there is no airport—so development is fairly moderate despite the island's improbable beauty and growing popularity.

Once here, boats connect you to the outlying islet of Koh Phi Phi Leh, recognized from its leading role in *The Beach* (2000), starring Leonardo DiCaprio. The island's remote beaches still represent an archetypal secret paradise today. Popular boat excursions to Koh Phi Phi Leh's famous bays run year-round. Join the day-trippers from nearby Krabi or Phuket (see next page and p. 631) to visit isolated coves, crystal-clear waters, and undeveloped beaches. The actual beach "discovered" by Leo in the film is Maya Bay, surrounded by towering cliffs and heartbreakingly beautiful. There are no accommodations on Koh Phi Phi Leh, but visiting the compact island makes for a wonderful day trip.

Despite an influx of day visitors, staying on the principal island of Koh Phi Phi Don still promises a compelling Thai island experience. The snorkeling is excellent right off the beach, and you can hop a boat trip to "James Bond Island" (see next page) in Phangnga Bay. Other options include superb diving around the island's shores, Thai cookery classes, and tours that include immense, cathedral-like caverns where Sea Gypsies harvest edible birds' nests (much loved by the Chinese). Stay at a resort with a private beach and you'll enjoy delicious seclusion. The island's most comfortable is the Phi Phi Village Beach Resort & Spa, with stylish hillside villas, plus 800 yards of its own stretch of shoreline, lined with palm trees and hammocks.

WHERE: 24 miles/39 km southwest of Krabi; 27 miles/43 km southwest of Phuket. **PHI PHI VILLAGE BEACH RESORT:** Tel 66/76-363-700; www.ppisland.com. *Cost:* from $225. **BEST TIME:** Dec–Apr for cooler, drier weather.

Thailand's Cosmopolitan Island Scene

KOH SAMUI

Thailand

The backpacker brigade first stumbled upon Koh Samui in the 1970s, and the island changed considerably once word got out. An airport was built in 1989, and Western tourists, drawn by talk of dazzling beaches, started to frequent a growing number of upscale hotels. Now Koh Samui continues to develop as one of Thailand's most cosmopolitan island getaways. But it's an exceedingly versatile slice of holiday heaven, with luxury villas, hip yoga and meditation retreats, and laid-back beach bars that still exude Samui's original counterculture vibe.

Nestled on the west coast is the Baan Taling Ngam resort, which opened during Koh Samui's pre-airport days on some of the island's best real estate and is still the island's ritziest property (it's privileged with great sunsets). From its terraced guest rooms and seven pools, the resort offers uncommonly lovely views of some of the small islands and jungle-clad outcroppings scattered across the Gulf of Thailand. They are part of the Ang Thong National Marine Park, a popular destination for world-class diving and snorkeling that encompasses 42 islands. The largest inhabited key, Koh Pha Ngan (7 miles north and accessible by daily boat runs), continues to draw budget travelers and scuba lovers the way Samui once did, though it's also showing signs of a more upmarket future. Farther north, tiny Koh Tao offers the best approximation of Koh Samui's former days as a shoestring-traveler's haven.

Long sweeps of white beaches encircle Koh Samui, while the middle of the island remains dense with coconut plantations. Coconuts were once a mainstay of the local economy, when 2 million fruits were shipped to Bangkok every month. The trade is now greatly reduced, but the coconut is still used widely in Koh Samui's increasingly sophisticated restaurants. The elegant Zazen on Bo Phut beach combines ocean views, a romantic ambience, and European-Thai fusion food. Try the crispy sea bass in a green-curry cream or silky smooth lemongrass crème brûlée. The restaurant's accompanying Zazen Boutique Resort & Spa features Asian minimalist décor and a beachfront location.

Where: 300 miles/480 km southwest of Bangkok. **Baan Taling Ngam:** Tel 66/77-423-019; www.baan-taling-ngam.com. *Cost:* from $280 (off-peak), from $530 (peak). **Zazen Boutique Resort & Spa:** Tel 66/77-425-085; www.samuizazen.com. *Cost:* from $190; dinner $50. **Best time:** Dec–Apr to avoid monsoon rains.

A Wonderland of Spectacular Limestone Peaks

Phangnga Bay

Krabi, Thailand

James Bond fans might recall Phangnga Bay as the spectacular island setting for *The Man with the Golden Gun,* parts of which were filmed on Koh Phing Kan, now known as "James Bond Island." Cinematic fame aside, this spectacular profusion of sheer limestone mountain peaks rising from the Andaman Sea's pistachio green waters is one of the world's most beautiful natural phenomena. Located just off the southern Thai coast near the city of Krabi, the bay's sharp outcroppings reach up 1,000 feet, many covered by dense mounds of jungle. On a gray day, these islands with their tiny lagoons and mangrove swamps have the mystical aura of Chinese watercolors.

The optimal way to explore the bay's secret caves is by boat.

Several of the humped and jagged islets are riddled with stalactite- and stalagmite-embellished caves. You can explore them along with idyllic beaches and fishing villages built on stilts via long-tail boats or sea kayaking excursions from Krabi, nearby Phuket, or Koh Phi Phi (see pp. 631 and 627). Paddle your way into narrow caverns with barely enough head room. An inky dusk descends at twilight creating shape-shifting shadows around these labyrinths of limestone and tangles of overgrown vegetation.

This unique topography is what you'll be gazing at during languid days spent in any of the 42 villas of the Tubkaak Boutique Resort, set on a beautiful remote beach north of Krabi town. But little can beat the well-known Rayavadee Resort, nestled within a tropical rain forest that's populated by wild monkeys and exotic birdlife. Accessible only by boat through the bay's towering karst outcroppings, it's one of the world's most unusual hotel locations. Three Andaman Sea beaches surround the property, one of which, Phra Nang, is renowned as one of the planet's most perfect.

One hour by boat from either Phuket or Krabi are two islands—Koh Yao Yai (Big Long Island) and Koh Yao Noi (Little Long Island)—that represent what Thailand was like when it was first discovered by backpackers decades ago. They are part of a national park, with simple beach-bungalow inns and village homestays—and one breathtakingly beautiful resort. The luxury on offer at the Six Senses Hideaway Yao Noi hints at what may be the island's not-so-distant future.

WHERE: 37 miles/60 km east of Phuket (90 scenic minutes by boat). **TUBKAAK BOUTIQUE RESORT:** Tel 66/75-628-400; www.tubkaakresort.com. *Cost:* from $250 (off-peak), from $510 (peak). **RAYAVADEE RESORT:** Tel 66/75-620-740; www.rayavadee.com. *Cost:* from $650 (off-peak), from $750 (peak). **SIX SENSES HIDEAWAY YAO NOI:** Tel 66/76-418-500; www.sixsenses.com. *Cost:* from $415 (off-peak), from $850 (peak). **BEST TIME:** Nov–Mar for cooler, drier weather.

"City of Mist"

MAE HONG SON

Thailand

Once you spend a morning in Bangkok's traffic, you may be ready to escape to Mae Hong Son, in the cool hills 600 miles to the northwest and near the border of Myanmar. Tourism has left few Thai towns free of Western impact, but the lovely town of Mae Hong Son, known as the "City of Mist," fits the bill better than most. (Venture to nearby riverside villages like Soppong and slow-paced Pai for an even more authentic ambience.)

Mae Hong Son was founded as an elephant training camp in the 1830s and remained cut off from the world until the late 1960s, when a paved road was built from Chiang Mai (see p. 624), 160 miles away. A distinct Burmese influence lingers, especially in the town's brightly colored and zinc-trimmed temples and stupas.

Dewy mist gives Mae Hong Son its nickname, the "City of Mist," or sometimes, the "City of Three Mists."

Local guides can arrange bamboo rafting trips down the gentle Pai River, bush trekking by elephant, or hiking to tribal villages. It's a wonderfully peaceful scene; the only time downtown Mae Hong Son really comes alive is for the early-morning market when hill tribe women arrive to buy from and barter with the locals. Things calm down again by breakfast, while the swirling mists that give the town its name lift by late afternoon. That's the time to motorbike to the top of Doi Kong Mu hill and the 19th-century Wat Phra That temple for a spectacular view of the Pai Valley and the surrounding mountains.

This area of Thailand is also home to a small but growing number of fine eco-resorts. Set among rice paddies and gentle streams just south of Mae Hong Son, Fern Resort features 40 bungalows built in the Shan style (an ethnic group from this part of Southeast Asia). Airy rooms and stand-alone suites are accented with silk, bamboo, and teak, and the resort's open-sided restaurant features excellent local food, including the unusual dish of fried tree fern. As for how to spend your days, bird-watching excursions and nature walks provide immersion in the local flora and fauna, while mountain biking and river trips offer gentle thrills.

WHERE: 160 miles/257 km northwest of Chiang Mai. **FERN RESORT:** Tel 66/53-686-110; www.fernresort.info. *Cost:* $85. **BEST TIMES:** Nov–Feb for cooler and drier weather; early Apr for Poi Sang Long, celebrating the initiation of young boys into Buddhist monkhood.

Island Trailblazer and Perennial Favorite

PHUKET

Thailand

Known as the Pearl of the Andaman Sea, Phuket—Thailand's largest island at 210 square miles—offers a cavalcade of gorgeous beaches, inspiring resorts, and more interesting heritage architecture than one might expect.

Although much of its innocence and character was diluted in the tourist boom of the 1980s and '90s, visitors continue to come, these days looking for luxury. In 1988, Amanpuri opened as the inaugural property of Amanresorts, the exclusive hotel chain that is now the standard-bearer of Asian luxury, and it remains the premier property on the island. On a coconut-palmed hillside, 40 open-sided teak pavilions with curved roofs and vaulted ceilings overlook the private Pansea Beach and create the one-with-nature solitude for which Aman is renowned.

The Banyan Tree, long considered one of Asia's finest spa hotel groups, was also the first-ever property of the prestigious chain to be built. Twenty open-air spa pavilions offer aromatic and hedonistic treatments, such as the 3-hour Banyan Indulgence, using methods such as Thai acupressure massage and ingredients including lemongrass and cucumber. Tre, the Banyan Tree's premier restaurant located beside the resort's private lagoon, showcases French-Vietnamese fusion food using such diverse ingredients as star anise and lotus seeds to accent dishes featuring Wagyu beef and scallops.

Travelers with deep pockets have long flocked here, but the island is also accessible to vacationers with more modest budgets. The Marina Phuket Resort, on jungle-backed Karon beach, has a can-do staff who gladly arrange day trips by boat to Phangnga Bay (see p. 629) and excursions to the twin islands of Koh Racha Noi and Koh Racha Yai, where divers swim among graceful manta rays and easily accessed wrecks.

WHERE: 430 miles/690 km southwest of Bangkok. **AMANPURI:** Tel 66/76-324-333; in the U.S., 800-477-9180; www.amanresorts.com. *Cost:* pavilions from $525 (off-peak), from $850 (peak). **BANYAN TREE PHUKET:** Tel 66/76-324-374; in the U.S., 800-591-0439; www.banyantree.com. *Cost:* villas from $485. **MARINA PHUKET RESORT:** Tel 66/76-330-625; www.marinaphuket.com. *Cost:* from $100 (off-peak), from $200 (peak). **BEST TIMES:** Dec–Apr for cooler, drier weather; late Sep–early Oct for Vegetarian Festival with colorful processions, fire walking, and body piercing.

Highland Honeymoon in the City of Eternal Spring

Da Lat

Vietnam

A cool retreat from the sweltering heat of Vietnam's coastal plains, Da Lat was a favorite hill station for royalty and the colonial French, who created their own *petit Paris* here almost 5,000 feet above sea level. Enjoying mild, springlike weather year-round, Da Lat is known as the "City of Love" to Vietnamese honeymooners, who come for the high-country landscape scattered with clear lakes, waterfalls, evergreen forests, and flowering gardens. You'll want to come for all that too—as well as for the lingering bohemian ambience. Expect to see a few Gauloises-smoking types amongst all the newlyweds. With pedal-your-own giant swan boats and horse-drawn carriages cruising around town, Da Lat can be kitschy, but the glorious scenery and a relative absence of Western visitors make it a delightful detour.

Daily flights arrive from Ho Chi Minh City, but opt instead to make the 4-hour journey by road, which traverses some of Vietnam's finest scenery, winding through villages lined with coffee drying at the roadside and eventually emerging in Da Lat's scenic valleys. Stay at the lakeside Dalat Palace Heritage Luxury Hotel, where traditional French elegance blends with Vietnamese graciousness. Built in 1922, the hotel features a world-class, 18-hole golf course. The Ana Mandara Villas Dalat Resort & Spa, which was built during the same period, comprises 17 renovated villas spread across 35 acres of parkland in the hills surrounding the city. The luxury and attention to detail are definitely 21st century, but an old-world ambience lingers, courtesy of a few telling touches: antique gramophones, period furniture, and the vintage Peugeots used to chauffeur guests around town.

Where: 191 miles/308 km northeast of Ho Chi Minh City. **Dalat Palace:** Tel 84/63-382-5444; www.dalatpalace.vn. *Cost:* from $175. **Ana Mandara Villas:** Tel 84/63-355-5888; http://anamandara-resort.com. *Cost:* from $125. **Best time:** Dry season is Nov–Mar; temperatures are consistent through the year.

The Mythical Bay of Dragons

Ha Long Bay

Vietnam

Vietnamese legend maintains that dragons once descended from heaven and spouted streams of jade droplets into the waters of Ha Long Bay (Vin Ha Long), forming thousands of islands to protect the bay and its people from invading marauders. Today this mysterious body of water on the edge of the Gulf of Tonkin is studded with more than 2,000 outcroppings of all shapes and sizes.

The soaring limestone monoliths resemble dogs, elephants, toads, and monkeys—creatures that have inspired the islands' names. It's an area that has the shimmering, surreal quality of classical Chinese and Vietnamese paintings, especially when the sails of sampans and junks are silhouetted like giant butterflies against the horizon.

Outcroppings and rock formations make for a unique bay backdrop.

More than 100 miles long, Ha Long Bay features mostly uninhabited islands and sandy, deserted beaches. Away from the mainland, the bay's chief population centers are the floating villages and fish farms of local Sea Gypsies. Wooden cruise boats ply the bay's waters, serving freshly grilled seafood—including huge tiger prawns—that is often caught just minutes before mealtime.

The largest island in the bay is Cat Ba, a popular overnight stopping point. The Cat Ba National Park features caves and grottoes to explore, including the multichambered Trung Trang Cave. To really experience Ha Long Bay's hidden lagoons, caves, and fantastic rock formations, consider joining a kayaking trip through the maze of jagged isles. Or sign up for a cruise. More than 300 boats make excursions ranging from a few hours to several days in length. An overnight adventure affords the chance to see craggy limestone peaks being slowly revealed in the indigo dawn of a misty morning. Cruise Halong runs three thoroughly retrofitted boats, including the *Halong Violet,* a stylish junk imbued with the glamour and style of 1930s Indochina.

WHERE: 103 miles/160 km east of Hanoi. **CRUISE HALONG:** Tel 84/4-3933-5561; www.cruisehalong.com. *Cost:* 2-day cruise from $700 per cabin, inclusive. Originates in Hanoi. **HOW:** U.S.-based Mountain Travel Sobek offers 13-day adventure trips that include 4 days kayaking on Ha Long Bay. Tel 888-831-7526 or 510-594-6000; www.mtsobek.com. *Cost:* $4,795, all-inclusive. *When:* Mar–Oct. **WHERE TO STAY:** The contemporary Novotel in Ha Long City has large rooms, most with views of the bay. Tel 84/3-3384-8108; in the U.S., tel 800-668-6835; www.novotelhalong.com.vn. *Cost:* from $80 (off-peak), from $160 (peak). **BEST TIMES:** Oct–Nov and Mar–Apr are the nicest months of the cooler, drier season.

A Culinary Outpost, Now a Hot Spot

THE FOOD SCENE IN HANOI

Hanoi, Vietnam

If diving headfirst into a country's local food culture is one of your reasons for traveling, Hanoi could be your perfect destination. Discerning locals expect the freshest food at their daily markets, and foreign visitors are spoiled for choice with great street food, outstanding local eateries, and well-priced restaurants serving international cuisine. Hanoi's iconic dish is *bun cha*—a bowl of fresh rice noodles, shredded herbs and vegetables, and grilled pork, served with a sweet-salty-spicy sauce, crispy crab spring rolls, and as much or little chile and garlic as you'd like. People from all walks of life flock to bun cha stalls, such as the humble Bun Cha Dac Kim.

The Doan family at Cha Ca La Vong has spent five generations serving up *cha ca*, or curried Red River fish, its famous solitary dish. The restaurant's longevity inspired the city to rename the lane out front in its honor. In the no-frills upstairs restaurant, diners cook themselves chunks of seasoned garrupa fish on a clay charcoal brazier, stirring in chives and dill before spooning it into bowls of vermicelli and topping it with shrimp sauce, fried peanuts, and pickled vegetables.

Among Hanoi's many excellent modern-Vietnamese, fusion, and international restaurants is the upscale La Verticale, where dishes like lamb with five spices innovatively blend European and Asian influences. More local but equally interesting is Highway 4, with fare inspired by Vietnam's northern mountain region; its four buzzing outlets serve dishes such as catfish spring rolls and chicken in passion fruit sauce—and, for adventurous palates, locusts roasted with lemon leaves.

To experience the full range of Vietnamese cuisine in one place, dine at the Spices Garden restaurant, in the Sofitel Legend Metropole. Restored to its original 1920s style, the Metropole sits amid the wide, tree-lined boulevards of Hanoi's French Quarter, built while the city was capital of French Indochina. In colonial times, the elegant hotel was a gathering place for artists, writers, and government officials, and today it's the city's top address again. Book a room in the original building, where the buffed hardwood floors, green-shuttered windows, and other European elements have been carefully preserved. Keen gastrotourists can sign up for Vietnamese cooking classes with the Metropole's skilled chefs, while everyone else repairs to the top-notch spa—possibly the finest in the city.

Bun Cha Dac Kim: Tel 84/4-828-5022. *Cost:* $5. **Cha Ca La Vong:** Tel 84/4-825-3929. *Cost:* $8. **La Verticale:** Tel 84/4-3944-6316; www.verticale-hanoi.com. *Cost:* dinner $70. **Highway 4:** Tel 84/4-3715-0577; www.highway4.com. *Cost:* dinner $25. **Sofitel Legend Metropole:** Tel 84/4-826-6919; in the U.S., 800-763-4835; www.sofitel.com. *Cost:* from $255; dinner at Spices Garden $35. **Best times:** Oct–Apr has the least rainfall; Dec–Jan can be cool.

A Street for Every Ware

Hanoi's Old Quarter

Vietnam

Tucked between the green oasis of Hoan Kiem Lake and the Red River, the ancient, mazelike Old Quarter of Hanoi has been a shopping venue since the 15th century. Forty of the quarter's narrow, crowded streets—Rice Street, Silk Street, and Gold Street among them—are named after the goods once sold there (Bootleg DVD Street and Fake iPad Street have yet to be designated). Open, dilapidated storefronts—compact cubbyholes sometimes just spacious enough to hold a wizened merchant surrounded by goods stacked to the ceiling—give new meaning to "window shopping." Noodles, flowers, antiques, and handicrafts are yours for the bargaining.

The Old Quarter is also one of the city's most charming neighborhoods. Tree-lined streets, centuries-old temples, and Colonial architecture, including the 19th-century St. Joseph Cathedral, all provide balance to its more mercantile thrust. When the weather is cooler, the Quarter is best explored on foot, but if the tropical heat roils, flag down a cyclo, the city's ubiquitous pedal-powered version of a rickshaw. When you're in need of refreshment, ask your driver to drop you at Green Tangerine. This haven from the area's enjoyable chaos fills a beautifully restored 1928 French town house and offers cuisine that skillfully combines Vietnamese and French flavors. Try the delicious mango tarte tatin.

If you want a coffee break, ignore the Western-style clones sprouting up around Hanoi, and instead pull up a (very small) plastic chair at a traditional neighborhood café. The sidewalk seating arrangements may be more suitable for preschoolers, but a robust Vietnamese-style *café den*—with or without a shot of condensed milk—is an adult treat. The Old Quarter also has many fine places to stay, including the trendy, design-conscious Maison d'Hanoi Hanova. The recently built 55-room hotel combines traditional Vietnamese design with modern comforts, and is just a short stroll from serene Hoan Kiem Lake.

The streets of the Old Quarter are flooded with fruit and vegetable merchants, some of them on wheels.

How: Hidden Hanoi offers 2-hour walking tours of the Old Quarter and beyond. Tel 84/91-225-4045; www.hiddenhanoi.com.vn. *Cost:* $20. **Green Tangerine:** Tel 84/4-3825-1286; www.greentangerinehanoi.com. *Cost:* lunch $15. **Maison d'Hanoi Hanova:** Tel 84/4-3938-0999; www.hanovahotel.com. *Cost:* from $100. **Best times:** Oct–Apr has the least rainfall; Dec–Jan can be cool.

Temples, Traders, and Terrific Food

Saigon's Bustling Markets

Ho Chi Minh City, Vietnam

Vietnam is a Communist country, but visitors would never know it from the explosive wave of commercial activity that has washed over the country since the 1990s, particularly in Ho Chi Minh City (still commonly called Saigon). Big money is evident in new construction and luxury-car showrooms, but it's the capitalistic drive on display in more than 40 local markets spread around the city that truly marks Saigon's entrepreneurial renaissance.

Ben Thanh Market, the French-built municipal marketplace, is the city's largest and oldest. Hundreds of merchants create a narrow maze of stalls touting everything from the latest Japanese and Korean electronic gizmos to bolts of silk, bottles of cobra wine, and conical "poem" hats. The traditional is stacked up alongside the modern, and animated haggling is a given. Go for the color and the exotic chaos, but realize that no matter how honed your negotiating skills, you'll still pay twice as much as a local. Culinary consolation is easily achieved at Ben Thanh's tasty array of food stalls. Tuck into a bowl of *pho* (pronounced fuh)—delicious beef noodle soup topped with fresh herbs—or the French-Vietnamese combo of *banh mi*, a crunchy baguette stuffed with pork pâté, cool cucumber, and spicy condiments.

Another of Ho Chi Minh's principal markets, Binh Tay, is in bustling Cholon, the epicenter of the city's traditional Chinatown. Follow your nose to the natural medicine and herb shops running between Luong Nhu Phuc and Trieng Quang Phuc streets before diving into the market; look for its Chinese-style architecture topped with a stately clock tower. Cholon is also home to two of the city's most interesting Buddhist temples. Huge, fragrant coils of incense burn in the Thien Hau pagoda, dedicated to seafarers, while Quan Am pagoda is decorated with ornate ceramics depicting traditional Chinese legends.

Binh Tay is one of Saigon's commercial hubs.

BEST TIMES: Dec–Apr for drier, cooler weather; Jan or Feb for annual Tet New Year Festival.

Colonial Echoes in an Emerging Metropolis

HERITAGE HOTELS IN SAIGON

Ho Chi Minh City, Vietnam

With a cityscape dominated by construction cranes and unrelenting motorcycle traffic, Ho Chi Minh City often feels like an emerging metropolis stuck on fast-forward. But explore the city's three most famous heritage hotels and a more gracious and relaxed atmosphere emerges. Nostalgia rules at the Rex Hotel's rooftop bar, once a home away from home for expats and wartime journalists and still among the city's most popular watering holes. With year-round Christmas lights, topiary, and singing birds, you won't mistake it for a sophisticated cocktail joint, but the Rex is dripping with history, and few Westerners pass through town without stopping by. And while the recently renovated rooms are not the city's most luxurious, they fit the bill for visitors in search of the Saigon Experience.

Before the escalation of the Vietnam War in the early 1960s, Saigon was home to a coterie of spies, drifters, and journalists. For British novelist Graham Greene, Room 214 at the venerable Hotel Continental was his second home, and the hotel is the adopted residence of protagonist Thomas Fowler in Greene's novel *The Quiet American*. Its gracious interiors and elegant verandas also appear in the lushly elegant film *Indochine* (1992).

Opened in 1880 as the city's premier hotel, the Continental housed the de facto Saigon bureau for *The New York Times* and *Newsweek* by the 1960s. Following the war, the elegant façade concealed a forlorn and rundown interior, but the refurbished Continental is again one of Saigon's best addresses, with spacious, wood-accented rooms.

From the Continental, it's a short stroll down tree-lined Dong Khoi Street to the Saigon River and the Majestic Hotel. Built in

1925, the Majestic offers value in a colonial ambience. Riverside rooms are slightly more expensive but provide expansive views of the energetic bustle of Saigon River life. Come evening, head up to the hotel's rooftop bar for a gin and tonic and a vista of the waterway crammed with rice barges and watch as the city's floating restaurants turn on their soft flickering lights.

Rex Hotel: Tel 84/8-3829-2185; www.rexhotelvietnam.com. *Cost:* from $125. **Hotel Continental:** Tel 84/8-3829-9201; www.continentalvietnam.com. *Cost:* from $150. **The Majestic Hotel:** Tel 84/8-3829-5517; www.majesticsaigon.com.vn. *Cost:* from $160. **Best times:** Dec–Apr for cooler, drier weather; Jan or Feb for Tet New Year Festival; May 19 for celebrations of Ho Chi Minh's birthday.

A Quaint Port with European Influences

Hoi An

Vietnam

For centuries a river port city that drew large numbers of Japanese, Portuguese, Dutch, Arab, Chinese, and French merchants and seafarers, Hoi An today clings to its charm and heritage despite growing numbers of tourists. Its 800-plus historic structures—including Chinese guildhalls, pagodas, and Japanese bridges—were miraculously left unscathed by the Vietnam War. Many have been converted to shops or restaurants or are open to the public free of charge.

Hoi An has a vibrant, eclectic food scene—Asian fusion, traditional Vietnamese, and even Italian restaurants often coexist on the same block. Try popular local dishes such as *cao lau,* made of Japanese-style soba noodles topped with a hearty helping of fresh herbs, sliced pork, and crunchy *banh da* rice crackers, in one of the bustling restaurants lining the Thu Bon River. One of the best is Morning Glory, housed in an atmospheric, spacious old shop house. You can join proprietress Trinh Diem Vy for cooking classes that begin with a trip to the large food market. After exploring Hoi An's surrounding pedestrian cobblestoned streets, stop at one of the town's cafés for a glass of *bia hoi*—fresh draft beer that's just 3 percent alcohol.

Hoi An locals are known for being excellent tailors and shoemakers. The streets are crammed with shops that can have you outfitted and ready to go in two days or less. Bring along a magazine clipping of your favorite designer look and prepare to be impressed.

For an escape from Hoi An's bustle, check in at the Life Heritage Resort, set beside the river on quiet, tree-shaded grounds. Fifteen minutes outside town, the low-key, high-design Nam Hai Villas sit on an 85-acre expanse of the legendary China Beach, famous during the Vietnam War. Set a day aside to see the abandoned Hindu temple complex at My Son, 30 miles southwest of Hoi An, and return to the Nam Hai's spa—one of Vietnam's best—and recharge with a Chedi Jade massage.

Where: 18 miles/28 km south of Da Nang and 603 miles/972 km north of Ho Chi Minh City. **Morning Glory:** Tel 84/510-224-1555; www.restaurant-hoian.com. *Cost:* dinner $20; cooking classes from $15. **Life Heritage Resort:** Tel 84/510-914555; www.life-resorts.com. *Cost:* from $175. **Nam Hai:** Tel 84/510-3940-000; www.thenamhai.com. *Cost:* from $600. **Best times:** Jan–Mar for the cooler season; monthly full moon festival.

Ghosts of the Nguyen Dynasty

The Imperial City of Hue

Hue, Vietnam

Modeled on Beijing's Forbidden City (see p. 480), Hue's Imperial City lies within a 1,300-acre citadel on the banks of the Song Huong (Perfume River), halfway between Hanoi and Ho Chi Minh City.

The Hue Citadel was the political, religious, and cultural center ruled by the 19 emperors of the Nguyen Dynasty from 1802 to 1945, when Vietnam's last emperor abdicated the throne. Its Imperial City once housed Vietnam's grandest temples and finest palaces. Many structures still stand, awash with Chinese-influenced design motifs. At the dynasty's height, the imperial complex contained hundreds of rooms in dozens of ornately decorated buildings, all protected by a 65-foot-wide moat and 6-foot-thick walls. Neither was enough to stop the destruction wrought by the French occupation or the Vietnam War (the 1968 Tet Offensive in particular), but ongoing restoration is gradually transforming moss-covered, crumbling ruins into evocative treasures.

A gateway leads into the Imperial City's Hien Lam Pavilion.

Within the Imperial City, separated by another battery of walls and moats is the even more impressive Forbidden Purple City. It once housed royal family members in an elaborate series of chambers, and the weapons, clothing, housewares, and ceremonial pieces now held by the Citadel's Museum of Royal Fine Arts illuminate the grand lives enjoyed by their owners. The extravagant mausoleums of the rulers of the Nguyen Dynasty are scattered south of Hue, along the banks of the Perfume River, easily reached by boat.

Across the river, built around a former colonial governor's Art Deco home, La Résidence Hôtel & Spa has 122 rooms and suites, many with balconies overlooking the water and the Citadel—an especially impressive sight at night, when the Imperial City is illuminated. Outside the city center is the comfortable resort Pilgrimage Village. Though just 10 minutes by car from central Hue, its thatch-roofed bungalows and villas exude a relaxed, rural ambience. Hue's cuisine is renowned for being Vietnam's finest, and both La Résidence and Pilgrimage Village have excellent dining rooms with traditional Hue food. But an essential experience is to eat at the city's simple shop houses, where you can try *banh khoai*—a delicate rice-flour pancake stuffed with pork, crunchy bean sprouts, and peanut sauce—with a locally brewed Huda beer.

Where: 434 miles/689 km south of Hanoi. **La Résidence:** Tel 84/54-383-7475; www.la-residence-hue.com. *Cost:* from $140. **Pilgrimage Village:** Tel 84/54-388-5461; www.pilgrimagevillage.com. *Cost:* from $150. **Best times:** Feb–Aug for least rainfall; Feb–Apr for cooler temperatures.

Vietnam through the Back Door

THE MEKONG DELTA

Vietnam

From its source high in the Tibetan Plateau, the Mekong River journeys for 3,050 miles through China, Myanmar, Laos (see p. 601), Cambodia, and Vietnam—where it fragments into nine main distributaries before finally entering the South China Sea. The Vietnamese call it Song Cuu Long, or "River of Nine Dragons." And upstream in Thailand and Laos, it's the Mae Nam Khong, or "Mother of All Rivers," a very accurate description for the sustaining labyrinth of land and water that forms the Mekong River delta.

Referred to as "Vietnam's rice bowl," the delta is one of the most fertile areas in southeast Asia, supplying the country with most of its rice, fruit, and seafood, and affording travelers wonderful insights into the real Vietnam. In riverside villages accessible only by boat, visitors can see a countryside little changed by the centuries—as well as experience the warmth of the local people and enjoy juicy tropical fruit, potent rice wine, and simple full-flavored meals. Like any of history's great trade thoroughfares, the delta is home to many different peoples, including Vietnamese, Chinese, Khmer, and Cham. Floating river merchants and city markets showcase the area's bounty, and delving into the Mekong's heartland reveals floating towns, villages on stilts, and the popular beaches of Ha Tien, just a few miles from the Cambodian border.

To best experience the languid rhythms of the delta, charter your own slow-moving boat. The Song Xanh is a minifleet of four intimate wooden sampans, each with an airy bedroom and living area—plus a chef and a river-savvy skipper. The Song Xanh's journey begins at Cai Be, about 60 miles southwest of Ho Chi Minh City, and meanders along canals and tributaries before stopping in the French-colonial port town of Sa Dec. Guests eat and sleep onboard before setting off to Can Tho, the delta's largest city and home to the enormous Phung Hiep floating market—a bustling affair where seven branches of the Mekong converge.

WHERE: Can Tho is 99 miles/159 km southwest of Ho Chi Minh City. **HOW:** Ann Tours offers 1- and multi-day tours of the delta region, departing from Ho Chi Minh City. Tel 84/8-3925-3636; www.anntours.com. *Cost:* 1-day tour $70. **SONG XANH:** Tel 84/9-7942-0204; www.songxanhcruisemekong.com. *Cost:* 2-day tour of the delta from $250 per person, inclusive. Originates in Ho Chi Minh City. **WHERE TO STAY:** The Colonial-style Victoria Can Tho Resort is an excellent base for exploring the area. Tel 84/710-381-0111; www.victoriahotels-asia.com. *Cost:* from $165. **BEST TIME:** Dec–Mar for cooler and drier weather.

Produce-filled boats act as storefronts of the Phung Hiep floating market.

Beachside R&R

NHA TRANG

Vietnam

Vietnam's beach capital is the perfect place to wind down after a whirlwind tour of Southeast Asia. Fringed with palm trees and unfurling for 4 miles, it is one of the most beautiful stretches of sand on the South China Sea.

From morning to night, the elegant promenade is infused with a lively but easygoing vibe. At dawn, legions of locals perform tai chi exercises; later in the day an expanding array of sophisticated restaurants and clubs spring to life. Until relatively recently, the city of around 350,000 was a favorite of the backpacker crowd, but they've moved on; it's now Vietnamese families who come en masse, keeping the atmosphere local and festive.

Spend a leisurely evening sampling excellent seafood at any of the town's outdoor restaurants (where lemongrass prawns, chili crabs, and abalone are in abundance), or, for a traditional experience, find a spot at Cho Dam, the central food market.

Crystal-clear waters off the coast make Nha Trang an ideal place for diving and snorkeling, especially around the two dozen smaller, scenic islands to the north and south of the beach. Many of them can be visited on a day trip by chartered boat or guided tour. If all that sounds too energetic, simply rent a beach chair from one of the many waterfront bars and restaurants, sit back, and enjoy the view of the lush islands from the mainland.

Six Senses is located on remote Ninh Van Bay, accessible only by a 20-minute boat ride. The resort emphasizes privacy and pampering—especially at its exceptional spa—making this one of Vietnam's most special hideaways. A more accessible sister property and Nha Trang's only beachfront resort is Evason Ana Mandara where guests stay in thatch-roofed villas. After enjoying the resort's private beach, the intoxicating treatments of its spa call, followed by a dinner of East-West fusion cuisine at the Pavilion restaurant.

WHERE: 280 miles/450 km north of Ho Chi Minh City. **SIX SENSES NINH VAN BAY:** Tel 84/58-372-2222; www.sixsenses.com. *Cost:* from $650 (off-peak), from $840 (peak). **EVASON ANA MANDARA:** Tel 84/58-352-2222; www.sixsenses.com. *Cost:* from $290. **BEST TIMES:** Jan–Sep for the dry season; Apr–Jun are the least windy months.

Untrammeled and Lovely, Vietnam's Largest Island

PHU QUOC

Vietnam

Overlooked for decades, Vietnam's largest island has finally caught the world's attention. Around 30 miles long—roughly the size of Singapore—Phu Quoc features long strands of pristine beach, a verdant and lush interior, and just a handful of resorts and inexpensive local eateries. No building is higher than two stories, most of the island's interior rain forest remains undisturbed, and the Phu Quoc National Park, established in 2001, covers 70 percent of the island, guaranteeing protection for future generations. Change is sure to come, though, as an international airport is slated to open soon. So try to go now, while the only way to get to Phu Quoc is still by hydrofoil or on the daily turboprops from Ho Chi Minh City.

La Veranda Resort, on Duong Dong Beach, is an oasis of luxury. Built recently but in French-Colonial style, the boutique property effortlessly evokes the past with whitewashed louvers, paddle fans, four-poster beds, and touches of white wicker. The resort's Peppertree and Beach Grill restaurants are excellent, but sooner or later everyone ends up at the family-run Palm Tree next door. This humble beach shack's combination of freshly caught seafood—squid, garrupa, and kingfish—and cold 333 beer is hard to beat. Many dishes are prepared using peppercorns and *nuoc mam*, a pungent fish sauce that is Phu Quoc's most famous export. On nearby Ong Lang beach, the beach-bungalow resort at Mango Bay cleverly uses solar electricity panels and has incorporated recycled, local materials to ensure that the airy accommodations blend in seamlessly with the lush grounds. Don't expect television or air-conditioning, but do look forward to a rustic, romantic ambience. Spend your lazy days discovering exceptional beaches with gin-clear water, where you can kayak, snorkel, and dive. This is your chance to experience a Southeast Asian idyll that has—so far—kept overdevelopment at bay.

WHERE: 28 miles/48 km off the southeast coast; boats leave from Rach Gia. **LA VERANDA:** Tel 84/77-398-2988; www.laverandaresort.com. *Cost:* from $150. **MANGO BAY:** Tel 84/903-382-207; www.mangobayphuquoc.com. *Cost:* from $70. **BEST TIME:** Nov–May for the dry season (Apr–May are the hottest months).

The island's beaches have a reputation for being quiet and unspoiled.

Tribal Markets in the Vietnamese Alps

SAPA

Vietnam

It's a shame the train journey from Hanoi to Lao Cai runs only at night, as the 8-hour journey traverses some of Vietnam's most stunning mountain country. It's a traveler's consolation, then, that the 90-minute journey by car from the Lao Cai train station up to Sapa wends through equally rugged and beautiful landscapes—especially when early morning banks of mist are beginning to lift from the surrounding valleys and peaks.

The northern Vietnam hill town of Sapa is

perched at 5,000 feet in the Hoang Lien Mountains (dubbed the Tonkinese Alps by the colonial French, who arrived in the 1920s). This craggy region abutting Laos and China is home to 30-odd minority hill tribes collectively known as Montagnards ("mountain people"). The Black Hmong and Red Dao dominate, filling the former hill station's marketplace on Saturdays to trade their homegrown produce, sell handicrafts, and share news. Later, on Saturday evenings, the Montagnard gather to socialize at a weekly "love market." Sunday is the day you want to head 4 hours north to the market in Bac Ha, a remote town that's home to the colorfully dressed Flower Hmong people.

Sapa is also the perfect base for day trips or overnight treks to 10,312-foot Mount Fansipan (the country's highest peak), or to Montagnard villages built around steep, terraced vegetable gardens and crystal-clear mountain streams. Trekking and mountain biking excursions can be arranged through the beautifully situated Topas Ecolodge, with 25 bungalows just 11 miles from Sapa. The Alpine-style Victoria Sapa Resort & Spa has incredible views of the town and emerald green valleys below and its staff will also help plan hiking excursions. To arrive in relative luxury, guests can take the hotel's overnight Victoria Express—a special carriage attached to the nightly departure from Hanoi. The opportunity to bed down in comfort should help overcome any disappointment about missing the exceptional scenery outside.

The Red Dao tribe is one of the most populous of the dozens who live in the hills surrounding Sapa.

Where: 23 miles/38 km southeast of the Chinese border; 211 miles/340 km northwest of Hanoi. **How:** U.S.-based Global Spectrum offers a 12-day trip to Sapa (with 5 days trekking). Tel 800-419-4446 or 703-671-9619; www.asianpassages.com. *Cost:* $1,945, inclusive. Originates in Hanoi. **Topas Ecolodge:** Tel 84/4-3715-1005; www.topasecolodge.com. *Cost:* from $90. **Victoria Sapa Resort:** Tel 84/20-387-1522; www.victoriahotels-asia.com. *Cost:* from $175; Victoria Express train from $180 round-trip. **Best times:** Mar–May for the warmest, most settled weather; Oct–Nov for minimal rain; late Nov–early Dec for Hmong New Year festival, celebrating the end of harvest.

AUSTRALIA,
NEW ZEALAND,
AND
THE PACIFIC
ISLANDS

PALAU
YAP
CHUUK ISLANDS
MICRONESIA
EQUATOR
N
W
E
S
EQUATOR
Bismarck Archipelago
PAPUA NEW GUINEA
BISMARCK SEA
New Ireland
New Britain
SOLOMON ISLANDS
0 200 400 MILES
0 322 644 Kilometers
Santa Isabel
Port Moresby
SOLOMON SEA
Guadalcanal
TIMOR SEA
Darwin
Arnhem Land
Gulf of Carpentaria
VANUATU
SAMOA
CORAL SEA
Vanua Levu
Viti Levu
FIJI
Kimberley Plateau
NORTHERN TERRITORY
GREAT DIVIDING RANGE
Great Barrier Reef
AUSTRALIA
TONGA
NEW CALEDONIA
GIBSON DESERT
QUEENSLAND
INDIAN OCEAN
SIMPSON DESERT
WESTERN AUSTRALIA
PACIFIC OCEAN
SOUTH AUSTRALIA
Brisbane
Lake Eyre
GREAT VICTORIAN DESERT
COOK ISLANDS
Nullarbor Plain
Lake Torrens
Darling
NEW SOUTH WALES
Perth
Great Australian Bight
Sydney
Adelaide
Canberra
AUSTRALIAN CAPITAL TERRITORY
VICTORIA
Melbourne
Auckland
North Island
Bass Strait
NEW ZEALAND
TASMANIA
Wellington
Tahiti
Marquesas Islands
Hobart
TASMAN SEA
SOUTHERN ALPS
Christchurch
Bora Bora
South Island
FRENCH POLYNESIA

AUSTRALIA AND NEW ZEALAND

Spectacular Scenery in Sydney's Backyard

The Blue Mountains

New South Wales, Australia

Microscopic droplets of oil from the leaves of densely growing eucalyptus trees hang in the air here, refracting the sunlight to create the misty blue haze that gave this park its name. Just 90 minutes away from Sydney, Blue Mountains National Park is a glorious playground of forest containing 26 small townships that offer everything from antiques shopping to bushwalking. The highlands surrounding them are not truly mountains but a vast sandstone tableland whose dramatic, eroded scenery is best enjoyed from lookouts such as Govett's Leap or Echo Point, a good vantage point from which to enjoy the park's famous sandstone pillars, the Three Sisters. Just to the west are two more of the park's highlights: the Scenic Skyway, a glass-floored gondola traveling 1,000 feet above the canyon, and the Katoomba Scenic Railway, an open-sided cog-rail incline that descends at 52 degrees but feels nearly twice as steep. The park also affords opportunities for rock climbing, horseback riding, spelunking, and canoeing, though most visitors are here for the dozens of walking paths. Explore them on your own or sign up for the Aboriginal Blue Mountains Walkabout, an intimate experience that combines a 4.4-mile nature walk with storytelling and lessons on Aboriginal culture.

You can get a quick overview of the area on a day trip from Sydney, but it really deserves a longer stay, and for that the country hotel–style Lilianfels Blue Mountains Resort is hard to beat. It's one of Australia's best getaway destinations, with a fantastic setting, magnificent panoramas, and Darley's, a smart, award-winning restaurant where your meal is created from produce sourced from the surrounding countryside. Looking every bit the gracious European manor, the hotel perches 3,300 feet above sea level, almost at the edge of the cliff at Echo Point, with the canyons and ravines of the Jamison Valley below. Guests at the nearby century-old Lurline House stay in one of seven rooms, all with four-poster beds, and awaken to a full English breakfast and bushwalking trails just outside their door.

Where: 75 miles/122 km west of Sydney. **Aboriginal Blue Mountains Walkabout:** Tel 61/408-443-822; www.bluemountainswalkabout.com. *Cost:* from $80. **Lilianfels Blue Mountains Resort:** Tel 61/247-801-200; www.lilianfels.com.au. *Cost:* from $300 (off-peak), from $450 (peak); tasting menu

Cable cars glide past the Three Sisters: Meehni, Wimlah, and Gunnedoo.

at Darley's $115. **Lurline House:** Tel 61/247-824-609; www.lurlinehouse.com.au. *Cost:* from $145. **Best times:** Mar–Apr for fall colors; Mar for the Blue Mountains Music Festival in Katoomba; Sep–Oct for spring weather.

Australia's Oldest Vineyards

The Hunter Valley

New South Wales, Australia

The scenic Hunter Valley, home to over 120 wineries, is Australia's oldest continuously planted region. Associated with the country's most famous varietals, it draws lovers of fine wine from across the globe. They find here some of the world's best shiraz and some of its most acclaimed sémillon, along with award-winning chardonnay and cabernet sauvignon. A vibrant gourmet food culture also flourishes, replete with artisanal cheeses and locally smoked meats, olives, and olive oil, plus stylish, contemporary restaurants showcasing the area's finest talents.

Visitors may recognize such international labels as Rosemount or Lindemans, but smaller, limited-production operations that do not export also enjoy respect at home. An easy 2-hour drive from Sydney, Hunter Valley can feel chockablock on weekends, but roads are quiet and dinner reservations easy to come by on weekdays. Gourmands partial to picturesque country hotels gravitate to Halls Road in Pokolbin, where two of Australia's favorite lodges are situated. Pepper's Convent is an impressive 17-room complex in the heart of the valley, occupying a turn-of-the-century former convent; your suite might be a former kindergarten or music room. Nearby Tower Lodge is a more intimate, 12-room Spanish Mission–style inn; its acclaimed Roberts restaurant serves leisurely meals in an 1876 settler's cottage, accompanied by vintages from vines you can practically reach out and touch. You can also dine at the lodge's exclusive Nine Restaurant, where you'll savor nine-course dinners matched with wines from Tower Estate. Pokolbin is also where you'll find the cozy Splinters Guesthouse, consisting of a few rooms and cottages with views of vines and mountains. Long a favorite of weekending Sydneysiders, it is within walking distance of boutique vineyards and small welcoming restaurants.

Vineyards first came to the valley during the 1830s.

Where: 125 miles/200 km north of Sydney. **Pepper's Convent:** Tel 61/249-984-999; www.peppers.com.au/convent. *Cost:* from $430; 9-course dinner at Nine $180 (weekends only). **Tower Lodge:** Tel 61/249-987-022; www.towerlodge.com.au. *Cost:* from $755; dinner at Roberts $85. **Splinters Guesthouse:** 61/265-747-118; www.splinters.com.au. *Cost:* from $190. **Best times:** Mar–Apr for the Harvest Festival; Jun for Hunter Valley Food & Wine Month; Sep–Oct for spring weather.

A Forgotten Paradise in the Tasman Sea

Lord Howe Island

New South Wales, Australia

Hailed as one of the most beautiful subtropical islands in the Pacific, the tiny crescent of Lord Howe Island boasts 90 species of coral on surrounding reefs—the world's southernmost—500 species of fish, and more than 130 recorded bird species, including the endemic wooden hen. Several of these had a close brush with extinction before a successful recovery program boosted their numbers. The island is home to approximately 350 human residents as well—also protected, although by just one policeman.

Known for its unique topography, Lord Howe Island is full of rocky cliffs, owing to marine erosion.

The tallest stack of volcano pinnacles in the world was formed here, millions of years ago, by massive eruptions. One of them, Ball's Pyramid, juts 1,800 feet out of the ocean 14 miles south of Lord Howe. It is one of countless spots nearby that lure divers with their access to a kaleidoscopic underwater world. Snorkelers can rent goggles and snorkels on the beach and simply walk into the surf from various points on the island to find themselves on the reef.

Given Lord Howe's size (it's 7 miles long and just 1.2 miles across at its widest), biking and walking are the preferred modes of transportation, and the networks of trails for both range from easy to rigorous. Most of the handful of accommodations on the island are owned by welcoming locals, including the beautifully sited all-inclusive Pinetrees Resort, which hosts jazz concerts from June through August. Luxurious Capella Lodge is perched above romantic Lover's Bay, with spectacular views of the ocean and mountains. Have your hotel prepare a picnic lunch for you to enjoy on the white sand of Ned's Beach; you'll discover that its crystal-clear waters are a favorite of tropical fish that will eat right out of your hand. No matter where you go, crowds on the island will never be an issue: Visitors are limited to 400 at a time.

Where: 445 miles/717 km east of Sydney. **Visitor info:** www.lordhoweisland.info. **Pinetrees Resort:** Tel 61/2-9262-6585; www.pinetrees.com.au. *Cost:* 5-night all-inclusive package from $1,065 per person (off-peak), from $1,760 (peak). **Capella Lodge:** Tel 61/2-9918-4355; www.capellalodge.com.au. *Cost:* from $650 per person, all-inclusive (off-peak), from $700 (peak). **Best time:** Dec–Mar for summer weather.

Great Icons of the Magnificent Waterfront City

Sydney Opera House and the Harbour

New South Wales, Australia

Sydney is Australia's largest, oldest, and brashest city, and its Opera House—initially lambasted for its startlingly modern, sail-like shape—has come to be as emblematic of the city as the Eiffel Tower is of Paris. Chosen from more than 200 submissions from world-famous architects in 1958, the design generated instant controversy. During the 15 years the building took to complete, its disillusioned Danish creator, Jørn Utzon, removed himself from the project. Today the opera house, commanding a prime spot on Sydney's busy harbor, is Sydney's cultural heartbeat. Those without tickets can repair to the Opera House's Guillaume at Bennelong restaurant for an elegant meal with magnificent views.

For even more stunning vistas, you can't do better than the elegant Park Hyatt Sydney. The hotel is conveniently located near Circular Quay, the launching point for hundreds of boats and ferries that zigzag across Sydney Harbour. On the east side of the Quay, the apartment-style accommodations of the Grand Quay Suites put you in the midst of the waterfront action with the Royal Botanic Gardens, a 70-acre green oasis offering some of the finest strolls in town, nearby.

The Rocks, the 19th-century haunt of brawling sailors and ex-convicts, is now home to restaurants, shops, galleries, exhibition spaces, and weekend markets. One of the few original buildings still standing is Lord Nelson, the city's oldest continuously operating pub, opened in 1841. For Sydney's most unusual tour, sign up for the BridgeClimb, a 200-step trek to the top of the Harbour Bridge—the largest (though not longest) steel-arch bridge ever built. It guarantees dramatic 360-degree views and bragging rights for life.

Climb back down and catch a ferry to Manly. Stroll or bike the 6-mile-long Manly Scenic Walk for spectacular harbor views, then head over to Doyles on Watsons Bay, a beloved waterfront seafood restaurant that opened in 1885. Five generations later, the Doyle family continues to serve plenty of fresh fish, best coupled with a fine Australian wine.

Visitor info: www.sydney.com.au. **Sydney Opera House:** Box office, tel 61/2-9250-7777; www.sydneyoperahouse.com. *When:* opera season New Year's Eve–Mar and Jun–Oct. **Guillaume at Bennelong:** Tel 61/2-9241-1999; www.guillaumeatbennelong.com

Jørn Utzon received the Pritzker Prize, architecture's highest honor, for his design of the Sydney Opera House.

.au. *Cost:* dinner $80. **Park Hyatt Sydney:** Tel 61/2-9256-1234; www.sydney.park.hyatt .com. *Cost:* harbor-view rooms from $695. **Grand Quay Suites:** Tel 61/2-9256-4000; www.mirvachotels.com. *Cost:* from $365. **BridgeClimb:** Tel 61/2-8274-7777; www .bridgeclimb.com. *Cost:* $190. **Doyles on the Beach:** Tel 61/2-9337-2007; www .doyles.com.au. *Cost:* dinner $75. **Best times:** Jan–Feb for summer weather and festivals, including Sydney Festival, Australia's largest celebration of the arts; Oct–Nov for spring flowers; New Year's Eve—Sydney's celebration is second only to New York's.

Aboriginal Rock Art and Bush Culture

Kakadu National Park and Arnhem Land

Northern Territory, Australia

The 8,000-square-mile Kakadu National Park is half the size of Switzerland, yet still remote and little known outside Australia. For now, its rugged frontier feel remains intact, while the resident population of 15-foot "saltie" and smaller "freshie" crocodiles still laze undisturbed in the shallows of its rivers and surrounding marshlands. In 1981, Kakadu received the rare double honor of being named a UNESCO World Heritage Site for its natural wonders as well as for culture: 5,000 rock paintings dating as far back as 50,000 years grace its sandstone caves. Ubirr, 27 miles north of park headquarters, is one of the most visited of these art sites; in its cave-like "galleries," images record life from the Stone Age to the early 20th century.

Adjacent to Kakadu sprawls a vast indigenous reserve known as Arnhem Land, a place of unspoiled bush country, eucalyptus forest, and coastal wilderness endowed with abundant wildlife. It is one of the few places in Australia where Aboriginal culture still dominates (around 15,000 people live here). Lords Safaris is the only accredited outfitter to offer access to Arnhem Land as well as to a pair of other outstanding regional attractions, Koolpin Gorge and the Mary River floodplains. The Mary River's vast coastal wetlands, rich in wildlife, is also home to the luxurious Bamurru Plains, an exclusive backcountry resort of just nine stylishly low-key safari suites on a working buffalo station. It is one of a handful of such stations on the western boundary of Kakadu, and is a 25-minute flight or a 3-hour drive from the territorial capital, Darwin. Mornings offer the chance to take an exhilarating airboat ride on the floodplains that form one of the most significant wetland ecosystems in Australia—keep your eyes peeled for blue-winged kookaburras. In the drier months, set off in open 4WD vehicles to view wallabies, wallaroos, dingos, and crocodiles.

Where: 150 miles/241 km east of Darwin. **Kakadu National Park:** Tel 61/8-8938-1120; www.environment.gov.au/parks/kakadu. **Lords Safaris:** Tel 61/8-8948-2200; www .lords-safaris.com. *Cost:* guided day trips to Arnhem Land from Darwin, $230; to Jabiru, $195; multiday tours also available. **Bamurru Plains:** Tel 61/2-9571-6399; www .bamurruplains.com. *Cost:* $990 per person, all-inclusive. *When:* Feb–Oct. **Best times:** May–Sep for dry season, though some prefer the greenness of wetter months, Nov–Apr.

Over the Top: Hunting and Gathering in Prehistoric Forests

The Tiwi Islands

Northern Territory, Australia

All but unknown to the outside world, Bathurst and its sister island, Melville, are the ancestral home of Australia's Tiwi Islanders, who originally came from mainland Australia and were isolated some 7,000 years ago when sea levels rose. As a result, the Tiwi (or "We People") developed a rich culture and language distinct from other Aboriginal groups, maintaining religious customs that absorbed bits of Catholicism introduced by missionaries in the late 18th century. Despite the islands' size—at 2,234-square-miles, Melville Island is Australia's second largest—their population is a sparse 2,700. Traditional ways prevail: Dugong (a cousin of the manatee) and turtle eggs are still hunted and gathered, essential to the islanders' diet.

Today, non-Tiwi can visit Bathurst Island only as part of a Tiwi-owned and -operated tour (Melville is closed to the public). Highlights include the Catholic church, which reveals the Tiwi's unique blend of their ancient culture with Christianity; artists' workshops and arts and crafts centers such as the Ngaruwanajirri Art Community; and a "boiling of the billy" tea with local Tiwi ladies who chat as they work on their weaving and painting. The proximity of the Indonesian archipelago is reflected in the use of batik patterns in the local textile crafts. And be sure to see the island's renowned *pukumani*—elaborately carved and painted poles adorned with mythological motifs that are erected at gravesites.

Where: 50 miles/80 km off the coast of Darwin. **How:** Darwin Day Tours leads 1-day tours from Darwin. Tel 61/8-8923-6523; www.darwindaytours.com.au. *Cost:* $498, includes air and lunch. *When:* Mar–Nov. **Best time:** May–Sep for nicest weather.

Spiritual Shrines in the Outback

Uluru and Kata Tjuta (Ayers Rock and the Olgas)

Northern Territory, Australia

Never mind how many times it has appeared in movies or on postcards: The great red monolith of Uluru (Ayers Rock) still stirs those who visit it. The sandstone formation rises 1,142 feet above the desert plain and has a circumference of nearly 6 miles. Revered as a center of spiritual power by the Anangu Aboriginal peoples—whose ancestors are believed to have lived here as long as 40,000 years ago—the orange-red rock subtly changes color during the day, seeming to glow from within at sunrise and sunset. Rich deposits of iron mean that Uluru actually rusts when it rains. Climbing the rock is discouraged because of its religious significance to the Aborigines, who have jointly managed the surrounding 511-square-mile national park since 1985. Maintain your respect—and your knees—and opt instead to walk the trail at its base.

Depending on the light, Uluru can appear to be anywhere from pink to dark red in color.

About 30 miles west of Uluru lies Kata Tjuta (the Olgas), a similarly spectacular group of 36 gigantic rock domes reaching as high as 1,800 feet and spread over an area of 15 square miles. The main walking trail here is the Valley of the Winds, a 4.6-mile loop best experienced in the cool of early morning.

This otherworldly landscape may seem far from upscale comforts, but Longitude 131° provides unexpected luxury in the Uluru outback. At this romantic (and astronomically priced) resort, the accommodations are elegant safari-style tents, filled with fine furniture and outfitted with air-conditioning, private bathrooms, and the plethora of amenities reserved for top-of-the-line hotels. If a traditional hotel is more your style, you'll find premium comfort at Sails in the Desert, highlighted by fine dining, stylishly appointed, art-filled rooms, and an extensive pool and patio area shaded by a series of canvas sails.

WHERE: 200 miles/322 km southwest of Alice Springs. **ULURU-KATA TJUTA NATIONAL PARK:** Tel 61/8-8956-1128; www.environment.gov.au/parks/uluru. **LONGITUDE 131°:** Tel 61/2-8296-8010; www.longitude131.com.au. *Cost:* 2-night package $4,100 per person, all-inclusive. **SAILS IN THE DESERT:** Tel 61/2-8296-8010; www.ayersrockresort.com.au/sails. *Cost:* from $480 (off-peak), from $580 (peak). **BEST TIMES:** Mar–May and Sep–Nov for pleasant weather.

Where Earth's Oldest Living Rain Forest Meets the Great Barrier Reef

CAPE TRIBULATION

Queensland, Australia

Queensland's Wet Tropics rain forest and the Great Barrier Reef come together on Australia's northeast coast at Cape Tribulation, named in 1770 by a peeved Captain James Cook, "because here began all my troubles," when his ship hit a coral reef. Protected within the Cape Tribulation and Daintree national parks and believed to have been the evolutionary cradle for much of Australia's unique wildlife, the rain forest here contains trees that are 3,000 years old, including 85 of the 120 rarest species on earth.

A number of locally based operators offer a

variety of adventure trips that take you snorkeling on the area's Mossman River (the only place in the world where you can do so in a rain forest river), rafting, biking, and night game viewing, among other activities. You'll cross the Daintree River by vehicle ferry, then continue to Cape Tribulation beach, where you can jungle surf (by means of a zip-line) through the rain forest canopy, then recharge with a picnic lunch on a tropical beach. Wildlife-watching is good on cruises along the forest-lined Daintree River—you'll spy crocodiles, tree snakes, and all manner of bird species.

Choose between two outstanding ecotourism properties that comfortably coexist within miles of each other; both have naturalists on staff to give guided walks through the wilderness. Silky Oaks Lodge offers luxurious lodging in river houses by the swift-flowing Mossman River or in tree houses reached by boardwalks high in the forest. The lodge's Healing Waters Spa relies on indigenous plants and herbs for its treatments. Daintree Eco Lodge and Spa features 15 beautifully furnished, elevated "bayan" houses that are equipped with every modern comfort. At the lodge's Julaymba Restaurant—perched at the edge of a freshwater lagoon—the exotic and unusual flavors of the rain forest are integrated with the cosmopolitan cuisine of modern Australia.

WHERE: 70 miles/113 km north of Cairns. **HOW:** Back Country Bliss Adventures! leads full-day tours from the Port Douglas area. Tel 61/7-4099-3677; www.backcountrybliss.com.au. *Cost:* from $250. **SILKY OAKS LODGE:** Tel 61/7-4098-1666; www.silkyoakslodge.com.au. *Cost:* from $530; dinner $70. **DAINTREE ECO LODGE:** Tel 61/7-4098-6100; www.daintree-ecolodge.com.au. *Cost:* from $250; dinner $80. **BEST TIME:** May–Sep for the "dry" season.

A Romp on the World's Largest Sand Island

FRASER ISLAND

Queensland, Australia

The Butchulla Aboriginal people called it K'Gari (Paradise)—and for good reason. Here on the world's largest sand island you can swim in freshwater lakes, walk through the ancient Valley of the Giants rain forest, join rangers to track down some of the island's 350 species of birds, or just enjoy the uninterrupted 75 miles of broad coastal beach—the world's most unusual "highway." Join a 4WD tour offered by the island's ecotourism hotel, the Kingfisher Bay Resort, or hire your own vehicle and follow the jeep tracks over the dunes. Or spend the day cruising the southernmost tip of the Barrier Reef with the Pacific Ocean on one side and 40-foot cliffs that resemble Gothic cathedrals on the other. The northern tip of the island, where huge sand mountains tower above a vibrant blue sea, offers more chance for endless exploration. Afterward, take your taste buds on an adventure at the resort's Seabelle Restaurant, where you'll find fresh seafood, traditional fare infused with "bush tucker" (plants that grow in the wild, which replace European herbs), and dishes inspired by the indigenous Butchulla tribe.

There are several superb walking trails that take you through idyllic scenery: This is the only place on earth where rain forests are rooted in sand dunes, at elevations above 500 feet. Top attractions include stunning Lake McKenzie, its clear blue water ringed by a snowy–white sand beach, and Lake Wabby, surrounded by eucalyptus forest on three sides. The 53-mile Fraser Island Great Walk links the island's highlights, but unless you have 6 to 8 days, plan to walk just a portion of it.

The surf fishing is exceptional on Fraser Island, as is the bird-watching, and Australia's purest breed of dingo lives here. Climb to a perch lookout for a chance to spot manatees, sharks, manta rays, and whales offshore. From August to late October, the Kingfisher Bay Resort offers cruises that allow you an up-close look at humpback whales during their magnificent annual migration south to the Antarctic.

Where: 230 miles/370 km northeast of Brisbane. **Kingfisher Bay Resort:** Tel 61/ 7-4120-3333; www.kingfisherbay.com. *Cost:* from $225 (off-peak), from $320 (peak); dinner $60. **Best times:** Weather is warm year-round; Aug–Nov for whale-watching.

Wondrous Undersea Panorama

The Great Barrier Reef and the Coral Sea

Queensland, Australia

It's often called the Eighth Wonder of the World, and that might be selling it short. The Great Barrier Reef is the only living organism on the planet that's visible from outer space. Located between 10 and 50 miles off the continent's northeast Queensland coast and stretching for more than 1,400 miles, actually it's not one coral reef but an association of approximately 2,900 separate fringing reefs, with about 600 tropical islands and 300 coral cays sprinkled among them. The largest marine preserve in the world, it's home to a stupefying profusion of sea creatures, including 360 species of brilliantly colored hard corals, one-third of the world's soft corals, 1,500 varieties of fish, and over 5,000 kinds of mollusks.

One of the most popular ways to explore it all is aboard the *Quicksilver*, a high-tech, high-speed wave-piercing catamaran that departs from Port Douglas for the 90-minute trip to an anchored glass-bottomed platform, where you can swim, snorkel, or scuba dive. Or you can ride in a semisubmersible vessel and listen to your guide's running commentary on the underwater spectacle outside your window. Dozens of smaller tour boat operators in Port Douglas and Cairns offer a more intimate half- or full-day experience on sailboats, yachts, and catamarans.

Those wanting a longer tour can spend 4 days aboard the luxurious mini cruise ships *Coral Princess* or *Coral Princess II*. The 115-foot ships offer snorkeling, scuba diving, guided coral-viewing excursions in small glass-bottomed boats, reef fishing, and evening presentations by trained marine biologists. If you've always dreamed of learning how to dive, the ships' qualified PADI instructors will have you logging your first underwater hours in no time.

Most people think of the Great Barrier Reef as the last word in deep-sea diving, but the waters of the lesser-known, less-dived Coral Sea, beyond the reef, are in some ways more wonderful yet. Highlights of this pristine wilderness of crystal-clear waters and its uninhabited coral atolls include huge perpendicular drop-offs and visibility as deep as 160 feet—not to mention giant clams and 300-pound groupers. Some live-aboard trips include a visit to the wreck of the SS *Yongala,* a 363-foot relic still largely intact and said to host the greatest concentration and diversity of marine life in the world—a mind-boggling underwater experience for experienced divers.

Of the 24 island resorts amid the emerald and turquoise waters of the Great Barrier Reef, Lizard Island is one of the farthest north, a scenic 1-hour flight from Cairns. The 40 villa-style bungalows sit on the justly famous Blue Lagoon, where 24 secluded white-sand, palm-fringed coves mean there's a good chance you'll have a beach to yourself. The resort is uninhabited save for staff and guests and lies within a 2,500-acre national park. Don't be surprised to see a 3-foot-long monitor lizard—after which Captain James Cook named the island in 1770—sunbathing on the palm-studded green lawn in front of your bungalow.

WHERE: Cairns is 1,219 miles/1,961 km north of Sydney. ***QUICKSILVER:*** Tel 61/7-4087-2100; www.quicksilver-cruises.com. *Cost:* $225, includes lunch and equipment. **CORAL PRINCESS CRUISES:** Tel 61/7-4040-9999; www.coralprincess.com.au. *Cost:* 4-day cruises from $1,660, all-inclusive, diving lessons and equipment extra. **LIZARD ISLAND:** Tel 61/2-8296-8010; www.lizardisland.com.au. *Cost:* from $1,550, all-inclusive. **BEST TIME:** May–Nov for ideal sea conditions and weather.

Jewel of the Reef

HERON ISLAND

Queensland, Australia

Unlike many of the other islands near the Great Barrier Reef, Heron Island, situated on the Tropic of Capricorn, is a coral cay—literally part of the reef itself. To see even more, all you have to do is wade out from the beach and look down. But to really appreciate it all, you'll want to strap on a tank and mask. There are 20 dive sites within 15 minutes of shore; snorkelers and those opting for a semi-submersible ride can catch their own glimpse of fish, turtles, mantas, reef sharks, and endless varieties of invertebrates.

One of the most dazzling events on the reef is the rarely witnessed coral spawning. It is difficult to predict, but typically happens a few days after the full moon on one night in late spring or early summer (November to early December), when the polyps emit billions of pink-and-purple bundles of eggs and sperm. It's like being inside a pink snowstorm, and divers from all over the world plan night dives around this time of year in hopes of witnessing the awe-inspiring event.

There's also important wildlife-watching on the 30-acre island itself, half of which is a national park. Hundreds of green and loggerhead sea turtles swim ashore from November to March to lay their eggs; the hatchlings scamper into the sea from January to late April. You're likely to see abundant birdlife as well, including the reef herons for which the island is named. Offshore, humpback whales pass through from June through October.

No day-trippers are allowed on the island, and its sole lodging, the low-key, eco-sensitive Heron Island Resort, is among the most special of the few hotels located on the Barrier Reef Islands. Join one of its reef walks at low tide, or enjoy diving and snorkeling off the private beach. At the end of a day spent exploring, enjoy a pampering visit to the Aqua

Soul Spa and a dinner of local seafood at the resort's Shearwater Restaurant.

WHERE: 40 miles/64 km northeast of Gladstone, which is 691 miles/1,113 km north of Sydney. **HERON ISLAND RESORT:** Tel 61/3-9413-6284; www.heronisland.com. *Cost:* from $400, inclusive. **BEST TIMES:** Jun and Jul for clearest water; coral spawns typically occur sometime between the 2nd and 6th nights following the full moon in Nov.

A Dazzling Archipelago in the Heart of the Great Barrier Reef

SAILING THE WHITSUNDAYS

Queensland, Australia

It would be hard to conjure a more splendid destination for setting sail than these idyllic islands in the Coral Sea, discovered by Captain Cook in 1770 on Whitsunday (49 days after Easter). Cradled by the Great Barrier Reef (see p. 653) midway along Australia's Queensland Coast, these 74 islands (of which only eight are inhabited) are a sailor's dream and also offer glorious, deserted palm-fringed beaches, scenic bushwalks, and superb snorkeling and diving amid teeming coral reefs. Visitors can sail these turquoise waters using a range of options, from crewed luxury craft to bareboats for DIY adventurers, or you can sign up for a half or full day of adventure on a dive or snorkeling boat.

Excellent resorts are scattered around the islands, though few match the glamorous Hayman Great Barrier Reef Resort, nestled on private, 726-acre Hayman Island in the northern reaches of the Whitsundays and the closest to the Outer Barrier Reef. Set in a lush tropical jungle, this longtime favorite offers 200-plus guest rooms and beach villas as well as restaurants, bars, and boutiques. Guests arrive by 1-hour boat transfer from the small airport on Hamilton Island, the busiest and most developed of the Whitsundays, with the widest range of hotel options. At the southern end of the archipelago sits the high-end qualia Resort, with 60 breezy and elegant, free-standing, one-bedroom pavilions (many with private plunge pools) that hint of Southeast Asia. Guests can take part in any number of activities, including kayaking, sailing on one of the property's two 16-foot Hobie Cats, exclusive treatments at Spa qualia, or a day at the 18-hole championship Hamilton Island Golf Club (on its own little island).

A range of less luxurious resorts can be found on the neighboring islands of Daydream, Long, South Molle, Hook, and Lindeman. Airlie Beach and Shute Harbor, on the mainland, provide transportation by boat to the reef and a host of islands, including Whitsunday Island, where you'll find Whitehaven Beach, a perfect wedding-white crescent of sand that is possibly Australia's finest.

The sugar-white sands of Whitehaven Beach stretch for 7 miles.

Where: Hamilton Island is 560 miles/900 km north of Brisbane. **Visitor info:** www.whitsundaytourism.com.au. **How:** Explore Whitsundays (tel 61/7-4946-5782; www.explorewhitsundays.com.au) and Whitsunday Sailing Adventures (tel 61/7-4940-2000; www.whitsundaysailingadventures.com.au) offer various sailing and diving options. **Hayman Resort:** Tel 61/7-4940-1234; www.hayman.com.au. *Cost:* from $635. **qualia Resort:** Tel 61/2-9433-3349; www.qualia.com.au. *Cost:* from $1,020. **Best times:** Jul–Sep for whale-watching; Oct–Nov for favorable sea conditions.

High Culture in South Australia

Adelaide

South Australia, Australia

Australia's fifth largest city is one of its best-kept secrets. Equal parts charming country town and sophisticated big city, it boasts multicultural flair, a thriving arts-and-music scene, and a packed lineup of year-round festivals and big-draw events.

Adelaide is known as "a city within a park." More than 45 percent of it is made up of green spaces, each with its own specialty: rare and exotic flowers and fountains at the Botanic Gardens; more than 50 varieties of roses at Veale Gardens; a Japanese-style oasis of peace and tranquility at Himeji Garden; and river paddleboats, tennis courts, and bike rentals at Elder Park.

Still, one of Adelaide's best-known landmarks isn't a park but the Central Market, where growers and producers from all over the state pack 250 stalls, selling gourmet cheeses, smoked meats, artisanal breads, fruits, and vegetables. Some of Australia's best-known wine producers hail from these parts too—with the Barossa (see next page), McLaren Vale, and Adelaide Hills wine regions on the doorstep and more than 200 wineries within an hour's drive. But it's a mere 15-minute drive to the historic Penfolds Magill Estate (its other facility is an hour's drive away in the Barossa Valley). In the tasting room and modern, glass-fronted restaurant that boasts views of the vineyards and the city beyond, you can enjoy world-renowned wines by the glass, as well as seasonal dishes prepared from home-grown produce. Back in the city, be sure to visit the Australian Aboriginal Cultures Gallery in the South Australian Museum: It contains the world's largest and most significant collection of Aboriginal artifacts.

With over 3,000 artifacts, the South Australian Museum chronicles millennia of Aboriginal history.

For 3 weeks in March of even-numbered years only, the Adelaide Festival, devoted to the performing arts, takes over the town. The annual Fringe Festival (usually mid-February to mid-March) is the second largest such festival in the world (after Edinburgh; see p. 35), while the world music festival WOMADelaide hosts some of the best acts from all over in mid-March.

For a unique overnight in Adelaide, get in touch with Regina and Rodney Twiss, who have lovingly restored 20 heritage-listed cottages, mews, and manor houses—even a firehouse and a chapel—dotted all over the upscale neighborhood of North Adelaide. Or try the history-steeped, close-to-everything Medina Grand Adelaide Treasury, a 19th-century treasury building turned hotel. Its 80 spacious rooms are imbued with a contemporary style.

WHERE: 886 miles/1,394 km southwest of Sydney. **VISITOR AND FESTIVAL INFO:** www.cityofadelaide.com.au. **PENFOLDS MAGILL ESTATE:** Tel 61/8-8301-5569; www.penfolds.com. *Cost:* dinner $100. **SOUTH AUSTRALIAN MUSEUM:** Tel 61/8-8207-7500; www.samuseum.sa.gov.au. **NORTH ADELAIDE HERITAGE ACCOMMODATION:** Tel 61/8-8272-1355; www.adelaideheritage.com. *Cost:* from $235. **MEDINA GRAND ADELAIDE TREASURY:** 61/8-8112-0000; www.medina.com.au. *Cost:* from $185. **BEST TIMES:** Sep–May for pleasant weather; "Mad March" for countless festivals.

Historic Homesteads Yield World-Class Wines

BAROSSA VALLEY

South Australia, Australia

The picturesque Barossa Valley is Australia's epicenter for all things gastronomic. Together with nearby Clare Valley, it produces over 40 percent of Australia's wines. Easy to reach from Adelaide (see previous page), it is a relatively compact area of small country towns connected by scenic back roads that are flanked by 150 vineyards. Over 70 cellar doors (tasting rooms) present the chance to sample the signature shiraz and other robust varieties of red wine, as well as riesling, sémillon, and chardonnay. They include household names such as Jacob's Creek, Penfolds, and Peter Lehmann as well as smaller brands such as Henschke, Rockford, and Charles Melton.

Barossa's early settlers brought their food traditions with them, instilling the region's cuisine with a strong German-Polish influence. Stop in at a Barossa butcher and you'll find smoked mettwurst, lachsschinken, and bratwurst sausages, while a visit to Angaston's Saturday Farmers Market will reward you with fresh-from-the-oven baked goods. As for where to stay, Angaston's nearby Collingrove Homestead was built in 1856 by one of the early settlers and today operates as a charming inn. It is listed on the National Trust, as is the home of wine pioneer Joseph Seppelt, built at approximately the same time. The rambling and aristocratic Lodge Country House, once the home of one of his 13 children, is now a handsome bluestone inn and restaurant, across the road from the Seppelts' sprawling showpiece vineyard.

Tanunda is the most important of the Barossa wine towns as well as the quaintest, with a clutch of antiques shops, wine stores, and cafés. The Louise, a contemporary all-suite hotel, draws crowds with its Apellation restaurant, which features regional cuisine served in a sophisticated dining room. Smart but more casual is the 1918 Bistro and Grill, where the inventive, seasonal menu may feature the likes of confit pork belly with prawn ravioli and sweet-and-sour turnips.

WHERE: 45 miles/72 km northeast of Adelaide. **COLLINGROVE HOMESTEAD:** Tel

61/8-8564-2061; www.collingrovehomestead.com.au. *Cost:* $200. **The Lodge Country House:** Tel 61/8-8562-8277; www.thelodgecountryhouse.com.au. *Cost:* from $365; dinner $90. **The Louise:** Tel 61/8-8562-2722; www.thelouise.com.au. *Cost:* from $475; 3-course prix-fixe dinner $120. **1918 Bistro and Grill:** Tel 61/8-8563-0405; www.1918.com.au. *Cost:* dinner $70. **Best times:** Feb–Apr for fall and harvest time; Oct–Dec for spring/summer weather. In odd-numbered years only, the Vintage Festival takes place following Easter.

Authentic Outback, Untamed and Raw

Flinders Ranges

South Australia, Australia

Fascinating in their rugged beauty and for their renowned geological formations, the Flinders Ranges are estimated to be 800 million years old and harbor some of the planet's oldest animal fossils. These desert mountains, which start about 125 miles north of Adelaide (see p. 656) and stretch for more than 265 miles, are known for their dramatic primeval colors and bold sedimentary lines. They are home to over half of Australia's 3,100 indigenous plants and to scores of birds and reptile species. Best of all, the Flinders is accessible—within the context of travel in Australia, that is—and its most stunning landscapes are preserved in one area, Flinders Ranges National Park.

The most impressive of these is Wilpena Pound, a 31-square-mile natural amphitheater that looks like a prehistoric world where dinosaurs still roam. An outpost of comfort in this rugged landscape is nearby Wilpena Pound Resort, the only lodging within the park. Accommodations range from campgrounds and permanent tents to simple hotel rooms, and they have a lovely swimming pool and a restaurant where outback flavors accent modern Australian cooking. The resort can also help plan backcountry tours that get you way off the beaten path.

Northwest of the park, where the desert and red dunes meet the Flinders Ranges, is Parachilna (population 7). The tiny hamlet is home to the Prairie Hotel, a former pub that dates to 1876 and is famous for its basic but comfortable accommodations, outback hospitality, and an outstanding restaurant that features a surprisingly innovative menu—think emu pâté, kangaroo tail soup, and quandong pie, made from a peachlike fruit.

Down the road is Angorichina Station, a 250-square-mile sheep ranch whose fourth-generation owners also welcome guests to their stone-walled 1860s homestead. While the surrounding landscape is austere, the homestead is like an oasis, and the two guest suites are charming and comfortable. Come at the right time of year and you can help with the shearing of the sheep.

Where: beginning 125 miles/201 km north of Adelaide. **Flinders Ranges National Park:** Tel 61/8-8648-0048; www.environment.sa.gov.au/parks. **Wilpena Pound Resort:** Tel 61/8-8648-0004; www.wilpenapound.com.au. *Cost:* tents from $100; rooms from $200; dinner $65. **Prairie Hotel:** Tel 61/8-8648-4844; www.prairiehotel.com.au. *Cost:* from $195; dinner $55. **Angorichina:** Tel 61/8-8354-2362; www.angorichinastation.com. *Cost:* $725 per person, all-inclusive. **Best times:** May–Oct for milder temperatures; Sep–Oct for wildflowers.

Australia's Galápagos in the Southern Ocean

Kangaroo Island

South Australia, Australia

Australia's third largest island, "K.I.," as it's known to the locals, is uncrowded and uncomplicated. The sheep outnumber the people 300 to one, and it boasts a trove of rarer animal life too—most notably the namesake kangaroos, plus koalas, Tammar wallabies (now extinct on the mainland), sea lions, and fairy penguins. They inhabit an unspoiled and surprisingly varied wilderness marked by bright-white sand dunes, wind- and sand-sculpted boulders that resemble abstract art (and are aptly called the Remarkable Rocks), sparkling seas, and the Admirals Arch, a natural limestone bridge carved by the elements and a gathering place for thousands of fur seals. Seal Bay is home to their cousins, one of the world's rarest species of seals, the Australian sea lion; they can be seen lounging by the hundreds, and you can approach them for up-close-and-personal encounters rarely possible in the wild. From the island's 300 miles of beaches, empty except for the resident wildlife, you can spot bottlenose dolphins and southern right whales.

Lichen is responsible for the red orange splashes of color on and around the Remarkable Rocks.

Most visitors on day trips from Adelaide underestimate the island's size (90 by 40 miles) and wind up wishing they could stay on at one of the charming local B&Bs such as the Stranraer Homestead, a meticulously restored 1920s limestone farmhouse on a 3,500-acre working sheep farm. In addition to tasteful guest rooms, the homestead has extensive gardens and two natural lagoons that are home to an abundance of birds (watch for the endangered black glossy cockatoo). At the Wanderers Rest inn, the nine balconied rooms are modest but the views across the American River to the mainland are not. Lodging takes a glamorous turn on the island's south coast, at the Southern Ocean Lodge, a sleek eco-luxe resort that's known for impeccable service within a secluded setting of pristine limestone cliffs and white sand beaches.

Where: 75 miles/121 km southwest of Adelaide. **How:** Exceptional Kangaroo Island offers 1- and multiple-day tours. Tel 61/8-8553-9119; www.exceptionalkangarooisland.com. **Stranraer Homestead:** Tel 61/8-8553-8235; www.stranraer.com.au. *Cost:* from $190. **Wanderers Rest:** Tel 61/8-8553-7140; www.wanderersrest.com.au. *Cost:* from $200. **Southern Ocean Lodge:** Tel 61/2-9918-4355; www.southernoceanlodge.com.au. *Cost:* from $2,150, all-inclusive. **Best time:** Oct–Feb for nicest weather and good wildlife-viewing.

Walks on the Wild Side

Cradle Mountain National Park

Tasmania, Australia

Lying 150 miles off the southern coast of mainland Australia, mountainous Tasmania—an island about the size of West Virginia—seems like the end of the earth even to mainland Aussies. Because of its isolation, much of its flora and fauna exist nowhere else in the world, and some of Australia's most spectacular alpine scenery is protected too within about 3 million largely wild acres of parkland.

The jewel in this natural crown is Cradle Mountain–Lake St. Clair National Park, which you can explore on the 4- to 6-day, 53-mile Overland Track, beginning in Launceston and linking the 5,068-foot peak with Australia's deepest freshwater lake. It's the trail many Aussies vow to do at least once in their life. Hardy trekkers follow it through dense rain forests past glacial lakes and waterfalls, and down through lakeside eucalyptus forests, camping along the way. A more comfortable option can be booked through Cradle Mountain Huts, an outfitter that provides guided treks covering 6 to 11 miles a day and overnights in huts with twin beds or bunk-style rooms, hot showers, and a three-course evening meal. Your trek ends with a 10-mile cruise on Tasmania's most beautiful lake.

The circuit around Dove Lake is one of the park's most popular trails.

For those who'd rather not hike the whole trail—or even hike at all—the Cradle Mountain Lodge, on the edge of the park, offers horseback riding, canoeing, and shorter walks through lush rain forests and along alpine lakes. Cozy, timber-built cabins (some with fireplaces) and a spa await at the end of the day. Tasmania has a reputation for producing some of the country's finest food, and you'll get a sampling at the lodge's restaurant.

The 4-day guided Maria Island Walk lets you tour the beaches of that island, a short boat ride from Orford, on Tasmania's east coast, as well as learn a bit about the history and natural features of the area. The island's first inhabitants were Aborigines, followed by whalers and sealers, convicts, and ultimately an eccentric Italian entrepreneur who planted vineyards. Its population now consists of only a few park rangers along with wallabies, wombats, kangaroos, and fairy penguins.

Where: Launceston is 120 miles/200 km north of the island's capital city of Hobart. **Cradle Mountain–Lake St. Clair National**

Park: Tel 61/3-6492-1110; www.parks.tas.gov.au. **Cradle Mountain Huts:** Tel 61/3-6392-2211; www.cradlehuts.com.au. *Cost:* 6-day hike from $2,750, all-inclusive. Originates in Launceston. *When:* Oct–Apr. **Cradle Mountain Lodge:** Tel 61/3-6492-1303; www.cradlemountainlodge.com.au. *Cost:* from $345. **Maria Island Walk:** Tel 61/3-6234-2999; www.mariaislandwalk.com.au. *Cost:* 4-day walk $2,315, all-inclusive. Originates in Hobart. *When:* Oct–Apr. **Best times:** Oct–Apr for pleasant weather; late Jun for Tastings at the Top, a food and wine extravaganza at Cradle Mountain Lodge.

Inspiring Nature and Sophistication Way Down Under

Freycinet National Park

Tasmania, Australia

Freycinet National Park is a dramatic combination of pink granite mountains (called the Hazards), white sand beaches, and lapis-blue ocean, all easily explored. A self-guided 2½-hour nature walk through fields of wildflowers up and over a spine of mountains leads to legendary Wineglass Bay, one of Australia's most beautiful panoramas. The athletic might opt for the 17-mile, 2- to 3-day Freycinet Peninsula circuit, taking in the stunning scenery of the coast with its rich array of wildlife. The area also lures a wide range of adventurers with opportunities for sea kayaking, rock climbing, rappelling, and scenic flights.

Nestled within the confines of the national park is the "disappearing" Freycinet Lodge, so carefully constructed that its 60 luxurious cabins with redwood terraces are barely visible from even a few feet away. Guests may choose from a host of nature-oriented activities, including visits to the breeding grounds of fairy penguins and black swans and guided walks through forests populated by marsupials, brilliant parrots, yellow wattlebirds, and laughing kookaburras. At the two on-site restaurants, you can sample Tasmania's bounty: grass-fed lamb, succulent game meats, just-caught crayfish, and plump Freycinet oysters, paired with local boutique wines.

The arrival of the deluxe, eco-sensitive Saffire Freycinet marked a new pinnacle of refinement on the island. With views across deep-blue Great Oyster Bay to the peaks of the Hazard Mountains, the exclusive Saffire boasts 20 stylishly furnished rooms and a sanctuary-like setting that both uplifts and unwinds. The spa specializes in restorative treatments featuring gold and jewel powders, and the restaurant serves the finest in Tasmanian seafood and wines. For a more modest stay, head to the small seaside town of Swansea, an hour's drive from the park, and check into the inviting hilltop Meredith House, a refurbished 1853 residence with 11 comfortable rooms—some with views of Great Oyster Bay—and attentive, affable owners always on hand.

Where: 115 miles/185 km northeast of Hobart. Tel 61/3-6256-7000; www.parks.tas.gov.au. **Freycinet Lodge:** Tel 61/3-6257-0101; www.freycinetlodge.com.au. *Cost:* from $240; dinner at the Bay Restaurant $80. **Saffire Freycinet:** Tel 61/3-6256-7888; www.saffire-freycinet.com.au. *Cost:* suites from $1,565, includes breakfast, lunch, and activities; dinner $110. **Meredith House:** Tel 61/3-6257-8119; www.meredith-house.com.au. *Cost:* from $180. **Best times:** Feb–Mar for pleasant weather; Jul–Sep for whale-watching.

An Inspirational Ride to the Twelve Apostles

THE GREAT OCEAN ROAD

Victoria, Australia

Ranking among the world's top scenic drives, this 150-mile-long highway hugs the cliffs on its way southwest of Melbourne along the rough-hewn southern coast of the Australian continent. Every bend of the journey reveals another breath-catching view of jagged bluffs, windswept beaches, or magnificent rain forest and parkland (keep your eyes peeled for koalas and kangaroos) along with glimpses of old whaling and fishing towns, inviting restaurants, and sweet B&Bs. The road will take you past prime surf spots, including world-famous Bell's Beach, and such extraordinary rock formations as Loch Ard Gorge and the entire Bay of Islands.

The Twelve Apostles continue to erode at a rate of 2 centimeters per year.

The most famous of all is the Twelve Apostles—eight limestone sea pillars (originally there were nine, but the sea claimed one) that reach as high as 230 feet. They can be seen off a stretch of shoreline known as the Shipwreck Coast for the number of vessels lost here during colonization in the 1800s. It is the most spectacular segment of the Great Ocean Road, especially dramatic when the weather turns windy and stormy.

If you prefer to leave the car behind, lace up your hiking boots and explore this rugged coastline on foot, along the 65-mile Great Ocean Walk trail, which includes some of the route's most scenic highlights. Sign on with a walking-tour operator for 4- to 6-day guided tours (34 miles and 65 miles respectively) with overnights in lodges along the way.

Of the small inns and resorts that can be found in the seafaring villages along the Great Ocean Road, two choices stand out. Just north of Apollo Bay, on 100 rolling acres at the edge of a secluded beach, Chocolate Gannets offers four very private, contemporary villas with spa baths, wood-burning fireplaces, and big picture windows affording breathtaking views. The Great Ocean Ecolodge is a more basic but comfortable five-room guesthouse on the grounds of the Cape Otway Centre for Conservation Ecology, a dedicated wildlife rehabilitation and ecological research center. You just might see grazing kangaroos or koalas climbing in eucalyptus trees outside your window. Venture out into the bush with wildlife researchers, or just relax at the lodge and enjoy the comforts of great cooking and a relaxing snooze in the hammock.

WHERE: starts at the surf-center town of Torquay, 49 miles/78 km southwest of Melbourne, and ends just outside Warrnambool. **VISITOR INFO:** www.visitvictoria.com. **HOW:** Bothfeet offers guided walks. Tel 61/3-5334-0688; www.bothfeet.com.au. *Cost:* 4-day hikes from $2,150, inclusive. Originate in Melbourne. **CHOCOLATE GANNETS:** Tel 61/1-3005-00-139; www.chocolategannets.com.au. *Cost:* from $345. **GREAT OCEAN ECOLODGE:** Tel 61/3-5237-9297; www.greatoceanecolodge.com. *Cost:* from $320. **BEST TIMES:** Mar–May for dry autumn weather; Jun–Oct for whale spotting; Sep–Nov for spring wildflowers.

Pearling Paradise on the Edge of the Continent

CABLE BEACH

Broome, Western Australia, Australia

Australians take their beaches seriously, so when they claim that Cable Beach in the town of Broome is among the continent's most beautiful, take note. Large and lustrous South Sea pearls (from *Pinctada maxima,* the world's largest pearl oysters) put Broome on the map in the early 1900s. Today it is both outback and a little bit glamorous, a free-and-easy town where gastro-tourists won't be disappointed. The beach is the reason to go, though—after you've spent a day there, top things off with a sunset camel ride, the finest way to appreciate the 14 miles of sandy expanse and the swath of reds and violets that fills the sky as the sun disappears into the Indian Ocean. If you visit between March and October, watch for the natural phenomenon called Staircase to the Moon that occurs when the rising full moon is reflected on the exposed mudflats at extremely low tide, creating a optical illusion of a flight of stairs reaching up to the heavens.

The town owes its distinctive architectural look to the pearling masters from the early days, who built their bungalow homes of corrugated iron, adding wooden latticework screens and colonial verandas. Nowhere has the style been more beautifully executed than at the luxurious Cable Beach Club, set amid gardens and pools, and the only hotel adjacent to the beach. The town's cosmopolitan mix of cultures inspires the resort's kitchen, where Asian, European, and Aboriginal food traditions intersect deliciously.

In town opt for Pinctada McAlpine House, which has been transformed from a historic, century-old master pearler's home to a charming boutique lodge. With room for just eight guests, it is an ideal spot in which to unwind and steep in the town's unique character. A much celebrated addition to the Broome beach scene is the five-star Pinctada Cable Beach Resort and Spa. Try a treatment containing native botanicals and essence of mother of pearl from the *Pinctada maxima,* then visit Selene Brasserie, the resort's

A telegraph cable laid between Broome and Java gives the beach its name.

sumptuous dining room, where local seafood is given an eastern Mediterranean twist.

Where: 1,481 miles/2,389 km north of Perth. **Cable Beach Club:** Tel 61/8-9192-0400; www.cablebeachclub.com.au. *Cost:* from $320 (off-peak), from $460 (peak). **McAlpine House:** Tel 61/8-9192-0510; www.mcalpinehouse.com.au. *Cost:* from $190 (off-peak), from $350 (peak). **Pinctada Cable Beach Resort and Spa:** Tel 61/8-9193-8388; www.pinctadacablebeach.com.au. *Cost:* from $290 (off-peak), from $385 (peak); dinner $60. **Best times:** Apr–Oct for the dry season and near perfect weather; during full moons for Staircase to the Moon; Aug for Festival of the Pearl.

Wildflowers and Vineyards

Margaret River

Western Australia, Australia

In the last 30 years, the wine industry has given a cosmopolitan veneer to this remote and beautiful southwestern corner of the country, with its dazzling landscape of stunning surf beaches, carefully tended vines, and dense forests.

Prestigious vintages by Vasse Felix, Cape Mentelle, Cullens, and the venerable Leeuwin Estate enjoy recognition around the world, and more than 90 cellar doors (tasting rooms and outlets) at these and other producers promise leisurely days spent vineyard hopping. Leeuwin Estate is well known for its program of alfresco concerts, a heralded summer event attracting world-class performers and ever-growing crowds.

But grapes aren't all that grow here. The Margaret River area is famous for its spring wildflowers, which are at their peak from mid-September to mid-November, filling the countryside to the horizon with a kaleidoscope of color. More than 2,500 species have been identified in this part of the country, including 150-plus species of orchid. Over 60 percent of the plant species in Australia's southwest are found nowhere else on earth, making it one of the world's 34 "biodiversity hot spots" and the only one in Australia.

Cape Lodge, one of Australia's most tasteful and relaxing country retreats, is nestled among the vineyards near the town of Yallingup and sits within earshot of the sparkling Indian Ocean. Its 22 rooms and suites (and a magnificent five-bedroom luxury private residence) are scattered over 40 acres of parkland that centers on a beautiful free-form swimming pool. At the internationally acclaimed Cape Lodge Restaurant, the menu changes daily, and superbly prepared dishes are matched with premium Margaret River–area wines. Stylish and beautifully furnished, the nearby Llewellin's Guest House is for wine-lovers seeking more intimate lodging. Offering just three guest rooms and set amid 8 tranquil acres of native bush habitat, the inn impresses with welcoming, friendly service and marvelous breakfasts.

From either lodging, it's a short drive to Margaret River, a delightful town full of antiques stores and craft shops as well as vineyard restaurants, where menus are designed "from the wine up" to highlight the special characteristics of each winery. A top choice is the marvelous lunch service at Voyager Estate, where the five-course tasting menu pairs the vineyard's top vintages with an inspired seasonal menu.

Where: 181 miles/291 km south of Perth.

Leeuwin Estate Concerts: Tel 61/8-9430-4099; www.leeuwinestate.com.au. *When:* Feb–Mar. **Cape Lodge:** Tel 61/8-9755-6311; www.capelodge.com.au. *Cost:* from $480; dinner $105. **Llewellin's Guest House:** Tel 61/8-9757-9516; www.llewellinsguesthouse.com.au. *Cost:* from $180. **Voyager Estate:** 61/8-9757-6354; www.voyagerestate.com.au. *Cost:* 5-course tasting menu lunch $130. **Best times:** Mar–Apr for grape harvest and Margaret River Wine Festival; mid-Sep–mid-Nov for wildflowers.

Where Gentle Giants Gather

Snorkeling with Whale Sharks

Ningaloo Reef, Western Australia, Australia

One of the few places you can swim with the world's largest fish is Ningaloo Reef, on Australia's west coast. Whale sharks are capable of growing up to 60 feet long, though here they usually measure a relatively petite 12 to 40 feet. These gentle giants are nearly impossible to spot in open waters; Jacques Cousteau came across only two in his lifetime. But at the 200-mile-long Ningaloo Reef and a handful of other spots around the world (notably Belize and Honduras; see pp. 963 and 972), whale sharks appear regularly, arriving from April to July to feed on huge shoals of plankton, with little interest in any humans swimming nearby. Or at least they do for the moment: The placid sharks have so dwindled in number that they are now listed as nationally threatened, and for this reason, local tour operators restrict the number of people who are allowed to join the sharks in the water at one time. Ningaloo Blue Dive in Exmouth has a specially designed 50-foot vessel that can take up to 20 guests at a time.

Whale sharks' spots—along with their extreme length—stand out to snorkelers.

Consider staying at Sal Salis Ningaloo Reef, a stunning tent camp hidden in the dunes of Cape Range National Park, where the beach meets the reef, about an hour's drive south of Exmouth. The main eco-sensitive camp rises above the dunes, and the open-air lodge building has views out to the reef. Alfresco dinners are served against a backdrop of a vivid sunset, when kangaroos and wallaroos arrive for their own evening graze. The reef in front of the camp is a major breeding ground for three kinds of turtles—hawksbill, green, and loggerhead.

Where: Exmouth is 780 miles/1,260 km north of Perth. **Ningaloo Blue Dive:** Tel 61/8-9949-1119; www.ningalooblue.com.au. *Cost:* 1-day dive $415. **Sal Salis:** Tel 61/2-9571-6399; www.salsalis.com.au. *Cost:* 3- and 4-night whale shark–viewing packages from $3,350, all-inclusive. *When:* Apr–Jul.

Ancient Mountain Range Hidden in the Outback

The Kimberley and the Bungle Bungle Range

Purnululu National Park, Western Australia, Australia

In the northwestern part of Australia, called the Kimberley, there are fewer people per square mile than almost any other place on earth. Until the 1980s, just a few local Aborigines and a handful of stockmen knew about the strange landscape at the heart of this region, where thousands of orange-and-black-banded, beehive-shaped sandstone formations protrude hundreds of feet out of the ground. Known as the Bungle Bungle Range or the Bungles, they are part of Purnululu National Park, which measures roughly 925 square miles.

Geologists say the range was formed hundreds of millions of years ago during the Devonian era, after a great marine deposit was eroded down to the present domes, cliffs, and gorges. Only a few visitors make the journey to this natural wonderland, and while the area is rich in Aboriginal art and sacred sites, its magnificence is best appreciated from a helicopter or plane, soaring above the seasonal waterfalls and pools.

Still, backcountry enthusiasts might want to join a camping safari or hire a local Aboriginal guide for a trek through the majestic gorges carved into the Bungle Bungle limestone by seasonal rivers and creeks. Noncamping types can repair to El Questro Wilderness Park, a million-acre cattle station and high-end outback experience to the north of Purnululu Park. Explore one of the property's many tropical gorges or remote water holes, or take a 4WD jaunt with a resident ranger, who will introduce you to the station's thermal springs, waterfalls, and ancient Aboriginal rock art. You have a choice of staying in safari tents, bungalows, or experiencing the glamour of the El Questro Homestead, a small boutique hotel perched on the edge of the Chamberlain River and Gorge. With six luxurious rooms it promises the highest standards of cuisine and service, available to just a dozen guests at a time.

A tight squeeze awaits at Echidna Chasm, part of the Bungles, which is only 2 yards wide at its narrowest points.

Where: Kununurra is the eastern gateway to the Kimberley, 525 miles/840 km southwest of Darwin. **Purnululu National Park:** 155 miles/250 km south of Kununurra. Tel 61/8-9168-4200; www.dec.wa.gov.au. **How:** Relaxing Journeys offers a 13-day camping tour that includes the Bungles. Tel 61/7-5474-3911; www.relaxingjourneys.com/au. *Cost:* $6,545. **El Questro Wilderness Park:** Tel 61/8-9169-1777; www.elquestro.com.au. *Cost:* safari tent cabins from $290 per person; bungalows from $325; homestead rooms from $1,350, all-inclusive. *When:* closed Nov–Mar. **Best time:** May–Oct for cooler weather.

In the Wake of Captain Cook

THE BAY OF ISLANDS

North Island, New Zealand

The nation of New Zealand was born along a knotty section of coast in the far north of the North Island, where more than 150 tiny islands known as the Bay Islands hopscotch across the deep blue waters, their tall Norfolk pines growing side by side with subtropical banana plants and fan palms. It was here in the town of Waitangi, in 1840, that British officers and Maori chiefs entered into a treaty that granted Queen Victoria sovereignty over New Zealand and made the Maori her subjects. The Bay of Islands is renowned as a recreational playground, particularly for its big-game fishing. The majority of fishing and kayaking trips, as well as those that take you to see the dolphins—and even swim with them—begin in the beachside town of Paihia. You can experience the region the way Captain James Cook did (he anchored here in 1769), with the wind in your hair and the flapping of sails overhead as you slip past hundreds of hidden coves and secret beaches aboard the schooner *R. Tucker Thompson,* anchoring for a swim and a barbeque lunch. (Watch for minke and Bryde's whales from August to January.)

Urupukapuka Island is the largest of the 150 Bay Islands.

The charming historic town of Russell is also a departure point for bay excursions. Formerly a rowdy whaling port and New Zealand's first capital, its picturesque waterfront is lined with quaint Colonial buildings, including the venerable old Duke of Marlborough Hotel, a good place to stay the night, enjoy a great meal, or simply stop for a drink with local yachtsmen on the veranda. For even more historic charm, head up to Arcadia Lodge, a hillside B&B with half a dozen rooms and an open deck with 180-degree water views and an elaborate breakfast. Or make a 90-minute coastal drive and check into one of the elegant suites dotted along the stunning championship golf course at the Lodge at Kauri Cliffs, in Matauri Bay. It is set on 6,500 coastal acres of a working farm with over 4,000 sheep and cattle, and has three private beaches and an inviting spa.

WHERE: Paihia is 143 miles/230 km north of Auckland. ***R. TUCKER THOMPSON:*** Tel 64/9-402-8430; www.tucker.co.nz. *Cost:* 5½-hour cruise with lunch $105. *When:* closed May–Sep. **DUKE OF MARLBOROUGH:** Tel 64/9-403-7829; www.theduke.co.nz. *Cost:* from $175; lunch $35. **ARCADIA LODGE:** Tel 64/9-403-7756; www.arcadialodge.co.nz. *Cost:* from $150. **LODGE AT KAURI CLIFFS:** Tel 64/9-407-0010; www.kauricliffs.com. *Cost:* suites from $1,000 (off-peak), from $1,575 (peak), inclusive. **HOW:** Seasonz Travel arranges personalized New Zealand itineraries. Tel 64/9-360-8461; www.seasonz.co.nz. **BEST TIMES:** Feb–Jun for game fishing; Nov–Apr for nicest weather.

A Paradise for Rainbow Trout and Those They Lure

Lake Taupo and Tongariro National Park

North Island, New Zealand

Local bumper stickers call Lake Taupo "The Rainbow Trout Capital of the Universe," and they're not exaggerating: Even by New Zealand standards, these fish are monsters, with the average catch weighing in at 4 pounds and 10-pounders causing barely a stir among the anglers who flock here. The nation's largest lake, measuring 20 by 25 miles, Taupo is the crater of an ancient volcano. It's located near the center of the North Island and framed by three active volcanoes in nearby Tongariro National Park.

Huka Lodge is the area's star resort, the ne plus ultra of European-flavored country sporting lodges. With its proximity to the lake (it's just 3 miles away) and the Waikato River running through its 17-acre grounds, its name is spoken with reverence among anglers around the world. Eighteen spacious rooms and suites and two exclusive private cottages are located along the serene, willow-draped banks of the river. Ask to have a gourmet lunch hamper prepared and spend an afternoon downstream at mighty Huka Falls, fed by a series of churning rapids formed by a sudden narrowing of the river. Then visit the nearby Volcanic Activity Center, which provides excellent insight into the area's geothermal activity, or take the hour's drive north to the bubbling spectacle of Rotorua (see p. 670) and see it for yourself.

The intrepid will want to set aside a day to tackle the 11-mile Tongariro Alpine Crossing, which traverses a stunning volcanic landscape within the Tongariro National Park. Considered by most to be the best one-day tramp in the country, PureORAwalks offers treks led by a Maori guide, who will make it the highlight of your visit. At the end of the day, kick back at the 1920s-era Bayview Chateau Tongariro, built at the base of Mount Raupehu, an active volcano. The grande dame of the park, the lodge fills with hikers in the summer and with those who come for the nearby Whakapapa Ski Field in the winter. It's worth dropping in for Devonshire tea, even if you're not spending the night.

Tongariro Alpine Crossing's high altitude brings trampers above the clouds.

Where: 174 miles/280 km south of Auckland. **How:** Chris Jolly Boats operates 4 vessels with crew and fishing guides. Tel 64/7-378-0623; www.chrisjolly.co.nz. *Cost:* from $135 per hour, or from $12 per person per hour. **Huka Lodge:** Tel 64/7-378-5791; www.hukalodge.co.nz. *Cost:* from $630 per person, inclusive (off-peak), from $1,095 (peak). **Volcanic Activity Center:** Tel 64/7-374-8375; www.volcanoes.co.nz. **PureORAwalks:** Tel 64/21-042-2722; www.pureorawalks.com. **Bayview Chateau Tongariro:** Tel 64/7-892-3809; www.chateau.co.nz. *Cost:* from $195. **Best times:** Oct–Apr for fishing; Jul–mid-Nov for skiing.

An Art Deco Time Capsule in a Wine-Lover's Enclave

Napier and Hawkes Bay

North Island, New Zealand

In 1931, a 7.8 magnitude earthquake struck the east coast of the North Island and fire tore the downtown of Napier apart. The residents rebuilt in the popular architectural style of the day, and now the port city stands alongside Miami Beach (see p. 752) as one of the world's great examples of an Art Deco community. February's annual Art Deco Weekend, replete with vintage cars and women dressed as flappers, attests to the locals' love of their hometown's history, but it's also one of their many excuses to indulge in their true passion: food and wine.

The Hawkes Bay area is the second largest wine-growing region in New Zealand—after South Island's Marlborough (see p. 675)—with more than 70 vineyards. French missionaries first planted vines here in 1851 and started the Mission Estate Winery, still immensely popular and offering both historical tours and some of the bay's finest bottles. The same missionaries built a nearby church that's now converted to a restaurant fittingly called the Old Church. It is one of the town's finest dining establishments and arguably the most beautiful building in which to sample fine food as well as local red wines and chardonnays. A more rustic (but sophisticated) experience awaits at the French-flavored Terroir, which sits on the scenic grounds of the Craggy Range winery.

While many would be happy to simply eat and drink their way through Hawkes Bay (plenty of local companies run vineyard tours), the mild weather demands that one venture away to breathe the coastal air—and maybe hit the links. *Golf Magazine* rated the championship course at Cape Kidnappers as one of the world's finest. Set atop rolling cliffs that plunge dramatically into the sea, it's 30 minutes south of Napier and part of a 6,000-acre sheep farm that includes an exclusive lodge and the largest, most easily glimpsed mainland colony of gannets in the world; around 17,000 of them nest here from September through May.

If you prefer to be closer to Napier and the vineyards, stay at the award-winning Master's Lodge, a converted plantation house with just two exquisite suites that sits upon Bluff Hill, a lush piece of property that used to be an island until the earthquake raised it 20 feet out of the water and connected it to the mainland. Your dollars will stretch further if you stay at the welcoming Havelock House, a luxurious B&B whose three suites and one apartment overlook flowering gardens, a pool, and tennis courts.

Where: Napier is 196 miles/315 km north of Wellington. **Mission Estate Winery:** Tel 64/6-845-9350; www.missionestate.co.nz. **Old Church:** Tel 64/6-844-8866; www.theoldchurch.co.nz. *Cost:* dinner $55. **Terroir:** 64/6-873-0143; www.craggyrange.com. *Cost:* 3-course tasting menu $70. **Cape Kidnappers:** Tel 64/6-875-1900; www.capekidnappers.com. *Cost:* from $1,010 (off-peak), from $1,450 (peak), inclusive; greens fees from $200 (off-peak), $270 (peak), discount for overnight guests. **Master's Lodge:** Tel 64/6-834-1946; www.masterslodge.co.nz. *Cost:* from $630. **Havelock House:** Tel 64/6-877-5439; www.havelockhouse.co.nz. *Cost:* from $145. **Best times:** Oct–Apr for good weather; Feb for Art Deco Weekend in Napier.

Seaside Sheep Station

Wharekauhau Country Estate

Palliser Bay, North Island, New Zealand

A sheep ranch is not the first thing that comes to mind when you think "luxurious getaway," but Wharekauhau ("the place where the gods meet" in the Maori language) is all about confounding expectations.

A sprawling 5,500-acre farm that includes miles of secluded black volcanic sand beaches, emerald green pastures, and dense forests rich with red deer, wild boar, and mountain goats, Wharekauhau welcomes guests with both homespun hospitality and top-drawer amenities. Of course, guests can roll up their sleeves and help with the sheep shearing, but they are also free to bliss out in the serene spa or to simply float in the indoor pool. And there's always horseback riding, strolls along the beach, surf casting, and trips to explore historic Maori sites and local wineries when you feel like venturing farther afield.

Set aside a day to visit Cape Palliser and its red-and-white lighthouse that rises from the rocks like a barber pole and marks the southernmost point of the North Island. The drive hugs cliffs and coast and serves up some unique sights, including a large fur seal rookery and some curious collections of beached fishing boats that locals drag ashore via bulldozers and trailers in order to protect them from the notoriously rough surf. On the way home, make a detour to the Putangirua Pinnacles for a short hike up a dry riverbed to one of the country's geological oddities, a maze of crumbling rock spires, or hoodoos, some up to 150 feet high. When you return to the farm, you'll be able to recount your adventures over a dinner of simple, elegantly presented country fare served with wonderful wines from the nearby Martinborough region.

Where: 66 miles/105 km southeast of Wellington. Tel 64/6-307-7581; www.wharekauhau.co.nz. **Cost:** from $515 per person, inclusive (off-peak), from $790 (peak). **Best time:** Nov–Apr for good weather.

The World Cracked Open

Bubbling Rotorua

North Island, New Zealand

At Rotorua, the center of the intense thermal field of the Taupo Volcanic Plateau, mud pools spit, geysers shoot high into the air, and sulfurous steam and gas hiss through crevices in the earth's surface, creating a bizarre geothermal spectacle that George Bernard Shaw called "the most hellish scene" he had ever witnessed. There are hot and cold rivers, otherworldly-looking natural silica terraces, and the unpredictable Pohutu Geyser, which sprays up to 100 feet in the air.

One-third of New Zealand's Maori live in the area, and their legends explain the strange geological phenomena as a gift of fire from the gods. It was a gift the first British settlers relished, as Rotorua became a booming spa town in the 1840s. And although it has become commercialized (some refer to it as Roto-Vegas), people are still drawn to its sometimes frightening natural wonders.

For over 125 years, the Polynesian Spa has been Rotorua's main draw for its complex of 26 communal and private mineral pools that offer an extensive menu of treatments. But for the best examples of these and other natural phenomena, head to Wai-O-Tapu, an active geothermal area 17 miles to the south, where you'll find Champagne Pool, an effervescent, blue-green pond rimmed with brilliant orange mineral deposits, and Lady Knox Geyser, which erupts every morning at roughly 10:15 A.M., thanks to the addition of some catalytic laundry detergent.

To recharge in luxury, stay at Solitaire Lodge, built on the elevated tip of a forested promontory overlooking the rainbow trout–rich Lake Tarawera and an extinct volcano of the same name. Closer to the city, the Hamurana Lodge is a sedate manor house and boutique hotel on Lake Rotorua that's known for great dining and a helpful staff. In town you'll find the Regent of Rotorua, where the high-style suites are all white save for the stylish wallpaper. Don't leave without a visit to the Mitai Maori Village, a living history museum where an evening of song, dance, and a traditional hangi feast introduces travelers to the area's indigenous culture.

WHERE: 143 miles/230 km southeast of Auckland. **POLYNESIAN SPA:** Tel 64/7-348-1328; www.polynesianspa.co.nz. **WAI-O-TAPU:** Tel 64/7-366-6333; www.waiotapu.co.nz. **SOLITAIRE LODGE:** Tel 64/7-362-8208; www.solitairelodge.co.nz. *Cost:* from $1,100, all-inclusive. **HAMURANA LODGE:** Tel 64/7-332-2222; www.hamuranalodge.com. *Cost:* from $350 (off-peak), from $580 (peak). **REGENT OF ROTORUA:** Tel 64/7-348-4079; www.regentrotorua.co.nz. *Cost:* $111 (off-peak), $224 (peak). **MITAI MAORI VILLAGE:** Tel 64/7-343-9132; www.mitai.co.nz. *Cost:* $85. **BEST TIMES:** Oct–Apr for summer weather; Jun–Jul for Matariki (Maori New Year).

The Alpine Training Grounds of Sir Edmund Hillary

AORAKI/MOUNT COOK NATIONAL PARK

South Island, New Zealand

While the South Island of New Zealand is known for its palm trees and hibiscus plants, one third of the dazzling national park found here is covered in permanent snow and ice. Aoraki/Mount Cook National Park—it bears names from both the Maori (Cloud Piercer) and the English—contains 72 named glaciers and 22 mountain peaks that top 9,840 feet, including the park's namesake, which is New Zealand's highest at 12,316 feet. This is the place to splurge on unforgettable flightseeing. Some flights include a snow landing on the 17-mile-long Tasman Glacier, the longest river of ice outside the Himalayas. In the deep silence of the roof-of-the-world panorama, you can occasionally hear a rumble as the glacier shifts ever so slightly. Very few glaciers lead to lakes and even fewer of those are accessible to the average person, but here you can explore two by boat tour and by kayak, drinking in views of towering ice cliffs and the huge icebergs that float in the opaque turquoise waters.

Skiing is the other activity of choice in this alpine park, with guided heli-skiing, an exhilarating 8-mile-long glacier run (the southern hemisphere's longest ski run), and downhill skiing available. And there's hiking as well: A number of guided and self-guided walks take anywhere from 30 minutes to 3 days along the well-known Copland Track. New Zealander Sir Edmund Hillary trained in this high-altitude park before his record-setting ascent of Mount Everest (see p. 563) in 1953.

Views from the picture windows at the Hermitage no doubt would impress even him. Among the world's best-sited hotels, it is also the location of the new Sir Edmund Hillary Alpine Centre, showcasing mementos of one of New Zealand's most admired citizens.

In front of the Hermitage hotel, a statue of Sir Edmund Hillary surveys the landscape.

WHERE: 160 miles/257 km northeast of Queenstown. **HOW:** Mount Cook Ski Planes offers plane and helicopter trips. Tel 64/3-430-8034; www.skiplanes.co.nz. *Cost:* trips with snow landings from $300. Glacier Explorer offers glacier lake boat trips. Tel 64/3-435-1641; www.glacierexplorers.co.nz. *Cost:* $110. *When:* Sep–May. **HERMITAGE:** Tel 64/3-435-1809; www.hermitage.co.nz. *Cost:* from $170. **BEST TIMES:** Jul–Sep for skiing; Nov–Apr for trekking and glacier tours.

A High-Country Stay in the Southern Alps

ARTHUR'S PASS

Canterbury, South Island, New Zealand

Shortcuts are rare in New Zealand. Roads typically follow switchbacks over mountains, or avoid them completely, skirting their edges and piling on the miles needed to get from point A to point B. This had posed a distinct problem in the South Island, where the Southern Alps run the length of the land like a chain of vertebrae, dividing the east coast from the west. So the Kiwis created three grand coast-to-coast shortcuts: Lewis Pass in the north, Haast Pass in the south, and the crown jewel, Arthur's Pass, in the center.

The tiny Arthur's Pass Village serves as a gateway to vast Arthur's Pass National Park, which is marked by sprawling beech forests on its eastern side and deeply gorged rivers and thick rain forest to the west. You can ski, hike, or mountain bike while reveling in the alpine scenery. Another way to drink in all the beauty is aboard the TranzAlpine Express, which since 1923 has offered one of the most scenic railroad journeys anywhere. Its 4-hour route stretches from Christchurch on the east coast to Greymouth on the west, passing gorgeous vistas along the way not visible from the road. With prior arrangement, the train will stop at the minuscule station of Cass (possibly the smallest town in the world, with a population of one), where a representative of the Grasmere Lodge will be waiting to whisk you off to one of the country's finest retreats.

Set within a high-country station (or ranch) covering roughly 15,000 acres, this traditional homestead began as a two-room hut in 1858. Added onto over the years and extensively renovated, the lodge now hosts guests, who can choose to take part in farming activities among the cattle and merino sheep that still roam the rugged range or to simply enjoy the manor's world-class country elegance, epitomized by the gemlike spa. The camaraderie of cocktail hour is followed by a communal five-course dinner of New Zealand fare, which may include beef or lamb raised on the farm. Grasmere spreads across more than four rivers, eight streams and creeks, and eight lakes, which allow for fishing, kayaking, and rafting, and there's endless terrain to explore by horseback as well.

WHERE: Arthur's Pass is 80 miles/130 km west of Christchurch. **TRANZALPINE EXPRESS:** Tel 64/4-498-3090; www.tranzscenic.co.nz. *Cost:* from $90 one-way between Christchurch and Cass. **GRASMERE LODGE:** Tel 64/3-318-8407; www.grasmere.co.nz. *Cost:* from $700 (off-peak), from $990 (peak), inclusive. **BEST TIMES:** Dec–early Apr for warm weather and wildflowers; Jul–Sep for skiing and winter activities.

The Spectacular Milford and Doubtful Sounds

FIORDLAND NATIONAL PARK

South Island, New Zealand

The Australians may claim the Great Barrier Reef as the Eighth Wonder of the World, but Rudyard Kipling gave the honor to New Zealand's Milford Sound. Kiwis disagree with both—they rank it first or second. Milford is the most famous and accessible of the 15 fjords that make up the majestic 3-million-acre Fiordland National Park (the country's largest) on the South Island's southwestern coast. The 9.3-mile-long inlet is hemmed in by sheer granite cliffs rising up to 4,000 feet, with waterfalls cascading from the high mountain ridges. Playful bottlenose dolphins, fur seals, and gulls call its waters home, and crested penguins nest here in October and November before leaving for Antarctica. Mitre Peak is the centerpiece, a 5,560-foot pinnacle whose reflection in the mirror-calm water is one of New Zealand's most photographed sites. Flightseeing is a great way to see it all, and boats leave frequently for 2- to 4-hour or overnight cruises.

It used to be that the only way to reach Milford Sound by land was along the Milford Track, once dubbed "the finest walk in the world," a description that has deservedly stuck. The strenuous guided trek, which takes 5 days and covers 33 miles, rewards with awesome scenery. You'll begin on the banks of Lake Te Anau, cut through glistening green valleys, and cross over the utterly gorgeous

MacKinnon Pass. Even if you're spent, don't skip the optional hike to 1,900-foot-high Sutherland Falls, a treat only Milford trekkers can enjoy up close. The final flourish is a cruise on Milford Fjord, after which you travel back to Te Anau along the incredibly scenic Milford Road and through Homer Tunnel, a marvel of engineering that took 20 years to build and first brought cars to the sound in 1954.

Doubtful Sound is the deepest and, some say, most beautiful of the park's fjords. When the engines are turned off, you'll be enveloped in the primeval silence of one of the world's most remote and magical places. (Captain Cook wasn't sure he would be able to navigate his way out, hence the name.) Ten times larger than Milford Sound and less known outside of the country, Doubtful Sound retains an element of mystery. And while rainfall in this area is over 300 inches a year, even a day filled with showers has its moody beauty, as spontaneous waterfalls sprout out of nowhere, filling the air with their soothing music.

Mitre Peak was so named because its shape resembles the mitre hats worn by some Christian clergymen.

Where: Most departures for Milford are from Te Anau, which is 107 miles/172 km southwest of Queenstown. **How:** Ultimate Hikes leads guided treks. Tel 64/3-450-1940; www.ultimatehikes.co.nz. *Cost:* 5-day Milford Track from $1,450. Originates in Queenstown. *When:* Nov–Apr. Real Journeys offers Milford and Doubtful Sound cruises. Tel 64/3-249-7416; www.realjourneys.co.nz. *Cost:* day trips from $60, overnight trips from $275. *When:* Sep–May. **Best time:** Oct–Apr for spring and summer weather.

Superb Tramps on the Routeburn and Greenstone Tracks

The Grand Traverse

South Island, New Zealand

Don't be offended if someone in New Zealand asks you if you enjoy a good tramp. It probably means you look fit. In a country where nature is king, it's no surprise that "tramping" (aka hiking) is a national pastime—and what remarkable scenery there is to tramp through, particularly along the Grand Traverse (a combination of the Routeburn and Greenstone Tracks), one of New Zealand's premier trekking experiences. The 24-mile Routeburn Track (which some connoisseurs find more awe-inspiring than the fabled Milford Track; see previous page) is its first leg. It crosses the Southern Alps over the breathtaking 3,900-foot Harris Saddle and descends through a world of moss-clad trees, giant ferns, mountain streams, rich birdlife, lakes, and waterfalls within Mount Aspiring National Park. One glimpse and it's obvious why this landscape stood in for the "Misty Mountains" in Peter Jackson's trilogy of fantasy films *The Lord of the Rings*. The trail picks up the 25-mile Greenstone Valley Walk, which follows an ancient Maori path through Fiordland National Park, crossing the main divide of the Southern Alps within a beautiful river valley encircled by towering mountains. The 6-day Grand Traverse requires that you be in top shape—it's not just the scenery that will take your breath away.

Guided treks offer a number of obvious advantages, not least being access to private lodges, with snug beds, hot showers, toilets, and hearty food; those short on time can book 1-day samplers. Visitors who choose to go solo stay in more rudimentary accommodations and must register with the Department of Conservation. The number of hikers is strictly controlled, accompanied or not, so book well in advance.

WHERE: Te Wahipounanu World Heritage Area, southwest corner of the South Island. **HOW:** Ultimate Hikes offers guided trek packages. Tel 64/3-450-1940; www.ultimatehikes.co.nz. *Cost:* 3-day Routeburn Track from $900, all-inclusive; 6-day Grand Traverse from $1,245, all-inclusive. Originate in Queenstown. *When:* Nov–Apr. **BEST TIME:** Jan-Feb for most comfortable temperatures and least precipitation.

On the Trail of the Grape

MARLBOROUGH SOUNDS

South Island, New Zealand

The Marlborough region of the South Island offers two irresistible reasons to visit: in the north, the grandeur of the unspoiled Marlborough Sounds, with dozens of secluded bays and beaches, and in the south, the award-winning vineyards encircling the town of Blenheim. This area, formerly occupied by sheep farms, is the country's largest and best-known center of viticulture, with more than 100 wineries producing internationally acclaimed chardonnay and sauvignon blanc and, more recently, pinot gris, riesling, and gewürztraminer. Marlborough is dominated by industry giant Brancott Estate (formerly known as Montana), but wine fans will also recognize names such as Cloudy Bay, Grove Mill, and Hunter's. A few vineyards, like Herzog, offer some of the country's finest dining experiences too.

The area was first settled by Maori over 1,000 years ago, and it was well documented in Captain Cook's diaries from his first landing at Ship Cove in the 1770s. Outdoor enthusiasts know about the hiking along the Milford Track (see p. 673) and the nearby Abel Tasman Coastal Track. But you'll find amazing views and far less foot traffic on the 42-mile coastal trail, known as Queen Charlotte Track, which can be done in 1- to 4-day segments. And the many bays, inlets, and sheltered coves of the Pelorus, Queen Charlotte, and Kenepuru sounds make this a sea kayaker's paradise. Local agencies can customize packages that include guided walks, stays at charming lodges, dolphin- and whale-watching cruises, and visits to local vineyards in the company of excellent guides.

West of Blenheim, on the grounds of the Barrows, makers of organic World's End sauvignon blanc and pinot noir, you'll find the Straw Lodge. Here, private suites and a tucked-away cottage are mere yards away from the vines, with the peaks of Mount Richmond Forest Park as their backdrop. Nearby, Timara Lodge hosts no more than eight guests; the elegant-but-cozy, Tudor-style manor house was built in the 1920s, and its

English-style gardens and small lake make an idyllic setting. Excellent dinners are complemented by wines from the owners' vineyards as well as from their well-stocked cellar.

If you prefer to be right in the heart of Blenheim, the Hotel d'Urville occupies a well-preserved building on Main Street. Each of the 11 rooms is tastefully decorated, but it is the welcoming downstairs bar and smart, always-abuzz restaurant that make this an all-around great pick.

Where: Blenheim is 169 miles/272 km north of Christchurch. **Straw Lodge:** Tel 64/3-572-9767; www.strawlodge.co.nz. *Cost:* from $270. **Timara Lodge:** Tel 64/3-572-8276; www.timara.co.nz. *Cost:* from $1,280, inclusive. *When:* closed Jun–Jul. **Hotel d'Urville:** Tel 64/3-577-9945; www.durville.com. *Cost:* $160 (off-peak), $235 (peak). **How:** Marlborough Sounds Adventure Company leads multiday guided walks. Tel 64/3-573-6078; www.marlboroughsounds.co.nz. *Cost:* 4-day trips from $1,300. **Best times:** Nov–Mar for nice weather; Feb for Brews, Blues, and BBQs and the Marlborough Wine Festival.

Thrill Seeking in the Adventure Capital of the World

The Home of Bungee Jumping and Jet Boating

Queenstown, South Island, New Zealand

If you want to learn something fundamental about the Kiwi character, you need only know that New Zealand is the recognized home of both bungee jumping and jet boating. The former act of madness originated as a coming-of-age ritual on the Pacific islands of Vanuatu (see p. 698). And while you may not have realized you had a burning desire to attach a thick rubber cord to your ankles before diving headfirst off a bridge, Queenstown's high-energy brand of fun is infectious, and so far—with a 100 percent safety record—everyone has lived to brag about it. The Kawarau Suspension Bridge, which affords a 143-foot drop, has hosted more than 500,000 jumps. Feeling more adventurous? Opt for Ledge Urban Bungy, which lets you leap 1,312 feet above the rooftops of Queenstown. And there's more for adrenaline junkies here. The canyon-walled Shotover River is the place for heart-stopping jet boat trips that fly you over the shallow waters—sometimes only inches deep—negotiating huge boulders and rushing rapids.

To recuperate from all that death defying, repair to Eichardt's Private Hotel, an impeccably restored historical residence on Lake Wakatipu, in the heart of Queenstown's shopping and restaurant district. Fireplaces and antique furnishings distinguish the five luxurious suites and four cottages, all with front-row views of the lake and the Remarkables mountain range in the distance. Its House Bar is a longtime favorite. A similar European ambience and lakeside views come with your cozy room at Brown's Boutique Hotel, a 5-minute stroll from downtown. Or check out Pencarrow, one of New Zealand's best-loved B&Bs. Hidden on a hillside above Lake Wakatipu just east of town, it has views, gardens, and service to rival any luxury lodge.

How: For bungee jumping, A. J. Hackett Bungy, named for the man who made a historic leap from the Eiffel Tower in 1987; tel 64/3-442-4007; www.bun.co.nz. *Cost:* $135. For jet boats, Shotover Jet, tel 64/3-442-8570; www.shotoverjet.co.nz. *Cost:* $90. **Eichardt's Private Hotel:** Tel 64/3-441-0450; www.eichardtshotel.co.nz. *Cost:* from $800. **Brown's Boutique Hotel:** Tel 64/3-441-2050; www.brownshotel.co.nz. *Cost:* from $245 (off-peak), from $325 (peak). **Pencarrow:** Tel 64/3-442-8938; www.pencarrow.net. *Cost:* from $380. **Best time:** Jan–Mar for summer weather.

THE PACIFIC ISLANDS

A Turquoise Carpet on an Indigo Sea

Aitutaki

Cook Islands

It seems strange that of the many islands Captain James Cook visited during his exploration of the South Pacific Ocean in the mid-18th century, he never saw Aitutaki, which is part of the island group that now bears his name. Instead, Captain William Bligh "discovered" Aitutaki in 1789, 17 days before the infamous mutiny aboard the H.M.S. *Bounty.* Today most of those taking it in for the first time are day-trippers from Rarotonga (see next page), the Cook Islands's capital, which can seem downright raucous compared to this sleepy outpost.

From the air, Aitutaki's shallow lagoon resembles a spectacular turquoise carpet spread out on the indigo sea. Ringing it is a 30-mile necklace of 15 tiny, palm-studded *motus* (small islands), whose empty shores are perfect destinations for picnicking and strolling, not to mention swimming and snorkeling.

The highlight of any visit here is a day tour across the lagoon to one of the deserted islets, where locals will prepare you a picnic lunch featuring barbecued fish, usually snagged on the way. One Foot Island is the only motu that is inhabited (albeit sparsely); photographers are lured by its flawless white beaches.

Unhurried days are the reason one comes, but plenty of activities can be arranged: In addition to the snorkeling among giant clams, there are bike or scooter rides to banana and coconut plantations and jeep tours to visit ancient *marae* (sacred communal spaces) or World War II ruins (the U.S. Army used this as a refueling station). The shallow, gin-clear waters of the lagoon make for some of the Cook Islands' best bonefishing, and big game like marlin and sailfish can be found farther afield.

Of the several hotels occupying the hilly main island, the finest is the Etu Moana, eight thatch-roofed villas along a dreamy stretch of

A coral lagoon overflowing with rich marine life surrounds the motus *of Aitutaki.*

sand. The only place to stay on a motu is Aitutaki Lagoon Resort & Spa, on Akitua—its 16 Polynesian-style guest accommodations include the only overwater bungalows in the Cook Islands. Indigenous touches abound: The staff at the small but lovely spa can introduce you to a coconut leaf scrub, while dinner might be *ika mata,* a local dish of marinated raw tuna with coconut sauce. Or enjoy your meal at one of the beachside restaurants where young island dancers perform nightly.

WHERE: 155 miles/249 km north of Rarotonga. **ETU MOANA:** Tel 682/31-458; www.etumoana.com. *Cost:* from $375. **AITUTAKI LAGOON RESORT:** Tel 682/31-201; www.aitutakilagoonresort.com. *Cost:* garden bungalows from $330. **BEST TIME:** Apr–Oct when weather is driest.

An Idyllic Island Dedicated to Dance

RAROTONGA

Cook Islands

Often compared to Tahiti, its larger and more famous French Polynesian neighbor to the east (see p. 690), Rarotonga packs more fun into less space than any other Pacific island. Most of the action in this little jewel of an island takes place in the famous Muri Lagoon, which is ideal for swimming, snorkeling, windsurfing, and sailing. Even better snorkeling can be found within the coral head off Titikaveka, on the south coast. Inland, the well-marked 3- to 4-hour Cross-Island Track scales the rugged central mountains, starting in the main town of Avarua and continuing to the south coast, passing along the way the base of the Te Rua Manga, a needlelike rock that is one of Rarotonga's distinguishing landmarks.

"Island night" dancers help keep national pride alive.

But what really sets the Cook Islands' capital apart is its lively nightlife, for every day except Sunday sees at least one "island night" feast and dance show. The Cook Islanders are considered the best dancers in the South Pacific, and these events, hosted by local hotels, are authentic displays of tradition and national pride. Like their Tahitian neighbors, they perform the suggestive, hip-twisting *tamure,* though the enthusiasm of the Cook Islanders will convince you that the dance belongs solely to them. So dazzling are their skills that you may want to consider planning your trip around the Te Mire Kapa (Dancer of the Year Competition) in April or May, when the crème de la crème of the islands' villages and school dance troupes travel to Rarotonga for a week of song and traditional dance that will leave you breathless.

VISITOR INFO: www.cookislands.travel. **WHERE TO STAY:** There's something for everyone at the Rarotongan Beach Resort and Spa, including a wide range of room categories. Tel 682/25-800; www.therarotongan.com. *Cost:* from $215. **BEST TIMES:** Apr–May for dance competition; Apr–Oct for dry weather.

A Ghost Fleet in the Graveyard of the Pacific

Chuuk Lagoon

Chuuk, Federated States of Micronesia

During World War II, the strategic island group of Chuuk, which was then known as Truk (the name is still commonly used), was the stronghold of the Japanese Imperial fleet and their South Pacific forces. Its 50-mile-wide lagoon served as a natural fortress—outsiders tagged this seemingly impregnable outpost as the Gibraltar of the Pacific. Then in a surprise attack on February 17, 1944, aircraft from the U.S. Navy's Task Force 58 appeared overhead and dropped more than 500 tons of bombs and torpedoes on Japan's Fourth Fleet, quickly turning Chuuk Lagoon into the graveyard of the Pacific.

Today Chuuk Lagoon holds the coral-encrusted hulls of 60 Japanese ships, one of the world's largest concentrations of sunken wrecks, in relatively shallow and calm waters. A combination of unusually warm temperatures, prolific marine life, and gentle lagoon currents has transformed them into a garden of magnificent artificial reefs, with brilliant coral displays that grow to exceptional size. But divers can see more than natural wonders here: The 437-foot *Fujikawa Maru* is the most famous relic, a Japanese aircraft ferry standing upright in water 90 feet deep. A gaping torpedo hole in her starboard side leads into her cargo hold and its intact fighter planes, while her well-preserved machine shop is still equipped with lathes, compressors, and hand tools. The nearby oil tanker *Shinkoku* also served as a hospital—the operating room makes for an eerie visit.

These remarkable war ruins, left with their guns, trucks, silverware, and sake bottles undisturbed, were brought to light by Jacques Cousteau in the 1960s, and in the 1970s a fledgling dive industry sprang up around them. One of the oldest dive operators is the Blue Lagoon Dive Shop, which is located in the Truk Blue Lagoon Resort on the largest of Chuuk's 40 islands. Divers occupy 54 rooms, surrounded by coconut palms and overlooking the lagoon.

Where: 600 miles/966 km southeast of Guam. **Blue Lagoon Dive Shop:** Tel 691/330-2796; www.truk-lagoon-dive.com. *Cost:* 2-dive boat trip $105. **Truk Blue Lagoon Resort:** Tel 691/330-2727; www.bluelagoondiveresort.com. *Cost:* from $150. **Best time:** Jan–Apr for best underwater visibility.

Grass Skirts, Stone Money, and Manta Rays

Yap

Federated States of Micronesia

The most traditional of the Federated States of Micronesia, Yap is home to one of the Pacific's last island cultures that is still resistant to modern Western ways. As in the time before Europeans discovered this group of

19 islands in the 16th century, bare-breasted women wear traditional grass skirts, and men and women alike chew betel nut, a subtle narcotic that produces stained red lips and a mild high. Other than the topless islanders, the most oft-photographed sights are *rai*, the wheel-shaped stone money units that line the roads and measure up to 10 feet in diameter. Their value is determined by size, shape, and the difficulty of acquisition.

Modern money is also used, but it is not of the utmost importance to the Yapese, who have rejected Japanese overtures to build first-class resorts and thus attract more tourists—and profits—to their languid islands. Most of the few visitors who do come are divers. They head straight underwater, for Yap is one of the world's top dive destinations, providing incredible visibility for swimming with 1,000-pound manta rays in their natural habitat. With wingspans of 10 to 20 feet, these fearsome-looking giants pose no threat to divers (unlike stingrays). They commonly return to the same spot every day, oblivious to the divers' presence. In mating season (late November through March) females pirouette and soar through the waters, leading trains that can include 15 or more males.

To discover the rays and other underwater creatures, contact Bill Acker, a Texas-born Peace Corps worker who came to Yap in the 1980s and stayed to pioneer the local dive industry. He built the harborfront Manta Ray Bay Hotel, which has its own microbrewer, and is the best dive operation in the islands.

A traditional currency, rai *stones change hands but generally are not moved.*

WHERE: 530 miles/850 km southwest of Guam. **MANTA RAY BAY HOTEL:** Tel 691/350-2300; www.mantaray.com. *Cost:* from $260; dive packages available. **BEST TIMES:** Nov–Mar for dry season, when mantas mate and underwater visibility is best; Mar 1–2 for Yap Day dance celebrations.

Kaleidoscopic Marine Life

BEQA LAGOON

Beqa Island, Fiji

Just off the south coast of Viti Levu, Fiji's main island, the legendary Beqa Lagoon lies enclosed by one of the world's longest barrier reefs—90 miles of dazzling coral where the kaleidoscopic marine life makes for one of the Pacific's premier diving and snorkeling sites. The larger sea creatures—including blue marlin, wahoo, swordfish, and black marlin—beckon big-game fishermen here, while the surf break known as Frigate Passage offers world-class waves for experienced surfers. A few miles away lies Shark Reef Marine Reserve, a top shark-diving venue, providing adrenaline-pumping encounters with bull, tiger, and five other species of shark.

As for action beyond the water, there isn't much: The sparsely populated 14-square-mile Beqa Island itself gives visitors a glimpse into Melanesian life, which has been barely touched by modern development. Because there are no roads, boats are the only way to travel between the traditional Fijian villages situated along a shoreline serrated by small bays. Those who live there are famous in Fiji for fire-walking across 1,200°F stones, but nowadays that skill is mostly on display at Viti Levu's big resort hotels.

Beqa Lagoon's nutrient-rich waters produce forests of coral.

Of the lagoon's few modern hotels, Lalati Resort & Spa, at the mouth of scenic Malumu Bay, affords an enviable vista, extending from a narrow, mountain-edged bay across the shimmering lagoon to the southern shore of Viti Levu, where the nighttime lights of Suva, the country's vibrant capital city, twinkle on the horizon. With snorkeling a short walk from the resort's 12 guest *bures* (bungalows) and three private villas, and with more than 100 dive sites just 5 to 20 minutes away by boat, the location is superb. New owners gave Lalati a facelift after taking over in 2009, including the addition of two honeymoon bungalows with their own plunge pools. While guests are drawn here first by the lagoon's fame, they're apt to return for the food, hospitality, and pampering. The small Loloma Spa features treatments using warm seashells, coconut oil, and raw sugarcane, as well as sea-salt scrubs.

WHERE: 9 miles/15 km off the southern coast of Viti Levu. **VISITOR INFO:** www.fijime.com. **LALATI RESORT:** Tel 679/368-0453; www.lalatifiji.com. *Cost:* bures from $400, inclusive. **BEST TIMES:** May–Sep for nicest weather; May–Dec for ideal diving conditions.

Overwater Bungalows, Fiji Style

LIKULIKU LAGOON RESORT

Malolo Island, Fiji

Tourists have been flocking to the Mamanuca Islands since jet airliners first began landing at the airport on the nearby island of Viti Levu in the 1960s. Fringed by fine beaches (think *Castaway,* with Tom Hanks, which was filmed here), the Mamanucas enjoy Fiji's driest climate. The original Mamanuca resorts were eclipsed in the 1990s and early 2000s by high-end luxury hotels that cropped up elsewhere on the island-dotted map of Fiji. But the limelight returned to this graceful arc of islands when Likuliku Lagoon Resort opened in 2007, bringing the country's first romantic, over-the-water guest bungalows.

Situated beside a half-moon bay at the northern end of hilly Malolo Island, the largest of the Mamanucas, Likuliku is the pet project of the local Whitten family, which has long owned Malolo Island Fiji, a more modest, family-friendly resort on the bay next door. Authentic Fijian style can be seen in everything from Likuliku's furnishings, hewn of native hardwood, to its handmade *masi* (tapa cloth) accents.

The resort's restaurant serves excellent Pacific Rim fare and occupies the second floor of a large, thatch-roofed central building, which overlooks the cobalt blue lagoon and opens onto a large outdoor swimming pool. Nine of the ten spacious, overwater *bures* (bungalows) are built near the edge of the fringing reef and have a private platform from which guests can step into the lagoon and easily reach deep water at all tides. On land, another 26 bures line the beach; all are large and breezy and a few have small plunge pools.

WHERE: 15 miles/25 km west of Nadi, Viti Levu. **LIKULIKU LAGOON RESORT:** Tel 679/672-0978; www.likulikulagoon.com. *Cost:* from $775, inclusive. **MALOLO ISLAND FIJI:** Tel 679/666-9192; www.maloloisland.com. *Cost:* from $320. **BEST TIME:** May–Sep when weather is driest.

Deserted Beaches on Horseshoe Bay

MATANGI ISLAND

Fiji

A gorgeous, horseshoe-shaped island, Matangi is all that remains of an ancient volcano, half of which fell away into the sea, leaving behind two of the finest beaches in Fiji. Palms fringe the submerged crater, now filled with deep sapphire waters, whose only visitors are guests of the 240-acre island's single accommodation, Matangi Private Island Resort. Owned by the Douglas family, which has been on the island for five generations, it has ten Polynesian-influenced *bures* (bungalows) at sea level and three Honeymoon Tree Houses, one actually perched in an enormous almond tree, two others chiseled into the side of a cliff, with superb views through the branches to the Tasman Straits separating Matangi from Taveuni (see next page).

Occupied by a private resort, Matangi Island has a distinctive horseshoe shape that makes it easy to spot by air.

Guests who head to Horseshoe Bay beach will find it one of the loveliest in Fiji; they can also have the staff arrange for hikes across the crater's rim or for boat rides to take them picnicking on farther-flung beaches. Back at the resort, fresh-air dining takes place under a soaring roof and beside a freshwater swimming pool. Because the owners live here and are actively engaged in the day-to-day operations, Matangi has more of a family feel than that of most other resorts in Fiji.

Scuba divers and snorkelers will discover why northern Fiji is known as the soft coral capital of the world: Swift currents bring rich nutrients upon which these colorful creatures feed, resulting in a huge, easily viewed abundance of them. Matangi is close to numerous dive sites, including the Purple Wall, which has a 200-foot drop and is covered with purple soft corals, sea whips, and large gorgonian fans. The nearby Somosomo Strait is world-famous among divers for the aptly named Rainbow Reef and for its Great White Wall, first-class diving sites that are also easily accessed from Taveuni Island.

WHERE: 6 miles/10 km east of Taveuni Island. Tel 679/880-0260; www.matangiisland.com. *Cost:* from $610, inclusive; diving extra. **BEST TIME:** May–Oct for perfect weather and diving conditions.

Colorful Coral Around a Garden Island

TAVEUNI ISLAND

Fiji

With the largest population of indigenous plants and animals in the South Pacific, lush Taveuni earns its nickname as the Garden Island. The fertile volcanic soil is responsible for the densely growing tropical flora, including the tagimaucia, a flower found only at the very highest elevations—the mountains here rise up to nearly 4,000 feet.

Flying here from Fiji's more populated and developed island of Viti Levu is like traveling back half a century. A string of small, traditional villages along the western side of the island is home to easygoing, friendly Fijians, who offer a warm welcome to Westerners (no longer a novelty since many have built retirement homes here).

Here and there the rocky shore is dotted with some of Fiji's finest white sand beaches, while on the island's northern end, hikers can refresh under rushing, three-level Bouma Falls, explore the jungle-clad Vidawa Rainforest Hike, and discover even more pristine beaches along the Lavena Coastal Walk. All are part of Bouma Falls National Heritage Park, which covers four-fifths of the island.

But it's the dive sites in the narrow Somosomo Straits, separating the islands of Taveuni and Vanua Levu (and also accessible from Matangi Island; see previous page), that have put this area of Fiji on the travel map. Premier among them is the 20-mile-long Rainbow Reef and its stunning Great White Wall—Taveuni's Mount Everest of reefs—but dive operators will also whisk you off to Purple Wall, Rainbow Passage, Vuna Reef, and farther afield to nameless sites where the profusion of dazzling marine life can be even more magnificent.

Taveuni Island Resort offers the most luxurious accommodations around. Sitting atop a bluff, its 12 *bures* and infinity pool command magnificent views of the straits. At Coconut Grove Beachfront Cottages, you'll find just three simple waterfront bungalows as well as one of the best places to eat on Taveuni. The laid-back resort's restaurant prides itself on its fresh and simple food served on a breezy, open-air veranda, where local singers sometimes perform to the accompaniment of ukeleles.

WHERE: 44 miles/70 km north of Nadi, Viti Levu. **BOUMA FALLS NATIONAL HERITAGE PARK:** www.bnhp.org. **TAVEUNI ISLAND RESORT:** Tel 679/888-0441; www.taveuniislandresort.com. *Cost:* bures from $830, inclusive. **COCONUT GROVE:** Tel 679/888-0328; www.coconutgrovefiji.com. *Cost:* from $175; dinner: $40. **BEST TIMES:** May–Sep for driest weather; May–Dec for diving.

Heaven for Kids and Grown-ups

Jean-Michel Cousteau Fiji Islands Resort

Savusavu, Vanua Levu, Fiji

It's difficult for a small, intimate resort to successfully host both couples seeking a romantic escape and families with small children. But Jean-Michel Cousteau Fiji Islands Resort, set within a 17-acre oceanfront coconut grove on the wedge-shaped island of northern Vanua Levu and resembling a traditional local village, manages to do both. Guests occasionally run into Cousteau, son of the late oceanographer Jacques Cousteau and owner of this award-winning resort and scuba operation. He designed the eco-resort's 37-foot state-of-the-art dive boat, *L'Aventure,* and staffs it with a crew that includes marine biologists who guarantee you the most informative dive experience possible in one of the most diverse and populous marine habitats on earth. One don't-miss destination is Namena Marine Reserve. An hour's ride away, this 44-square-mile home to endemic and rare species is regarded as one of the world's best dive sites.

Those not interested in diving will find plenty to love about this place too, including snorkeling, kayaking, nature hikes, yoga classes, village visits and cultural trips, windsurfing, and bird-watching. Parents will appreciate the resort's Bula Camp (*bula* means "hello" in Fijian and is as ubiquitous as "aloha" is in Hawaii). Guests younger than 13 are free to disappear here from early morning until evening to swim and play as well as learn about the local environment and Fijian customs.

Preserving that environment is a way of life here. Cousteau insists that the resort be eco-sensitive, and many recycling efforts are evident as are the absence of energy-intensive air conditioners—the one luxurious honeymoon villa is the exception. Ceiling fans suffice in the other, less spacious but extremely comfortable guest bungalows.

Where: 3.5 miles/6 km northeast of Nadi, Viti Levu. Tel 679/885-0188, in the U.S., 800-246-3454; www.fijiresort.com. **Cost:** from $700, inclusive; diving extra. **Best times:** May–Sep for good weather; May–Dec for ideal diving conditions.

A String of Blue Beads

The Yasawa Islands

Fiji

First charted in 1840 by a U.S. exploring expedition, whose commander described them as "a string of blue beads lying along the horizon," the Yasawas have only recently emerged from a century-and-a-half snooze.

The new daily service by catamaran from Denarau, near Nadi on the main island of Viti Levu, is the reason; they were previously accessible only by expensive seaplane or a very long and arduous boat ride. As a result, the Yasawas have become one of the most popular destinations in Fiji, especially among young travelers, who frequent more than a dozen barebones accommodations here.

This string of islands is home to many fine beaches set against a backdrop of volcanoes and green-clad hills.

Along with a smattering of low-key development, you'll find small Fijian villages nestled beneath palm trees along some of the South Pacific's loveliest beaches. Fiji's most spectacular, the beach at Nalova Bay on Nacula Island, offers a swath of white sand leading into a clear lagoon deep enough for swimming and snorkeling even at low tide—a rarity in Fiji. Beside it resides little Blue Lagoon Beach Resort, a modest but exceptional new hotel with eight guest bungalows. Half the cottages and the relaxed, sand-floor restaurant are adjacent to the brilliant white beach, a world-class setting that more than compensates for the resort's lack of high-end amenities.

The Yasawas are where Fiji opened its first top-end resort, Turtle Island, which remains one of its finest. It was already up and running in 1979 when Hollywood arrived to film the remake of *The Blue Lagoon*, putting this 500-acre sliver of paradise on the map. It has 14 beaches—one for each of the 14 couples here when the place is fully booked—and a 4-acre organic garden that provides almost all the fruits, vegetables, herbs, and flowers used at the resort.

Low-key and friendly, the Yasawa Island Resort & Spa occupies its own island and boasts one of Fiji's longest and whitest beaches, dotted by 18 thatched *bures*. The open-sided restaurant, with one of the best wine selections in Fiji, competes with a lovely beachfront spa as the nicest spot to unwind.

Those interested in seeing more of the 16-island chain without hopping on and off the catamaran shuttle can board one of the boats operated by Blue Lagoon Cruises, which ply this 56-mile stretch of islands on 3-, 4-, and 7-day tours. It began its operation in the 1950s (taking its name from the original 1949 version of the film) and is now one of the nicest small-ship operations in the South Pacific. None of its four vessels has more than 35 cabins. Sunset departures leave each day free for visits to a different island and local village, lunchtime barbecues, and sunning on secluded beaches, where the only tracks will be those left by you.

WHERE: 35 miles/56 km north of Nadi, Viti Levu. **VISITOR INFO:** www.fijime.com. **BLUE LAGOON BEACH RESORT:** Tel 679/666-6337; www.bluelagoonbeachresort.com.fj. *Cost:* from $105. **TURTLE ISLAND:** Tel in Australia 61/3-9823-8300; in the U.S., 800-255-4347; www.turtlefiji.com. *Cost:* from $2,080, all-inclusive. **YASAWA ISLAND:** Tel 679/672-2266; www.yasawa.com. *Cost:* $900, all-inclusive. **BLUE LAGOON CRUISES:** Tel 679/666-1622; www.bluelagooncruises.com. *Cost:* 3-day cruise from $830 per cabin, all-inclusive. **BEST TIME:** May–Sep for driest weather.

A Cruise to Wild Beauty

The Marquesas Islands

French Polynesia

For years the wild beauty of the little-visited Marquesas Islands—some of the most remote inhabited islands on earth—has drawn artists and writers, and that's hardly a surprise: This is the untainted tropics, where forest-cloaked cliffs plunge into the rocky sea and eerie volcanic spires tower so dramatically that Robert Louis Stevenson once likened them to "the pinnacles of some ornate and monstrous church." Of the six inhabited islands (of ten total), Fatu Hiva, the most isolated, is the most beautiful, due in large part to its dramatic Bay of Virgins, which is surrounded by steep cliffs on which grow lush groves of mangoes, oranges, and guavas. The wildlife is extraordinarily rich throughout, with many bird, plant, and marine species unique to the Marquesas, and you are never far from the scent of jasmine, plumeria, or ginger.

Paul Gauguin intended to live out his days on Fatu Hiva, but instead disembarked on Hiva Oa, the second largest of the Marquesas and perhaps the best known. He—and, more than 80 years later, Belgian singer Jacques Brel—chose never to leave. Both men's frangipani-shaded graves can be found in Calvary Cemetery, located in the small town of Atuona, which has a museum dedicated to each. Herman Melville jumped ship off Hiva Oa and later based his novel *Typee* on his time in the Marquesas, while Jack London was moved to write about Taiohae Bay, which lies below a majestic cliff on the largest island of Nuku Hiva, saying, "One caught one's breath and felt the pang that it almost hurt, so exquisite was the beauty of it."

The best way to see the Marquesas is on the 200-passenger, 355-foot *Aranui 3*, a half-passenger, half-cargo ship that links the Marquesas with the outside world, making brief stops at Fakarava and Rangiroa, in the Tuamotu atolls, on its way to and fro. Entire villages—sometimes entire islands—turn out to greet its arrival, bartering *copra* (pressed and dried coconut) and wood carvings for basic supplies and the occasional pickup truck. While the crew handles the cargo, an expert archaeologist, anthropologist, or historian leads *Aranui*'s passengers on excursions to green valleys famed for their wild horses and abandoned carved tikis (huge stone icons of Polynesian gods). A cruise ship could replicate the *Aranui*'s itinerary, but not the experience.

You can also fly from Papeete to Nuku Hiva and Hiva Oa, where the hotels are few but offer plenty of relaxation amid jagged volcanic peaks and crashing surf. At the Keikahanui Nuku Hiva Pearl Lodge, the 20 guest bungalows perch on stilts, overlooking Taiohae Bay and the black sand beach below, while those at the Hanakee Hiva Oa Pearl Lodge have even more spectacular views of 3,903-foot Mount Te Metiu and the Pacific.

Where: 830 miles/1,300 km northeast of Tahiti. **Visitor info:** www.tahiti-tourisme.com. ***Aranui 3*:** Tel 689/426-240; in the U.S., 800-972-7268; www.aranui.com. *Cost:* 13-day cruises from $2,079, all-inclusive. *When:* depart Papeete every 3 weeks. **Keikahanui Nuku Hiva Pearl Lodge:** Tel 689/920-710; www.pearlresorts.com. *Cost:* from $330. **Hanakee Hiva Oa Pearl Lodge:** Tel 689/927-587; www.pearlresorts.com. *Cost:* from $275. **Best time:** May–Oct for pleasant weather.

The World's Most Beautiful Island

Bora-Bora

Society Islands, French Polynesia

Grab a seat on the left side of the plane for your first glimpse of Bora-Bora, the dramatic, lagoon-surrounded rock that has mesmerized visitors since Captain James Cook saw it more than 200 years ago. Just 4 miles long and 2.5 miles wide, Bora-Bora consists of a palm-covered barrier reef of semi-connected *motus* (islets) encircling a deep lagoon that glows in a range of blues and greens. The island rises to the renowned, tombstone-shaped 2,379-foot Mount Otemanu, Bora-Bora's most famous landmark. In the 1950s James Michener called this "the most beautiful island in the world" and "the South Pacific at its unforgettable best." Look beyond today's tourists and you will no doubt agree.

Some of the Pacific's best sites for inshore snorkeling beckon with underwater traffic jams of trumpet fish, angelfish, and parrot fish, as well as the rarer Pinocchio and Napoleon fish. Shark feeding, which is now widespread but began here, promises even more drama: Willing visitors submerge themselves amid dozens of 5-foot blackfin lagoon sharks, which are hand-fed by local divers. Once back on dry land, take a four-wheel-drive up into the mountains and jounce and rattle across the lush terrain. It's worth it for the cliffside views over the lagoon.

The island's finest resorts are now out on the skinny islets that enclose the lagoon, affording more privacy for their often famous guests. Rows of thatch-roofed bungalows stand over the lagoon's impossibly clear water.

Of the major hotels that occupy the palm-fringed *motus*, the newest is the family-friendly Four Seasons Resort Bora Bora; its 120 rooms and over-the-water bungalows and seven beachside villas are built on three inter-linked islets and boast both the top beach and the best view of Mount Otemanu. The huge, cathedral-like Kahaia spa nestles at the ocean's edge. On the main island not far from the exquisite, sugar-white Matira Beach—one of the most idyllic spots in the Pacific—Le Maitai Polynesia Bora Bora has 74 spacious hotel rooms and bungalows, some of them over water, all with views of the lagoon, the offshore motus, and—on the horizon—the islands of Tahaa and Raiatea.

A lagoon encircles the island, with the Mounts Otemanu and Paihia ascending into the sky.

Where: 145 miles/233 km northwest of Tahiti. **Visitor info:** www.tahiti-tourisme.com. **Four Seasons Resort Bora Bora:** Tel 689/603-130; in the U.S., 800-819-5053; www.fourseasons.com/borabora. *Cost:* from $993. **Le Maitai Polynesia Bora Bora:** Tel 689/603-000; www.hotelmaitai.com. *Cost:* from $195. **Best times:** May–Oct for nicest weather; weekend closest to Jul 14 (Bastille Day) for Fêtes de Juillet.

Steeped in Polynesian Tradition

HUAHINE

Society Islands, French Polynesia

Steeped in tradition and a standout for its varied scenery, splendid beaches, and proliferation of *marae* (sacred spaces), Huahine is one of the few Polynesian islands Captain James Cook might recognize if he were to return today. Tourism has been slow to arrive to this beautiful place, which is still largely agricultural and is often compared to what Bora-Bora and Moorea (see previous page and next page) were before the luxury hotels arrived. There's not much going on in its picturesque main town, and tiny, charming villages—but that's the point.

Among the least changed parts of Huahine is Fare, the island's seaport and its only town of note. Facing west, with neighboring Raiatea, Tahaa, and Bora-Bora on the horizon, Fare is a great place to sit at sunset with a cold Hinano beer.

Make sure to visit the ancient marae, which comprise one of the most important archaeological sites in all of Polynesia. Most of these stone structures stand along the shore of Lake Fauna Nui, which is actually an inlet separating the main island from a long, flat peninsula. To get the most from your visit, take an Island Eco Tours excursion led by a local anthropologist.

Settle into Te Tiare Beach Resort, Huahine's only luxury hotel, located on a beach on the main island. The main structure stands on pilings over the lagoon, as do about half its 40 bungalows, and guests in the 11 "deep overwater" units can step from their wraparound deck into the clear lagoon. If Huahine isn't removed enough from the world, have the amiable French and British owners of the Au Motu Mahare B&B come to fetch you and whisk you off to a small private *motu*, where no more than five guests occupy their little slice of paradise at any one time.

WHERE: 175 miles/282 km northwest of Papeete, Tahiti. **ISLAND ECO TOURS:** Tel 689/687-967; pauljatallah@mail.pf. **TE TIARE BEACH RESORT:** Tel 689/606-050; www.tetiarebeach.com. *Cost:* from $427. **AU MOTU MAHARE:** Tel 689/777-697; www.aumotumahare.blogspot.com. *Cost:* $95. **BEST TIMES:** May–Oct for pleasant weather; mid-Oct, when Huahine is the starting point for the annual Hawaiki Nui Va'a Outrigger Race, which ends in Bora-Bora.

The Last Great Secret of French Polynesia

MAUPITI

Society Islands, French Polynesia

If you dream of visiting Bora-Bora as it was 50 years ago, nearby Maupiti fits the fantasy bill. Devoid of luxury resorts (local residents have flatly rejected just about every hotel proposition), this island gem, unknown to most tourists, remains blessedly quiet and laid-back.

Like its famous neighbor Bora-Bora (see p. 687), Maupiti consists of a high central island encircled by a lagoon and five, palm-studded, beach-fringed islets. The only pass into the shallow lagoon is so narrow and treacherous that large ships dare not enter, leaving the main means of sea transport to the Maupiti Express, a passenger ferry that travels to and from Bora-Bora three times a week, allowing for an easy day trip.

Bicycles are the best way to get around the main island, where the only road follows the mostly flat shoreline; it's just 5.5 miles around from start to finish. It passes near Plage Tereia, one of the finest beaches in all of French Polynesia, where you can wade across the shallow lagoon to one of the largest *motus*. It also skirts the base of Mount Hotu Parata, a sheer basaltic cliff towering over Vaiea, one of Maupiti's three villages. French-speaking guides will lead you to the 1,220-foot summit for a spectacular vista that needs little translation.

Accommodations can be found at simple pensions, which are mostly found on the reef islets. Motu Tiapaa has four, including Le Kuriri, the best of the bunch. Owned and operated by French expats, its five charming *fare*s (bungalows), built mostly of native materials, are on the ocean side of the islet, where they catch the cooling southeast trade winds.

WHERE: 25 miles/40 km west of Bora-Bora. **MAUPITI EXPRESS:** Tel 689/676-669; www.maupitiexpress.com. **LE KURIRI:** Tel 689/745-454; www.maupiti-kuriri.com. *Cost:* $310, inclusive. **BEST TIME:** May–Oct for good weather.

The Prodigal Beauty of Nature

MOOREA

Society Islands, French Polynesia

There is no South Pacific view as spellbinding as the one from Moorea's Le Belvédère, a lookout high on the wall of the extinct volcanic crater forming this extraordinarily beautiful island, whose jagged peaks and soaring spires have served as the backdrop for numerous Hollywood films. The 36-mile drive that rings the island can be traveled by bicycle, scooter, car, or on foot, and affords incredible views of Cook's and Opunohu bays, cut deep into the island's lush green interior.

Equally impressive is Moorea's lagoon. Several hundred acrobatic spinner dolphins live here year-round, and humpback whales can be spotted offshore from July through October. The best way to visit them in the wild is with Dr. Michael Poole, an American marine biologist who leads daily tours. At the Moorea Dolphin Center, you are guaranteed to come face-to-face with the creatures, which are kept in fenced-off areas of the lagoon.

Sofitel Moorea Ia Ora Beach Resort is a top hotel choice, with bungalows on Moorea's most gorgeous coconut grove–shaded beach and an additional 40 units over the water. Beyond is the cobalt blue Sea of Moon, and beyond that a postcard view of the green, cloud-topped mountains of Tahiti. A more modest but charming option, Hotel Les Tipaniers, sits in a coconut grove beside a fine beach on the other side of Moorea. It has comfortable if not overly spacious bungalows, a good Italian restaurant, and Moorea's best beachside bar. After sunset, head over to the open-air Tiki Theatre Village for an island-style dinner and the most authentic Tahitian dance show in French Polynesia.

Where: 12 miles/19 km northwest of Tahiti. **Dr. Michael Poole:** Tel 689/562-322; www.drmichaelpoole.com. *Cost:* half-day tour $88. **Moorea Dolphin Center:** Tel 689/551-948; www.mooreadolphincenter.com. *Cost:* 30-minute encounter $180. **Sofitel Moorea Ia Ora Beach Resort:** Tel 689/550-355; www.sofitel.com. *Cost:* from $500. **Hotel Les Tipaniers:** Tel 689/561-267; www.lestipaniers.com. *Cost:* from $160; dinner $45. **Tiki Theatre Village:** Tel 689/550-250; www.tikivillage.pf. *Cost:* $47 show only, $93 with dinner. **Best times:** May–Oct for good weather; Jul–Oct for whale-watching.

The Mother of All Island Festivals

Heiva i Tahiti

Papeete, Tahiti, Society Islands, French Polynesia

Tahiti has been the most famous South Pacific island since English captain Samuel Wallis became the first European to lay eyes on it in 1767. And these days everyone coming to French Polynesia must set foot on Tahiti, for its Faa'a airport is the country's only international gateway. But with few white sand beaches to keep them here, most visitors quickly move on to the outer islands. Those who do tarry spend only a day or so exploring Papeete—the traffic-clogged capital city—and making a quick tour around the island.

There is one time of year when everyone should consider sticking around: during Heiva (festival) i Tahiti, the 7-week mother of all island festivals that takes place in June and July and crescendos in its final 15 days. Originally a brief observance of Bastille Day, in honor of all things French, the locals have turned it into an extravagant celebration of all things Polynesian. From the country's 115 islands they converge upon Tahiti for singing, traditional sports, and especially for dancing, all rooted in their common heritage and performed with passion.

Teams of canoe racers fill Papeete harbor during the annual festival, celebrating music and dance in addition to sports.

Although not heavily attended by visiting foreigners, these colorful displays honor the local culture that is so sorely missing from many of the glitzy resorts across Polynesia. Missionaries suppressed the region's suggestive *tamure* dancing in the early 19th century, but it has been enthusiastically revived, as can be witnessed at this festival. Check with Tourisme Tahiti, the tourist information office, to get times for the dance-offs, especially the emotionally charged finals. (Note that the winners often tour some of the principal hotels in August, in case you miss the boat.) In addition to the dancing, there are fire walking and stone lifting contests, along with outrigger canoe races and golf tournaments.

When you're ready to visit the other islands, board the 332-passenger *Paul Gauguin* cruise ship, the only one to sail these waters year-round. Named for the French artist who found paradise in these islands, the vessel offers cruises ranging from 8 days spent exploring the Society Islands to the 15-day trip that takes you as far north as the remote Marquesas Islands (see p. 686).

VISITOR INFO: www.tahiti-tourisme.com. **WHEN:** Jun–Jul. **WHERE TO STAY:** Located in the center of town, the modern Hotel Tahiti Nui is a convenient choice. Tel 689/463-899; www.hoteltahitinui.com. *Cost:* from $215. **PAUL GAUGUIN CRUISES:** Tel in the U.S., 800-848-6172 or 425-440-6171; www.pgcruises.com. *Cost:* 7-night cruise from $3,997.

Wading with Baby Sharks

RANGIROA

Tuamotu Islands, French Polynesia

The world's second largest atoll, Rangiroa has been called "God's aquarium," and is a favorite of divers and snorkelers. Swimmers love its placid, breeze-brushed waters, while sun worshipers head for its gorgeous pink-hued beaches. Unlike Tahiti, Moorea, Bora-Bora, and the other Society Islands, Rangiroa is pancake flat. Here the attractions are on and under the water, and they are astonishing.

Tops among these are exhilarating dives in the rushing rip currents of Avatoru and Tiputa passes, the only deep-water entries into the vast lagoon. Considered the best dive sites in French Polynesia, they are famous as a gathering place for hammerhead sharks from December to March and large manta rays from July to October. Gray-tip, black-tip, and other species of shark can be seen year-round. For dolphins it is a playground, a place to soar, dive, and frolic. This profusion of aquatic life is the reason divers in-the-know come here from all over the world to "shoot the pass."

Nondivers can have their own shark encounters on day trips to the Blue Lagoon, located in the outer reef. The water is too shallow for boats to drop anchor, so passengers must wade ashore for about 50 yards to the alluring white beach—often through a school of baby black-tip reef sharks. Well-fed from picnic leftovers, the little creatures may appear menacing but are harmless to humans.

If and when it reopens after an ongoing renovation, the Hotel Kia Ora could once again offer a dose of great style and comfort, especially in its ten luxury overwater bungalows. In the meantime, visitors can stay at the lagoonside Le Maitai Rangiroa, which has 38 guest bungalows, including some built over the water, or the Tevahine Dream, with three thatched bungalows directly on the beach. The two exceptional, hands-on hosts care for you like family and impress with their talents in the kitchen as well.

WHERE: 218 miles/351 km northeast of Papeete, Tahiti. **HOTEL KIA ORA:** Tel 689/960-222; www.hotelkiaora.com. **LE MAITAI RANGIROA:** Tel 689/931-350; www.pacificbeachcomber.com. *Cost:* from $225. **TEVAHINE DREAM:** Tel 689/931-275; www.tevahinedream.com. *Cost:* bungalows $315, inclusive. **BEST TIMES:** May–Oct for good weather; Dec–Mar for diving.

Some of the Richest Marine Life on the Planet

Palau

Palau

Stretching 400 miles along the far western Pacific, Palau consists of 343 islands (only eight are inhabited), most surrounded by a giant, spellbinding lagoon that many cognoscenti say offers the best diving in the world. The reason is location, location, location. The meeting place of three major ocean currents, these warm, nutrient-rich waters support more than 1,300 species of fish and four times the number of coral species found in the Caribbean. The Ngemelis Drop-off, a Technicolor reef beginning at 2 feet and plummeting vertically to more than 1,000 feet, is widely considered the world's best, while Blue Corner is legendary for the sheer abundance, variety, and size of its fish life, including schooling gray reef and white-tip sharks. More than 50 World War II shipwrecks (the remains of an aircraft carrier attack), rare and exotic marine species, and visibility that can exceed 200 feet add to divers' wonderment.

Divers can examine the sea fans that make up Palau's Peleliu Wall.

And there's more. Sprouting like emerald mushrooms along a 20-mile swath of transparent waters, the 200 Rock Islands are limestone outcrops covered with palms and dense jungle growth, making them home to cockatoos, parrots, kingfishers, and reef herons. A few of the islands have inland waters, such as Jellyfish Lake, where you can swim with millions of the diaphanous, nonstinging invertebrates. Others are rimmed with white sand beaches, and the calm lagoon is especially appealing to kayakers.

The country's best hotel is the six-story Palau Pacific Resort, just 10 minutes' drive from the ramshackle capital of Koror and offering some of the island's best snorkeling just feet from its chaise longues. An hour's boat ride away, the rustic but newly renovated beach cottages at Carp Island Resort are a favorite of young divers from all over the world, who appreciate its proximity to the dive sites.

Where: 800 miles/1,300 km southwest of Guam. **How:** Sam's Tours runs various dive and eco-adventure trips. Tel 680/488-5003; www.samstours.com. *Cost:* 7-night hotel-and-dive packages from $1,065. **Palau Pacific Resort:** Tel 680/488-2600; www.palauppr.com. *Cost:* from $280. **Carp Island Resort:** Tel 680/488-2978; www.carpislandpalau.com. *Cost:* from $85. **Best time:** Nov–Apr is dry season with best underwater visibility.

Celebrating Stone Age Culture

The Highlands Sing-Sing Festivals

Papua New Guinea

Few places in the world fascinate anthropologists more than Papua New Guinea. Occupying the eastern half of the world's second largest island, "PNG" is known for its warm seas rich with marine life and sunken World War II ships. On land is a vast array of flora and fauna, including 762 species of birds (with over 400 unique to the island), the world's greatest variety of orchids, and more than 400 species of butterflies.

Local tribes come to celebrate their culture at the Mount Hagen Sing-Sing.

But it's the people of PNG who draw the curious. Living in steep valleys masked by mountains rising as high as 14,000 feet and first seen by Westerners in 1933, the highlands are home to hundreds of tribal groups, whose subsistence lifestyles have changed little since the Stone Age. They speak more than 750 distinct languages and are known for their highly unusual artwork.

In the Tari Basin, a picturesque valley in the Southern Highlands, you'll find the Huli people, who insert wild boar tusks through their pierced noses, paint their faces with bright primary colors, and wear ornate wigs made from human hair and translucent plumes plucked from Tari's 13 species of birds of paradise. You can easily visit the Hulis if you stay at the modern Ambua Lodge, which commands a splendid view of the basin from its 7,000-foot location. It is also said to be the finest place anywhere to spot birds of paradise.

Come during a "sing-sing," or cultural show, when drums thunder and hundreds of Huli adorned with lavish face and body paint as well as elaborate headdresses stomp and chant in friendly intertribal competition. The sing-sings began in the 1960s as a government effort to halt centuries-old tribal rivalry and warfare. The largest today is the Mount Hagen Sing-Sing, during which nearly 80 tribes come from all parts to "mock fight" on a soccer field in the Western Highlands trading town while some 500 tourists watch. At the much more intimate Tumbuna Sing-Sing, about 250 locals participate and only 60 tourist tickets are sold. It's held on a hilltop clearing near Rondon Ridge, a luxury eco-lodge 30 minutes from Mount Hagen. Although the shows have inevitably become more commercial since their early days, there's still nothing like them anywhere.

Where: Mt. Hagen is 320 miles/514 km northwest of the capital city, Port Moresby. **Visitor info:** www.pngtourism.org.pg. **How:** U.S.-based Asia Transpacific Journeys offers tours that coincide with the sing-sings. Tel 800-642-2742 or 303-443-6789; www.asiatranspacific.com. *Cost:* 14-night land packages from $8,595. Originate in Port Moresby. **Ambua Lodge/Rondon Ridge:** Tel 675/542-1438; www.pngtours.com. *Cost:* $510 per person, all-inclusive. **When:** May for Tumbuna Sing-Sing; Aug for Mount Hagen Sing-Sing. **Best time:** Apr–Oct is cooler and drier.

A Mysterious River, Tribal Art, and Birds Galore

SEPIK RIVER

Papua New Guinea

Winding across a vast delta before ending 685 miles from its headwaters in the soaring highlands, the Sepik River was once the domain of anthropologists, naturalists, and adventure seekers. Today, an expedition up this mysterious river is for anyone wanting to explore one of the world's last unspoiled reservoirs of nature, culture, and—most especially—tribal art.

Some native peoples here have only just emerged from isolation, and their customs and crafts are so unique that many collectors consider this region to be one of the world's best sources of primitive art. Unlike the members of Papua New Guinea's highland tribes, who express themselves in face and body painting (see previous page), the Sepik peoples do so through their wood carving. Their *tambaran* spirit houses, embellished with intricate posts and gables, are living museums of their past.

The Sepik Basin is included in most organized tours of Papua New Guinea, which are the only feasible ways to visit this remote region of few roads and limited air service. Most book you on the nine-cabin MV *Sepik Spirit*, a shallow-draft vessel that takes you on a trip along the river before depositing you at the Karawari Lodge, a handsomely rustic inn on a ridge overlooking the jungle-clad Karawari River, a tributary of the Sepik.

Karawari Lodge sits in the middle of Arambak country, one of the most unspoiled parts of the country. Dugout canoe is still the favored means of transportation for the local people, but the lodge's canopied motor launch transports guests to nearby villages, where you can see firsthand the collision of ancient and modern cultures. The bird-watching alone makes a late-afternoon boat ride unforgettable: Cormorants, cockatoos, hornbills, kingfishers, and parrots are regularly sighted on the quiet waterway. Birds of paradise are an elusive plus.

WHERE: The town of Timbunke is 444 miles/715 km northwest of Port Moresby. **HOW:** U.S.-based Asia Transpacific Journeys offers customized trips. Tel 800-642-2742 or 303-443-6789; www.asiatranspacific.com. **MV *SEPIK SPIRIT*:** Tel 675/542-1438; www.pngtours.com. 3-night cruises between Timbunke and Karawari, both accessible by air only. *Cost*: $2,342, all-inclusive. **KARAWARI LODGE:** Tel 675/542-1438; www.pngtours.com. *Cost:* $510 per person, all-inclusive. **BEST TIME:** Jul–Nov is cooler and drier.

Sacred objects and carvings can be found within tambaran spirit houses.

Lava Fields and a Cultural Storehouse

SAVAI'I

Samoa

Few easily accessible places in Polynesia have preserved their ways as Samoa has, and this is especially true of the island of Savai'i. While Western civilization has made its impact on Upolu, the country's main island, *fa'a Samoa*—the old way of life—is still very much alive on Savai'i. Just 8 miles across the scenic Apolima Straits from Upolu, this virtual storehouse of Samoan culture known as the "soul of Samoa" is home to a people who put great emphasis on extended family, ancient customs, and religion. Its traditional villages are made up of *fales* (oval houses) that appear much as they did centuries ago, except that the thatched roofs have been replaced with tin ones.

Traditional Samoan life thrives on Savai'i.

The basic, no-frills Safua Hotel still offers the best exposure to *fa'a Samoa.* A local women's rights and community leader, owner Vaasili Moelagi Jackson makes sure her guests have a chance to participate in village life as well as enjoy what other attractions Savai'i has to offer, including its many natural wonders. Beautiful, empty beaches are punctuated by lava blowholes, where, during high tide and in rough weather, columns of water can shoot up to 100 feet high. A hike inland reveals the Afu Aau waterfalls, surrounded by dense rain forest, and the 46-foot-high, pyramid-shaped Pulemelei Mound, the largest and most mysterious archaeological ruin in Polynesia.

You'll also see Matavanu, which is what's known as a shield volcano. Created almost entirely of fluid lava flows, it features a large, low profile that resembles a warrior's shield. It is dotted with more than 400 craters, and its last eruption, which lasted for 4 years and ended in 1911, deposited large lava fields across the northern side of the island.

It's here that you'll find some of Samoa's best beaches, including the one near Mansae village, a long stretch of white sand with a clutch of beach fales. Most offer an experience that's akin to camping out, but at Vacations Beach Fales you'll find several with air-conditioning. Nearby Le Lagoto Beach Resort offers the most comfortable accommodation on the island—12 modern but traditionally styled fales and a gorgeous infinity pool. "Lagoto" means sunset, and after a massage at the lovely Bodyworks spa, this is where you'll want to be to drink it in.

WHERE: 8 miles/13 km west of Upolu. **VISITOR INFO:** www.samoa.travel. **SAFUA HOTEL:** Tel 685/51-271. *Cost:* from $50. **VACATIONS BEACH FALES:** Tel 685/54-001; www.vacationsbeachfales.com. *Cost:* from $80, inclusive. **LE LAGOTO BEACH RESORT:** Tel 685/58-189; www.lelagoto.ws. *Cost:* from $95. **BEST TIME:** May–Sep for pleasant weather.

Telling Tales in Samoa

Robert Louis Stevenson Museum

Apia, Upolu, Samoa

The South Pacific islands have attracted plenty of writers, but none cherished them more than Scottish author Robert Louis Stevenson, who arrived in Samoa in 1889 in search of a climate that would help ease the symptoms of his tuberculosis. Stevenson and his wife, Fanny Osbourne, bought 314 acres on the lush slopes of Mount Vaea above Apia, Samoa's sleepy but picturesque capital city, where they built a Western-style mansion and called it Vailima (Five Waters). Now home to the Robert Louis Stevenson Museum, it has been restored to look as it did when he died on its back porch in 1894, most likely of a cerebral hemorrhage.

Great storytellers in their own right, the Samoans called Stevenson Tusitala, "Teller of Tales." When he died they hacked a winding Road of Loving Hearts to his grave high on Mount Vaea, which overlooks his home and the mountains and sea that had so captivated him. The obligatory pilgrimage here is a challenging but rewarding half-hour climb, offering one of the loveliest vistas in the South Pacific. You'll also find here the poignant epitaph Stevenson penned for himself:

Here he lies where he longed to be;
Home is the sailor, home from the sea,
And the hunter home from the hill.

Another literary light, James A. Michener, came to Samoa during World War II (he was also stationed in Vanuatu; see p. 698), whereupon he took notice of Aggie Grey, a clever Samoan woman who sold hamburgers and hot dogs to the U.S. Marines training on Upolu. Michener used Aggie as inspiration for the Tonkinese character Bloody Mary in his novel *Tales of the South Pacific*. Aggie went on to found Aggie Grey's Hotel & Bungalows, which still reigns as downtown Apia's leading inn, one of the most famous in the South Pacific. Come by for a cold Vailima beer—or perhaps a Bloody Mary—and don't miss Wednesday night's *fiafia* evening of Samoan entertainment and a sumptuous buffet. Aggie herself would often dance the graceful Samoan *siva* at these weekly events, a ritual now maintained by her granddaughter, also named Aggie. After the original Aggie's death in 1988, her family built the sprawling Aggie Grey's Lagoon, Beach Resort & Spa, on Upolu's west coast, where it is surrounded by the sea and an 18-hole golf course. Its *fiafia* nights take place Thursdays.

Samoa became the adopted home of Scotsman and Treasure Island *author Robert Louis Stevenson.*

Visitor info: www.samoa.travel. **Robert Louis Stevenson Museum:** Tel 685/20-798; www.rlsmuseum.com. **Aggie Grey's Hotel & Bungalows:** Tel 685/22-880; www.aggiegreys.com. *Cost:* from $130. **Aggie Grey's Lagoon, Beach Resort & Spa:** Tel 685/45-611; www.aggiegreys.com. *Cost:* from $190. **Best times:** May–Sep for good weather; 1st week of Jun for Independence Day celebrations; 1st week of Sep for Teuila Festival, Samoa's top event, with boat races, dance, and music.

Whale-Watching, Kayaking, and Sailing in the South Pacific

Vava'u

Kingdom of Tonga

You can see humpback whales off many tropical islands, but few places will allow you to get as close as the Kingdom of Tonga's enchanting Vava'u island group, where you can swim and snorkel with the mighty beasts almost as if you were one of them. The whales appear off Vava'u between July and November, making the 5,000-mile journey up from Antarctica to mate and bear their young. The females can weigh up to 44 tons, and the babies at birth can weigh as much as 2 tons and measure 5 feet long. To watch the interaction of the two is both exhilarating and touching.

Among the swim-and-snorkel tour operators, the best is Whale Watch Vava'u, which pioneered the day trips. Their two custom-built boats don't promise daily swims: You may only enter the water if the seas are calm and the conditions are safe. But even if you can't join the whales, you can listen. Male humpbacks are particularly vocal; their haunting melodies can be heard through the boats' hydrophones.

Whale-watching is not all Vava'u offers. With some 50 reef-encircled islands separated by narrow waterways and protected within a large, emerald lagoon, it is also one of the top destinations for kayaking and yachting in the South Pacific. On guided kayak trips, you'll visit hidden marine caves and secret beaches, where you may encounter sea turtles, porpoises, and numerous seabirds, such as the white-tailed tropic bird, lesser frigate, brown boobie, and crimson-crowned fruit dove. Guides will also introduce you to the local Polynesian culture in the small outer-island villages. Here you can experience the traditional *umu* feast, in which a suckling pig steamed in a covered pit is consumed to the accompaniment of Tongan song and dance. The uninhabited islands you'll visit are ideal spots for beachside barbecues or pitching camp under waving palms and the Southern Cross.

Top off your stay by relaxing at Mounu Island Resort, which has four guest bungalows and a restaurant often frequented by passing yachtsmen in the know. It is set on a tiny 6.5-acre coral islet that is completely surrounded by a glorious white sand beach from which you can commonly spot whales breaching offshore.

Where: 150 miles/240 km north of the principal island of Tongatapu; 50-minute flight. **Whale Watch Vava'u:** Tel 676/54-331; www.whalewatchvavau.com. *Cost:* day trips $150. **How:** Friendly Islands Kayak Company offers 5-, 9-, and 11-day trips. Tel 676/70-173; www.fikco.com. *Cost:* from $1,135. **Mounu Island Resort:** Tel 676/70-747; www.mounuisland.com. *Cost:* from $250. **Best times:** May–Sep for weather; Jul–Nov for whale-watching.

Wreck Diving, Volcanoes, and Ancient Bungee Jumping

VANUATU

Vanuatu

Of all the Pacific islands, the 82 that make up the archipelago of Vanuatu present the most fascinating mélange of cultures. Well-dressed Europeans dine in French restaurants in Port Vila, the sophisticated capital city found on the island of Efate, while tribes on other islands live as they have for ages.

Port Vila's modern vibe is the legacy of pre-1980 colonial times, when France and Britain jointly ruled what was then called the New Hebrides Islands. Named the happiest place on earth by an economic think tank in 2006, Vanuatu exudes a warm hospitality that is the archipelago's biggest attraction, and nowhere will you find more of it than in the capital. Port Vila lies beside a fine natural harbor, and white sand beaches skirt many of the hotels here and elsewhere on the island, including the Eratap Beach Resort: Its 12 luxury villas are about a 20-minute drive south of Port Vila and are the nicest on Efate.

Land diving during harvest season is a rite of passage for island men.

Modern civilization also exists on Espiritu Santo, the largest island, an hour's flight north, alongside a few relics from the not too distant past. During World War II, 100,000 U.S. troops were stationed here; one of their transport ships, the SS *President Coolidge*, hit a mine and sank, almost completely intact. It is among the world's most accessible large wrecks, and divers flock here to explore it. Another popular diving destination is Million Dollar Point, where thousands of tons of U.S. military equipment was dumped into the sea—including trucks, bulldozers, jeeps, and forklifts—before the troops returned home. (The name refers to the booty's worth.)

If you'd rather trek than dive, one of the world's most easily visited active volcanoes, Mount Yasur, is one of the highlights on the island of Tanna. Four-wheel-drive vehicles and hiking trails climb its cinder cone almost to the growling crater's rim. At dusk the molten magma below and the setting sun above paint the erupting gas clouds orange, pink, and red. At the modest Tanna Evergreen Resort you'll find simple bungalows and a friendly staff who can arrange island tours.

On Saturdays from April until June, check out the Naghol, or land-diving ceremony, on Pentecost Island. In this precursor to bungee jumping (that later surfaced in New Zealand; see p. 676) village males strap grapevines to their ankles and, accompanied by chanting and dancing, leap headfirst off 85-foot-high towers to within centimeters of the ground in order to prove their manhood and ensure a bountiful yam harvest. You'll be one of many tourists, who—thankfully—are forbidden to participate.

VISITOR INFO: www.vanuatu.travel. **ERATAP BEACH RESORT:** Tel 678/554-05007; www.eratap.com. *Cost:* from $535. **TANNA EVERGREEN RESORT:** Tel 678/68774; www.tevergreenresort-tours.vu. *Cost:* from $190. **BEST TIMES:** May–Oct for dry season; Apr–Jun for land diving on Pentecost Island.

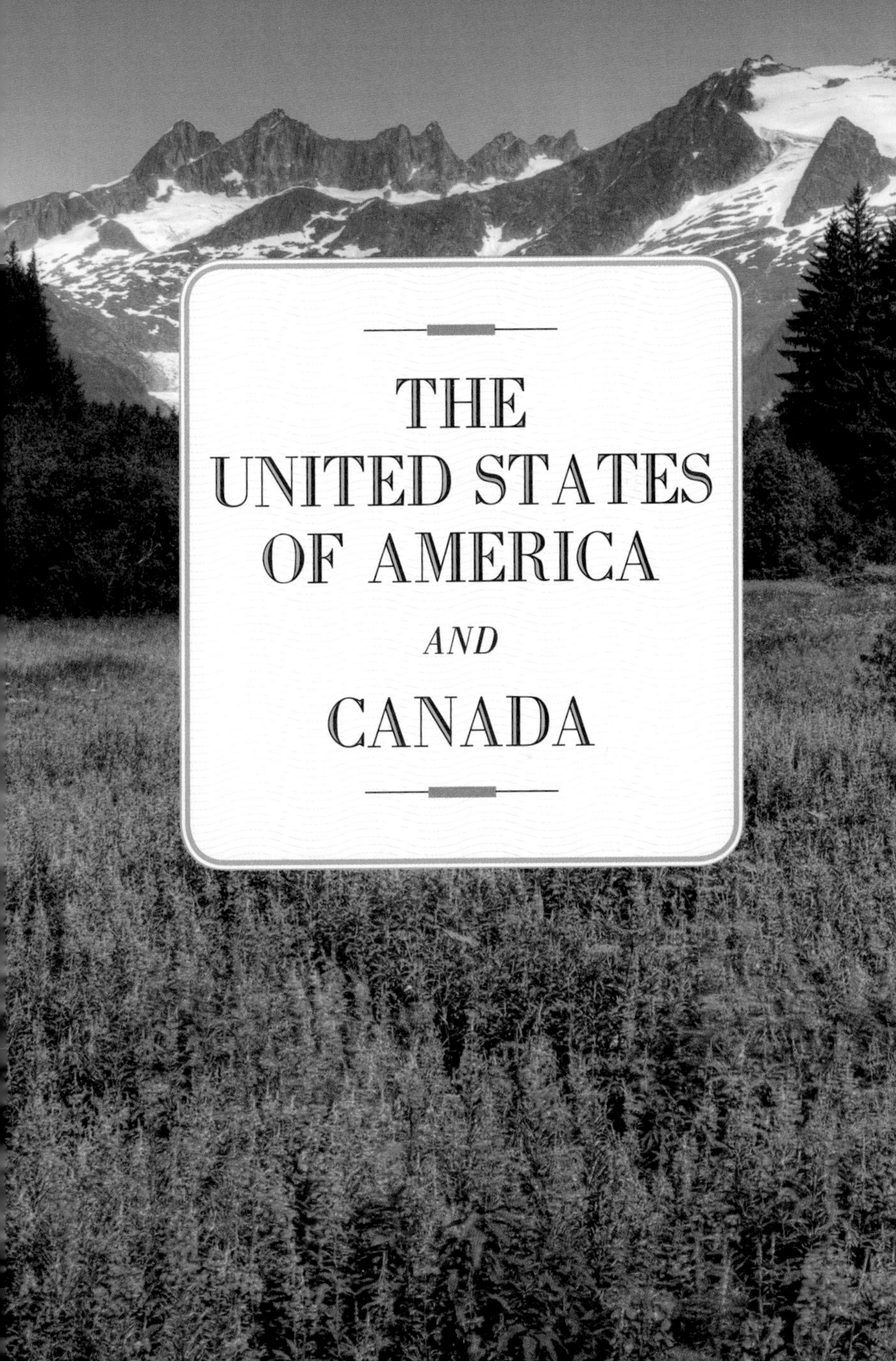

THE UNITED STATES OF AMERICA

AND

CANADA

ARCTIC OCEAN
AK (USA)
Yukon
Mt. McKinley
GULF OF ALASKA
PACIFIC OCEAN
YUKON
Great Bear Lake
NORTHWEST TERRITORIES
NUNAVUT
Great Slave Lake
HUDSON BAY
1 PRINCE EDWARD ISLAND
2 NEW BRUNSWICK
NEWFOUNDLAND & LABRADOR
Newfoundland
BRITISH COLUMBIA
ROCKY MOUNTAINS
ALBERTA
CANADA
MANITOBA
SASKATCHEWAN
ONTARIO
QUEBEC
NOVA SCOTIA
Great Lakes
Ottawa
HI (USA)
WA
OR
ID
MT
Missouri
ND
SD
WY
NV
Great Salt Lake
UT
CO
Colorado
CA
SIERRA NEVADA
AZ
NM
NE
KS
OK
TX
Rio Gra
MN
IA
MO
AR
LA
Mississippi
WI
IL
MI
IN
OH
KY
TN
MS
AL
GA
FL
SC
NC
VA
WV
PA
NY
VT
ME
NH
MA
RI
CT
NJ
DE
MD
Washington D.C.
UNITED STATES OF AMERICA
ATLANTIC OCEAN
N
S
E
W
0 200 400 MILES
0 322 644 Kilometers

THE UNITED STATES OF AMERICA

"The Last Great Race on Earth"

The Iditarod

Anchorage, Alaska, U.S.A.

Starting from Anchorage every March and ending 8 to 15 days later in Nome, the Iditarod is one of the great endurance tests in sport, with competitors mushing sled dogs across 1,150 miles of snow and ice in temperatures as low as 60°F below zero. It is Alaska's largest spectator sport, and few things celebrate the pioneering spirit of our 49th state better.

Now a National Historic Trail, the Iditarod began as a mail and supply route for miners. It winds across frozen rivers and desolate tundra, through dense forest and along miles of windswept coast from Seward, near Anchorage, to Nome, on the western Bering Sea coast. In 1925, part of the Iditarod Trail became a lifesaving highway for epidemic-stricken Nome. Diphtheria raged, and serum had to be brought in by intrepid mushers and their hard-driving dogs. In commemoration of those heroic feats, the route was turned into a race course in 1973, and today mushers come from as far away as Japan and Norway to compete for a share of the $600,000-plus purse.

You can get into the race yourself as a passenger, or "IditaRider," by bidding for a spot on a musher's sled for the first 11 miles (the auction begins in November, with a $7,500 offer guaranteeing your choice of musher). For a less competitive take, contact Raymie Redington, son of Joe "Father of the Iditarod" Redington Sr., who leads short trips on the Iditarod Trail. Winterlake Lodge, one of the remote fly-in outposts directly on the trail, offers four handsome guest cabins and opportunities to traverse the trail with a team of 24 Alaskan huskies (it's also one of the state's few wilderness lodges that stays open year-round). The dinner menu is remarkable even by big-city standards.

Teams of 12 to 16 huskies pull mushers through the snow.

Nome, the "end of the line" for the Iditarod (and almost everything else), stands on the coast of the Bering Sea. Its dirt streets and rough-and-tumble saloons are quiet until the month-long Iditarod celebration rolls into town every March. Along with the race fans come northern lights aficionados, as well as participants in the Bering Sea Ice Golf Classic, who hit orange golf balls onto Astroturf laid across the frozen sea.

Where: Headquarters in Wasilla, 40 miles north of Anchorage. Tel 907-376-5155 or 907-248-6874 (racetime); www.iditarod.com. *When:* early Mar. **IditaRiders auction:** Tel 800-566-7533 or 907-352-2202; www.iditarodauction.com. *When:* early Nov–Jan. **Raymie Redington:** Tel 907-376-6730. *Cost:* half-hour dog sled rides $50. *When:* beginning with 1st snow in Nov. **Winterlake Lodge:** Tel 907-274-2710; www.withinthewild.com. *Cost:* 2-night stay, $2,130 per person, all-inclusive with air transfer from Anchorage.

The American Safari

Denali National Park

Alaska, U.S.A.

At 20,320 feet, Mount McKinley stands as the tallest peak in North America. Named after the 25th U.S. president, it is also known by the indigenous Athabascans of central Alaska as Denali, "the high one."

Whatever you call the mountain, its grandeur transcends any language. It is the primary attraction of Denali National Park, but it's not the only draw.

Visitors return from the 6-million-acre park with tales of grizzlies, moose, and golden eagles; of sweeping vistas of subarctic tundra, glaciers, and the massive peaks of the Alaska Mountain Range that almost rival the great peak itself. In summer you'll enjoy 16–20 hours of light in which to take in all the dazzling scenery.

A floatplane awaits takeoff from one of Denali's many lakes.

Touring and camping are controlled to protect the park's fragile ecology. There's only one 90-mile road, and motorized traffic past the 15-mile point is limited to buses and official vehicles. For an eagle's-eye view, a number of operators will arrange plane or helicopter flightseeing excursions, while a more active and up-close experience can be had at Camp Denali or North Face Lodge. These sister properties, founded in 1951 by homesteaders at the heart of the not-yet-designated national parkland and currently run by third-generation owners, offer guests naturalist-guided hikes and educational programs. Alternative—and less pricey—accommodations can be found at the cluster of hotels at the park's entrance.

Drink in more of the 49th state's stark beauty aboard the *Denali Star* train, which takes you on a 365-mile journey from Anchorage to Fairbanks traveling through the frontier towns of Wasilla and Talkeetna—and also making middle-of-nowhere stops, where lumberjack types board the train with their huskies—and passes through the park. You'll marvel as verdant woodland, tundra, and snowy peaks slip by the picture windows.

Where: 125 miles south of Fairbanks. Tel 907-683-2294; www.nps.gov/dena. *When:* park road closed Oct–Apr. **Camp Denali** and **North Face Lodge:** Tel 907-683-2290; www.campdenali.com. *Cost:* 3 nights, $1,545 per person, all-inclusive. *When:* Jun–early Sep. **Alaska Railroad:** Tel 800-544-0552 or 907-265-2494; www.alaskarailroad.com. *Cost:* Anchorage to Denali, from $120 (off-peak), from $145 (peak). *When:* mid-May–mid-Sep. Aurora Winter Train runs weekends mid-Sep–mid-May. **Best times:** Jun for wildflowers and birding; Aug–Sep for fall foliage; Mar and late Sep for northern lights.

Land of Water and Ice

Inside Passage and Glacier Bay

Alaska, U.S.A.

Alaska has over 40,000 miles of coastline, and you can take in some of the most beautiful from your ship's deck while sailing the Inside Passage. It stretches through 500 scenic miles in the southeast of the state, from British Columbia's Queen Charlotte Islands in the south to the corner of Canada's Yukon Territory in the north (see p. 942). Thirty-plus cruise lines sail here every summer, and long-distance ferries depart from Bellingham, Washington, year-round.

The big draw is the astounding wilderness, with snow-capped mountains, deep rain forests, and a maze of islands that are the home of whales, sea lions, sea otters, harbor seals, porpoises, and seabirds. Tucked into all that bounty are the towns. Ketchikan may be the most touristy; pretty Sitka, midway up Southeast, is less so, despite its 19th-century heyday as the unofficial capital of Russian America and onetime nickname, "Paris of the Pacific." The icon-filled Russian Orthodox St. Michael's Cathedral, built in the 1840s, stands at the center of town, and the Russian Bishop's House now serves as a museum.

Farther north lie Juneau, Alaska's easy-going capital city, and the Mendenhall Glacier, which stretches for nearly 12 miles. Ferries travel the short distance northwest to Gustavus, gateway to Glacier Bay National Park, a 3-million acre wonderland at the northernmost point of the Inside Passage. Humpback whales arrive each summer, along with tourists who come to see them and the ten tidewater glaciers, some 4,000 years old, cascading down from the mountains. The popular park-run Glacier Bay Lodge sits at the park entrance; a 10-mile drive promises a more personal experience at the Gustavus Inn, a former homestead and farm. Both the Lodge and the Inn can arrange day trips into the park by foot, kayak, tour boat, or mountain bike. To the east of Glacier Bay is the charming town of Skagway, once the jumping off point for the Klondike Gold Rush of 1898. That was the year the 110-mile narrow-gauge White Pass and Yukon Route Railroad was built. You can still ride it to the 2,865-foot summit of White Pass.

Cruise options range from the less expensive 2,000-passenger megaships to expedition vessels (with 100 or fewer passengers) that can more easily access the bays, inlets, and coves and generally offer a more intimate glimpse of real Alaska. For a more independent experience, the Alaska Marine Highway ferries offer a hop-on/hop-off adventure along the coast.

Where: Most cruise ships sail from Seattle, Vancouver, or Anchorage. **How:** Lindblad Expeditions (tel 800-397-3348 or 212-765-7740; www.lindblad.com) and Regent Seven Seas Cruises (tel 877-505-5370 or 954-776-6123; www.rssc.com). *Cost:* expect to pay approximately $3,300 per person for 7 nights on larger ships; 8 nights from $4,450 on smaller ships. *When:* Cruises run May–Sep. **State ferries:** Tel 800-642-0066 or 907-465-3941; www.ferryalaska.com. **Glacier Bay National Park:** Tel 907-697-2230; www.nps.gov/glba. *When:* May–Sep. **Glacier Bay Lodge:** Tel 866-761-6634 or 907-264-4600; www.visitglacierbay.com. *Cost:* from $200. *When:* May–Sep. **Gustavus Inn:** Tel 800-649-5220 or

907-697-2254; www.gustavusinn.com. Cost: $425, inclusive. *When:* May–Sep. **White Pass and Yukon Route Railroad:** Tel 800-343-7373 or 907-983-9827; www.whitepassrailroad.com. *Cost:* from $115 round-trip. **Best times:** May–Jun is driest; Jul–Aug is warmest; May and Sep for lowest rates and smallest crowds; early Nov for annual Sitka Whale Festival.

A Majestic Microcosm of Alaska

The Kenai Peninsula and Prince William Sound

Alaska, U.S.A.

Lying across a narrow channel from metropolitan Anchorage, the Kenai Peninsula is like a movie trailer of Alaska highlights: incredible fishing, hiking, and kayaking opportunities; prolific wildlife; and to its east the stunning Prince William Sound, ringed by the steep and glaciated Chugach Mountains.

From Anchorage, the scenic Seward Highway skirts the glacial Turnagain Arm Waterway, passing through some of the most extraordinary natural beauty in the state before reaching the town of Girdwood, 40 miles away. Here, the Alyeska Resort, a 1,000-acre ski area and luxury hotel, is a year-round destination with a stunning indoor pool, full-service spa, and an aerial tram to the mountaintop Seven Glaciers restaurant. The riveting view makes it hard to concentrate on the menu, which runs from Alaskan king crab to reindeer hot dogs.

Continue on to Cooper Landing on the Kenai River, where fishermen pull in some of the world's biggest salmon. Keep going another 120 miles and you're in the artsy town of Homer (population 500). Set on a stunning 5-mile finger of land called The Spit, it fancies itself both a cultural and fishing hub. Drop into Homer's landmark Salty Dawg Saloon, an old trapper's hut where tourists hoist their beers with local fishermen and cannery workers.

From Homer, a kayak or boat outing across gorgeous Kachemak Bay provides glimpses of puffins, cormorants, and sea otters. On the fjordlike distant shore, the town of Halibut Cove perches on pilings above the water, its art galleries and houses connected by boardwalks. The enchanting, fly-in Kachemak Bay Wilderness Lodge offers six luxurious cabins, wilderness explorations, and meals featuring local Dungeness crab, salmon, and halibut, prepared to perfection.

An orca whale breaches in Kachemak Bay, off the coast of the Kenai Peninsula.

In Seward, named for the secretary of state who purchased Alaska from Russia in 1867 (it was known as "Seward's Folly" until gold was discovered), board a sightseeing boat to take you out to Kenai Fjords National Park, where the rugged coast is filigreed with caves and you can spot whales and brown bears. From Whittier and Valdez, tour boats and kayaks head out onto Prince William Sound, surrounded by fjords and tidewater glaciers and teeming with even more wildlife.

WHERE: Beginning about 50 miles southeast of Anchorage. **VISITOR INFO:** www.kenai peninsula.org. **ALYESKA:** Tel 800-880-3880 or 907-754-1111; www.alyeskaresort.com. *Cost:* from $149 (off-peak), from $240 (peak); lift tickets $55; dinner at Seven Glaciers $60. **SALTY DAWG SALOON:** Tel 907-235-6718; www.saltydawgsaloon.com. **KACHEMAK BAY WILDERNESS LODGE:** Tel 907-235-8910; www .alaskawildernesslodge.com. *Cost:* $875 per person, all-inclusive. *When:* late May–Sep. **BEST TIMES:** May and Sep for smaller crowds.

Sacred Outdoor Museum of the Navajo Nation

CANYON DE CHELLY

Arizona, U.S.A.

Owned by the Navajo Nation, one of 21 recognized tribes living in Arizona (and the largest in the U.S.), Canyon de Chelly (de-SHAY) exudes a quiet magic and spirituality that inspired mythology guru Joseph Campbell to call it "the most sacred place on Earth." Along with Monument Valley (p. 708), the canyon is considered one of the holiest places in the vast Navajo Indian Reservation.

The Ancestral Puebloans (also known as the Anasazi) began carving multistoried dwellings into the sandstone walls around A.D. 700. Mysteriously abandoned in the 1300s, they represent one of the oldest dwelling sites in North America and—paired with the canyon's natural beauty—the principal attraction of this 130-square-mile historic area.

The national monument's name comes from the Navajo word *tseyi*, meaning "rock canyon." Soaring cliffs glowing pink and orange are cut by the cottonwood-lined Rio de Chelly and decorated with ancient pictographs and petroglyphs. Near the visitor center you'll find the Thunderbird Lodge, built as a trading post in 1902. Sign up for one of the Navajo-led "shake-and-bake" jeep tours, named for the bumpy road and summer heat. (Most of the canyon bottom is off-limits to visitors; aside from the White House trail, the gorge is accessible by guided vehicle tour only.)

The paved 15-mile North Rim Drive follows the Canyon del Muerto (Canyon of the Dead) and leads to Navajo Fortress, where native warriors hid from U.S. troops in 1863 after being ordered to move to a barren reservation in eastern New Mexico. If time is limited, opt for the 16-mile South Rim Drive, which offers even more remarkable views. From the White House Overlook, take the steep trail a mile down to White House Ruins, the remains of an 80-room structure, the largest in the canyon. The last stop on the drive is the spectacular Spider Rock Overlook. Legend has it that the top of the sandstone pinnacle, rising 800 feet from the canyon floor, is home to a Navajo goddess called the

Inhabited from 1040 to 1275, the White House Ruins are the largest in the canyon.

Spider Woman. According to Navajo myth, she created the universe by tossing stars into the sky from her dew-laced web.

WHERE: 225 miles northeast of Flagstaff. Tel 928-674-5500; www.nps.gov/cach. **THUNDERBIRD LODGE:** Tel 800-679-2473 or 928-674-5841; www.tbirdlodge.com. *Cost:* from $75 (off-peak), from $130 (peak); tours from $55. **BEST TIME:** May–Oct for good weather and canyon conditions.

Nature's Masterpiece

GRAND CANYON

Arizona, U.S.A.

Few things in this world produce such awe as the Grand Canyon. "It will seem as novel to you, as unearthly in color and grandeur and quantity of its architecture as if you found it after death, on some other star," wrote a mesmerized John Muir, founder of the Sierra Club. The mile-deep chasm carved by the Colorado River is a staggering 277 miles long and up to 18 miles wide. Its striated walls change color by the hour, shifting from crimson to orange to purple. No matter what time of day you visit, you're in for a treat. Most of the 4 million visitors per year head to the South Rim, about an hour's drive north of Flagstaff, where the overlooks are the most dramatic and hiking trails wait to be explored. Here you'll find the main visitor center and a few lodges, anchored by the grand El Tovar, the park's man-made wonder. Built by Hopi craftsmen in 1905, with edge-of-the-world views, it is considered the crown jewel of national park lodges.

Two billion years of geological history are visible in the Grand Canyon's rock layers.

Guided rides on trail-savvy mules take you down to Plateau Point and back in a day. Or you can hike the Bright Angel Trail, which runs 9 miles to Phantom Ranch, the only accommodations below the rim. Other scenic options are South Kaibab Trail and the easy and mostly paved Rim Trail.

The more remote (and therefore less visited) but equally inspiring North Rim is a 210-mile drive or a 21-mile hike from the South Rim. Enjoy the views from the flagstone porches of the stone-and-log Grand Canyon Lodge, built in 1937, before striking off on the 14-mile North Kaibab trail to Phantom Ranch.

The area's newest attraction is the exhilarating 70-foot-long glass-bottomed Grand Canyon Skywalk, which juts 4,000 feet above the canyon floor. Located in Grand Canyon West, on the Hualapai Indian Reservation, it's a popular stop on most day trips leaving from Las Vegas (see p. 823), 120 miles away.

Adventurers looking for an insider glimpse of the masterpiece of nature should raft the swift-moving Colorado River—just be sure to book well in advance. Options include motorized or oar-powered boats and rafts, and trips take from a few hours up to 2 weeks through rapids ranging from Class I through V. Shore excursions let you explore side canyons, swimming holes, and waterfalls; nights are spent camping on sandy river beaches beneath a panoply of stars.

Many canyon visitors use Sedona (see p. 710) or Flagstaff as their base. If you set off from the latter, consider the Inn at 410, a nine-bedroom 1894 Craftsman bungalow–turned-B&B, two blocks from Flagstaff's renovated historic quarter. Be sure to check out the country dancing at Flagstaff's Museum Club (the Zoo Club to locals) and the stars at Lowell Observatory.

WHERE: South Rim is 80 miles north of Flagstaff; North Rim is 270 miles east of Las Vegas. Tel 928-638-7888; www.nps.gov/grca. **EL TOVAR:** Tel 888-297-2757 or 303-297-2757; www.grandcanyonlodges.com. *Cost:* from $180. **MULE RIDES:** Tel 888-297-2757 or 303-297-2757; www.grandcanyonlodges.com. *Cost:* from $137. *When:* year-round on the South Rim; mid-May–mid-Oct on the North Rim. **GRAND CANYON LODGE:** Tel 877-386-4383 or 480-337-1320; www.grandcanyonforever.com. *Cost:* from $115. *When:* mid-May–mid-Oct. **SKYWALK:** Tel 877-716-9378 or 702-878-9378; www.grandcanyonskywalk.com *Cost:* $70 (includes admission to Grand Canyon West). **RIVER RAFTING:** O.A.R.S. Tel 800-346-6277 or 209-736-4677; www.oars.com/grandcanyon. *Cost:* 4 days from $1,758. *When:* Apr–Oct. **THE INN AT 410:** Tel 800-774-2008 or 928-774-0088; www.inn410.com. *Cost:* from $160. **MUSEUM CLUB:** Tel 928-526-9434; www.museumclub.com. **LOWELL OBSERVATORY:** Tel 928-774-3358; www.lowell.edu. **BEST TIMES:** Mar–early May and Sep–Oct to avoid summer heat and crowds.

Man-Made Sea of the Southwest

LAKE POWELL

Arizona and Utah, U.S.A.

Imagine the Grand Canyon and then fill it with water. That is Lake Powell—the nation's second largest man-made lake, whose turquoise waters shimmer like a mirage in the red rock country of northern Arizona and southern Utah.

The 710-foot-high Glen Canyon Dam was first proposed in the 1920s and completed in the 1960s, but the lake wasn't completely filled by the Colorado River until 1980. Free tours from Carl Hayden Visitor Center take you inside the dam to see the gigantic turbines that generate power for states across the West.

Measuring 185 miles long and creating some 2,000 miles of more or less road-free shoreline, Lake Powell has become the "houseboat capital of America." The red cliffs let onto more than 90 canyons (from mere slots to nearly 10 miles wide). Countless sandy coves and beaches can be explored by day, while nighttime means spectacular stargazing. Houseboats (from bare bones to deluxe) and sea kayaks are for rent at Wahweap Marina, in the busy gateway town of Page, Arizona, where accommodations on terra firma are also available. Small powerboats can be rented—anglers come for the lake's year-round fishing—and cruises depart in the late afternoon for a scenic dinner on the water.

On the southern edge of the lake, Rainbow

Bridge is a site of deep spiritual significance to the Navajo, who call it "the rainbow turned to stone." At 290 feet high and 275 feet across, it is the longest natural arch in the world. The little-known Antelope Canyon, located within the Navajo Nation (see below), is a popular day trip from Page. A "slot canyon" measuring 120 feet deep and only yards wide in spots, it undulates with rust- and pink-colored curves that glow when lit by narrow shafts of light.

Travel just over the Utah border to Amangiri ("peaceful mountain"), the exquisite 600-acre property of the famously high-service Amanresorts. Ancient Navajo traditions are incorporated into its spa's extensive offerings. And the desert suites have astonishing views of dunes and plateaus.

WHERE: Page is 135 miles north of Flagstaff. **VISITOR INFO:** www.pagelakepowelltourism.com. **HOUSEBOATS:** Lake Powell Resorts & Marinas, tel 888-896-3829 or 928-645-1111; www.lakepowell.com. *Cost:* 3 days from $1,315 (off-peak), from $1,800 (peak) for a boat that sleeps 6. **HOW:** Overland Canyon Tours offers trips to Antelope Canyon. Tel 928-608-4072; www.overlandcanyon.com. **AMANGIRI:** Tel 877-695-3999 or 435-675-3999; www.amanresorts.com. *Cost:* from $1,000. **BEST TIMES:** Jun–Oct for water sports; Apr, Jun, and Oct–Nov for fishing.

The West Written in Stone

MONUMENT VALLEY NAVAJO TRIBAL PARK

Arizona and Utah, U.S.A.

The very embodiment of the old West, Monument Valley is a vast barren plain punctuated by towering red-rock formations straddling the Arizona-Utah border. A spectacularly scenic—and rough—17-mile dirt road runs from the visitor center past mesas and starkly eroded buttes, some reaching 1,000 feet above the valley floor with names like Totem Pole, the Mittens, and Elephant Butte. If you want to wander off the road, you must be in the company of a Navajo guide.

Millions of years of erosion shaped Yei Bi Chai and Totem Pole.

Monument Valley falls within the 27,000-square-mile Navajo Nation, roughly the size of West Virginia, where tribe members still live and farm among the skyscraper-size stone towers. To the Navajo all of *Tsébii´ nidzisgai* ("The Valley Within the Rocks") is sacred. It's special to Hollywood, too. Get an introduction to the area's celluloid history at Goulding's Lodge and Trading Post, established in 1924 by rancher Harry Goulding. It was Goulding who convinced director John Ford to use the setting as the location for his famous Westerns, beginning with the 1939 John Wayne classic *Stagecoach*. This 62-room hotel was the only game in town for the film crew and the legions of visitors who followed, but the recent arrival of the Navajo-owned and run View Hotel introduces a new option within the Navajo Tribal Park. The plate-glass walls of the View's atrium open onto the inspiring vista shared by the 95 guest rooms and a restaurant run by a talented Navajo chef. Watch how at sunset the entire valley seems to catch fire.

The small town of Window Rock is where you'll find the Navajo Nation Museum and the Navajo Nation Fair every September. From there it's not far to Tuba City, on one of the most eye-catching stretches of the Painted Desert. Come in October for the Western Navajo Fair and witness a town transformed by music, dancers, and a parade. Visitors are also welcome in the smaller Hopi Reservation, where 12 ancient villages are spread across three flat-topped mesas. The Hopi Cultural Center, in the heart of Second Mesa, is a combination museum, modest motel, and restaurant serving simple, traditional fare.

Where: 170 miles north of Flagstaff. Tel 928-871-6647; www.navajonationparks.org. **How:** Sacred Monument Tours leads horseback, jeep, and hiking tours. Tel 435-727-3218; www.monumentvalley.net. *Cost:* from $60. **Goulding's Lodge:** Tel 435-727-3231; www.gouldings.com. *Cost:* from $80 (off-peak), from $195 (peak). **View Hotel:** Tel 435-727-5555; www.monumentvalleyview.com. *Cost:* from $100 (off-peak), from $200 (peak); dinner $25. **Navajo Nation Museum:** Tel 928-871-7941; www.navajonationmuseum.org. **Navajo Nation Fair:** Tel 928-871-6478; www.navajonationfair.com. *When:* early Sep. **Hopi Cultural Center:** Tel 928-734-2401; www.hopiculturalcenter.com. *Cost:* from $85; lunch $10. **Best times:** late afternoon, sunset, or at night during a full moon; Apr–May and Oct–Nov when weather is cool and crowds are smaller; early Sep for Navajo Nation Fair, Oct for Western Navajo Fair.

A Desert Oasis Where Fairways Abound

Golfing the Valley of the Sun

Phoenix and Scottsdale, Arizona, U.S.A.

With over 200 golf courses and an average of 300 days of sun annually, the greater Phoenix area—known more poetically as the Valley of the Sun—has become one of America's most popular winter destinations.

Much of Scottsdale's reputation as a golfing mecca is thanks to Troon North and its two top-ranked daily fee courses: the Monument, designed by Tom Weiskopf and Jay Morrish, and Weiskopf's Pinnacle. Guests at the adjacent Four Seasons Resort Scottsdale at Troon North enjoy priority use of the facilities as well as lavish accommodations with terraces overlooking the cacti and après-golf wine tastings.

The crown jewel of the valley's top-ranked resorts is The Phoenician, with three nine-hole courses over 150 lush acres, the Centre for Well-Being spa, and a resident astronomer to interpret those clear desert skies. Not to be outdone, the oasislike Boulders Resort in nearby Carefree comes with breathtaking views of the Sonoran Desert, two 18-hole Jay Moorish–designed courses, and a Golden Door Spa.

Palms and tiled fountains give the Fairmont Scottsdale Princess the air of a Moorish-Spanish palacio. One of its two acclaimed courses, the TPC of Scottsdale, is host to the Waste Management Phoenix (originally Phoenix) Open.

The Arizona Biltmore, with its tricycle-borne room service, is luxurious but cheerier than many of its competitors. Designed by an apprentice of Frank Lloyd Wright, with the master's assistance, it is the stylish centerpiece to two 18-hole golf courses and a spa that knows few rivals. The Wigwam is the only resort in the area that claims three championship golf courses, including the classic Gold Course, designed by Robert Trent Jones Sr.

The state's largest infinity pool and an Asian-inspired spa are the stars at the chic Sanctuary on Camelback Mountain. Its panoramic views across Paradise Valley may make you consider ditching the clubs for a day.

VISITOR INFO: www.golfarizona.com. **TROON NORTH:** Tel 888-876-6687 or 480-585-5300; www.troonnorthgolf.com. *Cost:* greens fees from $45 (off-peak), from $145 (peak). **FOUR SEASONS RESORT:** Tel 888-207-9696 or 480-515-5700; www.fourseasons.com. *Cost:* from $195 (off-peak), from $525 (peak). **PHOENICIAN:** Tel 800-888-8234 or 480-941-8200; www.thephoenician.com. *Cost:* from $180 (off-peak), from $325 (peak); greens fees from $30 (off-peak), from $200 (peak). **BOULDERS RESORT:** Tel 888-579-2631 or 480-488-9009; www.theboulders.com. *Cost:* from $129 (off-peak), from $399 (peak); greens fees $200. **FAIRMONT SCOTTSDALE PRINCESS:** Tel 877-733-7485 or 480-585-4848; www.fairmont.com. *Cost:* from $149 (off-peak), from $279 (peak); greens fees from $100 (off-peak), from $140 (peak). **ARIZONA BILTMORE:** Tel 800-950-0086 or 602-955-6600; www.arizonabiltmore.com. *Cost:* from $129 (off-peak), from $299 (peak); greens fees from $39 (off-peak), from $99 (peak). **WIGWAM GOLF RESORT & SPA:** Tel 800-327-0396 or 623-935-3811; www.wigwamresort.com. *Cost:* from $110 (off-peak), from $260 (peak); Gold greens fees from $35 (off-peak), from $75 (peak). **SANCTUARY ON CAMELBACK MOUNTAIN:** Tel 800-245-2051 or 480-948-2100; www.sanctuaryaz.com. *Cost:* from $180 (off-peak), from $520 (peak). **BEST TIMES:** Dec–Apr; Jan–Feb for the WM Phoenix Open.

"Layer Cake" Terrain and Sandstone Skyscrapers

SEDONA AND RED ROCK COUNTRY

Arizona, U.S.A.

As if sculpted in crimson stone, the city of Sedona and its red rock towers stand tall against pine green hillsides and a cerulean sky. Getting there from Flagstaff is half the fun: Highway 89A takes you through Oak Creek Canyon and past eroded monoliths, and frequent pull-overs invite you to stop for photo ops or to splash about in the creek's refreshing swimming holes.

The Yavapai Apache tribe consider this area sacred, and seven supposed energy vortexes, known for their healing and cleansing properties, draw spiritualists and would-be shamans. Hiking and mountain biking opportunities abound, or you can gaze at the scenery from a hot-air balloon or one of the distinctive pink jeeps available for tours. The summer heat (moderated somewhat by the city's 4,500-foot altitude) drives many to swim in Slide Rock Canyon State Park or to take refuge in the air-conditioned galleries that line uptown's Main Street district and gave rise to Sedona's vibrant art scene.

Tlaquepaque Arts & Crafts Village, a re-created Mexican hamlet with leafy trees, fountains, and alfresco dining, has dozens of shops to explore. (It's across the street from the Center for the New Age, which offers guided tours of the vortexes.) The Chapel of the Holy Cross, another spiritual must-see, was built into the rock 200 feet above the valley. It features lovely views and a façade distinguished by a huge cross.

The Chapel of the Holy Cross, completed in 1956, offers views and inspiration.

Sedona is also known for its luxurious lodgings, with first prize going to the 70-acre Enchantment Resort on the outskirts of town. Most come for the hotel's Mii amo Spa, and its Boynton Canyon setting. End your day at the resort's acclaimed Yavapai Restaurant, and watch the moon rise over rust-colored cliffs.

A host of smaller and more intimate accommodations also invite you to linger. Garland's Oak Creek Lodge is a comfy 1930s getaway known for its down-home fare. Lush gardens and orchards surround its 16 rustic cabins, some with fireplaces and a few on the creek. In town, El Portal is a casual and pet-friendly hacienda within an easy stroll of Tlaquepaque.

Where: 120 miles north of Phoenix. **Visitor info:** www.visitsedona.com. **Pink Jeep Tours:** Tel 800-873-3662 or 928-282-5000; www.pinkjeep.com. **Slide Rock Canyon State Park:** Tel 928-282-3034; www.azstateparks.com. **Center for the New Age:** Tel 888-881-6651 or 928-282-2085; www.sedonanewagecenter.com. **Enchantment:** Tel 800-826-4180 or 928-282-2900; www.enchantmentresort.com. *Cost:* from $350 (off-peak), from $450 (peak); dinner $60. **Mii amo Spa:** Tel 888-749-2137 or 928-282-2800; www.miiamo.com. **Garland's Lodge:** Tel 928-282-3343; www.garlandslodge.com. *Cost:* from $245, inclusive. *When:* closed mid-Nov–late Mar. **El Portal:** Tel 800-313-0017 or 928-203-9405; www.elportalsedona.com. *Cost:* from $179 (off-peak), from $279 (peak). **Best times:** Mar–May and Sep–Oct for nicest weather; late Feb or early Mar for Sedona International Film Festival.

World-Class Wellness Trailblazers

Canyon Ranch and Miraval

Tucson, Arizona, U.S.A.

The beautiful saguaro-studded Sonoran Desert is home to two of the country's highest-rated destination spas. Although they may have different approaches to well-being, both Canyon Ranch and Miraval regularly make the best-of lists for treatments, accommodations, and location.

Since it opened in 1979 on 150 acres in the foothills of the Santa Catalina Mountains (with an equally plush facility in the Berkshires in Massachusetts), Canyon Ranch has become North America's most famous shrine to health, wellness, and extreme pampering. A seemingly endless roster of activities—from Pilates, guided desert hikes, and art classes to talks focused on medical issues—is presided over by a staff of specialists. Beyond simple relaxation, the goal is to take the lessons and benefits of the Canyon Ranch experience home with you, whether they involve managing stress or learning to prepare some of the restaurant's signature dishes. Their lemon blackberry pie is a favorite.

At nearby Miraval, you'll spend as much time on mental, emotional, and spiritual growth as on physical exercise or prickly pear sugar scrubs. Set in nearly 400 acres of serene desert in Catalina, Miraval offers the requisite fitness classes and spa treatments, but here you'll also participate in "challenge sessions," such as tightrope walking and soaring from a new 1,000-foot zip-line. Exploring a new way of life is what counts here.

Canyon Ranch: Tel 800-742-9000 or 520-749-9000; www.canyonranch.com. *Cost:* 4 nights from $2,860 per person (off-peak), from $4,070 (peak), all-inclusive. **Miraval Resort:** Tel 800-232-3969 or 520-825-4000; www.miravalresorts.com. *Cost:* $425 per person, all-inclusive.

Along El Camino Real

California Mission Trail

California, U.S.A.

On July 16, 1769, Father Junípero Serra, accompanied by a scraggly band of Spanish soldiers and missionaries, erected a brushwood shelter and founded Mission San Diego de Alcalá. It was the first of 21 Franciscan missions established along the coastal route dubbed El Camino Real ("The Royal Road"), extending from present-day San Diego (see p. 725) to the last and northernmost mission, founded in Sonoma (see p. 714) in 1823. Established for reasons both spiritual and military, these outposts are a cornerstone of California history, culture, and architecture. They are considered among the most beautiful buildings in the state and historically significant in the country.

Mission founder Junípero Serra is buried at San Carlos Borroméo.

Each mission serves as a snapshot of the state's early days, and all of them have their own appeal, but if you have to choose, here are the highlights. Mission San Juan Capistrano, "Jewel of the Missions," is as famous for its gardens as for its migrating swallows (*las golondrinas*) that return annually from Argentina around March 19 (St. Joseph's Day). Mission San Buenaventura, in Ventura, still looks much as it did when it was constructed, between 1792 and 1809. Visit the hilltop "Queen of the Missions" in Santa Barbara, for its distinctive twin bell towers and, on a clear day, its views of the Channel Islands. Finally, don't miss San Carlos Borroméo, in Carmel (see p. 724), founded in 1771 and once headquarters for the entire mission system in California. Pope John Paul II visited here in 1987 to beatify Father Serra, who died here in 1784 after establishing nine missions. Allowed to fall to ruins in the 19th century, it is now one of the most authentically restored mission churches in all of California.

Where: The mission trail runs for 600 miles south to north from San Diego to Sonoma. www.missionscalifornia.com. **San Diego de Alcalá:** Tel 619-281-8449; www.missionsandiego.com. **San Juan Capistrano:** Tel 949-234-1300; www.missionsjc.com. **San Buenaventura:** Tel 805-643-4318; www.sanbuenaventuramission.org. **Santa Barbara:** Tel 805-682-4713; www.sbmission.org. **San Carlos Borroméo:** Tel 831-624-1271; www.carmelmission.org. **Best times:** at Mission San Juan Capistrano: mid-Mar for migrating swallows with parade and festivities; Sat evenings Jun–Sep for Music Under the Stars summer concerts; Dec for Christmas celebration.

Napa and Sonoma: America's Premier Vineyards

California Wine Country

California, U.S.A.

If America has an answer to Tuscany—our own locus for great wine, great food, and the good life—Napa and Sonoma valleys are it. These fraternal twins, separated at birth by the Mayacamas Mountains, now bask in international recognition among oenophiles. Together they produce about 10 percent of the world's wines.

The 35-mile-long arc of Napa to the east is the better known and more densely populated: Three hundred–plus wineries lie along Highway 29 and the scenic Silverado Trail, taking advantage of the area's sunny days, cool nights, and long growing season.

Crowd-pleasing wineries include powerhouse Robert Mondavi Winery in Oakville; Francis Ford Coppola's Rutherford's Rubicon Estate; Yountville's Domaine Chandon; and Sterling Vineyards, near Calistoga. But don't overlook smaller gems like Schramsberg, in Calistoga, and Swanson Vineyards, in Rutherford. Board the Napa Valley Wine Train, a 3-hour journey in restored 1915-era Pullman cars, which runs 36 miles from Napa to St. Helena, past 27 wineries.

Visitors from San Francisco often come for the day, but to truly appreciate Napa, stay awhile. Rooms at Meadowood, with its rambling main lodge and cottagelike suites get snapped up the first week of June by attendees of the Napa Valley Wine Auction, the world's most soigné charity wine event.

The more intimate Auberge du Soleil is perched on a hillside dotted with olive trees and features both an excellent spa and an acclaimed restaurant. You won't want to leave the leafy 33-acre grounds, but to further enjoy the valley's gastronomy, there's perhaps no better choice than the legendary French Laundry. Neighboring competition is fierce these days, but Chef Thomas Keller's nine-course tasting menu is culinary theater, making it one of the top restaurants in the world. Its more relaxed sister restaurant, Bouchon, serves classic bistro fare. Other longtime wine country standouts include Mustard's Grill, in Yountville, and St. Helena's Terra and Tra Vigne.

Foodies share Napa with spa lovers, drawn by the famed mud baths of Calistoga. Its most luxurious option is Calistoga Ranch, with 46 cedar-shingle guest lodges and hot springs. Decidedly more low-key is the nonprofit Harbin Hot Springs, known as the birthplace of "watsu" (water shiatsu).

The Sonoma Valley is recognized as the birthplace of California's wine industry.

Sonoma, located to the west, is lusher, greener, and cooler than Napa, and known for California's best chardonnays and pinot noirs. It still retains many orchards and farms, which specialize in olive oil, lamb, and artisanal cheeses that complement the vintages produced by the county's 250-plus wineries.

Sonoma Valley's oldest city is Sonoma, centered around a shady plaza and an 1824 adobe mission. Buena Vista, one of California's first estate wineries, was established in 1857 a couple of miles northeast of here. Sonoma is also home to a host of popular eateries, such as the informal The Girl and the Fig, where fresh local ingredients occupy center stage.

A sprawling pink Fairmont Sonoma Mission Inn and Spa has been the region's most luxurious place to stay since it opened in 1927, one of a handful of resorts here to have its own hot springs. Nearby in Glen Ellen, Gaige House Inn, a Queen Anne Victorian dating to 1890, is now one of the country's finest B&Bs.

Sonoma's northern Russian River Valley is anchored by the lovely town of Healdsburg. Its historic town square is flanked by the Hotel Healdsburg, where guests come for the spa but particularly for acclaimed chef Charlie Palmer's Dry Creek Kitchen. Nearby, the exquisite Les Mars Hotel evokes the inns of France; add to that its excellent restaurant, Cyrus, and you have one of Sonoma's finest overnight addresses. Foodies flock to the less pricey Madrona Manor, surrounded by gardens and cool woods, for its cutting-edge restaurant.

WHERE: Napa and Sonoma are 40–70 miles north of San Francisco. **VISITOR INFO:** www.napavalley.com; www.sonomacounty.com. **NAPA VALLEY WINE TRAIN:** Tel 800-427-4124 or 707-253-2111; winetrain.com. *Cost:* from $50. **MEADOWOOD:** Tel 800-458-8080 or 707-963-3646; www.meadowood.com. *Cost:* from $475. **AUBERGE DU SOLEIL:** Tel 800-348-5406 or 707-963-1211; www.aubergedusoleil.com. *Cost:* from $550 (off-peak), from $750 (peak); dinner $60. **FRENCH LAUNDRY:** Tel 707-944-2380; www.frenchlaundry.com. *Cost:* 9-course tasting menu $240. **BOUCHON:** Tel 707-944-8037; www.bouchonbistro.com. *Cost:* dinner $50. **MUSTARD'S GRILL:** Tel 707-944-2424; www.mustardsgrill.com. *Cost:* dinner $50. **TERRA:** Tel 707-963-8931; www.terrarestaurant.com. *Cost:* dinner $60. **TRA VIGNE:** Tel 707-963-4444; www.travignerestaurant.com. *Cost:* dinner $50. **CALISTOGA RANCH:** Tel 800-942-4220 or 707-254-2800; www.calistogaranch.com. *Cost:* lodges from $565 (off-peak), from $750 (peak). **HARBIN HOT SPRINGS:** Tel 800-622-2477 or 707-987-2477; www.harbin.org. *Cost:* cottages from $170 (off-peak), from $230 (peak); day use from $25. **THE GIRL AND THE FIG:** Tel 707-938-3634; www.thegirlandthefig.com. *Cost:* dinner $45. **FAIRMONT SONOMA MISSION INN:** Tel 866-540-4499 or 707-938-9000; www.fairmont.com/sonoma. *Cost:* from $229 (off-peak), from $359 (peak). **GAIGE HOUSE INN:** Tel 800-935-0237 or 707-935-0237; www.gaige.com. *Cost:* from $200 (off-peak), from $350 (peak). **HOTEL HEALDSBURG:** Tel 800-889-7188 or 707-431-0330; www.hotelhealdsburg.com. *Cost:* from $275 (off-peak), from $360 (peak); dinner $45. **LES MARS HOTEL:** Tel 877-431-1700 or 707-433-4211; www.lesmarshotel.com. *Cost:* from $510. **CYRUS:** Tel 707-433-3311; www.cyrusrestaurant.com.

Cost: 8-course tasting menu $130. **Madrona Manor:** Tel 800-258-4003 or 707-423-4231; www.madronamanor.com. *Cost:* from $250; 4-course prix-fixe dinner $75. **Best times:** Apr–May for wildflowers; 1st week of Jun for the Napa Valley Wine Auction; Jul–Aug for Mondavi Summer Concert Series; Oct–Nov for harvest season.

As Low as You Can Go

Death Valley National Park

California, U.S.A.

Located in the northern reaches of the Mojave Desert, Death Valley National Park is the lowest, driest, and hottest spot in America, with scorching summers that reach 125°F and higher—in July 1913 it topped out at 134°F. Though the heat may be brutal, there's a striking beauty here, from the stark, parched Deadman Pass and Dry Bone Canyon to the soaring drama of Telescope Peak at 11,049 feet. Fifty-one species of mammals, 307 species of birds, and 1,000 species of plants are indigenous to this desiccated land that receives just 2 inches of rain a year.

Death Valley is actually not a valley but a plate of crusty salt flats that have been sinking between two slowly rising mountain ranges. Within the park confines (140 miles across), the most popular sights are Artist's Palette, where mineral deposits have colored the hills orange, pink, purple, and green, and Zabriskie Point, with its views of Sahara-like sand dunes. From mile-high Dante's View, you can see 360 degrees for 100 miles, taking in the highest and lowest points in the Lower 48: Mount Whitney, at 14,491 feet, and Badwater, at 282 feet below sea level. The park's most peculiar happenings take place on the flat, parched lakebed at Racetrack Playa, where boulders weighing as much as 700 pounds sometimes move hundreds of yards at night, with no witnesses or explanation.

Air-conditioned cars and luxury inns have improved on the experience of 19th-century pioneers that gave the area its name in 1849. The best place to stay in the park itself is the 1927 stone and adobe Mission-style Furnace Creek Inn, an oasis of hot springs and palm trees, with a welcoming, spring-fed pool, a restaurant offering cinematic views, and an 18-hole golf course (the lowest in the world). Continue your road trip south to Joshua Tree National Park: 800,000 acres of high desert and one of the most popular rock-climbing areas in the country, with more than 8,000 established routes. Nearby Desert Hot Springs drew the likes of Al Capone, who soothed his nerves at the Two Bunch Palms resort. You too can sink into its pure mineral water that comes out of the earth at 148°F but is cooled before reaching two stone pools set in a tree-shaded grotto.

Where: 120 miles northwest of Las Vegas. Tel 760-786-3200; www.nps.gov/deva. **Furnace Creek:** Tel 800-236-7916 or 760-786-2345; www.furnacecreekresort.com. *Cost:* from $315; greens fees $30 (off-peak), $55 (peak). *When:* mid-Oct–mid-May. **Joshua Tree National Park:** Tel 760-367-5500; www.nps.gov/jotr. **Two Bunch Palms:** Tel 800-472-4334 or 760-329-8791; www.twobunchpalms.com. *Cost:* from $160 (off-peak), from $230 (peak). **Best times:** Oct–May for good weather; mid-Feb–mid-Apr for wildflowers; dawn and late afternoon for dramatic views.

A Tale of Two Spas

Golden Door and Cal-a-Vie

Escondido and Vista, California, U.S.A.

Workaholics can recharge and reconnect with their minds and bodies at either of Southern California's top spa destinations, which are among the best in the country. The better known of the two is the venerable Golden Door, established in 1958 as the first wellness destination to combine nascent American fitness concepts with European body treatments, and long a top choice for Hollywood A-listers. Inspired by centuries-old ryokan-style Japanese inns, it's set on 377 decidedly Zen acres, complete with meditative sand gardens, elevated wooden paths, and koi ponds. It serves a mere 40 guests, usually all women, but men take over the place during a few special weeks each year. Activities range from hikes at sunrise to in-room massages and breakfast in bed (many ingredients come from the Door's own gardens). A staff-to-guest ratio of four to one helps guarantee a reinvigorated new you.

The even more blatantly luxurious Cal-a-Vie Health Spa accommodates only 30 guests at one time and promises a five-to-one staff-to-guest ratio, not to mention spectacular views of California hills from every vantage point. In addition to spa treatments, the 200-acre property promotes health through its state-of-the-art fitness pavilion loaded with enough contraptions to work out a lifetime's worth of wound-up minds and muscles. Like the Golden Door, it has all-inclusive rates—even providing workout clothes—but Cal-a-Vie offers shorter packages for those who can't disappear for a full week.

Golden Door: Tel 800-424-0777 or 760-744-5777; www.goldendoor.com. *Cost:* $7,750 per person per week, all-inclusive. **Cal-a-Vie:** Tel 866-772-4283 or 760-945-2055; www.cal-a-vie.com. *Cost:* 3 nights from $4,195 per person, all-inclusive. **Best time:** Sep–May for nicest weather.

"In Los Angeles, by the time you're 35, you're older than most of the buildings."—Delia Ephron

Los Angeles

California, U.S.A.

If one city characterizes the American Dream, it's Los Angeles. Over the years, it has been a magnet for countless dreamers who come here to remake themselves (for every hopeful starlet, there are scores of new immigrants) in the land of year-round sunshine and commercialized make-believe. As the entertainment capital of America, L.A. is filled with unexpected contrasts, but it's an equal-opportunity Dream Machine that celebrates the fine arts and kitsch with parallel enthusiasm, and embraces dining temples and food trucks with the same aplomb.

Top Attractions

Getty Center and Getty Villa—The 110-acre, six-building Getty Center, designed by architect Richard Meier and opened in 1997, holds the J. Paul Getty Museum's enormous collection of pre-20th-century European art as well as photography from all over the world. A commanding hilltop citadel of glass and off-white travertine, the center is a work of art itself and rates as one of the world's premiere art complexes.

The Getty Villa, near Malibu, was built by the American oil billionaire as a fantastic re-creation of Classical architecture: It is modeled after a majestic 2nd century B.C. villa near Pompeii. Set at the edge of the Pacific amid manicured gardens, it's now home to the J. Paul Getty Museum's extraordinary collection of Greek, Etruscan, and Roman antiquities. **Getty Center** and **Getty Villa:** Tel 310-440-7300; www.getty.edu.

Los Angeles County Museum of Art & Museum Row—The largest art museum in the western U.S., with a staggering trove of 150,000 objects dating from ancient times to the present, the Los Angeles County Museum of Art (LACMA) is undergoing an expansion and renovation known as the Transformation. With the recent debuts of an open-air pavilion and two new structures designed by architect Renzo Piano, the 20-acre, seven-building complex now features a host of rotating exhibits that draw from its collection of contemporary American art as well as its abundant holdings of historic art and artifacts from around the globe. LACMA is also a center for live music, with chamber concerts on Sunday evenings, jazz (Friday evenings April–November) and Latin (Saturday afternoons May–September), all free.

LACMA stands on a stretch of Wilshire Boulevard known as Museum Row, with four other excellent museums within two blocks, including the Architecture and Design Museum, the Craft and Folk Art Museum, and the Petersen Automotive Museum. But for an only-in-L.A. experience, head to the Page Museum at La Brea Tar Pits, where pools of bubbling liquid asphalt have trapped and preserved the remains of Ice Age mammals, such as the saber-toothed cats, dire wolves, ground sloths, and mammoths, who once roamed these parts. **Los Angeles County Museum of Art:** Tel 323-857-6000; www.lacma.org. **Page Museum and La Brea Tar Pits:** Tel 323-934-7243; www.tarpits.org.

Frank Gehry designed the Walt Disney Concert Hall's swooping curves and stainless steel exterior.

Walt Disney Concert Hall and the Los Angeles Philharmonic—Since its debut in 2003, the soaring Walt Disney Concert Hall has become downtown L.A.'s dazzling landmark, courtesy of architect Frank Gehry. An undulating mass of shiny steel that seems to billow like a ship at full sail, it offers marvelous state-of-the-art acoustics for the resident Los Angeles Philharmonic Orchestra, now under the youthful baton of superstar conductor Gustavo Dudamel. Visit the Disney in style: Come early for drinks or a meal at Patina, one of L.A.'s top French restaurants, then attend a concert and experience the hall at full throttle. In summer, follow the L.A.

Philharmonic as it heads outdoors for a series of evening concerts at the Hollywood Bowl, the fabulous amphitheater in the Hollywood hills that's been a Tinseltown tradition since 1922. **Walt Disney Concert Hall:** Tel 323-850-2000; www.laphil.com. **Patina:** Tel 213-972-3331; www.patinagroup.com. *Cost:* dinner $85. **Hollywood Bowl:** Tel 323-850-2000; www.hollywoodbowl.com.

Downtown L.A.—Long a snoozy high-rise business center, Downtown, in the best SoCal tradition, has had a makeover. The multivenue Music Center is the city's top performing-arts venue; its 11-acre campus comprises the Walt Disney Concert Hall (see previous page), the Dorothy Chandler Pavilion (home of the Los Angeles Opera and former site of the Academy Awards), the Ahmanson Theater, and the Mark Taper Forum, L.A.'s cutting-edge theater.

Just a block away is the two-building Museum of Contemporary Art (MOCA), which holds an outstanding permanent collection of American and European works, from abstract expressionism and pop art to the latest in conceptual and digital creations.

The imposing Cathedral of Our Lady of the Angels, opened in 2002, is considered a stunning example of modern ecclesiastical architecture. The interior is gloriously meditative, all soaring space and alabaster-filtered light.

Flanking Downtown are long-established immigrant neighborhoods—Chinatown, Little Tokyo, and the Mexican enclave along Olvera Street. Explore them for inexpensive, authentic ethnic food, or head to the Grand Central Market, L.A.'s largest and oldest open-air emporium, where bustling stalls and informal eateries draw an amazingly diverse crowd.

If you can score a ticket to an L.A. Lakers game, you'll see another cross section of Angelenos, including perhaps such courtside celebrities as Jack Nicholson and Leonardo DiCaprio. The Lakers play at the Staples Center, also adjacent to L.A. Live—a complex of restaurants, cinemas, and the very cool Grammy Museum. **Visitor info:** www.downtownla.com. **Music Center:** Tel 323-850-2000; www.musiccenter.org. **Museum of Contemporary Art:** Tel 213-626-6222; www.moca.org. **Our Lady of the Angels:** Tel 213-680-5200; www.olacathedral.org. **Grand Central Market:** Tel 213-624-2378; www.grandcentralsquare.com. **The Staples Center:** Tel 213-742-7340; www.staplescenter.com. **L.A. Live:** Tel 213-763-5483; www.lalive.com.

The iconic Hollywood sign is 350 feet long.

Hollywood—Show-biz pioneers Cecil B. DeMille, D. W. Griffith, and Jesse Lasky put Hollywood on the map in the 1920s as a town synonymous with glamour and ambition. In the 1930s, most of the city's production studios decamped north to the San Fernando Valley, and for a number of years the area largely traded on its glorious past. But like a faded star, Hollywood has had a face-lift.

Nevertheless, most of the stars you will see on Hollywood Boulevard (premieres aside) are those embedded in the sidewalk—the mile-long Hollywood Walk of Fame honors over 2,400 legends of entertainment. Revel in Old Hollywood glitz at Grauman's Chinese Theatre, an astonishingly ornate movie palace from 1927 that's still in business, but is most noted for its impressive collection of handprints and footprints of Hollywood heavyweights. Grauman's is also the pickup spot for Hollywood's most popular bus tour: Sure it's cheesy, but you know you can't resist Starline's 2-hour movie-star homes drive. Just up Hollywood Boulevard is where you can join another popular outing, the delightfully macabre (and rather naughty)

Dearly Departed Tour. Ride in the "Tomb Buggy" to visit sites of celebrity scandal (Hugh Grant, George Michael) and death (Michael Jackson, Janis Joplin, River Phoenix).

The Hollywood Museum, housed in the original Max Factor Building, offers another glimpse of the past. The Art Deco landmark is filled with over 10,000 items from the glory days: You'll see sets, costumes, and props from hundreds of movies, including Cleopatra's tunics and Hannibal Lecter's jail cell. Be sure to stop by the restored Max Factor salons and dressing rooms, where Marilyn Monroe went to have her roots touched up.

Breathing new life into Tinseltown is the Hollywood and Highland Center, a grand hotel, entertainment, and shopping complex. The center's focal point is the 3,400-seat Kodak Theatre, which opened in 2001 as the new home of the Academy Awards. Tours give you a chance to tread the red carpet, ogle an Oscar statuette, and peek into VIP rooms.

And don't forget to look for that famous "Hollywood" sign. The best view is from the corner of Sunset Boulevard and Bronson Avenue: Get your cameras out! **Hollywood Walk of Fame:** Tel 323-467-6412; www.hollywoodchamber.net. **Grauman's Chinese Theatre:** Tel 323-464-8111; www.manntheatres.com. **Starline Movie Stars' Home Tours:** Tel 800-959-3131 or 323-463-3333; www.starlinetours.com. **Dearly Departed Tour:** Tel 800-979-3370 or 212-209-3370; dearlydepartedtours.com. **Hollywood Museum:** Tel 323-464-7776; www.thehollywoodmuseum.com. **Hollywood and Highland Center:** www.hollywoodandhighland.com. **Kodak Theatre:** Tel 323-308-6300; www.kodaktheatre.com.

Beverly Hills—Though less than 6 square miles, Beverly Hills looms large in the world's collective imagination as the epitome of glamour and prestige. The city's commercial heart is the three-block-long "Golden Triangle" (bounded by Santa Monica Boulevard, Wilshire Boulevard, and Canon Drive). Here you'll find one of the world's most exclusive shopping districts, Rodeo (that's pronounced ro-DAY-oh) Drive, with such big-ticket jewelers as Tiffany & Co. and Harry Winston, plus every imaginable designer, from Armani to Zegna. The Paley Center for Media is a shrine to how most Beverly Hills residents made their fortunes. Visitors can request a favorite show from the archive of more than 150,000 television and radio programs and view or listen to them in a private cubicle.

Up on Sunset Boulevard, the legendary Beverly Hills Hotel, aka the "Pink Palace," has everything a fashionable and rich traveler could wish for, from a showy pool scene to bungalows with butler service. Its forever-popular Polo Lounge has long been the place where Hollywood makes and breaks its deals, and the Fountain Coffee Room, with its palm-patterned wallpaper, has that potent 1940s charm. **Visitor info:** www.lovebeverlyhills.org. **Paley Center for Media:** Tel 310-786-1000; www.paleycenter.org. **Beverly Hills Hotel:** Tel 800-283-8885 or 310-276-2251; www.beverlyhillshotel.com. *Cost:* from $450, dinner $65.

Santa Monica—Elegant, laid-back Santa Monica is a pedestrian-friendly city fronting onto the Pacific that feels much more than just 15 miles from central L.A. The downtown area, only minutes from the water, is centered on the Third Street Promenade, a pedestrian mall lined with shops, cafés, and movie theaters (and, on Wednesdays and Saturdays, a bustling farmers market). A block off the promenade is one of L.A.'s top Mexican restaurants, Border Grill, helmed by Mary Sue Milliken and Susan Feniger, the chef duo known through their TV shows and cookbooks as the Too Hot Tamales.

Head to the beach, dominated by the 1909 Santa Monica Pier, with its classic carnival rides, seashell souvenir shops, and, best of all, genuine 1920s carousel. Within sight of the pier—and one of only two hotels directly on the ocean—is the delightful Shutters on the Beach, which manages to combine the vibe of an upscale beach house (all rooms have balconies that let in the sound of the surf) with the amenities its VIP guests have come to expect, including a luxurious spa and seaside meals. The hotel's One Pico and Coast Beach Café and Bar are also ideal spots for drinks at sunset. **Third Street Promenade:** www.thirdstreetpromenade.com. **Border Grill:** Tel 310-451-1655; www.bordergrill.com. *Cost:* dinner $40. **Santa Monica Pier:** Tel 310-458-8900; www.santamonicapier.org. **Shutters on the Beach:** Tel 310-458-0030; www.shuttersonthebeach.com. *Cost:* from $495.

Venice and Venice Beach—While most of L.A. takes itself very seriously, Venice is indulgently bohemian and not just a little oddball. Famous for its beachfront spectacle, Venice was founded in 1905 by developer Abbott Kinney, who envisioned a suburban replica of Venice, Italy, complete with canals and gondolas. Though some canals still exist, they're not nearly as noteworthy as the city's famed 3-mile-long Venice Beach boardwalk, a paved promenade that runs alongside the white sand beaches. With its inexpensive cafés and its stalls selling sunglasses and tie-dyed clothes, it's a carnival of tattooed humanity, where street musicians, muscle men, Rollerbladers, bikini-clad posers, surfers, and a few classic Southern California freaks are perpetually on parade. Hipsters meet for roof-top drinks at the beach-view Hotel Erwin, a stylish, minimalist hotel that's as arty and high-spirited as the neighborhood. **Visitor info:** www.venicebeach.com. **Hotel Erwin:** Tel 800-786-7789 or 310-452-1111; www.jdvhotels.com. *Cost:* from $179.

Studio Tours—In L.A., it's simply called The Industry. Movies and TV are what make this town tick, and touring the film studios delivers fascinating insights into what goes on behind the camera. Hollywood is where it all started, but of the major studios, only Paramount Pictures still makes movies right in town. Two-hour VIP tours (by reservation only) of this last holdout take you behind the sets and soundstages where such classics as *I Love Lucy*, *Sunset Boulevard*, and *Friends* were created.

Universal Studios' backlot tour is one of its signature attractions.

Most of the other movie and TV studios are north of L.A., in the San Fernando Valley, where the big name in tours is Universal Studios. You can take an hour-long tram tour through sets for *Psycho*, *War of the Worlds*, and *Desperate Housewives*, among many others, as part of their all-in-one theme-park extravaganza (which also includes a 3-D film experience, a visit to a special-effects stage, TV- and movie-themed rides, plus a shopping, dining, and entertainment complex). At Warner Bros., the roughly two-and-a-half-hour Studio VIP Tour is customized whenever possible to include a visit to an active soundstage or film set. **Paramount Pictures:** Tel 323-956-1777; www.paramountstudios.com. **Universal Studios:** Tel 818-622-3801; www.universalstudioshollywood.com. **Warner Bros.:** Tel 818-972-8687; vipstudiotour.warnerbros.com.

Where to Stay

Hotel Bel-Air—The Mission-style Hotel Bel-Air is one of L.A.'s finest and most exclusive addresses, its allure intact after a multimillion-dollar refurbishment that added new canyon-view rooms and suites and a La Prairie spa. Since 1947, the hotel, with its 12 acres of junglelike gardens, swan-studded ponds, and hidden villas, has been the spot where the show-business elite come to seek anonymity and respite. **Info:**

Tel 800-648-4097 or 310-472-1211; www.hotelbelair.com. *Cost:* from $565.

Chateau Marmont—A long-standing favorite in lively West Hollywood, the Chateau Marmont is perched above Sunset Strip, at the very center of the action. Built in 1927 to resemble a Loire Valley castle, the Marmont is rambling and romantic, managing to seem at once old-school and hip. No wonder its quirky, apartment-like guest rooms and secluded bungalows are the top pick for young A-listers. The hotel's reputation for discretion even in the face of outrageous celebrity behavior (this is where comic John Belushi overdosed at age 33) hasn't changed since the days when studio boss Harry Cohn told William Holden and Glenn Ford, "If you must get into trouble, do it at the Marmont." **Info:** Tel 800-242-8328 or 323-656-1010; www.chateaumarmont.com. *Cost:* from $415.

Hollywood Roosevelt Hotel—While the Hollywood Roosevelt Hotel hails from 1927 (it even hosted the first Academy Awards in 1929), it recently underwent a massive face-lift from which it emerged still historic but happening. Among the updates: swank, bachelor-pad-like guest rooms, a bit of gloss added to the high-beamed Art Deco lobby, a David Hockney mural by the pool, and a pair of uberpopular bars brimming with Hollywood's young and lovely. **Info:** Tel 800-950-7667 or 323-466-7000; www.hollywoodroosevelt.com. *Cost:* from $259.

The Standard, Downtown L.A.—The Standard sets the (ahem) standard for chic downtown hotels, with a playful mid-century stylishness that's sexy and inviting. Hotelier-to-the-stars Andre Balazs took the 1955 former headquarters of Standard Oil and transformed it into a bastion of cool, injecting a decided bit of swagger into this once dowdy part of town. Best of all, there's a room type for nearly every budget (Medium, Huge, and Wow! are some of your options). Join the young, well-dressed types sipping trendy cocktails in the roof-top lounge amid a thicket of soaring towers. **Info:** Tel 213-892-8080; www.standardhotels.com/los-angeles. *Cost:* from $285.

Sunset Marquis Hotel and Villas—There are L.A. hotels with outsized reputations, where celebs (and wannabes) go to see and be seen, and then there's the Sunset Marquis in West Hollywood. The property made its name as a sanctuary for rock stars (in fact, award-winning artists still come here to lay down tracks in the on-site recording studio) and, decades later, it continues to uphold its reputation as a luxe-yet-low-key home away from home for the cognoscenti. The recent 5-acre expansion and top-to-toe renovation means there's a new restaurant and spa, plus coolly updated Mediterranean-style villas and suites. Who would know this secluded tropical oasis is just steps from Sunset Strip? **Info:** Tel 310-657-1333; www.sunsetmarquis.com. *Cost:* from $285.

Eating & Drinking

The Bazaar by José Andrés—Beverly Hills is the perfect backdrop for José Andrés's inventive cooking, a blend of tradition and fantasy that flawlessly fits the SoCal zeitgeist. Located in the splashy SLS Hotel, the playful Philippe Starck–designed dining room has multiple personalities, as does the menu, which offers straight-from-Seville-style tapas along with more avant-garde offerings, such as cotton candy fois gras and Caprese salad with liquid mozzarella. Andrés's sophisticated food is always vividly flavorful and exciting to look at: An evening at The Bazaar is equal parts gastronomy and theater. **Info:** Tel 310-246-5555; www.thebazaar.com. *Cost:* dinner $60.

Lucques/AOC—Contemporary Mediterranean-style cooking reaches its zenith at Lucques (pronounced LUKE), where chef Suzanne Goin uses farm-fresh produce and an instinctive finesse to create a cuisine that is at once classic and of-the-moment. Lucques is housed in the former carriage house of silent-era star Harold Lloyd—it's an atmospheric West Hollywood spot to enjoy such dishes as summer melon gazpacho with crispy prosciutto and mustard-grilled chicken with Parmesan pudding. Goin and sommelier/partner Caroline Styne operate a number of other restaurants in L.A., including a gem of a wine bar, AOC, which dazzles with exquisite small plates that rely on house-made charcuterie, wood-oven specialties, and a cheese selection to make you swoon. **Lucques:** Tel 323-655-6277; www.lucques.com. *Cost:* dinner $65. **AOC:** Tel 323-653-6359. *Cost:* dinner $45.

Nobu West Hollywood—While top Japanese chef Nobu Matsuhisa claims outposts around the world, his West Hollywood address just may be the most lushly atmospheric and romantic space in which to enjoy his famed mix of superb sushi and fish specialties (black cod and miso is a signature), served with a Latin American twist. Be sure to try the sashimi tacos. **Info:** Tel 310-657-5711; www.nobu restaurants.com. *Cost:* dinner $70.

Osteria Mozza/Pizzeria Mozza—The fruit of a collaboration among superstar baker Nancy Silverton (of La Brea Bakery and formerly of Campanile) and celebrity New York restaurateurs Mario Batali and Joseph Bastianich, this pair of eateries is an immensely popular one-two punch of Italian gastronomy. The Osteria offers an almost epic menu that's notable for its exuberant flavors and gusto—choices include tagliatelle with oxtail ragu and pancetta-wrapped quail with sage and honey. Around the corner, the always packed Pizzeria is an unpretentious spot to enjoy the slice of a lifetime: sublime crust and just-so toppings. **Osteria Mozza:** Tel 323-297-0100; www.mozza-la.com. *Cost:* dinner $70. **Pizzeria Mozza:** Tel 323-297-0101. *Cost:* pizza $15.

Sona/Comme Ça—Award-winning chef David Myers's flagship restaurant, Sona, grounded in the finest of local, organic products, shoots for the stars in terms of culinary experience. Myers employs strikingly unusual preparations and combinations of flavors to achieve his brand of transcendence: Seared foie gras is served with frozen banana and green tea crackers; fried lemon meringue pie comes with English peas and popcorn ice cream. Myers also operates the convivial brasserie Comme Ça, where he uses his protean creativity to update classic French comfort food. **Sona:** Tel 310-659-7708; www..sonarestaurant.com. *Cost:* dinner $70. **Comme Ça:** Tel 323-782-1178; www.comme carestaurant.com. *Cost:* dinner $45.

Spago Beverly Hills/CUT—The flagship of Wolfgang Puck's restaurant empire, Spago Beverly Hills continues to dazzle and set the standard for inventive California cuisine, a style of cooking that Puck (and Spago) played a large part in creating. Spago's most coveted tables are on the patio beneath the century-old olive trees, though the comfortably formal dining room is also an enchanting place to experience such stellar dishes as beet and goat cheese layer-cake salad or handmade agnolotti with sweet corn and mascarpone. Puck's new venture, CUT, reinvents the steak house in the Beverly Wilshire Hotel's stylish, Richard Meier–designed dining room. **Spago:** Tel 310-385-0880; www.wolf gangpuck.com. *Cost:* dinner $80. **CUT:** Tel 310-276-8500. *Cost:* dinner $95.

Classic L.A. Dining—L.A.'s motto is "Out with the old, in with the new"—except when it comes to much-loved dining establishments. Hollywood's oldest restaurant, Musso and Frank Grill, is a wood-paneled, red leather–boothed throwback to the city's glory days, a Hollywood hot spot that has been the place to get steak-house fare and straight-up martinis since 1919—served by waiters who just might have been working on opening day. Older still, the casual, sawdust-on-the-floors Philippe the Original claims to be the spot where, in 1908, the French Dip sandwich was invented. It certainly perfected it, with delicious thinly sliced beef (pork, ham, turkey, and lamb are options too) sandwiched in a French roll and accompanied by a savory dipping sauce. In the Fairfax area, experience L.A.'s diversity at the vibrant Farmers Market—the city's favorite open-air dining bazaar. Favorites include tacos at Lotteria Grill, classic pies at Du-par's, fresh seafood at the Gumbo Pot, and coffee at Bob's Donuts. Nearby, at Pink's hot dog shack, opened by Paul and Betty Pink in 1939, you can still order a hot dog drowned in Betty's secret chili sauce—it's one of nearly three dozen variations on the menu. In Beverly Hills, you'll find several great delis, including Nate & Al's, a favorite of Groucho Marx and Doris Day (and the breakfast choice of Larry King), and especially beloved for its roast beef brisket with potato pancakes. **Musso and Frank Grill:** Tel 323-467-5123; www.mussoandfrankgrill.com. *Cost:* dinner $50. **Philippe the Original:** Tel 213-628-3781; www.phillipes.com. *Cost:* lunch $8. **Farmers Market:** Tel 323-933-9211; www.farmersmarketla.com. **Pink's:** Tel 323-931-4223; www.pinkshollywood.com. *Cost:* lunch $6. **Nate & Al's:** Tel 310-274-0101; www.natenal.com. Cost: lunch $10.

Sleeping Beauty Castle provides a fairy-tale gateway to Disney's Fantasyland.

Day Trips

Disneyland and Disney California Adventure—Filmmaker Walt Disney's family-oriented theme park, established in 1955, was initially dismissed as "Walt's Folly." Today it's a vast resort attracting nearly 15 million visitors yearly and encompassing two amusement parks (Disneyland and the newer Disney California Adventure), a shopping and entertainment area (Downtown Disney), and three hotels. Join the lines for favorite rides, such as Pirates of the Caribbean, the Haunted Mansion, and the white-knuckle roller-coaster Space Mountain. Disney California Adventure, across from the entrance plaza, celebrates the state's history and natural splendor. Its new attractions include Toy Story Mania and the World of Color, a music-and-special-effects show, which plays against a backdrop of 1,200 fountains shooting water over 200 feet high. **Where:** 26 miles southeast of L.A. near Anaheim. Tel 714-781-7290; disneyland.disney.go.com. *Cost:* 1-day/1-park ticket $75 (ages 3–9), $80 (ages 10 and up).

Huntington Library, Art Collections and Botanical Gardens—One of the country's greatest cultural treasures, the Huntington Library, Art Collections and Botanical Gardens was founded in 1919 by rail baron Henry Huntington and his wife, Arabella, both inveterate collectors. Their 207-acre hilltop Italianate estate holds claim to an extraordinary array of treasures, including a Gutenberg Bible from the 15th century and the earliest-known manuscript of Chaucer's *Canterbury Tales*. Gainsborough's *Blue Boy*, Sir Thomas Lawrence's *Pinkie*, and other masterpieces of British, French, and American art are also on display. Head outside to drink in the lush landscaping, including the beautiful Japanese garden and the Rose Garden's 1,000-variety display, which you can also view from the museum's much loved tearoom. **Where:** 15 miles southwest of Downtown L.A. Tel 626-405-2100; www.huntington.org.

Highway to Heaven

The Pacific Coast Highway and Big Sur

California, U.S.A.

The Pacific Coast Highway is America's dream drive, offering two lanes through gorgeously isolated terrain, and frequent turnoffs and vantage points to soak in the astounding beauty. You can head south from L.A. (see p. 716) to San Diego (see next page), or take the traditionalist's route north to San Francisco (see p. 727) and beyond.

A landmark along the Pacific Coast Highway, the Lone Cypress is over 250 years old.

From L.A., head west to Santa Monica, then follow the coast to Malibu where you'll already feel a world away. Seventy miles up the road, you'll skirt the environs of Santa Barbara, known as the American Riviera, where the Queen of the Missions (see p. 712), founded in 1782, stands. Stop for divine tacos and tamales at La Super-Rica Taqueria or stay the night at the San Ysidro Ranch, a 500-acre rustic-chic hideaway of lush gardens, hillside bungalows, and a restaurant, the Stonehouse, that has won every award in the book. Here the fabled PCH begins to unfurl at its most majestic, an awesome ribbon of highway 500 to 1,000 feet above the roaring Pacific. The highlight: the 90-mile stretch from San Simeon, past Big Sur, and on to the Monterey Peninsula.

San Simeon's Hearst Castle, a 165-room Mediterranean Revival–style spectacle, was built by publishing titan William Randolph Hearst, and was the model for Orson Welles's over-the-top home in *Citizen Kane*. Spend the night in the nearby artists community of Cambria, where J. Patrick House B&B exudes a relaxed country-coastal vibe.

Fiercely protected by its 1,500 residents, Big Sur is a natural masterpiece with a staggering drama about it. Take it in at Pfeiffer State Beach and from your windshield as you snake along the edge of the Santa Lucia mountains. Stop for lunch at Nepenthe's outdoor patio, suspended 800 feet above the surf, or stay at the dramatically situated Post Ranch Inn, with its grand vistas of the Pacific 1,200 feet below. Across the highway, the Ventana Inn & Spa offers the same casual luxury and middle-of-nature feel. For an infinitely more affordable sum, consider Deetjen's Big Sur Inn, offering old-fashioned comfort since the 1930s.

Head north to the Monterey Peninsula and Carmel-by-the-Sea, home to the landmark 1771 Carmel Mission (see p. 712). Clint

Eastwood, former mayor and one-time proprietor of the Hog's Breath Inn, still owns the historic Mission Ranch Inn, housed in an 1850s farmhouse, and occasionally makes an appearance at its popular steak house.

Golfers adore Pebble Beach Resort's four courses, including the famed Pebble Beach Golf Links, consistently ranked the best public course in America. Guests staying at the Lodge at Pebble Beach are within earshot of the Pacific's crashing waves. Nongolfers can enjoy the same views by traveling the legendary 17 Mile Drive, a private toll road connecting the towns of Carmel and Monterey. Check into one of the 10 exquisite rooms at the Tudor-style Monterey Inn. Then head to the Monterey Bay Aquarium, home to over 550 aquatic species, including sea otters, sharks, octupuses, and the improbably beautiful jellyfish.

From Monterey, the PCH winds up to San Francisco, past rocky Point Reyes National Seashore and the 19th-century fishing-town-turned-artists-colony of Mendocino. Though the PCH technically ends in Leggett, it's worth the scenic 40-minute drive up Highway 101 to the Humboldt Redwoods State Park, where ancient, mist-cloaked trees line the 31-mile-long Avenue of the Giants.

WHERE: PCH runs approx 655 miles from Southern California north to Leggett. www.byways.org. **LA SUPER-RICA TAQUERIA:** Tel 805-963-4940. *Cost:* lunch $6. **SAN YSIDRO RANCH:** Tel 800-368-6788 or 805-565-1700; www.sanysidroranch.com. *Cost:* from $650; dinner $65. **HEARST CASTLE:** Tel 800-444-4445 or 916-414-8400; www.hearstcastle.com. **J. PATRICK HOUSE:** Tel 800-341-5258 or 805-927-3812; www.jpatrickhouse.com. *Cost:* from $170. **NEPENTHE:** Tel 831-667-2345; www.nepenthebigsur.com. *Cost:* dinner $40. **POST RANCH INN:** Tel 800-527-2200 or 831-667-2200; www.postranchinn.com. *Cost:* from $595 (off-peak), from $750 (peak). **VENTANA INN:** Tel 800-628-6500 or 831-667-2331; www.ventanainn.com. *Cost:* from $400. **DEETJEN'S:** Tel 831-667-2377; www.deetjens.com. *Cost:* from $90. **MISSION RANCH:** Tel 800-538-8221 or 831-624-6436; www.missionranchcarmel.com. *Cost:* from $135; dinner $45. **LODGE AT PEBBLE BEACH:** Tel 800-654-9300 or 831-624-3811; www.pebblebeach.com. *Cost:* from $715; greens fees from $110. **OLD MONTEREY INN:** Tel 800-350-2344 or 831-375-8284; www.oldmontereyinn.com. *Cost:* from $239. **MONTEREY BAY AQUARIUM:** Tel 831-648-4800; www.mbayaq.org. **HUMBOLDT REDWOODS STATE PARK:** Tel 707-946-2263; www.humboldtredwoods.org. **BEST TIMES:** Apr–May and Sep–Oct for nicest weather; mid-Sep for Monterey Jazz Festival; Dec–Feb for whale-watching.

Animal Attraction by the Sea

THE SAN DIEGO ZOO

San Diego, California, U.S.A.

The world-famous San Diego Zoo, with more than 4,000 animals representing 800 species, dates back to 1916, when it set the standard for wildlife conservation around the world. Two of the most popular exhibits spread among 100 well-tended acres are Elephant Odyssey (the playful Cha Cha is the draw) and the Giant Panda Research Center, whose main attraction, the adorable Yun Zi, was born in 2009. Other exotic residents of the zoo are the orangutans of Indonesia, and creatures rarely seen in captivity, including tree kangaroos, and giant tortoises from the Galápagos.

The zoo is the centerpiece of Balboa Park, a verdant 1,200-acre recreational area and the largest cultural park in the country. Its 14 museums, housed in beautiful Spanish-Moorish buildings, were constructed for the 1915 Panama-California Exposition. Wildlife viewing continues 35 miles away at the 1,800-acre San Diego Safari Park (a sister facility of the San Diego Zoo), home to hundreds of different species—African lions, white rhino, warthogs, and cheetah—that roam freely in vast enclosures, creating a safari-like experience. Wild creatures also abound at SeaWorld San Diego, where five species of dolphins, sea lions, and a number of orcas including Shamu all pirouette and perform in what is widely considered America's premier showplace for marine life.

Stay at the timeless Hotel del Coronado, famous for hosting 14 presidents and Marilyn Monroe (when *Some Like It Hot* was filmed here). Built in 1888, "The Del" towers like a Victorian wedding cake over 2 miles of pristine white beach on the "island" of Coronado that it shares with its sister property, Beach Village at the Del. Stop by the Crown Room, named for the Duke and Duchess of Windsor, who allegedly met there, and sample its world-famous Sunday Brunch. The nearby Glorietta Bay Inn offers a similarly elegant ambience if you reserve a room in the central 1908 mansion. The staff can arrange rentals for bicycles as well as boats for sailing on the bay across the street.

Just 15 miles north of San Diego, the "California Riviera" around La Jolla lures vacationers with its 17 miles of sandy coves sheltered by dramatic cliffs. The bluff-top vantage of the Mediterranean-style La Valencia Hotel overlooks La Jolla Cove, one of the area's most popular swimming spots (for people and sea lions alike). Golfers come here for Torrey Pines golf course, host of the PGA's Buick Invitational and the 2009 Samsung World Championship, and the lucky ones unpack at The Lodge at Torrey Pines, a Craftsman wonder overlooking the course (with an extensive spa for golf widows). Theater buffs enjoy the La Jolla Playhouse, founded in 1947 by Hollywood luminaries such as Gregory Peck, Dorothy McGuire, and Mel Ferrer, and winner of a Tony Award for America's Outstanding Regional Theater.

WHERE: 120 miles south of Los Angeles. **SAN DIEGO ZOO:** Tel 619-231-1515; www.sandiegozoo.org. **BALBOA PARK:** Tel 619-239-0512; www.balboapark.org. **SAFARI PARK:** Tel 760-747-8702; www.sandiegozoo.org/park. **SEAWORLD:** Tel 800-257-4268 or 619-226-3901; www.seaworld.com. **HOTEL DEL CORONADO:** Tel 800-468-3533 or 619-435-6611; www.hoteldel.com. *Cost:* from $249; brunch $75. **GLORIETTA BAY INN:** Tel 800-283-9383 or 619-435-3101; www.gloriettabayinn.com. *Cost:* from $190. **LA VALENCIA:** Tel 800-451-0772 or 858-454-0771; www.lavalencia.com. *Cost:* from $300. **TORREY PINES GOLF COURSE:** Tel 800-985-4653 or 858-453-3226; www.torreypinesgolfcourse.com. *Cost:* greens fees from $95. **THE LODGE AT TORREY PINES:** Tel 800-656-0087 or 858-453-4420; www.lodgeattorreypines.com. *Cost:* from $300 (off-peak), from $450 (peak). **LA JOLLA PLAYHOUSE:** Tel 858-550-1010; www.lajollaplayhouse.com. *When:* May–Nov. **BEST TIMES:** Zoo animals are most active in cooler months and early or late in the day; late Jun for La Jolla Festival of the Arts; Jul for U.S. Open Sandcastle Competition; early Aug for San Diego Street Scene; late Dec–mid-Mar for whale-watching.

Trained orcas perform at the 7-million-gallon Shamu Stadium, often splashing audience members seated in the "soak zone."

"One day if I do go to heaven, I'll look around and say, 'It ain't bad, but it ain't San Francisco.'"
—HERB CAEN

SAN FRANCISCO

California, U.S.A.

San Francisco is the city Americans fantasize about, sing about, and leave their heart in, a place of myth and magic on par with Paris and Venice. With a stunning waterfront setting that rivals that of Rio de Janeiro or Cape Town, it is America's most livable big city, with wonderful food, a raft of great hotels, and fascinating and unique neighborhoods, all beloved by its highly individualistic citizenry.

When it opened in 1937, the Golden Gate Bridge laid claim to the world's longest suspension span.

TOP ATTRACTIONS

ALCATRAZ ISLAND—Though closed as a penitentiary since 1963, Alcatraz ("the Rock") remains America's best-known prison, having once housed such notorious criminals as Al Capone, Robert "Machine Gun" Kelly, and Robert "The Birdman" Stroud. Located on a craggy, escape-proof island in San Francisco Bay, this former maximum-security prison, reachable via a 1.5-mile ferry ride, is now a popular half-day trip. For a truly eerie experience, take the night tour, which starts with an incomparable sunset view of the city and bay. **INFO:** Tel 415-561-4900; www.nps.gov/alca. **HOW:** Alcatraz Cruises offers ferries from San Francisco's Pier 33, tel 415-981-7625; www.alcatrazcruises.com.

GOLDEN GATE PARK—One of the country's greatest urban green spaces, 1,000-plus-acre Golden Gate Park is a magical place that brings together towering redwood forests, a Japanese tea garden, the world-class California Academy of Sciences (see p. 729), herds of American bison, and the outstanding de Young Museum (see next page), all linked by footpaths and shady thoroughfares. **INFO:** www.sf-recpark.org.

THE PRESIDIO & GOLDEN GATE BRIDGE—At the far northern end of the San Francisco peninsula, the Presidio has been a fortification since at least 1776, when the Spanish established a garrison here. It remained a military post after the U.S. took control (it was the headquarters of Western Defense Command during World War II), but in 1994 the Army transferred this parklike, 3-square-mile property to the National Park Service. The Presidio is now one of the city's favorite outdoor escapes, with beaches (Baker Beach is clothing optional), coastal trails, and new destinations such as the Disney Family Museum. Rising from the Presidio's tip is the massive 1.7-mile span of the Golden Gate Bridge. An engineering marvel, the bridge is named not for its color (an "international orange" that makes the bridge more visible in fog) but for the Golden Gate Strait it crosses. Traverse the east-side walkway of the bridge for an exhilarating, wind-blasted walk and an enthralling panorama of bay and city. **The Presidio:** Tel 415-561-4323; www.nps.gov/prsf. **Walt Disney Family Museum:** Tel 415-354-6800; www.disney.go.com/disneyatoz/familymuseum. **Golden Gate Bridge:** www.goldengatebridge.org.

San Francisco Ferry Building—The imposing 1898 Ferry Building, with its signature clock tower, is a mighty temple to the region's culinary delights and a showcase for many of Northern California's legendary food purveyors: Cowgirl Creamery, Hog Island Oyster Company, and the fantastic artisan chocolates of Recchiuti Confections, to name a few. At the outdoor farmers market, open Tuesdays, Thursdays, and Saturdays, shoppers jostle for produce just plucked from the field. The Ferry Building is also home to top restaurants such as the Slanted Door, where Charles Phan serves acclaimed Vietnamese cuisine, and Mijita, a taqueria serving crispy Baja-style fish tacos. Plus, it still acts as the hub for ferries to and from Bay Area destinations, including Sausalito. **Info:** Tel 415-693-0996; www.ferrybuildingmarketplace.com. **Slanted Door:** Tel 415-861-8032; www.slanteddoor.com. *Cost:* dinner $50. **Mijita:** Tel 415-399-0814; www.mijitasf.com. *Cost:* lunch $15.

de Young Museum—The de Young Museum's sleekly angular, copper-clad new home, designed by Herzog & de Meuron and opened in 2005, holds the West Coast's foremost collection of art from the Americas, Oceania, and Africa. In addition to these traditional strengths, it has impressive holdings of sculpture and American art—including works by Edward Hopper and Grant Wood—as well as costumes, beautiful Turkmen carpets, and medieval ecclesiastical vestments. **Info:** Tel 415-863-3330; www.deyoung.famsf.org.

Asian Art Museum—As befits a city where over a third of the population claims Asian and Pacific Islander heritage, the Asian Art Museum is the country's largest showcase of Eastern treasures, with 17,000 pieces in its permanent collection. In its new home, a 1917 Beaux Arts building (formerly the city's main library), the dazzling collection spans 6,000 years of works from China (its greatest strength), Japan, Korea, India, Afghanistan, Thailand, and Myanmar. **Info:** Tel 415-581-3500; www.asianart.org.

San Francisco Museum of Modern Art—The San Francisco Museum of Modern Art (SFMoMA), devoted solely to 20th-century art, is housed in a striking structure by Swiss architect Mario Botta, a landmark in the South of Market (SoMa) neighborhood. Among the stars of its collection: paintings by Matisse, O'Keeffe, and Picasso, and photographs by Alfred Stieglitz and Ansel Adams.

On the horizon: a 100,000-square-foot expansion, designed by Norwegian architecture firm Snøhetta to accommodate

SFMoMA moved to its new Mario Botta–designed home in 1995, 60 years after the museum was founded.

the prized contemporary art collection of Gap cofounders Doris and Donald Fisher. **INFO:** Tel 415-357-4000; www.sfmoma.org.

CALIFORNIA ACADEMY OF SCIENCES—In its new Renzo Piano–designed home, the California Academy of Sciences is one of the crowning glories of San Francisco. Located in Golden Gate Park (see p. 727), the Academy encompasses Steinhart Aquarium, Morrison Planetarium, Kimball Natural History Museum, and world-class research and education programs. Under one roof (and a "living" roof at that, with a 197,000-square-foot native plant gardenscape designed to provide natural insulation), you'll journey from a living rain forest to a coral reef ecosystem, and from the ocean depths to the boundaries of space. **INFO:** Tel 415-379-8000; www.calacademy.org.

CHINATOWN—In San Francisco's famed Chinatown—with one of the largest Chinese populations outside Asia—you'll hear more Cantonese and Mandarin than English. Enter this exotic world through a green-roofed, pagoda-style gate that opens onto Grant Avenue, the city's oldest street. Wander Stockton Street's back alleys to see butchers, fishmongers, Chinese herb and tea shops, and a fortune cookie factory on Ross Alley. For a counterpoint to the bustle of the streets, take the elevator in the Chinatown post office to the Kong Chow Temple. This spiritual refuge, filled with incense, gilded altars, and flowers, offers a marvelous view from the balcony. For the best dining, look for places packed with Chinese patrons, such as the R&G Lounge, or if you don't mind sharing a single long table, the House of Nanking, known for its noodles. **VISITOR INFO:** www.sanfranciscochinatown.com. **R&G LOUNGE:** Tel 415-982-7877; www.rnglounge.com. *Cost:* dinner $15. **HOUSE OF NANKING:** Tel 415-421-1429. *Cost:* dinner $18.

NORTH BEACH—This long-time Italian neighborhood is characterized by alfresco café tables, the aromas of garlic and freshly ground coffee, and the still-potent spirit of the Beat Generation. It's perfect for strolling, people-watching, and nursing cappuccinos. Along a busy stretch of Columbus Avenue, North Beach's main thoroughfare, is the landmark City Lights Books, cofounded in 1953 by poet Lawrence Ferlinghetti and once frequented by Alan Ginsberg. Climb the stairs up Telegraph Hill for some of the best vistas in town, particularly from the top of 212-foot-high Coit Tower. Watch the trees for flashes of color; flocks of parrots make their home on the hill. **CITY LIGHTS BOOKS:** Tel 415-362-8193; www.citylights.com.

FISHERMAN'S WHARF—Though a small fishing fleet still departs from Fisherman's Wharf, this hugely popular tourist mecca is largely dedicated to souvenir shops and take-away food. Brave the throngs and head to the bay front, where you can enjoy straight-from-the-boat fish-and-chips and freshly cracked Dungeness crab. Watch jostling and barking sea lions from Pier 39 and take in the stunning view of the Golden Gate Bridge (see p. 727) or Alcatraz (see p. 727). Top it off with a chocolate sundae at Ghirardelli Square or an Irish coffee at the Buena Vista café, which claims to have perfected the drink in 1952. **VISITOR INFO:** www.fishermanswharf.org. **GHIRARDELLI SQUARE:** Tel 415-474-3938; www.ghirardellisq.com. **THE BUENA VISTA:** Tel 415-474-5044; www.thebuenavista.com.

OTHER MUST-DOS

ONLY-IN-SAN-FRANCISCO ENTERTAINMENT—The Fillmore Theater, a cornerstone of the 1960s counterculture sound (think Jefferson Airplane), is still rocking out. So is the BooM BooM RooM, once owned by John Lee Hooker and still the best blues and funk club in the city. Hilarious Beach Blanket Babylon, a zany, ever-evolving musical revue, dates back to anything-goes 1970s San Francisco. Elaborate drag shows have their own long tradition in the city, and Harry Denton's

Starlight Room, atop the Sir Frances Drake Hotel, offers Sunday brunch featuring a high-energy variety show with a bevy of sparkling divas. **The Fillmore:** Tel 415-346-6000; www.thefillmore.com. **BooM BooM RooM:** Tel 415-673-8000; www.boomboomblues.com. **Beach Blanket Babylon:** Tel 415-421-4222; www.beachblanketbabylon.com. **Harry Denton's:** Tel 415-395-8595; www.harrydenton.com.

Riding the Cable Cars—Jump aboard one of San Francisco's iconic cable cars as it clangs up and down the city's insanely steep hills—it's the archetypal San Francisco experience. Of the three cable car routes, the most scenic is the Powell-Hyde line, which climbs past the mansions of Nob Hill and inches along Russian Hill with its Victorian homes. **Info:** www.sfcablecar.com.

San Francisco's cable cars are one of the few National Historic Landmarks that move.

AT&T Park & the San Francisco Giants—San Franciscans are devoted to Major League Baseball's Giants and their intimate AT&T Park. The stadium is one of the smallest but newest in the majors, with retro touches like a redbrick exterior and clock tower. The location is unique: Boats bob beyond the outfield on the sparkling bay, occupied by fans with fishing nets at the ready for a "splash hit." **Info:** Tel 415-972-2400 for tours; 415-972-2000 for tickets; www.sanfrancisco.giants.mlb.com.

Events & Festivals

Chinese New Year—Chinese New Year is celebrated on the lunar new year, and in San Francisco it's grown into the largest celebration of Chinese culture outside Asia. The highlight (on a Saturday, in January or February) is the New Year Parade, with surreal floats, colorful costumes, firecrackers, and the spectacular 250-foot Golden Dragon, which snakes through the streets held aloft by a team of more than 100 men and women. **Info:** Tel 415-986-1370; www.chineseparade.com.

San Francisco International Film Festival—The San Francisco International Film Festival attracts an annual audience of more than 80,000. The 2-week event takes place from late April to early May and features 200-plus films. There are premieres, retrospectives, and rarities in a wide variety of genres, including new digital media offerings. The Film Society also holds screenings and events throughout the year. **Info:** Tel 415-561-5000; www.sffs.org.

Lesbian, Gay, Bisexual, Transgender Pride Celebration—During the last full weekend in June, the nation's largest gay festival attracts a spirited crowd of over 1 million for 2 days of speeches, partying, and colorful entertainment. The highlight is the Pride Parade, which, in its sometimes outrageous glory, wends down Market Street to the Civic Center. You don't need to be gay to enjoy the fabulous, uninhibited fun. **Info:** Tel 415-864-0831; www.sfpride.org.

WHERE TO STAY

ARGONAUT HOTEL—A top hotel in the busy Fisherman's Wharf area (see p. 729), the Argonaut offers water-view rooms, a nautical motif, and extra-comfortable beds and it's just steps from the cable car, San Francisco Maritime National Park, Aquatic Park's small beach, and all the mayhem of the touristy Wharf neighborhood. **INFO:** Tel 866-415-0704 or 415-563-0800; www.argonauthotel.com. *Cost:* from $185.

THE FAIRMONT SAN FRANCISCO—As much a grand palace as a hotel, the Fairmont San Francisco stands atop Nob Hill, with fabulous views (particularly from the Tower Suites). The fashionable but unstuffy clientele comes for the first-class amenities and Euro-style chic. **INFO:** Tel 866-540-4491 or 415-772-5000; www.fairmont.com/sanfrancisco. *Cost:* from $229 (off-peak), from $369 (peak).

HOTEL DRISCO—Get away from the bustle and noise of downtown at this small, elegant hotel in Pacific Heights. Built in 1903 and fully renovated, this stately retreat offers the relaxed comfort of an upscale B&B but with the furnishings and impeccable service of a top hotel. Complimentary chauffeur services whisk you to Union Square and other destinations. **INFO:** Tel 800-634-7277 or 415-346-2880; www.jdvhotels.com. *Cost:* from $209 (off-peak), from $299 (peak).

HOTEL VITALE—This hotel, built in 2005, has everything going for it: a marvelous location across from the bustling Ferry Building market (see p. 728), expansive views of the waterfront and city, and a cool, modern aesthetic. The overall experience is of soothing elegance, perfect for a romantic retreat. **INFO:** Tel 888-890-8688 or 415-278-3700; www.hotelvitale.com. *Cost:* from $299 (off-peak), from $499 (peak).

THE RITZ-CARLTON—With its white-columned Classical façade, the Ritz-Carlton is a veritable paean to luxury and a favorite of visiting celebs and well-heeled travelers. Enjoy cocktails and a raw bar in the chandelier-hung Lobby Lounge. Called The Dining Room, the hotel's restaurant serves modern French cuisine that is lauded as the city's best. **INFO:** Tel 800-542-8680 or 415-296-7465; www.ritzcarlton.com. *Cost:* from $329 (off-peak), from $399 (peak); dinner $80.

THE ST. REGIS SAN FRANCISCO—The St. Regis is the pinnacle of contemporary design and unabashed swank. The 40-story bastion of luxury is both hip (with top-of-the-line entertainment systems) and old school (many rooms come with butler service). At Ame Restaurant, chefs Hiro Sone and Lissa Doumani, the duo behind Napa Valley's renowned Terra (see p. 713), showcase seafood that's part Japanese, part French, and 100 percent delectable. **INFO:** Tel 415-284-4000; www.stregissanfrancisco.com. *Cost:* from $349. **AME:** Tel 877-787-3447 or 415-284-4040; www.amerestaurant.com. *Cost:* 5-course tasting menu $85.

EATING & DRINKING

BOULEVARD—A touch of the Belle Époque on the Bay, Boulevard is a perfect spot for a romantic dinner. It occupies the Audiffred Building on the Embarcadero, the only waterfront building to survive the 1906 earthquake. Its Parisian-style interior is the ideal accompaniment to chef Nancy Oakes's modern take on French cooking, with such soul-satisfying dishes as pan-seared veal sweetbreads and porcini mushrooms with toasted carrot spaetzle. **INFO:** Tel 415-543-6084; www.boulevardrestaurant.com. *Cost:* dinner $75.

COI—Coi (pronounced kwa, from the antiquated French word for "tranquil") is an intimate, 48-seat restaurant serving brightly flavored, carefully crafted food full of the terroir of Northern California. Chef Daniel Patterson's ever-changing 11-course tasting menu reflects the best and freshest ingredients available. This is cooking of great distinction, in which even the simplest foods sing with flavor. **Info:** Tel 415-393-9000; www.coirestaurant.com. *Cost:* 11-course tasting menu $135.

Delfina—While more rarified Italian restaurants can be found in San Francisco, none is more beloved than Delfina. The food at this handsome trattoria is refreshingly straightforward, with chef-owner Craig Stoll relying on farm-to-table ingredients and the rich traditions of Tuscan cooking to create dishes that are at once homey, classic, and adventurous. **Info:** Tel 415-552-4055; www.delfinasf.com. *Cost:* dinner $55.

Foreign Cinema—Talk about a double feature: Stylish, beautifully prepared California-by-way-of-France bistro cooking is paired with classic films projected onto the back wall of the restaurant's lovely open-air courtyard. Perfect for Mission hipsters, actors, restaurant insiders, and families. **Info:** Tel 415-648-7600; www.foreigncinema.com. *Cost:* dinner $60.

Gary Danko—The epitome of San Francisco style, Restaurant Gary Danko offers a dazzling selection of seasonal dishes that each diner builds into his or her own multicourse tasting menu. Choose from glazed oysters with osetra caviar or branzini fillets with fennel puree to create a freestyle epicurean extravaganza. Reserve well in advance, as this is a special-occasion favorite. **Info:** Tel 415-749-2060; www.garydanko.com. *Cost:* 3-course dinner $68.

Quince—In stylish new digs on Jackson Square, Quince now offers its many fans more elbow room to enjoy chef Michael Tusk's full-flavored, Italian-influenced cuisine. Exquisite ingredients inspire the daily-changing menu, and Tusk's masterful technique never masks the heady natural flavors. Particularly good are fish and pasta dishes, such as house-made spaghetti with clams, melon, and a splash of espresso to mellow the flavors. **Info:** Tel 415-775-8500; www.quincerestaurant.com. *Cost:* dinner $80.

Zuni Café—A favorite on Market Street, Zuni Café has been a San Francisco landmark since 1987. Chef-owners Judy Rodgers and Gilbert Pilgram continue to craft marvelous Mediterranean-style dishes (such as their legendary brick-oven-roasted chicken for two) that helped revolutionize cooking across the nation. While the menu has evolved, the scene is the same as ever, with a crowd as diverse as the neighborhood. **Info:** Tel 415-552-2522. *Cost:* dinner $55.

Day Trips

Chez Panisse & the Berkeley Food Scene—Across San Francisco Bay, Berkeley is home to the first University of California campus and has long been known for its progressive politics and culture. The city has also been at the culinary vanguard since the early 1970s, when Alice Waters opened legendary Chez Panisse, the restaurant that helped create "California cuisine" and make "fresh, seasonal, and local" the mantra of American cooking. As well regarded as ever, the redwood-paneled Chez Panisse dining room serves prix-fixe menus, while upstairs the Panisse Café offers a less expensive à la carte menu—all from ingredients supplied by over 80 local farms.

And as goes Chez Panisse, so goes the neighborhood. Along Berkeley's Shattuck Avenue, dozens of restaurants, artisan food and wine shops, and other purveyors of deliciousness have taken root. Explore the bounty on a Gourmet Ghetto Culinary Tour. **Chez Panisse:** Tel 510-548-5525; www.chezpanisse.com. *Cost:* dinner $75; $30 at the café. **Gourmet Ghetto:** Tel 415-806-5970; www.inthekitchenwithlisa.com.

Sausalito—The 25-minute ferry ride between the Ferry Terminal and the quaint Mediterranean-like town of Sausalito is considered one of the most scenic in the world, with epic vistas of the Golden Gate Bridge and the San Francisco skyline. Stay at Inn Above Tide for that same inimitable view.

Sausalito is a profusion of shops and boutiques and bayfront restaurants: Sushi Ran's sushi may be the finest in the Bay Area. **Golden Gate Ferry:** Tel 415-455-2000; www.goldengateferry.org. **Inn Above Tide:** Tel 415-332-9535; www.innabove tide.com. *Cost:* from $305. **Sushi Ran:** Tel 415-332-3620; www.sushiran.com. *Cost:* dinner $30.

Point Reyes National Seashore—Stretching 30 miles along the rugged Marin County coastline, the Point Reyes National Seashore draws hikers, solitude seekers, and birders to its coastal wilderness; migrating gray whales can sometimes be spotted in winter from the 1870 landmark Point Reyes Lighthouse. One short, easy hiking loop traces the San Andreas Fault Zone. Point Reyes's gateway villages are loaded with good shops and restaurants; near Marshall, Hog Island Oyster Company is a working farm that serves fresh barbecued oysters alfresco. Stay in Inverness at Manka's Inverness Lodge, a 10-room lodge known for its food, available by room service only. **Where:** 35 miles north of San Francisco. Tel 415-663-8054; www.nps.gov/pore. **Hog Island Oyster Company:** Tel 415-663-9218; www.hogislandoysters.com. *Cost:* lunch $40. **Manka's Inverness Lodge:** Tel 415-669-1034; www.mankas.com. *Cost:* from $215; dinner $60.

A High Sierra Gem

Yosemite National Park

California, U.S.A.

"No temple made with hands can compare with Yosemite," wrote naturalist John Muir, who contributed to the 1890 founding of Yosemite National Park. The park's dramatic beauty has been famously captured in the photographs of Ansel Adams, from Half Dome, Yosemite's 8,842-foot trademark peak, to El Capitan, the largest single granite rock on earth. The magnificent Yosemite Falls, another of the park's highlights, are, at 2,425 feet, the highest on the continent.

Yosemite's waterfalls are best viewed in late spring, when they're at peak flow, and before summer crowds arrive.

Millions converge in high season on the mile-wide, 7-mile-long Yosemite Valley, cut by the Merced River and guarded by sheer granite cliffs and domes rising 2,000 to 4,000 feet. Avoiding the park's summertime people-jams is easy: Strike out, whether on foot, horseback, or mule, and explore the wilder 95 percent of the park along any of its 800 miles of trails. The moderately strenuous Mist Trail offers a close-up view of 317-foot Vernal Fall and 620-foot Bridalveil Fall. It is part of the more ambitious, 211-mile

John Muir Trail, which snakes through six passes with elevations higher than 11,000 feet as it crosses the backbone of the Sierra Nevada.

With close to 200 miles of paved roads, there are plenty of pull-offs, such as Glacier Point, that afford spectacular views. And for white-water rafters, almost every class of rapids awaits on a 28-mile stretch of the Merced River and, just outside the park, the Tuolumne River, with more than 18 miles of scenic Class IV rapids.

The Ahwahnee, a rustic but luxurious lodge (whose name roughly translates from the Miwok word as "valley that looks like a gaping mouth"), is a 1927 showpiece of stone and native timber, with heart-stopping views. Winter here is a special time, when the lodge's much loved Bracebridge Dinner brings Old English Yuletide cheer to snow-covered Yosemite. For over 80 years, it's been a family favorite. Château du Sureau, the area's other notable lodging, is 15 minutes south of Yosemite. It's an enchanting ten-room inn with the air of a European country estate, and its acclaimed restaurant, Erna's Elderberry House, is known for its six-course menu.

WHERE: 190 miles east of San Francisco. Tel 209-372-0200; www.nps.gov/yose. **JOHN MUIR TRAIL:** www.pcta.org. **THE AHWAHNEE:** Tel 209-372-1407; www.yosemitepark.com. *Cost:* from $299. **BRACEBRIDGE DINNER:** 801-559-5000; www.bracebridgedinners.com. *Cost:* $375. *When:* mid–late Dec. **CHÂTEAU DU SUREAU:** Tel 559-683-6860; www.chateau sureau.com. *Cost:* from $445; prix-fixe dinner $95. **BEST TIMES:** May for waterfalls; May–Jun and Oct–Nov to avoid crowds.

High-Society Glamour and Glorious Skiing

ASPEN

Colorado, U.S.A.

Strip away its celebrity veneer and Aspen shines as one of the country's best places to ski. Add in a few excellent restaurants, art galleries, and a year-round social scene and you'll realize why this town is the darling of the rich and famous. Streets are lined with late-19th-century gingerbread homes from the city's heady mining-town years. And while their price tags may be out of the average visitor's budget, the peerless views of the Rockies are free.

Aspen's four mountains offer nearly 5,000 skiable acres, and all are linked by free shuttle service and transferable lift tickets. Snowmass is the biggie, with 3,128 acres of wide-open groomed runs perfect for families. Aspen Mountain, "Ajax" to locals, is a challenging peak that has a vertical drop of 3,267 feet and 76 variable-terrain ski trails made more accessible by recently improved lift capacity. Aspen Highlands is a favorite with many locals, as much for the hike to the top of the Highland Bowl as for the Olympic bowls, while Buttermilk is the best for beginners.

After a day on Aspen Mountain, settle in at The Little Nell, the only ski-in/ski-out lodge in Aspen and a snowball's throw from the Silver Queen Gondola, the longest single-stage gondola in the country. The lodge's stylish Montagna restaurant beckons with a farm-to-table menu good enough to compete with the views of Aspen Mountain.

In town, the Hotel Jerome dates to the boom mining years. The Victorian décor is impeccably intact, modernized with Jacuzzis and a heated outdoor pool, and the historic J-Bar is still among the best places in town for people-watching and nightlife.

You won't go hungry in Aspen, with options that range from tapas bars to world-class sushi. But head out of the fray to Krabloonik, a tiny log cabin on Snowmass named for the owner's lead sled dog. Repeat visitors come for the succulent wild game—maybe caribou chops or elk fillets—and dogsled rides into the quiet woods.

Aspen also lays claim to the title "Festival Capital of the Rockies," though Telluride (see p. 739) might have something to say about that. A year-round roster of cultural events climaxes with the classical Aspen Music Festival, the Aspen Dance Festival, and Jazz Aspen Snowmass, big enough to warrant two different programs of rock, soul, reggae, and jazz in June and again around Labor Day. Gourmets from around the world lead the festivities when the Food and Wine Classic takes over for three days in June.

WHERE: 200 miles southwest of Denver. **ASPEN SNOWMASS:** Tel 800-525-6200 or 970-925-1220; www.aspensnowmass.com. *Cost:* lift tickets from $96. *When:* ski season late Nov–mid-Apr. **THE LITTLE NELL:** Tel 888-843-6355 or 970-920-4600; www.thelittlenell.com. *Cost:* from $330 (off-peak), from $810 (peak); dinner at Montagna $70. **HOTEL JEROME:** Tel 800-331-7213 or 970-920-1000; www.hoteljerome.com. *Cost:* from $249 (off-peak), from $1,055 (peak). **KRABLOONIK RESTAURANT:** Tel 970-923-3953; www.krabloonikrestaurant.com. *Cost:* dinner $65. **BEST TIMES:** Dec–Mar for skiing; Jun–early Sep for hiking; mid-Jun for Food and Wine Classic; late Jun–late Aug for Music Festival; mid-Jul–late Aug for Dance Festival; late Jun and early Sep for Jazz Aspen.

A Young-at-Heart Mountain Town

DURANGO

Colorado, U.S.A.

"It's out of the way and glad of it," cracked Will Rogers. Nestled in the Animas River Valley between the desert and the San Juan Mountains, Durango is not all that inaccessible these days, but its caught-in-time feel, along with plenty of modern-day activities, are a big part of its allure. Founded in 1881, Durango is also popular for its proximity to Mesa Verde National Park (see p. 736).

Students attending Fort Lewis College give Durango an upbeat air and keep dozens of ski, bike, and camping stores in business. The Durango Mountain Resort has 1,200 skiable acres and 85 trails on Purgatory Mountain, while kayakers can tackle Class II and III rapids on the Animas River, which flows right through the center of town. Durango is also one of the most popular mountain biking towns in the West; it hosted the first-ever national mountain bike championships in 1990, now held annually around the country. Motorcyclists get their chance when they converge by the thousands during the Rally in the Rockies in early September.

Mosey over to the Strater Hotel, a handsome redbrick Victorian where Wild West legends Bat Masterson and Butch Cassidy both stayed. Louis L'Amour wrote a few of his Western novels in room 222, and live ragtime music wafts from the Diamond Belle Saloon, decorated with crystal chandeliers and plush velvet curtains.

The biggest draw for all ages is the Durango & Silverton Narrow Gauge Railroad, the setting for the hair-raising robbery scene in *Butch Cassidy and the Sundance Kid.* In operation since 1882, it once transported workers and precious minerals to and from the former silver-mining camp of Silverton. Now it carries tourists in Victorian coaches along the 45-mile route, ascending 3,000 feet while crossing narrow bridges that span roaring whitewater canyons.

Durango is also a wonderful starting point for the San Juan Skyway. The 236-mile loop heads through the beautiful San Juan Mountains north to Ouray and Silverton, crossing five mountain passes. It links up with the Million Dollar Highway, built in 1884, the visual highlight of the journey, before turning back to town via Telluride (see p. 739), Rico, and Cortez.

WHERE: 336 miles southwest of Denver. **VISITOR INFO:** www.durango.org. **DURANGO MOUNTAIN RESORT:** Tel 800-982-6103 or 970-247-9000; www.durangomountainresort.com. *Cost:* lift tickets $65. *When:* ski season Dec–Mar. **STRATER HOTEL:** Tel 800-247-4431 or 970-247-4431; www.strater.com. *Cost:* from $109 (off-peak), from $179 (peak). **DURANGO & SILVERTON RAILROAD:** Tel 877-872-4607 or 970-247-2733; www.durangotrain.com. *Cost:* from $49 round-trip (off-peak), from $79 round-trip (peak). *When:* May–Oct. **SAN JUAN SKYWAY:** www.byways.org. **BEST TIMES:** last weekend in Jan for Snowdown Winter Festival; early Sep for Rally in the Rockies; early Oct for Durango Cowboy Gathering.

Awe-Inspiring Cliff Dwellings in Desert Canyons

MESA VERDE

Colorado, U.S.A.

Located in the area known as the Four Corners, where Colorado, New Mexico, Arizona, and Utah meet, Mesa Verde is the only national park in the U.S. devoted exclusively to archaeology: One glance at the centuries-old, intricately constructed homes in the rocky cliffs shows why.

Members of the Ancestral Puebloan culture (also known as the Anasazi) that flourished here between A.D. 600 and 1300 created masonry dwellings tucked into alcoves along the steep canyon walls. Many of these alcoves face south, allowing them to capture precious sunlight in winter and avoid the summer glare, but historians believe their orientation may have been as much for sacred reasons as for utility.

Though known to the neighboring Ute Mountain tribe, the empty dwellings went mostly unnoticed until local ranchers stumbled on them in 1888. The area was declared a park in 1906; since then a handful of the 600 or so multistory cliff dwellings spread over 52,000 acres have been stabilized and opened to the public. Cliff Palace, the highlight of the park and the largest cliff dwelling in North America, had over 150 rooms occupied by about 100 people at its peak. You'll have to get a ticket for a ranger-led tour of this and Balcony House, which requires climbing ladders and crawling through a 12-foot-long tunnel and is the most challenging in the park. Both are on Chapin Mesa, as is Spruce Tree House, with 130 rooms and eight kivas (circular ceremonial chambers). If you'd rather explore on your own, the 6-mile Mesa Top Loop Road affords easy access to dozens of overlooks.

The only place to hang your hat in the park is the modest Far View Lodge, where the restaurant offers pretty good Southwestern fare. Rooms, though modest, have private porches with Four Corners views for miles.

WHERE: 35 miles west of Durango. Tel

970-529-4465; www.nps.gov/meve. *When:* year-round, but certain sites open only Apr–Oct. **FAR VIEW LODGE:** Tel 800-449-2288 or 970-564-4300; www.visitmesaverde.com. *Cost:* from $120. *When:* Apr–Oct. **BEST TIMES:** Apr–Jun and late Aug–Oct for fewer crowds; late May for Mesa Verde Country Indian Arts and Western Culture Festival.

A Natural High

Rocky Mountain National Park

Colorado, U.S.A.

Housing three distinct ecosystems within 415 square miles, Rocky Mountain National Park is Colorado's natural showpiece, a place of sparkling streams, glacial lakes, and rugged peaks galore—Longs Peak stands at 14,259 feet. Most of the 3 million annual visitors begin at the picture-perfect town of Estes Park, 3 miles from the park's eastern edge. From here the only route through the park is Trail Ridge Road, traversing 48 miles of astonishing scenery as it crosses the Continental Divide in one of the country's most important long-distance treks. The two-lane route tops out at 12,183 feet before reaching Grand Lake, the park's western entrance.

In between, there are over 350 miles of hiking trails. Bear Lake, one of 150 in the park, is a popular starting point for the scenic trail to Emerald Lake; the trailheads to Glacier Gorge and the not-to-be-missed Mills Lake are nearby. Wildlife thrives in this Alpine setting, from elk, moose, and bighorn sheep to elusive mountain lions, bears, and coyotes; wildflowers bloom from May through August.

The full Continental Divide Trail stretches from Mexico to Canada, passing through the park.

While there aren't any accommodations inside the park, the town of Estes Park is home to the rambling Stanley Hotel, which inspired Stephen King's *The Shining*. A more intimate experience awaits at the Romantic RiverSong Inn, a ten-room hotel nestled among 27 acres of evergreens. For a dude ranch experience with a dollop of luxury, go no farther than the 8,000-acre C Lazy U Ranch near Grand Lake. You can ride horseback by day and tuck into Western cookout fare at night, or simply unwind around the main hall's big stone fireplace.

WHERE: Estes Park is 65 miles northwest of Denver. Tel 970-586-1206; www.nps.gov/romo. *When:* park, year-round; Trail Ridge

Rd., late May–mid-Oct. **STANLEY HOTEL:** Tel 800-976-1377 or 970-577-4000; www.stanleyhotel.com. *Cost:* from $119 (off-peak), from $159 (peak). **ROMANTIC RIVERSONG INN:** Tel 970-586-4666; www.romanticriversong.com. *Cost:* from $165. **C LAZY U RANCH:** Tel 970-887-3344; www.clazyu.com. *Cost:* from $275 per person, all-inclusive (off-peak, 2-night minimum); from $2,590 per week, all-inclusive (peak). **BEST TIMES:** mid-Jul for Estes Park's Rooftop Rodeo and Parade; Sep–early Oct for elk viewing.

Birthplace of Skiing in Colorado with an Old West Flair

STEAMBOAT SPRINGS

Colorado, U.S.A.

The place where it all started was named in the 1860s by French fur trappers who thought a gurgling hot spring sounded like a steamboat cruising the Yampa River. The town of Steamboat Springs began as a summer resort, but with the opening of Howelsen Hill in 1914, it became the first ski destination in the state. Equal parts ranching community and Ski Town, U.S.A. (its trademarked moniker), it's the hometown of more Winter Olympics athletes than any other place in the country, including Billy Kidd, the 1964 slalom silver medalist. Sign up for his clinic—you'll spot him on the slopes wearing his Stetson hat and famous grin.

Steamboat Ski Resort maintains 165 ski trails, ranging from beginner to advanced.

Steamboat stands 6,700 feet above the Yampa River Valley, surrounded by the Medicine Bow/Routt National Forest and two wilderness areas rising to just over 12,000 feet. In addition to Howelsen Hill, with three lifts and 15 trails, there's the far larger Steamboat Ski Resort 3 miles from town. Six peaks (the highest is 10,568-foot Mt. Werner) make up the resort where the term "Champagne Powder" was coined to describe its much ballyhooed eiderdown-soft snow. It's a friendly place with plenty of easy and intermediate terrain, and a pioneer of kid's programs.

It's no surprise that there are more than 150 mineral springs in the area, starting with the Steamboat Springs Health and Recreation Center in town, which offers three outdoor mineral pools, a 350-foot waterslide, and an Olympic-size lap pool. The Strawberry Park Hot Springs, on Hot Springs Creek, offers a more natural setting, where water as hot as 150°F flows into stone pools tucked into the snow-dusted forest.

For a cozy, out-of-the-way retreat, take a trip to tiny Clark, where you'll find the Home Ranch, one of the most outstanding guest ranches in the state. Here, gourmet meals are served at communal tables (Friday is BBQ night), and a day spent horseback riding can be followed by a soak in the private hot tub on your porch under a canopy of stars.

WHERE: 160 miles northwest of Denver. **HOWELSEN HILL:** Tel 970-879-4300. *Cost:* lift tickets from $16. *When:* ski season Dec–Mar. **STEAMBOAT SKI RESORT:** Tel 970-879-6111; www.steamboat.com. *Cost:* lift tickets from $91. *When:* ski season late Nov–early Apr. **STEAMBOAT SPRINGS HEALTH AND RECREATION**

CENTER: Tel 970-879-1828; www.sshra.org. **STRAWBERRY PARK HOT SPRINGS:** Tel 970-879-0342; www.strawberryhotsprings.com. **HOME RANCH:** Tel 970-879-1780; www.homeranch.com. *Cost:* 2-night stay from $950, all-inclusive (off-peak); from $5,655 per week, all-inclusive (peak). **BEST TIMES:** Jan–Feb for skiing; early Feb for Winter Carnival; May–Jun for wildflowers; early Jul for Cowboy Round-up Days.

Epic Scenery and Skiing Second to None

TELLURIDE

Colorado, U.S.A.

Start with one of the best-preserved gold- and silver-mining towns in the state and perhaps the prettiest setting in the Rockies. Add an outstanding ski resort, plus a cultural season with a dazzling year-round roster, and you have Telluride. Restored Victorian homes and chic boutiques stand in the shadow of 14,000-foot peaks—proving that things have definitely changed since Butch Cassidy robbed his first bank here in 1889.

Of the 115 ski trails on 2,000 acres of gorgeous terrain, more than two-thirds are given over to beginners and intermediates, while experts rank the steeps among the toughest in the country. On a crystalline day, the See Forever trail lives up to its name. And forget the crowds—Telluride's remote location guarantees virtually uninterrupted runs.

A breathtaking gondola ride takes you from town to the European-style Mountain Village. This is where you'll find the Peaks Resort, where you can soothe your slope-weary bones, or join the locals over live music at either the mining-era Last Dollar Saloon or the ever-popular Fly Me to the Moon Saloon.

Step back in time in nearby Dolores at the painstakingly restored 19th-century ghost town resort of Dunton Hot Springs. Idyllic days are spent fly-fishing, horseback riding, or enjoying early-morning yoga in a log cabin once used as a Pony Express stop.

Known for its festivals, Telluride hosts a plethora of events, including Mountainfilm (late May), the Jazz Celebration (early June), and the Bluegrass Festival (mid-June). The Telluride Film Festival, in September, was described by Roger Ebert as "like Cannes died and went to heaven"; Blues & Brews, a beer and music festival, takes place later the same month. With so many events crowding the calendar, the townsfolk understandably welcome No Festival Weekend, when nothing whatsoever is going on.

WHERE: 33 miles southwest of Denver. **VISITOR INFO:** www.visittelluride.com. **TELLURIDE SKI RESORT:** Tel 800-778-8581 or 970-728-6900; www.tellurideskiresort.com. *Cost:* lift tickets from $92. *When:* late Nov–early Apr. **PEAKS RESORT:** Tel 800-789-2220 or 970-728-6800; www.thepeaksresort.com. *Cost:* from $139 (off-peak), from $199 (peak).

Telluride's Main Street calls to mind its Wild West roots.

Dunton Hot Springs: Tel 970-882-4800; www.duntonhotsprings.com. *Cost:* cabins from $500 all-inclusive (off-peak), from $850 (peak). **Mountainfilm:** Tel 970-728-4123; www.mountainfilm.org. *When:* late May. **Jazz Celebration:** Tel 970-728-7009; www.telluridejazz.com. *When:* early Jun. **Bluegrass Festival:** Tel 800-624-2422 or 303-823-0848; www.bluegrass.com/telluride. *When:* mid-Jun. **Film Festival:** Tel 510-665-9494; telluridefilmfestival.org. *When:* early Sep. **Blues & Brews Festival:** Tel 866-515-6166 or 970-728-8037; www.tellurideblues.com. *When:* mid-Sep. **Best times:** Apr–Jun and Oct–Nov for nicest weather; Jun–Sep for cultural events; Dec–Mar for skiing.

Powder Bowls and Perfect Snow

Vail

Colorado, U.S.A.

The largest single ski resort in North America has over 10 square miles of skiable terrain—and what terrain it is. It boasts 5,289 acres of free-ride, including the seemingly endless majesty of the world-famous Back Bowls.

The town itself, built in the 1960s, lacks the character of other Colorado ski towns, but visitors are here for the skiing. Thirty-four lifts crisscross the slopes, including the biggest, fastest set of high-speed detachable quads on one mountain.

Seven natural bowls filled with dry, fluffy powder stretch 7 miles wide on the back side of the mountain. The Blue Sky Basin, as big as Aspen Mountain (see p. 734), is perhaps the most spectacular: Its 645 acres of gladed runs (and no groomed trails) are carved out of the pristine wilderness for a quieter and more isolated experience.

The deluxe Lodge at Vail has the best slopeside location in town (and the lodge's Mickey's Lounge leads the pack for après-ski entertainment). Another good choice is the Sonnenalp Resort of Vail in Vail Village, featuring a full-service spa and 88 luxury suites with an old-world ambience.

Nearby Beaver Creek offers 146 trails across three mountains and recalls a sheltered town in the Alps; the resort is close enough to Vail that you can ski one in the morning and the other in the afternoon. (Vail and Beaver Creek lift tickets are also valid at Breckenridge, Keystone, and Arapahoe Basin, all within 40 miles and linked by shuttle service.) The nearby Ritz-Carlton, Bachelor Gulch, named for a group of old-timers who settled here in the early 1900s, centers on a grand timber lodge like those in Yellowstone and Yosemite. The ski-in/ski-out resort has nearly 100 fireplaces and a 21,000-square-foot spa with three rock-lined grottoes and a river hot tub.

Where: 100 miles west of Denver. Tel 877-204-7881 or 970-476-5601; www.vail.snow.com. *Cost:* lift tickets from $97. *When:* ski season mid-Nov–early Apr. **Lodge at Vail:** Tel 877-528-7625 or 970-476-5011; lodgeatvail.rockresorts.com. *Cost:* from $200 (off-peak), from $500 (peak). **Sonnenalp:** Tel 800-654-8312 or 970-476-5656; www.sonnenalp.com. *Cost:* suites from $380 (off-peak), from $850 (peak). **Beaver Creek:** Tel 800-842-8062 or 970-845-9090; www.beavercreek.com. *Cost:* lift tickets from $97. **The Ritz-Carlton, Bachelor Gulch:** Tel 800-241-3333 or 970-748-6200; www.ritzcarlton.com. *Cost:* from $399 (off-peak), from $600 (peak).

The Perfect American Small Town

ESSEX

Connecticut, U.S.A.

A dignified, Revolutionary War–era spirit lingers in Essex, a mint-condition town on the Connecticut River, where Colonial and Federal houses hark back to a shipbuilding heyday. On Main Street, white picket fences frame landmark buildings, while sailboats bob in nearby marinas.

Learn about Essex's seafaring heritage at the Connecticut River Museum, an 1870s steamboat warehouse filled with maritime artifacts, including a full-scale replica of America's first submarine, *The Turtle*. Train buffs will enjoy riding in vintage 1920s Pullman cars on the Essex Steam Train north to Deep River, where a summertime Fife & Drum Muster of more than 70 units marches down Main Street. Passengers can either return to Essex by train or continue aboard a Mississippi-style riverboat to East Haddam.

One of the most celebrated buildings in picture-book Essex is the Griswold Inn, the oldest continuously operating inn in Connecticut. The "Gris" is most famous for its Tap Room, a 1738 watering hole with a potbellied stove at its center and wood-paneled walls lined with maritime memorabilia and Currier & Ives prints. Many of the guests come for the enormous Sunday Hunt Breakfast, which dates back to the War of 1812.

Just a few minutes' drive inland is tiny Ivoryton's Copper Beech Inn, where the 22 rooms are as charming as the surrounding gardens. The main house is the site of Brasserie Pip's, serving lots of French standards, such as steak frites, duck confit, and sweetbreads.

WHERE: 100 miles northeast of New York City. **VISITOR INFO:** www.essexct.com. **CONNECTICUT RIVER MUSEUM:** Tel 860-767-8269; www.ctrivermuseum.org. **ESSEX STEAM TRAIN:** Tel 860-767-0103; www.essexsteamtrain.com. **GRISWOLD INN:** Tel 860-767-1776; www.griswoldinn.com. *Cost:* from $99; dinner at the Tap Room $35, Sunday Hunt Breakfast $19. **COPPER BEECH INN:** Tel 888-809-2056 or 860-767-0330; www.copperbeechinn.com. *Cost:* from $175 (off-peak), from $239 (peak); dinner $60. **BEST TIMES:** mid-Jul for the Fife & Drum Muster in Deep River; Christmas for holiday decorations.

Home of a Literary Legend

THE MARK TWAIN HOUSE

Hartford, Connecticut, U.S.A.

Literary fans come from around the world to visit the home of beloved author Samuel Clemens, aka Mark Twain. "To us," Twain said, "our house . . . had a heart, and a soul, and eyes to see us with. . . . It was of us, and we were in its confidence, and lived in its grace and in the peace of its benediction."

Although more commonly associated with his birthplace of Hannibal, Missouri, Twain always held this home in Hartford in a special light. The custom-designed high-Victorian mansion was commissioned from well-known New York architect Edward Tuckerman Potter. Twain lived here with his family from 1874 to 1891, during which time he penned some of his most acclaimed works, including *The Adventures of Tom Sawyer*, *The Adventures of Huckleberry Finn*, and *A Connecticut Yankee in King Arthur's Court*. The beautifully restored 19-room mansion features decorative work by Louis Comfort Tiffany and some 10,000 Victorian-era objects. A striking contemporary museum stands adjacent to the house, further detailing the life and times of this master storyteller.

Nearby, the Harriet Beecher Stowe Center celebrates the legacy of the author of *Uncle Tom's Cabin*, considered by many the greatest antislavery novel of all time. The brick Gothic Victorian was the author's home from 1873 until she died in 1896.

Hartford's acclaimed Wadsworth Atheneum is the nation's first public art museum. Just minutes from the landmark state capitol, its highlights include a renowned collection of Hudson River School paintings by such artists as Thomas Cole and Frederic Church.

Mark Twain House: Tel 860-247-0998; www.marktwainhouse.org. **Harriet Beecher Stowe Center:** Tel 860-522-9258; www.harrietbeecherstowecenter.org. **Wadsworth Atheneum:** Tel 860-278-2670; www.wadsworthatheneum.org. **Best time:** Christmastime, when the Mark Twain House is decked out in holiday splendor.

Rural Sophistication Under the Elms

Litchfield Hills

Connecticut, U.S.A.

The notion that the real New England is an endless drive from the urban chaos of New York City is dispelled upon approaching the Litchfield Hills, where a landscape of 18th- and 19th-century saltbox farmhouses, red barns, and tidy villages unfolds in the northwestern corner of Connecticut.

The small town of Litchfield anchors the region with its elegant storefronts, while just beyond its outskirts you'll find Connecticut's largest nature preserve, the 4,000-acre White Memorial Foundation. Explore some of its 35 miles of leafy trails, then head to Litchfield's West Street Grill, everyone's favorite place to linger, thanks to a well-chosen wine list and eclectic menu.

An ultra-luxurious treat in this pristine corner of New England is the all-inclusive, 100-acre mini-resort Winvian, on the edge of the White Memorial Foundation. Cottage prices are over the top but so is the service.

Rooms are decidedly more affordable at the Bavarian Tudor-style Manor House B&B just north of Litchfield, in sylvan Norfolk. Built in 1898 by Charles Spofford, who designed London's subway system, it is distinguished by a parlor whose 20 stained-glass windows were supplied by his friend Louis Comfort Tiffany.

In the heart of Litchfield County, the charming town of Washington is dotted with restaurants, galleries, and an inviting bookstore. Its claim to fame is the stately Mayflower Inn & Spa, which sits on 58 manicured acres like an English country house; a newly added 20,000-square-foot spa provides the prelude to sweet dreams in four-poster featherbeds.

Located just 10 miles southeast, Woodbury has earned the title of Antiques Capital of Connecticut. Take a break from browsing at the Good News Café, where the seasonal menu features a few permanent favorites, including mac-and-cheese with lobster and spinach. Or head north out of Washington to Lake Waramaug, overlooked by the 1890s Boulders Inn. Inviting accommodations and a famous Sunday brunch make for the perfect weekend.

Litchfield's First Congregational Church was built in the Federal style.

Where: Litchfield is 110 miles north of New York City. **Visitor info:** www.litchfieldhills.com. **West Street Grill:** Tel 860-567-3885; www.weststreetgrill.com. *Cost:* dinner $45. **Winvian:** Tel 860-567-9600; www.winvian.com. *Cost:* cottages from $650. **Manor House B&B:** Tel 866-542-5690 or 860-542-5690; www.manorhouse-norfolk.com. *Cost:* from $180. **Mayflower Inn:** Tel 860-868-9466; www.mayflowerinn.com. *Cost:* from $550; dinner $50. **Good News Café:** Tel 203-266-4663; www.good-news-cafe.com. *Cost:* dinner $40. **The Boulders Inn:** Tel 800-455-1565 or 860-868-0541; www.bouldersinn.com. *Cost:* from $355; dinner $60. **Best times:** early Jul for Litchfield Open House Tour; Jul–Aug for chamber music in Norfolk; early Aug for Litchfield Jazz Festival in Kent; Oct for fall foliage; Dec for Christmas Show & Sale at Washington Art Association.

America's Maritime Museum

Mystic Seaport

Mystic, Connecticut, U.S.A.

Mystic is one of the Northeast's most visited villages, thanks to Mystic Seaport, the country's largest maritime museum. Much of its 17-acre riverfront site encompasses a re-created coastal village that brings salty 19th-century seafaring America to life. Among the many fully rigged sailing ships open for visits is the *Charles W. Morgan* (1841), the world's last surviving wooden whaling ship. The kid-popular Mystic Aquarium & Institute for Exploration offers some 70 live exhibits of sea life and a vast outdoor beluga whale exhibit.

Mystic's only waterfront hotel, the Steamboat Inn, is a charmer, stylishly blending nautical and contemporary design. Ten of its 11 rooms have romantic river views, while six feature fireplaces. Sip sherry in the cozy common room after spending the day antiquing or browsing the nearby shops and galleries.

It's just another 5 miles to little-known Stonington, one of New England's most endearing coastal communities. First settled in 1649, the town has leafy streets lined with sea captains' houses and churches. Follow the fragrance of the sea down Water Street, which leads to an early-19th-century lighthouse. Stop at Noah's, a homey spot known for its sweet rolls and homemade clam chowder, or have a drink at the dockside Dog Watch Café. Several of the 18 rooms at the posh Inn at Stonington overlook the harbor, some with private decks.

Where: 130 miles northeast of New York City. **Visitor info:** mysticcountry.com. **Mystic Seaport:** Tel 888-973-2767 or 860-572-5315; www.mysticseaport.org. **Mystic Aquarium:** Tel 860-572-5955; www.mysticaquarium.org. **Steamboat Inn:** Tel 860-536-8300; www.steamboatinnmystic.com. *Cost:* from $160 (off-peak), from $240 (peak). **Noah's:** Tel 860-535-3925; www.noahsfinefood.com. *Cost:* dinner $35. **Dog Watch Café:** Tel 860-415-4510; www.dogwatchcafe.com. **Inn at Stonington:** Tel 860-535-2000; www.innatstonington.com. *Cost:* from $160 (off-peak), from $180 (peak). **Best times:** late May for Lobsterfest; Jun for Sea Music Festival; Jul for Antique and Classic Boat Rendezvous; mid-Oct for Chowderfest; Dec for Lantern Light Tours.

Family Legacies of the du Ponts and Wyeths

Brandywine Valley

Delaware and Pennsylvania, U.S.A.

The lush Brandywine Valley, an area dotted with manicured gardens, historic estates, and fascinating small museums, straddles Delaware's border with Pennsylvania. No state is more closely associated with a single family than Delaware is with the du Ponts: The grand houses they built here gave rise to the area's nickname "Chateau Valley," and no trip to the region is worth taking without glimpsing the magnificence they left behind.

The du Pont story begins at the Hagley Museum. It was here in the early days of the 19th century that French émigré Eleuthère Irénée du Pont constructed a riverside house and the first of his gunpowder mills outside Wilmington, structures that eventually grew into a 235-acre complex. In 1910, just across the river, E. I.'s great-grandson Alfred Irénée du Pont built Nemours, his Louis XVI–style mansion, and filled it with imported furniture, rare rugs and tapestries, and museum-quality works of art. Its formal French garden is the largest of its kind in North America.

It was Henry Francis du Pont, another great-grandson of E.I.'s, who was responsible for Winterthur, perhaps the most visited of the family estates. In the late 1920s, he transformed what began as a rather modest 12-room home into an eight-story châteaulike spread. Today it is considered the world's premier museum of 17th- to 19th-century American antiques and decorative arts, with some 85,000 objects arrayed in 175 period rooms. Horticulture was his passion, and visitors today can also visit 60 acres of glorious gardens (a fraction of their original size) accessible via the Garden Tram, including the fairy-tale Enchanted Woods. Meticulously restored and flower-decked Montchanin Village, once part of the Winterthur estate and

Winterthur's Montmorenci Stair Hall contains an elegant spiral staircase that spans two stories.

home to du Pont powder-mill workers, has been reborn as a luxury inn and spa, with former residences divvied up into 28 suites, some with fireplaces and private patios. The old blacksmith shop now houses Krazy Kat's restaurant, where the décor is whimsical but the new-French menu is big-city sophisticated. Visitors looking for more swank can opt to stay at the gilded Hotel du Pont in nearby Wilmington. Fashioned after a Renaissance palazzo, it was built in 1903 for those who came to do business with the family.

The du Pont trail continues just 20 minutes across the Pennsylvania border at the Longwood estate and its 1,050-acre, fountain-studded gardens, the personal fantasy of Pierre's. Every season is celebrated here (with an emphasis on Christmas) in myriad outdoor as well as indoor displays.

A family legacy of another kind can be found a bit farther east, at the Brandywine River Museum. A Civil War–era gristmill here houses three generations worth of art by the Wyeths. At N. C. Wyeth's nearby house and studio, The Homestead, the painting he was working on at the time of his death is on display.

Connecting all the dots is the 25-mile Brandywine Valley Scenic Byway, which begins in Wilmington ("last stop to freedom" on the Underground Railroad) and winds not only past the du Pont estates but the Brandywine Battlefield, where the largest battle of the Revolutionary War took place on September 11, 1777.

WHERE: Wilmington is 28 miles southwest of Philadelphia. **VISITOR INFO:** www.visitwilmingtonde.com; www.thebrandywine.com. **HAGLEY MUSEUM:** Tel 302-658-2400; www.hagley.org. **NEMOURS:** Tel 800-651-6912 or 302-651-6912; www.nemoursmansion.org. *When:* closed Jan–Apr. **WINTERTHUR:** Tel 800-448-3883 or 302-888-4600; www.winterthur.org. **MONTCHANIN VILLAGE:** Tel 800-269-2473 or 302-888-2133; www.montchanin.com. *Cost:* from $192. **KRAZY KAT'S:** Tel 302-888-4200; www.krazykatsrestaurant.com. *Cost:* dinner $35. **HOTEL DU PONT:** Tel 800-441-9019 or 302-594-3100; www.hoteldupont.com. *Cost:* from $159 (off-peak), from $259 (peak). **LONGWOOD GARDENS:** Tel 800-737-5500 or 610-388-1000; www.longwoodgardens.org. **BRANDYWINE RIVER MUSEUM:** Tel 610-388-2700; www.brandywinemuseum.org. **BEST TIMES:** Apr–May for gardens; Sun of 1st full weekend in May for Winterthur Point-to-Point Steeplechase; Oct–Nov for foliage; Dec for holiday displays.

A Seaside Escape That's Not Always on the Map

AMELIA ISLAND

Florida, U.S.A.

Floating off the northeastern tip of Florida and measuring just 13 miles by 2 miles, Amelia Island has over the years been claimed by France, Spain, England, Mexico, the U.S., and the Confederacy. Everyone wanted it, with the exception of railroad tycoon Henry Flagler, who bypassed the island when he opened much of mainland Florida to tourism in 1890. While other Florida vacation spots became fun-in-the-sun theme parks, Amelia Island remained a serene place apart. Today it is a time warp of Victorian beauty.

Fernandina Beach, located at the barrier island's northern end, and Amelia's only town, features a 52-block center listed in the National

Register of Historic Places. Some of the nation's finest examples of Queen Anne, Victorian, and Italianate mansions are here, built for the same wave of wintering socialites who also left their mark on Georgia's Golden Isles (see p. 756) just north of here. Many of these structures have found a second life as handsome B&Bs, such as the gracious antebellum Williams House, where a large Southern-style breakfast is served on the veranda. On cobbled Centre Street you'll find galleries, restaurants, and the Palace Saloon, which bills itself as Florida's oldest bar. It's one of the unofficial headquarters during the Spring Shrimp Festival, which features boatloads of seafood and fireworks.

Two state parks showcase Amelia's unique blend of maritime forest and saltwater marsh. Explore their 13 miles of pristine, white sand beaches on bike or horseback. In late spring and early summer, loggerhead turtles lay their eggs here; in late fall and early winter, whales are frequently spotted on their way to the warm waters of the Caribbean.

Frequently voted one of the finest resorts in the South, the elegant but family-oriented Ritz-Carlton Amelia Island offers a wide beachfront, tennis, golf on the adjacent championship course at the Golf Club of Amelia Island, and exceptional dining-with-a-view at Salt, its acclaimed restaurant. The Omni Amelia Island Plantation, the Ritz's friendly rival, is situated on 1,350 beachfront acres and boasts its own golf courses designed by Pete Dye and Tom Fazio, along with 23 clay tennis courts and a tennis school. An alternative to the big resorts is the beachfront Elizabeth Pointe Lodge, an 1890s Nantucket-shingle–style inn. The emphasis here is on pure relaxation—of the rocking-chair-on-the-porch variety.

WHERE: 30 miles northeast of Jacksonville via causeway. **VISITOR INFO:** www.ameliaisland.com. **WILLIAMS HOUSE:** Tel 800-414-9258 or 904-277-2328; www.williamshouse.com. *Cost:* from $195. **PALACE SALOON:** 904-261-6320; www.thepalacesaloon.com. **RITZ-CARLTON:** Tel 800-241-3333 or 904-277-1100; www.ritzcarlton.com. *Cost:* from $250 (off-peak), from $380 (peak); dinner at Salt $55. **OMNI AMELIA ISLAND PLANTATION:** Tel 888-261-6161 or 904-261-6161; www.omnihotels.com. *Cost:* from $209 (off-peak), from $339 (peak); greens fees from $150. **ELIZABETH POINTE LODGE:** Tel 800-772-3359 or 904-277-4851; www.elizabethpointelodge.com. *Cost:* from $220. **BEST TIMES:** 1st weekend of May for the Shrimp Festival; spring and early summer for beach fun; spring, fall, and winter for golf and tennis.

"We choose to go to the moon."—JFK, September 12, 1962

KENNEDY SPACE CENTER

Cape Canaveral, Florida, U.S.A.

Set amid 140,000 acres of marshland and mangrove swamp, Kennedy Space Center has been the headquarters of American rocketry and space exploration since the launch of the unmanned *Bumper 8* research rocket in July 1950. Eleven years later, Alan Shepard lifted off Pad 5 to become the first American in space, and in July 1969 *Apollo 11* blasted off from Pad 39A, carrying Neil Armstrong, Buzz Aldrin, and Michael Collins to the moon. Since then, the base has been home to America's space shuttle and International Space Station programs; it is currently overseeing unmanned missions to Mars, Jupiter, and beyond.

Visitor tours begin at the Kennedy Space Center Visitor Complex, which houses a collection of NASA rockets and two IMAX theaters showing films about space exploration that will get your patriotic juices flowing. Various programs offer chances to meet astronauts and tour other sections of the facility. Self-guided tours visit the LC-39 Observation Gantry, with a 360-degree view of the space shuttle launch pads, and the Apollo/Saturn V Center, housing a 363-foot Saturn V, the most powerful rocket ever launched by the U.S.

The U.S. Astronaut Hall of Fame features the world's largest collection of astronaut personal memorabilia, plus historic spacecraft, hands-on activities, and astronaut training simulators. Sit at a mission control console or take a virtual ride on Mars in the G-Force Trainer and feel the pull of 4 G's.

WHERE: 45 miles east of Orlando. Tel 321-449-4444; www.kennedyspacecenter.com.

Rubenesque Mermaids on the Gulf Coast

SWIMMING WITH THE MANATEES

Crystal River, Florida, U.S.A.

Their bodies look like zeppelins and they've got faces like sad-sack hound dogs, so it must have been the manatees' plaintive, squealing murmurs that made old-time sailors think they were mermaids, giving them the name *sirenia*. Mermaids they are not, but these adorable, air-breathing, water-dwelling mammals are endearingly playful and amazingly graceful despite their average 10–12 foot length and 1,000- to 2,000-pound bulk.

Contact with humans has been devastating for the manatees, which are nearsighted and swim just below the surface, putting them in the deadly path of speedboats. In 1981, former Florida governor Bob Graham and singer/songwriter Jimmy Buffett established the Save the Manatee Club, a nonprofit organization dedicated to research, advocacy, and protection efforts. Though their numbers have increased, they're not out of danger yet.

The U.S. population of some 3,000 West Indian manatees, known as sea cows, lives almost exclusively in the warm waters off Florida's eastern and western coasts, wintering particularly near Citrus County, the only place in the world where you can swim with manatees on a guided tour. A number of outfitters in Crystal River equip visitors with snorkeling gear and provide boat transportation to nearby Kings Bay, where 100 to 250 of the area's 400 creatures tend to loll. Snorkelers must wait for the manatees to approach—which they almost always do, sometimes nudging their curious visitors as if to say they're ready for their playdate.

Gentle manatees find refuge in Kings Bay.

WHERE: 80 miles west of Orlando. **HOW:** Crystal Lodge Dive Center offers 2.5-hour guided tours. Tel 352-795-6798; www.manatee-central.com. *Cost:* $15, gear extra. **BEST TIMES:** Nov–Feb; morning, when the water is clearest.

The Home of Speed

Daytona Speedway

Daytona Beach, Florida, U.S.A.

NASCAR racing is said to be the most popular spectator sport in the U.S. In 1947, when racing resumed after the war, Daytona Beach mechanic Bill France organized the National Association for Stock Car Auto Racing (NASCAR), then opened the Daytona International Speedway in 1959 on a 480-acre property at the southern end of the eponymous beach. The first Daytona 500 ran in February of that year, with a field of 59 cars, a purse of $67,760, and more than 41,000 spectators. Today it's the most prestigious stock car race in America, marking the official start of the NASCAR season with 200,000 fans in the stands, another 30 million on TV, and a total purse in excess of $18 million. The two weeks prior, known as Speedweeks, attract thousands for half a dozen races (including the historic Rolex 24 at Daytona sports-car race and the Daytona 500 qualifying rounds) and race-related events galore.

Daytona has become a mecca for nearly all aspects of motorsports, hosting eight different race weekends annually. In early March, motorcycle enthusiasts gather for Bike Week, a 10-day festival leading up to the Daytona 200, the most important two-wheeled race in the U.S., held annually since 1937. In late December, go-kart enthusiasts flood in for Daytona KartWeek.

In 1996, the Daytona 500 Experience, "the Official Attraction of NASCAR," opened at Daytona International, with motion-simulator rides, IMAX movies, and behind-the-scenes tours. For the ultimate thrill, pony up for the Richard Petty Driving Experience. Named for the seven-time Daytona 500 winner, this ride lets race fans slip behind the wheel or be a passenger on the Daytona International track.

Where: 60 miles north of Orlando. Tel 800-748-7467 or 386-254-2700; www.daytonainternationalspeedway.com. *When:* Speedweeks starts late Jan and ends with the Daytona 500. Bike Week is in early Mar (www.officialbikeweek.com). **Daytona 500 Experience:** Tel 386-681-6530; www.daytona500experience.com. **Richard Petty Driving Experience:** Tel 800-237-3889; www.drivepetty.com. *Cost:* from $135.

River of Grass

Everglades National Park

Florida, U.S.A.

Covering 1.5 million acres and spanning the southern tip of the Florida peninsula, Everglades National Park is just a slice of the great wetland that once stretched north from Florida Bay and is today 120 miles long

The snowy egret lives in the Everglades year-round, along with hundreds of other species of birds.

and 50 miles wide. Called Pa-hay-okee ("grassy waters") by the Seminole Indians, it is a complex ecosystem that is half land and half water with a bird population that was once so numerous flocks would black out the sky as they rose into the air. Today this region, the only subtropical preserve in North America, is still home to thousands of animal and plant species, tangled mangrove thickets, labyrinthine channels, and hundreds of islands. But its integrity is hanging by a thread following decades of disastrous South Florida water projects and urban sprawl, which have effectively diverted and polluted the steady flow of water the Everglades needs to survive.

Fortunately, environmentalists have made their voices heard, and government, big agriculture, and conservation groups alike are working to restore the region's ecological balance. Visitors can explore the peripheral marshland, beginning almost in Miami's backyard, via air boat, wooden walkways, and bicycle trails, but ideally you'll want a kayak or canoe and a knowledgeable guide. Despite the drop in the avian population since the 19th century, bird-watching can still be outstanding, especially when the winter's migratory guests join about 350 resident species. Flora fanciers have some 1,000 species to study beyond the ubiquitous saw grass. You may even spot some of the swamp's alligators, hawksbill turtles, manatees, and—if you're exceedingly lucky—one of the rare Florida panthers who call the park home.

Where: 40 miles southwest of Miami; main park entrance and visitor center just south of Homestead and Florida City. Tel 305-242-7700; www.nps.gov/ever. **How:** North American Canoe Tours offers canoe and kayak rentals, with and without guides, departing from Everglades City. Tel 239-695-4666; www.evergladesadventures.com. *Cost:* from $35 a day for canoe rental; from $125 per person for 6-hour guided canoe trip. **Best time:** Dec–Apr, when the climate is relatively dry, the bugs minimal, and the wildlife—especially birds—abundant.

The American Caribbean

The Florida Keys

Florida, U.S.A.

Stretching in a graceful arc from mainland Florida southwest into the Gulf of Mexico, the 800 islands (30 of them inhabited) known as the Florida Keys are connected by the awe-inspiring 128-mile-long extension of Route 1 called the Overseas Highway.

Closest to the mainland, the Upper and Middle Keys attract anglers—particularly Islamorada, which stretches across four islands in a region known as the sportfishing capital of the world. Check into the 200-room Cheeca Lodge & Spa, a mid-Keys mainstay since 1946. Sign up for any of the charters heading off for the day: into the Atlantic for sailfish, tuna, and mahi mahi, or into Florida Bay for tarpon and bonefish. Glass-bottom–boat outings and diving and snorkeling trips are available at the John Pennekamp Coral Reef State Park in Key Largo, the first U.S. undersea park, designed to preserve the only living coral barrier reef in the country. Marathon's Dolphin Research Center, in Grassy Key, offers the chance to interact with 19 Atlantic bottlenose dolphins in their 90,000-square-foot natural-lagoon habitat.

Cross the Seven-Mile Bridge to reach the more protected Lower Keys, where you may spot an endangered Key deer. The most secluded and luxurious accommodations can be found at Little Palm Island Resort, once a fishing camp for President Harry Truman and today a 6-acre resort of 30 thatched-roof bungalows. Accessible only by boat shuttle or seaplane, it's still more convenient than Tahiti for anyone with a platinum credit card and a South Pacific dream.

Your final destination is Key West. The southernmost point of the continental United States (it is closer to Cuba, 90 miles away, than it is to Miami), this key is known for its fusion of Caribbean, Latin, and American culture and relaxed Margaritaville lifestyle. The population of locals (known as "Conchs")—snowbirds, freethinkers, artists, and a large gay community (the town's unofficial motto is "One Human Family")—mixes with thousands of cruise ship passengers who descend for a few hours every day in the high season. Mile-long Duval Street is home to buzzing restaurants, hand-rolled–cigar stands, ice-cream shops (try the Key Lime flavor), an impressive Butterfly Conservatory, souvenir stores, and a whole host of legendary

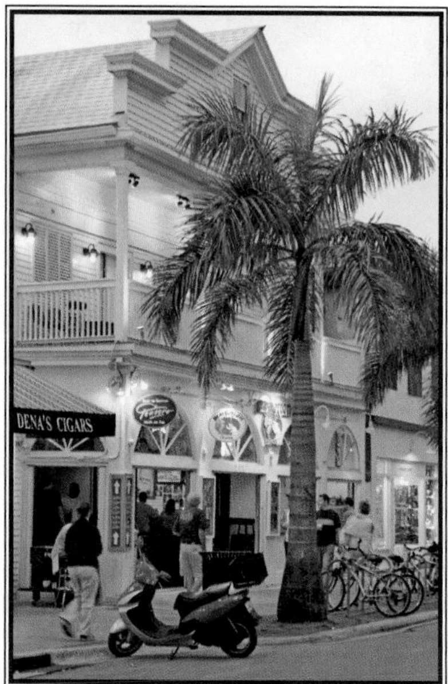

Key West's Duval Street teems with galleries, gift shops, saloons, and eateries.

bars. Sloppy Joe's draws hordes of tourists, though the original bar where Papa Hemingway used to drink is now known as Captain Tony's Saloon and is just around the corner. Hemingway aficionados can tour his house and studio, where descendants of his polydactyl, or "many-toed," cats still wander the grounds, and where Hemingway completed *For Whom the Bell Tolls* and *A Farewell to Arms.* History buffs can walk to the Little White House, waterfront vacation home of President Truman, preserved just as he left it.

Tool around town on the motorized Conch Tour Train to view one of North America's largest concentrations of 19th-century wooden houses, and wind up at Mallory Square pier for the daily sunset-watching ritual among buskers, fire-eaters, and musicians. Don't miss a chance to glimpse the ephemeral green flash, which allegedly occurs just as the sun sinks below the horizon. If you're lucky, you've found a room at the West Indian plantation-style Gardens Hotel just steps from Duval Street's hubbub. Lounge for a bit by the pool with a copy of Truman's or Hemingway's memoirs, cocooned by lush palms and orchids.

Where: Key West is 159 miles southwest of Miami. **Visitor info:** www.fla-keys.com. **Cheeca Lodge & Spa:** Tel 800-327-2888 or 305-266-7920; www.cheeca.com. *Cost:* from $199 (off-peak), from $399 (peak). **John Pennekamp State Park:** Tel 305-451-1202; www.pennekamppark.com. **Dolphin Research Center:** Tel 305-289-1121; www.dolphins.org. **Little Palm Island:** Tel 800-343-8567 or 305-515-4004; www.littlepalmisland.com. *Cost:* from $595 (off-peak), from $1,190 (peak). **Sloppy Joe's:** Tel 305-294-5717; www.sloppyjoes.com. **Hemingway Home:** Tel 305-294-1136; www.hemingwayhome.com. **Little White House:** Tel 305-294-9911; www.trumanlittlewhitehouse.com. **Conch Tour Train:** Tel 800-868-7482 or 305-294-5161; www.conchtourtrain.com. **Gardens Hotel:** Tel 800-526-2664 or 305-294-2661; www.gardenshotel.com. *Cost:* from $165 (off-peak), from $385 (peak). **Best times:** Nov–May for nicest weather. In Key West: late Jan for Yachting Race Week; Apr for Conch Republic Independence Celebration; early Jun for Pridefest; mid-Jul for Hemingway Days; late Oct for Fantasy Fest; New Year's Eve.

A South Beach Institution

Joe's Stone Crab

Miami Beach, Florida, U.S.A.

"Before SoBe, Joe be," touts Joe's Stone Crab, Miami Beach's (and possibly the nation's) number one crab institution, referring to its decades of renown prior to the rebirth of South Beach. Word of its tasty crustaceans spread quickly when the family-run place first opened in 1913, and the line to get in has been long ever since.

Today, in an expanded location, Joe's is still in the Weiss family's hands, and many of the employees have been around for decades. On the menu is just one entrée, the stone crab: a delicacy found only in southwestern Florida, the Keys, and along the Gulf of Mexico from mid-October to mid-May. Every day, crabbing boats head offshore to satisfy the daily demand for a ton of claws in the 450-seat indoor/outdoor restaurant. The crabs come in four sizes, medium to jumbo, served without fuss on a newspaper-covered table with mustard sauce or melted butter, hash browns or cottage-fried sweet potatoes, coleslaw, and creamed spinach. Save room for dessert: Joe's Key lime pie is the real thing.

Joe's crabs aren't cheap—Damon Runyon quipped that they were sold by the carat—and their no-reservations policy means there's always a wait for a table (the line for lunch moves more quickly and you'll see more locals). But it's all part of the experience, along with the formally dressed waiters and the lingering allure of nearly a century of Miami players, including Al Capone, Frank Sinatra, and Howard Cosell.

If you don't care about ambience—and want your crabs fast—head to Joe's Take Away, which is on-site. You can even get a meal shipped right to your door, whether you live in Chicago or across town.

Info: Tel 305-673-0365; www.joesstonecrab.com. **Cost:** $24 for medium claws. **When:** closed Aug–mid-Oct. **Best time:** Dinner lines tend to be shortest 5–6:30 P.M.

Art Deco on the American Riviera

South Beach

Miami Beach, Florida, U.S.A.

South Beach embodies the mash-up of fashion, celebrity, design, hip beach culture, and wealth that has come to define American fabulousness. The Miami area's location between Europe, New York, L.A., and South America no doubt contributed to its renaissance, but credit must also go to the city's architectural forefathers, who between the late '20s and early '40s built a backdrop as beautiful as today's bronzed and buffed denizens.

South Beach's Art Deco district crowds some 800 pastel-colored buildings in the Art Deco, Art Moderne, and Mediterranean Revival styles into a mere 1 square mile. Tours are available from the Miami Design Preservation League (MDLP). Afterward, repair to the 24-hour News Café for some of the best people-watching in town.

Miami Beach had its first incarnation as a glamorous playground back in the '40s, and then enjoyed a rebirth 50 years later that continues still. Although these days the epicenter of cool may change with the weather, some hotels keep appearing on the radar. The oceanfront Tides South Beach is a Deco queen dating from 1936, whose 2007 redesign helped it reclaim its legacy as the "Diva of Ocean Drive"; the luxurious oceanfront hotel's La Marea Restaurant is the place to indulge in the scene and cuisine. Less than a mile north, the Raleigh Hotel, built in 1940, is still loved for its Deco pool, tailor-made for the Esther Williams movies that were filmed there. The Delano, with its five restaurants and equally stylish swimming pool, has been a magnet for Miami's Beautiful People since its lavish 1995 redo by hotelier Ian Schrager and designer Philippe Starck. Art-Deco-meets-Asia at the beautifully recreated oceanfront Setai, which combines a replica of the '30s Dempsey Vanderbilt Hotel and a new 40-story tower for a Zen-infused escape. Prices are over-the-top, but so are the amenities. The low-profile Winter Haven Hotel is a restored 1939 classic on the quieter end of Ocean Drive; many of its 71 bright rooms have views of the ocean just across the street.

For the archetypal Miami Beach resort, head just north of South Beach to the Fontainebleau, a 1954 Neo-Rococo classic by architect Morris Lapidus. The favorite seaside palace of the '50s Rat Pack and Hollywood filmmakers (it was the setting of *Goldfinger*, Al Pacino's *Scarface*, and Jerry Lewis's *The Bellboy*), it draws crowds today for its Vegas-like past as well as new high-design towers, glass-walled spa, and state-of-the-art gym. Expect all these hotels to be booked to the gills when the annual Art Basel Miami Beach comes to town. Begun in 2002 (its Swiss counterpart dates to 1969; see p. 273), this prestigious 4-day art show features works from the world's top galleries, supplemented by cultural happenings all over the Art Deco district.

Miami Design Preservation League: Tel 305-531-3484; www.mdpl.org. *Cost:* tours $30. **News Café:** Tel 305-538-6397; www.newscafe.com. *Cost:* dinner $25. **The Tides:** Tel 800-439-4095 or 305-604-5070; www.tidessouthbeach.com. *Cost:* from $315 (off-peak), from $595 (peak); dinner at La Marea $45. **Raleigh:** Tel 800-848-1775 or 305-534-6300; www.raleighhotel.com. *Cost:* from $160 (off-peak), from $395 (peak). **Delano:** Tel 800-697-1791 or 305-672-2000; www.delano-hotel.com. *Cost:* from $435 (off-peak), from

$755 (peak). **Setai:** Tel 888-625-7500 or 305-520-6000; www.setai.com. *Cost:* from $695 (off-peak), from $1,500 (peak). **Winter Haven Hotel:** Tel 800-553-7739 or 305-531-5571; www.winterhavenhotelsobe.com. *Cost:* from $129 (off-peak), from $299 (peak). **Fontainebleau:** Tel 800-548-8886 or 305-538-2000; www.fontainebleau.com. *Cost:* from $249 (off-peak), from $429 (peak). **Best times:** Nov–Mar for nicest weather; 3 days in mid-Jan for Art Deco Weekend; early Dec for Art Basel.

America's Most Popular Resort

Walt Disney World

Orlando, Florida, U.S.A.

The brainchild of genius animator Walt Disney is an ever-expanding universe of escapism, celebrating magic, technology, nature, and Mickey Mouse. Along with Disneyland (see p. 723), Walt Disney World is among the most popular tourist attractions on the planet, transformed from a forgotten 30,000-acre pasture into four distinct parks, each demanding that you leave the real world at the gate.

The original Magic Kingdom, with Cinderella Castle at its center, has seven themed "lands" radiating outward. It is full of classic rides, including It's a Small World, and newer attractions like Buzz Lightyear's Space Ranger Spin.

Epcot Center, opened 16 years after Walt's death, presents a mix of science-oriented films, rides, and interactive experiences. Eleven countries and their cultures are represented in pavilions around a 40-acre lagoon. The thrill rides here include the Soarin' hang gliding adventure, the Mission: Space astronaut adventure, and Test Track, a car stress-test simulator.

Disney's Hollywood Studios is the most theatrical of the parks, with an American Idol experience that puts you into the show (audition for a chance to perform) and the Twilight Zone Tower of Terror, which drops you from 13 stories. At the 500-acre Animal Kingdom real jungle life and landscapes create a safari not unlike a trip to Botswana.

There are countless less expensive hotel options in and around Orlando, but the various Disney-owned and -run hotels are closer to the principal attractions and linked by complimentary transportation. The Grand Floridian Resort & Spa may be the nicest choice, with the air of a breezy turn-of-the-century summer resort.

The nearby Universal Studios Florida lets fans of all ages experience being smack dab in their favorite flick. True adventure junkies love the Islands of Adventure, 110 acres divided into five themed islands ranging from Dr. Seuss to Marvel Comics, and the Harry Potter "park within a park" that opened in 2010.

Where: 20 miles southwest of Orlando. Tel 407-934-7639; www.disneyworld.com. *Cost:* 1-day/1-park ticket $84 (ages 3–9), $91 (ages 10 and up). Resort stays from $100. **Grand Floridian:** Tel 407-824-3000; www.disneyworld.com. *Cost:* from $460 (off-peak), from $555 (peak). **Universal Studios:** Tel 800-837-2273 or 407-363-8000; www.universalorlando.com. *Cost:* 1-day/1-park ticket $79 (ages 3–9), $85 (ages 10 and up). **Best times:** Jan–Apr and Sep–Nov for small crowds; mid-Apr–early Jun for Epcot's Flower and Garden Festival; Oct–Nov for Epcot's International Food and Wine Festival; Oct for Halloween in Magic Kingdom; Dec for Christmas celebrations.

Where the Well-Heeled Winter

Palm Beach and The Breakers

Florida, U.S.A.

For a peek into the life of the landed gentry, look no farther than Palm Beach, a 13-mile barrier island enclave established as the winter home of America's uber-rich in the 1890s, and the essence of upper-crust prestige ever since. At its heart is the amusingly named Worth Avenue, where designer Lilly Pulitzer opened her little juice stand in 1958. Après shopping, drop in to Ta-boo, a '40s-era bistro with the air of an updated Victorian palm garden. The Bloody Mary was allegedly invented here to soothe heiress Barbara Hutton's hangover (a competing legend has its origin at the St. Regis hotel in New York; see p. 846).

Bike the 6-mile Lake Trail, which winds along the Lake Worth section of the Intracoastal Waterway, flanked by bobbing yachts and megamansions. On the Atlantic side of the island, Ocean Boulevard is home to another agglomeration of estates, including Donald Trump's Mar-a-Lago, the former home of heiress Marjorie Merriweather Post.

On the mainland, the social set gathers for the January start of polo season at Wellington's Palm Beach Polo and Country Club. The facility is also home to the Palm Beach Polo Equestrian Club; its winter festival (January through March) is the nation's largest equestrian show-jumping competition.

Set up camp at the Brazilian Court, which opened its doors in 1926, welcoming the likes of Greta Garbo and Cary Grant to its Spanish-style suites and courtyards. For dinner it's French-American cuisine at the hotel's Café Boulud, an outpost of celebrity chef Daniel Boulud's New York empire (see p. 847).

Or unpack at the fabled Breakers, built by railroad visionary Henry Morrison Flagler. Modeled after Rome's Villa Medici, the legendary 560-room, 140-acre resort has Venetian chandeliers and fountain-splashed grounds leading down to a half mile of white private beach. The Mediterranean-style indoor/outdoor spa is frequently named one of the country's finest, and dinner at L'Escalier is culinary theater. The decadent buffet Sunday brunch at The Circle is also a don't-miss.

Henry Flagler's heirs rebuilt The Breakers after a devastating fire in 1925.

Where: 70 miles north of Miami. **Ta-boo:** Tel 561-835-3500; www.taboorestaurant.com. *Cost:* lunch $30. **Palm Beach Polo and Country Club:** Tel 800-257-1038 or 561-798-7000; www.palmbeachpolo.com. *When:* peak polo season late Jan–Apr. **The Brazilian Court:** Tel 800-745-8883 or 561-655-7740; www.thebraziliancourt.com. *Cost:* from $220 (off-peak), from $325 (peak); dinner at Café Boulud $65. **The Breakers:** Tel 888-273-2537 or 561-655-6611; www.thebreakers.com. *Cost:* from $270 (off-peak), from $450 (peak); dinner at L'Escalier $100, brunch at The Circle $90. **Best times:** Nov–May for weather; Jan–Feb for the peak of the social season.

A Beachcomber's Bonanza

SANIBEL AND CAPTIVA ISLANDS

Florida, U.S.A.

Down on Florida's southern Gulf coast, Old Florida lives on. Of the more than 100 neighboring islands, the best known are Sanibel and Captiva, connected to the mainland by a 3-mile causeway and to each other by a reputation for palm-stenciled sunsets, romantic sugary-white beaches, and arguably the country's best shell collecting. A good northwest wind can fill the beaches with hundreds of varieties of shells, most in one piece. Collectors wake before dawn and patrol the sands with flashlights, scrunched over in what has become known as the "Sanibel Stoop" or the "Captiva Crouch" (head to secluded and beautiful Bowman's Beach for a little less competition). Rainy day? Get your fix at Sanibel's Bailey-Matthews Shell Museum. It has the most comprehensive collection of its kind in the country—some 150,000 specimens.

There's more than just gorgeous beach here. Visit Sanibel's J. N. "Ding" Darling National Wildlife Refuge, 6,390 cool acres of mangrove estuary, marshes, and West Indian hardwood hammock. Birders come to watch for more than 320 species, including bald eagles, wood storks, and peregrine falcons. Footpaths, bicycle trails, and kayak and canoe routes crisscross the area, or you can motor along the winding Wildlife Drive.

Captiva and Sanibel's three most interesting neighbor islands, located in Pine Island Sound, are car free and accessible only by boat. Cayo Costa State Park's deserted beaches offer yet more excellent shelling, while over at Cabbage Key Jimmy Buffett is said to have found inspiration for his song "Cheeseburger in Paradise." At the other end of the spectrum, Gatsby-esque Useppa Island is home to the Collier Inn, where Teddy Roosevelt vacationed with his tarpon-fishing friends. Today it operates as a private club that welcomes nonmembers for overnight stays and lunch through special charters. Nearby Boca Grande on Gasparilla Island hosts an annual big-purse tarpon tournament.

WHERE: 135 miles south of Tampa. **VISITOR INFO:** www.fortmyers-sanibel.com. **SHELL MUSEUM:** Tel 888-679-6450 or 239-395-2233; www.shellmuseum.org. **"DING" DARLING REFUGE:** Tel 239-472-1100; www.fws.gov/dingdarling. **COLLIER INN:** Tel 888-735-6335 or 239-283-1061; www.useppa.com. *How:* Nonmember overnights through Southwest Florida Yacht Charters. Tel 800-262-7939 or 239-656-1339; www.swfyachts.com. Lunch charters through Captiva Cruises. Tel 239-472-5300; www.captivacruises.com. **BEST TIMES:** May–mid-Jul for tarpon season; Dec–Apr for peak shelling (winter storms in Dec–Jan commonly drive shells ashore); Nov–May for weather and bird-watching.

Roseate spoonbills wade at the J. N. "Ding" Darling National Wildlife Refuge.

A 2,178-Mile Walk in the Woods

The Appalachian Trail

Georgia to Maine, U.S.A.

The Appalachian Trail, the world's longest continuously marked footpath, wends its way along the eastern states from Georgia to Maine. Completed in 1937, it attracts between 3 and 4 million people every year. Most just tackle a portion of the trail, while 500 to 600 "through-hikers" complete the entire journey, from Georgia's Springer Mountain to Maine's Mount Katahdin—a trek of about 5 million steps, passing through 14 states, 8 national forests, and 6 national parks.

The first leg traverses the Chattahoochee National Forest, threading through Tennessee, North Carolina, and Virginia to West Virginia's 4-mile-long section. The Appalachian Trail Conservancy headquarters is found in West Virginia's Harpers Ferry, perhaps best known as the site of John Brown's ill-fated slave rebellion in 1859 that sparked the Civil War.

The halfway mark is in Pennsylvania, where the trail heads through the Michaux State Forest and the Cumberland Valley before reaching the Delaware Water Gap. It then enters New Jersey, offering occasional Manhattan skyline views. New York's popular Harriman–Bear Mountain State Park contains the first portion of the trail completed, in 1923.

The trail continues through Connecticut's section of the scenic Taconic Range and Housatonic River Valley, the beautiful Berkshire Mountains of western Massachusetts (see p. 812), and Vermont, where it approaches tree line at Killington (see p. 885). The portion of the trail in New Hampshire's majestic White Mountains (see p. 826) attracts more back-country hikers than any other part of the trail, and the 281-mile homestretch through Maine ends in the famous "Hundred Miles," an isolated stretch of mountains, lakes, and forest between the town of Monson and Mount Katahdin.

Where: 2,178 miles from Georgia to Maine. Tel 304-535-6331; www.appalachiantrail.org. *When:* generally Mar–Sep (northbound) or Jun–Dec (southbound). **Best times:** mid-May in Damascus, Va., for Appalachian Trail Days; Jun–Jul in the southern Appalachians for flowering shrubs; Oct in New England for fall foliage.

History, Aristocrats, and Splendid Isolation

The Golden Isles

Georgia, U.S.A.

In the 19th century, Astors, Rockefellers, Vanderbilts, Goodyears, and Pulitzers, fleeing snowy northern winters, began the tradition of vacationing on Georgia's stunning barrier islands. Five of these getaways would come to be known as the Golden Isles, as much for their special light as their privileged lifestyle.

Reachable only by ferry, Cumberland is the largest and most enchanting. More than 90 percent of the 35-square-mile island is protected, home to sea turtles, wild horses, and more than 300 species of birds. Day visitors are limited, but a lucky few overnighters have the place to themselves at the only accommodation on the island, the plantation-style Greyfield Inn. Little has changed at steel baron Thomas Carnegie's former home, built in 1901 and still run by his descendants.

The 9-mile-long Jekyll Island, two-thirds of which is off-limits to developers, offers a network of paved bike paths past grand "cottages" from its gilded past. The Queen Anne–style Jekyll Island Club Hotel, the island's former elite social hub, is the anchor of the 240-acre historic district and retains the aura of an Edwardian millionaires' hangout.

On Sea Island, the legendary Cloister at Sea Island resort has two 18-hole championship courses that rank among the best in the Southeast. Designed in classic Mission style, the romantic resort is surrounded by live oaks dripping with Spanish moss and boasts a lavish spa and 5 miles of pinkish white sandy beach. Neighboring Simons Island is no less beautiful, but more accessible and affordable. Since 1872, the 104-foot-tall St. Simons Lighthouse has stood guard over the main village's clutch of specialty boutiques, antiques shops, and seafood restaurants. Its sister, Little St. Simon's Island, reached only by ferry, is the least visited of all. Explore this special 10,000-acre oasis of moss-draped forests with a guide, who will show you some of the 20 miles of winding trails and 7 miles of shell-strewn beach. At the Lodge, rustic Adirondack-style cabins are home to no more than 30 guests, though they'll be sharing the island with up to ten day-trippers from June through September.

WHERE: 80 miles south of Savannah. **VISITOR INFO:** www.comecoastawhile.com. **CUMBERLAND ISLAND:** Tel 877-860-6787 or 912-882-4335; www.nps.gov/cuis. **GREYFIELD INN:** Tel 888-243-9738 or 904-261-6408; www.greyfieldinn.com. *Cost:* from $395 (off-peak), from $475 (peak), all-inclusive. **JEKYLL ISLAND CLUB HOTEL:** Tel 800-535-9547 or 912-635-2600; www.jekyllclub.com. *Cost:* from $190. **THE CLOISTER AT SEA ISLAND:** Tel 800-732-4752 or 912-638-3611; www.seaisland.com. *Cost:* from $450 (off-peak), from $700 (peak); greens fees from $225 (off-peak), from $295 (peak) for Seaside, and $175 (off-peak) and $210 (peak) for Plantation. **THE LODGE AT LITTLE SIMON:** Tel 888-733-5774 or 912-638-7472; www.littlessi.com. *Cost:* from $475 (off-peak), from $625 (peak), all-inclusive. Day visitors, from $75 inclusive. **BEST TIMES:** Apr–May and Sep–Oct for mild weather.

Georgia's Jewel

SAVANNAH'S HISTORIC DISTRICT

Savannah, Georgia, U.S.A.

Savannah is America's best walking city, a living museum with the country's largest National Historical Landmark District: more than 2,300 Colonial and Victorian buildings within 2.5 square miles. The nation's first planned city, Savannah was laid out in 1733 on a grid by its founder, British general James Oglethorpe; 21 of the original 24 leafy 1-acre squares remain. "White gold" (King Cotton) subsequently filled the coffers of this port city and was responsible for the proliferation of mansions. At President Lincoln's request, Savannah was spared during Gen. William Tecumseh Sherman's scorched-earth military campaign in 1864.

Almost a hundred years later, the Historic Savannah Foundation was born to protect the city's architectural legacy. The Davenport House Museum, the first building saved by the foundation, dates to 1820 and is one of the nation's finest Federal-style urban houses.

Take in the city by horse-drawn carriage, trolley, bicycle, or on foot. Several companies offer tours that include highlights from the 1994 bestseller *Midnight in the Garden of Good and Evil*, as well as notable buildings by British architect William Jay. Among his best are the Owens-Thomas House, an 1819 mansion in stunning Oglethorpe Square, and the nearby Telfair Academy. Both are today part of the Telfair Museum of Art, the South's oldest public art museum.

Some of the city's most impressive historic homes are now charming B&Bs and inns. The genteel 17-room Gastonian consists of two Italianate town houses and a carriage house dating from the 1860s; its legendary Southern breakfast is a challenge to walk off. Mansion on Forsyth Park combines a regal, 1888 Victorian-Georgian mansion and a newer annex that blends harmoniously. It includes a spa, and the 700 Drayton, a restaurant as known for its hamburgers as it is for its more inventive fare.

Savannah celebrates its food with inimitable panache. Housed in an elegant turn-of-the-century Beaux Arts manse, Elizabeth on 37th has long been popular for its refined interpretation of classic lowcountry recipes. Meanwhile, over at Mrs. Wilkes's Boarding House, large communal tables disappear under platters of fried chicken, peppery crab stew spiked with sherry, and Savannah red rice. "The Lady" who owns The Lady & Sons restaurant is Food Network chef Paula Deen. Her enormous and forever full restaurant in a former 19th-century hardware store draws raves for what many say are the best crab cakes and fried chicken in town.

Where: 250 miles southeast of Atlanta. **Visitor info:** www.savannahvisit.com. **Davenport House:** Tel 912-236-8097; www.davenporthousemuseum.org. **Telfair Museum of Art:** Tel 912-790-8800; www.telfair.org. **The Gastonian:** Tel 800-322-6603 or 912-232-2869; www.gastonian.com. *Cost:* from $205. **Mansion on Forsyth Park:** Tel 888-711-5114 or 912-238-5158; www.mansiononforsythpark.com. *Cost:* from $160 (off-peak), from $310 (peak); dinner $50. **Elizabeth on 37th:** Tel 912-236-5547; www.elizabethon37th.net. *Cost:* dinner $60. **Mrs. Wilkes's Boarding House:** Tel 912-232-5997; www.mrswilkes.com. *Cost:* lunch $15. **The Lady & Sons:** Tel 912-233-2600; www.ladyandsons.com. *Cost:* dinner $37. **Best times:** late Mar for Tour of Homes and Gardens; mid-May for spring tour of historic gardens.

Locals call the Asendorf House, built in the Queen Anne style, the "Gingerbread House."

"I believe Hawaii is the most precious jewel in the world."—Don Ho

Hawai'i Island (Big Island)

Hawaii, U.S.A.

The youngest, largest, and most primal of the 1,500-mile-long Hawaiian archipelago, Hawai'i Island has all the necessary tropical delights and awe-inspiring natural attractions, including the world's most active volcano. This is the birthplace of the great warrior King Kamehameha I, who in 1812 conquered the other islands and created the Kingdom of Hawai'i. Though Hawai'i Island is the correct geographic name, it is best known as the Big Island because all the other islands could fit into it twice over. Whatever you call it, the island is a miracle of diversity, containing 11 of Earth's 13 climate zones—from lush tropical rain forests to desolate, black lava deserts and arctic tundra. Don't miss the thrilling spectacle of watching the molten lava of Kilauea make the island grow bigger before your eyes.

Top Attractions

Hawaii Volcanoes National Park—The island's most prominent features are its five volcanoes—the largest, Mauna Kea, extends from sea level to 13,796 feet. You can get a glimpse of their power in the 330,000-acre Hawaii Volcanoes National Park. Here, you'll be taken on a journey back to the creation of earth, as deep, smoldering calderas hiss and underground lava tubes cut their way through the jungle. Follow the Crater Rim Drive to Kilauea Volcano, the park's crown jewel and believed to be the home of fiery goddess Pele. It has been spewing lava almost continuously since 1983.

At night the streaming lava glows like an incandescent ribbon on the flank of the mountain. The modest but conveniently located Volcano Inn, just a mile from the park entrance, assures an early start or the chance to spend a late night watching the fiery flows. **Where:** 30 miles southwest of Hilo. **Volcanoes National Park:** Tel 808-985-6000; www.nps.gov/havo. **Volcano Inn:** Tel 800-628-3876 or 808-967-7773; www.volcanoinnhawaii.com. *Cost:* from $99.

The Mauna Kea Summit—To the ancient Hawaiians, the snow-covered summit of Mauna Kea ("White Mountain") was where the gods lived. To astronomers, the 13,796-foot mountain, with its close-to-the-equator location and unusually clear, pitch-black skies, is the best place on earth to view the cosmos. Its peak is home to a number of the world's largest telescopes, but even naked-eye stargazing here is fantastic. With a 4WD vehicle, it's possible to drive from sea level to the top in a few hours. Pack some warm gear and a picnic dinner, and watch out for signs of altitude sickness, which is not uncommon.

At 9,200 feet, the Onizuka visitor center offers free tours that take you through an observatory at the summit. You can also explore the heavens on your own, using the center's telescopes. Arrive at the summit before sunset to wander around the colony of observatories, where 11 nations have set up 13 of the world's most sophisticated telescopes for deep-space exploration.

In Hilo you'll find the titanium-clad cones of the 'Imiloa Astronomy Center of Hawaii, where a state-of-the-art planetarium explores the origin of the universe according to both astronomical calculations and the Hawaiian creation chant. **Where:** 70 miles east of Kailua-Kona. **Onizuka Visitor Center:** Tel 808-961-2180; www.ifa.hawaii.edu/info/vis. **'Imiloa Astronomy Center:** Tel 808-969-9700; www.imiloahawaii.org.

Parker Ranch—Home of the *paniolo,* the Hawaiian cowboy, Parker Ranch is among the oldest and largest of U.S. ranches, founded in 1847 by one of Hawaii's earliest Anglo immigrants. Patriarch John Parker jumped ship in 1809 and was hired by King Kamehameha to cull maverick cattle. Before long, salt beef had become the island's top export, and in the 1830s, vaqueros from California taught riding and roping skills to paniolos (from the Hawaiian pronunciation of "*español*"). Centered around the quiet cow town of Waimea, the Parker Ranch still has a cattle operation, producing 14 million pounds of beef annually. It's at its liveliest during the Independence Day and Labor Day Rodeos, when paniolos strut their calf-roping, bronc-busting, bull-riding stuff. Cowboys of Hawaii offers ranch tours by ATV and horseback. **Where:** Kamuela. Tel 800-262-7290 or 808-887-1046; www.parkerranch.com. **Cowboys of Hawaii:** Tel 808-885-5006; www.cowboysofhawaii.com.

Waipi'o Valley—A Garden of Eden dense with fruit trees, waterfalls, and a gorgeous beach of black sand, Waipi'o Valley is also a place of great *mana*, or spiritual power—many *ali'i* (royalty) rest in ancient burial caves in the cliffs of this "Valley of the Kings." At the turn of the 17th century, aqueducts and ingenious aquaculture ponds supported a population of 40,000; today, it's a sleepy, peaceful place. After taking in the majestic views from Waipi'o Valley Overlook, you can head down into the valley on guided 4WD tours or on foot, then ride horseback or take a mule-drawn wagon tour of the valley floor. Spectacular waterfalls cascade down the steep, jungled valley walls, including

Carved wooden images, known as ki'i, greet visitors at Pu'uhonua o Honaunau National Historic Park.

1,200-foot Hiilawe Falls, Hawaii's tallest. This is also the starting point for one of Hawaii's best drives. The 45-mile trip along the Hamakua Coast takes you through quaint villages, past plunging waterfalls, and over bridges spanning deep ravines, ending in Hilo. Make your base the Waipi'o Wayside Inn, a 1932 former sugar plantation bungalow commanding ocean views from the top of a 1,000-foot cliff. **Where:** 50 miles north of Hilo. **Waipi'o Wayside B&B:** Tel 800-833-8849 or 808-775-0275; www.waipiowayside.com. *Cost:* from $99.

Kealakekua Bay—At Kealakekua Bay, dramatic cliffs surround turquoise waters on the southern Kona Coast. Captain Cook was the first documented European to land here in 1779. Visitors come today for the underwater park and marine preserve, one of Hawaii's best snorkeling and diving locations and home to abundant populations of tropical fish, sea turtles, octopus, and visiting spinner dolphins that lend a magical note, especially if you see them by kayak. (The best chance of a sighting is first thing in the morning.) Calm conditions prevail all but a few days out of the year, and the turquoise water is warm and clear, with visibility up to 100 feet. **Where:** 16 miles south of Kailua-Kona.

Pu'uhonua o Honaunau—In ancient Hawaii, death was the penalty for breaking a *kapu* (law), but offenders who eluded the chief's warriors could find safety at a *pu'uhonua*, or place of refuge. At Pu'uhonua o Honaunau National Historic Park, a nearly 500-year-old Great Wall—10 feet high, 1,000 feet long, and 17 feet thick—circumscribes one of these legendary pu'uhonuas. Outside it lies a complex of archaeological sites, and within, a restored 1650 temple that holds the remains of 23 ancient Hawaiian chiefs. In late June and early July, the Cultural Festival celebrates Hawaiian traditions with a royal court procession, hula, and samples of traditional foods. **Where:** 22 miles south of Kailua-Kona. Tel 808-328-2288; www.nps.gov/puho.

Best Beaches

Hapuna Beach—A gorgeous half-mile-long swath of sand on brilliant blue waters, Hapuna is one of Big Island's largest and most popular beaches. It has shore breaks for body boarders, humpback whale viewing in winter, and great snorkeling in summer. Local families spend the day here, bringing their hibachis and coolers for picnicking in the green park nearby. **Where:** 9 miles north of Waikoloa Village.

Kauna'oa Beach—This palm-fringed slice of soft white sand fronting the Mauna Kea Beach Hotel on the Kohala Coast is, like its sister, Hapuna Beach to the south, one of the most beautiful seaside spots on the island. Sometimes referred to as Mauna Kea Beach, Kauna'oa is usually less crowded than Hapuna Beach because parking is limited. Unless you're staying at the hotel, arrive early to enjoy swimming, snorkeling, bodysurfing, and, in winter, the frequent appearance of humpback whales. **Where:** Kohala.

Anaeho'omalu Bay—This lovely coconut palm–lined beach (nicknamed A-Bay) fronting Waikoloa Resort is often calm even when the surf is rough elsewhere. A-Bay offers sailing and diving expeditions and boasts some of the best windsurfing in West Hawaii. Plus, it has a large petroglyph field and two ancient Hawaiian fishponds that once served Hawaiian royalty. The only thing lacking is surfable waves. **Where:** Waikoloa.

Kahalu'u Beach Park—Snorkelers and scuba divers come to the Kona coast to swim with angelfish, darting wrasses, yellow tangs, and the occasional dolphin. If you're a beginner, Kahalu'u Beach Park is an excellent place to start. A reef offshore keeps the waters calm, and much of the protected cove is only 3 feet deep. It couldn't be easier—vendors even sell plastic fish identification cards that you can take with you into the water. For the best experience, come early in the morning before the crowds arrive. **Where:** 5 miles south of Kailua.

Makalawena Beach—If it weren't so hard to get to, this spectacular piece of shoreline at Keahole would be the most popular beach on the island. Dotted with coves and protected by dunes, Makalawena requires that you hike a half hour through black lava fields to reach it, but handsomely rewards the effort with isolation and pristine beauty. The swimming, snorkeling, and body boarding are all excellent. **Where:** In Kekaha Kai State Park, 4 miles north of Kona International Airport.

Makalawena Beach lies along the island's Kona coast.

Events & Festivals

King Kamehameha Day—The oldest of Hawaii's festivals, King Kamehameha Day was proclaimed in 1871 to honor the great warrior-king who unified the Hawaiian archipelago. Though celebrated throughout the islands, it is here, on his home island, that it is most enthusiastically embraced every June 11. In North Kohala, where he was born, a lei-draping ceremony centers on the King Kamehameha Statue. In the oceanside village of Kailua-Kona, which Kamehameha named the capital of the Kingdom of Hawaii in 1812, an elaborate procession with Pa'u queens and princesses on horseback and their retinues from all eight islands parades through the streets. **Where:** North Kohala and Kailua-Kona. www.kamehamehafestival.org.

Merrie Monarch Hula Festival—Hawaii's largest and most prestigious hula competition, this gorgeous display of performance and pageantry, held the week after Easter in Hilo, features contestants from the best hula *halau* (schools) on the islands and the U.S. mainland, with hundreds of dancers and musicians taking the stage throughout the weeklong event. You must mail your request for tickets by Dec. 26 to even have a hope of attending. Festival highlights include the Miss Aloha Hula solo competition, as well as contestants competing in *kahiko* (ancient) and *'auana* (modern) styles. The "Merrie Monarch" was Hawaii's last king, David Kalakaua, who led the revival of the hula and other cultural traditions during his reign from 1874 to 1891. **Where:** Hilo. Tel 808-935-9168; www.merriemonarchfestival.org.

The Ironman Triathalon—There are many Ironman competitions around the world, but this is the original—and the world championship. It started in 1978 as a 1-day competition that included Honolulu's three most difficult races: the 2.4-mile Waikiki Rough Water Swim, the 112-mile Around Oahu Bike Race, and the 26.2-mile Honolulu Marathon. The winner would be called "Iron Man." That first year, just 15 people showed up. Today it's held on Hawaii Island the second Saturday in October, with some 100,000 athletes from around the world competing in qualifying races for 1,700 starting positions.

After swimming and biking to the town of Hawi and back, the participants wind up at the finish line, the seawall along Ali'i Drive, where the winners come in around three o'clock. **Where:** The best view of the start is on the Kailua Bay Seawall, Kailua-Kona. Tel 808-329-0063; www.ironman.com.

Kona Coffee Cultural Festival—The Kona Coffee Belt is a 20-mile stretch from Holualoa to Kealakekua, where the sunny mornings, humid afternoons, and daily rain showers create the perfect growing conditions for some of the world's most prized coffee beans.

First planted by a missionary in 1828, the Kona bean grows on 700 farms today, making its cultivation one of the few nontourism industries in Hawaii. Die-hards will want to explore the region in early November during the 10-day Kona Coffee Cultural Festival. Besides the all-important cupping competition (blind tasting judged by experts), which determines the best Kona coffee in the state, there's a coffee bean–picking contest, art exhibits, farm tours, and even a Miss Kona Coffee pageant. **Where:** Kailua-Kona and environs. Tel 808-326-7820; www.konacoffeefest.com.

The Hawaii International Billfish Tournament—With warm, deep waters and sunny skies, the Kona coast is renowned for its big-game fishing. Most coveted of all are the "granders" (Pacific blue marlin weighing more than 1,000 pounds) reeled in every year from the fleet of high-tech sportfishing boats based in Honokohau Harbor. The action is at its most competitive in late July or early August, when teams of anglers from all over the world converge in search of marlin and other prized fish. The team with the most pounds (and points) wins the coveted and prestigious Governor's Trophy. **Where:** Kailua Pier, Kona Coast. Tel 808-836-3422; www.hibtfishing.com.

Where to Stay

The Fairmont Orchid—Set on 32 oceanfront acres with a sugar-white sand lagoon, this luxury resort with its grand staircases and endless marble is the perfect old-school hotel. Its excellent dining options include Brown's Beach House and Norio's Japanese Sushi Bar & Restaurant. And every Saturday it's Broadway meets Hawaii at "The Gathering of the Kings," a theatrical luau. **Where:** Kohala Coast. Tel 800-845-9905 or 808-885-2000; www.fairmont.com/orchid. *Cost:* from $325 (off-peak), from $350 (peak); dinner at Brown's $65, dinner at Norio's $65, luau $99.

Four Seasons Resort Hualalai—The Four Seasons Resort Hualalai on the Kohala Coast is a plantation-chic oasis of low-rise town houses clustered around four oceanside swimming pools. Its 18-hole Jack Nicklaus–designed Hualalai Golf Course is a big draw; open only to guests, it lies atop an 1801 lava flow from the currently dormant volcano that rises dramatically in the background and that gives the resort its name. The sunsets here are considered the most thrilling in Hawaii, and there's no better place to view them than from the casually elegant, oceanfront Pahu i'a ("aquarium") restaurant, known for its seafood and use of island ingredients. Treatments that use Hawaiian sea salt, macadamia nuts, and volcanic pumice lure guests to the Hualalai Spa, which mingles tropical gardens with cool interior spaces. **Where:** Kailua-Kona. Tel 888-340-5662 or 808-325-8000; www.fourseasons.com/hualalai. *Cost:* from $625; greens fees $250 (guests only); dinner at Pahu i'a $56.

King Kamehameha's Kona Beach Hotel—Located right on the beach in the village of Kailua-Kona, this updated '60s hotel has a contemporary, nature-inspired aesthetic. It has a legitimate claim to the King Kamehameha name: This is the sacred spot where he restored the centuries-old temple Ahu'ena Heiau and dedicated it to Lono, the god of peace and prosperity. Four nights a week (weather permitting), outrigger canoes carrying actors playing the king's royal court glide past the temple to begin the hotel's popular luau. **Where:** Kailua-Kona. Tel 800-367-2111 or 808-329-2911; www.konabeachhotel.com. *Cost:* from $130, luau from $70.

Kona Tiki Hotel—This classic 1950s motel is so close to the ocean, the surf crashes right outside your window—bring earplugs! A mile south of the restaurants and shopping of Kailua Village, Kona Tiki is a no-frills option with simple but clean rooms (there are no TVs or air-conditioning). The beaches are just a short drive to the north and the south. **Where:** Kailua-Kona. Tel 808-329-1425; www.konatikihotel.com. *Cost:* from $80.

Off the Kona coast, snorkelers can see fish clean the shell of a sea turtle by feeding on the algae that covers it.

Mauna Kea Beach Hotel—Laurance S. Rockefeller, grandson of industrialist John D. Rockefeller, was touring the island when he spotted a long, crescent-shaped white sand beach called Kauna'oa. By 1965, he had built a luxury hotel on the spot for the then unheard-of sum of $15 million. Now the cornerstone of the Mauna Kea Resort in Kohala, the Mauna Kea Beach Hotel is a showcase of classic 1960s architecture with a world-class Pacific Islands art collection throughout, a new spa, and a legendary golf course. **Where:** Kohala Coast. Tel 866-977-4589 or 808-882-7222; www.princeresorts hawaii.com *Cost:* from $350.

Mauna Lani Bay Hotel & Bungalows—Twilight at Kalahuipua'a, a monthly Hawaiian cultural celebration, is reason enough to stay at this oceanfront resort on the Kohala Coast. Once a month, on the Saturday closest to the full moon, Hawaii's most skilled performers share their songs and lore on a grassy lawn. Guests bring blankets and settle in for the evening, which recalls the time when neighbors would gather to sing, dance, and "talk story." For more contemporary pleasures, there's a sophisticated seaside restaurant, two 18-hole golf courses (see below), and a spa resembling a Hawaiian village. **Where:** Kohala Coast. Tel 800-367-2323 or 808-885-6622; www .maunalani.com. *Cost:* from $395.

Golf

Mauna Kea Resort—The sunny Kohala Coast is the golf capital of Hawaii, and most duffers aspire to make the pilgrimage. The one course they never miss is the stunning Mauna Kea, challenging guests since 1964, when Robert Trent Jones Sr. designed it around an ancient oceanfront lava flow. The Mauna Kea Resort, spread over 1,800 acres, is also home to the newer, environmentally friendly Hapuna Beach course, designed by Arnold Palmer and Ed Seay in the '90s. It has spectacular views of the Kohala Coast and snow-capped Mauna Kea volcano. **Mauna Kea:** Tel 808-882-5400; www.maunakeagolf.com. *Cost*: greens fees $225 (resort guests), $250 (nonguests). **Hapuna:** 808-880-3000. *Cost:* greens fees $125 (resort guests), $165 (nonguests).

Mauna Lani Resort—Another Kohala Coast golf mecca, the course at Mauna Lani ("mountain reaching heaven") Resort offers a visual feast of pitch-black lava flows, white sand traps, manicured fairways, and turquoise ocean as you play its 36 holes. The South Course's dramatic over-the-water 15th hole is among the most photographed in the world. Built over lava beds, the North Course is slightly tougher, its rolling terrain punctuated by mesquite forests and roaming herds of feral goats. **Info:** Tel 808-885-6655; www.maunalani .com. *Cost:* greens fees $160 (resort guests), $260 (nonguests).

Waikoloa Beach Resort—While it encompasses the island's most lavish shopping and interesting archaeological sites (including fields of petroglyphs), this south Kohala resort on Anaeho'omalu Bay is best known for 36 holes of great golfing. The original Waikoloa Beach Golf Course, designed by Robert Trent Jones Jr., wends its way along oceanfront lava flows shaded by swaying coconut palms. Humpback whales can sometimes be spotted from its challenging seventh hole. The Kings Golf Club, a Tom Weiskopf and Jay Morrish creation, offers a Scottish links–style course. **Info:** Tel 877-924-5656 or 808-886-7888; www.waikoloabeachgolf.com. *Cost:* greens fees $130 (resort guests), $195 (nonguests).

Eating & Drinking

Bamboo—Housed in a handsomely restored plantation-era building decorated with retro tropical prints, this bastion of "real Hawaii" is famous for its chicken satay pot stickers, hand-wrapped by a local auntie. Sip on a passion fruit margarita (invented here) while you browse through the gallery of Pacific art and handicrafts. If you're in the market for an aloha shirt, they have one of the largest collections on the island. **Where:** Hawi. Tel 808-889-5555; www.bamboorestaurant.info. *Cost:* dinner $30.

MANAGO—When you've tired of the swank resort eateries, step back in time at this classic hole-in-the-wall at Hotel Manago, owned by the same Japanese American family since 1917. There are only a dozen or so daily entrées, all fried, including the celebrated pork chops served with a bowl of rice and three sides. Just don't expect dessert and don't be late: Last orders are taken at 7:30 P.M. **WHERE:** Captain Cook. Tel 808-323-2642; www.managohotel.com. *Cost:* dinner $10.

MERRIMAN'S RESTAURANT—Considered the founding father of Hawaiian regional cuisine, Peter Merriman is still serving up kalua pig quesadillas and his signature wok-charred ahi at his restaurant in Waimea, near Parker Ranch. The secret to its longevity is perfect ingredients—Waimea-raised beef and lamb, fish from Kawaihae Harbor, and organic vegetables from nearby farms, many of which are grown only for him. Merriman's commitment to local products carries over to his new restaurants, including the more casual Merriman's Market Café and Merriman's Kapalua in Maui. **RESTAURANT:** Waimea. Tel 808-885-6822; www.merrimanshawaii.com. *Cost:* dinner $60. **MARKET CAFÉ:** Waikoloa. Tel 808-886-1700. *Cost:* dinner $35.

"Here am I, your special island!"
—*RODGERS AND HAMMERSTEIN,* SOUTH PACIFIC

KAUAI

Hawaii, U.S.A.

The greenest and oldest of the main Hawaiian islands, Kauai is essentially a single massive volcano rising 3 miles from the ocean floor. Two-thirds impenetrable, it has provided a scene-stealing vision of tropical paradise for many Hollywood movies and TV shows, including *South Pacific, Blue Hawaii,* and *Fantasy Island.* More rain falls here than in the rest of Hawaii—Kauai is known in Hawaiian lore as the birthplace of the rainbow—and it's so extravagantly covered with flowers and dense vegetation that it effortlessly earns its nickname "The Garden Isle."

Colorful and full of traces of lava, Waimea Canyon is Hawaii's answer to the Grand Canyon.

TOP ATTRACTIONS

NA PALI CLIFFS—The Na Pali Coast is the Hawaii of your dreams: 22 miles of vibrant green valleys and thundering waterfalls plunging into the sea from cliffs as high as 4,000 feet. Hawaii's last true wilderness that no road will ever cross, this 6,500-acre area is protected as the Na Pali Coast State Park. You can view this piece of Eden by helicopter or boat, though a few diehards attempt the thickly jungled shore on foot.

Waves crash against cliffs in Poipu, a popular beach and park on Kauai's southern coast.

Even seasoned hikers find a challenge in the narrow and often grueling Kalalau Trail, an ancient 11-mile footpath that unfurls along imposing cliffs and winds up at Kalalau Beach. **WHERE:** 40 miles northwest of Lihu'e. **VISITOR INFO:** www.hawaiistateparks.org.

WAIMEA CANYON & WAIMEA TOWN—Ten miles long, more than a mile across, and 3,657 feet deep, Waimea Canyon is one of Kauai's most awe-inspiring sights. Dubbed "The Grand Canyon of the Pacific," the cavernous gorge was carved by the Waimea River, which channels heavy rainfall from Mount Waialeale, so expect vivid green vegetation and the occasional white stripe of a waterfall. In Koke'e State Park, a vast network of hiking trails snakes through some 6,200 acres of rain forest. Low-key Waimea (population 1,787), the original capital of Kauai, is the settlement closest to the canyon. Seemingly the town that time forgot, it's a great place to relax and wander. Stop by Jo-Jo's for a shave ice. **WHERE:** 32 miles west of Lihu'e. **WAIMEA CANYON AND KOKE'E STATE PARKS VISITOR INFO:** www.hawaiistateparks.org.

HELICOPTER SIGHTSEEING—You can drive around the accessible parts of Kauai in a half day or so—it's only about 30 miles across at its widest—but the only way to take in the whole island is via helicopter. Over the course of about an hour, you'll swoop past some of Kauai's most beautiful sights: Manawaiopuna Falls (also known as "Jurassic Park Falls"); Hanapepe Valley; Waimea Canyon; the cliffs of the Na Pali Coast; Makana Mountain, also known as Bali Ha'i from its role in *South Pacific*; the azure waters of Hanalei Bay; and the Hanalei River Valley. Weather permitting, you can even fly into the crater of the 5,148-foot Mount Waialeale, where waterfalls plunge down walls nearly a mile high. **HOW:** Jack Harter Helicopters. Tel 888-245-2001 or 808-245-3774; www.helicopters-kauai.com. *Cost:* $230 per person for 1-hour tour.

NATIONAL TROPICAL BOTANICAL GARDEN—Two world-class horticultural attractions that are run by the National Tropical Botanical Garden can be found in the Lawa'i Valley west of Poipu Beach. The 252-acre McBryde Garden claims the world's largest ex-situ collection of native Hawaiian plants, plus a raft of specimens from elsewhere in the tropics. The exquisite Allerton Garden occupies more than 80 adjacent acres, where Hawaii's Queen Emma lived in the 1860s.

On the island's north shore, the National Garden's Limahuli Garden and Preserve sits at the foot of Makana Mountain. Spread over 1,000 acres of tropical valley and built on lava rock terraces, the site was selected by the American Horticultural Society as the best natural botanical garden in the U.S. **INFO:** Tel 808-742-2623 (McBryde and Allerton); 808-826-1053 (Limahuli); www.ntbg.org.

BEST BEACHES

POIPU BEACH—At the center of Kauai's sunny southern coast is Poipu Beach, a spot legendary for its gardens and glamorous resorts as well as for its water sports and green picnic lawn. On the east side, a rocky outcrop protects Poipu Beach Park, fronted by a sandy-bottomed pool that's perfect for children, while the west side has open ocean for swimmers, snorkelers, and surfers. **Where:** 12 miles west of Lihue.

Hanalei Bay—The most dazzling beaches in Hawaii are strung out like jewels in a necklace along 7 miles of Kauai's north shore. One of the finest and most famous is Hanalei Beach, where Puff the Magic Dragon frolicked in the 1962 hit by Peter, Paul, and Mary. You've seen it in travel posters: Cliffs laced with waterfalls tower some 4,000 feet in the background as gentle waves roll onto the golden sands of half-moon Hanalei Bay. Protected from the strong currents that make waters dangerous elsewhere on the north shore, Kauai is surfing central in the winter and spring, with a wide variety of breaks that attract beginners to experts. Just west of here is Lumahai Beach, an idyllic crescent framed by lava-rock cliffs. It's where Mitzi Gaynor washed Rossano Brazzi right out of her hair in *South Pacific*. **Where:** 18 miles southeast of Lihue.

Kalihi Wai Beach—Set in a cove, Kalihi Wai is a perfect family beach, with soft, honey-hued sand, easy waves, and a stream (with rope swings dangling above) that empties into the ocean. During the summer months, the ocean is usually calm and swimming is good; in winter it's popular with surfers and boogie boarders. Kalihi Wai is a bit off the beaten path—there are no facilities or lifeguard—but the shade of the ironwood trees provides a great spot for a picnic. **Where:** 2 miles south of Princeville.

Surfers, swimmers, and divers prize picture-perfect Hanalei Bay.

Makua Beach—Nicknamed "Tunnels," for the underwater lava tubes that draw scuba divers, this is a picture-perfect beach on the North Shore. Two large offshore reefs border the wide bay, making Makua the premier snorkeling site on Kauai in the summer, when waters are calmest. But no reef protects the beach itself, so waves funnel directly onto the shore, creating thrilling but dangerous conditions for the surfers who flock here in winter. **Where:** 9 miles west of Princeville.

Where to Stay

Grand Hyatt Kauai Resort & Spa—Set on 50 oceanfront acres hugging the southern coast of Poipu, this classic Hawaiian low-rise is a handsome resort with lavishly landscaped grounds. Its Anara Spa has a tiki torch–lit wing where each teak and thatch-roofed hale (pronounced HAH-lay) features a garden, private lava-rock shower, and wild-ginger steam grotto. Other draws include Camp Hyatt for kids and a championship golf course designed by Robert Trent Jones Jr. Of its numerous restaurants and cafés, Dondero's is widely regarded as the best Italian restaurant on the island. **Where:** Koloa. Tel 800-554-9288 or 808-742-1234; www.kauai.hyatt.com (golf, tel 808-742-8711; www.poipubaygolf.com). *Cost:* from $290 (off-peak), from $460 (peak); greens fees $150 (guests), $220 (nonguests); dinner at Dondero's $50.

St. Regis Princeville Resort—On the lush, wild northern coast, the luxurious St. Regis Princeville is worthy of its royal name. Set into the side of a cliff overlooking Hanalei Bay, the hotel is built in tiers, with the lobby on the ninth floor offering dramatic views of Makana Mountain and the beach below. Haleale'a Spa customizes treatments while Kauai Grill offers a menu created by chef Jean-Georges Vongerichten. Two of the state's most challenging golf courses are here, the 18-hole Prince Golf Course and the 27-hole Makai Course, both originally designed by Robert Trent Jones Jr. The tiny, appealing hamlet of Hanalei is just 5 minutes away. **WHERE:** Princeville. Tel 808-826-9644; www.princeville.com (golf, tel 800-826-1105 or 808-826-5001). *Cost:* from $500; greens fees from $125.

WAIMEA PLANTATION COTTAGES—Once the modest homes of sugar plantation workers, these 50 restored century-old cottages have been relocated to a breezy beachside coconut grove. From the one-bedroom option to the sprawling five-bedroom manager's house, every structure has been remodeled with a modern kitchen and bath. The mahogany, rattan, and wicker furniture, inspired by styles from the 1930s, creates an old-time plantation atmosphere. **WHERE:** Waimea. Tel 800-992-4663 or 808-338-1625; www.waimea-plantation.com. *Cost:* from $225.

FESTIVALS

WAIMEA TOWN CELEBRATION—It was here that Captain James Cook became the first European to set foot in Hawaii, dropping anchor near a tiny village of grass shacks in 1778. This and just about every other culturally significant event that ever happened in Waimea are commemorated during Waimea Town Celebration, held the weekend after Presidents Day in February. More than 10,000 people converge on the otherwise sleepy town, heading to the Old Waimea Sugar Mill for food, fun, and music. **INFO:** www.wkbpa.org/events.html.

KOLOA PLANTATION DAYS—The sugar industry profoundly influenced Hawaii's culture and history, and it all started on Kauai in 1834, when Ladd & Co. signed a lease with King Kamehameha III and founded Koloa Plantation. Now the mills are idle but the island's sugar-growing heritage is celebrated with Koloa Plantation Days at the end of July. The highlight is the parade, a classic small-town event, complete with flower-bedecked floats and marching bands; it's followed by an all-day, ride-filled party with food and entertainment that blends the many cultures once found at the plantation camps. **INFO:** www.koloaplantationdays.com.

EATING & DRINKING

THE BEACH HOUSE—Although the famous sunset views at the Beach House ooze romance, this place on the South Shore is not just about the setting. The menu is equally swoonworthy, especially the seared macadamia-nut-crusted mahi-mahi. **WHERE:** Koloa. Tel 808-742-1424; www.the-beach-house.com. *Cost:* dinner $60.

HAMURA SAIMIN STAND—The service is notoriously bad, yet there's a long wait to get a counter seat at this cash-only hole-in-the-wall. Why do locals love it? Because, they'll tell you, it's "real Hawaii." Saimin—homemade noodles in broth—date to the plantation era, when Chinese, Filipino, Japanese, Korean, Hawaiian, and Portuguese laborers prepared communal meals with a melting-pot appeal. Try Saimin Specialty (noodles with wontons, roasted pork, chopped ham, vegetables, half a boiled egg, fish cake, and green onions), followed by a slice of the mile-high lilikoi (passion fruit) chiffon pie. **WHERE:** Lihu'e. Tel 808-245-3241. *Cost:* $12.

PUKA DOG—Hot dog aficionados line up to order this cult classic, the ideal treat when you've worked up an appetite boogie-boarding on nearby Poipu Beach. It's named for the *puka*, or the hole piercing the long, fresh-baked bun that's toasted on a hot metal spike. After a few generous squirts of three toppings—a lemon-garlic sauce, Hawaiian mustard, and a tropical relish (mango, papaya, pineapple, coconut, banana, or starfruit)—in slides a grilled Polish sausage. A glass of lemonade, squeezed and mixed before your eyes, completes the Puka experience. While this Koloa location is the original, the Puka dog can also now be found at Waikiki, on Oahu. **WHERE:** Koloa. Tel 808-742-6044; www.pukadog.com. *Cost:* $9.

From Pineapples to Posh Hotels

LANA'I

Hawaii, U.S.A.

Hawaii's most secluded island, tiny unhyped Lana'i was once the state's largest pineapple plantation, a Dole empire unimaginatively dubbed "Pineapple Island." Since then it has become both a luxury retreat for the rich and an adventure outpost for day-trippers from Maui (see next page), a short ferry ride away. At Lana'i's vaunted resorts, guests are spoiled to an almost unheard-of degree, while the great outdoors remains unspoiled, with few cars and no traffic lights.

The elegant Four Seasons Resorts Lana'i at Manele Bay is a Mediterranean-inspired pleasure palace on idyllic Hulopoe Bay, a marine preserve where spinner dolphins cavort in clear, blue waters. Considered one of the finest beaches in all Hawaii, palm-shaded white sand–carpeted Hulopoe Beach is excellent for swimming and snorkeling. For golfers, the resort's Jack Nicklaus–designed Challenge at Manele enchants with some of the most riveting ocean views in all of Hawaii. Four Season sister property the Lodge at Koele overlooks Lana'i City from the cool, wooded upland district at the center of the island. A handsome mix of old-Hawaii plantation and British country manor styles, the Lodge treats guests to croquet, lawn bowling, and three o'clock tea. But its main attraction is the Experience at Koele, a Greg Norman–designed championship golf course, known for its stunning layout and sweeping views.

Downhill from the Lodge, Lanai City is the quintessential 1920s plantation company town. Tin-roofed homes are painted in a rainbow of colors, and the charming village square is ringed by general stores, diners, and a handful of boutiques and art galleries. Hotel Lana'i, a historic landmark built to house Dole executives, is a modest but charming bungalow-style inn that's the perfect jumping-off point for one of Hawaii's toughest hikes, the 14-mile round-trip Munro Trail to the top of the island's highest peak, 3,370-foot Lana'ihale. On a clear day, you can see the islands of Oahu, Molokai, and Maui from the summit.

If you're coming for a day, rent a 4WD vehicle and explore the plateau of encrusted lava called Garden of the Gods. Its red, orange, ocher, and yellow hues are at their most mysteriously beautiful in the early morning or just before sunset.

VISITOR INFO: www.visitlanai.net. **MANELE BAY:** Tel 800-321-4666 or 808-565-2000; www.fourseasons.com/lanai. *Cost:* from $400; greens fees $210 (guests), $225 (nonguests). **LODGE AT KOELE:** Tel 800-321-4666 or 808-565-4000; www.fourseasons.com/lanai. *Cost:* from $295; greens fees $210 (guests), $225 (nonguests). **HOTEL LANA'I:** Tel 808-565-7211; www.hotellanai.com. *Cost:* from $100. **BEST TIME:** 1st weekend in Jul for Pineapple Festival.

"I went to Maui to stay a week and remained five."
—Mark Twain

Maui

Hawaii, U.S.A.

Who's to argue with the local saying "*Maui no ka oi*"—"Maui is the best"? The "Valley Isle" is named for the Polynesian demigod who, after having plucked all the Hawaiian islands up out of the sea, decided to make this one his home. Known for its miles of stunning beaches, lush rain forests, and mix of crowd-pleasing resorts and luxurious hideaways, Maui embodies the spirit of aloha, an expression used to say hello and good-bye that actually means love.

Top Attractions

Haleakala Volcano—Nothing beats the views of and from the hulking mass of 10,023-foot Haleakala (House of the Sun), the world's largest dormant volcanic crater, so big that Manhattan could fit inside. Many visitors make a predawn ascent through 38 miles of upcountry landscape to watch a sunrise that Mark Twain called "the sublimest spectacle I ever witnessed."

The most thrilling way down Crater Road is by bicycle, an hours-long ride that requires next to no pedaling. (Stop for a breakfast of justifiably famous banana–macadamia nut pancakes at Kula Lodge & Restaurant.) Or spend the day hiking through rain forest and alpine shrub land, realm of the rare Hawaiian goose, or nene. Sunset, when the lunarlike landscape glows fiery red, is just as awe inspiring, and you'll practically have the place to yourself. **Where:** 40 miles southeast of Kahului Airport. Tel 808-572-4400; www.nps.gov/hale. **Biking:** Maui Downhill, tel 800-535-2453 or 808-871-2155; www.mauidownhill.com. *Cost:* bike tours from $109; sunrise tours $149.

Hana Highway—Maui's other famous road show is the narrow, serpentine Hana "Highway," on the island's lush, isolated northeastern coast. Beginning at the laid-back former sugar-plantation town of Paia, the 50-mile drive takes 2 to 3 hours, the road climbing and dropping along some 617 curves, crossing 54 one-lane bridges, and wending past dozens of waterfalls and vistas before reaching the sleepy, eye-blink town of Hana. Hire a convertible, pack a picnic, and plan to spend at least one night (preferably more) in Hana. Just don't hurry to get there; Hana Highway is about the journey

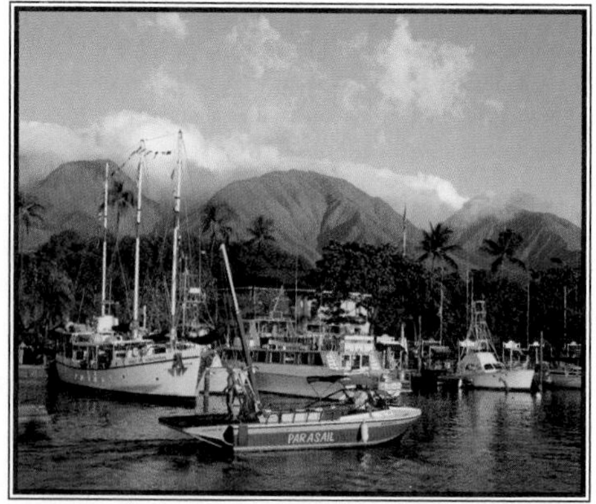

During the early-19th-century whaling boom, sailors packed Lahaina's harbor; today it's filled with pleasure craft.

and the incredible display of nature along the way. **Where:** 50 miles from Paia to Hana.

Hana Village—At the end of the serpentine Hana Highway lies "Heavenly Hana," a stronghold of local culture that is a throwback to the Hawaii of yesteryear. You can luxuriate on Hamoa Beach (see next page), climb the hill to Fagan's Cross for great views of the coast, then hike the ancient 6-mile trail of Wai'anapanapa State Park, winding past lauhala trees and coastal rock formations. Nearby, the National Tropical Botanical Garden's Kahanu Garden is home to Pi'ilanihale Heiau, an ancient lava rock temple that is the largest intact *heiau* in Hawaii. For the drive back, stop by the wonderfully old-timey Hasegawa General Store to stock up on cold drinks and sandwiches. **Where:** 64 miles southeast of Kahului Airport; www.hanamaui.com. **Wai'anapanapa State Park:** www.hawaii.gov. **Kahanu Garden:** Tel 808-248-8912; www.ntbg.org.

Humpback Whale National Marine Sanctuary—Humpback whales are Hawaii's largest visitors, and when they come, they come in force. Nearly two-thirds of the entire North Pacific population of humpbacks spend the winter here, migrating from their summer feeding grounds off Alaska to mate, calve, and fascinate curious humans. Book a cruise on a whale-watching boat (the nonprofit Pacific Whale Foundation has an underwater hydrophone that lets you hear humpbacks sing), hop a ferry to neighboring Molokai or Lanai, or simply scan the horizon from McGregor Point Lookout, Keawakapu Beach, or Big Beach. Calm conditions are ideal for sightings of breaching whales. Once you've seen the real thing, visit the sanctuary's Education Center in Kihei. You can also visit in February during the Great Maui Whale Festival for all sorts of whale-themed events. **Pacific Whale Foundation:** Tel 800-942-5311 or 808-879-8811; www.pacificwhale.org. It offers catamaran cruises and snorkel tours from Maalaea and Lahaina harbors. **Hawaii Humpback Whale Education Center:** Kihei. Tel 808-879-2818; www.hawaiihumpbackwhale.noaa.gov.

Lahaina & The Old Lahaina Luau—Maui's western coast is home to the picturesque 19th-century whaling village of Lahaina, which offers excursions to watch the whales its sailors used to harpoon. The first capital of the Kingdom of Hawaii is a delightfully walkable town, with restored Victorian buildings that now house art galleries, shops, and the island's liveliest dining scene. Take the town's Historical Walk, which includes 20-plus sites such as the 1836 Baldwin Home, built for the first missionary to Lahaina.

For Maui's best and most authentic luau, don't miss the nightly Old Lahaina Luau. Customary luau dishes include kalua (roast pork), laulau (pork wrapped in luau leaf), poi, and ahi poke (marinated raw tuna). After dinner a spellbinding program tells the story of Hawaii through hula and chant—it is far from the commercial clichés you'll catch on Waikiki. **Where:** 22 miles west of the Kahului Airport. **The Old Lahaina Luau:** Tel 800-248-5828 or 808-667-1998; www.oldlahainaluau.com. *Cost:* $95.

Best Beaches

Kapalua Bay—Maui is blessed with beaches—81 of them ring the island, all of them gorgeous. But with its perfect conditions for swimming, snorkeling, and kayaking, Kapalua Bay may be the most appealing: The sheltered, shallow beach lets you paddle a long way out before you hit deep water. And because it's part of Kapalua Resort, it has all the amenities, including vendors who rent scuba and snorkeling gear right on the beach. Once you're in the water, brilliantly colored parrotfish swim right up to you. **Where:** 10 miles north of Lahaina.

ONELOA BEACH—Oneloa Beach (also known as Big Beach) is widely considered one of the most beautiful stretches of sand on Maui. Three-quarters of a mile long and 100 yards wide, this tawny strand between two black lava points is just a few minutes' drive from the glitzy resorts of Wailea. Yet because it lacks facilities, it's rarely crowded. It's a pefect spot for lying in the sun, walking in the surf, and swimming or snorkeling. When you're hungry, head south on Makena Road to Makena Grill, a simple roadside cart, for great fish tacos, wood-grilled chicken, and teriyaki beef kabobs. **WHERE:** 1.5 miles south of Makena Beach & Golf Resort.

HOOKIPA BEACH—An early stop on the Hana Highway (see p. 770) just outside Paia, Hookipa ("hospitality") Beach Park is one of the greatest windsurfing spots on the planet. This pocket-size spot at the foot of a grassy cliff attracts only the best windsurfers and kiteboarders, along with the people who love to watch them from the bluff above. **WHERE:** 2 miles east of Paia.

HAMOA BEACH—One of Maui's most dramatic beaches, Hamoa, near Hana (see previous page) on the east side of the island, is a stretch of inky sand at the base of 30-foot lava sea cliffs. Called "Black Sand Beach" for its dark gray grains—a mix of coral and lava—Hamoa is especially popular with surfers and bodysurfers. But it's swept by strong currents, so less venturesome sorts are advised to simply enjoy its striking beauty from the shore. **WHERE:** 4.5 miles south of Hana.

GOLF

KAPALUA RESORT COURSES—The sun-drenched northwest coast of Maui is home to Kapalua Resort, a major destination with luxury accommodations (see the Ritz-Carlton, next page), shopping, beaches, and golf galore. With gentle rolling greens and wide fairways, the Bay Course (designed by Arnold Palmer and Francis Duane) is the more forgiving of its two championship courses. The clubhouse boasts one of Maui's best restaurants, the Pineapple Grill, known for its Pacific Island cuisine and almost exclusive use of Maui- or Hawaii-grown ingredients. The Plantation Course (designed by Ben Crenshaw and Bill Coore) unfurls across low rolling hills and offers, along with breathtaking views, a challenge worthy of the pros: The PGA Tour's SBS Championship is played here every January. And if your swing is a little rusty, the Kapalua Golf Academy is considered one of the best golf schools in Hawaii. **INFO:** Tel 877-527-2582 or 808-669-8044; www.kapaluamaui.com/golf. *Cost:* greens fees from $130 (guests), $185 (nonguests). **PINEAPPLE GRILL:** Tel 808-669-9600; www.pineapplekapalua.com. *Cost:* dinner $55. **KAPALUA GOLF ACADEMY:** Tel 808-665-5455; www.kapaluagolfacademy.com. *Cost:* from $195 for half day.

WAILEA COURSES—Spread over 2 miles of palm-fringed gold coast in southern Maui, the Wailea resort area has everything: sunny weather nearly every day; sandy beaches sloping into fish-filled waters; luxury hotels and shopping; and Wailea's greatest claim to fame, world-class golf. The area features three of Maui's best courses: the beginner-friendly Blue Course, designed by Arthur Jack Snyder; the challenging Gold Course, designed by Robert Trent Jones Jr.; and Jones's slightly more player-friendly Emerald Course. You can play them all from any of the area's best hotels, which offer every imaginable creature comfort. **WAILEA GOLF CLUB:** Tel 888-328-6284 or 808-875-7450; www.waileagolf.com. *Cost:* greens fees from $135.

FESTIVALS

KAPALUA WINE AND FOOD FESTIVAL—Attracting chefs, winemakers, critics, and food lovers by the thousands, this four-day festival held in June at the Kapalua Resort in West Maui is a high-end event, featuring guided tastings, cooking demonstrations, seminars—even golf with the winemakers. **Where:** 10 miles north of Lahaina Tel 808-665-9160; www.kapalua.com/index.php/kapalua-wine-food-fest. *Cost:* $699 for a 4-day pass; individual events from $50.

East Maui Taro Festival—The staple food of Hawaii, the taro root (the "potato of the tropics") is considered near-sacred, and this down-home festival, held each April in Hana Ball Park, gives it its due. Tourists and locals enjoy music, arts and crafts, and, of course, taro prepared every which way. But the real highlight is the taro pancake breakfast on Sunday morning. **Info:** Tel 808-264-1553; www.tarofestival.org.

Where to Stay

Four Seasons Resort Maui at Wailea—Known for its exceptional service, the Four Seasons is an elegant haven on the sandy crescent of Wailea Beach. The "Serenity Pool," with its swim-up bar, underwater music, and panoramic views of the ocean, is for adults only—for children, there's the fun-packed kids' camp. An exceptional spa offers seaside massage in thatched Hawaiian *hales,* and dining options include Wolfgang Puck's Spago and Ferraro's. **Where:** Wailea. Tel 800-334-6284 or 808-874-8000; www.fourseasons.com/maui. *Cost:* from $465.

The Grand Wailea Resort Hotel & Spa—Hawaii's first resort and spa and still one of its most lavish, the Grand Wailea is a family-friendly pleasure palace on Maui's southwestern shore. The opulent 40-acre resort is best known for Wailea Canyon, a water wonderland with nine pools, waterfalls, slides, a water elevator, and Tarzan swings. With a kids' camp that runs until 10 P.M., parents have plenty of time to relax in the enormous Spa Grande, and golfers can find three great courses just minutes away. **Where:** Wailea. Tel 800-888-6100 or 808-875-1234; www.grandwailea.com. *Cost:* from $725.

Old Wailuku Inn at Ulupono—Located in the island's lush center, the Old Wailuku Inn is a restored 1924 plantation manager's home. Renowned for its historic charm, island-born innkeepers, and home-cooked breakfasts, it is also near Iao Valley State Park, a verdant valley 750 feet above sea level. Hike past waterfalls and the Iao Needle, a tower of volcanic rock that rises to 1,200 feet. **Where:** Wailuku. Tel 800-305-4899 or 808-244-5897; www.mauiinn.com. *Cost:* from $165.

The Plantation Inn—In super-expensive Maui, the Plantation Inn in Lahaina is a find. Just two blocks from the waterfront, the 19th century–style B&B (built in the 1990s) is within walking distance of everything, and guests can get a taste of the island's best French cuisine at the inn's Gerard's, where chef Gerard Reversade combines Gallic traditions with fresh local ingredients. **Where:** Lahaina. Tel 800-433-6815 or 808-667-9225; www.theplantationinn.com. *Cost:* from $170. **Gerard's:** Tel 808-661-8939; www.gerardsmaui.com. *Cost:* dinner $60.

Ritz-Carlton Kapalua Hotel—Following its top-to-toe renovation in 2008, the Ritz-Carlton Kapalua, set on a knoll between two of Maui's best beaches, is now considered by some to be the island's best address. Part of the 23,000-acre Kapalua Resort, the Ritz-Carlton cultivates an elegant sense of place through the use of native hardwoods and displays of work by Hawaiian artists. Naturalists accompany guests on underwater photography missions while golfers can enjoy a 36-hole championship course (see previous page) and a glimpse of Molokai and Lanai across the channel. The spa's treatment rooms open onto private outdoor gardens and showers. **Where:** Kapalua. Tel 800-262-8440 or 808-669-6200; www.ritzcarlton.com. *Cost:* from $375.

Hotel Travaasa Hana-Maui—A cluster of hillside cottages on 66 secluded acres sloping down to a rugged seacoast, Hotel Travaasa Hana-Maui epitomizes the culture of old Hawaii. Built in 1946 and recently updated, it exudes low-key good taste. With no TVs or clocks in their rooms, guests quickly learn to slow down and relish their surroundings. Experiencing Hawaii's heritage is key here, from cooking to surfing lessons—maybe even learning the hula. **WHERE:** Hana.Tel 800-321-4262 or 808-248-8211; www.travaasa.com. *Cost:* from $325.

EATING & DRINKING

KŌ AT THE FAIRMONT—Inspired by Maui's rich past, Kō (which means "sugarcane") draws on the hearty culinary traditions of the Hawaiians, Chinese, Filipinos, Portuguese, Koreans, and Japanese who worked on the sugar plantations. Locals say they find Kō's food—Portuguese bean soup and lobster tempura, for instance—deeply familiar but greatly finessed. The restaurant is located at the all-suite Fairmont Kea Lani, Hawaii, footsteps from Wailea's Polo Beach. **WHERE:** Wailea. Tel 866-540-4456 or 808-875-4100; www.fairmont.com/kealani. *Cost*: dinner $55, rooms from $500.

LAHAINA GRILL—In the heart of historic Lahaina Town, Lahaina Grill has been winning "best restaurant in Maui" awards almost since it opened in 1990. You can always count on a crowd at this stylish bistro who come for the Kona-coffee-roasted rack of lamb and triple berry pie—raspberries, blueberries, and black currants in a cloud of whipped cream. **WHERE:** Lahaina. Tel 808-667-5117; www.lahainagrill .com. *Cost:* dinner $70.

MAMA'S FISH HOUSE—Tucked in a coconut grove on a secluded white sand beach, the eternally packed Mama's Fish House is the best (and one of the priciest) fresh-catch restaurants on Maui. With its Polynesian fantasy touches, the dining room recalls the set of *Gilligan's Island*, and the daily changing menu always features "Island Fish" that credits the name of the fisherman. The best place to spend the night is right next door, at the Inn at Mama's, in one of 12 plantation-style cottages on the beach, complete with hammocks. **WHERE:** Paia. Tel 808-579-8488 (restaurant), 800-886-4852 or 808-579-9764 (inn); www.mamasfishhouse.com. *Cost:* dinner $80, cottages from $175.

SANSEI SEAFOOD RESTAURANT & SUSHI BAR—Known for its imaginative sushi, fusion seafood, and lively atmosphere (there's late-night karaoke on Thursdays and Fridays), Sansei opened at the Kapalua Resort in 1996 and has been expanding ever since. Serious sushi lovers swoon over chef-owner D. K. Kodama's signature panko-crusted Ahi Roll. Prices are lower before 6 P.M. **WHERE:** Lahaina. Tel 808-669-6286; www.sansei hawaii.com. *Cost:* dinner $50.

Timeless Hawaii

MOLOKAI

Hawaii, U.S.A.

Blessed with lush vegetation and carved by eons of pounding waves that produced the world's tallest sea cliffs and some of Hawaii's longest waterfalls, Molokai is Mother Nature's wild and uninhibited work of art and one of Hawaii's least developed places. Fewer than 7,500 people live on the 10-by-38-mile island, the majority of them native Hawaiians who carry on traditional ways of fishing and hunting. Come to relax and recharge by hiking, kayaking, fishing, snorkeling, or walking on pristine white sand beaches.

The sleepy main town of Kaunakakai holds the island's only place to stay, the Hotel Molokai, a Polynesian classic circa 1968. Local singers croon here nightly, and on Fridays aunties and grandmas bring their ukeleles to the beachfront bar for a couple of hours of Molokai-style singing.

On the north side of the island is the dramatically beautiful Kalaupapa Peninsula, a former colony for people suffering from Hansen's disease, then known as leprosy. The colony was started by a Belgian priest named Father Damien, who ministered to the sufferers from 1873 until his death from the disease 16 years later. Today much of the peninsula is a National Historical Park. The Molokai Mule Ride, the most popular way to explore the park, follows a 3-mile trail with 26 switchbacks.

Though other islands take issue, Molokai considers itself the birthplace of the hula and each May stages a grand Hoʻolauleʻa (celebration) that features music, food, crafts, and graceful hula dancers undulating beneath the shade of the keawe trees.

Visitor info: www.molokai-hawaii.com. **Hotel Molokai:** Tel 877-553-5347 or 808-553-5347; www.hotelmolokai.com. *Cost:* from $139. **Kalaupapa National Historical Park:** Tel 808-567-6802; www.nps.gov/kala. **Molokai Mule Ride:** Tel 800-567-7550 or 808-567-6088; www.muleride.com. *Cost:* $175, includes lunch. **Best time:** 3rd weekend in May for Ka Hula Piko Festival, celebrating the birth of the hula.

"When I first moved to Oahu, I was thrilled by the softness and fragrance of the air, the steepness of the surrounding mountains, the profusion of flowers, the sense that I was suspended between air and water."

—Paul Theroux

Oahu

Hawaii, U.S.A.

Oahu has been a magnet for tourists almost since the days of Hawaii's last kings, and it's easy to understand why when you consider the daily rainbows that arch over its more than 125 beaches, the thundering waterfalls that cascade into crystal blue lagoons, and the perfect waves that roll steadily to shore. Home to Hawaii's most iconic destinations—Waikiki Beach, Diamond Head, and the North Shore's surfing waves—Oahu is the third-largest island in the chain but by far the most populated. More than just a tropical paradise, Oahu is Hawaii's urban center, state capital, nightlife and shopping mecca, commercial and culinary hub, and cultural hot spot.

Top Attractions

Pearl Harbor—At dawn on December 7, 1941, Japanese planes began bombing U.S. military installations in Oahu, including the Navy's Pacific fleet docked in Pearl Harbor. Ninety minutes later, 2,390 Americans had been killed, catapulting the U.S. into World War II.

Nearly half died on the 608-foot battleship

The USS Arizona *Memorial commemorates the lives lost in the attack on Pearl Harbor.*

USS *Arizona*, which sank in 9 minutes after its ammunition magazine exploded. Now part of the World War II Valor in the Pacific National Monument on Ford Island, the USS *Arizona* Memorial is a bone-white rectangular structure spanning the middle portion of the sunken ship, which lies untouched just a few feet below the surface. Each December 7, a commemorative ceremony takes place here that includes a 21-gun salute, a navy flyover, and the soon-to-disappear opportunity to shake the hands of Pearl Harbor survivors. Right next door, you can go below deck on the World War II submarine USS *Bowfin*, nicknamed the "Pearl Harbor Avenger" for its successful attacks on the Japanese. At the opposite end of Battleship Row sits the 58,000-ton battleship USS *Missouri*, where the war finally came to an end with the signing of the Japanese surrender on September 2, 1945. The Pacific Aviation Museum brings the war vividly to life with bombers, flight simulators, and an authentic Japanese Zero.

WHERE: 11 miles west of Waikiki in Honolulu. **USS *ARIZONA* MEMORIAL:** Tel 808-422-3300; www.nps.gov/usar. **USS *BOWFIN*:** Tel 808-423-1341; www.bowfin.org. **USS *MISSOURI*:** Tel 808-423-2263; www.ussmissouri.com. **PACIFIC AVIATION MUSEUM:** Tel 808-441-1000; www.pacificaviationmuseum.org.

BISHOP MUSEUM—For a peek at the world's greatest collection of Hawaiian and Pacific artifacts, spend a few hours at Honolulu's Bishop Museum, founded in 1889 by Charles Reed Bishop in honor of his late wife, Princess Bernice Pauahi Bishop. The core of the museum's holdings is Princess Pauahi's own collection, including royal family heirlooms, but it has been greatly expanded over the years to include more than 24 million cataloged items. A recent renovation of the historic Hawaiian Hall allows more access to the museum's treasures: ceremonial spears, calabash bowls, and King Kamehameha's magnificent feather cloak, to name but a few. In summer, the Bishop offers the Moonlight Mele (song), a series of concerts with some of Hawaii's top musicians. The multibuilding facility also includes a planetarium, and the Science Adventure Center specializing in oceanography, biodiversity, and volcanology (complete with a man-made volcano). **WHERE:** Honolulu. Tel 808-847-3511; www.bishopmuseum.org.

CHINATOWN—Chinese were first brought to Hawaii as indentured laborers for the sugarcane and pineapple plantations in 1789, and when their contracts were up, many stayed on and opened small shops and restaurants here around River Street, which by 1870 had become known as Chinatown.

Today, people from all over Asia call this well-preserved five-by-three-block area home, and visitors come to bargain for jade and antiques, worship in incense-filled temples, pick up high-quality leis for low prices, and eat authentic pho, pad thai, dim sum, and myriad other Asian delights. A tranquil spot adjacent to Chinatown is Foster Botanical Garden, which preserves a collection of rare and beautiful tropical plants on lush landscaped acres. **WHERE:** 4 miles from Waikiki. **VISITOR INFO:** www.chinesechamber.com. **FOSTER BOTANICAL GARDEN:** Tel 808-522-7066; www.honolulu.gov.

'IOLANI PALACE—Hawaii is an isolated archipelago, but it is also a crossroads of civilization, with a fittingly rich history. A voyaging canoe in Honolulu Harbor pays tribute to the oceangoing Polynesians who discovered the islands 1,500 years ago, and the extraordinary 'Iolani Palace is a reminder of how their descendants triumphed, then saw their long reign end. The only official state residence of royalty in the United States, the four-story palace was built by King David Kalakaua between 1878 and 1882 at a cost of $360,000. It was the first electrified building in Honolulu—wired even earlier than the White House and Buckingham Palace. The last member of Hawaiian royalty to occupy the palace was Queen Lili'uokalani, who was overthrown by European-Hawaiian and American-Hawaiian residents backed by U.S. forces in 1893, ending the Hawaiian monarchy. Today, the magnificent palace galleries include exhibits of the crown jewels and ancient feathered cloaks, among other items. **WHERE:** Honolulu. Tel 808-522-0832; www.iolanipalace.org.

DIAMOND HEAD STATE MONUMENT—Of all the state's volcanoes, the one that symbolizes Hawaii most famously is Diamond Head, an ancient cone rising at the end of Waikiki Beach. The name "Diamond Head" dates to the 1800s, when British sailors digging around in the crater found what they thought were diamonds—in fact, worthless calcite crystals, but the name stuck.

Visitors can reach the 760-foot summit, with its stunning 360-degree views of Oahu, via a steep, 1.5-mile path. Expect to see legions of other hikers—this is one of the most popular walks in all Hawaii. Less crowded is the unpaved trail to Diamond Head Beach, a small strip of sand at the volcano's base, with breathtaking views of the ocean. **INFO:** Tel 808-587-0300; www.hawaiistateparks.org/parks/oahu.

POLYNESIAN CULTURAL CENTER—Polynesia encompasses 16 million miles of ocean and thousands of islands, but you can get at least a glimpse of its people and culture in a single visit to the Polynesian Cultural Center. A kind of living museum in Laie, it illustrates the lifestyles, songs, dances, costumes, and architecture of a number of Pacific islands—Fiji, New Zealand, the Marquesas, Tahiti, Tonga, Samoa, Rapa Nui (Easter Island), and Hawaii—in re-created villages scattered throughout a 42-acre park. Operated by the Church of Jesus Christ of Latter Day Saints, the park also features stage shows celebrating the culture of Polynesia, and a luau every evening. Each May, competitors vie for the title of world's best fire knife dancer, spinning and tossing their flaming *nifo oti* as they dazzle sold-out crowds. **WHERE:** 35 miles north of Waikiki. Tel 800-367-7060 or 808-293-3333; www.polynesia.com.

BEST BEACHES

WAIKIKI BEACH—When Honolulu became the capital of the Kingdom of Hawaii in 1845, Hawaiian royalty built their homes on this 2-mile slice of sand. Moana Hotel (now the vastly expanded Moana Surfrider) dates to 1901, a white-columned "First Lady of Waikiki." Just after Hawaii was granted statehood in 1959, developers snapped up the rest of Waikiki Beach, leading to today's cheek-by-jowl profusion of high-rise hotels. Waikiki grew a bit tacky, but today it is dominated by handsomely renovated resorts, while the lavishly relandscaped outdoor shopping area on Kalakaua Avenue is lined with designer boutiques. The popular Waikiki Beachwalk is filled with shops and restaurants as well as live music and cultural performances daily.

Oahu's North Shore is legendary for its waves.

NORTH SHORE—Ever since Hawaiians revived the ancient

practice of surfing a century ago, riding the waves has been the quintessential Hawaiian sport, and the 6-mile stretch of Oahu's north shore, from the historic town of Haleiwa to Sunset Beach, is both its spiritual home and greatest testing ground. In winter, when monster swells from Pacific storms rush unimpeded toward reef breaks, cars line up bumper-to-bumper along the road to Waimea Bay, Sunset, and the fabled Banzai Pipeline off Ehukai Beach Park, the three beaches where the world's best surfers compete for the Vans Triple Crown of Surfing. When 20-foot breakers collapse here, the ground shakes. Yet from April to October these same tumultuous waters settle to a flat, glassy calm, inviting swimmers, kayakers, snorkelers, divers, and fishermen to play in the water. Stop at one of the many shrimp trucks in funky old Haleiwa, for local shrimp served plain or doused with seasonings. **Where:** Haleiwa is 28 miles northwest of Honolulu.

Lanikai Beach & Kailua Beach—Hawaii takes its beaches seriously, so even though gorgeous Lanikai Beach fronts a row of private homes, by state law there's public access every 400 yards. Set on Oahu's windward side, Lanikai is picture-perfect, with powdery white sand, jade green waters, and glimpses of offshore islands. All Lanikai lacks is facilities. For that, make the 2-minute drive to Kailua Beach, a local family favorite lined with palms and ironwoods and the perfect place to try kite boarding or kayaking.

A beach day here is not complete without a detour to Keneke's Plate Lunch in nearby Waimanalo Town, where folks line up for Asian-style barbecue, Filipino pork stew, and shave ice with ice cream. **Where:** 18 miles northeast of Waikiki, Honolulu. **Keneke's:** Tel 808-259-9811. *Cost:* lunch $13.

Sandy Beach—One of the most popular places to bodysurf on Oahu, Sandy Beach is right next to the Halona Blowhole, an unusual shore break that spits out water and causes waves to crash magnificently on the shore. While those who ride the waves (including traditional surfers) love it, it has earned the nickname "Break-Neck Beach" for all the injuries sustained here every year. Most folks come just for the view or to fly a kite, another of the big draws here. **Where:** 13 miles east of Waikiki.

Hanauma Bay—Oahu's most popular spot to don a mask and fins and ogle clouds of parrot fish is Hanauma Bay Nature Preserve, with its Hollywood-perfect palm-bordered beach. Most snorkelers explore reefs close to shore, in the safe 10-foot-deep inner bay. Serious scuba divers go farther out, shooting "the slot" through the reef's edge to get to turbulent Witch's Brew cove and see coral gardens, turtles, and sharks.

Before you put a toe in the water, though, visit the modern 10,000-square-foot Marine Education Center, which features a variety of informative marine exhibits. **Where:** 10 miles east of Waikiki. Tel 808-396-4229; www.co.honolulu.hi.

Festivals

Aloha Festivals—Since the 1970s, Hawaii has experienced a renaissance of its native culture. Hawaiian language is taught in public schools, and there has been a revival of traditional Hawaiian arts, including dancing the hula, weaving the strawlike leaf of the hala tree, making bark cloth known as tapa, building canoes, and navigating by the stars. All this and more is grandly celebrated during the Aloha Festivals, the state's largest cultural celebrations. Started in 1946 as Aloha Week, Oahu's Floral Parade makes for grand theater when extravagant floats covered with local blooms move in stately procession down Honolulu's Kalakaua Avenue from Ala Moana Park to Kapi'olani Park. **Where:** Honolulu and statewide. **Visitor info:** Tel 800-852-7690 or 808-545-1771; www.alohafestivals.com.

Prince Lot Hula Festival—Of all the native traditions, hula has had the greatest resurgence, with a proliferation of new *halau* (schools) teaching the ancient dance. To experience it, visit Honolulu's Moanalua Gardens in July, when dancers gather for the Prince Lot Hula Festival. Celebrating Native Hawaiian culture in all its forms, the all-day festival helps you understand the power nature holds in Hawaiian traditions. **WHERE:** Honolulu. Tel 808-839-5334; www.mgf-hawaii .com or www.moanaluagardensfoundation.org.

LANTERN FLOATING HAWAII—Lantern floating is a Buddhist tradition originating in Japan, but people of all backgrounds and beliefs gather on Ala Moana Beach in Honolulu every Memorial Day to send out their good wishes to the world. Participants write prayers, eulogies, and other messages on 2,000 lanterns, which, at dusk, after the hula dancing, the playing of the taiko drums, and the recitation of prayers, are gently released in the water, a spectacle that keeps everyone rapt. **WHERE:** Honolulu. www.lanternfloatinghawaii.com.

SPAM JAM—Foodies may scoff, but Hawaii, along with Guam and Saipan, accounts for the greatest per-capita consumption of Hormel's "spiced ham" (its popularity goes back to World War II days when fresh food was scarce). Spam is still so beloved that every April busy Kalakaua Avenue in Waikiki shuts down for a night to make room for a street festival where restaurants serve up their favorite canned ham dishes, the music goes nonstop, and the most ardent Spam fan on the island is crowned Mr. or Mrs. Spam. **WHERE:** Honolulu. Tel 808-255-5927; www.spamjamhawaii.com.

HONOLULU FESTIVAL—This three-day festival in March celebrates the cultures of the Pacific Rim. Aboriginal dancers from Australia painted with mud share the stage with silk-sheathed traditional Korean dancers, while artists, musicians, and craftsmen from Japan, the Philippines, China, mainland U.S., and Taiwan converge on Oahu to display and demonstrate their skills. The festivities culminate in an extravagant Grand Parade through Waikiki, along Kalakaua Avenue. **WHERE:** Honolulu. Tel 808-926-2424; www.honolulufestival.com.

WHERE TO STAY

HALEKULANI—Today the sumptuous, intimate Halekulani ("House Befitting Heaven") is the premier hotel on Oahu, a 5-acre oasis of elegance that first opened on Waikiki Beach in 1917. Of the 84 guest rooms, the best in the house is the expansive Vera Wang–designed suite and lanai. Treatments at SpaHalekulani are inspired by the healing traditions of Hawaii and other South Pacific islands. For the most romantic (and expensive) dining in town, visit its La Mer restaurant, which reinterprets the tenets of classic French cuisine. Downstairs, the hotel's less formal oceanfront Orchids dining room has a legendary Sunday brunch that draws as many Hawaiian families as visitors. **WHERE:** Honolulu. Tel 800-367-2343 or 808-923-2311; www.halekulani.com. *Cost:* from $450; dinner at La Mer $95; dinner at Orchids $75, brunch $55.

J. W. MARRIOTT IHILANI RESORT & SPA—Far removed from the tourist scene of Waikiki, this sleek, 17-story resort on Oahu's leeward coast is part of the 640-acre Ko Olina Resort and Marina. Set on a man-made lagoon, Ihilani offers easy access to a Ted Robinson–designed 18-hole golf course and a 35,000-square-foot spa specializing in water therapies. The Paradise Cove Luau is well known and well regarded. **WHERE:** Ko Olina. Tel 800-626-4446 or 808-679-0079. *Cost:* from $545. **PARADISE COVE LUAU:** *Cost:* from $80.

KAHALA HOTEL & RESORT—Set on a secluded beach in a Honolulu residential neighborhood, the Kahala has been attracting presidents, royalty, and celebrities since it opened in 1964. Swim in the natural lagoon that is home to six Atlantic bottlenose dolphins then book a table at Hoku, where the contemporary island cuisine and ocean views are among the best in Honolulu. Don't miss the Kahala Spa, known for its treatment rooms opening out onto a tropical courtyard. **WHERE:** Honolulu. Tel 800-367-2525 or 808-739-8888; www.kahalaresort.com. *Cost:* from $475; 3-course prix-fixe dinner at Hoku $50.

KE IKI BEACH BUNGALOWS—Located on Oahu's north shore, which is world famous for its surfing, Ke Iki Bungalows is the place to live out your beach-bum fantasies. Set on 1.5 acres fronting a strand of creamy beach, these five oceanfront and six garden rooms are simple but comfortable and have full kitchens. Swimming here is best in the summer, when the waters are calm. But outdoor grills, picnic tables, and the steps-from-the-water seating make this spot a laid-back haven year-round. **WHERE:** 38 miles northwest of Waikiki. Tel 866-638-8229 or 808-638-8229; www.keikibeach.com. *Cost:* from $135.

HOLIDAY INN WAIKIKI BEACHCOMBER—Just a shell's toss from Waikiki Beach on Waikiki's main street, this fresh, 23-story contemporary hotel offers surprisingly affordable rates. The completely refurbished Hawaiian-style rooms overlook lively Kalakaua Avenue, and Jimmy Buffett has been spotted at his namesake restaurant there. **WHERE:** Honolulu. Tel 888-465-4329; holidayinn.com. *Cost:* from $190.

ROYAL HAWAIIAN—Constructed on the site of a former royal beach house in Waikiki, the "Pink Palace of the Pacific" is an institution beloved since it opened in 1927. While the historic wing is romantic, rooms in the oceanfront tower up the ante with open-air lanais perfect for admiring sunsets. Every night, the Mai-Tai Bar serves up live island music, great burgers, and its signature high-octane cocktail. Impressive (and expensive) is the hotel's Monday-night Aha Aina Royal Celebration, a feast of food, music, and hula dancing, which serves as Waikiki's only oceanfront dinner and show. **WHERE:** Waikiki. Tel 800-325-3535 or 808-923-7311; www.royal-hawaiian.com. *Cost:* from $350. **AHA AINA:** from $145.

EATING & DRINKING

ALAN WONG'S—It wasn't long ago that foodies would hesitate to use "Hawaiian" and "cuisine" in the same sentence. But in the early 1990s, a band of creative local chefs combined Hawaiian ingredients with a variety of traditions to produce cross-cultural fusions—Euro-Asian and Indo-Pacific cooking. A revered figure in the world of Hawaiian regional cuisine, Alan Wong works his magic at two Honolulu hot spots: the restaurant bearing his name and its more casual branch, the Pineapple Room, inside Macy's at the Ala Moana Center. Here he combines tastes from all the ethnic groups of Hawaii with the organic, seasonal aesthetic of California cuisine to create signature dishes such as macadamia-coconut-crusted lamb chops with Asian ratatouille. **ALAN WONG'S:** Honolulu. Tel 808-949-2526; www.alanwongs.com. *Cost:* dinner $60. **THE PINEAPPLE ROOM:** Honolulu. Tel 808-945-6573; www.alanwongs.com. *Cost:* dinner $35.

CHEF MAVRO—Another of the original group of chefs who gave birth to Hawaiian regional cuisine, George Mavrothalassitis combines Hawaiian ingredients with influences from his native France at Chef Mavro, considered by some to serve the most sophisticated, elegant food in Honolulu. The emphasis here is on tasting menus. And instead of a wine list, every menu selection is presented with a wine pairing offered by the glass. **WHERE:** Honolulu. Tel 808-944-4714; www.chefmavro.com. *Cost:* 3-course dinner $70.

DUKE'S CANOE CLUB—Unabashedly touristy, this Waikiki icon is named for the Father of Surfing, Duke Kahanamoku. At sunset it's the perfect place to enjoy a cold beer or tropical drink like the Lava Flow, a piña colada with strawberry puree, while taking in one of its nightly Concerts on the Beach. Yes, the waits for dinner may be long, but no one leaves Waikiki without having been there. **Where:** Waikiki. Tel 808-922-2268; www.dukeswaikiki.com. *Cost:* dinner $40.

Helena's Hawaiian Food—"Local food" here means an exotic mélange of influences from Japan, the Philippines, Korea, China, and the mainland, and none serves it up as authentically as hole-in-the-wall Helena's, winner of a James Beard award. This family-owned shop in Kalihi smokes its signature pipikaula-style spareribs above the cooktop, and locals praise the cabbage for being just like Grandma used to make. With just a dozen tables, it's always packed. **Where:** Honolulu. Tel 808-845-8044; www.helenashawaiianfood.com. *Cost:* lunch $12.

'Ono Hawaiian Foods—Another deliciously authentic representation of Hawaiian cooking is the unassuming 'Ono Hawaiian Foods on the outskirts of Waikiki. It's the spot to try island dishes like laulau (pork wrapped in taro leaves and steamed), lomi salmon, and sweet haupia pudding. You know it's really Hawaiian because the combo plates come with a small cup of raw onion and 'alaea salt. **Where:** Honolulu. Tel 808-737-2275. *Cost:* lunch $15.

Roy's—One of the pioneers of Hawaiian regional cuisine, wonder chef Roy Yamaguchi has been the most spectacularly successful of them all, with a string of nearly 40 Roy's stretching from Guam to Pebble Beach and Orlando. The original site, a hectic, fun spot in Hawaii Kai (a largely residential area of Honolulu), opened in 1988 and still serves the signature blackened island ahi with spicy soy mustard butter. Comfortingly, so do all Roy's, including his Waikiki Beach location. **The Original Roy's in Hawaii Kai:** Tel 808-396-7697; www.royshawaii.com. *Cost:* dinner $65. **Roy's at Waikiki:** Tel 808-923-7697. *Cost:* 3-course prix-fixe dinner $40.

Where the Great Outdoors Meets the Great Indoors

Henry's Fork Lodge

Island Park, Idaho, U.S.A.

Idaho is one of America's most revered fishing destinations, with 2,000 lakes, 16,000 miles of streams, and 39 species of game fish. Angling for rainbow, brook, brown, and cutthroat trout on the Henry's Fork of the Snake River can be especially remarkable. The best fishing lodge in the area, Henry's Fork Lodge is just minutes from the renowned waters of Railroad Ranch State Park and an easy drive to fishing spots in nearby Yellowstone National Park (see p. 909) as well as such great fly-fishing rivers as the Madison, Gallatin, and South Fork of the Snake.

The modern, architecturally striking main house and cabins sit on an overlook where the peaks of Yellowstone and the Grand Tetons (see p. 907) dominate the horizon. Rooms are decked out with wood paneling, log beds, and fireplaces, and the dining room serves a low-key but refined dinner.

Those less captivated by world-class fly-fishing will enjoy 11,000-acre Harriman State Park 2 miles away, laced with hiking, biking, and horseback trails. As the Henry's Fork River leaves its high valley, about 25 miles south of the lodge, it drops nearly 114 feet through rainbow-misted Upper Mesa Falls before tumbling another 65 feet over Lower Mesa Falls in a series of rushing cascades.

Where: 81 miles northwest of Idaho Falls. **Henry's Fork Lodge:** Tel 208-558-7953; www.henrysforklodge.com. *Cost:* from $400 per person, inclusive; dinner for nonguests $35. *When:* mid-May–mid-Oct. **Harriman State Park:** Tel 208-558-7368; www.idahoparks.org. **Best times:** Jun–mid-Jul for dry-fly fishing and warm weather; Sep for fewer crowds, wildlife viewing, fall foliage, and hungry spawning fish.

A Pine-Forest-Enshrouded Gem

Lake Coeur d'Alene

Idaho, U.S.A.

Idaho's Panhandle, wedged between Washington, Montana, and Canada's British Columbia, is an enclave of dense forests, mighty rivers, and more than 60 deep glacial lakes. The town of Coeur d'Alene, named for the American Indian tribe that has lived along the Panhandle's waterways for millennia, stands at the head of the bewitchingly azure lake of the same name. Nestled in a glacier-dug channel between low mountains, the lake delights visitors with myriad water activities, from Chinook salmon and trout fishing to steamboat rides, water-skiing, and sunset dinner cruises.

Landlubbers can strike out on meandering bike trails and hiking paths, including one up to Tubbs Hill, a great vantage point from which to see the lake and its 135-mile shoreline, most of which has been protected from development. The Lake Coeur d'Alene Scenic Byway, along the eastern shore, lets you drink in windshield-wide lake views. The area is also home to bald eagles and one of the nation's largest populations of ospreys. The Coeur d'Alene Resort sprawls over 6 waterfront acres, and boasts a host of diversions. It claims one of the top resort golf courses in the U.S. with the world's first movable, floating green, and its state-of-the-art spa offers a Northwest-themed menu. Beverly's, the resort's restaurant, is a bastion of innovative regional cuisine with an award-winning wine collection.

Follow the scenic I-90 freeway east to Wallace, a well-preserved late-19th-century mining town. Its 1313 Club Historic Saloon & Grill serves the town's best burgers and fries. Or spend the day in pleasant Sandpoint, on the edge of 43-mile-long Lake Pend Oreille (pond-duh-RAY). Nearby Schweitzer Mountain Resort remains one of the region's best-kept secrets: its 2,900 skiable acres are uncrowded and offer magnificent lake views.

Where: 33 miles east of Spokane, WA. **Visitor info:** www.coeurdalene.org. **Lake Coeur d'Alene Scenic Byway:** www.byways.org. **Coeur d'Alene Resort:** Tel 800-688-5253 or 208-765-4000; www.cdaresort.com. *Cost:* from $140 (off-peak), from $200 (peak); dinner $55. **1313 Club:** Tel 208-752-9391; www.1313club.com. *Cost:* dinner $15. **Schweitzer Mountain Resort:** Tel 800-831-8810 or 208-265-0257; www.schweitzer.com. *Cost:* lift tickets $59. *When:* late Nov–mid-Apr. **Where to stay:** The slopeside Selkirk Lodge is in the heart of Schweitzer Village. Tel 877-487-4643 or 208-265-0257; www.schweitzer.com. *Cost:* from $155 (off-peak), from $295 (peak). **Best times:** Jul–Sep for best weather; late Nov–early Jan for the Coeur d'Alene Holiday Light Show.

America's Greatest White Water

Middle Fork of the Salmon River

Idaho, U.S.A.

Idaho has over 3,100 whitewater miles—more than any other state in the continental U.S.—and the Middle Fork of the Salmon River is ranked one of the top stretches of whitewater river in the world, a holy grail for river-runners.

The Middle Fork carves a mighty canyon through central Idaho's 2.36 million–acre Frank Church River of No Return Wilderness, the largest federally protected forest in the Lower 48 and home to bears, river otters, elk, Rocky Mountain bighorn sheep, and large birds of prey. The river drops some 3,000 feet in 100 miles, churning through 100 deep-rolling Class III and IV rapids and carrying you to sandy beaches for overnight camping and natural hot springs for soaking paddle-weary bones. Rafters can also enjoy superb fishing for rainbow, cutthroat, and Dolly Varden trout. Watch the canyon walls for vivid rock art, inscribed by the ancient Tukudeka people who once claimed these canyons as their homeland.

For the ultimate float on the Middle Fork—no motor craft are allowed—book a camping expedition with Rocky Mountain River Tours. On the river since 1978, owners Dave and Sheila Mills will pamper you with a 4- to 6-day trip that includes campfire dinners featuring favorite recipes from Sheila's popular *Outdoor Dutch Oven Cookbook*.

No matter how you navigate this scenic stretch, you'll probably wind up back in the old ranching community of Stanley, where the Sawtooth Mountains form a wall of pink granite behind spring-fed meadows and lakes within the 750,000-acre Sawtooth National Recreation Area. The nearby venerable Redfish Lake Lodge has been a recreation-oriented family favorite since 1926. Nine miles south of Stanley stands the 1,000-acre Idaho Rocky Mountain Ranch, established in 1930 as an exclusive hunting lodge and listed on the National Register of Historic Places. Don't head home without taking a drive along the 162-mile Salmon River Scenic Byway, a picturesque route along the river's upper reaches, much of it untouched since it was first explored by Lewis and Clark.

Middle Fork rafters enjoy alpine scenery when they're not navigating some of the country's best white water.

Where: Stanley is 130 miles north of Boise. **Rocky Mountain River Tours:** Tel 208-756-4808 (summer), 208-345-2400 (winter); www.rockymountainrivertours.com. *Cost:* 4 days from $995, all-inclusive. *When:* late May–Sep. **Redfish Lake Lodge:** Tel 208-774-3536 (summer), 208-644-9096 (winter); www.redfishlake.com. *Cost:* from $75. *When:* late May–early Oct. **Idaho Rocky Mountain Ranch:** Tel 208-774-3544; www.idahorocky.com.

Cost: from $300, inclusive. *When:* mid-Jun–mid-Sep. **Salmon River Scenic Byway:** www.idahobyways.gov. **Best times:** May–Jun for the spring melt and rafting thrills; Jul–Aug for good weather and great rapids; Sep for calm rapids and fly-fishing.

A Rockies Classic

Sun Valley

Idaho, U.S.A.

Sun Valley is America's original ski destination and is still beloved as one of the finest ski resorts on the continent. Averell Harriman was chairman of the board of Union Pacific Railroad in 1936 when he created the resort and its centerpiece, the Sun Valley Lodge, to fill his trains during the winter. He bet rightly that the Sawtooth Mountains could stand in for the Alps for Hollywood's A-list crowd; early visitors included Claudette Colbert and David O. Selznick.

The first of its kind, Sun Valley is still one of America's top ski resorts.

Since then, the 80 percent sunshine rate remains the same, though speedy lifts have replaced the world's first alpine chairlift (price back then: 25 cents). Bald Mountain (Baldy), the main ski slope, boasts a 3,400-foot vertical drop; of its 65 runs, 42 percent are an intermediate's dream. The resort also has its own Nordic and Snowshoe Center, with about 25 miles of groomed trails. One of the stars of the après-ski scene is the resort's Duchin Lounge, where live music and dancing create an ambience that is simultaneously relaxed, elegant, and just plain fun. The nearby Galena Lodge, a county-operated cross-country ski center, features 35 miles of trails, an informal restaurant, and 9 miles of snowshoe trails. Summertime devotees flock to the area for hiking and mountain biking.

The action continues a few miles down the road, in the old mining town of Ketchum, where Ernest Hemingway set up camp in 1939. He was buried here in 1961 and his memory lingers on at the unpretentious Pioneer Saloon, famous for its 32-ounce prime rib and Idaho potatoes. Papa never knew the small alpine-style Knob Hill Inn, a recently added Ketchum highlight. But he'd certainly recognize its soul-satisfying views of Sun Valley's slopes.

Where: 150 miles east of Boise. **Sun Valley Resort:** Tel 800-786-8259 or 208-622-4111; www.sunvalley.com. *Cost:* from $139 (off-peak), from $300 (peak); lift tickets $55 (off-peak), $80 (peak). *When:* ski season is late Nov–Apr. **Galena Lodge:** Tel 208-726-4010; www.galenalodge.com. *Cost:* lunch $12. **Pioneer Saloon:** Tel 208-726-3139; www.pioneersaloon.com. *Cost:* dinner $35. **Knob Hill Inn:** Tel 208-726-8010; www.knobhillinn.com. *Cost:* from $195. **Best time:** Feb–Mar for spring skiing.

"I give you Chicago. It is American in every chitling and sparerib. It is alive from snout to tail."
—H. L. Mencken

Chicago

Illinois, U.S.A.

Chicago is the quintessential American city, its soaring skyline on Lake Michigan a testament to its brawny roots and unbridled optimism. With its global sophistication, the "City of Big Shoulders" lives up to its reputation as a dining hotbed, a world-class center for art, and a showcase for jazz and blues.

Top Attractions

Art Institute of Chicago—Opened in 1893, the Art Institute of Chicago is famed for its collection of French Impressionist and Post-Impressionist paintings. It also holds masterpieces from this country, such as *American Gothic*, by Grant Wood, and Edward Hopper's *Nighthawks*. The new Modern Wing, opened in 2009 and designed by Renzo Piano, provides a new home for the museum's 20th- and 21st-century collection—and for Terzo Piano, a sleek, all-white dining room and roof-top terrace with views of Millennium Park and the Chicago skyline. **Info:** Tel 312-443-3600; www.artinstituteofchicago.org. **Terzo Piano:** Tel 312-443-8650. *Cost:* lunch $35.

Chicago Architecture Tour—After the Great Fire of 1871, Chicago rebuilt itself by reaching for the heavens. Steel-frame buildings rose to unprecedented heights, giving birth to a new form called the skyscraper. It's no surprise, then, that Chicago is unparalleled as a showcase of 20th-century architecture, and the Chicago Architecture Foundation makes it easy to tour the highlights, with guided walking or bus tours and—from May through November—boat cruises down the Chicago River. For a bird's-eye view of this city's soaring masterpieces, visit the Skydeck of the Willis Tower (formerly the Sears Tower and the tallest building in the U.S.), and take in the sights from the new glass-floored balconies floating 1,353 feet in the air. **Info:** Tel 312-922-3432; www.architecture.org.

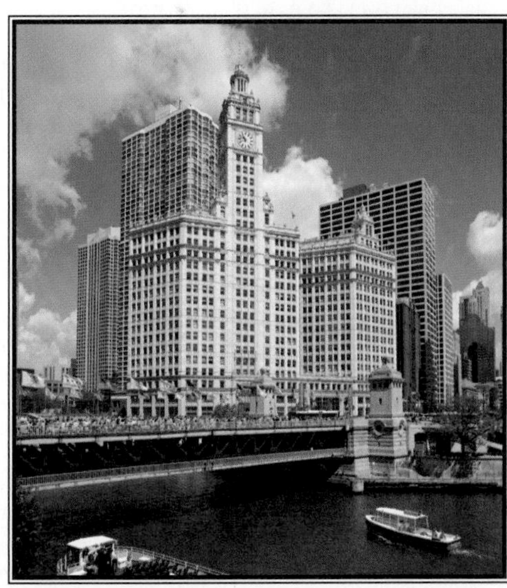

The Chicago River flows by the Loop, the city's downtown district.

MUSEUM CAMPUS—The 57-acre Museum Campus unites three of the city's oldest institutions. The vast lakefront Shedd Aquarium is home to 32,500 animals; it is the world's second-largest indoor aquarium. The Adler Planetarium and Astronomy Museum lets you explore the heavens in three state-of-the-art theaters. Established in 1893, the Field Museum's natural history collection covers subjects as wide-ranging as evolution, ancient Egypt, Great Plains Indian life, and dinosaurs, with top billing going to Sue, the biggest, best-preserved *Tyrannosaurus rex* ever unearthed. **SHEDD AQUARIUM:** Tel 312-939-2438; www.sheddaquarium.org. **ADLER PLANETARIUM:** Tel 312-922-7827; www.adlerplanetarium.org. **FIELD MUSEUM:** Tel 312-922-9410; www.fieldmuseum.org.

MUSEUM OF SCIENCE AND INDUSTRY—The Museum of Science and Industry provides more hands-on fun and wonder than any other destination in the city. Tour an authentic WWII German submarine, see your heart beat 13 feet tall, explore an Illinois coal mine, or find out how "Poop Happens." The museum's newest exhibit, Science Storms, explains the whys of seven megapowerful weather phenomena—and lets you stand in a simulated 40-foot tornado. **INFO:** Tel 773-684-1414; www.msichicago.org.

MILLENNIUM PARK—It opened too late for the actual millennium, but this grand park and public art and entertainment space has quickly become a focal point for the city. The centerpiece is the Frank Gehry–designed Jay Pritzker Pavilion, where the resident Grant Park Orchestra gives free summertime concerts from June to August. Don't miss the park's sculpture, such as the reflective "Bean"—officially titled *Cloud Gate*—by Anish Kapoor, or the McCormick Tribune Plaza, with its free ice skating rink (mid-Nov through mid-Mar) and dining at Park Grill (alfresco in summer). **INFO:** Tel 312-742-2963; www.millenniumpark.org. **PARK CITY GRILL:** Tel 312-521-7275; www.parkgrillchicago. com. *Cost:* lunch $22.

FRANK LLOYD WRIGHT HOME AND STUDIO—In 1889, 10 miles west of Chicago in Oak Park, the 22-year-old architect Frank Lloyd Wright began designing and building a house for his family. Completed in 1898, this showcase of Prairie School architecture, now open for tours, includes the studio where he designed more than 100 structures (roughly a quarter of his output). Other Wright masterworks, such as Unity Temple in Oak Park and Robie House on the University of Chicago campus, are also open to the public. **HOW:** Frank Lloyd Wright Preservation Trust organizes tours of the Wright Home and Studio and Robie House. Tel 708-848-1976; www.gowright.org. **UNITY TEMPLE:** Tel 708-848-6225; www.unitytemple.org.

OTHER MUST-DOS

CHICAGO'S COMEDY SCENE—Sketch and improvisational comedy reaches its zenith with Second City, a groundbreaking troupe from the Near North Side. Founded in 1959, the group has since spawned a TV show (*SCTV*) and supplied a bevy of *Saturday Night Live* cast members—it counts among its alumni Bill Murray, Tina Fey, and Steve Carrell as well as Joan Rivers. Catch today's rising stars in hilarious romps and revues in the 290-seat Mainstage or the 180-seat Second City e.t.c. theaters. **INFO:** Tel 877-778-4707 or 312-337-3992; www.secondcity.com.

WRIGLEY FIELD—The second-oldest ballpark in the majors (after Boston's Fenway Park; see p. 805), Wrigley Field is the quintessential place to take in a game. Opened in 1914, this legendary field, with its ivy-covered brick walls, retains a sense of intimacy lost in modern megastadiums. What Wrigley has never seen is a World Series victory by the Cubs, but their fans' contagious this-is-our-year optimism is a key part of the experience. **INFO:** Tel

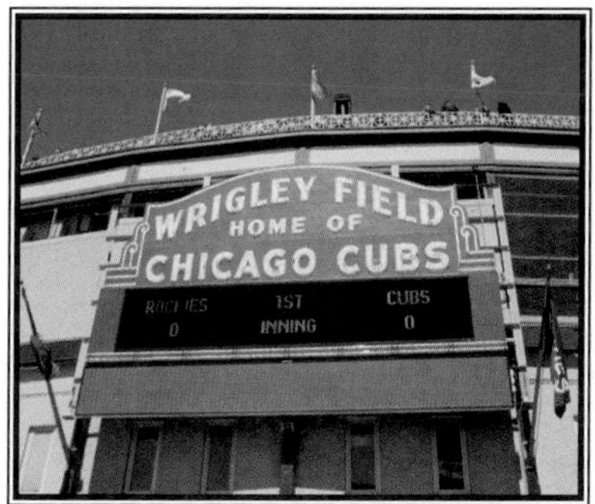

Wrigley Field takes its name from chewing gum tycoon and original owner William Wrigley Jr.

773-404-2827; www.cubs.com. *When:* regular-season games Apr–early Oct.

THE MAGNIFICENT MILE—The 14-block stretch of North Michigan Avenue north of the Chicago River is known as the Magnificent Mile, named for its architectural landmarks, but also for its high-end shopping and swank hotels. Stroll along the wide, bustling street, admiring such buildings as the John Hancock Center (from its 94th-floor observatory you can see 80 miles) and the castellated Water Tower, built in 1869 and a survivor of the Great Fire. Shop till you drop at Neiman Marcus, Bloomingdale's, and Saks Fifth Avenue, then refuel at a great restaurant such as Tru, which offers cutting-edge French cuisine, or the ultrarefined Spiaggia, the top Italian restaurant in the city. This is Chicago at its most glittering, and never more so than during winter's Magnificent Mile Lights Festival, when more than a million lights twinkle along the length of the avenue. **INFO:** www.themagnificentmile.com. **TRU:** Tel 312-202-0001; www.trurestaurant.com. *Cost:* 3-course prix-fixe dinner, $98. **SPIAGGIA:** Tel 312-280-2750; www.spiaggiarestaurant.com. *Cost:* dinner $120.

CATCHING THE BLUES—The blues may have been born in the Mississippi Delta, but Chicago is its home. In June, the Chicago Blues Festival draws throngs, but you can catch great performances anytime. Local legend Buddy Guy makes an occasional appearance at his namesake club on the South Loop, while on the North Side is Kingston Mines, the city's oldest and largest blues bar. The smoking-hot Rosa's Lounge is a Chicago institution. **BUDDY GUY'S LEGENDS:** Tel 312-427-0333; www.buddyguys.com. **KINGSTON MINES:** Tel 773-477-4646; www.kingstonmines.com. **ROSA'S LOUNGE:** Tel 773-342-0452; www.rosaslounge.com.

EVENTS & FESTIVALS

TASTE OF CHICAGO—Chicagoans are famed for their appetite, and one place they're sure to show up hungry is the Taste of Chicago food festival. A cookout to end all cookouts, this annual 10-day affair in late June and early July takes over Grant Park, with more than 50 restaurants serving a wide range of cuisine to some 3 million people yearly—the quality is as impressive as the quantity. **INFO:** Tel 312-744-3315; www.tasteofchicago.us.

RAVINIA FESTIVAL—Highland Park, located 23 miles north of Chicago, opened in 1904 as an amusement park, but today it's the site of North America's oldest and largest outdoor music festival, attracting some 600,000 listeners to as many as 150 events from June to mid-September. Classical concerts are the mainstay (the Chicago Symphony Orchestra is in residence), but the festival also includes jazz, dance, musical theater, and rock. **INFO:** Tel 847-266-5100; www.ravinia.org.

MILLENNIUM AND GRANT PARK MUSIC FESTIVALS—Chicago's lakefront Millennium Park serves as venue for both May's Celtic Fest Chicago and June's Gospel Music Festival, which features more than 50 performances on three stages. The Chicago Blues Festival—the nation's largest—follows in Grant Park later in June. Miles Davis, Ella Fitzgerald, and Herbie Hancock are just a few of the musical luminaries who have headlined at the Chicago Jazz Festival, which takes place in both Millennium and Grant parks on Labor Day Weekend. And not to be outdone is September's ¡Viva! Chicago Latin Music Festival in Millennium Park. **Info:** Tel 312-744-3315; www.explorechicago.org/specialevents.

Where to Stay

Hotel Burnham—One of Chicago's architectural gems dating from 1895, the Reliance Building by Daniel Burnham, was transformed in 1999 into the boutique Hotel Burnham. It maintains many of its original details, but the popular Atwood Café, done up in a mix of vintage and contemporary décor, provides a bit of modern sophistication. **Info:** Tel 312-782-1111; www.burnhamhotel.com. *Cost:* from $190; dinner at the Atwood Café, $40.

Drake Hotel—Anchoring the north end of the Mag Mile is the lavish Drake Hotel, Chicago's hallmark of vintage luxury—it's the kind of hotel that attracts both the British royal family and the Pope. Diners can loosen their ties in the informal Cape Cod Room, a classic seafood restaurant with killer crab cakes, or at its bar, where Marilyn Monroe and Joe DiMaggio once carved their initials. **Info:** Tel 800-553-7253 or 312-787-2200; www.thedrakehotel.com. *Cost:* from $179 (off-peak), from $269 (peak); dinner at the Cape Cod Room $60.

Four Seasons Hotel Chicago—Stylish décor, superb service, luxurious amenities, and the city and lake views are stunning to boot: Guest rooms perch 30 to 46 floors above nearby shop-lined North Michigan Avenue. The hotel's Spa and Fitness Club has a Roman-baths-like pool and a menu of specialty treatments. Just past the foyer's 18-foot marble fountain is Seasons, serving sophisticated New American cuisine. **Info:** Tel 800-819-5053 or 312-280-8800; www.fourseasons.com/chicagofs. *Cost:* from $420; dinner at Seasons $70.

Park Hyatt Chicago—A showpiece of the Hyatt empire, the Park Hyatt occupies a great location on the Magnificent Mile and features large rooms distinguished by their chic, modern design. The public spaces are dominated by attention-grabbing modern art, and the sleek NoMI restaurant wins top awards for its wine list and contemporary French cuisine. **Info:** Tel 312-335-1234; www.parkchicago.hyatt.com; www.nomirestaurant.com. *Cost:* from $275 (off-peak), from $525 (peak); dinner at Nomi $75.

The Talbott Hotel—The boutique-size Talbott combines old-fashioned elegance, excellent value, and an ideal location just off Michigan Avenue. Rooms are large and tastefully furnished and the mahogany-paneled lobby has the feel of a private club. **Info:** Tel 800-825-2688 or 312-944-4970; www.talbotthotel.com. *Cost:* from $180 (off-peak), from $259 (peak).

Eating & Drinking

Alinea and Next—At the cutting edge of the kitchen-as-laboratory school of cooking stands Alinea, where chef Grant Achatz presents a mind-boggling sequence of bite-size tastes (the full "tour" offers more than 25 courses). His highly anticipated Next, which opened in 2011, is inspired by a specific place and time (think Paris 1906) that changes every 3 months. **Alinea:** Tel 312-867-0110; www.alinea-restaurant.com. *Cost:* 12-course tasting menu $150. **Next:** Tel 312-226-0858; www.nextrestaurant.com. *Cost:* You have to bid for tickets online to Next, which start at $45 but have gone well over $1,000.

Arun's—Thai cooking reaches sublime heights with Arun's, a 12-course chef's menu that's personalized for each diner. Chef-owner Arun Sampanthavivat's presentation is exquisite, and the experience rivals what you'd find in Bangkok. **Info:** Tel 773-539-1909; www.arunsthai.com. *Cost:* prix-fixe dinner $85.

THE BAYLESS EMPIRE—Through their cookbooks, TV shows, and wildly popular restaurants, Rick and Deann Bayless helped introduce regional Mexican cuisine to the U.S. With flavors that practically jump off the plate, their cooking is inventive yet rooted in centuries-old traditions. Of their three side-by-side restaurants, Frontera Grill is casual, with a lively bar scene whereas Topolobampo (just "Topolo" to regulars) takes Mexican cooking upscale. On the corner is XOCO, a pocket-size dining room serving up zesty Mexican street food. **FRONTERA GRILL AND "TOPOLO":** Tel 312-661-1434. *Cost:* dinner at Frontera Grill, $45; at "Topolo," $65. **XOCO:** www.rickbayless.com. *Cost:* $25.

GIRL AND THE GOAT—The girl is thirty-something Top Chef–winner Stephanie Lizard, and she promises one of the hottest (butcher block) tables in town (there are seats at the bar too)—a fun and funky place in the West Loop with a vibrant vibe and wonderful food. The ever-changing menu is divided into Veggies, Fish, and Meat, but you can expect imaginative new American cuisine, infallibly prepared, with a Mediterranean bent. The ebullient staff reminds you that Lizard also makes her own desserts, so save room. **INFO:** Tel 312-494-6262; www.girlandthegoat.com. *Cost:* dinner $50.

MOTO—Chicago's foremost purveyor of what's known (rather unappetizingly) as molecular gastronomy, moto, which bills itself as a "multi-sensory science experiment" is set among the market stalls of the old Fulton Market. Dinner here is an adventure in culinary deconstruction and experimentation, and Homaro Cantu, whose role is equal parts chef and inventor, is as likely to prepare your meal using lasers and liquid nitrogen as a stove. Don't be put off by what seems like a gimmick: The food is always delicious as well as revelatory. **INFO:** Tel 312-491-0058; www.motorestaurant.com. *Cost:* 10-course dinner $135.

CHICAGO DINING INSTITUTIONS

CHICAGO-STYLE PIZZA—Chicagoans love pizza, particularly the hometown deep-dish version made with a thick crust and loads of cheesy topping. Texan Ike Sewell and Italian-born restaurateur Rick Riccardo came up with this Midwest-friendly twist on the classic Neapolitan pie and opened Pizzeria Uno in River North in 1943. The place became so popular that, 12 years later, they opened Pizzeria Due around the corner. While the city has seen pizza elevated to a gustatory art form (there are over 2,000 pizzerias), this is the Chicago-style original. **PIZZERIA UNO:** Tel 312-321-1000; www.unos.com. **PIZZERIA DUE:** Tel 312-943- 2400. *Cost:* large pizza $22.

HOT DOGS—For a taste of real Chicago, sample a Chicago-style hot dog, or "red hot," as they're known hereabouts: an all-beef frank with mustard on a poppy-seed bun that's been "dragged through the garden" —topped with dill pickle, chopped onion, relish, sport peppers, tomato wedges, and a dash of celery salt. Try the dogs at Superdawg Drive-In, where the magnificently retro exterior includes two 12-foot hot dog statues with blinking eyes, or at Gold Coast Dogs, where they're char-grilled with a side of the best cheese fries in town. For a haute dog, check out Hot Doug's, where you may choose to upgrade from the classic to a chicken sausage with duck-fat fries. **SUPERDAWG DRIVE-IN:** Tel 773-763-0660; www.superdawg.com. *Cost:* $5. **GOLD COAST DOGS:** Tel 312-917-1677. *Cost:* $5. **HOT DOUG'S:** Tel 773-279-9550. *Cost:* lunch $10.

BILLY GOAT TAVERN—Most famous as the inspiration for a *Saturday Night Live* sketch ("Cheezborger! Cheezborger! No fries, cheeps!"), the Billy Goat Tavern and Grill is also part of sports history. When his pet goat was ejected from Wrigley Field during the 1945 World Series, tavern founder Billy

Sianis declared that the Cubs would never win the championship as long as the goat wasn't allowed in the stadium. The "Curse of the Billy Goat" remains legendary, and so is the old-fashioned dive-bar charm of this beloved basement-level institution. **Info:** Tel 312-222-1525. *Cost:* double cheeseburger $5.

Italian Beef Sandwiches—One thing is certain: Italian beef sandwiches have little to do with Italy. Start with a thick white roll stuffed with shaved-thin slices of wet-roasted beef. Then top it all with pickled vegetables, peppers, and olives. Whether you take it wet (with extra roasting juice), hot (spicy peppers), or cheesy (mozzarella melted on top) is up to you. Always thronged, Al's No. 1 Italian Beef is, as the name suggests, a top spot to sample this Chicago staple, or check out Mr. Beef, where you eat at picnic tables amid photos of sandwich-munching celebrities. **Al's No. 1 Italian Beef:** Tel 312-226-4017; www.alsbeef.com. *Cost:* lunch $10. **Mr. Beef:** Tel 312-337-8500. *Cost:* lunch $10.

Honest Abe: A Man for the Ages

The Lincoln Trail

Springfield, Illinois, U.S.A.

The Lincoln Trail is the unofficially designated 1,000-mile string of sites that mark Abraham Lincoln's route from his Kentucky birthplace through Indiana to Springfield, Illinois, where the 28-year-old politician moved in 1837 as a freshly minted lawyer. Lincoln stayed in the central Illinois town, then the state capital, until February 1861, when he left for Washington, D.C., to become the nation's 16th president.

The newest Springfield attraction is the Abraham Lincoln Presidential Library and Museum, the largest repository of Lincoln artifacts anywhere. Opened in 2005, in time for the 2009 bicentennial of his birth, it contains must-see documents like a copy of the Emancipation Proclamation and a draft of the Gettysburg Address and personal items such as his stovepipe hat.

The New Salem Historic Site re-creates the Illinois of Lincoln's early years.

The city's other Lincoln sites are within easy walking distance of one another. The Old State Capitol is where Lincoln urged opposition to the expansion of slavery in 1858. Seven years later, he lay in state here, the first American president to be assassinated; he was just 56. Across the street are the Lincoln-Herndon Law Offices, which he shared with his partner, William Herndon.

The family home where Abraham and Mary Todd Lincoln raised their children is a favorite attraction. Two blocks away is the Great Western Railway's Lincoln Depot, where the president-elect boarded the train to Washington on the heels of the Civil War, not sure of his return. He did return, of course, to his final resting place, the Lincoln Tomb, an imposing granite structure in Springfield's Oak Ridge Cemetery, which also holds the remains of his wife and three of their four sons.

Twenty miles northwest of the city is the New Salem State Historic Site, an authentic re-creation of the village where a young Lincoln received an education in law and politics that would launch him on a history-changing trajectory. With its 23 rustic buildings, folks in period dress, and active farms using planting and harvesting methods from Lincoln's time, New Salem gets you as close as possible to frontier life in the 1830s.

WHERE: 213 miles southwest of Chicago. **VISITOR INFO:** www.visit-springfieldillinois.com. **LINCOLN LIBRARY:** Tel 800-610-2094 or 217-782-5764; www.alplm.org. **OLD STATE CAPITOL:** Tel 217-785-7960; www.illinoishistory.gov. **LINCOLN-HERNDON LAW OFFICES:** Tel 217-785-7289; www.illinoishistory.gov. **LINCOLN HOME:** Tel 217-391-3226; www.nps.gov/liho. **LINCOLN DEPOT:** Tel 217-788-1411. **LINCOLN TOMB:** Tel 217-782-2717; www.illinoishistory.gov. **NEW SALEM:** Tel 217-632-4000; www.lincolnsnewsalem.com. **BEST TIMES:** birthday celebrations on Feb 12; Tues evenings in summer, when Civil War reenactors perform a flag retreat ceremony at the Tomb.

A Lifestyle Going, Going . . .

SHIPSHEWANA

Indiana, U.S.A.

Horse-drawn buggies start arriving before daybreak at the weekly Miscellaneous & Antique Auction in Shipshewana, a time-locked town in the heart of America's third-largest Amish community. The auction and market draw dealers and bargain hunters from as far away as California and New York, but it's the Amish farmers, whose religion restricts their use of modern machines, who flock here to find crockery, kitchenware, and hand-powered tools—even old wringer washing machines.

Named for an Indian chief, Shipshewana is surrounded by the farm region of Elkhart and LaGrange counties, home to 20,000 Amish. Experience the bucolic beauty of this area with a slow meander along the 100-mile Heritage Trail, down narrow country lanes, behind unhurried clip-clopping horses pulling black buggies, and past well-tended orchards and horse-plowed farms.

Amish Acres, in Nappanee (south of Shipshewana), features tours of a restored Amish farm and homestead made up of 18 structures from the 19th century. The highlight here is the Thresher's Dinner, served family style in the round barn: farm-size platters of fried chicken, roast turkey, or beef, plus mashed potatoes, cornbread, and the must-sample molasses-based shoofly pie.

Horse-drawn buggies travel Shipshewana's country roads.

Thousands of acres of corn stretch as far as the eye can see. The bounty is put to good use at the Yoder popcorn shop in Topeka, 12 miles south of Shipshewana. Yoder's sells "popcorn the way you remember it," in various flavors scooped straight from the popper into paper sacks.

Where: 150 miles north of Indianapolis. **Visitor info:** www.backroads.org **Miscellaneous & Antique Auction:** www.tradingplaceamerica.com. *When:* Wed. **Amish Acres:** Tel 800-800-4942 or 574-773-4188; www.amishacres.com. *Cost:* dinner $18. *When:* closed Jan–Feb. **Yoder Popcorn:** Tel 800-892-2170 or 260-768-4051; www.yoderpopcorn.com. **Where to stay:** The welcoming Spring View B&B in Goshen sits on a pond 15 minutes from most sites. Tel 574-642-3997; www.springview.com. *Cost:* from $69. **Best times:** Tues–Wed, May–Oct for the Shipshewana Flea Market; mid-Jul for Elkhart County 4-H Fair; early Aug for Arts & Crafts Festival at Amish Acres; Sat after Labor Day for the Valparaiso Popcorn Festival.

America's Most Famous Ag-stravaganza

Iowa State Fair

Des Moines, Iowa, U.S.A.

Immortalized by the 1932 Phil Stong novel *State Fair*, which inspired Rodgers and Hammerstein's Broadway musical and three motion pictures, the Iowa State Fair is a true American classic. For 11 days in August, more than a million people enjoy all the signatures of the modern state fair: stomach-churning rides on the midway, sugar-dusted funnel cakes and deep-fried Oreos, and big-name entertainers. But the Iowa State Fair, which started in 1854 as a way to bring far-flung country folks together, has stayed close to its rural roots. It is one of the world's largest livestock exhibitions—after all, it was Iowa that invented 4-H, the educational organization for rural youth.

There's still hog- (and husband-) calling, cow-chip throwing, the Super Bull contest, and of course the Butter Cow, sculpted from 550 pounds of the stuff. For many, young and old alike, the fair is the place to strut their stuff, in competitions that judge everything from cattle to needlepoint to vegetables. The pie department is an old-time favorite, with butterscotch, strawberry, pumpkin, apple, and countless other subdivisions. A blue ribbon is the ultimate prize—and more than 5,000 of them are awarded every year.

Just about everyone comes to fatten up on deep-fried foods you can find only once a year—more than 40 kinds are served here on sticks. The trend started with the 1950s corn dog, and has since spread to pork chops (Iowa has 16 million hogs—that's 5 for every human), dill pickles, and even Twinkies. Other local favorites include caveman-size turkey drumsticks, Carl's two-handful sandwiches called Gizmos, and fresh strawberry and peach ice cream from Bauder Pharmacy, an establishment that has been making kids (and grown-ups) smile since 1923.

In addition to staples like pizza and soda pop, corn dogs and other foods that come on sticks are prevalent.

Info: Tel 800-545-4692 or 515-262-3111; www.iowastatefair.org. **When:** 11 days in mid-Aug.

Horse Heaven

Bluegrass Country

Kentucky, U.S.A.

Central Kentucky's bluegrass country is one of America's most genteel and elegant landscapes, spread over 15 counties and 8,000 square miles accented by Tara-style manor houses and oak plank fences. It is also the undisputed international center of Thoroughbred horse breeding, and horses live better here than most humans do, in cupola-topped barns with hand-forged gates and stained-glass windows.

Two of America's most scenic byways, the Old Frankfort Pike and the Paris Pike, wend past more than 400 farms, many home to former Kentucky Derby winners (four-legged gold mines earning their keep as studs).

Most of these farms are closed to the public, but north of Lexington, the 1,200-acre Kentucky Horse Park welcomes lovers of all things equine to the International Museum of the Horse and the American Saddlebred Museum. The park also hosts scores of annual happenings, including the prestigious Rolex Kentucky Three Day Event, in April, with everything from dressage to jumping contests.

Although Louisville's Churchill Downs hosts the storied Kentucky Derby (see p. 795), the Keeneland Race Course, in Lexington, is the South's most beautiful track, with elegant limestone grandstands and a tree-shaded setting. Watch workout sessions that begin at dawn, then breakfast at the Track Kitchen.

To experience Kentucky hospitality at its best, visit quaint Harrodsburg, which is the state's oldest town as well as the home of Kentucky's oldest family-owned and -operated inn, the renowned Beaumont. Today the three-story 1845 Greek-Revival inn draws visitors from far and wide for its hickory-smoked country ham dinners and Gen. Robert E. Lee cake, a four-layer orange-lemon wonder. Food is also the draw at the 19th-century Shaker Village at Pleasant Hill, where you can overnight and dine by candlelight on the impeccably restored 3,000-acre grounds.

The nearby town of Berea is an idyllic Appalachian arts and crafts center, where hundreds of potters, painters, and other artisans live and work. Stroll the tree-shaded streets or the campus of Berea College, a tuition-free school where traditional handicrafts have been taught since 1893. College students help run the handsome Boone Tavern Hotel and Restaurant, a gracious 1909 landmark that offers comfortable rooms and hearty Kentucky classics, like spoonbread and chess pie, and updated dishes like blue cheese grits.

Where: Lexington is 75 miles east of Louisville. **Visitor info:** www.visitlex.com. **Kentucky Horse Park:** Tel 800-678-8813 or 859-233-4303; www.kyhorsepark.com. **Keeneland Race Course:** Tel 800-456-3412 or 859-254-3412; www.keeneland.com. *When:* 3 weeks of racing in both Apr and Oct. **Beaumont Inn:** Tel 800-352-3992 or 859-734-3381; www.beaumontinn.com. *Cost:* from $120; dinner $25. **Shaker Village:** Tel 800-734-5611 or 859-734-5411; www.shakervillageky.org. *Cost:* from $100; dinner $35. **Boone Tavern:** Tel 800-366-9358 or 859-985-3700; www.boonetavernhotel.com. *Cost:* from $140; dinner $30. **Best times:** Apr and Oct for Thoroughbred racing; May, Jul, Oct for Berea crafts fairs; Jun for the Kentucky Horse Park's Egyptian Arabian horse show and annual Festival of the Bluegrass weekend.

America's Great Homegrown Spirit

THE BOURBON TRAIL

Kentucky, U.S.A.

Thanks to native corn and limestone-rich springs. Kentucky makes about 95 percent of the world's bourbon, its unique flavor defined mostly by the charred white-oak barrels where it is aged a minimum of 2 years (6 to 8 years for small-batch premium brands).

Bardstown is the de facto capital of Bourbon Country, with its cluster of seven distilleries open for guided tours, including Heaven Hill Distilleries' Bourbon Heritage Center; Jim Beam, 12 miles west; and Maker's Mark, the nation's oldest working distillery (1805), 17 miles south. World-famous Wild Turkey and Four Roses are 40 miles east of Bardstown near Lawrenceburg, and Labrot & Graham, established in 1812 in nearby Woodford County, produces an elixir that has been praised by everyone from Walt Whitman to Mark Twain.

Bourbon buffs are drawn to the annual Kentucky Bourbon Festival in September for its mix of live music, tastings, and lots of Kentucky hospitality. The Oscar Getz Museum of Whiskey traces American whiskey production from pre-colonial to post-Prohibition years with its displays of moonshine stills and even Abe Lincoln's liquor license.

Founded in 1780, Bardstown offers a number of nonalcoholic diversions. My Old Kentucky Home State Park includes a golf course and Federal Hill, the 1812 plantation that inspired Stephen Foster's folk tune "My Old Kentucky Home." Guests who travel aboard the My Old Kentucky Dinner Train are served gourmet fare in 1940s-era railcars while crossing the state's beautiful countryside. More nostalgia can be found across the street from Federal Hill at Kurtz Restaurant, which has been dishing out comfort food since 1937. Three generations of the Kurtz family keep loyal guests happy; many folks come just for the biscuit pudding with bourbon sauce. Or stop in the atmospheric Old Talbott Tavern, the oldest stagecoach stop in Kentucky, dating back to 1779. It's the perfect spot to savor a shot of the local elixir.

WHERE: Bardstown is 40 miles southeast of Louisville. **VISITOR INFO:** www.visitbardstown.com. **HEAVEN HILL:** Tel 502-337-1000; www.bourbonheritagecenter.com. **KENTUCKY BOURBON FESTIVAL:** Tel 800-638-4877 or 502-348-2999; www.kybourbonfestival.com. *When:* 6 days in mid-Sep. **OSCAR GETZ MUSEUM:** Tel 502-348-2999; www.whiskeymuseum.com. **MY OLD KENTUCKY HOME:** Tel 800-323-7803 or 502-348-3502; www.parks.ky.gov. **MY OLD KENTUCKY DINNER TRAIN:** Tel 866-801-3463 or 502-348-7300; www.kydinnertrain.com. *Cost:* dinner $75. **KURTZ RESTAURANT:** Tel 502-348-8964; www.bardstownparkview.com. *Cost:* dinner $15. **OLD TALBOTT TAVERN:** Tel 800-482-8376 or 502-348-3494; www.talbotts.com. *Cost:* dinner $25. **BEST TIMES:** Apr–May and Sep–Oct, especially during the Bourbon Festival.

Maker's Mark's historic warehouses each hold 4,000 barrels of bourbon.

Run for the Roses

KENTUCKY DERBY

Louisville, Kentucky, U.S.A.

"This Kentucky Derby, whatever it is—a race, an emotion, a turbulence, an explosion—is one of the most beautiful and violent and satisfying things I have ever experienced," wrote novelist John Steinbeck.

The Kentucky Derby marks the first leg of the Triple Crown.

Billed as "the greatest two minutes in sports," the Kentucky Derby is the oldest continuously held sporting event in America and one of the most prestigious races in the world. Although horse racing in Kentucky goes back to 1789, Louisville's Churchill Downs didn't officially open as the home of the Derby until almost 100 years later. By tradition, up to 20 three-year-old Thoroughbreds vie to be the winning horse draped with a blanket of red roses, its owner taking home the $2 million purse.

The two-week Kentucky Derby Festival that precedes the race attracts more than 1.5 million people annually when the Bluegrass State's dogwoods are in magnificent bloom. Thunder Over Louisville, the largest annual fireworks display in the country, kicks things off, followed by more than 70 events (most of them free), including hot-air balloons, the Pegasus Parade, and an old-fashioned steamboat race on the Ohio River.

During Dawn at the Downs, beginning the Saturday before the Derby and continuing through Thursday of Derby Week, visitors enjoy a Kentucky-style buffet breakfast while watching celebrity equines train. Finally, Oaks Day, held the day before Derby, is when crowds pack the paddocks, grandstands, and infield to celebrate the Kentucky Oaks and other races. If you can't afford grandstand seats for the big day or haven't purchased tickets months in advance, you can join the legions who fill the 40-acre infield. You won't see much of the race, but the mint julep–fueled crowd promises a good time. Or, if you have missed the Derby season entirely, relive the excitement at the Kentucky Derby Museum, then check into the Seelbach Hotel, open since 1905. Guests have included F. Scott Fitzgerald, who set a scene from *The Great Gatsby* here. Book a table at the hotel's opulent restaurant, the Oakroom, which was once a billiards room that hosted the likes of Al Capone.

INFO: Tel 502-636-4400; www.kentuckyderby.com. *Cost:* Grandstand seats from $172 (written requests must be received before Nov of previous year); standing-room-only general admission tickets sold the day of the race, $40; Kentucky Oaks general admission $25. *When:* 1st Sat in May. **KENTUCKY DERBY FESTIVAL:** Tel 502-584-6383; www.kdf.org. **KENTUCKY DERBY MUSEUM:** Tel 502-637-7097; www.derbymuseum.org. **SEELBACH HOTEL:** Tel 800-333-3399 or 502-585-3200; www.seelbachhilton.com. *Cost:* from $180 (off-peak), from $270 (peak); Derby weekend prices upon request; dinner in Oakroom $45. **BEST TIMES:** late Apr–early May for Derby events; late Apr–early Jul for racing; late Oct–Nov for fall meet.

A Gumbo of Pleasures in America's Least American City

The French Quarter

New Orleans, Louisiana, U.S.A.

Melding French, Spanish, Italian, and Afro-Caribbean cultures, New Orleans is a city that is at once elegant and debauched. And while it has profoundly changed since Hurricane Katrina in 2005, the Big Easy has shown formidable resiliance.

Many of the city's myriad pleasures are packed within the lively grid of streets that make up the Vieux Carré (aka the French Quarter). It is New Orleans's most touristy area, yet also its heart. The French laid out the Quarter's 90 blocks of narrow streets in the 1720s, and the Spanish—who ruled during the mid- to late 18th century—further developed it. Indeed, despite its name, the neighborhood looks more Spanish than French.

St. Louis Cathedral, the country's oldest continuously operating cathedral, faces Jackson Square.

Wherever you stroll, you risk sensory overload, from jazz on boisterous Bourbon Street to the smell of café au lait and beignets (deep-fried dough dusted with powdered sugar) wafting from Café du Monde in Jackson Square. Decatur Street offers souvenir stands, offbeat boutiques, and charming restaurants. It's also home to Central Grocery, an old-fashioned Italian deli whose claim to fame is having perfected (some say invented) one of the city's classic sandwiches, the muffuletta. Royal and Chartres streets are your best bets for upscale shopping. Be sure to pop into the tacky but fun Pat O'Brien's to sample their Hurricane, a fruity—and potent—rum cocktail in a glass shaped like a hurricane lamp.

Charming Soniat House is comprised of 30 antiques-filled rooms in a cluster of three 19th-century Creole town houses overlooking an interior courtyard garden where guests breakfast on warm biscuits and homemade preserves. For a big-hotel experience, and a big dose of history, it's hard to beat the lavish 600-room 1886 Hotel Monteleone. Stop by its revolving circus-themed Carousel Bar for a Sazerac cocktail before dinner. The Windsor Court, arguably the finest hotel in the Big Easy, is known for its palatial accommodations, award-winning restaurant, the Grill Room, and museum-quality art collection—yes, that's a Gainsborough.

Visitor info: www.neworleansonline.com. **Pat O'Brien's:** Tel 504-525-4823; www.patobriens.com. **Soniat House:** Tel 800-544-8808 or 504-522-0570; www.soniathouse.com. *Cost:* from $240. **Hotel Monteleone:** Tel 800-535-9595 or 504-523-3341; www.hotelmonteleone.com. *Cost:* from $100 (off-peak), from $190 (peak). **Windsor Court:** 888-596-0955 or 504-523-6000; www.windsorcourthotel.com. *Cost:* from $190 (off-peak), from $350 (peak); dinner at the Grill Room $50. **Best times:** Jan–Feb or Mar for Mardi Gras season; Mar–May and Oct–Nov for pleasant weather; early Apr for the 3-day French Quarter Festival; Christmas is magical and often overlooked.

The Essence of New Orleans High Society

THE GARDEN DISTRICT

New Orleans, Louisiana, U.S.A.

The epicenter of New Orleans high society and its architectural apogee, the Garden District was settled in the 19th century by wealthy Anglo-Saxons (as opposed to the Creoles living in the French Quarter), and many of their stunning Greek Revival, Second Empire, and Italianate mansions still stand.

Tour companies lead narrated rambles, describing the homes of many illustrious residents past and present, such as Sandra Bullock, Archie Manning, and novelist Anne Rice.

New Orleans has long been famous too for its above-ground burial vaults, or "cities of the dead." Visit the Lafayette Cemetery No. 1 with a guide from Save Our Cemeteries. (The group also gives tours of St. Louis Cemetery No. 1, opened in 1789 on the outskirts of the French Quarter, where Marie Laveau, the 19th-century Voodoo Queen of New Orleans, rests.)

Across the street from the Lafayette Cemetery, Commander's Palace, housed in a frothy turquoise-and-white Victorian and run by the Brennan family, has been drawing crowds since 1880. Chef Tory McPhail serves a daring mix of old-school Creole cuisine and more innovative fare, and fans come for the Jazz Brunch, a weekend tradition. Casamento's, the Garden District's other favored haunt, is an old-timey family-run seafood joint established in 1919. Stop in at lunchtime for its fresh-shucked Gulf oysters or fried-oyster loaf, with a bowl of delicious gumbo to start.

VISITOR INFO: www.neworleansonline.com. **HOW:** Historic New Orleans Tours, tel 504-947-2120; www.tourneworleans.com. **SAVE OUR CEMETERIES:** Tel 504-525-3377; www.saveourcemeteries.org. **COMMANDER'S PALACE:** Tel 504-899-8221; www.commanderspalace.com. *Cost:* dinner $45; jazz brunch $39. **CASAMENTO'S:** Tel 504-895-9761; www.casamentosrestaurant.com. *Cost:* lunch $12. **BEST TIMES:** Mar–May for blooming gardens; Oct–Nov for cooler temperatures.

Laissez les Bons Temps Rouler

MARDI GRAS

New Orleans, Louisiana, U.S.A.

Mardi Gras would be heaven without the multitudes of half-lit partygoers, but it also wouldn't be Mardi Gras, America's biggest, liveliest, and most showstopping party. Its larger-than-ever crowds provide a raucous heartfelt confirmation that post-Katrina New Orleans has bounced back with a vengeance.

Months before the late-winter festival, preparations begin with the creation of elaborate costumes and two- and three-story floats crescendoing during the 12-day leadup to

Mardi Gras itself. *Mardi Gras,* which means "Fat Tuesday," is the day before Ash Wednesday; it ushers in the 40 days of the somber Catholic period of Lent that culminates with Easter. Brought by French colonists to New Orleans in the 1700s, the event soon fused with the African and Caribbean traditions of the city's black population, eventually becoming as much a show to reap tourism dollars as a revered local tradition. Arrive early to stake out a spot along the parade routes of St. Charles Avenue and Canal Street, amid a sea of carnivalistas demanding "throws"—trinkets, doubloons, and coveted necklaces tossed by float-borne revelers. Of the many parades that begin in earnest two weeks prior to Fat Tuesday, the biggest and best take place on the days leading up to the big event.

VISITOR INFO: www.mardigrasguide.com. **WHEN:** Jan to Fat Tuesday (Feb or Mar).

The Lifeblood of the Big Easy

NEW ORLEANS'S MUSIC SCENE

New Orleans, Louisiana, U.S.A.

The music we know as jazz was born in late-19th-century New Orleans, derived from a confluence of European marching-band music and African rhythms. It evolved thanks to musicians such as cornetist Buddy Bolden, drummer Papa Jack Laine, and pianist Jelly Roll Morton, and was given a clear voice in the 1920s and '30s by hometown hero Louis "Satchmo" Armstrong. Then, in the late 1980s, another group of local virtuosos, including trumpeter Wynton Marsalis and his family, helped repopularize the New Orleans sound by nurturing their own version of modern jazz.

The Big Easy's annual Jazz and Heritage Festival (aka Jazz Fest) is one of America's great music parties. For ten days in late April and early May, hundreds of musicians perform on 12 stages at the Fair Grounds Race Course, offering a rich gumbo of jazz, Cajun, Latin, zydeco, R&B, rock, gospel, and African-Caribbean music. Recent years have drawn Bob Dylan, Etta James, Pearl Jam, and B.B. King. The best of Louisiana's culinary offerings (from crawfish Monica to alligator tail meat in a red pepper *sauce piquante*) share the spotlight at nearly 100 stalls. Sweet tooths should save room for shaved-ice Sno-balls, pralines (pecan, chocolate, or coconut), or Angelo Brocato's celebrated gelato.

Whether you're here at Fest time or not, be sure to visit the dark and spartan Preservation Hall, showcasing traditional New Orleans jazz and a world-famous institution since it opened in 1961. The musical pilgrimage continues at Tipitina's, an uptown club that once hosted legends like Dr. John and Allen Toussaint, and where jazz, Cajun, funk, and R&B continue to keep the dance floor hopping.

Bourbon Street is the home of what may be the world's most notorious traveling party, but it also offers a chance to hear a performance by one of New Orleans's rising stars, trumpeter Irvin Mayfield, at the plush Royal Sonesta Hotel. Or head to Frenchman Street, where Snug Harbor, a storefront jazz bistro in the hip Faubourg Marigny, headlines big names like Ellis Marsalis and Charmaine Neville. You can even bowl to zydeco, swing, blues, and jazz at Mid-City Lanes Rock 'n' Bowl. And then there are those days when it seems that the solitary sax player in front of the cathedral in Jackson Square is the best thing you've heard all week—and it's free.

Visitor info: www.neworleansonline.com. **Jazz and Heritage Festival:** Tel 504-410-4100; www.nojazzfest.com. *When:* Apr–early May. **Preservation Hall:** Tel 504-522-2841; www.preservationhall.com. **Tipitina's:** Tel 504-895-8477; www.tipitinas.com. **Royal Sonesta:** Tel 504-586-0300; www.royalsonesta-neworleans.com. **Snug Harbor:** Tel 504-949-0696; www.snugjazz.com. **Mid-City Lanes:** Tel 504-861-1700; www.rockandbowl.com. **Best times:** early Jul for Essence Music Festival; late Jul–early Aug for Satchmo Summerfest.

From Dives to Palaces of Haute Creole

The New Orleans Restaurant Scene

New Orleans, Louisiana, U.S.A.

Crescent City is a place where food is religion and the funkiest neighborhood joint is as beloved as the grandest restaurant. Its unique blend of influences—French, Spanish, Caribbean, and African—has no peers.

The French Quarter has many inviting options, starting with Galatoire's Restaurant, a New Orleans tradition for more than a century—even though its egalitarian no-reservations policy (for the main dining room) means that the line can stretch a long way down Bourbon Street. Tuxedoed waiters bear plates of chicken clemenceau and shrimp rémoulade; the food is surpassed only by the floor show, which peaks at the famously boozy Friday lunch that goes on till dinnertime. Antoine's first opened in 1840: Its walls are lined with old photographs and memorabilia, while its Hermes Bar has a modern flair. Emeril's, the high-energy Lagasse flagship, was a Warehouse District pioneer when it opened in 1990, and its barbecued shrimp and roasted rack of lamb are still getting raves. You're also in good hands at Bayona, where local darling Susan Spicer serves her pan-global fare in a Creole cottage setting.

If a white-linen locale is not your thing, consider the faux-dive Acme Oyster House where off-the-boat oysters and excellent fried-oyster-filled po'boys explain the line out the door. The weathered Napoleon House has been a favorite lunch spot since it opened in 1797 and is famed for its hot muffuletta sandwiches and local Abita beer. Or pair their spicy jambalaya with a Pimm's cup, a local tradition.

At his haute-Creole/New American restaurant Herbsaint, local celebrity chef/owner Donald Link wows patrons with crab meat and watermelon gazpacho and smothered pork belly. Cochon, which Link opened with Stephen Stryjewski, showcases their sophisticated take on down-home Cajun cooking.

At the atmospheric August, where diners sit beneath elegant chandeliers in a refurbished four-story French-Creole warehouse, award-winning chef John Besh serves up dishes such as gnocchi tossed with blue crab and truffles and whole suckling pig. And finally, no visit to the Big Easy is complete without a po'boy at the working-class Mother's, in the Central Business District.

Galatoire's: Tel 504-525-2021; www.galatoires.com. *Cost:* dinner $45. **Antoine's:** Tel 504-581-4422; www.antoines.com. *Cost:* dinner $50. **Emeril's:** Tel 504-528-9393; www.emerils.com. *Cost:* dinner $45. **Bayona:**

Tel 504-525-4455; www.bayona.com. *Cost:* dinner $45. **Acme Oyster House:** Tel 504-522-5973; www.acmeoyster.com. *Cost:* lunch $20. **Napoleon House:** Tel 504-524-9752; www.napoleonhouse.com. *Cost:* lunch $15. **Herbsaint:** Tel 504-524-4114; www.herbsaint.com. *Cost:* dinner $45. **Cochon:** Tel 504-588-2123; www.cochonrestaurant.com. *Cost:* dinner $35. **August:** Tel 504-299-9777; www.restaurantaugust.com. *Cost:* dinner $55. **Mother's:** Tel 504-523-9656; www.mothersrestaurant.net. *Cost:* lunch $12. **Best time:** late May for New Orleans Wine & Food Experience.

Rusticating Amid Nature's Glory

Acadia National Park

Maine, U.S.A.

Mount Desert Island is Maine's national treasure, a 12-by-14-mile domain of fir and spruce forests, lakes, and inns. It is all as captivating today as when the Rockefellers, Astors, Fords, Vanderbilts, and their fellow "rusticators" founded a summer colony here in the early 20th century. The government set aside 60 percent of the island as Acadia National Park in 1929, throwing a few neighboring islands in to create a 35,000-acre park of craggy grandeur. It's got extraordinary oceanside drives, surf-battered bluffs, off-island whale-watching, and lobster shacks with a view.

The timeless serenity of Mount Desert Island is tested by the ever-increasing traffic on the 27-mile Park Loop Road. Some of the nation's loveliest walking and bicycling paths (they become cross-country ski trails off-season) join 120 miles of moderate hiking trails, all offering great views. Most people will need a car to observe the park tradition of catching America's first rays of sun from Cadillac Mountain, the highest peak on the U.S. Atlantic coast at 1,530 feet.

Otter Cliff juts dramatically into the Atlantic Ocean.

Plan to arrive at the 100-year-old Jordan Pond House on the Park Loop Road in time for late-afternoon tea and popovers on the restaurant's front lawn, another island tradition. Then overnight at the family-run 1884 Claremont Hotel and Cottages, sitting quietly on 6 shorefront acres. Enjoy inspiring vistas of the Somes Sound from rockers on the porch or from window-side tables in the welcoming, unpretentious dining room.

Where: 36 miles southeast of Bangor, connected to the mainland by causeway. Tel 207-288-3338; www.nps.gov/acad. *When:* Park Loop Rd. closed Dec–mid-Apr. **Jordan Pond House:** Tel 207-276-3316; www.jordanpond.com. **Claremont Hotel:** Tel 800-244-5036 or 207-244-5036; www.theclaremonthotel.com. *Cost:* from $155 (off-peak), from $225 (peak). *When:* late May–mid-Oct. **Best times:** Jul–Aug for finest weather and whale-watching; May–Jun are also lovely; Oct for fall foliage.

George Bush Slept Here

THE KENNEBUNKS

Maine, U.S.A.

The Kennebunks are the quintessence of seaside Maine, brimming with magnificent architecture, rocky beaches, and top-notch dining. First settled in the early 17th century, the Kennebunks—Kennebunk, Kennebunkport, and Kennebunk Beach—prospered two centuries later as shipbuilding towns. That boom went bust, but its legacy—a profusion of grand Colonial- and Federal-style houses amid a picture-perfect landscape—helped transform the area into one of Maine's most popular destinations. President George H.W. Bush and his family have vacationed here for generations.

The Kennebunks are all about the sea.

Kennebunk Beach's White Barn Inn is one of New England's greatest, with 29 meticulously appointed European-style guest rooms in several 1820s-era buildings that are within walking distance of sandy Gooch's Beach. The inn's outstanding candlelit restaurant is widely considered the best dining north of Boston, seamlessly blending the rustic and refined. As a cozy, romantic alternative, the Federal-style Captain Lord Mansion has 16 guest rooms and a rooftop cupola with Kennebunk River views.

But the Kennebunks aren't all about luxury. Everyone eventually winds up at the Clam Shack, one of America's great seafood dives. Or tuck into a lobster roll at nearby Mabel's Lobster Claw—but save room for the peanut butter ice cream.

WHERE: 20 miles south of Portland. **WHITE BARN INN:** Tel 207-967-2321; www.whitebarn inn.com. *Cost:* from $310 (off-peak), from $465 (peak); dinner $95. **CAPTAIN LORD MANSION:** Tel 800-522-3141 or 207-967-3141; www.cap tainlord.com. *Cost:* from $200 (off-peak), from $240 (peak). **THE CLAM SHACK:** Tel 207-967-2560; www.theclamshack.net. *Cost:* $15. *When:* May–Oct. **MABEL'S LOBSTER CLAW:** Tel 207-967-2562. *Cost:* $20. **BEST TIMES:** May–Oct for lovely weather; early Dec for Christmas Prelude.

Of Wind, Waves, and Lobster

PENOBSCOT BAY

Maine, U.S.A.

Cutting a 35-by-27-mile gash in the center of the Maine coast, Penobscot Bay is a scenic wonder, circled by some of the state's prettiest towns and dotted with dozens of islands. Renowned for its craggy, pine-covered coastline, it has standout sunsets and lighthouses right out of an Andrew Wyeth painting.

Camden is the archetypal coastal village, its gorgeous old houses converted into B&Bs,

and antiques and craft shops lining its Main Street. Linger a moment in Harbor Park, laid out in the early 1900s by Central Park–designer Frederick Law Olmsted, and take in the stunning waterfront in all its glory.

Castine, first settled in 1613, is full of beautiful Federalist, Georgian, and Victorian architecture, and more than 100 historic sites, including Fort George, built by the British in 1779. Check into the Pentagöet Inn, a turreted 1894 Queen Anne Victorian and Castine's original summer hotel, or at the cozy 19th-century Castine Inn, just a block from the harbor.

The village of Deer Isle, on the island by the same name (accessible by bridge), maintains an active fishing and lobstering fleet and is home to many artists and artisans. Here you'll find the charming waterfront Pilgrim's Inn, built in 1793. There's superb sea kayaking along Merchant's Row, a string of islands and islets between the nearby village of Stonington and Isle au Haut, whose southern half is part of Acadia National Park (see p. 800).

The towns of Rockland, Rockport, and Camden are home to the bay's historic schooner fleet, including 12 of the Maine Windjammer Association's vessels, most of which are from the late 19th and early 20th centuries. They offer rustic 3- to 6-day sailing adventures during which passengers can help tack and jibe or just relax, enjoying lobster bakes and stargazing before bedding down in tiny, simple cabins. The Farnsworth Museum, in Rockland, is one of the country's finest regional museums, with works by artists such as Winslow Homer and Andrew Wyeth. Time your visit in early August for days of all-American fun at the Maine Lobster Festival, also in Rockland, the capital of the lobster universe in a state where the average annual catch generally exceeds 36 million pounds (festivalgoers devour an impressive 10 tons). There's music, homemade blueberry ice cream, lobster-eating contests, and even the coronation of a Sea Goddess.

Where: Camden is 86 miles northeast of Portland. **Visitor info:** www.therealmaine.com. **Pentagöet Inn:** Tel 800-845-1701 or 207-326-8616; www.pentagoet.com. *Cost:* from $140. *When:* May–Oct. **Castine Inn:** Tel 207-326-4365; www.castineinn.com. *Cost:* from $110. *When:* early May–mid-Oct. **Pilgrim's Inn:** Tel 888-778-7505 or 207-348-6615; www.pilgrimsinn.com. *Cost:* from $119. *When:* mid-May–mid-Oct. **Maine Windjammers:** Tel 800-807-9463 or 207-832-0810; www.sailmainecoast.com. *Cost:* 3 nights from $425, all-inclusive (longer cruises available). *When:* late May–mid-Oct. **Farnsworth Museum:** Tel 207-596-6457; www.farnsworthmuseum.org. **Best times:** Jun and Sep for fewer people; late Jul–early Aug for Maine Lobster Festival; Oct for fall foliage.

Crab Town's Gold Standard

Obrycki's and Faidley's

Baltimore, Maryland, U.S.A.

Seldom is a city more associated with a specific food than Baltimore is with the *Callinectes sapidus*, or blue crab. More than 2 million pounds of these spindly-legged side-crawlers are hauled in from nearby Chesapeake Bay (see next page) every year, and a sizable chunk of the catch is merrily consumed at Obrycki's, a family-run place in the historic Fells Point neighborhood that's been drawing crowds since 1944. Menu highlights include the broiled seafood combination, piled with enough fruits of the deep to sink a trawler. Kick it up a notch with the piquant Old Bay Seasoning, invented in Baltimore in 1939, or the secret, more peppery house blend.

For another take on no-frills epicurean delights, head to Baltimore's venerable Lexington Market. Started in 1782, the city's beloved grazing ground houses more than 140 merchants, of which Faidley's is its anchor and uncontested favorite. A seafood shop and raw bar, it is famed for its oversize, jumbo-lump crab cakes, which have been called the best in the Chesapeake (some say the best on the planet). This egalitarian, stand-and-eat hole-in-the-wall also serves scrumptious codfish cakes and shrimp. But save those for your next visit.

Obrycki's: Tel 410-732-6399; www.obryckis.com. *Cost:* dinner $40. *When:* Mar–Nov. **Lexington Market:** Tel 410-685-6169; www.lexingtonmarket.com. **Faidley's:** Tel 410-727-4898; www.faidleyscrabcakes.com. *Cost:* lunch $15. **Best times:** May–Jun for soft-shell crabs, Sep–early Oct for hard-shell.

American Charm and the Ubiquitous Blue Crab

Chesapeake Bay

Maryland, U.S.A.

Chesapeake Bay is the largest estuary on the continent, and its Eastern Shore owes its renown to miles of wetlands, coves, and quaint waterfront towns. The triangle formed by Easton, Oxford, and St. Michaels is the area's most popular destination, a charming enclave of pre-Revolutionary and Federalist houses. Browse the antiques stores in Easton, the unofficial capital of the region, before traveling to Oxford, one of the best-preserved colonial settlements in the country. Check in at the Robert Morris Inn, which dates to 1710 and is where James Michener wrote parts of *Chesapeake*.

A ferry links Oxford to the Victorian shipping village of St. Michaels, where the 1879 Hooper Strait Lighthouse stands vigil. The Chesapeake Bay Maritime Museum, at Navy Point, has a working boatyard, where you'll find expert builders restoring historic vessels. Head next door to the Crab Claw for hot, spiced Maryland blue crabs (Michener declared them "the best food under the sun").

St. Michaels is also known for the bay's most special getaway, the romantic Inn at Perry Cabin, an 1816 manor on the banks of the Miles River. At once elegant and relaxed, its bayside restaurant serves fish and seafood fresh from the local waters. Or head to any of the bay islands, particularly Tilghman, a working watermen's village first charted by Captain John Smith in the early 1600s. Home to the last commercial sailing fleet in North America, its pace is unhurried and its surroundings unspoiled. Bunk down at the Lazyjack Inn, an 1850s waterfront home with views of the boats bobbing in the sleepy harbor.

It's 40 minutes by boat from the hamlet of Crisfield to Smith Island and its small fishing communities. Here, the old-fashioned Inn of Silent Music is surrounded by water on three sides. Tuck into a slice of the island's namesake multilayered cake with chocolate icing, the official state dessert.

Complete your Chesapeake experience in Annapolis. Settled in 1649, the state capital has an enjoyably walkable historic district and is home to the U.S. Naval Academy. Take a class at the Annapolis Sailing School, then enjoy terra firma again at the Annapolis Inn, a

1770s Georgian and Greek Revival town house with just three sumptuous suites.

Where: Easton is 63 miles southeast of Baltimore. Annapolis is 30 miles south of Baltimore on the Western Shore. **Visitor info:** www.baygateways.net. **Robert Morris Inn:** Tel 888-823-4012 or 410-226-5111; www.robertmorrisinn.com. *Cost:* from $150. **Maritime Museum:** Tel 410-745-2916; www.cbmm.org. **The Crab Claw:** Tel 410-745-2900; www.thecrabclaw.com. *Cost:* lunch $15. **Inn at Perry Cabin:** Tel 800-237-1236 or 410-745-2200; www.perrycabin.com. *Cost:* from $390; dinner $50. **Lazyjack Inn:** Tel 800-690-5080 or 410-886-2215; www.lazyjackinn.com. *Cost:* from $160. **Inn of Silent Music:** Tel 410-425-3541; www.innofsilentmusic.com. *Cost:* from $110. *When:* Apr–mid-Nov. **Annapolis Sailing School:** Tel 800-638-9192 or 410-267-7205; www.annapolissailing.com. *When:* Apr–Oct. **Annapolis Inn:** Tel 410-295-5200; www.annapolisinn.com. *Cost:* from $260. **Best times:** May–Jun for soft-shell crabs; 3rd Wed in Jul for Crab and Clam Bake in Crisfield; last Sat in Jul for Chesapeake Folk Festival in St. Michaels; Sep–early Oct for hard-shell crabs; Oct in Annapolis for U.S. Sailboat Show and Powerboat Show; mid-Oct for Tilghman Island Day.

St. Michaels's 19th-century Hooper Strait Lighthouse today serves as a museum exhibit.

"And this is good old Boston / The home of the bean and the cod / Where the Lowells talk only to the Cabots / And the Cabots talk only to God."—John Collins Bossidy

Boston

Massachusetts, U.S.A.

Don't assume that because Boston is chock-full of history its personality is stodgy. Yes, it looks back proudly on its role in the American revolution, but it also strides youthfully forward, courtesy of the area's many elite universities (Boston is the biggest college town in the world) and the city's thriving art and culture scene.

Top Attractions

Museum of Fine Arts—The MFA's holdings are so vast—more than 450,000 pieces, from objects produced from around 6000 B.C. to works by contemporary artists—that you'll find treasures no matter where you wander. A major renovation and expansion culminated in 2010 with the opening of the new airy American Wing, which displays 5,000 treasures from across the New World. **Info:** Tel 617-267-9300; www.mfa.org.

Isabella Stewart Gardner Museum—Venture inside beyond the austere façade of this 1901 mansion to discover a romantic four-story re-creation of a 15th-century Venetian palazzo, with a central courtyard.

Once the home of Isabella Gardner, a turn-of-the-20th-century bohemian and art collector, the building now houses her idiosyncratic collection of European, Asian, and American fine and decorative art. The museum hosts chamber music concert series most Sunday afternoons from September through May. A Renzo Piano–designed wing is scheduled to open in 2012. **Info:** 617-566-1401; www.gardnermuseum.org.

Institute of Contemporary Art/Boston—This light-filled structure of glass and steel built in 2006, and cantilevered over the South Boston waterfront, showcases contemporary and avant-garde art in all media, not just visual art and installations, but music, film, video, and performance. There's always something intriguing to experience here. **Info:** Tel 617-478-3100; www.icaboston.org.

Fenway Park—Fenway Park is the oldest major league ballpark in America. Its appeal derives mostly from its quirky architecture and the history that oozes from every brick and board—a history that, to the despair of Red Sox fans, included only two World Series titles between 1918 and 2004. (They scooped up another trophy in 2007.) If you can't make a game, at least take a tour. **Info:** Tel 877-733-7699 (tickets) or 617-226-6666 (tour); www.redsox.com. *When:* games Apr–early Oct; tours year-round.

The Freedom Trail—The 2.5-mile self-guided Freedom Trail connects 16 of Boston's most important colonial and Revolutionary War landmarks. It begins at Boston Common, the nation's first park (created in 1634), and runs past the circa 1680 Paul Revere House and the "one if by land, two if by sea" Old North Church (1723). Also on the trail is Faneuil Hall, Boston's original market building and meeting hall. Today it's the centerpiece of a five-building complex of shops, bars, and eateries. The restaurants include Durgin-Park, open since 1827 and known throughout the years for hearty Yankee fare—including its Boston cream pie. **Info:** Tel 617-357-8300; www.thefreedomtrail.org. **Durgin-Park:** Tel 617-227-2038; www.durgin-park.com. *Cost:* lunch $25.

The Public Garden—This is America's first public botanical garden, with plantings dating back to 1837. At its verdant center is a small lagoon that's filled in the summer with Swan Boats pedaled by college students. In winter, ice-skaters pirouette on the pond's glassy surface. Near the corner of Beacon and Charles streets, *Make Way for Ducklings* is a string of tiny bronze statuettes of waterfowl eternally following their mother toward the pond, as they did in Robert McCloskey's children's book of the same name. Close to the exit onto Commonwealth Avenue, a landmark statue of George Washington gazes down from his horse. **Swan Boats:** Tel 617-522-1966; www.swanboats.com. *When:* late Apr–mid-Sep.

The city's 24-acre green heart was once a marsh.

Beacon Hill—One of Boston's oldest neighborhoods, Beacon Hill is a time capsule of elegant, early-19th-century architecture, with white-trimmed redbrick town houses, well-tended window boxes overflowing with flowers, and gas lamps lighting the cobbled streets. The steep streets lead up to the golden dome of the 1797 Massachusetts State House. The south slope of the hill is known as Boston Common, and the "flat of the hill," between Charles Street and the Charles River, adjoins the Public Garden. Or follow the Black Heritage Trail, which links 15 historically significant sites, including a stop on the Underground Railroad and the Museum of African American History. **Visitor info:** www.bostonusa.com. **Boston African American National Historic Site:** Tel 617-742-5415; www.nps.gov/boaf. **Museum of African American History:** Tel 617-725-0022; www.maah.org.

HARVARD SQUARE—No visit to Boston is complete without a side trip to "The People's Republic of Cambridge," the lively and unabashedly intellectual city across the Charles River that's home to two heavyweight seats of learning, the Massachusetts Institute of Technology (M.I.T) and Harvard University (founded in 1636). Life here revolves around Harvard Square, bustling with the tides of students, professors, and visitors, and crowded with trendy boutiques, restaurants, and bistros. Just adjacent lies Harvard Yard, where you'll see nearly three centuries' worth of architecture, including the university's oldest building, Massachusetts Hall (1720). The nearby Fogg, with its Italian Renaissance–style stone courtyard, is the best known of the university's three museums, which together hold more than 250,000 objects. (The Fogg and Busch-Reisinger Museums are closed for renovation through 2013; in the interim, selected pieces from these collections are on view at the nearby Arthur M. Sackler Museum.) **VISITOR INFO:** www.cambridge-usa.org. **HARVARD UNIVERSITY:** www.harvard.edu. **HARVARD ART MUSEUMS:** Tel 617-495-9400; www.artmuseums.harvard.edu.

Narrow, row house–lined Acorn Street epitomizes elite, historic Beacon Hill.

BOSTON'S NORTH END—Its narrow streets crammed with redbrick tenements, the North End is where many newly arrived immigrants made their first homes. Beginning in the mid-1800s, the area teemed with Irish families, followed by new arrivals from Eastern Europe, Portugal, and finally Italy. Today it remains one of the nation's most famous Italian-American communities, with a wealth of great restaurants, from Pizzeria Regina, with its thin-crust pies, to Caffè Vittoria, the oldest café in Boston, to the more formal Mamma Maria, known for northern Italian cuisine and romance. In summer, the North End fills with street fairs, peaking with the Fisherman's Feast in mid-August, which kicks off with a procession of the Madonna and continues with entertainment and lots of good food. **PIZZERIA REGINA:** Tel 617-227-0765; www.pizzeriaregina.com. *Cost:* large pie from $13. **CAFFÈ VITTORIA:** Tel 617-227-7606; www.vittoriacaffe.com. **MAMMA MARIA:** Tel 617-523-0077; www.mammamaria.com. *Cost:* dinner $55.

EVENTS & FESTIVALS

BOSTON HARBORFEST—Boston enjoys the Fourth of July far too much to confine its celebration to one day or one place: Its Harborfest lasts a full week and happens at various venues downtown and along the waterfront. Harborfest's 200-plus events—concerts, cruises, tours, performances, and more—include Children's Day and Chowderfest, where crowds vote on the region's signature soup. The climax of the festivities is the free concert by the Boston Pops (see next page) on the night of the Fourth, complete with church bells, cannon fire (during the finale of the 1812 Overture), and a thunderous display of fireworks set to music. **INFO:** Tel 617-227-1528; www.bostonharborfest.com. **POPS CONCERT:** Tel 888-484-7677 or 617-267-2400; www.july4th.org.

THE BOSTON MARATHON—The Boston Marathon is the world's oldest such race held annually, and the centerpiece of the city's celebration of Patriots Day, a state holiday that falls on the third Monday in April and commemorates the start of the Revolutionary War. Upwards of 20,000 official runners set out from the starting line in suburban Hopkinton and make their way along the 26.2-mile course, cheered on by a half million spectators lining nearly the entire route. Almost everyone eventually makes it to Boylston Street in the Back Bay, crossing the finish line near Copley Square. **Info:** Tel 617-236-1652; www.bostonmarathon.org.

Head of the Charles Regatta—The world's largest two-day rowing event, with 300,000-plus spectators, the Head of the Charles draws more than 8,000 athletes from colleges, high schools, and clubs in the U.S. and abroad to compete in 59 races. The curving 3.2-mile course stretches from Boston University's DeWolfe Boathouse to the finish just past the Eliot Bridge. Although the Regatta is not directly affiliated with any of the area's universities, there's an undeniable collegiate energy, with youthful supporters screaming themselves hoarse as the boats whiz by. **Info:** Tel 617-868-6200; www.hocr.org. **When:** 3rd weekend in Oct.

The Boston Symphony Orchestra and The Boston Pops—The Boston Symphony Orchestra is one of the world's very best, and if you're in the city from late September through April, you should plan to take in a concert in the acoustically perfect Symphony Hall. The Boston Pops Orchestra also performs here, most frequently during the holiday season and from May through early July. **Info:** Tel 888-266-1200 or 617-266-1200 (tickets), 617-266-1492 (info); www.bso.org.

Where to Stay

Boston Harbor Hotel—Location, location, location: Perched above Boston Harbor, this hotel has the city's best views, along with top-notch facilities (including a full-service spa). There's nothing demure about the façade, featuring an 80-foot arch topped by a rotunda, but in contrast, the 230 guest rooms have a relaxed elegance that's chic rather than stuffy. The Meritage dining room pairs its exquisite, full-flavored cuisine with wines from its 12,000-bottle collection. **Info:** Tel 617-439-7000; www.bhh.com. *Cost:* from $290; dinner at the Meritage $80.

Eliot Hotel—The Eliot is a refined and elegant boutique hotel, with personalized service and European-style luxury. The classically furnished one- and two-bedroom suites quickly become a home away from home. The sophistication extends to the hotel's restaurant Clio, where award-winning chef Ken Oringer interweaves the vivid, distinctive flavors of the freshest local produce with classic French techniques. **Info:** Tel 800-443-5468 or 617-267-1607; www.eliothotel.com. *Cost:* from $225 (off-peak), from $395 (peak); dinner $75.

Fairmont Copley Plaza—Boston's most romantic hotel is filled with all the grace and opulence you'd expect of its 1912 pedigree (it was designed by the same architect as New York's Plaza Hotel). Guest rooms are sinfully comfortable, but it's the gilded lobby and the Oak Bar (a clubby hideaway of leather furniture and excellent martinis) that make you feel like royalty. **Info:** Tel 800-257-7544 or 617-267-5300; www.fairmont.com/copleyplaza. *Cost:* from $270 (off-peak), from $380 (peak).

Four Seasons Hotel Boston—Four Seasons Hotel Boston combines discreet luxury with a gorgeous setting and award-winning dining. The Public Garden is a constant presence: It's visible through huge windows from the lobby, restaurant, guest rooms, and swimming pool. Accommodations are large, with marble-tiled bathrooms and a soothing modern décor. The convivial Bristol Lounge is where locals and guests alike gather to enjoy cocktails, live music, and memorable cuisine, including the famous Bristol Burger with truffle fries. **Info:** Tel 617-338-4400; www.fourseasons.com/boston. *Cost:* from $450 (off-peak), from $650 (peak); dinner $60.

Downtown Boston's Faneuil Hall (center) has long been a gathering site for debate and commerce.

Lenox Hotel—Blending vintage elegance with modern comforts, the Lenox offers great value, plus a superb location in the Back Bay. The 1901 hotel maintains its historic charms—many of the suites have working fireplaces—while receiving accolades as one of the "greenest" hotels in the nation. **Info:** Tel 800-225-7676 or 617-536-5300; www.lenoxhotel.com. *Cost:* from $185 (off-peak), from $345 (peak).

Taj Boston—Opened in 1927 as the Ritz-Carlton Hotel and purchased by Taj Hotels Resorts in 2007, the Taj Boston continues to occupy a special niche befitting its venerable pedigreed opulence. Decorated in classic style and outfitted with all the latest perks (call the front desk for the "Fireplace Butler"), it's the one truly legendary Boston hotel. Two of its longstanding draws are its traditional afternoon tea, accompanied by live harp music, and its location on Newbury Street, known for the city's best shopping. **Info:** Tel 877-482-5267 or 617-536-5700; www.taj hotels.com/boston. *Cost:* from $250 (off-peak), from $395 (peak); afternoon tea $32.

Eating & Drinking

Hamersley's Bistro—At this South Bay storefront, Gordon Hamersley helped pioneer the chef-owned restaurant scene. The menu changes seasonally, but a handful of stalwarts, including perfectly roasted chicken with garlic, lemon, and parsley, are standouts all year long. **Info:** Tel 617-423-2700; www .hamersleysbistro.com. *Cost:* dinner $50.

Legal Sea Foods—This beloved chain of seafood restaurants originated in the 1950s as a fish market (Julia Child was an early customer). Today Legal Sea Foods is a venerable institution, internationally renowned for the quality and freshness of its fish. There are more than a dozen locations in greater Boston, but the one most convenient to the Freedom Trail is the waterfront dining room on Long Wharf. Legal's chunky clam chowder is a must-sample, but so is the steamed or baked lobster, and a perfect rendition of Boston cream pie for dessert. **Info:** Tel 617-742-5300; www.leagalseafoods .com. *Cost:* dinner $40.

Locke-Ober—The ornate dining room at Locke-Ober, with its vintage carved mahogany paneling, Art Nouveau stained glass, and crystal chandeliers, evokes its 1860s roots. This well-loved landmark received a menu update from Lydia Shire, who revised the French menu and added lighter, more contemporary fare. Still, it's the classics like lobster Savannah (lobster stuffed with mushrooms and seafood) that keep the let's-dress-up-for-dinner crowd coming back for more. **Info:** Tel 617-542-1340; www .lockeober.com. *Cost:* dinner $75.

No. 9 Park—Sitting high on Beacon Hill, No. 9 Park sets the standard for contemporary fine dining. Chef-owner Barbara Lynch has won a James Beard Award for her refined cooking, which takes its cues from French and Italian cuisines but is the essence of New England in its flavors. The dining room, designed to evoke a 1940s supper club, looks out on the Common. Lynch also operates B&G Oysters, with fantastically fresh seafood, and Sportello, an American diner seen through an Italian lens. **No. 9 Park:** Tel 617-742-9991; www.no9park.com. *Cost:*

tasting menu $96. **B&G Oysters:** Tel 617-423-0550; www.bandgoysters.com. *Cost:* dinner $40. **Sportello:** Tel 617-737-1234; www.sportelloboston.com. *Cost:* dinner: $40.

Oleana—The sunny flavors of the eastern Mediterranean reign at this cozy Cambridge restaurant operated by chef-owner Ana Sortun. Complex blends of spices infuse her tamarind-glazed beef and grilled octopus with fennel conserve. Oleana's shady courtyard is perfect for alfresco dining. **Info:** Tel 617-661-0505; www.oleanarestaurant.com. *Cost:* dinner $55.

Ye Olde Union Oyster House—Established in 1826 near Faneuil Hall, in an atmospheric corner known as the Blackstone Block, Ye Olde Union Oyster House is the country's oldest restaurant in continuous service. Stop by its famous raw bar for oysters—and a full serving of old-time atmosphere. The path to your table, across sloping wooden floors, may take you past Booth 18, once favored by John F. Kennedy. **Info:** Tel 617-227-2750; www.unionoysterhouse.com. *Cost:* dinner $35.

Oldies but Goodies

Brimfield and Sturbridge

Massachusetts, U.S.A.

The country's largest and best-known antiques and collectibles market teems with more than 6,000 dealers and some 1 million visitors who come from all over the country and beyond. Materializing in central Massachusetts three times a year, the Brimfield Outdoor Antiques Show occupies a 1-mile stretch of former farmland along Route 20, blanketing the fields in tents and makeshift display areas. The air may be jovial, but the dealers aren't fooling around, and neither are the legions of buyers, who arrive as early as 4:30 A.M. on opening day (Tuesday), loaded for bear.

Each field keeps its own schedule; many are open between dawn and dusk throughout the show's six days. By the weekend, the prime merchandise has been snapped up, but latecomers to "the Brimfield fleas" can sometimes take advantage of slashed prices on items sellers don't want to haul home. Wear your most comfortable shoes, and be warned that it frequently rains during the May show.

It's just 6 miles from the hubbub to another remarkable collection of antiques—Old Sturbridge Village, the largest living history museum in the Northeast. This re-creation of a rural 1830s New England community is thoughtfully arranged across 200 acres; its 40 period buildings were transported from all over the region beginning in the mid-1940s. There are authentically furnished homes, a working farm, a small school, and water-powered mills, as well as a stagecoach to ride and costumed "residents" demonstrating their trades and crafts, and celebrating holidays and the seasons in traditional ways.

Where: 64 miles west of Boston. **Brimfield Outdoor Antiques Show:** Tel 413-283-2418; www.quaboag.com. *When:* 3 shows (Tues–Sun) yearly: 2nd Tues in May, 2nd Tues after July 4, 1st Tues after Labor Day. **Old Sturbridge Village:** Tel 800-733-1830 or 508-347-3362; www.osv.org. **Best times:** in Sturbridge: Apr for Barnyard Babies; early Jul for Independence Day events; Sep–Nov for harvest and Thanksgiving celebrations; Dec for Christmas festivities.

The Bay State's "Other Cape"

Cape Ann

Massachusetts, U.S.A.

Massachusetts's "Other Cape" juts out into the Atlantic just north of Boston. In 1623, European settlers of Cape Anne declared the waters around Gloucester the best fishing grounds in the New World, and descendants of early Portuguese and Italian fishermen still gather today for St. Peter's Fiesta, an enormous summer street fair that includes a blessing of the fleet.

Gloucester remains a scrappy seafaring town (it was the setting for the book *The Perfect Storm* and its film adaption), and today specializes in whale-watching cruises. Cape Ann's proximity to the National Marine Sanctuary at Stellwagen Bank, running from Gloucester to Provincetown (see next page) and a veritable banquet for migrating whales, led to its self-anointed role as "Whale-Watching Capital of the World." It's also home to the Rocky Neck Art Colony, the nation's oldest such colony. Nearby Rockport attracts visitors with its own vibrant artist community and a downtown that—even with its overflow of gift shops and B&Bs—retains its charm. The gracious 19th-century Emerson Inn by the Sea, named for the famous philosopher and onetime guest, sits north of town, with a columned back veranda and lovely restaurant that both enjoy water views. Nearby Essex's legacy is proudly preserved in the small Essex Shipbuilding Museum, which traces its story from the first shipyard in 1668 to the mid-19th century, when as many as 15 manufacturers worked around the clock to produce 50 or more vessels a year.

Cape Ann's greatest fame is arguably as the hallowed birthplace of the fried clam, thanks to Chubby Woodman's vision back in 1916. Today, Woodman's in Essex is a vacation ritual for the 2,000 people who show up on any given summer day. The red-and-white-striped Clam Box, a takeout in nearby Ipswich, opened in 1938 and maintains a friendly rivalry with the older eatery.

If you're heading south toward Boston, don't bypass Salem, perhaps better known for witches and Halloween than for its rich history, art, and architecture. The city, site of the infamous witch trials in 1692, abounds with "witch kitsch" and is home to a not-so-scary Salem Witch Museum. The Peabody Essex Museum is the city's cultural centerpiece, the oldest continuously operating museum in the country (since 1799). Don't miss the tour of the nearby rambling House of the Seven Gables, the setting for Salem native Nathaniel Hawthorne's novel of the same name.

Where: Gloucester is 36 miles northeast of Boston. **Visitor info:** www.capeannvacations.com. **Emerson Inn by the Sea:** Tel 800-964-5550 or 978-546-6321; www.emersoninnbythesea.com. *Cost:* from $135; dinner $35. **Essex Shipbuilding Museum:** Tel 978-768-7541; www.essexshipbuildingmuseum.org. **Woodman's:** Tel 800-649-1773 or 978-768-2559; www.woodmans.com. **Clam Box:** Tel 978-356-9707; www.ipswichma.com/clambox. **Salem Witch Museum:** Tel 978-744-1692; www.salemwitchmuseum.com. **Peabody Essex Museum:** Tel 866-745-1876 or 978-745-9500; www.pem.org. **House of the Seven Gables:** Tel 978-744-0991; www.7gables.org. **Best times:** late Jun for St. Peter's Fiesta in Gloucester; mid-Sep for Gloucester Seafood Festival; Oct for Halloween in Salem.

New England's Summer Playground

CAPE COD

Massachusetts, U.S.A.

Cape Cod National Seashore comprises a 40-mile stretch of rolling dunes and gorgeous beaches, from Chatham north to Provincetown. President John F. Kennedy granted the area federal protection in 1961, well over a century after Henry David Thoreau wrote this is where "a man can stand and put all America behind him." Here lighthouses overlook wonderful wide beaches, sand bars, and salt marshes, and kettle ponds dot the woodlands.

Cape Cod National Seashore boasts miles of coastline and towering dunes.

The old sea captains' town of Chatham is one of the Cape's most desirable destinations, with handsome clapboard buildings set off by white picket fences, ice-cream shops, and flowering gardens. Built in 1839, the Captain's House Inn has romantic rooms with four-posters and fireplaces, while the Chatham Bars Inn, a historic 200-plus–room oceanfront establishment, enjoys loyal return guests who come for the classic New England resort experience, complete with beach clambakes under the stars.

The two-lane Old King's Highway (Route 6A) passes a plethora of antiques shops and inviting eateries on its way north to Provincetown. Known as P-town, this longtime fishing and whaling port is now also home to an artists' colony and a vibrant gay community that throngs busy Commercial Street on weekend nights. The *Mayflower* landed here in 1620 before continuing across the bay to Plymouth (see p. 814). It's also just 6 miles from the krill-rich Stellwagen Bank, which explains the almost guaranteed sightings of migrating whales from mid-April through October. A busy cultural scene revolves around the numerous art galleries and the Provincetown Theater, which has been attracting luminaries since the early 1900s.

Of the town's host of seafood restaurants, the Lobster Pot is a perennial favorite for its award-winning clam chowder and Portuguese-inspired specialties. As for accommodations, the 1904 Land's End Inn is famed for its location and Bay Tower suite with a 360-degree view from its wraparound deck. In the heart of town, the larger Crowne Pointe Inn & Spa encompasses a late-19th-century sea captain's house and three renovated carriage houses, with a spa that is the best around.

WHERE: Chatham is 90 miles southeast of Boston. Provincetown is 35 miles north of Chatham. **VISITOR INFO:** www.capecodchamber.org. **CAPE COD NATIONAL SEASHORE:** Tel 508-255-3421; www.nps.gov/caco. **CAPTAIN'S HOUSE INN:** Tel 800-315-0728 or 508-945-0127; www.captainshouseinn.com. *Cost:* from $185 (off-peak), from $265 (peak). **CHATHAM BARS INN:** Tel 800-527-4884 or 508-945-0096; www.chathambarsinn.com. *Cost:* from $195 (off-peak), from $465 (peak). **PROVINCETOWN THEATER:** Tel 800-791-7487 or 508-487-7487; www.ptowntix.com. **LOBSTER POT:** Tel 508-487-0842; www.ptownlobsterpot.com. *Cost:* dinner $35. *When:* closed Dec–Mar. **LAND'S END INN:** Tel 800-276-7088 or

508-487-1145; www.landsendinn.com. *Cost:* from $170 (off-peak), from $330 (peak). **CROWNE POINTE:** Tel 877-276-9631 or 508-487-6767; www.crownepointe.com. *Cost:* from $100 (off-peak), from $240 (peak). **BEST TIMES:** May–Jun and Sep–Oct for pleasant weather and smaller crowds; mid-Apr–Oct for whale-watching; late Jun for P-town's Portuguese Festival; Jul–Aug for best beach weather.

A Gorgeous Setting for a Smorgasbord of Culture

BERKSHIRE SUMMER FESTIVALS

Lenox, Massachusetts, U.S.A.

When warm weather sets in, musicians from all over the world head to the Berkshires' rolling, wooded hills and the Tanglewood Music Festival, its marquee event. Summer home of the Boston Symphony Orchestra, Tanglewood's lush 500-acre estate encompasses four performance venues as well as the Lawn for picnicking under the stars. The concert-studded season culminates in early September with the Tanglewood Jazz Fest.

In nearby Becket, the internationally acclaimed Jacob's Pillow Dance Festival, with more than 200 free performances (from ballet to flamenco), is held at The Pillow, a 163-acre National Historic Landmark.

Shakespeare & Company focuses, not surprisingly, on the Bard, but also hosts contemporary works. The venerable Berkshire Theatre Festival in nearby Stockbridge takes place in the 1888 Stockbridge Casino, designed by Stanford White. In town, the Norman Rockwell Museum houses the largest collection of works by the beloved American artist, who lived here until his death in 1978.

Anchoring Stockbridge's Rockwell-perfect Main Street is the ever-popular 19th-century Red Lion Inn. More sumptuous accommodations await in surrounding mansions, harking back to the Gilded Age building boom that peaked in 1885. More than 70 of these "cottages" survive, including the 1902 Elizabethan-style Blantyre, presiding like a Scottish castle over 117 acres. Its friendly rival Wheatleigh, an Italianate palazzo built in 1893 has a fine restaurant and views of the 22-acre grounds designed by Frederick Law Olmsted of Central Park fame. Less baronial but no less comfortable, the 18th-century Old Inn on the Green in New Marlborough is a former stagecoach stop, welcoming guests with a candlelit dining room.

WHERE: Lenox is 130 miles west of Boston. **VISITOR INFO:** www.berkshires.org. **TANGLEWOOD:** Tel 888-266-1200 or 617-266-1492; www.tanglewood.org. *When:* late Jun–early Sep. **JACOB'S PILLOW DANCE FESTIVAL:** Tel 413-243-9919; www.jacobspillow.org. *When:* late Jun–late Aug. **SHAKESPEARE & COMPANY:** Tel 413-637-1199; www.shakespeare.org. *When:* mid-Jun–Nov. **BERKSHIRE THEATRE FESTIVAL:** Tel 413-298-5576; www.berkshiretheatre.org. *When:* late May–Dec. **NORMAN ROCKWELL MUSEUM:** Tel 413-298-4100; www.nrm.org. **THE RED LION INN:** Tel 413-298-5545; www.redlioninn.com. *Cost:* from $135 (off-peak), from $240 (peak). **BLANTYRE:** Tel 413-637-3556; www.blantyre.com. *Cost:* from $600. **WHEATLEIGH:** Tel 413-637-0610; www.wheatleigh.com. *Cost:* from $715; tasting menu $165. **THE OLD INN ON THE GREEN:** Tel 413-229-7924; www.oldinn.com. *Cost:* from $225; dinner $65.

Island Charm off the Coast of Cape Cod

Martha's Vineyard and Nantucket

Massachusetts, U.S.A.

Cape Cod's two celebrated islands float just off its southern shore. The 100-square-mile Martha's Vineyard is the larger and more serene, a place of beautiful beaches, woods, cranberry bogs, and charming inns, distinguished from its neighbor Nantucket by its proximity to the mainland and its variety of landscapes.

The offbeat, fun village of Oak Bluffs is one of six on the island, distinguished by its colorful Victorian homes and 1876 working carousel, said to be the oldest in the country. Vineyard Haven is known for the Black Dog Tavern, purveyor of ubiquitous T-shirts and tasty pub grub. In West Tisbury the Norman Rockwell–style Alley's General Store is a proud "Dealer in Almost Everything." The dramatic cliffs of Aquinnah (aka Gay Head) and its landmark lighthouse are the island's Land's End, while in Menemsha you'll find the hilltop Beach Plum Inn and Restaurant. It has an excellent water-view restaurant and access to some of the island's best beaches, perfect for sunset watching.

In Edgartown (the largest of the Vineyard's villages and the one with the most buzz) is Atria, a restaurant in an 1890s sea captain's house with a lively bar and famous burgers. The 19th-century Charlotte Inn is the finest hostelry on the island, with a fine Italian restaurant, Il Tesoro, and 23 antiques-filled guest rooms in five buildings enveloped by flowering gardens.

Thirty miles off the coast of Cape Cod, 49-square-mile Nantucket exists in its own insular world. Though its population of 10,000 swells to five times that every summer, the island retains a world-apart atmosphere. Stringent zoning laws help maintain the traditional New England appearance of the "Little Gray Lady of the Sea," whose historic district includes more than 800 Georgian, Federal, and Greek Revival houses. Nantucket was once the whaling capital of the world (part of *Moby Dick* was set here) and its Whaling Museum illustrates the island's importance in the "blubber-boiling" industry.

In the 19th century, Vineyard Haven was one of New England's busiest ports.

The posh, weathered-shingled Wauwinet stands in romantic end-of-the-world isolation adjacent to 26 miles of protected shoreline, with sweeping ocean vistas from most of the simply furnished, spacious rooms. At the inn's restaurant, Topper's, you'll find creative takes on regional favorites. The Wauwinet's sister property, The White Elephant, brings the same style and charm into town on the waterfront.

Where: Seasonal ferries for Martha's Vineyard depart from Woods Hole, New Bedford,

Hyannis, and Falmouth; ferries for Nantucket depart from Harwich Port and Hyannis. **VISITOR INFO:** *Martha's Vineyard:* www.mvy.com. *Nantucket:* www.nantucketchamber.org. **BLACK DOG TAVERN:** Tel 800-626-1991 or 508-693-4786; www.theblackdog.com. *Cost:* dinner $30. **BEACH PLUM INN:** Tel 508-645-9454; www.beachpluminn.com. *Cost:* from $195 (off-peak), from $295 (peak); dinner $65. *When:* closed Nov–Apr. **ATRIA:** Tel 508-627-5850; www.atriamv.com. *Cost:* dinner $60. *When:* closed Dec–Mar. **THE CHARLOTTE INN:** Tel 508-627-4151; www.charlotteinn.net. *Cost:* from $325; dinner $70. **WHALING MUSEUM:** Tel 508-228-1894; www.nha.org. *When:* closed Nov–Jun. **THE WAUWINET:**: Tel 800-426-8718 or 508-228-0145; www.wauwinet.com. *Cost:* from $350 (off-peak), from $550 (peak); prix-fixe dinner $85. *When:* closed mid-Oct–May. **WHITE ELEPHANT:** Tel 800-445-6574 or 508-228-2500; www.whiteelephanthotel.com. *Cost:* from $225. **BEST TIMES:** in Martha's Vineyard: mid-Jun for A Taste of the Vineyard; Jul for Edgartown Regatta. In Nantucket: late May for Figawi Sailboat Race; 1st weekend in Dec for Christmas Stroll and Dec for Nantucket Noel.

A Taste of History at America's Symbolic Doorstep

THANKSGIVING AT PLIMOTH PLANTATION

Plymouth, Massachusetts, U.S.A.

At Plimoth Plantation, it's always 1627. The living museum and its costumed "residents" re-create New England's first successful European settlement as well as a Native village. Thanksgiving dinner has its roots in a harvest celebration that 52 Pilgrims shared with 90 members of the Wampanoag tribe in 1621, one year after the settlers sailed from England. It included fowl (probably ducks and geese rather than turkey), venison, corn, and most likely fresh and dried fruits and vegetables. Every fall Plimoth Plantation re-creates a harvest meal from that period as well as serving a classic American Thanksgiving dinner.

Mayflower II *was completed in 1957.*

Make your way to the downtown waterfront to visit (the surprisingly small) Plymouth Rock and *Mayflower II*, a 106-foot-long replica of the ship that carried 102 Pilgrims (with their livestock and worldly goods) and took some 66 tempestuous days to cross the Atlantic.

Learn of the area's role in the whaling trade—which peaked in the mid-19th century—in New Bedford, a 45-minute drive southwest of Plymouth. The New Bedford Whaling Museum, the world's largest, displays a wide variety of artifacts, as well as an 89-foot half-scale model of the fully rigged whaling bark *Lagoda*, built in 1826, and Kobo, a 66-foot skeleton of a juvenile blue whale.

WHERE: 40 miles southeast of Boston. Tel 800-262-9356 or 508-746-1622; www.plimoth.org. *Cost:* dinner from $65. *When:* closed late Nov–late Mar. **NEW BEDFORD WHALING MUSEUM:** Tel 508-997-0046; www.whalingmuseum.org. **BEST TIMES:** selected dates in Oct and Nov for harvest and Thanksgiving meals.

Road Trip Filled with History and Culture

THE MOHAWK TRAIL

Williamstown and Deerfield, Massachusetts, U.S.A.

The Mohawk Trail (Route 2) unfurls for 63 miles through a rural corner of Massachusetts, Vermont, and New York. Originally a Native American footpath, it became the main route connecting the British colonists in Boston to the Dutch in Albany and is the only active motor road in the country that predates World War I. It twists and turns through gorgeous countryside and appealing towns, such as picturesque Williamstown, home to Williams College and a lively cultural scene. The Williamstown Theatre Festival has hosted prominent names from Broadway and Hollywood since 1955. The small but impressive Sterling and Francine Clark Art Institute ("the Clark") houses works by Renoir, Monet, Degas, and Pissarro as well as English silver and early photography.

On Deerfield's mile-long main street, 13 historic homes and a contemporary building make up an engaging museum complex devoted to the town's architectural history and American decorative arts. The 1884 Deerfield Inn has 24 rooms and the popular Champney's Restaurant & Tavern, featuring a market-driven menu and 101 types of martini.

No other erstwhile manufacturing community has reinvented itself quite so creatively as North Adams. Opened in 1999, MASS MoCA (Massachusetts Museum of Contemporary Art) is the largest contemporary arts center in the country. Housed mostly in converted 19th-century textile mills, it features specially commissioned pieces, revolving exhibits, and a dynamic performance schedule. Across the street, the homey Porches Inn blends high-tech amenities with flea-market touches.

WHERE: Williamstown is 153 miles northwest of Boston. **VISITOR INFO:** www.mohawktrail.com. **WILLIAMSTOWN THEATRE FESTIVAL:** Tel 413-597-3400; www.wtfestival.org. *When:* Jul–Aug. **THE CLARK:** Tel 413-458-2303; www.clarkart.edu. **DEERFIELD INN:** Tel 800-926-3865 or 413-774-5587; www.deerfieldinn.com. *Cost:* from $170 (off-peak), from $250 (peak); dinner $40. **MASS MoCA:** Tel 413-662-2111; www.massmoca.org. **THE PORCHES INN:** Tel 413-664-0400; www.porches.com. *Cost:* from $150. **BEST TIMES:** Jul–Aug for Williamstown Theater Festival and the Berkshires' full range of cultural offerings; mid-Sep–mid-Oct for foliage.

A Victorian Relic in the Great Lakes

MACKINAC ISLAND

Michigan, U.S.A.

The gilded Victorian era is preserved on Mackinac Island, with horse-drawn carriages clip-clopping down vehicle-free streets and pedestrians stopping in ice cream parlors and cafés. It can seem a bit touristy, but Mackinac

A true summer colony, the car-free island has just 500 year-round residents.

(MAK-i-naw) is also irrepressibly charming, especially when you leave downtown's cluster of trinket shops (only after sampling the fudge, an island specialty).

Mackinac Island lies in the Straits of Mackinac, where Lakes Michigan and Huron meet, and where the immense Lower and Upper Peninsulas of Michigan are linked at their closest point by one of the world's longest suspension bridges, the 4-mile-long Mackinac. Wealthy urbanites began arriving in the late 19th century and built the grandiose "cottages" you see today; farsighted locals banned the automobile almost as quickly as it arrived. Today more than 500 horses are stabled on the island and, aside from bikes, are the only way to get around.

Hike up to Fort Mackinac or wander the other 80 percent of the island that is protected as a state park. Mackinac's most famous landmark is the sprawling Grand Hotel, a white Greek Revival palace built in 1887 that movie fans will recognize as the setting for the 1980 cult classic *Somewhere in Time*. Perched on a bluff, the time-weathered dowager boasts a magnificent main dining room and expansive lake views to enjoy from a rocking chair on its 660-foot-long veranda.

Another of the island's architectural charmers is the Chippewa Hotel, a lovely Victorian landmark overlooking the marina. Its Pink Pony Bar & Grill enjoys a certain fame as the "finish line" of the 333-mile Chicago-Mackinac Yacht Race ("the Mac"), which has been a cause for celebration every July since 1898.

WHERE: 280 miles north of Detroit. **VISITOR INFO:** www.mackinacisland.org. **GRAND HOTEL:** Tel 800-334-7263 or 906-847-3331; www.grandhotel.com. *Cost:* from $500, inclusive. *When:* May–Oct. **CHIPPEWA HOTEL:** Tel 800-241-3341 or 906-847-3341; www.chippewahotel.com. *Cost:* from $95 (off-peak), from $155 (peak). *When:* May–Oct. **BEST TIMES:** early Jun for the 10-day Lilac Festival; mid-Jul for the Chicago-Mackinac Yacht Race; early Sep for the Bridge Walk.

Paddling—and Sledding—Through Paradise

BOUNDARY WATERS CANOE AREA WILDERNESS

Ely, Minnesota, U.S.A.

More than 1,000 lakes—ranging from 10 to 10,000 acres each—are scattered throughout the piney woods along the Minnesota-Ontario border. On the Minnesota side lie a staggering 1 million protected acres of land known as the Boundary Waters Canoe Area Wilderness (BWCA), the largest U.S. wilderness preserve east of the Rockies. Cross the border and another 1.2 million acres are yours in Ontario's Quetico Provincial Park.

Free of cars, largely free of motorboats, and with more than 1,500 acres of mapped canoe routes, the BWCA was first used by the Ojibwa and later by the French, Dutch, and British fur traders of the 17th century. Today it draws canoers who paddle and portage for days or weeks, camping on forested shores and pulling in walleye or pike for dinner.

Paddlers and anglers make the BWCA the most heavily used wilderness area in the nation. Nevertheless, a strictly enforced permit system keeps crowds manageable: You're more likely to encounter moose, loons, and the occasional wolf than other humans. After narrowly avoiding extermination in the 1930s, around 3,000 eastern timber wolves roam the woods here today. Learn more at the International Wolf Center in Ely, and get close to an "ambassador pack" of six wolves (all born in captivity) who live in a 1.25-acre enclosure next to the center.

Ely (population 4,000) is home base for outfitters providing everything from basic gear rental to fully equipped weeklong canoeing excursions. After several nights in the backcountry, treat yourself to a night in one of the handsome log cabins at the Burntside Lodge just outside town. An early-20th-century lakefront resort, it has a top-notch kitchen and well-chosen wine list—unexpected delights in this remote outpost. Winter, too, has its magic in these parts. This is when the snow-blanketed wilderness turns into a glittering wonderland, and Ely becomes the Sled Dog Capital of the U.S. At Wintergreen Lodge, renowned polar explorer Paul Schurke offers lodge-to-lodge or camping dogsled trips across the frozen landscape.

WHERE: 100 miles northwest of Duluth. Tel 218-626-4300; www.fs.fed.us. **HOW:** Williams & Hall help you plan and outfit your trip. Tel 800-322-5837 or 218-365-5837; www.williamsandhall.com. *Cost:* from $110 per person per day, all-inclusive. *When:* May–Sep. **INTERNATIONAL WOLF CENTER:** Tel 218-365-4695; www.wolf.org. **BURNTSIDE LODGE:** Tel 218-365-3894; www.burntside.com. *Cost:* cabins from $170. *When:* mid-May–Sep. **WINTERGREEN LODGE:** Tel 877-753-3386 or 218-365-6022; www.dogsledding.com. *Cost:* 4 nights from $875 per person, all-inclusive (off-peak), from $1,075 (peak). **BEST TIMES:** Jul–Aug for warmest weather; Sep for fall color and fewer bugs.

The BWCA lies within the Superior National Forest.

Antebellum Life in the Old South

NATCHEZ AND THE NATCHEZ TRACE

Mississippi, U.S.A.

Once a bustling port, Natchez, on the banks of the Mississippi, is a living museum of antebellum architecture. More than 500 historic treasures remain intact, many still inhabited and lovingly preserved by the original owners' descendants. Begun in 1932, the Natchez Spring Pilgrimage is an annual highlight when more than 30 private homes and gardens are open to the public and azaleas, camellias, and magnolias are in full bloom. The Confederate Pageant is also held at this time, with costumed volunteers re-creating a romanticized vignette of the Old South.

Eight historic homes welcome visitors year-round, including a few that serve as B&Bs. Monmouth is one of the best, a paean to Southern grandeur and the former residence of a Mississippi governor; its acclaimed 1818 restaurant takes its name from the year it was built. Another grand Greek Revival "temple" is the colonnaded 26-room Dunleith, built in 1856 and enveloped by 40 grassy acres.

The Cock of the Walk, a popular restaurant in town, serves local specialties such as skillet-fried catfish, fried dill pickles, and skillet cornbread. Over at Fat Mama's Tamales, try the signature Gringo Pie—tamales smothered with chili, cheese, onions, and jalapeños—and their Knock-You-Naked margarita.

Natchez is the southern terminus of the Natchez Trace Parkway, an old American Indian and trappers trail, later a colonial trading route, and today one of the country's best places to drive and bicycle. For 444 miles, "The Trace" stretches along the banks of the Mississippi River to the green hills surrounding Nashville, Tennessee (see p. 875). Designated a National Scenic Byway, the two-lane road is a pleasant and unhurried way to catch a glimpse of the Old South, refreshingly free of billboards and commercial development. The Trace Visitor Center is located midway in Tupelo, a sleepy town best known as the site of the two-room house where Elvis Presley was born. It's now a museum devoted to the King of Rock 'n' Roll.

Where: 115 miles southwest of Jackson. **Visitor info:** www.visitnatchez.org. **Natchez Pilgrimage Tours:** Tel 800-647-6742 or 601-446-6631; www.natchezpilgrimage.com. *When:* Spring Pilgrimage 5 weeks in Mar–Apr; Fall Pilgrimage 2 weeks in Sep–Oct. **Monmouth:** Tel 800-828-4531 or 601-442-5852; www.monmouthplantation.com. *Cost:* from $195; dinner $50. **Dunleith:** Tel 800-433-2445 or 601-446-8500; www.dunleith.com. *Cost:* from $130 (off-peak), from $175 (peak). **Cock of the Walk:** Tel 601-446-8920. *Cost:* dinner $20. **Fat Mama's Tamales:** Tel 601-442-4548; www.fatmamastamales.com. *Cost:* dinner $12. **Elvis Presley Birthplace & Museum:** Tel 662-841-1245; www.elvispresleybirthplace.com. **Best times:** 1st weekend in Jun for Tupelo's Elvis Presley Festival; late Mar–mid-Apr for peak azalea season.

A Culinary and Musical Mecca

Kansas City BBQ and Jazz

Kansas City, Missouri, U.S.A.

In K.C., barbecue is king—its millions of fans have included native sons like jazz legends Charlie Parker and Count Basie. Queue up at any one of the 100-plus joints in town for short ribs and "brownies" (crispy, coveted scraps of beef brisket) smothered in sauce. Unlike other barbecue meccas, Kansas City prides itself on its anything-goes attitude (pork, beef, mutton, sausage, and chicken), and that goes for sauces as well (ingredients can include any combination of tomatoes, vinegar, sugar, honey, molasses, mustard, and garlic).

Barbecue and K.C. had already nurtured a long love affair when Arthur Bryant's Barbecue and its signature hot, gritty, paprika-packed barbecue sauce were catapulted to fame in 1974 by hometown hero Calvin Trillin of *The New Yorker,* who declared the restaurant the best in the world.

George Gates founded his own BBQ empire in 1946 in the segregated black neighborhood around 18th & Vine, profiting from the birth of the jazz scene that thrives there today. That location is closed, but there are six others serving up a sweet style of barbecue under the revered name Gates Bar-B-Q.

In truth, you just can't get bad barbecue in K.C., and its variety is a gastronome's nirvana. People travel all the way to the suburb of Belton for Snead's famous log sandwich—a savory blend of smoked beef, pork, and ham chopped up together and stuffed into a long loaf of bread. For a full-tilt barbecue experience, visit K.C. in the fall during the 2-week American Royal Livestock, Horse Show and Rodeo, which hosts the American Royal Barbecue Competition, which ranks up there with the Memphis Barbecue Contest (see p. 873).

The American Jazz Museum sits at a famous jazz crossroads.

K.C.'s dual passions unite at the Rhythm and Ribs Jazz Festival, an annual barbecue contest accompanied by national and local jazz, blues, R&B, and gospel artists. The festivities are held behind the American Jazz Museum; its collection includes historic recordings and memorabilia such as Louis Armstrong's trumpet and the Blue Room, a 1930s-era night club that is museum exhibit by day, jazz club by night. Under the same roof, the Negro Leagues Baseball Museum chronicles the great players of the renowned Kansas City Monarchs. Jazz disciples shouldn't miss the rough-and-tumble Mutual Musicians Foundation, a former union hall where Charlie Parker and Dizzy Gillespie reputedly met and where musicians continue to jam, often till dawn.

Bryant's Barbecue: Tel 816-231-1123; www.arthurbryantsbbq.com. *Cost:* lunch $11. **Gates Bar-B-Q:** Tel 816-531-7522; www.gatesbbq.com. *Cost:* dinner $15. **Snead's:** Tel 816-331-7979. *Cost:* log sandwich $7. **American Royal Barbecue Competition:** Tel 816-221-9800; www.arbbq.com. *When:* 1st weekend of Oct. **American Jazz Museum:** Tel 816-474-8463; www.americanjazzmuseum.org. **Negro Leagues Baseball Museum:** Tel 888-221-6526 or 816-221-1920; www.nlbm.com. **Mutual Musicians Foundation:** Tel 816-471-5212; www.thefoundationjamson.org. **Best time:** 3rd Sun in Jun for Rhythm and Ribs.

Mountain Bliss Without the Crowds

Big Sky

Montana, U.S.A.

When it comes to Big Sky, Montana's premier ski and resort destination, "big" really is the operative word. At the head of a beautiful mountain valley an hour north of Yellowstone National Park (see p. 909), Big Sky was created in 1973 by Chet Huntley, the late NBC newscaster and Montana native.

Big Sky's 3,812 skiable acres, reaching across three mountains, have magnificent views of the Rockies and an average of only two skiers per acre. The recently opened Moonlight Basin, on the north and west faces of 11,166-foot Lone Peak, is even more deserted, and lifts have no lines to speak of.

Much of the annual 400-plus inches of snowfall is the bone-dry talc reverently called "cold smoke," and while there's extreme white-knuckle skiing (Lone Peak summit offers a 4,350-foot vertical drop, with some of the steepest chutes in the world), more than a quarter of Big Sky's 150-plus trails are perfect for intermediate skiers. The "Biggest Skiing in America" can be enjoyed with a joint lift ticket that allows you access to 5,512 acres of interconnecting ski trails between Moonlight Basin and neighboring Big Sky.

The elegant Lone Mountain Ranch is a year-round favorite for its 45 miles of cross-country ski trails, snowy horse-drawn sleigh rides to lantern-lit cabins and romantic dinners, and its Orvis-endorsed fly-fishing in summer. For plain value and friendliness, the Lodge at Big Sky is a winner.

More rustic luxury can be found at the stone-and-timber Big EZ Lodge, sitting at 7,500 feet. Most of the 12 spacious and woodsy-chic rooms have otherworldly views of the Madison Mountains. An enormous outdoor hot tub and the restaurant's Rocky Mountain–style cuisine are just icing on the cake.

Where: 45 miles south of Bozeman. **Big Sky Resort:** Tel 800-548-4486 or 406-995-5900; www.bigskyresort.com. *Cost:* lift tickets from $79. *When:* ski season late Nov–early Apr. **Moonlight Basin:** Tel 877-822-0432 or 406-993-6000; www.moonlightbasin.com. *Cost:* lift tickets from $55, *When:* ski season Dec–Apr. **Lone Mountain Ranch:** Tel 800-514-4644 or 406-995-4644; www.lmranch.com. *Cost:* from $2,565 per person per week, all-inclusive. Sleigh ride dinner $85 for nonguests. *When:* mid-Jun–mid-Sep; mid-Dec–Mar. **The Lodge at Big Sky:** Tel 406-995-7858; www.lodgeatbigsky.com. *Cost:* from $100 (off-peak), from $140 (peak). **Big EZ Lodge:** Tel 877-244-3299 or 406-995-7000; www.bigezlodge.com. *Cost:* from $595, all-inclusive. **Best times:** Jan–Feb for cross-country skiing, Jan–Mar for downhill; Jun–Jul for fly-fishing; early Jul for food festival; Sat nights in winter for fireworks on Lone Peak.

Home on the Range in the Bitterroot Valley

Triple Creek Ranch

Darby, Montana, U.S.A.

Tucked into the southern end of the scenic Bitterroot Valley, at the foot of 10,157-foot Trapper Peak, Triple Creek is a ranch-cum-luxury-hideaway bordered on three sides by national forest, where seclusion, beauty, and comfort are served up in Western-size portions. The remarkable cuisine and noteworthy wine list are best described as "France meets the Northern Rockies."

The ranch organizes cattle drives, trail rides, and fly-fishing for guests.

The ranch's 23 hand-hewn log cabins are scattered amid 600 Eden-like acres of towering ponderosa pines and meadows, where you'll also find its namesake three creeks, Baker, No Name, and House. Beyond are several million acres of pure wilderness in the Bitterroot Mountains. The property's 40 horses are at the ready, and between rides the guests can unwind in a pool or fitness center or partake of trout ponds, tennis courts, and a putting green. The three-story central lodge is tiered with balconies and houses the vaulted, wood-beamed dining room, library, and a rooftop bar-lounge. The ranch-proud staff outnumbers guests and delivers true luxury and friendly but sophisticated service.

Summer brings mountain biking, hiking, trail riding, and Orvis-endorsed fly-fishing, while winter months promise 300 inches of snowfall, cross-country skiing on the grounds, and short lift lines at nearby Lost Trail Powder Mountain ski area. Or just stay put and enjoy a hot buttered rum—a ranch specialty, concocted with a touch of ice cream—in front of a crackling fire.

WHERE: 75 miles south of the Missoula airport. Tel 800-654-2943 or 406-821-4600; www.triplecreekranch.com. **COST:** from $750, all-inclusive. **WHEN:** closed Mar–Apr and Nov. **BEST TIMES:** late Jul for Darby's Strawberry Festival; early Sep for the Ravalli County Fair in Hamilton.

Ice-Sculpted Majesty: the American Alps

GLACIER NATIONAL PARK

Montana, U.S.A.

The epic mountain scenery of Glacier National Park, believed by the Blackfeet Indians to be sacred ground, was described by John Muir as "the best care-killing scenery on the continent" and is called the "Crown of the Continent" for its staggeringly rugged skyline. Created by the movement of massive glaciers, this park claims one of the most intact ecosystems in the temperate zone, which is crisscrossed by more than 700 miles of maintained trails. Take a hike and you'll likely be rewarded with sightings of moose, bighorn sheep, mountain lions, lynx, and maybe even a glimpse of either a black bear or a grizzly: Glacier has one of the largest concentrations of grizzlies in the Lower 48.

The tiny island in the center of Lake Saint Mary is known as Wild Goose Island.

It also boasts one of the world's most spectacular mountain drives, the 50-mile, 3-hour Going-to-the-Sun Road, which bisects the million-acre wilderness, passing seasonal waterfalls and dense evergreen forests while climbing to the summit of the Continental Divide at 6,646-foot Logan Pass. There are currently 27 named glaciers within the park, down from about 150 in the mid-1800s, and experts believe they will all but disappear by 2030.

The Great Northern Railway built massive log-and-stone lodges here in the early 1900s, and of these, the Swiss-style lakeside Many Glacier Hotel is perhaps the most beautifully sited. About 60 miles west, the charming Lake McDonald Lodge sits beside a lake of the same name and features a game trophy–bedecked lobby and a vast walk-in fireplace. Of the cluster of lodgings found just outside the park's boundary, the cozy Alpine-style Izaak Walton Inn is among the most popular. Built in 1939 for rail workers, it offers easy access to excellent fishing and cross-country skiing.

There's not much that can top a visit to the park, unless you've booked at Paws Up, a 37,000-acre luxury wilderness resort that features 28 two-story pine homes and is a scenic 3-hour drive away. From mid-May through September, the lodging offers an American safari experience at its 12 riverside tents, replete with feather beds and butlers, giving new meaning to the expression "glamping." The plethora of summer activities, from horseback riding to fly-fishing in the Blackfoot River, is complemented by an impressive winter list including skiing on hundreds of miles of trails, snowshoeing, and dogsledding into the frosty surroundings.

Where: The park's west entrance is West Glacier, 30 miles northeast of Kalispell. Tel 406-888-7800; www.nps.gov/glac. *When:* open year-round, but much of Going-to-the-Sun Rd. is closed mid-Sep–mid-Jun. **Many Glacier Hotel** and **Lake McDonald Lodge:** Tel 406-892-2525; www.glacierparkinc.com. *Cost:* from $130. *When:* late May–Sep. **Izaak Walton Inn:** Tel 406-888-5700; www.izaakwaltoninn.com. *Cost:* from $120 (off-peak), from $150 (peak). **Paws Up:** Tel 800-473-0601 or 406-244-5200; www.pawsup.com. *Cost:* 2-bedroom homes from $890 (off-peak), from $1,175 (peak), inclusive; tents from $820, inclusive. *When:* tents late May–Sep. **Best times:** Jan–Mar for cross-country skiing; Jul–Aug for wildflowers; Sep for fewer crowds.

Big Sky, Big Country, Big Fish

Big Hole Country

Wise River, Montana, U.S.A.

The term "big hole" was frontier-speak for a wide, deep valley. Montana's Big Hole Country, in the state's southwest corner, is one of its most beautiful areas—a 6,000-foot-elevation prairie basin flanked by snowcapped peaks and drained by crystal-clear streams and rivers. Cattle ranches and pastures filled with loose, unbaled piles of hay gave rise to the Big Hole's epithet, the "Valley of 10,000 Haystacks." The tiny town of Wisdom (population 300) is the epicenter of the area, a spot known for its easygoing vibe and cowboy character, just an hour's drive from the more touristy Bitterroot Valley.

For fly-fishers, the focus is the Big Hole River, a blue-ribbon trout stream in a state blessed with superlative fishing. (Montana lakes and streams are home to brown, rainbow, brook, bull, and cutthroat trout, plus the trouts' cousins, Arctic grayling and the land-locked kokanee salmon.) Many visitors experience a near-mystic sense that Montana is the spiritual home of this sport, a sentiment captured in the first line of Norman Maclean's classic Montana novel, *A River Runs Through It*: "In our family, there was no clear line between religion and fly fishing." Along the river's banks, mule deer, moose, and elk are a common sight.

The Big Hole's most famous lodge is the Complete Fly Fisher outside the town of Wise River. Its location on the Big Hole River and proximity to the Wise, Beaverhead, Bitterroot, Clark Fork, and Missouri rivers guarantees unparalleled fishing, and its 14-guest limit promises personalized service and instruction—even novices can pull in the big ones.

Dining on the lovely riverside porch encourages camaraderie and is more sophisticated than you'd expect. Also on the Big Hole River in nearby Twin Bridges, the Great Waters Inn, one of Montana's original fly-fishing lodges, is a more modest operation. Unlike most other full-service lodges, this one allows its 18 guests to book shorter stays and can customize activities on a daily basis.

WHERE: Wise River is 40 miles south of Butte. **COMPLETE FLY FISHER:** Tel 866-832-3175 or 406-832-3175; www.completeflyfisher.com. *Cost:* 7 days with 5 days of guided angling $4,800 per person, all-inclusive. *When:* mid-May–mid-Oct. **GREAT WATERS INN:** Tel 406-835-2024; www.greatwatersinn.com. *Cost:* 5 days with 3 days guided fishing $1,395 per person, all-inclusive; nonguided use $175 per person per day, inclusive. **BEST TIMES:** May and Sep–Oct for good angling; Jun–Aug for nicest weather; mid-Jun for very active fly-fishing.

Where Megawatt Crass Marries Nouveau Class

THE LAS VEGAS STRIP

Las Vegas, Nevada, U.S.A.

The 4.5-mile stretch of Las Vegas Boulevard known as the Strip is the world capital of glitter, festooned with pleasure palaces, 24-hour casinos, and quick-hitch wedding chapels. But the tacky wackiness has slowly been ceding ground to top-of-the-line luxury, and these days the town's hotels are defined more by high-thread-count sheets and tasteful marble baths than faux-crystal chandeliers and neon.

When completed, the Bellagio was the most expensive hotel ever built.

Still, much of the Strip retains its outré roots, and you can't visit here without taking a drive and soaking in the flashy parade of hotels-cum-casinos, from the giant lion outside the MGM Grand to the half-scale copy of the Eiffel Tower at Paris Las Vegas.

In a class all its own is the Bellagio, an imposing Italianate palazzo with almost 4,000 rooms that appears to float on an 8.5-acre man-made lake. The resort's dancing fountains beckon visitors into its sumptuous casino. Across the way, Wynn Las Vegas and its new annex, Encore, offer guests every luxury imaginable, from high-tech-gadget-embellished rooms to the only golf course on the Strip.

Sin City's rebirth has brought with it some of America's—and the world's—premier chefs. At Paul Bartolotta's restaurant in Wynn Las Vegas, named for its chef-owner, you can dine outdoors on fish flown in daily from the Mediterranean. The Bellagio's multicourse prix-fixe wonders prepared by Julian Serrano are enjoyed under the gaze of the Picassos that give the haute eatery its moniker. And what about those all-you-can-eat buffets? They're still there, and the uncontested champion is at the Wynn, with everything from Kansas City–style barbecue to five kinds of ceviche.

Vegas's classic "showgirl" experience of bare breasts and big headdresses is all but gone, replaced by a wide array of big-name Broadway and Cirque du Soleil shows, the latter multimillion-dollar productions that elevate traditional big-top theatrics to high-concept performance art. But perhaps the pinnacle of Vegas's journey from crass to class is the new CityCenter, a visually stunning and architecturally sophisticated hotel/residential complex with high-end restaurants and a retail mall designed by Daniel Libeskind. At its center stands the ARIA Resort and Casino, its 61 stories filled with more than 4,000 rooms, a top-of-the-line Asian-themed spa, more than a dozen restaurants and bars, and a theater showing one of Cirque du Soleil's newer shows, *Viva ELVIS*.

Venture north along of the Strip to find the vestiges of the tacky Las Vegas of yore, like the busy Chapel of the Flowers, which, along with more than three dozen other Strip chapels, accounts for nearly 100,000 marriages every year.

Visitor Info: www.visitlasvegas.com. **Bellagio:** Tel 888-987-6667 or 702-693-7111; www.bellagio.com. *Cost:* from $160; 4-course prix-fixe dinner at Picasso $115. **Wynn Las Vegas:** Tel 877-321-9966 or 702-770-7100; www.wynnlasvegas.com. *Cost:* from $159; dinner at Bartolotta's $140, dinner at The Buffet $28. **Cirque du Soleil:** 866-241-2833 or 702-693-7722 for most shows; www.cirquedusoleil.com. **ARIA:** Tel 866-359-7757 or 702-590-7757; www.arialasvegas.com. *Cost:* from $130. **Best times:** Jun–Aug for low hotel rates; Apr or Oct for nice weather.

Luxury in the Heart of the Mountain Wilderness

The Great North Woods

Dixville Notch and Whitefield, New Hampshire, U.S.A.

Blankets of trees, picturesque lakes, and meandering streams envelop the northernmost part of New Hampshire—an area owned largely by lumber and paper companies, where moose are more common than people.

The scenic 98-mile Moose Path Trail offers excellent opportunities for wildlife sightings, running from Gorham to Pittsburg and taking motorists through the town of Dixville Notch into serene wilderness, where idyllic spots for camping, fishing, rafting, and hiking abound.

Nestled in an isolated mountain pass 16 miles south of the Canadian border, the Balsams, a magnificent, old-fashioned resort, stands at the center of 8,000 mountain acres. Opened in 1866, it has expanded to include over 200 guest rooms and offers loads of activities. For golfers there is the Donald Ross–designed 18-hole Panorama course on Keazer Mountain, a nine-hole executive course, and a top-notch golf school. Those who don't know drivers from 9-irons can swim in the heated outdoor pool, play tennis, mountain bike, fish, or boat on the resort's tranquil Lake Gloriette. Sixteen popular and not-too-challenging alpine runs and 59 miles of Nordic trails bring guests back in the winter months; ice-skating is available too. It's a four-season destination, and three-generation vacations aren't unusual here. Dinner is a festive affair, and jackets for men are a must.

Hidden in the small town of Whitefield is another landmark hotel, the Mountain View Grand Resort & Spa, with an award-winning spa, a 100-year-old golf course, and jaw-dropping views of the White Mountains from its enormous front porch. Whitefield's other claim to fame is Grandma's Kitchen, a beloved old-timey diner that serves breakfast all day long—and considers pie a reasonable choice first thing in the morning.

WHERE: Dixville Notch is 210 miles north of Boston. **VISITOR INFO:** www.northerngatewaychamber.org. **THE BALSAMS:** Tel 800-255-0600 or 603-255-3400; www.thebalsams.com. *Cost:* from $180 per person, all-inclusive (off-peak), from $310 (peak). **MOUNTAIN VIEW GRAND:** Tel 866-484-3843 or 603-837-2100; www.mountainviewgrand.com. *Cost:* from $140 (off-peak), from $200 (peak); greens fees from $25. **GRANDMA'S KITCHEN:** Tel 603-837-2525. *Cost:* breakfast $10. **BEST TIMES:** late Aug for the Moose Festival in Colebrook; mid-Sep–late Oct for foliage; late Dec for Christmas Celebration and New Year's Eve Blast at The Balsams.

Summer Playgrounds and Golden Ponds

The Lakes Region

Lake Winnipesaukee and environs, New Hampshire, U.S.A.

Rural villages, rustic summer colonies, extravagant "cottages," and family-friendly motels dot the shores of the 273 lakes and ponds that comprise New Hampshire's idyllic Lake Region. At 72 square miles, Lake Winnipesaukee ("Smiling Waters") is the largest lake in the state with one of its prettiest drives: the 97-mile Lakes Region Tour. Or explore it by boat aboard the popular 230-foot MS *Mount Washington*, which cruises around the lake's many islands en route to charming lakeside towns.

The elegant village of Wolfeboro claims to be America's oldest summer resort. Meredith is also a lovely town, in a gorgeous spot between lakes Winnipesaukee and Waukewan. Book a stay at the historic Inns & Spa at Mill Falls, a waterside complex partially housed in a renovated waterside textile mill that includes an appealing variety of shops and restaurants.

If Lake Winnipesaukee seems too bustling, consider quiet Squam Lake, storied location of the 1981 film *On Golden Pond*. A Yankee summer colony with an exclusive air sits on the pretty lake, which you can explore by canoe, kayak, or boat tour. Stay at the Manor on Golden Pond, an English-style country house built in the early 20th century, with inspiring views of the lake and the foothills of the White Mountains. Its romantic rooms and cottages, some with private decks and fireplaces, and an acclaimed dining room and wine cellar make it the area's standout inn.

The Lakes Region isn't all scenery and serenity. Family-friendly Weirs Beach, on the western shore of Winnipesaukee, lets you mix things up with water slides, souvenir shops, miniature golf, and one of the largest video arcades in the country. The nearby city of Laconia is famous for its rowdy, 9-day motorcycle rally held every June. Dating back to 1923, it draws more than 300,000 bikers and bike fans from all over the country.

WHERE: Wolfeboro is 100 miles north of Boston. **VISITOR INFO:** www.lakesregion.org. **INNS & SPA AT MILL FALLS:** Tel 800-622-6455 or 603-279-7006; www.millfalls.com. *Cost:* from $110. **MANOR ON GOLDEN POND:** Tel 800-545-2141 or 603-968-3348; www.manorongoldenpond.com. *Cost:* from $235; dinner $60. **BEST TIMES:** mid-Jun for Laconia Motorcycle Week; late Jul for Antique & Classic Boat Show in Meredith; late Sep–Oct for foliage.

The High Point of the Northeast

The White Mountains

North Conway and environs, New Hampshire, U.S.A.

The White Mountains inspire superlatives—tallest, coldest, windiest—and their crowning glory, Mount Washington, at 6,288 feet, claims the title of highest in the Northeast. From its summit you can take in the majesty of the Presidential Range, with its five peaks above 5,000 feet and, if you're not so lucky, encounter some of the most severe weather in the country.

Reach the top by car on an 8-mile private road (admission includes a "This Car Climbed Mt. Washington" bumper sticker) or by train. In operation since 1869, the Mount Washington Cog Railway (the first such railway in the world) pushes rather than pulls its cars up the mountain and in the winter transports local skiers up to trails that run parallel to the tracks. The Conway Scenic Railroad is a more horizontal train option, operating restored vintage cars that chug around the Mount Washington Valley and through the dramatic mountain gap of Crawford Notch.

At the magnificent Omni Mount Washington Resort at Bretton Woods, a sprawling white 1902 building with a cherry red roof anchors the 1,500-acre complex. Guests fill their days with golf, tennis, horseback riding, and treatments at the top-notch spa, though the resort is probably best known for its downhill and cross-country skiing.

The Appalachian Trail (see p. 756) is the most renowned of hundreds of picturesque driving and hiking routes that crisscross the White Mountains. As part of the 100-mile White Mountains Trail, the 26.5-mile section of the Kancamagus Highway that connects the towns of Lincoln and Conway has been designated a National Scenic and Cultural Byway and is a favorite New England drive.

Locomotives first climbed Mount Washington on the cog railway in 1869.

The "Kanc" twists and turns as it climbs to nearly 3,000 feet, passing the sparkling waterfalls and backcountry lakes of the White Mountain National Forest.

Where: 135 miles north of Boston. **Visitor info:** www.visitwhitemountains.com. **Mt. Washington Road:** Tel 603-466-3988; www.mountwashingtonautoroad.com. *When:* mid-May–mid-Oct. **Cog Railway:** Tel 800-922-8825 or 603-278-5404; www.thecog.com. *Cost:* $59. *When:* mid-Jun–Oct. **Conway Scenic Railroad:** Tel 800-232-5251 or 603-356-5251; www.conwayscenic.com. *When:* closed Jan–mid-Apr. **Mount Washington Resort:** Tel 877-873-0626 or 603-278-1000; www.mountwashingtonresort.com. *Cost:* from $130 (off-peak), from $270 (peak). **White Mountain National Forest:** Tel 603-528-8721; www.fs.fed.us/r9/white. **Best time:** Jun–Aug for summertime activities; late Sep–mid-Oct for foliage.

A Victorian-Era Town by the Sea

CAPE MAY

New Jersey, U.S.A.

Cape May is the oldest seaside resort in the U.S., but its real appeal is its juxtaposition of Victorian atmosphere and Jersey Shore location. The resort dates back to the mid-1800s, when the area's salty air, wide beaches, and cool breezes drew elite vacationers such as Abraham Lincoln, P. T. Barnum, and Henry Ford. Scores of homes were built, of which some 600 survived the great fire of 1879 and the century of development that followed.

Today the whole town of Cape May has National Historic Landmark status; its 2.5-square-mile historic district brims with grand Victorian-dowager houses, the largest such collection in the country. They are best seen via a rented bicycle or a horse-drawn buggy. Bird-watchers come from around the world for the Cape May Migratory Bird Refuge, where more than 400 recorded species pass through annually.

The Virginia Hotel, opened in 1879, continues to offer a sublimely Victorian hotel experience with 24 main guest rooms that are furnished in an updated classic style. The hotel's restaurant, the Ebbitt Room, serves regional American cuisine with international accents. Nearby, the Mainstay Inn was among the town's first B&Bs and remains one of its best. A dignified Italianate manor dating to 1872, it has 14-foot ceilings, airy rooms, and porch swings on a flower-decked veranda.

WHERE: 90 miles south of Philadelphia. **VISITOR INFO:** www.capemaychamber.com. **MIGRATORY BIRD REFUGE:** Tel 908-879-7262; www.nature.org. **VIRGINIA HOTEL:** Tel 800-732-4236 or 609-884-5700; www.virginiahotel.com. *Cost:* from $100 (off-peak), from $300 (peak); dinner $65. **MAINSTAY INN:** Tel 609-884-8690; www.mainstayinn.com. *Cost:* from $175 (off-peak), from $295 (peak). **BEST TIMES:** Mar–May and Nov for bird-watching; late Apr–early May for Spring Festival; mid-Oct for Victorian Week; Christmastime for holiday festivities and decorations.

Up, Up, and Away Through Technicolor Skies

ALBUQUERQUE INTERNATIONAL BALLOON FIESTA

Albuquerque, New Mexico, U.S.A.

At roughly the size of a house, the average hot-air balloon is mighty impressive. Now imagine more than 600 of them, slowly inflating and lifting off into the sky like the decorations for the world's biggest birthday party. This is the Albuquerque International Balloon Fiesta, the world's largest hot-air balloon rally.

Held every year since 1972, the Balloon Fiesta draws more than 800,000 people, who come to wander among the floating wonders on the 78-acre field. Nearly every morning of the 9-day event sees a dawn patrol—selected balloons launch before sunrise, glowing like giant colorful lightbulbs; a little later comes a mass ascension of all the balloons, a wondrous 2-hour polychromatic spectacle. Some pilots engage in distance competitions while others join the Special Shape Rodeos, an event in which balloons in fanciful forms such as mushrooms, witches, and cows are launched. Show up in the evening for the popular Balloon Glow (when the balloons fire up their burners and are lit up from within like giant ornaments) and the AfterGlow fireworks display.

Learn more about the technology and history of the sport at the Anderson-Abruzzo Albuquerque International Balloon Museum. If you've got your heart set on getting up in the air for real, Rainbow Ryders offers balloon rides year-round.

Another high-altitude option is the Sandia Peak Tram, which at 2.7 miles long is billed as the world's longest aerial tramway. It runs from the northeast corner of the city to the top of the Sandia Mountains, 10,378 feet up, where you can hike on trails, then grab a bite with a view at the High Finance Restaurant and Tavern.

Launch directors coordinate a mass ascent, when hundreds of balloons take off at once.

Info: Tel 888-422-7277 or 505-821-1000; www.balloonfiestacom. *When:* 9 days in early Oct. **Balloon Museum:** Tel 505-880-0500; www.balloonmuseum.com. **Rainbow Ryders:** Tel 800-725-2477 or 505-823-1111; www.rainbowryders.com. *Cost:* balloon rides $160; from $375 during Fiesta. **Sandia Peak Tram:** Tel 505-856-7325; www.sandiapeak.com. **High Finance Restaurant:** Tel 505-243-9742. *Cost:* lunch $18.

Underground Wonder in the Chihuahuan Desert

Carlsbad Caverns

Carlsbad, New Mexico, U.S.A.

One of the world's most complex, astounding, and easily accessible cave systems winds beneath the Guadalupe Mountains in southeastern New Mexico. Carlsbad Caverns National Park contains more than 100 known caves, the remains of a fossil reef from an inland sea that covered the area some 250 million years ago. Though discovered by settlers in the late 19th century, fascinating Native American pictographs covering the walls point to much earlier visits.

Above ground is the stark, unforgiving beauty of the northern Chihuahuan Desert. Beneath the surface, though, is another universe entirely. Take the steep walkway down 750 feet to the Big Room, one of the most enormous underground chambers on the planet, large enough to hold six football fields with room to spare. (You can also reach the Big Room by elevator, a ride that evokes a journey-to-the-center-of-the-earth sensation.) From here a mile-long trail winds past speleothems (cave formations), fantastic shapes sculpted by natural forces, resembling soda straws, draperies, frozen waterfalls, totem poles, and draped silk. Many have colorful, descriptive names, from the Rock of Ages to the Painted Grotto.

For more adventure, take a ranger-guided tour of some of the "wild" caves in the park, including the Queen's Chamber, part of the Kings Palace tour and a site of astounding beauty. The Left Hand Tunnel tour is the easiest, while trips to grottoes such as Spider Cave are the most strenuous and involve stooping, climbing, wading across pools, and even crawling on your stomach. Access to Lechuguilla Cave is limited to researchers and exploration teams, which have descended 1,604 feet into it and mapped more than 120 miles of passages, establishing it as the fifth-longest cave in the world.

Another Carlsbad treat happens nightly from spring to fall: the mass exodus of nearly 400,000 Mexican free-tailed bats, spiraling from the mouth of the cave for a frenzied night of insect hunting. Come for the prelaunch ranger talks where you'll learn that the animals, while astonishing, are hardly threatening and are vital to the area's ecosystem.

WHERE: 304 miles southeast of Albuquerque. www.nps.gov/cave. **GUIDED CAVE TOURS:** Tel 877-444-6777 or 518-885-3639; www.recreation.gov. **BEST TIMES:** Bat flights happen from Apr–Nov but are best Jul–Aug.

The park contains over 100 caves, whose unique shapes are due to their corrosive formation.

Train Buffs: All Aboard!

Cumbres & Toltec Scenic Railroad

Chama, New Mexico, U.S.A.

Pine-covered hillsides, alpine peaks, and one of the highest railroad summits in the western U.S. are all part of the Cumbres & Toltec Scenic Railroad, which winds its steam-powered way across the scenic New Mexico-Colorado border north of the small town of Chama.

The Denver and Rio Grande Railroad arrived in Chama in 1881, turning the riverside town into a lumber and mining center. Today trains on the Chama line still chug to Antonito, Colorado, offering one of the country's prettiest and most authentic Old West railroad experiences. The line stands as perhaps the finest example of remote Rocky Mountain railways and the engineering challenges their creators overcame.

At 128 miles round-trip, the Cumbres & Toltec is the longest narrow-gauge train route in the U.S. The 3-foot-wide train tracks were built more compactly than standard gauge to hug the sheer sides of Toltec Gorge, 600 feet above the Rio Chama, and to pass through two tunnels and over two 100-foot-high trestles. At Cumbres Pass, elevation 10,015 feet and the highest point in the U.S. reached by scheduled passenger trains, you can see the pastoral Chama Valley below, surrounded by the densely wooded Rio Grande, Carson, and Santa Fe national forests.

Quiet and unassuming Chama (with a population just above 1,000) is chock-full of souvenir shops and B&Bs. For luxury lodgings, head out of town to the 21-room Lodge and Ranch at Chama, with its rustic but sophisticated décor and dining, and 36,000 acres that are nirvana to anglers. Southwest of town, paddle on the pristine Rio Chama, a National Wild and Scenic River and a popular whitewater run, as it flows through a 1,500-foot-deep canyon lined with red cliffs and sage-covered grasslands.

WHERE: Chama is 168 miles north of Albuquerque. **CUMBRES & TOLTEC:** Tel 888-286-2737 or 719-376-5483; www.cumbrestoltec.com. *Cost:* $88 round-trip, includes lunch. *When:* mid-May–mid-Oct. **THE LODGE AND RANCH AT CHAMA:** Tel 575-756-2133; www.lodgeatchama.com. *Cost:* from $275 per person per day, inclusive. **BEST TIMES:** mid-May–Sep for wildlife ranch tours at the Lodge; late May–early Jun for high-water rafting; Jun–Sep for fishing; Jul–Aug for lower-water rafting and warmer weather.

Out of This World

ROSWELL

New Mexico, U.S.A.

Who knows what actually crashed to earth near sleepy Roswell on a July night in 1947? Local ranchers described finding pieces of purple metal inscribed with strange hieroglyphics; newspapers reported the recovery of "flying discs"; and the U.S. Army announced that a spaceship had crashed, then said it was a weather balloon and stonewalled further discussion.

Nevertheless, in the decades since "the incident," this city in southeastern New Mexico has become synonymous with unidentified flying objects. Roswell's notoriety has spawned movies, TV shows, conferences, and the International UFO Museum and Research Center downtown, where conspiracy theorists can peruse celestial paintings, models of alien spacecraft, and some of the thousands of books written about the subject.

Every July Fourth weekend, the annual Roswell UFO Festival features lectures, workshops, and abduction panels, plus lighthearted costume contests, fireworks, and a parade down Main Street. The infamous Hangar 84, where the government stored the debris from the mysterious crash, is open for tours during the festival.

The Roswell Museum and Art Center displays a small but world-class collection of New Mexico modernism, including works by Georgia O'Keeffe (see p. 832) and the budding artists of the Roswell Artist-in-Residence Program. Also on exhibit is a special collection of early rockets and engines created and developed by the "Father of Modern Rocket Science" Robert Goddard, who lived and worked here for 12 years beginning in the 1930s. The attached Robert H. Goddard Planetarium is the largest in the state, featuring a NASA-derived link to the Hubble Telescope called Viewspace.

WHERE: 200 miles southeast of Albuquerque. **INTERNATIONAL UFO MUSEUM:** Tel 800-822-3545 or 575-625-9495; www.roswellufomuseum.com. **ROSWELL UFO FESTIVAL:** Tel 575-625-9495; www.roswellufofestival.com. *When:* July 4 weekend. **ROSWELL MUSEUM:** Tel 575-624-6744; www.roswellmuseum.org.

Get Your Kicks on America's Mother Road

ROUTE 66

New Mexico and beyond, U.S.A.

There's no road more embedded in the psyche of America than Route 66. Commissioned in 1926, the 2,448-mile "Mother Road" epitomized the American dream and led Dust Bowl refugees and beatniks alike to California, spawning an unparalleled profusion of neon and drive-in Americana in eight states from Chicago to Los Angeles. Steinbeck and Kerouac wrote about it, Nat King Cole sang about it, and there were even a TV series (*Route 66* premiered in 1960) and an animated film (Pixar's *Cars*) inspired by it.

Although it was officially decommissioned in 1985, "America's Main Street" retains its hold on the nation's imagination. From the birthplace of the corn dog (Springfield, Illinois) to the Grand Canyon (see p. 706), this National Scenic Byway encompasses kitsch, natural wonders, and much else that defines America.

Portions of the two-lane black-topped route are gone, but 85 percent of it remains, with many long stretches drivable, particularly in the Southwest. Explore the roadside culture that cropped up on New Mexico's flatter eastern portion, starting at Glenrio. Half an hour east is Tucumcari and the Mesalands Dinosaur Museum, home of the world's largest collection of fossils, as well as bronze skeletons and other replicas of prehistoric creatures. Spend the night at the friendly Blue Swallow Motel, built in 1939, and don't miss Tom Coffin's huge tail-fin sculpture, *Roadside Attraction*, at the town's west end.

In Santa Rosa, 60 miles west, take a dip in the cool, clear waters of the Blue Hole and stop to ogle the classic cars at the Route 66 Auto Museum. The road once curved north to Santa Fe before heading south again to Albuquerque, where 18 miles are still lined with classic billboards and '50s architecture.

Fill up your tank and keep heading west to Gallup, commercial hub of the nearby Navajo Nation (see p. 708). Route 66 still serves as a neon-lined Main Street here, with the largest concentration of trading posts and galleries selling Native American crafts in the state. Stay at the tacky but cool, history-steeped El Rancho, a popular location for Western film shoots from 1929 through 1964.

ROUTE 66 FEDERATION: Tel 909-336-6131; www.national66.com. **MESALANDS DINOSAUR MUSEUM:** Tel 575-461-3466. **BLUE SWALLOW MOTEL:** Tel 575-461-9849; www.blueswallowmotel.com. *Cost:* from $50. **ROUTE 66 AUTO MUSEUM:** Tel 505-472-1966; www.route66automuseum.com. **EL RANCHO:** Tel 505-863-9311; www.elranchohotel.com. *Cost:* from $95.

An Artist's Love Affair with New Mexico's Beauty

Georgia O'Keeffe Trail

Santa Fe and Abiquiu, New Mexico, U.S.A.

"The colors are different up there," Georgia O'Keeffe wrote of the Land of Enchantment, a place she not only loved but became identified with. Although a Midwesterner who initially found inspiration in New York City, she has long been considered New Mexico's most celebrated artist. To see what moved her, start by spending time in Santa Fe's Georgia O'Keeffe Museum, which houses the world's largest permanent collection of the artist's work; a number of her paintings are also on display at the nearby New Mexico Museum of Art.

Abiquiu's adobe St. Thomas Church is in keeping with the southwestern style that inspired O'Keeffe.

But to really get a sense of O'Keeffe's world, travel to the little town of Abiquiu, 37 miles to the north, where she moved permanently in 1949, 3 years after the death of her husband, the acclaimed photographer Alfred Stieglitz. It's here that she developed her iconic style: colorful, almost surreal canvases that portray her adopted land, with sensual images that often include two of her favorite subjects—animal skulls and bones and large-scale flowers.

Despite the attention O'Keeffe's work has brought, Abiquiu remains a small village, with only about 1,000 residents. Today it is home to a number of artists, who make Abiquiu a quiet enclave of creativity. If you're spending the night, stay at the unpretentious Abiquiu Inn. Its Southwest-themed rooms and casitas sit next to the meeting place for tours of the Georgia O'Keeffe Home and Studio, both owned by the Georgia O'Keeffe Museum, which arranges a limited number of visits annually.

O'Keeffe divided her time between Abiquiu and nearby Ghost Ranch, an existence that provided her with what she called "the wideness and wonder of the world as I live in it." The ranch is now a retreat and an education center that offers seminars on topics ranging from spirituality to science to art. Accommodations are comfortable and basic, with no phones or TVs, but the views are those that gave birth to great art.

Georgia O'Keeffe Museum: Tel 505-946-1000; www.okeeffemuseum.org. **New Mexico Museum of Art:** Tel 505-476-5072; www.nmartmuseum.org. **Georgia O'Keeffe Tours:** Tel 505-685-4539. *When:* by appointment, mid-Mar–late Nov. **Abiquiu Inn:** Tel 888-735-2902 or 505-685-4378; www.abiquiuinn.com. *Cost:* from $90. **Ghost Ranch:** Tel 877-804-4678 or 505-685-4333; www.ghostranch.org. *Cost:* seminars from $220 per week; lodging from $90 per person.

Taking the Waters Under the Desert Sky

HOT SPRINGS AND SPAS

Santa Fe and Northern New Mexico, U.S.A.

New Mexico is brimming with places to indulge in a heavenly hot-water soak, from sandy-bottomed pools deep in the woods to a Zen-like destination spa that recalls Kyoto. The latter is Ten Thousand Waves, a favorite hideaway in a forested mountain setting just outside Santa Fe. Its low-key ambience, serene accommodations, and wooden outdoor pools, modeled after those found at Japanese *onsen* (hot-spring baths) promise to mend both body and mind. Treatments include everything from the signature "Four Hands, One Heart" massage to the centuries-old Japanese Nightingale facial.

An hour north of Santa Fe lies the 1,100-acre Ojo Caliente Mineral Springs Resort & Spa, one of the oldest health resorts in North America. The Mission Revival–style adobe hotel, built in 1916, houses the Artesian Restaurant along with 48 rooms and suites, found both in the main house and in several cottages. The private outdoor pools are filled with water from a number of mineral hot springs, all with the same restorative blend of minerals enjoyed by Native Americans centuries ago.

TEN THOUSAND WAVES: Tel 505-982-9304; www.tenthousandwaves.com. *Cost:* shared tubs $19; rooms from $200 (off-peak), from $240 (peak). **OJO CALIENTE:** Tel 800-222-9162 or 505-583-2233; www.ojospa.com. *Cost:* mineral springs from $16; rooms from $140 (off-peak), from $170 (peak).

A Fiesta for All Seasons

MARKETS AND FESTIVALS OF SANTA FE

Santa Fe, New Mexico, U.S.A.

On the north side of Santa Fe's historic central plaza stands the Palace of the Governors. The oldest continuously occupied public building in the U.S., it was built in 1610 by Spanish settlers who founded the nation's first capital. Learn about its history at the on-site New Mexico History Museum. Outside, Native Americans from throughout the state sit in the shade of the portico and sell handmade pottery, jewelry, and textiles.

The leafy plaza is the heart of Old Town Santa Fe and the site of some of the city's most popular events, including the Santa Fe Indian Market, which draws more than 1,000 Native artists, selling everything from beadwork to baskets. The Traditional Spanish Market offers Hispanic crafts from more than 200 local artisans, as well as food and music. July brings the Santa Fe International Folk Art

Market, with outstanding work by artisans from Armenia to Zimbabwe.

September's Fiesta de Santa Fe, the oldest continuously held celebration in the country, is an exuberant, music-filled festival that overflows with crafts for sale. A highlight is the burning of Zozobra, a 50-foot effigy symbolizing the travails of the past year.

Close to the plaza are two of the city's best upscale hotels. The Inn of the Anasazi is worth visiting for its décor and its award-winning Anasazi Restaurant. La Posada de Santa Fe Resort & Spa is a former artist colony spread, which, despite its many modern luxuries, retains an old Santa Fe feel.

Santa Fe's vibrant cultural life is highlighted by the summer season of the Santa Fe Opera. Its striking adobe home is set on a hilltop just north of the city, with nearly 360-degree views of the mountains and desert. Opening night includes a gala celebration and tailgate parties.

Palace of the Governors: Tel 505-476-5100; www.palaceofthegovernors.org. **New Mexico History Museum:** Tel 505-476-5200; www.nmhistorymuseum.org. **Santa Fe Indian Market:** Tel 505-983-5220; www.swaia.org. *When:* 3rd weekend in Aug. **Spanish Market:** Tel 505-982-2226; www.spanishmarket.org. *When:* Jul and early Dec. **Santa Fe International Folk Art Market:** Tel 505-476-1197; www.folkartmarket.org. *When:* mid-Jul. **Fiesta de Santa Fe:** Tel 505-988-7575; www.santafefiesta.org. *When:* early Sep. **Inn of the Anasazi:** Tel 800-688-8100 or 505-988-3030; www.innoftheanasazi.com. *Cost:* from $220 (off-peak), from $425 (peak); dinner $50. **La Posada de Santa Fe:** Tel 866-331-7625 or 505-986-0000; www.laposada.rockresorts.com. *Cost:* from $180 (off-peak), from $345 (peak). **Santa Fe Opera:** Tel 800-280-4654 or 505-986-5900; www.santafeopera.org. *When:* Jul–Aug.

The Unique Flavor of the Southwest

Santa Fe's Southwest Cuisine

Santa Fe, New Mexico, U.S.A.

While some might vote for spectacular sunsets or red-rock scenery, many would agree that there's nothing quite as emblematic of the Southwest as its food. One bite of a blue-corn chicken enchilada covered with a piquant blend of red and green chiles, and you're hooked.

America's oldest indigenous cuisine is an intriguing blend of ingredients brought by its many settlers, including beans, tomatoes, rice, and corn. Chiles are a cornerstone, and New Mexico is the country's largest grower and consumer. The question "red or green?" accompanies nearly every food order. ("Christmas" is local shorthand for both salsas.)

Start with the legendary *huevos motuleños* and smoked-trout hash at Café Pasqual's, decorated with hand-painted murals and named after the Mexican patron saint of cooks. Fans come for its fusion of Old Mexican, New Mexican, and Asian flavors.

But it's world-renowned chef Mark Miller who put the local cuisine on the national radar when he opened the Coyote Café in 1987. Today, chef Eric DiStefano still draws crowds here as well as to the less expensive Rooftop Cantina upstairs.

Come in September for the Santa Fe Wine & Chile Fiesta, which culminates in the Grand Food & Wine Tasting at the Santa Fe Opera, as fall colors tint the Sangre de Cristo Mountains.

Master some of the secrets and flavors of the region at the Santa Fe School of Cooking, where you'll make and eat delectable meals with the help of some of the city's top chefs. And stop by the vibrant Santa Fe Farmers Market, with more than 100 vendors from 15 counties hawking everything from fruit to flowers and offering countless places to snack on Southwestern specialties. The market is a key feature of the new Santa Fe Railyard Park and Plaza, a revitalization project that has created more than 12 acres of public spaces in downtown Santa Fe.

Café Pasqual's: Tel 800-722-7672 or 505-983-9340; www.pasquals.com. *Cost:* breakfast $12. **Coyote Café:** Tel 505-983-1615; www.coyotecafe.com. *Cost:* dinner $45; Rooftop Cantina $25. **Wine & Chile Fiesta:** Tel 505-438-8060; www.santafewineandchile.org. *When:* late Sep. **Santa Fe School of Cooking:** Tel 800-982-4688 or 505-983-4511; www.santafeschoolofcooking.com. *Cost:* from $42. **Farmers Market:** Tel 505-983-4098; www.santafefarmersmarket.com.

Extravagant Isolation, Forever Wild

The Adirondacks

New York, U.S.A.

The largest park in the continental U.S.—larger than the entire state of Massachusetts—the 6-million-acre Adirondack State Park is legally protected to remain "forever wild," thanks to the tireless efforts of 19th-century lawyer-turned-surveyor Verplanck Colvin.

Named after mountains that are among the world's oldest peaks, the park attracted 19th-century men with names like Whitney, Vanderbilt, and Rockefeller, who built themselves backwoods "Great Camps." Surrounded by primeval forests, abundant wildlife, and more than 3,000 lakes and ponds, their waterfront compounds blended luxury and a rustic charm that relied on rough-hewn logs and decorative twig work, a timeless style of décor known as Adirondack.

The Point, on Upper Saranac Lake, stands on the site of William Avery Rockefeller's Camp Wonundra and marries the tradition of the "Great Camps" with the creature comforts of today. Campers stay in one of 11 lavish guest rooms and spend idyllic days canoeing, fishing, or hiking, followed by candlelit meals with offerings from an exceptional wine list.

On the western shore of Lake Placid is the equally special (and slightly more affordable) Lake Placid Lodge. Built in 1882, it features 1920s-era lakeside cabins with stone fireplaces and huge soaking tubs. The 125-mile Jackrabbit Trail passes the lodge's front door, for those inclined to hike.

The picturesque village of Lake Placid, site of the 1932 and 1980 Winter Olympics (and the only U.S. city to host them twice), maintains its role as "Winter Sports Capital of the World." International athletes still train on its world-class skating rinks, ski jumps, and 30 miles of cross-country trails, all of which are also open to the non-Olympian public. Whiteface Mountain, scene of the 1980 alpine competitions, has the steepest vertical drop in the East (3,430 feet) as well as a trail system popular with families and beginners.

At 5,344 feet, Mount Marcy is one of the High Peaks of the Adirondacks.

Perfectly tucked away on 7 sylvan acres with a private lakefront beach, Mirror Lake Inn is a 131-room white clapboard resort that is a notch more refined than its counterparts. It is known for its signature Adirondack flapjacks, spa, the excellent View restaurant, and cozy pub.

Visit the region via the High Peaks Scenic Byway, a 48-mile stretch of Route 73 that climbs the park's tallest mountains, including Big Slide, in the north. Stop by the Adirondack Museum at Blue Lake to see works by Thomas Cole and Winslow Homer, pretty gardens, and awe-inspiring views a Rockefeller would enjoy.

WHERE: 250 miles north of New York City. **VISITOR INFO:** *Adirondacks:* www.visitadirondacks.com. *Lake Placid:* www.lakeplacid.com. **THE POINT:** Tel 800-255-3530 or 518-891-5674; www.thepointresort.com. *Cost:* from $1,375, all-inclusive. **LAKE PLACID LODGE:** Tel 877-523-2700 or 518-523-2700; www.lakeplacidlodge.com. *Cost:* from $575. **WHITEFACE MOUNTAIN:** Tel 518-946-2223; www.whiteface.com. *Cost:* lift tickets $74. **MIRROR LAKE INN:** Tel 518-523-2544; www.mirrorlakeinn.com. *Cost:* from $275. **THE ADIRONDACK MUSEUM:** Tel 518-352-7311; www.adkmuseum.org. *When:* late May–mid-Oct. **BEST TIMES:** mid-Sep for Rustic Furniture Fair at the Adirondack Museum; Sep–Oct for foliage.

A Manhattanite's Nirvana

THE CATSKILLS

New York, U.S.A.

Since their wild beauty first captured the imagination of great painters like Thomas Cole, the Catskills have lured growing numbers of weekenders and second-home hunters from New York City, who have found these gentle mountains an easy and idyllic escape from the oppressive summer heat and workaday life.

Ulster County's Woodstock has had a bohemian streak since the early 1900s, when artists and writers settled here. Today a tonier breed of culture vultures comes for the Woodstock Film Festival, one of the country's best independent film festivals.

Just south of here, in Sullivan County, is the Bethel Woods Center for the Arts, a venue for a variety of performing artists who play to a 4,500-seat summer pavilion with space on the lawn for 10,500 more. Sharing the 2,000-acre complex is the Museum at Bethel Woods, adjacent to the field where the legendary Woodstock concert took place in 1969; an enjoyable high-tech, music-infused exhibit explores that unique flower-child experience and its influence on American culture.

Those who bond with nature while hip-deep in cold water should visit the famous Beaverkill River, the birthplace of American dry-fly fishing. It is the raison d'être for the Beaverkill Valley Inn, a classic 20-room fishing lodge on 1 mile of private blue-ribbon river and only a quick cast away from the revered Wulff fly-fishing school, founded by Lee Wulff, an icon of the sport.

For more indoorsy types, the Emerson Resort and Spa offers luxury suites and a spa with a long roster of treatments. Its sister property, the Lodge, is family- and pet-friendly and just steps away from hiking, biking, fishing, and tubing. Although not officially within the boundaries of the Catskills, the Mohonk Mountain House has been an upstate favorite since it opened in 1869. Sprawling at the edge of a glacial lake, on 2,200 private acres ideal for strolling or rock climbing, this seven-story Victorian castle blends seamlessly with the adjacent spa of newer vintage—nirvana for weary Manhattanites.

WHERE: 100 miles north of New York City. **VISITOR INFO:** www.visitthecatskills.com. **BETHEL WOODS CENTER:** Tel 866-781-2922 or 845-454-3388; www.bethelwoodscenter.org. *When:* closed Jan–Mar. **BEAVERKILL VALLEY INN:** Tel 845-439-4844; www.beaverkillvalley.com. *Cost:* from $175. **WULFF SCHOOL OF FLY FISHING:** Tel 800-328-3638 or 845-439-5020; www.royalwulff.com. *Cost:* $625 for 3-day course. *When:* late Apr–Jun. **EMERSON RESORT & SPA:** Tel 877-688-2828 or 845-688-2828; www.emersonresort.com. *Cost:* inn from $299, lodge from $160. **MOHONK MOUNTAIN HOUSE:** Tel 800-772-6646 or 845-255-1000; www.mohonk.com. *Cost:* from $540, inclusive. **BEST TIMES:** Apr–mid-Oct for trout fishing; late Sep–early Oct for Woodstock Film Festival; Oct for foliage.

Baseball, Bel Canto, and Bucolic Charm

COOPERSTOWN

New York, U.S.A.

A gracious, tree-lined village in upstate New York's woodlands, Cooperstown sits proudly stuck in time on the southern tip of hill-ringed Otsego Lake. According to legend, it was here, in 1839, that Abner Doubleday created the game of baseball—a distinction that's made this town of 2,000 a pilgrimage site for baseball lovers and home of the National Baseball Hall of Fame and Museum. The museum's collection runs the gamut from Joe DiMaggio's locker to a 1909 Honus Wagner card—some 38,000 objects and 500,000 photos in all.

But there's much more to this town than baseball. Every summer since 1975, Cooperstown has hosted the prestigious Glimmerglass Festival, which blends classic operatic repertory with rarities, played in an acoustically perfect 900-seat house with views of surrounding farmland. Nineteenth-century novelist James Fenimore Cooper, son of the New Jersey transplant who founded Cooperstown in 1786, referred to Otsego Lake as "Glimmerglass" in his Leatherstocking Tales—hence the festival's name.

Artifacts from the novelist Cooper's life can be found at the Fenimore Art Museum, a 1930s neo-Georgian mansion on Lake Otsego, along with a renowned collection of North American Indian Art, and works of Hudson River school artists such as Thomas Cole.

Amid it all is the friendly Inn at Cooperstown, a fine 1874 example of Second Empire architecture just steps off Main Street. For something grander, head to the sprawling Federal-style Otesaga Resort Hotel, commissioned in 1909 and much admired for its 400 windows, unrivaled lakefront setting, and venerable 18-hole Leatherstocking Golf Course, designed in 1909 by Devereux Emmet.

WHERE: 228 miles northwest of New York City. **VISITOR INFO:** www.cooperstownchamber.org. **BASEBALL HALL OF FAME:** Tel 888-425-5655 or 607-547-7200; www.baseballhalloffame.org. **GLIMMERGLASS FESTIVAL:** Tel 607-547-2255; www.glimmerglass.org. *When:* Jul–Aug. **FENIMORE ART MUSEUM:** Tel 888-547-1450 or 607-547-1400; www.fenimoreartmuseum.org. *When:* closed Jan–Mar. **THE INN AT COOPERSTOWN:** Tel 607-547-5756; www.innatcooperstown.com. *Cost:* from $110 (off-peak), from $200 (peak). **THE OTESAGA RESORT HOTEL:** Tel 800-348-6222 or 607-547-9931; www.otesaga.com. *Cost:* from $420, inclusive; greens fees from $89. *When:* mid-Apr–mid-Nov. **BEST TIMES:** late Jul for the National Baseball Hall of Fame induction ceremonies; Christmastime for holiday decorations.

World-Class Wines and Small-Town Americana

FINGER LAKES

New York, U.S.A.

The Iroquois attributed these long, narrow lakes to the Great Spirit, who laid his hands in blessing on this particularly beautiful area of upstate New York, but it's more likely that glacial activity carved them out eons ago. Most are deep—Cayuga and Seneca, the largest, are 435 and 618 feet deep, respectively, and about 38 miles long. Together, these 11 parallel lakes cover an area no more than 100 miles across in a bucolic region where the sleepy Main Streets of waterfront towns like Geneva, Skaneateles, and Hammondsport invite strolling and antiques hunting.

The Finger Lakes are particularly known for their "boutique" vineyards—today numbering close to 100 and recognized for some of the country's best rieslings and chardonnays. Of the area's various trails, the most popular is the Keuka, named for what is widely considered the most beautiful of the lakes. The route takes in the pioneering Dr. Konstantin Frank's Vinifera Wine Cellars, outside Hammondsport, and nearby Pleasant Valley Wine Company, whose eight historic stone buildings add up to one of the best tours in the region.

Geneva on the Lake, a 1910 Roman villa–inspired hotel, has a beautiful expanse of parterre garden leading down to a pool on the shore of Seneca Lake. At Skaneateles Lake—among the cleanest in the country—the Mirbeau Inn and Spa is a Francophile's dream with a garden that would woo Monet.

Along Cayuga Lake Scenic Byway lies Aurora, a tidy little town of 650 that is experiencing a renaissance thanks to Pleasant Rowland, creator of the American Girl dolls. Rowland restored the lakeside Aurora Inn, a redbrick Federal-style inn from 1833, and its neighbor, the 7-room E. B. Morgan House. The Aurora Inn's dining room opens onto a waterfront veranda where American classics, like oven-crusted pork tenderloin, are paired with wines from neighboring vineyards.

WHERE: 20 miles southwest of Syracuse. **VISITOR INFO:** www.fingerlakes.org. **DR. FRANK'S WINE CELLARS:** Tel 800-320-0735 or 607-868-4884; www.drfrankwines.com. **PLEASANT VALLEY WINE COMPANY:** Tel 877-662-8833 or 607-569-6111: www.pleasantvalleywine.com. **GENEVA ON THE LAKE RESORT:** Tel 800-343-6382 or 315-789-7190; www.genevaonthelake.com. *Cost:* from $165 (off-peak), from $235 (peak). **MIRBEAU INN:** Tel 877-647-2328 or 315-685-5006; www

.mirbeau.com. *Cost:* from $220 (off-peak), from $350 (peak). **Aurora Inn** and **E. B. Morgan House:** Tel 866-364-8808 or 315-364-8888; www.aurora-inn.com. *Cost: Aurora Inn* from $150 (off-peak), from $225 (peak); dinner $50. *E. B. Morgan House* from $175 (off-peak), from $250 (peak). **Best times:** late Jul for Finger Lakes Wine Festival in Watkins Glen; last weekend of Jul for Antique Boat Show in Skaneateles.

Where "America the Beautiful" Began

Hudson Valley

New York, U.S.A.

In 1609, Dutch explorer Henry Hudson sailed up the scenic river that now bears his name, looking for a passage to the Orient. Known to Native Americans as the "two-way river" because salty ocean tides reach as far north as Albany, the Hudson begins in the Adirondack Mountains (see p. 835) before emptying into the Atlantic near New York City (see p. 841) 315 miles later. The Hudson has exerted such a profound effect on American history, art, and literature that Bill Moyers dubbed it "America's First River."

Alexander Liberman's Iliad *is among the Storm King Art Center's sculptures.*

A drive through the valley that cradles this timeless waterway won't disappoint: Take off on back roads past horse farms and orchards, then stop for lunch and antiquing in 18th- and 19th-century riverfront towns like Cold Spring or Hudson. Washington Irving, who set his "Legend of Sleepy Hollow" here, said of the area, "The Hudson Valley is, in a manner, my first and last love."

For a glimpse of the beauty that inspired the landscape painters of the Hudson River school, visit Olana, Frederick Church's 1874 hilltop Moorish mansion, then walk the nearby Poughkeepsie-Highland Railroad Bridge, completed in 1888. Reincarnated as a state historic park in 2009, it is still, at 1.28 miles, the world's longest pedestrian bridge.

In nearby Hyde Park, the prestigious Culinary Institute of America offers five student-staffed restaurants open to the public. Hyde Park is also home to Springwood, Franklin D. Roosevelt's 300-acre riverside home, where visitors can tour the FDR Presidential Library and Museum. Nearby is the Beaux Arts Vanderbilt Mansion—with 54 opulent rooms and extensive gardens, it's the showiest of the valley's historic pleasure palaces.

Many battles took place along the Hudson's banks during the Revolutionary War, leading the government to designate the valley a National Heritage Area. George Washington's most important stronghold at the river's narrowest point became the U.S. Military Academy at West Point, the nation's oldest military academy and its most beautifully sited.

Art lovers will discover that the Hudson Valley also hosts an impressive wealth of museums. Just north of West Point, the Storm

King Art Center, an outdoor sculpture park, invites guests to walk among the works by Louise Nevelson and Alexander Calder as well as a host of other monumental structures that grace its 500 acres. Across the river, you'll find gems by artists like Andy Warhol, Donald Judd, and Dan Flavin at Dia:Beacon, a gallery housed in a 1929 printing plant, where the focus is major (and often oversize) works from the 1960s to the present.

Where: 150 miles from New York City north to Albany. **Visitor info:** www.travelhudsonvalley.com. **Olana:** www.olana.org. **Walkway over the Hudson:** www.walkway.org. **Culinary Institute of America:** Tel 845-451-1588 (tours); www.ciachef.edu. **Springwood:** Tel 800-337-8474 or 845-486-1966; www.nps.gov/hofr. **Vanderbilt Mansion:** Tel 845-229-7770; www.nps.gov/vama. **West Point:** Tel 845-938-2638; www.usma.edu. **Storm King Art Center:** Tel 845-534-3115; www.skac.org. *When:* Apr–mid-Nov. **Dia:Beacon:** Tel 845-440-0100; www.diabeacon.org. **Best times:** May for spring beauty; Jul–Aug for a variety of festivals and events; Oct for fall foliage.

Summer Scene Where the Elite Meet and Greet

The Hamptons

Long Island, New York, U.S.A.

During the summer months, the seaside towns on eastern Long Island known as the Hamptons are inundated with city folk—you'll run into almost as many Manhattanites at the Candy Kitchen, Bridgehampton's 1920s-era soda fountain, as you would on Madison Avenue. But along with polo fields, there are still roadside honor-system farm stands and seafood stores stocked by local fishermen.

What lures the crowds are miles and miles of glorious beach, handsomely restored historical towns, and an active social scene. Southampton is the grande dame of old money and sweeping estates, but East Hampton is arguably the most fashionable town, once the haunt of artists and writers including Willem de Kooning, Jackson Pollock, Truman Capote, and Joseph Heller. Spend an afternoon in Sagaponack, where the region's last stretches of potato fields are fragrant with flowers in August, and you'll see why they were so inspired.

Restaurants in the Hamptons are as fine as their New York City peers. The intimate 1770 House, on East Hampton's Main Street, is best known for its elegant dining room, but many prefer the hearty fare served in the cozy basement tavern. Overnighters should book at the Maidstone, an elegant 19th-century white clapboard inn enjoying a recent Scandanavian makeover.

A few miles north is the former whaling port of Sag Harbor. Its shop-lined Main Street is anchored by the American Hotel, which has been welcoming guests since 1846. The 110-page wine list includes the best from the local vineyards and beyond. For flip-flop casual, try the juicy burgers at the Corner Bar.

At the end of Long Island lies Montauk, with its famous lighthouse and surfing, nominally part of the Hamptons but in atmosphere light-years apart. Seafood is the fare of choice in town, and you'll find none better than at Gosman's Dock, a Montauk institution that has evolved into a complex of open-air waterside restaurants.

Where: Southampton is 95 miles east of New York City. **Visitor info:** www.discover

Historic Mulford Farm can be found in East Hampton.

longisland.com. **Candy Kitchen:** Tel 631-537-9885. *Cost:* lunch $20. **The 1770 House:** Tel 631-324-1770; www.1770house.com. *Cost:* rooms from $229; dinner $60 (upstairs), $18 (tavern). **The Maidstone:** Tel 631-324-5006; www.themaidstone.com. *Cost:* from $280 (off-peak), from $580 (peak). **The American Hotel:** Tel 631-725-3535; www.theamericanhotel.com. *Cost:* from $150 (off-peak), from $250 (peak); dinner $50. **The Corner Bar:** Tel 631-725-9760; www.cornerbarsagharbor.com. *Cost:* lunch $15. **Best times:** May–Jun and Oct for fewer crowds; Jul–Aug for nicest beach weather and Mercedes-Benz Polo Challenge; last weekend of Sep for Montauk Surf Classic Tournament.

"New York . . . moves so fast, it takes energy just to stand still."—Barbara Walters

New York City

New York, U.S.A.

This is Metropolis. This is Gotham City. This is the one all the other cities wish they were—"the only real city-city," as Truman Capote put it. Its skyscrapers loom above canyonlike streets where some 8.3 million New Yorkers go about their daily business—walking fast, talking fast, and taking no lip, yet sharing that pride and sense of community that was displayed so unforgettably when terrorists targeted their home on September 11, 2001. They say it's the capital of the world . . . and maybe it is.

Top Attractions

American Museum of Natural History—The movie *Night at the Museum* was set here, but you don't need a talking Teddy Roosevelt to convince you of all the wonders on display, from the famed 94-foot model of a blue whale to the fossil composite of a *T. rex* skeleton to the 21,000-carat Brazilian Princess topaz. The futuristic Rose Center for Earth and Space is a four-story sphere encased in glass that holds the Hayden Planetarium, which features the world's largest and most powerful virtual reality simulator, seemingly able to send visitors to the Milky Way and beyond. **Info:** Tel 212-769-5100; www.amnh.org.

Central Park—Laid out between 1859 and 1870 according to a design by Frederick Law Olmsted and Calvert Vaux, Central Park's 843 acres are an urban miracle. Its highlights include Bethesda Fountain; the romantic Boathouse restaurant; the Trump Wollman Ice Skating Rink; the Sheep Meadow (an enormous lawn that's blanket-to-blanket with sunbathers by the time July rolls around); the carousel, with its 58 hand-carved horses; and the gemlike Conservatory Garden. In summer, visitors can take in free performances by the Metropolitan Opera and the New York Philharmonic on the Great Lawn; SummerStage concerts by a spectrum of international artists;

and Shakespeare in the Park. **Info:** Tel 212-310-6600; www.centralparknyc.org. **Boathouse Restaurant:** Tel 212-517-2233; www.thecentralparkboathouse.com. *Cost:* dinner $55. **Opera and Symphony:** www.centralpark.com. *When:* Jun–Sep. **SummerStage:** Tel 212-360-2756; www.summerstage.org. *When:* Jun–Aug. **Shakespeare in the Park:** Tel 212-260-2400; www.publictheater.org. *When:* Jun–Aug.

The Empire State Building is 102 stories tall.

Empire State Building—The Chrysler Building may be the most beautiful of New York's skyscrapers, but the Empire State Building is undoubtedly its most iconic, soaring 1,454 feet and bathed at night in lighting chosen to reflect occasions as diverse as Frank Sinatra's birthday (all blue) and New York Jets games (green and white). Completed in 1931, it reigned as the tallest building in the world until the World Trade Center surpassed it in the early '70s. It's now again the tallest in the city—for the moment. Visit the 86th floor's open-air observatory and see the sights up to 80 miles in all directions. **Info:** Tel 212-736-3100; www.esbnyc.com.

Lincoln Center—Since 1962, when the first of its theaters opened, the 16-acre Lincoln Center complex has been the centerpiece of New York's performing arts scene, with twelve resident companies that include the New York City Ballet, the American Ballet Theatre, the New York Philharmonic, and the Metropolitan Opera, the latter widely considered the best in the world. In recent years, architects Diller Scofidio + Renfro have been guiding a major (and sometimes controversial) transformation of the campus, modernizing the buildings to make them more welcoming. Inviting new public spaces include Illumination Lawn, a sloping grass roof above the high-concept Lincoln restaurant. In summer, dance bands from swing to salsa perform in the pocket-size Damrosch Park as part of the Midsummer Night Swing series. **Info:** Tel 212-875-2656; www.lincolncenter.org.

Metropolitan Museum of Art—With more than 2 million works created in the Stone Age, the digital age, and any time in between, the Metropolitan Museum ranks as one of the largest repositories of art and culture on the planet. Founded in 1870, this institution has expanded to such a degree that its Gothic Revival building is now completely surrounded by additions. Highlights include the Roman and Greek galleries; the Costume Institute; the impressive holdings of Byzantine and Chinese art; the collection of European paintings, with works by Tiepolo, Cézanne, Vermeer, and Monet; the Arms and Armor collection; and the Egyptian collection, with its mummies, sphinx, and the amazing 1st century B.C. Temple of Dendur, presented as a gift of the Egyptian government. The museum's Roof Garden Café is a popular summertime haunt, while the Neapolitan Christmas Creche in the Medieval Sculpture Hall is a holiday favorite. **Info:** Tel 212-570-3828; www.metmuseum.org.

Museum of Modern Art— Founded in 1929 to promote new approaches to artistic expression, MoMA was remodeled and enlarged in 2004 under the guidance of architect Yoshio Taniguchi. Nearly twice its original size, it is today home to the world's finest collection of works from the late 19th century to the present, including Van Gogh's *Starry Night*, and Picasso's 1907 *Les Demoiselles d'Avignon*. Other holdings

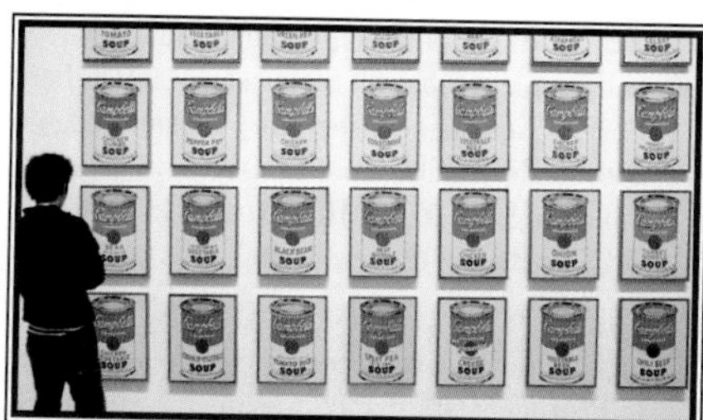

The MoMA displays Andy Warhol's 32 portraits of Campbell's Soup Cans, *one for each variety of the soup available in 1962.*

include the 3,000 objects in the Architecture and Design collection; the Film and Media collection, with its 4 million stills and 23,000 films; and 25,000 photographs, including works by Man Ray, Walker Evans, and Ansel Adams, among others. There's respite in the peaceful open-air Abby Aldrich Rockefeller Sculpture Garden—with pieces by Giacometti, Picasso, Rodin, and others—or in the sleek, much-lauded restaurant, The Modern. **INFO:** Tel 212-708-9400; www.moma.org. **THE MODERN:** Tel 212-333-1220; www.themodern nyc.com. *Cost:* 3-course prix-fixe dinner $88.

THE SOLOMON R. GUGGENHEIM MUSEUM—Designed by Frank Lloyd Wright and completed in 1959, this dramatic structure is shaped like a spiraling seashell. Take the elevator to the top and walk down through the uninterrupted, circling gallery to ground level (as Wright intended), and view works that span the late 19th century to the present, including Mr. Guggenheim's original collection of nonobjective art; niece Peggy Guggenheim's trove of Surrealist and abstract works; and examples from various other schools, including Impressionist, Post-Impressionist, German Expressionist, and Minimalist works. **INFO:** Tel 212-423-3500; www.guggenheim.org.

ROCKEFELLER CENTER AT CHRISTMAS—Built and financed in the 1930s by John D. Rockefeller, this complex of office buildings is a masterpiece of streamlined modern architecture, full of Art Deco relief work and sculpture that harks back to Greek mythology while paying homage to American optimism in the face of the Great Depression. The center looks its best at Christmastime, when a towering, brightly lit Norway spruce is displayed above the tiny but incredibly romantic ice-skating rink. The Top of the Rock observation deck offers stunning 360-degree midtown views from the 70th floor of 30 Rockefeller Plaza. In the evening, head to Radio City Music Hall, the complex's Deco masterpiece, for the annual Broadwayesque Christmas Spectacular, starring the Rockettes and Santa. **INFO:** Tel 212-632-3975; www .rockefellercenter.com. **RADIO CITY MUSIC HALL:** Tel 212-247-4777; www.radiocity.com.

STATUE OF LIBERTY AND ELLIS ISLAND—Lady Liberty was designed by Frédéric-Auguste Bartholdi and engineer Alexandre-Gustave Eiffel and was a gift from France to the United States in 1885. The 151-foot-tall copper-clad statue was dedicated on October 28, 1886, and received a remarkably effective face-lift in time for her centennial. Visitors can climb the 168 steps to Liberty's crown, though the less athletic may just want to view her steel skeleton through the glass ceiling in the 10th-floor observatory.

Between 1892 and 1954, Ellis Island was the gateway to America for roughly 12 million hopeful immigrants. Today, about 30 percent of Americans have an ancestor who stopped here on arriving to this country. Visitors can view moving, interactive exhibits, research their heritage, and stand in the same baggage and registry rooms as their forebears once did. Those who want a good view of the Statue of Liberty and the Manhattan skyline without visiting the monuments can hop on the Staten Island Ferry for a free ride to and from New York's outermost borough. **STATUE OF LIBERTY:** www.nps.gov/stli. *Ferry information:* tel 212-269-5755; www.statue cruises.com. **ELLIS ISLAND:** Tel 212-363-3200; www.ellisisland.org. **STATEN ISLAND FERRY:** Tel 718-815-2628; www.siferry.com.

Times Square can feel like the crossroads of the world.

TIMES SQUARE AND THE THEATER DISTRICT—By the 1970s, Times Square had degenerated into a swamp of peepshows, hustlers, and lowlifes. That all changed in the 1990s, when the city invited Disney and other business giants to redevelop the area. Broadway is once again the Great White Way, and Times Square a thriving family-entertainment and business district. Neon billboards are everywhere and theaters line the side streets. On New Year's Eve, this is party central, when upward of a million people brave what's sometimes single-digit weather, waiting for the famous ball to drop.

OTHER MUST-DOS

BIG ONION WALKING TOURS—This excursion company clearly thinks the Big Apple is more like a Big Onion—you could peel off layer after layer without ever reaching the core. Its 2-hour tours wend their way through Greenwich Village, Harlem, Chinatown, and many other neighborhoods. You can also book a historic walk or a specialty tour: for instance, one to explore and sample multiethnic foods. **INFO:** Tel 212-439-1090; www.bigonion.com.

BRONX ZOO AND NEW YORK BOTANICAL GARDEN—Opened in 1899, the Bronx Zoo is the largest metropolitan zoo in the U.S. and home to more than 5,000 animals, most in natural settings across 265 pleasant acres. Exhibits include Himalayan Highlands, complete with rare snow leopards; the 6.5-acre Congo Gorilla Forest, with one of the largest breeding groups of lowland gorillas in captivity; and Wild Asia, populated by elephants, tigers, and rhinoceroses. Nearby, the New York Botanical Garden is a sanctuary of another sort, the home of more than a million plants that fill 50 gardens and of the largest Victorian conservatory in America. **BRONX ZOO:** Tel 718-367-1010; www.bronxzoo.com. **NEW YORK BOTANICAL GARDEN:** Tel 718-817-8700; www.nybg.org.

BROOKLYN BOTANIC GARDEN—New York's most popular garden covers 52 acres adjacent to Prospect Park (which was designed by Frederick Law Olmsted and Calvert Vaux after their success with Central Park). The BBG has over 11,000 species of plants arranged in more than 20 specialty gardens, including the Cranford Rose Garden, the English-style Shakespeare Garden, and the Cherry Esplanade, one of the finest spots outside Japan to see cherry blossoms in spring. **INFO:** Tel 718-623-7200; www.bbg.org.

BROOKLYN BRIDGE—Completed in 1883 after 16 years of construction, this massive suspension bridge is undeniably one of the architectural gems of New York, connecting lower Manhattan with the 19th-century neighborhood of Brooklyn Heights, known for its handsome old brownstones and quiet, tree-lined streets. Stroll across the bridge's boardwalk-like central promenade, and admire up close its huge stone pylons and spiderweb of steel support cables along with the expansive views of the East River below. The elegant River Café, beneath the bridge's Brooklyn tower, offers one of the best restaurant views in town. **RIVER CAFÉ:** Tel 718-522-5200; www.rivercafe.com. *Cost:* 3-course prix-fixe dinner $100.

FRICK MUSEUM—Built in 1914 by the inordinately rich steel and railroad magnate Henry Clay Frick, this lovely French Neoclassical mansion houses a collection of mostly European masterpieces from the Renaissance to the 1900s. The opulent interior is resplendent with 18th-century French furniture and porcelain, and is much loved by New Yorkers for its intimacy and the relative absence of crowds. The museum's highlights include works by Rembrandt,

Vermeer, Holbein, Velázquez, Titian, El Greco, Bellini, and Goya. **Info:** Tel 212-288-0700; www.frick.org.

Grand Central Terminal—Grand Central is grand indeed, and it's one of the best places in the city to catch the spirit of early-20th-century New York and America. Its triumphant Beaux Arts exterior is adorned with statues of Hercules, Minerva, and Mercury. Inside, the ceiling covering its huge main concourse is lit with constellations, and lofty windows illuminate its marble interior with swaths of natural light. Have lunch at the Oyster Bar on the lower level. In business since 1913, it serves some 4,000 pounds of fresh seafood daily, including its famous New England clam chowder and dozens of different kinds of oysters. **Info:** www.grandcentralterminal.com. **Oyster Bar:** Tel 212-490-6650; www.oysterbarny.com. *Cost:* lunch $40.

Harlem Spirituals Tour—Out-of-towners have been increasingly common at Harlem's traditional Sunday morning services, home to the near-ecstatic black gospel tradition that was born during days of slavery. For those who want to be similarly stirred, the best bets are Mother A.M.E. Zion, founded in 1796 and with a history that connects it to the Underground Railroad; the Abyssinian Baptist Church, renowned for its choir; and the New Mount Zion Baptist Church, under the direction of much-loved pastor Carl L. Washington Jr. **Mother A.M.E. Zion Church:** Tel 212-234-1545; www.amez.org. **Abyssinian Baptist Church:** Tel 212-862-7474; www.abyssinian.org. **New Mount Zion Baptist Church:** Tel 212-283-2934; nmzbc.org. **How:** Harlem Spirituals Tours: tel 212-391-0900; www.harlemspirituals.com.

Yankee Stadium—"The House that Ruth Built" is technically no more, as the historic stadium was replaced in 2009 by a huge, swanky new one across the street, but architectural nods to the original (including the façade) would make the Babe feel right at home. There are about the same number of seats here as before but more of everything else, from leg room to concession stands, along with restaurants offering all kinds of fare, and a museum of Yankee memorabilia. If you can't make it to a game, take the 1-hour stadium tour and see the highlights, including the storied Monument Park, which was lovingly moved from its old home. **Info:** Tel 718-293-6000; newyork.yankees.mlb.com.

Yogi Berra threw the ceremonial first pitch at the new Yankee Stadium in 2009.

Where to Stay

The Bowery Hotel—Helping transform a once-seedy area, this trendy hotel is a favorite of the younger celebrity set. Although the building is new, the lobby's velvet sofas, wood paneling, and faded Oriental carpets evoke a vintage vibe. The 135 rooms aren't large, but floor-to-ceiling factory-style windows with city views compensate, and the galleries, shops, and cafés of SoHo, NoLita, and the East Village are all within walking distance. Dine on rustic Italian fare at the hotel's Gemma, or stroll two blocks downtown and sample Daniel Boulud's hip eatery, DBGB (see p. 847). **Info:** Tel: 212-505-9100; www.theboweryhotel.com. *Cost:* from $325 (off-peak), from $495 (peak); dinner $40.

The Four Seasons—Soaring 52 stories above one of the city's toniest shopping areas, the I. M. Pei–designed Four Seasons Hotel is the destination of the posh and powerful. The sleek lobby exudes an almost templelike quiet, and leads to several restaurants and bars, including L'Atelier de Joël Robuchon, the celebrated French chef's first venture in New York, with haute (and *très cher*) French cuisine. The hotel's 368 large, flawlessly decorated rooms and suites have 10-foot ceilings, opulent marble bathrooms, and soaring views over the city. **Info:** Tel 800-487-3769 or 212-758-5700; www.fourseasons.com. *Cost:* from $695. **L'Atelier de Joël Robuchon:** Tel 212-829-3844. *Cost:* dinner $100.

Grace Hotel—Tucked down a side street off Times Square, this boutique-on-a-budget hotel is a great find for young travelers who want to be in the thick of it all. The 139 small, quiet rooms are stylishly spartan but equipped with Wi-Fi and flat-screen TVs. Built-in furnishings make the most of the limited space, and some rooms even have bunk beds for traveling friends. A highlight is the lobby's 22-foot heated pool with a swim-up bar and DJs. **Info:** Tel 212-380-2700; www.room-matehotels.com. *Cost:* from $219.

The Inn at Irving Place—A little-known refuge of great charm and set a stone's throw from the genteel enclave of Gramercy Park, this 12-room inn was created by combining two 1834 town houses. It offers the gracious atmosphere of Edith Wharton's New York with luxurious period furnishings, Persian rugs, fireplaces, and flowers. Take afternoon tea in Lady Mendl's Tea Salon, or sip something stronger in the clubby Cibar Lounge. **Info:** Tel 800-685-1447 or 212-533-4600; www.innatirving.com. *Cost:* from $325 (off-peak), from $450 (peak).

Mandarin Oriental—For luxurious, five-star swank, it's hard to beat this modern hotel on the edge of Central Park. Occupying floors 35 to 54 in the sleek Time Warner Center, it makes the most of its lofty setting with walls of windows framing jaw-dropping views. Asian touches keep the sophisticated décor timelessly serene. Enjoy afternoon tea in the Lobby Lounge, dine on Asian–New American cuisine at Asiate or try one of the other restaurants in the Time Warner building (see p. 849). The exquisite, state-of-the-art spa is considered New York's best. **Info:** Tel 212-805-8800; www.mandarinoriental.com. *Cost:* from $695 (off-peak), from $1,055 (peak). **Asiate:** Tel 212-805-8881. *Cost:* dinner $70.

St. Regis Hotel—Built by John Jacob Astor in 1904 as his residence, this opulent Beaux Arts building still reflects that era's gilded grandeur, welcoming guests with top-hatted doormen, trompe l'oeil ceilings, and polished service. Upstairs, the 164 spacious rooms and 65 suites are done up in silk wall coverings, with marble baths, glamorous bedding, and 24-hour butler service adding to the indulgent feel. The King Cole bar, named for the Maxfield Parrish mural on one wall, claims to be the birthplace of the Bloody Mary, known here as the Red Snapper. The appropriate splurge is the sublime French fare at Adour, Alain Ducasse's raved-about restaurant. **Info:** Tel 800-759-7550 or 212-753-4500; www.stregis.com/newyork. *Cost:* from $895. **Adour:** Tel 212-710-2277. *Cost:* dinner $90.

The Standard—A glass-and-concrete creation perched on 56-foot stilts, this futuristic-looking newcomer from trendy hotelier Andre Balazs straddles the High Line, a pedestrian park built on a disused elevated railroad. The hotel towers above the hip Meatpacking District, so the floor-to-ceiling windows in all 337 rooms have stellar views of the downtown skyline or the Hudson River. Décor morphs from sleek, early-20th-century style in the lobby to mid-century modern in the middle and 21st-century wow in the glass-enclosed, celebrity-studded lounge on the 18th floor. Diners can enjoy creative American fare at the stylish Standard Grill; sip a cocktail in the Living Room; or hoist a stein in the outdoor Summer Biergarten over hearty German fare. **Info:** Tel 212-645-4646; standardhotels.com. *Cost:* from $295. **Standard Grill:** Tel 212-645-4100; www.thestandardgrill.com. *Cost:* dinner $48. **The High Line:** www.thehighline.org.

Eating & Drinking

Daniel—For years regarded by fellow chefs and devoted patrons as one of the country's most brilliant French-trained talents, Daniel Boulud remains a trailblazer. Refined fantasy describes his flagship restaurant Boulud and its menu, which features technically complicated, perfectly executed, and artistically presented dishes. You can revel in Boulud's inventive spirit less expensively at his stylish Café Boulud or at db Bistro Moderne, in the Theater District, justly famous for its sumptuous haute hamburger. More casual still are Bar Boulud, directly across from Lincoln Center, specializing in charcuterie and wines, with the Épicerie Boulud café next door, and downtown's hip, industrial-chic DBGB Kitchen and Bar, where the brasserie-style menu features house-made sausages and a broad selection of beers. **Daniel:** Tel 212-288-0033; www.danielnyc.com. *Cost:* 3-course prix-fixe dinner $105. **Café Boulud:** Tel 212-772-2600. *Cost:* dinner $65. **db Bistro Moderne:** Tel 212-391-2400. *Cost:* dinner $60. **Bar Boulud:** Tel 212-595-0303. *Cost:* dinner $45. **DBGB Kitchen and Bar:** Tel 212-933-5300. *Cost:* dinner $40.

Delis—Amid the city's sophisticated dining scene, a handful of genuine Jewish delis prevail, offering a glimpse of old-time New York. What keeps folks coming back is the frill-free classic fare, specifically the towering, thick-sliced pastrami sandwiches, meant to be washed down with a cream soda or an egg cream. The oldest of all is Katz's Delicatessen, a cavernous remnant of Jewish life on the Lower East Side that has been in business since 1888. The iconic Second Avenue Deli has relocated uptown to new black-and-white-tiled digs on East 33rd. There the nephew of the original owner continues to dish up the deli's famous chopped liver, matzoh ball soup, triple-decker corned beef sandwiches, and other genuine kosher fare. Just north of the Theater District, the legendary Carnegie Deli is known for elbow-to-elbow tables and pretend-grumpy waiters. Locals always ask to share their mile-high sandwiches, and they still never leave without a doggy bag. Save room for the cheesecake. **Katz's Delicatessen:** Tel 212-254-2246; www.katzdeli.com. *Cost:* $25. **Second Avenue Deli:** Tel 212-689-9000; www.2ndavedeli.com. *Cost:* $20. **Carnegie Deli:** Tel 212-757-2245; www.carnegiedeli.com. *Cost:* $30.

The Four Seasons—With stunning décor by Mies van der Rohe and Philip Johnson that's remained virtually unchanged since the place opened in 1959, the Four Seasons is one of Manhattan's legendary restaurants (and not part of the Four Seasons Hotel; see p. 845). At lunchtime, the city's power elite gather to graze in the Grill Room. At dinner, out-of-towners dine there and around the white marble pool in the elegant, aptly named Pool Room, enjoying exceptional, classic American food from enlightened chef Fabio Trabocchi. **Info:** Tel 212-754-9494; www.fourseasonsrestaurant.com. *Cost:* dinner $80.

The Italians—New York's constellation of Italian chefs promise an embarrassment of choices. Among the standouts, television personality Mario Batali's Babbo is a perennial hot spot, famous for introducing curious New Yorkers to such exotic delicacies as lamb's tongue and ravioli stuffed with beef cheek. There are eight other Batali eateries; if you are in the mood for opulent, palazzo-style surroundings, opt for Del Posto. Or stop by Cesare Casella's casual little wine-bar-cum-salumi shop, Salumeria Rosi, to sample his seasonal small-plate "assagi" of caponata and lasagna, and you'll revel in the authentic flavors of Casella's Tuscan hometown. Scott Conant brings dishes as simple as spaghetti with tomato and basil to new heights at Scarpetta, located in a stylish town house on the edge of the Meatpacking District. **Babbo:** Tel 212-777-0303; www.babbonyc.com. *Cost:* dinner $55. **Del Posto:** Tel 212-497-8090; www.delposto.com. *Cost:* 7-course dinner $125. **Salumeria Rosi:** Tel 212-877-4800;

www.salumeriarosi.com. *Cost:* dinner $40. **Scarpetta:** Tel 212-691-0555; www.scarpettanyc.com. *Cost:* dinner $65.

Jean-Georges—Unusual ingredients, innovative combinations, and artful presentations keep dazzling the foodies who have followed Jean-Georges Vongerichten since the early days at JoJo (still going strong), confirming his reputation as one of America's most creative culinary forces. His newest venture, the chic Mark Restaurant, in the Mark Hotel, offers Vongerichten's delectable take on comfort food, the likes of which your mom never made. **Jean-Georges:** Tel 212-299-3900; www.jean-georges.com. *Cost:* 3-course prix-fixe dinner $98. **JoJo:** Tel 212-223-5656; www.jean-georges.com. *Cost:* dinner $48. **The Mark Restaurant:** Tel 212-744-4300; www.themarkrestaurant nyc.com. *Cost:* dinner $75.

Le Bernardin—Considered Manhattan's ultimate seafood restaurant, this elegant, celebrated spot delights even those who think they don't care for fish. Chef Eric Ripert, the French-born culinary star who heads up the kitchen, divides his menu into Almost Raw, Barely Touched, and Lightly Cooked, and he presents an astonishing array of sublime fare while strictly enforcing his no-endangered-species rule. **Info:** Tel 212-554-1515; www.le-bernardin.com. *Cost:* prix-fixe dinner $115.

The Meyer Empire—Amiable restaurateur Danny Meyer now has so many acclaimed eateries, from high end to burger stand (he has opened multiple wildly popular Shake Shacks in the city), it's hard to keep track. His flagship Union Square Café is a New American–style bistro offering unfussy, Mediterranean-based comfort food. Meyer's formula for genuinely warm service and delicious food at good value also explains the sustained popularity of the handsome, highly rated Gramercy Tavern. Maialino is his first Italian venture, a charmingly atmospheric, Roman-style trattoria. The name means "little pig," and pork stars on a menu that also offers fresh takes on finger foods and pasta. **Union Square Café:** Tel 212-243-4020; www.unionsquarecafe.com. *Cost:* dinner $65. **Gramercy Tavern:** Tel 212-477-0777; www.gramercytavern.com. *Cost:* prix-fixe dinner $86. **Maialino:** Tel 212-777-2400; www.maialinonyc.com. *Cost:* dinner $55.

Peter Luger Steakhouse—A veritable shrine to Porterhouse, Peter Luger's is possibly the country's finest steak restaurant, drawing happy carnivores to its tavernlike, old–New York premises in Brooklyn beneath the Williamsburg Bridge since 1887. Each butter-tender prime beef steak is handpicked and dry aged on site. **Info:** Tel 718-387-7400; www.peterluger.com. *Cost:* dinner $65.

New York Pizza—Nothing beats a New York pizza, its smoky crust slightly charred, daubed with warm blobs of fresh mozzarella, tomato sauce, and basil, plus toppings like homemade meatballs, pepperoni, and kalamata olives. In what remains of Little Italy, Lombardi's still makes the original pizza of a century ago and serves it in classic, red-tablecloth digs. The pies are baked in a coal-fired oven.

Across the river, under the Brooklyn Bridge, Grimaldi's has had hordes lining up since it opened in 1990. No wonder, the pizza is probably the best in town.

Back in Manhattan, John's of Bleecker Street serves brick-oven pie in a setting that features booths and tables covered with carved initials and graffiti dating to the 1920s.

Among the newcomers is Co. ("Company"), where Roman-style pies featuring toppings like zucchini-anchovy puree with zucchini blossoms have pizza buffs swooning. **Lombardi's:** Tel 212-941-7994; www.firstpizza.com. *Cost:* large $20. **Grimaldi's:** Brooklyn. Tel 718-858-4300; www.grimaldis.com. *Cost:* large $16. **John's Pizzeria of Bleecker Street:** Tel 212-243-1680; www.johnsbrickovenpizza.com. *Cost:* large $14. **Co.:** Tel 212-243-1105; www.co-pane.com. *Cost:* $16.

TIME WARNER RESTAURANT COLLECTION—Two glass-and-steel towers on the western edge of Columbus Circle, the Time Warner Center contains a cluster of eateries, from eclectic to sublime, that's made it a destination for dedicated foodies. At Per Se, Thomas Keller of Napa Valley's French Laundry (see p. 713) has created a Gotham version of his celebrated flagship, with glorious views over Central Park. More stunning still is the cuisine (and the tab too): It is regularly voted the city's No. 1 spot. Keller's popular Bouchon Bakery, a café-patisserie, serves soups and sandwiches along with mouthwatering macaroons and pastries. The conspicuous-consumption award goes to Masa, where true sushi fans never question the cost of the multicourse delicacies presented by sushi god Masa Takayama. The costs are less stratospheric next door at Bar Masa. At A Voce, chef Missy Robbins takes Italian fare to new heights, serving up clever iterations of rustic-yet-refined classics, including heavenly fresh pasta dishes. **PER SE:** Tel 212-823-9335; www.perseny.com. *Cost:* 9-course prix-fixe dinner $275. **BOUCHON BAKERY:** Tel 212-823-9366; www.bouchonbakery.com. **MASA:** Tel 212-823-9800; www.masanyc.com. *Cost:* multicourse sushi for $450. **BAR MASA:** tasting menu $98. **A VOCE:** Tel 212-823-2523; www.avocerestaurant.com. *Cost:* dinner $55.

A 19th-Century Queen of Spas

SARATOGA SPRINGS

New York, U.S.A.

The name Saratoga Springs has long evoked images of thoroughbreds and genteel garden parties. Once known as the "Queen of Spas," the area has been a longtime summer playground for the moneyed, thanks to its natural springs and a horse-racing season considered one of the nation's best.

The elegant Saratoga Race Course, America's oldest sports venue, is the flower-bedecked town's top attraction with an impressive Victorian grandstand. Between races, spend an hour at the National Museum of Racing and Hall of Fame across the track, a repository of Triple Crown trophies, diamond-encrusted whips, and interactive exhibits.

In the summer months, the open-air Saratoga Performing Arts Center (SPAC) hosts the New York City Ballet, followed by the Philadelphia Orchestra. Big-name artists from opera to pop music fill out the season's roster.

The Adelphi Hotel, built in 1877, is the epitome of Victorian charm, with 39 rooms full of antiques of various periods and a décor that borders on theatrical. There's also a wealth of fine smaller inns and B&Bs to choose from, foremost among them the Batcheller Mansion Inn, a splendid example of high Victorian Gothic architecture and an old-world welcome.

About 10 miles east of town is the site of the Battle of Saratoga, the first significant military victory of the American Revolution. Replica British cannons and a self-guided tour at the Saratoga National Historical Park convey the story of how, in 1777, American forces met and defeated a major British army.

WHERE: 200 miles north of New York City. **VISITOR INFO:** www.saratoga.org. **SARATOGA RACE COURSE:** Tel 518-584-6200; www.nyra.com. **MUSEUM OF RACING:** Tel 800-562-5394 or 518-584-0400; www.racingmuseum.org.

SPAC: Tel 518-587-3330; www.spac.org. *When:* May–Sep. **ADELPHI HOTEL:** Tel 518-587-4688; www.adelphihotel.com. *Cost:* from $145 (off-peak), from $350 (peak). *When:* mid-May–late Oct. **BATCHELLER MANSION INN:** Tel 800-616-7012 or 518-584-7012; www.batchellermansioninn.com. *Cost:* from $165 (off-peak), from $345 (peak). **SARATOGA NATIONAL HISTORICAL PARK:** Tel 518-664-9821; www.nps.gov/sara. **BEST TIMES:** late Jun for the Saratoga Jazz Festival at SPAC; late Jul–early Sep for racing season.

America's Grandest Estate

BILTMORE

Asheville, North Carolina, U.S.A.

"Strange, colossal, heartbreaking . . . in effect, like a gorgeous practical joke," said Henry James upon visiting George Washington Vanderbilt III's new palace in the Blue Ridge Mountains. Designed by Richard Morris Hunt, who also conceived The Breakers, the family's "cottage" in Newport, Rhode Island (see p. 865), Biltmore was completed in 1895 after an eight-year construction. It took 1,000 laborers to lay the 11,000 bricks for this "weekend getaway," which was inspired by French châteaux and has hosted luminaries such as Edith Wharton, Henry Ford, and Woodrow Wilson. It ranks as the largest private home ever built in America, containing 35 bedrooms, 43 bathrooms, 65 fireplaces, and extravagances (telephones, hot and cold running water) unheard of at the turn of the century.

Biltmore—still owned by Vanderbilt descendants—can be visited on tours that explore about 100 of the 250 rooms (decorated with some 1,600 works of art, including pieces by Renoir, Whistler, and Sargent) as well as a bowling alley and a 10,000-volume library.

The estate represents the height of Gilded Age splendor.

Of the 8,000 acres of stunning grounds designed by Frederick Law Olmsted, of Central Park fame (see p. 841), more than 400 are gardens showcasing magnificent dogwoods, roses, and some 50,000 tulips and 1,000 azalea bushes. Tour the Biltmore Estate Winery, which produces several well-respected wines, then spend the night at the newly built Inn on Biltmore Estate and enjoy a meal served on Vanderbilt china in the elegant Dining Room.

The Grove Park Inn Resort & Spa once hosted Biltmore's overflow of high-society houseguests. Today, despite its size, the 500-room inn still promises a cozy feel, with a slew of restaurants, a Donald Ross golf course, and an award-winning spa. It also houses the world's largest collection of Arts and Crafts furniture, with names like Stickley and Morris adorning most chairs and lighting fixtures. In Asheville's Montford Historic District, the far more intimate Black Walnut Inn, designed in 1899 by Biltmore's supervising architect, offers eight tastefully appointed guest rooms.

BILTMORE: Tel 800-411-3812 or 828-225-1333; www.biltmore.com. **INN ON BILTMORE ESTATE:** Tel 800-411-3812 or 828-225-1600. *Cost:* from $199 (off-peak), from $399 (peak); prix-fixe dinner $48. **GROVE PARK INN:** Tel

800-438-5800 or 828-252-2711; www.groveparkinn.com. *Cost:* from $229 (off-peak), from $280 (peak). **Black Walnut Inn:** Tel 800-381-3878 or 828-254-3878; www.blackwalnut.com. *Cost:* from $150 (off-peak), from $325 (peak). **Best times:** Feb for the Arts & Crafts Fair Conference at Grove Park Inn; early Apr–mid-May for Biltmore's Spring Festival of Flowers; Jul weekends for Summer Evening Concerts; Nov–Dec for Christmas celebrations.

World's Longest Stretch of Barrier Islands

The Outer Banks

North Carolina, U.S.A.

Some of the most beautiful beaches on America's Atlantic coast are in North Carolina's Outer Banks, a string of skinny barrier islands that stretches 130 miles from the Virginia border south to Cape Lookout and Beaufort.

The northern stretch consists largely of seasonal beach towns popular with anglers, swimmers, and windsurfers, such as Kitty Hawk and Kill Devil Hills, where the Wright Brothers pioneered airplane flight. In nearby Duck, the Sanderling Resort & Spa sits along miles of lonely windblown beach adjacent to the 3,400-acre Pine Island Audubon Sanctuary. Eat at the inn's popular Left Bank restaurant, or—for more casual fare—at its restaurant housed in a restored 1899 U.S. Life-Saving Service station with a name to match.

The midportion of the Outer Banks is dominated by bustling Nags Head and Jockey's Ridge State Park, home to towering sand dunes and gateway to Roanoke Island. Its main town, Manteo, is famous as the location of the first British settlement in the New World, which vanished in 1590. The mystery is explored in the Waterside Theatre's production of *The Lost Colony*, a play performed outdoors here since 1937. Inarguably the nicest place to stay in town is the aptly named Tranquil House Inn, overlooking the waterfront and offering 25 sunny rooms and the nautical-themed 1587 Restaurant.

Continue south to Cape Hatteras National Seashore and check out the candy-striped Cape Hatteras Lighthouse, the tallest traditional lighthouse in North America, and tiny Ocracoke Island's exceptionally pretty beaches.

The southern end of the region encompasses Cape Lookout National Seashore, where wild horses have roamed for centuries. Skip inland to Beaufort, founded in 1713, and visit the North Carolina Maritime Museum. Then join the locals who frequent the white clapboard Beaufort Grocery Company for its homemade gumbo, a much-loved specialty.

Where: 225 miles east of Durham. **Visitor info:** www.outerbanks.org. **The Sanderling:** Tel 800-701-4111 or 252-261-4111; www.thesanderling.com. *Cost:* from $110 (off-peak), from $250 (peak); dinner at the Left Bank $85, at the Lifesaving Station $40. **Waterside Theatre:** Tel 252-473-3414; www.thelostcolony.org. *When:* late May–mid-Aug. **Tranquil House Inn:** Tel 800-458-7069 or 252-473-1404; www.1587.com. *Cost:* from $109 (off-peak), from $199 (peak); dinner $40. **North Carolina Maritime Museum:** Tel 252-728-7317; www.ncmaritime.org. **Beaufort Grocery Company:** Tel 252-728-3899; www.beaufortgrocery.com. *Cost:* lunch $20. **Best times:** Mar–Apr and Sep–Oct for pleasant weather; mid-Jul for the original Wright Kite Festival at Kill Devil Hills.

Cleveland Rocks!!

Rock and Roll Hall of Fame and Museum

Cleveland, Ohio, U.S.A.

Architect I. M. Pei admitted to knowing little about the music in question when he was commissioned to design Cleveland's Rock and Roll Hall of Fame and Museum. After some remedial listening, he set off to create a building that would embody rock's brash dynamism while incorporating several of his signature elements: The glass pyramid echoes his Louvre Pyramid in Paris (see p. 114). It's an ideal home for the living heritage of rock—and it guarantees a pretty fun afternoon besides.

Exhibits are interactive—there's lots of sound and videos—make sure not to miss the collage of the 250-plus inductees (the museum hosts the annual induction ceremony every 3 years; New York City does the honors in between). The permanent collection includes instruments and stage costumes from the likes of Jimi Hendrix and Iggy Pop, but also unexpected items, such as Jim Morrison's Cub Scout uniform. Also on display are Janis Joplin's psychedelic Porsche, ZZ Top's 1933 Ford coupe, and even school report cards once belonging to John Lennon and Keith Moon of The Who (the latter's reads "shows promise in music").

Although it's home to the esteemed Cleveland Orchestra and musicians from Phil Ochs to Trent Reznor, Cleveland is hardly the hub of the music industry. However, it was native DJ Alan Freed who supposedly coined the term "rock and roll," and put on the country's first rock concert in 1952. The museum is just one of the stops on what's known as Ohio's "Hall of Fame Corridor," which includes the National Inventors' Hall of Fame in Akron and the hugely popular Pro Football Hall of Fame in Canton.

Info: Tel 800-493-7655 or 216-781-7625; www.rockhall.com.

Where the Wild West Lives On

Oklahoma City's Cowboy Culture

Oklahoma City, Oklahoma, U.S.A.

When cattlemen and cowboys come to Oklahoma City, they head straight for Stockyards City Main Street, a retail district smack in the center of town and chock-full of saddleries and Western-wear clothing stores.

It's right next to the Oklahoma National Stockyards, the world's largest stocker/feeder market, where every Monday and Tuesday you can watch live cattle being auctioned.

With their business dealings done, everyone heads for Cattlemen's Restaurant, the consummate Western steak house and the state's busiest restaurant. The most popular cut is rib eye quickly broiled over hot charcoal and served in a salty jus with homemade Parker House rolls. The original 1910 café is popular for breakfast, but the dinner crowd likes the 1960s-era South Dining Room. Settle into a red vinyl booth and enjoy the backlit wall-size panorama of two ranchers herding Black Angus. One of them is Gene Wade, who won the place in a craps game in 1945 and ran it until 1990.

Oklahoma has more horses per capita than any other state, and Oklahoma City has more horse shows than any other city in America. Stockyards City Main Street is at its best and busiest during competitions such as November's American Quarter Horse Association World Championship Show, where competitors from around the world show off their cowboy skills.

The Old West comes alive at the National Cowboy & Western Heritage Museum. The American Cowboy Gallery follows the evolution of the working cowboy in America, and there's a good permanent collection of Western artists, particularly Charles M. Russell and Frederic Remington. On Memorial Day weekend, ranch hands rustle up cowboy food at the museum's annual Chuck Wagon Gathering & Children's Cowboy Festival.

Oklahoma is home to 39 Native American tribes. Visit in June for any of the powwows that take place here or for the annual 3-day Red Earth Native American Cultural Festival. More than 1,200 Native American artists and dancers from more than 100 tribes come from across the nation (and Canada) to participate in ceremonial dance competitions, parades in full traditional dress, and a marketplace where it is as much fun to browse as it is to buy.

WHERE: 106 miles southwest of Tulsa. **OKLAHOMA NATIONAL STOCKYARDS:** Tel 405-235-8675; www.onsy.com. **CATTLEMEN'S RESTAURANT:** Tel 405-236-0416; www.cattlemensrestaurant.com. *Cost:* dinner $25. **NATIONAL COWBOY & WESTERN HERITAGE MUSEUM:** Tel 405-478-2250; www.nationalcowboymuseum.org.

A Treasure Trove of Art and Artifacts Devoted to the American West

GILCREASE MUSEUM

Tulsa, Oklahoma, U.S.A.

An unsurpassed repository for the best of the Old West, the Gilcrease Museum is the lasting legacy of Thomas Gilcrease, a one-eighth Creek Indian who struck it rich in 1905 when oil was found on his 160-acre allotment 20 miles south of Tulsa. Gilcrease spent his profits gleefully amassing the world's largest collection (some 400,000 items) of fine art, artifacts, and archives devoted to the American West.

When the price of oil dropped in the 1950s, rather than break up the collection, Gilcrease deeded the entire lot to the city of Tulsa. It includes artwork by Charles M. Russell, Frederic Remington, George Catlin, and John Singleton Copley. The Gilcrease Museum also has a large anthropology collection, with thousands of items—from 12,000-year-old Paleo-Indian tools to 20th-century Plains Indian beadwork.

Oil money is also behind Tulsa's other world-class collection, the Philbrook Museum of Art. Housed in an ornate 72-room 1920s Italian Renaissance villa that once belonged to oilman Waite Phillips, it's known for its fine Italian Renaissance and Baroque paintings.

The town of Tulsa itself is a sort of open-air museum, thanks to all the grand Art Deco homes that were built here from the 1920s to the 1940s to remind the world of the town's status as "Oil Capital of the World." Stop by the Warehouse Market Building, which houses Lyon's Indian Store, a beloved Oklahoma tradition since 1916. The Indian Store is considered the best place around to buy all the turquoise, Pendleton blankets, and Oklahoma beadwork your heart desires.

GILCREASE MUSEUM: Tel 888-655-2278 or 918-596-2700; www.gilcrease.org. **PHILBROOK MUSEUM OF ART:**: Tel 800-324-7941 or 918-749-7941; www.philbrook.org. **LYON'S INDIAN STORE:** Tel 918-582-6372.

Much Ado About Ashland

OREGON SHAKESPEARE FESTIVAL

Ashland, Oregon, U.S.A.

"Gentles, perchance you wonder at this show; but wonder on, till truth make all things plain," wrote William Shakespeare about the magic of theater. And that magic is abundantly on display every year at the Oregon Shakespeare Festival (OSF), the largest and longest-running celebration of the Bard in America. Today, upwards of 130,000 theater lovers attend performances at the festival's three state-of-the-art venues, including the outdoor Elizabethan Stage, fashioned after the 16th-century Fortune Theatre. The Tony Award–winning festival, which has staged performances in Ashland since 1935, is the home of the biggest rotating repertory theater in the country.

In addition to 11 plays presented annually, from mid-February through October, there are outdoor concerts, backstage tours, lectures, and discussions led by actors and scholars.

The festival's success is aided by the charm of Ashland, a small, lively city 15 miles north of the California border that has become the cultural—and gastronomic—center of southern Oregon. From the town's central plaza, lovely Lithia Park winds along Ashland Creek; park trails meander for miles, and there are possibilities for day trips galore in the mountainous region of southern Oregon, from visits to nearby vineyards to skiing at Mount Ashland in the winter months.

Built in 1900 as a railroad workers' boardinghouse, the beautifully updated Peerless Hotel offers tasteful rooms with luxurious comforts. These take a backseat to its restaurant next door, one of the best in town. Even closer to the festival, the Winchester Inn offers polished accommodations in an 1886 Victorian mansion, carriage house, and two neighboring homes, all surrounded by an English cottage–style garden. Guests enjoy a sumptuous breakfast, but even if you're not staying there book a table for dinner at the Winchester's celebrated restaurant, where local ingredients and an award-winning wine list heavy on Oregon's best are the lures.

WHERE: 285 miles south of Portland. Tel

800-219-8161 or 541-482-4331; www.osfashland.org. *When:* mid-Feb–Oct. **Peerless Hotel and Restaurant:** Tel 541-488-1082; www.peerlesshotel.com. *Cost:* from $85 (off-peak), from $160 (peak); dinner $35. **The Winchester Inn:** Tel 800-972-4991 or 541-488-1113; www.winchesterinn.com. *Cost:* from $150 (off-peak), from $195 (peak); dinner $50. **Best times:** May–Oct for nicest weather; July 4 for live music and celebrations.

A Majestic Cleft in the Cascade Volcanoes

The Columbia River Gorge

Oregon and Washington, U.S.A.

The Columbia River's enormous 80-mile-long gorge through the Cascade Mountains is one of the most dramatic destinations in the Pacific Northwest, its splendor so remarkable that in 1986 Congress designated it the first of America's National Scenic Areas. The mile-wide river, flanked by volcanic sentinels Mount Hood (in Oregon) and Mount Adams (in Washington), flows between basalt walls rising 4,000 feet. And all this beauty—plus excellent hiking trails and world-class windsurfing—is just an hour's drive from Portland.

This awe-inspiring chasm is the only sea-level passage through the Sierra and Cascade ranges, making it a major transportation corridor for centuries. Lewis and Clark passed through the gorge in 1805–6. The gorge would later become the final challenge to pioneers on the Oregon Trail, and it was only opened up to automobiles in 1916, by means of the Historic Columbia River Highway. Although much of this route has been subsumed by fast-moving I-84, remnants of the winding roadway are by far the best routes for exploring the gorge.

The town of Hood River, the hub of the gorge, enjoys a certain renown as the windsurfing capital of the world. South of the city, above the Hood River Valley stands massive Mount Hood, the very symbol of Oregon. In 1906 a rail line was built to carry lumber and, later, the valley's bounty of fruit. The Mount Hood Railroad now ferries day-trippers between Hood River and Parkdale.

Benson Footbridge provides a spectacular view of Multnomah Falls.

West of Hood River, a segment of the Historic Columbia River Highway climbs past the greatest concentration of waterfalls in North America—77 on the Oregon side of the river alone. The most spectacular of all is Multnomah Falls, the second highest year-round waterfall in the U.S. (after Yosemite Falls; see p. 733), with a total drop of 620 feet.

Riverboat cruises aboard the *Columbia Gorge* sternwheeler depart from the town of Cascade Locks, offering modern-day travelers a chance to see the river as early pioneers did.

WHERE: The gorge follows the Washington-Oregon border for 80 miles, beginning 56 miles east of Portland, west to Biggs. **MT. HOOD RAILROAD:** Tel 800-872-4661 or 541-386-3556; www.mthoodrr.com. *When:* Apr–Dec. ***COLUMBIA GORGE* STERNWHEELER:** Tel 800-224-3901 or 503-224-3900; www.sternwheeler.com. *When:* May–Oct. **WHERE TO STAY:** Columbia Gorge Hotel is a landmark in Hood River, with river views. Tel 800-345-1921 or 541-386-5566; www.columbiagorgehotel.com. *Cost:* from $250. **BEST TIME:** May–Oct for nicest weather.

Nature's Theater in the Round

CRATER LAKE NATIONAL PARK

Oregon, U.S.A.

Most visitors are drawn to Crater Lake by its perfect, jewel-like beauty, unaware of its catastrophic geological origins. Oregon's only national park had its beginnings about 7,700 years ago when a phenomenal eruption caused the massive Mount Mazama (once 12,000 feet high) to collapse inward on itself. The resulting 6-mile-wide caldera slowly filled with water; its lowest point is 1,943 feet from the surface, making it the nation's deepest lake. The cold, calm, and exceptionally clear water doesn't fill the caldera all the way to its rim; a steep mile-long trail on the lake's north side leads down to the shore, where hikers can board a tour boat (the only boat aside from research vessels permitted on the lake) and cruise to Wizard Island. The 33-mile Rim Drive encircles the 21-square-mile lake and offers a dazzling view for motorists, hikers, and bicyclists. In winter, heavy snowfall closes the drive to vehicles, and it becomes a breathtaking place to cross-country ski or snowshoe on a ranger-guided tour.

Construction on Crater Lake Lodge began in 1909, and a 1990s renovation is responsible for its present rustic elegance. The Great Hall's massive stone fireplace and broad picture windows framing the cobalt blue lake are in the tradition of other great national park lodges and make it the finest in the Pacific Northwest.

Take in the present-day splendor of the Cascade Mountains' fierce past on the 500-mile Volcanic Legacy Scenic Byway, which starts at the park and heads south past the town of Klamath Falls into California, where it skirts Mount Shasta and terminates just south of Lassen Peak and Lassen Volcanic National Park.

WHERE: 181 miles south of Portland. Tel 541-594-3000; www.nps.gov/crla. *When:* park open year-round; boat tours mid-Jul–mid-Sep; Rim Drive late Jun–mid-Oct, depending on snowfall. **CRATER LAKE LODGE:** Tel 888-774-2728 or 541-830-8700; www.craterlakelodges.com. *Cost:* lake view from $200. *When:* late May–mid-Oct. **VOLCANIC LEGACY BYWAY:** www.volcaniclegacybyway.org. **BEST TIMES:** Jul–Aug for nice weather; mid-Jul for wildflowers.

Rugged Masterpiece of the Natural World

THE OREGON COAST

Oregon, U.S.A.

Sculpted by the turbulent waves of the Pacific, Oregon's 362-mile coastline is one of nature's masterworks. Thanks to a farsighted state government in the 1910s, the entire length was set aside as public land, with most of it still nearly undeveloped.

For one of the most awe-inspiring road trips in America, follow the Beaver State portion of Highway 101 from north to south. Begin at the northern outpost of Astoria, a richly historic city northwest of Portland where the Columbia River (see p. 855) flows into the Pacific. At Cannon Beach, northern Oregon's most beautiful seaside village, the sandy shore stretches for miles, interrupted by massive basalt sea stacks like the iconic 235-foot Haystack Rock. Cannon Beach has retained its weathered-shingle seaside charm, exemplified by the Stephanie Inn, a boutique inn that's arguably the coast's most romantic getaway. Its sister property, the Surfsand Resort, is a perennial favorite with families and a cozy place for wintertime storm-watching.

At Neahkahnie Mountain, Highway 101 edges around 700-foot cliffs that drop into the surging Pacific. Not long after dipping inland around Tillamook's dairy and artichoke farms, 101 deposits travelers at the much-loved Salishan Spa & Golf Resort, south of Lincoln City on Siletz Bay. Set on 760 acres, this eco-friendly retreat has a reputation built largely around its championship-caliber Peter Jacobsen–designed golf course, as well as a superior restaurant and wine cellar showcasing the best of the Pacific Northwest.

At Newport, the central Oregon coast's largest city, the Oregon Coast Aquarium ranks as one of the state's top attractions, providing a fascinating glimpse into the region's marine environment and intertidal life. Or join a whale-watching tour either at the end of December or in March, when about 20,000 gray whales pass close to shore. Newport's quirky Sylvia Beach Hotel is dedicated to book lovers, with 20 guest rooms that evoke the spirit and work of various authors; even nonguests are welcome at the hotel's well-regarded Tables of Content restaurant.

South of Yachats (pronounced YA-hots) is the most rugged stretch of the Oregon coast. There Cape Perpetua towers 830 feet above the roiling waters, providing scenic overlooks. A little farther south is Heceta Head Lighthouse, a stark white gem on a rocky headland 205 feet above the Pacific that is still in operation. The beautifully maintained 1894 lighthouse keeper's home is open as a B&B (and is particularly known for its breakfast). Take in the nearby Sea Lion Caves, the largest natural sea grotto in the country.

South of Florence, the Oregon Dunes extend along the coast for over 40 miles. Hiking trails explore the mighty, ever-shifting sand formations, some measuring 500 feet high. From Charleston south to the California border, the beaches are home to rookeries of puffins and penguin-like murres. Farther south is Bandon Dunes Golf Resort, equal parts New Age retreat and golf mecca (on the short list of the nation's best). There are three other top-ranked courses nearby: Pacific Dunes, Bandon Trails, and the newest, Old Macdonald. The state's most famous river, the fast-flowing Rogue, meets the Pacific at Gold River; follow the river upstream 7 miles to the excellent Tu Tu' Tun Lodge, offering opportunities for unmatched fishing and exhilarating jet-boat trips on the river's surging rapids.

Where: from Astoria, 95 miles northwest of Portland, to Brookings, 318 miles south of Portland. **Visitor info:** www.visittheoregon coast.com. **Stephanie Inn:** Tel 800-633-3466 or 503-436-2221; www.stephanie-inn.com. *Cost:* from $359. **Surfsand Resort:** Tel 800-547-6100 or 503-436-2274; www.surfsand .com. *Cost:* from $140 (off-peak), from $430 (peak). **Salishan Spa & Golf Resort:** Tel 888-725-4742 or 541-764-2371; www .salishan.com. *Cost:* from $160 (off-peak), from $180 (peak); greens fees from $60 (off-peak), from $99 (peak). **Oregon Coast Aquarium:** Tel 541-867-3474; www.aquarium .org. **Sylvia Beach Hotel:** Tel 888-795-8422 or 541-265-5428; www.sylviabeach hotel.com. *Cost:* from $100; dinner $25. **Heceta Head Lighthouse:** Tel 866-547-3696 or 541-547-3696; www.hecetalight house.com. *Cost:* from $135 (off-peak), from

In Oregon's northwest corner, colossal rocks break up Cannon Beach's peaceful coastline.

$210 (peak). **Bandon Dunes Golf Resort:** Tel 888-345-6008 or 541-347-4380; www .bandondunesgolf.com. *Cost:* from $100 (off-peak), from $200 (peak); greens fees from $75 (off-peak), from $220 (peak). **Tu Tu' Tun Lodge:** Tel 800-864-6357 or 541-247-6664; www.tututun.com. *Cost:* from $135 (off-peak), from $235 (peak); dinner $60. **Best times:** mid-Dec–mid-Jan and Mar–Jun for whale-watching; Jun–Sep for warmer weather; Apr–Sep for sea lion viewing at Sea Lion Caves.

The Way that Napa Used to Be

Willamette Valley

Oregon, U.S.A.

At the end of the historic Oregon Trail, close to 10,000 acres of rolling vineyards unfold in the northern Willamette Valley, less than an hour's drive south of Portland. It's one of two wine-producing regions that have helped make the state the envy of vintners from California to France.

The first vineyards were planted in the valley in the 1960s; today pinot noir is the undisputed leader, though pinot gris and chardonnay thrive here as well. Route 99W, the main road through Yamhill County—the heart of northern Oregon's wine country—is frequently clogged with traffic, but the back roads also wind through vineyards and oak groves and are ideal for bicycling or a lazy drive. Many of the area's 200 (mostly boutique) wineries operate tasting rooms, and most are open daily in summer and on weekends in winter.

Here you'll find the small towns of Newberg—home of Rex Hill, where the wines and gardens both warrant a stop—and Dundee, whose Argyle Winery produced one of the first Oregon wines served at the White House. Ponzi Vineyards, just south of Beaverton, turns out top-shelf pinot noirs, while the village of Dayton is the site of the area's most acclaimed dining room at the Joel Palmer House.

At Wine Country Farm B&B and Cellars, you'll enjoy sweeping views of the estate's vineyards from the 1910 farmhouse, along with access to their popular wine-tasting rooms. The chic and comfortable nine-suite Brookside Inn is situated on 22 tranquil acres, a former religious retreat that now draws visitors who revere wine and good food. The Allison Inn & Spa is a handsome newcomer with 85 rooms enveloped in 35 acres of gardens and pinot noir vineyards. The popular restaurant, JORY, along with the spa, entices guests never to leave the grounds. Don't give in to the temptation—the rest of this oenophile's paradise is too good to miss.

WHERE: Newberg is 15 miles southwest of Portland. **VISITOR INFO:** www.oregonwine country.org. **REX HILL:** Tel 800-739-4455 or 503-538-0666; www.rexhill.com. **ARGYLE WINERY:** Tel 888-427-4953 or 503-538-8520; www.argylewinery.com. **JOEL PALMER HOUSE:** Tel 503-864-2995; www.joelpalmerhouse.com. *Cost:* dinner $50. **WINE COUNTRY FARM:** Tel 800-261-3446 or 503-864-3446; www .winecountryfarm.com. *Cost:* from $150. **BROOKSIDE INN:** Tel 503-852-4433; www .brooksideinn-oregon.com. *Cost:* from $185. **THE ALLISON INN:** Tel 503-554-2525; www .theallison.com. *Cost:* from $295; dinner $60. **BEST TIMES:** last weekend in May and Nov for special tastings; late Jul for International Pinot Noir Celebration in McMinnville.

A Shrine to the Civil War's Fallen

Gettysburg National Military Park

Gettysburg, Pennsylvania, U.S.A.

If there is a home for the soul of America, it is almost certainly Gettysburg, the nation's most visited Civil War battlefield. Here, in July 1863, the Union and Confederate armies clashed in the bloodiest battle ever fought on American soil. In three days of fighting, more than 51,000 men were killed, wounded, captured, or went missing (nearly a third of all who fought there). Though the war dragged on for nearly two more years, Gettysburg was the turning point as the South's last major offensive drive in the North.

This monument memorializes the 1st Pennsylvania Cavalry.

Four months after the battle, Abraham Lincoln read the brief words of his Gettysburg Address at the dedication of the Soldier's National Cemetery, where 3,512 soldiers were interred. Today the battlefield's 6,000-acre grounds are protected as a national park, with more than 1,300 statues, monuments, and cannons marking 26 miles of roads that wend past the most legendary sites and the field on which the Confederate army sustained more than 5,000 casualties in 50 minutes. Stop by the Visitor Center to see the fully restored 42-foot-high 1884 *Battle of Gettysburg* cyclorama, which features a 360-degree view of General George Pickett's Confederate infantry charge, and a 22-minute film, *A New Birth of Freedom*, narrated by Morgan Freeman. The attached Gettysburg Museum of the American

Civil War shows highlights from a collection of more than 300,000 objects and artifacts.

Of the many commemorative events held during the week of July Fourth, the skirmishes reenacted near the park by uniformed volunteers are the highlight. Take some quiet time to recall the words of Col. Joshua Lawrence Chamberlain at the 1889 dedication of the monument to his troops: "Generations that know us not and that we know not of, heart-drawn to see where and by whom great things were suffered and done for them, shall come to this deathless field to ponder and dream."

WHERE: 30 miles south of Harrisburg. **VISITOR INFO:** www.gettysburgcvb.org. **GETTYSBURG CYCLORAMA & MUSEUM:** Tel 717-334-1124; www.nps.gov/gett. **WHERE TO STAY:** It's a 15-minute drive to the former plantation of Antrim 1844, Taneytown, MD. Tel 800-858-1844 or 410-756-6812; www.antrim1844.com. *Cost:* from $160 (off-peak), from $235 (peak). **BEST TIMES:** late May for Memorial Day commemoration; 1st week of Jul for anniversary events and battle reenactment; mid-Jun–mid-Aug for free ranger-guided programs.

Where the Plain People Live

PENNSYLVANIA DUTCH COUNTRY

Lancaster, Berks, and adjacent counties, Pennsylvania, U.S.A.

Pennsylvania's Amish and Mennonite communities have lived here peacefully since the 1720s, when they arrived as part of William Penn's grand experiment. Today the largely agricultural counties of southeastern Pennsylvania are home to some 50,000 of the "Plain People." Members of the strict Old Order Amish, about 25,000 strong, wear traditional dark clothing, get around on foot or in horse-drawn buggies, educate their own, and live mainly by farming. Those belonging to more liberal groups live less isolated from society.

The "English" (that means all outsiders) are expected to respect the communities' privacy. Area towns—with names like Paradise and Bird-in-Hand—each have attractions and B&Bs to recommend them. The city of Lancaster features the Lancaster Cultural History Museum, the Lancaster Quilt & Textile Museum, and a bustling Central Market built in 1889 on a site in use since the 1730s. Stop in for crafts and locally grown produce and shoofly pie. For an overnight, the Kings Cottage B&B provides eight classically elegant rooms in a 1913 Spanish-style mansion whose owners are helpful and friendly.

The small town of Lititz, to the north, was founded by Moravians in the late 1700s. Today its Main Street boasts Colonial buildings that house antiques shops and gift stores (where you might pick up a decorative hex sign) and the Sturgis Pretzel House, the oldest commercial pretzel bakery in the U.S.

Neighboring Ephrata is known for the cloister founded by Conrad Beissel and his followers, who built the settlement in the mid-1700s (a dozen restored buildings are open for tours) while practicing their blend of proto-mysticism, Anabaptism, and celibacy. The Historic Smithton Inn, originally a stagecoach stop here, has been welcoming guests since 1763. About 12 miles east, in Churchtown, the Inn at Twin Linden features bucolic grounds, country-elegant guest rooms, and a lovely Saturday night dinner.

Where: Amish heartland is 60 miles west of Philadelphia. **Visitor info:** www.padutchcountry.com. **Central Market:** Tel 717-291-4723. *When:* Tues, Fri, and Sat. **Kings Cottage:** Tel 800-747-8717 or 717-397-1017; www.kingscottagebb.com. *Cost:* from $160. **Ephrata Cloister:** Tel 717-733-6600; www.ephratacloister.org. **Historic Smithton Inn:** Tel 877-755-4590 or 717-733-6094; www.historicsmithtoninn.com. *Cost:* from $120. **Inn at Twin Linden:** Tel 866-445-7614 or 717-445-7619; www.innattwinlinden.com. *Cost:* from $130; Saturday dinner $55. **Best times:** early Jul for Kutztown Festival, the country's oldest folklife festival; Christmastime for lantern tours at Ephrata Cloister.

The Birthplace of American Democracy

Independence National Historical Park

Philadelphia, Pennsylvania, U.S.A.

The L-shaped swath surrounding the old Pennsylvania State House (now Independence Hall) stands as the most important historic district in any American city. Created by an act of Congress in 1948, Independence National Historical Park encompasses almost 55 acres, with 20 buildings open to the public.

Independence Hall, built between 1732 and 1753, is not only where the Declaration of Independence was debated and approved, but also where the Articles of Confederation were adopted in 1781 and the U.S. Constitution was finally enacted in 1787. Original copies of all three documents are displayed, along with the silver inkstand used in their signing.

Next door is Congress Hall, which served as the home of the U.S. Congress from 1790 to 1800, while nearby the new Liberty Bell Center houses the most famous bell in the world, inscribed with the words "Proclaim Liberty throughout all the land unto all the inhabitants thereof." It is believed that the 2,000-pound bell was rendered unringable in 1846 after it was sounded in honor of the late George Washington's birthday.

A block and a half east of Independence Hall, Carpenters Hall was the site of the first meeting of the Continental Congress in 1774, and a few blocks north lies Franklin Court, where Benjamin Franklin made his last home. It now houses several museums that include some of Franklin's possessions. The Betsy Ross House is nearby, where she is said to have created the original American flag; the house and workshop have been restored to their 1777 appearance.

Because it is famously cracked, the Liberty Bell hasn't rung since 1846.

The City Tavern was a regular haunt of Jefferson, Adams, and Franklin. Rebuilt in 1976, it offers an 18th-century dining experience, right down to the pepperpot soup and beers brewed using Washington's and Jefferson's own recipes.

The City of Brotherly Love blossoms in early March when the Philadelphia International Flower Show comes to town. Held every year since 1829, it transforms 10 acres into a fantasy of bursting buds and blooming trees.

INFO: Tel 877-444-6777 or 215-965-7676; www.independencevisitorcenter.com. **FRANKLIN COURT:** Tel 800-537-7676 or 215-965-7676. **BETSY ROSS HOUSE:** Tel 215-686-1252; www.betsyrosshouse.org. **CITY TAVERN:** Tel 215-413-1443; www.citytavern.com. *Cost:* dinner $40. **PHILADELPHIA INTERNATIONAL FLOWER SHOW:** Tel 215-988-8899; www.theflowershow.com. *When:* early Mar. **WHERE TO STAY:** from the Omni Hotel at Independence Park it's an easy stroll to historical sights. Tel 800-843-6664 or 215-925-0000; www.omnihotels.com. *Cost:* from $250. **BEST TIMES:** Mar–Oct for Lights of Liberty walking tour; on and around July 4 for city-wide celebrations.

Temples of Culture in the City of Brotherly Love

Philadelphia Museum of Art and the Barnes Foundation

Philadelphia, Pennsylvania, U.S.A.

Standing like a Roman temple at the head of the broad, tree-lined Benjamin Franklin Parkway, the Philadelphia Museum of Art is among the country's largest art museums and one of its best, with a permanent collection of more than 225,000 objects housed in more than 200 galleries. Still, the movie *Rocky* is on most visitors' minds when they arrive and many attempt the sprint up the 72 steps (Rocky's statue can be found at the foot of the steps).

The museum's outstanding American collection holds an impressive number of paintings by 19th-century Philadelphia artist Thomas Eakins. Its European galleries include masterpieces such as Van Gogh's *Sunflowers* and Cézanne's *Large Bathers*. Among the modern and contemporary pieces are works by Picasso, Dalí, Miró, Léger, de Kooning, and Pollock, plus the world's largest collection of works by Marcel Duchamp.

Another home to many of Philadelphia's art treasures, the Barnes Foundation, will soon move from suburban Merion to a more central location just minutes from the Philadelphia Museum of Art. The foundation was established in 1922 by Dr. Albert C. Barnes, a self-made millionaire, and has since amassed one of the world's premier private art collections. The new complex, scheduled to open in 2012, is intended to replicate the look of the original Merion site, with indoor gardens and masterworks alongside everyday items. The Barnes holds one of the most important collections of French Impressionist and post-Impressionist paintings anywhere, and you can expect to find 181 works by Renoir alone, and countless others by Cézanne, Matisse, and Picasso as well as Van Gogh, Degas, Monet, Manet, Goya, and El Greco.

Philadelphia Museum of Art: Tel 215-763-8100; www.philamuseum.org. **Barnes Foundation:** Tel 610-667-0290; www.barnesfoundation.org.

Life, Liberty, and the Pursuit of Cheesesteaks

Philly Food

Philadelphia, Pennsylvania, U.S.A.

Philadelphia's vibrant restaurant scene continues to gain recognition, but it will first and foremost be associated with—and loved for—its humble cheesesteak. Leaving Philly without sampling one would be like going to Napa and not sipping the wine.

Local legend has it that in 1930, South Philly hot dog vendor Pat Olivieri, tired of eating his own grub for lunch, tossed some shaved steak slices and onions onto his griddle and piled it on some Italian bread. In time, cheese entered the mix, and fans like Humphrey Bogart and Frank Sinatra pumped up the sandwich's cachet. Today you can visit Pat's, the restaurant Olivieri opened at Philly's famed 9th Street Italian Market, the country's oldest and largest working outdoor market. The ramshackle corner joint is still run by the Olivieri family, still open 24 hours, and still serving from a take-out window. Although American and provolone cheeses are available, the classic is "whiz, wit'," a steak smothered in gobs of molten Cheez Whiz with onions.

Geno's is open 24 hours a day.

Right across the intersection is Pat's nemesis since 1966, Geno's. Though bright compared to Pat's Depression-era authenticity, it offers essentially the same menu, fueling a friendly rivalry. Jim's Steaks (also known for their hoagies—Philly-speak for submarine sandwiches) is in the running too. Try all three if your arteries can bear it, or head over to the Reading Terminal Market, a huge late-19th-century railroad shed and wander among 80-plus food stalls manned by artisanal vendors and Amish farmers selling Pennsylvania Dutch specialties among others. Be sure to visit the marble counter at Bassett's, which has been selling rich ice cream since the market opened in 1892.

At the other end of the culinary spectrum are a number of the city's celebrated restaurants. Try the authentic Italian cuisine at celebrated chef Marc Vetri's Vetri Ristorante, a small, rustic place where dishes such as roasted capretto with soft polenta are served alongside fazzoletti ("little handkerchiefs") with duck ragu. Lacroix at the Rittenhouse is as favored for its elegant, special-occasion setting as for its food—a subtle mix of tried-and-true favorites and experimental creations from chef Jon Cichon. Nearby, the cozy Rittenhouse 1715 offers 23 luxuriously appointed guest rooms in a former 19th-century carriage house.

Pat's: Tel 215-468-1546; www.patskingofsteaks.com. **Geno's:** Tel 215-389-0659; www.genosteaks.com. **Jim's Steaks:** Tel 215-928-1911; www.jimssteaks.com. **Reading Terminal Market:** Tel 215-922-2317; www.readingterminalmarket.org. **Vetri Ristorante:** Tel 215-732-3478; www.vetriristorante.com. *Cost:* dinner $60. **Lacroix at the Rittenhouse:** Tel 215-790-2533; www.lacroixrestaurant.com. *Cost:* dinner $65. **Rittenhouse 1715:** Tel 877-791-6500 or 215-546-6500; www.rittenhouse1715.com. *Cost:* from $160. **Best time:** mid-May weekend for 9th Street Italian Market Festival.

Eleven Square Miles of Yankee Paradise

Block Island

Rhode Island, U.S.A.

Unpretentious Block Island is a barefoot-and-bicycle kind of place, with rolling green hills, hundreds of freshwater ponds, and dramatic 250-foot bluffs that remind many of Ireland. So bewitching is it that the Nature Conservancy was inspired to call the island "one of the last great places in the Western Hemisphere."

Not much happened here until tourists began arriving in the 1870s (leading to a boom in the construction of grand Victorian hotels). Today, on peak summer weekends, up to 16,000 tourists flock to this 11-square-mile New England gem.

Despite the island's popularity, there is no Martha's Vineyard–style social fuss. Residents and visitors tend to be quiet and protective of the natural beauty around them; a third of the island is set aside as wildlife refuge, with more than 30 miles of hiking trails and gorgeous cliffside biking paths. The island is ringed by some 17 miles of beach, while the Great Salt Pond harbors hundreds of pleasure boats, most from nearby Newport (see next page). Situated on the Atlantic flyway, it's a favorite of bird-watchers during the autumn migrations, when huge flocks representing more than 150 species pass through.

Dubbed the "Bermuda of the North" during its Victorian-era heyday, Block Island still boasts a number of rambling porch-fringed buildings, which wear their age with dignity. The Hotel Manisses is a big 1870s charmer that surprises by way of its upscale restaurant with garden seating. (Order the signature lobster mashed potatoes.) Of a number of sister properties, the nearby 1661 Inn is the most inviting while the ten-room Sea Breeze Inn is delightful: It sits on a bluff overlooking the ocean and is surrounded by flowering gardens.

Where: 12 miles south of mainland Rhode Island. **Visitor info:** www.blockislandchamber.com. **How:** Ferries depart from Pt. Judith year-round. Seasonal departures from Newport; New London, CT; and Montauk, NY. **Hotel Manisses and 1661 Inn:** Tel 800-626-4773 or 401-466-2421; www.blockislandresorts.com. *Cost:* Manisses from $75 (off-peak), from $220 (peak); dinner $40. 1661 Inn from $90 (off-peak), from $340 (peak). *When:* Hotel Manisses, Apr–Oct; 1661 Inn, year-round. **Sea Breeze Inn:** Tel 800-786-2276 or 401-466-2275; www.seabreezeblockisland.com. *Cost:* from $160 (off-peak), from $230 (peak). **Best times:** May–mid-Jun and mid-Sep–Oct for fewer crowds; Aug for nicest weather; Sep–Oct for bird-watching.

Seaside Cottages of the Gilded Age

NEWPORT MANSIONS AND THE CLIFF WALK

Newport, Rhode Island, U.S.A.

In the 19th century, wealthy, socially prominent families, such as the Vanderbilts and Astors, descended on Newport to escape the cities' summer heat in their seaside "cottages." Today about a dozen of these homes, each one grander than the last, are open to the public, including the undisputed showstopper The Breakers. A 70-room Renaissance-style palazzo completed in 1895 for Cornelius Vanderbilt II, it has a gilded 2,400-square-foot dining room lit by 12-foot chandeliers and a great hall that mimics an open-air courtyard.

Marble House was built for Cornelius's younger brother William between 1888 and 1892 in a style inspired by Marie Antoinette's Petit Trianon at Versailles. Rosecliff is another favorite, a relatively intimate 40-room manse built in 1902 by architect Stanford White. Newport's 8 square miles are filled with many other impressive examples of 18th- and 19th-century architecture, including 83 structures that are preserved by the Newport Restoration Foundation, created by tobacco heiress Doris Duke in 1968. Her own mansion, Rough Point, is also open for tours.

Enjoy wonderful mansion views along the 3.5-mile Cliff Walk that wends 30 feet above the shoreline. The Chanler at Cliff Walk was the first to be built on the historic trail, in 1873. After many reincarnations, it operates today as an opulent oceanfront inn, with 20 handsomely appointed rooms scattered between its French Empire Mansion and villas, and an elegant restaurant called the Spiced Pear. A more secluded rest awaits at the Gatsbyesque Castle Hill Inn, an 1874 waterfront mansion sitting on its own grassy peninsula just off the spectacular 10-mile Ocean Drive.

Influential architect Richard Morris Hunt designed The Breakers.

Newport is also the spiritual and physical center of the U.S. sailing universe, hosting more than 40 races annually. The New York Yacht Club sailors, who maintain their summer base here and have defended the America's Cup race title for 132 years, hold their annual regatta in June. You can also see the historic Annapolis to Newport Race during odd-numbered years and the famed Newport Bermuda Race in even-numbered years. When it's time to eat, boat folks gravitate to the boisterous Black Pearl, a waterfront mainstay, or the more refined White Horse Tavern, in business since 1687.

VISITOR INFO: www.gonewport.com. **PRESERVATION SOCIETY:** (info on visiting the mansions) Tel 401-847-1000; www.newportmansions.org. *When:* The Breakers closed early Jan–Apr; others closed seasonally. **THE**

Chanler: Tel 866-793-5664 or 401-847-2244; www.thechanler.com. *Cost:* from $320 (off-peak), from $800 (peak); dinner $60. **Castle Hill Inn:** Tel 888-466-1355 or 401-849-3800; www.castlehillinn.com. *Cost:* from $275 (off-peak), from $575 (peak); brunch $40. **Black Pearl:** Tel 401-846-5264; www.blackpearlnewport.com. *Cost:* dinner $35. **White Horse Tavern:** Tel 401-849-3600; www.whitehorsetavern.us. *Cost:* dinner $50. **Best times:** Jun and Jul for regattas; early–mid-Aug for JVC Jazz Festival & Newport Folk Festival; Dec for Christmas decorations at The Breakers and Marble House.

Where the Old Times Aren't Forgotten

Beaufort and the Lowcountry

South Carolina, U.S.A.

The honeycombed coastline south of Charleston stretches for 200 miles, dissolving into peninsulas, channels, and subtropical Sea Islands that make up the South Carolina lowcountry. Kiawah Island is a key player, enjoying proximity to Charleston and boasting one of the most talked-about golf resorts in North America (tennis and beach sports are also stellar). Its Sanctuary Hotel is a sumptuous choice for those who want to linger. Neighboring Hunting Island State Park, a nature reserve, is rife with loggerhead turtles, alligators, and herons.

The small waterfront town of Beaufort is the gateway to Sea Islands. Known for its many antebellum houses, Beaufort (pronounced BYEW-fert) has enjoyed something of a renaissance, thanks to its popularity with Hollywood: *The Big Chill*, *Forrest Gump*, and *The Prince of Tides* were all shot here, and many of the actors stayed at the Rhett House Inn. A short walk from the restored waterfront and main street, the white-columned 1820s inn epitomizes Southern hospitality.

St. Helena Island's Penn Center was established in 1862 as one of the first schools in the country for freed slaves. Its small museum is the cultural hub of the area's Gullah community. Members trace their roots to West Africa and their community was founded here in the early 18th century.

St. Helena's low-key Gullah Grub Restaurant is the perfect venue for red rice and shrimp, catfish chowder, and gumbo, or visit the roadside Shrimp Shack, where the fresh shrimp burgers explain the ever-present lines.

Not far from the Georgia border, Hilton Head Island presides as one of the most popular resort areas on the eastern seaboard. It's a seaside playground with 25 championship golf courses and some 300 tennis courts. A more authentic experience can be found inland at Palmetto Bluff; stay in one of 50 cabins on the moss-draped banks of the May River.

Where: Kiawah is 27 miles south of Charleston. **Visitor info:** www.beaufortsc.org. **Kiawah Island Golf Resort:** Tel 800-654-2924 or 843-768-2121; www.kiawahgolf.com. *Cost:* from $270 (off-peak), from $460 (peak); greens fees at Ocean Course $265 (off-peak), $360 (peak). **Rhett House Inn:** Tel 888-480-9530 or 843-524-9030; www.rhetthouseinn.com. *Cost:* from $175. **Penn Center:** Tel 843-838-2432; www.penncenter.com. **Gullah Grub Restaurant:** Tel 843-838-3841; www.gullahgrubs.com.

Cost: dinner $20. **Inn at Palmetto Bluff:** Tel 866-706-6565 or 843-706-6500; www.palmettobluffresort.com. *Cost:* from $475. **Best times:** Apr–Jun and mid-Sep–Jan for pleasant weather; May for Beaufort's Gullah Fest; early Oct for Beaufort's Shrimp Festival.

Nothing Could Be Finer

The Heart of Charleston

Charleston, South Carolina, U.S.A.

At the time of the American Revolution, Charleston stood as one of the young nation's largest, wealthiest, and most dynamic communities. Today this sultry and gracious metropolis at the confluence of the Cooper and Ashley rivers remains unparalleled in charm. Its wonderfully walkable historic district contains one of the nation's largest collections of Colonial architecture, and a fair share of distinctive Victorian buildings as well. Charleston also delights visitors with its antiques shops, amiable residents, and the city's emerging arts and food scenes.

Charleston became the symbol of Southern resistance when the first shots of the Civil War were fired at Union-occupied Fort Sumter, which still stands guard over Charleston Harbor. Take a crash course on the city's heritage at the Charleston Museum, the country's oldest (founded in 1773).

The city's architectural legacy can be traced to the days when cotton was king, and the fabulous wealth of planters and merchants financed the sumptuous antebellum homes that line the city's leafy streets. Tours of more than 150 private homes and walled gardens sell out well in advance of the annual springtime Festival of Houses and Gardens and the same goes for the equally popular Fall Tours of Homes and Gardens.

To truly experience a historic home, check into Two Meeting Street, the city's oldest continuously operating inn. The 1892 Queen Anne structure on the Battery waterfront is resplendent with Tiffany stained-glass windows and nine guest rooms brimming with antiques. Breakfasts are served in the shady pocket-size garden where magnolias bloom.

Another Charleston home turned inn is the spectacular 1886 Wentworth Mansion, which boasts Tiffany stained glass, marble fireplaces, and 21 spacious rooms and suites. Dine at Circa 1886 in the handsome carriage house just behind the inn, where chef Marc Collins creates artful lowcountry meals. The urbane Planters Inn is a quiet 64-room oasis despite its location alongside the bustling City Market. Its Peninsula Grill is considered a culinary temple of New South cuisine.

The city's role as cultural center of the pre–Civil War South continues today, with the Spoleto Festival U.S.A., a 17-day extravaganza featuring more than 120 performances

Antebellum homes line the Battery in Charleston.

from opera to dance. Started in 1977 as a sister event to the one in Spoleto, Italy (see p. 216), the festival ends with fireworks at the 18th-century Middleton Place plantation on the Ashley River. Dine early at its acclaimed restaurant, then stroll through America's first landscaped gardens.

VISITOR INFO: www.charlestoncvb.com. **FORT SUMTER:** Tel 843-883-3123; www.nps.gov/fosu. **CHARLESTON MUSEUM:** Tel 843-722-2996; www.charlestonmuseum.org. **FESTIVAL OF HOUSES AND GARDENS:** Historic Charleston Foundation. Tel 843-722-3405; www.historiccharleston.org. *When:* 4 weeks beginning mid-Mar. **FALL TOURS:** Preservation Society of Charleston. Tel 843-722-4630; www.preservationsociety.org. *When:* 5 consecutive long weekends beginning late Sep. **TWO MEETING STREET INN:** Tel 888-723-7322 or 843-723-7322; www.twomeetingstreet.com. *Cost:* from $230. **WENTWORTH MANSION:** Tel 888-466-1886 or 843-853-1886; www.wentworthmansion.com. *Cost:* from $330; dinner at Circa 1886 $60. **PLANTERS INN:** Tel 800-845-7082 or 843-722-2345; www.plantersinn.com. *Cost:* from $200; dinner at Peninsula Grill $55. **SPOLETO FESTIVAL:** Tel 843-579-3100; www.spoletousa.org. *When:* May–mid-Jun. **BEST TIMES:** Mar for blooms; Mar–May and Sep–Dec for pleasant weather.

A Marriage of the Old South and the New

LOWCOUNTRY CUISINE

Charleston, South Carolina, U.S.A.

The coastal areas of South Carolina and Georgia are the home of lowcountry cuisine, a harmonious blending of French, Spanish, African, and Caribbean influences, and Charleston is its culinary capital. Drawing upon traditional ingredients like shrimp, oysters, crab, rice, grits, okra, and fried greens, lowcountry food has enjoyed a creative spin in recent years.

At the city's most hallowed culinary institutions, such as the Peninsula Grill and Circa 1886 (see previous page), and the slightly more casual but still highly refined Magnolias, you'll find time-honored recipes alongside more innovative dishes. Similarly, at both Fig and Husk, the farm-to-table menus pay homage to the bounty of the lowcountry with an updated twist.

But to truly appreciate the high style of the new South, you've got to experience the homey excellence of the no-frills old South at Hominy Grill, a neighborhood restaurant whose devotees adore the breakfasts of buttermilk pancakes and biscuits with country ham and mushroom gravy. Lunch is great too.

Family-run Bowen's Island Restaurant is another down-home favorite, located on the outskirts of town and serving some of the best roasted oysters and the freshest shrimp around. Regulars wept when the original shack burned down in 2006. Luckily, you can still eat shovelfuls of bivalves, straight from Bowen's Island's own beds, in the new main dining room.

MAGNOLIAS: Tel 843-577-7771; www.magnolias-blossom-cypress.com. *Cost:* dinner $45. **FIG:** Tel 843-805-5900; www.eatatfig.com. *Cost:* dinner $45. **HUSK:** Tel 843-577-2500; www.huskrestaurant.com. *Cost:* lunch $20. **HOMINY GRILL:** Tel 843-937-0930; www.hominygrill.com. *Cost:* dinner $30. **BOWEN'S ISLAND:** Tel 843-795-2757; www.bowensislandrestaurant.com. *Cost:* dinner $15. **BEST TIMES:** late Jan–early Feb for Lowcountry Oyster Festival; early Oct for Taste of Charleston festival.

Nature's High Drama

Badlands National Park

South Dakota, U.S.A.

To the Lakota Sioux, they were the *mako shika*, the "bad lands." The French-Canadian fur trappers saw them as *"les mauvaises terres à traverser,"* "bad lands to travel across." But Frank Lloyd Wright described them as "an indescribable mysterious elsewhere . . . more spiritual than earth but created out of it."

This area once rested under an inland sea and later was a lush forest, and rich fossilized remains from both eras now lie beneath the surface. Above ground it's the "bones of the Badlands" that draw us. Sculpted by 75 million years of sedimentation and erosion and now preserved as a national park, the 244,000 acres are an eerily sparse yet spectacular landscape. Some rock formations rise more than 1,000 feet, while others wear bands of stratified mineral deposits—nature's brushstrokes.

Explore the Badlands by foot using either a quarter-mile loop or the little-used 10-mile Castle Trail. Or travel by car on the Badlands Loop. Nature's theatricality is most visible at dawn, dusk, and just after a rainfall, when the interplay of light and shadow is most poetic.

American Indians lived here for 11,000 years, but they were forced onto reservations when white homesteaders arrived in the late 19th century. In desperation, many became followers of the "Ghost Dance" religion. Fearing that the religious fervor could incite war, the Seventh Cavalry took a band of Sioux dancers into custody in December 1890. A scuffle at Wounded Knee Creek escalated into wholesale slaughter—nearly 300 Indians were killed. Today a simple memorial marks the site, approximately 45 miles south of the park.

Where: Northeast entrance is 88 miles southeast of Rapid City. Tel 605-433-5361; www.nps.gov/badl. **Best times:** Apr–Jun and Sep–Oct for nicest weather. Winter promises solitude.

Sacred Land of Heroes: Mount Rushmore and Crazy Horse

The Black Hills

South Dakota, U.S.A.

Named for the inky shade of their ponderosa pines, the Black Hills of South Dakota have been considered sacred by the Lakota Sioux for millennia. Today, because of the passions of a few artists, the land itself has become hallowed in a different way.

Conceived in 1924 by Danish-American sculptor Gutzon Borglum, the monument at Mount Rushmore was to be a "Shrine of Democracy," tracing the country's history by way of its leaders, from its birth (Washington) through its early growth (Jefferson), preservation (Lincoln), and later development (Teddy

Roosevelt). Seventeen years later Rushmore was transformed, with four enormous faces, six stories high, peering into the Black Hills.

The monument was an insult to native peoples. An 1868 treaty deeded the land to the Sioux "in perpetuity," but 6 years later, gold was discovered and the U.S. government reclaimed it. In 1876, when all Lakota bands were ordered onto reservations, the great chiefs Crazy Horse, Sitting Bull, and Gall organized a resistance that destroyed the Seventh Cavalry at General George Custer's Last Stand, at the Little Bighorn. But in less than two years Crazy Horse was dead, and the Sioux's fate was sealed.

The creation of the Crazy Horse Memorial is an ongoing project.

In 1939 the Sioux invited Boston-born sculptor Korczak Ziolkowski to carve the image of their own hero, Crazy Horse, into a Black Hills mountain 17 miles southwest of Rushmore. Unlike the monument at Mount Rushmore, Crazy Horse would be sculpted in the round: the great chief, sitting astride a horse, his arm outstretched. The memorial would also dwarf Rushmore at 563 feet high and 641 feet long, making it the largest monument on earth. Since Ziolkowski's death in 1982, his family has carried on with the work. A completion date is impossible to predict, but, as the project's motto says, "Never forget your dreams."

The monuments aren't the only reason to visit this region. The 71,000 rolling acres of Custer State Park hold one of the largest publicly owned buffalo herds, some 1,500 strong—though only a glimmer of the 60 million buffalo that once roamed the American prairie. The annual Buffalo Roundup brings the West's early days alive and includes a 3-day Buffalo Roundup Arts Festival and a popular chili cookoff. Drive the 18-mile Wildlife Loop Road, keeping an eye out for elk and eagles, or take in spectacular views on the scenic 14-mile Needles Highway.

Near the park's eastern border is the stone-and-pine State Game Lodge. Built in 1920, it was Calvin Coolidge's Summer White House in 1927. You can stay in his room, but less pricey options are also available.

WHERE: Mt. Rushmore is 25 miles southwest of Rapid City; www.nps.gov/moru. **CRAZY HORSE:** Tel 605-673-4681; www.crazyhorsememorial.org. **CUSTER STATE PARK:** Tel 605-773-3391; www.custerstatepark.info. **STATE GAME LODGE:** Tel 888-875-0001 or 605-255-4772; www.custerresorts.com. *Cost:* from $140. **BEST TIMES:** summer evenings for illumination ceremony of Rushmore, fireworks, and the Crazy Horse "Legends in Light" laser light show; late Sep for Buffalo Roundup.

Party!

STURGIS MOTORCYCLE RALLY

Sturgis, South Dakota, U.S.A.

For folks who like choppers, hogs, and all forms of motorbikes, there's no place like Sturgis, a small town (population 6,442) that annually hosts the biggest motorcycle rally in America. It was here, in 1936, that Clarence "Pappy" Hoel founded the Jackpine Gypsies Motorcycle Club, which held the first Black Hills Motor Classic, with nine participants, two years later. Today Sturgis attracts close to a half million people every August for a week of bike shows, concerts, races, demos, group rides, camaraderie, and plain old partying, with hundreds of vendors selling everything from food to tattoos. Attendees run the gamut from those who live by the Harley code to dentists and CEOs who don their leathers only on weekends. It's like Mardi Gras with chrome, though things have quieted down since the days when it was not unusual to see naked riders cruising down Main Street.

Yes, there's lots of booze (Jack Daniel's is a major sponsor); yes, there's a lot of rock 'n' roll (recent concerts have included ZZ Top and Kid Rock); and campgrounds like the Buffalo Chip get pretty wild; but Sturgis isn't all just one big party. Bike buffs can explore the Sturgis Motorcycle Museum and Hall of Fame or join posses of riders who hit the scenic byways of the Black Hills National Forest. Wall Drug Store, famous for its Great Depression marketing ploy of promising free water to customers, is nearby and sells everything from hand-tooled cowboy boots to horse liniment. Try a buffalo burger at the 520-seat restaurant and soak up the Western hospitality.

WHERE: 24 miles north of Rapid City. Tel 605-720-0800; www.sturgismotorcyclerally.com. *When:* early Aug. **BUFFALO CHIP CAMPGROUND:** Tel 605-347-9000; www.buffalochip.com. *Cost:* rally pass from $155, includes campsite, facilities use, and access to all concerts on the campground. **STURGIS MOTORCYCLE MUSEUM:** Tel 605-347-2001; www.sturgismuseum.com. **WALL DRUG STORE:** Tel 605-279-2175; www.walldrug.com. **WHERE TO STAY:** Holiday Inn Express is the newest and nicest of slim pickings. Tel 605-347-4140; www.hiexpress.com. *Cost:* from $155.

Cloaked in Blue Haze

THE GREAT SMOKY MOUNTAINS

Tennessee and North Carolina, U.S.A.

Rolling across 800 square miles of the southern Appalachians and straddling the Tennessee–North Carolina border, Great Smoky Mountains National Park is the most visited national park in the country. Visitors come to gaze at the 16 peaks rising higher than 5,000 feet and the plethora of native plant, fish, and animal species, which has led to the park's designation as an International Biosphere Reserve.

Among the world's oldest mountain ranges, the Smokies were named for the bluish haze that often shrouds them, water vapor emitted by the dense forests that cover 95 percent of the park. The 150 hiking trails range from easy walks to a rugged 70-mile stretch of the Appalachian Trail (see p. 756). About 550 miles of the park's approximately 800 miles of marked trails allow exploration on horseback, or you can enjoy it all by car on the Newfound Gap Road, whose 34 scenic miles link Gatlinburg, Tennessee, and Cherokee, North Carolina. The road's views encompass 6,593-foot Mount LeConte and Clingmans Dome, the park's highest peak at 6,643 feet.

Blackberry Farm is a kind of "Ritz-Carlton in the Woods," known for unparalleled country sophistication and luxe accommodations. Its 4,200-acre spread is an extension of the park's natural beauty; of the various activities on the menu, fly-fishing is king. Toast sundown with a shot of 20-year-old bourbon, then enjoy the southern-oriented "foothills cuisine" for which this upscale resort has won awards, served in its barnlike restaurants.

For a fraction of the cost, the contemporary, couples-only Butterfly Gap B&B offers five unique cottages on 900 acres that might lure you into thinking you have the Smokies to yourself. Those approaching from N.C. will be tempted to stop at the 250-acre hilltop retreat called The Swag. This charming 14-room inn, comprised of five historic buildings deftly outfitted in country-chic décor, has poetic views and a private hiking trail into the park.

Where: Tennessee's main park entrance is the Sugarlands Visitor Center, 2 miles south of Gatlinburg. Tel 865-436-1200; www.nps.gov/grsm. **Blackberry Farm:** Tel 800-648-2348 or 865-380-2260; www.blackberryfarm.com. *Cost:* from $395. **Butterfly Gap:** Tel 865-984-6021; www.butterflygap.com. *Cost:* from $195 (off-peak), from $215 (peak). **The Swag:** Tel 800-789-7672 or 828-926-0430; www.theswag.com. *Cost:* from $490, inclusive. *When:* late Apr–early Nov. **Best times:** May for spring flowers; Oct for foliage.

Newfound Gap is the lowest mountain pass through the Great Smokies.

The King's Castle on the Hill

Graceland

Memphis, Tennessee, U.S.A.

Elvis Presley's Graceland Mansion, where he lived from 1957 till his death on August 16, 1977, at the age of 42, is something of a hoot, but it is also intriguing and at times surprisingly moving. Most people have heard about the crystal chandeliers and the legendary Jungle Room, with its waterfall wall, shag-carpeted ceiling, and fake-fur upholstery. But irreverence soon fades: Graceland goes beyond simple kitsch.

Much of this experience has to do with the fans who travel thousands of miles to see the King's home and final resting place, in the Meditation Garden. It also has much to do with the greatness of Elvis himself, a poor boy from Mississippi who took the music of both the black and white South and ran them through a set of vocal cords that could get young girls, old women, and most likely God Himself all jittery. From the day the successful 22-year-old heartthrob moved in here with his mama and daddy in fulfillment of a boyhood promise to buy them the biggest house in town (it cost a whopping $102,500 at the time), Graceland was Elvis's escape and refuge, its lavishness a public display of the private excess that would be his downfall. Graceland today ranks as one of the nation's most visited homes, and its frozen-in-time living room, music room, dining room, kitchen, TV room, pool room, and Jungle Room are all open for visitors. Elsewhere within the 14-acre complex are a trophy hall lined with gold and platinum records, stage costumes, and mementos; Elvis's collection of 33 vehicles, including his famous 1955 pink Cadillac Fleetwood; and his two private jets. About 100 miles southeast of Memphis, true pilgrims can also visit Elvis's birthplace, a simple two-room home in Tupelo, Mississippi (see p. 818), where the King was born on January 8, 1935.

INFO: Tel 800-238-2000 or 901-332-3322; www.elvis.com. **WHERE TO STAY:** The kitsch-but-cool Heartbreak Hotel is across the street. Tel 877-777-0606 or 901-332-1000; www.elvis.com/epheartbreakhotel. *Cost:* from $140. **BEST TIMES:** Jan 8 for Elvis's birthday celebration; around Aug 16 (the anniversary of Presley's death) for Elvis Week.

It's All About the Pork

MEMPHIS BARBECUE

Memphis, Tennessee, U.S.A.

Though the competition is fierce among the various barbecue capitals in America, Memphis stands above the crowd. Unlike Texas barbecue, which is all about beef, BBQ in Memphis means pork, and it comes in two versions: pulled pork shoulder (shredded by hand) and ribs served either "wet" (with sauce) or "dry" (with a rub of spices and herbs).

The best of the smoky bunch just might be found at the Rendezvous, located in a busy cellar near the grand Peabody Hotel, known for the trained ducks that waddle through its lobby twice daily to the music of John Philip Sousa. For the full Rendezvous experience, order the dry charcoal-broiled ribs with red beans and rice. The other big Memphis name for dry ribs is Corky's Bar-B-Q, with a string of franchises across the country and a long list of well-loved dishes that keep the place packed.

The funkier, more down-home Payne's, housed in an old gas station near Graceland (see previous page), serves one of the most legendary chopped pork sandwiches in town. At another great casual joint, the paper-plate-style Cozy Corner, the specialties are BBQ Cornish hens and surprisingly tasty BBQ baloney sandwiches. Central BBQ, a relative newcomer, has developed a following for meaty ribs (both dry and wet) and thick-cut homemade potato chips. At the beloved Jim Neely's Interstate Bar-B-Que, tender pork ribs are slathered with a thick, sweet-and-tangy basting sauce, which also flavors the curiously delicious house specialty, barbecued spaghetti. This town even figured out how to barbecue pizza: Coletta's Italian Restaurant, open since 1923, is this category's self-proclaimed winner.

For all-around barbecue nirvana, show up at the cutthroat World Championship Barbecue Cooking Contest, part of the city's annual Memphis in May bash, where more than 200 teams from around the globe congregate to grill their secret recipes on the Mississippi waterfront.

RENDEZVOUS: Tel 901-523-2746; www.hogsfly.com. *Cost:* large ribs $18. **CORKY'S:** Tel 901-685-9744; www.corkysribsandbbq.com. **PAYNE'S:** Tel 901-272-1523. **COZY CORNER:** Tel 901-527-9158; www.cozycornerbbq.com. **CENTRAL BBQ:** Tel 901-272-9377; www.cbqmemphis.com. **INTERSTATE BAR-B-QUE:** Tel 901-775-2304; www.interstatebarbecue.com. **COLETTA'S:** Tel 901-948-7652; www.colettasrestaurant.com. **BARBECUE COOKING CONTEST:** Tel 901-525-4611; www.memphisinmay.org. *When:* mid-May.

Where Blues Legends Began Their Careers

The Memphis Music Scene

Memphis, Tennessee, U.S.A.

Hailed as home of the blues and the birthplace of rock 'n' roll, Memphis welcomes music enthusiasts from around the globe. They come to walk in the footsteps of Elvis Presley (see p. 872) and to see the haunts of blues legends Furry Lewis, Muddy Waters, B.B. King, and countless others. With its laid-back funk and unmistakable mojo, Memphis is the holy grail of American popular music.

Beale Street throbs with blues and rock bands every afternoon—and all night long. The best bets here for live music are B.B. King's Blues Club, named for the beloved guitarist who got his start here, and the Rum Boogie Café, which has a killer house band and a stellar guitar collection.

Beale Street's Rum Boogie Café dishes up Cajun and barbecue fare along with great music.

Elsewhere around town, hipsters jam at the grungy Hi-Tone Café, near the Memphis College of Art, while the no-frills juke joint Wild Bill's draws dancing-room-only crowds. Redemption awaits at the Full Gospel Tabernacle, where the Grammy Award–winning Reverend Al Green leads a hand-clapping, sing-out-to-Jesus service.

The Stax Museum of American Soul Music, on the site of the razed Stax recording studio, is chock-full of treasures, including vintage guitars, flashy threads, and Isaac Hayes's gold-trimmed Cadillac. The Memphis Rock 'n' Soul Museum offers a comprehensive look at the city's musical roots, from rural field hollers of the 1930s to the explosion of Sun, Stax, and Hi Records, as well as its global musical influence. Explore Elvis's early career at Sun Studio, where the King recorded his first hit, "That's All Right Mama," in 1954.

Today, artists and fans converge on the banks of the Mississippi for three rowdy days and nights in early May during the Beale Street Music Festival, which kicks off the annual monthlong extravaganza called Memphis in May. Rock, rap, gospel, country, and blues blare across the 33-acre Tom Lee Park, to host a rich array of hometown and visiting musical heroes.

B.B. King's Blues Club: Tel 800-443-0972 or 901-524-5464; http://memphis.bbkingclubs.com. **Rum Boogie Café:** Tel 901-528-0150; www.rumboogie.com. **Hi-Tone Café:** Tel 901-278-8663; www.hitonememphis.com. **Wild Bill's:** Tel 901-726-5473. **Full Gospel Tabernacle:** Tel 901-396-9192; www.algreenmusic.com. **Stax Museum:** Tel 888-942-7685 or 901-946-2535; www.soulsvilleusa.com. **Memphis Rock 'n' Soul Museum:** Tel 901-205-2533; www.memphisrocknsoul.org. **Sun Studio:** Tel 800-441-6249 or 901-521-0664; www.sunstudio.com. **Beale Street Music Festival:** Tel 901-525-4611; www.memphisinmay.org/music. **Best times:** mid-Aug for Elvis Week; early Sep for the Beale Street Labor Day Music Festival.

The Home of Country Music

THE GRAND OLE OPRY

Nashville, Tennessee, U.S.A.

Nashville has been known as "Music City, U.S.A." for the better part of a century, since the Grand Ole Opry began its weekend broadcast here in 1925. The world's longest-running live radio show, it was aired from downtown's Ryman Auditorium, revered as "the Mother Church of Country Music," from 1943 to 1974. The Ryman's stained-glass windows still attest to the building's original use as the Union Gospel Tabernacle; the concert hall's superior acoustics are favored by musicians of all genres.

The new incarnation of the Grand Ole Opry House is the modern 4,372-seat venue that dominates an area 20 minutes from town, known as Music Valley, where modern-day names and legendary old-timers perform traditional country, bluegrass, and rockabilly. But the Opry is the holy grail—from Hank Williams to Carrie Underwood, nearly every award winner has performed here. The Opry Museum is packed full of memorabilia that tells the story of the show that made country music famous.

Downtown, the Country Music Hall of Fame and Museum shows off an impressive hoard of artifacts, such as Elvis's 1960 "solid gold" Cadillac and Mother Maybelle Carter's 1928 Gibson guitar. From the museum, you can book a bus tour to the nearby Historic RCA Studio B, on Music Row, where Elvis, Chet Atkins, and others cut hit records.

For live music and a honky-tonk ambience, stop by the Bluebird Café, a small, unassuming venue that showcases new talent. On Lower Broadway, lovable dives include Robert's Western World Bar, Tootsie's Orchid Lounge, and the old-timey Ernest Tubb Record Shop. Nearby, big-name acts play B.B. King's Blues Club, and rowdy line dancers gather at the Wildhorse Saloon.

Everyone from Johnny Cash to Patsy Cline performed at the Ryman Auditorium, the original Grand Ole Opry.

Take a break at the Loveless Cafe, a Nashville institution since 1951. Favored by country music stars and foodies who endure the hour-long waits, the cramped house rewards with signature slow-cured country ham and red-eye gravy, and pancakes with molasses.

RYMAN: Tel 615-458-8700; www.ryman.com. **GRAND OLE OPRY AND OPRY MUSEUM:** Tel 615-889-3060; www.opry.com. **COUNTRY MUSIC HALL OF FAME:** Tel 800-852-6437 or 615-416-2001; www.countrymusichalloffame.com. **BLUEBIRD CAFÉ:** Tel 615-383-1461; www.bluebirdcafe.com. **ROBERT'S WESTERN WORLD:** Tel 615-244-9552; www.robertswesternworld.com. **TOOTSIE'S:** Tel 615-726-0463; www.tootsies.net. **ERNEST TUBB RECORD SHOP:** Tel 615-255-7503; www.ernesttubb.com. **B.B. KING'S BLUES CLUB:** Tel 615-256-2727; www.bbkingbluesclub.com. **WILDHORSE**

Saloon: Tel 615-902-8200; www.wildhorsesaloon.com. **Loveless Cafe:** Tel 615-646-9700; www.lovelesscafe.com. *Cost:* breakfast $10. **Where to stay:** The elegant and historic Hermitage Hotel is centrally located. Tel 888-888-9414 or 615-244-3121; www.thehermitagehotel.com. *Cost:* from $245. **Best times:** Jun for the CMA Music Festival; Thurs in Jun–Jul for Bluegrass Nights at the Ryman; mid-Oct for the Grand Ole Opry Birthday Bash.

The Lone Star State's Heartbeat

Austin's Live Music Scene

Austin, Texas, U.S.A.

Although Austin is the seat of state government and home to one of the largest universities in the nation, its soul resides in its music. Laid-back and fun-loving, the city bills itself as the Live Music Capital of the World and claims nearly 200 venues showcasing everything from rockabilly to Tejano year-round, from no-names to Texas greats like Willie Nelson and the Dixie Chicks.

No surprise, then, that the city's famous South by Southwest Music and Media Conference (aka "SXSW") is one of the biggest music showcases anywhere, with an amazing lineup of more than 1,900 music hopefuls performing on more than 85 stages. The city's other major music festival is Austin City Limits, which brings together bands both fresh and familiar (including Pearl Jam, Beastie Boys, and Dave Matthews Band) for 3 days of rock.

Austin's year-round music nerve center is on Sixth Street and in the Red River District immediately north of it, where rock, blues, jazz, country, and R&B emanate from formerly seedy doorways. This is where you'll find the world-renowned Antone's, Austin's "Home of the Blues," and Stubb's BBQ, beloved for great music and food, particularly its Sunday Gospel Brunch. Or head across the river to Threadgill's southern location. The restaurant is not far from the Broken Spoke, Texas's premier two-step dance hall, where Willie Nelson still stops for chicken fried steak. Big names perform at the Backyard, an open-air amphitheater surrounded by Texas Hill Country (see p. 880).

Visiting musicians make a beeline for the hip Hotel San José (if you can't get a room, go for a coffee or a cold Lone Star at Jo's, across the parking lot, where live bands play). The Hotel Saint Cecilia is its higher-end sister property, with nostalgia-imbued rooms in a historic Victorian mansion as well as more modern studios and poolside bungalows. Both hotels helped usher in the renaissance of the now trendy SoCo (South of Congress) entertainment district, whose cool and quirky boutiques and restaurants embody the city's unofficial motto: "Keep Austin Weird."

South by Southwest: Tel 512-467-7979; www.sxsw.com. *When:* mid-Mar. **Austin City Limits:** Tel 888-512-7469 or 512-389-0315; www.aclfestival.com. *When:* 3 days in early Oct. **Antone's:** Tel 512-320-8424; www.antones.net. **Stubb's BBQ:** Tel 512-480-8341; www.stubbsaustin.com. **Threadgill's:** Tel 512-451-5440; www.threadgills.com. **Broken Spoke:** Tel 512-442-6189; www.brokenspokeaustintx.com. **The Backyard:** Tel 512-263-4146; www.thebackyard.net. **Hotel San José:** Tel 800-574-7322 or 512-852-2350; www.hotelsanjose.com. *Cost:* from $165. **Jo's:** Tel 512-444-3800; www.joscoffee.com. **Hotel Saint Cecilia:** Tel 512-852-2400; www.hotelsaintcecilia.com. *Cost:* from $295.

Cultural Jewels in Big D

The Dallas Arts District

Dallas, Texas, U.S.A.

The Dallas Arts District is the centerpiece of the city's cultural life, a 68-acre, 19-block enclave built by some of the world's finest architects to hold some of the best collections of art anywhere. Begun in 1978, the area is now the nation's largest urban arts district and has undoubtedly altered the world's view of the city as cultural game player.

One of the early arrivals, in 1984, was the Edward Larrabee Barnes–designed Dallas Museum of Art, a treasure trove of more than 24,000 pieces from around the globe, representing 7,000 years of art. Only a block away, the Crow Collection of Asian Art holds another exemplary collection, including large architectural gems, such as a sandstone façade from an 18th-century home in India. Inside the Nasher Sculpture Center, a modern building designed by Renzo Piano, reside more than 300 pieces, including works by Rodin, Picasso, Matisse, and Degas. An inviting indoor/outdoor café overlooks a garden that showcases large-scale works from the permanent collection.

The district's architectural centerpiece is arguably the new AT&T Performing Arts Center (the second largest in the country after Lincoln Center in New York; see p. 842), which includes four venues designed by Norman Foster and Rem Koolhaas. Besides the 2,200-seat Winspear Opera House, which offers some of the best acoustics in the country, and the 600-seat Wyly Theater, the center also features an open-air performance space and a 5-acre public park in the heart of downtown. Across the street sits one of the first buildings on the block, the I. M. Pei–designed Meyerson Symphony Center, which has been delighting music lovers since 1989.

Rest your weary feet at the Adolphus, a neo-Baroque hotel in nearby downtown that was built by beer baron Adolphus Busch. Rooms are tastefully (sometimes dramatically) decorated, and the thoughtful touches and impeccable service are like those found at a posh English country house. Or join the list of discerning guests who love the Texas-size luxury of the Rosewood Mansion on Turtle Creek, a 1920s Italian Renaissance–style estate with a serene swimming pool, the-sky's-the-limit service, and one of the city's most respected restaurants.

Visitor info: www.thedallasartsdistrict.org. **Dallas Museum of Art:** Tel 214-922-1200; www.dallasmuseumofart.org. **Crow Collection:** Tel 214-979-6430; www.crowcollection.org. **Nasher Sculpture Center:** Tel 214-242-5100; www.nashersculpturecenter.org. **AT&T Performing Arts Center:** Tel 214-880-0202; www.attpac.org. **Meyerson**

The retractable chandelier is a highlight of the Winspear Opera House at the AT&T Performing Arts Center.

Symphony Center: Tel 214-670-3600; www.dallasculture.org/meyersonsymphonycenter. **Adolphus:** Tel 800-221-9083 or 214-742-8200; www.hoteladolphus.com. *Cost:* from $125 (off-peak), from $329 (peak). **Rosewood Mansion on Turtle Creek:** Tel 800-527-5432 or 214-559-2100; www.mansiononturtlecreek.com. *Cost:* from $250 (off-peak), from $395 (peak). **Best times:** 1st and 3rd Sat of the month for Arts District tours.

An Eclectic Collection of Texas Treasures

Houston's Art Museums

Houston, Texas, U.S.A.

When it first opened in 1924, the Museum of Fine Arts Houston was the first art museum in Texas and only the third in the American South. One of the most visited of the 18 venues that make up the city's Museum District, today it is the fifth largest museum in the country. Of its more than 40,000 works, those by Rembrandt, Van Gogh, Monet, and Picasso are perennial favorites, and you'll find here as well an excellent collection of Latin American art and one of most extensive photography collections in the nation. The centerpiece of the MFAH campus is the original neoclassical Caroline Wiess Law Building. Additions by Mies van der Rohe—his only museum design in America—hold even more items from around the globe, while the Isamu Noguchi–designed Lillie and Hugh Roy Cullen Sculpture Garden is an urban oasis filled with works by Matisse and Calder.

Also in the museum district is the Menil Collection, widely esteemed as one of the finest private museums in the United States. Containing some 17,000 objects amassed by the late legendary Houston arts patron Dominique de Menil and her husband, John, the museum opened in 1987 in an elegant low-rise building designed by Renzo Piano, who skillfully suffused the space with filtered natural light. At its heart is the Surrealism collection, with works by Man Ray, Duchamp, and Max Ernst, as well as one of the world's best collections of Magritte. The Menil also spotlights other 20th-century European painters and sculptors, such as Picasso, Giacometti, and Rodin, along with contemporary artists and photographers. Across the street, an annex comprises nine galleries displaying the work of Cy Twombly, one of the few museums designed for, built for, and devoted to the work of a single American artist.

For something utterly different, see the Orange Show Center for Visionary Art. Created by Houston postal worker Jeff McKissack between 1956 and 1979, the Orange Show is an architectural wonder and an ode to outsider art made from recycled tiles, concrete, steel, and found objects such as tractor seats and mannequins. Since McKissack's death in 1980, the Orange Show site has been preserved by various arts patrons, ranging from Dominique de Menil herself to ZZ Top. Kids love such installations as the Beer Can House and the fantastical Art Car Parade, as do all lovers of the strange and quirky.

Museum of Fine Arts Houston: Tel 713-639-7300; www.mfah.org. **Menil Collection:** Tel 713-525-9400; www.menil.org. **Orange Show:** Tel 713-926-6368; www.orangeshow.org. **Best time:** early May for the Orange Show's Art Car Weekend.

A Lively Oasis in a Multicultural Town

RIVER WALK

San Antonio, Texas, U.S.A.

Mark Twain rated San Antonio as one of America's most outstanding cities. Today he would recognize the city's historic showpiece, the Alamo, but not its other most-visited attraction, the Paseo del Rio, or River Walk, a lively flagstone esplanade that unfurls amid cypresses, oaks, flowering bushes, and willows along both banks of the lazy San Antonio River. Completed in 1941 as a Depression-era WPA project and since rejuvenated, it is now enjoyed by those who fill its lively sidewalk cafés, shops, hotels, and barge cruises, all one level below the city's streets. Boudro's is a fine command post: order a prickly pear margarita and a scrumptious lunch of smoked shrimp and gulf crab enchiladas and watch river life go by.

Considered a public park, the River Walk flows through 5 miles of the city.

At the prettiest of the river's horseshoe bends you'll find the La Mansión del Rio Hotel. Originally a Spanish-influenced 19th-century school, it was reborn in 1968 as an elegant respite of cool courtyard fountains and old-world ambience. Across the river, its sister property, Mokara Hotel & Spa, offers sumptuous interiors, a new rooftop pool with a view, and spa offering treatments using mesquite and wildflower blossoms.

It's an easy stroll to the Alamo, the very symbol of Texas's independence. Here 189 valiant defenders held off General Santa Anna's 2,600-strong Mexican army for 13 days in 1836. Catch the IMAX film *Alamo: The Price of Freedom* around the corner at the RiverCenter Mall, then visit the Alamo Cenotaph, a marble-and-granite sculpture in front of the mission that is carved with the names of the Alamo's heroes, including David Crockett's and Jim Bowie's.

The River Walk is particularly wonderful during the Christmas season, when more than 120,000 twinkling lights illuminate its vintage façades and bridges, and in late April, when the whole city stops for the Fiesta San Antonio, 11 days of events highlighted by three parades and set to the score of the city's signature Tejano music, a unique blend of Mexican and German influences. Indulge in more of the city's Hispanic heritage at Market Square, consisting of El Mercado, the largest Mexican market outside Mexico, and various farmers markets and restaurants, including the renowned Mi Tierra Café & Bakery. The chicken enchildadas are a favorite.

RIVER WALK: Tel 210-227-4262; www.thesanantonioriverwalk.com. **BOUDRO'S:** Tel 210-224-8484; www.boudros.com. *Cost:* dinner $40. **LA MANSIÓN DEL RIO:** Tel 800-843-6664 or 210-518-1000; omnihotels.com. *Cost:* from $170 (off-peak), from $310 (peak). **MOKARA HOTEL:** Tel 866-605-1212 or 210-396-5800; www.mokarahotels.com. *Cost:* from $300 (off-peak), from $500 (peak). **THE ALAMO:** Tel 210-225-1391; www.thealamo.org.

Market Square: Tel 210-207-8600; www.marketsquaresa.com. **Mi Tierra Café & Bakery:** Tel 210-225-1262; www.mitierracafe.com. *Cost:* dinner $12. **Best times:** Mar 2 for Texas Independence Day at the Alamo; mid-Apr for Fiesta San Antonio; mid-May for Tejano Conjunto Festival; late Nov–early Jan for various Christmas events.

Back Roads and Bluebonnets

Texas Hill Country

Texas, U.S.A.

Deep in the heart of Texas is an area of grassy pastures and limestone bluffs, crystal-clear streams, rivers, and lakes, a place that local boy President Lyndon B. Johnson called a "special corner of God's real estate." Visitors to the Hill Country have his wife, Lady Bird Johnson, to thank for the veritable blanket of wildflowers (especially bluebonnets) that cover the region every spring. After LBJ left office in 1969, the couple settled at their ranch 50 miles west of Austin, and Lady Bird's passion for wildflowers grew into the Austin-based 280-acre Lady Bird Johnson Wildflower Center. Stop and take in some 600 indigenous species before heading out to enjoy them in situ.

With a gently rolling landscape that never reaches more than 1,900 feet above sea level, Texas's Hill Country was settled in the mid-1800s, mostly by German immigrants, whose ethnic influence can still be felt in local Oktoberfest and Christmastime festivals in and around Fredericksburg, the area's prettiest town. Oenophiles should follow the Fredericksburg Wine Road (aka U.S. Highway 290) linking Hill Country wineries, including the popular Becker Vineyards. Fredericksburg has a bevy of historic inns and B&Bs, such as the Hoffman Haus with 14 beautifully furnished rooms one block off Main Street.

On Saturday afternoons between March and December, the town of Bandera, the self-appointed Cowboy Capital of the World, hosts Cowboys on Main, a street party with chuck wagons, barbecue booths, and roping trick demonstrations. Hill Country Equestrian Lodge, a 275-acre ranch, offers private lessons or simply a place to relax after a quiet ride in the adjacent Hill Country State Natural Area, where great birding is a welcome plus.

Gruene is the place to scoot your boots, beginning with Gruene Hall, the oldest continuously operating dance hall in Texas. The nearby Gruene Mansion Inn, an 1872 Victorian home, is within easy reach of the town's dance halls and the Guadalupe River, popular for tubing.

Where: Fredericksburg is 70 miles west of Austin. **Visitor info:** www.texashillcountry.com. **LBJ National Historical Park:** Tel 830-868-7128; www.nps.gov/lyjo. **Wildflower Center:** Tel 512-232-0100; www.wildflower.org. **Becker Vineyards:** Tel 830-644-2681; www.beckervineyards.com. **Hoffman Haus:** Tel 830-997-6739; www.hoffmanhaus.com. *Cost:* from $135. **Hill Country Equestrian Lodge:** Tel 830-796-7950; www.hillcountryequestlodge.com. *Cost:* from $180. **Gruene Dance Hall:** Tel 830-606-1281; www.gruenehall.com. **Gruene Mansion Inn:** Tel 830-629-2641; www.gruenemansioninn.com. *Cost:* from $190. **Best times:** Feb–May and Sep–Nov for pleasant weather; Mar–Apr for wildflower season; late May–mid-Jun for Kerrville Folk Festival; early Nov for WurstFest in New Braunfels.

Biking and Hiking Amid Arches and Canyons

MOAB AND RED ROCK COUNTRY

Utah, U.S.A.

The adventure-travel epicenter of canyon country is a surprisingly small town. But even with a population of just under 5,000, Moab affords enough great-outdoors options—plus enough movie-worthy scenery—to rival a town ten times its size. Begun as a Mormon settlement in 1855 and enjoying a boom as a uranium mining center in the 1950s, Moab reinvented itself in the 1980s, when proponents of a nascent sport called mountain biking discovered that the endless miles of colorful slickrock were perfect for fat-tired fun.

Moab has off-road trails galore, but the punishing 10-mile Slickrock Trail is a rite of passage for serious bikers. The city's unique location, in a narrow green valley split by the Colorado River, has made it perfect for prime river-rafting as well. Local outfitters will guide you through its white water or arrange multi-day float trips through the placid Labyrinth or Stillwater canyons on the Green River.

Moab is an easy 10 minutes from Arches National Park, famous for its extraordinary 2,000-plus salmon-colored sandstone spans sculpted by the elements. Enjoy magnificent vistas from the park's 18-mile scenic drive, or along easy trails such as the 3-mile one to Delicate Arch, the unofficial state symbol. Moab is also 40 minutes from Canyonlands National Park, Utah's largest park, it packs an abundance of reasons to visit into its 530 square miles that are divided into three distinct sections separated by the Green and Colorado rivers. The Island in the Sky district is the closest to Moab and, with 20 miles of paved road, the most accessible by car.

Hiking trails crisscross both parks, while prospectors' roads left over from the area's mining days bring in 4WD enthusiasts, who arrive for Jeep Safari on Easter weekend. September brings chamber music, jazz, and bluegrass during the world-renowned Moab Music Festival, while fat-tire fans gather in October for the Moab Ho-Down Bike Festival.

Among the many places in town to hang your hat, the Gonzo Inn offers a touch of retro 1970s charm and a pool for soaking your slickrock-weary body. Or drive half an hour to the Sorrel River Ranch, a 180-acre property set on a scenic bend in the Colorado River.

WHERE: 238 miles southeast of Salt Lake City. **VISITOR INFO:** www.discovermoab.com. **ARCHES NATIONAL PARK:** Tel 435-719-2299; www.nps.gov/arch. **CANYONLANDS NATIONAL PARK:** Tel 435-719-2313; www.nps.gov/cany. **GONZO INN:** Tel 800-791-4044 or 435-259-2515; www.gonzoinn.com. *Cost:* from $160. **SORREL RIVER:** Tel 877-359-2715 or 435-259-4642; www.sorrelriver.com. *Cost:* from $400. **BEST TIMES:** Apr–mid-May and Sep–mid-Nov for the nicest weather.

Turret Arch is framed here by North Window Arch in Arches National Park.

The Greatest Snow on Earth

Skiing the Wasatch Range

Park City and environs, Utah, U.S.A.

With 11 ski resorts within an hour's drive of Salt Lake City and an annual snowfall of 500 inches in some areas, it's no mystery why Utah was chosen to host the 2002 Winter Olympics. What's more, the charming century-old mining town of Park City is arguably the best little ski town in the country.

Only 4 miles north of downtown Park City sprawls The Canyons Resort, encompassing 3,700 family-friendly skiable acres, with diverse terrain and an arsenal of lifts that whisk skiers up to eight mountain peaks and 167 variable runs. U.S. ski and snowboard Olympic teams and wannabes train at Park City Mountain Resort, choosing among its 108 trails, 15 lifts, nine bowls, and seven peaks, as well as one of the biggest "superpipes" in North America. The 389-acre Utah Olympic Park keeps the excitement alive. Sports fans can take on the Olympic bobsled track and any of six Nordic jumps, stopping to watch Olympic hopefuls train.

Deer Valley is unquestionably Utah's plushest resort. Its four summits—the highest is 9,570 feet—were home to many Olympic events, and its 99 runs, served by 22 lifts, never seem crowded. The chic but unpretentious Norwegian-themed Stein Eriksen Lodge is a ski-in, ski-out Alpine treasure; of its host of pampering amenities, the award-winning spa and Glitretind restaurant hold the spotlight.

Climbing 5,500 feet in 11 dramatic glacier-cut miles, Little Cottonwood Canyon is home to the Alta and Snowbird resorts. Snowbird provides a newer, high-tech contrast to Alta's old-school atmosphere. Alta is Utah's oldest resort and prides itself on being a "skier's mountain" (read: no snowboards allowed). The funky, family-owned Alta Lodge has been open since 1939 and is practically a museum of ski memorabilia.

For a different vibe, drive to Sundance Resort, the creation of Robert Redford, who purchased these 6,000 acres of wilderness back in 1969. The modest 500 skiable acres echo Redford's "smaller is better" vision, which places emphasis on the environment and the arts. Sundance is most often associated with the indie film festival founded in 1981 and held here and in Park City every January, the leading event of its kind.

Where: Park City is 36 miles east of Salt Lake City. **Visitor info:** www.parkcity.com. **The Canyons Resort:** Tel 888-226-9667 or 435-649-5400; www.thecanyons.com. *Cost:* lift tickets $81. **Park City Mountain Resort:** Tel 800-222-7275 or 435-649-8111; www.parkcitymountain.com. *Cost:* lift tickets from $86. **Olympic Park:** Tel 435-658-4200; www.olyparks.com/uop. **Deer Valley:** Tel 800-558-3337 or 435-649-1000; www.deervalley.com. *Cost:* lift tickets $86. **Stein Eriksen Lodge:** Tel 800-453-1302 or 435-649-3700; www.steinlodge.com. *Cost:* from $195 (off-peak), from $830 (peak); dinner at Glitretind $50. **Snowbird:** Tel 800-232-9542 or 801-933-2222; www.snowbird.com. *Cost:* Cliff Lodge from $150 (off-peak), from $410 (peak); lift tickets from $65. **Alta:** Tel 888-782-9258 or 801-359-1078; www.alta.com. *Cost:* lift tickets from $65. **Alta Lodge:** Tel 800-707-2582 or 801-742-3500; www.altalodge.com. *Cost:* from $110 (off-peak), from $145 (peak). **Sundance Resort:** Tel 800-

892-1600 or 866-259-7468; www.sundanceresort.com. *Cost:* from $270; lift tickets $50. **Best times:** Jan–early Mar for ideal skiing; late Jan for the Sundance Film Festival.

Mormon Mecca and America's Choir

Temple Square

Salt Lake City, Utah, U.S.A.

"This is the place," declared Brigham Young, leader of the Church of Jesus Christ of Latter-day Saints (LDS), when he first gazed across the bleak Salt Lake Valley in July of 1847. The valley is now the epicenter of one of the world's fastest-growing religions (more than 70 percent of Utahns are Mormon, and of the creed's 13.5 million believers, over half live outside the U.S.).

The heart of this community and of Salt Lake City is Temple Square, as revered by Mormons as the Vatican is by Catholics. Enter on the south, west, or north side, where young guides offer free tours in 40 languages.

Young himself laid the cornerstone of the granite, six-spired Salt Lake Temple in 1853; a 12-foot statue of the angel Moroni tops the tallest spire. The interior of the temple is open only to LDS church members.

The famous Mormon Tabernacle Choir has its home in a distinctive domed building whose enormous 11,623-pipe organ is considered one of the finest in the world. The Grammy-winning, 360-member, all-volunteer choir performs Sunday mornings and rehearses on Thursday evenings; both events are open to the public. Try to make it for the annual Christmas concert, which can cheer even the stubbornest Scrooge and is televised around the world.

Info: Tel 801-240-4872; www.visittemplesquare.com. **Best time:** late Nov–Dec for Christmas festivities and lights.

The Quintessential Road Trip

Zion and Bryce National Parks

Utah, U.S.A.

It's hard to pick favorites among Utah's five stellar national parks. West-to-east park-hopping should begin with Zion National Park, the oldest and perhaps most beautiful—and that's saying a lot. It was first called Zion, the Hebrew word for "sanctuary," by early Mormons. The Virgin River, which carved these 2,000-foot walls of delicately hued sandstone, seems to have been named for the unspoiled landscape it wends through. The 10-mile Zion–Mount Carmel Highway (Highway 9) runs east–west across the 232-square-mile park. If the Grand Canyon (see p. 706) is all about standing at the rim and looking down, here inspiration comes from looking (or hiking) up. Only the adventurous tackle the trail up to Angel's Landing, which climbs 1,488 feet in 2.5 miles, but few miss the less arduous Narrows hike through the Virgin River. The only lodging in the park itself is the rustic, 1920s Zion Lodge. Across the road is the start of the popular Emerald Pools Trail, which leads through cool forests to three basins fed by small waterfalls and kept a deep, rich green by algae.

Eighty-six miles east of Zion is 56-square-mile Bryce Canyon National Park, known for its thousands of multihued hoodoos—tall, thin spires of rock that come in every possible shade of white, pink, red, and purple; just wait a minute as the light shifts, and the colors all change before your eyes. The views from the rim at 8,000 feet are astonishing, especially at sunrise. You can take the 18-mile scenic drive following the park's rim, or hike down among the formations on 60 miles of trails. The venerable Bryce Canyon Lodge, built of ponderosa timbers and native sandstone in the 1920s, has 114 guest rooms and a lively dining room filled with park lovers from all over the world.

A forest of eroded hoodoos makes up Bryce Canyon.

In the morning, head east on Highway 12, a designated "All American Road" that offers 124 of the prettiest driving miles in the country. After peaking at almost 10,000 feet, it crosses the 1.9-million-acre Grand Staircase-Escalante National Monument, a series of gigantic, colorful plateaus of sedimentary rock that stretch to the Grand Canyon. Continue past Escalante on the Million Dollar Road (that's how much it cost to build the highway's "missing link" in 1935) to Boulder and look for the turnoff to the stylish, eco-friendly Boulder Mountain Lodge. Food fans travel for hours to dine at Hell's Backbone Grill, a culinary outpost attached to the hotel.

WHERE: Zion is 307 miles southwest of Salt Lake City. Tel 435-772-3254; www.nps.gov/zion. Bryce is 267 miles south of Salt Lake City. Tel 435-834-5322; www.nps.gov/brca. **ZION LODGE:** Tel 888-297-2757 or 303-297-2757; www.zionlodge.com. *Cost:* from $170. **BRYCE CANYON LODGE:** Tel 877-386-4383 or 435-834-8700; www.brycecanyonforever.com. *Cost:* from $160. *When:* Apr–Oct. **GRAND STAIRCASE–ESCALANTE NATIONAL MONUMENT:** Tel 435-644-4680; www.ut.blm.gov/monument. **BOULDER MOUNTAIN LODGE:** Tel 800-556-3446 or 435-335-7460; www.boulder-utah.com. *Cost:* from $85. **HELL'S BACKBONE GRILL:** Tel 435-335-7464; www.hellsbackbonegrill.com. *Cost:* dinner $25. *When:* mid-Mar–late Nov. **BEST TIMES:** Apr–mid-May and Sep–mid-Nov for nice weather.

A Cheesemaking Village Stuck in Time

GRAFTON

Vermont, U.S.A.

A pitch-perfect Vermont village credited with restarting the state's handcrafted cheese industry, Grafton is an architectural showcase of historical buildings. It is not a living museum staffed by people in period costumes, but a real-life community with a population of 600, many of whom work in the well-stocked general store, the shops along the tree-lined main street, or at the renowned cheese company. Grafton's cheesemaking roots go back to 1892, and today the Grafton Village Cheese Company makes one of the world's finest cheddars, which you can sample as you watch it being made.

Founded in 1763, Grafton thrived in the early 1800s and it peaked in 1830 with a population of 1,482 people (and 10,000 sheep). After the wool industry collapsed, Grafton survived as a stagecoach stopover between Boston and Montreal, but the advent of the automobile left it a shell of its former self.

In 1963, the Windham Foundation was created to resuscitate the town. The foundation owns 25 buildings in the central village, including the Old Tavern, a classic white-clapboard, black-shuttered inn built in 1801. Today the three-story structure has 45 discreetly modernized rooms (11 in the main building and 34 in nearby cottages), with a guest registry that includes Rudyard Kipling, who honeymooned here in 1892. The dining room is a perennial draw, with an inviting selection of hard-to-find wines and cuisine featuring fresh ingredients gathered from the inn's organic gardens and local farms.

Drive to nearby Bellows Falls to catch the Green Mountain Flyer, a vintage sightseeing train that makes a 90-minute round-trip run to Chester, past covered bridges, small towns, and, in autumn, an explosion of colorful foliage. Half the point of visiting Grafton, though, is kicking back and enjoying the lazy pace of yesteryear.

WHERE: 59 miles northeast of Bennington. **VISITOR INFO:** www.graftonvermont.org. **GRAFTON VILLAGE CHEESE COMPANY:** Tel 800-472-3866 or 802-843-2222; www.graftonvillagecheese.com. **THE OLD TAVERN:** Tel 800-843-1801 or 802-843-2231; www.oldtavern.com. *Cost:* from $190 (off-peak), from $225 (peak). **GREEN MOUNTAIN FLYER:** Tel 800-707-3530 or 802-280-2295; www.rails-vt.com. *When:* Fri mid-May–mid-Oct. **BEST TIMES:** Jan–Mar for winter sports; Sep–Oct for foliage.

The King of East Coast Skiing and Top-Drawer Inns

KILLINGTON AND WOODSTOCK

Vermont, U.S.A.

The Aspen of the East Coast, Killington isn't the most classic or romantic Vermont ski destination (for that, head to Stowe; see p. 889), but it has plenty to brag about. It's the first to open (early November) and the last to close (May), has a vertical drop that falls just shy of Aspen's, and uses the largest snow-making system in the world. What's more, its extensive system of 22 lifts serve more terrain than any other resort in the East.

One hundred forty-one Alpine ski runs sprawl across six mountains, including Outer Limits, one of the steepest and most challenging mogul trails in the country, as well as such ominously named double black–diamond runs as Anarchy and Downdraft, which prove irresistible to thrill-seekers. Killington's very lively après-ski scene is equally alluring. For cozy accommodations that President Eisenhower enjoyed in 1955, try the Mountain Top Inn & Resort, which offers cross-country skiing (and horseback riding when warm weather arrives) on 350 acres surrounded by the Green Mountain National Forest.

If Killington's big-and-brash aesthetic wears thin, escape to nearby Christmas-card-darling Woodstock, a cosmopolitan village that claims the title of oldest ski resort in the country and site of the first ski tow. It owes its distinction as the "prettiest small town in America" to Laurance Rockefeller (grandson of John D. Rockefeller Sr.) and his wife, Mary Billings, who spent 60 years preserving its 19th-century feel. In 1969, they built the town's centerpiece, the genteel Woodstock Inn and Resort. The Colonial Revival retreat offers top-drawer amenities and easy access to the Woodstock Ski Touring Center, an 18-hole Robert Trent Jones Sr. course, and 37 miles of trails for cross-country skiing and snowshoeing.

Ten miles north is one of America's most luxurious and enchanting resort inns, Twin Farms, secluded on over 300 stunning acres. The former Colonial-era farmhouse—a wedding gift from Nobel prize–winning novelist Sinclair Lewis to his bride, Dorothy Thompson—is just part of a complex that boasts a small but excellent art collection, 20 individually designed rooms and suites, and endlessly inventive meals.

WHERE: Killington is 84 miles south of Burlington. **VISITOR INFO:** www.killington.com. *Cost:* lift tickets from $77. *When:* ski season Nov–May. **MOUNTAIN TOP INN & RESORT:** Tel 800-445-2100 or 802-483-2311; www.mountaintopinn.com. *Cost:* from $170 (off-peak), from $275 (peak). **WOODSTOCK INN & RESORT:** Tel 800-448-7900 or 802-457-1100; www.woodstockinn.com. *Cost:* from $200 (off-peak), from $329 (peak). **TWIN FARMS:** Tel 800-894-6327 or 802-234-9999; www.twinfarms.com. *Cost:* from $1,300, all-inclusive. **BEST TIMES:** Jan–Mar for skiing; Mar for the Bear Mountain Mogul Challenge; May–Oct for cycling, hiking; late Sep–early Oct for foliage; mid-Dec for Woodstock's Wassail Weekend.

An Archetypal New England Town

MANCHESTER

Vermont, U.S.A.

Ringed by Vermont's Green Mountains, this archetypal New England town, with its maple-shaded streets, has lured visitors since before Abraham Lincoln's family summered here. Manchester's impressive white mansions and marble sidewalks retain a peaceful historic feel, while the raft of high-end factory outlets on the edge of town lends a modern allure.

The village's star attraction, the 1,300-acre Equinox Resort & Spa, is a lavishly restored 195-room Federal-style property that has been a favorite of U.S. presidents from Taft to Roosevelt. Its championship 18-hole golf course was designed by Walter Travis in 1927 and updated in 1992 by Rees Jones. Upper-crust British pastimes prevail, with lessons in archery, falconry, and off-road driving all available. Stop by the state-of-the-art spa for a white-clay body mask, or sunbathe on the outdoor patio within sight of Mount Equinox, at 3,848 feet the highest peak in the Taconic mountain range.

Local sons Charles and Franklin Orvis started out here as hoteliers in the mid-1800s and found that tourists lured by the Battenkill and Mettawee rivers were a fine market for their handcrafted rods and tackle. Their empire lives on in the Manchester flagship store, which stands beside the popular Orvis fly-fishing school. Here, would-be enthusiasts can release their inner angler with field trips to the hallowed Battenkill, famed for its rainbow and brook trout.

The Equinox Resort & Spa began as a tavern in colonial times and has expanded over the years.

Today, Charles Orvis's home has been reincarnated as the Charles Orvis Inn, part of the Equinox Resort, along with the cozy 13-bedroom Federal-style 1811 House nearby, where Abraham Lincoln's granddaughter Mary Lincoln Isham lived. Hildene, the Lincoln family home, is not far away. The 24-room Georgian Revival mansion on 412 acres was built by Robert Todd Lincoln (Abraham and Mary's son) in 1905.

At least one morning should be spent at Up for Breakfast (named for its second-floor location), a local landmark famed for its delicious pancakes drizzled with Vermont maple syrup.

WHERE: 100 miles south of Burlington. **VISITOR INFO:** www.manchestervermont.net. **EQUINOX:** Tel 800-362-4747 or 802-362-4700; www.equinoxresort.com. *Cost:* from $230 (off-peak), from $600 (peak); greens fees from $85. *1811 House:* from $100 (off-peak), from $320 (peak). **ORVIS FLY-FISHING SCHOOL:** Tel 866-531-6213 or 802-362-4604; www.orvis.com/schools. *Cost:* $470 for 2-day session. *When:* mid-Apr–Oct. **HILDENE:** Tel 800-578-1788 or 802-362-1788; www.hildene.org. **UP FOR BREAKFAST:** Tel 802-362-4204. **BEST TIMES:** late Apr–mid-Sep for fishing; mid-Jul of even-numbered years for Hildene Antiques Show; 1st weekend of Aug for Southern Vermont Art & Crafts Fair.

Fall's Riotous Foliage, Unsurpassed

NORTHEAST KINGDOM

Vermont, U.S.A.

In 1949, a former U.S. senator from Vermont, struck by the timeless beauty of his state's three northeasternmost counties (Orleans, Essex, and Caledonia), dubbed them the Northeast Kingdom—and when fall's brilliant palette arrives, it's among the most stunning places in America. Here, thickly wooded hills give way to sleepy hamlets and the fjordlike Lake Willoughby, with its flanking, soaring cliffs.

The unofficial gateway to the region is St. Johnsbury ("St. Jay's"), but this uncrowded corner of Vermont is better known for small towns such as Peacham (population 611), which may well be Vermont's finest photo op during foliage season. Keep driving through valleys of tidy farmlands, where cows outnumber the proudly insular Yankee residents. Harsh winters and sheer remoteness have kept development and tourism at bay, making these roads a paradise for cyclists as well as motorists.

Winter sports enthusiasts are drawn to historic Craftsbury, home to the highly regarded Nordic Ski Center and its 50-mile network of ski trails, including a stretch of the 300-mile Catamount Trail, the longest cross-country ski trail in the U.S. In summer, no less beautiful a season, Big Hosmer Pond offers opportunities for rowing and paddling. Ringing it are miles of trails and dirt roads for biking, walking, and running.

In the time-forgotten village of Lower Waterford (whose population hovers around 50), the Rabbit Hill Inn, built in 1795 in the Federal style, complete with white colonnade, sits on 15 unspoiled acres with a commanding view of the White Mountains. Its 19 guest rooms are individually decorated, and dinner is an elegant farm-to-table three-course affair, while breakfast is every bit as scrumptious.

Where: St. Johnsbury is 75 miles east of Burlington. **Visitor info:** www.travelthekingdom.com. For info on New England's color scene: www.vermontfallfoliage.com. **Craftsbury Nordic Ski Center:** Tel 802-586-7767; www.craftsbury.com/skiing. **Rabbit Hill Inn:** Tel 800-762-8669 or 802-748-5168; www.rabbithillinn.com. *Cost:* from $199; dinner $50. **Best times:** late Sep–early Oct for peak foliage and local foliage festivals.

Like Guests at a Vanderbilt Estate

Shelburne Farms

Shelburne, Vermont, U.S.A.

On a bluff overlooking 100-mile-long Lake Champlain, with New York's Adirondacks beyond, sits the Inn at Shelburne Farms, surrounded by 1,400 acres designed by Frederick Law Olmsted, the landscape architect who designed New York City's Central Park (see p. 841). The redbrick Queen Anne–style country mansion, built in 1886 by Lila Vanderbilt and her husband, William Seward Webb, welcomes guests into a bygone era of turrets, fireplaces, oil portraits, and floral wallpaper. Its 24 guest rooms are appointed with family-heirloom antiques and are dripping with character. The inn's candlelit restaurant offers a menu that might include roasted rack of locally raised lamb complemented by organic produce from the property's garden. The inn is the crown jewel of Shelburne Farms, a non-profit conservation center run by the Webbs' great-grandchildren.

Staying at the inn supports Shelburne Farms's educational programs.

In addition to the inn and the working farm, there's a hands-on children's farmyard and a dairy known for its excellent cheddar cheese. Some 140,000 pounds are produced annually from the farm's herd of Brown Swiss cows. At the Shelburne Museum, the nearly 40 structures (25 of them historic) scattered across 45 grassy acres hold one of the finest collections of Americana in the country. Dubbed "the Smithsonian of New England," the museum's holdings include some 150,000 pieces, amassed by the family a century ago, including cigar-store Indians, pewterware, glass dolls, quilts, and even a carousel.

Where: 7 miles south of Burlington. **Inn at Shelburne Farms:** Tel 802-985-8498; www.shelburnefarms.org. *Cost:* from $160; dinner $45. *When:* early May–mid-Oct. **Shelburne Museum:** Tel 802-985-3346; www.shelburnemuseum.org. *When:* mid-May–Oct. **Best times:** late May for Lilac Festival; mid-summer for Vermont Cheesemaker's Festival; Jul–early Aug for the 5-week Vermont Mozart Festival; mid-Sep for Shelburne Farms Harvest Festival.

Where the Hills Are Alive

Stowe

Vermont, U.S.A.

Considered the queen of Northeast ski areas, Stowe Mountain Resort was created in the 1930s, making it one of the oldest in the country. Despite its reputation for quaintness, Stowe has reinvented itself as a resort to rival the nation's best, complete with 116 trails over 485 skiable acres and the new Over Easy gondola linking the Mount Mansfield and Spruce Peak ski areas. Stowe has more mile-long lifts than any other Eastern resort and slopeside accommodations worthy of its name, Ski Capital of the East. Warm-weather activities like the 2,300-foot Alpine slide and extensive hiking trails draw visitors once the powder's gone.

Stowe Mountain Lodge, the exposed-timber and stonework centerpiece of Stowe's renaissance, is the mountain's only ski-in, ski-out hotel. With floor-to-ceiling windows that overlook the dazzling winterscape, the 139-room lodge caters to skiers who come to tackle the famously steep Front Four trails on Mount Mansfield, at 4,395 feet, Vermont's highest peak. In summer months, golfers head for the Bob Cupp–designed course, designated as an Audubon International Signature Sanctuary. The 200-year-old town of Stowe, with the requisite white steepled church and a folksy Main Street that features the old-fashioned Shaw's General Store, is the quintessence of charm.

Stowe is also home to the country's first cross-country ski center. The 2,400-acre Trapp Family Lodge was opened in 1950 by the Austrian family of *Sound of Music* fame, who settled here after coming to America in 1942. The resort's Tyrolean ambience, old-world service, and menu of Wiener schnitzel and spaetzle make this chalet-style lodge one of the coziest this side of the Alps.

Most skiers reach Stowe via Route 100, a highly scenic two-lane road that stretches some 200 miles along the rugged spine of the Green Mountains, connecting several major ski resorts and a string of picturesque villages. Stop in Weston, where the biggest attraction is the jam-packed Vermont Country Store, founded in 1946 and famous as "purveyors of the practical and hard-to-find." Nearby, the small town of Warren is best known for its vital cultural scene and the luxurious Pitcher Inn, originally opened in the 1850s. It has 11 rooms, each distinct, a restaurant that has been showered with superlatives, and an extensive wine list. Visit the old-fashioned Warren Store for penny candy, baked goods, and the locally brewed Lawson's Finest beer, sold exclusively here.

Where: 45 miles east of Burlington. **Visitor info:** www.gostowe.com. *When:* ski season Nov–Apr. **Stowe Mountain Resort:** Tel 800-253-4754 or 802-253-3000; www.stowe.com. *Cost:* lift tickets from $57 (off-peak), from $89 (peak). **Stowe Mountain**

Lodge: Tel 888-478-6938 or 802-253-3560; www.stowemountainlodge.com. *Cost:* from $179 (off-peak), from $400 (peak). **Trapp Family Lodge:** Tel 800-826-7000 or 802-253-8511; www.trappfamily.com. *Cost:* from $215 (off-peak), from $325 (peak). **Vermont Country Store:** Tel 802-824-3184; www.vermontcountrystore.com. **Pitcher Inn:** Tel 888-867-4824 or 802-496-6350; www.pitcherinn.com. *Cost:* from $425; dinner $30. **Best times:** Jan–Mar for winter sports; late Jan for Stowe Winter Carnival; Feb for Stowe Derby.

In Pursuit of Life, Liberty, and Luxury

The Thomas Jefferson Trail

Monticello and environs, Virginia, U.S.A.

Monticello was the dream house of Renaissance man Thomas Jefferson—visionary, principal author of the Declaration of Independence, founder of the University of Virginia, and America's third president. He designed the house—you've seen it on the back of the nickel—over a 40-year period and said of it, "I am as happy nowhere else." Set on a hilltop overlooking Charlottesville and the 2,500 remaining acres of the Jefferson family's plantation, Monticello (meaning "small hill" in Italian) is one of America's outstanding architectural achievements.

Jefferson began planning the three-story Palladian-style structure in 1769, when he was just 26. The resulting design, influenced by Italian architecture and his five-year stay in France as U.S. Minister, includes the first dome on a residence in North America and an entrance hall filled with objects from Lewis and Clark's expedition, which Jefferson himself had commissioned.

After serving as U.S. president from 1801 to 1809, Jefferson retired to Monticello and founded the University of Virginia, just 2 miles away. Today, his beloved "academical village" is one of the nation's top public universities. The impeccably curated U.Va. Art Museum, opened in 1935, houses a permanent collection that includes Asian, African, and pre-Columbian pieces as well as European and American works that range from pre-Renaissance to contemporary. It is a block north of the distinctive Rotunda, designed by Thomas Jefferson and modeled after the Pantheon in Rome. Jefferson died at Monticello at age 83 on July 4, 1826, and is buried on the extensive grounds. Overnighters can stay nearby at the elegant 18-room Clifton Inn, built in 1799 by Jefferson's son-in-law, and dine at its well-regarded restaurant.

Continue in Jefferson's footsteps by heading 100 miles west to Hot Springs and soaking in the town's mineral-rich, 98°F waters.

Jefferson is buried on the grounds of Monticello, site of his family's 18th-century plantation.

Jefferson bathed in these springs, for centuries reputed by the native people to possess restorative powers. Today the pools are part of The Homestead, a venerable 483-room Georgian-style resort founded in 1766 as one of the first European-style spas in the U.S. Guests can choose among a host of activities, from falconry to fishing a 4-mile stocked stream to hiking and biking over 100 miles of scenic trails through the property's 3,000 verdant acres. The resort's three golf courses are consistently ranked among the country's best, and the Old Course offers the oldest first tee in continuous use in the U.S.

WHERE: Monticello is 115 miles south of Washington, D.C. **MONTICELLO:** Tel 434-984-9822; www.monticello.org. **U.VA. ART MUSEUM:** Tel 434-924-3592; www.virginia.edu/artmuseum. **CLIFTON INN:** Tel 888-971-1800 or 434-971-1800; www.cliftoninn.net. *Cost:* from $195 (off-peak), from $525 (peak); 4-course dinner $65. **THE HOMESTEAD:** Tel 866-354-4653 or 540-839-1766; www.thehomestead.com. *Cost:* from $225 (off-peak), from $300 (peak). **BEST TIMES:** July 4, the anniversary of Jefferson's death, for Monticello Independence Day Celebration and Naturalization Ceremony; Oct for foliage.

A Scenic Highway Runs Through It

SHENANDOAH VALLEY

Virginia, U.S.A.

Shenandoah is the name of the mountainous region in western Virginia, the fertile, 200-mile-long valley west of it, and the lazy river that flows between them to the Potomac. Beyond its historical importance (numerous military campaigns were waged here during the Civil War), Shenandoah is one of the state's most enchanting regions.

While riding horseback through what is today the nearly 300-square-mile Shenandoah National Park in the Blue Ridge Mountains, Herbert Hoover was said to have remarked, "These mountains are made for a road." That came to pass in 1939 with the completion of the 105-mile Skyline Drive, which winds among some 60 peaks, running alongside the Appalachian Trail (see p. 756) for 100 miles. It hooks up with the Blue Ridge Parkway, a 469-mile moving postcard running south from Waynesboro, Virginia, to Great Smoky Mountains National Park (see p. 871) in North Carolina. In autumn, the sycamores, hickories, oaks, and maples of the Blue Ridge Mountains put on a riotous display of color, which can be savored from any of the roadway's 75 scenic overlooks or from the park's 500 miles of hiking trails.

The Shenandoah Valley is awash in early American history, as is delightfully obvious in towns such as Staunton, where five National Historic Districts brim with 19th-century architecture that escaped Civil War destruction. Woodrow Wilson was born here, and visiting his presidential library makes for an interesting afternoon.

And then there are the area's subterranean attractions found at the U.S. National Landmark Luray Caverns. In addition to its amazing rock formations, guests can hear music played by the Great Stalacpipe Organ—actually a lithophone, an instrument made of rock that is struck to produce haunting, bell-like sounds. Covering more than 3.5 acres, it has earned a listing in Guinness World Records as the world's largest musical instrument.

Where: The valley runs from Front Royal (90 miles southwest of Washington, D.C.) in the north to Roanoke in the south. Staunton is 158 miles southwest of Washington, D.C. **Visitor info:** www.visitstaunton.com. **Shenandoah National Park:** Tel 540-999-3500; www.nps.gov/shen. **Blue Ridge Parkway:** www.nps.gov/blri. **Luray Caverns:** Tel 540-743-6551; www.luraycaverns.com. **Best times:** May for blooming wildflowers; mid-Oct for vibrant foliage and Front Royal's Festival of Leaves.

A Gourmet Sanctuary in the Middle of Hunt Country

The Inn at Little Washington

Washington, Virginia, U.S.A.

The Inn at Little Washington, opened in 1978 in a converted garage with a self-taught chef in the kitchen, is today considered one of the best, most romantic restaurants and country inns in the world. The setting, of course, helps. Laid out in 1749 by a 17-year-old George Washington, "Little Washington" (population 158) is a place of timeless rustic charm tucked into the foothills of the Blue Ridge Mountains and just over an hour's drive from Washington—big Washington.

Celebrated chef and owner Patrick O'Connell oversees every aspect of the Colonial-style inn himself. The sumptuous décor evokes a fantasy atmosphere, a distillation of the world's great country-house traditions that impresses a steady stream of D.C. types and world-traveled gourmands.

O'Connell's sublime cuisine defies pigeonholing, at times leaning toward traditional regional fare and at others taking on a more "*haute Américaine*" flair. Order from the 14,000-bottle wine list and prepare to be amazed. The dining room is a Venetian-inspired dream, with 30 intimate tables and striped-silk wall coverings. Repair to any of the inn's exquisite bedrooms and suites, where Victorian eclecticism mixes with a splash of theatricality. If there's no room at the inn, the Middleton Inn is an easy stroll away. This beautifully appointed brick estate home was built in 1840 by Middleton Miller, later known as the man who designed and manufactured the Confederate uniform.

The Inn at Little Washington sits in the middle of Virginia hunt country, a landscape laced with long wooden fences and stone walls hiding grand ancestral homes. The 18th-century town of Middleburg is its hub—equal parts quaint and upscale. Stop by the Red Fox Inn and Tavern, which claims to be the oldest continuously operated tavern in the country, for crabcakes and a bowl of rich peanut soup in the dark, timbered restaurant. A meandering drive outside Middleburg eventually leads you to the bucolic Goodstone Inn, a luxurious 265-acre country estate established in 1768. It offers handsomely furnished rooms and suites in restored buildings, including the carriage house and stables, and a wonderful restaurant and scenic cocktail deck.

Where: Washington is 67 miles west of Washington, D.C. **Inn at Little Washington:** Tel 540-675-3800; www.theinnatlittlewashington.com. *Cost:* rooms from $425 (off-peak), from $525 (peak); prix-fixe dinner from $168. **Middleton Inn:** Tel 800-816-8157 or

540-675-2020; www.middletoninn.com. *Cost:* from $275. **Red Fox Inn:** Tel 800-223-1728 or 540-687-6301; www.redfox.com. *Cost:* lunch $20. **Goodstone Inn:** Tel 877-219-4663 or 540-687-4645; www.goodstone.com. *Cost:* from $285. **Best times:** late May for Hunt Country Stable Tour; Oct for foliage and Virginia Fall Races in Middleburg.

Life in 18th-Century America

Colonial Williamsburg

Williamsburg, Virginia, U.S.A.

Colonial Williamsburg meticulously re-creates the crucial period in America from 1750 to 1775, the end of the colonial era and the eve of the Revolutionary War. The level of detail is astonishing, from the actors who channel statesmen and merchants, to the authentically replicated workshops. It's the country's largest, most popular living history museum and one of the world's finest.

Interpreters portray real and imagined colonial figures.

The cultural and political capital of Virginia (England's largest colony) from 1699 to 1780, Williamsburg was home to a lively aristocratic social scene; Thomas Jefferson and George Washington both spent time here debating the merits of independence. In 1926, John D. Rockefeller Jr. initiated a $68 million restoration of the 300-acre site, including 88 original buildings and 90 acres of period gardens. Hundreds more structures have harmoniously been added since.

Williamsburg is a treat for both adults and kids. Walking its cobbled streets, you might have an impromptu discussion with "Thomas Jefferson" or the rabble-rousing "Patrick Henry"; attend the trial of a pig thief; or follow the town's Fife & Drum Corps parading down Main Street. Tour the Georgian-style Governor's Palace or the Courthouse of 1770 with its pillories and stocks out front. Stop for a tipple and traditional alehouse fare at any of the four historic taverns.

The elegant 1937 Regency-style Williamsburg Inn has hosted notables from presidents to queens (Queen Elizabeth II stayed here in 1957 and 2007). The inn is now a full-service upscale resort, with a lavish spa using colonial-era herbs like pennyroyal and angelica, and the nearby Golden Horseshoe Golf Club (including the Gold Course, considered one of Robert Trent Jones Sr.'s finest). Simple accommodations are also available in 26 restored 18th-century buildings scattered across town.

It's only 3 miles south to Williamsburg Winery, one of the largest in the state and an important player in Virginia's flourishing viticultural scene. You can also pick up the 24-mile Colonial Parkway, a winding wooded road that connects Williamsburg with the other two towns that make up Virginia's "Historic Triangle": Jamestown, founded in 1607 and the original capital of colonial Virginia, and Yorktown, one of the colony's major ports in the 18th century and the site of the last battle of the American Revolution.

Where: 150 miles south of Washington, D.C. Tel 800-447-8679 or 757-220-7645; www.colonialwilliamsburg.com. **Williamsburg Inn & Colonial Houses:** Tel 800-447-8679 or 757-220-7978; www.colonialwilliamsburg.com. *Cost:* Inn from $320 (off-peak), from $450 (peak); houses (1 to 8 bedrooms) from $240. **Williamsburg Winery:** Tel 757-229-0999; www.williamsburgwinery.com. **Best times:** mid-May for Drummers Call weekend; late Nov–early Jan for Williamsburg's exceptional Christmas decorations; early Dec for the Grand Illumination.

"It is sometimes called the City of Magnificent Distances, but it might with greater propriety be termed the City of Magnificent Intentions."—Charles Dickens

Washington, D.C.

District of Columbia, U.S.A.

While Washington is all about politics all the time, it's also a spectacularly beautiful city of monumental museums, parks, and broad boulevards. French planner Pierre L'Enfant divided the city into quadrants centered around the U.S. Capitol; he also created the city's open grid of lettered and numbered streets, intersected by diagonal avenues named for states. These factors, along with the city's height limit on buildings, add up to Thomas Jefferson's vision of a city crisscrossed by "light and airy" thoroughfares.

Top Attractions

Historic Georgetown—Georgetown has hosted D.C.'s social and diplomatic scene since the early 19th century. Its brick sidewalks are lined with historic Georgian and Federal homes and tidy Victorian-era row houses; come in late April or early May for house and garden tours that allow an inside look. The oldest building in the District, the Old Stone House, from 1765, is a snapshot of colonial middle-class life. Up the hill, the 1920 Federal-style house known as Dumbarton Oaks is where diplomats met in 1944 to plan the United Nations; its formal gardens are a highlight. To the west is the turreted campus of Georgetown University, the oldest Catholic university in the country.
Old Stone House: Tel 202-426-6851; www.nps.gov/olst. **Dumbarton Oaks:** Tel 202-339-6401; www.doaks.org. **Georgetown House and Garden Tours:** www.georgetownhousetour.com, www.georgetowngardentour.com.

National Gallery of Art—Founded in 1937, the National Gallery enjoys a dual personality. In John Russell Pope's original Neoclassical West Building, the European and American art ranges from early Italian altar panels to works by Dutch masters and French Impressionists, plus the only painting by Leonardo da Vinci in the New World. I. M. Pei's modernist East Building, opened next door in 1978, houses gems by Calder, Matisse, Picasso, Pollock, and Rothko, while a masterwork-studded 6-acre sculpture garden awaits just outside.
Info: Tel 202-737-4215; www.nga.gov.

In springtime, cherry blossoms surround the Washington Monument.

THE NATIONAL MALL—Washington's centerpiece, a two-mile greensward running west from the U.S. Capitol, holds some of the nation's most important monuments. The Washington Monument, the first presidential memorial, is at its center and offers a spectacular view from the top. To the west is the Neoclassical Lincoln Memorial, where Daniel Chester French's massive sculpture of the brooding president sits, the wrenching words of his Gettysburg Address etched behind him. To feel its power, visit at night, when the monuments are illuminated and the crowds have thinned out. The elegant Thomas Jefferson Memorial is on the south side of the Tidal Basin; the third president's bronze likeness stands beneath a Pantheon-inspired dome. The memorial dedicated to Franklin Delano Roosevelt in 1997 comprises four outdoor galleries, one for each of the president's terms in office. Northeast of the Lincoln Memorial, the riveting Vietnam Veterans Memorial consists of a simple V-shaped wall of polished black granite inscribed with the names of almost 60,000 soldiers who died in action. Nearby is the evocative Korean War Veterans Memorial and on the east end of the Reflecting Pool is the stately National World War II Memorial. The Mall is spectacular in early spring, when thousands of Japanese cherry trees burst into bloom around the Tidal Basin. **INFO:** www.nps.gov/nama.

THE NATIONAL ZOO—Giant pandas have made their home at the Smithsonian's National Zoo ever since President Nixon was given two by China following his 1972 goodwill trip there. They are part of the zoo's new Asia Trail. Another recently added highlight is the Elephant Trek, where you'll meet the zoo's three Asian pachyderms, Shanthi, Ambika, and Kandula. All told, some 2,400 animals roam these leafy grounds. **INFO:** Tel 202-673-4800; www.nationalzoo.si.edu.

THE NATION'S MEMORY—Between them, the Library of Congress and the National Archives preserve the documents that created this country and the printed and digital matter that chronicles its history. The LOC is the country's official library and the world's largest—it contains close to 30 million books, including a Gutenberg Bible, and millions of photographs, maps, and recordings. The star attraction: the Main Reading Room of the Jefferson Building, topped by an ornate 160-foot dome. In the rotunda of the Archives, display cases hold the original handwritten copies of the Declaration of Independence, the Constitution, and the Bill of Rights. **LIBRARY OF CONGRESS:** Tel 202-707-5000; www.loc.gov. **NATIONAL ARCHIVES:** Tel 866-272-6272; www.archives.gov.

SMITHSONIAN MUSEUMS—Most of the 19 national museums that make up the Smithsonian Institution line the National Mall, holding some 137 million objects. The two most popular are the Air and Space Museum, with everything from the Wright Brothers' glider to the *Apollo 11* command module, and the century-old Museum of Natural History with its dinosaurs and diamonds, such as the 45½-carat dark blue Hope Diamond. The American History museum includes as much pop culture as serious history. One of the newest additions is the gallery that holds the Star-Spangled Banner, the flag that inspired the national anthem, but you'll also find here an original Kermit the Frog Muppet, a sampling of First Ladies' inaugural gowns, and Julia Child's kitchen. **Smithsonian Info:** Tel 202-633-1000; www.smithsonian.org.

U.S. Capitol—At the east end of the National Mall is the Capitol Building, one of the first structures conceived by city planner Pierre L'Enfant; George Washington laid the cornerstone in September 1793. Guided tours include the Rotunda, under the building's dome; in the dome itself, an 1865 fresco depicts the first president rising into the heavens. The Capitol's south and north wings contain the House and Senate chambers, where visitor galleries are open to anyone who obtains a gallery pass in advance from their senator or congressperson. **Info:** Tel 202-225-6827; www.aoc.gov.

White House—The exterior of this grand Neoclassical building is still as architect James Hoban designed it in 1792. Visitors lucky enough to join a tour (make advance arrangements through your congressperson) can see a number of rooms inside the executive mansion, including the State Dining Room (once Thomas Jefferson's office); the Blue Room, with furniture selected by James Monroe after the British torched the house in the War of 1812; and the East Room, where seven presidents have lain in state. **Info:** Tel 202-456-7041; www.whitehouse.gov/history/tours.

Many famous speeches, most notably Martin Luther King's "I Have a Dream" speech, were delivered at the Lincoln Memorial.

Other Must-Dos

American Art—Of course America's capital showcases American art. D.C.'s oldest museum, founded in 1869, is the Corcoran Gallery. Its collection includes works from 19th-century greats such as Mary Cassatt and John Singer Sargent as well as modern and contemporary artists like Edward Hopper and Jacob Lawrence. Three other American-oriented museums are part of the Smithsonian constellation. The Portrait Gallery and American Art Museum share a historic 1836 building; the former owns the famous "Lansdowne portrait," Gilbert Stuart's full-length painting of George Washington, while the latter encompasses the largest collection of American art in the world. Finally, the Renwick Gallery holds the premier collection of American craft objects and decorative arts. **Corcoran Gallery of Art:** Tel 202-639-1700; www.corcoran.org. **American Art Museum:** Tel 202-275-1500; www.americanart.si.edu. **National Portrait Gallery:** Tel 202-275-1738; www.npg.si.edu. **Renwick Gallery:** Tel 202-633-2850; www.americanart.si.edu/renwick.

Hillwood Estate, Museum & Gardens—Among the city's unsung gems is the Georgian mansion of Marjorie Merriweather Post, the late cereal heiress and socialite. Set on 25 acres, the home holds Post's important cache of Russian porcelain and icons (plus the Catherine the Great Easter Egg by Fabergé), which she acquired when the Soviet government endorsed the selling off of Russia's imperial art treasures. **Info:** Tel 202-686-5807; www.hillwoodmuseum.org.

Phillips Collection and Hirshhorn Museum—The Phillips was the country's first museum to pay homage to the world of modern art and is known for its Impressionist and Post-Impressionist paintings, including Renoir's monumental *Luncheon of the Boating Party*. The Hirshhorn Museum and Sculpture Garden, unmistakable for its resemblance to a large cylindrical tank, is part of the Smithsonian Institution on the National Mall. Its collection includes works by Picasso, Giacometti, de Kooning, Pollock, Warhol, Rodin, and hundreds of others. **Phillips Collection:** Tel 202-387-2151; www.phillips collection.org. **Hirshhorn Museum:** Tel 202-633-4674; www.hirshhorn.si.edu.

Holocaust Museum—Between 1939 and 1945, Europe saw the slaughter of 6 million Jews, 1.9 million Poles, and 500,000 others. The U.S. Holocaust Memorial Museum is dedicated to not letting us forget: Its permanent exhibit follows the Nazis' rise to power and the subsequent genocide they perpetrated, with a haunting collection of photos, reconstructions, and personal effects of the doomed prisoners. **Info:** Tel 202-488-0400; www.ushmm.org.

The International Spy Museum and the Newseum—The only thing more thrilling than reading about spies is learning how to be one. The Spy Museum leads visitors through spy school, where they learn the history of espionage and how spies function in the 21st century—complete with displays of miniature cameras, lipstick-tube pistols, and a shoe-phone with heel transmitter (courtesy of the KGB). The Newseum celebrates both the news itself and American journalism's role in covering it. A 90-foot wall flashes the day's events, and objects on display include sections of the Berlin Wall, the Unabomber's cabin, and a remnant of the World Trade Center. **Spy Museum:** Tel 202-393-7798; www.spymuseum.org. **Newseum:** Tel 888-639-7386 or 202-296-6100; www.newseum.org.

Unofficial Monuments—The largest railroad station in the world when it opened in 1907, Washington's Union Station has been meticulously restored, and while it is still an active railroad and Metro station, it is now studded with shops and restaurants. The National Building Museum celebrates American architecture; its spectacular home is the old U.S. Pension Building, whose Great Hall flaunts double loggias, a central indoor fountain, and eight colossal Corinthian columns supporting its 159-foot ceiling. Its museum gift shop has been called the best in the country. You can visit the John F. Kennedy Center for the Performing Arts for a play, the opera, or the symphony orchestra, or you can take a daytime tour. The center is a "living memorial" to the assassinated 35th president. **Union Station:** Tel 202-289-1908; www.unionstationdc.com. **National Building Museum:** Tel 202-272-2448; www.nbm.org. **Kennedy Center:** Tel 202-416-8727; www.kennedy-center.org.

Day Trips

Arlington Cemetery—With more than 300,000 white marble headstones, this is the final resting place for American military personnel, from the Revolutionary War to the war in Iraq. Graveside services are held every day—your visit may be punctuated by the crack of a rifle salute and the sound of "Taps." The most visited grave is that of President John F. Kennedy, with its eternal flame; his wife, Jacqueline Kennedy Onassis, lies next to him. Atop the hill is Arlington House, Robert E. Lee's mansion. **Where:** in Virginia, directly across Arlington Memorial Bridge from the Lincoln Memorial. Tel 703-607-8000; www.arlingtoncemetery.org. **Arlington House:** Tel 703-235-1530; www.nps.gov/arho.

Mount Vernon—George Washington himself designed his Georgian-style plantation home on the banks of the Potomac River. Ongoing restoration has uncovered the original, surprisingly lively interior wall colors, and restored the first president's whiskey distillery. You can also see quarters for the 316 slaves he owned at the time of his death in 1799, along with his grave and that of his wife, Martha. Arrive at Mount Vernon the way Washington's friends often did—from the river. Spring through fall, Spirit Cruises offers passage from D.C.'s southwest marina. **Where:** 16 miles south of D.C. in Virginia. Tel 703-780-2000; www.mountvernon.org. **How:** Spirit Cruises, tel 866-211-3811; www.cruisetomountvernon.com.

Old Town Alexandria—The historic heart of this 18th-century Potomac River port town has lots of 18th- and 19th-century buildings plus lively streets lined with shops, art galleries, antiques stores, and restaurants. The Founding Fathers frequented Gadsby's Tavern, a circa 1785 building that is now both a museum to eating and drinking in colonial America and a restaurant housed in the original dining room. **Where:** 8 miles south of Washington in Virginia. www.alexandriava.gov. **Gadsby's Tavern Museum:** Tel 703-548-1288; www.gadsbystavern.org. *Cost:* dinner $45.

Where to Stay

Four Seasons—At the entrance to Georgetown, this hotel's discreet brick façade does not hint at what awaits within: arguably the most luxurious digs in town. Amenities are top-of-the-line, including the power dining at Michael Mina's handsomely appointed Bourbon Steak restaurant. **Info:** Tel 800-332-3442 or 202-342-0444; www.fourseasons.com. *Cost:* from $595 (off-peak), from $795 (peak). **Bourbon Steak:** Tel 202-944-2026; www.michaelmina.net. *Cost:* dinner $75.

The Hotel George—This Kimpton hotel—convenient to Union Station, the Capitol, and the National Mall—is distinguished by a modern décor that blends a dash of glitz with a heaping dose of wit. Chef Jeffrey Buben's in-house Bistro Bis offers a French menu, a comfortable bar, and the chance to glimpse Capitol Hill bigwigs at the next table. **Info:** Tel 800-546-7866 or 202-347-4200; www.hotelgeorge.com. *Cost:* from $179 (off-peak), from $300 (peak). **Bistro Bis:** Tel: 202-661-2700; www.bistrobis.com. *Cost:* dinner $55.

Hay-Adams Hotel—If your invitation for a night in the Lincoln Bedroom didn't come through, stay right across Lafayette Square at the Italian Renaissance–style Hay-Adams Hotel, a favorite of diplomats and visiting heads of state. **Info:** Tel 800-853-6807 or 202-638-6600; www.hayadams.com. *Cost:* from $330 (off-peak), from $525 (peak).

The Jefferson—A 2009 overhaul turned the cozy 90-room Jefferson, up the street from the White House, into a real jewel, with the well-turned-out Plume restaurant, the more casual Greenhouse for lunch and brunch, and a new spa with treatments based on the botanicals Thomas Jefferson grew in his Monticello gardens. Exquisite details are matched by flawless service. **Info:** Tel 202-448-2300; www.jeffersondc.com. *Cost:* from $375 (off-peak), from $450 (peak); lunch at Greenhouse $40. **Plume:** Tel 202-448-2322. *Cost:* dinner $65.

Hotel Tabard Inn—The Tabard Inn, named for the inn in Chaucer's *Canterbury Tales,* has 40 rooms in three attached Victorian town houses near Dupont Circle. The parlor leads to The Restaurant, a venerable, modern-American favorite with a busy bar and a roaring fire. It is filled with locals for dinner and especially for weekend brunch. **Info:** Tel 202-785-1277; www.tabardinn.com. *Cost:* from $165; dinner at The Restaurant $50.

Willard InterContinental—Abraham Lincoln held staff meetings in the voluptuous lobby here before his inauguration—and paid his hotel bill with his first presidential paycheck. Presidents Grant and Hayes spent the night too. You'll learn this and more in the "museum" at the back of the lobby, which is as much a history of Washington as of the Willard. The lobby, folklore has it, is also where lobbyists got their name. The K Street bunch still hangs out in the storied Round Robin Bar. **Info:** Tel 866-487-2537 or 202-628-9100; www.washington.intercontinental.com. *Cost:* from $349.

Eating & Drinking

Central Michel Richard—After enjoying immediate success with Georgetown's innovative, French-flavored Citronelle, chef Michel Richard created the more casual Central, a New American–French brasserie serving comfort food with playful twists. **Info:** Tel 202-626-0015; www.centralmichel richard.com. *Cost:* dinner $50.

City Zen—Iowa native Eric Ziebold is known for experimenting with New American cuisine, and the results have foodies filling this exquisite spot in the Mandarin Oriental hotel by the Maine Avenue marina. The menu might promise mille feuille of prime beef or buttered Maine lobster. **Info:** Tel 202-787-6006; www.mandarinoriental.com. *Cost:* 3-course prix-fixe dinner $80.

Clyde's—Clyde's of Georgetown is the original, but the Clyde's Restaurant Group has 13 reliably great places around town, and all run seasonal menus—from just-in produce from local farms to softshell crabs. Clyde's is also behind the clubby Old Ebbitt Grill downtown, a classic Victorian-style saloon frequented by businesspeople and Secret Service agents. **Clyde's:** Tel 202-333-9180; www.clydes.com. *Cost:* dinner $34. **Old Ebbitt Grill:** Tel: 202-347-4800; www.ebbitt.com. *Cost:* lunch $30.

José Andrés—Young Spanish chef and beloved local fixture José Andrés brought Spain's famed tapas to Washington, at Jaleo, then stuck around to help create a downtown empire: Café Atlántico for Caribbean; Oyamel for Mexican small plates; Zaytinya for Mediterranean meze; and his tiny (six-seat!) uberexperiment in molecular gastronomy, Minibar by José Andrés. **Info:** www.thinkfood group.com. **Jaleo:** Tel 202-628-7949. *Cost:* dinner $30. **Café Atlántico:** Tel 202-393-0812. *Cost:* dinner $50. **Oyamel:** Tel 202-628-1005. *Cost:* dinner $30. **Zaytinya:** Tel 202-638-0800. *Cost:* dinner $35. **Minibar:** upstairs from Café Atlántico. *Cost:* prix-fixe dinner $120.

Komi—Thirty-something chef-owner Johnny Monis is at the helm in this small Mediterranean-inspired restaurant, where a dazzling parade of petite but mind-blowing dishes is served in an unadorned space and enhanced by service that is charming, smooth, and smart. **Info:** Tel 202-332-9200; www .komirestaurant.com. *Cost:* tasting menu $125.

The Monocle—This solid 50-year-old Capitol Hill favorite serves reliably good fare that is a throwback to earlier times—you'll find steak, seafood, and signature crab cakes here, and often enough, senators and congressmen schmoozing in the convivial, red-walled dining room. **Info:** Tel 202-546-4488; www.themonocle.com. *Cost:* dinner $45.

Washington's Ferry Land

The San Juan Islands

Washington, U.S.A.

In the northwest corner of Washington State, the waters of Puget Sound, the Strait of Georgia, and the Strait of Juan de Fuca mingle, forming the Salish Sea, home to the forested, rock-faced San Juan Islands. Although the archipelago is composed of more than 750 islands scattered across 10,000 square miles, only 170 of them are named. Of those, only about 40 are inhabited, and just four are served by Washington State Ferries.

Despite their proximity to Seattle, the

islands have significantly better weather than the city and have retained their bucolic allure. Lopez is the most rural, and with few hills and friendly drivers, it's a great island to explore on two wheels. Many consider the mountainous Orcas Island the most beautiful. From the top of 2,409-foot Mount Constitution, in rugged Moran State Park, views on a clear day stretch from Mount Rainier to Vancouver. Weekenders appreciate a sophisticated but casual eating scene, such as the dinner of fresh-from-the-greenhouse vegetables and locally caught seafood at the Inn at Ship Bay Restaurant. Turtleback Farm Inn strikes that same balance between refinement and rustic charm. The inn, a working farm set on 80 country acres, offers lodging in both a beautifully restored 19th-century green-clapboard farmhouse and the Orchard House, which offers glimpses of Mount Wollard. Work off prize-winning breakfasts by hiking the nearby 1,575-acre Turtleback Mountain Preserve.

San Juan Island is the most distant from the mainland, and the only one with an incorporated town, Friday Harbor. A bustling port, it's also the place for kayak trips and unmatched whale-watching. Three pods of orcas, one of the highest concentrations anywhere, call these chilly waters home, as do seals and porpoises. Stay overnight at the Friday Harbor House, a contemporary hotel with a restaurant and sweeping views of the marina, and spend a morning at the Whale Museum, with informative displays of the San Juan marine ecosystem.

Lime Kiln Lighthouse, on San Juan Island's rocky coast, is popular with whale-watchers.

WHERE: 90 miles north of Seattle; www.visitsanjuans.com. **WASHINGTON STATE FERRIES:** Tel 888-808-7977 or 206-464-6400; www.wsdot.wa.gov/ferries. **INN AT SHIP BAY:** Tel 877-276-7296 or 360-376-5886; www.innatshipbay.com. *Cost:* dinner $50. *When:* closed Dec–Jan. **TURTLEBACK FARM INN:** Tel 800-376-4914 or 360-376-4914; www.turtlebackinn.com. *Cost:* from $115. **FRIDAY HARBOR HOUSE:** Tel 866-722-7356 or 360-378-8455; fridayharborhouse.com. *Cost:* from $130 (off-peak), from $200 (peak); dinner $35. **WHALE MUSEUM:** Tel 360-378-4710; www.whalemuseum.org. **BEST TIMES:** late Apr for the Tour de Lopez bicycling event; Jun–Sep for sighting orcas; early Sep for the Deer Harbor Wooden Boat Rendezvous on Orcas.

The Gastronomic Heart of Seattle

PIKE PLACE MARKET

Seattle, Washington, U.S.A.

Not all roads in Seattle lead to Pike Place Market, but it sure feels that way. The site opened in 1907—making it one of the oldest continuously operating farmers markets in the U.S.—so growers could sell directly to customers, eliminating the middleman. Today, this always busy, always freewheeling marketplace's circuslike atmosphere is underscored by street entertainers and the spectacle of fishmongers tossing whole salmon across the counters for the amusement of passersby.

The market is at the edge of bluffs overlooking the Seattle waterfront and extends across seven city blocks, filling 23 multilevel buildings with 600 vendors and as many as 40,000 daily visitors. Seafood reigns, with spot prawns (Northwest shrimp), halibut, geoduck clams, and oysters from a variety of Northwest bays all chilling atop mountains of shaved ice. But though the heart of the market remains its wondrous food, there's a lot more than eats for sale in this assemblage of shops, stalls, and warren-like underground arcades, from magicians' supplies to wind-up toys to vintage clothes. The market is also home to some of Seattle's best-loved restaurants and watering holes, many of them tucked into narrow offshoots such as Post Alley. A revered point of pilgrimage is 1912 Pike Place, site of the world's first Starbucks, which began in 1971 as a plain-Jane hole-in-the-wall coffee shop before spawning a coffee mania that spread worldwide.

In addition to 70 luxurious guest rooms with views over the market and Elliott Bay, the cozy but elegant Inn at the Market, the only accommodation within Pike Place, delivers delicious southern-French room service dishes from the Campagne restaurant, while the more informal Café Campagne offers lighter meals and a wine bar. Next to the market, Etta's Seafood Restaurant is a valentine to lovers of fish and shellfish, serving oysters on the half shell, signature Dungeness crab cakes, and smoked sake salmon. For this (and a bevy of other culinary delights such as Dahlia, Palace Kitchen, and Lola) you can thank local chef extraordinaire Tom Douglas. Another option is worth the 15-minute taxi ride to the city's best-known waterside restaurant, Ray's Boathouse, a real Seattle classic. It's a fun spot for happy hour upstairs on the popular summertime deck, and there's a more refined eatery downstairs. For a romantic Seattle sunset over Shilshole Bay, this is the best place to be.

INFO: Tel 206-682-7453; www.pikeplacemarket.org. **STARBUCKS:** Tel 206-448-8762; www.starbucks.com. **INN AT THE MARKET:** Tel 800-446-4484 or 206-443-3600; www.innatthemarket.com. *Cost:* from $185 (off-peak), from $245 (peak). **CAMPAGNE:** Tel 206-728-2800; www.campagnerestaurant.com. *Cost:* dinner $55. **CAFÉ CAMPAGNE:** Tel 206-728-2233. *Cost:* dinner $40. **ETTA'S:** Tel 206-443-6000; www.tomdouglas.com. *Cost:* dinner $50. **RAY'S BOATHOUSE:** Tel 206-789-3770 (restaurant) or 206-782-0094 (deck); www.rays.com. *Cost:* dinner $55.

Running the Rivers of the Mountain State

West Virginia's Whitewater Rafting

West Virginia, U.S.A

With some of the highest thrills-per-rapid ratios anywhere in North America, West Virginia's rivers are regularly ranked among the top ten whitewater runs in the world, passing through a landscape so rugged that it's often referred to as the West of the East. Most outfitters suggest getting your feet wet in the curiously named New River (it's purportedly the world's second oldest river, after the Nile; see p. 381), which offers a range of rafting experiences along its 53 scenic miles, as well as opportunities for hiking, mountain biking, fishing, and rock climbing. The lower river, aptly called the "Grand Canyon of the East," drops 250 feet in 16 miles, with rapids ranging from Class II to Class V. Toward the end of the run looms the enormous 876-foot-high New River Gorge Bridge, which is the longest single-arch span in the northern hemisphere and the highest after Colorado's Royal Gorge Bridge. Completed in 1977, it's at its wildest during Bridge Day, in October, when 450 BASE jumpers, from as far away as Russia and Australia, don parachutes and jump from it for the 8.8-second ride of a lifetime.

North of the New River, the Gauley River is one of the country's most challenging runs. In the 1960s, the U.S. Army Corps of Engineers built a 40-story, 2,280-foot-wide dam in the river's upper reaches, creating Summersville Lake. In summer the serene lake is kept full at an elevation of 1,652 feet above sea level, enabling a wide range of watersports. Rafting enthusiasts live for September and early October, though, when millions of gallons of excess lake water are released, turning the Gauley into a roaring beast with more than 60 steep Class IV and V rapids that have earned names like "Heaven Help You" and "Pure Screaming Hell." The Upper Gauley is the more difficult section, flowing through a narrow canyon with drops averaging 32 feet per mile. On the Lower Gauley, tough rapids are followed by calm pools, giving you a chance to catch your breath and take in the utter beauty of the wooded Appalachian terrain.

Where: 50 miles southeast of Charleston. **Visitor info:** www.newrivercvb.com. **How:** Lansing-based Wildwater Expeditions offers New River and Lower Gauley river rafting trips. Tel 800-982-7238 or 304-658-4007; www.wvaraft.com. *Cost:* from $129. **When:** Mar–Oct on the New River, early Sep–mid-Oct on the Gauley. **Best times:** Oct for foliage; 3rd Sat of Oct for Bridge Day.

Paddling against the New River's rapids affords rafters thrills and views of gorges, cliffs, and other natural wonders.

Where Presidents Take the Waters

The Greenbrier

White Sulphur Springs, West Virginia, U.S.A.

Like West Virginia's wealth of river-rafting venues, The Greenbrier owes its fame to water—in this case the sulfur-rich springs that made it the summer capital of the Old South. With a guest registry whose names include Davy Crockett, Daniel Webster, and 26 U.S. presidents, the landmark white-columned property continues to attract pilgrims eager to "take the cure." Begun as a cluster of cabins in the 1800s and later transformed into a stately 634-plus-room hotel, The Greenbrier today stands grandly amid 6,500 acres in a scenic valley of the Allegheny Mountains, as proud of its remarkable roster of more than 50 activities as of its pedigree.

There's no mistaking that golf is the leading attraction, with three 18-hole championship courses plus a respected golf academy. The Greenbrier Course, site of both the Ryder (1979) and Solheim (1994) Cups, was laid out in 1924 and redesigned by Jack Nicklaus in 1977. The 40,000-square-foot spa continues the Greenbrier's 230-year tradition of hydrotherapy with a vast menu of services. Tennis on indoor and outdoor courts, horseback riding, fishing, mountain biking, croquet, and the new guests-only underground casino complex ensure that nongolfers will not feel neglected.

A staff of 1,300 exemplifies the resort's characteristic graciousness and decorum—they'll gently remind you that a jacket-and-tie dress code still prevails in the high-ceilinged, chandeliered dining room. A clubby steak house, Prime 44 West, pays homage to former Los Angeles Laker and West Virginia native Jerry West. The Greenbrier's most unusual feature is its underground bunker, a huge complex built during the Eisenhower administration and intended to house members of Congress in the event of a Cold War–era nuclear war. It was declassified in 1992 and is open for the curious to visit.

Catch the nearby Midland Trail (U.S. Route 60), once a buffalo trail used by Indians and pioneers. It offers beautiful vistas of wooded mountains and travels the entire length of the state. The trail will lead you to Lewisburg, arguably the most beautiful town in the state, with a 236-acre National Register Historic District. Check in to the family-owned General Lewis Inn, a 1929 addition to an 1834 home, with 25 rooms and a restaurant renowned for its refined country cooking. Also make time to hike some of the 79-mile Greenbrier River Trail, which you can pick up nearby. If it's August, it may feel like the entire state is in town to enjoy carnival rides, livestock shows, and blue-ribbon produce competitions at the annual state fair.

WHERE: 120 miles southeast of Charleston. **THE GREENBRIER:** Tel 800-624-6070 or 304-536-1110; www.greenbrier.com. *Cost:* from $295 (off-peak), from $370 (peak); greens fees from $185; dinner at Prime 44 West $50. **MIDLAND TRAIL:** Tel 866-768-7360 or 304-343-6001; www.midlandtrail.com. **GENERAL LEWIS INN:** Tel 800-628-4454 or 304-645-2600; www.generallewisinn.com. *Cost:* from $135; dinner $30. **GREENBRIER RIVER TRAIL:** www.greenbrierrivertrail.com. **STATE FAIR:** Tel 304-645-1090; www.statefairofwv.com. *When:* mid-Aug. **BEST TIMES:** Oct for foliage; 2nd weekend in Oct for Taste of Our Town festival in Lewisburg.

Sanctuary on North America's Largest Lake

THE APOSTLE ISLANDS

Bayfield, Wisconsin, U.S.A.

Strewn across 450 square miles of Lake Superior's crystalline waters, the 21 Apostle Islands are tiny jewels on an immense inland sea, the largest freshwater body in the world. With the exception of Madeline, the biggest of the Apostles, all the islands are undeveloped and uninhabited, a showcase for craggy shorelines, old-growth hemlocks and hardwoods, and sculpted sandstone cliffs and caves. From minuscule 3-acre Gull to 10,000-acre Stockton, the islands are protected as the Apostle Islands National Lakeshore, along with 12 miles of shoreline on the adjacent Bayfield Peninsula. Although more than 50 miles of trails crisscross the islands, which are home to black bears, bald eagles, and more than 200 species of migratory birds, the best exploration is done by boat. The Apostle Islands Cruise Service and captained sailboat charters offer a variety of options that revolve around beachcombing, hiking, and swimming in sun-warmed bays. The national lakeshore includes eight historic lighthouses—more than any other national park—some of which offer tours in summer. Kayaks are perfect for open-water passages between islands and for ducking in and out of the sea caves that pock the sandstone shoreline.

With sweeping island vistas and a yacht-filled marina, the gateway village of Bayfield (population 600) makes a great base camp from which to explore and arrange island excursions. After your adventures, you'll be happy to rest your head at the Old Rittenhouse Inn, where guests are pampered in a lovingly restored Queen Anne–style showcase that also serves some of the best meals in town.

WHERE: 90 miles east of Duluth, MN. **VISITOR INFO:** www.nps.gov/apis. **APOSTLE ISLANDS CRUISE SERVICE:** Tel 800-323-7619 or 715-779-3925; www.apostleisland.com. *When:* mid-May–mid-Oct. **OLD RITTENHOUSE INN:** Tel 888-611-4667 or 715-779-5111; www.rittenhouseinn.com. *Cost:* from $115 (off-peak), from $140 (peak); prix-fixe dinner $55. **BEST TIMES:** Feb–early Mar for hiking to the ice-coated caves along Bayfield Peninsula; Jul–Aug for warm weather and calm waters; early Aug–Sep for annual lighthouse celebration.

Millennia of waves have carved natural sea caves into the islands' coasts.

Elegant Escape Deep in the North Woods

CANOE BAY

Chetek, Wisconsin, U.S.A.

The spring-fed lakes, deep pine forests, and clean air of northwestern Wisconsin's Indianhead region have long made it a getaway for everyone from industrial-era tycoons to U.S. president Calvin Coolidge. Near Chetek, the 280-acre Canoe Bay resort brings alive that era of back-to-nature luxury for those seeking solitude and respite. With no children, telephones, jet skis, or motorboats to pierce the serenity, Canoe Bay frequently makes the list of "most romantic" getaways. Nature and the architectural aesthetic are the lure here, with 23 elegant lakeside rooms and cottages promising stone fireplaces, double whirlpools, and wilderness views at every turn. Wisconsin native Frank Lloyd Wright's protégé and collaborator on New York City's Guggenheim Museum (see p. 843), John Rattenbury, designed the Rattenbury Cottage and Edgewood, a 2,000-square-foot showpiece of stone, wood, and glass with a 1,500-square-foot wraparound deck. Couples at Canoe Bay enjoy breakfast in bed, in-room massages, and innovative dining in a lakeside restaurant with an unpretentious but sophisticated menu inspired by seasonal picks from local markets and an award-winning wine list.

Guests can hike around three private glacial lakes via 4 miles of scenic trails that snake through Canoe Bay's 280 acres of hardwood forest, and the resort provides canoes, kayaks, and rowboats for gliding across the crystal-clear Lake Wahdoon. Largemouth bass and pan fish provide catch-and-release fishing opportunities, and swimmers enjoy warm waters and a sandy beach on summer afternoons. Come winter, Canoe Bay rents snowshoes for traipsing around the snow-blanketed property, and Nordic skiers can explore 20 miles of groomed trails nearby.

WHERE: 120 miles east of Minneapolis, MN. Tel 800-568-1995 or 715-924-4594; www.canoebay.com. *Cost:* from $350; 3-course prix-fixe dinner $75. **BEST TIMES:** Jun–Aug for water sports; 1st half of Oct for peak foliage.

From Company Town to Luxe Golf Resort

The American Club

Kohler, Wisconsin, U.S.A.

Sure, it sounds odd to build an exclusive resort around a plumbing factory, but that's exactly what happened in the Village of Kohler, a name known for its stylish, high-end bathroom fixtures. In 1918, company president (and later governor of Wisconsin) Walter J. Kohler commissioned an impressive, block-long redbrick Tudor building directly opposite his factory as a boardinghouse for his immigrant workforce. In the 1980s, the dormitory was transformed into a high-end inn, and the property was gradually expanded to encompass four restaurants and 240 guestrooms fitted with (not surprisingly) lavish bathrooms. Today, one of Kohler's favorite quotes is etched in stained glass in the handsome Wisconsin Room restaurant, once the workers' dining hall and now part of the American Club Resort Hotel: "Life without labor is guilt; labor without art is brutality."

Golf is the primary—but far from the only—draw at the American Club: Four magnificent championship courses designed by Pete Dye frame the resort. Blackwolf Run's two 18-hole courses (River and Meadow Valleys, top-notch enough to host the 2012 Women's Open) take advantage of the region's naturally undulating glacier-scoured terrain. Dye also created Whistling Straits, evoking the windswept, rough-hewn courses of Scotland and Ireland. Complete with grazing sheep, it stretches along a flat bluff above the blue expanse of Lake Michigan. Built in 1998, Whistling Straits hosted the 2004 and 2010 PGA Championships (a rare honor for such a new course) and is slated to do so again in 2015.

The 500-acre River Wildlife private nature preserve provides 25 miles of hiking trails, horseback riding, and pheasant hunting; 7 miles of salmon-filled rivers and trout streams; and the excellent Lodge restaurant. At the 24,000-square-foot Kohler Waters Spa, you can choose from more than 50 treatments. Settings are designed to showcase Kohler's plumbing marvels, such as the RiverBath room, which features a waterfall and whirlpool jets that mimic river currents.

WHERE: 55 miles north of Milwaukee. Tel 800-344-2838 or 920-457-8000; www.destinationkohler.com. *Cost:* from $180 (off-peak), from $285 (peak); greens fees from $165; dinner at the Lodge $70. **BEST TIMES:** late May for Festival of Beer; Jun for the Kohler Golf Expo; Oct for the Kohler Food and Wine Experience.

The Daddy of All Rodeos

Cheyenne Frontier Days

Cheyenne, Wyoming, U.S.A.

The Cowboy State's capital city was once nicknamed Hell on Wheels, and during its annual Frontier Days you'll understand why. This celebration of all things Western was first held in 1897, a mere 15 years after William F. Cody, aka "Buffalo Bill," created the rodeo tradition with his traveling Wild West Show. Today it's a 10-day carnival of rodeos, wild-horse races, marching bands, intertribal Indian dancing, and a parade that's been led by some memorable names over the years—including Buffalo Bill himself in 1898 and an enthusiastic Teddy Roosevelt in 1910.

Frontier Days is known among rodeo aficionados as "The Daddy of 'em All," bringing upward of 550,000 visitors every year, plus more than 1,800 of the toughest cowboys and cowgirls from across the nation. The event's rollicking atmosphere extends to its famous free pancake breakfasts, at which 10,000 guests consume more than 100,000 flapjacks, 475 gallons of syrup, and 520 gallons of coffee.

If you have a hankering for more genteel pursuits, the celebration has included an art show and sale of works by Western artists, carvers, and Navajo weavers. Cheyenne's Victorian opulence is on display in the stretch of 17th Street known as "Cattle Baron's Row." Indulge like a gentleman rancher from another age by staying at Nagle Warren Mansion B&B, situated in the meticulously restored home of a former governor and U.S. senator.

Where: 100 miles north of Denver. Tel 800-227-6336 or 307-778-7222; www.cfdrodeo.com. *When:* late Jul. **Nagle Warren Mansion B&B:** Tel 800-811-2610 or 307-637-3333; www.naglewarrenmansion.com. *Cost:* from $145.

Cowboys have been drawn to Cheyenne since the 1890s, when Buffalo Bill's show attracted a crowd of thousands.

Horse Heaven

Bitterroot Ranch

Dubois, Wyoming, U.S.A.

Fifty wild, mountainous miles from Yellowstone, Bitterroot Dude Ranch rests in a remote valley flanked by the Shoshone National Forest on one side and a 52,000-acre wildlife refuge on the other. Mel and Bayard

Fox own and operate this 1,300-acre rider's paradise, with a dozen hand-hewn log cabins—some a century old—scattered along the trout stream that runs through it. The magnificent Arabians they breed and train here make up the majority of a herd that is 160 strong and kept exclusively for their 30 guests.

Visitors can sign up for riding lessons or take part in cattle drives; riders are expertly matched with horses and assembled into groups by skill. Trails meander over sagebrush plains, along rocky gorges, and across alpine meadows, with snow-capped mountains in view. For the experienced, there's even a cross-country course with more than 70 jumps.

Nonequestrians fill their days by hiking, fishing, or just relaxing, while kids can spend time with the lambs, foals, and other animals on Bitterroot's farm. Evenings feature some of the finest and freshest eating in the area, and Dubois, half an hour away, offers shops and galleries, plus square dancing in the summer. It's also home to the National Bighorn Sheep Center, thanks to the country's largest such herd, which roams the mountains above the town.

WHERE: 85 miles east of Jackson. Tel 800-545-0019 or 307-455-3363; www.bitterrootranch.com. *Cost:* from $1,785 per person per week, all-inclusive (off-peak), from $2,100 (peak). *When:* late May–Sep. **NATIONAL BIGHORN SHEEP CENTER:** Tel 888-209-2795 or 307-455-3429; www.bighorn.org. **BEST TIMES:** Jun–Jul for wildflowers; Sep for aspens.

The West's Most Scenic Mountains

GRAND TETON NATIONAL PARK

Wyoming, U.S.A.

Craggy, glacier-chiseled, and rising to 7,000-plus feet above the floor of Wyoming's Jackson Hole Valley (itself more than 6,000 feet above sea level), the dramatic peaks of Grand Teton National Park win America's topographical beauty pageant. With no foothills to mar the view, the oft-photographed Tetons dominate the skyline with a grandeur that's starkly primeval.

The Tetons are the youngest mountains in the Rockies. Legend has it that French Canadian trappers in the early 19th century gave the Teton peaks their lasting name—*les Grand Tetons*, or "the big breasts." Winters could be harsh, but enterprising landowners soon realized that marketing the beauty of the area to aspiring "dudes" provided the best hope of making a living. Today, at the Triangle X Ranch, the only working dude ranch within the park (though one of many in the area; see Jackson, next page), guests enjoy Western hospitality in a laid-back family atmosphere with lots of outdoor adventures such as fly-fishing or rafting on the Snake River.

At the foot of the range, glaciers gouged a string of deep, cold, sapphire blue lakes, of which Jenny Lake is among the most beautiful and most visited. The popular Jenny Lake Lodge, one of the park's nicest and best situated, originated as a dude ranch for the eastern effetes who came west to rough it.

The largest lake, Jackson Lake, is 15 miles long, with cruises to Elk Island and its mountainous western shore. Guided float trips meander down a calm stretch of the Snake

River from Deadman's Bar to Moose, and local outfitters offer whitewater trips as well. A 45-mile loop drive from Moose by way of Moran Junction presents much of the same spectacular scenery seen from the comfort of your car.

Adjacent to the park's southern border, the 24,700-acre National Elk Refuge is the winter home for up to 8,000 migrating elk, the largest herd in North America. From mid-December through March you can get an up-close look at them via a horse-drawn sleigh ride.

Where: 12 miles north of Jackson. Tel 307-739-3300; www.nps.gov/grte. **Triangle X Ranch:** Tel 307-733-2183; www.trianglex.com. *Cost:* cabins from $250 (off-peak) per night, $3,200 per week (peak), all-inclusive. **Jenny Lake Lodge:** Tel 800-628-9988 or 307-733-4647; www.gtlc.com. *Cost:* cabins from $620, all-inclusive. *When:* early May–early Oct. **National Elk Refuge:** Tel 307-733-9212; www.nationalelkrefuge.fws.gov. **Best times:** Jul–Aug for warmest weather; Sep for foliage and fewer crowds.

American Grandeur and Awesome Skiing

Jackson Hole

Wyoming, U.S.A.

One of the art, recreation, and lifestyle capitals of the New West, Jackson has evolved from a fur-trading cow town into a bustling tourist center that borders on being cosmopolitan. While the scenic 50-mile-long Jackson Hole area (the "hole" is a high, enclosed mountain valley) is full of trophy homes and gated communities, Jackson itself draws an egalitarian mix of ski bums, the moneyed elite, hikers and climbers, and even a real Wyoming cowboy or two.

Jackson's tree-lined town square, anchored at each corner with arches made from elk antlers, is surrounded by bars, restaurants, quirky boutiques, and art galleries. Drop by timeworn hangouts like Bubba's Bar-B-Que; the Million Dollar Cowboy Bar, popular since 1937; and the Silver Dollar Bar and Grill in the historic Wort Hotel, famous for the 2,032 silver dollars embedded in its bar.

The Spring Creek Ranch, above town, has elegant log cabins scattered about a 1,000-acre wildlife sanctuary and a restaurant-with-a-view, the Granary. The Zen-like Amangani ("peaceful home") is down the road, but it feels worlds away. A beguiling mix of Asian aesthetic and understated Western cool, it offers a sweeping panorama of the Grand Tetons through 40-foot-high picture windows, an infinity pool, and a heavenly spa.

Jackson's true glory is location, location, location. Grand Teton National Park's lofty peaks rise just to the north (see previous page); it's a day trip away from Yellowstone (see next page); and minutes away from the 2,500 acres of "steep and deep" skiing at Jackson Hole Mountain Resort. Passionate skiers come for the stunning vertical drop of 4,139 feet down the east face of 10,450-foot Rendezvous Mountain and for outstanding intermediate skiing on the Apres Vous Mountain run. Swing by the boisterous Mangy Moose restaurant and saloon before retiring to the slopeside Teton Mountain Lodge & Spa. Nearby Grand Targhee Ski Resort has an incredible 500 inches of snow annually, making it one of skidom's holy grails.

If the area's cowboy vibe has awakened your inner dude, head an hour north of

Jackson to Moran and the Heart Six Ranch, whose trail rides and stream fishing are summer mainstays. In winter, guests explore a virgin wonderland aboard snowmobiles or bliss out in the solitude of the snowbound Rockies.

WHERE: Jackson is 275 miles northwest of Salt Lake City, UT. **VISITOR INFO:** www.jacksonholechamber.com. **SPRING CREEK RANCH:** Tel 800-443-6139 or 307-733-8833; www.springcreekranch.com. *Cost:* from $175 (off-peak), from $340 (peak); dinner at the Granary $55. **AMANGANI:** Tel 877-734-7333 or 307-734-7333; www.amanresorts.com. *Cost:* from $595 (off-peak), from $875 (peak). **JACKSON HOLE MOUNTAIN RESORT:** Tel 888-333-7766 or 307-733-2292; www.jacksonhole.com. *Cost:* lift tickets from $55 (off-peak), from $91 (peak). *When:* ski season Dec–early Apr. **TETON MOUNTAIN LODGE & SPA:** Tel 800-631-6271 or 307-734-7111; www.tetonlodge.com. *Cost:* from $119 (off-peak), from $359 (peak). **GRAND TARGHEE RESORT:** Tel 800-827-4422 or 307-353-2300; www.grandtarghee.com. *Cost:* lift tickets $69. *When:* ski season Dec–mid-Apr. **HEART SIX RANCH:** Tel 888-543-2477 or 307-543-2477; www.heartsix.com. *Cost:* from $120 per person per night (off-peak), from $1,095 per person for 3 days (peak), all-inclusive. **BEST TIMES:** Jan–Mar for skiing; late May for Old West Days; July 4 for Music in the Hole Concert; mid-Sep for Fall Arts Festival.

The Earth's Extravagant Showcase

YELLOWSTONE NATIONAL PARK

Wyoming, U.S.A.

Established in 1872, Yellowstone National Park is America's oldest national park, known worldwide for the geysers and geothermal pools that hark back to its volcanic past. Yellowstone's 3,500 square miles encompass rugged plateaus and heavily forested peaks, steaming hot springs, crystalline lakes, and 290 thundering waterfalls. Over 3 million people visit every year, so if you plan to go between June and September, expect plenty of company in the park's popular areas.

Castle Geyser erupts every 10 to 12 hours.

The legendary geyser known as Old Faithful is just the beginning of the attractions here. The park offers incredible natural diversity and abundant wildlife, all amid breathtaking scenery. The rainbow-hued Grand Canyon of the Yellowstone River, 20 miles long and up to 1,200 feet deep, begins at the showpiece 308-foot Lower Falls. Bears and herds of bison roam the Hayden Valley, while moose and elk linger near the hot springs terraces at Mammoth, and some 322 bird species flit from spruce to fir. White and gray wolves, reintroduced to the park in 1995, hunt in the Lamar Valley.

A highlight of any visit is a stay at the Old Faithful Inn, a huge, century-old pine lodge designed in a rugged Craftsman style that subsequent park lodges have imitated. It sits right next to its namesake geyser, which sprays steaming water up to 184 feet into the air every 65 to 92 minutes. The less reliable Steamboat is the highest-gushing geyser in the world.

The park's 300-plus active geysers (60 percent of the earth's geysers are found here) and the bubbling mud pools, hissing fumaroles, and hot springs—over 10,000 hydrothermal features in all—make up the world's largest geothermal system.

Winter is the serene season, when the park is open to cross-country skiers, snowshoers, and guided tours on snowmobiles and snowcoaches (vanlike vehicles with ski runners and snowmobile-like treads). Snowcoaches also run to Old Faithful Snow Lodge, completed in 1999, the perfect base for wintertime visitors to the park.

WHERE: The park has 5 entrances: 3 in Montana and 2 in Wyoming. www.nps.gov/yell. *When:* most park roads open mid-Apr–early Nov; north entrance (Gardiner, MT) open year-round. **OLD FAITHFUL INN:** Tel 866-439-7375 or 307-344-7311; www.travelyellowstone.com. *Cost:* from $100. *When:* mid-May–mid-Oct. **OLD FAITHFUL SNOW LODGE:** Tel 307-344-7311; www.travelyellowstone.com. *Cost:* from $100. *When:* May–mid-Oct and mid-Dec–early Mar. **BEST TIMES:** May–mid-Jun and Sep–mid-Oct for nice weather without crowds; Sep–mid-Oct for fall foliage; winter for cross-country skiing.

CANADA

The Wild West, Canadian Style

CALGARY STAMPEDE

Calgary, Alberta, Canada

Calgary goes Western during its world-famous stampede, kicking up its (boot) heels for ten rodeo-filled days in July. Rodeos have been a part of Calgary summers since 1886, soon after the city was founded as an outpost for the Royal Canadian Mounted Police.

The Calgary Stampede is the world's largest and most prestigious rodeo, with more than 400 of the world's elite rodeo contestants entered in six major events, competing for a total prize topping nearly $2 million. More than 1 million visitors come for live music and dance performances, parades, a Western art showcase, free pancake breakfasts served from chuckwagons, a carnival and midway, and native powwow dance competitions—just a few of the spectacles that take over the city.

The rodeo is the indisputable heart of the stampede with competition in bareback, saddle bronc, and bull riding; tie-down roping; steer wrestling; and barrel racing. One of the stampede's unique competitions is the Chuckwagon Race, in which old-time horse-pulled cook wagons—not built for speed or grace—contend for the fastest time around the track in a fury of dust and pounding hooves.

To keep in the Western spirit, make your hotel reservations at the Fairmont Palliser, built in 1914, just two years after the first official stampede was held. Cattle barons hung their hats at this oasis of gentility, with a columns-and-marble lobby, luxurious guest rooms, and a palpable sense of period grandeur. Enjoy a juicy Alberta steak in the Rimrock Restaurant, amid authentic Canadiana décor.

Info: Tel 800-661-1767 or 403-269-9822; www.calgarystampede.com. **When:** 10 days in mid-Jul. **Fairmont Palliser:** Tel 800-441-1414 or 403-262-1234; www.fairmont.com/palliser. *Cost:* from $155 (off-peak), from $340 (peak); dinner $55.

Canada's Rocky Mountain High

Banff, Jasper, and Yoho National Parks

Alberta and British Columbia, Canada

Spanning the crown of the majestic Canadian Rockies are Banff, Jasper, and Yoho National Parks, collectively known as the Rocky Mountain Parks. Banff was Canada's very first national park and is now a 2,656-square-mile giant and Canada's No. 1 tourist destination. The park's pride is a pair of shimmering jade green lakes: the stunning Moraine Lake, nestled beneath soaring 10,000-foot peaks, and Lake Louise, known for its dramatic setting at the base of Victoria Glacier. It's also the location of the Fairmont Château Lake Louise, the lakeside luxury-hotel-cum-storybook-castle. All this scenic drama whets the appetite; luckily one of western Canada's top hotels and restaurants can be found in the nearby village of Lake Louise. Its dining room is helmed by stellar chef Hans Sauter.

Banff, at the highest elevation of any town in Canada, offers great dining, shopping, and opulent hotels in a primordial setting. The Fairmont Banff Springs was built in 1888 by the Canadian Pacific Railway to resemble a Scottish baronial castle. The hotel's Stanley Thompson golf course is one of Canada's best (and one of the world's most spectacularly sited) as is the sumptuous, European-style Willow Stream Spa.

One of the world's most scenic roadways, the 142-mile Icefields Parkway links Banff and Jasper National Park, passing through an unbroken panorama of glacier-topped peaks, waterfalls, and turquoise lakes flanked by spruce and fir forests. The literal high point is 11,450-foot Mount Athabasca, surrounded by the Columbia Icefield, which covers more than 200 square miles at the crest of the Continental Divide.

The parkway ends in Jasper National Park (Canada's largest at more than 4,200 square miles), where year-round outdoor adventures abound: Raft the roiling white water of the Athabasca and Sunwapta rivers, hike narrow Maligne Canyon, saddle up for trail rides

Moraine Lake is surrounded by the Valley of the Ten Peaks.

around Patricia Lake, or canoe mirror-still Maligne Lake, the largest of the Rockies' glacier-fed lakes. The Fairmont Jasper Park Lodge is the park's most exclusive resort; accommodations range from comfortable to sumptuous with a mix of cabins, chalets, and cottages in a woodsy 700-acre lakeside setting. With its Stanley Thompson–designed course, the Lodge has been named Canada's No. 1 golf resort.

Adjacent to Banff, on the steep western slopes of the Rockies, Yoho National Park lies in the steep drainage of the Kicking Horse River, which boasts Class III and IV rapids, making it one of Canada's most exciting whitewater destinations. A popular short hike leads to a viewpoint overlooking Takakkaw Falls, Canada's second highest at 1,250 feet. At Emerald Lake Lodge, the rooms' private lakefront balconies overlook deep-green waters and the reflection of soaring mile-high peaks.

WHERE: Banff is 80 miles/129 km west of Calgary. **BANFF NATIONAL PARK:** Tel 403-762-1550; www.pc.gc.ca/banff. **FAIRMONT CHÂTEAU LAKE LOUISE:** Tel 800-441-1414 or 403-522-3511; www.fairmont.com/lakelouise. *Cost:* from $330 (off-peak), from $450 (peak). **POST HOTEL & DINING ROOM:** Tel 800-661-1586 or 403-522-3989; www.posthotel.com. *Cost:* $250; dinner $75. **FAIRMONT BANFF SPRINGS:** Tel 800-441-1414 or 403-762-5755; www.fairmont.com/banffsprings. *Cost:* from $305 (off-peak), from $455 (peak). **JASPER NATIONAL PARK:** Tel 780-852-6176; www.pc.gc.ca/jasper. **FAIRMONT JASPER PARK LODGE:** Tel 800-441-1414 or 780-852-3301; www.fairmont.com/jasper. *Cost:* from $179 (off-peak), from $539 (peak). **YOHO NATIONAL PARK:** Tel 250-343-6783; www.pc.gc.ca/yoho. **EMERALD LAKE LODGE:** Tel 800-663-6336 or 403-410-7417; www.emeraldlakelodge.com. *Cost:* from $215 (off-peak), from $300 (peak). **BEST TIMES:** Jul–Aug for hiking and Banff Summer Arts Festival; Sep–Oct for foliage; Dec–Apr for skiing.

Rail Adventure Through Mountain Majesty

THE CANADIAN ROCKIES BY TRAIN

Alberta and British Columbia, Canada

When railroads first crossed Canada in 1885 ("an act of insane recklessness," read the headlines), they did more than bring in settlers: They opened up western Canada to tourism. "If we can't export the scenery," declared William Van Horne, president of the Canadian Pacific Railroad, "we'll import the tourists." Lavish hotels were constructed in the wilderness with breathtaking views of ancient glaciers, snowcapped peaks, roaring waterfalls, and tranquil mountain lakes.

Traveling by train through the Rockies is still one of the best—and most relaxing—ways to explore this massive and inspiring country. VIA Rail Canada, Canada's national passenger rail network, offers a year-round 4-night, 2,775-mile trip between Toronto and Vancouver. It passes through Jasper National Park (see previous page), over the Continental Divide, and past the Canadian Rockies' highest peak, 12,972-foot Mount Robson. In winter, VIA Rail's Snow Train packages offer passengers transportation in vintage stainless-steel railcars to Jasper from all points along the same route.

A seasonal alternative is the Rocky Mountaineer, the largest privately owned passenger rail service in North America and deservedly popular for its 2-day all-daylight train trips to and from Vancouver and Jasper, Banff, or Calgary. For those seeking a shorter yet just as spectacular journey, the Rocky Mountaineer also offers daily service between Vancouver and Whistler (see p. 922) along the Sea-to-Sky route and seasonal service between Whistler and Jasper via Quesnel. All travel is during daylight hours only, so you won't miss a single scenic wonder, and in lieu of a jostling railcar, you'll sleep in a comfortable hotel.

VIA Rail Canada: Tel 888-842-7245 or 514-871-6000; www.viarail.ca. *Cost:* 4-night Toronto–Vancouver $1,040 (off-peak), from $1,825 (peak) per person, double occupancy cabin. **Rocky Mountaineer:** Tel 800-665-7245 or 604-606-7245; www.rockymountaineer.com. *Cost:* 2-day tour from $925, inclusive. *When:* mid-Apr–mid-Oct. **Best times:** Apr–Jun for wildlife; Sep–Oct for pleasant weather, foliage, and smaller crowds.

A Rustic Getaway with Idyllic Country Inns

The Gulf Islands

British Columbia, Canada

The rock-faced Gulf Islands lie sprinkled between the mainland city of Vancouver and Vancouver Island (see pp. 916–922), in the Strait of Georgia. These deep-forested islands are a haven for celebrities, eco-farmers, artists, and travelers seeking gorgeous nature, classy country inns, and top-flight culinary outposts.

Five of the islands are easily reached on BC Ferries, from Tsawwassen on the mainland or Swartz Bay on Vancouver Island—the narrow passage between these islands is considered one of the most beautiful ferry rides on earth. Each of the almost 100 islands exudes its own unique character. Take Galiano, a long string bean of an island whose cliff-lined southern reaches drop straight into the churning waters of Active Pass. Or bucolic Mayne Island, once an agricultural center known for its apples, tomatoes, and sheep farms and today popular for kayaking.

Mount Maxwell rises over Salt Spring Island.

Salt Spring Island is the largest in the archipelago, with 82 miles of coastline and a population of 10,000. The main town, Ganges, hosts a thriving artist colony, well represented at the boisterous Salt Spring Saturday Market. Perched above Ganges and standing in delightful contrast to the island's bohemian vibe is Hastings House, an exemplary luxury retreat and spa enveloped by flowering English gardens and towering Douglas firs. The rural estate's centerpiece is the imposing Manor House, built to resemble a centuries-old Sussex country manse; it's now home to the renowned Manor Dining Room.

The Pender Islands are another Gulf highlight, two rural islands joined by a short bridge and reached by ferry or water taxi from Victoria (see p. 921). Just a mile north of the watery U.S.-Canada border, Poets Cove Resort and Spa is the primary port of call for pleasure boats passing between the two countries. Tucked into a secluded cove and overlooking a busy marina in Pender Island's Bedwell Harbour, the large wood-beamed resort features elegant guest rooms, cottages, and villas scattered along the forested headland. Relax with an alfresco dinner of fresh oysters and a glass of tart pinot gris from the vineyards of nearby Saturna Island.

VISITOR INFO: Tel 250-754-3500; www.vancouverisland.travel. **BC FERRIES:** Tel 888-223-3779 or 250-386-3431; www.bcferries.com. **HASTINGS HOUSE:** Tel 800-661-9255 or 250-537-2362; www.hastingshouse.com. *Cost:* from $300 (off-peak), from $505 (peak); 3-course dinner $70. **POETS COVE RESORT AND SPA:** Tel 888-512-7638 or 250-629-2100; www.poetscove.com. *Cost:* from $185 (off-peak), from $300 (peak). **BEST TIME:** Apr–Oct for pleasant weather.

High-Altitude Nirvana in Remote Backcountry

Heli-Skiing and Heli-Hiking

British Columbia, Canada

Just west of the Canadian Rockies lie waves of mountains: The Cariboo, Bugaboo, Monashee, Selkirk, Galina, and Purcell ranges are unknown to many but famous to fans of high-mountain hiking and powder skiing. These remote peaks are beyond the reach of roads and ski lifts, but getting to the mountaintop is possible—and exhilarating—with CMH Heli-Skiing and Summer Adventures. CMH ferries skiers and outdoor enthusiasts aboard its fleet of helicopters to any of its 12 modern and very comfortable backcountry lodges in the heights of southeastern British Columbia. Each accommodates only 40-some guests at a time, assuring exclusive access to a wilderness area half the size of Switzerland—all without a chairlift in sight.

High-country skiing requires intermediate to advanced skills, but the rewards are unmatched. Over the course of one mind-boggling powder-filled week helicopters set skiers down for 8 to 15 different runs per day, all on snow uncrossed by another human's tracks. Back at the lodge, skiers can expect mountain-man breakfasts and epicurean dinners, with soothing massages for slope-weary limbs.

As soon as the snows melt, heli-tourists can pursue summer hiking and trekking in these same unbelievable mountains. The high country is transformed into a primeval world of alpine wildflowers and monumental views of dozens of snowcapped mile-high peaks. Two of the lodges remain open, enticing adventurers to remote and rarely visited backcountry for hiking, mountaineering, and climbing. Some heli-hiking ambles are gentle enough to be suitable for multigeneration family groups, but others require some technical climbing skill and mountaineering training, which guides can provide.

CMH: Tel 800-661-0252 or 403-762-7100; www.canadianmountainholidays.com. *Cost:* 7-day ski trips from $6,590, all-inclusive. Originates in Calgary. 3-day hiking trip from $2,530, all-inclusive. Originates in Banff. **WHEN:** ski trips Dec–May; hiking trips early Jul–late Sep. **BEST TIMES:** Jan–Feb for ideal ski conditions; early Jul–mid-Aug for wildflowers; early Sep for fall foliage.

Wilderness Sophistication at the Edge of the Map

Nimmo Bay Resort

British Columbia, Canada

The helicopter whisks you away, soaring above the islands of Queen Charlotte Strait and nosing toward the craggy peaks of the Coast Mountains on Canada's Pacific edge. Your destination is Nimmo Bay Resort, an 18-guest wilderness retreat carved into the Great Bear Rain Forest. No roads lead to Nimmo Bay; at this pocket-size enclave of luxury and ecological stewardship, guests experience the serenity of a verdant waterfront paradise with opportunities for adventures in unspoiled wilderness, from sea level to 7,000 feet.

Nimmo Bay Resort is a pioneer in "heli-ventures"—using helicopters for adventure tourism. Ascend over ancient rain forests to the toe of Silverthrone ice field for a gourmet picnic hike; or head to pristine rivers and streams in remote backcountry for catch-and-release fishing. Guests can also enjoy the amenities and activities at the resort, such as massage or yoga rain forest hikes, or taking a guided sea kayaking trip for a seal's-eye view of coastal inlets.

The resort's nine elegantly furnished, cedar-paneled chalets are built on stilts above a fjordlike bay. The dining room competes with Vancouver's best: locally grown organic produce, fish, and shellfish pulled that morning from neighboring bays, all paired with fine wines from around the world.

Where: 200 miles/322 km north of Vancouver. Tel 800-837-4354 or 250-956-4000; www.nimmobay.com. **Cost:** 3-night heli-venture package from $6,990 per person, all-inclusive; 3-night resort-based trip (without heli-ventures) from $3,850 per person, all-inclusive. **When:** May–Oct. **Best times:** May–Sep for outdoor activities.

The Napa Valley of Canada

The Okanagan Valley

British Columbia, Canada

The arid yet fertile Okanagan Valley (with 125 miles of interconnected lakes—think Napa Valley with Lake Tahoe in the middle) is Canada's second largest wine-producing area (its foremost is Niagara-on-the-Lake; see p. 929). Its 100 wineries comprise almost 10,000 acres, producing wines that rival nearby Washington State's in power, richness, and finesse. Okanagan's wine-growing area begins immediately north of the U.S.-Canada border at Osoyoos and extends to Vernon, an expanse of more than 100 miles. Kelowna—a bustling city of 110,000—is an excellent base for tasting expeditions, with more than 18 wineries within a half hour's drive.

Wineries not to miss include CedarCreek Estate, where you can drink in the view—and a magnificent pinot noir—at the Vineyard Terrace Restaurant while savoring a Mediterranean-style lunch. At Mission Hill Family Estate Winery, established in 1981 and one of the valley's first serious vineyards, sample their award-winning chardonnay, merlot, icewine, and the estate's signature Bordeaux-inspired Oculus. Mission Hill's restaurant, Terrace, offers courtyard dining, with regional cuisine made to pair perfectly with wines. Try the pinot noir and chenin blanc in the tasting room at Quail's Gate Estate or at the winery's Old Vines Patio Restaurant, with alfresco dining and views over vineyards and Okanagan Lake. You just might spot Ogopogo, the lake's own Loch Ness monster.

Where: Kelowna is 245 miles/395 km east of Vancouver. **Visitor info:** www.tourismkelowna.com. **Okanagan Wine Country tours:** Tel 866-689-9463 or 250-868-9463; www.okwinetours.com. *Cost:* 3-hour tour from $67. **CedarCreek Estate:** Tel 250-764-8866; www.cedarcreek.bc.ca. *When:* tasting room Jun–Sep. *Cost:* lunch $25. **Mission Hill Winery:** Tel 250-768-7611; www.missionhillwinery.com. *Cost:* dinner $40. **Quails' Gate:** Tel 800-420-9463 or 250-769-4451; www.quailsgate.com. *Cost:* dinner $40. **Where to stay:** Foodies love the aptly named A View of the Lake B&B in Kelowna. Tel 250-769-7854; www.aviewofthelake.com. *Cost:* from $130. **Best times:** May–Oct for good weather; early Oct for Fall Okanagan Wine Festival.

First Nations Art and Modern Architecture

Museum of Anthropology

Vancouver, British Columbia, Canada

Rising from a cliffside meadow above the Strait of Georgia, the Museum of Anthropology at the University of British Columbia houses phantasmagorical carvings by British Columbia's indigenous artists: towering totem poles; squat tree-trunk sculptures of ravens, sea wolves, and bears; and intricately painted masks of cedar and feathers. One of North America's leading collections of Northwest Coast First Nations art, it highlights haunting figures and artifacts that are both historical—many of the carvings served as house poles at remote coastal villages—and contemporary, as wood carving remains a vital art form among the Native populations in British Columbia.

Hand-carved canoes and totem poles are on display in the museum's Great Hall.

The soaring, light-filled space, designed by Canadian architect Arthur Erickson, is as dramatic as the art it holds. From the 50-foot windows of the Great Hall, carved creatures and totem poles stare out across the forests and waters, while in the rotunda, the massive yellow cedar sculpture *The Raven and the First Men* by the late Haida artist Bill Reid is a potent expression of spiritual wonder.

Info: Tel 604-822-5087; www.moa.ubc.ca.

Eastern Roots in Canada's West

Sun Yat-Sen Classical Chinese Garden

Vancouver, British Columbia, Canada

Canada's multiculturalism, a fascinating mosaic of peoples and customs, finds its zenith in Vancouver, with one of the highest concentrations of ethnic Chinese residents outside Asia. Just east of downtown is Vancouver's historic Chinatown, where nearly all of the signs are in Chinese and storefront windows are filled with hanging ducks, bales of dried fish, and unlikely looking medicinal potions.

An island of calm in this otherwise frenetic community is the Sun Yat-Sen Classical Chinese Garden, the first full-scale classical Chinese garden ever built outside China. Named after the founder of China's first republic, the 2.5-acre Sun Yat-Sen is an exquisite re-creation of a typical 15th-century Ming garden. Its complex network of corridors and courtyards seems like an intricately chambered jewel box, a pocket-size otherworld.

Completed in 1986, the garden is designed in the style of Suzhou (see p. 494), Vancouver's sister city in Eastern China's Jiangsu Province, long famed for its exquisite gardens. A team of 52 Suzhou artisans and horticulturists spent more than a year building the garden, and almost all its materials were brought from China, including the pagoda roof tiles, the naturally sculpted rocks, and the worn pebbles that create the mosaics covering the winding foot paths. Don't miss the complimentary tours that provide perspectives on Chinese culture, architecture, horticulture, and life during the Ming Dynasty, as well as on the art of feng shui.

Info: Tel 604-662-3207; www.vancouverchinesegarden.com. **Best times:** Jan or Feb for Chinese New Year; Mar–May for blooms; Sep–Oct for foliage.

The Culinary Capital of Western Canada

Vancouver's Top Restaurants and Granville Island Public Market

Vancouver, British Columbia, Canada

Vancouver is wedged between the chilly waters of the Pacific, the farmlands of the Fraser River valley, and misty mountains whose meadows abound with wild mushrooms and berries. A natural nexus for an exuberant food culture, Vancouver enjoys one of North America's most exciting and cosmopolitan dining scenes.

The city's predilection for all things eastern finds its showcase at Tojo's, a popular Japanese restaurant named for its much-admired chef-owner, Hidekazu Tojo. The most coveted seats are at the convivial omakase ("in the chef's hands") counter, where the chef prepares the finest sushi and sashimi with the precision of a surgeon and a dash of Vegas swagger, along with cooked items that are simultaneously traditional and highly inventive. Boasting a decades-long career, Tojo holds bragging rights for helping to introduce sushi to North America (his original Tojo Roll from 1971 is now ubiquitously found under the name California Roll).

West Restaurant focuses on a contemporary reinterpretation of classic cuisine. In a sleek, jewel-box-like dining room along fashionable South Granville Street, executive chef Warren Geraghty performs a kind of kitchen alchemy, transforming pristine local ingredients into dishes packed with flavor and artful high style. For the complete experience, book a "chef's table" in the kitchen, order a multicourse tasting menu, and marvel as the masterfully trained kitchen professionals perform their own version of dinner theater.

Raincity Grill, overlooking English Bay from Vancouver's West End, was one of the first purveyors of Pacific Northwest cuisine, a style of cooking that brings classic European techniques to the freshest of Northwest fish, meats, and produce. While this style is no longer news, Raincity Grill's dedication to locavore interpretations has kept this restaurant at the cutting edge of Vancouver dining.

To see Vancouver's rich bounty at its source, go to bustling Granville Island Public Market, the epicenter of the city's burgeoning food scene. Tucked beneath the Granville Street Bridge, it is a veritable cornucopia where stalls brim with local fruit, vegetables, flowers, just-caught fish, artisanal sausages and cheeses, still-warm baked goods, and wines from the province's vineyards—all in all, the cream of British Columbia's crop.

Tojo's: Tel 604-872-8050; www.tojos.com. *Cost:* dinner $80. **West Restaurant:** Tel 604-738-8938; www.westrestaurant.com. *Cost:* dinner $65. **Raincity Grill:** Tel 604-685-7337; www.raincitygrill.com. *Cost:* dinner $63. **Granville Island Public Market:** Tel 604-666-5784; www.granvilleisland.com.

Wilderness and Luxury on the North Pacific Coast

Pacific Rim National Park

Vancouver Island, British Columbia, Canada

The coastal rain forests, cliff-lined islands, and broad, sandy beaches of Vancouver Island's remote western flank are preserved as the three-unit Pacific Rim National Park Reserve, a maritime wilderness that's hallowed ground for ecotourists, long-distance hikers, and sea kayakers. In the first unit you'll find the West Coast Trail, a 47-mile track hailed as one of the most spectacular and challenging hikes on the continent.

At the mouth of Barkley Sound is the park's second unit, centered on the Broken Group Islands, a rocky archipelago rich with wildlife and popular with sea kayakers. The park's third unit is its most accessible: the 9-mile curve of Long Beach, some 500 yards wide at low tide and popular in summer, when the weather is sunny and breezy. Winter brings the curious Northwest pastime of winter storm-watching, best done from the Wickaninnish Inn. Located just north of the park, the rustically elegant and sophisticated "Wick" is built of local cedar, stone, and glass, that rare modern structure that blends harmoniously with the glories of its natural surroundings. Don't miss the Northwest specialties—or the 240-degree views—at the inn's Pointe Restaurant, or the relaxing body treatments at its handsome, award-winning Ancient Cedars Spa.

A few miles north, the little seafaring village of Tofino feels like the edge of the earth and, at the same time, the center of the universe. This quirky, unpretentious harbor town thrives on contrasts—young ecotourists rub shoulders with grizzled fishermen, while upscale European visitors share tables with tattooed surfer dudes.

Tofino is literally the end of the road on Vancouver Island's wild west coast—unless you've got reservations at the Clayoquot Wilderness Resort, an eco-safari resort located within the fragile Clayoquot Sound Biosphere Reserve and accessible only by water taxi from Tofino or floatplane from Vancouver. Twenty white canvas tents serve as guest rooms: think wooden floors, opulent rugs, antiques, and otherworldly comforts. The dining, library, and massage tents connected by cedar boardwalks offer visitors a taste of upscale safari life, along the water's edge.

Where: About 85 miles/138 km northwest of Victoria. Tel 250-726-7721; www.pc.gc.ca/pacificrim. *When:* West Coast Trail open May–late Sep; the rest of park open year-round. **Wickaninnish Inn:** Tel 800-333-4604 or 250-725-3100; www.wickinn.com. *Cost:* from $300 (off-peak), from $500 (peak); dinner $90. **Clayoquot Wilderness Resort:** Tel 888-333-5405 or 250-726-8235; www.wildretreat.com. *Cost:* from $4,825 for 3-nights, all-inclusive with floatplane transfer from Vancouver. *When:* mid-May–late Sep. **Best times:** Jun–Jul for warm weather and long days; Nov–Feb for storm-watching; Mar for Pacific Rim Whale Festival; 1st weekend in Jun for Tofino Food and Wine Festival.

Home of the Mighty Orcas

Stubbs Island Whale-Watching

Vancouver Island, British Columbia, Canada

Separating Vancouver Island from the cedar-flanked coast of British Columbia, Johnstone Strait near Telegraph Cove is home to the world's largest concentration of orcas. Over 200 of these black-and-white whales inhabit these waters, and they have good reason to gather here. In addition to congregating to socialize and mate, the orcas come here to eat: The confines of Johnstone Strait force migrating salmon into a narrow channel, which means easy hunting and an all-you-can-eat fish buffet. The area also features the "rubbing beaches" at the Robson Bight Ecological Reserve, where the orcas gather at shallow, pebbly beaches to rub their bellies on rocks and gravel—a kind of whale massage. Although the rubbing beaches are off-limits to human visitors, wildlife-viewing tour boats visit nearby areas where passengers can watch these magnificent creatures as they dive, breech, and spy-hop—the whale equivalent to treading water.

Stubbs Island Whale Watching operates two 60-foot Coast Guard–certified vessels, with an on-board marine biologist to explain and interpret wildlife behaviors, plus hydrophones that allow passengers to listen to the orcas' vocalizations. Although Mother Nature is unpredictable, the company has over a 90 percent success rate with orca sightings.

WHERE: Telegraph Cove is 250 miles/402 km north of Victoria. **STUBBS ISLAND WHALE WATCHING:** Tel 800-665-3066 or 250-928-3185; www.stubbs-island.com. *Cost:* from $74. *When:* late May–mid-Oct. **BEST TIME:** Jul–Sep.

Local Bounty off the Continent's Coast

Vancouver Island's Gastro Havens

Vancouver Island, British Columbia, Canada

With its diversity of Pacific seafood, generous rainfall, and mild coastal climate creating some of the best growing conditions in North America, Vancouver Island was a culinary revolution waiting to happen.

So it's no surprise to find internationally acclaimed restaurants, inns, and resorts in this corner of Canada, minutes from Victoria, BC's intimate, very British capital (see next page).

On a quiet wooded promontory overlooking the Strait of Juan de Fuca and the distant Olympic Mountains sits a tidy white 1929 clapboard inn that has played a leading role in changing how we eat and think of food today. Sinclair and Frederique Philip's Sooke Harbour House is justly famed as an epicenter for authentic regional cuisine showcasing resolutely local ingredients.

Its dining room features inventive, delicious cuisine prepared with just-caught fish and seafood from local waters, produce and meats from nearby organic farms, and a wide selection of wild mushrooms from the area. Growing herbs, vegetables, and edible flowers, the inn's organic garden plays a major role in the menu's ever-changing, one-of-a-kind dishes. Served in a candlelit dining room overlooking the rocky coastline, dinner is complemented by a stellar list of more than 2,000 wines. End your evening in one of the inn's serene and unpretentious guest rooms.

Continue west, along the winding, ever-wilder coastline to reach Point-No-Point Resort, another outpost of fine dining and gracious hospitality. Perched above a rocky, wave-crashed headland, it offers 22 delightfully woodsy cabins with hot tubs and fireplaces on 40 forested acres. The restaurant serves excellent meals focused on seafood (don't miss the local wild salmon, halibut, and spot prawns) and organic produce, and the views from the dining room can't be beat—just pick up the binoculars on your table to watch orcas, otters, dolphins, and bald eagles.

The region's top restaurants procure much of their local produce and delicacies from the nearby Cowichan Valley, a burgeoning center for cheese- and wine-making, organic farming, and ranching. Drive the lovely back roads to visit wineries, and be sure to stop at Merridale Estate Cidery, a charming farm with orchards of centuries-old apple varieties, for a tasting and a marvelous bistro lunch.

From the Cowichan Valley, take the slow road back to Victoria, via the Mill Bay Ferry to Brentwood Bay on the Saanich Peninsula. The famed Butchart Gardens is your destination, with 55 acres of formal plantings in a former limestone quarry. Over a million bedding plants in some 700 varieties throughout the gardens ensure uninterrupted bloom from March through October.

Sooke Harbour House: Tel 800-889-9688 or 250-642-3421; www.sookeharbourhouse.com. *Cost:* from $166 (off-peak), from $256 (peak); 5-course prix-fixe dinner $67. **Point-No-Point Resort:** Tel 250-646-2020; www.pointnopointresort.com. *Cost:* from $140; dinner $45. **Merridale Cidery:** Tel 250-743-4293; www.merridalecider.com. *Cost:* lunch $18. **Butchart Gardens:** Tel 250-652-4422; www.butchartgardens.com. **Best times:** Jun–Sep for pleasant weather; Mar–Apr for spring bulbs and Jul–Sep for roses at Butchart Gardens.

Victoria's Magnificent Waterfront

The Inner Harbour

Victoria, Vancouver Island, British Columbia, Canada

Replete with beautifully preserved Victorian-era architecture, British Columbia's capital has always enjoyed its reputation as being "more British than Britain." Today's traveler is probably less impressed by the opportunity to eat crumpets or go lawn bowling than by the city's lively street life and magnificent setting on the Strait of Juan de Fuca, with Washington's Olympic Mountains rising to the south. The Inner Harbour is Victoria's centerpiece, a pocket-size inlet flanked by historic buildings and bustling with sea-going vessels—skittering water taxis, bobbing seaplanes, and the mammoth car ferry from Port Angeles, Washington.

The Fairmont Empress, built between 1904 and 1908, honors British traditions.

The ivy-covered Fairmont Empress is an unlikely backdrop to the busy harborscape. The larger-than-life regal landmark, distinguished by marvelous Edwardian architecture and filled with sumptuous detail, is a grand lodging with the style and furnishings of another, more gracious era and all the comforts and conveniences of modern times. Sit in the opulent Tea Lobby and enjoy a Victorian tradition, partaking of the hotel's secret blend of tea, accompanied by freshly baked raisin scones served with Devon-style double clotted cream and strawberry preserves.

For less historic splendor, the boutique Magnolia Hotel is just steps from the Inner Harbour; its elegant guest rooms are havens of good taste.

Overlooking the harbor, the Royal BC Museum sits between the Fairmont Empress and the ornate British Columbia Parliament Building. It is an exceptional regional museum with three permanent galleries focused on British Columbia's natural environment, its settlement history, and the rich art and culture of its First Nation peoples. Perhaps most compelling, and always the most visited, is the First Peoples Gallery, dedicated to the region's several distinct indigenous nations. Displays of hand-carved masks, ceremonial garb and headdresses, decorative accessories and textiles, and totem poles bring to life Native cultures dating back thousands of years.

FAIRMONT EMPRESS: Tel 888-705-2500 or 250-384-8111; www.fairmont.com/empress. *Cost:* from $200; tea $45. **MAGNOLIA HOTEL AND SPA:** Tel 877-624-6654 or 250-381-0999; www.magnoliahotel.com. *Cost:* from $175. **ROYAL BC MUSEUM:** Tel 888-447-7977 or 250-356-7226; www.royalbcmuseum.bc.ca. **BEST TIMES:** late Jul for International Flower and Garden Festival; early Sep for Classic Boat Festival.

The 2010 Winter Olympics Showcase

WHISTLER BLACKCOMB SKI RESORT

British Columbia, Canada

The giant twin peaks of Whistler and Blackcomb, just 75 miles north of Vancouver on the stunningly scenic Sea-to-Sky Highway (Highway 99), comprise North America's largest ski and snowboard resort, regularly rated No. 1 by polls and magazines. After a major construction boom prior to cohosting (together with nearby Vancouver) the 2010 Winter Olympic Games, Whistler Blackcomb is now even more incredible than ever.

The resort's numbers do a lot of the talking: Whistler Blackcomb has the greatest vertical drop (more than 5,000 feet) of any ski resort on the continent; 8,100 acres of skiable terrain; more than 200 marked trails; 17 massive alpine bowls; an unfathomable average of 33 feet of snowfall per year; and a ski season that runs from late November through May.

Whistler and Blackcomb are separated by a deep valley, and the new Peak 2 Peak gondola carries skiers and snowboarders (and in summer, thrill seekers) directly between the two summits: it is the world's longest unsupported cable span.

Whistler Blackcomb has acquired a cult reputation with advanced and extreme skiers and snowboarders, but more than half the trails are rated intermediate, with a host of other winter activities to keep guests busy, such as dogsledding, snowshoeing, snowmobiling, and cross-country skiing.

The peaks are linked at their base by the Tyrolean-style and surprisingly cosmopolitan Whistler Village, a pedestrian zone with café-lined plazas, boutiques, restaurants, and bars.

The top hotel choice goes to the Four Seasons Resort Whistler, a *très* elegant monument to refinement in a town with its share of faux alpine hominess. Its urbane good taste extends to the sumptuously appointed guest rooms and marvelous spa (Whistler's largest and most luxurious), with a heated outdoor pool and three whirlpool baths.

Whistler Blackcomb's best ski-in/ski-out property, however, is the grand, gabled Fairmont Château Whistler, a resort-within-a-resort at the base of Blackcomb Mountain. With 550 luxury-level rooms it's not exactly intimate, but it's the place to ski and be seen. The resort segues effortlessly into a summertime playground, with a beautiful 18-hole

Robert Trent Jones Jr. course and three other fine courses lying within striking distance.

Not all Whistler hotels are grand and imposing; sleekly minimalist Adara Hotel has urban-chic furnishings in a modern Scandinavian style in the heart of Whistler Village.

WHERE: 75 miles/120 km north of Vancouver. **VISITOR INFO:** Tel 866-218-9690 or 604-932-3434; www.whistlerblackcomb.com. *Cost:* 3-day lift tickets from $210. *When:* ski season Nov–May. **FOUR SEASONS RESORT WHISTLER:** Tel 888-935-2460 or 604-966-2700; www.fourseasons.com/whistler. *Cost:* from $310 (off-peak), from $410 (peak). **FAIRMONT CHÂTEAU WHISTLER:** Tel 800-441-1414 or 604-938-8000; www.fairmont.com/whistler. *Cost:* from $240 (off-peak), from $395 (peak); greens fees $110 (off-peak), $175 (peak). **ADARA HOTEL:** Tel 866-502-3272 or 604-905-4009; www.adarahotel.com. *Cost:* from $135 (off-peak), from $285 (peak). **BEST TIMES:** Jan–Mar for best skiing; mid-Jul for Whistler Music & Arts Festival; early Nov for Cornucopia, a celebration of food and wine.

Kings of the Tundra in the Far North

POLAR BEAR SAFARI

Churchill, Manitoba, Canada

Since long before Churchill had a human history (with stints as an Inuit settlement and armed forces base), it was the polar bear capital of the world. Today, every October and November, up to 1,000 of these generally solitary creatures gather just outside Churchill, making it the world's greatest concentration of polar bears. Expectant bears come here to fatten up on seals before taking to their dens and bearing young. Come witness the timeless drama played out by some of the largest of all terrestrial predators (some weighing in at 1,500 pounds), and come soon, as a warming climate and melting polar ice threaten the future of polar bears. The Churchill denning area was placed under the protection of Wapusk National Park in 1996, and travelers are permitted to visit only as part of an authorized tour group. Outfitters will ensure that you get up close in the comfort and safety of a tundra buggy.

Wapusk National Park takes its name from the Cree word for "white bear."

Beyond the excitement of seeing roving polar bears, the late-fall night skies frequently put on a show of their own, pulsing with the aurora borealis. These are the northern lights, shifting curtains of multicolored light that swirl across the sky, an astral dance between the earth's magnetic fields and electrons and protons brought in by gusts of solar wind.

Whereas polar-bear viewing is best in fall, the arctic summer brings a brief but astonishing display of flora and wildlife to the tundra. Summer trips to Churchill, a town with fewer than 1,000 inhabitants, allow you to journey on to Hudson Bay or along the coast—under nearly-24-hour daylight—in search of beluga whales (nearly 3,000 congregate near here in summer), caribou, and seals, or to join a birding trip to search out the more than 200 species of rare arctic waterfowl and shorebirds.

You can't reach Churchill by road; most travelers fly in from Winnipeg, but VIA Rail Canada offers passenger rail service through the vast open tundra between Winnipeg and Churchill year-round, a 43-hour journey each way.

Where: 630 miles/1,014 km north of Winnipeg. **Wapusk National Park:** Tel 888-748-2928 or 204-675-8863; www.pc.gc.ca/wapusk. **How:** Natural Habitat Adventures offer 6- and 7-day polar-bear-viewing trips and 7-day summer excursions. Tel 800-543-8917 or 303-449-3711; www.nathab.com. *Cost:* from $4,995, includes air from Winnipeg; summer excursions from $4,595. *When:* polar-bear trips mid-Oct–mid-Nov; summer excursions mid-Jun–mid-Aug. **VIA Rail Canada:** Tel 888-842-7245 or 514-871-6000; www.viarail.ca. *Cost:* Winnipeg–Churchill round-trip seats from $610; sleepers from $1,960 per person, double-occupancy. **Best time:** Feb for Northern Manitoba Trappers' Festival.

A Marine Wonder of the World

Bay of Fundy

New Brunswick and Nova Scotia, Canada

The Bay of Fundy boasts the world's highest tides, rising as much as 48 feet in six hours—more than 22 times greater than the average tide in open seas. The hard, rapid tides have sculpted the bay's cave-pocked coastline, reducing huge boulders to fantasy shapes, such as the Hopewell Rocks, which jut from the sand with miniature forests on their summits. The bay is best observed at Fundy National Park, established in 1948 to protect 80 square miles of coastline and forested mountains on the bay's New Brunswick coast.

So dramatic is the difference between low and high tide that, at the park's Alma Beach, almost three quarters of a mile of tidal flats are exposed at low tide. Then, when the water comes rushing back in, it produces a roar at mid-tide called "the voice of the moon." Explore the dramatic coastal cliffs, sea caves, and hidden beaches by sea kayak. In addition to more than 250 species of seabirds, you may see the rare right whales, just one of eight whale species that call these food-rich waters home. Stay in Alma, where hotels like the Cliffside Suites provide views of the bay from a peaceful and secluded perch.

Those wanting to explore the bay by car can take the scenic Fundy Coastal Drive, stretching from Aulac to St. Stephen, near the Maine border. This scenic 5-hour route takes in great stretches of natural beauty and quaint towns such as the seaside village of St. Andrews at the mouth of the St. Croix River, a favorite summer playground for the wealthy and fashionable at the turn of the 20th century. Lined with tasteful shops and galleries, historic Water Street parallels the bay and its bustling harbor, while gorgeous Kingsbrae Garden offers 27 acres of formal plantings and woodland trails. Enjoy a view of the gardens or the bay when you overnight at the Kingsbrae Arms, built in 1897 as a "cottage-style" manor house and later converted into a stylish ten-room country-house hotel. The chef has made the dining room a destination offering world-class cuisine that bursts with contemporary flavors.

The most imposing option is the hilltop Algonquin Hotel and Resort, with 234 rooms. Built in 1889 overlooking the bay, its Tudor-style turrets, red-tile roof, top-ranked seaside golf course, and kilt-wearing staff might convince you that you've woken up on the other side of the Pond.

Where: 84 miles/135 km northeast of Saint John. **Fundy National Park:** Tel 506-887-6000; www.pc.gc.ca/fundy. **Cliffside Suites:** Tel 866-881-1022 or 506-887-1022; www.cliffsidesuites.com. *Cost:* from $110. **Kingsbrae Arms:** Tel 506-529-1897; www.kingsbrae.com. *Cost:* from $230. **Algonquin Hotel:** Tel 506-529-8823. *Cost:* from $120 (off-peak), from $175 (peak). **Best times:** a new or full moon for the most dramatic tides; mid-Jul–mid-Sep for peak bird migration and best kayaking weather; Sep–Oct for foliage and whale-watching.

Fjords, Beaches, Mountains, Bogs, and Meadows

Gros Morne National Park

Newfoundland and Labrador, Canada

Gros Morne National Park is sometimes called the "Galápagos of Geology" because its rocks provide fascinating evidence for plate tectonics—a theory that is to geology what evolution is to biology. A place of immense splendor and forlorn beauty, it is eastern Canada's most renowned hiking and adventure destination. Roughly translated as "big lone hill," the term "Gros Morne" refers to the park's highest point: a barren, mist-draped mountain that can inspire a mild case of melancholy even on a sunny day.

Start your exploration at the Discovery Centre with exhibits on the geology, plant and animal life, and diverse history of the Northern Peninsula. Then move on to the Bonne Bay region of the park, where kayaks and tour boats ply the double-armed fjord, a 15-mile-long inlet in a steep, cliff-lined glaciated valley. One of the park's indisputable highlights is the rugged massif called the Tablelands, where hiking trails meander over rocks jutting up from the ancient mantle in the earth's interior. The boulders have such an unusual chemistry that many plants cannot easily grow in their orange-brown terrain.

Steep rock walls enclose Western Brook Pond.

To the north, coastal lowlands bordering the Gulf of St. Lawrence are covered with expanses of boreal forest and bog; inland is the wilderness plateau of the Long Range Mountains—part of a severed mountain range whose other half is across the Atlantic in Scotland. Western Brook Pond is among the park's most popular stops, a landlocked fjord that offers travelers a combination of hiking trails and boat trips into the heart of the billion-year-old mountains.

Where: Park entrance at Wiltondale is 186 miles/300 km from Port aux Basques. Tel 709-458-2417; www.pc.gc.ca. **When:** Most park facilities and services are available late May–mid-Oct. **Where to stay:** Neddies

Harbour Inn offers Scandinavian-style charm and a good restaurant. Tel 877-458-2929 or 709-458-3089; www.theinn.ca. *Cost:* from $160. *When:* closed Dec–mid-May. **Best times:** late May–early Oct for hiking and wildlife and Trails, Tales and Tunes festival, the Gros Morne Theatre Festival, and Writers at Woody Point; Sep–early Oct for foliage.

Beautiful Drives and Auld Culture in New Scotland

Cape Breton Island

Nova Scotia, Canada

"I have traveled the globe. I have seen the Canadian and American Rockies, the Andes and the Alps and the Highlands of Scotland: But for simple beauty, Cape Breton outrivals them all." So wrote Alexander Graham Bell, who summered and worked here for 35 years.

As it juts northward between the Atlantic Ocean and the Gulf of St. Lawrence, Nova Scotia's Cape Breton Island becomes increasingly mountainous and barren. Cape Breton Highlands National Park protects much of the island's northern tip, a region so remote it wasn't even accessible by automobile until the 1930s. Today, you can take one of the world's great drives here: the 184-mile-long Cabot Trail. Follow the picturesque, craggy coastline around the 365-square-mile national park, passing centuries-old French Acadian and Scottish fishing villages before pushing up and over the island's central plateau, between Pleasant Bay and Cape North—a striking moorland with stunted old-growth hardwood forests and tundralike meadows.

Cape Breton must have looked just like home to the Scottish immigrants who streamed into Nova Scotia (Latin for "New Scotland") between 1770 and 1850. The island is home to the only native Gaelic-speaking population outside the British Isles, along with a thriving Celtic music and art scene. Overlooking St. Ann's Bay, the Gaelic College of Celtic Arts and Crafts hosts summer ceilidhs (pronounced KAY-lees), or musical gatherings, with fiddling and traditional dancing, and its Great Hall of Clans museum depicts the exodus of the Scottish people to the New World. The annual Gaelic Mod, a day of Gaelic language, song, and workshops held every August, ends with a traditional codfish supper.

The island-wide 9-day Celtic Colours festival in October is the largest celebration of all things Gaelic in North America with over 300 artists from around the Celtic world. In the village of Ingonish Beach, the British influence holds strong at the Keltic Lodge, a Tudor-style resort with a historic patina and knockout ocean views. You'll find unusually good dining and proximity to the nearby Highlands Links, considered one of Canada's must-play golf courses.

Where: 175 miles/282 km northeast of Halifax. **Cape Breton Highlands National Park:** Tel 902-224-2306; www.pc.gc.ca. **Gaelic College:** Tel 902-295-3411; www.gaeliccollege.edu. *When:* open Jun–Sep. **Keltic Lodge:** Tel 800-565-0444 or 902-285-2880; www.kelticlodge.ca. *Cost:* from $148 (off-peak), from $265 (peak), inclusive. *When:* mid-May–Oct. **Highlands Links Golf Course:** Tel 800-441-1118 or 902-285-2600; www.highlandslinksgolf.com. *Cost:* greens fees from $75. *When:* Jun–Oct. **Best times:** mid-Aug for Gaelic Mod; Sep for fall foliage and nice weather, with fewer crowds; Oct for the Celtic Colours International Festival.

A Colonial Town Perfectly Preserved

OLD TOWN LUNENBURG

Nova Scotia, Canada

In the 1750s, lured by the prospect of free land, nearly 1,500 Protestant pioneers from Germany, Switzerland, and France set sail under protection of the British Crown to establish a colony on the coast of Nova Scotia. With them was a set of town plans drawn up by the London-based Board of Trade and Plantations. As part of the agreement with their British sponsors, the colonists would use these plans to build a predesigned "model town" in the Canadian wilderness.

The Lunenburg colony survived and prospered as a well-known shipbuilding and fishing center. Little change has come to its Old Town and waterfront since the 1700s, and two and a half centuries after its establishment, the tiny coastal hamlet is still in near-pristine condition. Dignified homes and buildings have been beautifully maintained—70 percent of the structures date to the 18th and 19th centuries—and the streets of the Old Town still follow the original plan, though accommodations were made for the unexpectedly steep hills the settlers found upon arrival.

While it's fascinating to wander the picturesque streets with colorful Victorian and Georgian houses marching up the hillside from the bay, the heart of the village remains its waterfront. The sprawling Fisheries Museum of the Atlantic combines an aquarium of local sea life with exhibits on Lunenburg's seafaring past. Moored off the museum wharf (and part of its operation) are a number of historic ships to visit. They were built right here in Lunenburg, among them a replica of the legendary 1921 racing schooner *Bluenose*, which you might recognize from the back of the Canadian dime.

Once a shipbuilding hub, Lunenburg is quiet today.

The bustling harbor is filled with fishing boats (scallop fishing is still an important industry) and a number of both new and old wooden tall ships, which call here for repair, fitting, or provisions. Catch the spirit of Lunenburg's wooden boat heritage aboard the *Eastern Star*, a 48-foot wooden ketch that offers tours of Lunenburg harbor. Setting out with the sails snapped taut and the hull cleaving the water, you'll relive the days when sailing ships ruled the seas and Lunenburg was one of colonial North America's most important ports of call.

WHERE: 62 miles/100 km southwest of Halifax. **VISITOR INFO:** www.explorelunenburg.ca. **FISHERIES MUSEUM:** Tel 866-579-4909 or 902-634-4794; www.museum.gov.ns.ca/fma. ***EASTERN STAR:*** Tel 877-247-7075 or 902-634-3535; www.novascotiasailing.com. *When:* Jun–Oct. **WHERE TO STAY:** The charming Lunenburg Arms has harbor views and a good restaurant. Tel 800-679-4950 or 902-640-4040; www.eden.travel/lunenburg. *Cost:* from $130. **BEST TIME:** early Aug for Lunenburg Folk Harbour Festival.

Rugged Beauty at the Top of the World

NUNAVUT

Canada

The North is like no other place. Far from a frigid wasteland, the Arctic is a land of profound though alien beauty. It is homeland to the Inuit; habitat for wildlife such as wolves, musk oxen, wolverines, and caribou; and temporary home to millions of migratory birds. Nunavut is Canada's eastern Arctic and its newest and largest territory—approximately the size of Western Europe. Created in 1999 as a territory for the Inuit people, it has a human population of 30,000, which is outnumbered 30 to 1 by caribou.

Few visitors travel to the Arctic, but those who do experience the subtle yet powerful splendor of the landscape and, during the Arctic summer, witness the explosion of life that occurs when 24-hour daylight ignites a kaleidoscope of wildflowers.

Given the precipitous seasonal changes, lack of roads, and minimal infrastructure for tourism, visiting the Arctic isn't always easy, but a handful of backcountry lodges offer comfortable accommodations and guided adventures.

For millennia, the area around Bathurst Inlet has been home to the Kingaunmiut people, Inuits who live off the bounty of this harsh but beautiful land. As a young Royal Canadian Mounted Police staff sergeant, Glenn Warner patrolled the area in the 1960s, often by dogsled. When the community's Hudson's Bay Company trading-post buildings and the Catholic mission church were offered for sale, Warner and his wife, Trish—smitten by the area's pristine natural beauty—bought the motley collection of structures. They transformed them into the Bathurst Inlet Lodge, which has become one of the Arctic's foremost destinations for lodging, outfitting, and naturalist programs, offering a level of personal comfort rarely found in such remote and rugged territory. The lodge opened in 1969, and in 1984, the local Inuit residents of Bathurst Inlet joined the Warners as full partners in the operation, one of the first such joint ventures in the North. Glenn's son Boyd now manages the property.

Bathurst Inlet Lodge is dedicated to the natural history of the north and is noted worldwide for the excellence of its weeklong programs, offered in July, the best time for birding and setting eyes on an abundance of arctic wildflowers. Naturalists and local Inuit guides lead guests on day trips to visit rocky islands where musk oxen graze and barren-ground caribou gather. Guests might watch as grizzly bears, Arctic wolves, and foxes seek their prey or a peregrine falcon brings food to a mate.

During the brief Arctic summer, yellow-billed and red-throated loons, Lapland longspurs, golden eagles, and numerous other birds migrate here, luring bird-watchers from all over. The lodge also offers day trips to 1,000-year-old stone camps built by the Thule people, ancestors of the Inuit, and provides a window on the proud and vibrant culture of the local Inuit.

VISITOR INFO: www.nunavuttourism.com. **BATHURST INLET LODGE:** 30 miles/48 km north of the Arctic Circle, and 360 air miles/580 km northeast of Yellowknife. Tel 867-873-2595; www.bathurstarctic.com. **COST:** $5,850 per person per week all-inclusive with air charter from/to Yellowknife. **WHEN:** Jul.

Thunderous Grandeur and Sophisticated Vintages

Niagara Falls and Niagara Wine Country

Ontario, Canada, and New York State, U.S.A.

The Niagara River draws water from four of the five Great Lakes and flings it down 20 stories at the rate of 42 million gallons a minute, creating waterfalls that are by volume the largest and most powerful in North America. Almost a mile wide in total, the falls straddle the U.S.-Canada border and are divided by islands into three sections: the 1,060-foot American Falls, which includes a smaller section called Bridal Veil Falls, and the 2,600-foot Horseshoe Falls on the Canadian side.

To get up close to this incredible force of nature, start your visit in New York's Three Sisters Islands, where visitors can stand within a few feet of the brink of the falls, or at the Cave of the Winds tour. Here a series of decks and stairs leads to the Hurricane Deck, just 20 feet from the pounding waters at the base of Bridal Veil Falls. Take a trip on the *Maid of the Mist*, a sturdy 600-passenger boat that's accessible from both sides. Don a plastic poncho and sail right into the maelstrom at the base of Horseshoe Falls.

The Canadian side offers the best views, including nighttime illumination shows. At Journey Behind the Falls, descend via elevator through 150 feet of rock for views from behind the cascading water of Horseshoe Falls.

The Maid of the Mist *took its maiden voyage in 1846.*

For creature comforts, the Canadian side also wins out—it has better facilities—nightclubs, restaurants, upscale hotels, and the Niagara Fallsview Casino Resort, which offers spacious rooms with incredible views.

After taking in the falls, leave the honeymooning crowds behind and travel north to the lovely little 19th-century town of Niagara-on-the-Lake, full of elegant historic homes, Victorian storefronts, wine shops, beautiful parks and gardens, B&Bs, and the Prince of Wales Hotel and Spa. Presiding over the center of town, this beautifully restored Victorian hotel is especially popular during the town's acclaimed Shaw Festival, dedicated to presenting plays by or about George Bernard Shaw and his contemporaries.

Niagara-on-the-Lake is also, along with the neighboring communities of St. Catharines, Jordan, and Vineland, at the heart of the Niagara wine region. The Niagara Peninsula, a neck of land that separates Lake Erie from Lake Ontario and shares Tuscany's latitude, is the largest viticultural area in Canada, with some 60 wineries that account for 80 percent of Canada's grape-growing volume. Favorite stops include Peller Estates, Château des Charmes, Vineland Estates Winery, and Inniskillin Winery, a leading producer of icewine, the honeylike dessert wine made from grapes left to freeze on the vine.

One of Ontario's top country hotels, the Inn on the Twenty, is a welcoming and convenient base in Jordan for touring the wine country. Foodies gather at this renovated sugar warehouse for the innovative cuisine and fine wines of the well-known dining room.

WHERE: 82 miles/132 km southeast of Toronto. *Ontario visitor info:* www.niagarafallstourism.com. *New York visitor info:* www.niagara-usa.com. **CAVE OF THE WINDS:** Tel 716-278-1730; www.niagarafallsstatepark.com. *When:* May–Oct. ***MAID OF THE MIST:*** Tel 905-358-5781 (Ontario), 716-284-8897 (New York); www.maidofthemist.com. *When:* Apr–Oct. **JOURNEY BEHIND THE FALLS:** Tel 905-354-1551; www.niagaraparks.com. *When:* May–Oct. **NIAGARA FALLSVIEW CASINO RESORT:** Tel 888-325-5788 or 905-374-6928; www.fallviewcasinoresort.com. *Cost:* from $210. **PRINCE OF WALES:** Tel 888-669-5566 or 905-468-3246; www.vintageinns.com. *Cost:* from $180 (off-peak), from $300 (peak). **GEORGE BERNARD SHAW FESTIVAL:** Tel 800-511-7429 or 905-468-2172; www.shawfest.com. *When:* Apr–Nov. **INN ON THE TWENTY:** Tel 800-701-8074 or 905-562-5336; www.innonthetwenty.com. *Cost:* from $150 (off-peak), from $260 (peak); dinner $55. **BEST TIMES:** weekends in mid-May–Aug for fireworks at the falls; Sep for Niagara Wine Festival.

Celebrating the Canadian Winter

WINTERLUDE AND THE RIDEAU CANAL

Ottawa, Ontario, Canada

If nature gives you snow and ice, celebrate the joys of winter. That's exactly what Canada's capital city has done every February since 1979, during Winterlude, Ottawa's paean to skating, family activities, and fun in the snow.

More than 650,000 visitors show up every year for the celebration, which includes a whole host of events: a winter triathlon (skiing, skating, and running), a hot stew cook-off, figure-skating performances, and outdoor concerts. Across the Ottawa River, in Quebec, Gatineau's Jacques-Cartier Park hosts the world's largest snow playground—complete with a snow maze and dozens of snow slides. This is Snowflake Kingdom, the site of the National Snow Sculpture Competition, a crowd favorite that displays giant works prepared by professional snow sculptors from each province and territory. Gatineau feels like a winter wonderland for those exploring its 124 miles of groomed cross-country ski trails through hardwood forests. Meanwhile, back at Ottawa's Confederation Park, the Crystal Garden International Ice-Carving Competition is peopled by imposing ice statues that take on an eerie luminescence when lit at night.

Snow and ice sculptures enthrall visiting families.

The Rideau Canal is the centerpiece of Winterlude. Built in the 1830s as a 126-mile military route linking the Ottawa River and Lake Ontario, North America's oldest continuously operated canal becomes Winterlude's main drag when 5 miles of its length, in the heart of Ottawa, are groomed for skating. During the rest of winter, the canal doubles as an ice thoroughfare—and the world's largest naturally frozen ice rink. It fills with businesspeople commuting by skate between home and office; schoolchildren zipping along, carrying lunch boxes; and skaters and sledders who stop at food concessions along the way for hot chocolate, beavertails (wedges of deep-fried dough covered with cinnamon sugar), and maple syrup on shaved ice.

The imposing Fairmont Château Laurier, on the spot where the Rideau Canal meets the Ottawa River, is the best place to hang your skates. At the least, come for a cup of tea, served with Nova Scotia salmon and fresh-baked scones. Built in 1912, the Laurier offers a historic castlelike setting, handsome furnishings, and one of the most European hotel experiences this side of the Atlantic.

WINTERLUDE: Tel 800-465-1867 or 613-239-5000; www.winterlude.ca. *When:* 1st 3 weekends in Feb. **FAIRMONT CHÂTEAU LAURIER:** Tel 613-241-1414; www.fairmont.com/laurier. *Cost:* from $205 (off-peak), from $305 (peak); high tea $35.

The Bard—and More—on Canada's Avon River

THE STRATFORD FESTIVAL

Stratford, Ontario, Canada

"The play's the thing," according to Shakespeare—a philosophy that has guided the highly acclaimed Stratford Festival of Canada since the early 1950s, when Stratford-born journalist Tom Patterson established a summer theater festival in this scenic and appropriately named city. Now the largest classical repertory theater in North America, the venue offers over a dozen productions yearly, from mid-April through early November. In addition to world-class productions of Shakespeare, it mounts a broad range of classic plays, musicals, and cutting-edge dramas on its four stages. Visitors can also attend a full program of fringe events, including concerts, discussions, and readings.

Apart from its dynamic thespian activity, Stratford is a charming and romantic place to visit any time of year. The downtown core is a well-preserved bastion of ivy-covered Victorian storefronts centered on a market square, with excellent antiques stores, bookshops, art galleries, and restaurants. Call ahead for reservations at the Church Restaurant, a (now deconsecrated) house of worship built in 1873, where excellent modern French cuisine matches the unique setting, or take the stairs to its Belfry bar, a popular place for light meals and pre- and post-theater drinks.

With ten quirky yet luxurious guest rooms in three historic 19th-century homes and a carriage house, the Three Houses Bed and Breakfast Inn perfectly captures Stratford's sophistication and good-natured sense of high drama. The stylish décor partakes equally of whimsy and refined good taste, and breakfasts have the festive spirit of a dinner party.

WHERE: 93 miles/149 km west of Toronto. Tel 800-567-1600 or 519-273-1600; www.stratfordfestival.ca. *When:* mid-Apr–early Nov. **THE CHURCH RESTAURANT:** Tel 519-273-3424; www.churchrestaurant.com. *Cost:* 3-course tasting menu $55. **THREE HOUSES INN:** Tel 519-272-0722; www.thethreehouses.com. *Cost:* from $195. **BEST TIMES:** Jul–Aug for the peak of the theater festival; late Jul–mid-Aug for Stratford Summer Music Festival.

Temples of Canadian Art and Culture

Art Gallery of Ontario and the Royal Ontario Museum

Toronto, Ontario, Canada

With a striking new Frank Gehry–designed expansion that increased gallery space at the Art Gallery of Ontario (AGO) by almost half, one of the largest and most important collections of visual art in Canada is bigger and better than ever. The expansion didn't just enlarge the august 1918 Beaux Arts building physically, it also brought an additional 10,000 new works of art to the permanent collection and added FRANK, a contemporary, chic restaurant with locally sourced comfort food and an all-Ontario wine list. Named after the Toronto-born, Los Angeles–based architect, the restaurant also throws a nod to Frank Stella, whose installation adorns the space.

The AGO expansion was triggered when Kenneth Thomson, a leading Canadian businessperson, donated nearly 2,000 works from his private art collection to the museum—the largest gift ever made to a Canadian cultural institution. The Thomson collection spans the centuries, from Medieval and Baroque ivories and classics of 17th- and 18th-century European painting to Canadian art from the 19th and 20th centuries. It joined the museum's already impressive collection of works by European masters from Brueghel to Van Gogh, and more-contemporary artists like Andy Warhol and Claes Oldenburg. The AGO also has the finest collection of Inuit art in Canada and the world's largest collection of works by British sculptor Henry Moore.

The Royal Ontario Museum's "Crystal" addition was designed by Daniel Libeskind.

Also newly expanded, the Royal Ontario Museum (ROM) is Canada's largest museum of natural history and world culture. More than 6 million objects comprise an overview of natural history from the dawn of time, with art and artifacts of human cultures from around the world. The exhibits are diverse and captivating, ranging from a remarkable selection of Chinese art and a wing dedicated to European decorative arts to dinosaur skeletons and a Canadian heritage gallery.

Further reason to visit can be found in the Daniel Libeskind–designed "Crystal"—300,000 square feet of new and renovated gallery space defined by the jagged, multifaceted form adjoining the museum's neo-Romanesque façade. It helped reinvent the venerable museum, while expanding gallery space for the display of never-before-seen collections.

Art Gallery of Ontario: Tel 416-979-6648; www.ago.net. **Royal Ontario Museum:** Tel 416-586-8000; www.rom.on.ca.

Hollywood Glamour on Lake Ontario

Toronto International Film Festival

Toronto, Ontario, Canada

Established in 1976, and showing more than 330 films from over 65 countries, the Toronto International Film Festival is the top film festival in North America. Widely considered second only to Cannes (see p. 127) on the world stage, it is regarded by many filmmakers as the premier opportunity for launching new films. Little wonder, Canada in general, and Toronto specifically, has become Hollywood North, a major filmmaking center minus the high costs of southern California.

The September festival began as an assemblage of films from other showcases, a "festival of festivals," but quickly became a platform for film premieres, idiosyncratic retrospectives, and the introduction of international films to North America. For 10 intensive days, the films are screened in 23 different venues in downtown Toronto, attracting an audience of over 300,000 filmgoers. The presence of so many cinephiles, Hollywood executives, and movie stars in a relatively compact area makes for a real *People*-magazine-goes-to-the-carnival atmosphere.

When the film world's glitterati finish gracing the red carpets, chances are excellent that they'll take their limos to Yorkville and the Four Seasons Hotel, the Canadian company's flagship property and still one of Toronto's most fashionable. Some rooms offer views of the city skyline, with the 1,815-foot Canadian National (CN) Tower—the world's tallest freestanding structure and the symbol of the city.

For those who prefer their lodgings a little more eclectic, there's the Drake, a small design-aware hotel that serves as a hip crossroads for Toronto's creative types.

Visitor info: Tel 416-968-3456; www.tiff.net/thefestival. *When:* 10 days in early to mid-Sep. **Four Seasons Hotel:** Tel 800-268-6282 or 416-964-0411; www.fourseasons.com/toronto. *Cost:* from $300 (off-peak), from $445 (peak). **Drake Hotel:** Tel 866-372-5386 or 416-531-5042; www.thedrakehotel.ca. *Cost:* from $190.

Green Gables and the Founding of Canada

Prince Edward Island

Canada

Canada's smallest province, Prince Edward Island (PEI) is a low-lying, richly agricultural isle in the Gulf of St. Lawrence. PEI is as pastoral as a postcard, with tiny farm towns set amid rolling green hills and coastal villages on rocky bays where fishermen pull lobsters, clams, scallops, and oysters from the sea. Its self-reliant lifestyle was nurtured by isolation—until 1997, when the 9-mile Confederation Bridge was completed, ferries were the only link to the mainland. The northern shores of PEI don't just look storybook, they are storybook: This is the bucolic setting of *Anne of Green Gables*, Lucy Maud Montgomery's famed novel of a spunky, red-haired orphan girl coming of age at the turn of the 20th century. The inspiration for the book's setting was Green Gables House, the Cavendish farm belonging to Montgomery's cousins, now preserved for all to enjoy as part of Prince Edward Island National Park and drawing 350,000 visitors annually to the island and its many Anne-related sights.

But Prince Edward Island National Park is more than just Anne's Land. The park also protects 25 miles of the island's north-central coast, a unique maritime shoreline of sand spits, dunes, islands, and beaches, plus coastal wetlands and forests. Stay at the gracious Dalvay-by-the-Sea National Historic Site and Heritage Inn, a seaside Victorian mansion turned summer resort, built in 1895 and today administered by the park. It offers beaches, hiking trails, and golf nearby.

Even Charlottetown, PEI's capital and a delightful small city on the island's southern coast, gets caught up with Green Gables fever during the Charlottetown Festival, held every summer at the Confederation Centre of the Arts. The festival offers a showcase of live performances but the perennial audience favorite is *Anne of Green Gables—the Musical.*

Charlottetown (population of 35,000) is PEI's one true hub, though it feels more like a well-to-do and friendly small town. Its waterfront, with Peake's Wharf at its center, is a lively place to visit, with its brick warehouses converted to shops, restaurants, and open-air cafés. Above the waterfront, the old town center is more stately, with Georgian-era homes and storefronts: Wander up Great George Street, lined with old churches and majestic maples, for an especially evocative glimpse of old Charlottetown. Fifteen of the historic buildings on this street are part of the Great George, a unique set of lodging options with guest rooms that range from traditional to stylishly modern.

Charlottetown celebrates its fishing heritage during September's International Shellfish Festival. Those prized Malpeque oysters, shipped worldwide, taste twice as sweet here.

WHERE: Cavendish is 24 miles/39 km from Charlottetown. www.pc.gc.ca. **GREEN GABLES HOUSE:** Tel 902-963-7874; www.pc.gc.ca. **DALVAY-BY-THE-SEA:** Tel 902-672-2048 (summer), 902-672-1408 (winter); www.dalvaybythesea.com. *Cost:* from \$205. *When:* mid-Jun–Oct. **THE GREAT GEORGE:** Tel 800-361-1118 or 902-892-0606; www.thegreatgeorge.com. *Cost:* from \$180. **BEST TIMES:** Jul–Sep for nicest weather; late May–mid-Oct for Charlottetown Festival; mid-Jul for Summerside Lobster Carnival; early Aug for Highland Games in Eldon; mid-Sep for International Shellfish Festival.

Wilderness Grandeur in the Newport of the North

CHARLEVOIX

Quebec, Canada

An hour northeast of Quebec City, along the north shores of the St. Lawrence River, the land grows rugged; forests of fir, cedar, and spruce edge into farmland, and the banks of the river rise into rock-faced cliffs. This is

Charlevoix, an area of astonishing natural beauty, long famed for its upscale resorts and bucolic recreational pursuits.

Although the first French traders arrived here in the 1670s, it was in the next century, after the English began driving the French Acadians from the Maritime Provinces, that Charlevoix was truly settled. Charlevoix's beauty began to attract travelers, and during the Gilded Age of the late 1800s, a summer influx of wealthy American families began streaming into the Charlevoix villages known collectively as Murray Bay (in French, La Malbaie and Pointe-au-Pic), making this the "Newport of the North."

The clifftop Fairmont Le Manoir Richelieu has stood above the river since 1899 (the current structure was built after a fire in 1928). This 405-room castlelike hotel perfectly captures Charlevoix's blend of quiet countryside charm, wilderness grandeur, and world-class resort life. Spacious guest rooms, a tunnel connection to the Casino de Charlevoix, a pampering spa, and a number of dining choices are luxurious complements to the outdoor activities that have long lured return guests.

The area has become a year-round destination and offers a myriad of opportunities for hiking, biking, kayaking, and wildlife-watching (particularly for beluga whales). The resort's golf club maintains 27 scenic holes on a bluff above the river. In the white months, the region's deep snowfalls lure snowmobilers and both downhill and Nordic skiers, while ice-skaters glide and twirl at the hotel's river-facing outdoor rink.

A delicious air of country elegance prevails at the 18-room Auberge La Pinsonnière. Expect marvelous views (some overlooking Murray Bay), cozy-but-elegant furnishings, an impressive art collection, and impeccable service. Topping it all is the hotel's famous restaurant, widely considered the best in Charlevoix (and beyond), with an award-winning 12,000-bottle wine cellar.

Where: 50 miles/80 km northeast of Quebec City. **Fairmont Le Manoir Richelieu:** Tel 800-441-1414 or 418-665-3703; www.fairmont.com/richelieu. *Cost:* from $155 (off-peak), from $200 (peak). **La Pinsonnière:** Tel 800-387-4431 or 418-665-4431; www.lapinsonniere.com. *Cost:* from $295 (off-peak), from $350 (peak); dinner $80. **Best times:** May–Oct for outdoor activities and whale-watching; Dec–Mar for skiing and snowmobiling.

Idyllic Retreats and Gourmet Adventures in the Quebec Heartland

Lake Massawippi and the Eastern Townships

Quebec, Canada

Quebec's Eastern Townships feature wide valleys, glacial lakes, and low mountains (the northern extension of the Appalachians) snuggled between the St. Lawrence River and the borders of Maine, New Hampshire, and Vermont. The region's many farms and vineyards provide the produce, wines, and traditional foods that lend a French je ne sais quoi to fine cuisine across the province of Quebec.

At the turn of the 20th century, Lake Massawippi, a narrow, 10-mile-long glacier-dug lake flanked by hardwood forests, had become a favorite summer vacation destination

A round red barn is part of the charming scenery of West Brome, one of the Eastern Townships.

for wealthy families; train lines brought America's captains of industry, who built grand lakefront estates here.

Today, Lake Massawippi is still an idyllic place. Small prim villages such as North Hatley sit at the lake's edge, their narrow streets lined with galleries, antiques shops, and excellent restaurants. Many of the old lakeside mansions have been converted to boutique hotels and country inns, all exuding an inimitable mix of Quebecois charm and New England character.

Built in 1899, Manoir Hovey stands amid 25 hillside acres, an elegant country inn with English-style gardens sloping down to a heated pool, clay tennis court, and two small lakefront beaches. Diners enjoy award-winning Quebecois food and an acclaimed wine list by the dining room's inglenook fireplace.

At the southern end of Massawippi, in the town of Ayer's Cliff, the Ripplecove Inn sits on a 12-acre peninsula, a testament to its beginnings as a 1940s fishing resort. Today, this well-loved inn offers luxurious accommodations, fine dining, and easy access to outdoor recreation.

The village of Dunham is at the center of the "Route des Vins"—a circuit of 16 wineries that's popular with cyclists. Artisanal cheeses are another local specialty, none more revered than the award winners made by the small community of monks at the Abbey of St. Benoit-du-Lac, on Lake Memphremagog.

A marvelous way to take in the scenery and enjoy regional cuisine is to board the Orford Express, a vintage excursion train that offers 3.5-hour sightseeing and culinary trips that travel past farms, vineyards, orchards, and lakes—the countryside whose bounty appears on the menu.

WHERE: 100 miles/161 km southeast of Montreal. **VISITOR INFO:** www.easterntownships.org. **MANOIR HOVEY:** Tel 800-661-2421 or 819-842-2421; www.manoirhovey.com. *Cost:* from $350, inclusive. **RIPPLECOVE INN:** Tel 800-668-4296 or 819-838-4296; www.ripplecove.com. *Cost:* from $280, inclusive. **ABBEY OF ST. BENOIT-DU-LAC:** Tel 819-843-4080; www.st-benoit-du-lac.com. **ORFORD EXPRESS:** Tel 866-575-8081 or 819-575-8081; www.orfordexpress.com. *When:* early May–Oct. **BEST TIMES:** Jun–Sep for fishing and boating; last 2 weekends in Sep for Knowlton Duck Festival; late Sep–early Oct for foliage.

A Festival City par Excellence

Montreal's Summer Festivals

Montreal, Quebec, Canada

Montreal loves a party, as its reputation as Canada's "capital of festivals" makes clear. By far the city's most important event is the 11-day early-summer Montreal International Jazz Festival, the world's largest and most prestigious. In the entertainment district anchored by the Place des Arts, 10 outdoor stages present 450 free concerts, while 200 indoor concerts are held in clubs and theaters around town. An annual tradition since 1979, the festival attracts an audience of 2.5 million jazz lovers and brings together some 3,000 world-class musicians from more than 30 countries, who fill the city with jazz as well as blues, reggae, electronica, and Latin and African music. In recent years, the festival has hosted international luminaries ranging from Wynton Marsalis and Tony Bennett to Stevie Wonder and Diana Krall.

Starting with a bang—quite literally—the Montreal International Fireworks Competition lights up the city's night skies from mid-June through late August. National teams of fireworks designers from around the world launch their biggest, newest, and most revolutionary creations to the accompaniment of brilliant musical arrangements.

The Just for Laughs Festival is the world's largest comedy event. In July, more than 1,600 comedians from over 20 countries come to Montreal for the two-week festival, cracking up 2 million festivalgoers at over a thousand shows and performances, many of them in English. There's also a huge free outdoor street fair and quirky events like the annual Twins Parade, where thousands of twins and multiples march through Montreal.

In late August and early September, the World Film Festival brings together more than 450 international films, with entries from nearly 80 countries, as well as a growing number of world premieres. Other standouts of Montreal's summer lineup include Les FrancoFolies de Montréal, celebrating French music from around the world, and the Festival Nuits d'Afrique, promoting music of the African diaspora with indoor and outdoor concerts that really get the city in party mode.

Montreal Jazz Festival: Tel 888-515-0515 or 514-871-1881; www.montrealjazzfest.com. *When:* late Jun–early Jul. **International Fireworks Competition:** Tel 514-397-2000; www.internationaldesfeuxloto-quebec.com. *When:* mid-Jun–Jul. **Just for Laughs Festival:** Tel 888-244-3155 or 514-845-3155; www.hahaha.com. *When:* mid-Jul. **World Film Festival:** Tel 514-848-3883; www.ffm-montreal.org. *When:* late Aug–early Sep. **Les FrancoFolies de Montréal:** Tel 800-361-4595 or 514-790-1245; www.francofolies.com. *When:* early Jun. **Festival Nuits d'Afrique:** Tel 514-499-9239; www.festivalnuitsdafrique.com. *When:* mid-Jul.

Both classic and "pyromusical" (musically synchronized) fireworks light up the Jacques Cartier Bridge.

Paris Without Jet Lag

Vieux-Montréal

Montreal, Quebec, Canada

Montreal got its start in 1642, when a group of French missionaries arrived by river and set up camp, intent on converting the local Iroquois to Christianity. By 1759, after the British defeated the French for the rule of Canada, the growing city was centered along a narrow stretch of headland above the busy port on the St. Lawrence River. Today, this is Montreal's old city center, known as Vieux-Montréal, and despite almost 250 years of British rule and the influence of *anglais*-speaking Canada and the United States, it remains a bastion of French diaspora culture. After Paris, Montreal is the second largest French-speaking city in the world.

Place Jacques-Cartier is the epicenter of Montreal summer life, with its street performers, cafés, flower merchants, and horse-drawn caleches—you'll see why it is commonly used by North American film crews as a stand-in location for Europe. Place d'Armes is another popular gathering spot, with views of some of the city's most beautiful and historic sites, including the 1829 Basilica of Notre Dame, and the adjacent Sulpician Seminary, Montreal's oldest building. Amid all this history, the Place d'Armes Hôtel and Suites strikes a note of majestic refinement, with swanky modern rooms and chic dining options all behind a grand and stately façade.

Near the riverfront, Rue St-Paul is the city's oldest, a winding street lined with gaslights and early-19th-century storefronts, now housing art galleries and boutiques. Along the St. Lawrence, the Old Port has been transformed from a gritty warehouse district into a promenade full of parks, exhibition spaces, skating rinks, and playgrounds. In keeping with the spirit of transformation is the stylish Auberge du Vieux-Port, an 1882-warehouse-turned-hotel with brass beds and luxury bedding, as well as an elegant bistro and wine bar.

A short distance from the busy Vieux-Port is the always popular Auberge Les Passants du Sans Soucy, a fur warehouse built in 1723, now converted into a delightful B&B whose nine rooms—with their stone walls, polished wood floors, and traditional Quebecois furniture—also have all the modern comforts. Nearby, Toqué! is one of Montreal's most acclaimed contemporary French restaurants, serving up dazzling food and friendly, unpretentious service. Celebrity chef Normand Laprise's constantly changing menu reflects the long-standing relationships he has built with local purveyors. For a quick bite, head north of the Old Quarter and join *tout Montréal* at L'Express, a popular spot for authentic French bistro fare.

VISITOR INFO: www.vieux.montreal.qc.ca. **PLACE D'ARMES HÔTEL:** Tel 888-450-1887 or 514-842-1887; www.hotelplacedarmes.com. *Cost:* from $160 (off-peak), from $230 (peak). **AUBERGE DU VIEUX-PORT:** Tel 888-660-7678 or 514-876-0081; www.aubergeduvieuxport.com. *Cost:* from $180. **AUBERGE LES PASSANTS DU SANS SOUCY:** Tel 514-842-2634; www.lesanssoucy.com. *Cost:* from $135. **TOQUÉ!:** Tel 514-499-2084; www.restaurant-toque.com. *Cost:* dinner $70. **L'EXPRESS:** Tel 514-845-5333. *Cost:* dinner $35. **BEST TIMES:** Feb–Mar for High Lights Winter Festival; Jun–Sep for nice weather.

Eastern Canada's Top Mountain Resort

Mont Tremblant Resort and the Laurentian Mountains

Quebec, Canada

Mont Tremblant, North America's second oldest ski resort (after Idaho's Sun Valley; see p. 784) stands atop the highest peak (3,001 feet) of Quebec's Laurentian Mountains. Established in 1939, Mont Tremblant is often ranked the No. 1 ski area in eastern North America, attracting skiers from around the world with more than 47 miles of trails (broken up into 94 runs). The mountain receives more than 150 inches of snow in winter, and a full 50 percent of its trails are classified expert, including the daunting double–black diamond Dynamite with its 42-degree incline, the steepest in eastern Canada.

At the mountain's base lies Mont Tremblant Village, a pedestrian-only area designed to resemble Quebec City's historic district, right down to its cobbled streets, wrought-iron balconies, and tin roofs, and its countless bars, restaurants, and shops. Le Shack, located on the St. Bernard Plaza, is Tremblant's most popular après-ski spot, with a laid-back atmosphere that's shared by the whole resort. The ski-in/ski-out Fairmont Tremblant sits just above the village, harmoniously integrated into its natural setting. It exudes the feel of a rustic château on a grand scale, with a fitness center, year-round indoor and outdoor swimming pools, whirlpools overlooking the ski slopes, and a European-style spa. At the resort's top restaurant, the Windigo, chef Daniel Tobien brings traditional French savoir-faire to fresh local products.

Mont Tremblant is as busy in summer as in winter—families come for the water sports on Lake Tremblant, hiking and mountain biking in the Laurentians, and golf at two world-class 18-hole golf courses—the par-71 Le Diable and par-72 Le Géant—that are arguably Quebec's best. July brings a popular nine-day blues festival; in September the Laurentian Mountains are ablaze with colorful autumn foliage, particularly the fiery red of native sugar maples.

Where: 75 miles/121 km north of Montreal. **Mont Tremblant:** Tel 888-736-2526 or 819-681-2000; www.tremblant.ca. *Cost:* lift tickets $70; greens fees from $75 (off-peak), from $115 (peak). *When:* ski season mid-Nov–mid-Apr. **Fairmont Tremblant:** Tel 819-681-7000; www.fairmont.com/tremblant. *Cost:* from $180 (off-peak), from $230 (peak). **Best times:** Dec–Mar for ski conditions; Jul for Blues Festival; Sep for foliage and Symphony of Colours Festival.

A Toast to Winter's Chill

Carnaval de Québec

Quebec City, Quebec, Canada

In winter's frosty midst—partly in defiance, partly in celebration—Quebec City springs to life during the Carnaval de Québec (Quebec Winter Carnival). The world's largest winter carnival and the Mardi Gras of the north, it promises 17 festive days of dancing, music, parades, winter sports, and high spirits—much of the latter due to a traditional beverage called the Caribou, a mixture of brandy, vodka, sherry, and port. Plenty of events that cater to the whole family round out the roster.

Presiding over the carnival is Bonhomme, a snowmanlike creature who serves as festival ambassador and mythical resident of the Ice Palace, an enormous castle built entirely of ice near the Quebec Parliament building. A high point of the carnival is the International Snow Sculpture Competition at Place Loto-Québec. The narrow streets of Vieux-Québec (Old Quebec; see next page) ring with the mushers' cries as La Grande Virée dogsledding competition circles the city; adults and children alike whiz down icy chutes on toboggans; and after downing a fortifying Caribou (or many), hardy Quebecois engage in the annual Snow Bath by stripping down to their Speedos in front of a raucous crowd and diving into a snowdrift. The annual canoe race is even more daring: Paddlers have raced across the ice-choked St. Lawrence River since 1894.

The St. Lawrence River is the only place in the world where canoes are raced through the ice.

While all Vieux-Québec hotels put on a festive air, there's no more appropriate place to check in than the Hôtel de Glace, a 32,000-square-foot hotel constructed of ice and snow. Located 30 minutes west of Quebec City, this "icetablishment" offers 36 guest rooms and suites and includes a wedding chapel, an art gallery, an ice slide, a Nordic-style spa with hot tubs and sauna, plus a bar and nightclub—all fashioned anew each year from 15,000 tons of snow and 500 tons of ice. Admittedly the Ice Hotel's accommodations don't appeal to everyone (and few reserve for more than one night), but at least make time to come for a drink—in an ice glass, of course—at the Ice Bar.

If you'd prefer a Carnaval nightcap with a bit less chill, ask for a Neige (a cider made like icewine) at the Auberge Saint-Antoine, an intimate hotel fashioned from an 1820s stone warehouse in Quebec City's old port district. The Auberge's restaurant, Panache, is one of the city's top spots for fine dining, serving updated traditional Quebecois cuisine. Its lavish guest rooms, beautifully appointed in a mix of modern and historic themes, are likewise a contemporary iteration of a great classic.

INFO: Tel 866-422-7628 or 418-626-3716; www.carnaval.qc.ca. *When:* late Jan–early Feb. **HÔTEL DE GLACE:** Tel 877-505-0423 or 418-875-4522; www.icehotel-canada.com. *Cost:* from $350. *When:* Jan–mid-Mar. **AUBERGE SAINT-ANTOINE:** Tel 888-692-2211 or 418-692-2211; www.saint-antoine.com. *Cost:* from $155 (off-peak), from $290 (peak); dinner at Panache $80.

Old France in the New World

VIEUX-QUÉBEC

Quebec City, Quebec, Canada

Once the capital of New France, Quebec City is one of the oldest European settlements in North America and the continent's only walled city north of Mexico. Perched on Cap Diamant, a rocky promontory above the St. Lawrence River, it was established in 1608 by French explorer Samuel de Champlain. The walls of Vieux-Québec (Old Quebec) didn't stop the British from taking the city in 1759, ending France's colonial aspirations in eastern North America. Spend some time in this charming old-world enclave and you'll wonder if the French ever got the memo.

Vieux-Québec is divided into the Haute-Ville and Basse-Ville (Upper and Lower Towns), designations that are now simply geographic but were once economic and strategic. Haute-Ville is the fortified city that occupies the crest of Cap Diamant. Brimming with atmosphere, it is best explored on foot. Winding, hilly streets lined by vintage stone houses and chic boutiques lead to leafy public squares, with glimpses of the St. Lawrence in the distance. Constructed by the British to defend against U.S. invasion during the War of 1812 and occupying the highest crag of Cap Diamant, the Citadel is still a military fortification. At the center of Haute-Ville, the Auberge Place d'Armes bridges history by occupying two buildings—one from the 1640s, the other from 1853. The lovingly restored inn balances the genuinely old—antique stone walls and one-of-a-kind period details, such as furnishings from Versailles—with every modern comfort. A few steps down Rue St-Louis is Aux Anciens Canadiens, a venerable restaurant in a 1677 structure known for its home-style Quebecois fare, such as savory meat pies, maple-glazed duck, and platters of local cheese.

Château Frontenac is named for a governor of the colony of New France.

From the Terrasse Dufferin viewpoint, take the Escalier Casse-Cou (the aptly named Breakneck Stairs) or the funicular to Basse-Ville, the old port district at the base of Cap Diamant. The heart of Basse-Ville is Place Royale, the city's public market area in the 17th century, now a charming cobblestone plaza flanked by stone houses, cafés, and the Église Notre-Dame-des-Victoires, dating from 1688. Amid the historic shops, galleries, and flower-bedecked squares of Basse-Ville is an updated gem, the Hôtel Le Germain-Dominion, whose vintage stone façade masks a stylish, contemporary boutique hotel. Formerly a warehouse, it has been transformed into a strikingly attractive place, the rooms all appointed with quiet good taste. An equally stylish experience awaits just around the corner at Laurie Raphaël Restaurant, where chef Daniel Vézina charts the frontiers of modern French-Canadian cooking, with bold flavors and exuberant presentations that are excitingly new yet grounded in Quebec's hearty terroir.

Towering above all of Vieux-Québec with green-copper turrets, and in many ways the symbol of the city, is the Fairmont Le Château Frontenac. Designed in the style of a Loire Valley château, it was built in 1893 on the highest point in town. Book an odd-numbered room in the main tower for a view of the St. Lawrence River, or an even-numbered room for a panorama of the city's rooftops—probably the most European vista this side of Paris.

VISITOR INFO: www.bonjourquebec.com. **AUBERGE PLACE D'ARMES:** Tel 418-694-9485 or 866-333-9485; www.aubergeplacedarmes.com. *Cost:* from $120 (off-peak), from $190 (peak). **AUX ANCIENS CANADIENS:** Tel 418-692-1627; www.auxancienscanadiens.qc.ca. *Cost:* dinner $55. **HÔTEL LE GERMAIN-DOMINION:** Tel 888-833-5253 or 418-692-2224; www.hoteldominion.com. *Cost:* from $220. **LAURIE RAPHAËL RESTAURANT:** Tel 418-692-4555; www.laurieraphael.com. *Cost:* 6-course tasting menu $85. **FAIRMONT LE CHÂTEAU FRONTENAC:** Tel 800-441-1414 or 418-692-3861; www.fairmont.com/frontenac. *Cost:* from $195. **BEST TIMES:** late Jan–early Feb for Carnaval de Québec; Jul–Sep for best weather; mid-Jul for Festival d'Été de Quebec; Dec for Christmas Market.

Catching Gold Fever in the Klondike

Dawson City and the Yukon River

Yukon, Canada

In 1896, the cry went up: Gold! A small party of prospectors panning for nuggets on a remote tributary of the Yukon River discovered gold, and lots of it. Word of the Klondike gold fields spread like wildfire, and by 1898, Dawson City, just 165 miles south of the Arctic Circle, counted more than 30,000 inhabitants, a boomtown if ever there was one. While some early prospectors made easy fortunes, many other "Stampeders" eked out livings without ever holding a pan, working as merchants, suppliers, cardsharps, bankers, saloonkeepers, and dance-hall girls. By the 1910s, industrial dredging replaced prospecting, but not before the Klondike shipped out more than $360 million in gold.

In 1896, news of a gold rush traveled down the Yukon River.

Unlike many gold rush towns, Dawson City refused to die. It served as the capital of Yukon Territory until 1953, and with its late-Victorian hotels, saloons, false-fronted stores, and residences from mansions to miner's shacks, Dawson City, with a year-round population of 1,300, eventually became an interesting open-air museum. Peer into Bombay Peggy's Victorian Inn and Pub. Built in 1900 as the town brothel, it now peddles more reputable hospitality as a stylish inn with boudoiry guest rooms.

Stop by to view a replica of novelist Jack London's log cabin (where he lived during his stint as a gold miner) or hear actors recite the verses of Robert Service, including "The Cremation of Sam McGee." Or drop in Diamond Tooth Gertie's Gambling Hall, Canada's northernmost casino, replete with honky-tonk piano and dancing girls.

Nearly all 1898 gold rushers reached Dawson City via the mighty Yukon River—the fabled "River of Gold," one of the most powerful rivers in North America. The most exhilarating way to enter town is still by river, perhaps even on a guided multiday canoe trip—you'll pass rugged pristine wilderness, First Nation fishing camps, and abandoned mining sites before paddling into Dawson. Outfitters in Whitehorse offer a range of Yukon River expeditions (from a week to 17 days, depending on where you begin) that revive the Stampeders' river journey, but with modern comforts and much better food.

Where: 333 miles/537 km north of Whitehorse. **Dawson National Historic Site:** Tel 867-993-7200; www.pc.gc.ca. **How:** Up North Adventures offers multi- and 1-day guided Yukon River canoe trips. Tel 867-667-7035, www.upnorthadventures.com. *Cost:* 7-day trip from $1,620. **Bombay Peggy's Victorian Inn:** Tel 867-993-6969; www.bombaypeggys.com. *Cost:* from $135 (off-peak), from $155 (peak). **Best times:** Jun–mid-Sep for long summer days; mid-Aug for Discovery Days celebrating the finding of Klondike gold.

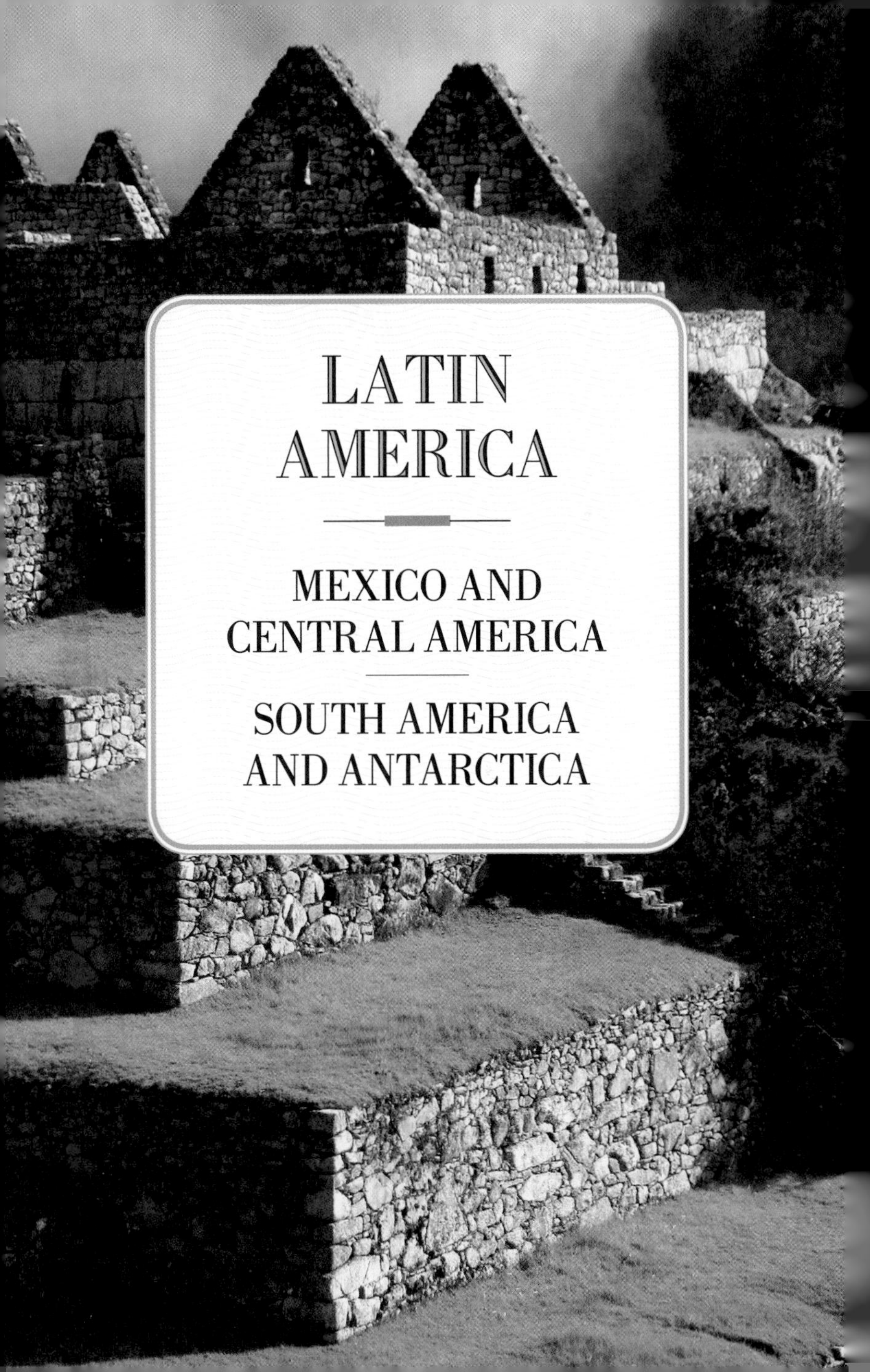

LATIN AMERICA

MEXICO AND CENTRAL AMERICA

SOUTH AMERICA AND ANTARCTICA

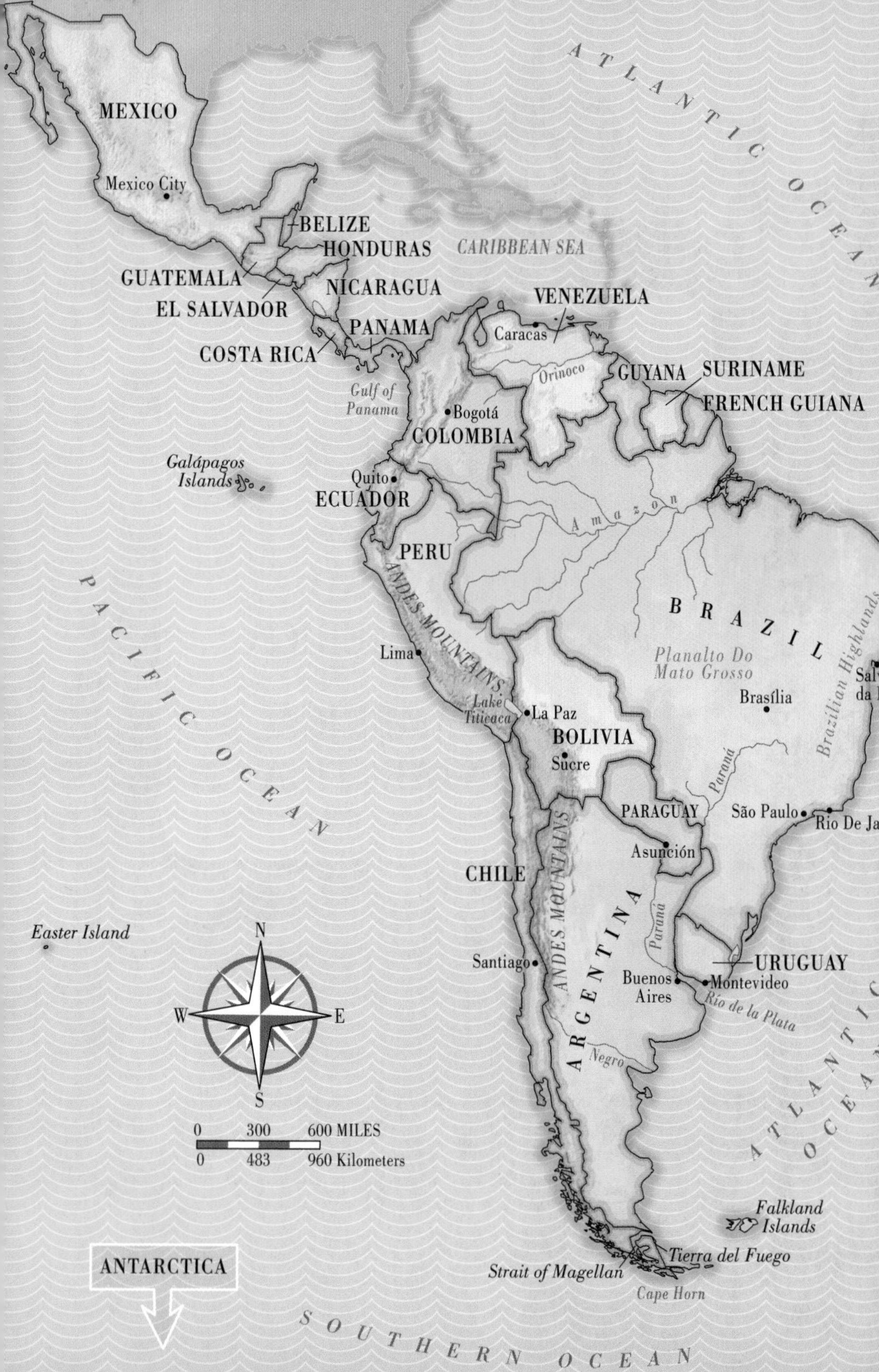
ATLANTIC OCEAN
MEXICO
Mexico City
BELIZE
HONDURAS
CARIBBEAN SEA
GUATEMALA
NICARAGUA
EL SALVADOR
VENEZUELA
Caracas
PANAMA
COSTA RICA
Orinoco
GUYANA
SURINAME
FRENCH GUIANA
Gulf of Panama
Bogotá
COLOMBIA
Galápagos Islands
Quito
ECUADOR
Amazon
PERU
ANDES MOUNTAINS
PACIFIC OCEAN
BRAZIL
Brazilian Highlands
Planalto Do Mato Grosso
Lima
Brasília
Lake Titicaca
La Paz
BOLIVIA
Sucre
Paraná
PARAGUAY
São Paulo
Asunción
CHILE
ANDES MOUNTAINS
ARGENTINA
Paraná
Easter Island
N
W
E
S
Santiago
URUGUAY
Buenos Aires
Montevideo
Río de la Plata
Negro
ATLANTIC OCEAN
0 300 600 MILES
0 483 960 Kilometers
Falkland Islands
ANTARCTICA
Tierra del Fuego
Strait of Magellan
Cape Horn
SOUTHERN OCEAN

MEXICO AND CENTRAL AMERICA

Where the Sea of Cortez and the Pacific Meet

Los Cabos

Baja California Sur, Mexico

At the tip of the 775-mile-long Baja Peninsula, where the Pacific Ocean meets the Sea of Cortez, the resort area of Los Cabos (the capes) stretches over a 25-mile corridor that joins the desert towns of Cabo San Lucas and San José del Cabo. Development began in the 1980s, and Cabo San Lucas quickly earned a reputation as a wild, cerveza-drenched spring break destination. It became equally famous for its world-class fishing, with marlin and sailfish the top prizes.

Cabo turned high-end when a cluster of world-class resorts arrived, led by Las Ventanas al Paraíso, cushioned between sea and desert sands on 12 acres along the corridor. It has become a celebrity darling with its breezy suites, seaside drop-edge pool, an 18-hole Robert Trent Jones Jr. golf course, and a spa offering services from a torch-lit couple's massage to cactus cleansing wraps.

More relaxed and traditional than Cabo is the colonial town of San José del Cabo, with its pink church, shady town square, and old adobe homes. Its slow siesta-time pace is epitomized at the stylish Casa Natalia, tucked away in a lush enclave in the historic center. European owners decorated the 16 high-ceilinged rooms with handmade furniture, local art, and brightly painted walls. Its restaurant, Mi Cocina, is a perennial favorite.

Sensational rock formations tower over the sandy beaches of Cabo San Lucas.

Just north of Cabo San Lucas on the Pacific coast lies Todos Santos, an oasis and artists' colony with no resorts, golf courses, or strip malls—just a walkable little town with sophisticated galleries, boutiques, cafés, and restaurants. Café Santa Fe is renowned for Italian food (ask for the lobster and shrimp ravioli). There are beautiful, almost deserted beaches nearby and the best surf breaks in Baja California. Just outside of town, Rancho Pescadero is a cozy, luxurious inn where guests can read or snooze in a swaying hammock and spend nights listening to the gentle sound of the surf.

Where: About 1,000 miles/1,609 km south of San Diego. **Visitor info:** www.visitloscabos.travel. **Las Ventanas:** Tel 52/624-144-2800; in the U.S., 888-767-3966; www.lasventanas.com. *Cost:* from $550 (off-peak), from $815 (peak). **Casa Natalia:** Tel 52/624-146-7100; in the U.S., 888-277-3814; www.casanatalia.com. *Cost:* from $150; dinner $30. **Café Santa Fe:** Tel 52/612-145-0340. *Cost:* lunch $30. *When:* closed Sep–Oct. **Rancho Pescadero:** Tel 52/612-135-5849; in the U.S., 910-300-8891; www.ranchopescadero.com. *Cost:* from $185 (off-peak), from $250 (peak). **Best times:** Dec–Apr for whale-watching; Oct for international fishing tournaments.

The Aquarium of the World

Sea of Cortez and San Ignacio Lagoon

Baja California Sur, Mexico

Separating the 775-mile-long Baja Peninsula and the Mexican mainland, the Sea of Cortez brims with pristine, plankton-rich waters that create an amazing ecosystem like no other on earth. Jacques Cousteau called it the "aquarium of the world." The uninhabited islands of Espíritu Santo, Isla Partida, and Isla Santa Catalina present a remarkable opportunity to snorkel in the midst of sea lions, dolphins, manta rays, and massive schools of fish. Boaters, kayakers, and snorkelers will find plenty to enjoy as well.

The Baja Peninsula's Pacific coast is famed for one of nature's most remarkable annual migrations. Gray whales swim 5,000 miles from their chilly Arctic feeding grounds to the safety of Baja's warm, shallow waters in order to breed and calve from December to March. Hundreds of dolphins accompany the whales, sometimes along with humpback, finback, Bryde's, sperm, and even blue whales, the largest animals on the planet.

One of the whale calving refuges is San Ignacio Lagoon, visited by several thousand whales every winter—it can host up to 400 at one time. Calves are about 15 feet long and can weigh up to 1,500 pounds at birth. The whales regularly approach small motorboats, called *pangas,* to be stroked by awed spectators.

How: U.S.-based Lindblad Expeditions offers Sea of Cortez cruises from La Paz with kayaks. Tel 800-397-3348 or 212-261-9000; www.expeditions.com. *Cost:* boat trips of 4 nights or more from $1,990. *When:* Dec. Baja Expeditions operates safari-style camps at San Ignacio. Tel 800-843-6967 or 858-581-3311; www.bajaex.com. *Cost:* cabanas $420 per night, all-inclusive. *When:* Jan–Apr. **Best times:** Oct–May for nicest weather; Dec–Mar for whale-watching.

Maya Cities, Ancient and Modern

Palenque and San Cristóbal de las Casas

Chiapas, Mexico

One of the most extraordinary ruins of Maya culture occupies a high, strategically situated plateau surrounded by dense virgin jungle. Palenque blossomed during the 6th to 9th centuries as a center of art, religion, and astronomy and was one of the first Maya sites to be discovered. It remains one of the most majestic and best preserved, still dazzling with its elegant architecture, stucco carvings, calligraphy, and highly artistic decorative friezes. The star attraction is the Templo de las Inscripciones (Temple of the Inscriptions), the massive pyramid housing the carved tomb of King Pacal, who died in A.D. 683 (his burial mask, made of 200 fragments of jade, resides in the Museum of Anthropology in Mexico City; see p. 952). Palenque's best lodging is Chan-Kah Resort Village, featuring stone and wooden bungalows spread over 50 acres of primordial jungle.

The descendants of more than 30 different tribes of ancient Maya live in the high-altitude, red-tile-roofed city of San Cristóbal de las Casas, in the highlands of Chiapas. This pretty colonial town is a stronghold of indigenous culture, as proven by a visit to the Saturday market, where locals come to sell their wares, most notably brightly colored woven textiles. You might hear near-extinct tribal languages and see vendors wearing distinctive headdresses and ornately embroidered *huipiles* (blouses). A centuries-old amalgam of Maya and Catholic rituals is commonly carried out by shamans at any of several churches, including Santo Domingo, where you'll also find one of the city's best crafts markets.

The dinner bell rings at 7 P.M. at Na Bolom, the 19th-century home of late archaeologist Frans Blom and his wife, ethnologist-photographer Gertrude Blom. Now a guesthouse and museum, it is also the headquarters for continuing research and support of the area's highland indigenous villages. The 16 rooms have fireplaces and are decorated with local crafts, and you're guaranteed an interesting mix of guests at the communal dinners in a salon filled with art and artifacts.

WHERE: Palenque is 88 miles/142 km southeast of Villahermosa. San Cristóbal is 142 miles/229 km southwest of Palenque. **CHAN-KAH:** Tel 52/916-345-1134; www.chan-kah.com.mx. *Cost:* from $150. **NA BOLOM:** Tel 52/967-678-1418; www.nabolom.org. *Cost:* rooms from $88; dinner $15. **BEST TIMES:** Dec–Feb for nicest weather. In San Cristóbal, Semana Santa (the week before Easter) for festivities and processions.

A Breathtaking Train Ride Through Rugged Splendor

COPPER CANYON

Chihuahua, Mexico

Northwestern Mexico's Sierra Madre mountain range encompasses one of the greatest canyon complexes in the world, Barrancas del Cobre. Though called the Copper Canyon in English, it is actually a series of six major intertwined canyons, plus 200 minor ones. Cumulatively, the Barrancas are four times larger (and often deeper) than the Grand Canyon.

Crossing this vast wilderness is the Ferrocarril Chihuahua Pacifico—"El Chepe"—one of the most scenic train rides in the world. The rail line is a 400-mile engineering marvel and takes passengers on a 13-hour journey from Los Mochis, on the Pacific coast, to the city of Chihuahua. It snakes through pine-forested highlands, across 39 bridges, and through 86 tunnels, with the most spectacular scenery between El Fuerte and Creel. (Take the train east from Los Mochis; if you travel westbound from Chihuahua, you'll pass the gorgeous views in the dark.)

At Divisadero the train stops briefly for seemingly endless vistas of the canyons. Another heart-stopping view is provided at the Hotel Mirador, perched at the rim at the Barrancas stop so that each room's private balcony appears to hang over the canyon edge. From Creel, it's 20 minutes to the charming, rustic Sierra Lodge, which offers a variety of backcountry hikes with native guides. A hair-raising, 5-hour van ride of 140 miles includes a vertiginous 6,000-foot descent to the old silver-mining town of Batopilas on the canyon floor. The Riverside Lodge, an antiques-filled Victorian-era hacienda, makes for a memorable stay.

WHERE: Los Mochis is 543 miles/874 km south of Tuscon, AZ. **"EL CHEPE":** Tel 52/614-439-7211; in the U.S., 888-484-1623; www.chepe.com.mx. *Cost:* $159 one way. **HOW:** U.S.-based California Native offers escorted canyon tours and independent itineraries. Tel 800-926-1140 or 310-642-1140; www.calnative.com. *Cost:* from $860 for a 4-night program, all-inclusive. **HOTEL MIRADOR:** Tel 52/668-812-1613; in the U.S., 888-528-8401; www.hotelesbalderrama.com. *Cost:* from $250, inclusive. **SIERRA LODGE** and **RIVERSIDE LODGE:** In the U.S., tel 800-648-8488 or 435-259-3999; www.coppercanyonlodges.com. *Cost:* Sierra Lodge from $145, inclusive; Riverside Lodge from $125, room only. *When:* Oct–Apr for Riverside Lodge. **BEST TIMES:** Mar–Apr and Oct–Nov for nicest weather.

Colonial Gems in the Central Highlands

SAN MIGUEL DE ALLENDE AND GUANAJUATO

Guanajuato, Mexico

Artists and writers first started arriving in the colonial city of San Miguel de Allende in the 1930s, drawn by its Old Mexico charm and the purity of its seductive light. Founded in 1542 by wealthy Spanish cattle barons, today San Miguel attracts well-heeled Mexico City weekenders and has a large community of American residents attracted to the city's vibrant artistic and cultural scene. Cobblestone streets are lined with galleries, as well as restored mansions, 18th-century churches, boutiques, outdoor cafés, and excellent restaurants. Grab a bench in tree-shaded El Jardín, the central plaza, and watch the light change at dusk against the salmon-colored Parroquia, the whimsical neo-Gothic parish church.

Built in 1580 and now a refined hotel, Casa de Sierra Nevada consists of seven adjoining colonial-era manor homes two blocks from El Jardín. Of the town's many romantic bed-and-breakfasts, the Casa Schuck is a stylish choice, housed in a Colonial home with beamed ceilings and fireplaces, and a small but beautiful swimming pool.

Many a Spaniard made a fortune by extracting silver from these hills, and Guanajuato, 60 miles west of San Miguel, is another historic city full of centuries-old architecture paid for by these mines. Its narrow, hilly cobblestone lanes resonate with the music of strolling *estudiantinas* (university students), who dress as 16th-century troubadours to perform for passersby. In October, the city holds the world-renowned Cervantes Arts Festival, celebrating music, dance, theater, and the visual arts. One of its many venues is the opulent turn-of-the-century Teatro Juárez, which Caruso deemed one of the finest performance

Built during colonial times, La Parroquia church got a Gothic makeover in 1880.

spaces in the Americas. It overlooks the Jardín de la Unión, the former mining capital's main square and a gathering place for mariachis. Museo Casa de Diego Rivera, the restored home where the artist was born in 1886, houses a good collection of his early works.

Guanajuato's greatest claim to fame is its pivotal role in Mexican history. A funicular climbs a steep hill to the foot of the gargantuan statue honoring *"El Pípila,"* the miner who set fire to the Spanish-controlled granary in 1810. His action allowed the insurgents to attack the Spanish soldiers barricaded inside and was the first major military victory for the independent forces.

Villa María Cristina, in a handsomely restored 19th-century building, is the most sophisticated of the city's hotels. It has just 13 spacious suites with a sunken pool that is perfect for a swim after a day of sightseeing.

WHERE: San Miguel de Allende is 180 miles/290 km northwest of Mexico City. **CASA DE SIERRA NEVADA:** Tel 52/415-152-7040; in the U.S., 800-701-1561; www.casadesierranevada.com. *Cost:* from $250. **CASA SCHUCK:** Tel 52/415-152-0657; in the U.S., 937-684-4092; www.casaschuck.com. *Cost:* from $195. **VILLA MARÍA CRISTINA:** Tel 473-731-2182; in U.S., 866-424-6868; www.villamariacristina.net. *Cost:* from $290. **BEST TIMES:** In San Miguel: Semana Santa (week before Easter) for processions and festivities; Sep 15–16 for Independence Day; Sep 29 for Fiesta de San Miguel. In Guanajuato: Oct for Cervantes Festival.

Where Hollywood Came to Play

ACAPULCO

Guerrero, Mexico

Much of Acapulco's onetime sultry reputation as Hollywood's south-of-the-border beach club has been eclipsed by that of Mexico's other resorts, but the heart-stopping beauty of its horseshoe-shaped bay is eternal. Add in the legendary Pacific sunsets, a flashy, all-night party scene, and those thrilling La Quebrada cliff divers who jump from dizzying heights into a terrifyingly small inlet, and it's no wonder this city has staying power.

A recent renaissance has introduced several new hotels, including the 1950s stylish Hotel Boca Chica, which, thanks to a recent renovation, recalls the glamorous days when John Wayne, Rita Hayworth, and Elvis Presley stayed here (the latter while filming *Fun in Acapulco*). Thirty retro-modern rooms have views of lush Isla La Roqueta, a popular island for snorkeling and sunbathing.

Las Brisas is the hilltop doyenne in this consummate resort town. Secluded bougainvillea-draped casitas, each with a private pool filled with floating hibiscus flowers, sprawl across a hillside commanding eye-popping bay views. The hotel's hallmark pink jeeps transport guests through expansive gardens.

For something removed from Acapulco's bustle, head to the serene Banyan Tree Cabo Marques, a sophisticated newcomer featuring Asian-inspired villas with private pools and dramatic panoramas. Or try the sleepy fishing village of Pie de la Cuesta, where a stroll along the powdery beach will take you back to a time before Acapulco was a glimmer in Hollywood's eye.

Where: 240 miles/386 km south of Mexico City. **Boca Chica:** Tel 52/744-482-2879; in the U.S., 800-337-4685; www.hotel-bocachica.com. *Cost:* from $120. **Las Brisas:** Tel 52/744-469-6900; in the U.S., 866-427-2779; www.brisashotelonline.com. *Cost:* from $225. **Banyan Tree:** Tel 52/744-434-0100; in the U.S., 800-591-0439; www.banyantree.com. *Cost:* from $600. **Best times:** Nov–May for ideal weather; Dec 12 for Virgin of Guadalupe feast day and diving at La Quebrada.

A Best-Kept Secret No Longer

Zihuatanejo

Guerrero, Mexico

It's not easy to pronounce Zihuatanejo, let alone find it on a map, but veteran travelers discovered long ago that the colorful old fishing village is one of Mexico's treasures. Low-key "Zihua," backed by the foothills of the Sierra Madre, lies on a horseshoe-shaped bay ringed by sparkling beaches. No wonder it's a destination some would rather not share.

The palm-fringed Playa la Ropa and Playa las Gatas feature calm, clear waters that are perfect for swimming and snorkeling, along with simple, thatch-roofed seafood restaurants.

A pair of hotels here are counted among Mexico's top beach resorts: The Tides Zihuatanejo, on Playa la Ropa, offers an attention to detail, design, and décor that is more typical of a private home than a hotel; it has long been showered with accolades as an ideal romantic hideaway. Palm-shrouded villas are done up in warm colors, and king-size beds come swathed in sheer mosquito netting. La Casa Que Canta (The House That Sings) perches on a rocky hillside nearby. Made from molded adobe to resemble a traditional pueblo, the mood is both romantic and relaxed, beginning with the infinity pool, whose blues of sky, horizon, and bay blend into one magnificent seascape. Many of the sea-view suites have open-air living rooms, small private pools, and thatch-roofed terraces.

For a sublime end to the day, arrive in time for sunset at the dining terrace overlooking the bay at Kau-Kan, where Parisian-trained chef-owner Ricardo Rodriguez serves up delicious fresh-caught seafood—his signature dish is potato stuffed with lobster and shrimp—under a canopy of starry skies. Rodriguez also oversees the boutique Casa Kau-Kan, a small hotel facing miles of pristine beach outside town.

Where: 357 miles/576 km southwest of Mexico City. **The Tides:** Tel 52/755-555-5500; in the U.S., 866-905-9560; www.tideszihuatanejo.com. *Cost:* from $355 (off-peak), from $500 (peak). **La Casa Que Canta:** Tel 52/755-555-5050; in the U.S., 888-523-5050; www.lacasaquecanta.com. *Cost:* from $490. **Kau-Kan:** Tel 52/755-554-8446; www.casakaukan.com/kaukan. *Cost:* dinner $50. **Casa Kau-Kan:** Tel 52/755-554-6226; www.casakaukan.com. *Cost:* $120. **Best time:** Nov–Apr for nicest weather.

"In Mexico City, there is a god under every stone, and when the stones speak, they are the memory of our people."—Elena Poniatowska

Mexico City

Mexico

More than 1,000 years ago, the Aztecs built their capitol of Tenochtitlán on an island in a vast lake here; it was the largest metropolis in the world when the Spanish arrived in 1519. Mexico City, or often D.F. for *Distrito Federal,* built on top of the ancient city, is again one of the most populous on the planet, where all the disparate strains of Mexican culture come together in a fusion of ancient civilizations and contemporary urbanity. Immense and bustling, sophisticated, and human-scaled, ringed by snow-peaked volcanoes now visible through newly clear air, this much-maligned but gracious Latin American city is fast gaining recognition as one of the world's increasingly stylish capitals of culture.

The Zócalo has been a public gathering site since Aztec times.

Top Attractions

THE ZÓCALO—Mexico City's massive zócalo, also known as Plaza Mayor, is second in size only to Moscow's Red Square. This was the heart of the Aztec empire, razed by the conquistador Hernán Cortés who recycled its grand temples to build the monuments that now stand atop it. These buildings include the largest and most impressive cathedral in Latin America, Catedral Metropolitana, and beside it the Museo Templo Mayor, which occupies the first floor of a sacred Aztec temple that was accidentally discovered in 1978 and is now a brilliant showcase of the capital's preconquest past. The 17th-century Palacio Nacional, Mexico's seat of government, houses Diego Rivera's epic murals that depict the sweep of Mexican history. The best views of the plaza are from the Holiday Inn's rooftop terrace, which occupies the site where Moctezuma's palace once stood. **MUSEO TEMPLO MAYOR:** Tel 52/55-5542-4943; www.templomayor.inah.gob.mx. **HOLIDAY INN:** Tel 52/55-5130-5130; www.holidayinn.com. *Cost:* from $120.

PALACIO DE BELLAS ARTES—Situated on the rim of D.F.'s colonial core, the opulent Palacio de Bellas Artes is both the venue for the Ballet Folklorico and the country's oldest and most important art museum: The murals by Diego Rivera that grace the interior walls are second only to his work in the Palacio Nacional, and the early-20th-century murals by Mexican artists Tamayo, Orozco, and Siqueiros are unequaled. Together with the magnificent 1907 Palacio

Postal across the street, the Palacio faces the 10-acre Alameda, a leafy park that's popular with lovers and families. **Info:** Tel 52/55-5325-9000; www.bellasartes.gob.mx.

The Palacio de Bellas Artes's Art Nouveau exterior reflects what visitors will find inside.

Plaza Garibaldi and Tlatelolco—On weekends, you'll find swaying crowds of singers and vendors offering tequila shots in the Plaza Garibaldi—an open-air mariachi market filled with impeccably suited bands playing their hearts out to land a wedding gig or *quinceañera* ("sweet fifteen" party). Ten blocks away, the ruins of Tlatelolco, an ancient Aztec market center, testify to the natives' last stand against Cortés under 16th-century Aztec ruler Cuauhtémoc, nephew of Moctezuma. The site also has modern significance: In 1968, government troops squelched a spate of student protests by firing on a rally in the plaza, killing hundreds. Many Mexicans trace the opposition to the ruling Institutional Revolutionary Party (PRI) to "Tlatelolco."

Paseo de la Reforma and the Museo Nacional de Antropología—One of the few accomplishments of Austrian-born Maximilian I, short-lived emperor of mid-19th-century Mexico, was to build an answer to Paris's Champs Élysées. Paseo de la Reforma is one of the most elegant boulevards in the Americas. A stroll west from the center of town lets you take in major embassies as well as the Monument of Independence, and the Zona Rosa neighborhood's banyan-canopied streets. The Chapultepec Park, a mammoth plot of forest, has two mandatory stops: The hilltop Castillo de Chapultepec, where the city's last defenders surrendered to U.S. troops in 1847, looms over the park's central lake; and on the other side of the park stands Mexico's largest museum, the Museo Nacional de Antropología. One of the world's finest, it is the repository of the country's pre-Hispanic past, counting pyramids and a 12-foot-wide, 25-ton Aztec sun stone among its thousands of artifacts. The building itself is stunning, an inspiring example of mid-20th-century Modernism, with an open courtyard and a fountain designed by Mexican sculptor Chavez Morado. **Museo Nacional de Antropología:** Tel 52/55-5553-6381; www.mna.inah.gob.mx.

Coyoacán—Cortés once kept his native mistress (the national antiheroine La Malinche) in this Aztec market town turned genteel suburb. This slow-paced colonial enclave, famed for decades as an intellectual hub, is home to Casa Azul, the "Blue House," where painter Frida Kahlo was born in 1907. It is now a museum dedicated to her art and life—including her marriage to master muralist Diego Rivera, whose work and personal items also appear throughout. A few blocks away is the fortresslike Casa León Trotsky, where the Russian revolutionary took refuge from Stalin's purges and was assassinated in 1940. A stroll around Coyoacán's central market and three cheerful public squares is best fueled with a stop at El Jarocho, an outdoor café famous for serving some of the best—and surely the strongest—coffee in the city. **Casa Azul:** Tel 52/55-5444-5999; www.museofridakahlo.org.mx. **Museo Casa de León Trotsky:** Tel 52/55-5554-0687; http://museocasadeleontrotsky.blogspot.com. **El Jarocho:** Tel 52/55-56-58-50-29; www.cafeeljarocho.com.mx.

UNAM—Universidad Nacional Autónoma de México is the oldest university in North

America and, with an enrollment of 270,000, one of the largest in the world. Its sprawling campus offers a rare chance for city residents to bask in wide-open green space, and to admire the enormous murals by David Alfaro Siqueiros and Diego Rivera. Juan O'Gorman's 43,000-square-foot mural wrapping the 12-story Central Library (Biblioteca Central) illustrates 400 years of Mexico's history. **Edificio de la Biblioteca Central:** Tel 52/55-5622-1603; www.unam.mx.

Basilica de Guadelupe—On this spot in 1531, a poor Mexican Indian named Juan Diego reputedly saw the Virgin Mother, who filled his cloak with rose petals and left her image imprinted on it. Today there are two basilicas on the site, which is locally called "La Villa." Construction of the first started immediately and was completed in 1709. The adjacent basilica, built in 1976 to accommodate the masses of pilgrims who come here—more than any Catholic site except the Vatican—holds the original cloak. Hundreds of thousands converge here to honor the country's patron saint on December 12. Juan Diego, canonized in 2002, is the first indigenous saint of the Americas. **Info:** Tel 52/55-5577-6022; www.virgende guadalupe.org.mx.

Xochimilco—In Xochimilco, Aztecs once grew produce on reed islands that floated on a now-buried lake. Only a few canals remain, where families and groups of friends today come for weekend fun among the floating gardens—if you visit, you're sure to see at least one waterborne wedding party seated at the long central table of a brightly painted, flower-bedecked *trajinera* (flatboat). Revelers stop at tiny island liquor stores or the pavilion restaurant located at the heart of the watery maze, or they buy beer, corn, and tacos from vendors who ply the canals in canoes. Mariachi bands will float up and take requests, and after sundown, the festively lit scene turns enchantingly romantic. **Where:** 17 miles/28 km south of city center.

Where to Stay

Camino Real—With nearly 700 rooms on 8 gardened acres, the Camino stands out for both its sheer scale and its luxurious features, including fountain-splashed lobbies under soaring cathedral ceilings and five restaurants. All this, plus a truly unbeatable location—steps from Chapultepec Park and Reforma's string of embassies and international headquarters—gives guests the sense of being at the very nexus of the city. **Info:** Tel 52/55-5263-8888; www .caminoreal.com. *Cost:* from $180.

La Casona—Housed in an imposing two-story mansion built at the end of the 19th century, this diminutive hotel features rooms decorated with floral-print wallpaper, Oriental rugs, and lovely antiques. It delivers gracious hospitality and first-class service without any big-hotel ceremony, plus the opportunity to enjoy the Roma neighborhood's fine, old-world ambience simply by stepping outside the door. **Info:** Tel 52/55-5286-3001; www.hotellacasona.com.mx. *Cost:* from $140.

Condésa DF—Opening in 2004 on lush Parque España, Condésa DF immediately injected style into this trendy neighborhood-on-the-rise. The combination of economical yet sophisticated design and haute cuisine was revolutionary, and this sleek oasis in the middle of the city's urban chaos still feels fresh. The four-story hotel surrounds a bright atrium, where a popular patio restaurant serves terrific breakfasts and weekend brunches. **Info:** Tel 52/55-5241-2600; www.condesadf.com. *Cost:* from $195.

Las Alcobas—This hotel took Condésa DF's approach north to tonier Polanco and laid on state-of-the-art extras. Its staff provides service reminiscent of an old-world grand hotel, while its 35 wired rooms and public areas are showcases of cutting-edge design. Celebrated restaurateur Marta Ortiz runs the intimate Barroco, which offers traditional fine dining, and the outdoor Dulce

Patria, for more casual, cantina-style Mexican fare. As for shopping, step outside the front door and you are on the country's most fashionable street. **Info:** Tel 52/55-3300-3900; www.lasalcobas.com. *Cost:* from $290.

Distrito Capital—French interior designer Joseph Dirand's stylish-yet-cozy retreat of just 30 rooms starts at the 26th floor of a modern highrise and gazes across at the Valley of Mexico's twin volcanoes, Popocatépetl and Iztaccíhuatl. The hotel is located outside traditional boutique territory, in the Santa Fe business and shopping district, part of the city's tony west side. Among the amenities are a restaurant run by local celebrity chef Enrique Olvera (Pujol restaurant; see below). **Info:** Tel 52/55-5257-1300; www.hoteldistritocapital.com. *Cost:* from $150; dinner $45.

El Patio 77—This eight-guest-room, mid-19th-century villa was restored with eco-conscious flair and recycled materials, and the results are truly inviting: handsome dark wood doors, burnished long-plank floors, high ceilings. two peaceful courtyards where breakfast is served. The neighborhood is equidistant from the Centro and Reforma, and, tucked above swank Polanco, has become the latest stalking grounds for the city's chic bohemians. **Info:** Tel 52/55-5592-8452; www.elpatio77.com. *Cost:* from $75.

Eating & Drinking

Bistrot Mosaico—A single glance at this classic French bistro's deli case will lure you inside. From omelets to cutlets to soups, sandwiches, and salads, everything delights and goes well with a glass of wine. It's a perfect place to stop while taking in the Art Deco Hipódromo neighborhood. Lunch is busy and loud, dinner quiet and candlelit, and while the room looks casual, you'll need reservations if you're not willing to wait. **Info:** Tel 52/55-5584-2932; www.bistrotmosaico.com.mx. *Cost:* lunch $20.

El Califa—There are no pretensions at this always-busy institution loved for its Mexican comfort food. Most *chilangos* (local residents) agree it serves the best tacos in town, made fresh until the place closes down in the wee hours. Clean, bright, and efficient, it offers many to choose from, but the tacos *al pastor,* made with bits of marinated pork topped with onion, cilantro, and pineapple, may be the most irresistible. **Info:** Tel 52/55-5271-6285; www.elcalifa.com.mx. *Cost:* $15.

Izote—This small and minimalist restaurant owned by cookbook author and chef Patricia Quintana, reigning queen of Mexican dining, is so good it can afford to be casual. The menu straddles the new-light/old-heavy divide and favors indigenous ingredients given a contemporary spin. You'll find a sampler ceviche (fish, onions, and peppers marinated in lime juice) in three variations, soups and steaks, and a tender lamb that's barbecued in banana leaves. **Info:** Tel 52/55-5280-1671. *Cost:* lunch $30.

Pozolería Tixtla—*Pozole* is the beloved national soup of pork, cheese, chilies, and grits, commonly served on Thursdays in Mexico but available here daily—the only respect in which this awning-fronted neighborhood treasure breaks tradition. Choose straight *blanco* or *verde* (with green mole), add in avocados, *chicharrones* (fried pork rinds), and fresh tortilla strips, and go straight to Mexican heaven. The rest of the menu is a primer in local cuisine: tacos, *chiles japones* (Japanese chiles), *tostadas con pato* (duck), or *cecina* (dried, salted, thinly sliced meat) from the owners' home state of Guerrero. **Info:** Tel 52/55-5564-2859. *Cost:* lunch $16.

Pujol—At this modern and consistently top-ranked restaurant, chef Enrique Olvera creates sophisticated dishes that are small but perfect, marrying European-influenced style with indigenous foods. Try the tamales stuffed with *huitlacoche* (sometimes called corn

A mariachi band performs aboard a trajinera *in the canals of Xochimilco, one of the city's boroughs.*

mushroom or the Aztec truffle), a duck carpaccio with mescal foam, and venison served on a purple banana puree. **INFO:** Tel 52/55-5545-4111; www.pujol.com. *Cost:* dinner $65.

SOBRINOS—This newcomer isn't trendy, but with a deft approach to food, a charmingly retro bistro ambience, and an unbeatable location, it was an immediate favorite. Specializing in simple French fare, it also offers artfully prepared Mexican dishes, such as the *torta de pato* (duck sandwich) in red salsa. Desserts are gemlike, and the selection of wine, tequila, and mescal may be unequaled in the city. Sidewalk seating puts you right in the midst of the vibrant Roma Norte neighborhood. **INFO:** Tel 52/55-5264-7466. *Cost:* dinner $40.

TAQUERÍAS—Tacos, the national food, are available from street vendors on every commercial block in Mexico City—for lunch, for dinner, then late at night—and might include any edible part of a pig, cow, goat, lamb, or chicken. They shatter class distinctions: Members of every social stratum eat them almost daily, on or off the street. Street food here is some of the most reliable in the country (still, visitors feel safer by adding plenty of lime and chili, which are strongly antiseptic *and* enhance flavors). Tacos Speed (at Carlos B. Zetina 118) in Tacubaya, a neighborhood long famous for its taquerías, has the city's best *alambre*—divine layers of shredded beef, onions, and peppers wrapped in flour tortillas. Los Parados, in Roma Sur, is part of a chain that does high late-night volume, but there is nothing cookie-cutter about its output of simple, fresh tacos. The variety of *pico de gallo*—the standard "dry" salsa made with chopped tomato, onions, and hot peppers—is legion, and best ingested with care. La Fonda Argentina, in elegant Independencia between the Centro and Coyoacán, is so good it opened an annex across the street, serving the original establishment's beef tacos as well as other street fare. **LOS PARADOS:** Tel 52/55-5564-6941. **LA FONDA ARGENTINA:** Tel 52/55-5539-1617; www.fondaargentina.com.

PULQUE—This thick variant of mescal, brewed from the maguey cactus, is rarely available outside central Mexico: It can't be refrigerated without breaking down and must be drunk within 24 hours. Taken straight and milky or blended with strawberry, guava, oatmeal, nuts, and a host of other flavors, pulque (POOL-kay) was the poor man's drink until World War II, when it was displaced by beer. Hundreds of tile-walled, men-only *pulquerías* have been reduced to a convivial, mixed-gender few today. Open from mid-morning until the late evening meal, they allow visitors to meet a friendly cross-section of middle- and lower-class Mexico. Indeed, pulque, once a drink the ancient Aztecs gave to sacrificial victims on the way to their deaths, is winning a growing number of young devotees. The last *pulquería* in the Centro is tiny La Risa, (Mesones 71), full of old men and young students sitting elbow to elbow.

You'll find foreigners here too, thanks to its tourist-heavy location. Stronger brew flows at La Hija de los Apaches (Dr. Claudio Bernard 149, Col. Doctores), a cavernous student hangout near Romita, where grandfatherly '50s middleweight boxing champ Epiphano "Pifas" Leyvas reigns over the affectionately rowdy clientele. The first new *pulquería* to open in a decade is Los Insurgentes (Insurgentes Sur 226, Col. Roma Norte), where clay jars full of the sweet, strong concoction are served in a room with old-fashioned décor. The young owners are reinventing a tradition that nearly vanished before they were born.

Day Trips

TEOTIHUACÁN—Centuries before the Aztecs arrived, this massive, ancient city of black rock was Mesoamerica's most powerful social and political center. Built between 100 B.C. and A.D. 250, it was a sophisticated, rigorously planned, 8-square-mile city of more than 200,000. Abandoned around A.D. 750, it lay forgotten until the Aztecs arrived in 1200, naming it "place where gods are born" and using it as a pilgrimage center. You can climb the landmark Pyramid of the Sun, second largest in the world, or the similar but slightly smaller Pyramid of the Moon, which dominates the city's broad Avenue of the Dead. Spend the morning contemplating one of the most excavated and researched archaeological sites in the world, then escape the heat for a few hours in the site's excellent museum. **WHERE:** 30 miles/48 km north of the Mexico City center.

TEPOZTLÁN—Tepoztlán is a beautiful town of terra-cotta buildings tucked into the base of rugged cliffs that tower over a valley reputed to have mystical powers. This is the mythical birthplace of Quetzalcóatl, the feathered serpent god of Aztec, Toltec, and Maya lore. Hikers who trek to the Aztec pyramid dedicated to him at the top of nearby Tepozteco mountain are rewarded with spectacular views. Still a sleepy village, unspoiled Tepoztlán attracts devotees of yoga, astrology, meditation, and other New Age pursuits. One of Mexico's Magic Pueblos, it has become a favorite place for Mexico City residents to unwind and de-stress, so cafés and shops are in good supply. The Tepoznieve ice-cream parlor is famous for flavors that range from classic vanilla to tequila, carrot, and chile. The town center becomes an open-air market on weekends, while the *pastorelas,* or nativity plays, attract crowds the week before Christmas. **WHERE:** 57 miles/92 km south of Mexico City center; 10 miles/16 km north of Cuernavaca.

CUERNAVACA—Cortés was the first in a long line of V.I.P. Mexico City residents to keep a vacation home in the "City of Eternal Spring," where temperatures hover around 72°F year-round. The conqueror's fortresslike retreat is now the Museo Regional Cuauhnáhuac (the city's Aztec name), displaying an excellent array of colonial and pre-Hispanic artifacts, a Diego Rivera mural, and remnants of the ancient pyramid Cortés razed. Malcolm Lowry's 1947 classic *Under the Volcano* was set here, but fans won't recognize much beyond leafy Plaza de Armas, picturesque in its wrought-iron finery and lively with local families, vendors, and visitors. Stop by the Museo Robert Brady, which exhibits native art, colonial antiques, and paintings by prominent Mexican artists. Las Mañanitas, often lauded as one of Mexico's finest hotels, is a 15-minute walk from the zócalo. The hacienda-style retreat has hosted presidents and princes since 1950; its 20 suites are set in a paradise of tropical plants, peacocks, and macaws, with an inviting pool and alfresco restaurant. **WHERE:** 50 miles/81 km south of Mexico City center. **BRADY MUSEUM:** Tel 52/77-7318-8554; www.bradymuseum.org. **LAS MAÑANITAS HOTEL:** Tel 52/77-7314-1466; www.lasmananitas.com.mx. *Cost:* from $200 (off-peak), from $450 (peak).

Home to Native Arts and Monarch Butterflies

Morelia and Pátzcuaro

Michoacán, Mexico

Michoacán, one of Mexico's most culture-rich states, is the land of the Tarascans, a native people known for their melodic Purépecha language and for their brilliantly colored handicrafts and folk art. Much of the latter is showcased at the Casa de Artesanías de Michoacán, a museum and store, housed in a former convent in the stately capital of Morelia. Here you'll also find rose-colored stone Colonial buildings and a glorious twin-towered cathedral dating to 1640—the second largest in the Americas.

On Morelia's main square, Hotel Los Juaninos, a palatial, 17th-century bishop's residence, epitomizes the city's old-world charm. Rooms are clustered around a courtyard and feature wood-beam ceilings and elaborately carved doors. The rooftop bar-restaurant enjoys wonderful views of the cathedral, which is dramatically lit at night. In the leafy hills south of the city, guests at the antiques-filled Villa Montaña enjoy an enchanting maze of gardens and cobbled walkways with sweeping city views.

Time a trip mid-November through March to witness some of the tens of millions of orange-and-black monarch butterflies that make the 2,000-mile migration from the eastern United States and Canada to Mexico's central highlands. At El Rosario Butterfly Sanctuary, 2 hours from Morelia, butterflies are so numerous you can hear their wings beating. The weight of so many tiny bodies clustered in dense layers sometimes breaks limbs from the trees; when they fly, the sky appears flecked with golden confetti.

Michoacán's second city is the picturesque colonial town of Pátzcuaro, near a lake of the same name and about 30 miles from Morelia. Friday is market day when native women in bright traditional dress stream in from the neighboring villages that specialize in various crafts: hand-hammered copperware from Santa Clara del Cobre, guitars from Paracho, exquisite lacquerware from Uruapán. Pátzcuaro itself is famous for high-quality serapes and other hand-woven textiles.

No visit is complete without a boat ride to Isla Janitzio, in the middle of the long lake. It is especially fascinating during Día de los Muertos (Day of the Dead), November 1 and 2, when Mexicans celebrate life while remembering those who have died. The festivities here are some of the most famous and well-attended in the country.

Pátzcuaro's La Mansión de los Sueños, a renovated 17th-century home with thick adobe walls, wood-beam ceilings, and courtyards with original fountains, transports you to colonial times. Twelve singularly decorated suites are filled with painted murals, antiques, and fireplaces, a cozy touch on cool evenings.

Where: Morelia is 190 miles/306 km west of Mexico City. **Hotel Los Juaninos:** Tel 52/443-312-0036; www.hoteljuaninos.com.mx. *Cost:* from $150. **Villa Montaña:** Tel 52/443-314-0231; www.villamontana.com.mx. *Cost:* from $210. **How:** Mex Mich Guides offers full-day guided tours of El Rosario Monarch Butterfly Sanctuary, departing from Morelia. Tel 52/443-340-4632; www.mmg.com.mx. *Cost:* $40. *When:* mid-Nov–Mar. **Mansión de los Sueños:** Tel 52/434-342-5708; www.mansiondelossuenos.com. *Cost:* from $165. **Best times:** mid-Nov–Mar for butterflies; Nov 1–2 for Day of the Dead celebrations.

A Cultural and Gastronomic Field Day

OAXACA

Oaxaca, Mexico

A remarkable blend of Old World and deep-rooted Zapotec and Mixtec traditions are gloriously at play in the cobblestoned historic center of Oaxaca. You can spend days visiting the city's 27 ornate churches—which include the Baroque Templo de Santo Domingo de Guzmán and its gold-ornamented Rosario Chapel—as well as its overflowing markets. Wander the side streets around the *zócalo* and browse the art galleries and crafts shops, such as the Mercado de Artesanías, which brims with embroidered clothing from the region. The Museo Regional de Oaxaca, housed in a convent from the 1600s, is one of Mexico's finest museums, tracing the development of the Oaxaca area from the Olmec period in 1200 B.C.

Fresh vegetables are a market staple.

Oaxaca is surrounded by villages that specialize in crafts: black pottery (San Bartolo), woolen textiles (Teotitlán del Valle), and brightly painted wood carvings (Arrazola). The city is also a culinary mecca, known for its empanadas, hot chocolate, and seven varieties of the delectable mole sauce. Sample the finest mezcal, the region's famed smoky distilled spirit, at the atmospheric Mezcalería los Amantes. For adventurous palates, spicy, fried *chapulines*—grasshoppers—are another local specialty. Food appreciation classes, such as those offered through Casa de los Sabores, have become almost de rigueur for visiting food lovers.

One of Mexico's most important archaeological sites lies just outside Oaxaca. Ancient Monte Albán was the center of Zapotec culture, which flourished from A.D. 300 to 800. From its Great Plaza, you can see the remains of ball courts, plazas, and more than 170 tombs, including Tomb 7, where approximately 500 pieces of gold and precious gems were found (the most prized artifacts are in the Museo Regional).

The 16th-century Convent of Santa Caterina de Siena is now the Camino Real, Oaxaca's most elegant hotel. Guests enjoy ancient frescoes, jasmine-scented patios, and Los Lavaderos—a water fountain surrounded by 12 stone laundry basins. Another top choice: chic and minimalist Casa Oaxaca, a seven-room inn with local art adorning its white walls. The owner, chef Alejandro Ruiz, ingeniously updates Oaxacan cuisine, served in a candlelit courtyard at the inn and as well as at a restaurant with a romantic rooftop terrace two blocks away.

WHERE: 340 miles/547 km south of Mexico City. **MUSEO REGIONAL:** Tel 52/951-516-2991. **CASA DE LOS SABORES:** Tel 52/951-516-5704; in the U.S., 201-255-6105; www.casadelossabores.com. *Cost:* $65 for 1-day cooking class. **CAMINO REAL:** Tel 52/951-516-0611; in the U.S., 800-722-6466; www.camino-real-oaxaca.com. *Cost:* from $240. **CASA OAXACA:** Tel 52/951-514-4173; www.casaoaxaca.com.mx. *Cost:* from $170. **CASA OAXACA EL RESTAURANTE:** Tel 52/951-516-8531; www.casaoaxacaelrestaurante.com. *Cost:* dinner $40. **BEST TIMES:** Easter week; late Jul for Guelaguetza Dance Festival; Nov 1–2 for Day of the Dead; Dec 23 for Night of the Radishes.

The Maya's Only Seaside City

Tulum and the Riviera Maya

Quintana Roo, Mexico

At the southern end of Mexico's Riviera Maya, the string of fishing-villages-turned-sophisticated-resort-towns that dot the Caribbean coastline south of Cancún, stands the only ancient Maya city on the coast. What Tulum lacks in archaeological significance it compensates for in beauty, evident in its spectacular fine-white-sand beaches and its temple dramatically poised on a coastal bluff. The walled complex of ruins dates from A.D. 1000, the most impressive of which, besides the temple, is El Castillo (the castle), the shrine and watchtower whose carvings of serpents recall of those at Chichén Itzá (see p. 960).

Like the rest of the Yucatán Peninsula, the region is laced with thousands of cenotes. The underground freshwater sinkholes and rivers, such as those at Gran Cenote and Hidden Worlds, are unearthly, located in giant limestone rooms where sunlight streaming through breaches in the ceiling (or artificial light from within) illuminate stalagmites, stalactites, and cool, clear water. Taking a plunge is the perfect antidote to a hot afternoon.

Other cenotes can be found along 62 miles of undeveloped coastline just south of Tulum. This is the Sian Ka'an Biosphere Reserve, 1.3 million acres of protected tropical forests, mangroves, coral reefs, and an array of wildlife that includes 100 species of mammals—notably, jaguars, pumas, and spider and howler monkeys—and over 300 bird species.

Once the province of wandering backpackers, Tulum now hosts an influx of well-heeled but still environmentally minded travelers. The boom in "eco-chic" hotels can be traced to secluded Ana y José, run by the Soto family. The 23 suites and cottages have simple, contemporary décor, including bright artwork splashed against whitewashed walls. Yesteryear's budget offerings live on at the simple Posada Dos Ceibas, where yellow, blue, and pink cottages with solar-generated electricity and ceiling fans are set amid dense jungle.

Of the coastline's ultraluxurious accommodations, Maroma knows few rivals. Set in a 600-acre ecological preserve on a crescent-shaped beach and backed by mangroves and coconut palms, it has thatch-roofed terraces and sea views that stop the most world-weary travelers in their tracks.

Tulum is most known for its unique coastal location.

Where: Tulum is 80 miles/130 km south of Cancún. **Ana y José:** Tel 52/998-880-6022; www.anayjose.com. *Cost:* from $248. **Posada Dos Ceibas:** Tel 52/984-877-6024; www.dosceibas.com. *Cost:* from $65. **Maroma:** Tel 52/987-28200; in the U.S., 866-454-9351 or 843-937-9066; www.maromahotel.com. *Cost:* from $450 (off-peak), from $765 (peak). **Best time:** Dec–Apr for best weather and bird-watching at Sian Ka'an.

Into the Yucatán's Maya Heartland

Chichén Itzá and Mérida

Yucatán, Mexico

The magnificent metropolis of Chichén Itzá, the most spectacular, and consequently most visited, of Mexico's ancient sites, was the principal ceremonial center of the Yucatán, the heartland of the Maya. The complex of grand pyramids, temples, and ornate palaces was inhabited for about 800 years, beginning in roughly A.D. 432 during the Classic Period, when the Maya empire reached into present-day Belize and Guatemala.

If you are lucky enough to be here on the spring or autumnal equinox, you will marvel at the mastermind who positioned the temple of El Castillo de Kukulcán: The late-afternoon light and shadow creates a moving serpent representing the leader Kukulkán that, over the course of 34 minutes, slithers down the steps to the base of the pyramid's principal façade before disappearing. Although it's an easy day trip from Mérida, you can have the place to yourself by staying overnight in the thatch-roofed bungalows at the Lodge at Chichén Itzá, set on 100 private acres at the edge of the ruins that are shared with its more touristy sister hotel, Mayaland.

Mérida, the bustling capital of the Yucatán, is full of history, culture, and music. Free concerts and cultural events take place every night in the leafy main plaza and around the rest of the town. You might catch the traditional and achingly romantic *trova* music or 1940s Cuban big-band music.

This four-sided pyramid is named for Kukulcán, the ancient leader-turned-diety, represented by a snake.

A few steps from the plaza stands San Ildefonso, North America's oldest cathedral. Construction started in 1561 and incorporated ancient stones from the ruins of Tiho, the Maya city that was razed by the Spaniards to build their own. Of the beautifully restored haciendas just outside town built during Mérida's heyday as the source of the world's sisal, many have been converted into guest houses. Xcanatún (sh-kana-TOON) is the most elegant, with 18 rooms done up in exquisite colonial-Caribbean décor. The hacienda's Casa de Piedra restaurant is a local favorite for its sumptuous Caribbean-Yucatecan-French fusion meals.

Don't leave Mérida before visiting Uxmal, (oosh-MAHL), one of the best-preserved Maya ceremonial centers. The vast complex of ruins, 50 miles south of the city, dates from the period between the 7th and 10th centuries. Its highlights are the Pirámide de Adivino (Pyramid of the Magician) with its steep, 115-foot sides and crowning temple, and the Palace of the Governor, renowned for its sculptures of serpents and Chac, the god of rain.

Where: Chichén Itzá is 74 miles/120 km east of Mérida. **Lodge at Chichén Itzá:** Tel 52/998-887-2495; in the U.S., 800-235-4079; www.mayaland.com. *Cost:* from $250. **Xcanatún:** Tel 52/999-930-2140; in the U.S., 888-883-3633; www.xcanatun.com. *Cost:* from $230; dinner $35. **Best times:** Nov–Feb for nice weather; Mar or Sep equinox at Chichén Itzá for Kukulkán phenomenon.

Superb Diving Among a Necklace of Cays

BELIZE'S BARRIER REEF

Ambergris Caye, Belize

Belize is part of the longest barrier reef system in the Western Hemisphere. The coral mountains and canyons of the Great Mesoamerican Reef stretch unbroken for 750 miles, from Isla Contoy, on the tip of Mexico's Yucatán Peninsula, to the Bay Islands of Honduras (see p. 972). Only Australia's Great Barrier Reef (see p. 653) is longer. Connoisseurs consider the 185-mile Belize Barrier Reef, with more than 450 offshore islets and cays and 500 species of fish, one of the world's ultimate dive sites.

Endangered hawksbill turtles swim freely in the protected areas of the barrier reef.

Almost 25 miles long and only 1 mile wide, Ambergris Caye is by far the largest and most popular of the cays. Its laid-back town of San Pedro is the reef's most important starting point for more than 40 snorkeling and dive sites. Stylish Victoria House, a 42-room plantation-style inn, has a sandy beachside location, infinity pool, and quarters that range from modest rooms to luxury villas. Don't miss Elvi's Kitchen, a former hole-in-the-wall that still serves its famous burgers for lunch but now also draws crowds with fine dinner fare, such as roasted garlic chipotle lobster.

Off the southern tip of Ambergris, the Hol Chan Marine Reserve offers one of the best diving and snorkeling sites for its sheer variety of marine life—here you'll find 40 kinds of grouper, a forest of coral, and sponge as dense and varied as the mainland's jungle mantle. Nearby, the sandy-bottomed, 8-foot-deep Shark Ray Alley is home to a thriving population of gentle nurse sharks and stingrays that you can visit up close. Take a day trip to smaller, less developed Caye Caulker and dine on banana leaf–steamed snapper with papaya sauce at Habanero's or nurse a rum punch all day at the Lazy Lizard, a scruffy, open-air bar and grill by the Split, a channel formed in the 1960s by Hurricane Hattie.

Head to Belize's three (of the Caribbean's four) ring-shaped coral atolls. Lighthouse Reef is the most accessible, owing to a small airstrip, and is nearest to two of the reef's most stellar dives: the fabled Blue Hole (called "one of the four must-dive locations on this blue planet" by Jacques Cousteau in 1970) and Half Moon Caye National Park.

Turneffe Island Atoll is famous for its wall dives, and the Elbow is the ultimate, with hawksbill turtles, hammerhead sharks, and the largest sea fans imaginable. It's also a good place for snorkeling in shallow lagoons, and the saltwater fly-fishing is world-class. With palm-shaded cottages on its own private island, Turneffe Island Resort—35 miles offshore and reachable by air—is the ideal base.

VISITOR INFO: www.travelbelize.org. **VICTORIA HOUSE:** Tel 501/226-2067; in the U.S., 800-247-5159; www.victoria-house.com. *Cost:* from $185. **ELVI'S KITCHEN:** Tel 501/226-2176; www.elviskitchen.com. *Cost:* dinner $30. **HABANERO'S:** Tel 501/226-0486. *Cost:* lunch $20. **TURNEFFE ISLAND RESORT:** Tel 501/220-4142; in the U.S., 713-236-7739; www.turneffe resort.com. *Cost:* from $900 per person for 3 nights, inclusive (diving extra). **BEST TIMES:** Dec–Mar for nicest weather; Feb–Jul for fishing; mid-Jun for Lobsterfest in San Pedro.

A Sojourn into the Lost World of the Maya

CAYO DISTRICT

Belize

The tropical broadleaf forest of western Belize's mountainous Cayo District was the heart of the ancient Maya world. Of the 600 ruins buried in the jungle near the Guatemalan border—reachable by horseback or jeep—none compare to Caracol. Though not as well excavated as Tikal in Guatemala (see p. 970), it was one of the great Maya city-states, occupied from the 1st to the 11th centuries and known for its 140-foot-high "sky palace." In its heyday there were thousands of buildings across a 30-square-mile area that supported a population of more than 150,000. Set off with a guide to explore Caracol and other nearby treasures, such as underground river cave systems and natural pools and waterfalls that are perfect for a swim. Or spend the day zip-lining, trekking, kayaking, exploring butterfly gardens, or spotting the birdlife for which the country is famous.

The riverside Lodge at Chaa Creek features thatch-roofed cottages, an excellent hilltop spa, horses for jungle treks, and a large, airy restaurant. It is set on a private 365-acre riverside nature preserve, where guests can enjoy a butterfly farm, visit a Maya medicine center, and hike miles of trails. Guides point out exotic jungle residents, such as quarrelsome howler monkeys and some of the 300 species of tropical and migratory birds.

A few miles away at the more rustic Mountain Equestrian Trails (MET), horseback riding is the specialty. A guide will lead you along 60 miles of narrow, winding trails into the Mountain Pine Ridge Forest Reserve, pointing out wildlife and recounting jungle lore. Back at the lodge, repair to a kerosene-lamp-lit cabana, and in the morning feast on banana pancakes.

Set by a scenic creek and a series of gentle falls, the nearby Blancaneaux Lodge, owned by filmmaker Francis Ford Coppola, is the most stylish in the district, with 20 detail-rich accommodations ranging from modest cabanas to a sprawling villa. Amenities include a riverside spa and a restaurant with the jungle chorus in the background.

Worth the detour north of Cayo to Orange Walk, the jungle-enveloped Chan Chich Lodge lets you feel as if you've stepped into the ancient world. Built on a Maya plaza dating to the Classic Period (A.D. 300–900), Chan Chich's elegant thatch-roofed bungalows are surrounded by 130,000 acres of vine-tangled wilderness teeming with more jaguars, jaguarundi, pumas, ocelots, and margays than you'll find in any other part of Belize. Nine miles of trails wend around temples concealed under grass-covered mounds, and local guides are as well versed in the region's flora and fauna as they are in the history of its ancient peoples.

LODGE AT CHAA CREEK: 70 miles/113 km southwest of Belize City. Tel 501/824-2037; in the U.S., 877-709-8708; www.chaacreek.com. *Cost:* from $300. **Mountain Equestrian Trails:** Tel 501/669-1124; in the U.S., 800-838-3918; www.metbelize.com. *Cost:* from $75. **Blancaneaux Lodge:** Tel 501/824-4912; in the U.S., 800-746-3743; www.coppolaresorts.com/blancaneaux. *Cost:* from $230 (off-peak), from $330 (peak). **Chan Chich Lodge:** Tel 501/223-4419; in the U.S., 800-343-8009; www.chanchich.com. *Cost:* from $205 (off-peak), from $250 (peak). **Best times:** Nov–Jun for dry season; Jan–Apr for coolest months.

Whale Sharks, Jaguars, and Other Natural Wonders

Placencia

Belize

With long, sleepy stretches of white sand shoreline and turquoise water, the 11-mile-long skinny peninsula of Placencia parallels the coast of southern Belize near the Guatemala border. These are the country's best beaches, without the bustle of Ambergris Caye (see p. 961) to the north, but with equally fine diving and snorkeling. Head 27 miles out to sea to Glover's Reef Marine Reserve, on the southernmost of Belize's three atolls; inside its 20-by-8-mile lagoon, splendid coral gardens invite endless snorkeling.

Huge whale sharks, which can measure up to 50 feet in length, are one of the most prized sightings in the Gladden Spit Marine Reserve, 45 minutes out by boat. There's nothing to fear about diving or snorkeling with these gentle giants, which converge here in late spring.

At the peninsula's southernmost tip, Placencia Village provides easy access to dive outfitters and tours of wildlife habitats. Spot manatees in the mangroves of Placencia Lagoon, or ride a boat up Monkey River, a bird-watchers' paradise that's also a good place to glimpse crocodiles and howler monkeys. Make an inland excursion to Cockscomb Basin Wildlife Sanctuary, home to one of the world's densest concentrations of jaguars.

Set on 22 acres near Placencia Village, the Inn at Robert's Grove has 52 rooms and suites, a reputable dive shop, and a fun beachside bar that is always abuzz. Or ask to be dropped off at either of its two private islands, complete with cook, so you don't have to lift a finger while playing castaway.

Turtle Inn is nearby, one of Francis Ford Coppola's three Central American eco-resorts (see previous page and p. 970). Inspired by a Balinese village, its thatched cottages and villas have private gardens, outdoor showers, and large screened porches. Guests can amble over to De Tatch, known for its friendly staff, beautiful beachfront location, and mouthwatering seafood that pairs perfectly with a few cold Belikins, the local beer.

Where: Placencia Village is 144 miles/184 km south of Belize City. **How:** Seahorse Diving leads a variety of dives and snorkel trips. Tel 501/523-3166; www.belizescuba.com. *Cost:* $80 for snorkeling at Glover's Reef; $160 for whale shark dives. **Inn at Robert's Grove:** Tel 800-565-9757 or 501/523-3565; www.robertsgrove.com. *Cost:* from $175; private island rates from $930, all-inclusive. **Turtle Inn:** Tel 501/824-4912; in the U.S., 800-746-3743; www.coppolaresorts.com/turtleinn. *Cost:* from $285 (off-peak), from $375 (peak). **De Tatch:** Tel 501/503-3385; www.seasprayhotel.com. *Cost:* dinner $25. **Best times:** Nov–Jun for dry season; late Mar–Jun for whale sharks.

Costa Rica's Fiery Streak

Arenal Volcano

La Fortuna, San Carlos, Alajuela, Costa Rica

Costa Rica, famous for its rain forests and beaches, also has a serious hot streak: It is part of the Pacific Ring of Fire, an arc of intense seismic and volcanic activity that stretches from the coast of the Americas to just off the coast of Asia. In fact, Costa Rica is home to one of the world's most active volcanoes. The magnificent Arenal, a 5,366-foot behemoth that erupted suddenly and violently in 1968, is the youngest of the country's nine active volcanoes. It is so dangerous it must be viewed from a distance—in contrast to neighboring Poás Volcano, where you can drive to the top and peer in during an easy day trip from the capital city, San José. By day you can see smoke and hear rumbles, but Arenal is most dramatic at night, when red-hot rocks shoot hundreds of feet into the sky and incandescent lava cascades down its north side.

Arenal is responsible for the area's many hot springs.

Tabacón Grand Spa Thermal Resort is located near a river heated by the volcano. Set within dense vegetation are mineral pools, falls, and lagoons of varying temperatures: The farther upstream you go, the hotter the water gets. At the Grand Spa's outdoor treatment rooms, you can be massaged and slathered in detoxifying volcanic mud to the blissful sounds of wildlife, rushing water, and occasional volcanic rumblings.

The best place from which to view Arenal's dramatic activity is Arenal Observatory Lodge, a mile from the volcano's restless northern side. A former research station, the rustic lodge is less glamorous than Tabacón but offers more drama, especially if you book one of the volcano-facing rooms, which have enormous picture windows and terraces.

Farther east and within easy driving range of Arenal, Chachagua Rainforest Hotel & Hacienda consists of simple but spacious bungalows nestled by a clear mountain stream in the Monteverde range, one of the most biologically diverse areas in this verdant country. Half of Chachagua's 247-acre spread abuts forest reserves, and the potential for bird and wildlife viewing here is tremendous; a resident naturalist is on hand to serve as your guide. The other half is a working cattle ranch with horses available to guests. The area also provides abundant opportunity for spelunking, whitewater rafting, and rappelling.

Where: 87 miles/140 km northwest of San José. **Tabacón:** Tel 506/2519-1999; in the U.S., 877-277-8291; www.tabacon.com. *Cost:* from $225 (off-peak), from $330 (peak); day passes from $85. **Arenal Observatory Lodge:** Tel 506/2290-7011; www.arenalobservatorylodge.com. *Cost:* from $120. **Chachagua Hotel:** Tel 506/2468-1010; www.chachaguarainforesthotel.com. *Cost:* from $120. **Best time:** Nov–Mar for dry season.

Where Turtles Come to Nest

Tortuguero National Park

Limón, Costa Rica

A lowland wilderness on Costa Rica's northern coast, Tortuguero National Park lies between the Caribbean and a dense maze of jungle canals. Its 22 miles of protected black sand beaches are one of the world's greatest sea turtle nesting sites. (*Tortuga* means "turtle.") Loggerhead sightings are the rarest, and giant leatherbacks the most magnificent. Growing as long as 6 feet and weighing 1,000 pounds, the latter nest from October to March. Though endangered, green and hawksbill turtles are the most common—they can be seen from July through October. Hundreds clamber ashore at the same time, dig a nest and lay their eggs, and disappear back into the sea. The hatchlings crawl out 7 to 10 weeks later and make a scramble to the sea. Very few will make it past the birds, crabs, sharks, and human pollution to reach adulthood. And yet that some of them do—and return to lay the next generation—is the magic of Tortuguero.

Reachable only by small plane or boat, the 47,000-acre Tortuguero National Park has charms that go beyond turtles. You can tour its warren of canals and inland waterways, home to manatees, river otters, spider monkeys, three-toed sloths, and 300 species of birds. Indeed, this park features a biodiversity that is often dubbed the "Amazon in miniature."

Though the area is remote, comfortable lodging is available, most notably Tortuga Lodge & Gardens, which lures guests with its great food, a beautiful pool, and rich wildlife in the 50 acres that surround the lodge. The newest accommodation is the Manatus Hotel, with stylish, air-conditioned rooms and amenities you won't find anywhere nearby, including an excellent restaurant and a lovely little spa.

Where: 140 miles/225 km northwest of San José. **How:** Il Viaggio Travel in San José arranges customized trips. Tel 506/2289-8225; in the U.S., 360-283-5266; www.ilviaggiocr.com. **Tortuga Lodge:** Tel 506/2257-0766; www.costaricaexpeditions.com. *Cost:* from $250, inclusive. **Manatus Hotel:** Tel 506/2709-8197; www.manatuscostarica.com. *Cost:* 2-day package from $685, all-inclusive with transfer from San José. **Best time:** Jul–Oct for opportunites to view turtle nesting and hatching.

Into the Coastal Wild

Corcovado National Park

Osa Peninsula, Puntarenas, Costa Rica

Costa Rica boasts one of the world's best systems of reserves and national parks; its 35 wildlife refuges protect more than 25 percent of the country's territory, so deciding where to head first is a visitor's toughest choice.

The largest, wildest, and most pristine is Corcovado National Park, the last great tract of tropical rain forest on the Pacific coast. Covering one third of the remote Osa Peninsula, in the country's southwest corner, Corcovado has no roads to link its 103,000 acres of virgin rain forest, uninhabited beaches, jungle-rimmed rivers, and large swamplands. Within its boundaries live more than 140 species of mammals, with Baird's tapirs and jaguars the rarest and most sought-after by wildlife spotters. Corcovado also has the largest population of scarlet macaws in Central America, which—together with the 375 other species of birds that live here in more than 850 kinds of trees—vie with four species of monkeys to be heard above the jungle cacophony.

The Bosque del Cabo is a 750-acre rain forest lodge that puts you in the midst of the primal magic. It's a 45-minute drive into the park, but why bother? Stay in any of the comfortable thatched bungalows and watch for scarlet macaws and howler monkeys overhead or an off-shore whale from your porch's hammock.

One of the first to discover this area's treasure trove of wildlife diversity was Lapa Ríos, a pioneering luxury eco-lodge that has won praise from conservationists, hotel critics, and guests alike. Perched 350 feet above the Pacific in its own lush 930-acre nature reserve, it overlooks three panoramic ridges. Sixteen thatched bungalows feature lacquered bamboo walls and polished tropical wood floors; the lodge also boasts a bar-restaurant, infinity pool, and spa, along with open-air observation platforms from which wondrous expanses of ocean and forest are visible. Days revolve around nature, beginning with a sunrise hike and ending with shaman-guided tours that reveal the area's natural medicinal plants. Excellent meals in the middle of the wilderness are as much a revelation as the nocturnal jungle walk that follows.

Where: 231 miles/368 km southwest of San José, on the Osa Peninsula. **Bosque del Cabo:** Tel 506/2735-5206; www.bosquedelcabo.com. *Cost:* from $175 per person, all-inclusive (off-peak), from $210 (peak). **Lapa Ríos:** Tel 506/2735-5130; www.laparios.com. *Cost:* $270 per person, all-inclusive (off-peak), $360 (peak). **Best times:** Nov–Apr is dry season, though many also like the "green" or rainy season of May–Oct.

White Sand Beaches and Rain Forest–Clad Mountains

Manuel Antonio National Park

Puntarenas, Costa Rica

Of Costa Rica's constellation of national parks, Manuel Antonio is a pocket-size gem. Though just 1,680 acres, it is one of the country's most heavily visited parks, with idyllic, easily accessible white sand beaches that offer snorkeling and diving in rich coral reefs, surfing, and fishing, all in addition to access to rain forest–clad mountains. The park is one of the last remaining habitats for the red-backed squirrel monkey and home to 200 species of birds and 100 kinds of mammals, including sloths and bold, white-faced capuchin monkeys that love to pester beachgoers.

La Mariposa, one of the first hotels in the area, nabbed the best location—a dramatic aerie above the sea. Many of the rooms and the split-level Mediterranean-style villas have magnificent mountains-to-sea panoramas, which can also be enjoyed by nonguests who come for drinks or an alfresco meal at sunset.

The area's most stylish hotel is Arenas Del Mar, newly built on a forested hillside sloping down to the ocean. The brainchild of Teri and Glenn Jampol, two of the leaders of Costa Rica's sustainable tourism movement, the 38-room hotel offers spectacular beach and nature activities and the highest levels of comfort and sustainability—along with a small but perfect spa. Contemporary Costa Rican cuisine served at the open-air El Mirador restaurant might include spiced pumpkin soup, fresh snapper with green plantain and tomato sauce, and a rich coconut–macadamia nut tart. The Jampols' first property is the Finca Rosa Blanca Coffee Plantation & Inn, a half-hour drive north of the capital city of San José. The eccentric 13-room inn is surrounded by 30 acres of certified organic, shade-grown coffee; guests can tour the plantation and join in a *catación*—coffee-tasting—to learn more about the taste and quality of Costa Rican beans.

WHERE: 116 miles/180 km south of San José. **HOTEL LA MARIPOSA:** Tel 506/2777-0355; in the U.S., 800-549-0157; www.hotelmariposa.com. *Cost:* from $155 (off-peak), from $215 (peak). **ARENAS DEL MAR:** Tel 506/2777-2777; www.arenasdelmar.com. *Cost:* from $260 (off-peak), from $330 (peak). **FINCA ROSA BLANCA:** Tel 506/2269-9392; in the U.S., 305-395-3042; www.fincarosablanca.com. *Cost:* from $250 (off-peak), from $295 (peak). **BEST TIMES:** Dec–Mar and Jun–Aug are dry months.

Quakers and Quetzals in the Cloud Forests

MONTEVERDE

Puntarenas, Costa Rica

Named for its lush mountains, known as the Tilarán, Monteverde is one of Costa Rica's most visually arresting natural attractions, a cool, highland forest 4,600 feet above sea level that is perennially cloaked in clouds and rich in biodiversity. This extraordinary tangle of greenery is home to 450 varieties of orchids, 500 types of butterflies, and 400 bird species, including 30 species of hummingbirds and the rare, gorgeously plumed quetzal that keen-eyed guides can often spot.

Instead of government-owned national parks, private forests and wildlife reserves make up Monteverde, encompassing almost 70,000 acres of protected land. The largest (at 26,000 acres) and most famous, Monteverde Cloud Forest Reserve was established by Quakers who emigrated from Alabama in 1951 as conscientious objectors to the Korean War.

To mix thrills with exotic scenery, explore Monteverde on a zip-line canopy tour, a high-adrenaline attraction invented here in the 1970s that has since spread throughout the world. The daring are strapped into a harness attached to an overhead cable that lets them whiz along above the treetops and through clearings; the less adventurous can amble along elevated

The concept of the high-flying zip-line is said to have originated here.

walkways. The only operator located within the Monteverde Cloud Forest Reserve is Selvatura Park. Its 2-mile treetop walk takes you across eight bridges of varying heights and lengths (up to 510 feet), while its zip-line canopy tour sends you flying (alone or with a guide) along 15 cables and 18 platforms.

Hotel Fonda Vela is a tidy Swiss chalet–style property with 40 comfortable rooms a walkable mile from the Monteverde Cloud Forest Reserve. For those who simply want to hike along quiet trails, the 27-room Monteverde Lodge near the less-visited 765-acre Santa Elena Reserve, is a longtime favorite owned by ecotourism leader Costa Rica Expeditions.

A casual but surprisingly refined restaurant in the area is the small, American-owned Sofia's. After a successful day of quetzal sighting in the cloud forest, toast your good fortune with a ginger mango mojito, then dine on seafood chimichangas or beef tenderloin with chipotle butter sauce. The banana bread pudding is so rich you'll need to share.

WHERE: 104 miles/167 km northwest of San José. **HOTEL FONDA VELA:** Tel 506/2645-5125; www.fondavela.com. *Cost:* from $110. **MONTEVERDE LODGE:** contact Costa Rica Expeditions in San José, tel 506/2521-6099; www.costaricaexpeditions.com. *Cost:* from $158. **SOFIA'S:** Tel 506/2645-7017. *Cost:* dinner $25. **BEST TIME:** Dec–Apr is dry season and offers the best birding.

Colonial Monuments, Poetic Ruins

ANTIGUA

Guatemala

Gorgeously set in a green mountain- and volcano-rimmed valley, Antigua is one of the Western Hemisphere's best-preserved Spanish colonial cities. Founded in 1543, it was Spain's prosperous capital of the middle Americas until the earthquake of 1773. The crown ordered everyone out and moved the seat of government to Guatemala City, but the poorer families remained and Antigua never died.

Today's strict preservation ordinances protect what remains of its Spanish Renaissance and Baroque churches, monasteries, and homes, built between the 16th and 18th centuries. Some have been reconstructed, others remain evocative ruins, but they are all part of the lure for the wealthy weekend homeowners from nearby Guatemala City and the artistically inclined expats who flock here. The town center revolves around Plaza Mayor and Convento de las Capuchinas, so solidly built in 1736 that the earthquake damage was minor. It now serves as a museum dedicated to the history of the nuns who once lived there.

Distinguished by stucco pilasters, the brilliantly restored Baroque church Iglesia y Convento de Nuestra Señora de la Merced (known simply as La Merced) serves as the starting point for the city's elaborate processions during Semana Santa (Holy Week), one of the most lavishly celebrated in Central America. When the Lenten season arrives, the city becomes one huge passion play, as processions pass over intricate carpets of flowers and colored sawdust called *alfombras,* a tradition that originated in the 16th century.

Standing amid the fashionable cafés and shops and the poetically decaying ruins, the Casa Santo Domingo is Antigua's showpiece hotel. It is set within the remains of what was once the city's richest and most powerful convent, built in 1642. It is large for Antigua (with 128 rooms), and its museum-quality exhibits attract the curious, so those looking for more intimate accommodations should consider the Posada Del Angel boutique hotel. With just seven sumptuously decorated rooms, each graced with a wood-burning fireplace and fresh flowers, the inn is unpretentious, considering President Clinton and members of European royalty have stayed here.

The most-climbed of Guatemala's volcanoes is 7,388-foot Pacaya, east of Antigua, which erupted in 1961 without warning and has been continuously active ever since—from minor steam emissions to explosions that have forced evacuations. A 2- to 3-hour trek takes you to the rim for a peek.

WHERE: 15 miles/25 km west of Guatemala City. **CASA SANTO DOMINGO:** Tel 502/7820-1220; www.casasantodomingo.com.gt. *Cost:* from $170. **POSADA DEL ANGEL:** Tel 502/7832-0260; in the U.S., 305-677-2382; www.posadadelangel.com. *Cost:* from $195. **BEST TIMES:** Dec–Apr for nice weather; Semana Santa (week before Easter); Sep 24 for La Merced festival; Christmas and New Year's.

Agua Volcano looms above Arco de Santa Catalina.

Ancient Beauty, Ancient Ways

LAKE ATITLÁN

Panajachel, Altiplano, Guatemala

The Altiplano, Guatemala's western highlands, is the country's most stunning region, and blue-green Lake Atitlán—mirroring three Fuji-like volcanoes—its most perfect snapshot. Those who have seen it would agree with writer Aldous Huxley, who called it "the most beautiful lake in the world." In certain seasons, the lake, under siege from human pollution, has experienced algae blooms, but international teams of scientists are working to alleviate the problem.

In the highlands surrounding the lake (a collapsed volcano cone that covers 50 square miles), descendants of the ancient Maya still live off the ash-rich land, their simple maize-farming methods unchanged over time. A dozen lakeside villages and numerous mountain towns, where life and customs have changed little over the centuries, promise interesting day trips, particularly on market day, which varies from village to village.

The best jumping-off point is still Panajachel, the largest and most touristy of the towns. With a population of 14,000, it retains some characteristics of its 1970s hippie heyday, but the finest accommodations in the lake region are found here, including lakeside Hotel Atitlán, whose 60 rooms all have private balconies and splendid views of lush gardens and the lake beyond. A few miles outside of town is the ultracharming Casa Palopó, which feels more like a rich uncle's estate than a small luxury inn. Its seven rooms and two-bedroom villa all command some of the lake's most gorgeous vistas. Boat tours and water taxis leave Panajachel regularly for the lake's more traditional towns, such as the popular Santiago Atitlán, where proud Tzutujil Maya residents still cling to their old customs. At the Friday and Sunday markets women wearing colorfully hand-embroidered *huipiles* (blouses) sell hand-woven textiles. Posada de Santiago, nestled on a lagoonlike offshoot of the lake, is the place to stay. Of its 17 rooms, six are small stone cottages, with gardens and a well-known kitchen that brims with local flavor.

WHERE: 92 miles/147 km west of Guatemala City. **HOTEL ATITLÁN:** Tel 502/7762-1441; www.hotelatitlan.com. *Cost:* from $140. **CASA PALOPÓ:** Tel 502/7762-2270; www.casapalopo.com. *Cost:* from $175. **POSADA DE SANTIAGO:** Tel 502/7721-7366; www.posadadesantiago.com. *Cost:* from $65. **BEST TIMES:** Nov–Apr for dry, clear weather; Oct 4 for Fiesta de San Francisco de Asis in Panajachel.

Ghost Metropolis of the Maya

TIKAL

El Petén, Guatemala

In a vast empire that once encompassed Mexico, Belize, Honduras, El Salvador, and Guatemala, Tikal was the most resplendent of all Maya cities. A mighty religious, political, and military center, Tikal represented the apogee of Classic Maya civilization. Its pyramids and acropoli were the highest structures in the western hemisphere, and an estimated 100,000 people lived among them in a 10-square-mile area. It was abandoned by A.D. 1000, when its civilization collapsed. Only a small portion of Tikal has been excavated; nevertheless, more than 3,000 temples, ceremonial platforms, ball courts, and plazas now make up Guatemala's most famous and impressive Maya ruin, which is less crowded than the better-known sites of the Maya Heartland in Mexico's Yucatán (see p. 960).

Tikal Temple I is also known as the Temple of the Great Jaguar.

Tikal's centerpiece is the Plaza Mayor (Great Plaza), flanked by tall, well restored temples. Soaring to 186 feet and 212 feet respectively, Temple V and Temple IV are the highest on the grounds, each an ideal perch from which to watch the sun set. Special passes are granted to visit the Great Plaza after hours on nights with a full moon, when Tikal is at its most magical. The ruins lie within the Tikal National Park, 222 square miles of dense jungle that, with over 400 species, ranks as a world-class birding destination, especially at dawn. The most comfortable lodging within the park is Jungle Lodge, with modest bungalows and easy access to the ruins.

Forty miles to the southwest and surrounded by the waters of lovely Lake Petén Itzá, the island village of Flores, reachable by causeway, is a popular stop for lunch and a boat tour of the lake. At its northeastern edge, the town of El Remate is the location of La Lancha, one of Francis Ford Coppola's three eco-lodges in Central America (see pp. 962 and 963). Half of the ten quaint rooms face the lake, with balconies sometimes visited by friendly howler monkeys.

Lakeside Ni'tun is another of Guatemala's most appealing eco-lodges. Its four stone-and-thatch cottages and two-story open restaurant are set on a wild 86-acre preserve; the compound is the launching pad for Monkey Eco Tours, whose organized day excursions include Tikal and other rarely visited Maya ruins.

Where: 40 miles/64 km northeast of Flores. **Visitor info:** www.tikalpark.com. **Jungle Lodge:** Tel 502/2477-0570; www.junglelodgetikal.com. *Cost:* $150, inclusive. **La Lancha:** Tel 501-824-4912; in the U.S., 800-746-3743; www.coppolaresorts.com. *Cost:* from $110 (off-peak), from $145 (peak). **Ni'tun and Monkey Eco Tours:** Tel 502/5201-0759; www.nitun.com. *Cost:* from $195. **Best times:** Dec–Feb for nicest weather; Feb–early Apr for birding.

A Still-Thriving Pre-Columbian Trading Town

Market at Chichicastenango

Quiché, Guatemala

Guatemala's largest market takes place in Chichicastenango, one of the country's most colorful and accessible highland towns and an important trading center since pre-Columbian times. "Chichi" is famous for its indigenous arts and crafts, hand-woven textiles and blankets, and wooden masks. It draws tourists by the busload every Thursday and Sunday, who wander the market's myriad stalls and head to the maze of *comedores* (open-air food stalls) to sample fried chicken and blue corn tortillas.

Chichi's market is a popular day trip from Lago Atitlán and Antigua (see pp. 969 and 968), but stay overnight to get the full experience of the market. Watch as Maya families from the highlands set out their wares and exchange news the night before, then settle in to sleep under the stars. Rise at dawn to watch the market swing into action, making sure to visit the inner nucleus around the fountain to find the most traditional goods. If you've come for Sunday's market, visit the whitewashed 16th-century Church of Santo Tomás, where the *cofradías*, or traditional Catholic brotherhoods, often stage processions or ceremonies.

Opened in 1932 just a block from the market, the Mayan Inn was the first hotel in town and is still its most famous. The Quiché-Maya staff wear traditional dress, and the 30 rooms are accented with local crafts. The larger, Colonial-style Hotel Santo Tomás, built around a courtyard fountain, offers simple luxuries like quiet rooms with fireplaces and views of the countryside.

To see where the locals shop for everything from chickens and sacks of beans to alarm clocks, head to San Francisco el Alto, whose name refers to its perch atop a rocky escarpment overlooking the plain of Quetzaltenango. Thousands flock here every Friday for the largest market in Guatemala's western region, conducting their business with a quiet politeness that is distinctively Maya.

Where: 40 miles/65 km northwest of Antigua. **Visitor info:** www.visitguatemala.com. **Mayan Inn:** contact Clark Tours, tel 502/2412-4753; www.clarktours.com.gt. *Cost:* from $110. **Hotel Santo Tomás:** Tel 502/7756-1061; www.centralamerica.com/guatemala. *Cost:* from $99. **Best times:** Thurs or Sun for market; Dec for Feast of Santo Tomás and Christmastime.

A Diver's Paradise in the Western Caribbean

THE BAY ISLANDS

Honduras

The lovely coral reefs off the lush, mountainous Bay Islands (Islas de la Bahía) are the southernmost extension of Belize's barrier reefs (see p. 961), world famous as the largest after Australia's Great Barrier Reef (see p. 653). But the unparalleled marine life here seems even more beautiful than Down Under because it is less touristed and less developed (at least for the moment: The islands are poised to become a full-blown tourist destination).

Scuba divers revel in the extensive coral reefs that surround the Bay Islands.

Along with the three principal Bay Islands—Roatán, Utila, and Guanaja—there are four lesser ones and 60 small cays, stretching 70 miles in a northeasterly arc, all of which offer countless diving and snorkeling opportunities. Reefs fringing the Bay Islands support the greatest diversity of corals, sponges, and invertebrates in the Caribbean. It's heaven to divers, from scuba snobs avoiding overtrafficked destinations elsewhere in the Caribbean to newbies who have heard that these islands are one of the best and least expensive places to earn dive certification.

Roatán is the largest, most popular, and most developed. Still, it's a good base for diving or snorkeling, and even nondivers come for Roatán's Institute for Marine Sciences, a research and educational facility with dolphin-training demonstrations open to the public. Located on the periphery of Anthony's Key Resort—the island's best sited and best all-around hotel—the institute also offers a chance to swim, snorkel, or dive with dolphins in the open ocean or inside the lagoon.

Utila, the smallest of the three major Bay Islands, is what Roatán used to be: an inexpensive, unspoiled diving paradise. It's best known for its thriving population of whale sharks, gentle plankton-eating behemoths which can be observed up close on 4-hour snorkeling outings organized by the Whale Shark & Oceanic Research Center. Guanaja, the third major island, lies to the north of Roatán and is the quietest of all.

Even closer to La Ceiba, the mainland's big port city where the ferry departs for the Bay Islands, are the two small Cayos Cochinos (Hog Islands), surrounded by some of the most pristine coral reefs in the entire barrier reef system. For those willing to trade some creature comforts for a near-perfect location, Plantation Beach Resort has ten rustic rooms and one of the best dive operations in the country. If Roatán is your base, boats can whisk you here for a day of superlative diving.

WHERE: Roatán is 35 miles/56 km off the

northern coast of Honduras. **Anthony's Key Resort:** Tel 504/445-3003; in the U.S., 800-227-3483; www.anthonyskey.com. *Cost:* diving packages from $135 per person, per night, all-inclusive (off-peak), from $165 per person (peak). **Whale Shark & Oceanic Research Center:** Tel 504/425-3760; www.wsorc.org. **Plantation Beach Resort:** Tel 504/3371-7556; www.plantationbeachresort.com. *Cost:* rooms $200, inclusive; $300 for all-inclusive dive package. **Best times:** Mar–Sep for dry season; year-round for whale sharks in Utila.

Wildlife and Whitewater Rafting

Pico Bonito National Park

Honduras

A mighty mountain that stands outside the port city of La Ceiba and towers nearly 8,000 feet high, Pico Bonito (beautiful peak) is the heart of 270,000 acres of tropical rain forest that represents Honduras's greatest preserve, much of it wild and inaccessible. Though the mountain is steep and much of it is off-limits, the park that surrounds it offers plenty of hiking trails that wend through verdant, varied forests at different elevations. No fewer than 22 rivers carve through this dense habitat, creating spectacular waterfalls; the most popular hiking path leads to La Ruidosa, "The Noisy One."

Pico Bonito National Park is home to more than 400 species of birds, including extravagantly plumed purple and blue cotingas, toucans, motmots, and hummingbirds. Jaguars, ocelots, and pumas roam the hills, though sightings are rare. Tapirs, deer, and white-faced and spider monkeys are more common, as are countless species of reptiles, amphibians, and butterflies.

The most luxurious place to hang your binoculars is the Lodge at Pico Bonito, an eco-resort made up of 22 stone and native-pine cabins with verandas and with hammocks scattered among old cacao groves. Set on 200 acres right at the park's edge, where two fast-moving rivers meet, it offers ample access to natural wonders and adventures; though just a half-hour's drive from La Ceiba, it feels remote. Swim in the rock pools on the Río Cordalito, spot birds from high wooden towers, visit a butterfly sanctuary where 40 species flutter about, or hike into the forested hills before unwinding in the spa. Adrenaline junkies can take on the Río Cangrejal, which offers some of the best Class II to V rapids in Central America.

Another jewel is the unassuming Casa Cangrejal bed-and-breakfast, whose warm and engaging Canadian owner serves robust Honduran coffee and luscious home-baked breads for breakfast. Its four spacious and tastefully designed rooms are nestled in the fragrant rain forest, within earshot of a babbling creek. The inn is close to the Cuero y Salado Wildlife Refuge, 20 miles west of La Ceiba, where three mountain-fed rivers meet in a massive estuary brimming with wildlife, including the elusive and endangered West Indian manatee.

Where: 5 miles/8 km south of La Ceiba. **Visitor info:** www.letsgohonduras.com. **The Lodge at Pico Bonito:** Tel 504/440-0388; in the U.S., 888-428-0221; www.picobonito.com. *Cost:* from $205 (off-peak), from $265 (peak). **Casa Cangrejal:** Tel 504/408-2760; www.casacangrejal.com. *Cost:* $65 (off-peak), $90 (peak). **Best time:** Feb–Apr for dry, cool weather.

The Caribbean of Yesteryear

The Corn Islands

Nicaragua

The sweet, unspoiled Caribbean of the 1950s lingers on the Corn Islands, off the eastern coast of Nicaragua. On Big Corn, the attractions are many: fine diving and snorkeling in turquoise water, cheap lobster, affordable digs, deep-sea fishing trips, and gloriously undeveloped, palm-fringed beaches like Picnic Beach, which you'll often have to yourself. Despite its name, Big Corn is just 4 square miles, so you can zip around easily by golf cart, bike, or moped.

At the small-scale hotels of the island, air conditioning and hot water are considered high-end amenities, and that's part of its back-in-time charm. Arenas Beach Hotel is the nicest, with 22 comfortable rooms and bungalows right on Southwest Bay Beach, one of the island's most beautiful stretches of white sand. Lounge on a cushy sofa sheltered by a white tent while sipping the hotel's signature Sand Fly.

On Little Corn, a 30-minute boat ride to the northeast, there are no golf carts—or roads, for that matter. Dirt paths crisscross the 1-square-mile island, and you can walk everywhere. Still, there's plenty to do, from beach hikes to swinging in a hammock with a good book to diving in a healthy reef system blessed with an abundance of marine life. The best place to play castaway is at Little Corn Beach and Bungalow, eight simple cabanas tucked among the palm trees on pretty Cocal Beach. The resort serves great margaritas and food that is delicious and unpretentious—think ribs, fish tacos, and homemade coconut ice cream. Snorkel on the reef in front of the hotel, or ask the American owners to set you up with a morning of ocean fishing. With few bars and good places to eat and limited electricity, Little Corn is for travelers who are happy with ceiling fans and mosquito netting, and who understand when primitive is bliss.

Where: Big Corn is 50 miles/80 km east of Bluefields. **Visitor info:** www.bigcornisland.com. **Arenas Beach Hotel:** Tel 505/2222-6574; www.arenasbeachhotel.com. *Cost:* from $90; dinner $10. **Little Corn Beach Bungalow:** Tel 505/8333-0956; www.littlecornbb.com. *Cost:* $70; dinner $9. **Best times:** Nov–May for fine weather. On Big Corn: May for Palo de Mayo; late Aug for Crab Soup Festival and celebration of emancipation of slaves.

Colonial Grandeur on a Great Lake

Granada

Nicaragua

Lack of tourism has helped keep both Nicaragua's natural environment and its heritage intact. Nowhere is this more evident than in Granada, an elegant and captivating colonial city on the western shores of

Lake Cocibolca (also called Lake Nicaragua), the largest freshwater lake in Central America.

Today the heart of the city is still the lively tree-lined Parque Central (also known as Parque Colón), dominated by the magnificent yellow Cathedral of Granada. Enjoy the view from the polished-wood balconies of Hotel Plaza Colón, an exquisitely restored 27-room colonial mansion overlooking the park. Three blocks away is Central America's oldest church, the massive, sky-blue San Francisco with its attached convent (now a museum); it's home to a display of towering black basalt statues, carved about 1,000 years ago and discovered in the 1880s on the ancient ceremonial island of Zapatera. Stroll to nearby El Zaguan for some of the best dining in town. The courtyard restaurant serves succulent fire-grilled meats, fresh rainbow bass from the lake, and sea bass from the Pacific.

Since 1583, the Cathedral of Granada has been destroyed and rebuilt many times.

Just offshore from Granada are some 365 diminutive islands called Las Isletas, formed 20,000 years ago by an eruption of the now dormant Volcán Mombacho. Many of the islands are privately owned, including the one where you'll find the luxurious Jicaro Island Ecolodge, with nine sleek, two-story casitas that look across the water to the volcano.

So wide is Lake Nicaragua that it takes 4 hours by boat to reach Ometepe, the exquisitely beautiful, twin-peaked island formed by two volcanoes. Ometepe is a mosaic of small farms producing plantains, corn, avocados, and coffee, and home to two lazy commercial centers, Moyogalpa and Altagracia. In addition to climbing the volcanoes, visiting secluded beaches, and hiking trails that wind among trees ruled by monkeys, you can view more than 70 ancient petroglyph sites and numerous stone idols scattered across the island.

A perfect day trip from Granada is to Masaya, long a center of art and culture and well known for its market; this is the place to find handmade hammocks, intricate pottery, wood carvings, and leather goods. Not much farther is Masaya Volcano National Park, where a road and trails lead directly to the most accessible live volcano in Nicaragua and, some say, the world. This low, gaping gas-belching volcano and its fiery eruptions inspired the Spanish to call it the Gates of Hell.

Nicaragua's main seaside resort, San Juan del Sur, is just an hour's drive south of Granada, a perfect spot for those seeking idyllic beaches or great surfing, sailing, deep-sea fishing, and scuba diving in the Pacific. Fifteen bungalows at Morgan's Rock Hacienda & Ecolodge enjoy magnificent views of the ocean, particularly at sunset. Guides can help you explore the 5,000-acre jungle-meets-beach property, home to howler, spider, and capuchin monkeys, as well as sloths, countless birds, and sea turtles.

Where: 27 miles/45 km southeast of Managua. **Visitor info:** www.visitnicaragua.com. **Hotel Plaza Colón:** Tel 505/2552-8489; www.hotelplazacolon.com. *Cost:* from $100. **El Zaguan:** Tel 505/2552-2522. *Cost:* dinner $15. **Jicaro Ecolodge:** Tel 505/2552-6353; www.jicaroecolodge. *Cost:* $380 (off-peak), $480 (peak), all-inclusive. **Morgan's Rock:** Tel 505/8670-7676; www.morgansrock.com. *Cost:* from $320 (off-peak), from $370 (peak), inclusive. **Best times:** Dec–May for good weather; Easter week for celebrations.

An Unspoiled Archipelago of Eco-Surprises

Bocas del Toro

Panama

Sixty-eight islands off the northwest coast of Panama comprise a complex and diverse ecosystem where you can experience a wealth of natural wonders both on land and in the water. Trek through wildlife-filled rain forests, glimpse endangered turtles on white sand beaches, and surf the world-famous waves off Isla Bastimentos and Isla Carenero, where Columbus made landfall in 1502.

Isla Colón is the largest of the islands; its Bocas Town is the region's main hub, though even that is a relative term. The smattering of inns and rustic eco-lodges exude a laid-back vibe and a strong local flavor. One example is Punta Caracol Acqua-Lodge, nine over-the-water bungalows connected by a wooden walkway. Step out of your room to enjoy swimming, kayaking, and snorkeling. Marvel at the sunset from your wraparound terrace, then dine on seafood paella at the open-air restaurant or take a water taxi into Bocas Town to Guari Guari, where the European owners create an inspired six-course menu from local ingredients.

Much of 20-square-mile Isla Bastimentos is home to the National Marine Park (the country's first). It measures more than 30,000 acres that range from dense virgin rain forest to a marine sanctuary, where you'll find clear waters and a barrier reef. Dive or snorkel the coral forests of the two Cayos Zapatillas (Slipper Islands), or sunbathe on Red Frog Beach. Make your base the friendly La Loma Jungle Lodge, a 57-acre working farm at the park's edge, complete with cacao, coconut, and banana groves. The highest of its four open-air thatched "ranchos" are worth the aerobic climb, offering sweeping views of the bay. The young owners make their own chocolate, which shows up in their famous chocolate-coconut cake; candlelight dinners might feature local grilled yellow jack with passion fruit *pico de gallo*.

A dock extends out from the coast of Isla Bastimentos, one of the larger Panamanian islands and only reachable by boat.

Al Natural provides a beach alternative; its seven round, thatch-roofed bungalows were built using the traditional techniques of the Ngöbe-Buglé Indians and rest perched on stilts at the edge of the Caribbean's crystal blue water. The Belgian owners are known for their excellent food, served in a two-story dining space with an observation tower.

Where: Isla Colón is 19 miles/32 km off the coast of Panama's northwest corner, and 341 miles/550 km northwest of Panama City. **Visitor info:** www.visitpanama.com. **Punta Caracol:** Tel 507/757-9410; www.puntacaracol.com. *Cost:* from $344 (off-peak), $430 (peak), all-inclusive. **Guari Guari:** Tel 507/6627-1825. *Cost:* dinner $25. **La Loma:** Tel 507/6619-5364; www.thejunglelodge.com. *Cost:* $200, all-inclusive. **Al Natural Resort:** Tel 507/757-9004; www.alnaturalresort.com. *Cost:* from $240, all-inclusive. *When:* closed May–Jul 15. **Best times:** Dec–Apr for nicest weather; Sep for International Festival of the Sea in Isla Colón.

In Search of the Resplendent Quetzal

Chiriqui Highlands

Panama

Forming a land bridge between Central and South America, Panama is slightly smaller than the state of South Carolina, yet it is home to more bird species than all of North America. King of them all is the resplendent quetzal, whose 2-foot-long, iridescent green tail feathers were used in the headdresses of Aztec rulers and were considered more valuable than gold. Today sighting a quetzal is a highly treasured experience in Central America, and Panama's Chiriqui Highlands, which rise to 10,000 feet in the westernmost part of the country, is where you're most likely to find them, together with blue cotingas, trogons, silver-throated tanagers, and toucans.

The misty, mountainous rain forests of Parque Nacional Volcán Baru are home to nearly 250 bird species, abundant orchids, and countless plants that grow in the shadow of the 11,401-foot dormant volcano. The 35,000-acre park's famed 5-mile Quetzal Trail is the country's most popular day hike for its panoramic lookouts and chances of spotting the bird for which it is named. Also here are the Chiriqui and Chiriqui Viejo rivers, revered by serious rafters for their Class III to V rides and lush scenery.

Boquete, the charming colonial town at the foot of the eastern slope of Baru Volcano, is a good place from which to strike out into the wilderness. Its landmark hotel, the 25-room Panamonte Inn & Spa, dates from 1914 and offers luxurious country-inn accommodations, beautiful gardens, and a renowned restaurant overseen by chef-owner Charlie Collins. Another nearby option is the Coffee Estate Inn, which offers three charming bungalows on a 6-acre shade-coffee farm rich with birdlife as well as beans.

Indeed, the volcanic soil and microclimates make the highlands one of the world's finest producers of coffee, including "geisha beans," reputed to be the very best. North of Boquete sits the highly photogenic Finca Lérida, a 650-acre working coffee plantation that you can tour, established in 1922 by a Norwegian engineer involved in building the Panama Canal (see p. 979). The family home is a bed-and-breakfast, and a new eco-lodge offers outstanding views of the lush, mountainous landscape.

On the western slope of Volcán Baru, Panama's highest peak, the village of Cerro Punta provides the best Panamanian access to La Amistad International Park (PILA), which spills over into neighboring Costa Rica. It's enormous—511,508 acres on the Panama side alone—and a refuge for jaguars, ocelots, tapirs, and 400 bird species.

Where: Boquete is 280 miles/450 km west of Panama City. **How:** U.S.-based International Expeditions leads a 9-day trip that includes Chiriqui Highlands. Tel 800-633-4734 or 205-428-1700; www.ietravel.com. *Cost:* from $4,098. Originates in Panama City. **Panamonte Inn:** Tel 507/720-1324 or 800-525-4800; www.panamonte.com. *Cost:* from $340; dinner $40. **Coffee Estate Inn:** Tel 507/720-2211; www.coffeeestateinn.com. *Cost:* $145. **Finca Lérida:** Tel 507/720-2285; www.fincalerida.com. *Cost:* $150. **Best times:** Nov–Apr for finest weather. In Boquete: mid-Jan for Flowers and Coffee Festival; Feb for Jazz Festival; mid-Apr for Orchid Festival.

An Independent Community Follows Its Ancient Ways

San Blas Islands

Comarca Kuna Yala, Panama

In a gorgeous seascape of small, idyllic islands along the northeastern Caribbean coast of Panama, the Kuna Indians, considered one of the most intact indigenous societies in the Americas, still live according to their ancient ways. Also known as the San Blas archipelago, this semiautonomous region (*comarca*) is officially called Kuna Yala, or "Land of the Kuna Indians." They are a proud, tightly knit people who number some 50,000, and who are governed by three tribal chiefs, or *caciques*. Kuna society is a matriarchal one, and the women are known for their elaborate adornment: gold jewelry, beads covering their legs and arms, and vividly colored, hand-stitched blouses appliquéd with *molas,* multiple layers of colorful fabric whose geometric designs are meant to mimic the body art that early European missionaries forced them to give up.

The brightly colored molas *are an integral part of Kuna culture.*

The Kuna Yala homeland consists of a narrow strip of coastal mainland and some 365 coral islands and keys, most of them uninhabited. Guests can stay with local island families in simple dwellings with limited or no electricity for next to nothing, or in a growing number of small, rustic inns owned and run by the Kuna. Some offer no more than a hammock to sleep in and lack even hot water, while the most modern, such as Kuna-owned and -run Yandup Island Lodge and Akwadup Lodge, each on its own small island, feature comfortable, thatched cabins, some over water. No diving is allowed within the protected waters of the comarca, but guests can spend languid days swimming, snorkeling, and visiting deserted, white sand beaches, as well as traditional Kuna villages, cemeteries, and markets. Simple but satisfying meals are generally based on fresh fish from the sea.

Sea kayaking is the most adventuresome way to explore the less visited islands, and Mountain Travel Sobek was the first of the few "outside" outfitters allowed to lead overnight kayaking trips in Kuna Yala. A motorboat whisks you to a remote outer archipelago, where you'll board a kayak and set off to find the best spots for snorkeling, camp on uninhabited islands, and visit far-flung Kuna villages as an honored guest.

If diving is a must, stay outside the comarca at the mainland Coral Lodge, where you can swim and snorkel right off your bungalow's sundeck or arrange for diving trips outside the protected waters, as well as day trips to the Kuna Yala islands. The six traditional thatch-roofed bungalows sitting over water also offer the rare commodity of air-conditioning.

Where: 50 miles/81 km northeast of Panama City. **Yandup Island Lodge:** Tel 507/394-1408; www.yandupisland.com. *Cost:* from $185, all-inclusive. **Akwadup Lodge:** Tel 507/396-4805; www.sanblaslodge.com. *Cost:* $300, all-inclusive. **Mountain Travel Sobek:** In the U.S., tel 888-831-7526 or 510-594-6000; www.mtsobek.com. *Cost:* 8 days (5 nights camping), $2,495, inclusive. Originates in Panama City. *When:* Dec–Mar. **Coral Lodge:** In the U.S., 800-950-2862 or 305-383-8071; www.corallodge.com. *Cost:* $220. **Best times:** Dec–Mar for nicest weather; Jul–Oct is rainy season but diving is good.

The World's Most Famous Shortcut

Panama Canal

Panama City to Colón, Panama

Built across the narrowest point between the Pacific and Atlantic oceans, the Panama Canal is one of the greatest engineering achievements of the 20th century. It stretches 50 miles from Panama City to Colón, and took first France, then the U.S., 65,000 workers and 20 years to build. Centuries of bankruptcy, mismanagement, and malaria delayed the project a number of times after the idea was first proposed in 1524 by King Charles V of Spain. But nearly 400 years later, on August 15, 1914, the SS *Ancon* became the first ship to sail from one side to the other. Today countless cruise and commercial ships line up for the 8- to 10-hour journey. Today's ships are so big that the canal is being expanded by 2014, in time for its centennial.

The comprehensive museum at the Miraflores Visitors Center, just yards from the locks, features interactive displays and a mesmerizing view from its restaurant. To truly enjoy the canal, though, consider a partial or full transit boat tour lasting 4 to 8 hours.

Located at the canal's southern end, cosmopolitan Panama City is a rich base for exploring the area. The romantic, 17th-century Casco Viejo (Old Quarter) is a city-within-a-city gradually being revived; of the growing number of boutique hotels occupying restored buildings here, the first was the Canal House, an 1893 mansion whose three elegantly appointed suites deliver contemporary style and plenty of amenities. Stroll through Plaza Bolívar, known for its charming sidewalk cafés, and dine at Manolo Caracol, popular for its ever-changing 12-course menu.

Just 10 minutes from the modern downtown, Natural Metropolitan Park is the world's only tropical rain forest within city limits. The birding opportunities are impressive here, but it gets even better at Soberania Park, the species-rich rain forest that runs alongside the canal and is an easy 15-mile drive from Panama City. Pipeline Road, the canal's former service road, is unmatched for birding; it holds the world's record for the greatest numbers of bird species identified in a 24-hour period—a staggering 360 (of the 500 known to thrive here). In the heart of the park is Gamboa Rainforest Resort, a luxurious, 107-room riverside hotel that includes 38 villas from the 1930s that once served as homes for Canal administrators. Both of its nearby sister properties—Canopy Tower (a refurbished, five-story former U.S. radar station, also within the park) and the more comfortable Canopy Lodge—serve avid birders with tree-top viewing platforms and expert guides.

Info: Tel 507/276-8325; www.pancanal.com. **Miraflores:** Tel 507/232-3120. *Cost:* lunch $40. **How:** Canal & Bay Tours offer partial and full transits. Tel 507/209-2009; www.canalandbaytours.com. **The Canal House:** Tel 507/228-1907; in the U.S., 888-593-5023; www.canalhousepanama.com. *Cost:* from $205. **Manolo Caracol:** Tel 507/228-4640; www.manolocaracol.net. *Cost:* dinner $25. **Gamboa Rainforest Resort:** Tel 507/314-9000; in the U.S., 877-800-1690; www.gamboaresort.com. *Cost:* from $250. **Canopy Lodge** and **Canopy Tower:** Tel 507/264-5720; in the U.S., 800-930-3397; www.canopytower.com. *Cost:* from $300 (off-peak), from $440 (peak), inclusive. **Best times:** Dec–Apr for dry season; Jan for Jazz Festival; Feb–Mar for Carnaval in Panama City.

SOUTH AMERICA AND ANTARCTICA

"Hard to believe Buenos Aires had any beginning. I feel it to be as eternal as the air."
—*Jorge Luis Borges*

Buenos Aires

Argentina

Buenos Aires is the sultry capital of Argentina, a cosmopolitan hub rising where the Pampas meet the Río de la Plata. A heady mix of Italian, French, Spanish, and other cultural influences, this vibrant, elegant city sometimes makes you wonder where you are. The rhythm is definitely Latin America, but the architecture and the glamour will have you thinking Europe.

Top Attractions

San Telmo Antiques Market—Known as the Feria de San Pedro Telmo, this Sunday-only event spills out from Plaza Dorrego, the heart of San Telmo, one of Buenos Aires's oldest neighborhoods. Antiques stalls, souvenir vendors, and street performers fill the plaza and continue up and down Calle Defensa, the area's main thoroughfare, which is lined with antiques stores and cafés. The real highlights are the tango dancers who perform in a corner of the plaza, holding the crowds in thrall with dancing that can go on till night. **Info:** www.feriadesantelmo.com.

Cemetario Recoleta—The most visited location in all of Buenos Aires, Recoleta Cemetery (which opened in 1822) is the final resting place for Argentina's elite and, with unmistakable irony, the woman most famous for challenging them: María Eva Duarte de Perón, better known to the world as Evita. Most tourists come only to catch a quick glimpse of her simple black granite tomb, covered in plaques, including one imploring Argentina not to cry for her, then head to the nearby neighborhood of Palermo, where the Museo Evita puts her love of her people on display. The café is worth an hour of your time. **Museo Evita:** Tel 54/11-4807-9433; www.museoevita.org.

Though she died in 1952, Evita's body wasn't buried for over 20 years.

Museo de Arte Latinoamericano de Buenos Aires (MALBA)—A vast, steel-and-glass, light-filled space, MALBA, as it's known, is as much a work of art as anything it exhibits. Departing from the Eurocentric thrust of so many of Argentina's museums, this one is devoted to Latin American art, including works by Frida Kahlo, Diego Rivera, Antonio Siguí, Antonio Berni, and contemporary Argentine artists. **Info:** Tel 54/11-4808-6500; www.malba.org.ar.

Museo Nacional de Bellas Artes—The National Fine Arts Museum has utilitarian roots—it was originally a water pumping station—but now contains the largest collection of Argentine art in the world, along with surprisingly varied holdings by European masters such as Rodin, Renoir, and Toulouse Lautrec, along with a broad range of Picasso drawings. Opened in 1930, the museum reflects the tastes of the wealthy Argentines who roamed the world at the beginning of the 20th century, looking to augment their art collections. **Info:** Tel 54/11-5288-9900; www.mnba.org.ar.

Teatro Colón—When it opened in 1908 the Teatro Colón opera house was Buenos Aires's pronouncement to the world that she was ready to compete with the best of Europe. The building features abundant marble, bronze, wood carvings, and stained glass imported from Europe. The centerpiece of the main (3,000-seat) theater is an enormous chandelier hanging from a domed ceiling adorned with frescoes by Argentine artist Raúl Soldi. In 2010 architect Victor Meano completed a sumptuous renovation. But the building is merely a magnificent backdrop: Some of the world's greatest singers and performers have graced this stage, from Enrico Caruso to Maria Callas to Plácido Domingo. **Info:** ticket office, tel 54/11-4378-7344; www.teatrocolon.org.ar.

Teatro Colón, considered to be among the finest acoustic venues in the world, opened in 1908 with a performance of Aida.

El Metejón Polo Club—You'd never know Argentina didn't invent polo if you drive an hour southwest of Buenos Aires to El Metejón, one of the country's top polo resorts. If you're game, sign up for the intensive classes run by the resort's instructors; you'll find it strenuous, but that's why the resort has a spa, pool, and 12 luxury suites on the grounds of this estancia-style getaway. If you'd rather sit on the sidelines, come any time from October to December, when the championships take place in Buenos Aires's Palermo district, and watch professionals practice. **Where:** Cañuelas, 30 miles/48 km southwest of B.A. Tel 54/2226-432-260; www.elmetejon.com.ar. *Cost:* from $600 (off-peak), from $800 (peak), all-inclusive.

Feria de Mataderos—Held opposite the National Cattle Market in the Mataderos neighborhood, this spirited street fair brings a nostalgic taste of the *campo,* or countryside, into the city. The *feria* takes place on Sundays year-round, but it is so popular that in late summer (February and March) it is held on Saturdays as well. Antiques dealers and food vendors fill the streets, folkloric dancers entertain the crowds, and gauchos in full regalia ride into town performing the Carrera de Sortija, a wild ride of a game in which they attempt to use a small stick to spear hanging rings at full gallop. **Info:** Tel 54/11-4342-9629; www.feriademataderos.com.ar.

Where to Stay

The Alvear Palace Hotel—All luxury hotels in Buenos Aires are compared to the Alvear, the city's classic 1929 grande dame in the center of exclusive Recoleta. The hotel brims with multicolored marble, gilded bronze, Louis XV furniture, and other precious details that somehow manage to escape stuffiness. Each room comes with round-the-clock butler service, and the hotel's La Prairie spa sprawls for over 8,000 square feet. La Bourgogne, overseen by chef Jean Paul Bondoux, is the city's finest French dining venue, while brunch at L'Orangerie is a scrumptious local tradition. **Info:** Tel 54/11-4808-2100; www.alvearpalace.com. *Cost:* from $450; dinner at La Bourgogne $100.

The BoBo Hotel—You have to love a hotel that can make fun of itself—BoBo is short for "bourgeois bohemian," the ironic term for members of the privileged classes who adopt countercultural pretensions. Still, you'll find plenty of elegance at this 1920s mansion in the very heart of trendy Palermo Soho. Step into the tranquil lobby—and you'll feel instantly transported, though upstairs you'll still see evidence of the hip neighborhood beyond: Each of the seven well-designed rooms is uniquely styled and named to reflect modern art movements. **INFO:** Tel 54/11-4774-0505; www.bobohotel.com. *Cost:* from $175.

THE FOUR SEASONS HOTEL—Located in the well-heeled Recoleta neighborhood, this hotel is built in two sections—there's the 12-story Park Tower, which houses all the guest rooms, distinguished by their elegant refinement, some with beautiful views over Nueve de Julio Boulevard. Then there's the 1916 La Mansión, whose seven private suites are popular with movie stars and dignitaries (the mansion's balcony is where Madonna practiced "Don't Cry for Me, Argentina" when filming *Evita*). The restaurant Le Mistral is known for its Mediterranean-influenced international cuisine. **INFO:** Tel 54/11-4321-1200; www.fourseasons.com. *Cost:* from $545; dinner at Le Mistral $75.

HOME HOTEL—This unconventional hotel fits perfectly among the lively nightclubs, bars, and restaurants of the very hip Palermo Hollywood neighborhood that serves as its setting. With a playful, of-the-moment aesthetic, a spa, poolside bar and restaurant, and seriously stylish rooms, Home is in fact home to many visiting celebs and entertainment execs (one of the owners is a DJ and record producer). Despite its in-the-know clientele, the hotel maintains its cool—the vibe here is mellow and the emphasis is on the comfortable side of high design. **INFO:** Tel 54/11-4778-1008; www.homebuenosaires.com. *Cost:* rooms from $140.

LEGADO MITICO—Each of the 11 large guest rooms here is meant to evoke a different historic Argentine personality, from Eva Perón to tango singer extraordinaire Tita Morello, and the results are showcases of design filled with sumptuous furnishings. Public rooms—a huge library, fireplace nook, and two terraces—are no less extraordinary, adding to the rich distinctive ambience. **INFO:** Tel 54/11-4833-1300; www.legadomitico.com. *Cost:* from $240 (off-peak), from $300 (peak).

THE PALACIO DUHAU PARK HYATT—Incorporating the former 1930s mansion of the aristocratic Duhau family, this hotel quickly became popular for the unique way it bridged old and new. Accommodations in the mansion have such classic touches as heavy wooden French doors with brass trim, while the second building, a 17-story tower, maintains a warm modernity and offers fantastic views from many of the rooms. The hotel has four restaurants, including the Duhau, known for its Argentine steaks and farm-to-table cuisine; the Oak Bar is decorated with 17th-century carvings from a castle in Normandy. And there's always afternoon tea, an elaborate affair so abundant you may well have to cancel your dinner reservation. **INFO:** Tel 54/11-5171-1234; www.buenosaires.park.hyatt.com. *Cost:* from $425; dinner at the Duhau $75.

EATING & DRINKING

BUENOS AIRES STEAK HOUSES—Argentina is world famous for the quality of its beef, and Buenos Aires's most characteristic dining experience is found at *parillas* (grills), where excellent steaks (as well as *asado*, a mixed grill of a variety of meat, including sweetbreads, kidneys, and brains) are grilled over glowing coals. A long-time favorite with local VIPs and discerning out-of-towners, La Cabaña Las Lilas serves some 90 tons of steak annually from steers raised on its 17,000-acre estancia along with an excellent selection of local wines. Founded in 1905, today's restaurant occupies a converted waterfront warehouse in the gentrified docks area of Puerto Madero. Dark-paneled, two-story La Cabaña is another Buenos Aires classic, with a dining room that feels like a swank Patagonian lodge. The grill is front and center—you pass it as you enter the restaurant, and its location allows you to watch your food being prepared. La Cabrera represents a more casual and contemporary *parilla* experience, in keeping with its address in trendy Palermo Soho. The whimsically decorated dining room is always bustling and the beef is excellent—as are the abundant side dishes, from salads to mushrooms to pumpkin puree. **La Cabaña Las Lilas:** Tel 54/11-4313-1336; www.laslilas.com.ar. *Cost:* dinner $65. **La Cabaña:** Tel 54/11/4814-0001; www.lacabanabuenosaires.com.ar. *Cost:* dinner $85. **La Cabrera:** Tel 54/11-4831-7002; www.parrillalacabrera.com.ar. *Cost:* dinner $45.

Café Tortoni—Bronze fixtures, stained-glass windows, a polished-wood bar, bow-tied waiters, and the patina of history are all part of the allure at Café Tortoni. Founded in 1858, this is Argentina's oldest café and still a favorite with locals and tourists alike, whether for conversation over a cappuccino, an appetizer or steak, or the intimate tango show in the back room. **Info:** Tel 54/11-4342-4328; www.cafetortoni.com.ar. *Cost:* dinner $30.

Casa Felix—The hot trend in Buenos Aires dining is *puertas cerradas,* or "closed door" restaurants, tiny dining rooms in homes or other private spaces where top chefs prepare sumptuous meals just a few days a week for a handful of guests (reservations required). One of the best is Casa Felix, where on Thursday, Friday, and Saturday evenings no more than 16 diners are welcomed into chef Diego Felix's home for an expertly prepared five-course meal featuring organic and local products. Casa Felix is a marvelous place to share a lively evening with new friends and the perfect destination for adventurous diners weary of the region's beef-rich diet: Meals are red-meat-free, focusing on fish, vegetables, and local fruit. **Info:** www.colectivofelix.com. *Cost:* $45.

The Germán Martitegui Experience—With its chi-chi nightclub atmosphere and menu of nouvelle Mediterranean and updated Argentine classics, no restaurant epitomizes Palermo Soho glamour quite like Casa Cruz. Polished wood, red walls, and warm lighting conspire to show patrons—heavy on fashionistas and visiting celebrities—at their stylish best. Its star chef, Germán Martitegui, also owns the Scandinavian-themed Ølsen, with sleek Nordic design, a huge selection of vodkas, and a popular weekend brunch featuring smoked fish, bagels, and caviar. Tegui, his most recent opening, offers a prix-fixe menu focused on Mediterranean-style seafood and seasonal produce. Less overtly showy than his other restaurants (the entrance is unmarked and graffiti on the walls is the work of local street-art provocateurs), Tegui is an excellent choice if you are looking for creative, contemporary Argentine cuisine. **Casa Cruz:** Tel 54/11-4833-1112; www.casacruz-restaurant.com. *Cost:* dinner $100. **Ølsen:** Tel 54/11-4776-7677. *Cost:* dinner $35. **Tegui:** Tel 54/11-5291-3333. *Cost:* dinner $55.

Gran Bar Danzón—This moody-but-sophisticated wine bar is the perfect place to gather with friends and sample Argentine wines by either the glass or the bottle. Many *porteños* (residents of Buenos Aires) gather here before heading out to clubs and other nightlife spots; some make a night of it and stay for dinner. Argentine favorites such as grilled steak and Italian cuisine top the list, but there's good sushi too. **Info:** Tel 54/11-4811-1108; www.granbardanzon.com.ar. *Cost:* dinner $30.

De Olivas i Lustres—This trendsetting restaurant helped establish high standards in the Palermo neighborhood and continues to enchant with its 14-dish menu of Mediterranean-style tapas served in an antiques-filled dining room. Or choose from the selection of savory pies, cannelloni, and roast meats, all infused with Argentina's Latin culinary heritage. **Info:** Tel 54/11-4667-3388; www.deolivasilustres.com.ar. *Cost:* 14-course tapas $20.

Oviedo—Despite Argentina's 2,900-mile coastline, good seafood is surprisingly hard to find in beef-crazed Buenos Aires. At formal, clubhouselike Oviedo, however, the focus is on fresh fish and shellfish, beautifully presented and prepared with a Mediterranean accent. Grilled shrimp and baby squid, oysters on the half shell, the fresh catch served with pumpkin gnocchi, and seafood-rich risottos are all accompanied by gracious service and a vast wine list that delves deeply into the best vintages of Mendoza (see p. 988) and Europe. **Info:** Tel 54/11-4821-3741; www.oviedoresto.com.ar. *Cost:* dinner $45.

Where to Tango

El Viejo Almacén—Founded by legendary tango singer Edmundo Rivero, El Viejo Almacén offers a show that is among the city's most intimate, with little of the Hollywood feel found elsewhere. Grandfatherly tango crooners belt out songs by Carlos Gardel, the fabled singer who made the tango famous the world over before dying in a 1935 plane crash, while sensual young dancers perform in costumes recalling the early days of tango's dark bordello roots. **Info:** Tel 54/11-4307-6689; www.viejo-almacen.com.ar. *Cost:* $100.

Casa Blanca—The unassuming doors of this building on a cobblestone street in San Telmo are a portal to another time. Casa Blanca's shows are a mix of folkloric dances and tango, distilling the best of the two traditions. Dressed in the clothes of the Pampas, the men try to seduce their partners by way of the zamba, a step dance in which each participant coyly waves a white handkerchief as they did when tango was first performed here in the early 20th century.

Tango originated in 19th-century Argentina.

Info: Tel 54/11-4331-4621. *Cost:* $80, including drinks.

Bar Sur—A sepia-toned throwback to old Buenos Aires, Bar Sur is a *milonga* (a place where locals dance) that puts on an intimate show for *porteños* and tourists alike. The small, turn-of-the-last-century bar offers lessons before each performance, beginning at 8 P.M. Later, the sleekly dressed tango dancers weave their way around the tables, bringing the action to patrons who sit, mesmerized, waiting for their own turn on the dance floor. It's easy to pop in and out of the casual show at any time for drinks or dinner. **Info:** Tel 54/11-4362-6086; www.bar-sur.com.ar. *Cost:* $50.

Confitería Ideal—The glory of old Buenos Aires shines from every bronze sconce and gilded flourish in this classic, century-old *milonga,* aglow with polished woods, well-worn marble, and stained glass. Patrons sit at tables on either side of the dance floor, usually separated by gender, with men and women exchanging stares and using subtle gestures, such as nods of the head or a flick of the hand, until the man approaches a woman to dance. It's here that Madonna and Antonio Banderas famously danced for the movie *Evita.* While it's open all day, the real action begins around midnight and goes on into the wee hours. Friday is the only day for shows, which are performed by professional dancers and musicians. **Info:** Tel 54/11-5265-8069; www.confiteriaideal.com. *Cost:* daily *milonga* $8 (entry only); Friday dinner show $50.

Tango Festivals—Tango is popular year-round in Buenos Aires, but for 18 days in

August events and competitions overtake the city for a few mid-winter weeks with the arrival of Tango Festival y Mundial: This is when theaters along Corrientes host impassioned performances by some of the world's best dancers and the *milongas* echo with stiletto heels and sultry rhythms. Indeed, from San Telmo to the Microcentro, the streets themselves become open-air dance spectacles, to the delight of the crowds that gather there each night. **INFO:** www.tango buenosaires.gov.ar.

A Gaucho Lifestyle Minutes from Busy Buenos Aires

LAS PAMPAS AND ESTANCIAS

Buenos Aires Province, Argentina

The pampas—"the only place on earth where God can roam large" wrote Argentinian poet Jorge Luis Borges—are the vast, flat grasslands stretching for hundreds of miles from where Buenos Aires abruptly stops. These open, empty plains are the source of Argentina's wealth—here, golden wheat and soy are grown and stout grass-fed cattle raised. This is the birthplace of the legendary gaucho, Argentina's cowboy, and of estancias, which were originally a combination of fortress, farm, and ranch, and played a bloody role in the conquest of the Indians. Now many welcome tourists.

Most estancias surround the leafy San Antonio de Areco, known for its silversmiths and the Museo Gauchesco Ricardo Güiraldes, which is dedicated to the author whose novel *Don Segundo Sombra* helped make gauchos a respected part of the collective culture. The sleepy town comes to life in early November for the annual gaucho festival, Día de la Tradición.

Visiting an estancia lets you witness the birth of animals, the harvest, and rural life in general, or to simply sit back and sip *mate* (the bitter Argentine herbal tea) or a glass of red wine with the gauchos or estancia owners. Most of the homes of the cattle barons—often quite opulent—were built during the 19th century, and many today lure guests with swimming pools, *asados* (barbecues), and sunset horseback rides. If you need a short break from the urban pace of Buenos Aires, some estancias are even within day-trip range.

The Colonial-style Estancia La Porteña, near San Antonio, is a beautiful bed-and-breakfast that is set on 500 acres and dates back to 1800. It was once owned by Ricardo Güiraldes, the famous novelist, and still oozes literary allure. Guests can enjoy polo lessons, gaucho-led rides on the grounds, and generous home-cooked meals of Argentine specialties.

Close to Buenos Aires's Ezeiza Airport and also easily day-trippable is Villa María, a Gothic-and-Tudor confection created by Alejandro Bustillo, the architect behind the Llao Llao resort and other Bariloche landmarks (see p. 990). The sprawling mansion, once owned by the Anchorenas, a wealthy cattle family, sits on exquisite grounds and is more genteel resort than estancia, with polo matches, a spa, and golf on offer.

WHERE: San Antonio is 70 miles/113 km northwest of Buenos Aires. **ESTANCIA LA PORTEÑA:** Tel 54/9-11-5626-7347; www.la porteniadeareco.com. *Cost:* $310, inclusive; day rate $85. **ESTANCIA VILLA MARÍA:** Tel 54/11-4832-8737; www.estanciavillamaria.com. *Cost:* $350, all-inclusive; day rate $100. **BEST TIMES:** Apr–May and Sep–Oct for best weather; Nov for Día de la Tradición.

The Patagonian Atlantic

Península Valdés

Chubut, Argentina

Jutting into the Atlantic from Argentine Patagonia, the Valdés Peninsula was, until recently, the country's best-kept secret. Its grassy expanses and 250 miles of rugged, cliff-lined coast are one of the world's most spectacular marine mammal and bird habitats. Puerto Madryn is the base for those who come to explore this unique environment.

Indeed, more than 180 kinds of marine and shore birds make their home on and around the peninsula, from Magellanic penguins at Punto Tumbo Nature Reserve to herons, kelp gulls, and egrets that are found throughout the cliffs and muddy tidal basins on the ocean's edge. At Punta Norte, in the peninsula's northeast corner, orcas prey on the birds, sea lions, and elephant seals by letting the tide carry them onto the beach, then snapping up their quarry, and rolling back into the water. The beach on the Attack Channel is off-limits to humans, but platforms are built in February and March overlooking the violent feeding frenzy. You'll also find nearly 2,000 southern right whales, half the world's population, congregating in the sheltered Golfo Nuevo, south of the peninsula.

The area's most comfortable lodge is El Pedral, a former sheep farm at the edge of Punta Ninfas, 30 miles from Puerto Madryn. It's a vast property that stretches up to the cliffs overlooking Golfo Nuevo. Located on its own secluded beach, the 1904 Tudor-style lodge has just eight rooms. The staff arranges private animal- and whale-viewing tours.

Where: Puerto Madryn is 870 miles/1,400 km south of Buenos Aires. **How:** U.S.-based Borello Travel offers a variety of Península Valdés tours. Tel 800-405-3072 or 212-686-4911; www.borellotravel.com. **El Pedral Lodge:** Tel 54/11-4311-1919; www.elpedrallodge.com. *Cost:* from $220 per person, all-inclusive (off-peak); from $290 (peak). **Best times:** all year for penguins and sea lions; Jun–Dec for right whales; Oct–Apr for orcas.

A City's Intellectual Center, Then and Now

Córdoba's Jesuit Block

Córdoba, Argentina

Now the country's second-largest city, Córdoba was established in 1573 by Jerónimo Luis de Cabrera, and the Jesuits arrived soon after. The city's romantic stucco-and-cobblestone heart is the Manzana Jesuítica, or Jesuit Block, anchored by the University of Córdoba. This is Argentina's first university, opened in 1613, and one of the oldest in the Americas. Within the "block" are the architecturally stunning Iglesia Compañia de Jesús (Church of the Society of Jesus), Argentina's first church and the city's oldest surviving building; the Colegio Nacional de Monserrat, the country's oldest high school; and the Capilla Doméstica (Domestic Chapel). These buildings, along with the flourishing estancias the Jesuits established outside of town, serve as one large historic museum. Nearby Plaza San Martín is graced with a number of cafés and several of its own historically significant buildings. The Cabildo, or Old City Hall, is now an arts center whose various cultural events include a Friday evening tango performance. The eclectic Cathedral of Córdoba next door, known for its angels with Native American faces, was started in 1577 and worked on for more than 200 years in a charming pastiche of styles. A few blocks away is the Museo Histórico Provincial Marqués de Sobre Monte, housed in what was once a private home; dating from 1722, it is the city's oldest residence still standing and an excellent example of Colonial architecture. Stay within the city's historic district by checking into its first design-minded hotel, the 14-room Azur Real Hotel Boutique, set in a 1915 town house just blocks from the main plaza.

La Cañada, a man-made canal lined with oak trees, meanders through town; its walkways and cafés are popular gathering points at night. On weekends, the Feria Artesanal del Paseo de los Artes bustles with handicrafts and antiques vendors.

Entire towns have grown up around the former Jesuit estancias surrounding Córdoba, the oldest of which is Caroya (1616). Alta Gracia, dominated by a Baroque church that is reached by an imposing staircase, is the closest (16 miles southwest); the young Ernesto Che Guevara lived in a house on its outskirts. In early January, visit Jesús María (31 miles north of Córdoba) for the gaucho-themed Festival Nacional de Doma y Folklore. Later that month, nearby Cosquín (32 miles northwest of Córdoba) hosts the Festival Nacional de Folklore, followed by the Cosquín Rock music festival in February. With its polo fields, extensive grounds overlooking the Córdoba Mountains, and spa, the elegant Estancia El Colibrí, a nine–guest room property 20 miles west of Córdoba, will make you feel like you're starring in an Argentine-style Ralph Lauren ad. Along with polo lessons and long rides accompanied by gaucho guides across the 420-acre tract, there's a juicy steak and a glass of Malbec to enjoy at the end of the day.

WHERE: 388 miles/624 km northwest of Buenos Aires. **AZUR REAL:** Tel 54/351-424-7133; www.azurrealhotel.com. *Cost:* from $125. **ESTANCIA EL COLIBRÍ:** Tel 54/352-546-5888; www.estanciaelcolibri.com. *Cost:* from $575 (off-peak), from $725 (peak), inclusive. **BEST TIME:** Jan–Feb for festivals and pleasant summer weather.

Nature's Mightiest Show of Sound and Fury

IGUAZÚ FALLS

Argentina and Brazil

Emerging from the jungle in a mist-covered fury, Iguazú is the world's widest waterfall, so impressive that Eleanor Roosevelt is said to have murmured "poor Niagara" upon witnessing its might. More than 60,000 cubic feet of water per second plunge over 200-foot cliffs, creating 275 separate falls (as many as 350 during rainy season) in a broad horseshoe that forms northern Argentina's natural border with Brazil.

Walkways drenched by Iguazú's spray provide the best encounter, taking travelers through dense tropical jungle and alongside and over the falls. More than 80 percent lie within Argentina, including the most impressive cascade, the U-shaped, 270-foot-high and nearly half-mile-long Garganta del Diablo (Devil's Throat). Exhilarating rafting excursions take you along the Garganta del Diablo canyon and into the watery spray, and to San Martín Island to climb the cliffs and look down onto the water from their precarious edge. Visiting the Brazilian side by bus or ferry is easy and lets you determine whether the view can possibly be better. (Helicopter rides, which launch from here, include special full-moon flights.)

If you long to fall asleep to the thunder of the falls, the pink Colonial-style Hotel das Cataratas in Brazil is your best (and most luxurious) choice. If awakening or dining to an awesome panorama is your pleasure, go for the Sheraton Iguazú Hotel & Spa in Argentina, with rooms and a restaurant, Garganta del Diablo, that overlook the waters. The small Argentine town of Puerto Iguazú, 11 miles from the falls, has a raft of modest, cheaper accommodations. Tours depart from there into the nearby rain forest, where you can see some 400 feathered species, including parrots, toucans, and manakins. To truly experience the luxuriant jungle depths, stay in Argentina's Yacutinga Lodge, 37 miles and worlds away from the falls. Its ten rustic but comfortable lodges blend organically with the leafy surroundings, where you may spot many of the 562 species of butterflies native to the region.

WHERE: 960 miles/1,094 km north of Buenos Aires. **HOTEL DAS CATARATAS:** Tel 55/45-2102-7000; in the U.S., 800-837-9051; www.hoteldascataratas.com. *Cost:* from $405. **SHERATON IGUAZÚ:** Tel 54/37-5749-1800; in the U.S., tel 800-325-3535; www.sheraton.com. *Cost:* rooms with falls view from $245 (off-peak), $335 (peak). **YACUTINGA LODGE:** www.yacutinga.com. *Cost:* 2-night "Yacutinga Experience" from $440 per person, all-inclusive. **BEST TIMES:** Sep–Nov to avoid heat, rain, and crowds; May–Jul for viewing the falls at their most impressive.

The name Iguazú is derived from a Guarani word meaning "great water."

Where Malbec Is King

MENDOZA

Argentina

Rich soil, intense sunlight, and a charmed, high-altitude location at the foot of the snow-capped Andes make Mendoza Province Argentina's premier wine capital. The signature grape is the Malbec, originally brought by the Spaniards 500 years ago and now as emblematic of Argentina as the tango.

Mendoza produced simple table wines until the 1990s, when technological changes and local determination improved the quality. Today, tens of thousands of acres and close to 1,000 bodegas (wineries) throughout the valleys surrounding Mendoza—Lujan de Cuyo, Maipu, and the Uco Valley—are planted with Malbec and other grapes. The best time to experience Mendoza's wine culture is in early March, during the Vendimia, the harvest festival that brings the city of Mendoza alive for a week of parades and beauty pageants that culminate with one young Mendocina selected *Reina Vendimia,* the Harvest Queen.

Mendoza abounds in outdoor adventure, from rafting in the Mendoza River to climbing Mount Aconcagua—at 23,000 feet, the highest peak outside the Himalayas—to skiing at Andean resorts. Much of the activity is concentrated along *los caminos del vino* (the wine roads) that link the dozens of vineyards that are open for visits. Or follow the local stretch of Ruta 40, the country's iconic highway that originates 1,100 miles to the north at Jujuy Province's border with Bolivia and continues through southern Patagonia, traversing some of the continent's most beautiful scenery.

With a prestigious perch over beautiful Plaza Independencia, the Park Hyatt Mendoza offers modern amenities behind its restored 19th-century façade. Its Bar Uvas is a popular meeting point, and its first-rate restaurant, Bistro M, offers elegant Mendozan food with a French accent. Isolation, tranquility, and a view of nothing but mountains and vineyards are the lures at Cavas Wine Lodge, 40 minutes outside of town. Each of the 14 adobe-style villas has a private pool, and there's a spa with treatments that include a Malbec-seed scrub.

To truly experience wine country, head two hours from Mendoza to San Rafael and the historic Finca Los Alamos, a working cattle ranch and viticulture enterprise dating back to 1830. The sprawling white adobe main house was once a retreat for Argentina's literary luminary Jorge Luis Borges.

Dining is unforgettable at Argentine star chef Francis Mallmann's 1884 Restaurant in nearby Godoy Cruz. Located in the manor house of the historic Bodega Escorihuela, the sumptuous restaurant features grilled steak, the perfect partner for the local Malbec. Learn about wine in town at the tasting room Vines of Mendoza, which offers samples of more than 90 wines from this region that locals call La Tierra de Sol y Buen Vino, "the Land of Sun and Good Wine."

WHERE: 600 miles/965 km southwest of Buenos Aires. **PARK HYATT MENDOZA:** Tel 54/261-441-1234; www.mendoza.park.hyatt.com. *Cost:* from $210; dinner $50. **CAVAS WINE LODGE:** Tel 54/261-410-6927; www.cavaswinelodge.com. *Cost:* from $325 (off-peak), from $560 (peak). **FINCA LOS ALAMOS:** Tel 54/2627-442-350; www.fincalosalamos.com. *Cost:* from $250, inclusive. *When:* closed May–Sep. **1884 RESTAURANTE:** Tel 54/261-424-2698; www.1884restaurante.com.ar. *Cost:* dinner $75. **VINES OF MENDOZA:** Tel 54/261-438-1031; www.vinesofmendoza.com. **BEST TIMES:** Feb–Apr and Oct–Dec for nicest weather; late Feb–Mar for the Fiesta Nacional de la Vendimia (harvest festival).

Spellbinding Land of Mountains, Rock, and Ice

GLACIERS NATIONAL PARK

Patagonia, Argentina

Characterized by a barren but beautiful landscape that is pocked by 50 major glaciers and more than 200 lesser ones, Parque Nacional Los Glaciares (Glaciers National Park) seems like another planet. While most glaciers are receding, Perito Moreno—the park's centerpiece, and four times the size of Manhattan—is still growing; its imposing 3-mile-wide wall of ice rises 200 feet above Lake Argentino. You can watch in awe from viewing platforms as icebergs grumble, crack, and calve off the face to plunge into the lake, or you can strap on crampons and walk a surface wrinkled by icy blue crevices and crossed by snowmelt rivers. Mount Fitz Roy looms more than 11,000 feet over Lake Viedma, which anchors the north end of the park. Argentines call it Cerro Chaltén, a mix of Spanish and Tehuelche for "Smoking Mountain," which refers to the cloud ring around its sheer, granite summit. Rising just across the border in Chile and at times visible from the park are the magnificent Torres del Paine peaks (see p. 1023).

Unlike most Patagonian glaciers, which are receding due to global warming, Perito Moreno is growing.

Los Glaciares exemplifies Patagonia, among the world's most sparsely populated areas. Santa Cruz Province, where the park lies, is almost as big as Texas but has a population of only 160,000. But you needn't explore the End of the World under the same harsh conditions that Darwin endured when he visited in the 1830s. The handsome Hostería Alta Vista offers luxury and is 20 miles from El Calafate, the rapidly expanding and relatively charmless gateway to the area. This 155,000-acre working sheep farm, dating to 1910, now offers a seven-room antiques-filled inn, along with stables of horses that let guests explore their inner gaucho. The only hotel within the park, almost touching Perito Moreno, is Los Notros. From every room, you can see—and sometimes hear—the glacier. Or try the luxurious 17-room Eolo, which was built in the style of an old Patagonian estancia in the empty windswept Anita Valley. A 7,400-acre property, it sits an hour outside El Calafate at the foot of a starkly beautiful mountain.

Where: El Calafate is 1,690 miles/2,720 km southwest of Buenos Aires. **Hostería Alta Vista:** Tel 54/2902-499-902; www.hosteria altavista.com.ar. *Cost:* from $475. *When:* closed May–mid-Sep. **Los Notros:** Tel 54/2902-499-510; www.losnotros.com. *Cost:* from $630, all-inclusive. *When:* closed Apr–Sep. **Eolo Lodge:** Tel 54/2902-492-042; www.eolo.com .ar. *Cost:* from $740, all-inclusive (peak), off-peak rates on request. *When:* closed May–mid-Sep. **Best times:** late Nov–early Mar for finest weather; Mar–Apr for fall foliage; Dec for a chance to help shear Alta Vista's 22,000 sheep.

The Switzerland of South America

The Lake District

Patagonia, Argentina

At the wet and wild northwestern edge of Patagonia, the windswept steppes rise into mountain foothills, pushing up against the soaring Andes and their glacial-melt lakes. This skier's dream, 1,000 miles southwest of

Buenos Aires, is the region of Bariloche, named for its main city of San Carlos de Bariloche, and owing its distinctive character to the Swiss and German immigrants who settled here and the Argentine architect Alejandro Bustillo, who designed many of the characteristic gingerbread buildings.

San Carlos de Bariloche (or simply Bariloche) stands on the shores of Lake Nahuel Huapi which sits within the 2-million-acre park of the same name and whose cool, crystalline rivers and lakes offer some of the world's best fly-fishing. Still, most come here to ski, and the place to do it is Cerro Catedral's 50-plus trails. Snowfall averages 16 inches at the base and more than 16 feet at the top, where the drop is nearly 3,400 feet. Ski season is June through October and the crowds are relatively small.

Rustic luxury is the dominant theme of the area's resorts, including Llao Llao, on a hill overlooking the lake. Designed by Bustillo, it's owned by the same family as Buenos Aires's Alvear Palace (see p. 981) and cared for with the same attention to detail. Los Césares, its restaurant, and its roster of amenities are the best in the area. Just beyond the city limits is Villa Huinid, featuring 12 pine cabins with stone fireplaces, 50 country-luxe rooms, many of which overlook the lake, and the Batistin restaurant.

Nahuel Huapi is the most important of the region's lakes.

Take a scenic drive 50 miles north of Bariloche and you'll find Villa La Angostura, a small town on a peninsula jutting into the lake and the place where well-to-do *porteños* (residents of Buenos Aires) build their vacation homes. The aptly named Correntoso ("fast-flowing") Lake and River Hotel sits at the juncture of river and lake, taking full advantage of the incredible views. A former fishing lodge, now newly refined, it is favored by hikers and fly-fishers, but many guests opt instead to relax in the hammam and spa or to enjoy memorable meals on the restaurant's wraparound terrace. About 70 miles farther north is San Martín de los Andes, the low-key and picturesque capital of Neuquén province, which offers many amenities for travelers.

This magnificent Patagonian countryside can be explored while staying at either of two of Argentina's most hospitable estancias, both about an hour's drive east of San Martín. The Estancia Quemquemtreu has just five guest rooms and is set on a 250,000-acre cattle ranch. A private stream and proximity to three of the region's best-stocked rivers make it especially appealing to anglers, but any guest will be enticed by traditional barbecues and wildlife viewing with the Andes's awe-inducing granite peaks as a backdrop. The estancia is also a polo ranch, and in summer months guests can watch some of the country's best players practice and train the 40 resident polo ponies.

For a real cowboy experience, stay at the Estancia Huechahue, a 15,000-acre Anglo-Argentine cattle ranch. Guests can travel on horseback through lake-dotted rolling hills, dense forests, and high ridges where condors nest, and can also participate in rounding up, herding, and branding the livestock. Or they may opt for simply enjoying the day's delicious *asado* (barbeque) lunch.

WHERE: San Carlos de Bariloche is 1,001 miles/1,615 km southwest of Buenos Aires. **LLAO LLAO:** Tel 54/2944-448-530; www.llaollao.com. *Cost:* from $265 (off-peak), from $635 (peak). **VILLA HUINID:** Tel 54/2944-523-600; www.villahuinid.com.ar. *Cost:* from $175. **CORRENTOSO LAKE AND RIVER HOTEL:** Tel 54/2944-1561-9728; www.correntoso.com. *Cost:* $380. **ESTANCIA QUEMQUEMTREU:** Tel 54/2972-424-410; www.quemquemtreu.com. *Cost:* from $500 per person, all-inclusive. **ESTANCIA HUECHAHUE:** Tel 54/2972-491-303; www.huechahue.com. *Cost:* $715, all-inclusive. *When:* closed Jun–Sep. **BEST TIMES:** Dec–Feb for warm weather; Jun–Aug for skiing; Nov–Apr for fishing.

Argentina's Tuscany

CAFAYATE

Salta, Argentina

Manuel Fernando de Aramburu founded the town of Cafayate in 1840, but today's population includes descendants of the Inca, who lived in the area long before that. Once considered an excursion from the colonial city of Salta (see next page), which is 115 miles and a four-hour drive north, Cafayate has become a destination in its own right. The layered red-rock terrain surrounding it, among the country's most striking, is a paradise for hikers and horseback riders. But the true star is the dry and aromatic white wine produced from torrontés grapes, which flourish in the sandy, pink-and-tan hills of the area. The climate, elevation, and constant sunshine give the grapes their distinctive color, flavor, and sugar content.

The Quebrada de las Conchas (Gorge of the Shells) took its name from the shell fossils found here.

The town hit the international radar in 2005 with the opening of the luxurious spa resort Patios de Cafayate, on the Bodega (winery) El Esteco. The 1892 main house, which encompasses flowering courtyards, is full of antiques and artwork recalling the region's rustic history. You can drink the local wine—even bathe in it, with full-body immersion vinotherapy—or experience massage treatments using grape seeds and pulp. Just outside the center of Cafayate you'll find the simple, 12-room Viñas de Cafayate. It allows guests to take in magnificent views of the surrounding mountains and features a pool set amid the grapevines.

North of Cafayate along Ruta 40, Argentina's answer to U.S. Route 66, lie portions of the beautiful Calchaquíes Valley, whose landscape ranges from dense vegetation to multicolored desert reminiscent of the United States' Southwest. Within the valley, the town of Cachi, ancient home of the Chicoanas Indians, boasts a cactus-wood–roofed church and one of the region's finest archaeological museums as well as several shops featuring the work of local artisans. The valley's biggest surprise is nearby Colomé, a vast (100,000-acre) high-tech winery and nine-suite luxury lodge, complete with its own helipad and riveting mountain scenery. The estancia, founded in 1831 but now owned by the Swiss master vintner Family Hess (their first vineyards opened in the Napa Valley), has some of the highest-altitude vineyards in the world. The James Turrell Museum opened on the property in 2009 and houses works by the celebrated California-born artist, famous for exploring the relationship of light and space.

WHERE: 797 miles/1,283 km northwest of Buenos Aires. **PATIOS DE CAFAYATE:** Tel 54/3868-421-747; www.patiosdecafayate.com. *Cost:* from $300. **VIÑAS DE CAFAYATE:** Tel 54/3868-422-272; www.cafayatewineresort.com. *Cost:* from $135. **BODEGA COLOMÉ:** Tel 54/3868-494-044; www.bodegacolome.com. *Cost:* from $300 (off-peak), from $390 (peak). **BEST TIMES:** Feb for Serenade to Cafayate Folklore Festival; Feb–Apr for grape harvest; Nov for Torrontés Wine Festival.

Romantic Respite and a Breathtaking Train Ride

SALTA

Salta, Argentina

Argentines call it Salta la Linda: "Salta the Pretty." Set in the distinctive and incredibly varied landscape of Argentina's northwest, the country's best-preserved colonial city is uniquely proud of both its Spanish and indigenous heritage. Its heart beats in the charming café-ringed Plaza de Nueve de Julio, which dates from the city's founding in 1582 and is flanked by the pink Salta Cathedral and the former Cabildo (City Hall), the city's oldest government building. The new and fascinating Museo de Arqueología de Alta Montaña (Museum of High Altitude Archaeology), or MAAM, houses exhibits on pre-Columbian culture, the highlight of which are three mummified, 500-year-old Inca children, found frozen atop an Andean peak and believed to be sacrifices to the Inca gods. In Salta, food (the city is known for its savory empanadas) and music come together at atmospheric *peñas folkloricos,* or folk clubs, such as El Boliche Balderrama or the Cason del Molino where the zamba (Salta's answer to the samba) and chacarera rhythms are contagious.

Salta's stunning countryside is dotted with pre-Columbian ruins, the vineyards that produce its well-known wines, and artisan villages, and is characterized by its deep, mineral-streaked, polychromatic *quebradas* (gorges) carved by rivers running down the nearby snow-draped Andes. (You'll witness more of this spectacular landscape if you keep going 4 hours south across spectacular high-desert plateau to Cafayate; see previous page.) For an unforgettable view of this terrain along the Chilean border, board the seasonal El Tren a las Nubes (Train to the Clouds), one of the highest railroads in the world. The highlight of this 15-hour, 269-mile round-trip adventure is the 200-foot-high viaduct over a yawning chasm that you'll glimpse just before the train turns around at an old Indian mining town 13,800 feet above sea level.

While in Salta, stay at Legado Mítico, an 11-room treasure of a hotel housed in a former private residence a 5-minute walk from the main square. Or head 15 minutes south of town to House of Jasmines, a 300-acre ranch where guests enjoy rustic luxury and lounging by the pool or in the small spa, as well as horseback riding along the Arenales River. About an hour northeast of Salta, the 11,000-acre El Bordo de las Lanzas was the home of Martín Miguel de Güemes, who fought with gauchos against Spanish royalists in the early 1800s. Today it is run as an estancia by the gregarious Arias family.

WHERE: 787 miles/1,265 km northwest of Buenos Aires. **MAAM:** Tel 54/387-437-0499; www.maam.culturasalta.gov.ar. **EL TREN A LAS NUBES:** Tel 54/387-4223-033; www.trenalasnubes.com.ar. *Cost:* $160, includes lunch. *When:* closed Dec–Mar. **LEGADO MÍTICO:** Tel 54/387-4228-786; www.legadomitico.com. *Cost:* from $155 (off-peak), from $210 (peak). **HOUSE OF JASMINES:** Tel 54/387-497-2002; www.houseofjasmines.com. *Cost:* from $215. **ESTANCIA EL BORDO DE LAS LANZAS:** Tel 54/387-4903-070; www.turismoelbordo.com.ar. *Cost:* $400, all-inclusive. **BEST TIMES:** Apr–Jun and Aug–Nov to avoid the rainy season and the crowds; Apr for Culture Festival; Jun for Semana Salta (Salta Week), a popular gaucho festival; Jun 17 for Güemes Gauchos Festival.

Southernmost City in the World

Ushuaia and Tierra del Fuego

Argentina

Nothing feels more like the end of the earth than Ushuaia, the final stop on the Pan American Highway and the city closest to the South Pole. Situated at a latitude of 55 degrees south and squeezed between the Beagle Channel and the Andes, this city is the starting point for most Antarctic expeditions (see p. 1053). Yet Ushuaia, which means "bay looking to the west" in the language of the Yámana Indians who once populated the area, supports a population of 70,000 hardy souls and is a marvelous underexplored destination in its own right. It is the capital of Tierra del Fuego province, comprised of the large Isla Grande and an archipelago of hundreds of lesser islands that are shared by Chile and Argentina. The Spanish called this area Tierra del Fuego (Land of the Fire) after seeing the flames the Yámana kept constantly burning to keep warm.

Nature is the star attraction here—mountains, forested plains, glaciar Martial, and the rocky, frozen coastline along with birds such as the rare Andean condor, black-browed albatrosses, and Magellanic penguins. This beauty—and the 18 hours of summer sunlight—was once the sole consolation for Argentina's most hardened prisoners, first sent here in the late 1800s. The old jail is now the Museo Maritimo; today's rickety Tren del Fin del Mundo (Train of the End of the World), which makes a picturesque 40-minute ride into the Parque Nacional Tierra del Fuego, is a replica of the one used to shuttle them to their hard labor of chopping down the now-protected lenga trees.

The frontier town's dining and lodging options surpass expectations. Las Hayas, located on the road to the glaciar Martial, affords sweeping views of the town and surrounding bay. Closer to town, the hilltop Tierra de Leyendas is a cozy hostería with just five stylish rooms and a small but top-notch restaurant with large windows facing the Beagle Channel. Staying here will also put you close to Kaupe, a restaurant famed for its king crab and its stunning views.

Many visitors use Cruceros Australis for 4-day cruises from Punta Arenas (see p. 1024), the main city at the icy end of Chilean Patagonia. Comfortable, 130-person passenger ships sail between icebergs and Zodiac boats make landings that allow for visits with penguins, sea lions, and other wildlife in the Beagle and Murray channels. The ships also stop at Cape Horn National Park, the last

The Beagle Channel is named for the ship Charles Darwin sailed on during his exploration of the region.

piece of land before the open ocean and Antarctica, 600 miles away.

Where: 1,473 miles/2,372 km south of Buenos Aires. **Las Hayas:** Tel 54/2901-430-710; www.lashayas.com.ar. *Cost:* from $300. **Tierra de Leyendas:** Tel 54/2901-443-565; www.tierradeleyendas.com.ar. *Cost:* from $125 (off-peak), from $189 (peak). **Kaupe:** Tel 54/2901-422-704; www.kaupe.com.ar. *Cost:* dinner $50. **Cruceros Australis:** In the U.S., tel 877-678-3772 or 305-695-9618; www.australis.com. *Cost:* 4-day cruises from $1,500 (off-peak), from $1,895 (peak), all-inclusive. *When:* Jan–Apr and Sep–Dec. **Best time:** Nov–Mar (austral summer), with temperatures in the 50s and waterways clearest of ice.

Subantarctic Galápagos

Falkland Islands

British Overseas Territory

The British-administered Falkland Islands, called the Islas Malvinas by Argentines, may currently be most renowned for being the point of contention that sparked a war in 1982. Yet these nearly 800 tiny islands, still part of the British empire, are also a common stopping-off point for expeditions to South Georgia Island and Antarctica (see pp. 1054 and 1053). They are home to more sheep than people (650,000 vs. 3,000), though potential offshore oil reserves, not woolen sweaters, might have been the real reason for the war.

A British character is pervasive in the tidy capital "city" of Stanley—pubs and teatime are commonplace. It is dominated by a quaint Victorian stone church and a gilded whalebone arch and located on the hauntingly barren island of East Falkland, where two-thirds of the island chain's people live. Independent tourists are few (the majority are cruise-ship day-trippers), and most choose to stay at the cozy Malvina House Hotel, near the town's cathedral.

The Falklands are famous for their biological diversity—they're known as the cold Galapágos—and in particular for their five species of friendly penguins. Like their Pacific counterparts, the animals are utterly unafraid of visitors. Three-foot-tall gold-throated king penguins hold court on bleakly beautiful Volunteer Beach, a 2-hour drive from Stanley, while gentoo and Magellanic penguins roam Leopard Beach on Carcass Island, in the northwest of the archipelago. Along with some 180 other bird species (and the world's largest colonies of the huge black-browed albatross), they make this remote land a bird-watcher's wonderland.

For even more wildlife, head to Sea Lion Island, where aptly named elephant seals and sea lions swim ashore while killer whales circle in pursuit. The 12-room Sea Lion Lodge is both the Falklands' best hotel and the world's southernmost British one. From here, nothing but cold ocean separates you from the Antarctic.

Where: 1,200 miles/1,931 km southwest of Buenos Aires. **How:** U.S.-based Ladatco Tours offers 14-day wildlife tours. Tel 800-327-6162 or 305-854-8222; www.ladatco.com. *Cost:* from $10,900, all-inclusive. *When:* Oct–Mar. **Malvina House Hotel:** Tel 500/21355; www.malvinahousehotel.com. *Cost:* from $95. **Sea Lion Lodge:** Tel 500/32004; www.sealionisland.com. *Cost:* $145 (off-peak), $230 (peak). *When:* closed May–Aug. **Best times:** Oct–Feb is austral summer, with temperatures in the mid-50s and optimal bird-watching; Sep–Apr for best animal-watching.

A Pilgrimage City on the Banks of a Sacred Lake

Copacabana and Lake Titicaca

Bolivia

This is the original Copacabana—not the beach in Rio de Janeiro (see p. 1013), but a sunny little town up in the Andes, blooming with red-tile roofs and set on the southern shores of Lake Titicaca. One of South America's most important Roman Catholic pilgrimage sites, Copacabana is best known for its 400-year-old Moorish-style basilica, which houses the shrine of the Dark Virgin of the Lake, Bolivia's beloved patron saint. The famous statue has been believed to be responsible for a spate of miracles since being carved by the native artist Tito Yupanqui in 1592. Foremost among the town's various feast days in her honor is the Fiesta de la Virgen de la Candelaria, celebrated the first two days of February, when Aymara dancers arrive from all over Bolivia and Peru. Holy Week soon follows, bringing throngs of the faithful who make the multiday walk from La Paz to pay homage to the Virgin, with a candlelight procession on Good Friday.

For the best views of the lake, hike to the replica of Calvary Hill, El Cerro Calvario, and try to plan your trek for sunset. Back in town the charming colonial Hotel Rosario del Lago stands a few blocks from the main plaza and is popular for its restaurant, Kota Kahuana (View of the Lake), which specializes in fresh Titicaca trout.

Boats leave regularly from Copacabana to some of the 36 mostly uninhabited islands that float on Lake Titicaca, considered the cradle of the Inca civilization, the "womb of the world." Isla del Sol (Island of the Sun) and Isla de la Luna (Island of the Moon) were sacred to the Incas, whose ancient temples and ruins are found on these islands. The largest, the tranquil and sparsely inhabited Isla del Sol, is said to be the birthplace of the Inca sun god—its terraced, hilly terrain and incredible views overlooking the lake to the Cordillera Real mountains are what draw visitors today. You can drink in the same vista from most of the 20 handsomely furnished rooms at the Posada del Inca, housed in a former hillside hacienda, then have the staff arrange an excursion to one of the lake's numerous reed islands, such as Uros-Irutos, created by the Aymara Indians who, while escaping invasion by the Incan armies, wove giant spongey refuges from the lake's *totora* reeds.

Copacabana's basilica stands on the site of a long-gone Inca temple.

The deep, crystalline blue lake is accessible from both Bolivia and bordering Peru, via the port town of Puno (see p. 1046). While most visitors head out to enjoy its attractions, don't overlook the most popular land excursion. Tiwanaku (Tiahuanaco in Spanish), known as the City of the Gods, is the ancient capital of a pre-Incan civilization believed to date back to 500 B.C. Its Sun Portal might have been part of a calendar, and monumental sculptures abound, whose purposes still baffle archaeologists.

WHERE: Copacabana is 93 miles/150 km northwest of La Paz. **HOTEL ROSARIO DEL LAGO:** Tel 591/2-862-2141; www.hotelrosario.com/lago. *Cost:* $60; dinner $12. **POSADA DEL INCA:** Tel 591/2-233-7533; www.titicaca.com. *Cost:* $85. **HOW:** Crillon Tours offers a variety of Titicaca tours. Tel 591/2-233-7533; in the U.S., 888-848-4323; www.titicaca.com. *Cost:* 2-day all-inclusive tour $300 per person. Originates in La Paz. **BEST TIMES:** May–Dec is dry season; early Feb for festivals; Semana Santa (the week before Easter).

Fascinating and Peculiar Finds

WITCHCRAFT MARKET

La Paz, Bolivia

La Paz's daily Witchcraft Market, known locally as either the Mercado de Hechicería ("sorcery") or Mercado de Brujas ("witches"), is a fascinating place, brimming with everything from herbal tea infusions to homeopathic folk cures as old as the Andes themselves. Coca leaves are ubiquitous—the rest of the world might find the remedy controversial, but for those suffering from *soroche*, or altitude sickness, in the world's highest capital (11,913 feet above sea level), a tea made from the crushed leaves is a local cure. Other peculiar offerings include fertility and shamanic figurines, dried toucan beaks, snake skins, slabs of llama lard to be burned as offerings to the gods, amulets to guarantee a long and happy sex life, and even llama fetuses, thought to bring good luck and often buried in backyards or in the cornerstones of new buildings as a *cha'lla* (offering) to the earth goddess Pachamama.

Ingredients that can be used in a variety of spells are available at the market.

If you believe the locals, the market is where to find the best ways to keep you on the good side of Pachamama and the dozens of other spirits who oversee the fates of mortals. Given the growing number of gringo curiosity seekers, booths selling colorful alpaca sweaters and woven textiles do a brisk business too. But the proud, indigenous women, known as *cholas*, sit among their witchcraft goods like queens. You'll recognize them by their custom of wearing two braids fastened behind them and bowler hats adopted from the Europeans generations ago. With as much as 60 percent of the population of pure Indian blood, La Paz is home to more indigenous people than any other Latin American capital. Alongside Spanish, you'll find that Aymara and Quechua, ancient languages predating the conquest, are freely spoken here.

BEST TIME: Apr–Oct, with Jun and Jul the least rainy months.

Overlooked and Untrammeled in the Amazon Rain Forest

MADIDI NATIONAL PARK

Bolivia

With its towering mountains and the world's highest capital, Bolivia has deservedly been nicknamed "the Tibet of the Andes," yet nearly two-thirds of the country is covered in Amazon jungle. One of the best places to experience it is in Parque Nacional Madidi, a protected ecosystem encompassing nearly 5 million acres of dense forest that is accessible via the jungle town of Rurrenabaque, a 1-hour flight from La Paz.

The Beni River meanders through the park, ultimately connecting to other tributaries that feed into the mighty Amazon. Along its banks you might spot jaguars and howler monkeys, along with pink river dolphins that frolic alongside the small tour boats. Nearly 10 percent of the world's species of flora and fauna lie within the park's borders, and breaking this number down leads to some unbelievable statistics: Nearly 44 percent of all American mammal species live here, along with 38 percent of all known tropical amphibian species and 10 percent of all known bird species. The jungles of Bolivia might be off the radar to most tourists, but in many ways they outdo larger, more famous destinations such as those in Brazil (see p. 1000). Throughout the preserve, Indian tribes exist much as they have for thousands of years, many still hunting with bows and arrows.

The perfect place from which to experience it all is the Chalalán Ecolodge. The oldest and most famous of the country's eco-lodges, it is owned and run by the Quechua-Tacana Indians and is accessible from Rurrenabaque by motorized dugout canoe, a manner of jungle transport not far removed from that used by the first Europeans to arrive here. Fourteen well-marked nature trails surrounding the rustic, riverside lodge allow you to trek through the jungle at your leisure, on your own or with the lodge's guides. Return to rest in hammocks beneath the canopy as night falls and the sounds of the forest envelop you.

WHERE: Rurrenabaque is 255 miles/410 km north of La Paz. **CHALALÁN ECOLODGE:** Tel 591/2-231-1451; www.chalalan.com. *Cost:* 4-day stays $350 per person, all inclusive. **HOW:** America Tours offers 4- and 5-day customized tours of Madidi, originating in La Paz. Tel 591/2-237-4204; www.america-ecotours.com. **BEST TIME:** Apr–Oct for dry season.

A White City and Former Capital

SUCRE

Bolivia

Proud, genteel Sucre is Bolivia's original capital and one of the first Latin American cities to declare independence from Spain. A prestigious and wealthy place that attracted great artists and architects, it eventually lost

San Felipe Neri Convent, whitewashed to match the rest of Sucre's Colonial buildings, has a lovely view of the city.

its status as the seat of government to La Paz in 1898. Though it has just 250,000 residents, it still claims position as judicial capital and its reputation as the country's prettiest city.

Sucre, quite intentionally, is Bolivia's White City; by government decree, all buildings in its historical heart must be whitewashed every year, creating beautiful contrasts with the red roof tiles that seem to cascade down the gentle hills. Sucre also retains vestiges of its colonial heritage: With its many descendants of the Spanish colonists from centuries ago, and its wealth of centuries-old architecture, it has a palpable European feel.

The city was founded as Ciudad de la Plata de la Nueva Toledo (Silver City of New Toledo) by Pedro Anzures in 1538. Twenty-one years later, construction began on La Catedral Metropolitan, which is located near the tree-lined Plaza 25 de Mayo, one of South America's largest and loveliest city squares. Built over the course of a century and a half, it is one of the best examples of architecture from this period and is famous for its Virgin of Guadelupe, Sucre's patron saint, dripping with jewels left by the faithful. A small museum holds colonial art and religious objects made from silver mined in nearby Potosí. The thoughtfully organized Museo de Arte Indígena, or Textile Museum, offers insights into the region's ancient crafts and culture.

El Hostal de Su Merced, in a former home dating from the 1700s, is the city's finest inn when it comes to charm and character. The 16 small rooms are full of antiques, and the rooftop terrace has stunning views of the cathedral and city. Nearby is Hotel La Posada, where several of the 24 rooms open onto a garden courtyard, and the popular restaurant is an ideal choice for sampling local specialties. A pleasant year-round climate means almost any time is good to visit Sucre. Day trips include one to the busy Tarabuco Sunday market (30 miles east), one of the country's best, where indigenous women wearing coin-festooned hats sell their wares.

Where: 460 miles/740 km southeast of La Paz. **El Hostal de Su Merced:** Tel 591/4-644-2706; www.desumerced.com. *Cost:* $55. **Hotel La Posada:** Tel 591/4-646-0101; www.hotellaposada.com.bo. *Cost:* from $50; dinner $10. **Best times:** Jan, Jun, and Sep for best weather; 3rd Sun in Mar for Tarabuco's traditional Pujllay festival; Sep 8 for Fiesta de la Virgen de Guadalupe.

An Eerie Sea of Salt in the Altiplano

Uyuni Salt Flat

Bolivia

The world's highest and largest salt flat, and the only remnant of a prehistoric salt lake that once covered much of Bolivia, the Salar de Uyuni feels like another planet. The white expanse, lying 11,975 feet above sea level, is crystalline and vast, punctuated by freshwater lakes that glow like emeralds and sapphires, fed by copper deposits filtering up through the ground. Just as brilliant are the flocks of pink flamingos that feast on the red algae that grows in the scattered water deposits. A highlight of the region is the Sol de la Mañana, an area of geysers, fumaroles, and patches of boiling mud. It is best seen in the magical light of sunrise.

During the dry season, it's easy to cross the expanses in 4WD vehicles. And during the rainy season, the area is transformed into a majestic wonderland as floods convert the flats into a giant mirror, reflecting an almost disorienting panorama of the surrounding volcanic mountains of nearby Sajama National Park against the vastness of sky. Spending time here requires some fortitude: Salar de Uyuni can be intensely cold, especially at night, even in the summer months, and salt-flat crossings are rough, as there are no real roads in the area, so hiring an experienced tour operator is a must. Many of those based in the southwest corner of Bolivia's Altiplano can organize trips that continue over the border into the Atacama Desert of Chile (see p. 1026).

Not surprisingly, accommodations here are basic. The most unusual place to stay is the Hotel Luna Salada (Salty Moon Hotel). Much of it is made of salt, from the beds to the floors and tables. And every room has a fantastic view of the flats.

WHERE: 260 miles/402 km south of La Paz. **HOTEL LUNA SALADA:** Tel 591/4-453-0672; www.lunasaladahotel.com.bo. *Cost:* $110. **HOW:** Crillon Tours leads 3-day trips. Tel 591/22-337-533; in the U.S., 888-848-4323; www.titicaca.com. *Cost:* from $660, all-inclusive. Originates in La Paz. **BEST TIMES:** Nov–Dec for driest, warmest climate; Jan–Mar to view in the rain.

The Mother of All Rain Forests

BRAZILIAN AMAZON

Amazonas, Brazil

The vast kingdom of the Amazon, known as Amazonia, stretches across nine South American nations. At 1.4 billion acres it is the largest and densest rain forest on earth, roughly the size of the contiguous United States, and contains over 1,000 bird species, 300-plus mammal species, and roughly 45,000 species of plants. Freshwater dolphins, manatees, jaguars, macaws, toucans, and squirrel monkeys are just a few examples of Amazonia's incredibly varied wildlife. And the statistics associated with the water that runs through it, once known as "the River Sea," are just as staggering. As it gathers strength from more than 1,000 tributaries, the Amazon's volume becomes ten times greater than that of the Mississippi and is responsible for one-fifth of all the water that pours into the world's oceans. The area claimed by Brazil comprises 60 percent of this hot, steamy region, with coastal Belém (see p. 1009), at the mouth of the great river, and Manaus, in the heart of Amazonia and accessible only by air, the popular starting points for exploring it. (Other common entry points to the Amazon are Iquitos, in northern Peru, see p. 1037; Ecuador's El Oriente, see p. 1034; and Parque Nacional Madidi in Bolivia, see p. 998.)

Manaus is home to the famed Teatro Amazonas, a Belle Époque opera house built in 1896 at the height of the rubber boom. Just as historic are the corridors of the century-old Mercado Adolfo Lisboa, an iron-and-glass replica of the now-defunct market hall in Les Halles, Paris. It brims with the region's bounty of fresh fish (including piranha), fruits (like the sweet/sour bacuri), and vegetables as well as ancient herbal remedies used by the river communities for countless ailments. Boats leave Manaus to visit the Encontro de Águas (Meeting of the Waters), where two tributaries—the dark waters of the Rio Negro and those of the muddy Rio Solimões—meet to form the Amazon. (Peru, where the Ucayali and Marañón rivers join and also form the Amazon, claims to be the great river's birthplace as well.)

Human destruction of the area continues, but there are still many ways to experience the Brazilian Amazon. Hotel Tropical is popular for its convenient location on the shores of the Rio Negro, 10 miles from Manaus. A more enlightening experience awaits deeper in the jungle at the Pousada Uakari, which is affiliated with the Mamirauá Institute's pioneering conservation project. Guests stay in thatch-roofed cabins on rafts anchored on the river within the Mamirauá Reserve. The 18-suite Anavilhanas Lodge, a study in minimalist jungle décor, is set in the eponymous riverine archipelago—with 400 mostly deserted islands, it is the largest in the world. Another way to explore the river is via Amazon Clipper Premium's expeditions. Air-conditioned, old-style riverboats carry 18–32 passengers who can watch for pink dolphins at Janauaca Lake, fish for piranha, and canoe into the lesser tributaries.

One of the longest rivers in the world, the Amazon winds through its namesake rain forest.

The biggest festival in the region is Boi Bumba, as eagerly awaited as Carnaval is in Rio (see p. 1012); revelers come from all parts for music, theater, and dancing. It takes place in late June in Parintins, a 1-hour flight or 10-hour boat ride from Manaus.

WHERE: Manaus is 1,666 miles/2,681 km northwest of São Paulo. **HOTEL TROPICAL:** Tel 55/92-3656-1246; www.tropicalmanaus.com.br. *Cost:* from $195. **MAMIRAUÁ/POUSADA UAKARI:** Tel 55/97-3343-4160; www.uakarilodge.com.br. *Cost:* 3-night stay from $760 per person, all-inclusive with round-trip transfer to/from Tefé airport. **ANAVILHANAS LODGE:** Tel 55/92-3622-8996; www.anavilhanaslodge.com. *Cost:* 2-night package from $850 per person, all-inclusive with transfer to/from Manaus. **AMAZON CLIPPER:** Tel 55/92-3656-1246; www.amazonclipper.com.br. *Cost:* 3-day cruise from $810, all-inclusive, with transfer to/from Manaus. **BEST TIMES:** Jul–Nov for dry season; late Apr–May for Festival Amazonas de Ópera in Manaus; late Jun for Boi Bumba.

Hidden Corners of the Wild Cocoa Coast

ITACARÉ

Bahia, Brazil

The small town of Itacaré has the best waves in northeastern Brazil, so it's no coincidence that surfers were among the first travelers to discover this sun-drenched destination in the 1970s. They kept it off the radar until the end of the 1990s, when the road linking the village to Ilhéus, to the south, was paved, securing Itacaré's role as an eco hot spot on what is called Bahia's Cocoa Coast.

Vacationers of all ages looking to improve their wave-riding skills (or those trying it for the first time) enroll at the EasyDrop Surf School, where programs range from single-day lessons to a surf camp that includes stays in beachfront pousadas. Visitors may also take classes in yoga, Portuguese, rappelling, and tree climbing, and can trek through the Mata Atlântica, an unspoiled forest ecosystem full of waterfalls and rare tropical flora and fauna. Pathways meander through the rain forest–covered hills to many of Itacaré's coveted outer beaches.

These days, more affluent travelers have been showing up, and they invariably find their way to the low-profile Txai Resort, 20 minutes outside town. On the site of a former 6,000-acre coconut plantation, Txai (pronounced chai, like the tea) consists of breezy, luxuriously simple bungalows that are tiered up the jungly hillside overlooking Itacarezinho beach. Add in multiple swimming pools and the hilltop Shamash spa, and it's easy to see why most guests spend their days moving from bed to pool to lunch to beach.

Ilhéus, 40 miles to the south, was built on the wealth of the cocoa trade, but is better known as the hometown of Jorge Amado, who immortalized the region in his ribald and comical tales of Bahian life in such novels as *Gabriela, Cravo e Canela* (*Gabriela, Clove and Cinnamon*).

WHERE: 273 miles/440 km south of Salvador. **EASYDROP SURF SCHOOL:** Tel 55/73-3251-3065; www.easydrop.com. *Cost:* from $600 for a 4-day surfing course. **TXAI RESORT:** Tel 55/78-3634-6936; www.txairesort.com.br. *Cost:* from $695 (off-peak), from $770 (peak). **BEST TIMES:** Sep–Apr for nicest weather. In Ilhéus: early Jan for Gincana da Pesca, a fishing event; mid-Jan for Festa de São Sebastião street festival; Apr 23 for Festa de São Jorge, a religious ceremony that combines Catholic and Afro-Brazilian traditions.

Surfers find powerful waves at the protected São José beach.

Proud Heart and Soul of an Afro-Brazilian City

CIDADE ALTA

Salvador da Bahia, Brazil

The colorful Pelourinho district, architectural jewel of this former capital's hilltop Cidade Alta (Upper City), has been restored and transformed into the cultural heart of a city long famous for its rich Afro-Brazilian heritage.

In the 18th century, sugarcane as well as gold and diamonds from interior mines brought enormous riches here, as evidenced by the gold-drenched Baroque churches in the city's Colonial center. These outstanding religious landmarks are clustered in the

Pelourinho (pillory) district—one of many reminders of the city's historical and emotional ties to Africa. More than 4 million slaves were brought to Brazil from Africa (by contrast, about 600,000 were brought to the United States).

Pelourinho was home to Salvador's affluent European descendants until the beginning of the 20th century, when it descended into squalor and physical collapse. With a massive restoration that began in 1992, the district is now the haunt of poets and artists as well as a showplace for Bahian craftsmanship. Landmark buildings in Easter-egg colors now house museums, art galleries, cafés, and restaurants.

Largo do Pelourinho, a small plaza commemorating the day in 1888 when Princess Isabel signed the decree that ended slavery, boasts lovely Colonial architecture and nightly music on public stages. Make sure to visit Terreiro de Jesus, the historic and beautiful main square surrounded by four polychrome churches. Dominating the square is the 17th-century Catedral Basílica, an eclectic mix of Neoclassical, Baroque, and Rococo styles, flanked by the 1808 Faculdade de Medicina building and the excellent Museu Afro-Brasileiro da Bahia, which documents the evolution of Afro-Brazilian culture.

The best time to visit the elaborately Baroque São Francisco complex—two churches and a convent built between 1686 and 1750—is on Tuesday, when a lively street party follows the 6 P.M. mass. Also on Tuesdays, the steps of the Igreja do Santíssimo Sacramento do Passo fill with performing musicians.

Some of Salvador's most entertaining performances are the gracefully competitive acrobatics of capoeira, a martial art from the state of Bahia that is as much about music and dance as about combat. You can see it weekly at Mestre Bimba, a local capoeira school.

Like its religious and cultural traditions, Salvador's cuisine is a mélange of African, indigenous, and European elements. Coconut, cassava, peppers, and fresh seafood are staples at Casa da Gamboa, a longtime favorite.

Colonial buildings date back to when Salvador de Bahia served as Brazil's first capital, from 1549 to 1763.

Flavorful Bahian dishes (like *moquecas*, or seafood stews) and Italian-influenced ones highlight the menu at the upscale Jardim das Delicias, set in an antiques-laden dining room with a lovely bougainvillea-shaded courtyard. Traditional cuisine, such as *acarajé*—deep-fried bean cakes—is plentiful at the souklike Feira São Joaquim, the city's oldest and biggest daily market. A short cab ride away is Trapiche Adelaide, a contemporary restaurant where Italian, French, and Bahian cuisine come deliciously together on a pier overlooking the island-studded Bay of All Saints.

Afterward, check in at the Convento do Carmo just steps away from the Igreja da Ordem Terceira do Carmo, a Carmelite church built in 1636 on a dramatic hilltop location and refashioned with Neoclassical details following a fire in 1786. Dating to 1586, the Convento is an atmospheric hotel and restaurant that welcomes guests with its luxurious ambience. At the charming Solar dos Deuses, each of the nine rooms is named after one of the Afro-Brazilian gods, called *orixas*, and many of the rooms overlook the Church of São Francisco. Another lodging option with architectural character is the Hotel Catharina Paraguaçu in Rio Vermello, 15 minutes away. A pink, art-filled, 30-room Colonial mansion, it has lovely gardens and rooftop views of the beach.

WHERE: 749 miles/1,206 km northeast of Rio. **MUSEU AFRO-BRASILEIRO:** Tel 55/71-3283-5540; www.ceao.ufba.br/mafro/. **MESTRE BIMBA:** Tel 55/71-3322-0639; www.capoeira

mestrebimba.com.br. **Casa da Gamboa:** Tel 55/71-336-1549; www.casadagamboa.com. *Cost:* lunch $18. **Jardim das Delicias:** Tel 55/71-3321-1449. *Cost:* dinner $12. **Trapiche Adelaide:** Tel 55/71-3326-2211; wwww.trapicheadelaide.com.br. *Cost:* dinner $20. **Pestana Convento do Carmo:** Tel 55/71-3327-8400; www.pestana.com. *Cost:* from $430. **Solar dos Deuses:** Tel 55/71-3320-3251; www.solardosdeuses.com.br. *Cost:* from $80 (off-peak), $160 (peak). **Hotel Catharina Paraguaçu:** Tel 55/71-247-1488; www.hotelcatharinaparaguacu.com.br. *Cost:* from $140. **Best times:** Dec–Mar is peak season, although sunny weather year-round makes the off-peak Jun–Sep equally attractive.

Bahia's Special Heritage

The Festivals of Salvador

Salvador da Bahia, Brazil

Rio's Carnaval is a carnal, seething, pulsating extravaganza that attracts all the notoriety (see p. 1012), but these days many travelers are heading north to Salvador da Bahia for an authentic, more participatory, and no less indefatigable pre-Lenten blowout. The people of Bahia are known as the most festive and musical of their countrymen, and Rio's samba is replaced here by African-based *axé* music played on *trio eléctricos* (motorized floats) that make their way along various parade routes all across town. Salvador has the highest percentage of people of African descent of any large city outside Africa, and elements from both Portuguese Catholicism and the Afro-Brazilian Candomblé religion come together during this feverish, unending street party that lasts a full seven days.

Drummers perform in the city's squares year-round.

Preparations start months in advance; several *blocos* (bands) stage rehearsals open to the public, making it easy for off-season visitors to absorb some of the myth and magic (for example, the prominent *bloco afro* called Ilê Aiyê welcomes visitors to its rehearsals, which begin as early as November). Founded in 1979 as a recreational organization for residents of the neighborhood, Olodum is Salvador's most innovative Carnaval percussion group. It stages weekly public practices at Casa do Olodum for those who can't make it during Carnaval season.

With more than 20 festivals and processions each year, Salvador has much more than Carnaval on offer, especially in December, January, and February. Candomblé is fervently practiced here, yet 70 percent of the population is Catholic. On December 4, worshippers join the procession through the Pelourinho neighborhood to the sound of sirens and live music, in honor of Santa Bárbara, who is also known as Iansa, the Candomblé goddess of the winds. The Festa de Nosso Senhor dos Navegantes takes place on New Year's Eve, with a maritime procession and beachside revelry on Praia da Boa Viagem. Lavagem da Igreja do Bonfim, an 8-day celebration in mid-January, brings African hymns to Salvador's most famous church, the 18th-century Nosso Senhor do Bonfim, as local women perform a ritual washing (*lavagem*) of the steps to symbolically cleanse sins away. Follow the faithful inside to the Sala dos Milagros (Room of Miracles), where worshippers hang haunting casts and replicas of body parts as thanks for miraculous healings. Then, on February 2, Iemanjá, the Afro-Brazilian protectress and goddess of the sea (a counterpart to the Virgin Mary), is honored with the massive Festa de Iemanjá.

CASA DO OLODUM: Tel 55/71-3321-4154; www.olodum.com.br. **BEST TIMES:** Carnaval is in Feb or Mar, culminating the 7 days prior to Ash Wednesday; Aug or Sep for Festin Bahia, which celebrates international music; Dec–Feb for more festivals.

A Seaside Town Where Simplicity Rules

TRANCOSO

Bahia, Brazil

Much more than just a gateway to the beautiful, untouched beaches for which southern Bahia is known, the laid-back village of Trancoso represents a way of life. Visitors and locals coexist in harmony, whether beachside or during long, lively nights spent listening to reggae and world-music-spinning DJs. There are few ATMs and no traffic lights, just dusk-to-dawn parties along magnificent stretches of virgin sand, a cluster of rustic-meets-stylish inns, and plenty of high-profile types who arrive by helicopter, willing to pay big to live an unpretentious beach-getaway dream.

The heart of the village is the blufftop Quadrado de Trancoso, an expansive, grassy town square anchored by a whitewashed 17th-century church, the second oldest in Brazil, and ringed by colorful old one-story houses that have been converted into pousadas, boutiques, and restaurants. The Quadrado overlooks the Praia dos Nativos, a 2-mile stretch of sand that is the town's main beach, where visitors sip beer and passion-fruit caipirinhas at open-air cafés. For more time at the shore, there's Arraial d'Ajuda to the north, the tranquil village famous for its Pitinga and Taípe beaches. Half an hour south of Trancoso, day-trippers stroll peaceful Praia do Espelho (Mirror Beach), perhaps sampling the catch of the day at Sylvinha's Place, an easygoing seaside restaurant open only for lunch.

In Trancoso, Capim Santo, one of the first and still one of the best restaurants in town and right on the Quadrado, has an inspired menu of Brazilian dishes with an Asian accent. Check into any of its crisp white guest rooms, with outdoor soaking tubs surrounded by a pool and gardens. Also on the Quadrado, villas at Uxua Casa blend a rustic vibe with sleeker touches and are decorated with works of Bahían artisans; days center on the hotel's quartz-lined pool. The décor at Etnia Pousada reflects a global sensibility; names of its colorful, themed bungalows include Kyoto, Goa, Tribal, and Mediterraneo. One of the few good hotels directly on the water, Estrela D'Água, was built around the former home of legendary Brazilian singer Gal Costa. It is now a 28-room luxury resort with a tiered swimming pool and the best bar on the beach.

WHERE: 460 miles/741 km south of Salvador. **SYLVINHA'S PLACE:** Tel 55/73-9985-4157. *Cost:* lunch $30. **CAPIM SANTO:** Tel 55/73-3668-1122; www.capimsanto.com.br. *Cost:* from $125 (off-peak), from $175 (peak); dinner $20. **UXUA CASA:** Tel 55/73-3668-2277; www.uxua.com. *Cost:* from $750. **ETNIA POUSADA:** Tel 55/73-3668-1137; www.etniabrasil.com.br.

Cost: from $310 (off-peak), from $400 (peak). **Estrela D'Água:** Tel 55/73-3668-1030; www.estreladagua.com.br. *Cost:* from $535 (off-peak), $750 (peak). **Best times:** Mar–Apr for nicest weather and fewest crowds; winter months Jun–Aug are pleasant and less of a scene; Jan 20 for Festa de São Sebastião with fireworks and processions.

Capital City and Oasis of Modernism

Brasília

Distrito Federal, Brazil

Oscar Niemeyer, born in 1907 in Rio de Janeiro, has been called the Pablo Picasso of architecture and a living legend of Modernism. The biggest concentration of his work is in Brazil's capital of Brasília.

Calls to move Brazil's capital from Rio de Janeiro to the nation's unpopulated geographic center began in the late 19th century. But not until the 1950s did anyone make good on those plans, when President Juscelino Kubitschek selected a large, empty stretch of land to create what would be the world's first and most ambitious master-planned 20th-century capital. The city was inaugurated in 1960. Lúcio Costa was responsible for the city's urban planning, and Niemeyer—a protégé of Le Corbusier—was the man behind its most important buildings. A window seat on a Brasília-bound flight provides the best glimpse of the city's eye-catching shape, which resembles an airplane or a bird with outstretched wings. The less dramatic view from the iconic TV tower illustrates that, although dominated by concrete, Brasília is poetic and surprising, whether in the gentle curves of the Palácio do Planalto, the president's office, or in the daring, almost impossibly angled 16 columns of the Catedral Metropolitana. The public buildings are open to visitors and are relatively close to each other; most stand along the Eixo Monumental, with the exception of the slightly removed Palácio da Alvorada, the president's official residence.

The capital is also home to an impressive culinary scene, including one of the best French restaurants in the nation: Alice, across from the presidential palace, where a cozy, unpretentious ambience attracts the political elite and visiting dignitaries, who savor the masterful creations of chef Alice de Castro. Or try the decidedly stylish Zuu, whose tasting menu might include such dishes as fresh sesame tuna and mint-marinated lamb.

The unique design of the Catedral Metropolitana is emblematic of the capital city's enclave of Modernist architecture.

Where: 468 miles/754 km northwest of Rio de Janeiro. **Restaurante Alice:** Tel 55/61-3248-7743; www.restaurantealice.com.br. *Cost:* dinner $40. **Zuu:** Tel 55/61-3244-1039. *Cost:*

dinner $35. **Where to stay:** Royal Tulip Hotel Alvorada is located on the shore of Lake Paranoá, near the president's residence. Tel 55/61-3424-7000; www.royaltulipbrasilia alvorada.com. *Cost:* from $230. **Best times:** Oct–May for the dry season; Jan for International Music Summer Course; Jun for National Fair.

A Wildlife-Watching Wonderland

Pantanal

Mato Grosso do Sul, Brazil

The largest freshwater wetland in the world, a place where more than 100 rivers meet, the Pantanal is an oasis for wildlife of staggering variety. It supports the greatest concentration of fauna in the western hemisphere and constitutes one of the most diverse ecosystems on the planet. On a typical multiday excursion you might spy various species of monkeys, giant river otters, tapirs, giant anteaters, marsh deer, caimans, and anacondas, plus macaws and toucans (just two of the 600 bird species). And there are the creatures you've never heard of—jabiru (a large stork), chachalaca (a turkeylike game bird), capybaras (the world's largest rodent), and coati (a relative of the raccoon). If you're very lucky, you might even see a maned wolf or the elusive jaguar.

Collared anteaters forage in the wetlands of the Pantanal.

Most of the South Dakota–size region is privately owned and devoted to huge cattle *fazendas* (ranches) tended by horseback-riding *pantaneiros* that have turned to ecotourism in recent days. The Caiman Ecological Refuge—a family-run, sustainable ranch that pioneered the movement here—is an ideal base for exploring the Pantanal. Located about 150 miles from Campo Grande, the state capital, it offers guided field excursions (on foot or by boat, jeep, or horseback) throughout the 131,000-acre refuge. Nature's spectacle continues into the night, when millions of fireflies twinkle like Christmas lights, and the eerie sounds of evening predators fill the air.

Life on this working fazenda centers on the main pousada, a handsome, Mediterranean-style building that was originally the manor house of the owner's family. Together with the nearby lodges, the accommodations offer total immersion in this unique wildlife reserve, with air-conditioning, a pool, and great home cooking thrown in for good measure.

Where: Campo Grande is 199 miles/319 km northwest of São Paulo. **Caiman Ecological Refuge:** Tel 55/67-3242-1450; www.caiman.com.br. *Cost:* from $1,170, all-inclusive; 3-night minimum. *When:* Jul–Sep. **How:** U.S.-based International Expeditions organizes a 10-day program that includes the Pantanal. Tel 800-234-9620 or 205-428-1700; www.ietravel.com. *Cost:* from $5,000, all-inclusive. Originates in Rio de Janeiro. *When:* Jun–Aug. **Best times:** Jul–Sep is dry season with the best bird-watching; Sep–Oct for spotting jaguars.

Baroque Splendor in the Mountains

Gold Towns of Minas Gerais

Minas Gerais, Brazil

Brazil's early economy, based heavily on sugar revenue, took a sharp turn in 1690, when huge deposits of gold were discovered in what is now the state of Minas Gerais. With trade enriching the region like never before, towns showcasing stunning Baroque architecture and unprecedented wealth proliferated.

Visitors who stroll the cobblestone streets of Brazil's famous gold towns quickly discover why Minas Gerais (General Mines) is home to more UNESCO World Heritage sites than any state in Brazil. Treks into the surrounding hills can be followed by meals at atmospheric restaurants serving tasty cuisine and some of the nation's best *cachaça,* a sugarcane-based liquor.

A beautifully preserved 18th-century town tucked into the mountains 2 hours east of Belo Horizonte, the state capital, Ouro Preto ("black gold") is one of Brazil's greatest enclaves of Baroque architecture. Like a stage set of decorative wrought-iron balconies, pastel-colored mansions, and steep cobblestone streets, the town is home to 13 Baroque churches harking back to Brazil's gold boom.

The name and work of native son Antônio Francisco Lisboa, the architect and sculptor known as Aleijadinho, aka the "Little Cripple," is synonymous with Ouro Preto. Deformed and so debilitated at the age of 40 that his assistants had to tie his chisels to his hands, he went on to become Brazil's premier Baroque sculptor, and Ouro Preto was his showcase. The church of São Francisco de Assis, begun in 1766, is his most masterful solo project. Almost all the sculptures in the church are his, including those carved directly onto the ceiling. Next door is one of the town's best places to stay, the finely furnished 18th-century Pousada do Mondego, some of whose 24 rooms have views of the church and city rooftops. Continue your tour of the city's churches at the lavish Nossa Senhora de Pilar, with more than 1,000 pounds of locally mined gold used in homage to the Madonna.

While Ouro Preto was the affluent 19th-century provincial capital, Tiradentes, 140 miles to the south, remained remote and rustic, much as it is today. Situated between the picturesque Rio das Mortes and the Atlantic forest at the foot of the mighty Serra São José mountain, this town of 6,000 residents and nine winding streets has seven impressive Baroque churches and a lost-in-time charm. A smattering of contemporary art studios, galleries, and small but top-notch restaurants have made the town a favored weekend getaway for visitors from Rio and Belo Horizonte.

Mineira cuisine is among the most popular in the nation, a rich blend of Portuguese, African, and indigenous flavors. Traditional dishes like *frango ao molho pardo* (chicken with a brown gravy-like sauce) are served at Viradas do Largo—also called Restaurante da Beth, after the owner and chef. Aficionados of cachaça head to Confidências Mineiras, a candlelit restaurant and bar that carries some 500 artisanal brands. The charming Solar da Ponte is a rustic but elegant country inn with an airy dining room that overlooks landscaped gardens.

Where: Ouro Preto is 250 miles/400 km north of Rio de Janiero. **Pousada do Mondego:** Tel 55/31-3551-2040; www.mondego.com.br. *Cost:* from $135. **Viradas do Largo:** Tel 55/32-3355-111. *Cost:* dinner $25. **Confidências**

Mineiras: 55/32-3355-2770. *Cost:* dinner $40. **Solar da Ponte:** Tel 55/32-355-1255; www.solardaponte.com.br. *Cost:* from $315. **How:** U.S.-based Borello Travel & Tours offers a 5-day trip to Belo Horizonte and Ouro Preto. Tel 800-405-3072 or 212-686-4911; www.borellotravel.com. *Cost:* from $2,000. **Best times:** Nov–Apr for good weather. In Tiradentes: Apr 21 for Tiradentes Day; Aug for a culinary festival.

Color and Culture at the Mouth of the Amazon

Belém's Old City

Belém, Pará, Brazil

Founded by the Portuguese in 1616, Belém benefited greatly from its strategic location at the meeting of the Amazon River and the Atlantic Ocean. It was here that locals first showed colonials the Amazon's bounty, resulting in the rubber boom of the late 1800s that brought fabulous wealth to the city. You'll see vestiges of those days in Cidade Velha (Old City), Belém's oldest neighborhood, a mélange of faded elegance and revitalization.

Belém—Portuguese for Bethlehem—is the Amazon's most historic city. For centuries the boats sailing down from the depths of the Amazon have unloaded their goods at the noisy and chaotic daily market known as Ver-o-Peso, for the colonial-era sales pitch "See the weight!" The main attraction of the market—one of the country's largest—is its cornucopia of the Amazon's most unusual kinds of fish (piranha!), meat (armadillo), vegetables, and ice cream, which is made from exotic rain-forest fruits like cupuaçu and açaí. Next to the market, a group of 19th-century warehouses have in recent years been reborn as Estação das Docas, a complex of modern boutiques, galleries, and restaurants.

Taste the region's blend of European and African influences at Lá Em Casa, a good place to try the city's premier dish, *pato no tucupi,* duck in an aromatic herb sauce. Market-fresh fish is on the menu at the Manjar da Garças, scenically set in a thatch-roofed bungalow at the river's edge, inside the Mangal das Garças ecological park.

Belém is especially known for October's unique Cirio de Nazaré, the largest and most important religious festival in the North. More than one million people join the 5-hour procession honoring the Virgem de Nazaré (Virgin of Nazareth), who is said to be responsible for many miracles here.

Get away on a 3-hour boat ride that takes you to Ilha de Marajó, the world's largest river island and home to dense vegetation, water buffaloes, caimans, monkeys, and seemingly endless flocks of colorful birds. Fazenda Sanjo, a 50-minute boat ride from the ferry dock in the delightful small town of Soure, is a family-run buffalo ranch that provides a comfortably rustic experience: Guests ride water buffaloes and horses and take guided trail walks.

Where: 1,227 miles/1,974 km north of Rio. **Lá Em Casa:** Tel 55/91-223-1212; www.laemcasa.com. *Cost:* dinner $25. **Manjar da Garças:** Tel 55/91-3242-1056; www.manjardasgarcas.com.br. *Cost:* dinner $25. **Where to stay:** Crowne Plaza Belém is the city's newest and best choice. Tel 55/91-3202-2000; in the U.S., 877-227-6963; www.crownebelem.com.br. *Cost:* from $310. **Fazenda Sanjo:** Tel 55/91-3228-1385; www.sanjo.tur.br. *Cost:* $225 per person for 2 nights, all-inclusive. **Best time:** Jun–Nov is less rainy.

Island Paradise of Dolphin Ballets and Spectacular Beaches

FERNANDO DE NORONHA

Pernambuco, Brazil

One of the last great, little-visited ecotourist destinations, the impossibly beautiful archipelago of Fernando de Noronha promises an unusual, Galápagos-like experience with Brazilian flair. With about 75 percent of its territory designated a national marine park (Brazil's first), its waters provide an ecological sanctuary to hundreds of species of wildlife.

The island's highest point, Morro do Pico, can be seen from anywhere on Fernando de Noronha.

This 21-island paradise also offers some of the world's best diving and snorkeling, with year-round visibility that can surpass 100 feet, and miles of pristine beaches (*praias*). Colorful coral, manta rays, and 14 species of sharks can be found here, as well as a community of more than 600 whitebelly spinner dolphins which has made the Baía dos Golfinhos (Dolphin Bay) its home since the 1700s. The dolphins' famous acrobatics can be glimpsed during boat excursions or from the bay's escarpments.

A rented dune buggy is the best way to tour the hilly, 10-square-mile main (and only inhabited) island, Ilha Fernando de Noronha. Bumping along the beautiful coastline, you'll come upon the beach at Baía do Sueste, where the shallow, calm waters are ideal for families and snorkelers, who might find sea turtles swimming alongside them at high tide. If you prefer to surf, head to Cacimba do Padre, a beach that hosts surf championships and boasts waves up to 12 feet between December and March. And for gorgeous seclusion, brave the iron ladders scaling sheer, 100-foot red-rock cliffs to Baía do Sancho. Tidal pools at Praia do Atalaia are perfect for snorkeling.

Celebrity sightings, limited accommodations, and restrictions on the number of visitors have only added to the islands' allure, keeping prices high and requiring reservations far in advance. The top lodging is Pousada Maravilha, a minimalist eco-chic hideaway; guests sway in hammocks outside their private bungalows or gaze at the horseshoe-shaped Baía do Sueste from the infinity pool at the main lodge. Close by, the somewhat more modest Solar dos Ventos is within walking distance of the beach and claims some of the most spectacular views on the island. The best of the limited dining options are Palhoça da Colina and Restaurante Ekologiku, the latter known for its delicious *moquecas* (coconut-based seafood stews).

WHERE: 223 miles/360 km northeast of Natal. **HOW:** Atlantis Divers offers a variety of diving packages. Tel 55/84-3206-8840; www.atlantisdivers.com.br. In the U.S., Marnella Tours offers a variety of tour options. Tel 866-993-0033 or 919-782-1664; www.marnellatours.com. **POUSADA MARAVILHA:** Tel 55/81-3619-0028; www.pousadamaravilha.com.br. *Cost:* from $715, inclusive. **POUSADA SOLAR DOS VENTOS:** Tel 55/81-3619-1347; www.pousadasolardosventos.com.br. *Cost:* from $535 (off-peak), from $625 (peak). **BEST TIMES:** Oct–Apr for best weather; Dec–Mar for surfing and championships; Sep for International Regatta Recife; Oct for best underwater visibility.

The Rich Musical Traditions of the Northeast

Recife and Olinda

Pernambuco, Brazil

The developed waterfront city of Recife and its more tranquil colonial neighbor, Olinda, are home to some of Brazil's most fascinating music and dance traditions, best seen during festivals that are held throughout the year. Recife, which still bears signs of its early Dutch roots, is the cultural and gastronomic hub of Brazil's northeast, and home to the 4-mile-long, palm-lined Boa Viagem, an attractive beach by urban standards and the location of some of the city's best eating and drinking spots. Indulge in freshly caught seafood while enjoying ocean views at Bargaço. After dark, you'll find some great settings to hear live bands here as well as in Recife Antigo, a historic neighborhood whose narrow streets and cobblestoned squares are lined with shops, bars, nightclubs, and restaurants set in centuries-old town houses.

Make time to admire the fanciful work of Brazil's most famous ceramic artist at the workshop/museum called Oficina Cerâmica Francisco Brennand just outside the city center.

Only 10 minutes from Recife (and perched on a series of hilltops overlooking it) sits this city's historic and artsy counterpart, the charming enclave of Olinda. It was founded in 1537 by Portuguese nobleman Duarte Coelho, who supposedly uttered *"O, linda . . . !"* ("Oh, beautiful . . . !") upon first sight. And the city's collection of Baroque architecture ensures that its reputation continues as one of the prettiest colonial cities in Brazil. The Igreja da Sé (Church of the See), built in 1537, offers excellent views, but the greatest architectural treasure is the Mosteiro (Monastery) de São Bento, which dates to 1582 and has a 46-foot Baroque altar gilded to its last square inch. A walk down Rua do Amparo leads past colorful former homes that now serve as ateliers for artists and artisans. Nestled among them is the Pousada do Amparo, set in two Colonial buildings. Antique furniture, a gorgeous garden with views over the town, and the romantic Flor de Coco, one of Olinda's best restaurants, are among its highlights.

The pre-Lenten Carnaval celebrations in Recife and Olinda are among the most exuberant—and longest—in the nation. This is the time to experience a multiplicity of music and dance styles that blend European, African, and indigenous elements. Among them are *forró* (featuring accordion, triangle, and a drum called the zabumba), the fast-paced, brassy *frevo* (its name comes from the Portuguese word *ferver*, to boil, which makes instant sense upon seeing whirling dancers), and dazzlingly costumed *maracatu nação* groups (which hark back to an 18th-century slave tradition). Olinda's Carnaval is still free of the commercialized feel of Rio's celebration, and people of all ages, colors, and inclinations fill the streets and plazas to celebrate it, joining in parades behind the enormous trademark *bonecos* (papier-mâché dolls) and dancing to *afoxé* (an Afro-Brazilian musical genre) and the Brazilian samba.

For post-Carnaval recuperation, head an hour south to the former fishing village of Porto de Galinhas, renowned for its white sand beaches. In the town's charming pedestrian center you'll find a cluster of shops and good restaurants, such as Beijupira. Don't let its funky ambience fool you: The kitchen is serious about such creative fare as *camarulu*—shrimp brushed with a sugarcane glaze in a passion-fruit sauce. For lodgings, head a few miles out to either of two beachfront inns, Tabapitanga or its less expensive sister property, Tabajuba. Rooms at both are spacious and colorful, and the vibe is friendly, relaxed, and romantic.

WHERE: 1,165 miles/1,874 km northeast of Rio. **RESTAURANTE BARGAÇO:** Tel 55/81-3465-1847; www.restaurantebargaco.com.br. *Cost:* dinner $40. **OFICINA CERÂMICA:** www.brennand.com.br. **POUSADA DO AMPARO:** Tel 55/81-3439-1749. *Cost:* from $125 (off-peak), from $195 (peak). **BEIJUPIRA:** Tel 55/81-3552-2354; www.beijupira.com.br. *Cost:* dinner $35. **TABAPITANGA** and **TABAJUBA:** Tel 55/81-3352-1037; www.tabapitanga.com.br and www.tabajuba.com. *Cost:* from $85 (off-peak), from $135 (peak). **BEST TIMES:** Sep–Apr are driest; Feb or Mar for Carnaval; late Oct–Nov for Recifolia, an off-season Carnaval in Recife; late Nov–early Dec for Arte em Toda Parte, an art festival in Olinda.

The World's Most Decadent Party

CARNAVAL!

Rio de Janeiro, Brazil

Say "Carnaval" and the world thinks Rio de Janeiro. Each year, in the weeks before Lent, the whole city becomes a stage and throws one of the world's great free-for-all street parties. What began as a pre-Lenten celebration has grown into a series of street parties, masquerades, and samba parades during the height of Rio's summer, beginning at least a week before the official event, which runs from the Friday before Ash Wednesday until Shrove (Fat) Tuesday.

Lavish costumes are a Carnaval tradition.

Rio's more than 70 samba "schools" (neighborhood social groups, not educational institutions) spend the entire year preparing for this moment, and many open to visitors beginning in September for those who come outside of Carnaval season. For those who come for the Carnaval itself, though, the centerpiece is the samba parades, made up of lavishly costumed troupes and over-the-top floats from Grupo Especial (the 12 top-tier schools)—each accompanied by a pounding, 150-member-strong drum corps—who perform and compete on the Sunday and Monday before Ash Wednesday. The parades are televised from 9 P.M. to dawn, at the filled-to-capacity, 75,000-seat Sambódromo (a stadium built specifically for this purpose). Here, the flamboyantly—often scantily—dressed teams fill the air with music, passion, and unbridled frenzy as they compete for the year's coveted championship.

Indoor samba balls (often attended by guests in full costume) are held in nightclubs, bars, and some hotels around town. But the most authentic experience of all is to join the open-air concerts and tag-along bands that snake through the beachside neighborhoods of Copacabana, Ipanema, and Leblon and the hilltop Bohemian district of Santa Teresa, forming a kind of citywide street party. A glitzy and outrageous bacchanal of flesh and fantasy, Rio's Carnaval is not for the prudish or crowd-fearing.

For those who want to escape the chaos of Carnaval, there's the grand Copacabana Palace, which hosts the most exclusive black-tie ball in Rio. Built in 1923, "The Palace" overlooks the famous beach from which it takes its name, and its elegant pool makes a beautiful setting for a dip or an afternoon caipirinha, while its top-rated restaurants serve excellent meals. This was the backdrop for *Flying Down to Rio,* the 1933 film that first paired Fred Astaire and Ginger Rogers; the movie made the Palace a Hollywood favorite. The myth of yesteryear lives on in the ornate Golden Room; its famous glass dance floor, lit from below, is where the famous Magic Ball takes place during Carnaval.

Visitor info: www.rcvb.com.br. **When:** Carnaval begins in the weeks before Ash Wednesday (Feb or Mar), culminating the Thurs–Tues before Ash Wednesday. **How:** Some Rio-based travel agencies and high-end hotels can help arrange tickets to the parade or private balls. **Copacabana Palace:** Tel 55/ 21-2548-7070; www.copacabanapalace.com .br. *Cost:* $7,805 for 5 nights (minimum) during Carnaval; from $430 the rest of the year. Magic Ball tickets from $1,199.

Surf, Sand, and Samba in the Cidade Maravilhosa

Copacabana and Ipanema

Rio de Janeiro, Brazil

With 45 miles of glorious beaches fringing Guanabara Bay, Rio de Janeiro is famed for its magnificent setting, a combination of tropical beauty and big-city excitement. Its beachside neighborhoods are as known for their individual character and energy as for their natural beauty.

Hectic, democratic, and glorious, Copacabana is 2.5 miles long, lined with hotels, apartments, and open-air restaurants. Sun-lovers take to the sands for pickup soccer and volleyball games, jogging and cycling along the beach path, frolicking in the waves, or simply soaking up rays with a cold *agua de coco* (coconut water) in hand.

Ipanema, immortalized in the 1960s by Antônio Carlos Jobim and Vinícius de Moraes in their famous bossa nova hit, "The Girl from Ipanema," is Rio's most sophisticated beach. It's a showcase for gorgeous bodies, dental-floss swimwear, and hedonistic attitudes to match. The beach is divided into *postos,* or sections—visit Posto 9 to bask with local bathing beauties, or more sedate Posto 12 in neighboring Leblon for a family outing. Designer boutiques, parks, and outdoor cafés beckon within a few blocks of the sand.

To fully understand why *cariocas* (Rio residents) call their city the "*cidade maravilhosa*" (marvelous city), head for the hills. The mesmerizing, 360-degree panorama from atop Corcovado Mountain puts Rio de Janeiro's heart-stopping beauty at your feet: a unique, overpowering tableau of curving beaches, skyscrapers, and dense rain forest–covered mountains. Corcovado's summit is crowned by the city's legendary symbol, a 124-foot-high soapstone figure of Christ, his outstretched arms measuring 98 feet across. The passenger train to the summit makes its steep 2.3-mile ascent through leafy Tijuca National Park, the world's largest urban park—an 8,151-acre forest with blue morpho butterflies the size of salad plates and dozens of waterfalls.

The dramatic oceanfront Pão de Açúcar

(Sugarloaf Mountain) offers its own inspiring views, from the minute you board the aerial tram at the Urca base station until you glide toward the peak, where you're treated to a superb panorama 1,299 feet above the sea.

Several of Rio's best hotels are also on the waterfront. One of the newest is the Fasano, a Philippe Starck–designed gem in Ipanema, where the rooftop infinity pool's vista of the beach just across the street is unforgettable. At Ipanema's Caesar Park Rio, even the fitness center has floor-to-ceiling ocean views. A few blocks away, in Leblon, the oceanfront Marina All Suites Hotel features chic, modern décor, and its ultrahip restaurant provides both a spectacular beachscape and delicious and innovative Italian cuisine.

The most exciting way to experience Rio's beach scene is during one of the city's annual celebrations. The wild and raucous Carnaval (see p. 1012) is the grandest event, but Reveillon, which takes place first, isn't far behind. Each New Year's Eve, 2 million revelers dance barefoot on Copacabana Beach to samba bands while fireworks fill the midnight sky. Book a room months in advance at the JW Marriott; the beach party unfolds right across the street. The mysterious and quintessentially Brazilian Festa Iemanjá unfolds on December 29. Iemanjá is the beloved African goddess of the sea, conflated with the Virgin Mary in the Afro-Brazilian Condomblé religion. Thousands of her white-clad followers head to the beach and send their petitions to her for good fortune out to sea in little boats.

Corcovado: Tel 55/21-2558-1329; www.corcovado.org.br. **Caminho Aéreo Pão de Açúcar:** Tel 55/21-2546-8400; http://bondinho.com.br. **Hotel Fasano:** Tel 55/21-3202-4254; www.fasano.com.br. *Cost:* from $585. **Caesar Park Rio:** Tel 55/21-2525-2525; www.caesar-park.com. *Cost:* from $320. **Marina All Suites Hotel:** Tel 55/21-2172-1100; www.marinaallsuites.com.br. *Cost:* from $400. **JW Marriott:** Tel 55/21-2545-6500; www.marriott.com. *Cost:* from $490. **Best times:** Nov–Mar for nice weather; Feb or Mar for Carnaval; Dec 29 and 31 for Festa Iemanjá and Reveillon.

Goal!

Maracanã Stadium

Rio de Janeiro, Brazil

One of Brazil's biggest passions is soccer, and one of the best places to experience it firsthand is Maracanã Stadium, Rio de Janeiro's enormous shrine to "the beautiful game." When Rio inaugurated Maracanã in 1950 to host the FIFA World Cup, it was touted as the finest soccer stadium in the world. Many other great facilities have been built since then, but Rio's home base for *futebol* remains an icon. It was here that Brazil suffered a heart-stopping loss during the 1950 World Cup final to Uruguay and where in 1969, more gloriously, Pelé scored his 1,000th goal.

Maracanã seats more than 90,000 for soccer games, and even more people pack in, sitting on the playing field, for concerts and other special events (including a mass led by Pope John Paul II in 1980). The stadium is undergoing an upgrade as it prepares for its high-profile role as part of the 2014 World Cup and the 2016 Summer Olympics.

The best time to visit Maracanã—or simply "Maraca" in Rio slang—is when rival local teams (Flamengo, Fluminense, Botafogo, or Vasco da Gama) face off there. Crowds arrive hours in advance, enjoying beer and samba before entering the stadium (alcohol isn't allowed inside). The pregame joviality is only a precursor to the high emotion that swirls around each match; events on the playing field often pale in comparison to the audience reaction—there's nothing like sitting in a sea of humanity screaming "goooooal!" If you can't make it for a match, take a guided tour of the stadium including the playing field, locker rooms, and the corridors used by clubs. The on-site sports museum exhibits photographs, uniforms, and other memorabilia, including plaster casts of the feet of the most famous players, and Pelé's number 10 shirt.

Info: Tel 55/21-2299-2942; www.suderj.rj.gov.br/maracana.asp. **How:** Most hotel concierges can help procure tickets to games; guided tours are available daily, except when there is a game.

Barefoot Chic in Brazil's Most Glamorous Beach Town

Búzios

Rio de Janeiro State, Brazil

Those looking for the St-Tropez of South America flock to this coastal town's famously gorgeous beaches, sophisticated inns, and buzzy dining and nocturnal scene. (Those looking for a quieter hideaway head to Paraty; see p. 1017.) A former fishing village, Búzios was launched to stardom when Brigitte Bardot and her Brazilian boyfriend-of-the-moment basked in the sun here in the 1960s. Today the region is a magnet for Rio's glitterati, many of whom have second homes here. Soccer players and *novela* (soap opera) stars mingle with well-heeled foreign travelers, who come for the lively nightlife and fill the stylish oceanfront restaurants.

The 5-mile-long peninsula comprises some 20-odd idyllic beaches with something for everyone. Ferradura is a wide, horseshoe-shaped beach with blissfully calm, deep waters perfect for snorkeling. Large, open Geriba is the best pick for surfing and enjoying the scene. The warm, gentle tides of Azeda beach are reached by boat or via a trail from Ossos beach, where small boats dot the water and cafés invite you to sit and watch the world go by. Would-be castaways hop aboard schooners or private water taxis for day trips to various beaches and secluded island hideaways, some of which offer ideal conditions for diving. Nights are filled with a variety of live-music bars, jazz clubs, and open-air cafés that invite lingering until the wee hours, thanks in no small part to the free-flowing cachaça and the DJs spinning a wide variety of beats. The cobbled Rua das Pedras is lined with chic boutiques and casual but excellent restaurants.

One of the best of the town's Colonial-style inns, or pousadas, is Casas Brancas (White Houses), where guests sleep in cool, airy hilltop rooms—some with balconies and Praia de Armação views—indulge in spa treatments or lounge by the pool, and dine on Brazilian-Mediterranean cuisine in the laid-back terrace restaurant.

Where: 105 miles/169 km northeast of Rio de Janeiro. **Visitor info:** www.buziosonline.com.br. **Casas Brancas:** Tel 55/22-2623-1458; www.casasbrancas.com.br. *Cost:* from $210 (off-peak), from $315 (peak); dinner $45. **Best times:** Sep–Feb for good weather; Jul for Búzios Jazz e Blues Festival.

A Magical, Verdant Island

Ilha Grande

Angra dos Reis, Rio de Janeiro State, Brazil

A shimmering jewel in Brazil's Costa Verde (Green Coast), Ilha Grande (Big Island) is the largest in a constellation of 360 islands that dot the beautiful Angra dos Reis (Bay of Kings). This rain forest–covered idyll with empty beaches and a do-nothing vibe is a relative newcomer to the tourist scene. It was a pirate hideout during the colonial era, and later a leprosarium and the infamous maximum-security penitentiary Candido Mendes, which closed in 1994. Largely untamed, the island has lately become a favorite for Brazilian sun seekers and a handful of foreign beach cognoscenti.

Fine sand, shallow waters, and few people make Lopes Mendes Beach one of Ilha Grande's—and the country's—best.

A ferry from mainland Angra dos Reis whisks visitors to the colorful village of Vila do Abraão, the gateway to Ilha Grande's tropical seclusion. You'll find no cars, no neon lights, and no ATMs on the 74-square-mile island; instead there are miles of walking trails that meander through a protected rain forest chock-full of birds, sloths, howler monkeys, and other wildlife. You'll also find waterfalls—and ruins from the island's dark past: Along with the pirates, the slave trade was a part of the island's history. You can catch a boat to untouched beaches, including Caxadaço and Saco do Céu, which are among the finest strands in all of Brazil. Good visibility year-round makes for excellent snorkeling in the Green and Blue lagoons, where warm currents harbor starfish and sea anemones and nearby shipwrecks create dramatic scenery. Forest-lined dirt roads take hikers to several great beaches, such as Lopes Mendes and Dois Rios.

After long days on the sandy shores, travelers can hang their hats at simple but captivating inns such as Pousada Naturália, a shady retreat where suites are graced with polished wood and private balconies with hammocks. Or take a speedboat from Abraão to the elegant Sagú Mini Resort, where the Restaurante Toscanelli Brasil, featuring Brazilian and Italian cuisine, is a major draw.

Where: a 90-minute ferry ride from Angra dos Reis, which is 91 miles/168 km west of Rio de Janeiro. **Visitor info:** www.ilhagrande.com.br. **Pousada Naturália:** Tel 55/24-3361-5198; www.pousadanaturalia.net. *Cost:* from $85 (off-peak), from $135 (peak). **Sagú Mini Resort:** Tel 55/24-3361-5660; www.saguresort.com. *Cost:* From $190 (off-peak), from $250 (peak); dinner $35. **Best times:** Dec–Feb is peak season, although late Feb–Mar is less crowded and less humid.

Colonial and Charismatic on the Lush Costa Verde

PARATY

Rio de Janeiro State, Brazil

During the gold rush of the 18th century, Paraty flourished as a port for galleons carrying precious cargo from inland Minas Gerais (see p. 1008) to Rio and on to Portugal's royal court. Its cobblestone streets are lined with colorful remnants of its colonial past. Paraty's location on Brazil's lush Costa Verde (Green Coast) is stunning, with jungle-clad mountains rising behind the town and white sand beaches a short drive or boat ride away. In the historic, car-free center, you can stroll waterfront lanes lined with casually stylish boutiques and elegant restaurants. Admire the fine houses and elaborate churches that wealthy merchants erected for themselves, along with a church built by and for slaves. The Casa da Cultura provides a valuable, multimedia explanation of Paraty's role in the past and present. One of the area's biggest draws, however, is its dozens of outlying islands; their deserted beaches are reachable by guided boat trips departing daily.

Paraty has countless inns; one of the first is still among the most charming. Pousada Pardieiro is set among a group of 18th-century former homes, its simple old-world architecture offset by a stylish selection of modern artwork. For lunch, catch a boat for the 10-minute crossing to Kontiki, a seafood restaurant set on a tiny, idyllic island in the bay with views of Paraty.

On the town's growing list of annual events, the Festival da Pinga is a highlight, a four-day gathering dedicated to locally produced *cachaça* (also called *pinga*), a sugarcane-based liquor. This region produces some of the nation's best, making Paraty an ideal spot to linger in a café for some people-watching over a smooth, sweet caipirinha—the cool, mint-infused drink associated most with Brazil and once called a Paraty.

WHERE: 150 miles/241 km southwest of Rio. **VISITOR INFO:** www.paraty.com.br. **POUSADA PARDIEIRO:** Tel 55/243-371-1370; www.pousadapardieiro.com.br. *Cost:* from $175. **KONTIKI RESTAURANTE:** Tel 55/243-371-1666; www.ilhakontiki.com.br. *Cost:* lunch $20. **BEST TIMES:** Nov–Jun for good weather; Feb–Mar for Carnaval; Jul for Festa Literária.

Beach Buggy Adventure in the North

CRUISING THE SAND DUNES OF NATAL

Rio Grande do Norte, Brazil

Located in the easternmost region of the South American continent, Natal—the capital of Rio Grande do Norte—is the gateway to an expanse of enormous white sand dunes as well as some of the world's most beautiful beaches. Fifteen miles north of the city is Genipabu, a protected area where ocean swimming, sunset strolls, camel rides, and sand surfing are the pastimes of choice; you can also hire a *jangada* (balsa wood raft) to visit offshore reefs, or sign up for a roller-coaster-style ride in a four-wheel-drive *bugue* (buggy). The buggies can also be rented by the intrepid, but no one knows the shifting sands and adrenaline-rushing turns of these hair-raisingly steep dunes—which top 300 feet—like the local professional *bugueiros* (buggy drivers). They will whisk you away to secluded lagoons, palm-fringed lakes, or a funky beach hut selling grilled shrimp and cold Brahma beer—a well-deserved reward after braving one of their wild rides. Guided four-day journeys trace a sandy route through 500 miles and 85 beaches, from Natal north to Fortaleza.

About an hour north of Natal is Maracajaú, where low tide creates excellent snorkeling conditions among the shallow coral reefs. An hour south of Natal, gorgeous Praia da Pipa is a scenic beach community, known for dolphin-watching and a vibrant nightlife thriving along cobblestone streets, that is often likened to the Búzios (p. 1015) of 20 years ago. This is where you'll find Toca da Coruja, a collection of bungalows that are rustic yet infused with a refined blend of Brazilian-Victorian style. The pousada is set away from the beach, amid lush gardens where tiny monkeys bound from tree to tree. Nearby, on the pristine beach of Praia de Sibaúma, fishermen are a more common sight than tourists.

WHERE: 184 miles/297 km north of Recife. **HOW:** Buggy & Cia offers rentals with or without driver. Tel 55/84-9416-2222; www.buggyecia.com.br. **TOCA DA CORUJA:** Tel 55/84-3246-2226; www.tocadacoruja.com.br. *Cost:* from $360. **BEST TIME:** Nov–Apr for balmiest weather.

Creativity on a Grand Scale

São Paulo's Art Scene

São Paulo, Brazil

São Paulo, Brazil's economic engine—a metropolis of more than 19 million—is South America's biggest city and among the largest on earth. It is a sprawling concrete jungle in some respects, but its reputation for artistry and design shines through in everything from galleries and museums to cuisine and hotels.

One of the city's most recognizable landmarks is the Museu de Arte de São Paulo (MASP), a glass-and-concrete behemoth perched on four red pillars on the grand Avenida Paulista. In addition to permanent exhibits of 14th- to 20th-century pieces by the likes of Raphael, Matisse, and Dalí, MASP shows work by Brazilian artists. More Brazilian art from the 19th and 20th centuries is set against beautifully simple brick walls in another of São Paulo's famed art museums, the Pinacoteca do Estado, housed in a building that dates to 1900 and is surrounded by the verdant gardens of Jardim da Luz. Oscar Niemeyer, Brazil's most famous architect and the force behind the city of Brasília (see p. 1006), created a more modern setting for the Monument to Latin America complex, which contains a small art gallery and an iconic concrete sculpture of a giant hand stained with a bloodred map of Latin America.

In October and November of even-numbered years, São Paulo becomes a stage for one of the most important art expositions in the

Americas: the Bienal Internacional de São Paulo, which takes place in a Niemeyer-designed building set in the massive Parque do Ibirapuera. It is the permanent home of the Museu de Arte Contemporânea (MAC), a contemporary art gallery. Also in Ibirapuera Park is the Museu de Arte Moderna (MAM), which displays local and international contemporary art, and the white-domed OCA Pavilion, another stunning Niemeyer creation, which hosts rotating exhibits and music and dance performances.

São Paulo's boutique hotels are sure to impress design-conscious visitors. Located near Ibirapuera Park is Hotel Unique, easily the city's most architecturally ambitious hotel. Shaped like a gigantic slice of watermelon, the structure houses 95 sleek white-on-white rooms, two trendy bars, and a popular restaurant-with-a-view. In the heart of the upscale Jardins district is the chic Emiliano, with 19 spacious suites distinguished by original artwork and stylish décor, and the Fasano, an outpost of the local family-owned brand that has expanded from fine dining (see next page) to include sublime, streamlined hotels. Just off busy Avenida Paulista, the 80-room L'Hotel is the most elegant of the city's boutique options, appealing for its traditional design and its museum-quality antiques.

Niemeyer's bleeding open hand is the somber centerpiece of the Monument to Latin America.

MASP: Tel 55/11-3251-5644; www.masp.art.br. **Pinacoteca do Estado:** Tel 55/11-5576-7600; www.pinacoteca.sp.gov.br. **MAC:** Tel 55/11-3091-3039; www.mac.usp.br. **MAM:** Tel 55/11-5085-1300; www.mam.org.br. **Pavilhõ da Bienal de Arte:** Tel 55/11-5573-5255; www.fbsp.org.br. **Hotel Unique:** Tel 55/11-3055-4710; www.unique.com.br. *Cost:* from $555. **Emiliano:** Tel 55/11-3068-4399; www.emiliano.com.br. *Cost:* from $690. **Fasano:** Tel 55/11-3896-4000; www.fasano.com.br. *Cost:* from $650. **L'Hotel:** Tel 55/11-2183-0500; www.lhotel.com.br. *Cost:* from $295.

Groundbreaking Cuisine from Brazil and Beyond

São Paulo's Food Moment

São Paulo, Brazil

Dining is a serious pastime for *paulistas,* and they stay well informed about the best places to savor the countless cuisines in this diverse metropolis. To understand firsthand something of the local bounty, start by visiting the Mercado Municipal, which is set in a 1928 neo-Baroque building. More than 300 stalls overflow with fresh fruits, vegetables, meat, fish, and other goods. Sample the *caju* (cashew apple), *maracuja* (passion fruit), or *pitaya* (dragon fruit), then stop at the Hocca Bar, where patrons line up for *bolinhos de bacalhau* (cod-filled croquettes).

There's a galaxy of superb restaurants in São Paulo, but many gourmands believe that D.O.M. is the best in Brazil. (D.O.M. is an acronym for *Domus Optimus Maximus,* a Latin phrase asserting that this is the optimum, maximum dining experience.) Here, groundbreaking celebrity chef Alex Atala blends classic French elements with exotic Amazonian ingredients: Foie gras is paired perfectly with crispy wild rice, and breaded oysters are enhanced with tapioca marinade. Atala is also the mastermind behind Dalva e Dito, across the street, a paean to simple Brazilian fare, such as the classic *prato feito* of rice, beans, and meat.

At Brasil a Gosto, chef Ana Luiza Trajano does a creative take on traditional comfort food from Brazil's backwaters, while at Mocotó, cow's-foot soup and other time-honored specialties from northeastern Brazil are prepared with modern panache under the watchful eye of rising chef Rodrigo Oliveira. Celebrities are frequent guests at Maní, claiming seats in either the garden or dining room to sample the panethnic creations of forward-thinking chef Helena Rizzo.

Figueira Rubaiyat is known as much for the gnarled trunk of a magnificent old fig tree that reaches skyward from its front patio as for its cuisine, the highlights of which are meat from the owner's ranch, as well as a rich, traditional paella and simply prepared fish-of-the-day. The finest choice for Italian cuisine in the city is the elegant, uberfashionable Fasano, in the hotel of the same name (see previous page).

Restaurants that serve contemporary cuisine open and close in the blink of an eye in São Paulo. But Carlota has thrived since the 1990s thanks to Chef Carla Pernambuco's talent for reinvention. Set in an old brick pousada, the restaurant features such globe-spanning dishes as crispy shrimp risotto with ham and sweet pepper chutney.

Mercado Municipal: Tel 55/11-3228-0673; www.mercadomunicipal.com.br. **D.O.M.:** Tel 55/11-3088-0761; www.domrestaurante.com.br. *Cost:* dinner $95. **Dalva e Dito:** Tel 55/11-3068-4444; www.dalvaedito.com.br. *Cost:* dinner $40. **Brasil a Gosto:** Tel 55/11-3086-3565; www.brasilagosto.com.br. *Cost:* dinner $35. **Mocotó:** Tel 55/11-2951-3056; www.mocoto.com.br. *Cost:* lunch $30. **Maní:** Tel 55/11-3085-4148; www.manimanioca.com.br. *Cost:* dinner $35. **Figueira Rubaiyat:** Tel 55/11-3063-3888; www.rubaiyat.com.br. *Cost:* lunch $40. **Fasano:** Tel 55/11-3896-4000; www.fasano.com.br. *Cost:* dinner $65. **Carlota:** Tel 55/11-3661-8670; www.carlota.com.br. *Cost:* dinner $35.

At Home with Internationally Acclaimed Vintners

The Wine Roads of Chile

Central Valley, Chile

Winemaking was brought to Chile by the Spanish conquistadors and missionaries, who cultivated the grape for sacramental purposes, but the wines really came into their own when noble French cuttings were planted in the mid-19th century. Chile escaped the plagues that later blighted France's vines; it is the only country besides Australia still planted with its original rootstock.

The fifth-largest exporter in the world, Chile has plenty of traditional wineries on century-old, hacienda-like properties, such as Cousiño Macul, Errazuriz, and Concha y Toro. But it is home to many boutique wineries too, which produce some of the country's most exciting varietals, such as Clos Apalta, Altair, Casa Marin, Almaviva, and Neyen. The principal wine regions, from north to south, are the Aconcagua, Casablanca, Maipo, Colchagua, and Maule, which together form the Central Valley, or Valle Central, region. Casablanca, located near the Pacific, is renowned for its chardonnay and sauvignon blanc; Colchagua, for bold reds that include cabernet sauvignon, carmenère, and syrah; and Maipo, Chile's oldest wine valley, located on the outskirts of Santiago, for its cabernet sauvignons.

It's easy to visit vineyards on a day trip from Santiago, but anyone with the time should consider spending the night. The earthquake that struck central Chile in 2010 took its toll on wine production here and closed some of the hotels temporarily, but most reopened quickly with refreshed and updated amenities and services.

Colchagua is often compared to the Napa Valley of California. The low, vineyard-covered hills with their traditional *finca* homesteads boast some 56,700 acres of vines and some of the best wineries in Chile. This area also has the best touring infrastructure and lodging options. For contemporary ambience, Casa Lapostolle is an exclusive getaway set on the grounds of the state-of-the-art Clos Apalta winery. One of the country's most distinctive hotels, it is composed of four casitas named for the primary red grape varietals on the property. The Colonial-style Hotel Santa Cruz Plaza is located on the attractive main square of that town, the epicenter of the valley's winemaking and vineyard-touring scene. The Spanish-inspired property, with wrought-iron details and heavy chandeliers, has 116 rooms situated around a large common area, an outdoor swimming pool, a spa with an impressive menu of treatments, and a well-stocked wine cellar. Its owner, Carlos Cardoen, is the force behind the spectacular Colchagua Museum, the largest private museum in Chile.

The grapes grown in Chile's Valle de Aconcagua replicate French flavors.

WHERE: Santa Cruz is 112 miles/180 km southwest of Santiago. **HOW:** Santiago Adventures offers custom-planned trips that allow visitors to meet with winemakers in Chile's various wine regions; it also arranges wine tours by bike. Tel 56/2-244-2750; in the U.S., 802-904-6798; www.santiagoadventures.com. **CASA LAPOSTOLLE:** Tel 56/7-295-3360; www.casalapostolle.com. *Cost:* from $1,000, all-inclusive. **HOTEL SANTA CRUZ PLAZA:** Tel 56/72-209-600; www.hotelsantacruzplaza.cl. *Cost:* from $330. **BEST TIMES:** Oct–Apr for nicest weather; mid-Feb–Apr for harvest; Mar for Fiesta de la Vendimia wine festival in Santa Cruz.

The Thousand Mysteries of Rapa Nui

EASTER ISLAND

Chile

The tiny, windswept speck of land called Rapa Nui, aka Easter Island, continues to captivate a curious world long after its "discovery" by the Dutch West India Company on Easter Sunday 1722. It's the world's most remote inhabited island—over 1,200 miles from its nearest populated neighbor, Pitcairn Island. Easter Island is best known for its *moai*, more than 800 huge, elongated stone figures, 50 of them standing like giant chess pieces staring eyeless at the distant horizon. Measuring an average of 14 feet tall and weighing 10 tons apiece, they were carved from the island's volcanic tufa stone by early Polynesian settlers sometime between the 9th and 17th century, transported for miles by means that have confounded modern-day observers, and raised onto great stone altars.

No written record exists to explain the meaning or history of the moai.

The best are part of Ahu Tongariki, the largest excavated and restored series of *moai* on the island. Relatively little is known about their purpose or history, although possible clues are on exhibit at the nearby Museo Antropológico Sebastián Englert and its affiliated library and bookstore.

The mystery—as well as the statues themselves—are so engrossing that few visitors leave enough time to take advantage of the island's adventure options: biking, trekking, and horseback riding. Not to mention the beaches, which include Anakena, where the white sand lies within view of several *moai*, and Ovahe, which features pink-tinged sand and dramatic rock formations.

Despite its world renown, 63-square-mile Easter Island retains an old–South Pacific air, with just one main road and a cluster of modest hotels in and around Hanga Roa, the small town where nearly all the island's population of 4,700 live. The nearby eco-sensitive Explora is the first luxury resort on the island, its spaceshiplike profile gracing a hilltop 4 miles from town. Guests can expect fiery sunsets, staggering views of the mighty Pacific, and memorable meals. The twice-daily excursions led by trained Rapa Nui guides are timed to allow visitors to feel as if they are the only ones on the island. Of the handful of good lodging options in town, the Hotel Taura'a is a popular choice, a simple-but-clean bed-and-breakfast in a converted home.

WHERE: 2,350 miles/3,781 km west of Santiago. **HOW:** U.S.-based Maxim Tours offers 4-day trips. Tel 800-655-0222 or 973-927-0760; www.maximtours.com. *Cost:* from $550, all-inclusive, air extra. Originates in Santiago. **EXPLORA RAPA NUI:** Tel 56/2-206-6060; in the U.S., 866-750-6699; www.explora.com. *Cost:* 3-night packages from $2,385 per person, all-inclusive. **HOTEL TAURA'A:** Tel: 56/2-255-1310; www.taurraahotel.cl. *Cost:* from $180. **BEST TIMES:** Jul–Aug for cool weather and fewer crowds; late Jan or early Feb for Tapati Festival, the island's largest celebration of local culture.

Filigreed Channels at the End of the World

CRUISING CHILE'S FJORDS

Patagonia, Chile

Two-thirds of the way down its coastline, beyond Puerto Montt, Chile crumples into archipelagos of thousands of islets, covered with flourishing vegetation, that slowly give way to eerie ice fields. This spectacularly filigreed coast is home to icy channels opened by seismic and glacial activity millions of years ago, and its waters are full of elephant seals and sea lions, humpback whales and dolphins. It is best appreciated by ship.

Board one of the red-and-white ships that belong to the Kochifas family, the pioneers who opened the area to international tourism in the late 1970s. The 110-passenger *Skorpios III*, the most upscale of the fleet, sails from Puerto Natales, a gateway to Torres del Paine National Park (see below). Heading to the southern ice field, it takes in more than a dozen glaciers, including the imposing Glaciar Amalia, which soars as high as 328 feet, and Glaciar Bernal, one of five visible in the Montañas Fjord.

The 130-passenger *Skorpios II* sails from Puerto Montt to Chiloé, one of only three inhabited islands in a region where humankind has barely left a mark. Among the most photographed sites are its peaceful fishing villages and more than 50 reverently maintained wooden churches that date to the 18th and 19th centuries. From Chiloé, the cruise heads south to the breathtaking, neon-blue Glaciar San Rafael, in Chile's northern Patagonia region. The mile-wide, 9-mile-long glacier, the closest to the equator, rivets the attention as its 200-foot ice spires calve off with thunderous roars.

Alternatively, voyagers may ply the southernmost reaches of Chilean Patagonia and explore the wild scenery and isolated glaciers of Tierra del Fuego, South America's largest island. Weather permitting, guests can disembark and pay a visit to the end of the world at Cape Horn. Cruceros Australis offers a 4-night journey that leaves from Punta Arenas, the southernmost city in Chile, and ends in Ushuaia, Argentina (see p. 994), and a 3-night journey that does the reverse. Visits to the penguin colonies at Isla Magdalena, with 50,000 breeding pairs, and Seno Otway, a sanctuary for 2,000 breeding pairs, are always a highlight. The line's two compact ships carry a maximum of 136 passengers and thread waterways that are off-limits to most larger ships. The utter silence of the labyrinthine seas inspires the same awe that must have overcome Magellan when, in 1520, he stumbled upon these as yet uncharted waters; Antarctica (see p. 1053) is just 500 miles away.

WHERE: Puerto Montt is 631 miles/ 1,016 km south of Santiago; Punta Arenas is 1,360 miles/2,190 km south of Santiago. **TURISMO SKORPIOS:** Tel: 56/2-477-1900; in the U.S., 305-484-5357; www.skorpios.cl. *Cost:* 3-night sailings from $1,400 all-inclusive (off-peak), from $1,550 (peak). *When:* Sep–Apr. **CRUCEROS AUSTRALIS:** Tel 56/2-442-3115; in the U.S., 877-678-3772; www.australis.com. *Cost:* 4-night sailings from $1,500 all-inclusive (off-peak), from $1,895 (peak). *When:* Sep–Apr. **BEST TIME:** Jan–Feb, when days are long and temperatures are warmest.

Wilderness and Civilization on the Continent's Tip

TORRES DEL PAINE NATIONAL PARK

Patagonia, Chile

This remote outpost in the heart of Chilean Patagonia is one of nature's last virtually untrammeled wildernesses. Unmapped before the 1930s, the Torres del Paine park is a 600,000-acre network of aquamarine lakes, rushing rivers, groaning glaciers, pampas, and fjords. But it is perhaps best known for the Cuernos del Paine, spectacular 10,000-foot "horns" or towers of rose-colored granite that are part of the Cordillera Paine mountains.

This wonderland contains more than 200 species of plants and 25 species of mammals, including the tall, orange-and-white guanaco, a cousin of the llama, and the ever-elusive mountain puma. The Andean condor, with its fabled 10-foot wingspan, occasionally appears against the sky above the surreal landscape; it is but one of some 100 different species of native birds found here.

Hardy travelers head for the "W," a 35-mile trail that runs from east to west that starts at Laguna Amarga and takes 4 to 5 days to complete. The more demanding "Circuit" wends through 37 miles of scenic territory, requiring between 4 and 11 days to cover. But far easier hikes await the less ambitious, and kayaking and horseback riding provide their own perspectives on the park.

Estancia Cerro Guido is one of the few upscale lodges with a view of the Torres. It is composed of 20 historic buildings that date to when this property was a sheep ranch, in the early 20th century. Travelers seeking maximum luxury should opt for the Explora's Hotel Salto Chico, on the southeast corner of Lago Pehoé. One of the most upscale wilderness lodges in all of South America—with perhaps the most striking setting of any hotel on the planet—it serves up impeccable style and service, with full-time naturalists on staff offering guided park excursions.

The Torres del Paine mountains look out over Lake Pehoé.

Although most visitors fly into Punta Arenas, the true gateway to the region is 150 miles northwest, in Puerto Natales, a picturesque town on a fjord dramatically called Ultima Esperanza (Last Hope). Founded in 1911 as a meatpacking town and fishing port, this settlement of some 20,000 residents provides easy access to adventures afield and a growing array of cozy restaurants and inns. Handsome and reasonably priced, the Indigo Hotel offers views of the Mount Balmaceda glacier and the Paine Grande peak, as well as a rooftop Jacuzzi and spa and a well-liked restaurant that serves a variety of pisco sours.

WHERE: Punta Arenas is 1,360 miles/2,190 km south of Santiago. **CERRO GUIDO:** Tel 56/2-196-4807; www.cerroguido.cl. *Cost:* from $200. *When:* closed May–Sep. **EXPLORA:** Tel 56/2-228-4665; in the U.S., 866-750-6699; www.explora.com. *Cost:* 4-night all-inclusive package from $2,780 per person, all-inclusive. **INDIGO:** Tel 56/61-413-609; www.indigopatagonia.com. *Cost:* from $150 (off-peak), from $260 (peak). **BEST TIMES:** mid-Mar–Apr for fewer visitors and less wind; early Oct–Nov for spring wildflowers.

Skiing the Formidable Andes

PORTILLO AND VALLE NEVADO

Chile

A jaunt down to Chile's ski resorts can seem an irresistible choice for North Americans and Europeans; when slopes north of the equator are snow-free, visitors here find the Western hemisphere's highest peaks, the finest deep-powder snow, no lift lines or slope traffic, plus resorts offering plenty of Chilean hospitality and breathtaking scenery.

The most developed and largest of these are Portillo and Valle Nevado, and while both are top-notch, with the best snow, on average, in South America, they serve different kinds of Alpine enthusiasts. Portillo (Little Pass), renowned as the site of the 1966 World Alpine Ski Championships, perches high above the tree line at 9,233 feet. Overlooking the sapphire waters of Lake Inca and facing a bowl of spectacular Andean peaks, its 14 lifts access 2,200 acres of snowy diversion, some at an elevation of 11,000 feet, while helicopters open thousands of additional acres of powder skiing. Some slopes are notoriously steep, such as the Roca Jack, which makes Portillo ideal for advanced skiers. As for where to bunk down when the last run's been made, the brilliant yellow Hotel Portillo and its less expensive annexes are the only game in town. They offer weekly packages for every budget, and the hotel's design encourages camaraderie among the guests, creating the sense that you are all members of your own private club.

Valle Nevado boasts dramatic Andean scenery, the continent's most modern lift system, and more than 2,000 acres of terrain suitable for every skill level—as well as plenty of off-piste runs and a terrain park for those who enjoy doing tricks. Heli-skiing from Valle Nevado is widely considered the best in South America, allowing skiers access to peaks rivaled only by the Himalayas. Valle Nevado's complex includes three hotels, and various restaurants and shops for nonskiers and skiers alike. Its 1-hour proximity to Santiago makes day skiing a possibility for those with limited time.

WHERE: Portillo is 88 miles/132 km northeast of Santiago. **PORTILLO:** Tel 56/2-263-0606; in the U.S., 800-829-5325; www.skiportillo.com. *Cost:* 1-week packages at the Double Valley Hotel, from $1,700 per person (off-peak), from $3,200 (peak), all-inclusive. **VALLE NEVADO:** Tel 56/2-477-7705; in the U.S., 800-669-0554; www.vallenevado.com. *Cost:* Hotel Tres Puntas from $350 (off-peak), from $575 (peak), all-inclusive. **BEST TIMES:** mid-Jun–early Oct for ski season with Jul and Aug offering best conditions; Jul for family weeks.

Outdoor Adventures amid Picture-Perfect Scenery

Chile's Lake District

Pucón, Chile

Bordered by Lake Villarrica on one side and the snow-capped Villarrica Volcano on the other, the town of Pucón is the portal to the pristine Regiòn de los Lagos (Lake District). Unofficially known as the adventure capital of Chile, it is one of the country's major destinations for boaters, water-sports enthusiasts, and sport fishermen. From Pucón, excursions lead visitors to areas such as Lake Caburga, Coñaripe, Lican Ray, and beyond; active types can raft, kayak, or fish the Río Trancura, trek through Huerquehue National Park, or join canopy tours to soar among the treetops there. More adventurous souls may try climbing the 9,341-foot volcano (you can ski it in the winter), where molten magma offers surreal photo opportunities.

Chile is filled with not only volcanoes but geological faults; the latter create ideal conditions for the natural hot-springs spas that dot the Lake District. Few are as inviting as Termas

Geométricas, 40 minutes outside of Pucón, where a maze of wooden walkways leads through lush vegetation to a series of slate-tiled pools of various temperatures, simultaneously providing soothing relaxation and minimalist—almost Japanese—style.

When Queen Elizabeth II and Neil Armstrong each visited Chile's Lake District, they stayed at the family-run Hotel Antumalal, one of its most intriguing hotels. Dating to 1945, the inn blends Bauhaus design with abundant gardens and offers guests use of a private beach on Lago Villarrica. Each of the 22 guest rooms is graced with handmade wood furnishings, a fireplace, and huge windows that frame panoramic views of the lake. The hotel's restaurant, Parque Antumalal, is one of the best in the region. Start with a signature Cran Sour cocktail, move on to the Chilean lobster, and end with sweet *kuchenes* (a nod to the German immigrants who settled the area)—all served with spectacular water views.

Where: 490 miles/789 km south of Santiago. **Antumalal:** Tel 56/45-441-011; www.antumalal.com. *Cost:* from $265 (off-peak), from $360 (peak); dinner $45. **Best times:** mid-Dec–Feb for nicest summer weather; Jan–Feb for Muestra Cultural Mapuche festival in Villarrica.

Surreal Odyssey to the Driest Place on Earth

The Atacama Desert

San Pedro de Atacama, Chile

Stretching over nearly one-third of Chile's surface, the Atacama Desert is so otherworldly that NASA has conducted experiments here. But word of its austere yet striking natural beauty has traveled far, and intrepid spirits now come for its year-round promise of adventure as well as its many natural wonders. The base for exploring this, the driest desert on earth, is the village of San Pedro de Atacama, which stands 7,000 feet above sea level. Built mostly from adobe brick, San Pedro offers convenient access to hiking, mountain biking, horseback riding, sand-boarding, and other activities.

Valle de la Luna, shaped by millennia of erosion, takes its name from its resemblance to the surface of the moon.

The Museo Arqueológico Padre Le Paige, an archaeological museum with an excellent collection of pre-Columbian artifacts preserved by the arid climate, provides a valuable introduction to visitors before they head out on one of the many guided excursions. Early morning is best for striking out to see the Geysers del Tatio, the highest in the world, which come to life in the early light; en route are the Termas de Puritama, hot springs that offer an enticing way to unwind in eight warm pools descending a narrow, lush gorge.

Afternoons are ideal for viewing dozens of flamingos grazing in the mineralized lake that sprawls across the tremendous salt flat at Salar de Atacama, part of a national flamingo reserve. At the end of the day, the setting sun casts shades of gold, violet, and red across the lunarlike landscape of the aptly named Valle de la Luna (Valley of the Moon). Multiday tours from San Pedro visit Bolivia's Salar de Uyuni, the world's largest salt flat (see p. 999).

In recent years, hotels have sprouted up around San Pedro, ranging from simple hostels to full-service luxury lodges. Among the top-of-the-line choices is the low-slung Alto Atacama Desert Lodge, a pioneer in eco-sustainability and one of Chile's most attractive nature lodges. It was designed to blend into the terra-cotta cliffs of the Catarpe Valley, near Atacama and Inca ruin sites and just minutes from San Pedro. The lodge offers lots of guided excursions, six inviting pools that spread out like an oasis, a spa with sauna, and gourmet-in-the-middle-of-nowhere dining. Those looking for individualized service in a smaller setting choose Awasi, with its eight spacious, thatch-roofed bungalows that surround a courtyard, pool, and lovely open-air lounge, with handmade wooden furniture. For a stay in the center of San Pedro, Kimal is a well-run 19-room inn; the staff greets new arrivals with a pisco sour and warm welcome.

WHERE: 1,038 miles/1,670 km north of Santiago and 61 miles/98 km from Calama, the nearest commercial airport. **ALTO ATACAMA:** Tel 56/2-957-0300; www.altoatacama.com. *Cost:* 2 nights from $940 per person, all-inclusive. **AWASI:** Tel 56/2-233-9641; in the U.S., 888-880-3219; www.awasi.cl. *Cost:* 3 nights from $1,885 per person, all-inclusive. **KIMAL:** Tel 56/5-585-1030; www.kimal.cl. *Cost:* from $185. **BEST TIMES:** year-round for sunny weather; nights are coldest (about 30°F/–1°C) Jun–Aug; Jun 29 for patron saint festivities during Fiesta de San Pedro y San Pablo.

Irresistible Contrasts in Chile's Twin Cities

VIÑA DEL MAR AND VALPARAÍSO

Valparaíso, Chile

Few cities are so close geographically but so different in looks and personality as Valparaíso and Viña del Mar. Visitors to Chile's central coast can travel from the wonderfully quirky, Victorian-era ambience of the former to the upscale beachfront pleasures of the latter in just a few minutes.

During the 19th century, Chile's Pacific port city of Valparaíso was one of the wealthiest places on the continent, attracting new residents who built grand Neoclassical and Victorian mansions overlooking the water. The 1914 opening of the Panama Canal, which provided a more efficient shipping route, spelled an end to the city's boom, but Valpo (as locals call it) remains one of Chile's most enjoyable destinations. Perched on a series of 45 hills (*cerros*) above a huge bay, it is often compared to San Francisco: Visitors spend their days wandering the tangle of cobbled backstreets that line the steep slopes and enjoying small restaurants, shops, and inns set in colorful former homes. The obligatory stop is the hilltop La Sebastiana, which in 1961 became one of the late poet Pablo Neruda's three homes. Share

Neruda's love for Valparaíso's charms with a stroll through the city's 19th-century cemeteries with their Baroque mausoleums or with a ride aboard one of the *ascensores,* rickety funicular railways that connect the downtown area with the streets above.

Set in a beautifully restored 1920s mansion in the Cerro Alegre district, where English and German immigrants built their homes, Hotel Casa Higueras has 20 guest rooms, many with private terraces and panoramic views of Valparaíso Bay. To see where the city's local gastro revival began, take a table at lively Pasta e Vino, or on the terrace of Café Turri, where you can enjoy excellent seafood along with the stunning vistas.

For the yin to this urban yang, head next-door to Viña del Mar, founded in 1874 by well-to-do *santiaguinos* and *porteños* (residents of Santiago and Valparaíso, respectively) who decided they needed a seaside getaway. Since then Viña, as it's known to locals, has grown into Chile's largest and most popular beach resort, a high-profile destination for Latin American and foreign travelers alike. You'll find broad, sandy beaches, luxury apartment buildings, and grand private homes. The Casino Municipal, built in 1930, is a throwback to the days when gamblers dressed to the nines. Glimpses of the city's posh past are also on view at the Museo Palacio Rioja, an opulently furnished 1910 Belle Époque mansion that hosts performances of classical music and theater as well as movie screenings. Swank accommodations include Hotel del Mar, a contemporary Greco-Roman confection attached to the casino, with views of the sea. A devoted following comes to the hotel to dine at Savinya, which serves international cuisine with Mediterranean flair.

Some call bohemian Valparaíso the "Pearl of the Pacific."

Stop in the Casablanca Valley wine region en route back to Santiago; Viña Indomita offers guided tours and spectacular views from its hilltop bodega and restaurant.

WHERE: Valparaíso is 61 miles/98 km northwest of Santiago. **CASA HIGUERAS:** Tel 56/32-249-7900; www.hotelcasahigueras.cl. *Cost:* from $245. **PASTA E VINO:** Tel 56/32-249-6187; www.pastaevinoristorante.cl. *Cost:* lunch $25. **CAFÉ TURRI:** Tel 56/32-225-2091; www.cafeturri.cl. *Cost:* dinner $30. **HOTEL DEL MAR:** Tel 56/32-250-0800; www.enjoy.cl. *Cost:* from $215 (off-peak), from $285 (peak). **VIÑA INDOMITA:** Tel: 56/32-275-4400; www.indomita.cl. **BEST TIMES:** Nov–Mar for warm weather; New Year's Eve for fireworks and celebrations in Valparaíso; mid-Feb for the Festival Internacional de la Canción in Viña del Mar.

A Reborn City and Its Treasures

CANDELARIA AND GOLD MUSEUM

Bogotá, Colombia

Once known primarily for drug cartel–driven crime, Colombia's capital has cleaned up its bad-boy image. A bohemian element that endured through the dark times has turned the heart of the city into a cultural and artistic center and infused the place with a forward-looking spirit. Indeed, Bogotá is fast becoming one of Latin America's most progressive and prosperous cities.

La Candelaria, also known as Zona C, leads this renaissance. The formerly seedy area is now a place where locals and visitors enjoy its pedestrian-only cobblestone streets lined with Colonial mansions and churches. It is also home to a stylish new cultural center and a dozen popular museums.

Its highlight, located on the edge of the neighborhood, is the Museo del Oro, the world's largest and finest gold museum. Only 15 percent of its collection of more than 30,000 artifacts is on display in a bright and airy new building. The sophisticated workmanship of the items on exhibit, not to mention the sheer magnitude of the collection, is staggering. The stunning displays, representing every major pre-Columbian culture in the region at the time of the Spanish conquest, will make you believe the legends of El Dorado. The museum also houses the world's largest uncut emerald, testament to Colombia's role as the world's foremost producer of the beautiful green gems.

Colombia's foremost artist, Fernando Botero, donated 123 of his pieces to create the nearby Donación Botero, the largest museum of his works anywhere. His signature art—whimsically corpulent people and animals, rendered in paintings and sculpture—shares space with works by Chagall, Picasso, and other artists from Botero's private collection.

The boutique Hotel de la Opera, created from two restored Colonial buildings next to the famous 19th-century Teatro Colón, is just steps from the expansive Plaza de Bolívar, the neighborhood's main square. Some of its rooms are decorated in a Colonial style and others with Deco lines. Either way, you'll enjoy a pool, spa, and a rooftop restaurant with city views.

For dinner, digress to Zona G, one of Bogotá's trendiest and most vibrant neighborhoods. Or consider Andrés Carne de Res, in Chia, 40 minutes from downtown, a longtime institution. Wandering musicians and get-up-and-move soundtracks effortlessly fill more than one dance floor. Thick grilled steaks, imported from Argentina, take up just one of the menu's 30 pages; don't miss the traditional *ajiaco*, a potato and chicken soup.

MUSEO DEL ORO: Tel 57/1-343-2222; www.banrep.gov.co/museo. **DONACIÓN BOTERO:** Tel 57/1-343-1212; www.lablaa.org/museobotero.htm. **HOTEL DE LA OPERA:** Tel 57/1-336-2066; www.hotelopera.com.co. *Cost:* $185 (off-peak), $250 (peak). **ANDRÉS CARNE DE RES:** Tel 57/1-863-7880; www.andrescarnederes.com. *Cost:* dinner $60. **BEST TIMES:** Dec–Apr for summer weather; Mar of even years for Ibero-American Theater Festival.

A Riot of Color, a Caribbean Vibe

OLD CARTAGENA

Colombia

When the Spanish came looking for the kingdom of El Dorado in 1533, they landed at Cartagena and built its wealth on slavery, gold, and sugar. Today this coastal gem of Colonial architecture is beautifully restored, particularly within its authentic and lively 16th- and 17th-century Ciudad Vieja (Old City), helping to make Colombia again a global destination. The city's elaborate *murallas*—nearly 7 miles of walls, up to 25 feet thick and 83 feet high—enclose flowering patios, wooden balconies, narrow back streets, stately and vividly painted mansions housing hotels and fine restaurants, café- and palm-lined plazas, and centuries-old churches. The walls, together with an impregnable chain of outer forts such as San Sebastián de Pastelillo and San Felipe de Barajas, protected Colombia's most important city from plundering pirates, most famously Sir Francis Drake. They took more than 200 years to complete and are the only such fortifications in South America.

Cartagena is a riot of color, its houses splashed in red, blue, and orange and cloaked in flowers. Resounding with *cumbia, vallenato, champeta,* and other Afro-Caribbean rhythms, the city can feel more like Old Havana (see p. 1075) than anywhere in South America. *Palenqueras*—women balancing pans filled with fruit on their heads—linger in Plaza Santo Domingo, with its voluptuous reclining nude by Colombian artist Fernando Botero, and in the triangular Plaza de los Coches, where shops, restaurants, and bars occupy handsome balconied houses.

Cartagena's finest hotel is the early-17th-century Convento de Santa Clara, luxuriously refurbished by the French hotel company Sofitel. Guests can swim in an oversize pool and dine in the nuns' former refectory just off the cloister, filled with a flowering garden. The city now has dozens of boutique hotels, but one of the first remains one of the finest: The intimate Hotel Agua offers just six individually decorated rooms in a Colonial 17th-century mansion. Its rooftop pool provides great views of the city and the sea.

The best place for sunset drinks is the Café del Mar, right on top of the city walls and overlooking the water, while La Vitrola, one of the most atmospheric restaurants in town, serves excellent Cuban-Caribbean cuisine. Its ceiling fans, crisply jacketed waiters, and live Cuban jazz quartet will take you back to a more elegant era.

For all-out romance, have an alfresco dinner at Club de Pesca, which overlooks the marina in the working-class Getsemaní neighborhood and serves contemporary Caribbean-inspired dishes. Nearby, the stately Hotel Monterrey offers moderate rates for simple but spacious, comfortable rooms in a 19th-century building. The view of the walled city from the fifth-floor terrace, where you can relax with a drink, is among the best in town.

Hotel Santa Clara: Tel 57/5-650-4700; in the U.S., 800-763-4835; www.hotelsantaclara.com. *Cost:* $350 (off-peak), $495 (peak). **Hotel Agua:** Tel 57/5-664-9479; www.hotelagua.com.co. *Cost:* $340 (off-peak), $390 (peak). **Café del Mar:** Tel 57/5-664-6513. *Cost:* dinner $45. **La Vitrola:** Tel 57/5-660-0711. *Cost:* dinner $60. **Club de Pesca:** Tel 57/5-660-4594; www.clubdepesca.com. *Cost:* dinner $50. **Hotel Monterrey:** Tel 57/5-650-3030; www.hotelmonterrey.com.co. *Cost:* $155. **Best times:** Dec–Apr for dry season; early Jan for Cartagena International Music Festival; Jan 20 for Fiesta de la Candelaria; mid-Mar for Caribbean Music Festival and Festival Internacional de Cine; late Mar–early Apr for Ibero-American Theater Festival.

Palenqueras *famously carry fruit in bowls balanced atop their heads.*

The Coffee Triangle

EJE CAFETERO

Colombia

One of the most beautiful areas to visit in all of Colombia is the one that produces coffee, the country's most famous product. Nearly 10 percent of the world's crop is grown here, making Colombia the second largest producer after Brazil. Rising as high as 5,900 feet above sea level, the region comprises three departments: Caldas, Quindio, and Risaralda, that together form the Eje Cafetero (Coffee Axis, aka Coffee Triangle). Armenia, the capital of Quindio, serves as a regional hub, as does Pereira, where the main airport is located.

Nature is king here, and the region's national parks include the slightly Disney-like Parque Nacional del Café, with its train, mechanical rides, and vignettes about coffee cultivation, and the Parque Nacional Natural Los Nevados, near Pereira, a large water and land reserve occupying more than 144,000 acres. The highlight is the 17,440-foot-high Los Nevados peak, a particular lure for trekkers and ecotourists. Agritourism has made the area one of Latin America's top rural destinations, thanks to nearly 700 traditional coffee haciendas, or *fincas*, working farms that provide lodging and a glimpse of traditional life. Many offer horseback tours with the Andes as a dramatic backdrop, allowing you to glimpse waterfalls and ride across endless plantations and lush countryside, where birds and butterflies drift through the air. Other possibilities are kayaking, whitewater rafting, trekking, treetop canopy tours, or dipping into mud baths and hot springs near Santa Rosa del Cabal. For now, most tourists here are Colombians enjoying long weekends.

Luxury has come to the region with the opening of Sazagua, on the outskirts of Pereira, a boutique hotel with ten suites, a spa surrounded by lush gardens, and a restaurant that is the gastronomic highlight of the area.

WHERE: 100 miles/160 km west of Bogotá. **PARQUE NACIONAL DEL CAFÉ:** Tel 57/6-741-7417; www.parquenacionaldelcafe.com. **PARQUE NACIONAL NATURAL LOS NEVADOS:** 57/1-243-1634; www.parquesnacionales.gov.co. **SAZAGUA:** Tel 57/6-337-9895; www.sazagua.com. *Cost:* from $180. **BEST TIMES:** Mar–Jun and Oct–Dec for coffee harvest season.

Highland Colonial Charm

CUENCA

Ecuador

The historical center of Cuenca, Ecuador's third largest city, oozes colonial charm, with cobblestone streets, balconies, and buildings no higher than a church steeple per zoning regulations. The best days to visit are Thursdays and Sundays, when the central plaza becomes a marketplace filled with local women, known as *cholas cuencanas* and dressed in *polleras,* colorful woolen dresses. Many stalls overflow with Panama hats, which are actually made here and not in Panama; the best are made by Homero Ortega P. & Hijos. Overlooking the city are the Iglesia El Sagrario (Sanctuary Church), aka Catedral Vieja, its oldest structure, and the Catedral de la Inmaculada Concepción (aka New Cathedral), modeled on the Italian Baptistry in Florence. Museo del Banco Central (aka the Museo Pumapungo) highlights local culture, while Museo del Monasterio de la Concepción is a 16th-century Colonial structure filled with religious art. Nearly as revered by locals is Villa Rosa, a restaurant in the enclosed courtyard of a lovingly restored Cuencan home near the central plaza. Owner Berta Vintimilla uses old family recipes to delight her loyal clientele—her empanadas are not to be missed. Antiques and fine art are highlights of any stay at the Mansion Alcazar, built in the 1870s as the home of Luis Cordero, then president of Ecuador. Today it is one of the most inviting of the new crop of recently restored hotels in the historic quarter.

One exciting way to experience the mountains is by taking the *Spirit of the Andes* train ride, until recently called the famous Chiva Express. Get ready for dramatic views along a route that follows the Avenue of the Volcanoes, passing the active Cotopaxi and extinct Mount Chimborazo. It soon reaches the legendary Nariz del Diablo (Devil's Nose), a feat of engineering that follows a hair-raising series of switchback turns, before delivering you to Riobamba, the old market town 4 hours south of Quito.

Riobamba's well-known weekend Indian market sprawls across the town's five squares; you can identify the various communities of Indians by the women's distinctive hats. Spend an hour in the Museo de Arte Religioso whose remarkable collection of art and gold objects is displayed in a restored convent and cloisters.

If it's Sunday, head to Cuenca's outlying villages for the markets, especially to Gualaceo, about a half hour east. The most popular excursion from Cuenca is to Ingapirca, Ecuador's largest pre-Columbian ruin. This was a religious site, unusual for its round and oval structures, built by the Cañari people before they were conquered by the Incas.

WHERE: 265 miles/442 km south of Quito. **VILLA ROSA:** Tel 593/7-2837-944. *Cost:* dinner $25. **MANSION ALCAZAR:** Tel 593/7-2823-889; www.mansionalcazar.com. *Cost:* from $205. **HOW:** U.S.-based Ladatco Tours offers custom itineraries that include Cuenca, Riobamba, and the train ride. Tel 800-327-6162 or 305-854-8422; www.ladatco.com. *Cost:* 7-day tour from $2,325. Originates in Quito. **BEST TIMES:** Jan, Sep–Nov for good weather; Nov 3 for Independence Day in Cuenca; Sun for markets in and around Cuenca.

Evolutionary Miracles Above and Under Water

GALÁPAGOS ISLANDS

Ecuador

A modern-day traveler's rules of thumb: Visit the most fragile places first; stay on the trails; disturb nothing. Nowhere does this apply more than to the 58 islands and cays of the Galápagos archipelago, which straddle the equator 600 miles off the coast of Ecuador. They were essentially unknown until Charles Darwin's arrival in 1835. It was here that he first developed his theory of evolution, using as evidence an amazing roster of wildlife that thrived on these islands, each remarkably individual in its topography, flora, and fauna. They are still home to the greatest proportion of endemic species in the world. The one most associated with the area is the 400-pound land tortoise, whose shell resembles a riding saddle, known to the early Spaniards as a *galápago*—thus their name for the archipelago. Marine iguanas (the only lizard in the world that lives in the ocean), blue-footed boobies, and 13 species of finches are also peculiar to these volcanic islands. In their isolation from predators, the animals of the Galápagos have no instinctive fear of man—their curiosity may surpass your own.

Blue-footed, red-footed, and masked boobies can all be found on the islands.

The Galápagos Islands are as stunning underwater as above. Declared UNESCO's first Natural World Heritage Site in 1978 and then a UNESCO Biosphere Reserve in 1984, they host an astonishing variety of marine life: Scuba divers will see the hemisphere's northernmost population of penguins (thanks to the cooling Humboldt Current), sea lions, fur seals, dolphins, and even the odd migrating whale. Some fully equipped live-aboards head for the remote and uninhabited islands of Wolf and Darwin, where you can expect to be surrounded by enormous schools of hammerheads and manta rays, for which the Galápagos are famous.

The most popular way to visit the islands is by boat; you can choose among more than 80 options carrying 12 to 100 passengers each. Landlubbers can stay in one of a clutch of very comfortable resorts, such as the Royal Palm Hotel, occupying a 400-acre site on Santa Cruz; of the 18 main islands, it is one of the largest (380 square miles) and is the most populated. The resort's private boat takes guests on wildlife-viewing day trips, delivering them back in time for a spa treatment followed by a candlelight dinner. Santa Cruz is also the site of the Darwin Research Station, which many giant tortoises call home.

WHERE: 618 miles/966 km west of Guayaquil. **HOW:** U.S.-based INCA offers 11-day trips that include an 8-day cruise on a 12–16-passenger ship. Tel 510-420-1550; www.inca1.com. *Cost:* from $4,895. Originates in Quito. U.S.-based Caradonna Dive Adventures offers an all-inclusive 7-day diving package. Tel 800-328-2288 or 407-774-9000; www.caradonna.com. *Cost:* from $4,150. Originates in Santa Cruz. **ROYAL PALM HOTEL:** Tel 593/5-527-408; in the U.S., 800-528-6069; www.royalpalmgalapagos.com. *Cost:* from $375. **DARWIN RESEARCH STATION:** Tel 593/5-526-146; www.darwinfoundation.org. **BEST TIMES:** mid-Apr–Jun and Sep–Dec for nicest weather and fewest crowds.

Rain Forest Luxe and Wildlife to Match

MASHPI LODGE

Ecuador

Ecotourism has reached new heights of comfort just 2 hours from Quito on the western slopes of the Andes with a modern masterpiece that might have won the approval of Frank Lloyd Wright. Built with cutting-edge, environmentally sound methods, the 18-suite Mashpi Lodge features contemporary, clean lines and natural materials that blend effortlessly into the 2,620-acre private rain-forest reserve—part of the Tumbez-Chocó-Darién biodiversity hot spot—in which it nestles. The lodge's glass walls present breathtaking views of the forest and valleys from nearly every angle. Only electric vehicles are allowed within the reserve, so as not to disturb the wildlife.

Learn about the rain forest's wild beauty in the company of local guides and naturalists along miles of trails that pass by waterfalls and blooming orchids (Ecuador is home to 4,000 species). The area boasts 500 species of birds, including 36 endemic ones. Travel into the upper tree canopy via a mile-long aerial tram or take a nocturnal walk that offers a completely different, more mystical experience. Back at the lodge, a serpentarium and saparium will increase your appreciation for the snakes and toads of the rain forest.

Families who live in the vicinity welcome guests to visit and learn about their methods of raising cocoa and other crops. Watch the beans being processed into dark chocolate and sample the goods, then strike off for the restored archaeological site of Tulipe, where the Yumbo civilization thrived between 800 and 1660. Finish your day at the lodge's restaurant, which specializes in refined dishes complemented by a carefully selected wine list from South America and beyond. And don't forget to visit the spa, which incorporates local traditions and herbs into its rejuvenating treatments. Going green is all pleasure here.

WHERE: 71 miles/114 km northwest of Quito. Tel 593/9-2298-8200; in the U.S., 877-500-9402; www.mashpilodge.com. *Cost:* 2 nights from $1,300 per person, all-inclusive, with transfer from Quito. **BEST TIMES:** Jan–May for dry season; the solstices and equinoxes in Mar, Jun, Sep, and Dec, when ceremonies are performed at Tulipe.

Exuberant World of Biodiversity

El Oriente, Ecuador's Amazon

Ecuador

El Oriente ("The East") is Ecuador's vast, wild region of tropical Amazon forest. Among the world's most biodiverse regions, it occupies more than one-third of Ecuador but holds only 4 percent of the population. It is here that snowmelt spreads from the base of the Andes, mixing with volcanic soil and making the rich earth that sustains this area's varied plant and wildlife. You'll glimpse everything from monkeys and birds to caimans. In the Cuyabeno, Pastaza, and Putumayo rivers—all tributaries of the Amazon—pink freshwater dolphins can sometimes be spotted. Nine native tribes inhabit the area too, including the Quechua, Huaorani, and Shuar.

Sacha Lodge, set on a lake in 5,000 acres teeming with hundreds of species of birds, fish, and mammals, is one of the originals. The view from the virgin property's 135-foot observation tower, where you can discover a world of treetop bromeliads and the exotic birds they attract, includes the snow-topped peak of Sumaco, an extinct volcano 100 miles away. Local English-speaking naturalists lead daily jungle walks.

Kapawi Ecolodge and Reserve, among the area's most remote lodges, has 20 eco-friendly cabins built on stilts over a lagoon cocooned by jungle that stretches for more than 2 million acres. The Achuar tribe helped to build the lodge and became its owners in 2008. The Napo Wildlife Center Amazon Lodge is another environmentally sensitive option, with 12 lakefront cabañas sitting on more than 82 square miles of forest within Yasuni National Park. Two observation towers allow you to see over the jungle canopy. Built with the assistance of the Añangu-Quichua community, who have owned the lodge since 2007, it's also a birder's paradise. Some of the most colorful of the more than 560 species recorded in the region are parrots and macaws, attracted to the mineral-rich clay licks.

Where: Lago Agrio is 161 miles/259 km northeast of Quito. **How:** U.S.-based Andean Treks can customize all-inclusive 4- to 8-day packages at any of the various lodges. Tel 800-683-8148 or 617-924-1974; www.andeantreks.com. **Sacha Lodge:** Tel 593/2-256-6090; www.sachalodge.com. **Kapawi Ecolodge and Reserve:** Tel 593/2-600-9333; www.kapawi.com. **Napo Wildlife Center Amazon Lodge:** Tel 593/2-600-5893; in the U.S., 866-750-0830; www.napowildlifecenter.com. **Cost:** all lodges charge from $695 to $800 per person, for a 4-day stay, all-inclusive with canoe transfer. **Best time:** Dec–Apr for dry season.

The Continent's Most Famous Indigenous Market

Otavalo

Ecuador

The oldest, best-known, and most important Indian market in South America takes place every Saturday high in the Andes. Otavalo's market has always served as the social and economic heartbeat of the northern highlands; today it is one of Ecuador's most popular destinations, after the Galápagos Islands (see p. 1032). The otherwise sleepy town awakens at dawn to a cacophony of chickens, cows, and sheep and the trading of hemp, saddles, vegetables, grain, and textiles. There are also tourist trinkets galore—pottery, weavings, jewelry, carved wooden animals—but what most visitors are seeking is the authentic local atmosphere as the brightly dressed *otavaleños* converge to barter. Early birds should ideally arrive before the animal market bedlam ends at around 8 A.M., or at the very least before day-trippers arrive on buses rolling in from Quito (see p. 1036) at around 10 A.M.

Bartering for goods at the local market is a tradition among otavaleños.

Spend Friday night at the nearby Hacienda Cusín, a 17th-century colonial plantation reincarnated as a first-class rural inn. Rooms have a rustic, old-world charm—some with romantic fireplaces and wrought-iron balconies opening onto lovely vistas of the surrounding mountain scenery. Fifteen minutes away is the more sophisticated La Mirage, a lush flower- and vine-draped oasis perched high on an Andean hillside that combines the best of local culture and artistry with the owners' love of European aesthetics and luxury. The staff at the impeccably run inn's working farm can send you off with a guide on horseback through ancient Indian towns and unspoiled high country to the shores of a volcanic lake. Dining at La Mirage is as memorable for the view of the snow-capped Cotacachi and Imbabura mountains as it is for the excellent menu, enhanced by local Ecuadoran wines and served by young Otavalo Indian girls in traditional embroidered dress.

Midway on the 2-hour drive from Quito to Otavalo is Mitad del Mundo, the "Middle of the World" monument celebrating Ecuador's equatorial position. (Ecuador is Spanish for "equator.") The equator actually lies 984 feet to the north of the monument, which was placed on the basis of measurements made during the 1736 French Geodesic Mission. Still, straddling the line here for a photo op is hard to resist.

WHERE: 80 miles/120 km north of Quito. **HACIENDA CUSÍN:** Tel 593/6-2918-013; in the U.S., Myths & Mountains, 800-670-6984; www.haciendacusin.com. *Cost:* $120. **LA MIRAGE:** Tel 593/6-2915-237; in the U.S., 800-327-3573; www.mirage.com.ec. *Cost:* from $350. **BEST TIMES:** Sat for best market, though markets take place almost daily; Jun 24–Jul 6 for celebration of the patron saints of Cotacachi.

Latin America's Best-Preserved Center

QUITO

Ecuador

At 9,200 feet above sea level, Quito is among the world's highest capitals. Ringed by mountains and volcanoes that are often crowned with snow, this city is as spectacular and welcoming as its year-round temperature (an average of 70°F despite its just-south-of-the-equator location). The ancient heart of Quito, the first city center to be declared a UNESCO Heritage Site, is rich with Colonial buildings built on Incan foundations, much like Cuzco, in Peru (see p. 1040). In fact, Quito was the ancient capital of the Inca's northern realm long before it became the capital of the new Republic of Ecuador in 1830. The Quito School of Art, developed in the 1500s, combined European and indigenous influences, many of which can still be seen today.

The Jesuit order is the "company" behind La Iglesia de la Compañia de Jesús.

Among the most imposing buildings in Quito is the Iglesia de San Francisco (honoring the city's patron saint), which rises over Plaza San Francisco. An immense Spanish Baroque church dating from 1535, it is one of South America's oldest, built over the ruins of an Inca temple. Even more stunning is the Iglesia de la Compañia de Jesús, a late-18th-century masterpiece that combines Baroque and Mudejar design. With virtually no surface left unembellished, it is possibly the most beautiful of the capital's 86 churches (95 percent of the population is Catholic). The 16th-century cathedral Iglesia de la Catedral can be found on the Plaza de la Independencia, also called Plaza Grande, the Spanish colonial administrative heart. Hotel Plaza Grande, in the opulent former home of Juan Díaz de Hidalgo, a founder of Quito, provides 15 luxury rooms in an unmatched plazaside location. Patio Andaluz, a Colonial boutique hotel designated a national treasure, also allows you to stay within walking distance in an ambience that mixes old-world charm with modern fittings.

Handicrafts proliferate in Quito. For an incomparable display of those harking back to pre-Columbian times, as well as wares from contemporary artisans, drop by Olga Fisch Folklore, a crafts store-cum-museum.

Cotopaxi, at 19,347 feet the world's highest continuously active volcano, is an hour's drive southeast. The climb to the summit is serious business and requires acclimation, so don't attempt it on your first day. Or settle for the view of the snow-capped summit from Hacienda San Agustín de Callo. Built in the 15th century on the site of an Inca palace and owned today by a descendant of early 20th-century president Leonidas Plaza, the atmospheric inn offers 11 comfortable guest rooms, some of which still feature ancient masonry. It is a working farm, the source of much of the traditional Andean cuisine enjoyed by guests.

HOTEL PLAZA GRANDE: Tel 593/2-2510-777; in the U.S., 888-790-5264; www.plazagrandequito.com. *Cost:* from $550. **HOTEL PATIO ANDALUZ:** Tel 593/2-2280-830; www.hotelpatioandaluz.com. *Cost:* $200. **OLGA FISCH FOLKLORE:** Tel 593/2-2541-315; www.olgafisch.com. **HACIENDA SAN AGUSTÍN DE CALLO:** Tel 593/3-2719-160; www.incahacienda.com. *Cost:* from $350, all-inclusive. **BEST TIMES:** Jun–Aug for nicest weather; Semana Santa (the week before Easter); 1st week of Dec for Fiestas de Quito.

Where the Mighty River Begins

PERUVIAN AMAZON

Amazonas, Peru

The confluence of the Ucayali and Marañón rivers in Loreto, Peru, forms the legendary head of the mighty Amazon, 2,400 miles from where it flows into the Atlantic. Though Brazil garners most of the fame as the home of the Amazon (see p. 1000), Peru is one of the best places to see it. Flying into Iquitos provides a peek at the region's largest city, established by the Jesuits in the 1750s and a flourishing rubber tree plantation hub in the late 1800s. It's the launchpad for exploring the headwaters of the longest river in the Americas (and, by recent calculations, in the world) and the 5-million-acre biodiversity-rich Pacaya-Samiria National Reserve. Twice the size of Yellowstone Park (see p. 909), it is the largest wetland reserve in the world.

International Expeditions, one of the first to establish a presence in the region more than 30 years ago, takes travelers deep into the jungle aboard the 28-passenger *La Amatista,* built in the style of a 19th-century riverboat. It stops at small settlements along the way, allowing you to visit the local shaman or one-classroom schools. Local naturalists point out the wealth of wildlife: More species of primates have been recorded in this region than anywhere else in the new world, and gray and pink river dolphins can be glimpsed swimming beside the ship. Small excursion boats penetrate narrow passages, flooded forests, and backwater lakes, allowing guided hikes through dense Amazon jungle. A new company, Aqua Expeditions, brings unprecedented comfort to Amazon explorations with its contemporary luxury cruisers, the 24-passenger *Aqua* and the 32-passenger *Aria*. Guests return from jungle forays to meals from a kitchen supervised by Lima chef Pedro Schiaffino, then repair to spacious suites with enormous picture windows.

If you prefer to overnight on land, unpack at any of Explorama's five lodges in the 250,000-acre Amazon Biosphere Reserve, all within 1 to 3 hours by boat from Iquitos. The 72-room Ceiba Tops, opened in 2004, is their newest and most luxurious—in these parts, that means air-conditioning and a large pool. A trip to the nearby nonprofit Swiss Family Robinson–style camp called the Amazon Center for Environmental Education and Research reveals a treetop system of ladders, cables, and netting. Visitors ascend 125 feet—about 13 stories—to explore the rain forest via an ingenious multi-level system of aerial platforms and suspended pathways. From here you might spy one of the estimated two-thirds of the rain forest species that live in, and never descend from, the canopy. Many of them have yet to be identified.

Where: Iquitos is 1,153 miles/1,860 km northeast of Lima (1.5 hours by air; Peru's largest jungle city is accessible by air only). **International Expeditions:** In the U.S., tel 800-633-4734 or 205-428-1700; www.ietravel.com. *Cost:* $3,498 for 10-day trip (7 days sailing), all-inclusive, air extra. Originates in Lima. **Aqua Expeditions:** Tel 51/65-601-053; in the U.S., 866-603-3687; www.aquaexpeditions.com. *Cost:* 7-night cruises $5,950, all-inclusive, air extra. (3- and 4-night also available.) Originate in Lima. **Explorama Tours and Lodges:** Tel 51/65-252-530; in the U.S., 800-707-5275; www.explorama.com. *Cost:* $630 per person, all-inclusive for 4-night Ceiba excursions with Canopy Walkway Special. Originates in Iquitos. **Best times:** May–Nov for least rain; Jan–Feb for most rain and better animal viewing.

A Little-Known Valley of Wonders

Colca Canyon

Arequipa, Peru

Just a few bumpy but highly scenic hours from Arequipa, at the heart of what writer Mario Vargas Llosa described as "the Valley of Wonders," lie two of the world's deepest canyons: Colca and Cotahuasi. Both measure 11,000-plus feet deep—twice the depth of the Grand Canyon, but with more gradually sloping walls.

More accessible from Arequipa (see next page), Colca Valley welcomes greater numbers of tourists, who often come to visit the 14 villages founded in Spanish colonial times that are now home to the descendants of pre-Inca ethnic groups. Outdoor enthusiasts are drawn to the hiking, rafting, and other adventurous pursuits amid the snowcapped volcanoes and soaring mountains scored by agricultural terraces.

In the morning, visitors gather at the Cruz del Cóndor, on what has become Peru's most famous lookout point, to marvel at the Andean condors. Among the canyon's most impressive sights is the condors leaping from the high cliffs to catch the valley's rising currents of warm air, soaring with wings outstretched to nearly 10 feet.

Until roads were built in the surrounding valley in the 1970s, the Colca Canyon was largely unexplored.

Amid this remote, unspoiled beauty, in an unparalleled canyon setting, Orient-Express has opened Las Casitas del Colca's 20 rustic-luxe "little houses." Guests here can continue to marvel at condors swooping below them and at the alpacas that roam the grounds. Or they can choose to indulge in treatments that use the valley's indigenous herbs and plants at the hotel's Spa Samay. Each casita has a private heated plunge pool for nighttime swims beneath the brilliant star-filled skies. The Colca Lodge is a more modest option deep within the valley that nevertheless impresses with an awe-inspiring view of the surrounding mountains and access to natural thermal hot springs. In Chivay, the canyon's largest town, Casa Andina welcomes guests to make one of its individual stone houses their home base. The hotel's attached observatory, associated with Maria Reiche, the German mathematician who studied Peru's Nazca Lines (see p. 1045), offers guests the chance to study the Southern Hemisphere's constellations.

WHERE: 102–133 miles/165–215 km north of Arequipa. **LAS CASITAS DEL COLCA:** Tel 51/1-610-8300; www.lascasitasdelcolca.com. *Cost:* from $1,000, all-inclusive. **COLCA LODGE:** Tel 51/54-531-191; www.colca-lodge.com. *Cost:* from $155. **CASA ANDINA:** Tel 51/1-213-9739; in the U.S., 866-447-3270; www.casa-andina.com. *Cost:* from $90. **HOW:** Lima Tours offers customized itineraries to the area. Tel 51/1-619-6900; in the U.S., 305-792-0085; www.limatours.com.pe. **BEST TIMES:** Apr–Nov for dry season, with Apr–Jun the lushest; Jun–Aug for spotting condors.

An Island of Serenity in Peru's White City

MONASTERIO DE SANTA CATALINA

Arequipa, Peru

Known as La Ciudad Blanca (the White City) for the pearly volcanic stone called *sillar* used to build its elaborate 16th- and 17th-century Spanish homes and churches, Arequipa is Peru's second largest city. It was founded in 1540 and retains a small-town charm that is set against a backdrop of three majestic snow-covered volcanoes: El Misti, Pichu Pichu, and Chachani, each nearly 20,000 feet high.

Little prepares the wanderer who stumbles upon this lovely city's greatest secret, the cloistered world of the Monasterio de Santa Catalina. In this miniature city within a city, which opened to the public only in 1970, visitors meander along narrow, twisting streets, admiring the pastel-painted buildings and stopping in the tiny fruit tree–shaded plazas. The few elderly Dominican nuns still in residence have moved to the northern corner of the convent; the rest of the grounds offer a glimpse of an earlier age. The original convent was built in 1580 by a rich widow, María de Guzmán, and soon gained a reputation as a sort of exclusive club where aristocratic families sent their daughters for an education, safe haven, or a spiritual vocation. Many brought large dowries and lived in pure luxury, with servants or slaves in tow. Of the nearly 500 women living there, only one-third were nuns—until the Vatican sent Sister Josefa Cadena to put a halt to the hedonistic lifestyle in 1871.

The restaurant La Trattoria del Monasterio is housed within the monastery's outer walls. Peru's star chef based in Lima, Gastón Acurio (see p. 1044), oversees the menu, a mix of Italian specialties and Peruvian comfort food served in three elegant whitewashed dining rooms. Stay nearby in the Vallecito residential district at the Casa Arequipa, a Neocolonial mid-20th-century mansion reinterpreted as a boutique hotel. Rooms offer old-world charm with deluxe touches, and a sumptuous breakfast is served on the rooftop with a view of snow-tipped Andean peaks. Walk it off when you head into the center of town—the Plaza de Armas is 15 minutes away.

WHERE: 632 miles/1,020 km southeast of Lima. **MONASTERIO DE SANTA CATALINA:** Tel 51/54-608-282; www.santacatalina.org.pe. **LA TRATTORIA DEL MONASTERIO:** Tel 51/54-204-062. *Cost:* dinner $30. **CASA AREQUIPA:** Tel 51/54-284-219; www.arequipacasa.com. *Cost:* $75. **BEST TIMES:** Weather is springlike year-round; Aug 15 is the city's founding day, with parades, celebrations, and concerts.

At the Center of the Inca Universe

CUZCO AND THE SACRED VALLEY

Peru

An obligatory stop for those setting out for Machu Picchu (see p. 1042) and other sites in the Sacred Valley, Cuzco—steeped in ancient culture and surrounded by the beauty and mysticism of the Andes—is sometimes overlooked as a unique destination unto itself.

Founded in the 12th century (it is the oldest continuously inhabited city in the Americas), Cuzco sits 11,000 feet above sea level. It was the birthplace and center of the Inca empire; in the Quechua language, *qosqo* means "the Earth's navel." Today, the Old City, which spreads in a 10-block radius around the central Plaza de Armas, is a historical repository of the years following Pizarro's arrival in 1532—an event that led to the eventual destruction of what was once the Western Hemisphere's greatest empire.

The plaza's centerpiece is the ornate Baroque cathedral—one of the most splendid examples of religious Colonial architecture in the Americas. It is surrounded by other churches, mansions, and colonnades, all built upon the stone foundations of Inca palaces and temples. Vestiges of these sloping foundations, their impeccable masonry fitted without mortar, are still visible; some extend as high as two stories.

The Hotel Monasterio, mere steps from the plaza, is housed in the 16th-century San Antonio de Abad seminary and built on the

Special hand-woven hats, shoulder scarves, and skirts distinguish traditional Quechua women.

remains of the palace of the ancient Inca Emperor Amaru Qhala. One of Latin America's most important seminaries from the 1700s to the late 1970s, the site retains its Colonial patios, vaulted arches, stone water fountains, and religious artwork. The former monks' cells have been enlarged into comfortable rooms outfitted with antique furniture and marble baths. In the nearby Plaza Nazerenas stands one of the city's earliest Spanish houses, Inkaterra La Casona. Now Cuzco's first luxury boutique hotel, this beautifully restored manor home features 11 suites with stone fireplaces that surround a quiet courtyard. A budget alternative is the Niños Hotel, a 10-minute walk from the Plaza de Armas, where 19 basic but spacious rooms occupy two renovated historical buildings a block apart. Established in 1996, the inn uses a portion of its proceeds to provide schooling and medical care to hundreds of children throughout the city.

Just outside town lie the towering ruins of Sacsayhuamán, a fortress complex of enormous interlocking stones—one alone can weigh up to 360 tons—and the site of one of the Incas' last attempts to reclaim their empire from the Spanish in 1556. Inti Raymi (the Inca Sun Festival), greatest of all Inca celebrations, is held among these ruins every June 24 around the time of the Winter Solstice, with parades and special ceremonies.

The Urubamba (aka Sacred) Valley, was the heart of the Inca Empire. Stretching from the town of Pisac to Ollantaytambo, it is full of terraced farms and ancient ruins, as well as atmospheric colonial towns and incomparable vistas of the surrounding Andes. Wending through it is the Urubamba River, famous for its whitewater rafting, and the Inca Trail (see p. 1043), which leads hikers on an awe-inspiring journey to Machu Picchu. Ollantaytambo, with its well-preserved, formidable fortress, is one of the most popular starting points for the Inca Trail hike and is the valley's other most-visited spot. An authentic Inca town and important stronghold during the empire, "Ollanta" has retained its original street names, layout, irrigation system, and houses—among the oldest occupied buildings in South America. The Sunday market and the Quechua mass held in the Colonial church San Pedro Apostál in Pisac draw vendors, worshippers, and tourists from all parts. Just as memorable is a trek up to Pisac's ruins and the network of linked hilltop Inca strongholds above the town. And be sure to visit the shimmering, terraced salt pans of Maras; the enigmatic Inca crop circles of Moray; and the Sunday market at hilltop Chinchero and its Inca ruin–cum–Catholic church. Among the growing number of inns in the valley, one of the most delightful is the secluded Sol y Luna Lodge, in Urubamba. The collection of 28 circular stone-and-adobe bungalows, surrounded by gardens and mountain scenery, has a first-rate dining room and a small spa.

Where: Cuzco is 715 miles/1,153 km southeast of Lima. **Hotel Monasterio:** Tel 51/84-604-000; in the U.S., 800-237-1236; www.monasteriohotel.com. *Cost:* from $520. **Inkaterra La Casona:** Tel 51/84-245-314; in the U.S., 800-442-5042. *Cost:* from $490. **Niños Hotel:** Tel 51/84-231-424; www.ninos hotel.com. *Cost:* $95. **Sol y Luna Lodge:** Tel 51/84-201-620; www.hotelsolyluna.com. *Cost:* $250. **Best times:** Apr–Oct for dry season; Semana Santa (week before Easter); Jun 24 for Inti Raymi; early Sun for Pisac Market.

The Lost City of the Incas

MACHU PICCHU

Urubamba Valley, Cuzco Region, Peru

On a continent endowed with magnificent pre-Columbian archaeological sites, this "lost city of the Incas" is the supreme showpiece. Machu Picchu's strategic and isolated setting more than 7,800 feet above sea level, coupled with its mysterious significance in the ancient Inca universe, make this remote site one of the world's most beautiful and haunting destinations. Abandoned by the Inca and reclaimed by the jungle, the 100-acre complex of temples, warehouses, homes, irrigation terraces, and stairs cascades down the mountain. It remained hidden from outsiders until a 10-year-old local boy led American explorer Hiram Bingham to it in 1911. Inexplicably, it had been unaccounted for in the Spanish conquistadors' otherwise meticulous records, and speculation about the age and significance of Machu Picchu (Old Mountain) continues. Current thinking suggests the site was a retreat for Inca nobility most likely built in the 15th century, during the Inca Empire's golden age. What is certain is that the vistas from Machu Picchu are dumbfounding, especially at sunrise or sunset.

At Machu Picchu, the Incas made architectural use of the naturally mountainous landscape.

On a clear day, the very fit should consider climbing Huayna Picchu (Young Mountain), where the near-vertical one-hour scramble to the summit is breathtaking in more ways than one. The truly ambitious can arrive at sunset at Machu Picchu's 500-year-old Gate of the Sun after a 4- or 5-day trek along the Inca Trail (see next page).

There is no direct road from Cuzco to Machu Picchu, though PeruRail runs several train options (approximately 3½ hours each way) geared to tourists leaving from Cuzco. The Hiram Bingham Orient Express train is the fastest and smoothest ride, with elegant, 1920s Pullman-style décor. Passengers are pampered with brunch en route, private guides at the ruins, and cocktails and a four-course dinner on the return. All runs end at Aguas Calientes (also called Machu Picchu Pueblo) and connect with shuttle buses that zigzag up to Machu Picchu.

The high-end Machu Picchu Sanctuary Lodge will get you as close as possible to the ruins' entrance. Its rustic simplicity is as welcome as its location, and it allows guests the unique privilege of wandering about the moonlit ruins after the crowds leave. Down in Aguas Calientes and farther from the ruins the less pricey Inkaterra Machu Picchu Pueblo Hotel lets you bed down in whitewashed casitas scattered along lushly landscaped, riverside grounds. The resort's 12-acre reserve is laced with paved paths and hiking trails and blessed with inspiring views that can best be enjoyed from the glass-walled restaurant at sunset.

WHERE: 69 miles/112 km northwest of Cuzco. **HOW:** U.S.-based Andean Treks offers a variety of trips to Machu Picchu. Tel 800-683-8148 or 617-924-1974; www.andeantreks.com. **PERURAIL:** www.perurail.com. *Cost:* from $96 round-trip; Vistadome $175 round-trip; Hiram Bingham $588 round-trip, all-inclusive. **MACHU PICCHU SANCTUARY LODGE:** Tel 51/84-211-039; in the U.S., 800-237-1236; www.sanctuarylodgehotel.com. *Cost:* from $825, all-inclusive. **INKATERRA MACHU PICCHU PUEBLO HOTEL:** Tel 51/84-245-314; in the U.S., 800-442-5042; www.inkaterra.com. *Cost:* from $490, all-inclusive. **BEST TIME:** Jun–Sep for dry weather, but expect crowds.

The Andes' Sacred Highways

THE INCA TRAILS

Peru

The Inca built a complex and extensive network of mountain trails through their empire, which centered on the Andean mountain range from Colombia to Chile. Though many of them have been reclaimed by the jungle, a number of ancient paths still offer a journey through the unparalleled splendor of the fertile valleys and mountain passes outside the former capital of Cuzco to the trails' end, where the sacred city of Machu Picchu awaits (see previous page).

Each of the local trail options varies in length, scenery, and required stamina, while accommodations range from basic tents to newly built lodges offering every comfort. The so-called Inca Trail—the old "Royal Highway"—is the best known and most popular, offering a number of segments. The full 26-mile hike is the trophy approach and requires trekkers to tolerate thin air in order to appreciate the drama of the scenery, with its wealth of Inca outposts, fortresses, and mysterious, terraced ruins. Centuries-old, hand-hewn staircases scale the mountains, many covered with exotic orchids that hummingbirds feed on while condors soar overhead. Of the trail's many highlights is the stretch up and over the 13,800-foot-high "Dead Woman's Pass," the highest point. Four-day hikes end by descending the Inca staircase from the Sun Gate as the day's first light reveals Machu Picchu. However long your tour, spend a few enjoyable days in Cuzco (see p. 1040) first, adjusting to the high altitude, before picking up the trail outside town. (No more than 500 people can hike the trail per day and tickets can sell out months in advance.)

For an alternative to the Inca Trail that also leads to Machu Picchu, Salcantay is the way to go: Though there are slight variations, this 5-day, approximately 35-mile journey begins in Mollepata, a few hours northwest of Cuzco. Salcantay is more physically demanding than the classic Inca Trail, but there are no permits needed, and no limits on the number of hikers (save for availability at the lodges). You have the option of overnighting at the Mountain Lodges of Peru, a relatively new and supremely comfortable lodge-to-lodge option, though camping remains popular as well.

A third trekking option takes you not to Machu Picchu but to the much less visited—and much less excavated—sister site of

Choquequirao, "cradle of gold" in Quechua. The trek, typically 5 days, begins and ends in the town of Cachora, four hours from Cuzco by road. Between the arresting beauty and blessed isolation from the masses, these ruins are undoubtedly worth the arduous trek. Likely dating from the 1400s, this was one of the sites visited by Hiram Bingham and forgotten after he found Machu Picchu. You'll practically have them to yourself.

Where: Cuzco is 715 miles/1,153 km southeast of Lima. **How:** U.S.-based Mountain Travel Sobek offers various trekking options. Tel 888-831-7526 or 510-594-6000; www.mtsobek.com. *Cost:* 10-day trips from $4,395. **Mountain Lodges of Peru:** Tel 51/1-421-6952; in U.S., 510-525-8846; www.mountainlodgesofperu.com. *Cost:* 7-day trips via Salcantay from $2,560. **Best times:** May–Sep for dry weather; May sees fewer trekkers.

Gastronomic Revolution

Lima's Food Scene

Lima, Peru

American chef Todd English has hailed Lima as the culinary capital of Latin America—recognition that its distinctive, inventive cuisine is leaving an imprint around the world. It's a cuisine as cosmopolitan as its population: founded on centuries-old indigenous cooking, enriched with Spanish and European traditions, emboldened with Asian flavors courtesy of 20th-century Chinese and Japanese immigrants, then set to simmer with Creole spices brought by Caribbean workers.

Countless *chifas* (slang for Chinese-Peruvian restaurants) line the streets, where you'll find spicy dim sum. Line up for a table at a *cebichería,* where the Peruvian national dish ceviche (raw fish chunks marinated in citrus and tossed with fresh herbs and seasonings) is served at lunchtime. At tiny, unpretentious Sankuay (everyone calls it Chez Wong), chef Javier Wong doesn't bother with a menu (or a sign outside)—you get the day's ceviche as a first course, plus whatever Chef Wong thinks you might like, based on the freshest of fish and vegetables and created in front of your eyes.

At Rafael, chef Rafael Osterling brings together the flavors and ingredients of Peru using sophisticated techniques gained from long apprenticeships in top French and British restaurants. Located in a historic mansion, Rafael offers eclectic, innovative fare that's firmly grounded in local tradition.

Commander in chief of Peru's culinary revolution is Gastón Acurio, who was trained in some of Europe's finest restaurants. His flagship restaurant Astrid y Gastón is widely considered Peru's top dining spot; Peruvian ingredients are flecked with French, Asian, and Creole flavors. Acurio has a fleet of other eateries in Lima, including Cebichería La Mar, which offers both traditional and Asian-influenced ceviche. With additional restaurants in Peru, across Central and South America, as well as in Madrid and San Francisco, Acurio is doing his share to expand the reach of Peruvian cuisine.

Sankuay: Tel 51/1-470-6217. *Cost:* lunch $15. **Rafael:** Tel 51/1-242-4149; www.rafaelosterling.com. *Cost:* dinner $50. **Astrid y Gastón:** Tel 51/1-242-5387; www.astridygaston.com. *Cost:* dinner $55. **Cebichería La Mar:** Tel 51/1-421-3365; www.lamarcebicheria.com. *Cost:* dinner $35.

A Bird- and Wildlife-Watcher's Utopia

Manu National Park

Peru

In the southeastern corner of Peru, at nearly 4.5 million acres, Manu National Park is the largest tropical rain forest reserve in South America, unrivaled for its biodiversity. Manu encompasses radically different ecological zones, ranging from Andean peaks of more than 13,000 feet down through the cloud forest and into the vast lowland Amazon rain forests that rest below 1,000 feet. No other reserve on earth compares for sheer biodiversity: Here you'll find an estimated 15,000 plant species, 1,000-plus species of birds (more than in the United States and Canada combined and one-tenth of all the world's), and 13 species of monkeys, from capuchin and spider to the mustachioed emperor tamarin. Its 200 mammal species include the elusive jaguar; Manu offers one of your best chances to spot one in all of South America.

The trade-off is that Manu is difficult to get to, occasionally almost impossible. Trips are time-consuming and tours typically involve camping or other rustic accommodations. Manu Expeditions, the region's first tour operator, is still the best choice. The owners, ornithologist Sir Barry Walker, who doubles as the British Consul in Cuzco, and his wife, Cuzco native Rosario Velarde, have been leading rain forest and mountain tours since 1983. Among the places they take travelers is the Manu Wildlife Center Lodge, which requires a plane trip followed by a two-hour boat ride. The remote riverside retreat features 22 cabins enveloped by rain forest, 30 miles of nature walks, and canopy-viewing platforms.

Where: 100 miles/161 km southwest of Cuzco. **Manu Expeditions:** Tel 51/84-225-990; www.manuexpeditions.com. *Cost:* 6-day trips $1,650, all-inclusive (shorter expeditions available), air extra. **When:** Apr–Dec, when there is less rain.

Age-Old Mysteries Etched into the Desert Floor

The Nazca Lines

Nazca, Peru

Peru's desert coast is the setting for the mysterious, ancient Nazca lines, a vast series of furrows in the earth that depict stylized human and animal forms as well as geometric shapes. The full impact of their 193-square-mile expanse sets in only when they are seen from the air, which is how they were discovered in the 1920s. Faithful to the motifs of the Nazca culture, some of these simple, perfect triangles, trapezoids, and crisscrossing lines run for miles across the desert. There's also a 540-foot-long lizard, a 360-foot-long monkey with a tightly curled tail, and a condor with a 440-foot wingspan. The geoglyphs are believed to have been "etched" by the removal of rocks and topsoil to reveal lighter soil underneath between 2,000 and 5,000 years ago.

So what, exactly, are they? Though every theory from extraterrestrial landing strip to astronomical calendars has been postulated, these extraordinary pre-Inca cultural artifacts remain veiled in mystery. But a visit to the Italian-run Museo Antonini may shed some light through its archaeological displays, trophy skulls, textiles, and artifacts that have been found in the area.

From 1946 until her death in 1998, the German-born mathematician Maria Reiche dedicated her life to researching the lines and the Nazca culture. The simple room in the village of Pascana, where she lived for much of that time, is now a tiny museum. Reiche spent most of her last decade as a guest in the Hotel Nazca Lines, about 5 miles from the site. Today, this Colonial hacienda's 32 rooms are modest yet comfortable. It has a pleasant patio and welcoming pool, and the staff presents nightly lectures. For a more luxurious stay, there's the newly reincarnated seaside Hotel Paracas, which has the excellent bonus of access to the amazing Ballestas Islands, promoted as Galápagos-in-miniature for their enormous populations of sea lions, pelicans, and penguins. The parent company's private plane, which trumps local competitors for newness and comfort, offers flights over the Nazca lines.

Along with monkeys, living creatures depicted by the lines include hummingbirds, spiders, and whales.

WHERE: 280 miles/450 km south of Lima. **HOW:** U.S.-based Andean Treks offers trips to Nazca and throughout Peru. Tel 800-683-8148 or 617-924-1974; www.andeantreks.com. *Cost:* 3-day trip $675. Originates in Lima. **MUSEO ANTONINI:** Tel 51/56-523-444; www.digilander.libero.it/mdantonini. **HOTEL NAZCA LINES:** Tel 51/56-522-293; www.peru-hotels.com. *Cost:* from $100. **HOTEL PARACAS:** Tel 51/56-581-333; www.starwoodhotels.com. *Cost:* from $200. **BEST TIME:** Dec–Apr for warm, dry weather.

Mythical Birthplace of the Incas

LAKE TITICACA

Puno, Peru

Set in the Andes at 12,500 feet above sea level, legendary Lake Titicaca is the highest navigable lake in the world and, at 3,200 square miles, it is the continent's largest. Ancient myth holds that Manco Cápac and his sister-consort, Mama Ocllo, emerged from these magical Andean waters, known for their luminescence and calm, to found Cuzco and the Inca Empire. The Uros Indians first created the lake's 50-odd floating islands and their boats of totora reeds as early as the 15th century to escape conflicts with the land-dwelling Inca. The two natural islands of Taquile and Amantani are peopled by Quechua-speaking Indians, whose brightly colored, handwoven textiles fill the markets in the islands' main plazas. There are no cars here, no bicycles or roads.

The lakeside town of Puno, while not big on charm, is Peru's capital of folklore. Its mythical founding is the reason for November's fascinating Semana de Puno (Puno Week) festivities, with ornate and imaginative costumes, wild dancing, masks, and music that are rooted in Inca culture. But February 2 marks the beginning of the biggest event of the year, the festival of the Virgen de la Candelaria. It ostensibly figures on the Roman Catholic calendar, but witness the famous *diablada* (devil's dance) and the *kallahuaya* (medicine man's dance) before deeming the celebration strictly Christian. The flamboyant Trajes de Luces (Suits of Lights) dances are considered the festival's main draw.

The gleaming white Hotel Libertador sits on its own island, connected by causeway to Puno. Most of its 120 comfortable and spacious rooms offer views of the lake, as does the hotel's popular restaurant. Well off the beaten path, about 45 minutes by boat from Puno, the new, all-inclusive Hotel Titilaka looks stark and almost Scandinavian in design. Each of its 18 stylish lakeview suites is labeled Dusk or Dawn, depending on whether its windows open to the rising or the setting sun.

Peru shares the ancient lake with Bolivia; regular boat service links Puno to that country's picturesque shoreside town of Copacabana (see p. 996). The *Andean Explorer,* one of the world's highest railways, runs along the shore of Lake Titicaca, connecting the ancient Inca capital of Cuzco (see p. 1040) to Puno. Jointly overseen by the Orient Express and PeruRail, the 10-hour scenic journey carries passengers in luxurious 1920s Pullman cars, some with open-air observation cabins.

Where: 243 miles/389 km southeast of Cuzco. **Hotel Libertador:** Tel 51/1-518-6500; in the U.S., 877-778-2281; www.libertador.com.pe. *Cost:* from $150. **Hotel Titilaka:** Tel 51/1-700-5100; in the U.S., 866-628-1777; www.titilaka.com. *Cost:* $530, inclusive. ***Andean Explorer:*** Tel 51/1-612-6700; www.perurail.com. *Cost:* from $220 one-way from Cuzco to Puno or reverse; includes lunch. **Best times:** May–Nov for pleasant weather; early Feb for Festival de la Virgen de la Candelaria; 1st week in Nov for Puno Week.

A Little-Known Getaway

Colonia del Sacramento

Uruguay

A tiny colonial outpost on the Río de la Plata surrounded by rolling gaucho country and vineyards and an easy ferry ride away from Buenos Aires (see p. 980), Colonia is the unappreciated gem of Uruguay—itself vastly underrated among South American countries. Founded by the Portuguese and fought over by the Spanish, Colonia is a beguiling collection of whitewashed buildings, tile-and-stucco homes, and historic landmarks such as Iglesia Matriz, Uruguay's oldest church. The sycamore-shaded, cobblestoned Barrio Histórico, the town's colonial core, is among the continent's most carefully restored urban areas. Tiny museums, smart bars, and romantic, candlelit restaurants cluster around the ancient Plaza Mayor (visit the Sunday market here); more line Calle de los Suspiros, which leads to the old port.

While you can certainly see the most important sights in a day, an overnight stay allows you to steep in Colonia's history. The charming 19th-century Posada Plaza Mayor's flowering patio and simple Colonial-style guest rooms are matched only by its location, the best in town. Dine at nearby La Florida: Owned by a French Argentine and housed in a former brothel, this restaurant lets you choose between overlooking the water or eating in a pretty, secluded courtyard for full-on romance.

More than 270 wineries surround Colonia, offering a less crowded, quaint alternative to Argentina's wine scene (see Mendoza, p. 988). Locally produced Tannat, known for its soft tannins and fruity essence, is the national wine. The perfect place to sample it, as well as Albariño and other varietals, is at the family-owned Bodega Bouza, on the road from Colonia to the capital city of Montevideo. Guests can dine in rustic splendor after touring the vineyards.

Just an hour away from Colonia, on the Río de la Plata, is Uruguay's most award-winning hotel, the Four Seasons Carmelo. Secluded in a pine and eucalyptus forest, it mixes Asian and regional elements in its enormous private bungalows, outdoor patios, and expansive Zen-like spa. Spend time on the 18-hole golf course and then lose yourself in the gardens on an afternoon stroll. The nearby town of Carmelo delights with a century-old serenity and charm.

Where: 113 miles/182 km west of Montevideo. **Posada Plaza Mayor:** Tel 598/522-3193; www.posadaplazamayor.com. *Cost:* from $110. **La Florida:** Tel 598/94-293036. *Cost:* dinner $40. **Bodega Bouza:** Tel 598/2-323-7491; www.bodegabouza.com. *Cost:* lunch $50. **Four Seasons Carmelo:** Tel 598/542-9000; www.fourseasons.com. *Cost:* from $275. **Best times:** Mar–Apr for fall weather, foliage, and grape harvest; Sep–Nov for spring weather.

Like Bohemian Summer Camp with Celebrities and Soccer Stars

José Ignacio

Uruguay

A 40-minute drive east of Punta del Este (see next page) but a world away from its high-rise development is the small peninsula of José Ignacio and the stylish Playa Brava beach. A former fishing village set around a rocky promontory, its most prominent landmark is Faro José Ignacio, a century-old lighthouse where surfers catch waves at sunset. The area draws a boho-chic crowd that gathers for house parties, dines in restaurants tucked into beachside pine groves, and feasts on the day's catch, sipping wines from nearby vineyards. The vibe in this laid-back, off-the-radar getaway is like summer camp with celebrities, soccer stars, and their supermodel friends.

La Posada del Faro sits on a hilltop perch, overlooking José Ignacio Bay. Many of the whitewashed rooms have ocean views and balconies, while the pool is a favorite spot for people-watching. Afternoons, everyone gathers at Parador La Huella, on Playa Brava. The informal gourmet spot, with tables on a deck that opens onto the sandy beach, offers fresh fish and local wines. Or brave the sandy road winding through the pines to find Namm, where just-caught seafood and grilled beef are prepared with an Asian flair. It's so well hidden that many call it "the tree house," but it's well worth the quest.

A working cattle ranch with an ocean view is no oxymoron at Estancia Vik, offering the ultimate in privacy and luxury on Laguna José Ignacio. Surrounded by 4,000 acres of rolling plains, its 12 rooms range from simple quarters to cutting-edge suites, each uniquely designed with artwork by Uruguayan and international artists. Lounge by the granite pool or ride horses down to the estancia's new sister property, Playa Vik, at the beach. The dusty town of Garzón took on a new sophistication when celebrity chef Francis Mallmann transformed the old general store into an inn and candlelit restaurant, where magic happens every night. He splits his time between the dining room here and 1884, his restaurant in Argentine wine country (see p. 989).

WHERE: 25 miles/35 km north of Punta del Este. **POSADA DEL FARO:** Tel 598/4-862-110; www.posadadelfaro.com. *Cost:* from $250 (off-peak), $375 (peak). **PARADOR LA HUELLA:** Tel 598/4-862-279; www.paradorlahuella.com. *Cost:* lunch $30. **NAMM:** Tel 598/4-862-526. *Cost:* dinner $40. **ESTANCIA VIK:** Tel 598/94-605-212; www.estanciavik.com. *Cost:* from $490 (off-peak), $1,000 (peak), all-inclusive. **GARZON INN:** Tel 598/4-102-811; www.restaurantegarzon.com. *Cost:* from $820, inclusive; dinner $75. **BEST TIMES:** Nov–mid-Dec and Feb–Apr for warm weather and fewest crowds.

South America's St-Tropez

PUNTA DEL ESTE

Uruguay

Straddling a peninsula flanked by the Atlantic Ocean and the Río de la Plata, "Punta," as South Americans call it, has reigned for decades as the continent's premiere jet-set mecca. A former fishing village now full of high-rise hotels and condominiums, it has lost some of its exclusive air. Yet it still has a whiff of St-Tropez about it with its long stretches of white sandy beaches, elegant designer boutiques, and chic nightclubs. To escape the crowded central beaches and towering condos, try neighboring Punta Ballena and Barra de Maldonado (simply known as La Barra) or a day trip to Isla Gorriti or Isla de Lobos to glimpse sea lions instead of beautiful people.

Where to eat is the day's pressing decision. Of the plethora of possibilities, La Bourgogne, overseen by Jean-Paul Bondoux, is a favorite. This casual Provençal outpost, with an outdoor garden patio, is the sister to the more formal version in Buenos Aires's grand Alvear Palace Hotel (see p. 981). Simple, French-inspired cuisine emphasizes local ingredients—many from the chef's own

Mediterranean influences are visible in the façade of Casa Pueblo, designed by a local sculptor and artist.

farm—and a wildly popular bakery features French bread and pastries.

One of the most surreal hotels in South America is Casa Pueblo in Punta Ballena, a cliff-top Gaudiesque structure built over a period of 36 years by the Uruguayan sculptor and painter Carlos Páez Vilaró. Rooms are small and simple but all have magnificent views of the sunset over the Río de la Plata and the Atlantic waters famous for migrating whales (*ballenas* in Spanish) that give this area its name. For a glamorous beach holiday, the sophisticated Mantra Resort is the grande dame of Punta. Situated right on the coast, in the relatively less congested La Barra area, it features a spa, a lively pool scene, a casino, and its own cinema.

Join local families and knowing Argentines who show up at L'Auberge for late-afternoon tea and the legendary Belgian waffles drizzled with warm dulce de leche. Think about unpacking your bag here: The redbrick, Tudor-style mansion in a secluded residential neighborhood enchants with 36 cozy rooms, a popular barbecue lunch pavilion, and a pool surrounded by immaculate grounds. All make you feel a world away from Punta's beach scene.

Where: 60 miles/96 km east of Montevideo. **La Bourgogne:** Tel 598/42-482-007; www.labourgogne.com.uy. *Cost:* dinner $75. **Casa Pueblo:** Tel 598/42-578-041; www.clubhotelcasapueblo.com. *Cost:* from $150 (off-peak), from $290 (peak). **Mantra Resort:** Tel 598/42-776-100; www.mantraresort.com. *Cost:* from $250 (off-peak), from $1,100 (peak). **L'Auberge:** 598-42-488-888; www.laubergehotel.com. *Cost:* from $125 (off-peak), from $300 (peak). **Best times:** Nov–Apr for summer weather; mid-Dec–Jan for peak season.

Earth's Highest Waterfalls Deep in the Lost World

Angel Falls

Puerto Ordaz, Gran Sabana, Venezuela

American bush pilot Jimmie Angel was searching for gold when he "discovered" these wondrous falls—the highest in the world—in 1935. Plunging from 3,212 feet, and with an uninterrupted drop of more than 2,600 feet, the thundering water nearly dissolves into mist by the time it hits bottom. The falls are a staggering 19 times taller than Niagara Falls (see p. 929) and more than twice as tall as the Empire State Building.

Clouds frequently deter hopeful falls viewers aboard sightseeing planes, so an in-person excursion at its base is the best bet.

The setting is impressive as well. Angel Falls—in Spanish called Salto Ángel and known locally by the native name Kerepakupai-meru—spring from the summit of the sheer-sided Auyantepuy (Devil's Mountains), formed by the confluence of tributaries from three of South America's greatest rivers, the Amazon, Essequibo, and Orinoco. La Gran Sabana (the Great Savanna), a grassy plateau in Venezuela's remote southeastern Bolívar state and the main jumping-off point for a visit to the falls, is dotted with more than 100 massive sandstone mesas or *tepuys* (from a Pemón Indian word meaning "mountain"). Formed more than 130 million years ago, they are some of the oldest and—with heights reaching 9,000 feet—most impressive rock formations on earth. They cover roughly 65 percent of Canaima National Park, the sixth largest national park in the world. The highest of the formations and easiest to hike, Mount Roraima, served as the setting for Sir Arthur Conan Doyle's *The Lost World*, his 1912 classic about dinosaurs and pterodactyls that would eventually inspire Michael Crichton's bestselling novel *Jurassic Park*. In this primeval land of unimaginably lush forests live giant anteaters, three-toed sloths, tapirs, and the elusive jaguar. The official tally of bird species stands at 550.

Overlooking a lagoon and ringed by soft sandy beaches, the Pemón Indian village of Canaima is the gateway to La Gran Sabana and about 30 miles from the falls. Dutch adventurer and trailblazer Rudy Truffino, aka Jungle Rudy, established a 15-room nature lodge here in 1956 and called it Campamento Ucaima. Rudy is long gone, and his daughters now run the lodge, helped by a loyal staff, as well as a satellite camp at the base of the falls. They can arrange flyover tours when clouds obscure the tops of the falls from lower vantages.

Where: 450 miles/725 km southeast of Caracas. **Campamento Ucaima (Jungle Rudy):** Tel 58/289-808-9251; www.junglerudy.com. *Cost:* 2-day stay per person $360 (off-peak), 3 days $940 (peak), all-inclusive. **Best time:** Jun–Jan is the unofficial season when the falls are voluminous, although frequently covered by clouds.

The Caribbean's Oldest and Largest Marine Park

Islas los Roques

Venezuela

Venezuela's offshore islands are so little known that few but Venezuelans talk about them—and they rave. Islas los Roques form a remarkable archipelago of 40 largish coral islands (only three are inhabited—sparsely) and more than 250 islets and cays, all surrounded by healthy reefs that promise snorkeling and diving in conditions that haven't existed elsewhere in the Caribbean for decades: over 280 species of fish, schools of fish numbering in the thousands, massive forests of soft coral, long stretches of virgin hard coral, perpendicular drop-offs, caverns, and pinnacles. At 850 square miles, Los Roques Archipelago National Park, created in 1972, is the Caribbean's oldest and largest marine national park. Nondivers will find talcum-soft beaches with no trace of a footprint and 92 bird species, including the largest concentration of scarlet ibises on earth, along with red-footed boobies and pink flamingos.

There's a small airport on the ambitiously named Gran Roque (Big Rock), a traffic-free island with about a thousand residents and a main fishing village all of three blocks long. A few dozen simple, Venezuelan-owned island *posadas* (guesthouses) are done up in tropical tones, mixing with the more stylish ones owned by the large number of Italians living on the island. Among them is the intimate, whitewashed Posada Movida, with only six rooms and a boat that can whisk you to some of the archipelago's remotest islands for sunbathing and snorkeling. Return to the posada for some of the best cuisine on the island. Los Roques is also the ideal spot for kite boarding and sea kayaking, and is one of the best places in the world for fly-fishing (bonefish and tarpon are abundant). Posadas can arrange boat trips into the coral-strewn inlets, where the prized fish congregate in crystal-clear waters.

On Los Roques, flamingos enjoy an unspoiled, protected habitat.

WHERE: Gran Roque is 125 miles/201 km north of Caracas. **POSADA MOVIDA:** Tel 58/237-221-1016; www.posadamovida.com. *Cost:* $260 (off-peak), $320 (peak), all-inclusive. **BEST TIME:** Apr–Dec for nicest weather.

The Serengeti of South America

LOS LLANOS

Venezuela

The grassland region of Los Llanos, "the Plains," covers more than 115,000 square miles, nearly one-third of Venezuela, stretching from the foothills of the Andes through the lowlands of the Orinoco Delta and into neighboring northeast Colombia. This spectacularly diverse area is one of the top spots on the planet for bird-watching: home to nearly 475 species, including seven species of ibis, the Orinoco goose, 20 species of heron, and endangered jabiru storks that grow up to 5 feet tall. More than 148 mammal species make this their habitat too, perhaps most notably the capybara, the world's largest rodent, weighing in at up to 175 pounds, while dolphins, crocodiles, and piranhas swim in the Orinoco and Apure rivers. Los Llanos has only two seasons. In the extreme wet season, running from May to October, the plains flood, making travel difficult and spotting the capybara and other mammals easier. The dry season, from November to March, leads to improved roads while forcing birds and animals to congregate around sparse water sources.

Cowboys in Venezuela are called *llaneros,* or "plainsmen," and their culture dates from the mid-1500s and the Spanish settlement. Many large ranches, or *hatos,* have taken up the torch of ecotourism and are now open to the public, with naturalist guides who explain the agricultural way of life and lead tours of the nearby nature reserves. One of the best is Hato Cedral, in the lowlands of Los Llanos. These sprawling grounds are home to 390 species of birds (best seen in the dry season, when massive flocks are common) and an astonishing variety of wildlife. The anaconda is commonly spotted here in the dry season; the jaguar and ocelot are only rarely seen.

WHERE: The access point of Barinas is 250 miles/402 km southwest of Caracas. **HATO CEDRAL:** Tel 58/416-502-2757; www.elcedral.com. *Cost:* from $175, all-inclusive. **HOW:** Lost World Adventures offers an 8-day Andes and Los Llanos tour. Tel 58/212-577-0303; in the U.S., 800-999-0558; www.lostworldadventures.com. *Cost:* $1,827, all-inclusive; with domestic air. Originates in Caracas. **BEST TIME:** Nov–Mar for dry season, when birding is good and roads are best.

Terra Australis Incognita

THE WHITE CONTINENT

Antarctica

Antarctica—*Terra Australis Incognita,* "the unknown land of the south"—is the surreal seventh continent at the bottom of the world, a place of ethereal beauty and unequivocal grandeur that inspired the great explorers of old and captures the hearts of adventurers today. The limitless landscape of ice, sea, and sky comes in a million shades of blue, and jagged, snowy mountain peaks and glistening glaciers dwarf anything ever made by man. It is the ultimate, end-of-the-earth expedition, the world's most inaccessible continent.

The nearly total absence of humans means you might be the first to leave footprints in a centuries-old snowbank, while the peaceable wildlife welcomes you into its habitat with childlike curiosity. Orca, humpback, fin, and right whales—even the giant blue whale—are known to swim right up to passing ships, while Weddell and leopard seals may stare at you from their lazy perch on floating icebergs.

But it's the penguins that draw so many travelers; to stand inside a wild, thriving rookery of tuxedoed Adélies or much larger, iconic emperors, is a once-in-a-lifetime experience: You will be outnumbered by 10,000 to one.

Trips to the warmer, animal-rich Antarctic Peninsula are the most popular; they sometimes include ports of call in the Falklands and South Georgia Island (see p. 995 and next page). Zodiac launches allow for quick landings on remote islands, including Deception Island, a collapsed but still active caldera where visitors take a dip in Pendulum Cove's volcano-heated water so they can tell the folks back home that they went swimming in the Antarctic. Despite the chill, nature's never-ending show keeps you out on deck, mesmerized by this year-round winter wonderland. If you travel during December and January, the sun shines for nearly 24 hours.

Sign up for a tour that offers a high number of shore landings to optimize wildlife encounters and choose a line whose ships have reinforced hulls to break through the ice. A veteran crew that includes geologists, zoologists, polar explorers, historians, ecologists, and oceanographers will help make the incredible real.

WHERE: Hobart, Tasmania (Australia), and Ushuaia, Argentina, are the most common points of embarkation. **HOW:** U.S.-based Abercrombie & Kent offers 14-day expeditions. Tel 800-554-7016 or 630-725-3400; www.abercrombiekent.com. *Cost:* from $10,465, all-inclusive. Originates in Buenos Aires. *When:* Dec and Jan. **BEST TIMES:** Nov–Feb (austral summer), when temperatures average a balmy 28°F; late Nov–Dec for nesting penguins; Jan–Feb for baby fur seals and baby penguins.

Icebergs form when glacier pieces break off into the ocean; Antarctica boasts among the world's largest.

South Atlantic Bird Paradise

SOUTH GEORGIA ISLAND

South Georgia and the Sandwich Islands (British Overseas Territory)

Windswept and largely unknown, the utterly isolated isle of South Georgia stands days away from any civilized shore, a white crest of carved ice rising from the cold subantarctic waters that surround the South Atlantic mountains nearly 1,300 miles east of Tierra del Fuego and 800 miles southeast of the Falkland Islands (see pp. 994 and 995). Deemed unlivable by Captain James Cook, the first explorer to land on the island, in 1775, and still virtually uninhabited, the 100-mile-long island nevertheless delights intrepid visitors with impossibly high sea cliffs, dazzling fjords, and snowy alpine peaks sloping down to wave-whipped beaches of fine-grained salt-and-pepper sand.

These seemingly desolate shorelines harbor one of the world's largest and most important penguin colonies: More than a half million breeding pairs of king penguins, the second largest penguin in the world, serve as the island's biggest draw. Arriving at the glacial valley of the Salisbury Plain, you instantly find yourself surrounded by at least 100,000 of them, all braying in chorus and waddling to and from the sea.

Bird-watchers find heaven in the 81 other rare and wonderful species too, including the million-plus macaroni penguins, with their distinctive yellow crest, and petrels of all kinds. Albatross Island and Prion Island provide a close-up view of the regal wandering albatross, whose 12-foot wingspan is the largest of any bird on earth.

Expedition cruises typically sail the length of the narrow, steep-walled Drygalski fjord, then follow the island's calmer northern coast, where protected bays allow for smooth Zodiac landings and easy access to the wildlife. In summer, some 3 million fur seals breed on the shores of South Georgia, giving birth to playful pups. Enormous elephant seals loll in muddy pools, whales dominate the surrounding ocean, and up in the hills you can glimpse members of the world's southernmost reindeer herd, introduced by 19th-century Norwegian whalers who longed for a taste of home.

Vestiges of the area's whaling days remain at the "capital" of Grytviken, home to a cozy museum and fewer than 20 souls, mostly research scientists and the British government officers who manage this crown colony. A prim wooden church built in 1913 is open so that visitors can climb the belfry and ring the dolorous iron bell. Nearby lies the grave of legendary explorer Sir Ernest Shackleton, who perished here on his final voyage to Antarctica (see previous page). His wife back in England insisted the hero's body remain in South Georgia. Today, hikers can follow in his footsteps by crossing the high pass between Fortuna Bay to Stromness—the final leg of his daring rescue from the doomed *Endurance*.

WHERE: Expedition ships typically depart from Ushuaia, Argentina. **HOW:** U.S.-based Lindblad Expeditions offers a 24-day expedition that also includes the Falklands. Tel 800-397-3348 or 212-765-7740; www.expeditions.com. *Cost:* from $13,780, all-inclusive. Originates in Buenos Aires. **WHEN:** Oct. **BEST TIMES:** Nov–Mar (austral summer) when temperatures hover around 40°F; late Nov for penguins nesting with eggs; Dec for hatching baby penguins; Jan–Mar for baby fur seals and fledgling penguins.

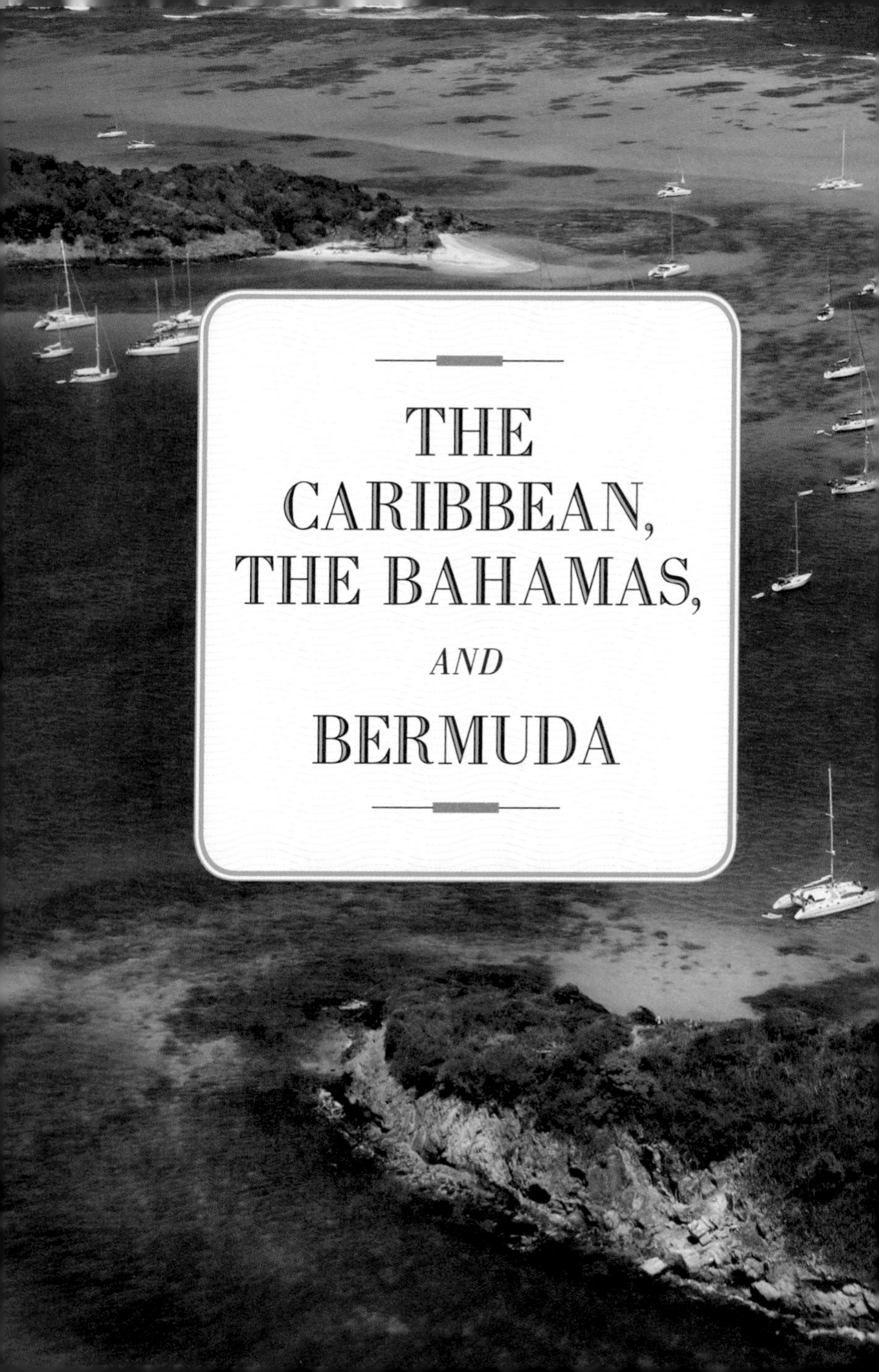
THE
CARIBBEAN,
THE BAHAMAS,
AND
BERMUDA

BERMUDA
ATLANTIC OCEAN
Nassau
Havana
THE BAHAMAS
CUBA
TURKS AND CAICOS ISLANDS
GREATER ANTILLES
CAYMAN ISLANDS
HAITI
DOMINICAN REPUBLIC
Port-au-Prince
Santo Domingo
JAMAICA
Kingston
SABA
ANGUILLA
ST. MARTIN
ST. BARTHÉLEMY
BRITISH VIRGIN ISLANDS
San Juan
PUERTO RICO
U.S. VIRGIN ISLANDS
ST. KITTS AND NEVIS
ANTIGUA AND BARBUDA
GUADELOUPE
DOMINICA
MARTINIQUE
ST. LUCIA
ST. VINCENT AND THE GRENADINES
BARBADOS
GRENADA
TRINIDAD AND TOBAGO
Port of Spain
LESSER ANTILLES
CARIBBEAN SEA
CURAÇAO
BONAIRE
N
S
E
W
0 100 200 MILES
0 161 322 Kilometers

33 Spectacular Beaches

ANGUILLA

Lesser Antilles

Anguilla is a flat, scrubby island that's light on interior scenery, but take a look at its confectionery 12-mile perimeter: These are some of the most picture-perfect white-sand beaches and crystal-clear waters you'll find anywhere. Some of the finest of its 33 beaches are anchored by special hotels with celebrated in-house restaurants, making the island an unrivaled choice for an indulgent stay-put vacation. Venture beyond your hotel grounds and you'll find friendly towns undisturbed by cruise ships, casinos, or strip malls.

Sensual, romantic Cap Juluca was an early arrival on the island, attracting Hollywood moguls and financiers with whitewashed Moorish turrets, arches, and domes on Maunday's Beach, a magical, mile-long crescent of sugary white sand that all 98 luxurious suites overlook. It manages Anguilla's first and only golf course, an 18-hole links-style creation by Greg Norman. The only place guests wear anything more elaborate than a swimsuit and a suntan is in its Pimm's Restaurant, whose menu features Eurobbean cuisine—think Anguillan lobster bisque drizzled with spiced Cognac or green peppercorn–marinated swordfish.

Just a few beaches east on Rendezvous Bay, CuisinArt Resort & Spa is another whitewashed Mediterranean vision on a long stretch of perfect beach. Lie back in a beach chair and enjoy the dreamy views of the volcanic slopes of St. Martin. Dinner at Santorini, the resort's restaurant, is a major draw; its famous grilled tuna and johnnycakes are served with herbs and vegetables grown on the hotel's hydroponic farm. The two-story Venus Spa is one of the largest in the Caribbean.

Stroll down the shoreline to the Dune Preserve, a fantastical beach bar owned by local reggae legend Bankie Banx, who sometimes performs, especially during the full-moon parties and March's music festival, Moonsplash.

On the island's northern side, the bluff-top Malliouhana Hotel & Spa on Meads Bay was the first luxury hotel on Anguilla when it opened in 1984, and it wears its age beautifully. It offers hands-on involvement by the gracious British owners and staff and a highly regarded spa. Nonguests are welcome to dine at the island's most refined restaurant, which offers classic French dishes with an island accent, as well as one of the most extensive wine lists in the Caribbean. A boutique alternative is the Mediterranean-style Anacaona Hotel, just paces from Meads Beach. Save an evening for nearby Blanchard's, a trailblazer in Anguilla's impressive food scene where choices like chunky lobster cakes and warm lemon-buttermilk pound cake with homemade ice cream explain its popularity.

Anguilla's 12 miles of coastline are home to some of the world's most beautiful beaches.

Shoal Bay might be the beauty pageant winner of Anguilla's can't-go-wrong beaches, a 2-mile strip on the northeast coast known for food shacks such as Uncle Ernie's, famous for grilled chicken, ribs, and special cole slaw, and Gwen's, another rib specialist, with hammocks in a shady palm grove and a reggae colada–fueled Sunday afternoon jump-up. Or play castaway on Gorgeous Scilly Cay, a popular beach-shack restaurant on its own coral-sand islet. The alfresco feast of simple grilled Anguilla lobster marinated in a curry-based sauce is legendary, so reserve ahead.

VISITOR INFO: www.anguilla-vacation.com. **CAP JULUCA:** Tel 888-858-5822 or 264-497-6666; www.capjuluca.com. *Cost:* from $495 (off-peak), from $995 (peak); dinner $75. *When:* closed Sep–Oct. **CUISINART RESORT:** Tel 800-943-3210 or 264-498-2000; www.cuisinartresort.com. *Cost:* from $440 (off-peak), from $815 (peak); dinner $75. *When:* closed Sep–Oct. **MALLIOUHANA HOTEL:** Tel 800-835-0796 or 264-497-6111; www.malliouhana.com. *Cost:* from $430 (off-peak), from $860 (peak); dinner $80. *When:* closed Sep–Oct. **ANACAONA HOTEL:** Tel 877-647-4736 or 264-497-6827; www.anacaonahotel.com. *Cost:* from $150 (off-peak), from $300 (peak). **BLANCHARD'S:** Tel 264-497-6100; www.blanchardsrestaurant.com. *Cost:* $60. **GORGEOUS SCILLY CAY:** Tel 264-497-5123; www.scillycayanguilla.com. *Cost:* lobster lunch $75. **BEST TIMES:** Nov–Apr for finest weather; Mar for Moonsplash; May for Anguilla Regatta; Nov for Tranquility Jazz Festival.

A Nautical Kentucky Derby and Stellar Beaches

ANTIGUA

Lesser Antilles

In 1784, a young Horatio Nelson arrived in Antigua, the premier Caribbean naval base for the British fleet during the Napoleonic Wars. He'd still recognize the restored dockyard, now a national park bearing his name and one of a few British Georgian–style naval dockyards left in the world. Antigua remains one of the most British of the Caribbean isles and reveres its rapport with the sea. Every April some 200 boats from 25 countries descend on this otherwise quiet outpost for Antigua Sailing Week, one of the top regattas in the world.

The Admiral's Inn, a Georgian brick building dating back to 1788, is the unofficial headquarters for the Sailing Week hubbub and the architectural centerpiece of the Dockyard. Known as the Ads, it's the island's most interesting historic hotel, with 13 rooms and the ambience of an old ship. The well-tanned yachting crowd comes here to cool off in the shady terrace bar/restaurant, their carefully tended pleasure craft and racing yachts bobbing nearby. For a quiet retreat from the sailing scene, a loyal clientele repairs to the time-honored Curtain Bluff resort, flanked by two perfect beaches in one of the prettiest spots in Antigua. Guests are lulled to sleep at night by the pounding surf on the windward side, while the lagoon-smooth leeward beach serves as the launching place for the hotel's host of water activities. Tennis buffs come to participate in the prestigious Antigua Tennis Week held here every May.

The newest and chicest hotel on Antigua, Carlisle Bay, swept the island scene into the 21st century: Its sleek and soothing suites

A traditional English telephone booth sits on Dickenson Bay.

overlook a lovely crescent of white and golden sand backed by rolling hills, with not a neighboring hotel in sight. Guests rarely leave the grounds, with everything you could want available—kids club, water sports, spa, yoga pavilion, tennis, fabulous food—and all offered with restrained good taste.

The largest of the Leeward Islands, Antigua is rightly known for its abundant beaches (365 of them)—and the snorkeling that goes with them. The most popular are Dickenson Bay in the northwest, a wide strip of powder-fine sand with blissfully calm turquoise waters, and Half-Moon Bay, which stretches for a sandy mile on the eastern coast. The most fashionable, however, and only five minutes from the Dockyard, is Pigeon Point.

Wherever you are (the island is only 14 miles long and 11 miles wide), it's never very far to Shirley Heights, the highest point in Antigua (where the remains of General Shirley's 17th-century fort still stand), for a sunset party on Sunday nights.

Antigua's sister island to the north, flat and rocky Barbuda, is a bird-watcher's paradise, best known for a rookery of frigate birds some 5,000 strong, outnumbering the local human population threefold. With seemingly endless stretches of white and pink sand beaches, Barbuda can bring tears to the eyes of beach aficionados.

VISITOR INFO: www.antigua-barbuda.com. **NELSON'S DOCKYARD:** Tel 268-460-1379; www.antiguamuseums.org/nelsonsdockyard.htm. **ADMIRAL'S INN:** Tel 268-460-1027; www.admiralsantigua.com. *Cost:* from $105 (off-peak), from $170 (peak). *When:* closed late Aug–Oct 20. **CURTAIN BLUFF:** Tel 888-289-9898 or 268-462-8400; www.curtainbluff.com. *Cost:* from $715 (off-peak), from $1,100 (peak), all-inclusive. *When:* closed Aug–late Oct. **CARLISLE BAY:** Tel 866-502-2855 or 268-484-0002; www.carlisle-bay.com. *Cost:* from $425 (off-peak), from $920 (peak). *When:* closed early Sep–mid-Oct. **BEST TIMES:** Nov–Apr for good weather; Apr for Classic Yacht Regatta and Sailing Week; Aug for Summer Carnival; Dec for Yacht Show.

A Mini-Archipelago Lures Boaters, Diners, and Anglers

SAILING THE ABACOS

The Abacos, The Bahamas

Among the most affluent of the Out Islands, the Abacos are known as "the sailing capital of the world." Although that's a title it might share with the British Virgin Islands and the Grenadines (see pp. 1071 and 1106), the Abacos promise a fine collection of 25 cays off the eastern coast of the long, thin, boomerang-shaped Great Abaco Island. Some are uninhabited, while others are home to small resorts and inviting towns that date to the American Revolution, when Loyalists from the Carolinas resettled here. Sail from one cay to the next, dropping anchor for snorkeling, swimming, excellent fishing, diving, or island exploration. With the exception of Eleuthera's Harbour Island (see p. 1062), you'll find more 18th-century charm here than anywhere else in the Bahamas.

The prime launch pad is Great Abaco's

Marsh Harbour, an easy harbor to enter and equipped with several full-service marinas—this is the place to rent a boat, with or without a crew. Before setting off, stop by the Jib Room for conch burgers and their signature Bilge Burner drink. The popular harbor-view spot really jumps with music and dancing on the two nights it serves dinner—barbecued baby-back pork ribs on Wednesdays, and juicy New York strip steaks on Saturdays.

Built in 1838, Hope Town's Elbow Reef Lighthouse is powered by kerosene, one of the last lighthouses of its kind in the world.

There are beautiful beaches and harbors aplenty, but some are not to be missed. Elbow Cay is best known for its 120-foot-tall, peppermint-striped lighthouse built in 1838 in the charming village of Hope Town.

Hotels in the Abacos tend to be small and casual. Elbow Cay's Abaco Inn draws return guests to its cheerful island-style rooms nestled among sand dunes and coconut palms. Perched at the crest of a sandy ridge with views of both the Atlantic Ocean and Sea of Abaco, the inn's restaurant has a reputation for the best seafood around (try the grilled wahoo or crispy, pan-fried coconut grouper). Leave room for the desserts by Miss Belle, a fourth-generation Hope Town Bahamian whose fresh-squeezed key lime, coconut, and chocolate silk pies are a local legend. At the very tip of Elbow Cay is Tahiti Beach, a gorgeous curve of sand whose utterly placid, clear turquoise waters are so remote you can only get there by foot, bike, golf cart, or boat.

With pastel clapboard homes and white picket fences, Man-O-War Cay takes you back in time. Residents are justly proud of their 200-year history of shipbuilding, and continue to craft their famous fiberglass boats today. Great Guana, the longest of the Abaco cays, stretches nearly 7 miles tip to tip but has just 100 full-time residents. Its endless beach, alluringly deserted and with grassy dunes, runs the entire length of the island and is one of the loveliest in the Bahamas. It's home to Nippers, one of the best (and most family-friendly) beach bars around. A multilevel structure perched high on a 40-foot dune, it offers snorkelers and divers easy access to the outstanding Great Abaco Barrier Reef Beach, which starts less than 50 feet from shore. Adults indulge in frozen Nipper Trippers—a frozen concoction of five rums and two juices—while kids can splash about in small swimming pools. Sunday is an all-day party disguised as a pig roast.

Some of the best fishing grounds border Treasure Cay. It's also the place to be for golf. Treasure Cay Hotel Resort & Marina has a Dick Wilson–designed 18-hole course that is one of the best in the Bahamas. The property is just steps from the surprisingly uncrowded Treasure Cay Beach, a 3.5-mile-long stretch of incredibly powdery sand, which is perfect for swimming. On Green Turtle Cay, New Plymouth is another historic village settled in 1783 when Loyalists fled America to find a new home. Now it's best known for Miss Emily's Blue Bee Bar—a shack, really—hung with Junkanoo masks and home of the Famous Goombay Smash. The top secret recipe is believed to contain coconut rum, dirty rum, apricot brandy, and pineapple juice. Get one to go and amble over to Coco Bay beach, shaded by casuarina pines and, amazingly, almost always empty.

The fishing in the Abacos is renowned: Find yellowtail and grouper on the reefs, marlin and tuna in the deeps, and fast, canny bonefish in the Marls, 400 square miles of lush mangrove islands and sandy cays on the western side of Great Abaco.

VISITOR INFO: www.myoutislands.com. **HOW:** The Moorings rents bareboats and crewed yachts. Tel 888-952-8420 or 242-367-4000; www.moorings.com. **JIB ROOM:** Tel 242-367-2700; www.jibroom.com. *Cost:* dinner $25. **ABACO INN:** Tel 800-468-8799 or 242-366-0133; www.abacoinn.com. *Cost:* from $160; dinner $50. *When:* closed mid-Aug–mid-Oct. **NIPPERS:** Tel 242-365-5143; www.nippersbar.com. *Cost:* lunch $15. **TREASURE CAY HOTEL RESORT & MARINA:** Tel 800-327-1584 or 954-525-7711; www.treasurecay.com. *Cost:* from $130; greens fees $65 (guests), $90 (nonguests). **BEST TIMES:** Nov–May for nicest weather; Apr–Jun for Bahamas Billfish Championship; early Jul for Bahamas Cup and Regatta Time in Abaco; May–Aug for blue marlin fishing.

Blue Holes, Bonefish, and Beaches

ANDROS ISLAND

The Bahamas

Because of shallow channels called "bights" that indent and cut across the island, most of Andros, the Bahamas' largest island, remains sparsely inhabited, little visited, and largely unexplored—except by in-the-know visitors drawn here by its gin-clear waters and the world-class diving and fishing they provide.

Running parallel to its east coast, Andros's 142-mile barrier reef is the third longest in the world after those in Australia and Central America (see pp. 653 and 961). Venture beyond the reef for a wall that plunges 6,000 feet to a narrow underwater canyon known as the Tongue of the Ocean (aka TOTO). There, divers also find dozens of cathedral-like caves called blue holes (first made famous by Jacques Cousteau)—there are more in the Bahamas than anywhere else in the world.

All this lies just 1 mile offshore from the Bahamas' oldest (and arguably best) diving and fishing resort, Small Hope Bay Lodge. If you don't know how to dive or snorkel, they'll teach you at your own pace (you can even get certified), while nondiving guests are happy with a book or a beer in a hammock among the coconut palms. No one puts on airs at this easygoing beachfront cottage colony—no one even puts on shoes very often, except perhaps at dinner, a hearty, convivial affair that might include fresh conch fritters and chowder, lobster, and warm home-baked johnnycakes. Guests also come for the fishing: Marlin and bluefin tuna are plentiful, but Andros is known as the bonefishing capital of the world. With large numbers of trophy-size bonefish (often topping 12 pounds), Andros provides some of the most exciting light-tackle fishing there is. Cargill Creek is the place to hire a local specialist to guide you through the sandy, shallow flats.

Amp up the luxury quotient at Kamalame Cay, one of the few private-island resorts in the Bahamas' Out Islands. A 96-acre hideaway off the northeast coast of Andros with a 19th-century British colonial atmosphere, Kamalame ranges from relatively affordable marina rooms to breezy beachfront villas. Only 3 dozen people enjoy this off-the-grid experience at any one time. And with the barrier reef just a mile away, divers and snorkelers are promised exceptional underwater thrills.

Visitor info: www.myoutislands.com. **Small Hope Bay Lodge:** Tel 800-223-6961 or 242-368-2013; www.smallhope.com. *Cost:* from $470, inclusive. **Kamalame Cay:** Tel 800-790-7971 or 876-632-3213; www.kamalame.com. *Cost:* from $400. *When:* closed late Aug–mid-Oct. **Best times:** Nov–Apr for nicest weather; Nov and May for fishing.

Out-Island History and Pink Sand

Harbour Island

Eleuthera, The Bahamas

The Martha's Vineyard of the Caribbean and one of the oldest settlements in the Bahamas, Harbour Island is known for its colonial charm and barefoot glamour. It's so diminutive at 3.5 miles long and less than a mile wide that everyone zips around in golf carts or on beach bikes. Celebrities and fashionistas arrive via the 5-minute water-taxi ride from Eleuthera, the narrow 100-mile-long island whose name is Greek for "freedom," a reference to Puritan pilgrims who settled here in 1648 after being expelled from Bermuda.

Harbour Island ("Briland," as it's known by locals) is best known for its 3-mile pink sand beach, which runs the length of the island. The postcard-perfect crescent, whose color comes from flecks of red plankton mixed with finely crushed white coral, is languidly lapped by calm, turquoise waters that are protected by a reef, making for some of the safest and most enjoyable swimming in the Bahamas. It's an unpretentious spot, unobtrusively lined with small villas and resorts, happily void of crowds. Along with barefoot R&R, the quietly posh island is favored for bonefishing and for diving the Current Cut Dive, an exciting underwater gully that ranks among the world's finest.

Looking startlingly like a Cape Cod village, charm-packed Dunmore Town was laid out in 1791 by Lord Dunmore, governor of the Bahamas, after having lost the same job in Virginia during the American Revolution. Eating is excellent here, from the dive-y to the inspired. Start at Queen Conch, a simple shack right off the fishermen's dock on Bay Street, where there's just one thing on the menu: fresh-caught, -cracked, and -diced conch salad (be forewarned that locals consider conch an aphrodisiac), revved up with Scotch bonnet peppers and cooled down with a cold Nassau-brewed Kalik beer. Spicy conch chili is the draw at a lime green–painted beachside spot called Sip Sip—lobster quesadillas and rum-spiked carrot cake round out the simple menu.

A little slice of Miami Beach has arrived on a low bluff above the harbor, where the Rock House, a former Catholic schoolhouse, has been transformed into a very chic British-Mediterranean inn and sophisticated restaurant, with a centerpiece pool surrounded by thatch-roofed cabanas. Wonderfully stylish rooms can also be found at the Landing, set right at the ferry dock and dating from 1800. It is one of the island's stately old mansions, with original Abaco pine floors, limestone walls, and wraparound verandas where diners enjoy a globally inspired menu and fine harbor views.

At the heart of it all and setting the standard since it opened in 1951, Pink Sands Resort (formerly owned by Chris Blackwell, founder of Island Records) is still a glamorous destination for a young and decidedly cool crowd. Perched on one of the finest beaches in all of the Bahamas, its 25 pastel-colored cottages are spread over 20 tropical acres. Guests and nonguests alike frequent the Blue Bar for its Caribbean fusion menu. The elegant informality of the place is deliberately and deceptively unassuming, in keeping with the island's vibe.

VISITOR INFO: www.myoutislands.com. **SIP SIP:** Tel 242-333-3316. *Cost:* lunch $40. **ROCK HOUSE HOTEL:** Tel 242-333-2053; www.rockhousebahamas.com. *Cost:* from $300; dinner $75. *When:* closed Aug–Oct. **THE LANDING:** Tel 242-333-2707; www.harbourislandlanding.com. *Cost:* from $250; dinner $70. *When:* closed Sep–Oct. **PINK SANDS RESORT:** Tel 800-407-4776 or 242-333-2030; www.pinksandsresort.com. *Cost:* cottages from $495 (off-peak), from $750 (peak); dinner $55. **BEST TIMES:** Nov–May for pleasant weather; Jul for Eleuthera Pineapple Festival; Oct for North Eleuthera/Harbour Island Sailing Regatta.

Swimming Pigs! Plus Spectacular Sailing and a Marine Preserve

THE EXUMA CAYS

The Bahamas

If you arrive in the Exumas by air, book a window seat. Swooping in over the 110-mile-long, spiny chain of 365 cays, which start about 30 miles southeast of Nassau, provides one of the most stunning sights in all of the Caribbean, and a first glimpse of why these mostly undeveloped islands are often considered the crown jewels of the Bahamas. Like a sand painting rising out of the sea, elaborate channels and sandbars are surrounded by waters in every imaginable shade of blue.

While the Abacos (see p. 1059) are traditionally touted as the Caribbean's best sailing, many claim the Exuma chain steals the show. Its centerpiece is the Exuma Cays Land and Sea Park, a 176-square-mile, breathtakingly beautiful "no take" marine preserve where coral gardens flourish with conch, grouper, and lobster populations that are so abundant they're helping to repopulate the whole archipelago. Established in 1959 and accessible only by boat (your own or a tour company's), this is the oldest land and sea park on the planet. But while the land is pretty, providing habitat for turtles, iguanas, and birds, it is the sea that truly dazzles, offering some of the best sea kayaking, yachting, snorkeling, and diving in all the Bahamas.

The closest civilization is an hour away at Staniel Cay Yacht Club. It is a perfect home base for access to the park and other attractions, like Thunderball (a beautiful marine cave excellent for snorkeling and named for the 1965 James Bond movie shot there), and friendly swimming pigs (they paddle out to greet boaters who often bring them food). It may sound swanky, but the yacht club is a congenial social center of just nine unpretentious cottages in fun colors right on the water, an 18-slip marina for boaters, and a small landing strip. It becomes the yachting world's preferred place to be during the New Year's Day Cruising Regatta.

Great Exuma Island anchors the southern end of the Exuma archipelago; George Town is its charming pink capital. The popular Augusta Bay Bahamas is a freshly updated property whose 16 spacious suites enjoy sweeping views of a perfect white beach. Check in and then check out the local Fish Fry, a collection of colorful beach shacks at the pier where everyone hangs out, playing cards and listening to music while dining on conch salad, fried fish, and just-caught lobster. Or join the models, photographers, and sailors who make the short trip to nearby Stocking Island for its especially gorgeous beaches and the legendary Chat 'N' Chill, a beach bar known for its grilled conch burgers, barbecued ribs, and on Sundays, a rowdy pig roast with music.

VISITOR INFO: www.myoutislands.com. **EXUMA CAYS LAND & SEA PARK:** www.exumapark.com. **STANIEL CAY YACHT CLUB:** Tel 242-355-2024 or in the U.S., 954-467-8920; www.stanielcay.com. *Cost:* from $145 (off-peak), from $210 (peak). **AUGUSTA BAY BAHAMAS:** Tel 242-336-2251; www.augustabaybahamas.com. *Cost:* from $175 (off-peak), from $225 (peak). **CHAT 'N' CHILL:** Tel 242-336-2700. *Cost:* dinner $30, pig roast $20. **BEST TIMES:** Dec–May for nicest weather; late Apr for Family Island Regatta in George Town.

Enchanting Creatures, Face-to-Face

DOLPHIN DIVE

Little Bahama Bank, The Bahamas

The Bahamas is a vast archipelago of 750 sun-soaked islands with 2,500 cays, stretching over 100,000 square miles of green and cobalt blue seas. It's so close (but with a faraway vibe) to Florida that many visitors launch their island-hopping on private sailboats, yachts, or planes from there. How convenient, then, that one of the Bahamas' finest attractions—a weeklong encounter with wild dolphins, strictly on their terms—actually departs from Palm Beach.

Wild spotted dolphins have become habituated to sharing their waters with humans.

A pod of wild spotted dolphins congregates regularly north of Grand Bahama Island in spring and summer to play and swim and interact with people; they come without the enticement of food or reward, apparently charmed by their human playmates. Captain Scott of Dream Team, who has spent over 30 years leading weeklong expeditions, is an honorary member of the pod. Upon hearing the sound of his 86-foot boat, the *Dolphin Dream,* the dolphins appear, riding the bow waves of the boat. The dolphins have learned it's "zoo time" and come to see who Scott has dropped into the crystal-clear waters. Baby dolphins play with these strange but harmless creatures while the mothers circle nearby, keeping a watchful eye. They may stay a few minutes or a few hours. You'll usually have one or two encounters a day (or perhaps at night) over the weeklong trip on the boat, which serves as a hotel for 8 to 12 passengers. The water over the Little Bahama Bank—shallow, calm, and with excellent visibility—is perfect for nondiving snorkelers and swimmers, who can enjoy themselves even after the dolphins slip away.

DREAM TEAM: Tel 888-277-8181 or 561-848-5375; www.dolphindreamteam.com. **COST:** weeklong trips from $1,595 per person, based on 8 passengers, all-inclusive. **WHEN:** Apr–Aug.

Extravagance Both Showy and Discreet

Clubs Paradise

Paradise Island and New Providence Island, The Bahamas

Paradise Island is the tiny neighbor of busy Nassau, the capital of the Bahamas on New Providence Island. The long and narrow island is the home of Atlantis megaresort and the most developed, priciest stretch of gorgeous white beach in the Bahamas. Yet you can still manage to feel like you've gotten away from it all at the One&Only Ocean Club.

Now one of the most beautiful resorts in the Caribbean, it began as the private estate of A&P heir Huntington Hartford II. Its terraced hillside gardens were inspired by Versailles and decorated with a 12th-century French cloister purchased by William Randolph Hearst and brought piece by piece to the U.S. One&Only became such an ultraposh, British Colonial–style enclave that the James Bond film *Casino Royale* found its perfect location here.

With just 105 rooms and suites, situated on 35 acres, honeymooners love its quiet and intimate feel, while enjoying big-resort amenities, including an 18-hole championship golf course designed by Tom Weiskopf; six tennis courts; and a beachfront restaurant, Dune, by celebrity chef Jean-Georges Vongerichten. Eight exquisite Balinese-style spa pavilions open onto gardens and offer private waterfall showers.

Atlantis looms next door, a 3,000-plus–room theme park, like Vegas in the tropics, that is both loved and hated by locals and tourists. The 141-acre Aquaventure water park includes a man-made lagoon for encounters with dolphins and the world's largest open-air marine habitat, home to over 50,000 sea creatures, while adult pleasures include a casino and the celebrity-chef outposts of Nobu Matsuhisa, Bobby Flay, and Jean-Georges Vongerichten. Of Atlantis's many towers, two are recently built hotels-within-hotels: the swank all-suite Cove Atlantis, which appeals to couples, and the family-friendly Reef Atlantis. When the need for escape calls, nearby Cabbage Beach still retains some of its glitz-free vibe, unfolding for 2 miles of broad white sand and lined with palms and casuarinas before morphing into Paradise Beach.

Across the bridge, urban Nassau is best known for its casinos, megaresorts, and endless parade of cruise ships, but the aptly named A Stone's Throw Away provides welcome respite outside town. Though recently built, this small hideaway evokes a handsome old Bahamian plantation home, with wood floors, louvered shutters, and a wraparound porch. Or keep driving west for a romantic sundowner drink at Compass Point Beach Resort's oceanfront bar, a few steps from justly famous Love Beach. Crayola-colored clapboard cottages provide steady breezes and views of one of Nassau's few unadulterated stretches of beach. Their colors evoke Junkanoo, the lavish Afro-Bahamian carnival that originated when plantation owners gave their slaves a rare holiday between Christmas and New Year's—it's still celebrated today with elaborate parades.

Visitor info: www.bahamas.com. **One&Only Ocean Club:** Tel 888-528-7157 or 242-363-2501; http://oceanclub.oneandonlyresorts.com. *Cost:* from $515 (off-peak), from $1,030 (peak). **Atlantis:** Tel 800-285-2684 or 242-363-3000; www.atlantis.com. *Cost:* from $280 (off-peak), from $480 (peak) for Atlantis; from $590 (off-peak), from $790 (peak) for Cove Atlantis; from $465 (off-peak), from $705 (peak) for Reef Atlantis. **A Stone's Throw Away:** Tel 242-327-7030;

www.astonesthrowaway.com. *Cost:* from $190. **Compass Point:** Tel 866-431-2874 or 242-327-4500; www.compasspointbeachresort.com. *Cost:* from $300; dinner $50. **Best times:** Dec 26–Jan 1 for Junkanoo; Jun and Jul for Nassau/Paradise Island Junkanoo Summer Festival.

The Caribbean's "Little England"

Platinum Coast

Barbados, Lesser Antilles

More than 300 years of British rule have left their mark on this beautiful isle of pink and white sand beaches. Although independent since 1966, Barbados has retained a *veddy* British atmosphere. Afternoon tea is a tradition, cricket is the national sport, and most of the tourists are Brits, many of whom flock to "the Platinum Coast," named for the ritzy hotels and condos found along this western shoreline that faces the Caribbean Sea. It is home to the calmest waters and best beaches, and there is snorkeling with sociable well-fed sea turtles just offshore.

The jewel of the West Coast, Sandy Lane nabbed some of the finest waterfront early on. It has long been one of the resort world's classiest (and priciest) acts, its house-proud Bajan staff treating every guest as they did Queen Elizabeth when she visited. Its 45 holes of golf include the Tom Fazio–designed Green Monkey course, considered one of the best in the region. The Spa is known for its highly skilled therapists and top-quality aromatherapy treatments. Dressing up for dinner has always been a tradition here, so the more casually inclined now drift to the open-air, oceanfront Bajan Blue.

Proof that Barbados has grown to be a culinary destination can be found at the Fish Pot, known for its stylish outdoor dining (it's practically on top of the waves) and inventive dishes like chicken and foie gras pâté with guava-and-ginger marmalade. If you want to go more local, try the island specialty, a flying fish sandwich. The best place to snag one is the Friday night Fish Fry in Oistins, a fishing village on the southern coast, where vendors serve up grilled or fried fish, paired with cold Banks beer. It's the best party on the island, with lots of loud music, dancing, and rum-drinking.

Barbados's most popular attraction is Harrison's Cave, site of a jaw-dropping collection of well-lit stalactites and stalagmites. From here, head to the more rugged, windy eastern coast, which faces the Atlantic, an area so quiet that locals call it "the country." The beaches around Bathsheba are beautiful, though cooler and rougher than others—which makes for excellent surfing, especially at "Soup Bowl," where you'll find the island's biggest waves and an annual surf competition in November. Within walking distance is Sea U Guest House, a charmer built in the style of a Colonial Caribbean home, with mahogany

The subterranean drama of Harrison's Cave remained unexplored until the 1970s.

furniture, batik art, and hammocks strung between palm trees. It's an easy uphill stroll to the Andromeda Botanic Garden, a lush, 6-acre tropical garden overlooking the sea. Its 600 species of plants include an extensive collection of heliconia, orchids, and palms and a massive, native bearded fig tree for which the Portuguese reputedly named the island "Los Barbados"—"the bearded ones."

VISITOR INFO: www.visitbarbados.org. **SANDY LANE:** Tel 866-444-4080 or 246-444-2000; www.sandylane.com. *Cost:* from $1,190 (off-peak), from $1,450 (peak). **THE FISH POT:** Tel 246-439-3000; www.littlegoodharbourbarbados.com. *Cost:* dinner $60. **HARRISON'S CAVE:** Tel 246-438-6640; www.harrisonscave.com. **SEA U GUEST HOUSE:** Tel 246-433-9450; www.seaubarbados.com. *Cost:* from $120. **ANDROMEDA BOTANIC GARDEN:** Tel 246-433-9384; andromeda.cavehill.uwi.edu. **BEST TIMES:** Nov–Apr for nicest weather; Jul–Aug for Crop Over Festival.

So Much More Than Shorts and Triangles

BERMUDA

Bermuda

Considerably cooler than the Caribbean islands that lie south of here, Bermuda is best known for its stunning pink sand beaches (the result of sand mixed with the crushed red skeletons of reef-dwelling protozoa), Bermuda shorts (standard business dress for men when worn with a blazer, tie, and knee socks), and "the Bermuda Triangle" (a debunked myth about the not-so-mysterious disappearances of ships and aircraft in a huge swath of ocean that includes Bermuda).

Bermuda is a 21-square-mile archipelago of 7 major islands and 143 smaller ones interconnected by bridges and causeways. When the British sailing ship *Sea Venture* wrecked here in 1609 en route to Jamestown, Virginia. (very likely inspiring Shakespeare's play *The Tempest*), a few stalwarts stayed on to claim it, making it England's oldest colony.

The beaches alone were reason enough to stay behind. Typically, South Shore beaches—postcard-perfect Horseshoe Bay is one of the most popular—are more scenic than those on the north side. No hotels sit directly on Bermuda's beaches, but the venerable 50-acre Elbow Beach Hotel, built in 1908, is as close as you can come. Now a Mandarin Oriental, the 235-room property has the island's finest spa, afternoon tea, and excellent dining that runs from the romantic Lido restaurant to Mickey's, the best bistro-on-the-beach—sample the island's signature Dark 'n' Stormy (Black Seal rum and Barritt's ginger beer) here.

For utter serenity from sunrise to sunset, set off by scooter (there are no car rentals in Bermuda) to the soft and truly pink Warwick Long Bay. With over 200 square miles of near-virgin reef and clear waters, Bermuda offers excellent diving and is one of the world's great shipwreck diving capitals. Easily reached historic wrecks include everything from the *Sea Venture* to Civil War paddle wheelers and the 1930s luxury cruise liner *Cristóbal Colón*.

But it is perhaps golf that Bermuda is most famous for: There are more golf courses per square mile here than anywhere else in the world. Six public and two private golf clubs offer spectacular scenery, challenging courses (seven are championship standard), and wind—plenty of wind—plus a tradition of excellence not easy to find outside Scotland (see p. 45). Riddell's

Bay, established in 1922, is the island's oldest and most picturesque club. Belmont Hills, challenging and undulating, opened a year later. The private Mid Ocean Club, long considered the island's finest, has a rival in beauty and challenge in the Tucker's Point Golf Course, dramatically refashioned out of a 1932 champion course at Castle Harbour. Next door is the 88-room Rosewood Tucker's Point, the first luxury hotel to be built in Bermuda since 1970. The flawless Point restaurant and some of Bermuda's most beautiful seafront are two of its many boons.

Bermuda's popular "cottage colonies" are a local tradition best exemplified by the hillside 1920s-era Cambridge Beaches Resort & Spa, a refined country-club–like property on the island's extreme western edge. It occupies a 30-acre peninsula edged with coves and four powder (but not pink) sand beaches. Daily afternoon tea is observed punctiliously, and the formal Tamarisk Restaurant is a long-time favorite.

Situated on a dramatic limestone cliff overlooking a perfect pink beach, the Reefs is small, all-inclusive, and boasts a fanatically loyal following. A reservation-with-a-view at Coconuts is among the most coveted on the island, while its Royston's restaurant is a more formal choice.

Staying right in the small capital city of Hamilton is an unexpected delight when you've checked into the Rosedon Hotel, a 1906 home expanded into an impeccable 44-room inn that serves a large teatime spread and an equally wonderful breakfast. All it lacks is a pink beach—but Elbow Beach is just a 10-minute scooter ride away.

Visitor info: www.bermudatourism.com. **Elbow Beach Hotel:** Tel 800-223-7434 or 441-236-3535; www.mandarinoriental.com/bermuda. *Cost:* from $295 (off-peak), from $715 (peak). **Bermuda Golf Association:** Tel 441-295-9972; www.bermudagolf.org. **Rosewood Tucker's Point:** Tel 888-767-3966 or 441-298-4010; www.tuckerspoint.com. *Cost:* from $395 (off-peak), from $650 (peak); dinner at the Point $70. **Cambridge Beaches Resort & Spa:** Tel 800-468-7300 or 441-234-0331; www.cambridgebeaches.com. *Cost:* from $385 (off-peak), from $475 (peak). **The Reefs:** Tel 800-742-2008 or 441-238-0222; www.thereefs.com. *Cost:* from $410 (off-peak), from $650 (peak), inclusive. **Rosedon Hotel:** Tel 441-295-1640; www.rosedon.com. *Cost:* from $250 (off-peak), from $290 (peak). **Best times:** May–Oct for nice weather; Jan–Feb for Bermuda Festival; Jun for sailboat racing; late Sep–early Oct for Bermuda Music Festival; late Oct for Bermuda Tattoo.

Underwater Forests of Coral Reefs and Round-the-Clock Diving

Bonaire National Marine Park

Bonaire, Lesser Antilles

An island almost completely surrounded by teeming coral reefs, Bonaire is one big dive site. Eighty-six marked diving spots are scattered off the 24-mile, boomerang-shaped shoreline, and bright yellow painted rocks on the side of the road indicate where you can pull over and walk in. No other island has so many first-rate sites so close to shore nor such a conservation-sensitive dive industry and forward-thinking government.

The latter's unprecedented creation of the

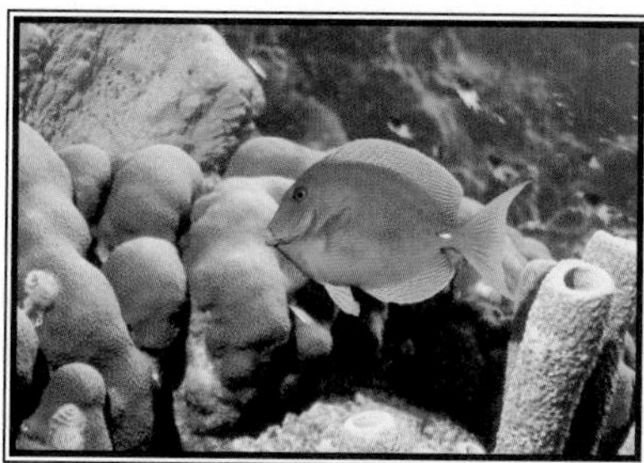

Blue tangs are part of Bonaire's technicolor underwater world.

island-encircling Bonaire National Marine Park in 1979 has resulted in some of the world's healthiest and most magnificent hard- and soft-coral reef gardens, harboring vast schools of tropical fish; over 370 species call these waters home. It's a veritable underwater Eden rife with doctorfish, sergeant majors, trumpet fish, and four-eye butterfly fish. It's paradise for snorkelers, but it's really divers who witness the best of Bonaire's treasures. Reef-damaging activities like anchoring, spearfishing, and touching coral are strictly prohibited in the park. Special dive moorings allow easy access all around Bonaire and Klein Bonaire, the small, uninhabited island off the western leeward coast. And since Bonaire is exceptionally arid with minimal freshwater runoff, underwater visibility (60–100 feet) is among the Caribbean's clearest.

On the western coast, within easy reach of Klein Bonaire, Captain Don's Habitat is the nerve center for visiting scuba divers. Californian Captain Don is a salty island legend and was instrumental in the dive industry's early days of conservation and sustainable tourism. The oceanfront rooms and villas have a laid-back, relaxing atmosphere, and this full-service PADI (Professional Association of Diving Instructors) diving center offers 50 world-class dives within a 15-minute boat ride. Bonaire is still largely untouched by big development, but divers looking for more luxurious digs will find them at nearby Harbour Village Beach Club, with Mediterranean-style villas, a private palm-fringed white sand beach, and divemasters at your service.

Bonaire also has much to offer above the surface, including some of the best windsurfing and kayaking in the Caribbean on the shallow, calm waters of Lac Bay (the warm trade winds confirm Bonaire's name, meaning "good air"). And between December and March, on the island's northwestern tip, enjoy the sight of the brilliantly colored pink flamingos on the salt flats in Washington-Slagbaai National Park.

Visitor info: www.tourismbonaire.com. **Bonaire Marine Park:** Tel 599-717-8444; www.bmp.org. **Captain Don's:** Tel 800-327-6709 or 599-717-8290; www.habitatbonaire.com. *Cost:* from $150 (off-peak), from $190 (peak). **Harbour Village:** Tel 800-424-0004 or 599-717-7500; www.harbourvillage.com. *Cost:* from $275 (off-peak), from $385 (peak). **Washington-Slagbaai Park:** Tel 599-788-9015; www.washingtonparkbonaire.org. **Best times:** Jan–Oct for diving; Jun for Bonaire Dive Festival.

The Caribbean's Party Central

Jost Van Dyke

British Virgin Islands, Lesser Antilles

This rugged, hilly island may be small (about 4 square miles), but it is big in personality. Purportedly named for a Dutch pirate who made it his hideaway, Jost Van Dyke is where the sailing crowd (see Sailing the BVI, next page) pulls into port when they're ready for serious fun. While there are many beach bars here, the most famous is Foxy's Tamarind Bar, located near the dock in Great Harbour and founded in 1968 by Foxy Callwood, owner, troubadour, wit, and Member of the Order of the British Empire (awarded in person by Queen Elizabeth II for his contributions to local culture and tourism). One sign that you have arrived as a Caribbean traveler is having Foxy improvise a song about you when you walk up to the bar. Foxy's absolutely explodes on New Year's Eve, when the entire harbor is filled with boats gathered for one gigantic party under the stars.

You'll want to while away the day at White Bay, a perfect, white sand beach with great snorkeling and its own collection of beach bars, including Seddy's One Love (owned by Foxy's son) and Ivan's Stress Free Bar. But it is the Soggy Dollar Bar everyone knows about. You can get there by cab or by foot from the ferry, but the most dramatic entrance is by boat. There's no dock, so yachties simply drop anchor, swim to shore, and use wet money to pay for their drinks—hence the Soggy Dollar. The bar is part of Sandcastle Hotel, made up of four cottages and two rooms, all on or near the water. Wear to dinner what you wore to breakfast, and spend the day moving from one hammock to another with a Painkiller in hand. The drink is now famous throughout the islands—this spruced-up piña colada made with dark rum and fresh nutmeg can vary from mild to lethal.

Settle in for a stay at White Bay Villas and Seaside Cottages, ten hillside retreats perched above the beach and offering spectacular views of St. Thomas, St. John, and Tortola.

For outstanding snorkeling and remote beaches, sail over to Sandy Cay, Green Cay, and Sandy Spit, islets off the eastern end of the island. If you don't have your own boat, just hitch a ride with your new best friends from the bar.

Visitor info: www.bvitourism.com. **How:** Ferry service from West End, Tortola, and Charlotte Amalie, St. Thomas. **Foxy's Tamarind Bar:** Tel 284-495-9258; www.foxysbar.com. **Sandcastle Hotel and Soggy Dollar Bar:** Tel 284-495-9888; www.soggydollar.com. *Cost:* from $190 (off-peak), from $290 (peak). **White Bay Villas & Seaside Cottages:** Tel 800-778-8066 or 410-571-6692; www.jostvandyke.com. *Cost:* from $250 (off-peak), from $315 (peak), 5-night minimum. **Best times:** Nov–Apr for finest weather. At Foxy's: Sat night for barbecue, Memorial Day for Foxy's Wooden Boat Regatta, and New Year's Eve.

Gigantic Boulders a Stone's Throw from Luxury

The Baths and Little Dix Bay

Virgin Gorda, British Virgin Islands, Lesser Antilles

One of the most fabled beaches of the Caribbean, the Baths of Virgin Gorda look like something out of a fairy tale—huge, time-sculpted granite boulders that dwarf mere humans. Pushed up from the seafloor some 20 million years ago and haphazardly scattered about, they create a tantalizing maze that brings out the child in everyone. You can wade between them, pose alongside them, even swim in shallow pools and grottoes, as well as in one water-filled boulder that is the inspiration for the name "The Baths." The site is on every visitor's list, so avoid the boatloads of in-and-out tourists by strolling the less trafficked coastline on either side, where the massive boulders continue.

Virgin Gorda, whose undulating 10-by-2-mile form looked like a reclining "fat virgin" to Columbus, is known for its yacht clubs, quiet coves, and plentiful, safe anchorages. The island's blue-blood connections date to 1964, when Laurance Rockefeller—who also fell for nearby St. John in the USVI (see p. 1113)—opened a 500-acre resort on a perfect half-mile crescent of white beach. Now called Rosewood Little Dix Bay, the resort remains a luxurious classic, both romantic and good for (well-behaved) families. Nestled amid the lush grounds, native stone and hardwood cottages have an Asia-meets-the-tropics style. Dress up for dinner at the Sugar Mill, which combines Asian and European cuisines in dishes such as Mediterranean sea bass with soba noodles and Himalayan truffles. Its spa is one of the Caribbean's most intoxicating, with views of the bay and body scrubs using brown sugar, fresh mango, and papaya. One may feel insulated, but not isolated: It's just a half mile to Spanish Town.

The more couples-oriented Biras Creek Resort is a romantic hideaway of old-school Caribbean charm set on a narrow 140-acre peninsula. With just 31 light-filled suites with verandas, privacy and off-the-grid seclusion are guaranteed: It is accessible only by boat (the resort has a private launch). Dining at the Hilltop Restaurant is a draw, with a signature four-course menu that includes such dishes as grilled mahi-mahi with basil risotto followed by cream-filled blueberry shortcake.

Volcanic activity resulted in the Baths' artful maze of house-size boulders.

VISITOR INFO: www.bvitourism.com. **ROSEWOOD LITTLE DIX BAY:** Tel 888-767-3966 or 284-495-5555; www.littledixbay.com. *Cost:* from $450 (off-peak), from $650 (peak); dinner at the Sugar Mill $80. **BIRAS CREEK RESORT:** Tel 877-883-0756 or 248-364-2421; www.biras.com. *Cost:* from $495 (off-peak), from $690 (peak); prix-fixe dinner $85. *When:* closed late Aug–mid-Oct. **BEST TIMES:** Dec–Apr for good weather; Mar or Apr for Easter Festival.

Cruising Capital of the World

SAILING THE BVI

British Virgin Islands, Lesser Antilles

The craggy peaks of a submerged chain of volcanoes form the British Virgin Islands, scattered across miles of incomparably blue sea. The islands have been considered prime cruising grounds since the 1600s, when pirates found the perfect hiding place among their endless coves. Today, seven out of ten visitors come here for sailing, and those three unsuspecting landlubbers don't know what they're missing.

Some sixty islands, islets, and cays offer sailors the chance to drop anchor in inviting, deserted coves, walk empty beaches, and swim in turquoise water. Divers can check out the wreck of the 310-foot RMS *Rhone,* a royal mail steamer that sank in a hurricane near Salt Island in 1867. It broke into two pieces, providing unusually fine access and making it one of the great wreck-diving sites of the Caribbean.

If you don't have your own boat, you can rent one at the Moorings. This world-famous yacht operation has its Caribbean headquarters in Tortola, the largest of the BVIs and charter boat central. The 72-slip charter dock and 70-slip visitors dock are a destination in themselves. Stroll the boards and meet interesting boat lovers and owners from around the world. Many stay at the Mariner Inn Hotel, which accommodates Moorings customers before and after they hit the high seas.

West of the Moorings, Bomba's Shack is the island's oldest, most memorable, and most uninhibited watering hole, and it is one of the Caribbean's most famous. The colorful makeshift décor, including a collection of bras and panties that hang from the ceiling, helps camouflage a powerful sound system that gets things jumpin' even before Bomba's Punch (made with homemade rum) kicks in.

Boat people love the Bitter End Yacht Club, on Virgin Gorda's North Sound. Guests at the family-oriented resort have access to 100 vessels (including dinghies, catamarans, kayaks, and motorboats), as well as windsurfing gear, but you needn't be experienced upon arrival. Just sign up for lessons in their highly regarded and accredited Sailing School—all levels and ages are welcome.

The Moorings: Tel 888-952-8420 or 284-494-2332; www.moorings.com. *Cost:* bareboat rentals from $350 per day (off-peak), from $745 per day (peak). Crewed yachts available. **The Mariner Inn:** Tel 284-494-2333; www.bvimarinerinnhotel.com. *Cost:* from $180. **Bomba's Shack:** Tel 284-495-4148; www.bombassurfsideshack.com. **Bitter End Yacht Club:** Tel 800-872-2392 or 284-494-2746; www.beyc.com. *Cost:* from $570 (off-peak), from $770 (peak). *When:* closed mid-Aug–mid-Oct. **Best times:** Nov–Apr for nice weather; late Mar–early Apr for BVI's Spring Regatta & Sailing Festival; Jul for BVI Billfish Tournament.

Treasure, Romance, and Splendid Isolation

A Tour of BVI's "Other Islands"

British Virgin Islands, Lesser Antilles

This necklace of islands brings out the adventurer, lover, or pirate in folks. These are the BVI's "other islands," perfect for hideaways, getaways, honeymoons, or simply delicious alone time on pristine beaches.

Uninhabited Norman Island is said to be the inspiration for Robert Louis Stevenson's *Treasure Island* because of an 18th-century mutiny by pirates who buried 55 chests of booty here—most of them still undiscovered. The island's watery caves still hold a fascination for treasure-hunting snorkelers. But the real magnet is the bar/restaurant on the 100-foot schooner *Willy T,* permanently moored in a sheltered bay and popular anchorage called the Bight. There is no ferry to the *Willy T,* and Norman Island has no hotels, so it helps to have a boat.

Peter Island is the largest of the BVI's private islands.

Next up is a 1,800-acre private island occupied primarily by the luxurious Peter Island Resort, whose overnight guests have the place to themselves: five empty beaches, miles of hiking and biking trails, prime diving sites, an alluring beachfront spa, and an excellent restaurant (day-trippers from Tortola are welcome though with limited access).

The most northeasterly of the BVI, Anegada ("drowned island") is one of the least visited and least known despite having Horseshoe Reef, the third-largest barrier reef in the world, and the best snorkeling in all of the Virgin Islands. The only BVI that is not volcanic, Anegada is a flat coral and limestone atoll. The bonefishing here can be phenomenal, as can the beachcombing—there's nothing but 3,000 miles of open water off the northern shore. The Cow Wreck Bar is the place to go for an ice-cold Carib beer, conch fritters, and grilled just-caught rock lobster, a combination so heavenly the owners built three modest villas called the Cow Wreck Beach Resort for guests who refused to leave.

North of Virgin Gorda is Necker Island, 74 private, previously uninhabited acres where Virgin Airways founder Richard Branson established a fantasy escape. The Balinese Great House, complete with its 360-degree seascape and staff of 60, could be rented out in its entirety—accommodating up to 28 people—when Branson himself wasn't staying there. It burned down in 2011 after a lightning strike, but don't abandon hope of ever enjoying this heaven on earth: Branson vowed to quickly rebuild an equally special getaway.

Those who want untrammeled nature all to themselves head to Guana, a privately owned 850-acre wildlife sanctuary with one of the richest varieties of flora and fauna on any island its size in the region, including 100 species of birds—among them roseate flamingos, black-necked stilts, herons, and the endangered masked booby. In the 18th century, the island was a sugarcane and cotton plantation owned by two American Quaker families, and today that classic simplicity is still evident in the 15 rooms at Guana Island Club, the island's only hotel. The panoramic sweep from the whitewashed ridge-top cottages is spectacular. Reached only by boat, the hilly island, with its 20 nature trails, bountiful orchard, and seven white powder beaches, is for guests' use alone. For once yachties don't have the run of the place: "Drop-ins" are discouraged.

VISITOR INFO: www.bvitourism.com. ***WILLY T:*** Tel 284-494-0183; www.williamthornton.com. *Cost:* dinner $35. **PETER ISLAND RESORT:** Tel 800-346-4451 or 284-495-2000; www.peterisland.com. *Cost:* from $590 (off-peak), from $950 (peak), all-inclusive. **COW WRECK BEACH RESORT:** Tel 284-495-8047; www.cowwreckbeach.com. *Cost:* villas from $275; dinner $68. **NECKER ISLAND:** Tel 877-577-8777 or 212-994-3070; www.neckerisland.virgin.com. *Cost:* Celebration Weeks in Sep and Oct from $26,850 per couple per week, all-inclusive; whole island rental prices upon request. **GUANA ISLAND CLUB:** Tel 284-494-2354; www.guana.com. *Cost:* from $695 (off-peak), from $1,250 (peak), all-inclusive. *When:* closed Sep. **BEST TIME:** Nov–Apr for pleasant weather.

Iguanas, Stingrays, and Bloody Bay Wall

Cayman Islands

Greater Antilles

Cayman, a mostly flat British Crown Colony that consists of Grand Cayman, Little Cayman, and Cayman Brac, sits atop an ancient undersea mountain chain. On the surface, the translucent turquoise waters are serene, but just below you'll find dramatic walls and drop-offs only feet from shore, like an underwater Grand Canyon. It's one of the world's best dive sites, with an astonishing diversity of underwater life residing among coral-encrusted reefs and walls. The finest site in the area, though, is the 6,000-foot plunging coral garden known since pirate days as Bloody Bay Wall, off Little Cayman's north shore. Snorkelers can experience the top of the wall, and divers who go deep can explore the gorge, which teems with sea fans, anemones, and tropical fish.

Twelve-square-mile Little Cayman is relatively undeveloped and reigns popular among naturalists. Iguanas far outnumber the 100 full-time human residents, and a colony of 20,000 red-footed boobies populates the Caribbean's largest bird sanctuary. Little Cayman is also famous for Texas-born Gladys Howard—a student of Julia Child's—who caters to guests' every diving and dining need at her beachside inn, Pirate's Point Resort. She also offers a custom-built dive boat with a staff of experienced instructors.

Grand Cayman is larger (though still just 22 by 8 miles) and more cosmopolitan. And while tourism is more developed here, it's still welcomingly mellow. Offshore attractions include diving (over 100 sites) and Stingray City, a spot where throngs of sociable large-winged marine creatures eat from your hand (the famous "stingray kiss"). Even though it's a 25-minute boat ride from shore, the transparent waters are shallow—3 to 12 feet—and perfect for both divers and snorkelers.

Grand Cayman's famous Seven Mile Beach on the west side of the island is a gorgeous stretch of white sand lined with condos and plush resorts. With swimming-pool calm waters, it's the perfect beach for nonswimmers. The most luxurious accommodations can be found at the family-friendly Ritz-Carlton Grand Cayman—kids can learn about reef protection through Jean-Michel Cousteau's Ambassadors of the Environment program while parents indulge in the pleasures of a Greg Norman–designed golf course and a La Prairie spa. Blue by Eric Ripert (chef of Manhattan's Le Bernardin; see p. 848) serves caught-that-day yellowfin tuna and seafood specialties. Go in January to meet Ripert (and some fellow celebrity chefs), who hosts the Cayman Cookout, a celebration of Cayman and global cuisine on the beach.

When the sun goes down, Seven Mile Beach is where you want to be. The Reef Grill is fun and casual, serving fresh local seafood prepared with an innovative twist. Drift over to the cozy lounge when the soca and calypso music start to heat up the night.

Visitor info: www.caymanislands.ky. **Pirate's Point:** Tel 345-948-1010; www.piratespointresort.com. *Cost:* $500, inclusive; diving extra. **Ritz-Carlton:** Tel 800-542-8680 or 345-943-9000; www.ritzcarlton.com. *Cost:* from $299 (off-peak), from $569 (peak); prix-fixe dinner at Blue $110. **Reef Grill:** Tel 345-945-6360; www.reefgrill.com. *Cost:* dinner $50. **Best times:** early May for Carnival Batabano; Dec for Jazz Fest.

A Capital's Intoxicating Historic Quarter

La Habana Vieja

Havana, Cuba, Greater Antilles

Anchored by the gracious Plaza de la Catedral, Havana's Old Quarter (La Habana Vieja) is a magnificent architectural ensemble of monuments, fortresses, cobblestone streets, and grandiose townhouses that once belonged to an affluent bourgeoisie. With some 800 buildings dating from the 16th to 19th centuries, it is the most extensive and best-preserved colonial city in the hemisphere.

Paradoxically, the 1959 revolution responsible for the island's decades-long isolation has helped keep the city's finest architecture intact by banning private investments and real estate development—there's barely an incongruous modern structure to be found among the arcades and palm-shaded courtyards of the old Spanish core. Foreseeing a great future in tourism, Cuba has tidied up parts of the Old Quarter to mirror the Colonial Havana that was once the richest (and most heavily fortified) city in the Americas. Even its dilapidated corners have a charmed melancholy about them and a sense of decaying glory. Lovingly maintained classic American cars from the 1950s still cruise the streets, making you feel like you've stepped onto a movie set.

The Old Quarter's swankiest place to stay is Hotel Saratoga, whose 19th-century façade conceals a stylish 96-room hotel built in 2005. Set right on Parque de la Fraternidad near the must-visit Capitol, the famous Partagas Cigar Factory, and Havana's Gran Teatro (the most important opera and ballet house in this lively city's unrivaled arts scene), the hotel has a glamorous rooftop pool and bar from which to take it all in. Another impressive metamorphosis is the Hotel Raquel, a 1908 former bank that today provides surprisingly affordable splendor.

The grand Hotel Nacional is the city's best-known accommodation, built in 1930 to look like The Breakers in Palm Beach (see p. 754) and still more palace than hotel. Overlooking the Malecón, Havana's great 4-mile waterfront drive, this landmark was spruced up to recapture its glory days by restoring the opulent beauty of its Moorish arches and hand-painted tiles. Its Cabaret Parisien evokes 1950s Old Havana, when mobster Meyer Lansky operated Cuba's most glamorous casinos here. But there's no topping a show at the open-air Tropicana Cabaret. Since 1939 it has offered the city's most over-the-top spectacle of color, sound, and movement, with scantily and spectacularly clad showgirls strutting their stuff to son and salsa. For the everyday Habaneros who love to dance, Casa de la Musica is one of countless places to hear good music and try out your own moves. The apex of Havana's music scene comes with its International Jazz Festival, when musicians from around the world perform alongside many of Cuba's revered old-time stars.

Classic American cars from the 1950s populate one of the oldest cities in the Caribbean.

Ernest Hemingway spent most of the 1940s and 1950s in Havana, creating some of his greatest works between time at La Bodeguita del Medio (The Little Bar in the Middle) and the slightly more formal El Floridita. A visit to these unabashed tourist-trap watering holes is de rigueur, to sample two of Cuba's classic rum-based cocktails: La Bodeguita's refreshing mojito and El Floridita's frozen daiquiri, which Papa is said to have helped perfect. Hemingway's home, La Vigía, is 10 miles outside Havana, in the village of San Francisco; it has been left untouched and is open to the public.

Havana's historic bars are atmospheric and great fun, but Cuba cannot be considered a food destination—yet. Things have improved considerably with the arrival of *paladares,* private homes that serve traditional rustic fare at a handful of tables. One of the best is La Cocina de Lilliam, known for its romantic garden setting and *ropa vieja* (which means old clothes), a traditional, long-simmered dish made with beef or lamb.

HOTEL SARATOGA: Tel 53-7-868-1000; www.hotel-saratoga.com. *Cost:* from $230 (off-peak), from $350 (peak). **HOTEL RAQUEL:** Tel 53-7-860-8280; www.hotelraquel-cuba.com. *Cost:* from $120. **HOTEL NACIONAL:** Tel 53-7-833-3564; www.hotelnacionaldecuba.com. *Cost:* from $170; Cabaret Parisien, $35. **TROPICANA:** Tel 53-7-267-1010. *Cost:* show $65. **LA BODEGUITA DEL MEDIO:** Tel 53-7-866-8857. **EL FLORIDITA:** Tel 53-7-867-1300; www.floridita-cuba.com. **LA COCINA DE LILLIAM:** Tel 53-7-209-6514. *Cost:* dinner $15. **HOW:** U.S.-based Marazul Charters has been organizing trips to Cuba for American travelers for over 30 years. Tel 800-223-5334 or 201-319-1054; www.marazulcharters.com. **BEST TIMES:** Nov–Apr for nicest weather; Mar for Celebration of Classic Cars; Nov for Festival Internacional de Ballet; mid-Dec for International Jazz Festival.

Prehistoric, Surreal, and Quintessentially Cubano

VIÑALES VALLEY

Pinar del Rio, Cuba, Greater Antilles

The fertile Viñales Valley is Cuba's Shangri-la, a rare landscape of enormous steep-sided, round-topped limestone formations called *mogotes,* dramatically rising out of a rich rural landscape that grows some of the best tobacco in the world. Yet this magical 50-square-mile area was once completely flat; these massive tree-covered hummocks are the result of tectonic upraising and erosion by water over the ages.

The entire valley is a gorgeous, almost surreal setting for hiking, biking, horseback riding, and rock climbing that (although discouraged) draws climbers from around the globe. Inside the mogotes, an expansive network of caves and underground rivers provides tremendous spelunking and cave exploration. The most accessible is Gran Caverna de San Tomás, Cuba's largest cave system, with more than 28 miles of galleries studded with spiky stalactites and stalagmites. Explore underground streams by boat at Cueva del Indio, 9 miles west of Viñales; just don't expect to be the only tourist in the know.

Much of the region's appeal lies in its traditional rural culture and friendly *campesinos* (peasant farmers), whose way of life and farming methods have changed little for hundreds of years. Life revolves around tobacco here—more than 30 brands of highly coveted hand-rolled cigars are made from its prized crop, with world-famous *marquillas* (labels) such as Cohiba, Montecristo, and Partagas.

Unpack your bags in the unspoiled town of Viñales. Hotel Los Jazmines is one of only a few proper hotels in the area, with extraordinary views from most rooms. To sample Cuban hospitality at its best, stay with a local family in government-approved *casas particulares;* Villa Cristal is one of the nicest. The English-speaking owners can help organize trekking, biking, or horseback riding, and it's a 2-minute walk into the center of town where you can spend an evening listening to live music over a cold *cerveza*.

On the return to Havana, stop at Las Terrazas, a vibrant eco-village of artisan shops and small organic farms built in the lush, reforested landscape that was once the domain of the old French coffee plantations in the foothills of the Sierra del Rosario. Las Terrazas's remarkably diverse forests draw visitors for the best hiking and bird-watching in Cuba—the bee hummingbird, the world's smallest bird, is a resident here. Everyone stays at the comfortable 31-room Hotel La Moka, a hillside sanctuary so sensitive to the environment it was built around trees. You can walk to the nearby Buena Vista Restaurant, housed in a renovated hilltop French coffee estate for a lunch of barbecued pork.

Hotel Los Jazmines: Tel 53-48-79-6205. *Cost:* from $60. **Villa Cristal:** Tel 53-52-70-1284; www.villacristalcuba.com. *Cost:* $25. **Hotel La Moka:** Tel 53-48-57-8600 (reservations, 53-7-204-3739; www.hotelmokala terrazzas.com). *Cost:* from $60 (off-peak), from $110 (peak). **Buena Vista Restaurant:** *Cost:* lunch $15. **How:** For a *casa particular*, go to www.bbinnvinales.com. **Best times:** Oct–Apr for pleasant weather; Mar for Carnival in Viñales.

A Colonial Gem That Sugar Built

Trinidad

Sancti Spiritus, Cuba, Greater Antilles

Founded in 1514, the town of Trinidad was one of the original seven cities established by Spanish conquistador Diego Velázques. It is the best-preserved of the seven, packed with architectural treasures from the 18th and early 19th centuries when the city flourished from a thriving sugar trade. The prosperity of this golden era ended dramatically in the 1860s, giving the city a suspended-in-time feel that was secured in 1965 when the entire city was named a national monument.

Set on a breeze-swept hill overlooking the sea, Trinidad is a maze of narrow cobblestone streets lined with Colonial houses in soft pastel colors with massive wooden doors. Sugar barons built their mansions around Plaza Mayor, the heart of the old town. The star among them is the Museo Romantico, which showcases the once opulent lifestyle of this still-handsome city. The plaza is also the location of the city's most refined hotel, the 40-room restored Iberostar Grand.

By day Trinidad is sleepy, but at night the town pulses with live music around the Plaza Mayor. Trinidadians gather on the broad, deep steps of Casa de la Musica, an outdoor gathering spot beside the 19th-century Iglesia Parroquial de la Santissima (the largest church in the country), and dance to live music, mostly salsa, or watch the show. Rumba fans flock to Palenque de los Congos Reales, another alfresco venue, at Echerri and Ave. de Jesús Menéndez (be there at 10 P.M. for the fire-eating dancers), while Casa de la Trova at Plazuela de

Trinidad's Iglesia y Convento de San Francisco rises above a cityscape of Colonial architecture.

the Sierra del Escambray. You'll travel past abandoned plantations—the homes, slave quarters, and sugar mills in ruins—to an estate whose most dramatic attraction is the soaring 146-foot Iznaga Tower. Built around 1816, its bells once tolled the beginning and end of the workday in the fields.

Nearby Playa Ancón is easily the finest beach along Cuba's southern shore, a ribbon of white sand and blue-green waters with excellent diving. The 240-room

Segarte is the place for those who want to sit and listen to the town's finest musicians.

To truly immerse yourself in local life, stay in *casas particulares,* rooms in private houses, and eat in *paladares,* family homes that may or may not be official restaurants. Sol y Son is one of the best, serving traditional dishes like rum-soaked *cerdo borracho* (drunk pork) in a romantically lit courtyard.

To see the gorgeous countryside that gave rise to the country's wealth, go to the Valle de los Ingenios (Valley of the Sugar Mills). Buses and a wheezing 1907 Baldwin steam train make the journey daily through the green plains backed by the mountains of Hotel Brisas is the best choice for those who prefer to stay by the beach, and it's just a scooter ride away from this town stuck in time.

VISITOR INFO: www.gocuba.com. **MUSEO ROMANTICO:** Tel 53-41-99-4363. **IBEROSTAR GRAND HOTEL:** Tel 53-41-99-6070; www.iberostar.com. *Cost:* from $170 (off-peak), from $220 (peak). **PALADAR SOL Y SON:** dinner $20. **HOTEL BRISAS TRINIDAD DEL MAR:** Tel 53-41-99-6500; www.dtcuba.com. *Cost:* from $120, all-inclusive. **CASAS PARTICULARES:** www.casaparticular.info. **BEST TIMES:** Jan for Semana de la Cultura (Culture Week); week before Easter for Semana Santa; end of Jun for Carnival-like Fiestas Sanjuaneras.

An Enclave of Culture in the ABC Islands

CURAÇAO

Lesser Antilles

The three tiny islands known as the ABCs have a common Dutch heritage but couldn't be more different: Aruba is a party and beach destination; Bonaire (see p. 1068) a laid-back diving mecca; and the largest, Curaçao, the trio's sophisticated cultural enclave.

Beachside R&R is the Caribbean's stock-in-trade these days, but its less sunny history is told at Museum Kura Hulanda, the finest in the Caribbean and known for its superb but chilling displays about the slave trade. Having vanquished the native Caribs, Europeans established vast sugar plantations throughout the Caribbean in the 17th and 18th centuries and imported African slaves to work the fields. Curaçao was arid and unsuitable for agriculture, but its development as the Caribbean's busiest slave-trading depot began soon after the Dutch West India Company eyed its deep, protected harbors and claimed the island in 1643. The company sent rising star Peter Stuyvesant to be its governor long before he ever set foot in Manhattan. The Dutch traders built Curaçao into a prosperous financial center and trading port, a status it still enjoys.

The vision of Dutch businessman Jacob Gelt Dekker, Museum Kura Hulanda ("Dutch Courtyard" in Papiamentu, the ABCs' Creole tongue) is a 16,000-square-foot museum in Willemstad, housed in 16 restored Dutch Colonial homes gathered around a central courtyard where slaves were once sold. Along with a life-size reconstruction of a slave ship's hold, the museum has significant collections of pre-Columbian gold, Mesopotamian relics, Antillean art, and West African artifacts that explore the island's many cultural influences. It sparked the rebirth of the neighborhood's 65 historic buildings, which have been transformed into a living, breathing 18th-century village, with small shops, cafés, excellent restaurants such as the Astrolab Observatory, and the luxurious Hotel Kura Hulanda Spa & Casino. With 80 individually decorated rooms, the hotel is effortlessly integrated into this quiet corner of cobblestoned streets and lush tropical trees.

A cosmopolitan and charming city with polycultural riches, including the oldest active Jewish synagogue in the western hemisphere (the congregation has been here since 1651; the synagogue since 1732), Willemstad's greatest attribute is its Dutch-in-the-Caribbean culture. Its pastel-colored Colonial architecture (think Amsterdam gone tropical) along the Handelskade provides one of the most stunning and photographed waterfronts in the Caribbean. And its floating market is always bustling with merchants who sell their fresh seafood and produce from small fishing boats that have sailed in from Venezuela, just 44 miles south of here.

Curaçao offers more than culture and history. Its dozens of beaches, mostly scattered along the southwestern coast, are known for their calm, translucent waters, and the marine life ringing the island is rich and spectacular. Excellent snorkeling (including sunken ships and gardens of hard and soft coral) can be found in the Curaçao Underwater Marine Park, which stretches for 12 miles along the southern coastline. At the remote westernmost tip of the island, the sumptuous Lodge Kura Hulanda & Beach Club, another Dekker property, is perched on rugged cliffs overlooking Curaçao's prime diving sites (there are 65 around the island, with the *Superior Producer* shipwreck site being the most popular) and promising sunsets that enhance the island's spectrum of colors.

Visitor info: www.curacao.com. **Museum Kura Hulanda:** Tel 5999-434-7765; www.kurahulanda.com. **Hotel Kura Hulanda Spa & Casino:** Tel 877-264-3106 or 5999-434-7700; www.kurahulanda.com. *Cost:* from $180 (off-peak), from $370 (peak). **Lodge Kura Hulanda & Beach Club:** Tel 877-264-3106 or 5999-839-3600; www.kurahulanda.com. *Cost:* from $155 (off-peak), from $360 (peak). **Best times:** Oct–Apr for nicest weather; Jan 1–Ash Wednesday for Carnival; Easter Monday for Seu Folklore Parade; May for International Jazz Festival and Dive Festival; late Aug for Salsa Festival.

Boutiques, galleries, and cafés inhabit the vividly colored 18th-century Dutch buildings of the Handelskade.

A Lush Oasis for Eco-Adventurers

Morne Trois Pitons National Park

Dominica, Lesser Antilles

Wild and primeval, Dominica is likely the only landfall Columbus would recognize from 1493, when he landed here on a Sunday (hence the island's name). Lush and rugged Dominica claims nine potentially active volcanoes (more than any other Caribbean island), which may not be spewing lava but are heating up boiling lakes and sulfur springs. It is the Caribbean of centuries ago, with the purest population of indigenous Caribs (more accurately called Kalinago). With mountain defenses, they held out the longest against the world's colonizing powers and still reside in the Kalinago Territory on the island's northeast side.

Untrammeled and with few beaches to tout, Dominica draws naturalists and ecotourists to explore Morne Trois Pitons National Park—an ungovernable refuge of huge ferns, ancient trees, wild orchids, and bright anthuriums—named for the three-pronged mountain at its center. Much of Dominica's fame as the Caribbean's "Nature Island" derives from this 25-square-mile slice of wilderness that looks and feels more like Hawaii than the Caribbean.

Waterfalls (like the one feeding the Emerald Pool grotto) hide among verdant peaks. Those who want a little less Shangri-la and a little more sulfur can make the strenuous 8-hour trek to Boiling Lake, the earth's second-largest flooded fumarole, through the Valley of Desolation's steaming vents and boiling mud.

Far easier is the 15-minute stroll to Trafalgar Falls, a remarkable 200-foot twin cataract, from Papillote Wilderness Retreat, an ecotourism pioneer on the park's borders. Take a dip in a cool mountain river, tour the 12-acre botanical garden of bromeliads and begonias, and dine at the retreat's unfussy, thatch-roofed terrace restaurant.

At Champagne, a dive and snorkel spot just off the beach near the capital, Rouseau, volcanic gases are released from the ocean floor, creating an intoxicating and sensuous blend of warm bubbles. Top wildlife encounters include leatherback turtles laying their eggs and year-round sightings of sperm whales socializing, mating, and playing.

Not known for being high-end, Dominica is edging toward sophistication. On its remote southeast coast, the eco-sensitive Jungle Bay Resort & Spa's 35 cottages perched on wooden posts are stylish treehouses for adults, with stream-fed outdoor showers. Diving, snorkeling, kayaking, and waterfall treks fill the day. The starstruck can bask in the glow at Silks, a boutique hotel in a former rum distillery where Johnny Depp and Orlando Bloom stayed while filming *Pirates of the Caribbean: Dead Man's Chest*.

Visitor info: www.discoverdominica.com. **Kalinago Barana Aute:** Tel 767-445-7979; www.kalinagobaranaaute.com. **Papillote Wilderness Retreat:** Tel 767-448-2287; www.papillote.dm. *Cost:* from $115. *When:* closed Sep–Oct. **Jungle Bay:** Tel 767-446-1789; www.junglebaydominica.com. *Cost:* from $195 **Silks:** Tel 767-445-8846; www.silkshotel.com. *Cost:* from $120. **Best times:** Dec–May for dry season; late Oct for World Creole Music Festival.

World-Class Courses Designed by the Masters

THE REPUBLIC OF GOLF

Dominican Republic, Greater Antilles

Bermuda, move over. The Dominican Republic has claimed the title as the finest golfing destination in the region. In the last decade world-class golf courses have opened up across the island, following the 7,000-acre trailblazing resort Casa de Campo, famous for its three 18-hole, Pete Dye–designed courses. The best known is Teeth of the Dog, a windy masterpiece that skirts the sea, whereas the inland Links Course and Dye Fore are more forgiving. Home to the prestigious Golf Academy run by David Leadbetter, Casa de Campo also boasts a polo and equestrian center, a spa with invigorating plunge pools, and Altos de Chavón, a painstaking re-creation of a 16th-century hill town that houses a colony of artists and artisans.

Casa de Campo helped spark the massive development of golf resorts on the easternmost tip of the island, in Punta Cana, renowned for its 20-mile strip of oyster-white sands and turquoise sea along the "Coconut Coast." The area's pioneer is the long-established Puntacana Resort & Club, where Pete Dye designed the gorgeous oceanside La Cana Course. The resort is also home to Tom Fazio's thrilling new Corales Course, which works its way down to the water and an 18th dubbed "the Mother of All Golf Holes." It also features horseback riding, the especially beautiful Six Senses spa, and access to 3 miles of white beaches. Its Tortuga Bay, an exclusive resort within a resort, has 15 elegant Colonial-Caribbean villas designed by native son Oscar de la Renta. Golfers also gravitate to the nearby major resort of Cap Cana, one of the most ambitious developments in the works, centered around a challenging Jack Nicklaus course, the Punta Espada.

On the developed North Coast, treat yourself to Playa Grande, one of Robert Trent Jones Sr.'s last executed designs and considered by many to be the Pebble Beach of the Caribbean. With 12 ocean-side holes on a high plateau at the edge of a rain forest, Playa Grande remains surprisingly less known, though it is easily accessible from Puerto Plata, the major resort area an hour to the west. In a region known for large, all-inclusive resorts, the exception is the Casa Colonial Beach & Spa, an impeccable, privately owned all-suites boutique hotel that effortlessly fuses old-world elegance with sophisticated modern style and gracious service.

VISITOR INFO: www.godominicanrepublic.com. **CASA DE CAMPO:** Tel 800-877-3643 or 809-523-3333; www.casadecampo.com.do. *Cost:* from $250 (off-peak), from $495 (peak); greens fees from $85 (off-peak), $130 (peak). **PUNTACANA RESORT & CLUB:** Tel 888-442-2262 or 809-959-2262 (hotel), 809-959-4653 (golf); www.puntacana.com. *Cost:* PR&C from $125; Tortuga Bay from $710 (off-peak), from $830 (peak); La Cana greens fees $125 (for guests), $165 (nonguests); Corales greens fees $300 (guests), $380 (nonguests). **PUNTA ESPADA AT CAP CANA:** 809-227-2262 (for hotel reservations), 809-688-5587 (for golf); www.capcana.com. *Cost:* from $390 (off-peak), from $525 (peak) per person, all-inclusive; greens fees $195 (guests), $375 (nonguests). **PLAYA GRANDE:** Tel 809-582-0860; www.playagrande.com. *Cost:* greens fees from $110. **CASA COLONIAL:** Tel 866-376-7831 or 809-320-3232; www.casacolonialhotel.com. *Cost:* from $285 (off-peak), from $350 (peak). **BEST TIME:** Nov–Apr for good weather.

Unsurpassed Whale-Watching and (for the Moment) Undiscovered Beaches

Samaná Peninsula

Dominican Republic, Greater Antilles

Even if it weren't one of the world's top breeding grounds for humpback whales, the Samaná Peninsula in northeast DR would still draw travelers for its white sandy beaches and the near absence of resorts along its pristine coastline. Yet it is at its most thrilling from January to March, when more than 10,000 30-ton North Atlantic humpback whales, almost the entire population, migrate here to mate and calve. Courtship inspires the bulls' breaching, fin slapping, and lob tailing, all attempts to attract a female. You can enjoy the scene from any seaside café in the sleepy town of Samaná, but a day cruise will get you up close to the action.

Whale-watching boats leave from both Samaná, on the peninsula's southern coast, and Cayo Levantado, also known as "Bacardi Island" from a 1970s ad campaign that immortalized the idyllic location. Victoria Marine pioneered whale-watching in the area and is still the best tour operator around. There's less human presence at the Silver Banks Nursery, 100 miles west and 70 miles offshore, one of a very few places in the world where you can snorkel with humpback whales.

Of Samaná Peninsula's string of wonderful beaches, its showpiece is El Rincón, more than 2 miles long and backed by stately coconut palms. Located near the town of Las Galeras, it is the perfect place to sunbathe, swim, and lunch on freshly caught fish grilled at a waterside shack. At the peninsula's farthest point, Playa Frontón may have the best diving and snorkeling on the island, but you'll have to hire a boat or trek through the jungle to get there.

Along the north shore, Playa Las Terrenas is a former fishing village turned laid-back small-scale resort town. Its long, sandy seafront is just the place to hang out, soak up the sun, and then head for some good merengue and one of the legendary mojitos at Syroz Bar. To reach the remote and thundering El Limón waterfalls, head by horseback through fragrant forests up a rocky trail. The sheer 165-foot curtain forms a large swimming hole with cool, crystal-clear water at its base.

From Las Terrenas, head to Playa Bonita, a seemingly unending soft, sandy beach. Keep going and you'll come to Playa Cosón, an unspoiled and uninterrupted strip of white sand dropping down into a turquoise ocean, with even fewer visitors. This is the surprise location for the Peninsula House, one of the best small luxury properties in the Caribbean. Situated on a 15-acre bluff overlooking the Atlantic, the stately plantation-style inn has six suites whose verandas have sweeping views of the ocean. For gentler prices, Villas Eva Luna is a collection of five Mexican-style casitas and pool, a stone's throw from the beach.

Visitor info: www.godominicanrepublic.com. **Victoria Marine:** Tel 809-538-2492; www.whalesamana.com. **The Peninsula House:** Tel 809-307-1827; www.thepeninsulahouse.com. *Cost:* $580; dinner $70. **Villas Eva Luna:** Tel 809-978-5611; www.villa-evaluna.com. *Cost:* from $190. **Best times:** mid-Jan–mid-Mar for whale-watching; Feb 27 for Independence Day; every weekend in Feb for Carnival; Semana Santa (the week before Easter).

Spain's First Foothold in the New World

Zona Colonial

Santo Domingo, Dominican Republic, Greater Antilles

Wander the 500-year-old cobblestone streets of Zona Colonial and you're traveling in the footsteps of the first explorers to set their sights on the "New World." In 1492 Christopher Columbus first spotted the island of Hispaniola, now shared by the Dominican Republic and Haiti (see p. 1087), dubbing it "the fairest ever looked upon by human eyes." By 1496 his brother, Bartholomew, had founded Santo Domingo where the Ozama River empties into the Caribbean Sea. In 1509 his son Diego became the first viceroy of a colony that would flourish as the main staging ground for Spain's earliest forays into the Americas.

Santo Domingo has many of the New World's "firsts"—the first cathedral, fort, hospital, monastery, nunnery, customs house, university, paved road, even the first sewer system in the Americas. Most of these can be found in the 12-block Zona Colonial, a treasure trove of historic architecture and the heart of Santo Domingo. Climb the crenellated Tower of Homage, part of the Ozama Fortress, built in 1502, and enjoy a sweeping 360-degree view of the city and the sea. Catedral Santa María la Menor boasts vaulted ceilings and 14 interior chapels, while Alcazar de Colón, a palace completed in 1517 as a residence for Columbus's son, is now a museum displaying possessions of the Columbus family and genuine 16th-century furnishings.

Spanish expansion came at the expense of the native Taino, who were wiped out by war, slavery, and disease within 30 years. The Tainos' ancient ways are explored in Museo del Hombre Dominicano, which holds the Caribbean's finest collection of their artifacts. Located in the modern Plaza de la Cultura, it's one of four major museums here.

Catedral de Santa María la Menor is the oldest cathedral in the Americas.

The vibrant Zona Colonial's nerve center is the always crowded El Conde café and restaurant. Order a cold Presidente beer or a Morir Soñando (literally, "to die dreaming"), a mix of orange juice, milk, sugar, and chopped ice, and take in the sights of the Parque Colón, a leafy square in the heart of the quarter. Street stalls sell tasty empanadas but for fine dining and live music you can't do better than Mesón D'Bari, where grilled crab, spicy shrimp, and live music are the specialties.

Zona Colonial has loads of nightclubs along the Malecón, a breezy palm-lined seaside boulevard where suave, sexy merengue is on display. Merengue was born in the DR (along with its bluesy country cousin, bachata), and the island's obsession reaches its height every summer when the Malecón turns into a 4-mile-long dance floor as the country's best bands play live music during Festival del

Merengue. The best place to watch the masters year-round and try out your own moves is Mauna Loa, an opulent Art Deco nightclub from the 1920s.

A 1502 mansion built (and named) for the Americas' first governor, the Hostal Nicolas de Ovando is still the nicest in the colonial quarter, with handsome rooms and a tree-shaded swimming pool just 5 minutes from the sea. It's located right on the historic Calle las Damas ("Street of Ladies"), which was the first paved road in the new world and was named for the elegant ladies of the court who promenaded.

VISITOR INFO: www.godominicanrepublic.com. **MUSEO DEL HOMBRE DOMINICANO:** Tel 809-687-3623; www.museodelhombredominicano.org.do. **MESÓN D'BARI:** Tel 809-687-4091. *Cost:* dinner $30. **HOSTAL NICOLAS DE OVANDO:** Tel 800-515-5679 or 809-685-9955; www.accorhotels.com. *Cost:* from $130 (off-peak), from $175 (peak). **BEST TIMES:** Feb 27 for Independence Day; 1st Sun in Mar for Carnival; last 2 weeks of Mar for musical Son Festival; late Jul–early Aug for Festival del Merengue; Oct for Latin Music Festival; New Year's Eve along the Malecón.

A Fragrant Spice Island with Scenic Allure

ST. GEORGE'S HARBOUR AND GRAND ANSE BEACH

St. George's, Grenada, Lesser Antilles

This postcard-perfect horseshoe-shaped port—actually the crater of an inactive volcano—is one of the most scenic in all the Caribbean, flanked by early-18th-century forts and hugged by the raffishly charming port town, St. George's. A cheerful hodgepodge of West Indian and French colonial influences, it is known for its "fish scale"–roofed rainbow-hued homes climbing the steep, green hills behind it. The crescent-shaped waterfront district, the Carenage, is the colorful commercial hub of the naturally landlocked inner harbor.

Beyond St. George's horseshoe-shaped harbor lie charming buildings, green hills, and beaches.

Grenada is both lush and fertile, making it an extravagant producer of spices since nutmeg took off in the 1850s—today the Spice Island produces more than one third of the world's supply of nutmeg. Stop by the daily open-air market to listen to the turbaned ladies sell their fragrant cloves, bay leaves, cinnamon, and nutmeg, along with colorful piles of *pawpaw* (papaya), red and gold mangoes, and exotic vegetables.

This 21-by-12-mile island boasts one of the Caribbean's lushest rain forests in its mountainous interior. Grand Etang National Park, named for a picturesque lake or "big pond" formed from a volcanic crater, is a trekker's paradise, with wild nutmeg, long-tailed monkeys, and powerful waterfalls. Trails range from an easy excursion to the Seven Sisters waterfalls to more serious treks.

Grenada attracts snorkelers and divers with its unique and magically captivating Underwater Sculpture Park—65 works of art installed underwater in Molinere Bay, off the island's west coast. It also has one of the world's best wreck dives—the 600-foot luxury liner *Bianca C.*, which sank in 1961 and is hailed as the *Titanic* of the Caribbean.

St. George's is not recommended for action seekers or casino devotees, but beach lovers need look no further than Grand Anse, south of town. This 2-mile curve of perfect sand is the most famous of the island's 45 beaches, with gentle surf that sets the scene for water sports. Most of the island's best hotels are on or near Grand Anse, including Spice Island Beach Resort. This stylish all-inclusive breaks the mold, with eco-friendly design, a salt water pool, and 64 suites with Jacuzzi.

For creative local cuisine, amble across the road to La Belle Creole restaurant in the Blue Horizons Cottage Hotel. Sunset views accompany family-recipe classics like chilled lobster mousse, cream of tannia soup, or veal à la Creole. Listen to steel drums on Fish Fridays in Gouyave, a wonderfully scenic 30-minute drive up the coast, where the fresh, spicy fish is some of the island's best.

Small nonresorty and sophisticated hostelries have been popping up around the island, led by the Bali-inspired Laluna with 16 thatch-roofed cottages nestled into the hillside. Nearby, the offbeat Aquarium Restaurant sits right on the beach but built back into the forest. This cool, open-air retreat is known for its scallops wrapped in bacon with a bitter orange sauce and fresh bread from the oven. On the island's less developed northern coast, Petite Anse Hotel is a comfortable rustic-Colonial 11-room property tucked into the vegetation right above a gorgeous beach with views of the Grenadine Islands.

Grenada's two sister islands to the northwest are a ferry ride away. Undeveloped Carriacou is West India the way it used to be, where goats outnumber cars and the locals fish, build boats, and farm. Its stand-out white sand Anse la Roche joins with pristine reefs to make snorkeling and diving here world class. At nearby Petite Martinique, you can circumambulate the quiet, undeveloped island by foot in just a few blissful hours.

Visitor info: www.grenadagrenadines.com. **Spice Island Beach Resort:** Tel 845-628-1701 or 473-444-4258; www.spicebeachresort.com. *Cost:* from $800 (off-peak), from $1,308 (peak), all-inclusive. **La Belle Creole:** Tel 473-444-4316; www.grenadabluehorizons.com. *Cost:* dinner $50. **Laluna:** Tel 866-452-5862 or 473-439-0001; www.laluna.com. *Cost:* from $365 (off-peak), from $545 (peak). **Aquarium Restaurant:** Tel 473-444-1410; www.aquarium-grenada.com. *Cost:* dinner $50. **Petite Anse Hotel:** Tel 473-442-5252; www.petiteanse.com. *Cost:* from $125 (off-peak), from $260 (peak). **Best times:** Dec–May for nice weather; late Jan–early Feb for Grenada Sailing Festival; mid-Feb for Carriacou Carnival; Aug for Grenada Carnival and Carriacou Regatta; week before Christmas for the Big Drum Dance in Carriacou's Parang Festival.

Creole Cuisine and Tropical Adventures

Guadeloupe

Lesser Antilles

Called *l'île papillon* (butterfly island) by locals, Guadeloupe's two "wings" possess different but equally compelling personalities. To the east, Grande-Terre is flatter and more developed, with former plantations

In Basse-Terre, three levels of cascades form Carbet Falls.

and inviting beaches; the best are found on the southern shore in and around Sainte Anne. Guadeloupe is one of the great culinary destinations of the Caribbean, and Grande-Terre's 200 restaurants serve a marriage of African, French, and West Indian cuisine that rivals that of St. Martin and Martinique (see pp. 1103 and 1092).

For lively Creole ambience, the West Indian décor of the Iguane Café sets a relaxed tone. Begin with one of the two dozen rum punches, then follow with an intriguing menu of local and international dishes. Some of the best classic French dining can be found at the somewhat formal La Vieille Tour, a hotel resort built around an old sugar mill.

The food scene comes to a peak every August during the annual Fête des Cuisinières, when hundreds of the island's women, lavishly dressed in traditional madras costumes, parade through the streets of Grande-Terre's principal city, Pointe-à-Pitre, balancing baskets of the island's exotic bounty on their heads. After High Mass at the 19th-century Cathédrale de St-Pierre et St-Paul, a cook-off feast follows, and the streets fill with music, song, and dance.

Dominated by the large, brooding volcano La Soufrière, Basse-Terre is the verdant western wing of the butterfly, a less developed land (two-thirds of it is protected as national park) that offers more adventure. Follow the transcoastal Route de La Traversée through the rain forest for one of the most scenic highways in the Caribbean. A detour to the west coast brings you to Plage Malendure, a sliver of dark volcanic sand that is the departure point for tiny Pigeon Island, where good snorkeling and diving await in a park created by Jacques Cousteau.

Stay at Le Jardin Malanga, a chicly restored 1927 plantation house and cottages on the southern shore near Trois Rivières, offering easy access to the park and a trek to three waterfalls known as Chutes du Carbet (the largest of which plunges 410 feet). The inn offers views of Les Saintes, the mini-archipelago of seven islands (only two of which are inhabited) where Terre-de-Haut is the favorite stop. Or choose the charmingly funky Auberge Les Petits Saints—guests enjoy delightful views of Les Saintes Bay and a very special dinner—the lobster here is famous.

Nearby Marie Galante (not one of the Îles des Saintes) is even more pastoral; scores of tended plantations, windmills, and oxcarts attest to the importance of sugarcane and rum. At Petite Anse beach, enjoy a deliciously simple meal at any of the Creole shacks.

Visitor info: www.lesilesdeguadeloupe.com. **Iguane Café:** Tel 590-590-88-61-37. *Cost:* dinner $45. **La Vieille Tour:** Tel 590-590-84-23-23. *Cost:* dinner $60. **Le Jardin Malanga:** Tel 590-590-92-67-57; www.jardinmalanga.com. *Cost:* from $390. *When:* closed Jun–early Jul and Sep–mid-Oct. **Auberge Les Petits Saints:** Tel 590-590-99-50-99; www.petitssaints.com. *Cost:* from $125 (off-peak), from $175 (peak); dinner $65. **Best times:** Nov–Apr for good weather; early Jan–Ash Wednesday for Carnival; May for Creole Blues Festival on Marie Galante; 2nd Sat in Aug for Fête des Cuisinières in Pointe-à-Pitre.

Where African Spirits Come to Earth

Voodoo Nights at the Hotel Oloffson

Port-au-Prince, Haiti, Greater Antilles

Simply called *bagay la* ("the thing") by Haitians, the earthquake of 2010, centered 20 miles from capital Port-au-Prince, brought devastating destruction. But the Haitian people have a long history of determination and resilience: In 1801, a slave revolt defeated the mighty French army, and the newly formed nation became the first to abolish slavery in the Western Hemisphere. Despite persistent poverty and the slow pace of rebuilding, the Haitian spirit beats strong.

You can get a rum-flavored taste of that spirit every Thursday at Voodoo Night at the Hotel Oloffson, a ramshackle Victorian gingerbread that survived the earthquake. Crowds dance all night to *musique racine* (French for "roots music"), a potent blend of traditional music performed on indigenous instruments, such as the *rara* horn and *petwo* drums, combined with a dose of rock 'n' roll.

The Oloffson has a grand history—novelist Graham Greene fictionalized it in *The Comedians* as the Hotel Trianon, and affixed to the doors are plaques bearing the names of luminaries who have stayed there, including Mick Jagger, Ann-Margret, and Greene himself.

Vodou uniquely blends the religions brought by slaves from West Africa and the Catholicism of the French sugar plantation owners. With their native religions forbidden, slaves honored their ancestral spirits by assigning each its own corresponding Catholic saint; today's Vodou altars are rich blends of African and Christian iconography.

Vodou followers worship God, whom they call Gran Met or Bondye, but believe he is distant from the physical plane, so they summon lwa (or loa, "spirits," pronounced low-AH) through prayer, drumming, and song.

Everyone is welcome at Vodou ceremonies, where an offering to the *houngan*, or Vodou priest, is traditional. (A bottle of Barbancourt five-star rum will do.) Most visitors to Haiti hire a guide to find such ceremonies, but there's no better place to start than Thursday night at the Oloffson.

Hotel Oloffson: Tel 509-2223-4000; www.hoteloloffson.com. *Cost:* from $75. Thurs night entertainment free to guests, $10 for non-guests. **Where else to stay:** Karibe Hotel; tel 509-2256-9808 or 305-432-9696 in the U.S.; www.karibehotel.com. *Cost:* from $150. **How:** Voyages Lumière offers personalized excursions in Port-au-Prince and beyond. Tel 509-3557-0753; www.voyageslumiere.com. *Cost:* full-day tours from $90. **Best time:** the week before Lent (usually Feb or Mar) for Carnival.

Music and dance inspired by Vodou culture infuse the Oloffson's nightly celebration.

On Top of the World

Strawberry Hill and the Blue Mountains

Irish Town and Beyond, Jamaica, Greater Antilles

With some of the most beautiful views in the Caribbean, Strawberry Hill's 3,100-foot perch in the cool Blue Mountains is for those who relish sitting on a veranda and watching the late-afternoon mist settle on the green hills while the tree frogs begin their serenade. Surrounded by plantations that still produce the rare Jamaican Blue Mountain coffee, declared by the famous spy character James Bond to be "the most delicious in the world," Strawberry Hill is a former-plantation-turned-hotel. This is your own private Jamaica, with twelve Colonial-inspired cottages spread across 50 Edenic acres. The rooms evoke the daily lives of 19th-century planters, with mahogany four-poster beds, mosquito netting, and plank floors. A small but excellent spa (sign up for the coffee scrub) and a soothing minimalist design sense are modern flourishes. Strawberry Hill's restaurant turns out exotic, full-flavored reinventions of traditional Jamaican dishes, like jerk lamb loin with garlic guava glaze, and has long been famous for its elegant Sunday brunch.

Take time to explore the Blue Mountains, a lush, biodiverse forest that delights both birders and botanists with more than 500 species of flowering plants, including Jamaican bamboo, which flowers across the island only once every 33 years (the next bloom is due around 2017). Old mule tracks are now hiking trails that lead you to staggering views—if the mists cooperate you'll get a glimpse of Blue Mountain Peak, at 7,402 feet the island's highest. Or do it the easy way: Blue Mountain Bicycle Tours sets you up with bikes at 5,600 feet; just shove off and coast down past coffee plantations, stopping along the way for photo ops and a local lunch and finishing it off with a refreshing dip in a waterfall.

Where: Irish Town is 25 miles/40 km from the Kingston Airport. **Strawberry Hill:** Tel 800-688-7678 or 876-944-8400; www.islandoutpost.com. *Cost:* from $195 (off-peak), from $295 (peak). **Blue Mountain Bicycle Tours:** Tel 876-974-7075; www.bmtoursja.com. *Cost:* $98. **Best time:** Dec–Apr for good weather.

Great Reggae, Great Golf, and Great Houses

Montego Bay

Jamaica, Greater Antilles

Jamaica's second largest city after Kingston, Mo Bay is charged, hip, and gritty, with a lively music scene that reaches its frenzied height at Reggae Sumfest, a reggae and dancehall marathon that showcases star performers from dusk till dawn. Jamaica is the birthplace of reggae, its heartbeat, soul, and inspiration, and of all Mo Bay's music festivals, this is the one that locals save up for all year. Evolved from ska (a heady combination of African traditions with rhythm and blues) and the slower rocksteady and infused with the "one love" message of Rastafarianism, reggae still owes its greatest debt to the late Bob Marley, a national (and international) folk hero.

For those who have come to loll in the lap of luxury, staying put in Mo Bay means great golfing and fine resorts. Half-Moon is one of the Caribbean's best big resorts: With 400 well-manicured acres and almost as many rooms, not to mention 54 swimming pools, a 2-mile private beach, and 13 lit tennis courts, it feels more like a town—albeit one with an equestrian center, dolphin lagoon, and thrilling Robert Trent Jones Sr. 18-hole golf course. It's also home to Fern Tree, one of the island's newest and largest spas, where local elders helped integrate traditional Jamaican healing practices into the treatments.

The most serious (and seriously wealthy) golfers shortlist Tryall Club, a 2,200-acre former sugar plantation whose 18-hole golf course is known for its difficult, unpredictable holes. Designed by Ralph Plummer in the 1950s, it is considered by many to be the island's best and is open only to guests who book privately owned villas centered around an 1834 Georgian-style great house.

Jamaica's most famous—and infamous—great house is Rose Hall, built in the 1700s in the heyday of the sugar-plantation era and occupied in the 19th century by Annie Palmer, the "White Witch" of the region. Local lore says Annie was a cruel voodoo-practicing slave owner who murdered several husbands and eventually was herself murdered by one of her slaves. The beautifully restored house, alleged to be haunted, is set on a hill with sweeping lawns overlooking the sea.

And lastly, don't miss Mo Bay's spicy, succulent fare at the Pork Pit, a longtime local institution. The beach crowd arrives around noon, when the fiery jerk is ready to be lifted from its bed of coals and fragrant wood and slapped down on the communal picnic tables.

VISITOR INFO: www.visitjamaica.com. **REGGAE SUMFEST:** Tel 876-953-2933; www.reggaesumfest.com. *Cost:* festival passes from $135. **HALF-MOON:** Tel 888-830-5974 or 876-953-2211; www.halfmoon.com. *Cost:* from $270 (off-peak), from $440 (peak). **TRYALL CLUB:** Tel 800-361-9949 or 876-956-5660; www.tryallclub.com. *Cost:* villas from $395 (off-peak), from $550 (peak), per night, based on weekly minimum. Greens fees $50 (off-peak), $100 (peak), guests only. **ROSE HALL GREAT HOUSE:** Tel 876-953-9982. **PORK PIT:** Tel 876-952-1046. *Cost:* lunch $12. **BEST TIMES:** Nov–Apr for nice weather; late Jan for Jazz & Blues Festival; mid-Jul for Reggae Sumfest.

A Beach's Wild Reputation and Its Quieter Side

NEGRIL

Jamaica, Greater Antilles

It's always party time in hedonistic Negril, set on the northwestern tip of Jamaica and one of the country's most affordable destinations. The developed but still lovely Seven Mile Beach (also known as Long Bay) is the source of all the action, with sprawling all-inclusive resorts and the occasional nudist section. Negril's quieter side can be found in Country Country's 20 sherbet-colored gingerbread cottages—

Negril's pride and joy is its Seven Mile Beach, the country's longest stretch of sand.

wraparound porches and lovely gardens promise a mellow respite right in the middle of the action. True seclusion can be found a quick cab ride away at Rockhouse Hotel, a stylish but unpretentious retreat of thatch-roofed cottages atop a rocky waterfront promontory just outside town. Book a massage or a mocha and rum body wrap in cliff-edge treatment cabanas or snorkel in the sheltered waters of Pristine Cove below. In the evening enjoy Negril's legendary sunsets from the 60-foot cliff-top pool that seems suspended in air, then dine either at Pushcart, whose menu draws from Jamaica's street food—seafood fritters, jerk sausage, and warm sweet potato pudding—or the Rockhouse Restaurant, which specializes in lighter and modern interpretations of Jamaican cuisine.

For the island's most renowned sunset scene, go to nearby Rick's Café, inspired by the film *Casablanca* and the most famous bar on the island since it opened in 1974. Everyone watches divers do backflips off the cliffs 35 feet above the sea below, while waiting for the sun to sink beneath the horizon, when a lucky few will glimpse the elusive green flash.

WHERE: 50 miles/80 km west of Montego Bay. **COUNTRY COUNTRY:** Tel 876-957-4273; www.countrynegril.com. *Cost:* from $150 (off-peak), from $210 (peak). **ROCKHOUSE HOTEL:** Tel 876-957-4373; www.rockhousehotel.com. *Cost:* from $125 (off-peak), from $160 (peak); dinner at Pushcart $25, at Rockhouse $35. **RICK'S CAFÉ:** Tel 876-957-0380; www.rickscafejamaica.com. **BEST TIME:** Nov–Apr for pleasant weather.

A Genteel Inn and a James Bond Legacy

OCHO RIOS

Jamaica, Greater Antilles

Beyond the cruise ship attractions at Ocho Rios, Jamaica's popular port of call, lies a quieter, hidden side worth seeking out. Some of Jamaica's most intriguing inns can be found here, including the venerable Jamaica Inn, the most beloved of the island's old guard and the classic that all others try to emulate. Its 47 suites are tastefully furnished with Jamaican antiques, and spacious balconies serve as open-air living rooms with sofa, writing table, rocking chair, and inspiring ocean views. There's a smooth transition from the daytime's relaxed schedule of water sports, spa treatments, and croquet to the evening's retro, old-fashioned rhythm, when guests gather on the lamplit lower terrace for cocktails and dancing under the stars. The White Suite—favored accommodation of Winston Churchill—stands on a promontory overlooking the hotel's impeccably groomed beach, considered one of the island's prettiest.

The hotel GoldenEye breathes intrigue; reggae mogul and hotelier Chris Blackwell now owns the 15-acre property that centers around the three-bedroom home of James Bond author Ian Fleming (himself a British intelligence agent posted to Jamaica during World War II); all 14 of his thrillers were written here after the war. (No wonder the super-suave spy spends so much time in the Caribbean!) Guests can choose from the lush garden villas, sexy lagoon suites, or cottages on James Bond Beach—each a perfect place to tryst with the spy who loves you.

In Fleming's day GoldenEye was such a celebrity scene that playwright Noël Coward made his home just up the hill at Firefly House, a magical setting worth visiting for the views alone and where groups are sometimes allowed to take a peek inside. Pay homage to another icon by making the day trip to Nine Mile, the village where reggae genius Bob Marley was born. His home (and final resting place, where he is buried with his guitar) is now a shrine to his life, music, and message of "One World, One Love."

Back in Ochi, you may shun the touristy Dunns River Falls, but it's a wonderful place to join hands with a chain of strangers (and lots of them, when the cruise ships are in) and climb 600 feet of steplike rocks through cold, clear mountain water. After that it's time to refuel, so follow the aroma to Faith's Pen, where 30 ramshackle huts sell traditional Jamaican fare, including jerk chicken and pork, fried fish, ackee and saltfish (Jamaica's national dish), and fresh corn on the cob.

Where: 62 miles/100 km east of Montego Bay. **Jamaica Inn:** Tel 800-837-4608 or 876-974-2514; www.jamaicainn.com. *Cost:* from $290 (off-peak), from $500 (peak). **GoldenEye:** Tel 876-975-3354; www.goldeneye.com. *Cost:* from $670 (off-peak), from $840 (peak). **Bob Marley Centre & Mausoleum:** Tel 876-978-2929. **Best times:** Nov–Apr for fine weather; Jan for Accompong Maroon Festival; Jun for Ocho Rios International Jazz Festival.

An Errol Flynn Favorite and the Birthplace of Jerk

Port Antonio

Jamaica, Greater Antilles

Called "the most exquisite port on earth" by American poet Ella Wheeler Wilcox and "Porty" by locals, this quiet, historic former banana port is still the best place to get an authentic sense of Old Jamaica.

With its twin harbors, gorgeous white sand beaches, and verdant hillsides, Port Antonio charmed Errol Flynn and his cronies back in the 1940s. Its most lasting contribution to modern culture, however, is as the birthplace of jerk. "Maroons" (escaped slaves living in the Blue Mountains) are believed to be the first to have prepared jerk, by smoking seasoned wild boar, back in the 17th century.

Rustic stands started serving jerk at nearby Boston Bay Beach in the 1930s, and although the beach is not award winning, the jerk is. Six or so open-air jerk stands, each with its own special recipe, serve up fiery pork, chicken, fresh fish or lobster, and the less common jerk sausage. Must-include ingredients are allspice (called pimento), thyme, and the super-hot chili Scotch bonnet, with the meat slow-cooked over a wood fire, usually in steel drums cut lengthwise. Roll up your sleeves and tuck into the spicy fare with all the trimmings—sweet baked yams, "festival" (deep-fried cornbread) fritters, and the requisite Red Stripe beer—and there's always reggae music playing somewhere.

In Port Antonio, Woody's Low Bridge Place is famous for burgers (including great veggie burgers) and charming service courtesy of Woody Cousins and his wife, Cherry. But if you call ahead they'll make jerk chicken and curried goat to order. It's one of the highlights of staying at nearby Hotel Mocking Bird Hill, a ten-room eco-friendly inn on six tropical hilltop acres (with more than 40 endemic species, it's excellent for birders), far removed from the hustle of the island's mass tourism. Its restaurant, Mille Fleurs, is known for using local, organic ingredients and a daily-changing menu that serves innovative fare like soufflé made with ackee fruit or chicken in plum sauce, with an orange custard drizzled with wild orange liqueur for dessert. The two hands-on owners encourage you to explore the area, with trips to the closeby sandy beaches of Frenchman's Cove, the spring-fed Blue Lagoon—a 180-foot-deep indigo hole—or the Rio Grande for slow-moving, poled bamboo rafting, a method once used to transport bananas.

WHERE: 60 miles/97 km northeast of Kingston. **WOODY'S LOW BRIDGE:** Tel 876-436-5624. *Cost:* dinner $18. **HOTEL MOCKING BIRD HILL:** Tel 876-993-7267; www.hotelmockingbirdhill.com. *Cost:* from $175; dinner $50. **BEST TIMES:** Nov–Apr for good weather; Jul for Jerk Festival.

Island Cuisine—C'est Magnifique

THE FLAVORS OF MARTINIQUE

Martinique, Lesser Antilles

Unspoiled corners of this mountainous island look much as they did when Napoleon's empress, Josephine, was growing up here on the family sugar plantation in the late 18th century; the same lush islandscape inspired Paul Gauguin long before his better-known journey to Tahiti. It is the most French of the Caribbean islands, so it is little wonder, then, that local gastronomy—a mélange of classic French and Creole's fusion of local ingredients with Indian and African influence—plays a major role in the island's heritage and allure as a stroll through the local spice market in Fort-de-France will confirm.

Martinique is famous for its rums, which have been awarded the prestigious French designation Appellation d'Origine Contrôlée (AOC) and have long been the foundation of many traditional island recipes. The Route de Rhum will bring you to 12 of the island's best distilleries, including the historic Habitation Clément in Le François.

Rum ages in barrels at Habitation Clément, a distillery dating back to 1887.

The island's east coast has emerged as the best destination for fine dining. A front-runner in Martinique's vital food scene is the chic and intimate Hotel Plein Soleil, set on a hilltop offering gorgeous views of the Atlantic. Sixteen brightly colored rooms, some with a private plunge pool, accommodate those who come for the innovative cuisine prepared by Nathanael Ducteil, trained by French master Alain Ducasse in Paris and known here for his contemporary flavors. Nearby Cap Est Lagoon

Resort & Spa is the pinnacle of the luxury scene in Martinique, with 50 coolly minimal suites housed in 18 multihued villas reminiscent of Creole design. Restaurant Le Belem is known for its expansive buffet breakfasts and elegant dinners as well as for having the country's best wine cellar.

For stellar beaches, head south to Les Salines, a mile-long cove of soft white sand with perfectly calm waters, and Diamant Beach, more than 6 miles of bright shoreline that's perfect for picnicking and lazy beachcombing.

Martinique's interior is lush and hilly, as a drive north along the Route de Trace from Fort-de-France reveals. Springtime is the best time to see the wild displays of lotus, red ginger, and West Indian jasmine that gave Martinique the nickname "Isle of Flowers." Pull over at Le Jardin de Balata for a close-up of 3,000 plant species on 7 artfully planted acres. Continue north to Mont Pelée (Bald Mountain), a massive and still smoldering 4,583-foot volcano that in 1902 literally vaporized the colonial capital, St. Pierre, in the century's first and worst volcanic disaster. Bare and beautiful, Mont Pelée is a dramatic setting for hikes and bird-spotting around its base.

VISITOR INFO: www.martinique.org. **HOTEL PLEIN SOLEIL:** Tel 596-596-38-07-77; www.hotelpleinsoleil.fr. *Cost:* from $155 (off-peak), from $230 (peak); dinner $65. **CAP EST:** Tel 596-596-54-80-80; www.capest.com. *Cost:* from $580 (off-peak), from $870 (peak); dinner $70. **BEST TIMES:** late Feb or Mar for Carnival; mid-May for Sainte-Marie Culinary Week; early Dec for Sainte-Marie Rum Festival.

Puerto Rico's Wild West and Most Beautiful Back Road

RINCÓN AND LA RUTA PANORAMICA

Puerto Rico, Greater Antilles

Puerto Rico's wild and wonderful west coast is one of the world's top surfing destinations, and its town of Rincón was put on the map when the World Surfing Championships were held here on Domes Beach in 1968. Rincón means "corner"—this is where the Atlantic and Caribbean meet, giving rise to waves that can break at heights of up to 25 feet. The secret has long been out—this California-vibe town attracts a steady flow of transient surfers from around the globe—but it's a revelation to most.

Standing in contrast to Rincón's casual beach culture is the elegant and curiously named Horned Dorset, a sumptuous getaway for the smart set from San Juan. Situated on 7 acres with its own secluded beach, the 39-suite Spanish Neocolonial property maintains an ambience of quiet pampering. You'll feel as if this were the aristocratic home of a Spanish grandee whose coddled houseguests lounge in exotic gardens by a beautiful palm-flanked freshwater pool, between one superb meal and the next.

In nearby Mayagüez begins La Ruta Panoramica, a 165-mile drive that traverses the island, twisting and turning its way through lush, mountainous Corillera Central, dipping into valleys and passing small villages and farms before ending at Maunabo in the east. Plan at least 2 days for a one-way trip, with lots of photo ops of both the Atlantic and the Caribbean; brown *ruta* ("route") signs connect an assemblage of

40-plus roads. A good midway resting place is the charming Hacienda Gripiñas, an 1858 plantation house turned inn that helps steep you in the coffee culture that still thrives along this route. Just up the hill on one of the island's highest peaks, visit the forest preserve Toro Negro, more remote and less crowded than El Yunque (see p. 1096). Take a hike, then head back to the inn for dinner—perhaps choosing their excellent *carne guisada*, a traditional beef stew made with tomatoes and pigeon peas.

Where: Rincón is 100 miles/161 km west of San Juan. **Visitor info:** www.rincon.org. **Horned Dorset:** Tel 800-633-1857 or 787-823-4030; www.horneddorset.com. *Cost:* from $360 (off-peak), from $596 (peak); dinner $80. **Hacienda Gripiñas:** Tel 787-828-1717; www.haciendagripinas.com. *Cost:* from $135, inclusive. **Best times:** Nov–Apr for surfing and good weather; Feb for whale-watching; mid-Feb for the Coffee Festival in Maricao; Mar for Whale Festival in Rincón.

A Sizzling Arts Scene amid Architectural Treasures

Old San Juan

Puerto Rico, Greater Antilles

El Viejo San Juan, the seven-square-block landmark zone of the island's capital, is a perfectly preserved microcosm of Spanish Colonial architecture and a walk back through history. In fact, were it not for the chaotic traffic jams that are its liaison with reality, this nearly 500-year-old open-air theater set would look almost too beautiful to be authentic. Its narrow streets are paved with adoquine (a blue stone used as ballast on Spanish galleons), and its 16th-century fortresses, particularly the impregnable six-level El Morro rising 150 feet above the sea, still strike one as engineering marvels. This showcase of protected old-world landmarks is also chockablock with fashionable bistros, designer shops, art galleries, churches, and Colonial town houses with flowering wrought-iron balconies.

In Old San Juan's main square, Plaza de Armas, four statues represent the seasons.

The elegant El Convento was one of the first historic boutique hotels in the heart of Old San Juan, helping transform the district into one of the most vibrant historic and artistic communities in the Caribbean. The imposing 1651 Carmelite convent (which later served as a dance hall, a Howard Johnson's, and even a flophouse) has original details such as wooden beams and handmade tiles. Stop by Cana, its small and popular jazz bar.

High atop the Old City's North Wall sits the Gallery Inn, six interconnecting town houses that combine to create a quiet, quirky labyrinth of tilted staircases, open-air patios, and small pocket gardens. Owner Jan D'Esopo decorated each of the 22 eclectic rooms, lending an artist's sensibility while respecting the traditional setting. Its Wine Deck commands the highest point in the city, offering the best views of Old San Juan, the Atlantic Ocean, and San Juan Bay. For those who like Latin music and late nights and don't mind the noise, Da House (a hotel housed in a former Franciscan monastery) is right above the Nuyorican Café, which is the best spot for live salsa and Caribbean-influenced jazz with a mixed-age crowd.

By day, stroll the side streets of the historic district, grazing on street food and local dishes like *mallorcas* (grilled pastries filled with ham and cheese), *mofongo* (mashed plantains, garlic, and herbs with chicken), *bacalaitos* (salted cod fritters), and *piragua* (mounds of flavored shaved ice). By night, head to the lively SoFo district (South of Calle Fortaleza) for a music and dance scene that includes bomba, danza, salsa, and reggaeton—the hybrid of rap and reggae—pouring out into the streets from the raft of late-night clubs.

Visitor info: www.gotopuertorico.com. **El Convento:** Tel 800-468-2779 or 787-723-9020; www.elconvento.com. *Cost:* from $180 (off-peak), from $260 (peak). **The Gallery Inn:** Tel 866-572-2783 or 787-722-1808; www.thegalleryinn.com. *Cost:* from $140 (off-peak), from $210 (peak). **Da House:** Tel 787-366-5074; www.dahousehotelpr.com. *Cost:* from $80. **Best times:** Nov–Apr for nice weather; Jan for Festival de la Calle San Sebastian; mid-Feb–mid-Mar for Festival Casals; late Jun for Fiesta de San Juan Bautista; Jul for Puerto Rico Salsa Congress.

Off-the-Radar in the Spanish Virgin Islands

Vieques and Culebra

Puerto Rico, Greater Antilles

Puerto Rico's small sister island Vieques is distinctive both for what it lacks (souvenir shops, spas, stoplights, and most other signs of tourist development) and what it possesses (a bioluminescent bay, dozens of nearly deserted beaches, and a thriving population of free-roaming horses).

The 62-year presence of the U.S. Navy, which occupied more than half the 21-mile island, kept the island from being developed. When it departed in 2003, the base became a national wildlife refuge (much of it is still closed to the public because of the ongoing cleanup of unexploded ammunition). Vieques is a remarkable throwback to the old days of the Spanish Virgin Islands, and the perfect escape for wound-up mainlanders and San Juaneros, who travel here for natural beauty and the restorative pleasures of doing next to nothing.

An all-natural psychedelic experience is to be had at Mosquito Bay, the best and brightest bioluminescent bay in the world. The combination of nutrients from mangroves and nearly landlocked waters has created a massive concentration of dinoflagellates (called pyrodiniums or "whirling fire") that create a blue-greenish glow visible at night around anything that touches the water. The phenomenon is best viewed on dark, moonless evenings either aboard an electric boat (gasoline exhaust harms the creatures) or even better, by kayak, the eerie luminescence appearing with each paddle stroke. Trolling your hand overboard and "making angels" by swimming in the water are part of the magic.

In Vieques's growing selection of inns and small hotels (a W hotel made news as the first big name to arrive on the island in 2010), Hacienda Tamarindo was one of the first and is still one of the most satisfying, thanks to the hands-on approach of the owners. Named for the ancient tamarind tree that anchors the patio, the villa is set atop a hill with bright rooms open to the refreshing trade winds and sweeping views of the Caribbean.

Vieques's most popular beaches are east of Esperanza and include the beautiful Sun Bay, backed by trees and grasses where descendants of the paso fino horses left by the Spanish centuries ago roam freely. Cap your day with crab empanadas, *habichuelas* (a rice and beans staple), and a cold Medalla *cerveza* at El Resuelve, a casual restaurant run by locals. The longtime hot spot Chez Shack has the best barbecued ribs and crab cakes on the island and a great Reggae Grill night on Mondays in high season.

For even less of a scene, the tiny 7-by-4-mile island of Culebra to the north possesses one of the world's most beautiful beaches, Playa Flamenco. This brilliant white sand crescent with stunning turquoise waters is the best spot to encounter hawksbill turtles and angelfish among the reefs. A 20-minute walk to the west is the island's hidden jewel, Carlos Rosario Beach, where the shallow reef and calm, protected bay make for the island's best snorkeling. When your appetite rises, head to Dewey (the only town on the island) for waterside dining at Mamacita's, justly famous for its frozen cocktails and live conga band on Saturday nights.

Visitor info: www.gotopuertorico.com. **Mosquito Bay:** Numerous operators lead tours, including Island Adventures Biobay Eco-Tours. Tel 787-741-0720; www.biobay.com. **Hacienda Tamarindo:** Tel 787-741-8525; www.haciendatamarindo.com. *Cost:* from $135 (off-peak), from $195 (peak). **El Resuelve:** 787-741-1427. *Cost:* dinner $15. **Chez Shack:** Tel 787-741-2175. *Cost:* dinner $40. **Mamacita's:** Tel 787-742-0090; www.mamacitasguesthouse.com. *Cost:* dinner $35. **Best time:** Nov–Apr for pleasant weather.

America's Only Tropical Rain Forest

El Yunque National Forest

Puerto Rico, Greater Antilles

A popular day trip from San Juan, El Yunque combines all the magic of a rain forest—majestic trees, giant ferns, and mysterious peeps and trills emanating from the dense foliage in the rugged Luquillo Mountains.

As the only tropical rain forest in the United States National Forest System, El Yunque provides paved trails that are easy on children and inexperienced hikers. It even offers a drive-through option for windshield tourists who can enjoy the misty landscape and roadside waterfalls along Route 191, the only road through the 28,000-acre forest.

But El Yunque, considered sacred by the Taino Indians, is indubitably best experienced on foot. Home to thousands of plants, including 240 tree species (23 of which are found nowhere else) and 70 orchids, El Yunque has 13 hiking trails covering 23 miles of varied terrain. The hardy can summit El Toro and take in spectacular 360-degree views of the forest, but even small children can handle the less-than-a-mile-long Big Tree Trail that wends past La Mina Falls, whose cascades plummet 35 feet into a cool, refreshing pool of water—the perfect plunge on a hot day. The 3-mile El Yunque Trail is considered the most rewarding. The farther away you can get from the cruise-ship crowds, the more jungle magic you'll find.

There are no large creatures here such as monkeys or panthers, but there are plenty of small ones that you may not see but will certainly hear. Millions of tiny coqui, the endemic tree frog that is Puerto Rico's mascot, live here, trilling "co-KEE" sporadically until evening approaches, or after a rainfall, when it turns into a full-blown chorus. The most prized sighting is the bright-green Puerto Rican parrot, once abundant but now quite rare and highly endangered.

After the rain forest, it's only 8 miles north to Luquillo Beach, a much photographed palm-lined crescent of white sand and calm turquoise waters that attracts lots of local families from San Juan. Follow them: They know which roadside stand sells the best *alcapurrias,* plantain fritters stuffed with seafood.

Where: 22 miles/35 km southeast of San Juan. Tel 787-888-1880; www.fs.usda.gov/elyunque. **Best time:** Dec–Apr for the least rain.

Underwater Alps Draw Divers In-the-Know

Saba

Lesser Antilles

With just 1,200 (extremely friendly) inhabitants, diminutive Saba is neither chic nor fancy. It has no beaches or nightlife to speak of (one reason it's known as "the Unspoiled Queen"), but those with a thing for mountains—above or below the water—consider it a regular heaven on earth. Trekkers take to Mount Scenery, the 3,000-foot forest-clad tip of an extinct volcano, whose walls plunge into the sea, while divers are as astonished by what they don't see as what they do; with little tourism, Saba and its offshore waters remain uncrowded and uncorrupted.

Gum drop–shaped Saba (pronounced SAY-ba, and named for the Arawak word meaning "rock") is encircled by Saba Marine Park, the result of a farsighted government that safeguarded its pristine ecosystem. Coral-encrusted rocks, boulders, and reefs draw less experienced divers and snorkelers, but it's the spectacular pinnacles rising from the ocean floor to about 90 feet below the surface that make Saba a world-class destination for experienced divers. Saba's 29 seamounts include the dramatically named Shark Shoals, Twilight Zone, and Third Encounter.

Saba's 5 square miles are mostly vertical, with 12 great trekking trails that vary in distance and difficulty and just one paved road ("The Road") that switchbacks up one side of the island and down the other. Its airport has the shortest commercial runway in the world, flanked by two sheer cliffs. The incredibly situated Shearwater Resort promises some high-altitude drama: At 2,000 feet, the views from its pool are heart-stopping, taking in the immense sea and Saba's five neighboring islands, which are often enveloped in the clouds. You can spend the night or just go for sunset cocktails or dinner at the hotel's Bistro del Mare.

On the other side of the island is Queen's Gardens Resort, a charming cluster of red-roofed bungalows angled for sweeping views of the Caribbean Sea and two rain forest–covered mountains. Surrounded by lush gardens, it's known for its acclaimed restaurant and the beach-deprived island's largest pool. It's just a

5-minute walk to The Bottom, a Dutch village of gabled roofs and the island's capital.

Rainforest Restaurant is part of Ecolodge Rendez-Vous, whose charming Saban-style cottages stand deep in the rain forest. The quaintly decorated candlelit restaurant specializes in unfussy Caribbean classics like jerk chicken, locally caught seafood, and vegetables and fruits from its own garden. Enjoy hummingbirds by day and the lilting ring of tree frogs at night.

Most of the action takes place in Windwardside, where locals and tourists gather at Brigadoon for Chef Michael's wonderful Caribbean-influenced cooking and his wife Tricia's huge personality and homemade rums.

Visitor info: www.sabatourism.com. **Shearwater Resort:** Tel 599-416-2498; www.shearwater-resort.com. *Cost:* from $185. **Queen's Gardens Resort:** Tel 599-416-3494; www.queensaba.com. *Cost:* from $220 (off-peak), from $280 (peak); dinner $70. **Ecolodge & Rainforest Restaurant:** Tel 599-416-3348; www.ecolodge-saba.com. *Cost:* from $85 (off-peak), from $105 (peak); dinner $25. **Brigadoon:** Tel 599-416-2380. *Cost:* dinner $30. **How:** Sea Saba Dive Center leads diving excursions. Tel 599-416-2246; www.seasaba.com. *Cost:* from $90 per day. **Best times:** Diving is great year-round; Nov–Apr for best weather; Oct for Sea & Learn, when naturalists give presentations and lead field trips.

The Caribbean's Star-Studded Riviera

St. Barths

St. Barthélemy, Lesser Antilles

Chic, cool, very French, and only about half the size of Manhattan, St. Barths captivates with its amazing views of the sea and surrounding islands, wonderful markets and wine shops, excellent restaurants, and quiet French flair. For the 2 weeks around Christmas and New Year's Eve, it becomes the destination of choice for *le beau monde* who converge from France, Hollywood, and New York, sunning on topless and au naturel beaches, and filling stylish but casual cafés and killer villas.

But when things quiet down, an infectious serenity resurfaces and the island's nickname of "the Provence of the Caribbean" again applies. Private yachts anchor in the storybook-quaint harbor of Gustavia, St. Barths's only town and seaport. It's so tiny that only boutique cruise ships can anchor offshore, avoiding the ship and passenger overload common in nearby St. Martin or St. Thomas. Take it all in from the glamorous Hotel Carl Gustaf's outdoor bar and restaurant, perched high above the harbor and at its most enchanting during sunset. The same unencumbered panorama can be enjoyed round-the-clock from any of its luxurious suites, each with its own plunge pool.

Set on Anse de Public, right by the water just outside Gustavia, Maya's is the most famous of the island's many restaurants, serving Creole specialties in a relaxed and breezy setting. Maya's waterfront terrace is the perfect spot for sundowner cocktails and people-watching, while ready-made feasts for picnics are the reason for a bike ride to Maya's to Go, located across from the airport. Another favorite spot for drinks and burgers in town is the unpretentious Le Select.

St. Barths's beaches are spectacular. St. Jean Beach, on the northern side of the island, is most popular for celebrity-spotting and offers the best swimming. It's actually two beaches, separated by a small promontory occupied by Eden Rock, the first hotel on the island and still the most famous. Surrounded on three sides by water, this much-photographed landmark was originally built as the home of pilot and playboy Rémy de Haenen, who landed here in 1947 and "made" the island; soon Greta Garbo, David Rockefeller, and Baron Rothschild were arriving as guests at Eden Rock. The hotel is still the place to be near the action for those who can afford it. Otherwise, go for lunch at the atmospheric and legendary open-air Sand Bar café.

At dusk, Gustavia's enchanting harbor lights up.

Hotel Guanahani is the island's largest property, with 68 brightly colored bungalow-style rooms and suites scattered among bougainvillea, hibiscus, and palms. But, set on its own 16-acre peninsula with two private beaches, it doesn't feel big. Even though it's the only St. Barths hotel that offers a resortlike experience, complete with a stylish spa, it still has a low-key (but pampering) ambience—as if it were for people who don't want to be part of the scene—at least some of the time.

Salines Garden Cottages dispels the notion that St. Barths is only for those with very deep pockets. It's a 10-minute walk to the secluded and underveloped Saline Beach.

VISITOR INFO: www.st-barths.com. **HOTEL CARL GUSTAF:** Tel 866-297-2153 or 590-590-29-79-00; www.hotelcarlgustaf.com. *Cost:* cottage suites from $500 (off-peak), from $1,450 (peak); dinner $70. *When:* closed Sep–Oct. **MAYA'S:** Tel 590-590-27-75-73; www.mayasstbarth.com. *Cost:* dinner $70. *When:* closed mid-Jun–mid-Jul, Sep–Oct. **EDEN ROCK:** Tel 855-333-6762 or 590-590-29-79-99; www.edenrockhotel.com. *Cost:* from $750 (off-peak), from $1,050 (peak); dinner $75. **HOTEL GUANAHANI & SPA:** Tel 800-216-3774 or 590-590-276-660; www.leguanahani.com. *Cost:* from $590 (off-peak), from $980 (peak). **SALINES GARDEN:** Tel 590-590-51-04-44; www.salinesgarden.com. *Cost:* from $200. **BEST TIMES:** Jan for St. Barths Music Festival; Mar or Apr for the annual St. Barths Bucket Regatta; last 2 weeks of Dec for celebrity-spotting.

Plantation Inns Promise Romance and History

NEVIS

St. Kitts and Nevis, Lesser Antilles

Columbus imagined the clouds around the island's highest peak to be snow and named the island "Nuestra Señora de las Nieves" (Our Lady of the Snows), shortened over the years to Nevis. Nature enthusiasts hike into verdant rain forests, 3,200-foot Nevis Peak being the island's ultimate destination. Smaller than its nation-mate St. Kitts (see below), Nevis was another rich, important British sugar colony. But where St. Kitts (the "Mother Island") today is busier and more touristed with casinos and golf and big expansion plans for its future, lush and unhurried Nevis offers simple pleasures and not a single traffic light.

Alexander Hamilton was born here, and the legendary Admiral Horatio Nelson married local girl Fanny Nisbet on Montpelier Estate in 1787 when he was just a young captain. Perched on a hilltop with breathtaking views, the site is now home to Montpelier Plantation, a stylish 19-room inn offering a modern interpretation of plantation life. While the great house is gone, some structures on the 60-acre estate date to the 1700s; others are new but so tastefully interwoven it's hard to tell the difference. There are only 16 seats in the Mill, a renowned restaurant set in the estate's 18th-century stone mill, whose menu features produce grown on the property and specialties like mahi-mahi roasted in plantain leaves and desserts using one of the 50 varieties of mango that grow on the island.

There's an altogether different feel at Hermitage Plantation Inn, a delightful mélange of 11 pastel-painted gingerbread cottages, some brought from other sites around Nevis and painstakingly restored. The main house, completed in 1740 and believed to be the oldest wooden home in the Caribbean, serves as a lively social center where everyone gathers for cocktails before dinner. The beach is a 15-minute drive away, but guests can lounge by the pool, go horseback riding into the hills, or fill lazy afternoons waiting for dinner, the highlight of the day.

The Caribbean's only historic-plantation inn directly on the water fills out this trio of choices. The Nisbet Plantation Beach Club's broad palm-tree-flanked lawn sweeps down from the 1778 great house where Fanny once lived to a half-mile-long white sand beach. A hotel since the 1950s, Nisbet Plantation has 36 rooms, including charming cottages tucked amid 30 acres of tropical foliage. Although Nevis is not famous for its beaches, nearby Pinney's is the exception—a 3-mile reef-protected stretch of sugar-fine white sand by historic Charlestown. Located on the island's western side, it's perfect for sunsets, best seen from the open-air Sunshine's Bar and Grill, with a famously potent Killer Bee rum punch in hand.

VISITOR INFO: www.nevisisland.com. **MONTPELIER PLANTATION:** Tel 888-334-7609; www.montpeliernevis.com. *Cost:* from $345 (off-peak), from $550 (peak); dinner $75. **THE HERMITAGE PLANTATION INN:** Tel 800-682-4025 or 869-469-3477; www.hermitagenevis.com. *Cost:* from $185 (off-peak), from $395 (peak). **NISBET PLANTATION BEACH CLUB:** Tel 800-742-6008 or 869-469-9325; www.nisbetplantation.com. *Cost:* from $385 (off-peak), from $670 (peak), inclusive. **SUNSHINE'S BAR:** Tel 869-469-5817; www.sunshinenevis.com. **BEST TIMES:** Jan–Mar for good weather; late Jul–early Aug for the carnival-like Culturama; Aug for International Food Fair.

Where Sugar Was King

ST. KITTS

St. Kitts and Nevis, Lesser Antilles

This cloud-crowned volcanic island so enchanted Christopher Columbus that he named it after his patron saint—only later did locals shorten the name from St. Christopher's to St. Kitts. England's first settlement in the

Caribbean and once its wealthiest sugar colony, St. Kitts shares rich history and scenery with its smaller sister island Nevis (see previous page). St. Kitts is the livelier of the two, with resorts and gaming to go along with water sports and hikes into its dense rain-forest interior; windshield tourists can follow the road that encircles the 18-by-5-mile island. Feast your eyes on the panorama from Brimstone Hill, an 18th-century stone fortress built 800 feet above sea level, with views of six neighboring islands. Known as the Gibraltar of the West Indies, it protected colonial St. Kitts's sugar plantations—68 of them at the industry's height, one for every square mile of the island.

Many of the historic estates built by sugar barons have been tastefully restored to serve as inns and restaurants. One of the most captivating is the 17th-century Ottley's Plantation Inn, set on 35 acres in the foothills of majestic Mount Liamuiga, a dormant volcano. The inn's 24 rooms are handsomely decorated in English Colonial style, with gorgeous gardens for strolling. Its Mango Orchard Spa overlooks a rain-forest ravine, while the romantic Royal Palm Restaurant is renowned for culinary highlights such as the artfully presented coconut cream cheesecake.

The Rawlins Plantation is another 17th-century charmer. Gingerbread cottages surround the main house, with its wide veranda overlooking flower-splashed grounds. A wondrous West Indian buffet lunch draws both the local elite and nonislanders. Save room for the sensational chocolate terrine with passion fruit sauce.

Backed by hills, Frigate Bay is home to a popular beach.

Dining is a casual affair at Mr. X's Shiggidy Shack in Frigate Bay, a great sunset spot where you can dine on grilled lobster or lemon snapper with thyme. On Thursday nights let loose at the beach party with a bonfire, live music, and the amazing, blazing Fire Man. During the day, check out Reggae Beach, a kayaking, snorkeling, and sailing paradise on the South East Peninsula. Refuel on coconut shrimp and frozen reggae coladas and the justly famous banana chocolate chip cake with whipped cream at Reggae Beach Bar & Grill.

VISITOR INFO: www.stkittstourism.kn. **OTTLEY'S PLANTATION INN:** Tel 800-772-3039 or 869-465-7234; www.ottleys.com. *Cost:* from $220 (off-peak), from $300 (peak); dinner $66. **RAWLINS PLANTATION INN:** Tel 869-465-6221; www.rawlinsplantation.com. *Cost:* from $185 (off-peak), from $280 (peak); dinner $55. *When:* closed late Aug–mid-Oct. **MR. X'S SHIGGIDY SHACK:** Tel 869-762-3983; www.mrxshiggidyshack.com. *Cost:* dinner $25. **REGGAE BEACH BAR & GRILL:** Tel 869-762-5050; www.reggaebeachbar.com. *Cost:* dinner $40. **BEST TIMES:** Nov–Apr for pleasant weather; Jun for St. Kitts Music Festival; Dec 15–Jan 2 for Carnival.

Villas and Views Beyond Extraordinary

THE PITONS

St. Lucia, Lesser Antilles

The towering twin peaks known as the Pitons, abruptly rising side by side out of the sea, make lush St. Lucia one of the Caribbean's most dramatically beautiful islands. These volcanic remnants—the Gros Piton at 2,619 feet and the steeper-sided Petit Piton at 2,461 feet—are reminiscent of the jagged mountains of Bali Ha'i, lending an exotic South Pacific air to the island. Located in the southwestern corner of the island, these forest-swathed wonders are ubiquitous silhouettes that have appeared on everything from postcards to the label of the locally brewed beer and the national flag.

For the moment still largely undeveloped, the 27-by-14-mile former British and French property was better known for bananas than for tourism until the arrival of Anse Chastanet, a 600-acre resort that is beyond romantic, with hillside guestrooms hidden amid verdant foliage and bursts of color, harmonizing seamlessly with the natural surroundings. Some are even missing a wall, bringing the outside—and the twin-peaked views—in. The secluded palm-fringed soft-sand beach below has its own scuba center and school, and some of the Caribbean's best snorkeling and diving are along the Anse Chastanet Reef just a few feet offshore.

Anse Chastanet boasted the island's best views of the Pitons until owners Nick and Karolin Troubetzkoy outdid themselves by ingeniously building Jade Mountain into the cliff above—a resort-within-a-resort—with 22 enormous "sanctuaries" that are entirely and permanently open on one side yet completely private. With the fourth wall absent, there's nothing between you and mesmerizing views of the Pitons, pink-and-lavender sunsets, cool breezes, and the not infrequent flourish of a bird flying through. Each one-of-a-kind sanctuary is appointed with restrained luxury, including an extravagantly sized infinity pool lined with iridescent glass tiles (five "sky suites" have everything but the pool). There's the beach below (you can walk or grab the hotel shuttle) and a modern and stylish spa, but with a view this hypnotic, it's little wonder that some guests never venture out.

For a more down-to-earth experience, try Fond Doux ("sweet valley" in Lucian patois), a working cocoa plantation that has been in continuous production since French colonials established it in 1745. It's a deeply charming family-owned and -run place that exudes a distinctly St. Lucian experience, with stays in restored 19th-century wooden bungalows. See how cocoa is made, walk estate trails over 135 lush acres, and be back in time for a lunch of Creole specialties in one of the hotel's two open-air restaurants, then repair to the pool for an afternoon of idling.

The island's ultimate challenge is a guided hike to the top of Gros Piton, the Kilimanjaro of the Caribbean. (Petit Piton is too steep to climb.) Or learn more about St. Lucia's volcanic origins and ongoing activity at La Soufrière's "drive-in volcano" (a misnomer, as you can drive up to, but not directly into, it), a rocky, lunar landscape with bubbling, smelly, sulfur mud baths that are open to the public.

A Soufrière beach overlooks one of the dormant volcanic Pitons.

Visitor info: www.stlucia.org. **Anse Chastanet and Jade Mountain:** Tel 800-223-1108 or 758-459-7000; www.ansechastanet.com, www.jademountainstlucia.com. *Cost:* Anse Chastanet rooms from $330 (off-peak), from $495 (peak). Jade Mountain sky suites from $950 (off-peak), $1,200 (peak); sanctuaries from $1,250 (off-peak), from $1,550 (peak). **Fond Doux Estate:** Tel 758-459-7545; www.fonddouxestate.com. *Cost:* from $200 (off-peak), from $350 (peak). **Best times:** Dec–Apr for good weather; 1st week of May for Jazz Fest.

A Gastronomic Hot Spot in the Caribbean

St. Martin's Food Scene

St. Martin, Lesser Antilles

A 37-square-mile island peacefully divided between the French and the Dutch since 1648, St. Martin/St. Maarten is starkly different depending on which side you visit. Dutch St. Maarten, in the south, is known for cruise ships, casinos, and condos, whereas St. Martin, being French, focuses on the art of gastronomy.

On an island dense with the Caribbean's highest concentration of restaurants, the small resort town of Grand Case is the hot spot for fine dining. Le Pressoir is one of the best, specializing in classic French cuisine. Spiga is *pura Italiana,* down to the ebullient Italian-born chef who prepares homemade pasta daily, along with favorites like pancetta-wrapped roast pork tenderloin. For down-home Creole cooking, try Le Ti Coin Creole; chef/owner Carl Phillips serves up simple dishes such as fish fritters and conch cocktail. A stay at Le Petit Hotel puts you in the heart of it all. This tasteful, ten-room beachside inn oozes charm; it is also near the island's seaside "lolos" (barbecue shacks). These side-by-side eateries (look for Talk of the Town) will cost you next to nothing and include a Technicolor sunset free of charge.

The island has plenty of beautiful white-sand beaches to keep sunbathers elated, and Baie Longue, at the western tip of St. Martin, is a stunner. It is the site of La Samanna, a Mediterranean-style resort that is the island's most sybaritic place to stay. Dining reaches its opulent peak at Le Réservé, the hotel's open-air restaurant.

Baie Orientale is one of the largest and most popular beaches, with restaurants, hotels, boutiques, water sports, and a clothing-optional section in the south. Set on a hill overlooking the bay, the romantic, Provençal-inspired Sol e Luna Inn's six charming rooms adjoin a fine restaurant known for classic dishes with a French flourish.

Gourmet restaurants line Grand Case's shores.

The calm waters ringing the shallow reefs make the island a snorkeler's delight, but the very best sights are found in an underwater nature reserve off the coast. Take the 5-minute ferry to the uninhabited (but never deserted) Îlet Pinel (Pine Island), where two beach bars prepare lobsters plucked from the sea, and a snorkeling trail leads you to alluring underwater spots.

Visitor info: www.st-martin.org. **Le Pressoir:** Tel 590-590-87-76-62; www.lepressoir-sxm.com. *Cost:* dinner $60. **Spiga:** Tel 590-590-52-47-83; www.spiga-sxm.com. *Cost:* dinner $45. **Le Ti Coin:** Tel 590-590-87-92-09; www.grandcase.com/ticoincreole. *Cost:* dinner $30. **Le Petit Hotel:** Tel 590-590-29-09-65; www.lepetithotel.com. *Cost:* from $300 (off-peak), from $475 (peak). **La Samanna:** Tel 800-957-6128 or 590-590-87-64-00; www.lasamanna.com. *Cost:* from $995; dinner $80. *When:* closed Sep–Oct. **Sol e Luna Inn:** Tel 590-590-29-08-56; www.solelunarestaurant.com. *Cost:* from $130; dinner $40. **Best times:** Dec–Apr for good weather.

The Grenadines' Favorite Jump-up and a Hillside Retreat

Bequia

St. Vincent and the Grenadines, Lesser Antilles

Hilly, green, and just 7 square miles in size, Bequia (pronounced BECK-way) is the largest and northernmost of the Grenadine Islands. Once the region's busiest whaling station (back in the days of *Moby-Dick*), it still maintains traces of its seafaring heritage as well as a glimmer of how the Caribbean was not so long ago—no high-rises, no golf courses, no pretense. The wildest it gets is Thursday night, when the Frangipani Hotel's open-air barbecue and jump-up (who could stay seated?) is the place to be with live steel-drum music. Any sunset is reason enough to drop by for the famous Frangi Fever cocktail, which keeps hotel guests, locals, and the yacht set happy. The latter use this casual raffish gingerbread guesthouse as their nerve center, a convenient hub located right on picturesque Admiralty Bay, where they can keep an eye on their moored craft. The sailing is excellent in the Grenadines (see p. 1106) and this is one of its safest harbors.

Bequia has begun to go upmarket with the transformation of a formerly modest hillside inn into Firefly Plantation Bequia. Set on a 30-acre, 18th-century sugar plantation with orchards of mango, guava, and Bequia plums, it's as small and luxurious as its sister property Firefly Mustique (see below), with four lovely guest rooms in three buildings of hand-cut stone. It's perfect if your ideal vacation is one spent reading in a balcony hammock, listening to cows lowing and palm fronds rustling, turning your head occasionally to catch the glorious views. Take a dip in the pool or take a short, pleasant stroll to the deserted but stunning beach at Spring Bay, where the snorkeling is excellent. In the evenings, candlelit dinners feature ingredients fresh from the grounds or netted in the nearby waters.

Visitor info: www.bequiatourism.com. **Frangipani:** Tel 784-458-3255; www.frangipanibequia.com. *Cost:* from $120 (off-peak), from $190 (peak); dinner $35. *When:* closed Aug–mid-Oct. **Firefly Plantation Bequia:** Tel 784-458-3414; www.fireflybequia.com. *Cost:* from $395, all-inclusive. *When:* closed mid-Jun–Oct. **Best times:** Dec–May for good weather; late Jan for Bequia Music Festival; Easter for Regatta, Sand Castle Competition, and other events.

An Exclusive Enclave, Always Refined, and Now Welcoming

Mustique

St. Vincent and the Grenadines, Lesser Antilles

Join the rich, famous, and royal on the privately owned Grenadine island of Mustique, a regular stop for the sailing crowd and best known for its beauty, relaxed vibe, and utter exclusivity. Mythically beautiful Macaroni Beach,

Sailing enthusiasts are drawn to Mustique's exclusive waters.

on the eastern side, is almost always empty, and the picture-perfect village on Britannia Bay enjoys a strict no-cruise-ship policy. The 2.2-square-mile island has just 100 charmingly named villas ranging from the modest to the lavish, the latter owned by a rarefied group of royalty and pop stars. Many of the villas can be rented by the week, fully staffed. Renters are often high-profile glitterati, so if you're hoping for celebrity or rock star sightings, you may not need to look far. Celebs have been coming here since Scottish baron Colin Tennant bought the island in 1958 and gave 10 acres to a young Princess Margaret.

The elegant but charmingly low-key Cotton House is the island's only true hotel, an 18th-century coral warehouse and sugar mill that has been transformed into 20 guest rooms, recently revamped and glammed up to accommodate the overflow of the villas' house guests. Come for dinner at the first-rate Veranda Restaurant, or Tuesday's fun-yet-refined cocktail party in the plantation-style Great Room.

More intimate and romantic is Firefly, a once private villa transformed into an inn with just five exquisite rooms and some of the best dining on the island. On a dramatic hilltop overlooking Britannia Bay, Firefly is popular with residents as well as visitors—expect a lively bar scene and come in time for sunset.

That is, of course, unless you're nursing a Hurricane David at Basil's Bar, the heart of the island and magnet for locals and boldfaced names alike. Basil Charles, the Caribbean's answer to Casablanca's Rick, has been a Mustique legend since Princess Margaret's days. Drinking the night away here is something of a ritual, but thatch-roofed Basil's, which stands on a pier facing the turquoise waters of Britannia Bay, is also a great place for dinner. His famous bar is at its liveliest during the Wednesday-night jump-up barbecue, with lots of loud live music, the famed New Year's Eve celebration, and the 2-week-long Mustique Blues Festival.

VISITOR INFO: www.discoversvg.com. **HOW:** The Mustique Company handles villa rentals. Tel 784-488-8000; www.mustique-island.com. *Cost:* fully staffed 2 BR villas from $5,500 weekly (off-peak), from $9,000 (peak). **COTTON HOUSE:** Tel 800-223-1108 or 784-456-4777; www.cottonhouse.net. *Cost:* from $520 (off-peak), from $815 (peak). **FIREFLY:** Tel 784-488-8414; www.fireflymustique.com. *Cost:* from $995, inclusive. **BASIL'S BAR:** Tel 784-488-8350; www.basilsbar.com. *Cost:* lobster dinner $85. **BEST TIMES:** Nov–Apr for pleasant weather; late Jan–early Feb for Mustique Blues Festival.

A Private Island Resort Where There's Little to Do

PETIT ST. VINCENT

St. Vincent and the Grenadines, Lesser Antilles

Those who really, really want to get away from it all should drop anchor at this privately owned 113-acre luxury island resort. Encircled by white sand beaches, covered with palm trees, and washed by the impossibly clear waters of the fabled Grenadine archipelago, it's a castaway fantasy for a few privacy-seeking guests. They're drawn not only by what the island offers—a quiet, natural setting, superlative service, and remarkable dining—but also for what's missing: television, telephones, air-conditioning, casinos, beach vendors, even room keys.

Twenty-two large, breeze-cooled stone cottages are situated for maximum views and privacy. Room service works like a charm: Run up the red flag and the staff gives you a wide berth; raise the yellow flag, stick your request in your mailbox—a mango daiquiri, extra suntan lotion, dinner on your private terrace—and it arrives in record time. Weary CEO types in need of a retreat love it here. So do newlyweds—who can choose to make an appearance or not. Some people bring their children along now that there's more to do than in the early days: spa treatments in your cottage, tennis courts, and a dock house with everything you need to sail, snorkel, kayak, windsurf, or fish. Take a picnic lunch to the sandbar just off the island for a total castaway experience. Guests who fear they've become dangerously relaxed can arrange for deep-sea fishing, scuba diving, or a sailing trip (day or overnight) to Tobago Cays (see next page) aboard a 49-foot sailing sloop called *Beauty*.

WHERE: Tel 800-654-9326 or 954-963-7401; www.psvresort.com. **COST:** cottages $1,050 (off-peak), $1,350 (peak), all-inclusive. **WHEN:** closed Sep–Oct. **BEST TIME:** Nov–Apr for nice weather.

Idyllic Waters and Castaway Cays

SAILING THE GRENADINES

St. Vincent and the Grenadines, Lesser Antilles

Revered by yachtsmen and wannabes, the 32 islands and hundreds of dotlike cays that form the Grenadines archipelago enjoy near-constant breezes and a reputation as one of the world's best sailing grounds.

Strung like a necklace of gems across 40 miles of pristine waters between St. Vincent and Grenada (see p. 1084), they're blessed with powdery white sand beaches and gorgeous coral reefs. Many islands are uninhabited and accessible only by boat. Some (such as privately owned Mayreau) have tiny populations, mostly descended from African slaves, while others, like the larger Bequia (see p. 1104), are quietly awakening to tourism, with a small-town ambience that has drawn a thriving ex-pat community.

Daily schooners, ferries, and passenger-carrying mail boats sail from St. Vincent (locally known as "the mainland"), serving the half-dozen populated Grenadines. But the ideal way to go, for those in search of a different picnic-perfect, beach-ringed island every day (and who know their main from their genoa) is to charter a self-skippered bareboat through the Moorings in Canouan. The nonsailing set can book a cabin aboard a luxury catamaran (or round up a group of friends and charter the whole yacht) with their own private captain and chef.

Luxurious suites and two- to six-bedroom villas spread over 300 acres at Canouan Resort at Carenage Bay. One of the Caribbean's most elite retreats, its major draws include lovely beaches, challenging golf at the Jim Fazio–designed 18-hole course, and a spa with treatment rooms literally over the sea. The more casual Tamarind Beach Hotel, with 32 beachfront hideaways, is the only other place to stay on this unspoiled island.

Many consider this chain of islands a sailor's paradise.

Sailors head for the Tobago Cays, five uninhabited islands that form the heart of the Tobago Cays Marine Park, which offers superb snorkeling and diving and excellent anchorage. If you saw *Pirates of the Caribbean* and wondered where Johnny Depp was marooned on an island too beautiful to be true, this is it.

How: Charter a bareboat or book a berth via the Moorings. Tel 727-535-1446; www.moorings.com. *Cost:* weekly bareboat accommodating 4 from $1,970 (off-peak), from $2,400 (peak) per person. Weekly berths on crewed yachts accommodating 4 from $3,300 (off-peak), from $4,200 (peak). **Canouan Resort at Carenage Bay:** Tel 866-589-2450 or 784-458-8000; www.canouan.com. *Cost:* from $1,250 (off-peak), from $2,000 (peak); greens fees $220 (guests), $300 (nonguests). **Tamarind Beach Hotel:** Tel 784-458-8044; www.tamrarindbeachhotel.com. *Cost:* from $300 (off-peak), from $430 (peak). **Best time:** Nov–Apr for pleasant weather.

Eden's Aviary

Asa Wright Nature Centre and Lodge

Arima, Trinidad and Tobago, Lesser Antilles

Sitting on this former plantation's screened-in veranda is like sitting in an enormous aviary. From your ringside seat you can see toucans, squirrel cuckoos, tufted coquettes, and ten types of hummingbird—and that's all before breakfast. Visitors are in seventh heaven in this nature and wildlife sanctuary known to birders around the world, located on 1,500 acres in the island's Northern Range, rich, rain forest–covered coastal mountains believed to be the northernmost edge of the Andes Mountains.

Trinidad and sister island Tobago are home to a cornucopia of South American flora and fauna unknown elsewhere in the Caribbean. Approximately 460 species of birds are found on these two islands thanks to their proximity to Venezuela. You can see hundreds of species here in the Arima Valley alone—not to mention innumerable varieties of mammals, reptiles, butterflies, and flowering plants that make you feel you've found the Garden of Eden.

The sanctuary is named for Asa Wright, who, with her husband Newcome, moved to Trinidad in 1946 from England to buy what was then a coffee-and-cocoa plantation. She helped create the sanctuary in 1967. Day guests are welcomed on guided tours or for lunch, but only those staying in the simple guest rooms of the large, airy 1912 plantation house or in cottages scattered around the grounds get in on all the activity at dawn and

Green honeycreepers favor the tropical forests of Trinidad, which they often match in color.

dusk. Experienced guides take guests birding on a network of rain forest trails, always on the lookout for the most coveted sighting—the rare oilbird. This large nocturnal bird feeds on the oily fruit of a variety of palm (hence its name), and a sizeable nesting colony is found in a cavelike grotto in the sanctuary.

Adding to Trinidad's renown as an ornithological wonderland is the sunset spectacle when thousands of scarlet ibis return to their roost in nearby Caroni Swamp, a 40-acre wetland and mangrove preserve. For years their flaming red plumage was so prized for hats and Carnival costumes that they nearly disappeared, but they have made a comeback. Boats pass slowly through the swamp, also home to herons, egrets, and 150 other bird species.

Naturalists trek to Trinidad's northern shores, the beaches of Matura and Grand Rivière, the western hemisphere's best place to spot leatherback turtles as they clamber out of the ocean, dig a nest, and go into a trance as they lay their collection of precious eggs.

Where: 24 miles/39 km east of Port of Spain. Tel 868-667-4655; www.asawright.org. **Cost:** rooms from $300 (off-peak), from $430 (peak), inclusive. **How:** Caligo Ventures in the U.S., tel 800-426-7781 or 305-292-0708; www.caligo.com. **Best times:** Jan–May for dry weather; Mar–Sep for ibis in Caroni Swamp and leatherback turtle nesting.

A Riotous Celebration Where Soca Is King

Carnival

Port of Spain, Trinidad and Tobago, Lesser Antilles

You can't really understand Trinidad unless you come for Carnival, or mas (for masquerade), as it's locally known. Trinidad is a melting pot of West African, East Indian, Chinese, South American, and European, which has influenced both its music and Carnival itself. The country's West African roots gave birth to the steel pan (or steel drum, originally made from empty oil barrels), calypso music, and its more recent souped-up version, soca ("soul-calypso"), which makes this Carnival the loudest and wildest in all the Caribbean. It's the national obsession, with Port of Spain at its heart.

Bands and masqueraders begin their preparations a year in advance. Things start to hum after Christmas, gradually building to a crescendo of rehearsals, concerts, open-air fêtes, and calypso duels. The final 2-day explosion of color, music, and unbridled excess officially kicks off at 4 A.M. on Carnival Monday with the "opening day" parade called J'Ouvert (pronounced joo-VAY). Fueled by copious amounts of beer, revelers covered in mud, grease, body paint, and chocolate form a mass of happy humanity as they follow trucks blasting soca and "chip" (dance) until sunrise.

Monday ("old mas") continues with bands and dancers along a 6-mile parade route. The glitter and glamorous costumes of "pretty mas" are saved for Shrove Tuesday (Mardi Gras), the day before Ash Wednesday. Tens of thousands take to the streets in costume (often sequined bikinis and feather headdresses), with groups as large as 3,000 in identical costume following flatbed trucks carrying steel bands competing for the title of "Masquerade Band of the Year." Getups are at their most extravagant for the Kings and Queens Costume Competition—some can weigh up to 200 pounds (and are attached to wheels for mobility) and incorporate fog, fireworks, and other special effects.

"Pan" bands with as many as 100 musicians perform nonstop in a riotous celebration of King Carnival. Each band has a headquarters, or panyard, and rehearsals and preliminary playoffs are worth searching out. The pinnacle of the steel band competition, the Panorama Finals, is staged at Queen's Park Savannah (ground zero for mas) the Saturday before the parades.

Trinidad's two dominant cultures—West African and Indian—are evident in the array of street food, from spicy doubles (curried chickpeas and chutney between two fluffy fried flatbreads) and roti (soft flatbreads wrapped around various curries—goat and crab are favorites)—to *pelau,* a distinctly African dish where meat is fried in oil and sugar, then combined with pigeon peas and rice. For a more elegant dining experience, visit Veni Mange ("come and eat") for the best lunch on the island, a quintessentially Trinidadian feast that might start with traditional callaloo-pumpkin soup (which, according to legend, when well prepared can make a man propose marriage) and end with homemade soursop ice cream or coconut mousse.

Hotels sell out well in advance for Carnival, but try for Coblentz Inn, which is charming and close to the action—with 16 rooms whimsically decorated along a cultural theme: "the Rum Shop," "Cocoa House," "Cricket"—and a popular restaurant whose name, Battimamzelle, means dragonfly.

Though Carnival officially ends Tuesday at midnight, everyone heads to Maracas Beach an hour north of the city for a cool-down party on Wednesday, "limin'" (hanging out) on this long idyllic stretch of sand beneath towering mountains.

Trinidad's mas (for masquerade) is the largest Carnival in the Caribbean.

Visitor info: www.gotrinidadandtobago.com. **National Carnival Commission:** Tel 868-627-1357; www.ncctt.org. *Cost:* grandstand tickets from $20 and way up. *When:* week before Lent, usually Feb or Mar. **Veni Mange:** Tel 868-624-4597; www.venimange.com. *Cost:* lunch $30. **Coblentz Inn:** Tel 868-621-0541; www.coblentzinn.com. *Cost:* from $145 (off-peak), from $300 during Carnival; dinner $45.

Drift Diving and Bird-Watching on Robinson Crusoe's Island

TOBAGO

Trinidad and Tobago, Lesser Antilles

Mostly hilly and of volcanic origin, Tobago is a breathtaking rural treasure trove of stunning beaches, verdant rain forest, and a wealth of marine life and unspoiled coral reefs. Believed to be the island on which Robinson Crusoe was marooned in the classic 1719 novel by Daniel Defoe, Tobago is the beneficiary of the outflow of Venezuela's mighty Orinoco River. This nutrient-rich current is swept through the 20-mile channel between Trinidad and Tobago, creating astonishingly rich reefs with at least 44 species of hard and soft coral (including the world's largest brain coral) and the best drift diving in the Caribbean.

Though considerably more inhabited than it was the year the fictional Crusoe washed ashore (1649), Tobago is still Trinidad's sleepy country cousin, with just 4 percent of the population, no heavy industry, and no buildings taller than a palm tree.

At the island's southwestern tip, powdery white-sand Pigeon Point Beach is a popular strip and the jumping-off point for cruises to Buccoo (pronounced boo-COO) Reef, a splendid natural aquarium with easy access for novice divers, snorkelers, and the glass-bottom boat crowd. Don't miss Buccoo's "Sunday School," a massive nondenominational block party on Sunday evenings, providing street-food stalls and soca and calypso echoing well into the night.

You can even stay where Crusoe is said to have first landed (and where *Swiss Family Robinson* was filmed): the dark-sand Bacolet Beach, on the island's southern shore. Blue Haven Hotel is an updated 1940s-era property surrounded by water on three sides. Rooms have mahogany floors, four-poster beds, and the same great ocean views that Robert Mitchum and Deborah Kerr enjoyed when they stayed here during the filming of *Fire Down Below* and *Heaven Knows, Mr. Allison*.

Your best chance of seeing Tobago's famous giant manta rays, though they have dwindled in number, is in the waters off Speyside, in the island's remote northeastern reaches. The family-run Manta Lodge offers comfortable accommodations and the on-site Tobago Dive Experience, a year-round school specializing in drift dives past the giant rays as well as southern stingrays, nurse sharks, and turtles. Staying at Manta Lodge also means proximity to Jemma's Seaview Kitchen, where you can dine practically in the arms of a 200-year-old almond tree. The Creole-style food is rivaled by an unbelievable view from the lucky tables that overlook the ocean.

Tobago is also a world-class birding destination: Some 200 varieties have been recorded here. The avian-rich Tobago Forest Reserve, in the mountainous interior, was established in 1776, and is the oldest protected rain forest in the Western Hemisphere. It promises lots of sightings as well as the splendid Argyll Waterfall. Or head a mile offshore from Speyside to Little Tobago Island, one of the most important seabird sanctuaries in the Caribbean.

Charlotteville has a Crusoe-quiet beach called Man-O-War with one convenience he didn't have—a beach stall with ultrafresh fish and chips. Englishman's Bay is Tobago's jewel, an empty mile-long stretch of white sand and palm trees on the island's northern shore, at its most magical when magnificent leatherback turtles come to nest here.

VISITOR INFO: www.gotrinidadandtobago.com. **BLUE HAVEN HOTEL:** Tel 868-660-7400; www.bluehavenhotel.com. *Cost:* from $185 (off-peak), from $238 (peak). **MANTA LODGE:** Tel 866-486-2246 or 868-639-7034; www.mantalodge.com. *Cost:* from $110 (off-peak), from $135 (peak). **TOBAGO DIVE EXPERIENCE:** Tel 868-660-4888; www.tobagodiveexperience.com. **JEMMA'S SEAVIEW KITCHEN:** Tel 868-660-4066. *Cost:* dinner $60. **BEST TIMES:** Nov–Apr for nicest weather; Feb or Mar for Carnival; Nov for Diwaali (Festival of Lights).

Twelve Uninterrupted Miles of Pristine Beach

GRACE BAY

Turks and Caicos

The jewel in the crown of Turks and Caicos—an archipelago of 40 islands—Grace Bay boasts a staggering 12-mile arc of powdery white sand lapped by turquoise waters that teem with marine life. It's considered one of the most beautiful beaches in the world. Located on the northern shore of the main island of Providenciales ("Provo" to locals), it is protected by a coral reef just 1,650 feet off the coast, creating diving, snorkeling, and swimming conditions that are second to none.

A slew of new, stylish hotels and condo-style resorts have opened near the world-famous strand. But Grace Bay Club still reigns supreme in the luxury market, in part because it was early to the game and nabbed 11 choice acres, making it the lowest-density resort on the island. The original Mediterranean-style hotel has 21 suites for adults only, while families tend to stay in villas. All enjoy a host of amenities, including the breezy Anacaona restaurant by the beach.

Beach lovers revel in Grace Bay's miles of immaculate shoreline.

Island life at its basic best awaits those who make the trek to Da Conch Shack, an open-air landmark restaurant where the conch is harvested right in front of you and served every way imaginable—as salad, chowder, fritters, stir-fried, or as ceviche.

Or consider total isolation, via the 35-minute boat ride to Parrot Cay, a 1,000-acre private island with just one uberexclusive resort. It has a pared-down aesthetic and swish villas (owned by A-list celebrities) that can be rented. Guests staying in either the hotel or villas can book at what is arguably the best spa in the Caribbean, the COMO Shambhala Retreat ("shambhala" is related to the Sanskrit word for "center of peace and harmony"), a veritable temple of the soothing arts that brings in top therapists from around the globe.

One of the best places to experience the excellent snorkeling and diving is the appealingly undeveloped and sparingly populated Salt Cay. The dives here take you to forests of elkhorn coral, past a British frigate that wrecked back in 1790. In winter there's a good chance of spotting—and swimming among—migrating humpback whales.

Visitor info: Tel 800-241-0824 or 649-946-4970; www.turksandcaicostourism.com. **Grace Bay Club:** Tel 800-946-5757 or 649-946-5050; www.gracebayclub.com. *Cost:* from $570 (off-peak), from $980 (peak); dinner $75. **Da Conch Shack:** Tel 649-946-8877; www.conchshack.tc. *Cost:* $40. **Parrot Cay:** Tel 877-754-0726 or 649-946-7788; www.parrotcay.como.bz. *Cost:* from $450 (off-peak), from $775 (peak). **Best times:** Nov–Apr for nicest weather; Jan–Mar for whale-watching; late Nov for Conch Festival.

An Unrivaled Underwater Nature Trail

Buck Island

St. Croix, U.S. Virgin Islands, Lesser Antilles

At this uninhabited satellite island off St. Croix, a national monument where only 176 of the park's 19,000 acres are above ground, the snorkeling is legendary. The elkhorn coral reef that surrounds two-thirds of the island has extraordinary formations and deep grottoes in crystal-clear waters (think 100-foot visibility) at an average depth of 13 feet.

Off Buck's northeast end, a meandering snorkeler's trail is marked with explanatory plaques. The park supports all sorts of wildlife, including hawksbill turtles, brown pelicans, and more than 250 species of fish.

When the Kennedy family visited Buck Island in the 1950s, John F. Kennedy was so enchanted that in 1961, as president, he helped make it into one of the few fully protected underwater U.S. National Monuments; it was greatly expanded by President Bill Clinton in 2001. While Buck Island is considered one of the most important snorkeling sites in the Caribbean, St. Croix is also known for wall diving, satisfying to divers of varied ability. At Salt River Canyon and Cane Bay, lush coral gardens at 30 feet lead to "The Wall," 2,000 feet deep.

Tours for Buck Island leave from Christiansted, the historic Danish town on St. Croix's northern coast just 5 miles away. It's a 5-minute drive east to the Buccaneer, a pink palazzo beach resort that was once a sugar plantation and the boyhood home of Alexander Hamilton. It opened as an 11-room inn in 1947, and the same family still runs what is now a family-friendly 138-room resort spread over 340 acres with all the classic amenities.

Though St. Croix is the largest of the U.S. Virgin islands, it's still just 84 square miles, and much of it is still rural and dotted with the ruins of old sugar mills. It's worth a drive over to Frederiksted, at the western end of the island, to Blue Moon, a colorful waterfront bistro known for its Cajun-inflected food, fine wine, and live jazz on Wednesday, Friday, and at Sunday brunch. Order a Cruzan Confusion, made with local Cruzan rum, considered one of the world's best and still distilled on St. Croix.

Visitor info: www.nps.gov/buis. **How:** Big Beard's Adventure Tours offers full-day tours to Buck Island in a glass-bottomed boat, as well as half-day snorkeling trips, departing from Christiansted. Tel 866-773-4482 or 340-773-4482; www.bigbeards.com. *Cost:* half day $68. **The Buccaneer:** Tel 800-255-3881 or 340-712-2100; www.thebuccaneer.com. *Cost:* from $325 (off-peak), from $360 (peak). **Blue Moon:** Tel 340-772-2222; www.bluemoonstcroix.com. *Cost:* dinner $50, Sunday brunch $15. **Best times:** Nov–Apr for nice weather; Dec 5–Jan 2 for Crucian Christmas Festival (St. Croix's Carnival).

Trailblazers of Ecotourism in the American Caribbean

Virgin Islands National Park

St. John, U.S. Virgin Islands, Lesser Antilles

With more than half the island a national park, St. John puts the "virgin" back in Virgin Islands. More than 18,000 acres of coral seascapes are protected when you include the Virgin Islands Coral Reef National Monument. With 20 hiking trails wending through 7,000 tropical acres, and blissfully free of casinos or cabana boys, the 19-square-mile island is reachable only by ferry, appealing to travelers who care more about a star-studded night sky than five-star hotels.

This pristine landscape exists thanks to the foresight of wealthy conservationist Laurance Rockefeller, who bought up much of the island and then gave it away. While sailing in 1952, he spotted Caneel Bay, a 170-acre peninsula with seven stunning beaches, snapped it up, and built an estate. To protect the island he loved he added it to his holdings and in 1956 deeded 5,000 acres of sugary white coves, teal blue bays, and shady mountains to the federal government.

Trunk Bay is the showstopper of this extraordinary tropical estate, a picture-perfect, quarter-mile-long beach considered one of the world's most beautiful. It is famous for a 670-foot snorkeling trail with labeled underwater features, the perfect snorkeling debut for kids and other novices. Snorkeling snobs get their kicks at Haulover Bay and Leinster Bay, dramatic sites that are inaccessible from shore.

Above ground, the Reef Bay Trail is one of the park's most popular (and frequented). It's all downhill, beginning at 800 feet above sea level and winding past spectacular views, ancient petroglyphs, and the ruins of 18th-century Danish plantation houses before ending about 3 hours later on the southern shore.

Reachable only by ferry, most of St. John will never be touched by development.

Rockefeller's estate became the "it" resort with the wealthy in the '60s, and Caneel Bay is still the island's most luxurious place to stay. Today the Rosewood resort has expanded to 166 airy, spacious rooms and claims the island's most romantic dining at the Equator, which sits atop 18th-century sugar-mill ruins. The Self Centre's focus is on wellness, with offerings that include sound healing and guided stargazing.

The work of ecotourism pioneer Stanley Selengut, Maho Bay Camps and sister property Estate Concordia Preserve are set in the midst of St. John's verdant national parkland, providing easy access to both the beach and hiking trails. Maho Bay Camps' hand-constructed tent-cottages are linked by wooden walkways so as not to disturb the natural environment. They lack some amenities (private bathrooms) but the 114 tents tucked among the foliage all have their own decks, screened windows, electricity, and cooking facilities. Just up the hill are 12 Harmony Studios, which combine sustainability with creature comforts. Experiencing Maho Bay Camps' pristine parkland and its white-beached cove, guests may feel like privileged interlopers in paradise. Half an hour away at Estate Concordia Preserve, the 25 "eco-tents" are bigger, more substantial, and have bathrooms, while 13 spacious studios are built around a freshwater pool.

Don't leave the island without a stop at Woody's Seafood Saloon in Cruz Bay, known for its conch fritters and Bushwackers, potent milk shakes made with Cruzan light rum, Baileys, Kahlua, amaretto, vodka, and cream of coconut, blended with ice and sprinkled with fragrant nutmeg.

VISITOR INFO: www.nps.gov/viis. **CANEEL BAY:** Tel 888-767-3966 or 340-776-6111; www.caneelbay.com. *Cost:* from $450 (off-peak), $550 (peak); dinner at the Equator $65. **MAHO BAY CAMPS:** Tel 800-392-9004 or 340-776-6240; www.maho.org. *Cost:* Harmony Studios from $130 (off-peak), from $225 (peak). Maho Bay Camps from $80 (off-peak), from $140 (peak). Estate Concordia Preserve from $120 (off-peak), from $165 (peak). **WOODY'S SEAFOOD SALOON:** Tel 340-779-4625; www.woodysseafood.com. **BEST TIMES:** Nov–Apr for pleasant weather; mid-Jun–July 4 for St. John Festival.

Virgin Sands

MAGENS BAY BEACH

St. Thomas, U.S. Virgin Islands, Lesser Antilles

A thick fringe of palms lines this mile-long, horseshoe-shaped strip of white sand and turquoise waters—a prime contender on any short list of the world's most beautiful beaches. With alluring views of other islands just beyond where it opens to the sea, the beach is so shallow that you can wade out hundreds of feet without getting your shorts wet. Finding it is half the fun: Ask an island local to point you in the direction of the Magens Bay Discovery Trail.

St. Thomas, purchased from Denmark in 1917, is the most developed of the three U.S. Virgin Islands and one of the most popular stops for cruise ships: Duty-free shopping, a little Danish architecture, and a trip to Magens Bay Beach are all de rigueur. To avoid the legions, go when the ships aren't in port or do what the locals do: Hang out on Hull Bay Beach, the island's most popular surfing beach, just one bay to the west; it offers niceties, such as a restaurant and bar, along with your own private stretch of sand.

VISITOR INFO: www.usvitourism.vi. **BEST TIMES:** Nov–Apr for nicest weather; Mar for International Rolex Regatta; Apr for Virgin Islands Carnival; Jun–Oct for blue marlin angling; Aug for U.S. Virgin Islands Open/Atlantic Blue Marlin Tournament.

INDEX

NOTE: Items in SMALL CAPS refer to entry titles.

Visit www.1000places.com/indexes to access 12 special indexes that break the destinations down by theme. They are: ACTIVE TRAVEL, WILDLIFE, AND ADVENTURE • ANCIENT WORLDS: PYRAMIDS, RUINS, AND LOST CITIES • CULINARY EXPERIENCES • FESTIVALS AND SPECIAL EVENTS • GLORIES OF NATURE: GARDENS, PARKS AND WILDERNESS PRESERVES, AND NATURAL WONDERS • GORGEOUS BEACHES AND GETAWAY ISLANDS • HOTELS, RESORTS, ECO-LODGES, AND INNS • LIVING HISTORY: CASTLES AND PALACES, HISTORICAL SITES • ROADWAYS, RAILWAYS, AND WATERWAYS • SACRED PLACES • SPLENDOR IN THE GLASS: BARS AND PUBS, VINEYARDS AND WINERIES, BREWERIES AND DISTILLERIES • UNRIVALED MUSEUMS.

A

B

C

D

E

F

G

H

I

J

K

L

M

N

O

P

Q

R

T

U

V

W

X

Photo Credits

Unless otherwise specified, copyright on the works reproduced lies with the respective photographers, agencies, and museums. Despite extensive research, it has not always been possible to establish copyright ownership. Where this is the case, we would appreciate notification.

COVER: Front cover composite: globe stand **Photodisc Inc.;** globe **Fotolia/design56.**

BACK COVER AUTHOR PHOTO: **Gabrielle Revere** (www.gabriellerevere.com). Location courtesy of **Snack Taverna,** New York, N.Y. (www.snackny.com).

TABLE OF CONTENTS: **age fotostock:** p. iv Lee Frost, p. vii top The Print Collector, p. vii bottom SuperStock, p. viii top Kim Sullivan, p. viii bottom Sylvain Grandadam, p. ix top Janicek Ladislav, p. ix middle Ed Scott, p. x top Richard Maschmeyer, p. x bottom World Pictures. p. ix bottom Courtesy of **Monticello: Mary Porter.**

MAPS: pp. 2, 374, 444, 478, 644, 700, 944, 1056 Scott MacNeill (www.macneillandmacintosh.com).

Special thanks to **age fotostock** (www.agefotostock.com), and in particular to Susan Jones, who was always terrific to work with.

EUROPE

age fotostock: p. 1 Frank Chmura, p. 3 Peter Adams, p. 5 Tony Waltham, p. 7 David Lyons, p. 10 mrp, p. 12 Markus Keller, p. 14 Tibor Bognár, p. 15 H & D Zielske, p. 16 David Lyons, p. 17 Mickael David, p. 18 Eric Nathan, p. 20 Held Jürgen, p. 23 Steve Vidler, p. 26 Atlantide S.N.C., p. 30 Jevgenija Pigozne, p. 32 Stephan Goerlich, p. 34 Jason Friend, p. 36 Doug Pearson, p. 37 Fenneke Wolters-Sinke, p. 40 José Antonio Moreno, p. 42 Steve Vidler, p. 44 Douglas Houghton, p. 46 Graham Lawrence, p. 49 SuperStock, p. 51 Roy Shakespeare, p. 52 Keirsebilck Patrick, p. 54 Kevin Galvin, p. 55 The Irish Image Collection, p. 58 K. Stange/Arco Images, p. 61 The Print Collector, p. 62 Vito Arcomano, p. 64 The Irish Image Collection, p. 66 Daniel Acevedo, p. 68 Hoffmann Photography, p. 72 Martin Siepmann, p. 74 Sergio Pitamitz, p. 77 Philippe Renault, p. 78 Peter Adams, p. 79 David Lyons, p. 80 Xandi Kreuzeder, p. 82 José Fuste Raga, p. 83 Günter Flegar, p. 85 Ernst Wrba, p. 87 Josef Mullek, p. 88 Klaus-Peter Wolf, p. 91 Ivan Vdovin, p. 92 EKA, p. 93 Christian Handl, p. 96 Juergen Ritterbach, p. 97 Michael Zegers, p. 99 Bernhard Schmerl, p. 100 Bertrand Gardel, p. 104 H. Richter, p. 107 R Kiedrowski/Arco Images, p. 109 Rene Mattes, p. 110 Eymagic/Zoonar, p. 111 Juan José Pascual, p. 112 Steve Vidler, p. 113 Kord.com, p. 117 Sylvain Sonnet, p. 120 Jose Antonio Moreno, p. 123 Marc Dozier, p. 126 J. D. Heaton, p. 128 McPhoto, p. 131 Michel Philippe, p. 135 Hubertus Blume, p. 137 Mark Henley, p. 140 Andreas Strauss, p. 141 Alexander Kupka, p. 143 Andreas Rose, p. 146 Kevin Galvin, p. 148 Adam Eastland, p. 149 Jurgen Henkelmann, p. 151 Walter G. Allgöwer, p. 152 Carola Koserowsky, p. 154 José Fuste Raga, p. 157 Ulysses, p. 160 Evgeny Ivanov, p. 161 Alvaro Leiva, p. 162 Funkystock, p. 165 M. Von Aulock, p. 166 Ken Gillham, p. 168 Kozalides/IML, p. 169 Alamer, pp. 170 and 171 Patrick Frilet, pp. 172 and 174 Funkystock, p. 176 Bowman, p. 178 Guido Alberto Rossi, p. 181 Danilo Donadoni, p. 183 Alvaro Leiva, p. 184 Neil Emmerson, p. 185 Luke Hayes/VIEW, p. 188 Alvaro Leiva, p. 189 Giovanni Mereghetti, p. 190 Tommaso Di Girolamo, p. 193 gianni congiu, p. 194 Angelo Cavalli, p. 196 Atlantide S.N.C., p. 197 Philippe Michel, p. 198 Jean Du Boisberranger, p. 199 S. Lubenow, p. 201 Renato Bordoni, p. 203 José Fuste Raga, p. 204 JTB Photo, p. 205 Nico Tondini, p. 206 Raimund Kutter, p. 209 Lee Frost, p. 211 JTB Photo, p. 213 Erwin Wodicka, p. 214 Stefano Torrione, p. 215 Danilo Donadoni, p. 217 R. Nobbio/DEA, p. 218 Alvaro Leiva, p. 219 H & D Zielske, p. 220 Bertrand Gardel, p. 223 allOverTPH, p. 224 Karl F. Schofmann, p. 225 Sylvain Grandadam, p. 226 André Gonçalves, p. 227 Jean-Baptiste Rabouan, p. 228 Ingolf Pompe, p. 231 Roy Rainford, p. 233 Roland, p. 235 dreamtours, p. 237 José Elias, pp. 238 and 241 José Antonio Moreno, p. 242 Paul Seheult, p. 244 Alena Brozova, p. 245 Richard Semik, p. 247 Javier Larrea, p. 248 Jean-Pierre Degas, p. 249 José Fuste Raga, p. 250 Alena Brozova, p. 253 José Fuste Raga, p. 255 J.D. Dallet, p. 256 José Fuste Raga, p. 257 Ruth Tomlinson, p. 258 Ivern Photo, p. 259 Luis Castañeda, p. 260 Jean-Pierre Lescourre, p. 261 T. A. Hoffmann, p. 262 Juergen Richter, p. 264 Oscar García Bayerri, p. 265 Daniel P. Acevedo, p. 267 Hervé Hughes, p. 268 Sergio Pitamitz, p. 269 John Greim, p. 272 Doug Pearson, p. 273 Bertrand Rieger, p. 274 Norbert Eisele-Hein, p. 275 Patrick Frischknecht, p. 277 Thomas Bron, p. 278 Meinrad Riedo, p. 279 Haltmeier Herbert, p. 280 Neil Harrison, p. 282 Andy Selinger, p. 284 Henryk T. Kaiser, p. 286 Eva Parey, p. 287 Egmont Strigl, p. 292 Lucas Vallecillos, p. 293 Lydie Gigerichova, p. 294 Egmont Strigl, p. 297 Michael Runkel, pp. 299 and 301 Funkystock, p. 303 Tibor Bognár, p. 305 Walter Bibikow, p. 308 Wojtek Buss, p. 311 Ian Trower, p. 312 Peter Erik Forsberg, p. 313 Walter Bibikow, p. 315

Wojtek Buss, p. 316 Marco Cristofori, p. 320 Keribar/IML, p. 322 Fotosearch RM, p. 325 G. Lenz/Arco Images, p. 327 Alvaro Leiva, p. 330 Peter Adams, p. 332 Martin Bobrovsky, p. 335 Christophe Boisvieux, p. 336 Nils-Johan Norenlind, p. 339 Christophe Boisvieux, p. 340 Christian Kober, p. 343 Adam Woolfitt, p. 344 John Elk III, p. 350 Peter Widmann, p. 351 Dallas & John Heaton, p. 353 McPhoto/FSC, p. 354 Michele Falzone, p. 356 SuperStock, p. 357 Iain Masterton, p. 361 Christophe Boisvieux, p. 364 Frank Chmura, p. 366 SuperStock, p. 368 Christophe Boisvieux, p. 372 Christophe Boisvieux.

p. 346 Courtesy of **Uri Golman/Greenland Tourism,** p. 362 Courtesy of **Visti Flam/ Morten Rakke.**

AFRICA

age fotostock: p. 373 Uwe Skrzypczak, p. 375 Jonathan Carlile, p. 377 Blaine Harrington, p. 378 Christian Goupi, p. 380 J.D. Dallet, p. 381 Graham Mulroo/Zoonar, p. 384 Heeb Christian, p. 388 Walter Bibikow, p. 391 Alan Keohane, p. 392 Alistair Laming, p. 393 Saldari, p. 395 Jenny Pate, p. 396 Aldo Pavan, pp. 397 and 399 McPhoto, p. 401 Franck Guiziou, p. 402 Morales, p. 404 Wojtek Buss, p. 407 Jack Jackson, p. 408 Sylvain Grandadam, p. 409 Bernd Zoller, p. 410 Zoonar, p. 411 Paul Miles, p. 412 Ann & Steve Toon, p. 415 Peter Adams, p. 416 Suzanne Long, p. 418 Yadid Levy, p. 419 Kim Sullivan, p. 421 Frank van Egmond, p. 423 SuperStock, p. 425 Sybil Sassoon, p. 426 Gavriel Jecan, p. 427 Guido Alberto Rossi, p. 429 L. Fohrer, p. 430 Alvaro Leiva, p. 431 Paul Hobson/FLPA, p. 432 Ivan Vdovin, p. 434 Marek Patzer, p. 437 C. Hutter/Arco Images, p. 439 Angelo Cavalli, p. 440 Yann Guichaoua, p. 442 David Koster.

MIDDLE EAST

age fotostock: p. 443 Michele Falzone, p. 445 Aldo Pavan, p. 446 JTB Photo, p. 450 C. Albatross, p. 452 Nimrod Aronow/Albat, p. 455 Alison Wright, p. 457 Christian Kober, p. 458 Didier Forray, p. 459 Michele Falzone, pp. 463 and 464 Tibor Bognár, p. 466 Giovanni Mereghetti, p. 469 SuperStock, p. 471 Sylvain Grandadam, p. 473 José Fuste Raga, p. 474 Ember Stefano, p. 475 Sergio Pitamitz, p. 476 Tony Waltham.

ASIA

age fotostock: p. 477 Carol Buchanan, p. 479 S. Tauqueur, p. 480 Franck Guiziou, p. 481 Best View Stock, p. 483 Angelo Cavalli, p. 484 Horizon, p. 486 Steve Vidler, p. 488 PhotoStock-Israel, p. 490 Peter Adams, p. 492 Christian Goupi, p. 494 JTB Photo, p. 497 Christian Reister, p. 498 Eric Tam, p. 501 Mark Henley, p. 503 Christian Goupi, p. 507 JTB Photo, p. 509 JTB Photo, pp. 510 and 512 Gavin Hellier, p. 515 Travel Pix Collection, p. 517 JTB Photo, p. 519 Tibor Bognár, p. 520 Paul Quayle, p. 524 Patrick Frilet, p. 525 JTB Photo, p. 526 Olaf Schubert, p. 528 Philippe Michel, p. 530 Christophe Boisvieux, p. 531 Blaine Harrington, p. 532 Keith Rushforth/FLPA, p. 534 Dinodia, p. 535 Jordi Camí, p. 537 Dinodia, p. 538 Stuart Pearce, p. 539 Kim Sullivan, p. 540 Bildgentur-Online, p. 541 Ivan Vdovin, p. 542 Giovanni Mereghetti, p. 544 Christian Hütter, p. 545 Philippe Michel, p. 546 Tibor Bognár, p. 547 Patrick Frilet, p. 548 Dhritiman Mukherjee, p. 550 Jochen Tack, p. 551 Bernard Castelein, p. 552 Chris Caldicott, p. 553 Vision, p. 554 José Fuste Raga, p. 555 Jane Sweeney, p. 556 dreamtours, p. 557 Tibor Bognár, p. 558 Wojtek Buss, p. 559 Iñaki Caperochipi, p. 563 José Fuste Raga, p. 564 Peter Giovannini, p. 565 Colin Monteath, p. 566 Peter Baker, p. 567 Tibor Bognár, p. 569 José Fuste Raga, p. 571 Gavin Hellier, p. 572 Michael Runkel, p. 574 A. Hartl, p. 577 Movementway, p. 578 Philippe Michel, p. 579 Yadid Levy, p. 581 Santi Román, p. 583 Philippe Michel, p. 585 Patrick Forget, p. 586 Jane Sweeney, p. 587 Therin-Weise, p. 588 Egmont Strigl, p. 589 R. Philips/Arco Images, p. 590 Tim Hall, p. 591 Janek, p. 592 Piotr Powietrzynski, p. 595 Malherbe Marcel, p. 598 Steve Vidler, p. 601 Janicek Ladislav, p. 603 Stefano Baldini, p. 604 Georgie Holland, p. 607 José Fuste Raga, p. 608 Luca Invernizzi Tetto, p. 611 David Bowden, p. 612 Gavin Hellier, p. 614 OTHK, p. 616 Philippe Michel, p. 618 José Fuste Raga, p. 620 Christophe Boisvieux, p. 621 Rozbroj, p. 622 Laurence Simon, p. 624 Steve Vidler, p. 626 Stefano Torrione, p. 627 Ray Evans, p. 629 Luca Invernizzi Tetto, p. 630 Heeb Christian, p. 633 José Fuste Raga, p. 635 McPhotos, p. 636 Gonzalo Azumendi, p. 638 Philippe Michel, p. 639 Alvaro Leiva, p. 641 Wolfgang Herzog, p. 642 Stu Smucker.

p. 536 Courtesy of **Chapslee Hotel.**

AUSTRALIA, NEW ZEALAND, AND THE PACIFIC ISLANDS

age fotostock: p. 643 Ingo Schulz, p. 645 R. Gemperle, p. 646 Andrew Watson, p. 647 Don Fuchs, p. 648 José Fuste Raga, p. 651 Per-Andre Hoffmann, p. 655 Gerhard Zwerger-Schon, p. 656 Giovanni Rivolta, p. 659 Holger Leue, p. 660 S. Sailer/A. Sailer, p. 662 Konrad Wothe, p. 663 Bjorn Svensson, p. 665 Stephen Wong, p. 666 R. Gemperle, p. 667 Doug Pearson, p. 668 Don Fuchs, p. 672 Christian Kober, p. 674 Colin Monteath, p. 677 SuperStock, p. 678 Stuart Pearce, p. 680 Michael DeFreitas, p. 681 Daniela Dirscherl/W., p. 685 Raffaele Meucci, p. 687 Ed Scott, p. 690 Michel Renaudeau, p. 692 Reinhard Dirscherl, p. 693 Tuul, p. 694 Luca Invernizzi Tetto, p. 695 Jochem Wijnands, p. 696 Raffaele Meucci, p. 698 Upperhall.

p. 682 Courtesy **Mantangi Private Island Resort.**

UNITED STATES OF AMERICA AND CANADA

age fotostock: p. 699 Mike Criss, pp. 701, 702 and 704 Alaska Stock, p. 705 Heeb Christian, p. 706 Christian Beier, p. 708 Angelo Cavalli, p. 711 Chris Parker, p. 712 Nedra Westwater, p. 714 Anthony Dunn, p. 717 Ludovic Maisant, p. 718 Chris Cheadle, p. 720 Mattes Rene, p. 723 Topic Photo Agency, p. 724 Philippe Renault, p. 726 Egon Bomsch, p. 727 Michele Falzone, p. 728 Carlos S. Pereyra, p. 730 JTB Photo, p. 733 Ignacio Palacios, p. 737 Tom Till, p. 738 SuperStock, p. 739 Norbert Eisele-Hein, p. 743 Roy Rainford, p. 744 Barry Winiker, p. 747 Wayne Lynch, p. 749 Don Johnson, p. 750 Heeb Christian, p. 754 Johnny Stockshooter, p. 755 M. Delpho, p. 758 Jeff Greenberg, p. 760 Douglas Peebles, p. 761 Brigitte Merz, pp. 763 and 765 Masa Ushioda, p. 766 Elfi Kluck, p. 767 Tom Till, p. 770 José Fuste Raga, p. 776 Holger Leue, p. 777 Karl Weatherly, p. 783 Photolibrary, p. 784 SuperStock, p. 785 Philippe Renault, p. 787 SuperStock, p. 790 Dennis MacDonald, p. 791 Robert W. Ginn, p. 792 Joseph Sohm, p. 794 Walter Bibikow, p. 795 Scott Smith, pp. 796 and 800 SuperStock, p. 804 Walter Bibikow, p. 805 Michael Neelon, p. 806 Bilderbuch, p. 808 Sergio Tafner Jorge, p. 811 Raymond Forbes, p. 813 Walter Bibikow, p. 814 SuperStock, p. 816 Natalie Tepper, p. 817 Heeb Christian, p. 819 Walter Bibikow, p. 821 Gerhard Zwerger-Schon, p. 823 Ignacio Palacios, p. 826 Terrance Klassen, p. 828 Steve Vidler, p. 829 Jules Cowan, p. 832 Martin Barlow, p. 836 SuperStock, p. 839 GreenStockCreative, p. 841 Walter Bibikow, p. 842 Sylvain Grandadam, p. 843 Bartomeu Amengual, p. 844 Anton J. Geisser, p. 845 Donald Nausbaum, p. 850 SuperStock, p. 855 Egmont Strigl, p. 858 Gavriel Jecan, p. 859 Dennis MacDonald, p. 861 Kord.com, p. 863 John Greim, p. 865 Ernst Wrba, p. 867 G R Richardson, p. 870 Jim West, p. 872 SuperStock, p. 874 Patrick Frilet, p. 875 Andrea Forlani, p. 879 Robert B. Yarbrough, p. 881 Lee Frost, p. 884 McPhoto, p. 887 Fraser Hall, p. 893 Barry Winiker, p. 895 Garry Black, p. 896 Chuck Pefley, p. 906 Karl Johaentges, p. 909 Michael Just, p. 911 Josh McCulloch, p. 913 J. A. Kraulis, p. 916 Klaus Lang, p. 923 Thorsten Milse, p. 925 Barrett & MacKay, p. 927 Ron Watts, p. 929 Richard T. Nowitz, p. 930 Garry Black, p. 932 Oleksiy Maksymenko, p. 936 Barrett & Mackay, p. 937 Jeff Greenberg, p. 940 Philippe Renault, p. 941 Randa Bishop, p. 942 Stefan Wackerhagen.

p. 902 Courtesy of **Adventures on the Gorge:** p. 877 Courtesy of **AT&T Performing Arts Center: Nigel Young/Foster + Partners;** p. 921 Courtesy of **Fairmont Hotels & Resorts;** p. 890 Courtesy of **Monticello: Mary Porter;** p. 900 Courtesy of the **San Juan Visitors Bureau: Robin Jacobson;** p. 888 Courtesy of **Shelburne Farms;** p. 904 Courtesy of **The National Park Service;** p. 820 Courtesy of **Triple Creek Ranch, Darby, Montana, www.triplecreekranch.com.**

LATIN AMERICA

age fotostock: p. 943 Caroline Webber, p. 945 Michael Nolan, p. 949 Walter Bibikow, p. 951 Leonardo Diaz Romero, p. 952 Ritterbach, p. 955 José Fuste Raga, p. 958 Carlos S Pereyra, p. 959 Wojtek Buss, p. 960 Mel Longhurst, p. 961 Stuart Westmorland, p. 964 McPhoto, p. 967 Yadid Levy, p. 969 Kraig Lieb, p. 970 Richard Maschmeyer, p. 972 Larry Dale Gordon, p. 975 Carver Mostardi, p. 976 Richard Maschmeyer, p. 978 Corbis, p. 980 Fabian von Poser, p. 981 Tibor Bognár, p. 984 Guy Christian, p. 988 Stefano Paterna, p. 990 Jon Díez Beldarrain, p. 991 SuperStock, p. 992 Heeb Christian, p. 994 Dan Leffel, p. 996 Topic Photo Agency Inc., p. 997 Larry Dale Gordon, p. 999 M. Borchi/DEA, p. 1001 SuperStock, p. 1002 vittorio sciosia, p. 1003 Z. Alfredo Maique, p. 1004 Bruce Bi, p. 1006 Florian Kopp, p. 1007 Wayne Lynch, p. 1010 Ricardo Azoury, p. 1012 Bildagentur RM, p. 1016 Stefano Paterna, p. 1019 Pietro Scozzari, p. 1021 Holler Hendrik, p. 1022 McPhoto, p. 1024 Topic Photo Agency Inc., p. 1026 Gardel Bertrand, p. 1028 Luis Padilla, p. 1030 Jean-Baptiste Rabouan, p. 1033 Christian Kapteyn, p. 1035 SuperStock, p. 1036 Ryan Fox, p. 1039 SuperStock, p. 1041 Gonzalo Azumendi, p. 1042 Caroline Webber, p. 1046 SuperStock, p. 1049 Ximena Griscti, p. 1050 JTB Photo, p. 1052 Roberto Rinaldi, p. 1053 Michael Nolan.

CARIBBEAN

age fotostock: p. 1055 PetePhipp/Travelshots, p. 1057 Sylvain Grandadam, p. 1059 Gavin Hellier, p. 1060 Sylvain Grandadam, p. 1064 Joe Dovala/WaterFrame, p. 1066 Hans-Peter Merten, p. 1069 Georgie Holland, p. 1071 SuperStock, p. 1073 Kreder Katja, p. 1075 Alfredo Maiquez, p. 1078 Urs Flueler, p. 1079 Henry Beeker, p. 1083 Alfredo Maiquez, p. 1084 Angelo Cavalli, p. 1086 Philippe Michel, p. 1090 Picture Contact Bv, p. 1092 Jean-Daniel Sudres, p. 1094 Atlantide S.N.C., p. 1099 Michel Renaudeau, p. 1101 Gavin Hellier, p. 1102 World Pictures, p. 1103 Walter Bibikow, p. 1105 Angelo Cavalli, p. 1107 Fiore, p. 1108 J. & C. Sohns, p. 1109 Angelo Cavalli, p. 1111 Jochen Tack, p. 1113 SuperStock.

p. 1087 Courtesy of **Daniel Morel.**